PRIME FOCUS

View-D™

Create stereo 3D imagery from your 2D source with unprecedented speed, interactivity and quality.

View-D™ from Prime Focus is a proprietary system for the conversion of 2D moving images to stereo 3D images. It offers many advantages over alternative conversion methods, including superior quality of converted imagery, significantly shorter production timeframes, more iterations and control over virtually every pixel in the frame.

Prime Focus
Global Visual Entertainment Services.

E: sales.view-d@primefocusworld.com
North America: +1 323 461 7887 | UK: +44 207 565 1000 | India: +91 22 6715 5000
www.primefocusworld.com

MUMBAI | LONDON | LOS ANGELES | NEW YORK | VANCOUVER | WINNIPEG | HYDERABAD | CHENNAI | GOA | BANGALORE

PUBLISHING DIRECTOR

Jayne Hatfield

CHIEF EXECUTIVE

Bernard L Kay

SALES EXECUTIVES

James Hayward Jonathon Rigby

ACCOUNTS

Jacqueline Shepherd

DESIGN & ARTWORK

Alan Thompson @ BGA Design

Charlie Bone Samantha Miller

KAYS LIMITED

A Publisher of Directories, Websites & Apps for

the Commercial, Broadcast and Film Industry

Pinewood

Pinewood Studios, Pinewood Road

Iver Heath, Bucks SL0 0NH

London

Trinity Mews, Cambridge Gardens

London W10 6JH

Manchester

The Heart, MediaCityUK

Salford Quays, Manchester M50 2TH

Advertising Enquiries: 020-8226 8910

Tel: 020-8960 6900 Fax 020-8960 6700

Email: info@kays.co.uk

www.kays.co.uk®

ISBN 978-0-9540511-4-3

INDEX

INDEX

INDEX

INDEX

INDEX

INDEX

INDEX

ACCOMMODATION

Absolute Property	**020-7372 7272**
2-3 Coleridge Gardens	Fax 020-7372 8484
London NW6 3QH	Amanda Mitchell
Access Bookings	**0870-855 5777**
53A Tamworth Road	Fax 0870-950 5907
Lichfield, Staffs WS14 9HG	Patricia Barnes
www.accessbookings.com	
Andre Lanauvre Property	**020-7245 0788**
93 Knightsbridge	Fax 020-7245 0792
London SW1X 7RB	Janie Andre
The Apartment Service	**0870-080 2303**
5-6 Francis Grove	Fax 020-8944 6744
London SW19 4DT	Melanie Degand
www.apartmentservice.com	
Apartments4london	**020-8878 0990**
10-12 Barnes High Street	Fax 020-8876 0260
London SW13 9LW	Emmie Caesar
Big City Reservations	**020-8324 2729**
Elstree Studios, Shenley Road	Chrissy Phillips
Borehamwood, Herts WD1 1JG	
Bunkabin	**0845-456 7899**
Tweedale Way	Fax 0845-456 6899
Oldham, Lancs OL9 7LD	Luke Rothwell
www.bunkabin.co.uk	
Finchlea Estates	**01753-591559**
The Old Council Offices, The Green	020-7823 1530
Datchet, Berks SL3 9EH	Mark Leader
www.finchleaestates.com	
Go Native	**020-7221 2028**
United House	Fax 020-7221 2088
9 Pembridge Road, London W11 3JY	Faye Hand
Media Monkeys	**020-8324 2782**
42A Athenaeum Road	Clare Arnold
London N20 9AH	

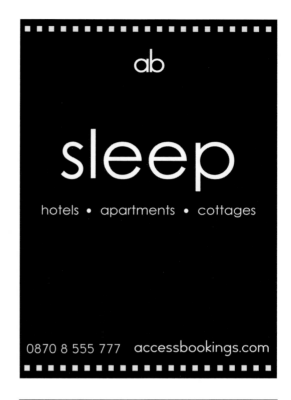

ACCOMMODATION

Mediacom 24-7	**01753-656218**
Pinewood Studios, Pinewood Road	Fax 01753-656416
Iver Heath, Bucks SL0 0NH	Steve Garner
Premier Booking Services	**020-7470 8720**
11-15 Betterton Street	Fax 020-7470 8780
London WC2H 9BP	Nigel Walker

ACCOUNTANTS

Addis & Co	**0161-432 3307**
Emery House, 192 Heaton Moor Road	Fax 0161-432 3376
Stockport, Cheshire SK4 4DU	Anthony Addis
Alexander James & Co	**020-8398 4447**
Admirals Quarters, Portsmouth Road	Fax 020-8398 9989
Thames Ditton, Surrey KT7 0XA	Andrew Nicholson
Arram Berlyn Gardner	**020-7330 0000**
30 City Road	Fax 020-7330 0001
London EC1Y 2AB	Gary Jackson
Baker Tilly	**020-7413 5100**
2 Bloomsbury Street	Fax 020-7413 5101
London WC1B 3ST	David Blacher
Barnes Roffe	**020-8988 6100**
Leytonstone House	Fax 020-8532 9020
3 Hanbury Drive, London E11 1GA	Paul Hughes
BDO	**01707-255888**
Prospect Place, 85 Great North Road	Fax 01707-255890
Hatfield, Herts AL9 5BS	Marios Brooks
Beechams	**020-7427 5700**
167 Fleet Street	Fax 020-7427 5701
London EC4A 2EA	Ravi Parmar
Berg Kaprow Lewis	**020-8922 9222**
35 Ballards Lane	Fax 020-8922 9223
London N3 1XW	Lesley Alexander
Berley Chartered Accountants	**020-7636 9094**
76 New Cavendish Street	Fax 020-7636 4115
London W1G 9TB	Mark Levy
The Blue Skies Partnership	**01767-690425**
Skyview House, 10 St Neots Road	Fax 01767-691707
Sandy, Beds SG19 1LB	Kenny Harrison
Bradley Foreman Accountants	**020-8950 4450**
60 Sparrows Herne	Fax 020-8950 1451
Bushey, Herts WD23 1FY	Selwyn Foreman
Breckman & Co	**020-7499 2292**
49 South Molton Street	Robert Breckman
London W1K 5LH	
Christopher Lunn & Co	**01892-665311**
The Pines, Boars Head	Fax 01892-655428
Crowborough, E Sussex TN6 3HD	Tracey Kimber

Clayman & Co	**020-7935 0847**
189 Bickenhall Mansions	Fax 020-7224 2216
Baker Street, London W1U 6BX	Michael Kabel
Collards	**020-8247 4480**
2 High Street	Fax 020-8247 4481
Kingston-upon-Thames, Surrey KT1 1EY	Walter Benzie
Deloitte	**020-7936 3000**
Hill House	Fax 020-7583 1198
1 Little New Street, London EC4A 3TR	Gavin Hamilton-Deeley
Duncan & Toplis	**01205-310250**
5 Resolution Close, Endeavour Park	Fax 01205-365405
Boston, Lincs PE21 7TT	Adrian Reynolds
Ernst & Young	**020-7951 2000**
1 More London Place	Fax 020-7951 1345
London SE1 2AF	Alan Flitcroft
Fat Cat Media Finance	**020-8890 0828**
85 Shelson Avenue	Fax 020-8890 0703
Feltham, Middx TW13 4QT	Nicholas Elliott
Grant Thornton	**020-7728 2343**
Grant Thornton House	Fax 020-7728 2480
Melton Street, London NW1 2EP	Terry Back
Harold Everett Wreford	**020-7535 5900**
32 Wigmore Street	Fax 020-7535 5901
London W1U 2RP	Michael Isaacs
Harris & Trotter	**020-7467 6300**
65 New Cavendish Street	Fax 020-7467 6363
London W1G 7LS	Ronnie Harris
Hays MacIntyre	**020-7969 5500**
Fairfax House	Fax 020-7969 5600
15 Fulwood Place, London WC1V 6AY	Simon Wilks
HW Fisher & Co	**020-7388 7000**
Acre House	Fax 020-7380 4900
11-15 William Road, London NW1 3ER	Steve Blackman
Kingston Smith	**020-7304 4646**
141 Wardour Street	Fax 020-7304 4647
London W1F 0UT	David Childs
KPMG	**020-7311 1000**
8 Salisbury Square	Fax 020-7311 3311
London EC4Y 8BB	Richard Bawden
Lee Associates	**020-7025 4600**
5 Southampton Place	Fax 020-7025 4666
London WC1A 2DA	
Levy & Co	**01342-835612**
Eastbourne House, 2 Saxbys Lane	Fax 01342-836213
Lingfield, Surrey RH7 6DN	Hilary Barrett
Lindford & Co	**020-7637 2244**
1 Duchess Street	Fax 020-7637 2999
London W1W 6AN	Terence Lindford

It's ok in the movies but why take real life risks with your finances....?

Call now and quote reference FTV123 for a free financial performance review. We will also prepare your first personal tax return with us **Free of Charge.**

For over 50 years Silver Levene has been the definitive name in film and television accounting and financial advice.

We're the film and television industry specialists which means we will save you more tax and help create more value from the work you do - Guaranteed!

We act for hundreds of professionals in the industry from writers, directors and producers to cameramen, editors and photographers and we'd like to work with you.

Call or email Tony Silver today:
tony.silver@silverlevene.co.uk

7 Warren Street, London W1T 6AD
Tel: 020 7383 3200 - www.silverlevene.co.uk

Silver Levene (SL)

Lubbock Fine — 020-7490 7766
Russell Bedford House
250 City Road, London EC1V 2QQ
Fax 020-7490 5102
Jeff Gitter

Mansfield & Co — 020-7482 2022
55 Kentish Town Road
London NW1 8NX
Fax 020-7482 2025
David Mansfield

Mazars — 020-7063 4000
Tower Bridge House
St Katharines Way, London E1W 1DD
Fax 020-7063 4001
Fiona Hotston Moore

Media Finance — 020-8237 1074
Riverside Television Studios
Crisp Road, London W6 9RL
Fax 020-8237 1071
Christopher Spurgeon

Michael Martin Partnership — 01233-633336
3 Queen Street
Ashford, Kent TN23 1RF
Fax 01233-633399
Martin Ades

Newman & Co — 020-7554 4840
Regent House
1 Pratt Mews, London NW1 0AD
Fax 020-7388 8324
Colin Newman

Northern Alliance — 020-7886 0730
19 Bolsover Street
London W1W 5NA
Fax 020-7665 8201
Mike Kelly

Nyman Libson Paul — 020-7433 2400
Regina House
124 Finchley Road, London NW3 5JS
www.nlpca.co.uk
Fax 020-7433 2401
Anthony Pins

Nyman Libson Paul — 01753-656428
Pinewood Studios, Pinewood Road
Iver Heath, Bucks SL0 0NH
www.nlpca.co.uk
Fax 01753-656428
Anthony Pins

OJK — 020-7792 9494
6 Lansdowne Mews
London W11 3BH
Fax 020-7792 1722
Patrick Savage

Postsums — 01932-563486
Shepperton Studios, Studios Road
Shepperton, Middx TW17 0QD
Fax 01932-571987
Tarn Harper

PricewaterhouseCoopers — 020-7583 5000
1 Embankment Place
London WC2N 6RH
Fax 020-7822 4652

RSM Tenon — 020-7535 1400
66 Chiltern Street
London W1U 4JT
Fax 020-7535 1401
John Graydon

Sargent-Disc — 01753-630300
The Coach House, Pinewood Studios
Pinewood Road, Iver Heath, Bucks SL0 0NH
www.sargent-disc.com
Fax 01753-655881
Laurence Sargent

Sedley Richard Laurence Voulters — 020-7287 9595
1 Conduit Street
London W1S 2XA
Fax 020-7287 9696
Stephen Marks

Shipleys — 020-7312 0000
10 Orange Street
London WC2H 7DQ
Fax 020-7312 0022
Ken Roberts

Silver Levene — 020-7383 3200
37 Warren Street
London W1T 6AD
www.silverlevene.co.uk
Fax 020-7383 4165
Tony Silver

Sloane & Co — 020-7221 3292
36-38 Westbourne Grove
London W2 5SH
Fax 020-7229 4810
David Sloane

Sopher + Co — 01753-652030
Pinewood Studios, Pinewood Road
Iver Heath, Bucks SL0 0NH
www.sopherco.com
Jeanette Lipscombe

Sopher + Co — 020-7493 0100
38 Berkeley Square
London W1J 5AE
www.sopherco.com
Fax 020-7493 3668
Robert Goodwin

Sopher + Co — 020-8207 0602
5 Elstree Gate, Elstree Way
Borehamwood, Herts WD6 1JD
www.sopherco.com
Fax 020-8207 6758
Neela Chauhan

Steele Robertson Goddard — 020-7269 9700
28 Ely Place
London EC1N 6AA
Fax 020-7269 9701
David Skeet

Thornton Springer — 020-8771 8661
67 Westow Street
London SE19 3RW
Fax 020-8771 4623
Nigel Springer

Vantis — 020-7467 4000
66 Wigmore Street
London W1U 2SB
Fax 020-7467 4040
Cliff Crown

West Wake Price — 020-7588 3541
4 Chiswell Street
London EC1Y 4UP
Fax 020-7638 7099
Mike Peters

SOPHER + CO

Sopher + Co is one of the most entrepreneurial and progressive firms of accountants, business advisors and tax consultants in the UK, with offices in Elstree, Pinewood and Central London.

What sets us apart is our personal approach. Our attention and approachability combined with experience and expertise will help you grow and prosper, giving you more time to concentrate on your business and relieve you of the burdens of compliance and bureaucracy.

With over 35 years experience in the entertainment and media industry, we understand your individual needs and are able to build our response and service around them. Our prime goal is to play a positive and creative role in the financial planning of our client's business and personal affairs and to maximise profits. We also have considerable networking skills which enable us to call on numerous banks, institutions and high net worth families and individuals to help raise finance and assistance. This is the kind of close working relationship for which we are known and the kind of relationship that works best for our clients.

There is no charge for your initial consultation. Once we have established the amount and scope of the work you would like us to undertake we will be pleased to give an indication of our charges. These will reflect our commitment to providing the highest quality of advice and service, combined with value for money.

For an initial no-fee consultation please call: +(44) 20 8207 0602
email: accountants@sopherco.com
web: www.sopherco.com

5 Elstree Gate Elstree Way	Pinewood Studios	38 Berkeley Square
Borehamwood Hertfordshire	Pinewood Road	London
WD6 1JD	Iver Heath	W1J 5AE
Tel: +(44) 20 8207 0602	Bucks SL0 0NH	Tel: +(44) 20 7493 0100
Fax: +(44) 20 8207 6758	Tel: +(44) 1753 652 030	Fax: +(44) 20 7493 3668

ADVERTISING AGENCIES

23red   **020-7843 5900**
20 Northdown Street   Fax 020-7843 5923
London N1 9BG
Creative Director: Sean Kinmont

Abbott Mead Vickers BBDO   **020-7616 3500**
151 Marylebone Road   Fax 020-7616 3580
London NW1 5QE
Head of TV: Francine Linsey

Abraham Ellis & Partners   **020-7580 1806**
76-78 Charlotte Street
London W1T 4QS
Directors: Christopher Abraham, Frances Abraham

Addiction   **020-7462 1400**
36 Percy Street   Fax 020-7462 1401
London W1T 2DH
CEO: Jeremy Rainbird Managing Director: Max Garner
Creative Director: Alan Grove

Agency   **020-7964 8200**
76-80 Whitfield Street   Fax 020-7964 8300
London W1T 4EZ
Managing Director: Chris Walker

archibald ingall stretton...   **020-7467 6100**
Berners House   Fax 020-7467 6101
47-48 Berners Street, London W1T 3NF
Creative Director: Steve Stretton

Arcplc   **01753-785620**
Pinewood Studios, Pinewood Road
Iver Heath, Bucks SL0 0NH
Managing Director: Paul Maloney

Armando Testa   **020-7851 4800**
Gainsborough House   Fax 020-7851 3638
81 Oxford Street, London W1D 2EU
Managing Director: Alexis Jacobs

The Bank   **020-7612 8000**
16-18 Berners Street   Fax 020-7612 8001
London W1T 3LN
Creative Director: Ian Cassie

Banner Corporation   **020-7349 2200**
Harbour Yard   Fax 020-7349 2300
Chelsea Harbour, London SW10 0XD
Director of Project Management: Louise Burrough

Bartle Bogle Hegarty   **020-7734 1677**
60 Kingly Street   Fax 020-7437 3666
London W1B 5DS
Head of TV: Frances Royle Producer: Helen Powlette

Beattie McGuinness Bungay   **020-7632 0400**
16 Shorts Garden   Fax 020-7632 0401
London WC2H 9AU
Creative Directors: Jeremy Green, Trevor Beattie

Blac   **020-7379 7799**
1 Mercer Street   Fax 020-7379 3077
London WC2H 9QJ
Managing Director: Neil Campbell
Creative Director: Murray Blackett

Bygraves Bushell Valadares & Sheldon   **020-7734 4445**
15 New Burlington Street   Fax 020-7434 0213
London W1S 3BJ
Managing Director: Daz Valadares Media Buyer: Sandy O'Sullivan

Cheetham Bell - JWT   **0161-832 8884**
Astley House   Fax 0161-832 2198
Quay Street, Manchester M3 4AS
Head of TV: Julia Gaffey

CHI & Partners   **020-7462 8500**
7 Rathbone Street   Fax 020-7462 8501
London W1T 1LY
Creative Director: Ewan Paterson

Cogent Elliott   **0121-627 5040**
Heath Farm, Hampton Lane   Fax 0121-627 5038
Meriden, W Midlands CV7 7LL
CEO: Tim Pile Creative Director: Richard Payne

CST   **020-7423 4610**
Devon House   Fax 020-7907 1201
58 St Katharines Way, London E1W 1LB
Creative Directors: Dave Trott, Gordon Smith
Producer: Carrie Moores

Dare   **020-7299 3000**
13-14 Margaret Street   Fax 020-7299 3001
London W1W 8RN
New Business Managers: Ellie Lucas, Liza Wostmann

DDB London   **020-7258 3979**
12 Bishops Bridge Road   Fax 020-7402 4871
London W2 6AA
Head of TV: Maggie Blundell Creative Director: Jeremy Craigen
Producers: Richard Chambers, Lucy Westmore, Lucinda Kerr,
Sarah Browell, Natalie Powell

Delaney Lund Knox Warren   **020-7836 3474**
25 Wellington Street   Fax 020-7240 8739
London WC2E 7DA
Head of TV: Susie Innes Producer: Christian Lobo

Dentsu   **020-7529 9000**
10 Hills Place   Fax 020-7529 9099
London W1F 7SD
CEO: Simon North Managing Director: Ida Rezani

DeWynters   **020-7321 0488**
48 Leicester Square   Fax 020-7321 0104
London WC2H 7LT
Managing Director: Anthony Pye-Jeary Creative Director: Bob King

Dialogue 141   **020-7470 5800**
121-141 Westbourne Terrace
London W2 6JR
New Business Director: Neil Jenkinson

Different   0191-261 0111

6-8 Ravensworth Terrace   Fax 0191-221 1122
Newcastle-upon-Tyne NE4 6AU
Managing Director: Ben Quigley   Creative Director: Mark Martin

Doner Cardwell Hawkins   020-7632 7600

26-34 Emerald Street   Fax 020-7632 7601
London WC1N 3QA
Managing Director: Andrew Hawkins
Creative Director: Paul Cardwell

Doremus & Co   020-7360 6700

10 Regents Wharf   Fax 020-7360 6701
All Saints Street, London N1 9RL
Managing Director: Alasdair Morrison

DraftFCB   020-3048 0000

84 Eccleston Square   Fax 020-3048 0400
London SW1V 1PX
Head of Production: James Osborn

EHS Brann   020-7017 1000

6 Briset Street   Fax 020-7017 1001
London EC1M 5NR
CEO: Matt Atkinson

Euro RSCG London   020-7240 4111

Cupola House   Fax 020-7467 9210
15 Alfred Place, London WC1E 7EB
Creative Director: Gerry Moira

Euro RSCG Riley   020-7022 4000

6 Briset Street   Fax 020-7022 4005
London EC1M 5NR
Creative Director: Peter Rice   Art Director: Duncan James

Fallon   020-7494 9120

Elsley Court   Fax 020-7494 9130
20-22 Great Titchfield Street, London W1W 8BE
Head of TV: Nicky Barnes

Farm   020-7874 6550

7 Midford Place   Fax 020-7383 4725
London W1T 5BG
Head of TV: David Clark
Creative Directors: Owen Lee, Gary Robinson

Finch Partnership   0151-236 2134

20 Chapel Street   Fax 0151-236 3774
Liverpool L3 9AG
Managing Director: Duncan Frazer   Creative Director: Paul Brown

First City Advertising   020-7436 7020

22 Goodge Place   Fax 020-7637 3277
London W1T 4SL
Managing Director: Andrew Ackland

Fold7   020-7251 0101

47 Underwood Street   Fax 020-7251 0202
London N1 7LG
General Manager: Sam Balderstone

G2 UK   020-7453 7900

Wells Point   Fax 020-7453 7999
79 Wells Street, London W1T 3QN
Managing Director: Nick Hoaldey
Business Development Manager: Dick Bloomfield

The Gate Worldwide   020-7423 4500

Devon House   Fax 020-7423 4597
58 St Katharines Way, London E1W 1LB
CEO: Philip Gregory   Managing Director: Philip Hawkins
Creative Director: Jeremy Baker

Genesis Advertising   028-9031 3344

1 Lower Crescent   Fax 028-9031 2245
Belfast BT7 1NR
Managing Director: Steven Bogan

glue London   020-7739 2345

31 Old Nichol Street   Fax 020-7920 7381
London E2 7HR
Managing Director: Jo Hagger

Golley Slater   0121-384 9700

205 Fort Dunlop, Fort Parkway   Fax 0121-384 9790
Erdington, Birmingham B24 9FD
Media Director: Ian James   Creative Director: Joe Ivory

Golley Slater   029-2038 8621

Wharton Place   Fax 029-2023 8729
Wharton Street, Cardiff CF10 1GS
Creative Director: Martin Bush   Creative Manager: Lisa Jackson

Grey Advertising   020-3037 3000

The Johnson Building   Fax 020-3037 3001
77 Hatton Garden, London EC1N 8JS
Head of TV: Stephanie Wellsley   Producers: Mark Bond, Ian Randle

Gyro HSR   020-7351 1550

The Chambers   Fax 020-7351 3318
Chelsea Harbour, London SW10 0XF
New Business Manager: Paul Neal

Hive Advertising & Marketing   0161-660 3620

The Pie Factory, 101 Broadway
Salford Quays, Manchester M50 2EQ

Wunderman	**020-7611 6333**
Greater London House	Fax 020-7611 6668
Hampstead Road, London NW1 7QP	
Creative Director: David Harris	

ADVERTISING AGENCY PRODUCERS

Hilary Bright	**020-8881 4363**
47 Princes Avenue	Fax 020-8881 4363
London N22 7SB	
Nicky Bystram	**020-8874 3111**
11 Herondale Avenue	Fax 020-8874 3111
London SW18 3JN	
Sarah Shaw	**020-8672 8612**
80 Selkirk Road	Fax 020-8672 8612
London SW17 0EP	
David Shute	**07770-431590**
32 Hatfield Road	
London W4 1AF	
Susie Stock	**020-8888 1146**
62 Woodfield Way	
London N11 2NS	

AGENTS - ARTISTES

A & B Personal Management	**020-7434 4262**
PO Box 64671	Bill Ellis
London NW3 9LH	
A & J Management	**020-8342 0542**
242A The Ridgeway	Fax 020-8342 0842
Enfield, Middx EN2 8AP	Jackie Michael
Actors Alliance	**020-7407 6028**
Disney Place House	Fax 020-7407 6028
14 Marshalsea Road, London SE1 1HL	
Actors Ireland	**028-9024 8861**
Crescent Arts Centre	Fax 028-9024 8861
2-4 University Road, Belfast BT7 1NH	Geraldine O'Dwyer
Actorum	**020-7636 6978**
9 Bourlet Close	Fax 020-7636 6975
London W1W 7BP	
Alan Field Associates	**020-8441 1137**
3 The Spinney, Bakers Hill	Fax 020-8447 0657
Hadley Common, Herts EN5 5QJ	Alan Field
Alpha Personal Management	**020-7241 0077**
Studio B4	Fax 020-7241 2410
3 Bradbury Street, London N16 8JN	

AM:PM The Actors Agency	**028-9023 5568**
52 Central Park	Fax 028-9023 5568
33 Alfred Street, Belfast BT2 8ED	
Amanda Howard Associates	**020-7287 9277**
21 Berwick Street	Fax 020-7287 7785
London W1F 0PZ	
Amputees In Action	**01635-31890**
23 Kingsley Close	Fax 01635-38001
Newbury, Berks RG14 2EB	John Pickup
www.amputeesinaction.co.uk	
Anita Alraun Representation	**020-7379 6840**
28 Charing Cross Road	Fax 020-7379 6865
London WC2H 0DB	Anita Alraun
APM Associates	**01753-639204**
Pinewood Studios, Pinewood Road	Fax 01753-639205
Iver Heath, Bucks SL0 0NH	Linda French
Associated International Management	**020-7831 9709**
Fairfax House	Fax 020-7242 0810
Fulwood Place, London WC1V 6HU	Nicola Mansfield
Big Chief Productions	**020-8996 0300**
81 Duke Road	Fax 020-8996 0400
London W4 2BN	Angie Fernandes
Billy Marsh Drama	**020-3178 4748**
20 Garrick Street	Fax 020-3178 5488
London WC2E 9BP	Linda Kremer
Brunskill Management	**020-7581 3388**
Suite 8A	Fax 020-7589 9460
169 Queens Gate, London SW7 5HE	Geoff Stanton
The BWH Agency	**020-7240 5299**
117 Shaftesbury Avenue	Fax 020-7240 2287
London WC2H 8AD	Joe Hutton
CA Artistes Management	**020-8834 1608**
26-28 Hammersmith Grove	Laila Debs
London W6 7BA	
Chatto & Linnit	**020-7352 7722**
123A Kings Road	Fax 020-7352 3450
London SW3 4PL	
Circus Maniacs	**07977-247287**
Office 8A, Kingswood Foundation	Fax 0117-947 7042
Britannia Road, Bristol BS15 8DB	Jacqueline Wellbourne
Conway Van Gelder Grant	**020-7287 0077**
8-12 Broadwick Street	Fax 020-7287 1940
London W1F 8HW	Jeremy Conway
Creative Artists Management	**020-7292 0600**
55-59 Shaftsbury Avenue	Fax 020-7734 3205
London W1D 6LD	Michael Wiggs
Dealers Agency	**028-9020 9761**
Belfast Business Centre	Kris Wall
23-31 Waring Street, Belfast BT1 2DX	

Dennis Lyne Agency	**020-7272 5020**
503 Holloway Road	Fax 020-7272 4790
London N19 4DD	Dennis Lyne
Devine Artiste Management	**0844-884 4578**
Mayfair House	Fax 0844-884 5083
14 Heddon Street, London W1B 4DA	
Eric Glass	**020-7229 9500**
25 Ladbroke Crescent	Fax 020-7229 6220
London W11 1PS	Janet Glass
Essanay	**020-8998 0007**
PO Box 44394	Nicholas Young
London SW20 0YP	
Ethnics Artiste Agency	**020-8523 4242**
86 Elphinstone Road	Fax 020-8523 4523
London E17 5EX	Pauline Oni
Excellent Talent Agency	**0845-210 0111**
118-120 Great Titchfield Street	Fax 020-7637 4091
London W1W 6SS	
Features	**020-7637 1487**
1 Charlotte Street	Fax 020-7637 0328
London W1T 1RD	Jenni Clarke
Felix De Wolfe	**020-7242 5066**
Kingsway House	Fax 020-7242 8119
103 Kingsway, London WC2B 6QX	
Galloways One	**020-7376 2288**
15 Lexham Mews	Fax 020-7376 2416
London W8 6JW	Jill Moore
Gardner Herrity	**020-7388 0088**
24 Conway Street	Fax 020-7388 0688
London W1T 6BG	Andy Herrity
Garricks	**020-7738 1600**
Angel House	Fax 020-7801 0088
76 Mallinson Road, London SW11 1BN	Megan Willis
Gavin Barker Associates	**020-7499 4777**
2D Wimpole Street	Fax 020-7499 3777
London W1G 0EB	Katie Harper
Genuine Arab Casting	**07799-063726**
78 York Street	Abu Jameel
London W1H 1DP	
GMA	**020-7278 1054**
Panther House	James Cooper
38 Mount Pleasant, London WC1X 0AP	
Hamilton Hodell	**020-7636 1221**
66-68 Margaret Street	Fax 020-7636 1226
London W1W 8SR	Christian Hodell
The Harris Agency	**01923-211644**
71 The Avenue	Fax 01923-211666
Watford, Herts WD17 4NU	Sharon Harris

Hobsons Actors	**020-8995 3628**
62 Chiswick High Road	Fax 020-8996 5350
London W4 1SY	Christina Beyer
Insanity Artistes Agency	**020-7927 6222**
5 Little Portland Street	Fax 020-7927 6223
London W1W 7JD	Andy Varley
International Artistes	**020-7025 0600**
Holborn Hall	Fax 020-7404 9865
193-197 High Holborn, London WC1V 7BD	Mandy Ward
J Gurnett Personal Management	**020-7440 1850**
12 Newburgh Street	Fax 020-7287 9642
London W1F 7RP	Jo Gurnett
Jacque Evans Management	**020-8699 1202**
14 Holmesley Road	Fax 020-8699 5192
London SE23 1PJ	Jacque Evans
Jaffrey Management	**01708-732350**
74 Western Road	Kim Barry
Romford, Essex RM1 3LP	
JB Agency	**0845-638 4984**
26 Onslow Gardens	Darrel Minton
London SW7 3AG	
John Doe Management	**020-8960 2848**
123 Hanover Road	Hannah Potter
London NW10 3DN	
John Miles Organisation	**01275-856770**
Cadbury Camp Lane	Fax 01275-810186
Clapton-in-Gordano, Bristol BS20 7SB	John Miles
Lovett Logan Associates	**020-7495 6400**
40 Margaret Street	Fax 020-7495 6411
London W1G 0JH	Dolina Logan
Mad Dog Casting	**020-7269 7910**
Holborn Hall	Fax 020-7831 7267
193-197 High Holborn, London WC1V 7BD	Maziar Yazdanian
www.maddogcasting.com	
Markham & Froggatt	**020-7636 4412**
4 Windmill Street	Fax 020-7637 5233
London W1T 2HZ	

MPC Entertainment	020-7624 1184
MPC House	Fax 020-7624 4220
15-16 Maple Mews, London NW6 5UZ	Michael Cohen
Nancy Hudson Associates	020-7499 5548
PO Box 1344	Nancy Hudson
High Wycombe, Bucks HP11 9ER	
The Narrow Road Company	020-7379 9598
76 Neal Street	Fax 020-7379 9777
London WC2H 9PL	Richard Ireson
New Faces	020-7439 6900
The Linen Hall	Fax 020-7287 5481
162-168 Regent Street, London W1B 5TB	Val Horton
Ordinary People	020-7267 7007
16 Camden Road	Fax 020-7267 5677
London NW1 9DP	Sarah Robbie
Oriental Casting Agency	020-8671 8538
60 Downton Avenue	Peggy Sirr
London SW2 3TR	
PC Theatrical	020-8381 2229
10 Strathmore Gardens	Fax 020-8933 3418
Edgware, Middx HA8 5HJ	Sandra Mooney
Peter Charlesworth & Associates	020-7792 4600
67 Holland Park Mews	Fax 020-7792 1893
London W11 3SS	Peter Charlesworth
Pineapple Agency	020-7241 6601
Montgomery House	Fax 020-7241 3006
159-161 Balls Pond Road, London N1 4BG	David Paton
www.pineappleagency.com	
Prime Performers	020-7251 8222
1-2 Faulkners Alley	Sally Dellow
Cowcross Street, London EC1M 6DD	
Re | animator Management	01444-447020
The Priory, Syresham Gardens	Fax 01444-447030
Haywards Heath, W Sussex RH16 3LB	Piers Gielgud
Red Door Management	0161-425 6495
The Pie Factory, 101 Broadway	
Salford Quays, Manchester M50 2EQ	
Richard Stone Partnership	020-7497 0849
2 Henrietta Street	Fax 020-7497 0869
London WC2E 8PS	Meg Poole
Scott Marshall Partners	020-7637 4623
15 Little Portland Street	Fax 020-7636 9728
London W1W 8BW	Manon Palmer
Screenlite	01932-561388
Shepperton Studios, Studios Road	Kerry Tovey
Shepperton, Middx TW17 0QD	
Shane Collins Associates	020-7470 8864
11-15 Betterton Street	Fax 0870-460 1983
London WC2H 9BP	Shane Collins

Stella Richards Management	020-7736 7786
42 Hazlebury Road	Fax 020-7731 5082
London SW6 2ND	Stella Richards
Talent Artists	020-7923 1119
59 Sydner Road	Fax 020-7923 2009
London N16 7UF	Jane Wynn Owen
Uni-VersalEXTRAS	0845-370 0884
Pinewood Studios, Pinewood Road	Wayne Berko
Iver Heath, Bucks SL0 0NH	
www.universalextrascasting.co.uk	
VSA	020-7240 2927
186 Shaftsbury Avenue	Fax 020-7240 2930
London WC2H 8JB	Andrew Charles

AGENTS - CHILDRENS

Abacus Agency	01306-877144
The Studio, 4 Bailey Road	Fax 01306-877813
Westcott, Dorking, Surrey RH4 3QS	Linda Davies
Barbara Speake Agency	020-8743 6096
Barbara Speake Theatre School	Fax 020-8740 6542
East Acton Lane, London W3 7EG	June Billham
Bizzykidz	0845-520 0400
Bizzy House, 73A Mayplace Road West	Fax 0845-520 0401
Bexleyheath, Kent DA7 4JL	Geraldine Mullins
Bonnie & Betty	020-8676 6294
County House, 221-241 Beckenham Road	Bonnie Breen
Beckenham, Kent BR3 4UF	
Bruce & Brown	020-8968 5585
Canalot Studios	Fax 020-8964 0457
222 Kensal Road, London W10 5BN	Kipsey Owen
Bubblegum	01753-632867
Pinewood Studios, Pinewood Road	Fax 01753-652521
Iver Heath, Bucks SL0 0NH	Jay Burnham
Doreen English 95	01243-825968
4 Selsey Avenue, Aldwick	Fax 01243-825968
Bognor Regis, W Sussex PO21 2QZ	Gerry Kinner
Elisabeth Smith	0845-872 1331
8 Dawes Lane	Charlotte Evans
Sarratt, Herts WD3 6BB	
Finchs Agency	01702-202149
3 The Mews	Fax 01702-202149
Hockley, Essex SS5 4RB	Nicola Hurdle
GP Associates	020-8886 2263
4 Gallus Close	Fax 020-8882 9189
London N21 1JR	Katie Hinde
Italia Conti Agency	020-7608 7500
23 Goswell Road	Fax 020-7253 1430
London EC1M 7AJ	Carrie Newton

Cooling & Heating Solutions	01590-682579
Marlwood House, Silver Street	Fax 01590-682900
Lymington, Hants SO41 6DG	Graham Jordan

Energyst Rental Solutions	01902-797000
4 Ashes Industrial Estate, Station Road	Fax 01902-797001
Wolverhampton, W Midlands WV10 7DB	Dave Curry

RapidHeatbusters	0800-977 8499
423 Becontree Avenue	Fax 020-8598 4027
Dagenham, Essex RM8 3UH	Bob Eager

AIR FREIGHT & COURIERS

Agony Aunts	01784-880482
Garden House, 41 Coleridge Road	Fax 01784-889513
Ashford, Middx TW15 2QS	Debbie Parr

Air Courier International	01753-561300
Colndale Road	Fax 01753-561301
Colnbrook, Berks SL3 0HQ	Darren Winter

Associated Air Services	020-8844 0805
Units 4-6, Feltham Business Complex	Fax 020-8844 0878
Browells Lane, Feltham, Middx TW13 7EQ	Ruth Parmenter

City Air Express	028-9078 1878
Unit B1	Fax 028-9078 1788
West Bank Drive, Belfast BT3 9LA	Stephen Wallace

Clover Shipping	01932-571460
Pinewood Studios, Pinewood Road	Fax 01932-560593
Iver Heath, Bucks SL0 0NH	Colin Christie

Davies Turner	01753-688053
Unit A1, Calder Way	Fax 01753-680648
Colnbrook, Slough, Berks SL3 0BQ	Clive Robertson
www.daviesturneraircargo.com	

Delivered On Time	020-8890 5511
Unit 4, The Mercury Centre	Fax 020-8890 5533
Central Way, Feltham, Middx TW14 0RN	Bob Brewster

DHL Global Forwarding	020-8754 5300
Danzas House, Kestrel Way	Fax 020-8754 5006
Dawley Park, Hayes, Middx UB3 1HJ	John Meller

EFM Management	01932-590322
Downside Mill, Cobham Park Road	Fax 01932-590323
Cobham, Surrey KT11 3PF	Mark Dooner

Geodis Wilson	020-8831 4200
145 Faggs Road	Fax 020-8890 5532
Feltham, Middx TW14 0LZ	John Baker

Heritage Media Services	01932-592634
Shepperton Studios, Studios Road	Robin Frith
Shepperton, Middx TW17 0QD	

Ivey International Freight Services	**01753-685008**
McMillan House, Units 7 & 8, Polygon Business Centre	Fax 01753-687008
Blackthorne Road, Colnbrook, Berks SL3 0QT	George Ivey
www.ivey-international.com	
Jetstream Logistics	**01753-682500**
Unit 12, Coln Industrial Estate	Fax 01753-681111
Old Bath Road, Colnbrook, Berks SL3 0NJ	Fiona Hancox
Mapcargo	**01895-432555**
365 Stockley Close	Fax 01895-432554
West Drayton, Middx UB7 9BL	Lee George
Media Onboard	**0844-700 7747**
Lufthansa Building, 557 Shoreham Road	Fax 0871-247 4468
Heathrow Airport, Hounslow, Middx TW6 3RJ	Craig Burdett
Media World Logistics	**020-8573 9999**
Media House, Springfield Road	Fax 020-8573 9592
Hayes, Middx UB4 0DD	Richard Clark
Midnite Express	**020-8607 5530**
Unit 16, Saxon Way	Fax 020-8607 5531
Harmondsworth, Middx UB7 0LW	Errol Grant
Precision Cargo Services	**01753-650551**
Pinewood Studios, Pinewood Road	Fax 01753-650601
Iver Heath, Bucks SL0 0NH	Gary Green Les Taylor
www.precisioncargo.co.uk	
Precision Cargo Services	**01932-593377**
Shepperton Studios, Studios Road	Fax 01753-650601
Shepperton, Middx TW17 0QD	Gary Green Les Taylor
www.precisioncargo.co.uk	
Production Freight	**01784-472600**
Crabtree Road, Thorpe Industrial Estate	Fax 01784-472666
Egham, Surrey TW20 8RS	Derek Hale
Renown Freight	**01753-685008**
McMillan House, Units 7 & 8, Polygon Business Centre	Fax 01753-687008
Blackthorne Road, Colnbrook, Berks SL3 0QT	George Ivey
Rock-It Cargo	**01784-431301**
Delta Way	Fax 01784-471052
Egham, Surrey TW20 8RX	Matthew Wright
www.rock-itcargo.com	
Team Air Express	**01895-448855**
Unit 8, Crown Way	Fax 01895-448851
Horton Road, West Drayton, Middx UB7 8HZ	Martin Gigg
Team Global	**01753-686393**
Units 1-4, Britannia Industrial Estate	Fax 01753-684115
Poyle Road, Colnbrook, Berks SL3 0BH	Martin Lovell
Watkins & Sole Transport	**01753-683647**
Units 6 & 11, Galleymead Road	Fax 01753-682405
Colnbrook, Berks SL3 0EN	Michael Higgins
World Courier (UK)	**0800-289839**
Sea Containers House	Fax 020-7928 7105
20 Upper Ground, London SE1 9PD	

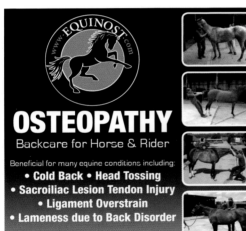
ANIMAL WELFARE

Beech House Veterinary Centre	**01932-220768**
16 Queens Road	Fax 01932-245672
Hersham, Surrey KT12 5NH	Jamie Crittall
Equinost	**020-8922 9870**
Pinewood Studios, Pinewood Road	Jonathan Cohen
Iver Heath, Bucks SL0 0NH	
www.equinost.com	
Hall Place Veterinary Centre	**01628-622086**
Lee Farm, Lee Lane	Fax 01628-634393
Pinkneys Green, Maidenhead, Berks SL6 6PE	Antony Collins
Priory Veterinary Group	**01737-242190**
10 Evesham Road	Fax 01737-222474
Reigate, Surrey RH2 9DF	John Baart
Richard Best Veterinary Surgeon	**01628-825203**
Hill Cottage, Bath Road	Richard Best
Knowle Hill, Reading, Berks RG10 9UU	
Stephen Ware	**01993-811890**
25 Oxford Road	Stephen Ware
Woodstock, Oxon OX20 1UN	
Thorsten Feddern	**01908-366400**
31 Station Road, Bow Brickhill	Fax 01908-365125
Milton Keynes, Bucks MK17 9JU	Thorsten Feddern
Vet On Set	**01962-813554**
Keanter, Stoke Charity Road	Fax 01962-877412
Kings Worthy, Winchester, Hants SO23 7LS	Peter Scott
Vetcetera	**01932-860564**
Brookers Cottage, Downside Common Road	Fax 01932-860564
Downside, Cobham, Surrey KT11 3NP	Adrian O'Meara
www.vetcetera.org.uk	

ANIMALS

1st Choice Animals	**01753-683773**
147 Coppermill Road	Fax 01753-683773
Wraysbury, Middx TW19 5NX	Jill Clark
www.1stchoiceanimals.com	
Al Animals	**01608-683954**
Wattel Hill Farm, Ledwell	Fax 01608-683954
Duns Tew, Oxon OX7 7AN	Liz Thornton
Abbies Animals	**0870-241 8463**
Greystones, Spirthill	Fax 0870-241 8463
Calne, Wilts SN11 9HW	Abbie Withers
Action Stunt Dogs & Animals	**01869-338546**
3 The Chestnuts, Clifton	Fax 01869-338546
Deddington, Oxon OX15 0PE	Gill Raddings
Agricultural Animals	**01460-281207**
Manor Farm, Hambridge	Fax 01460-281207
Langport, Somerset TA10 0AY	Paul Masters

Almost Human Animals	**01452-720459**
Yew Tree Farm	Pam Weaver
Moreton Valence, Glos GL2 7NA	
Amazing Animals	**01608-683389**
Heythrop Zoological Gardens, Heythrop	Fax 01608-683420
Chipping Norton, Oxon OX7 5TU	Jim Clubb
www.amazinganimals.co.uk	
Amey Zoo	**01442-834446**
12 High Street	Mark Amey
Bovingdon, Herts HP3 0HG	
www.ameyzoo.co.uk	
Animal Actors	**020-8654 0450**
95 Ditchling Road	Sam Davies
Brighton, E Sussex BN1 4ST	
Animal Ambassadors	**01635-200900**
Old Forest, Hampstead Norreys Road	Fax 01635-200021
Hermitage, Berks RG18 9SA	Kay Weston
Animal Celebrities	**07836-691110**
45 St Thomas Road	Martin Lacey
Spalding, Lincs PE11 2XT	
Animal Dramatics	**0118-981 5934**
Porkers Cottage, Baughurst Road	Fax 0118-981 1965
Aldermaston, Berks RG7 4PJ	Jackie Rowberry
Animal Enterprises	**01889-504300**
New House Farm, Uttoxeter Road	Fax 01889-504265
Blithbury, Rugeley, Staffs WS15 3HY	Stephen Swinnerton
Animal House	**07973-155671**
8 Burcott Close	Nigel Skeet
Bierton, Bucks HP22 5DH	
Animal Man	**01235-512501**
51 Halse Water	David Corke
Didcot, Oxon OX11 7TX	
Animal Promotions	**01732-762913**
White Rocks Farm, Underriver	Fax 01732-763767
Sevenoaks, Kent TN15 0SL	Sue Woods
Animals Galore	**01342-842400**
208 Smallfield Road	Cindy Newman
Horley, Surrey RH6 9LS	
Animals O-Kay	**01923-291277**
16 Queen Street	Fax 01923-269076
Chipperfield, Herts WD4 9BT	Kay Raven
Aquarep	**01608-683389**
Heythrop Zoological Gardens, Heythrop	Fax 01608-683420
Chipping Norton, Oxon OX7 5TU	Jim Clubb
www.amazinganimals.co.uk	
Aquatic Design Centre	**020-7580 6764**
107-111 Great Portland Street	Fax 020-7631 2033
London W1W 6QG	Nicholas Lloyd

Birds & Animals UK	**01923-681085**
Leavesden Studios, South Way	07977-988188
Leavesden, Herts WD25 7LT	Julie Tottman
www.birdsandanimals.com	
Brookleas Fish Farm	**01235-820500**
East Hendred	Fax 01235-820500
Wantage, Oxon OX12 8LN	Tim Lobb
Celebrity Reptiles	**020-8659 0877**
11 Tramway Close	07958-796210
London SE20 7DF	Martin Southcombe
www.celebrityreptiles.co.uk	
Charlotte Wilde	**07753-641230**
charlotte@charlottewilde.co.uk	Charlotte Wilde
www.charlottewilde.co.uk	
Cop & Dog Services	**01489-893028**
25 Gunners Park	Fax 01489-893028
Bishops Waltham, Hants SO32 1PD	Peter Whitear
Creature Feature	**01387-860648**
Gubhill	Fax 01387-860648
Ae, Dumfries DG1 1RL	David Stewart
Debbie Kaye Horses & Carriages	**01409-211312**
Higher Coombeshead Farm, Virginstow	Fax 01409-211312
Beaworthy, Devon EX21 5EA	Debbie Kaye
The Devils Horsemen	**01296-720854**
Wychwood Stud, Salden	Fax 01296-720855
Mursley, Bucks MK17 0HX	Gerard Naprous
www.thedevilshorsemen.com	
dogs-on-camera.com	**020-8678 9604**
22 Thornton Road	Sandra Strong
London SW12 0LF	
www.dogs-on-camera.com	
Dolbadarn Film Horses	**01286-870277**
High Street	Fax 01286-870277
Llanberis, Gwynedd LL55 4SU	Dylan Jones
Funky Fish	**01932-761878**
Squires Garden Centre, Halliford Road	Fax 01932-244515
Shepperton, Middx TW17 8RU	Nick Yianni

Hasholme Working Horses	**01430-860393**
Hasholme Carr	Geoff Morton
Holme-on-Spalding Moor, York YO43 4BD	

Heart Of England Falconry	**01789-298365**
Hatton Country World, Dark Lane	Fax 01789-298365
Hatton, Warwicks CV35 8XA	Richard Wall

Heythrop Zoological Gardens	**01608-683389**
Heythrop	Fax 01608-683420
Chipping Norton, Oxon OX7 5TU	Jim Clubb
www.amazinganimals.co.uk	

International Centre For Birds Of Prey	**01531-820286**
Newent	Fax 01531-821389
Glos GL18 1JJ	Jemima Parry-Jones

Janimals	**01753-683773**
147 Coppermill Road	Fax 01753-683773
Wraysbury, Middx TW19 5NX	Jill Clark
www.1stchoiceanimals.com	

Lloyd & Rose Buck	**01275-853728**
34 Cleveden Road	Lloyd Buck
Tickenham, Somerset BS21 6RA	

Paradise Wildlife Park	**01992-470490**
White Stubbs Lane	Fax 01992-440525
Broxbourne, Herts EN10 7QA	Steve Sampson

The **Animal Consultants and Trainers Association** comprises of twenty-three of the most highly regarded and experienced companies specialising in the casting, preparation, provision and expert supervision of Animals for filming and photography and was founded in 1989.

A.C.T.A was founded to promote and ensure the highest standards of safety and welfare in the preparation and supervision of Animals for filming and photography, and its members subscribe to and actively promote the following Aims:

www.acta4animals.com

1. At all times to ensure correct planning and preparation for each assignment, prior to any Animal being provided and expertly supervised for film and photography.

2. At all times to examine in detail the requirements of each assignment and to advise prospective clients of the suitability and viability of the assignment, with respect to the capabilities and welfare of the Animal(s) envisaged.

3. At all times to ensure the highest quality Animal husbandry when providing and supervising Animals for filming and photography.

A.C.T.A. members are:

1st Choice Animals	Contact: Jill Clark	Tel: 01753 683773
A1 Animals	Contact: Liz Thornton	Tel: 01608 683954
Academic Animals	Contact: Roger Farr	Tel: +420 325 598 888
Action Stunt Dogs	Contact: Gill Raddings	Tel: 01869 338546
Amazing Animals	Contact: Jim Clubb	Tel: 01608 683389
Amey Zoo	Contact: Mark Amey	Tel: 01442 834446
Animal Celebrities	Contact: Martin Lacey	Tel: 07836 691110
The Animal Company	Contact: Nathan Anderson Dickson	Tel: 0845 050 5805
Animal Man	Contact: David Corke	Tel: 01235 512501
Animalation	Contact: Bob Head	Tel: 01344 890830
Animals Galore	Contact: Cindy Newman	Tel: 01342 842400
Animals O-Kay	Contact: Kay Raven	Tel: 01923 291277
A-Z Animals	Contact: Gerry Cott	Tel: 01372 377111
The Cairngorm Reindeer Centre	Contact: Tilly Smith	Tel: 01479 861228
Celebrity Reptiles	Contact: Martin Southcombe	Tel: 020 8659 0877
Chariots Of Fire	Contact: Amanda Saville	Tel: 01576 610248
Charlotte Wilde	Contact: Charlotte Wilde	Tel: 07753 641230
Creature Feature	Contact: David Stewart	Tel: 01387 860648
Spirit Of The Horse	Contact: Nikki Fossett	Tel: 07899 766395

VETERINARY MEMBERS

Beech House Veterinary Centre	Contact: Jamie Crittall	Tel: 01932 220768
Hall Place Veterinary Centre	Contact: Antony Collins	Tel: 01628 622086
Priory Veterinary Group	Contact: John Baart	Tel: 01737 242190
Stephen Ware	Contact: Stephen Ware	Tel: 01993 811890

147 Coppermill Road, Wraysbury, Middlesex, TW19 5NX
Tel 0845 257 2986   Fax 01753 683773   Email members@acta4animals.co.uk

Screen & Stage SOLUTIONS
SUPPLYING FILM HORSES, STUNT TEAMS & WEAPONS
01690 760248
key@screenstagesolutions.com
www.screenstagesolutions.com

Parrot & Seal	**01206-305040**
East End, Green Farm	Fax 01206-308103
Brightlingsea, Colchester, Essex CO7 0SX	Anthony Bloom
Prop Farm	**01909-723100**
Grange Farm, Elmton	Fax 01909-721465
Creswell, Derbys S80 4LX	Les Powell
R & S Dent	**01923-779603**
Fieldways Farm, Harefield Road	Fax 01923-776256
Rickmansworth, Herts WD3 1PE	Steve Dent
Raphael Falconry	**01986-873928**
	Mike Raphael
Reediehill Deer Farm	**01337-828369**
Auchtermuchty	Fax 01337-827001
Fife KY14 7HS	John Fletcher
Rockwood Animals On Film	**029-2088 5420**
Lewis Terrace, Llanbradach	Martin Winfield
Caerphilly, Mid Glam CF83 3JZ	
Rona Brown & Associates	**01264-781804**
9 King Lane Cottages, Over Wallop	Fax 01264-782471
Stockbridge, Hants SO20 8JF	Rona Brown
Screen & Stage Solutions	**01690-760248**
Ty Coch Farm	Kevin Smith
Penmachno, Conway LL25 0HJ	
www.screenstagesolutions.com	
Special Action Horses	**01344-424531**
Parkview, Maidenhead Road	Fax 01344-360548
Billingbear, Wokingham, Berks RG40 5RR	Tony Smart
Stratford Butterfly Farm	**01789-299288**
Tramway Walk, Swans Nest Lane	Fax 01789-415878
Stratford-upon-Avon, Warwicks CV37 7LS	John Calvert
Sue Clark Animals	**01977-620374**
Timbertops, Jackson Lane	Fax 01977-621039
Wentbridge, Pontefract, W Yorks WF8 3HZ	Sue Clark
West Country Film Horses	**01566-775543**
St Leonards Equitation Centre, Polson	Fax 01566-774926
Launceston, Cornwall PL15 9QR	Andy Reeve

ANIMATICS

MGV	**020-7287 2176**
10 Frith Street	Fax 020-7287 8534
London W1D 3JF	Mark Cookman
Storyboards Animatics UK	**020-7734 1437**
18 Greek Street	Fax 020-7734 1088
London W1D 4JD	Ralph White

ANIMATION

A Large Evil Corporation	**01225-461122**
1 Saville Row	Fax 01225-461133
Bath BA1 2QP	Guy Thomson
A Productions	**0117-929 9005**
52 Old Market Street	Fax 0117-929 9004
Bristol BS2 0ER	Maggie Hughes
Aardman Animation	**0117-984 8485**
Gas Ferry Road	Fax 0117-984 8486
Bristol BS1 6UN	Heather Wright
Acme Animation	**020-8395 5130**
35 Wick Road	Fax 020-8395 5129
Teddington, Middx TW11 9DN	Nick Hellman
www.acmefilms.co.uk	
Adam Inskip Digital Animation	**01992-450060**
16 Croft Walk	Adam Inskip
Wormley, Herts EN10 6LD	
Airside	**020-7354 9912**
339 Upper Street	Fax 020-7354 5529
London N1 0PB	Natalie Wisdom
Animage	**020-7435 3883**
62 Westcroft Close	Fax 020-7435 3883
London NW2 2RR	Ruth Beni
Animation People	**020-8449 1601**
22 Churchmead Close	Fax 020-8449 1601
Barnet, Herts EN4 8UY	Brian Larkin
AnimNation	**07739-385526**
Studio 3A, Gloucester House	Sarah Bird
45 Gloucester Street, Brighton, E Sussex BN1 4EW	
Annix Studios	**01753-656728**
Pinewood Studios, Pinewood Road	Daniel Pickering
Iver Heath, Bucks SL0 0NH	
Architech Animation Studios	**01463-222201**
25 Baron Taylors Street	Alan MacDonald
Inverness IV1 1QG	
Arthur Cox	**0117-953 9788**
16 Whitehouse Street	Hilary Light
Bristol BS3 4AY	

Flying Cameras	01579-344087
Southview, Trehunist Quethiock	Simon Werry
Liskeard, Cornwall PL14 3SD	

Helimanx	01937-833448
Wilton House, Station Road	Don Copley
Tadcaster, N Yorks LS24 9SG	

MPL Aerial Filming Services	01362-684135
Ash Barns, Stone Lane	Mike Parker
Twyford, Norfolk NR20 5NA	
www.mpl-aerialfilming.co.uk	

SIS LIVE	01908-865500
2 Whitehall Avenue, Kingston	Fax 01908-865501
Milton Keynes, Bucks MK10 0AX	Donna Palumbo
www.sislive.tv	

Tenthirteen	01494-729873
60 Sheepfold Lane	Fax 01494-729873
Amersham, Bucks HP7 9EJ	David McKay
www.tenthirteen.co.uk	

AVIATION - AIR CHARTER

Air Charter Service	020-8339 8588
Millbank House, 171-185 Ewell Road	Fax 020-8339 8572
Surbiton, Surrey KT6 6AP	Joel Fenn

air charter

is our business

so when you need a credible logistics solution for your production, whether it is for cast, crew, set or equipment, trust the experts to deliver 24/7...

trust Hunt&Palmer

Media Aviation Division
T +44 1293 558000
F +44 1293 558099
E executive@huntandpalmer.com
www.huntandpalmer.com

Hunt&Palmer®
air charter and travel connections

• Hot Air Ballooning-Aerial Filming

• Cost Effective Stable Platform

• Film, Ad & TV Experience
Including Stunts & Crane Work

• BBC Approved Supplier

• Featured Cloud Hopper & Pilot
In Freelander 2 Advert

Tel: 01275 375300
www.baileyballoons.co.uk

Air Partner   **01293-844888**
Platinum House, Gatwick Road   Fax 01293-844859
Crawley, W Sussex RH10 9RP   Celine Shabbas

Amadeus Aviation   **01737-823707**
Hangar 5, Redhill Aerodrome   Fax 01737-823737
Redhill, Surrey RH1 5JY   Philip Amadeus

Amsair Executive Aviation   **020-3225 5666**
Sterling House, Langston Road   Fax 020-3225 5678
Loughton, Essex IG10 3TS   Daniel Sugar

Business Air Centre   **01452-859500**
Terminal Building, Gloucestershire Airport   Fax 01452-715010
Staverton, Glos GL51 6SR   James Shotton

The Charter Company (UK)   **020-7404 9030**
84 Kingsway   Fax 020-7404 9031
London WC2B 6AE   Neil Turnbull

Cool Air Charter   **01444-831794**
3 Hill Crest Lane, Scaynes Hill   Fax 01444-831048
Haywards Heath, W Sussex RH17 7PH   Christine Preston

Eurojet   **028-9442 2646**
Executive Jet Centre   Fax 028-9442 2640
Belfast International Airport, Belfast BT29 4AB

Harrods Aviation   **01279-665300**
First Avenue   Fax 01279-665389
Stansted Airport, Essex CM24 1QQ

Hunt&Palmer   **01293-558000**
The Tower, Goffs Park Road   Fax 01293-558099
Crawley, W Sussex RH11 8XX   Mark Jenkinson
www.huntandpalmer.com

International Air Charter   **020-8897 8979**
Quayside House, Standard Quay   Fax 020-8897 8969
Faversham, Kent ME13 7BS   Alison Wressell
www.privatejetcharter.com

JetAir   **01293-566040**
3 City Place, Beehive Ring Road   Fax 01293-566099
Gatwick Airport, W Sussex RH6 0PA

London Executive Aviation   **01708-688420**
Stapleford Airport   Jane Gross
Stapleford Tawney, Essex RM4 1SJ

Ocean Sky Jet Centre   **0161-436 6666**
Hangar 7, Faireys Way   Fax 0161-436 3450
Manchester Airport West, Manchester M90 5NE   Lewis Jones

Oxygen 4 Aviation   **01403-782700**
Unit 2, Foundry Court   Fax 01403-237011
Foundry Lane, Horsham, W Sussex RH13 5PY   James Alexis

Premier Aviation (UK)   **01293-852688**
Unit 2, Newhouse Business Centre, Old Crawley Road   Fax 01293-852699
Faygate, Horsham, W Sussex RH12 4RU   Adrian Whitmarsh

Supreme Aviation   **01795-870333**
62 Pennycress Road   Fax 01795-870333
Minster-on-Sea, Kent ME12 3AQ   Hakeem Jimoh

AVIATION - BALLOONS

Aerial Camera Systems (ACS)   **01483-426767**
Innovation House, Douglas Drive   Fax 01483-413900
Godalming, Surrey GU7 1JX   Matthew Coyde
www.acsmedia.com

Bailey Balloons   **01275-375300**
44 Ham Green   Fax 01275-375660
Bristol BS20 0HA   Jo Bailey
www.baileyballoons.co.uk

AVIATION - CO-ORDINATION

Aerial Broadcast ONE   **01305-775050**
17 Rodwell Avenue   Fax 01305-775050
Weymouth, Dorset DT4 8SH   Trevor Bassett Matthews

Aerial-Helicopter Film Services   **01895-833365**
Denham Aerodrome, Hangar Road   Fax 01895-834523
Uxbridge, Middx UB9 5DF   Jeremy Braben
www.helicopterfilm.tv

Aerobatic Displays   **01844-351585**
Wykehams Barn, Sydenham   Fax 01844-351585
Chinnor, Oxon OX39 4LY   Hilary Lamb

BROADCAST - RENTAL

24-7 Drama	**020-8614 8560**
Units 3 & 4, Teddington Business Park	Fax 020-8943 5307
Station Road, Teddington, Middx TW11 9BQ	Graham Hawkins
24-7 North	**0161-877 6700**
The Pie Factory, 101 Broadway	Fax 0161-877 0817
Salford Quays, Manchester M50 2EQ	Matt Turnbull
The 400 Company	**020-8746 1400**
B5/B6 West 12 Studios	Fax 020-8749 3755
2A Askew Crescent, London W12 9DP	Christian Riou
Acorn Film & Television	**028-9024 0977**
13 Fitzwilliam Street	Fax 028-9022 2309
Belfast BT9 6AW	Roger Fitzpatrick
Aerial Camera Systems (ACS)	**01483-426767**
Innovation House, Douglas Drive	Fax 01483-413900
Godalming, Surrey GU7 1JX	Matthew Coyde
www.acsmedia.com	
Alias Smith & Singh	**020-7436 3060**
40-44 Newman Street	Fax 020-7436 3030
London W1T 1QD	Danny Dawson
www.aliashire.co.uk	
ARRI Media	**01895-457100**
3 Highbridge, Oxford Road	Fax 01895-457101
Uxbridge, Middx UB8 1LX	Bill Lovell
Bluefin Television	**020-7622 0870**
70 St Alphonsus Road	Fax 020-7720 7875
London SW4 7AS	Anthony Leake
www.bluefintv.com	
Blueroom AV	**020-7987 2087**
Regatta Point	Richard Brade
Manilla Street, London E14 8JZ	
Boris TV	**01276-61222**
Bridge House, Branksome Park Road	Fax 01276-61549
Camberley, Surrey GU15 2AQ	Christopher Smith
www.boris.tv	
Broadcast RF	**01322-520202**
Unit 16, Acorn Industrial Park	Fax 01322-520204
Crayford Road, Dartford, Kent DA1 4AL	Chris Brandrick
Broadcast Services	**0845-130 3950**
The Coach House, Ruxbury Road	Fax 01932-570443
Chertsey, Surrey KT16 9EP	Peter Scrutton
www.broadcast-services.co.uk	
Broadcast Television Facilities	**0161-926 9808**
Acuba House, Lymm Road	Fax 0161-929 9000
Little Bollington, Altrincham, Manchester WA14 4SY	Robert Foster
www.broadcast-tv.co.uk	
Brownian Motion	**020-7820 8746**
3 Richborne Terrace	Fax 020-7820 8746
London SW8 1AS	Jeff Brown

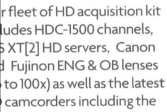

Camera Corps	**01932-592299**
Shepperton Studios, Studios Road	Fax 01932-592674
Shepperton, Middx TW17 0QD	Matt Frost
www.cameracorps.co.uk	
Central Rental	**020-7631 4455**
28 Newman Street	Fax 020-7631 3400
London W1T 1PR	Greg Woznica
www.centralrental.co.uk	
The Cruet Company	**020-8874 2121**
11 Ferrier Street	Fax 020-8874 9850
London SW18 1SN	Will Wilkinson
CueBox London	**0845-880 1270**
Unit 11, Dares Farm	Fax 0845-880 1280
Farnham Road, Ewshot, Surrey GU10 5BB	Ros Ince
www.cuebox.com	
Dan Greenway Minicam Specialist	**020-856 00 856**
dg@dangreenwayltd.co.uk	07711-903990
www.dangreenwayltd.co.uk	Dan Greenway
Decode	**020-8735 9170**
Unit 3, Parkside	Fax 020-8741 8952
Ravenscourt Park, London W6 0UU	Samuel Martin
www.decodeuk.com	
Digital Media Rentals	**0845-607 6635**
179 Wardour Street	Fax 020-7534 3411
London W1F 8WY	Duncan Napier-Bell
www.digitalmediarentals.co.uk	
Dreamtek	**0845-600 6122**
The Orchard, Elvetham Lane	Tristan Blakley
Elvetham Estate, Hartley Wintney, Hants RG27 8AJ	
Electra Film & Television	**020-8232 8899**
Wharf House, Brentwaters Business Park	Fax 020-8232 8877
The Ham, Brentford, Middx TW8 8HQ	Douglas Urquhart
Elite Television	**0113-262 3342**
248 Meanwood Road	Fax 0113-262 3798
Leeds LS7 2HZ	Stuart Josephs
www.elitetv.co.uk	
Extreme Facilities	**020-7801 9111**
Extreme Studios	Fax 020-7801 9222
15-17 Este Road, London SW11 2TL	Andrew Schaale
Film Band	**020-8707 6485**
68 Hanover Avenue	Ghandi El-Chamaa
Feltham, Middx TW13 4JP	
Filmscape Media	**01753-785554**
Pinewood Studios, Pinewood Road	Fax 01753-785953
Iver Heath, Bucks SL0 0NH	Anthony Holt Kevin Harvey
www.filmscapemedia.com	
Finepoint Broadcast	**0800-970 2020**
Hill House, Furze Hill	Fax 0800-970 2030
Kingswood, Surrey KT20 6EZ	Giles Bendig

First Take Autocue   **020-8898 8807**
info@first-take.tv   Chris Myers
www.first-take.tv

Focus24   **020-7033 6555**
30 Hoxton Square   Ben Mitchell
London N1 6NN
www.focus24.tv

Fuel Film & Television   **01923-233956**
30 Kingsfield Road   Fax 01923-224289
Watford, Herts WD19 4PS   Allen Della-Valle
www.fuelfilm.co.uk

GearBox London   **020-8380 7433**
23 Shield Drive, West Cross Industrial Estate   Fax 020-8380 7410
Brentford, Middx TW8 9EX   Richard Eastwood
www.gearbox.com

GearBox Midlands   **01527-854222**
Priory Mill, Castle Road   Fax 01527-857666
Studley, Warwicks B80 7AA
www.gearbox.com

GearBox North   **01772-433144**
Unit 7, Chandlers Business Park   Fax 01772-433177
Talbot Road, Leyland, Lancs PR25 2ZG
www.gearbox.com

GearBox Scotland   **0141-564 2710**
Unit 1, Millennium Court   Fax 0141-564 2719
Burns Street, Glasgow G4 9SA
www.gearbox.com

GearBox South West   **029-2067 0546**
The Television Centre   Fax 029-2067 9408
Culverhouse Cross, Cardiff CF5 6XJ
www.gearbox.com

Gearhouse Broadcast   **0845-820 0000**
Unit 12, Imperial Park   Fax 01923-691499
Imperial Way, Watford, Herts WD24 4PP   Jakki Hewitt

Genesis Plus   **020-7391 9200**
Suffolk House   Fax 020-7391 9201
1-8 Whitfield Place, London W1T 5JU   Tim Banks
www.genesis-plus.com

Green Door Films — 01844-217148
38 Glenham Road — Fax 01844-217148
Thame, Oxon OX9 3WD — John Hadfield
www.greendoorfilms.co.uk

Hammerhead TV Facilities — 020-8646 5511
Unit 19, Liongate Enterprise Park — Fax 020-8646 6163
80 Morden Road, Mitcham, Surrey CR4 4NY — Darrin Dart
www.hammerheadtv.com

Hammerhead TV Facilities — 0131-229 5000
9 Merchiston Mews — Fax 0131-229 2831
Edinburgh EH10 4PE — Phil Mews
www.hammerheadtv.com

Hammerhead TV Facilities — 0141-429 4200
Unit 1, The Tollgate — Fax 0141-429 4211
21 Marine Crescent, Glasgow G51 1HD — Phil Mews
www.hammerheadtv.com

Hammerhead TV Facilities — 0161-431 6400
Unit 2, Rugby Park, Battersea Road — Fax 0161-431 6300
Heaton Mersey, Stockport, Manchester SK4 3EB — John Dardis
www.hammerheadtv.com

Hire A Camera — 01435-873028
Unit 5, Wellbrook Farm — Fax 01435-874841
Berkeley Road, Mayfield, E Sussex TN20 6EH — Sales Team
www.hireacamera.com

The Hire Company (UK) — 0117-927 7473
The Picture House — Fax 0117-923 0862
4 Lower Park Row, Bristol BS1 5BJ — Andy Bennett

The Hiredesk — 020-7255 3455
Suffolk House — Mike Humphries
1-8 Whitfield Place, London W1T 5JU

HotCam — 020-8742 1888
Unit 14, Bell Industrial Estate — Fax 020-8742 8833
50 Cunnington Street, London W4 5HB Vicky McMahon Mary Hoffmann
www.hotcam.co.uk

Hyperactive Broadcast — 01252-519191
5 The Royston Centre, Lynchford Lane — Fax 01252-513939
Ash Vale, Surrey GU12 5PQ — James Gander Liam Wife
www.hyperactivebroadcast.com

Interbroadcast — 020-7580 5524
10-11 Percy Street — Terry Bettles
London W1T 1DN

Kit & Crew — 0845-224 4473
ben@kitandcrew.co.uk — Ben Manning-Wade
www.kitandcrew.co.uk

Kitroom Monkey — 0845-166 2597
Ealing Studios — Oliver Hickey
Ealing Green, London W5 5EP
www.kitroommonkey.co.uk

Electronic Visuals	**01784-483311**
20 Ferry Lane	Fax 01784-483918
Wraysbury, Middx TW19 6HG	Peter Goldman
ERA	**020-7851 7475**
162-170 Wardour Street	Fax 020-7734 6534
London W1F 8ZX	
First Choice Solutions	**01483-302333**
1L Merrow Business Centre, Merrow Lane	Fax 01483-306789
Guildford, Surrey GU4 7WA	Jim Inskip
www.firstchoicesolutions.co.uk	
Frontniche	**01949-851486**
Frontniche Stables, Stone House Farm	Fax 07092-362114
Main Street, Flawborough, Nottingham NG13 9PA	Stephen Bone
GV Multi-Media	**020-8814 5950**
Unit 1, Inwood Business Park	Fax 020-8569 6616
Whitton Road, Hounslow, Middx TW3 2EB	Dominic Hall
Hamlet Video International	**01494-729728**
Maple House, 11 Corinium Business Centre	Fax 01494-723237
Raans Road, Amersham, Bucks HP6 6FB	Stephen Nunney
HD Broadcast	**07801-389649**
81 Christchurch Avenue	Dilip Rudani
Harrow, Middx HA3 8LZ	
Hitachi Kokusai Electric UK	**0845-121 2177**
Windsor House, Britannia Road	Fax 0845-121 2180
Waltham Cross, Herts EN8 7NX	Paddy Roache
IDX Technology Europe	**01753-547692**
Unit 9, Langley Park	Fax 01753-546660
Waterside Drive, Langley, Berks SL3 6EZ	Robert Watson
www.idx-europe.co.uk	
Ikegami Electronics UK	**01932-769700**
Unit E1, Brooklands Close	Fax 01932-769710
Sunbury-on-Thames, Middx TW16 7EB	Ian O'Connor
Jigsaw Systems	**03332-400222**
The Old Mill	Fax 03332-409202
High Church Street, Nottingham NG7 7JA	Lewis Brown
www.jigsaw24.com/broadcast	
JVC Professional Europe	**020-8208 6200**
JVC House, JVC Business Park	Fax 020-8208 6260
12 Priestley Way, London NW2 7BA	Liz Cox
Kramer Electronics UK	**01296-330011**
Unit 2, Premus Business Park	Fax 01296-330055
Coldharbour Way, Aylesbury, Bucks HP19 8AP	Nick Mawer
LEQ	**020-8770 7790**
	Tony Covell
Libra Professional Broadcast	**01527-853305**
The Studios, The Old Vicarage	Fax 01527-852086
Coughton, Warwicks B49 5HU	Richard Whitehouse

Lightning Media	**020-8998 9977**
Unit 32, Sheraton Business Centre	Fax 020-8998 2781
20 Wadsworth Road, Perivale, Middx UB6 7JB	Lee Patel
www.lightningmedia.co.uk	
Lumavec	**01954-260595**
Stanton House, Station Road	Fax 01954-260595
Longstanton, Cambs CB24 3DS	Gill Ashby
Markertek	**020-8687 9700**
Unit 15, Liongate Enterprise Park	Fax 020-8687 9707
Morden Road, Mitcham, Surrey CR4 4NY	Tim Bennett
Microvideo	**01223-834119**
Copley Hill Farm	Fax 01223-834471
Cambridge Road, Cambridge CB22 3GN	Ian Hudson
Mitcorp UK	**020-8380 7400**
23 Shield Drive, West Cross Industrial Estate	Fax 020-8380 7410
Brentford, Middx TW8 9EX	Mark Forth
www.mitcorp.co.uk	
ON-AIR Systems	**0845-094 2612**
131-151 Great Titchfield Street	Fax 0845-094 2613
London W1W 5BB	Mark Errington
Panasonic PBITS	**01344-853747**
Panasonic House, Willoughby Road	Fax 01344-706919
Bracknell, Berks RG12 8FP	Adrian Clark

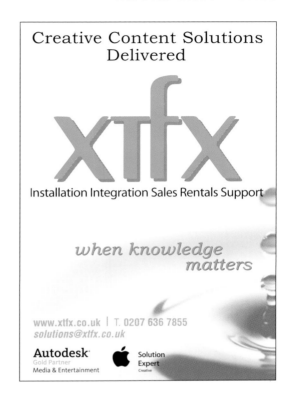

71

PEC Video	**020-7437 4633**
65-66 Dean Street	Fax 020-7025 1320
London W1D 4PL	Derek Morgan
Pharos Communications	**0118-950 2323**
83-85 London Street	Fax 0118-950 2525
Reading, Berks RG1 4QA	Roger Heath
Pixel Power	**01223-721000**
College Business Park	Fax 01223-721111
Coldhams Lane, Cambridge CB1 3HD	Richard Jones
Planet PC	**01274-713400**
The Old School, 690 Bradford Road	Fax 01274-713422
Birkenshaw, W Yorks BD11 2DR	Celia Shaw
Planet Video	**01753-422750**
Pinewood Studios, Pinewood Road	Fax 01753-656683
Iver Heath, Bucks SL0 0NH	Rod Gammons
www.planetvideosystems.co.uk	
PRECO (Broadcast Systems)	**020-8644 4447**
Unit 3, Four Seasons Crescent	Fax 020-8644 0474
Kimpton Road, Sutton, Surrey SM3 9QR	
Prestons	**01684-575486**
103 Worcester Road	Fax 01684-575594
Malvern, Worcs WR14 1EP	John Preston
Proactive UK	**01442-292929**
1 Eastman Way	Fax 01442-292930
Hemel Hempstead, Herts HP2 7DU	Neil Hart
Production Gear	**020-8236 1212**
Studio 2000, 5 Elstree Way	Fax 020-8236 1414
Borehamwood, Herts WD6 1SF	Edward Catton-Orr
Prokit	**020-8995 4664**
Unit 4	Fax 020-8995 4656
111 Power Road, London W4 5PY	Mark Holmes
Quantel	**01635-48222**
31 Turnpike Road	Fax 01635-815815
Newbury, Berks RG14 2NX	Roger Thornton
Raycom	**01789-777040**
Langton House, 19 Village Street	Fax 01789-881330
Harvington, Worcs WR11 8NQ	Chris Pemberton

Root 6	**020-7437 6052**
4 Wardour Mews	Fax 0870-094 0783
London W1F 8AJ	Dave Watson
Sentinel Broadcast	**01344-861566**
79 Qualitas, Roman Hill	Fax 01344-861744
Bracknell, Berks RG12 7QG	Paul Froom
www.sentinelbroadcast.co.uk	
Shootview	**01932-782823**
87 Cadbury Road	Fax 01932-772824
Sunbury-on-Thames, Middx TW16 7LS	Cliff Ford
Snell	**01799-523817**
Business & Technology Centre, Shire Hill	Fax 01799-508209
Saffron Walden, Essex CB11 3AQ	Stephen Hatch
Soft Tel	**0118-984 2151**
Unit 7, Horseshoe Park	Fax 0118-984 3939
Pangbourne, Berks RG8 7JW	Diane Ford
Sony Europe	**01932-816000**
The Heights, Brooklands	Fax 01932-817000
Weybridge, Surrey KT13 0XW	Carl Pring
Stanley Productions	**020-7439 0311**
147 Wardour Street	Fax 020-7437 2126
London W1F 8WD	Steve Langston Mick Pruce
www.stanleysonline.co.uk	
Tektronix UK	**01344-392000**
The Western Peninsula, Western Road	Fax 01344-392001
Bracknell, Berks RG12 1RF	
TNP Broadcast Sales	**01923-712712**
PO Box 2035	Fax 01923-712777
Watford, Herts WD18 9WZ	Howard Rose
Top-Teks	**01895-825619**
Bridge House, Royal Quay	Fax 01895-822232
Park Lane, Harefield, Middx UB9 6JA	Mike Thomas
TV-BAY	**01635-237237**
PO Box 6090	Fax 01635-529966
Newbury, Berks RG14 9BB	Matt Robbins
Van Diemen Films	**01276-61222**
Bridge House, Branksome Park Road	Fax 01276-61549
Camberley, Surrey GU15 2AQ	Christopher Smith
www.vandiemenbroadcast.co.uk	
Verity Systems	**01252-317000**
2 Eastern Road	Fax 01252-316555
Aldershot, Hants GU12 4TD	Keith Skinner
Videobrokers	**+33 6 09 84 13 86**
133 avenue St Michel	Fax +33 1 53 01 29 02
45160 Olivet, France	Alexandre Villegoureix
www.videobrokers.fr	
Visual Impact	**020-8977 1222**
Units 3 & 4, Teddington Business Park	Fax 020-8943 5307
Station Road, Teddington, Middx TW11 9BQ	Tim Sparrock

Vitec Group Communications	01223-815000
7400 Cambridge IQ, Beach Drive	Fax 01223-815001
Waterbeach, Cambridge CB25 9TP	Tracy Robinson

WTS Broadcast	020-8594 3336
Media Park, 40B River Road	Fax 020-8594 3338
Barking, Essex IG11 0DW	Mike Lippert

XTFX	020-7636 7855
12 Stephen Mews	Fax 020-7908 7240
London W1T 1AH	James Hamilton-Hislop
www.xtfx.co.uk	

BROADCAST SYSTEMS INTEGRATION

Dega Broadcast Systems	01256-816220
1 Newton Court, Rankine Road	Fax 01256-843952
Basingstoke, Hants RG24 8GF	John Cleaver

Feltech	01727-834888
Feltech House, 7 Longspring	Fax 01727-848704
St Albans, Herts AL3 6PE	Peter Fell

GAS Electronic Systems	020-7223 1125
72 Chatham Road	Fax 07050-801339
London SW11 6HG	Simon Baker

Planet Video	01753-422750
Pinewood Studios, Pinewood Road	Fax 01753-656683
Iver Heath, Bucks SL0 0NH	Rod Gammons
www.planetvideosystems.co.uk	

SIS LIVE	01908-865500
2 Whitehall Avenue, Kingston	Fax 01908-865501
Milton Keynes, Bucks MK10 0AX	Donna Palumbo
www.sislive.tv	

T4 Group	0845-500 6644
The Farmhouse, Latchford Farm	Fax 0845-500 6645
Latchford, Ware, Herts SG11 1QZ	Paul Vanlint

TTL Video	01737-767655
38 Holmethorpe Avenue	Fax 01737-767665
Redhill, Surrey RH1 2NL	Nigel Cubbage

CAMERA - RENTAL

Aerial Camera Systems (ACS)	01483-426767
Innovation House, Douglas Drive	Fax 01483-413900
Godalming, Surrey GU7 1JX	Matthew Coyde
www.acsmedia.com	

Aimimage Camera Company	020-7482 4340
Unit 5, St Pancras Commercial Centre	Fax 020-7267 3972
63 Pratt Street, London NW1 0BY	Mark Puffett

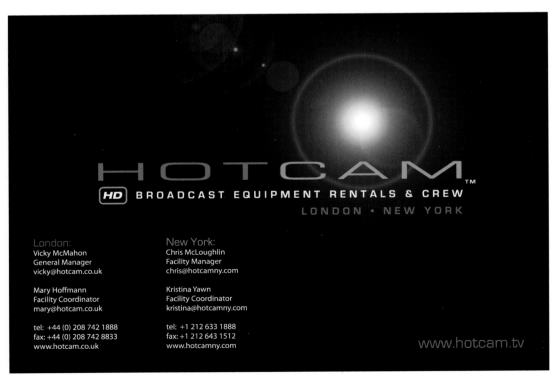

Alias Smith & Singh	020-7436 3060
40-44 Newman Street	Fax 020-7436 3030
London W1T 1QD	Danny Dawson
www.aliashire.co.uk	

ARRI Media	01895-457100
3 Highbridge, Oxford Road	Fax 01895-457101
Uxbridge, Middx UB8 1LX	Philip Cooper

ARRI Rental	0161-736 8034
Units 6-8	Fax 0161-745 8023
Orchard Street Industrial Estate, Manchester M6 6FL	Bob McGrego

Axis London	01932-592244
Shepperton Studios, Studios Road	Fax 01932-592246
Shepperton, Middx TW17 0QD	Paul Carter

Bluefin Television	020-7622 0870
70 St Alphonsus Road	Fax 020-7720 7875
London SW4 7AS	Anthony Leake
www.bluefintv.com	

Boris TV	01276-61222
Bridge House, Branksome Park Road	Fax 01276-61549
Camberley, Surrey GU15 2AQ	Christopher Smith
www.boris.tv	

Brian Drysdale - Steadicam	028-9065 3223
6 Richhill Park	Fax 028-9065 3223
Belfast BT5 6HG	

Broadcast Services   **0845-130 3950**

The Coach House, Ruxbury Road   Fax 01932-570443
Chertsey, Surrey KT16 9EP   Peter Scrutton
www.broadcast-services.co.uk

Broadcast Television Facilities   **0161-926 9808**

Acuba House, Lymm Road   Fax 0161-929 9000
Little Bollington, Altrincham, Manchester WA14 4SY   Robert Foster
www.broadcast-tv.co.uk

Camera Revolution   **01932-592322**

Shepperton Studios, Studios Road   Fax 01932-592202
Shepperton, Middx TW17 0QD   Ian Speed
www.camerarevolution.com

CCD - Camera Crew & Digital   **020-8960 8777**

Pinewood Studios, Pinewood Road   Fax 020-8960 6700
Iver Heath, Bucks SL0 0NH   Zoe Smith

Central Rental   **020-7631 4455**

28 Newman Street   Fax 020-7631 3400
London W1T 1PR   Greg Woznica
www.centralrental.co.uk

Computerised Timelapse   **020-8802 8791**

27 Birstall Road   Maxim Ford
London N15 5EN

Dan Greenway Minicam Specialist	**020-856 00 856**
dg@dangreenwayltd.co.uk	07711-903990
www.dangreenwayltd.co.uk	Dan Greenway
Decode	**020-8735 9170**
Unit 3, Parkside	Fax 020-8741 8952
Ravenscourt Park, London W6 0UU	Samuel Martin
www.decodeuk.com	
Film Band	**020-8707 6485**
68 Hanover Avenue	Ghandi El-Chamaa
Feltham, Middx TW13 4JP	
Filmways	**07770-321940**
hugh.fairs@ntlworld.com	Hugh Fairs
www.underwater-camera.com	
Fuel Film & Television	**01923-233956**
30 Kingsfield Road	Fax 01923-224289
Watford, Herts WD19 4PS	Allen Della-Valle
www.fuelfilm.co.uk	
Genesis Plus	**020-7391 9200**
Suffolk House	Fax 020-7391 9201
1-8 Whitfield Place, London W1T 5JU	Tim Banks
www.genesis-plus.com	
Green Door Films	**01844-217148**
38 Glenham Road	Fax 01844-217148
Thame, Oxon OX9 3WD	John Hadfield
www.greendoorfilms.co.uk	
Hammerhead TV Facilities	**020-8646 5511**
Unit 19, Liongate Enterprise Park	Fax 020-8646 6163
80 Morden Road, Mitcham, Surrey CR4 4NY	Darrin Dart
www.hammerheadtv.com	
Hammerhead TV Facilities	**0131-229 5000**
9 Merchiston Mews	Fax 0131-229 2831
Edinburgh EH10 4PE	Phil Mews
www.hammerheadtv.com	
Hammerhead TV Facilities	**0141-429 4200**
Unit 1, The Tollgate	Fax 0141-429 4211
21 Marine Crescent, Glasgow G51 1HD	Phil Mews
www.hammerheadtv.com	
Hammerhead TV Facilities	**0161-431 6400**
Unit 2, Rugby Park, Battersea Road	Fax 0161-431 6300
Heaton Mersey, Stockport, Manchester SK4 3EB	John Dardis
www.hammerheadtv.com	
Hire A Camera	**01435-873028**
Unit 5, Wellbrook Farm	Fax 01435-874841
Berkeley Road, Mayfield, E Sussex TN20 6EH	Sales Team
www.hireacamera.com	
HotCam	**020-8742 1888**
Unit 14, Bell Industrial Estate	Fax 020-8742 8833
50 Cunnington Street, London W4 5HB	Vicky McMahon Mary Hoffmann
www.hotcam.co.uk	

Hyperactive Broadcast	**01252-519191**
5 The Royston Centre, Lynchford Lane	Fax 01252-513939
Ash Vale, Surrey GU12 5PQ	James Gander Liam Wife
www.hyperactivebroadcast.com	

ICE	**020-7278 0908**
Bridge Wharf	Fax 020-7278 4552
156 Caledonian Road, London N1 9UU	Peter Bryant

Immages	**07860-544417**
www.scubacam4hire.com	Michael Barnes

Kit & Crew	**0845-224 4473**
ben@kitandcrew.co.uk	Ben Manning-Wade
www.kitandcrew.co.uk	

Kitroom Monkey	**0845-166 2597**
Ealing Studios	Oliver Hickey
Ealing Green, London W5 5EP	
www.kitroommonkey.co.uk	

Lightning Media	**020-8998 9911**
Unit 32, Sheraton Business Centre	Fax 020-8998 2781
20 Wadsworth Road, Perivale, Middx UB6 7JB	Lee Patel
www.lightningmedia.co.uk	

The London Filter Company	**020-7735 1900**
Unit 107, Canterbury Court	Fax 020-7820 1718
Kennington Business Park, 1-3 Brixton Road, London SW9 6DE	Carey Duffy
www.camerafilters.co.uk	

MGCR	**0113-257 4834**
Unit E1, St Catherines Business Centre	Mike Gaunt
Broad Lane, Leeds LS13 2TD	

MK-V Europe	**0161-850 0658**
The Pie Factory, 101 Broadway	Fax 0161-850 0729
Salford Quays, Manchester M50 2EQ	Rachael Ingrim

Movietech Camera Rentals	**01753-650007**
Pinewood Studios, Pinewood Road	Fax 01753-650006
Iver Heath, Bucks SL0 0NH	John Buckley
www.movietech.co.uk	

Optical Support	**020-7281 0999**
203 Belgravia Workshops	Fax 020-7561 0115
157-163 Marlborough Road, London N19 4NF	Chris Edwards
www.opticalsupport.co.uk	

Panavision Europe	**020-8839 7333**
Metropolitan Centre, Bristol Road	Fax 020-8839 7300
Greenford, Middx UB6 8GD	Jeff Allen

Panavision Manchester	**0161-872 4766**
Unit 3, Littlers Point	Fax 0161-872 6637
2nd Avenue, Trafford Park, Manchester M17 1LT	Dean Oram

Picture Canning North	**0191-265 0061**
156 Brinkburn Street	Jamie Hutchinson
Newcastle-upon-Tyne NE6 2AR	
www.picturecanningnorth.co.uk	

ROGUE ELEMENT
FILMS   DIGITAL FILM RENTAL

Digital Cinematography Services

DIGITAL FILM RENTAL

- 2D/3D Photography rentals •
- On Set colour timing systems •
- File based digital workflows
  F35/F23/Viper/Arri/5D/7D •
- DPXs • Cineform • H264 • AVCIntra •
- Codex • Stwo • Sony CineTal • 3CP •
- Iridas • Filmlight • Tangent •
- Astro • Full DPX processing Lab •
- Data location truck/facilities •

www.rogueelementfilms.com
+44 7866 447564 UK

Pirate	**020-8930 5000**
Disraeli Road	Fax 020-8930 5001
London NW10 7AX	Michael Ganss
www.pirate.co.uk	
Prime Focus	**020-7565 1000**
37 Dean Street	Shail Shah
London W1D 4PT	
www.primefocusworld.com	
ProVision	**0113-222 8222**
96 Kirkstall Road	Fax 0113-222 8110
Leeds LS3 1HD	Danny Howarth
Rogue Element Films	**07866-447564**
U12 Basepoint, Crab Apple Way	Dan Mulligan
Vale Park, Evesham, Worcs WR11 1GP	
www.rogueelementfilms.com	
South London Video	**020-7720 6464**
70-74 Stewarts Road	Fax 020-7622 3666
London SW8 4DE	Anthony Dow
Super 8 Camera Company	**07973-225506**
10 Granville Gardens	Alan Doyle
London W5 3PA	
Take 2 Film Services	**020-8992 2224**
Unit 10, West Point Trading Estate	Fax 020-8992 2204
Alliance Road, London W3 0RA	Vince Wild

Transmission (TX)	**020-8783 1972**
Shepperton Studios, Studios Road	Fax 01932-592571
Shepperton, Middx TW17 0QD	Steve Lloyd
www.ttx.co.uk	
Video Europe	**020-7494 1818**
8 Golden Square	Fax 020-7494 1717
London W1F 9HY	Matt Marner
www.videoeurope.co.uk	
Video Europe Wales	**029-2059 5111**
The Television Centre	Fax 029-2059 5222
Culverhouse Cross, Cardiff CF5 6XJ	Tom McNally
www.videoeurope.co.uk	
VMI	**020-8922 1222**
Unit 1, Granville Industrial Estate	Fax 020-8922 1114
146-148 Granville Road, London NW2 2LD	Barry Bassett
www.vmi.tv	

CAMERA - RENTAL : DIGITAL FILM

ARRI Media	**01895-457100**
3 Highbridge, Oxford Road	Fax 01895-457101
Uxbridge, Middx UB8 1LX	Philip Cooper
www.arrimedia.com	
Digital Media Rentals	**0845-607 6635**
179 Wardour Street	Fax 020-7534 3411
London W1F 8WY	Duncan Napier-Bell
www.digitalmediarentals.co.uk	
Movietech Camera Rentals	**01753-650007**
Pinewood Studios, Pinewood Road	Fax 01753-650006
Iver Heath, Bucks SL0 0NH	John Buckley
www.movietech.co.uk	
Red Digital Cinema	**01753-785454**
Pinewood Studios, Pinewood Road	Fax 01753-785453
Iver Heath, Bucks SL0 0NH	Alan Piper
Rogue Element Films	**07866-447564**
U12 Basepoint, Crab Apple Way	Dan Mulligan
Vale Park, Evesham, Worcs WR11 1GP	
www.rogueelementfilms.com	
Video Europe	**020-7494 1818**
8 Golden Square	Fax 020-7494 1717
London W1F 9HY	Matt Marner
www.videoeurope.co.uk	
Video Europe Wales	**029-2059 5111**
The Television Centre	Fax 029-2059 5222
Culverhouse Cross, Cardiff CF5 6XJ	Tom McNally
www.videoeurope.co.uk	

CAMERA - RENTAL : HIGH SPEED

Green Door Films	01844-217148
38 Glenham Road	Fax 01844-217148
Thame, Oxon OX9 3WD	John Hadfield
www.greendoorfilms.co.uk	

Hyperactive Broadcast	01252-519191
5 The Royston Centre, Lynchford Lane	Fax 01252-513939
Ash Vale, Surrey GU12 5PQ	James Gander Liam Wife
www.hyperactivebroadcast.com	

Lake Image Systems	01442-892700
The Forum, Icknield Way	Fax 01442-892792
Tring, Herts HP23 4JX	David Rudeforth

Pirate	020-8930 5000
Disraeli Road	Fax 020-8930 5001
London NW10 7AX	Michael Ganss
www.pirate.co.uk	

CAMERA - RENTAL : MINICAM

Bluefin Television	020-7622 0870
70 St Alphonsus Road	Fax 020-7720 7875
London SW4 7AS	Anthony Leake
www.bluefintv.com	

Dan Greenway Minicam Specialist	020-856 00 856
dg@dangreenwayltd.co.uk	07711-903990
www.dangreenwayltd.co.uk	Dan Greenway

Prime Television	020-8969 6122
Unit 7	Fax 020-8969 6144
Latimer Road, London W10 6RQ	Chris Earls
www.primetv.com	

Skarda - Miniature Cameras	020-7734 7776
7 Portland Mews	Fax 020-7734 1360
London W1F 8JQ	Martin Davidson

VMI	020-8922 1222
Unit 1, Granville Industrial Estate	Fax 020-8922 1114
146-148 Granville Road, London NW2 2LD	Barry Bassett
www.vmi.tv	

CAMERA - SALE

ARRI (GB)	01895-457000
2 Highbridge, Oxford Road	Fax 01895-457001
Uxbridge, Middx UB8 1LX	

Leica Geosystems	01908-256500
Davy Avenue, Knowlhill	Fax 01908-256509
Milton Keynes, Bucks MK5 8LB	Stephen Cox

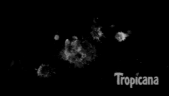

Lightning Media   020-8998 9977
Unit 32, Sheraton Business Centre   Fax 020-8998 2781
20 Wadsworth Road, Perivale, Middx UB6 7JB   Lee Patel
www.lightningmedia.co.uk

The London Filter Company   020-7735 1900
Unit 107, Canterbury Court   Fax 020-7820 1718
Kennington Business Park, 1-3 Brixton Road, London SW9 6DE   Carey Duffy
www.camerafilters.co.uk

Movietech Camera Rentals   01753-650007
Pinewood Studios, Pinewood Road   Fax 01753-650006
Iver Heath, Bucks SL0 0NH   John Buckley
www.movietech.co.uk

Planet Video   01753-422750
Pinewood Studios, Pinewood Road   Fax 01753-656683
Iver Heath, Bucks SL0 0NH   Rod Gammons
www.planetvideosystems.co.uk

Red Digital Cinema   01753-785454
Pinewood Studios, Pinewood Road   Fax 01753-785453
Iver Heath, Bucks SL0 0NH   Alan Piper

Van Diemen Films   01276-61222
Bridge House, Branksome Park Road   Fax 01276-61549
Camberley, Surrey GU15 2AQ   Christopher Smith
www.vandiemenbroadcast.co.uk

Videobrokers   +33 6 09 84 13 86
133 avenue St Michel   Fax +33 1 53 01 29 02
45160 Olivet, France   Alexandre Villegoureix
www.videobrokers.fr

Vision Research   01234-834850
Bedford i-lab, Priory Business Park   Fax 01234-834851
Stannard Way, Bedford MK44 3RZ   John Hannaford

CAMERA & ARTISTE FLYING-WIRE SYSTEMS

Aerial Camera Systems (ACS)   01483-426767
Innovation House, Douglas Drive   Fax 01483-413900
Godalming, Surrey GU7 1JX   Matthew Coyde
www.acsmedia.com

Cev-Cam Corporation   01753-522219
Black Potts, Pococks Lane   07552-698621
Eton, Windsor, Berks SL4 6HW   Kevin Welch
www.cev-cam.com

Flywire   020-8522 4347
Unit 7, Sugar House Business Centre   Gavin Weatherall
24 Sugar House Lane, London E15 2QS
www.flywiretrp.co.uk

Specialist Camera Systems	01753-785352
Pinewood Studios, Pinewood Road	07767-775760
Iver Heath, Bucks SL0 0NH	Kevin Mathews
www.specialist-wire-rigs.co.uk	

CAMERA 3D & 360 SPHERICAL SYSTEMS

Transmission TX	020-8783 1972
Shepperton Studios, Studios Road	Fax 01932-592571
Shepperton, Middx TW17 0QD	Steve Lloyd
www.ttx.co.uk	

CAMERA SUPPORT SYSTEMS

Aerial Camera Systems (ACS)	01483-426767
Innovation House, Douglas Drive	Fax 01483-413900
Godalming, Surrey GU7 1JX	Matthew Coyde
www.acsmedia.com	
Camera Dynamics	01284-752121
Western Way	Fax 01284-750560
Bury St Edmunds, Suffolk IP33 3TB	Peter Harman
The Camera Store	020-8891 8910
Unit 2, Heathlands Close	Fax 020-8891 8902
Twickenham, Middx TW1 4BP	Tim Highmoor
High Level TV	0845-094 4640
Building D1, Fairoaks Airport	Fax 0845-094 4670
Chobham, Surrey GU24 8HU	Ian Leslie
www.highlevel.tv	
Miller Fluid Heads (Europe)	07973-642555
Unit A2, Ford Lane Industrial Estate	Mike Lippmann
Ford, Arundel, W Sussex BN18 0DF	
Ronford Baker	020-8428 5941
Braziers, Oxhey Lane	Fax 020-8428 4743
Watford, Herts WD19 5RJ	Jeff Lawrence
www.ronfordbaker.co.uk	

CAMERA TRACKING RAIL SYSTEMS

Aerial Camera Systems (ACS)	01483-426767
Innovation House, Douglas Drive	Fax 01483-413900
Godalming, Surrey GU7 1JX	Matthew Coyde
www.acsmedia.com	
Camera Corps	01932-592299
Shepperton Studios, Studios Road	Fax 01932-592674
Shepperton, Middx TW17 0QD	Matt Frost
www.cameracorps.co.uk	

CAMERA TRACKING VEHICLES

99 Cars   01923-266373
Hyde Meadow Farm, Hyde Lane   Fax 01923-260852
Hemel Hempstead, Herts HP3 8SA   David Hammatt
www.nineninecars.com

Action Vehicles   0845-888 7000
Hangar 5, Redhill Aerodrome   Darren Litten Gary Litten
Redhill, Surrey RH1 5JY
www.actionvehicles.com

Advanced Camera Car Systems   01895-833365
Denham Aerodrome, Hangar Road   Fax 01895-834523
Uxbridge, Middx UB9 5DF   Jeremy Braben
www.advancedcameracars.com

Aerial Camera Systems (ACS)   01483-426767
Innovation House, Douglas Drive   Fax 01483-413900
Godalming, Surrey GU7 1JX   Matthew Coyde
www.acsmedia.com

All Terrain Camera Tracking   07979-026024
Adelphi House, Adelphi Gardens   Guy Dewdney
Slough, Berks SL1 2RG

Anglo American Filming Vehicles   0115-985 0986
Kings Meadow Campus   Fax 0115-985 0986
Lenton Lane, Nottingham NG7 2NR   Wayne Ridal

Barbour All Terrain Tracking   01620-892189
Lyndhurst West, Dirleton Road   Fax 0131-777 8036
North Berwick, E Lothian EH39 5DF   Duncan Barbour

Bickers Action   01449-761300
Ivy Farm Workshops, High Street   Fax 01449-760614
Coddenham, Ipswich, Suffolk IP6 9QX   Paul Bickers

HD On The Move   01395-272411
Osbourne House, The Strand   Michael Wright
Lympstone, Exmouth, Devon EX8 5JS

MGM Cars   020-8324 2664
Elstree Studios, Shenley Road   Fax 020-8324 2345
Borehamwood, Herts WD6 1JG   Ben Dillon Tom Dillon
www.mgmcars.com

Off Trax   020-8232 8822
Wharf House, Brentwaters Business Park   Fax 020-8232 8877
The Ham, Brentford, Middx TW8 8HQ   Crispin Kyle

SIS LIVE   01908-865500
2 Whitehall Avenue, Kingston   Fax 01908-865501
Milton Keynes, Bucks MK10 0AX   Donna Palumbo
www.sislive.tv

Track That   07941-234254
  Lee Bagley

Trackshot	**07802-264486**
181 Walderslade Road	Robert Boggis
Chatham, Kent ME5 0ND	

Wheel 2 Reel	**01992-450209**
40 New Road	Fax 01992-450209
Broxbourne, Herts EN10 7LW	Paul Weekes

CASES

5 Star Cases	**0845-500 0555**
Broadend Industrial Estate, Broadend Road	Fax 01945-427015
Wisbech, Cambs PE14 7BQ	Keith Sykes

ABS Cases	**020-7474 0333**
Unit 2, Pylon Trading Estate	Fax 020-7473 2548
Cody Road, London E16 4SP	Barry Smith

Amazon Cases	**020-8568 1881**
Unit 11, Worton Hall Industrial Estate	Fax 020-8568 1141
Worton Road, Isleworth, Middx TW7 6ER	Peter Johnston

Appleworld Distribution	**01753-422744**
Pinewood Studios, Pinewood Road	Fax 01753-656683
Iver Heath, Bucks SL0 0NH	Rod Aaron
www.appleworld-distribution.com	

Buster Cases	**0161-761 2040**
Unit 16C, Pimhole Business Park	Fax 0161-761 6040
Pimhole Road, Bury, Lancs BL9 7ET	James Wicks
www.bustercases.com	

Case Design	**01753-889969**
Chiltern Hill	Fax 01753-889855
Chalfont St Peter, Bucks SL9 9UQ	Charles Smith

CP Cases	**020-8568 1881**
Unit 11, Worton Hall Industrial Estate	Fax 020-8568 1141
Worton Road, Isleworth, Middx TW7 6ER	Fiona Haggerty

Doggybags	**020-8695 5686**
Unit B2, Broomsleigh Business Park	Fax 020-8695 9412
Worsley Bridge Road, London SE26 5BN	Jeff Hawkins

Justin Case Company	**0131-555 4466**
23 Water Street	Fax 0131-555 6901
Edinburgh EH6 6SU	Allan Brereton

Kaat Cases	**0191-237 6888**
Unit 13B, Delaval Trading Estate	Fax 0191-237 6999
Seaton Delaval, Whitley Bay, Tyne & Wear NE25 0QT	Peter Simpson

KT Systems (UK)	**023-8027 0981**
124 Brownhill Road	Fax 0560-209 3002
Chandlers Ford, Hants SO53 2FR	Ian Fraser

Lemsford Cases	**01707-323725**
24 Hyde Way	Fax 01707-373059
Welwyn Garden City, Herts AL7 3UQ	Phil Davis

Oakleigh Cases	**01707-655011**
Unit 10, The Summit Centre	Fax 01707-646447
Summit Road, Potters Bar, Herts EN6 3QW	Edward Nicorici

Peli Products (UK)	**01457-869999**
Peli House, Peakdale Road	Fax 01457-869966
Brookfield, Glossop, Derbys SK13 6LQ	Craig Hastings

QED Design & Manufacture	**01622-859988**
Fairbourne Manor, Harrietsham	Fax 01622-859119
Maidstone, Kent ME17 1LH	Andrew Richardson

Road Cases	**0114-272 8666**
Unit 15B, Clarence Works	Fax 0114-272 8666
Effingham Road, Sheffield S4 7YS	Eddie Pulford

Seddon MFG	**01924-410040**
Swallow Street	Fax 01924-411944
Heckmondwike, W Yorks WF16 0LA	Richard Seddon

TVCases	**01902-764000**
9 Elmsdale, Wightwick	Fax 0871-714 6633
Wolverhampton, W Midlands WV6 8ED	Tim Jones

Zero Cases (UK)	**0121-558 2011**
Unit 5, Alpha Park	Fax 0121-565 2115
Bevan Way, Smethwick, W Midlands B66 1BZ	Mike Dimmock

CASTING

Pippa Ailion	**020-8670 4816**
3 Towton Road	Fax 020-8670 4816
London SE27 9EE	

Dorothy Andrew	**0151-737 4044**
Campus Manor	Fax 0151-737 4006
Childwall Abbey Road, Liverpool L16 0JP	

Maureen Bewick	**020-8450 1604**
104A Dartmouth Road	
London NW2 4HB	

Hannah Birkett	**020-8960 2848**
123 Hanover Road	Fax 020-8960 2848
London NW10 3DN	

At Home Catering   01932-862026

40 High Street   Marilyn Newman
Cobham, Surrey KT11 3EB

Big Portion   01753-542631

23 Kennett Road   Fax 01753-592698
Langley, Berks SL3 8EQ   Ronnie Aujla

Blas Ar Fwyd   01492-640215

25 Heol Yr Orsaf   Fax 01492-642215
Llanrwst, Conwy LL26 0BT   Deiniol ap Dafydd

Bread & Honey Catering   020-8964 5255

Unit 3   Fax 020-8963 1726
13-15 Sunbeam Road, London NW10 6JP   Rob Voce
www.breadandhoney.net

Cafe Cio   01422-249482

Holdsworth Hall, 37 Holdsworth Road
Holmefield, Halifax, W Yorks HX2 9TB

The Catering Company   07973-499641

12 Claycorn Court, Station Way   Vincent Morse
Claygate, Surrey KT10 0QR
www.thecateringcompany.uk.com

Celestine Catering   01494-882479

Pentire House, Park Lane   Fax 01494-882479
Lane End, High Wycombe, Bucks HP14 3LB   Paul Roche

Chefs On Location	**01932-788430**
Unit E, Manor Farm	Fax 01932-788430
Charlton Road, Shepperton, Middx TW17 0RJ	Ian Kluth
Chorley Bunce	**0845-308 0062**
2 Mill Lane, Pannal	Fax 01423-810775
Harrogate, N Yorks HG3 1JX	Mark Bunce
Clarkson Catering	**020-8500 2431**
45 Colvin Gardens	Fax 020-8252 8268
Hainault, Essex IG6 2LH	Mark Soar
Crazy Chefs TV & Film Catering	**0161-286 8482**
940 Chester Road	Peter Craig
Stretford, Manchester M32 0PA	
Crew Catering	**07836-636252**
14 Victoria Street	Fax 01753-574878
Slough, Berks SL1 1PR	Vince Jordan
www.crewcatering.com	
Delicious Film Catering	**07823-880444**
4B Jebb Street	Michele Gould
London E3 2TL	
Dick Conisbee's Take Five	**01442-259560**
1 Woodfield Gardens, Leverstock Green	Fax 01442-259560
Hemel Hempstead, Herts HP3 8LZ	Dick Conisbee
Eat To The Beat	**01494-790700**
Preston Hill	Mary Shelley-Smith
Chesham, Bucks HP5 3HE	
Eat Your Heart Out Catering	**020-7289 9446**
The Basement	Fax 020-7266 3160
108A Elgin Avenue, London W9 2HD	Kim Davenport
En Route Catering	**028-9039 2183**
11 Kingscourt	Austin Sheeran
Belfast BT10 0AF	
Executive Catering	**01753-650103**
PO Box 3405	Fax 01753-655899
Iver, Bucks SL0 9WX	Ian Beagle
Fayre Do's	**020-7237 6691**
Unit 7, The Tower Workshops	Fax 020-7252 2851
Riley Road, London SE1 3DG	Annie Foley Jamie Cook
www.fayredos.co.uk	
Fill Your Boots Location Catering	**01276-855501**
60 Chertsey Road	Mat Beadle
Chobham, Surrey GU24 8PJ	
Food For Thought	**01934-842801**
Fuchsia Cottage, Hollow Road	Fax 01934-842801
Shipham, Somerset BS25 1TJ	Jules Shergold
Glenns Star Catering	**020-8397 7921**
31 Ellingham Road	Glenn Sheppard
Chessington, Surrey KT9 2JA	

Jack Murphy	**07904-272985**
45 Ifield Road	
London SW10 9AX	

Pineapple Agency	**020-7241 6601**
Montgomery House	Fax 020-7241 3006
159-161 Balls Pond Road, London N1 4BG	David Paton
www.pineappleagency.com	

Caroline Pope	**020-7722 4468**
177 Gloucester Avenue	Fax 020-7722 4468
London NW1 8LA	

Paul Roberts	**07970-256532**

Ryan Francois' Swing X-Treme	**020-7557 6654**
Dancers Inc, INC Space	07747-030422
9-13 Grape Street, London WC2H 8ED	Ryan Francois
www.ryanfrancois.com	

Sophies People	**0870-787 6446**
40 Mexfield Road	Fax 0870-787 6447
London SW15 2RQ	Sophie Pyecroft

United Production	**020-7498 6563**
6 Shaftesbury Mews	Lyndon Lloyd
London SW4 9BP	

CLEANING SERVICES

Chrispy Clean	**01932-858171**
25 Pear Tree Road	Fax 01932-858171
Addlestone, Surrey KT15 1SR	Debbie Millis
www.chrispyclean.co.uk	

COLLECTION ACCOUNT MANAGEMENT

Compact Collections	**020-7874 7480**
8-12 Camden High Street	Fax 020-7383 7868
London NW1 0JH	Alun Tyers

National Film Trustee Company   020-7242 3831
44-45 Chancery Lane   Fax 020-7242 6764
London WC2A 1JB

COMMUNICATIONS

2CL Communications   023-8033 6411
Unit C, Woodside Trade Centre   Fax 023-8072 0038
Parham Drive, Eastleigh, Hants SO50 4NU   Mike Baker

AAA Wavevend Radio Communications   020-7266 1280
17B Pindock Mews   Fax 020-7266 1290
London W9 2PY   Melvin Lind
www.wavevend.co.uk

Audiolink   020-8955 1101
17 Iron Bridge Close   Fax 020-8955 1111
London NW10 0UF   Andrew Morgan John Morgan
www.audiolink.co.uk

Audiolink   01753-656692
Pinewood Studios, Pinewood Road   Fax 020-8955 1111
Iver Heath, Bucks SL0 0NH   Andrew Morgan John Morgan
www.audiolink.co.uk

Communication & Surveillance   020-7486 3885
3 Portman Square   Fax 020-7486 2655
London W1H 6LB   Lee Marks

Communication & Technical Services   020-7252 1849
17 Pages Walk   Fax 020-7252 3241
London SE1 4SB   Loraine Kitcher

Event Communication Services   01256-474734
Unit D, Loddon Business Centre   Fax 01256-473370
Roentgen Road, Basingstoke, Hants RG24 8NG   Simon Brown

Headset Services   01273-234181
7 Cecil Pashley Way, Shoreham Airport   Fax 01273-234190
Shoreham-by-Sea, W Sussex BN43 5FF

London Communications   020-7483 6400
134 Gloucester Avenue   Fax 020-7483 6401
London NW1 8JA   Paul Rawlings

The Loop Communication Agency   0117-311 2040
Suite 302 QC30   Fax 0117-311 2041
30 Queen Charlotte Street, Bristol BS1 4HJ   Kami Lamakan

Melvin Lind Radio Communications   020-7266 1280
17B Pindock Mews   Fax 020-7266 1290
London W9 2PY   Melvin Lind
www.wavevend.co.uk

Radio Europe   01582-481114
Communications House, 17-21 Hastings Street   Fax 01582-481115
Luton, Beds LU1 5BE   John French

Radio Links Communications	**01480-217220**
Eaton House, Great North Road	Fax 01480-406667
Eaton Socon, Cambs PE19 8EG	Jenny Griffiths
Radiocoms Systems	**020-8680 1585**
170A Oval Road	Fax 020-8686 9433
East Croydon, Surrey CR0 6BN	Mark Blythe
Relcom Communications	**020-8965 2333**
Unit 1, Oliver Business Park	Fax 020-8965 2323
Oliver Road, London NW10 7JB	Jez Alexander
www.relcom.co.uk	
Riedel Communications	**01753-785805**
Pinewood Studios, Pinewood Road	Fax 01753-785806
Iver Heath, Bucks SL0 0NH	Simon Beesley
www.riedel.net	
Rocket Radio	**01462-675481**
Unit 1, Business Centre West	Mark Russell
Avenue One, Letchworth, Herts SG6 2HB	
Shoot Communications	**028-9046 6300**
B114 Portview Trading Estate	Fax 028-9046 6331
310 Newtownards Road, Belfast BT4 1HE	Chris Patterson
Wall To Wall Communications	**020-8770 1007**
Unilink House, 21 Lewis Road	Fax 020-8770 9700
Sutton, Surrey SM1 4BR	Laura Dagg

COMPLETION GUARANTORS

Film Finances	**020-7629 6557**
14-15 Conduit Street	Fax 020-7491 7530
London W1S 2XJ	James Shirras
International Film Guarantors	**020-7636 8855**
19 Margaret Street	Fax 020-7323 9356
London W1W 8RR	Luke Randolph

COMPUTER - RENTAL

Compuhire	**020-3137 0599**
mark@compuhire.com	Fax 020-8819 6010
www.compuhire.com	Mark Jordan
Digital Media Rentals	**0845-607 6635**
179 Wardour Street	Fax 020-7534 3411
London W1F 8WY	Duncan Napier-Bell
www.digitalmediarentals.co.uk	
Hire Intelligence	**0845-600 7272**
Unit 5, Acton Park Estate	Fax 020-8740 4004
The Vale, London W3 7QE	Jon Richards
www.hire-intelligence.co.uk	
MicroRent	**01494-768768**
Unit 6, The Gateway Centre, Coronation Road	Fax 01494-768700
Cressex Business Park, High Wycombe, Bucks HP12 3SU	Jinny Lambert
Rent IT	**0800-298 5186**
Geoscan House, Denmore Industrial Estate	Fax 01224-853101
Bridge Of Don, Aberdeen AB23 8JW	Hamish Forbes
SD TEC	**01753-639000**
The Coach House, Pinewood Studios	Fax 01753-639003
Pinewood Road, Iver Heath, Bucks SL0 0NH	Laurence Sargent
www.sd-tec.com	
Universal Rentals	**020-7720 8787**
Unit 31, Spaces Business Centre	Fax 020-7627 4586
Ingate Place, London SW8 3NS	Mark Stiles-Winfield
www.universalrentals.co.uk	

COMPUTER & IT SYSTEMS & SUPPORT

4S Systems	**01932-592345**
Shepperton Studios, Studios Road	Fax 01932-568448
Shepperton, Middx TW17 0QD	David Crane
AA Mac	**0844-357 9879**
110 Stafford Road	Fax 020-8647 0330
Wallington, Surrey SM6 9AY	Kerrie Lee
Appleworld Distribution	**01753-422744**
Pinewood Studios, Pinewood Road	Fax 01753-656683
Iver Heath, Bucks SL0 0NH	Rod Aaron
www.appleworld-distribution.com	
Computers Unlimited	**020-8200 8282**
Technology Park	Fax 020-8200 3788
Colindeep Lane, London NW9 6BX	James Sanson
Jigsaw Systems	**03332-400222**
The Old Mill	Fax 03332-409202
High Church Street, Nottingham NG7 7JA	Lewis Brown
www.jigsaw24.com/broadcast	
Mac Universe	**01753-422750**
Pinewood Studios, Pinewood Road	Fax 01753-656683
Iver Heath, Bucks SL0 0NH	Rod Gammons
www.macuniverse.com	
Moviesoft	**020-7060 9025**
26 York Street	Fax 0845-094 6061
London W1U 6PZ	Francois Farrugia
www.moviesoft.co.uk	
NetTel Media Services	**01920-443820**
Unit 15, Crane Mead Business Park	Fax 01920-487350
Crane Mead, Ware, Herts SG12 9PZ	Jason Panayiotou
OptivITy	**01753-651656**
Pinewood Studios, Pinewood Road	Fax 01753-651653
Iver Heath, Bucks SL0 0NH	Peter Bhachu
SD TEC	**01753-639000**
The Coach House, Pinewood Studios	Fax 01753-639003
Pinewood Road, Iver Heath, Bucks SL0 0NH	Laurence Sargent
www.sd-tec.com	

COMPUTER & ON-SCREEN GRAPHICS

Compuhire	**020-3137 0599**
mark@compuhire.com	Fax 020-8819 6010
www.compuhire.com	Mark Jordan
pleasefindattached	**0845-644 1874**
54 Chertsey Road	Fax 020-8891 4537
Twickenham, Middx TW1 1JQ	Stephen Holland

COMPUTER BUDGETING & SCHEDULING SOFTWARE

KAI Computer Services	**020-7383 3700**
Greendon House	John Chang
7C Bayham Street, London NW1 0EY	
Moviesoft	**020-7060 9025**
26 York Street	Fax 0845-094 6061
London W1U 6PZ	Francois Farrugia
www.moviesoft.co.uk	
Open Brolly	**01309-678100**
Horizon-Scotland, The Enterprise Park	Geoff Wilcock
Forres, Moray IV36 2AB	
Sargent-Disc	**01753-630300**
The Coach House, Pinewood Studios	Fax 01753-655881
Pinewood Road, Iver Heath, Bucks SL0 0NH	Laurence Sargent
www.sargent-disc.com	
ScheduALL	**020-7636 0707**
Princess House	Fax 020-7436 3555
50 Eastcastle Street, London W1W 8EA	Barry Lyne
The Screenwriters Store	**0845-094 6061**
Unit 3.02, Lafone House, The Leathermarket	Fax 0845-094 3846
11-13 Weston Street, London SE1 3HN	Rinaldo Quacquarini

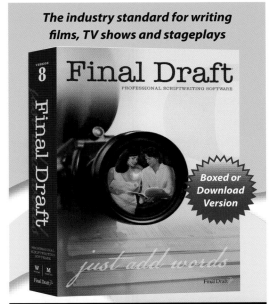

CONSTRUCTION

3D Creations	**01493-652055**
9A Bells Road	Fax 01493-443124
Gorleston, Norfolk NR31 6BB	Ian Westbrook
www.3dcreations.co.uk	
3D Set Company	**0161-273 8831**
8 Temperance Street	Fax 0161-273 6786
Ardwick, Manchester M12 6HR	Tony Walsh
3rd Generation Sets	**01932-226341**
Halliford Studios, Manygate Lane	Fax 01932-246336
Shepperton, Middx TW17 9EG	Callum Andrews Rigby Andrews
www.hallifordfilmstudios.co.uk	
A Construction Production	**07971-009015**
9 Alpha Street	Cameron Eccles
London SE15 4NX	
www.aconstructionproduction.com	
Advanced Fabrications	**020-8795 1188**
500 Sunleigh Road	Fax 020-8795 1171
Wembley, Middx HA0 4NF	Michael Wright
ADze Construction	**07702-241246**
The Garth, Marriotts Avenue	Paul Sansom
South Heath, Bucks HP16 9QN	
Alan King Construction	**01449-674126**
29 Old Street, Haughley	Fax 01449-674126
Stowmarket, Suffolk IP14 3NT	Alan King
Andy Knight Set Construction	**020-7252 5252**
2-6 Occupation Road	Fax 020-7252 5111
London SE17 3BE	Andy Knight
Armordillo Design & Construction	**01989-566102**
Unit 10, Newent Business Park	Rod Vass
Newent, Glos GL18 1DZ	
ATV Scenic Services	**01603-745892**
12 West End	Fax 01603-745892
Old Costessey, Norwich NR8 5AG	Nigel Rust
Brandon Thatchers Film Services	**0845-260 0899**
info@brandonthatchers.co.uk	Fax 0871-989 6378
www.brandonthatchers.co.uk	Dicken Warner
Brilliant Stages	**01462-455366**
Unit 2, Hillgate	Fax 01462-436219
Hitchin, Herts SG4 0RY	Tony Bowern
Canning Conveyor	**01909-486166**
Sandy Lane Industrial Estate, Sandy Lane	Fax 01909-500638
Worksop, Notts S80 1TN	Andrew Canning
www.canningconveyor.co.uk	
Concept Staging	**01282-777600**
Wellington Mill, Ribble Street	Fax 01282-777602
Padiham, Burnley, Lancs BB12 8DQ	Gary Hilton
www.conceptstaging.co.uk	

Construct Scenery	**07961-428510**
Unit 8, Boundary Business Centre	Fax 0871-989 5820
92-94 Church Road, Mitcham, Surrey CR4 3TD	Warren Lever
www.constructscenery.co.uk	

Creffields Timber & Boards	**0118-945 3533**
Unit 6, Marcus Close	Fax 0118-945 3633
Tilehurst, Reading, Berks RG30 4EA	Nigel Creffield
www.creffields.co.uk	

Cutting Edge	**020-8522 0886**
22 Sugar House Lane	Fax 020-8522 0586
London E15 2QS	Andrew Crimin

D:D Set Construction	**07866-758285**
Trinity Mews	David Deacon
Cambridge Gardens, London W10 6JH	

DRS Construction	**020-7231 7067**
Unit J210, Tower Bridge Business Complex	Fax 020-7231 7635
100 Clements Road, London SE16 4DG	Jono Moles

Dunnford	**01707-335558**
43 Elmwood	Roger Tyrrell
Welwyn Garden City, Herts AL8 6LD	

Estdale Scenex	**01895-233000**
Island Site, Eskdale Road	Fax 01895-233001
Uxbridge, Middx UB8 2RT	Andy Ivey
www.estdale.tv	

LEIGH GILBERT

FILM & TELEVISION SET
CONSTRUCTION

TEL:01628 669388 / 07836 580222

Fabry Trading	**01784-433962**
Unit 1, Omega Way	Fax 01784-437895
Thorpe Industrial Estate, Egham, Surrey TW20 8RD	David Gray
www.fabrytrading.com	
Factory Settings	**020-8988 1418**
Unit B	Lucien Mansell
97 Lea Bridge Road, London E10 7QL	
First Imperial Services	**01753-656779**
Pinewood Studios, Pinewood Road	Fax 01753-785679
Iver Heath, Bucks SL0 0NH	Bob Ash
Freeform Design & Construction	**020-8896 3131**
159 Dukes Road	Fax 020-8896 3232
London W3 0SL	Matt Crib
Harry Metcalfe	**020-7702 7337**
128 Chapman Street	Fax 020-7702 7334
London E1 2PH	Harry Metcalfe
Hedgehog Construction	**020-8561 4108**
Unit 3, Chailey Industrial Estate	Dan Crandon
Pump Lane, Hayes, Middx UB3 3NB	
www.hedgehogconstruction.co.uk	
Helix 3D	**020-8855 6888**
Unit 11, Gateway Business Centre	Fax 020-8855 9888
Tom Cribb Road, London SE28 0EZ	Brian Dowling
Hinge & Brackett	**07956-324566**
228 Chertsey Lane	Perry Cella
Staines, Middx TW18 3NF	
J Foster Construction	**01924-505830**
Mountain House, Overthorpe Road	Jonathan Foster
Dewsbury, Wakefield, W Yorks WF12 0BZ	
John Frost Scenery	**020-8898 0190**
15 Maswell Park Road	Fax 020-8755 3838
Hounslow, Middx TW3 2DL	Mike Parker
John Maher Film Construction	**01753-654157**
Pinewood Studios, Pinewood Road	Fax 01753-654157
Iver Heath, Bucks SL0 0NH	John Maher

JW Woodbridge Design	01932-562611	**Model Solutions**	020-8881 2333
Shepperton Studios, Studios Road	Fax 01932-568989	72X Clarence Road	Fax 020-8881 2233
Shepperton, Middx TW17 0QD	Jeffrey Woodbridge	London N22 8PW	Danny Brook
		www.modelsolutions.co.uk	

Keep For Series 020-8607 8769

Twickenham Film Studios, St Margarets — Fax 020-8607 7284
Twickenham, Middx TW1 2AW — Tony Harris
www.keepforseriesltd.com

O & A Associates 020-7635 9155

198 Drakefell Road — Fax 020-7277 5120
London SE4 2DS — Dave Allen

KH Fabrication 01252-879400

Unit 2, Leafy Oak Workshops — Fax 01252-879543
Cobbetts Lane, Blackwater, Surrey GU17 9LW — Keith Huggins

Palace Scenery 020-8658 8977

1 Tollgate Drive — Fax 020-8402 9290
London SE21 7LS — Steve Bohan

Leigh Gilbert Film & TV Set Construction 01628-669388

Unit 1, Hitcham Place — Fax 01628-667143
Taplow Common Road, Burnham, Bucks SL1 8NW — Leigh Gilbert
www.leighgilbert.co.uk

Parker Butler 028-9070 5678

8 Prince Regent Road — Fax 028-9079 4567
Belfast BT5 6QR — Valerie Butler

Lesters TV & Film Services 01494-448689

Lane End Road, Sands — Fax 01494-527552
High Wycombe, Bucks HP12 4HG — Mick Piggot
www.lesterstvandfilm.com

Postmill UK 01753-573115

6 Red Lion Cottages, Stoke Green — Malcolm Roberts
Stoke Poges, Bucks SL2 4HP

RDW Scenery Construction 020-8965 4413

Unit A, Genesis — Fax 020-8965 4414
Rainsford Road, London NW10 7RG — Iain Hill
www.rdwscenery.com

Lignarius 07973-918570

Exhibition House, North View — Fax 0117-957 2400
Soundwell, Bristol BS16 4NT — Don Smith
www.lignarius.co.uk

Rocket Creative Solutions 020-8740 5225

Sun Studios — Fax 020-8740 7450
30 Warple Way, London W3 0RX — Mark Walters

Rogers & Rogers	**01932-241523**
165 Manygate Lane	Simon Rogers
Shepperton, Middx TW17 9ER	
S2 Events	**020-7928 5474**
3-5 Valentine Place	Fax 020-7928 6082
London SE1 8QH	Wolter Dammers
www.s2events.co.uk	
Sam Mercer Construction	**07970-371897**
Unit 40, Cromwell Industrial Estate	Sam Mercer
Staffa Road, London E10 7QZ	
Scena Projects	**020-7703 4444**
240 Camberwell Road	Fax 020-7703 7012
London SE5 0DP	David Thompson
Scenex	**01895-251200**
Island Site, Eskdale Road	Fax 01895-251205
Uxbridge, Middx UB8 2RT	Wayne Melling
Scenic Projects	**01502-575000**
The Studios, London Road	Fax 01502-575840
Brampton, Suffolk NR34 8DQ	Martin Wilson
Scott Fleary Productions	**0870-444 1787**
Units 1-4, Vale Industrial Park	Fax 0870-444 8322
170 Rowan Road, London SW16 5BN	Matthew Scott
The Set Company	**01753-656669**
Pinewood Studios, Pinewood Road	Fax 01753-656669
Iver Heath, Bucks SL0 0NH	Spencer Reid
Set The Scene	**01296-682344**
Home Field House, Burcott	Fax 01296-682197
Wing, Leighton Buzzard, Beds LU7 0JW	Stephen Hargreaves
Set Supermarket	**020-8133 0573**
Chase 55	Michael Mulligan
55 Chase Road, London NW10 6LU	
www.setsupermarket.com	
Set-One	**01227-763653**
The Studio	Fax 01227-266855
Pean Hill, Kent CT5 3BD	Bill Collom
Sets In The City	**0117-955 5538**
Location House	Fax 0117-955 2480
5 Dove Lane, Bristol BS2 9HP	David Garbe
Shape Construction & Design	**07958-526148**
Totom House	Fax 020-8749 7347
70 Stanley Gardens, London W3 7SZ	James Westney
SIA Trading	**020-8578 2627**
5 Fairway Drive	Fax 020-8578 2425
Greenford, Middx UB6 8PW	Ken Ryan
www.sia-trading.co.uk	
Square One	**01525-374078**
Production House, Enterprise Way	Fax 01525-371663
Leighton Buzzard, Beds LU7 4SZ	Anthony Joseph

Steel Monkey	**0117-953 9984**
The Gas Works, Malago House	Fax 0117-953 8345
Bedminster Road, Bristol BS3 5PE	Annie French
Stephen Hayward Film & TV Construction	**020-8953 1745**
Estate Yard, High Canons	Fax 020-8953 9044
Borehamwood, Herts WD6 5PL	Stephen Hayward
Thames Valley Construction	**01753-867017**
Oakley Green Lodge, Oakley Green Road	Fax 01753-867057
Windsor, Berks SL4 4PZ	Peter Leavy
Thames Wire Productions	**01784-479949**
Unit 1, Omega Way	Fax 01784-437434
Thorpe Industrial Estate, Egham, Surrey TW20 8RD	Neil Duke
www.thameswire.co.uk	
Theme Traders	**020-8452 8518**
The Stadium	Fax 020-8450 7322
Oaklands Road, London NW2 6DL	David Jamilly
www.themetraders.com	
Totom Construction	**020-8742 9292**
Totom House	Fax 020-8749 7347
70 Stanley Gardens, London W3 7SZ	Hugo Slight
www.totom.co.uk	
Visionworks	**0114-281 9889**
9 Garden Street	Fax 0114-281 9889
Sheffield S1 4BJ	Trevor Fearnley
Watson Brown	**01895-234441**
Unit 1, Electron Works	Fax 01895-271520
Willow Avenue, Denham, Bucks UB9 4BG	Stuart Watson
Weld.Tec UK	**020-8847 4175**
Fabrication House, The Ham	Fax 020-8847 4176
Brentford, Middx TW8 8EL	Frank James
Wingfield Studios	**01442-832951**
126 Flaunden	Fax 01442-834519
Hemel Hempstead, Herts HP3 0PL	Michael Fleming
www.wingfield-studios.com	

CONSTRUCTION - CNC CUTTING

Advanced Fabrications	**020-8795 1188**
500 Sunleigh Road	Fax 020-8795 1171
Wembley, Middx HA0 4NF	Michael Wright
The CNC Factory	**01753-656975**
Pinewood Studios, Pinewood Road	Edward Hladio
Iver Heath, Bucks SL0 0NH	
www.thecncfactory.com	
Cnc-It	**01403-823628**
CNC House, Guildford Road	Fax 01403-823857
Bucks Green, Rudgwick, W Sussex RH12 3JJ	Paul Godden
www.cnc-it.co.uk	

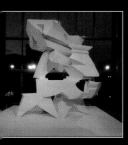

CUTcnc specialise in providing cnc cutting & cnc routing services, cutting simple or complex curves & shapes in a variety of sheet materials.

With accuracy to 0.2mm & large bed sizes up to 3 metres x 2 metres, our large format cnc routers are ideally suited to many industries.

ALICE IN LITTLE GREEN

CUTcnc's large cnc machines are also complimented by a small laser engraver which is suited to cutting, engraving & etching, enabling us to fulfill almost any criteria.

If your cnc routing needs are for small batches, prototypes or larger production runs we offer a fast & flexible service to meet your exact requirements.

Based in our 6500 square ft workshop in Uxbridge, Middlesex, we offer a national delivery service throughout the UK.

tel **01895 237 668**
fax **01895 237649**
email **mark@cutcnc.co.uk**
web **www.cutcnc.co.uk**

Bay D, Bridge Works, Iver Lane, Uxbridge UB8 2JG

CAMOUFLAGE

CAMOUFLAGE keep a catalogue of some 700 moulds available in PVC, ABS, Fibreglass and Plastic. For specific jobs we offer a mould making service. We also fit up sheets and can create virtually any surface in situ if required.

TOTOM
totom.co.uk

camouflage-it.com   Tel: 020 8742 9292

www.wingfield-studios.com

Bespoke Plaster & Glass Fibre Props & Scenery for the Film-TV-Exhibition Industries

Bringing your ideas to life

T: 01442 832951 F: 01442 834519 E: micky@wingfield.co.uk
126 Flaunden, Hemel Hempstead, Hertfordshire HP3 0PL

Concept Profiles	**01628-481642**
Bencombe Farm	Fax 01628-481645
Marlow, Bucks SL7 3LT	Adrian Houlder
Cordek	**01403-799600**
Spring Copse Business Park	Fax 01403-791718
Slinfold, W Sussex RH13 0SZ	Sarah Teversham
www.cordek.com	
CUTcnc	**01895-237668**
Bay D, Bridge Works	Fax 01895-237649
Iver Lane, Uxbridge, Middx UB8 2JG	Mark Davis
www.cutcnc.co.uk	
RDW Scenery Construction	**020-8965 4413**
Unit A, Genesis	Fax 020-8965 4414
Rainsford Road, London NW10 7RG	Iain Hill
www.rdwscenery.com	

CONSTRUCTION - GLASS FIBRE

All Propped Up	**01923-726955**
Unit 1, Woodcock Hill Estate	Fax 01923-896080
Harefield Road, Rickmansworth, Herts WD3 1PQ	Laurence Maguire
Camouflage	**020-8742 9292**
Totom House	Fax 020-8749 7347
70 Stanley Gardens, London W3 7SZ	Ray Churchouse
www.camouflage-it.com	
Creative Glassfibre Models	**0121-744 9226**
266 Ralph Road, Shirley	Fax 0121-744 9226
Solihull, W Midlands B90 3LF	Steve Watts
Peter Evans Studios	**01582-725730**
12-14 Tavistock Street	Fax 01582-481329
Dunstable, Beds LU6 1NE	Peter Evans
Totom Construction	**020-8742 9292**
Totom House	Fax 020-8749 7347
70 Stanley Gardens, London W3 7SZ	Hugo Slight
www.totom.co.uk	
Wingfield Studios	**01442-832951**
126 Flaunden	Fax 01442-834519
Hemel Hempstead, Herts HP3 0PL	Michael Fleming
www.wingfield-studios.com	

CONSTRUCTION - GLAZING

Pentagon London	**0800-907 1254**
Unit 4, Hazel Green Works	Fax 020-8275 8551
Edward Road, Barnet, Herts EN4 8AZ	Martin Westney
www.pentagonlondon.co.uk	

CONSTRUCTION - STANDBY

Set The Scene 01296-682344
Home Field House, Burcott   Fax 01296-682197
Wing, Leighton Buzzard, Beds LU7 0JW   Stephen Hargreaves

CONSTRUCTION GROUNDWORK & LANDSCAPING

AJ Hawes & Family 01491-571571
The Manse, Pheasants Hill   Fax 01491-571571
Hambleden, Henley-on-Thames, Oxon RG9 6SD   Andrew Hawes

The English Garden Company 01707-645069
The Meadows, Blanche Lane   Fax 01707-649814
South Mimms, Herts EN6 3PB   Harriet Bagge

Filmscapes 020-8398 9151
Ditton Nursery, Summerfield Lane   Fax 020-8398 6260
Surbiton, Surrey KT6 5DZ   Lucinda Mclean
www.filmscapes.co.uk

Lesters TV & Film Services 01494-448689
Lane End Road, Sands   Fax 01494-527552
High Wycombe, Bucks HP12 4HG   Mick Piggot
www.lesterstvandfilm.com

Living Props 01895-835100
Sevenhills Road   Fax 01895-835757
Iver Heath, Bucks SL0 0PA   Karen Maychell Michael Lambert
www.livingprops.co.uk

Ruskins Trees & Landscapes 01277-849990
The Rose Garden, Warley Street   Fax 01277-849991
Great Warley, Essex CM13 3JH   Robert Wilkins

CONSTRUCTION PLANT HIRE

A-Plant 01753-689099
Heathrow Traffic Depot (133), Colnbrook By Pass Fax 01753-687513
Colnbrook, Berks SL3 0ET   Matthew Homewood

BB Conveyors 01777-711111
Unit 5, Aurillac Way   Fax 01777-711501
Hallcroft Industrial Estate, Retford, Notts DN22 7PX   Shaun Barker

Bob Wiesinger 07000-wirefx (947339)
10 Blaydon Court, Sussex Crescent   Fax 07968-253071
Northolt, Middx UB5 4DW   Bob Wiesinger

Brandon Tool Hire 0117-971 9119
72-75 Feeder Road   Fax 0117-972 0116
Bristol BS2 0TQ

STEPHEN HARGREAVES
SET BUILDERS AND DESIGN
STANDBY CONSTRUCTION

M 07970 753142
T 01296 682344
F 01296 682197

setthescene@mac.com

Canning Conveyor 01909-486166
Sandy Lane Industrial Estate, Sandy Lane   Fax 01909-500638
Worksop, Notts S80 1TN   Andrew Canning
www.canningconveyor.co.uk

Charles Wilson Plant Hire 020-8756 6312
1366 Uxbridge Road   Fax 020-8573 6500
Hayes, Middx UB4 8JJ   Andrew Sutliff

Elliott Hire 01525-844070
Station Road, Station Industrial Estate   Fax 01525-406625
Amphill, Beds MK45 2RB

Global Film Supplies Crane & Planthire 01753-785351
Pinewood Studios, Pinewood Road   07810-510005
Iver Heath, Bucks SL0 0NH   Tim Ambridge
www.globalfilmsupplies.com

Grassform Plant Hire 01277-353686
Little Woodbarns Farm Yard, Green Street   Fax 01277-356890
Fryerning, Ingatestone, Essex CM4 0NT   Mark Dunning
www.grassform.co.uk

HSS Hire 020-8965 5443
19 Abbey Road   Fax 020-8965 5490
London NW10 7SJ   Martin Matterson

Lesters TV & Film Services 01494-448689
Lane End Road, Sands   Fax 01494-527552
High Wycombe, Bucks HP12 4HG   Mick Piggot
www.lesterstvandfilm.com

Men At Work 020-8893 5569
90-95 Waterside Centre   Fax 020-8571 6505
Trumpers Way, London W7 2QD   Gerard Boath
www.menatwork.co.uk

Plantire 01784-247463
36 Feltham Road   Fax 01784-247167
Ashford, Middx TW15 1DH   John Tocher

Poulsom Plant Hire 01252-792614
Glenroona, Batts Corner   Fax 01252-795707
Dockenfield, Farnham, Surrey GU10 4EX   Katy Poulsom

Speedy Hire	**0845-601 5129**
Chase House, 16 The Parks	Fax 01942-402870
Newton-le-Willows, Merseyside WA12 0JQ	

Thames Valley Hire Services	**01784-433984**
193-194 High Street	Fax 01784-472876
Egham, Surrey TW20 9ED	Stephen Storey

CONSTRUCTION SUPPLIES

Adhesive Brokers	**01494-868870**
3 Whitefield Lane	Fax 0560-047 8208
Great Missenden, Bucks HP16 0BH	Nicola Brown
www.adhesivebrokers.co.uk	

Amari Plastics	**020-8961 1961**
2 Cumberland Avenue	Fax 020-8961 9194
London NW10 7RL	Chris Simonette

AW Smith & Partner (Calor Gas)	**01895-236781**
41 Oxford Road	Fax 01895-233026
New Denham, Middx UB9 4DB	John Smith
www.awsmith-calorgas.co.uk	

British Harlequin	**01892-514888**
Festival House, Chapman Way	Fax 01892-514222
Tunbridge Wells, Kent TN2 3EF	Monica Arnott

Brodie & Middleton	**020-7836 3289**
68 Drury Lane	Fax 020-7497 0554
London WC2B 5SP	Andrew Milne Home
www.brodies.net	

Bryan & Clark	**020-8206 2200**
Units 2 & 3, Bowman Trading Estate	Fax 020-8206 2929
Westmoreland Road, London NW9 9RL	Dilip Pattni

Bryson Products	**020-8660 9119**
Unit D, Redlands	Fax 020-8660 9118
Coulsdon, Surrey CR5 2HT	Dan Reiner
www.bryson.co.uk	

Camouflage	**020-8742 9292**
Totom House	Fax 020-8749 7347
70 Stanley Gardens, London W3 7SZ	Ray Churchouse
www.camouflage-it.com	

Colorite Paint Company	**020-8579 3381**
169 Boston Road	Fax 020-8567 5158
London W7 3QJ	Irene Condon
www.colorite.co.uk	

Corevista	**01388-775157**
Unit 11, All Saints Industrial Estate	Fax 01388-776674
Shildon, Co Durham DL4 2RD	Geoff Layland

Creffields Timber & Boards	**0118-945 3533**
Unit 6, Marcus Close	Fax 0118-945 3633
Tilehurst, Reading, Berks RG30 4EA	Nigel Creffield
www.creffields.co.uk	

Dirty Down	**07926-196471**
screenproducts@yahoo.co.uk	Fax 0845-299 2299
www.dirtydown.co.uk	Alan Taylor
Dresser Mouldings	**01204-667667**
Unit 3, Blackrod Mill	Fax 01204-667600
Station Road, Bolton, Lancs BL6 5GP	Simon McDonnell
Edmundson Electrical	**01923-245066**
Unit 2, Imperial Park	Fax 01923-240463
Imperial Park Road, Watford, Herts WD24 4PP	Roy London
Flint Hire & Supply	**020-7703 9786**
Queens Row	Fax 020-7708 4189
London SE17 2PX	Alasdair Flint
www.flints.co.uk	
Gibbs & Dandy	**01628-600743**
462 Bath Road	Fax 01628-600744
Slough, Berks SL1 6BQ	Mark Wheatley
Honeysuckle Bottom Sawmill	**01483-282394**
Honeysuckle Bottom, Green Dene	Fax 01483-282394
East Horsley, Surrey KT24 5TD	Stuart Dale
Jacobson Chemicals	**01420-86934**
Unit 4, Newman Lane Industrial Estate	Fax 01420-549574
Alton, Hants GU34 2QR	Mike Cooper
www.jacobsonchemicals.co.uk	

James Mansfield Timber	**01753-656317**
Pinewood Studios, Pinewood Road	Fax 01753-785882
Iver Heath, Bucks SL0 0NH	James Chancheong
James Mansfield Timber	**01932-564418**
Shepperton Studios, Studios Road	Fax 01932-567923
Shepperton, Middx TW17 0QD	Floyd Farrer
Jewson	**01483-715371**
Arthurs Bridge Wharf, Horsell	Fax 01483-763680
Woking, Surrey GU21 4NQ	Michael Dyer
John Myland	**020-8670 9161**
26 Rothschild Street	Fax 020-8761 5700
London SE27 0HQ	Dominic Myland
Lesters TV & Film Services	**01494-448689**
Lane End Road, Sands	Fax 01494-527552
High Wycombe, Bucks HP12 4HG	Mick Piggot
www.lesterstvandfilm.com	
Lookin' Glass	**020-8896 1920**
389 Uxbridge Road	Fax 020-8992 5779
London W3 9SA	Ken Seager
www.lookin-glass.co.uk	
Mask It	**020-7460 6484**
31 Lancaster Road	Fax 020-7460 6484
London W11 1QJ	

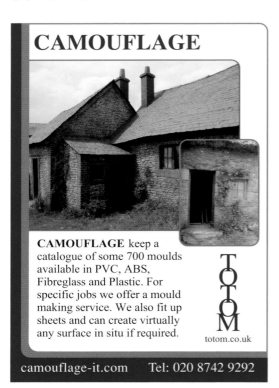
Paris Hose & Ducting	01344-758600
Unit 22, Wellington Business Park	Fax 01344-758610
Dukes Ride, Crowthorne, Berks RG45 6LS	David Kemp
Protective Textile Company	**020-8974 1271**
Canvas Works, Cox Lane	Fax 020-8974 1957
Chessington, Surrey KT9 ISG	Claire Prosser
PT Corkill - Fibrous Plasterers	**0151-638 1005**
McKennas Building, Dock Road	Fax 0151-630 6434
Birkenhead, Merseyside CH41 IDQ	Phil Corkill
Range Master Supplies	**01690-710497**
Bodlondeb, Pentrefelin	Fax 01690-710497
Betws-y-Coed, Conwy LL24 0BB	Robert Scott
S2 Events	**020-7928 5474**
3-5 Valentine Place	Fax 020-7928 6082
London SE1 8QH	Wolter Dammers
www.s2events.co.uk	
Saint-Gobain	**024-7656 0700**
Saint Gobain House	Fax 024-7656 0705
Binley Business Park, Coventry CV3 2TT	Alun Oxenham
Scenery Salvage	**01494-866110**
Middlegrove Farm, Chesham Road	07831-455583
Great Misenden, Bucks HP16 0RD	Hugo Keating
www.scenerysalvage.com	

The Stockyard	020-8963 9944
Unit A, Genesis	Fax 020-8963 9955
Rainsford Road, London NW10 7RG	Ron Painter
www.stockyard.tv	

Thames Valley Building Supplies	01753-652929
Poveys Yard, Uxbridge Road	Fax 01753-653934
Iver Heath, Bucks SL0 0LR	James Crockett

Totom Construction	020-8742 9292
Totom House	Fax 020-8749 7347
70 Stanley Gardens, London W3 7SZ	Tom Overton
www.totom.co.uk	

Trevor Howsam	020-8838 6166
182 Acton Lane	Fax 020-8838 6167
London NW10 7NH	Marcus Howsam
www.retrowallpaper.co.uk	

Trevor Howsam	01205-356010
The Granary, Grove Street East	Fax 01205-366411
Boston, Lincs PE21 6TE	Trevor Howsam Tim Howsam
www.retrowallpaper.co.uk	

Vacuum Coatings	020-8520 5353
66 Barrett Road	Fax 020-8520 5353
London E17 9ET	Terry Pearce
www.scientificmirrors.co.uk	

Yarwood Leather	0113-252 1014
Treefield Industrial Estate, Gelderd Road	Fax 0113-252 7391
Morley, Leeds LS27 7JU	Matthew Nicholls

CONSTRUCTION SUPPLIES - ADHESIVES

Adhesive Brokers	01494-868870
3 Whitefield Lane	Fax 0560-047 8208
Great Missenden, Bucks HP16 0BH	Nicola Brown
www.adhesivebrokers.co.uk	

CONSTRUCTION SUPPLIES - GLASS & MIRRORS

1st Glass & Mirror	020-8595 1666
Sterling Industrial Estate, Rainham Road South	Fax 020-8595 1660
Dagenham, Essex RM10 8TX	Bobbi Schneider

Lookin' Glass	020-8896 1920
389 Uxbridge Road	Fax 020-8992 5779
London W3 9SA	Ken Seager
www.lookin-glass.co.uk	

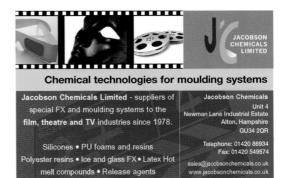

CONSUMABLES

Aerofoam	**020-8204 8411**
30 Dalston Gardens	Fax 020-8204 7072
Stanmore, Middx HA7 IBY	Mike Rawlings
ARRI Media Camstore	**01895-457100**
3 Highbridge, Oxford Road	Fax 01895-457101
Uxbridge, Middx UB8 ILX	Dan Gruenpeter
Consumables Superstore	**07818-061108**
Shepperton Studios, Studios Road	Damien Thomas
Shepperton, Middx TW17 0QD	
Dirty Down	**07926-196471**
screenproducts@yahoo.co.uk	Fax 0845-299 2299
www.dirtydown.co.uk	Alan Taylor
Fujifilm Motion Picture UK	**020-3040 0400**
56 Poland Street	Fax 020-7494 3425
London WIF 7NN	Steve Jones
www.fujifilm.co.uk/motion	
Fujifilm Recording Media UK	**01234-572702**
Unit 10A, St Martins Business Centre	Fax 01234-572650
St Martins Way, Bedford MK42 0LF	Ruth Senna
www.fujifilm.co.uk/recmedia	
Le Mark Group	**01480-494540**
Houghton Hill Industries, Houghton	Fax 01480-494206
Huntingdon, Cambs PE28 2DH	Mark Gibbons
Movietech Camera Rentals	**01753-650007**
Pinewood Studios, Pinewood Road	Fax 01753-650006
Iver Heath, Bucks SL0 0NH	John Buckley
www.movietech.co.uk	
Pinewood Studios	**01753-651700**
Part of the Pinewood Studios Group	Fax 01753-656219
Pinewood Road, Iver Heath, Bucks SL0 0NH	
www.pinewoodgroup.com	
Stanley Productions	**020-7439 0311**
147 Wardour Street	Fax 020-7437 2126
London WIF 8WD	Steve Langston Mick Pruce
www.stanleysonline.co.uk	

COPYRIGHT CLEARANCE

Arthouse Hire	**020-8838 0436**
Studio 10, Europa Studios	Fax 020-8453 0920
Victoria Road, London NW10 6ND	Jane Henwood
www.arthousehire.com	
The Clearing House	**020-7262 7670**
38 Coniston Court	Fax 020-7681 1317
Kendal Street, London W2 2AN	Ruth Halliday

COSTUME EFFECTS

Artem	**020-8997 7771**
Perivale Park, Horsenden Lane South	Fax 020-8997 1503
Perivale, Middx UB6 7RH	Frank Steggall
www.artem.com	
Artem (Scotland)	**0141-427 5775**
64-68 Brand Street	Fax 0141-427 1199
Govan, Glasgow G51 1DG	Joanna Dewar Gibb
www.artem.com	
Dirty Down	**07926-196471**
screenproducts@yahoo.co.uk	Fax 0845-299 2299
www.dirtydown.co.uk	Alan Taylor
Jacobson Chemicals	**01420-86934**
Unit 4, Newman Lane Industrial Estate	Fax 01420-549574
Alton, Hants GU34 2QR	Mike Cooper
www.jacobsonchemicals.co.uk	
Robert Allsopp & Associates	**020-8654 4391**
4 Woodside Avenue	Fax 020-8654 4391
London SE25 5DJ	Robert Allsopp
www.raprops.com	
Schultz & Wiremu Fabric Effects	**020-8469 0151**
Unit B202, Faircharm Trading Estate	Fax 020-8469 0151
8-12 Creekside, London SE8 3DX	Miriam Schultz

COSTUME EMBROIDERY

Diane Holmes Embroidery	**020-8977 8421**
108 Broom Road	Fax 020-8977 8421
Teddington, Middx TW11 9PF	Diane Holmes
Embroidery By Design	**020-8998 1983**
Studio 3, 24 Wadsworth Road	Jazz Dhanjal
Perivale, Middx UB6 7JD	
Hand & Lock	**020-7580 7488**
86 Margaret Street	Fax 020-7580 7499
London WIW 8TE	Sana Volden
Props Galore	**020-8746 1222**
1-17 Brunel Road	Fax 020-8354 1866
London W3 7XR	Naomi Leigh
www.farley.co.uk	
Ron Briggs Design	**020-8444 8801**
1 Bedford Mews	Ron Briggs
London N2 9DF	
www.ronbriggs.com	

COSTUME HIRE

1920's-70's Crazy Clothes Connection	**020-7221 3989**
134 Lancaster Road	Fax 020-7221 3989
London W11 1QU	

CameraCrews   01749-343231

Mill Masters House, 11 Lower Silk Mill   Ian Careless
Darshill, Shepton Mallet, Somerset BA4 5HF

Camm Facilities   0115-932 1913

87 Ilkeston Road   Fax 0115-944 0011
Trowell, Notts NG9 3PY   George Camm

Capital Crewing   020-8467 9842

Downline, Southill Road   Mark Bourdeaux
Chislehurst, Kent BR7 5EE

Central Rental   020-7631 4455

28 Newman Street   Fax 020-7631 3400
London W1T 1PR   Greg Woznica
www.centralrental.co.uk

Crewed Up   0161-952 0738

Granada Television   Fax 0161-952 0740
Quay Street, Manchester M60 9EA   Mike Turnbull

Debrouillard   0114-220 0667

74 Ashland Road   Jonathan Young
Sheffield S7 1RJ

Edit 123   0141-248 3123

123 Blythswood Street   Fax 0141-248 3423
Glasgow G2 4EN   Jenny Matthews

The Electronic Camera Company   020-7734 5021

1 Greenbank   John Tarby
London E1W 2PA

Eugene J McVeigh Television   07860-364649

21 Knockmoyle   Eugene J McVeigh
Cookstown, Co Tyrone BT80 8XS

Eurocrew Worldwide   020-3100 7700

1-7 Livonia Street   Fax 020-3100 7701
London W1F 8AD   Peter Britten

Extra Veg Camera Crews   0131-446 0444

Glenlockhart House   Fax 0131-446 0222
6 The Steils, Edinburgh EH10 5XD   Cindy Thomson

Fuel Film & Television   01923-233956

30 Kingsfield Road   Fax 01923-224289
Watford, Herts WD19 4PS   Allen Della-Valle
www.fuelfilm.co.uk

Gemini Production Services   01243-575710

20 Rowan Avenue   David Tozer
Waterlooville, Hants PO8 8AZ

Goldmoor Television   01908-370516

Unit L31, MK2 Business Centre   Peter Rimington
Milton Keynes, Bucks MK2 3HU

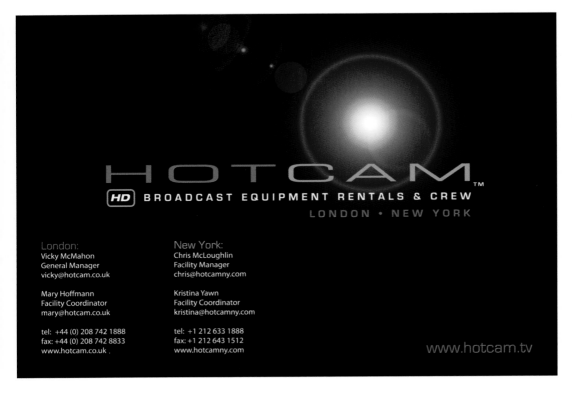

Hammerhead TV Facilities	**020-8646 5511**
Unit 19, Liongate Enterprise Park	Fax 020-8646 6163
80 Morden Road, Mitcham, Surrey CR4 4NY	Darrin Dart
www.hammerheadtv.com	
Hammerhead TV Facilities	**0131-229 5000**
9 Merchiston Mews	Fax 0131-229 2831
Edinburgh EH10 4PE	Phil Mews
www.hammerheadtv.com	
Hammerhead TV Facilities	**0141-429 4200**
Unit 1, The Tollgate	Fax 0141-429 4211
21 Marine Crescent, Glasgow G51 1HD	Phil Mews
www.hammerheadtv.com	
Hammerhead TV Facilities	**0161-431 6400**
Unit 2, Rugby Park, Battersea Road	Fax 0161-431 6300
Heaton Mersey, Stockport, Manchester SK4 3EB	John Dardis
www.hammerheadtv.com	
Hoi Polloi Film & Video	**0191-233 0050**
PO Box 5052	Andy Greenwood
Newcastle-upon-Tyne NE99 1LR	
HotCam	**020-8742 1888**
Unit 14, Bell Industrial Estate	Fax 020-8742 8833
50 Cunnington Street, London W4 5HB	Vicky McMahon Mary Hoffmann
www.hotcam.co.uk	
Howl At The Moon	**01895-631635**
Hill Lane	Rick Manzanero
Ruislip, Middx HA4 7JJ	
Huntley Visual Communications	**01245-225803**
The Conifers, 16 Barley Mead	Stephen Huntley
Danbury, Chelmsford, Essex CM3 4RP	
Infinite Vision	**020-8874 7233**
5 Morie Street	Fax 020-8875 0261
London SW18 1SL	Abigail Theodosiou
Kit & Crew	**0845-224 4473**
ben@kitandcrew.co.uk	Ben Manning-Wade
www.kitandcrew.co.uk	
Kitroom Monkey	**0845-166 2597**
Ealing Studios	Oliver Hickey
Ealing Green, London W5 5EP	
www.kitroommonkey.co.uk	
Mac Film & Video Services	**07831-890802**
37 The Chase	Robin McDonald
Sutton Coldfield, W Midlands B76 1JS	
Magpie Film Productions	**01527-60264**
471 Birmingham Road	Jim Knights
Redditch, Worcs B97 6RL	
MD Camera Services	**020-8567 4482**
21 Claygate Road	Martin Doyle
London W13 9XG	

Miracle International Crews	**020-7391 9203**
Suffolk House	Maria Sohlen
1-8 Whitfield Place, London W1T 5JU	
www.genesis-plus.com	
Monkshood Television	**01553-670066**
9 Monkshood	Merv Gagen
Kings Lynn, Norfolk PE30 3HG	
MU Crew	**07866-758285**
21:05 The Heart, MediaCityUK	Victoria Jones
Salford Quays, Manchester M50 2TH	
PI Communications	**028-9029 8124**
19 Church Avenue	Fax 028-9091 4571
Dunmurry, Belfast BT17 9RF	
Picture Canning North	**0191-265 0061**
156 Brinkburn Street	Jamie Hutchinson
Newcastle-upon-Tyne NE6 2AR	
www.picturecanningnorth.co.uk	
Prima Vista	**020-8549 0200**
75 Sigrist Square	Andy Fairgrieve
Kingston-upon-Thames, Surrey KT2 6JY	
Prime Television	**020-8969 6122**
Unit 7	Fax 020-8969 6144
Latimer Road, London W10 6RQ	Chris Earls
www.primetv.com	
Purplecrew	**0161-380 0075**
The Pie Factory, 101 Broadway	Fax 07970-880720
Salford Quays, Manchester M50 2EQ	Ferdia de Buitlear
Redapple	**01483-455044**
214 Epsom Road, Merrow	Fax 01483-455022
Guildford, Surrey GU1 2RA	Nigel Reynolds
Redwood TV	**01903-884441**
Old Bank House, 1 High Street	Chris Evans
Arundel, W Sussex BN18 9AD	
Shooters	**020-7737 6651**
Unit 10, Eurolink Business Centre	Stephen Norris
49 Effra Road, London SW2 1BZ	
Shooting Box (UK)	**020-7682 1071**
12 Parmoor Court	Janusz Szczerek
Gee Street, London EC1V 3RP	
SIS LIVE	**01908-865500**
2 Whitehall Avenue, Kingston	Fax 01908-865501
Milton Keynes, Bucks MK10 0AX	Donna Palumbo
www.sislive.tv	
Spectra Television	**020-8871 0050**
Unit 14, Earlsfield Business Centre	Fax 020-8871 0010
9 Lydden Road, London SW18 4LT	Andrew Craig
Spot-on-Sound	**01328-829353**
Manor Farmhouse, Stibbard Road	Ian Savage
Fulmodeston, Norfolk NR21 0LX	

Steeplepin	**020-8997 0676**
16 Glencairn Drive	Fax 020-8997 2406
London W5 1RT	Paul Kanwar
Tarmak Films	**020-7100 7458**
585A Fulham Road	Dana Trometer
London SW6 5UA	
Three S Films	**01736-367912**
12 Regent Square	Fax 01736-367912
Penzance, Cornwall TR18 4BG	Mitch Adams
Transmission (TX)	**020-8783 1972**
Shepperton Studios, Studios Road	Fax 01932-592571
Shepperton, Middx TW17 0QD	Steve Lloyd
www.ttx.co.uk	
Video Europe	**020-7494 1818**
8 Golden Square	Fax 020-7494 1717
London W1F 9HY	Matt Marner
www.videoeurope.co.uk	
Video Europe Wales	**029-2059 5111**
The Television Centre	Fax 029-2059 5222
Culverhouse Cross, Cardiff CF5 6XJ	Tom McNally
www.videoeurope.co.uk	
Videoheads	**020-8743 0412**
Unigate House, Depot Road	David Symmons
Wood Lane, London W12 7RZ	

VMI   **020-8922 1222**
Unit 1, Granville Industrial Estate   Fax 020-8922 1114
146-148 Granville Road, London NW2 2LD   Barry Bassett
www.vmi.tv

Widescreen   **020-8324 2634**
Elstree Studios, Shenley Road   Fax 020-8324 2684
Borehamwood, Herts WD6 1JG   Shirley Taylor

zero db   **020-7604 4100**
10-14 Lonsdale Road   Fax 020-7604 4144
London NW6 6RD   Dionne James

DATA MANAGEMENT

Rogue Element Films   **07866-447564**
U12 Basepoint, Crab Apple Way   Dan Mulligan
Vale Park, Evesham, Worcs WR11 1GP
www.rogueelementfilms.com

Sohonet   **020-7292 6900**
60 Poland Street   Fax 020-7292 6901
London W1F 7NT   Richard Linecar
www.sohonet.co.uk

DIALOGUE & ACCENT COACHES

Roisin Carty   **07870-636944**

Mel Churcher   **07778-773019**

Constantine Gregory   **020-3239 8939**

Brendan Gunn   **07710-242529**

Andrew Jack   **07836-615839**

Paula Jack   **07836-615839**

Representation Upson Edwards   **01782-827222**
   Sarah Upson

Julia Wilson-Dickson   **020-7586 5854**

Neville Wortman   **020-8994 8886**

DIARY SERVICES

ARRI Crew   **01895-457180**
3 Highbridge, Oxford Road   Fax 01895-457101
Uxbridge, Middx UB8 1LX   Kate Collier

Art Department   **020-7428 0500**
51 Pratt Street   Deborah Randall-Cutler
London NW1 0BJ

Bookends   **01727-841177**
83 Maynard Drive   Sharon Gold
St Albans, Herts AL1 2JX

Callbox   **01932-592572**
Shepperton Studios, Studios Road   Patsy Brinkworth
Shepperton, Middx TW17 0QD

The Camera Crew   **0845-634 5910**
The Field, Rectory Lane   Helen Brown
Saltwood, Hythe, Kent CT21 4QA

Carlin Crew   **01932-568268**
Shepperton Studios, Studios Road   Fax 01932-571109
Shepperton, Middx TW17 0QD   Lynne Hames

Connections   **020-8420 1444**
The Meadlands, 11 Oakleigh Road   Fax 020-8428 5836
Hatch End, Middx HA5 4HB   Barbara Roberts

Crews Up North   **07946-197835**
Ceulan House   Becky Barrett
Talybont, Dyfed SY24 5HE

The Diary Agency   **020-8899 6695**
Building 3, Chiswick Park   Janie Willsmore
566 Chiswick High Road, London W4 5YA

The Digital Garage   **01932-569874**
Shepperton Studios, Studios Road   Lynne Hames
Shepperton, Middx TW17 0QD

Exec Answering Service   **01753-646677**
6 Travis Court   Fax 01753-646770
Farnham Royal, Berks SL2 3SB   Sue Jones

The Firm Booking Company   **020-8840 6030**
8 St James Avenue   Fax 020-8840 8285
Brighton, E Sussex BN2 1QD   Kirsty Howe

GAS (The Guilds Answering Service)   **020-8813 1999**
Panavision Building, Metropolitan Centre   Fax 020-8813 2111
Bristol Road, Greenford, Middx UB6 8GD

Linkline   **020-8426 2200**
64 Cecil Park   Fax 020-8429 2216
Pinner, Middx HA5 5HH   Nick Hunter

Production Switchboard   **020-7434 2647**
82 Berwick Street   David Rudland
London W1F 8TP

Red Diary Service   **020-8374 3074**
49 Woodfield Way   Fax 020-8889 4411
London N11 2NR   Lynne Hurley

Stellas Diary   **020-8994 1199**
39 Oxford Gardens   Stella Rooke
London W4 3BN

Suz Cruz   **01932-252577**
Halliford Studios, Manygate Lane   Fax 01932-246004
Shepperton, Middx TW17 9EG   Zoe Matthews

TOVS	020-7287 6110
The Linen Hall	Fax 020-7287 5481
162-168 Regent Street, London W1B 5TB	Irene Hanley
Warpaint	**020-7700 5777**
16B Witherington Road	Josephine Pierre
London N5 1PP	
Wizzo & Co	**020-7437 2055**
47 Beak Street	Fax 020-7437 2066
London W1F 9SE	Victoria Cameron

DIGITAL ASSET MANAGEMENT

Jigsaw Systems	03332-400222
The Old Mill	Fax 03332-409202
High Church Street, Nottingham NG7 7JA	Lewis Brown
www.jigsaw24.com/broadcast	
Prime Focus	**020-7437 2626**
58 Old Compton Street	
London W1D 4UF	
www.primefocustechnologies.com	
Sohonet	**020-7292 6900**
60 Poland Street	Fax 020-7292 6901
London W1F 7NT	Richard Linecar
www.sohonet.co.uk	

DINING BUSES

Ace Flush	01753-840777
17 St Andrews Close	Paul Jones
Old Windsor, Berks SL4 2QU	
www.aceflushltd.com	
Andy Dixon Facilities	**01656-725560**
3 Squire Drive, Brynmenyn Industrial Estate	Fax 01656-725194
Bridgend, Mid Glam CF32 9TX	Andy Dixon Steve Haines
www.andydixonfacilities.co.uk	
Andy Dixon Facilities	**07768-436768**
Longcross Studios, Chobham Lane	Andy Dixon
Chertsey, Surrey KT16 0EE	
www.andydixonfacilities.co.uk	
Delux Diners	**0845-072 2998**
Unit 6, Hendham Vale Industrial Estate	Fax 0161-202 2299
Hazelbottom Road, Manchester M8 0GF	Mark Cohen
Dining Bus Services (DBS)	**01895-672381**
7 The Mallows	Fax 01895-636101
Ickenham, Middx UB10 8BX	Martin Porter
www.diningbusservices.com	
Film Flow	**020-8438 9919**
The Yard	Fax 020-8438 9929
Adrian Avenue, London NW2 1LX	Alan Hayter Karen Hayter
www.filmflow.co.uk	

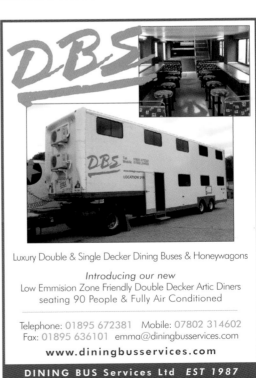

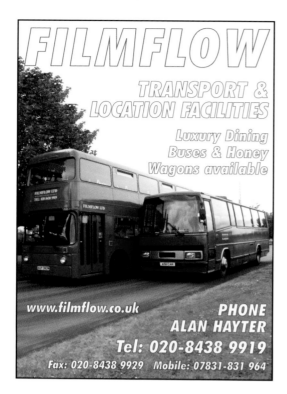

FILMFLOW

TRANSPORT & LOCATION FACILITIES

Luxury Dining Buses & Honey Wagons available

www.filmflow.co.uk

PHONE ALAN HAYTER
Tel: 020-8438 9919
Fax: 020-8438 9929 Mobile: 07831-831 964

GT Caterers & Facilities	**0113-253 7773**
Unit 2, Howley Park Close	Fax 0113-252 6773
Morley, Leeds LS27 0BW	Danny Janes
www.gtcaterers.com	
Location Facilities	**01784-436444**
Delta Way, Thorpe Industrial Estate	Fax 01784-430117
Egham, Surrey TW20 8RX	Ray Redrup
www.locationfacilities.com	
Movie Makers Facilities	**01932-828888**
Woburn Park Farm, Addlestone Moor	Fax 01932-844738
Addlestone, Surrey KT15 2QF	Mel Dunne
www.mmuk.tv	

DISTRIBUTION

III Pictures	**020-7758 0690**
111 Wardour Street	Fax 020-7734 2819
London W1F 0UH	Alki David
All 3 Media International	**020-7845 4350**
Berkshire House	Fax 020-7845 4360
168-173 High Holborn, London WC1V 7AA	Rachel Glaister
Altadena Films	**020-7424 7280**
Linton House	Fax 020-7428 8936
39-51 Highgate Road, London NW5 1RS	Ildi Toth Davy

ARD Films	**020-7256 8349**
22-25 Finsbury Square	Alastair Dickinson
London EC2A 1DX	
Arrow Film Distributors	**01923-858306**
Orchard Villa, Porters Park Drive	Fax 01923-859673
Shenley, Herts WD7 9DS	Neil Agran
Artificial Eye Film Company	**020-7438 9534**
20-22 Stukeley Street	Fax 020-7240 5242
London WC2B 5LR	Louisa Dent
Arts Alliance Media	**020-7751 7500**
9-11 North End Road	Howard Kiedaisch
London W14 8ST	
Avalon Distribution	**020-7598 8000**
4A Exmoor Street	Fax 020-7598 7300
London W10 6BD	Carly Hardman
Beckmann International	**01624-816585**
Milntown Lodge, Lezayre Road	Fax 01624-816589
Ramsey, Isle Of Man IM8 2TG	Joanna White
BFI Distribution	**020-7957 8902**
21 Stephen Street	Margaret Deriaz
London W1T 1LN	
Boulton-Hawker Films	**01449-616200**
Combs Tannery, Tannery Road	Fax 01449-677600
Combs, Stowmarket, Suffolk IP14 2EN	Jan Fellingham
Cake	**020-7307 3230**
76 Charlotte Street	Fax 020-7494 9107
London W1T 4QS	Edward Galton
Capers-MatCine	**01424-812436**
Wild Meadows, Chapel Lane	Tony Carr
Guestling Green, E Sussex TN35 4HP	
CBS International Studios	**020-7318 6400**
49 Charles Street	Fax 020-7491 2086
London W1J 5EW	Stephen Tague
Channel 4 Learning	**0870-124 6444**
Code Storm House, Walton Road	Fax 0844-335 8871
Farlington, Hants PO6 1TR	Vicki Salusbury
Cinefile	**0131-225 6191**
12 Sunbury Place	Fax 0131-225 6971
Edinburgh EH4 3BY	Ilona Morison
City Screen	**020-7734 4342**
Hardy House	Fax 020-7734 4027
16-18 Beak Street, London W1F 9RD	Lyn Goleby
Classic Media	**020-8762 6200**
Royalty House	Fax 020-8762 6299
72-74 Dean Street, London W1D 3SG	Paul Ashworth
Delanic Films	**020-7025 7420**
6 Heddon Street	Fax 020-7025 7406
London W1B 4BT	Joe Simpson

Diffusion Pictures	**020-7729 9987**	**ITV Global Entertainment**	**020-7157 3000**
108 Leonard Street	Nick Crossley	London Television Centre	Fax 020-7157 6063
London EC2A 4XS		Upper Ground, London SE1 9LT	Tobias De Graass
Digital Rights Group	**020-7494 5828**	**Lions Gate UK**	**020-7299 8800**
21-25 St Annes Court	Fax 020-7494 8046	60 Charlotte Street	Fax 020-7299 8801
London W1F 0BJ	Patrick Roberts	London W1T 2NU	Christopher Bailey
Dogwoof Pictures	**020-7833 3599**	**London Films**	**020-7499 7800**
Studio 211, Hatton Square Business Centre	Fax 020-7900 3270	77 South Audley Street	Fax 020-7491 7725
16 Baldwins Gardens, London EC1N 7RJ	Andy Whittaker	London W1K 1JG	Gary Mitchell
Double Take	**020-8788 5743**	**Mercury Media International**	**020-7221 7221**
21 St Mary Grove	Fax 020-8785 3050	6 Baseline Studios	Fax 020-7221 7228
London SW13 0JA	Maya Kemp	Whitchurch Road, London W11 4AT	Tim Sparke
EI Entertainment	**020-7907 3773**	**Metrodome Group**	**020-7766 8600**
120 New Cavendish Street	Fax 020-7907 3789	48 Leicester Square	Fax 020-7766 8620
London W1W 6XX	Richard Bridgewood	London WC2H 7LT	Sara Frain
Eros International	**020-7935 2727**	**MGM Television (Europe)**	**020-7632 4600**
13 Manchester Square	Fax 020-7935 5656	Orion House	Fax 020-7240 3208
London W1U 3PP	Kishore Lulla	5 Upper St Martins Lane, London WC2H 9EA	
Espresso TV	**01273-730929**	**Momentum Pictures**	**020-7534 0400**
25 York Villas	Fax 01273-730929	20 Soho Square	Fax 020-7383 0404
Brighton, E Sussex BN1 3TS	David Hooper	London W1D 3QW	Xavier Marchand
Eureka Entertainment	**020-8459 8054**	**MovieVentures**	**020-7493 7920**
9 Iron Bridge Close	Ron Benson	Hill House	Fax 020-7493 8088
London NW10 0UF		1 Little New Street, London EC4A 3TR	Karen Cuccaro
Exclusive Film Distribution	**020-3002 9510**	**Network Releasing**	**020-7605 4445**
52 The Haymarket	Fax 020-3002 9519	346 Kensington High Street	Tim Beddows
London SW1Y 4RP	Andy Mayson	London W14 8NS	
Filmbank	**020-7984 5950**	**Optimum Releasing**	**020-7534 2700**
Warner House	Fax 020-7984 5951	50 Marshall Street	Fax 020-7534 2701
98 Theobolds Road, London WC1X 8WB	Gary Martin	London W1F 9BQ	
G2 Pictures	**020-7479 7890**	**Outright Distribution**	**020-7239 1060**
187 Wardour Street	Fax 020-7734 9333	2 Holford Yard	Fax 020-7239 1061
London W1F 8ZB	Alan Partington	London WC1X 9HD	Chris Bonney
High Point Media Group	**020-7424 6870**	**Passion Distribution**	**020-7981 9801**
Suite 16, Deane House Studios	Fax 020-7485 3281	182 Hercules Road	Fax 020-7401 7801
Greenwood Place, London NW5 1LB	Carey FitzGerald	London SE1 7LD	Sally Miles
Hit Entertainment	**020-7554 2500**	**Revolver Entertainment**	**020-7243 4300**
Maple House	Fax 020-7388 9321	48-49 Princes Place	Fax 020-7243 4302
149 Tottenham Court Road, London W1T 7NF	Fiona Ross	London W11 4QA	Justin Marciano
Hollywood Classics	**020-7424 7280**	**Seven Arts Pictures**	**020-3006 8222**
Linton House	Fax 020-7428 8936	38 Hertford Street	Fax 020-3006 8220
39-51 Highgate Road, London NW5 1RS	Melanie Tebb	London W1J 7SG	Peter Hoffman
ICA Cinema	**020-7930 0493**	**Soda Pictures**	**020-7377 1407**
12 Carlton House Terrace	Tejinder Jouhal	17 Blossom Street	Fax 020-7377 1406
London SW1Y 5AH		London E1 6PL	Edward Fletcher
Indigo	**020-7424 1980**	**Sony Pictures Entertainment**	**020-7533 1000**
31 Oval Road	Fax 020-7424 1985	25 Golden Square	Fax 020-7533 1015
London NW1 7EA	David Lawley	London W1F 9LU	

Target Entertainment Group	**020-7535 7200**
Garfield House	Fax 0870-164 7475
86-88 Edgware Road, London W2 2EA	Sarah Walker
Transmedia International Releasing	**07000-434567**
Landmark House	Fax 01932-839978
17 Hanover Square, London W1S 1HU	Simon Caplan
TVF International	**020-7837 3000**
375 City Road	Fax 020-7833 2185
London EC1V 1NB	
United International Pictures	**020-3184 2500**
Building 5, Chiswick Park	Fax 020-3184 2501
566 Chiswick High Road, London W4 5YF	Eileen Por
Universal Pictures	**020-7079 6337**
Prospect House	Helen Parker
80-110 New Oxford Street, London WC1A 1HB	
Verve Pictures	**020-7436 8001**
79-80 Margaret Street	Fax 020-7436 8002
London W1W 8TA	Colin Burch
Walt Disney Studios (Europe)	**020-8222 1231**
3 Queen Caroline Street	Fax 020-8222 1105
London W6 9PE	Daniel Frigo
Wienerworld	**020-8206 1177**
Unit 7, Freetrade House	Fax 020-8206 2757
Lowther Road, Stanmore, Middx HA7 1EP	Anthony Broza
Works Media Group	**020-7612 0030**
Portland House	Fax 020-7612 0031
4 Great Portland Street, London W1W 8QJ	John Bullen
Yash Raj Films International	**0870-739 7345**
Regus House, 268 Bath Road	Fax 0870-739 7346
Slough, Berks SL1 4DX	Navraj Panesar
Yume Pictures	**020-7099 6024**
2-6 Curtain Road	Patrizia Raeli
London EC2A 3NQ	

DRAPES

Acre Jean	**020-8877 3211**
Unit 7, The Kimber Centre	Fax 020-8877 3213
54 Kimber Road, London SW18 4PP	Colin Hannah
www.acrejean.com	
Alexander Furnishings	**020-7935 7806**
51-61 Wigmore Street	Fax 020-7224 3275
London W1U 1PU	Alison Herman
Anthony Szuch	**07543-630313**
The Old Coach House, 51 Montague Road	07795-418317
Uxbridge, Middx UB8 1QN	Anthony Szuch
www.anthony-szuch.com	

Black Velvet Hire	**01932-560175**
Shepperton Studios, Studios Road	Fax 01932-560175
Shepperton, Middx TW17 0QD	Gary Handley
www.sheppertondrapes.co.uk	
Blackout	**020-8687 8400**
280 Western Road	Fax 020-8687 8500
London SW19 2QA	Lucy Akillian
Blitz Hire	**07931-377502**
3 Mills Studios	Fax 020-8534 4221
Sugar House Lane, London E15 2QS	Paul Skipper
www.blitz-rigging.co.uk	
Chromakey-Hire.com	**07831-871565**
15 Glenham Road	Graham Caulfield
Thame, Oxon OX9 3WD	
www.chromakey-hire.com	
Don Speake & Co	**020-8992 8668**
49 Churchfield Road	Fax 020-8992 8678
London W3 6AY	Eileen Driscoll
www.donspeake.4t.com	
Elstree Drape Hire	**020-8324 2666**
Elstree Studios, Shenley Road	Fax 020-8324 2694
Borehamwood, Herts WD6 1JG	Karl Wilson
www.elstreedrapes.com	

Entertainment Drapery Services	**01753-654403**
Unit 6, Bangor Park Farm	Fax 01753-654403
Bangor Road South, Iver Heath, Bucks SL0 0AZ	Colin Pearce
Hawthorn Theatrical	**01664-821101**
Crown Business Park	Fax 01664-821119
Old Dalby, Leics LE14 3NQ	Leisa Tomaselli
www.hawthorns.uk.com	
House Couturier	**020-7371 9255**
285 New Kings Road	Anne Thompson
London SW6 4RD	
Interior FX	**01455-612744**
Unit 2, Maizefield	Fax 01455-613412
Hinckley Fields Industrial Estate, Leics LE10 1YF	William Day
J & C Joel	**01422-833835**
Corporation Mill, Corporation Street	Fax 01422-835157
Sowerby Bridge, Halifax, W Yorks HX6 2QQ	Suzanne Wynne
Ken Creasey	**020-7277 1645**
34 Queens Row	Fax 020-7277 1701
London SE17 2PX	Graham Creasey
Metro Rigging & Drape Hire	**07973-115216**
metrorigging@hotmail.com	Fax 020-8341 1318
www.metrorigging.co.uk	Vince Shaw Lee Sherlock
Pinewood Studios Drapery	**01753-656245**
Part of the Pinewood Studios Group	Fax 01753-656202
Pinewood Road, Iver Heath, Bucks SL0 0NH	Frank Howe
www.pinewoodgroup.com	
Rex Howard Drapes	**020-8955 6940**
Unit F, Western Trading Estate	Fax 020-8955 6901
Trading Estate Road, London NW10 7LU	Sam Hooper Wayne Swann
www.rex-howard.co.uk	
Russell & Chapple	**020-7836 7521**
11 Garman Road	Fax 020-7497 0554
London N17 0UR	Andrew Milne Home
www.randc.net	
Russell & Chapple	**020-7836 7521**
68 Drury Lane	Fax 020-7497 0554
London WC2B 5SP	Andrew Milne Home
www.randc.net	
S2 Events	**020-7928 5474**
3-5 Valentine Place	Fax 020-7928 6082
London SE1 8QH	Wolter Dammers
www.s2events.co.uk	
Screens UK	**01932-560175**
Shepperton Studios, Studios Road	Fax 01932-560175
Shepperton, Middx TW17 0QD	Gary Handley
www.screensuk.com	
Seasons Textiles	**020-8965 6161**
9 Gorst Road	Fax 020-8961 6433
London NW10 6LA	Sue Toone
www.seasonstextiles.co.uk	

Shepperton Drape Shop	**01932-560175**
Shepperton Studios, Studios Road Shepperton, Middx TW17 0QD www.sheppertondrapes.co.uk	Fax 01932-560175 Cleo Nethersole
The Stockyard	**020-8963 9944**
Unit A, Genesis Rainsford Road, London NW10 7RG www.stockyard.tv	Fax 020-8963 9955 Ron Painter

DRY CLEANING & LAUNDRY SERVICES

Blue Dragon (Hillingdon)	**01895-236571**
Whiteleys Parade, Uxbridge Road Hillingdon, Middx UB10 0NZ www.bluedragon.uk.com	Fax 01895-812950 Colin Hill

DVD & BLU-RAY AUTHORING

Adaptatech	**020-8987 6161**
Unit 2, Bell Industrial Estate Cunnington Street, London W4 5HB www.adaptatech.co.uk	Fax 0870-458 2659 John Farrant
The Allotment	**0117-973 7003**
Downfield Villa 1D Downfield Road, Bristol BS8 2TG	Fax 0117-973 7003 Laurie Jones
Chapel Media	**020-7938 5329**
The Studios 8 Hornton Place, London W8 4LZ	Fax 020-7937 4326
DARE Post	**020-7734 5370**
16 Dufours Place London W1F 7SP	
Deluxe Digital Studios	**020-7437 4402**
7-11 Lexington Street London W1F 9AF	Fax 020-7437 4403 Willl Morley
Elite Television	**0113-262 3342**
248 Meanwood Road Leeds LS7 2HZ www.elitetv.co.uk	Fax 0113-262 3798 Stuart Josephs
Eyeframe	**020-7534 4888**
25-26 Poland Street London W1F 8QN	Fax 020-7287 8796 James Greenwall
ITFC	**020-8752 0352**
28 Concord Road London W3 0TH www.itfc.com	Fax 020-8993 6393 Liz Clarke
Lightning Media	**020-8998 9911**
Unit 32, Sheraton Business Centre 20 Wadsworth Road, Perivale, Middx UB6 7JB www.lightningmedia.co.uk	Fax 020-8998 2781 Lee Patel

Meedja	**020-8742 2792**
Unit 9, Bell Industrial Estate	Fax 020-8742 1038
Cunnington Street, London W4 5HB	Sarah Bradley
Metropolis DVD	**020-8742 1111**
The Power House	Fax 020-8742 3777
70 Chiswick High Road, London W4 1SY	Richard Osborn
Northern Pro-Media Services	**07890-452236**
PO Box 232	Steve Cooper-Bagnall
Manchester M32 2AQ	
PIMC	**0871-789 6810**
26 Eastfield Avenue	Cliff Oxlade
Basingstoke, Hants RG21 4BQ	
Pink Pigeon	**020-7439 3266**
34-35 Berwick Street	Fax 020-7439 3277
London W1F 8RP	Will Timbers
Printout	**020-7387 1325**
92 Cleveland Street	Stuart Livesey
London W1T 6NN	
Re:fine	**020-8962 2600**
316-318 Latimer Road	Fax 020-8962 2626
London W10 6QN	Symon Roue
Sonic Arts	**020-8962 3000**
Unit 1, Shaftesbury Centre	Fax 020-8962 6200
85 Barlby Road, London W10 6BN	Avi Landenberg

Sonic Solutions	**020-7437 1100**
22 Warwick Street	Fax 020-7437 1151
London W1B 5NF	
Sony DADC UK	**01403-739600**
Southwater Business Park, Worthing Road	Fax 01403-739601
Southwater, W Sussex RH13 9YT	Georg Schafrath
Stanley Productions	**020-7439 0311**
147 Wardour Street	Fax 020-7437 2126
London W1F 8WD	Steve Langston Mick Pruce
www.stanleysonline.co.uk	
Two Plus Two Multimedia	**01753-708500**
268 Bath Road	Fax 01753-708458
Slough, Berks SL1 4DX	Barry Tyler

DVD & BLU-RAY COPY PROTECTION

Rovi	**01628-677300**
Malvern House, 14-18 Bell Street	Fax 01628-677392
Maidenhead, Berks SL6 1BR	Pablo Rojas
Stanley Productions	**020-7439 0311**
147 Wardour Street	Fax 020-7437 2126
London W1F 8WD	Steve Langston Mick Pruce
www.stanleysonline.co.uk	

DVD & BLU-RAY DUPLICATION

10th Planet	**020-7434 2345**
68-70 Wardour Street	Fax 020-7287 2040
London W1F 0TB	Richard Lamb
4B Martinvest	**0845-644 1869**
Unit 3, Tring Business Park	Fax 0845-166 2869
Icknield Way, Tring, Herts HP23 4JX	Steve Bridson
Adaptatech	**020-8987 6161**
Unit 2, Bell Industrial Estate	Fax 0870-458 2659
Cunnington Street, London W4 5HB	John Farrant
www.adaptatech.co.uk	
AG Studios	**01727-762300**
15-17 Central Drive	Arif Gardner
St Albans, Herts AL4 0UX	
Amstore CD & DVD Production	**020-7232 5820**
Block J, Tower Bridge Business Complex	Fax 020-7237 6097
100 Clements Road, London SE16 4DG	James Roth
BDI Imaging	**0113-238 1031**
11 Primley Park Mount	David Benedict
Leeds LS17 7JL	

Bright Spark Studios   0845-257 7278

Sparkhouse Studios   Andrew Deptford
Ropewalk, Lincoln LN6 7DQ
www.brightsparkstudios.com

Copydisk (UK)   01992-446396

Unit 29, Plumpton House   Fax 01992-470131
Plumpton Road, Hoddesdon, Herts EN11 0LB   Geoff Long

Copymaster International   020-8543 9223

14 Lombard Road   Fax 020-8543 3419
London SW19 3TZ   Dave Atkinson

Copytrax   01954-212200

Unit 35, Dry Drayton Industries   Fax 01954-211950
Scotland Road, Cambs CB23 8AT   Philip Arlingham

dBMasters   01795-597755

9 Waterside Close, Upper Brents   Fax 01795-597766
Faversham, Kent ME13 7AU

The Digital Audio Company   01756-797100

Unit 3, Carleton Business Park   Fax 01756-797101
Carleton New Road, Skipton, N Yorks BD23 2AA   Dave Aston

Disc Wizards   020-8861 2349

Unit 11, Raymac House
Harrow, Middx HA3 7RR

Discus Group   0871-220 0199

PO Box 500   Fax 0871-715 0304
Northampton NN3 3WQ   Andrew Roberts

Downstream   01270-625125

44 Marsh Lane   Fax 07006-077212
Nantwich, Cheshire CW5 5LH   Edward Leetham

DQC   01442-262900

John Dickinson Centre, London Road   Fax 01442-262990
Hemel Hempstead, Herts HP3 9QU   Gavin McBride Wilson

DVD Plus Multimedia   01582-404146

18-26 Latimer Road   Fax 01582-400764
Luton, Beds LU1 3UZ

Friendly Mouse   0870-900 0016

194 Red Lion Road   Fax 0870-900 0016
Surbiton, Surrey KT6 7RA   John Deane

Lightning Media   020-8998 9911

Unit 32, Sheraton Business Centre   Fax 020-8998 2781
20 Wadsworth Road, Perivale, Middx UB6 7JB   Lee Patel
www.lightningmedia.co.uk

Media Heaven   0113-244 3550

Unit 12, Castleton Close Industrial Estate   Fax 0113-244 3994
Armley Road, Leeds LS12 2DS   Paul Lines

Mint Copies   0161-432 9012

South Manchester Studios, Battersea Road   Fax 0161-477 9191
Heaton Mersey, Stockport, Cheshire SK4 3EA   Martin Tetlow

MRH Duplication   0845-130 7475

The Old School House   Rob Hadley
Wroxeter, Shropshire SY5 6PH

Multi Media Replication   01264-336330

Unit 4, Balksbury Estate   Fax 01264-336694
Upper Clatford, Andover, Hants SP11 7LW   Philip Hall

Music Ventures   01743-884567

5-6 Vennington, Westbury   Fax 01743-885123
Shrewsbury, Shropshire SY5 9RG   Andrew Smales

One Stop Media   020-8991 2610

Hazelwood, Perivale Lane   Fax 020-8997 0180
Perivale, Middx UB6 8TL   Phil Stringer

Peak White   0845-874 1922

1 Latimer Road   Richard Bonfield
Teddington, Middx TW11 8QA

Ram Peripherals   020-8543 9222

14 Lombard Road   Fax 020-8543 3419
London SW19 3TZ   Martin Pickard

Software Logistics   01494-455545

Unit 7, The Valley Centre   Fax 01494-455556
Gordon Road, High Wycombe, Bucks HP13 6EQ   Barry Hurley

Sounds Good   0118-930 1700

12 Chiltern Enterprise Centre, Station Road   Fax 0118-930 1709
Theale, Reading, Berks RG7 4AA   Henry Smithson

Stanley Productions   020-7439 0311

147 Wardour Street   Fax 020-7437 2126
London W1F 8WD   Steve Langston Mick Pruce
www.stanleysonline.co.uk

TC Soho   020-7851 9180

1A Poland Street   Fax 020-7287 5323
London W1F 8PR   Sandra Rumble

TV Set   020-7637 3322

22 Newman Street   Fax 020-7637 1011
London W1T 1PH

VT Group   0845-257 1510

Portland Gate   Fax 0871-522 7267
21 Portland Square, Bristol BS2 8SJ   Amy Lewis

DVD & BLU-RAY PACKAGING

Adaptatech	020-8987 6161
Unit 2, Bell Industrial Estate	Fax 0870-458 2659
Cunnington Street, London W4 5HB	John Farrant
www.adaptatech.co.uk	

AGI Amaray	01536-274800
Amaray House, Arkwright Road	Fax 01536-274902
Corby, Northants NN17 5AE	William Millen

Stanley Productions	020-7439 0311
147 Wardour Street	Fax 020-7437 2126
London W1F 8WD	Steve Langston Mick Pruce
www.stanleysonline.co.uk	

EDITING EQUIPMENT - RENTAL

Broadcast Television Facilities	0161-926 9808
Acuba House, Lymm Road	Fax 0161-929 9000
Little Bollington, Altrincham, Manchester WA14 4SY	Robert Foster
www.broadcast-tv.co.uk	

Coach House Studios	020-8740 8000
2A Frithville Gardens	Fax 020-8743 8088
London W12 7JN	John Walbeoffe

Digital Media Rentals	0845-607 6635
179 Wardour Street	Fax 020-7534 3411
London W1F 8WY	Duncan Napier-Bell
www.digitalmediarentals.co.uk	

Edit Heaven	020-8949 8949
99 Cambridge Road	Bryan Comley
New Malden, Surrey KT3 3QP	

Hammerhead TV Facilities	020-8646 5511
Unit 19, Liongate Enterprise Park	Fax 020-8646 6163
80 Morden Road, Mitcham, Surrey CR4 4NY	Darrin Dart
www.hammerheadtv.com	

Hammerhead TV Facilities	0131-229 5000
9 Merchiston Mews	Fax 0131-229 2831
Edinburgh EH10 4PE	Phil Mews
www.hammerheadtv.com	

Hammerhead TV Facilities	0141-429 4200
Unit 1, The Tollgate	Fax 0141-429 4211
21 Marine Crescent, Glasgow G51 1HD	Phil Mews
www.hammerheadtv.com	

Hammerhead TV Facilities	0161-431 6400
Unit 2, Rugby Park, Battersea Road	Fax 0161-431 6300
Heaton Mersey, Stockport, Manchester SK4 3EB	John Dardis
www.hammerheadtv.com	

Hireworks	01753-656248
Pinewood Studios, Pinewood Road	Fax 01753-656145
Iver Heath, Bucks SL0 0NH	Lawrie Read

Hyperactive Broadcast 01252-519191

5 The Royston Centre, Lynchford Lane Fax 01252-513939
Ash Vale, Surrey GU12 5PQ James Gander Liam Wife
www.hyperactivebroadcast.com

Prime Focus 020-7437 2626

58 Old Compton Street
London W1D 4UF
www.primefocusworld.com

Salon

020-8746 7611 Fax 020-8746 7613
Email: hire@salonrentals.com
www.salonrentals.com
Salon House, Swainson Road, London W3 7XB
Contact: Nick Long
The UK's longest established editing equipment hire firm
supplying the latest post production kit including Avid's and
Final Cut's, HD/SD VTR's and shared storage solutions plus
traditional linear film equipment. Competitively priced with
full ACSR support as standard. Worldwide credits include:
Inception, Clash Of The Titans and Strike Back.

Video Europe 020-7494 1818

8 Golden Square Fax 020-7494 1717
London W1F 9HY Matt Marner
www.videoeurope.co.uk

Video Europe Wales 029-2059 5111

The Television Centre Fax 029-2059 5222
Culverhouse Cross, Cardiff CF5 6XJ Tom McNally
www.videoeurope.co.uk

XS Broadcast Equipment Hire 01932-454040

Bramshill, Guildford Road Fax 01932-454045
Ottershaw, Surrey KT16 0QN Stephanie Taylor

XTFX 020-7636 7855

12 Stephen Mews Fax 020-7908 7240
London W1T 1AH James Hamilton-Hislop
www.xtfx.co.uk

EDITING EQUIPMENT - SALE

Apple Computers (UK) 020-8218 1000

2 Furze Ground Way, Stockley Park Fax 020-8569 2957
Uxbridge, Middx UB11 1BB

Autodesk 020-7851 8000

Ingeni Building Fax 020-7851 8001
15-17 Broadwick Street, London W1F 0DE Kirsten Cameron

Avid Technology Europe 01753-655999

Pinewood Studios, Pinewood Road Fax 01753-654999
Iver Heath, Bucks SL0 0NH Dawn Egerton

Cypher Ams 01825-766665

148 High Street Fax 01825-760704
Uckfield, E Sussex TN22 1AT Bob Johnson

Film Guernsey	**01481-234567**
Raymond Falla House, Longue Rue	Fax 01481-235015
St Martins, Guernsey GY1 6AF	Jason Moriarty
Film Hampshire	**01962-846381**
Economic Development Office	Fax 01962-878131
The Castle, Winchester SO23 8UJ	Alexa Dugmore
www.filmhampshire.org.uk	
Film London	**020-7613 7676**
Suite 6.10, The Tea Building	Fax 020-7613 7677
56 Shoreditch High Street, London E1 6JJ	Helen Mackenzie
Glasgow Film Office	**0141-287 0424**
City Chambers	Fax 0141-287 0311
George Square, Glasgow G2 1DU	Jennifer Reynolds
Highlands Of Scotland Film Commission	**01463-702955**
The Highland Council	Fax 01463-702298
Glenurquhart Road, Inverness IV3 5NX	Trish Shorthouse
www.scotfilm.org	
Kent Film Office	**01622-696822**
Invicta House, County Hall	Fax 01622-221073
Maidstone, Kent ME14 1XX	Gabrielle Lindemann
Liverpool Film Office	**0151-233 6380**
Liverpool City Council, PO Box 2008	Fax 0151-233 6333
Municipal Buildings, Dale Street, Liverpool L2 2DH	Kevin Bell
Northern Film & Media	**0191-275 5942**
Studio 3, The Kiln	Fax 0191-275 5931
Hoults Yard, Newcastle-upon-Tyne NE6 1AB	Gayle Woodruffe
Northern Ireland Screen	**028-9023 2444**
Alfred House	Fax 028-9023 9918
21 Alfred Street, Belfast BT2 8ED	Andrew Reid
Portsmouth Film Office	**023-9283 4116**
Civic Offices, Guildhall Square	Fax 023-9283 4159
Portsmouth, Hants PO1 2AD	Louise Rodwell
Scottish Screen	**0141-302 1700**
249 West George Street	Fax 0141-302 1711
Glasgow G2 4QE	Amy Fairbairn
www.scottishscreen.com	
Screen East	**01603-776920**
2 Millennium Plain	Fax 01603-767191
Norwich NR2 1TF	Laurie Hayward
Screen East	**01923-495051**
Leavesden Studios, South Way	Fax 01923-333007
Leavesden, Herts WD25 7LT	Kerry Ixer
Screen South	**01303-259777**
The Wedge, 75-81 Tontine Street	Fax 01303-259786
Folkestone, Kent CT20 1JR	Jo Nolan
www.screensouth.org	
Screen South	**01753-656412**
Pinewood Studios, Pinewood Road	Fax 01753-657029
Iver Heath, Bucks SL0 0NH	Jenny Cooper
www.screensouth.org	

Screen WM	**0121-265 7120**
9 Regent Place	Fax 0121-265 7180
Birmingham B1 3NJ	Lee Thomas
Screen Yorkshire	**0113-294 4410**
Studio 22	Fax 0113-294 4989
46 The Calls, Leeds LS2 7EY	Hugo Heppell
South West Scotland Screen Commission	**01387-263666**
Gracefield Arts Centre	Mark Geddes
28 Edinburgh Road, Dumfries DG1 1JQ	
South West Screen	**0117-952 9977**
St Bartholomews Court	Fax 0117-952 9988
Lewins Mead, Bristol BS1 5BT	Joe Wheatley
TayScreen	**01382-432483**
DCA	Fax 01382-432471
152 Nethergate, Dundee DD1 4DY	Julie Craik
UK Film Council	**020-7861 7861**
10 Little Portland Street	Fax 020-7861 7862
London W1W 7JG	Colin Brown
www.ukfilmcouncil.org.uk	
UK Film Council (US)	**+1 310 652 6156**
329 North Wetherly Drive, Suite 206	Andy Weltman
Beverly Hills, CA 90211, USA	
www.ukfilmcouncil.org.uk/usa	
Vision+Media	**0844-395 0385**
100 Broadway	Anna Cousins
Salford Quays, Manchester M50 2UW	
Wales Screen Commission	**029-2043 5385**
33-35 West Bute Street	Fax 029-2043 5380
Cardiff CF10 5LH	Penny Skuse
West London Film Office	**020-8825 7575**
Perceval House	Mike Liddall
14-16 Uxbridge Road, London W5 2HL	

FILM MARKETING

Creative Partnership	**020-7439 7762**
13 Bateman Street	Fax 020-7437 1467
London W1D 3AF	Sally Chapman

FILM NETWORK

Shooting People	
info@shootingpeople.org	

FILM RESTORATION & TREATMENT

Film Preservation Centre	**01646-687737**
	Katrina Loftin

RTI (UK)	**01895-252191**
Unit 6, Swan Wharf Business Centre	Fax 01895-274692
Waterloo Road, Uxbridge, Middx UB8 2RA	Caroline McGuire

FILM TO DVD TRANSFER

Cine To DVD Transfers	**0117-987 7711**
Portland Film Studios	Fax 0871-522 7267
21 Portland Square, Bristol BS2 8SJ	Karren James

FILTERS - CAMERA

Calmar Filters	**01844-352651**
13 Mill Lane	Martin Lafferty
Chinnor, Oxon OX39 4QU	
The London Filter Company	**020-7735 1900**
Unit 107, Canterbury Court	Fax 020-7820 1718
Kennington Business Park, 1-3 Brixton Road, London SW9 6DE Carey Duffy	
www.camerafilters.co.uk	
Tiffen International	**0870-100 1220**
Unit 5, Avonbury Business Park	Fax 01869-321766
Howes Lane, Bicester, Oxon OX26 2UA	
Calmar Filters	**01844-352651**
13 Mill Lane	Martin Lafferty
Chinnor, Oxon OX39 4QU	
Van Diemen Films	**01276-61222**
Bridge House, Branksome Park Road	Fax 01276-61549
Camberley, Surrey GU15 2AQ	Christopher Smith
www.vandiemenbroadcast.co.uk	

FILTERS - LIGHTING

Chris James & Co	**020-8896 1772**
43 Colville Road	Fax 020-8896 1773
London W3 8BL	Barry Frankling
Cotech	**01495-725276**
Units 13-16, Tafarnaubach Industrial Estate	Fax 01495-725765
Tredegar, Gwent NP22 3AA	Daniel Llovet
Lee Filters	**01264-366245**
Central Way, Walworth Industrial Estate	Fax 01264-355058
Andover, Hants SP10 5AN	Ralph Young
Rosco	**020-8659 2300**
Kangley Bridge Road	Fax 020-8659 3153
London SE26 5AQ	Gordon Tomkins
White Light	**020-8254 4840**
20 Merton Industrial Estate	Fax 020-8254 4841
Jubilee Way, London SW19 3WL	Andrew Stringer

FINANCE - EQUIPMENT

Audio Visual Asset Management	**01737-830084**
Little Orchard House, Bears Den	Fax 01737-830063
Kingswood, Surrey KT20 6PL	Duncan Rushmer

Azule	**0845-260 2300**
2-4 High Street	Fax 0845-260 2301
Datchet, Berks SL3 9EA	Peter Savage

Clockwork Capital	**020-7287 3132**
14 Livonia Street	Fax 020-7292 0630
London W1F 8AG	Albert Seaward

European Asset Finance	**0844-800 3670**
Vine House, 7 Vine Lane	Fax 01252-794184
Farnham, Surrey GU10 4TD	John Mulheron

Fineline Media Finance	**020-8334 2100**
Heron House, 5 Heron Square	Fax 020-8334 2101
Richmond, Surrey TW9 1EL	Gareth Wilding
www.fineline.co.uk	

MediaLease	**01327-872531**
Nene House, Sopwith Way	Fax 01327-828360
Drayton Fields, Daventry, Northants NN11 8EA	Paul Robson Matt Vaughan
www.medialease.com	

Plus Finance	**01494-783773**
The Old Perfumery, 24 Higham Road	Fax 0870-013 4055
Chesham, Bucks HP5 2AF	Steve Pullen

Soho Media Finance	**020-3388 0212**
77B Berwick Street	John Edwards
London W1F 8TH	

FINANCE - FILM

4G Media Partners	**01753-422740**
Pinewood Studios, Pinewood Road	07711-668121
Iver Heath, Bucks SL0 0NH	Helen Gammons

Aquarius Films	**020-7291 1065**
9 Wimpole Street	Terence Potter
London W1G 9SR	

Aramid Capital	**020-7291 5250**
2 Cavendish Square	Fax 020-7291 5251
London W1G 0PU	Simon Fawcett

Baker Street Media Entertainment	**020-7637 0272**
25 Weymouth Street	Fax 020-7143 4211
London W1G 7BP	Keith Evans

Bank Leumi UK	**020-7907 8000**
20 Stratford Place	Fax 020-7907 8192
London W1C 1BG	Daniel Barr

Barclays Asset & Sales Finance	**0800-616169**
Churchill Plaza, Churchill Way	Fax 01256-791950
Basingstoke, Hants RG21 7GP	

Barclays Bank	**020-7445 5778**
27 Soho Square	Lee Dellar
London W1D 3QR	

BBC Films	**020-8576 7265**
Room 6023, Television Centre	Fax 020-8576 7268
Wood Lane, London W12 7RJ	Jane Wright

Cinemanx	**01624-662666**
Murdoch Chambers, South Quay	Fax 01624-678680
Douglas, Isle Of Man IM1 5PA	Marc Samuelson

Coutts & Co	**020-7753 1268**
440 Strand	Fax 020-7753 1069
London WC2R 0QS	Neil Phelps

Credo Capital	**020-8458 9003**
83 Pall Mall	Martin Churchill
London SW1Y 5ES	

Film4	**020-7306 5190**
124 Horseferry Road	Fax 020-7306 8368
London SW1P 2TX	Katherine Butler

Future Film Group	**020-7009 6767**
10 Old Burlington Street	Fax 020-7009 6766
London W1S 3AG	Stephen Margolis

Grosvenor Park Media	**020-7486 4639**
47 Queen Anne Street	Daniel Taylor
London WIG 9JG	
Howard Kennedy	**020-7546 8889**
19 Cavendish Square	Fax 020-7664 4489
London WIA 2AW	Brian Eagles
Imperial Media	**020-7467 1700**
31 Harley Street	Yanni Koutsomitis
London WIG 9QS	
Ingenious Media	**020-7319 4000**
15 Golden Square	Fax 020-7319 4001
London WIF 9JG	Jim Reeve
Investors In Film	**020-7638 8750**
1 Carthusian Street	Fax 020-7250 3559
London ECIM 6DZ	Albert Collins
Isle Of Man Film	**01624-687173**
Hamilton House, Peel Road	Fax 01624-687171
Douglas, Isle Of Man IMI 5EP	Hilary Dugdale
Limelight Media	**020-7478 9144**
139 Piccadilly	Michael Henry
London WIJ 7NU	
Matador Pictures	**020-7734 4544**
159 Wardour Street	Fax 020-7734 7794
London WIF 8WH	Nigel Thomas
Millennium Film Finance Corporation	**01865-858529**
Riverbank House	Fax 01491-413910
1 Putney Bridge Approach, London SW6 3JD	Graham Duffield
Premiere Picture	**01273-766399**
Hanover House, 118 Queens Road	Fax 01273-326077
Brighton, E Sussex BNI 3XG	Adam Betteridge
Premiere Productions	**020-7255 1650**
3 Colville Place	Peter Fudakowski
London WIT 2BH	
Prescience Film Finance	**01494-670737**
Canon House, 27 London End	Fax 01494-670740
Beaconsfield, Bucks HP9 2HN	Tim Smith

Prime Focus	**020-7565 1000**
37 Dean Street	Shail Shah
London WID 4PT	
www.primefocusworld.com	
Reach Up High Entertainment	**0845-330 5155**
86 Seymore Grove	Fax 0845-330 5156
Manchester M16 0WL	Demetris Kyriacou
Royal Bank Of Scotland	**020-7290 4626**
65 Piccadilly	Fax 020-7290 4692
London WIA 2PP	Chris Pell
Scion Films	**020-7851 5740**
50 Broadwick Street	Fax 020-7851 7541
London WIF 7AG	Beverley Reid
Spice Factory	**01273-739182**
14 Regent Hill	Fax 01273-749122
Brighton, E Sussex BNI 3ED	Michael Cowan
UK Film Council	**020-7861 7861**
10 Little Portland Street	Fax 020-7861 7862
London WIW 7JG	Colin Brown
www.ukfilmcouncil.org.uk	
Wales Creative IP Fund	**029-2033 8131**
Oakleigh House	Fax 029-2033 8198
Park Place, Cardiff CFI0 3DQ	Bethan Bannister

FIRE SAFETY

1st Defense Fire & Rescue Services	**01483-200911**
The South Wing, Building 140	Fax 01483-200994
Dunsfold Park, Cranleigh, Surrey GU6 8TB	Peter Edwards
www.1stdefensefire.co.uk	
Eurosafety (DDA Fire)	**01753-656181**
Pinewood Studios, Pinewood Road	Fax 01753-632820
Iver Heath, Bucks SL0 0NH	
www.ddafire.co.uk	

Firehouse UK	**0161-339 1362**
21 Peterborough Close	Fax 0161-330 3084
Ashton-under-Lyne, Lancs OL6 8XW	Jonathan Carter
www.firehouseuk.com	

Midland Fire Protection Services	**024-7636 7766**
Unit 6	Fax 024-7645 0923
Bayton Way, Coventry CV7 9ER	Liam Smith
www.midlandfire.co.uk	

Rapid Fire Cover	**07825-302402**
Unit 4, Boscomoor Industrial Estate	Matt Owens
Penkridge, Staffs ST19 5QY	
www.rapidfirecover.co.uk	

Thruxton Fire & Rescue Service	**01264-773388**
Unit 12B, Thruxton Industrial Estate	Rob Porter
Thruxton Airport, Hants SP11 8PW	

GOVERNMENT

COI	**020-7261 8349**
Hercules House	Paul Grice
6 Hercules Road, London SE1 7DU	

Department For Culture Media & Sport	**020-7211 6200**
2-4 Cockspur Street	Fax 020-7211 6337
London SW1Y 5DH	Jeremy Hunt

GRAPHICS

422 Manchester	**0161-839 6080**
South Central	Fax 0161-839 6081
11 Peter Street, Manchester M2 5QR	Damien Lynch

422 South	**0117-946 7222**
St Johns Court	Fax 0117-946 7722
Whiteladies Road, Bristol BS8 2QY	Ben Risk

Adams Trainor	**020-7278 5711**
199 Kings Cross Road	Fax 020-7278 6809
London WC1X 9DB	Jon Adams

Air - CGI	**01299-896110**
Brookend	Fax 01299-896110
Abberley, Worcs WR6 6BU	Hannah Morton

Atomic Arts	**020-7419 4190**
49 Goodge Street	Brooke Stanford
London W1T 1TE	

Attik	**020-7864 4747**
9 Lower John Street	James Sommerville
London W1S 9DZ	

Bernard Heyes Design	**020-7287 0202**
7 Meard Street	Fax 020-7434 9334
London W1F 0EW	Linda Thomson

Big Squid	01225-336990
1-2 Queens Parade Place	Richard Higgs
Bath BAI 2NN	
The Bionic Group	01753-653456
Pinewood Studios, Pinewood Road	Fax 01753-654507
Iver Heath, Bucks SL0 0NH	Andrew Eio
Burrell Durrant Hifle	0117-973 7575
71 South Parade	Fax 0117-923 7823
Oakfield Road, Bristol BS8 2BB	Pic Haywood
Cat & Mouse	01293-538358
Unit 10, Lloyds Court	Fax 01293-538469
Manor Royal, Crawley, W Sussex RH10 9QX	Simon Lucas
www.catandmouse.tv	
CelAction	020-7226 3649
PO Box LB608	Fax 020-7354 8868
London WIA 9LB	Andy Blazdell
Cinesite (Europe)	020-7973 4000
Medius House	Fax 020-7973 4040
2 Sheraton Street, London WIF 8BH	
www.cinesite.com	
Clockwork Digital	020-8211 3855
Studio A, 55 Alverstone Avenue	Simon Winstanley
East Barnet, Herts EN4 8ED	
Component Graphics	020-7631 4477
5 Berners Mews	Mike Kenny
London WIT 3AJ	
DeathtothePixels	07919-358277
62A Oldham Street	Chris Howart
Manchester M4 ILE	
Eclipse Creative	0845-643 6404
74-78 Park Road	Fax 0845-643 6405
Cardiff CF14 7BR	
Elite Television	0113-262 3342
248 Meanwood Road	Fax 0113-262 3798
Leeds LS7 2HZ	Stuart Josephs
www.elitetv.co.uk	
G2 Video Systems	01252-737151
5 Mead Lane	Fax 01252-737147
Farnham, Surrey GU9 7DY	Greg Hollidge
Gizmo Animation	01243-543697
19 Brittens Cottages, Brittens Lane	Fax 01243-543697
Fontwell, W Sussex BN18 0ST	Steve Whiteley
www.gizmoanimation.co.uk	
Graphix Asset	0117-911 3889
Tyndall House	Chris Gledhill
17 Whiteladies Road, Bristol BS8 IPB	
Huge Designs	020-7637 4843
9 Bourlet Close	Fax 020-7637 4846
London WIW 7BP	Hugo Moss

I-BOX	07958-942270
1 Holly Bush Lane	Jon Underwood
Hampton, Middx TW12 2QR	
Inferno	028-9033 1220
7-11 Linenhall Street	Colin Williams
Belfast BT2 8AA	
Ionoco	01962-810555
The Old Drill Hall, Hyde Close	Fax 01962-810666
Winchester, Hants SO23 7DT	Chris Goss
ISO	0141-572 9150
41 St Vincent Place	Fax 0141-572 9151
Glasgow G1 2ER	Suzy Glass
Jump Design & Direction	020-7253 1191
Unit 25	Fax 020-7253 5526
112 Tabernacle Street, London EC2A 4LE	Kate Norley
Kinemato	020-7350 2919
36 Bolingbroke Grove	Chris Allies
London SW11 6EJ	
Liquid TV	020-7437 2623
1-2 Portland Mews	Fax 020-7437 2618
London W1F 8JE	Asra Alikhan
Loose Moose Productions	020-7287 3821
74 Berwick Street	Fax 020-7734 4220
London W1F 8TF	Glenn Holberton
www.loosemoose.net	
Mainframe	020-7833 5546
Studio 10, The Piano Factory	Fax 020-7833 4893
117 Farringdon Road, London EC1R 3BX	Adam Jenns
mediahouse	020-8233 5400
3 Burlington Lane	Fax 020-8233 5401
London W4 2TH	Cherry Portbury
www.mediahouse.tv	
mediahouse FX	020-8233 5716
3 Burlington Lane	Andrew Gould
London W4 2TH	
www.mediahousefx.com	
Mercury FX	07974-823289
3 Cwrt Morgan	Craig Higgins
Caerwent, Monmouths NP26 5QZ	
Moov	020-8994 5333
Power Road Studios	Nevil Appleton
114 Power Road, London W4 5PY	
Nuts	020-7734 1674
Wedgwood Mews	Fax 020-7734 1391
12-13 Greek Street, London W1D 4BA	Sarah Mackay
The Pavement Studios	020-7220 2990
1 Lexington Street	Fax 020-7437 5402
London W1F 9AF	

Skaramoosh London	020-7240 1507
8-10 Neals Yard	Fax 020-7100 8225
London WC2H 9DP	Daniel Slight
Streetmonkey	028-9032 3662
Cotton Court	Ian Patton
38-42 Waring Street, Belfast BT1 2ED	
Studio Alba	01851-701125
54A Seaforth Road	Fax 01851-701094
Stornoway, Isle Of Lewis HS1 2SD	Willie Macleod
www.studioalba.com	
Thinkfarm	020-7383 8838
84 Marchmont Street	Stephen Izatt
London WC1N 1AG	
Useful Companies	01753-657200
Pinewood Studios, Pinewood Road	Fax 01753-657240
Iver Heath, Bucks SL0 0NH	Justin Owen
Wurmser Aids	020-8961 4005
Unit 23, Cumberland Business Park	Fax 020-8961 3886
17 Cumberland Avenue, London NW10 7RT	Jeremy Tidy

GRIP ENGINEERING

Bee's Engineering Company	020-8863 5666
Unit 5, Tudor Enterprise Park	Fax 020-8863 5563
Tudor Road, Harrow, Middx HA3 5JQ	Brian Busby
Doughty Engineering	01425-478961
Crow Arch Lane	Fax 01425-474481
Ringwood, Hants BH24 1NZ	Julian Chiverton
SSE Grip Gear	020-8449 8950
19 Sutton Crescent	Fax 020-8449 8950
Barnet, Herts EN5 2SW	Alan Saul

GRIP EQUIPMENT

Alpha Grip	01753-639200
Pinewood Studios, Pinewood Road	Fax 01753-783888
Iver Heath, Bucks SL0 0NH	Eugene McDonagh
www.alphagrip.co.uk	
ARRI Media Grip	01895-457100
3 Highbridge, Oxford Road	Fax 01895-457101
Uxbridge, Middx UB8 1LX	Dean Amor
Camera Revolution	01932-592322
Shepperton Studios, Studios Road	Fax 01932-592202
Shepperton, Middx TW17 0QD	Ian Speed
www.camerarevolution.com	
CCD Rental	020-8960 8777
Pinewood Studios, Pinewood Road	Fax 020-8960 6700
Iver Heath, Bucks SL0 0NH	Kerry Jones

Chapman UK	**01923-265953**
Unit 5, Kingley Park	Fax 01923-268315
Station Road, Kings Langley, Herts WD4 8GW	Dennis Fraser
www.chapmanleonard.com	
Decode	**020-8735 9170**
Unit 3, Parkside	Fax 020-8741 8952
Ravenscourt Park, London W6 0UU	Samuel Martin
www.decodeuk.com	
Focus24	**020-7033 6555**
30 Hoxton Square	Ben Mitchell
London N1 6NN	
www.focus24.tv	
The Grip Firm	**020-8977 5005**
24 Oxford Road	Fax 020-8977 9388
Teddington, Middx TW11 0PZ	Jimmy Mullins
Grip Unit	**01923-775785**
Pendeen, Copthorne Close	Fax 01923-721328
Croxley Green, Herts WD3 4AJ	Barry Read
Gripack	**01277-656759**
106 Noak Hill Road	Stuart Godfrey
Billericay, Essex CM12 9UH	
Gripology	**01372-452107**
65 Eastwick Drive	Mark Ellis
Great Bookham, Surrey KT23 3PU	

Hammerhead TV Facilities	**020-8646 5511**
Unit 19, Liongate Enterprise Park	Fax 020-8646 6163
80 Morden Road, Mitcham, Surrey CR4 4NY	Darrin Dart
www.hammerheadtv.com	
Hammerhead TV Facilities	**0131-229 5000**
9 Merchiston Mews	Fax 0131-229 2831
Edinburgh EH10 4PE	Phil Mews
www.hammerheadtv.com	
Hammerhead TV Facilities	**0141-429 4200**
Unit 1, The Tollgate	Fax 0141-429 4211
21 Marine Crescent, Glasgow G51 1HD	Phil Mews
www.hammerheadtv.com	
Hammerhead TV Facilities	**0161-431 6400**
Unit 2, Rugby Park, Battersea Road	Fax 0161-431 6300
Heaton Mersey, Stockport, Manchester SK4 3EB	John Dardis
www.hammerheadtv.com	
High Level TV	**0845-094 4640**
Building D1, Fairoaks Airport	Fax 0845-094 4670
Chobham, Surrey GU24 8HU	Ian Leslie
www.highlevel.tv	
Independent Grip Company	**01932-242910**
Halliford Studios, Manygate Lane	Fax 01932-246336
Shepperton, Middx TW17 9EG	Adam Young
www.independentgrip.co.uk	
Lightning Media	**020-8998 9911**
Unit 32, Sheraton Business Centre	Fax 020-8998 2781
20 Wadsworth Road, Perivale, Middx UB6 7JB	Lee Patel
www.lightningmedia.co.uk	
Movietech Camera Rentals	**01753-650007**
Pinewood Studios, Pinewood Road	Fax 01753-650006
Iver Heath, Bucks SL0 0NH	John Buckley
www.movietech.co.uk	
Optical Support	**020-7281 0999**
203 Belgravia Workshops	Fax 020-7561 0115
157-163 Marlborough Road, London N19 4NF	Chris Edwards
www.opticalsupport.co.uk	
Panavision Grips	**020-8578 2382**
Metropolitan Centre, Bristol Road	Fax 020-8578 1536
Greenford, Middx UB6 8GD	Mark Furssedonn
Picture Canning North	**0191-265 0061**
156 Brinkburn Street	Jamie Hutchinson
Newcastle-upon-Tyne NE6 2AR	
www.picturecanningnorth.co.uk	
Polecam	**01234-855222**
10 Sunbeam Road, Woburn Road Industrial Estate	Fax 01234-855270
Kempston, Beds MK42 7BY	Steffan Hewitt
ProVision	**0113-222 8222**
96 Kirkstall Road	Fax 0113-222 8110
Leeds LS3 1HD	Danny Howarth

R & M Prop Rentals	020-8232 9701
97-99 Worton Road	Fax 020-8232 9738
Isleworth, Middx TW7 6EG	Mike Pratt
www.rmtv.co.uk/prophire	

HOTEL BOOKING SERVICES

Access Bookings	**0870-855 5777**
53A Tamworth Road	Fax 0870-950 5907
Lichfield, Staffs WS14 9HG	Patricia Barnes
www.accessbookings.com	
The Apartment Service	**0870-080 2303**
5-6 Francis Grove	Fax 020-8944 6744
London SW19 4DT	Melanie Degand
www.apartmentservice.com	
Dovetail Foks	**020-7025 1515**
35 Soho Square	Dean Borg
London W1D 3QX	
Executive Status	**0161-613 9300**
Darnell House	Fax 0161-613 9310
14A Kenworthy Lane, Manchester M22 4EJ	Lynda Cronshaw

INSURANCE

Allan Chapman & James

01206-500000 Fax 01206-752216
Email: insurance@acjltd.co.uk
www.acjltd.co.uk
7 Phoenix Square, Wyncolls Road, Severalls Business Park,
Colchester, Essex CO4 9AS
Contact: Simon Miller
Allan Chapman & James have provided an insurance service
to the film, TV and media industry since 1988. Please contact
us for further details.

Aon	**0118-926 1100**
Alexander House, 205-207 Kings Road	Fax 0118-966 7458
Reading, Berks RG1 4LW	Tina Drakeford
Culpeck Insurance Services	**01733-208278**
Vinpenta House, 4 High Causeway	Fax 01733-208610
Whittlesey, Cambs PE7 1AE	Debbie Atkins
IMS London	**020-8805 2211**
Dean House, 193 High Street	Fax 020-8805 2218
Enfield, Middx EN3 4DZ	Turul Brown
Kerry London	**020-8560 1111**
Clare House, Worton Court	Fax 020-8569 7331
Worton Road, Isleworth, Middx TW7 6ER	Paul Samways
Media Insurance Brokers	**020-7287 5054**
Palladium House	Fax 020-7287 0679
1-4 Argyll Street, London W1F 7TA	Boyd Harvey

performance
film & media insurance

the A-list choice for film and media insurance, offering unrivalled cover for freelancers, production/post-production companies, film-makers, studios and equipment suppliers.

Call us now for personal, expert advice on
845 112 0104
or visit our website
www.performance-insurance.tv

Designed for your needs, our flexible approach provides fast, instant cover for annual policies, and you can even buy your short-period insurance online today!

You don't just need insurance-you need... Performance

COLLIER
MEDIA LAW

**Specialising in Media
and Entertainment Law**

Ealing Studios Ealing Green London W5 5EP
+44 (0) 20 8993 5577 Info@CollierMediaLaw.com
www.CollierMediaLaw.com

Blake Lapthorn	**020-7405 2000**
Watchmaker Court	Fax 020-7814 9421
33 St Johns Lane, London EC1M 4DB	Simon Stokes
Butcher Burns	**020-7713 7100**
Beaumont House	Fax 020-7713 6121
47 Mount Pleasant, London WC1X 0AE	Jonathan Krestin
Carr & Co	**01295-275168**
9 Broughton Road	Fax 01295-257870
Banbury, Oxon OX16 9QB	Richard Carr
Charles Russell	**020-7203 5000**
5 Fleet Place	Fax 020-7203 0200
London EC4M 7RD	Cathy Taylor
Clifford Chance	**020-7006 1000**
10 Upper Bank Street	Fax 020-7006 5555
London E14 5JJ	
Clintons Solicitors	**020-7379 6080**
55 Drury Lane	Fax 020-7240 9310
London WC2B 5RZ	
CMS - Cameron McKenna	**020-7367 3000**
Mitre House	Fax 020-7367 2000
160 Aldersgate Street, London EC1A 4DD	
Collier Media Law	**020-8993 5577**
Ealing Studios	Nikki Collier
Ealing Green, London W5 5EP	
www.colliermedialaw.com	
Collyer Bristow	**020-7242 7363**
4 Bedford Row	Fax 020-7405 0555
London WC1R 4DF	Howard Ricklow
Davenport Lyons	**020-7468 2600**
30 Old Burlington Street	Fax 020-7437 8216
London W1S 3NL	Richard Moxon
Denton Wilde Sapte	**020-7242 1212**
1 Fleet Place	Fax 020-7246 7777
London EC4M 7WS	Howard Morris
DLA Piper	**0870-011 1111**
3 Noble Street	Fax 020-7796 6609
London EC2V 7EE	Helen Obi

Eversheds	**0845-497 9797**
Eversheds House	Fax 0845-497 8888
70 Great Bridgewater Street, Manchester M1 5ES	
Field Fisher Waterhouse	**020-7861 4000**
35 Vine Street	Fax 020-7488 0084
London EC3N 2AA	Tim Johnson
Finers Stephens Innocent	**020-7323 4000**
179 Great Portland Street	Fax 020-7580 7069
London W1W 5LS	Mark Stephens
Hammonds	**020-7655 1000**
7 Devonshire Square	Fax 020-7655 1001
London EC2M 4YH	Peter Crossley
Harbottle & Lewis	**020-7667 5000**
Hanover House	Fax 020-7667 5100
14 Hanover Square, London W1S 1HP	Evette Elliott
Lee & Thompson	**020-7935 4665**
Green Garden House	Fax 020-7563 4949
15-22 St Christophers Place, London W1U 1NL	Jeremy Gawade
Lewis Silkin	**020-7074 8000**
5 Chancery Lane	Fax 020-7864 1200
Cliffords Inn, London EC4A 1BL	Ian Jeffery
Michael Simkins	**020-7874 5600**
Lynton House	Fax 020-7874 5601
7-12 Tavistock Square, London WC1H 9LT	Nigel Bennett
Mishcon de Reya	**020-7440 7000**
Summit House	Fax 020-7404 5982
12 Red Lion Square, London WC1R 4QD	
Olswang	**020-7067 3000**
90 High Holborn	Fax 020-7067 3999
London WC1V 6XX	Mark Devereux
Penningtons	**020-7457 3000**
Abacus House	Fax 020-7457 3240
33 Gutter Lane, London EC2V 8AR	Lewis Tolaini
Richard Howard & Co	**020-7831 4511**
Central Court	Fax 020-7831 4512
25 Southampton Building, London WC2A 1AL	Richard Howard
Ross & Craig	**020-7262 3077**
12A Upper Berkeley Street	Fax 020-7258 0104
London W1H 7QE	Ian Bloom
Russell Jones & Walker	**020-7657 1555**
50-52 Chancery Lane	Fax 020-7657 1547
London WC2A 1HL	Clive Howard
Schillings	**020-7034 9000**
11 Bedford Avenue	Fax 020-7034 9200
London WC1B 3AS	
Seddons	**020-7725 8000**
5 Portman Square	Fax 020-7935 5049
London W1H 6NT	

Sheridans	020-7079 0100
Whittington House	Fax 020-7079 0200
Alfred Place, London WC1E 7EA	Robin Hilton
SJ Berwin	**020-7111 2222**
10 Queen Street Place	Fax 020-7111 2000
London EC4R 1BE	
Taylor Wessing	**020-7300 7000**
5 New Street Square	Fax 020-7300 7100
London EC4A 3TW	Paul Mitchell
Wiggin	**020-7612 9612**
22 Percy Street	Fax 01242-224223
London W1T 2BU	Charles Moore

LENSES

Abakus	01778-590117
Grange Farm, Bourne Road	Kenneth Pollitt
Carlby, Stamford, Lincs PE9 4LU	
Canon Broadcast Division	**01737-220539**
Woodhatch Lodge, Cockshot Hill	Fax 01737-220599
Woodhatch, Reigate, Surrey RH2 8BF	Peter Luck
Cooke Optics	**0116-264 0700**
Cooke Close	Fax 0116-264 0707
Thurmaston, Leicester LE4 8PT	Geoffrey Chappell

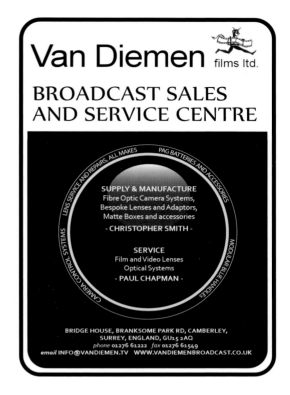

LENSES

Movietech Camera Rentals   01753-650007
Pinewood Studios, Pinewood Road   Fax 01753-650006
Iver Heath, Bucks SL0 0NH   John Buckley
www.movietech.co.uk

Optical Support   020-7281 0999
203 Belgravia Workshops   Fax 020-7561 0115
157-163 Marlborough Road, London N19 4NF   Chris Edwards
www.opticalsupport.co.uk

Pyser - SGI   01732-864111
Fircroft Way   Fax 01732-865544
Edenbridge, Kent TN8 6HA   Paul Goodwin

True Lens Services   01455-848411
20 Bank Terrace   Fax 01455-848311
Barwell, Leics LE9 8GG   Keith Truslove

Van Diemen Films   01276-61222
Bridge House, Branksome Park Road   Fax 01276-61549
Camberley, Surrey GU15 2AQ   Christopher Smith
www.vandiemenbroadcast.co.uk

Video Europe   020-7494 1818
8 Golden Square   Fax 020-7494 1717
London W1F 9HY   Matt Marner
www.videoeurope.co.uk

Video Europe Wales   029-2059 5111
The Television Centre   Fax 029-2059 5222
Culverhouse Cross, Cardiff CF5 6XJ   Tom McNally
www.videoeurope.co.uk

LIBRARIES - FOOTAGE

Adventure Archive   01395-446242
Fudge Cottage, Dalditch Lane   Mandy Dickinson
Budleigh Salterton, Devon EX9 7AH

Aerial Camera Systems (ACS)   01483-426767
Innovation House, Douglas Drive   Fax 01483-413900
Godalming, Surrey GU7 1JX   Matthew Coyde
www.aerialvideolibrary.com

Airtime Television   01628-482763
PO Box 258   Martin White
Maidenhead, Berks SL6 9YR

All Clear Films   020-3137 0599
55 Kewferry Road   Fax 020-8819 6010
Northwood, Middx HA6 2PQ   Mark Jordan
www.allclearfilms.com

AP Archive   020-7482 7482
The Interchange   Fax 020-7413 8327
Oval Road, London NW1 7DZ   Alan Bradshaw

Archive Film Agency   020-8670 3618
49 South Croxted Road   Fax 020-8670 3618
London SE21 8AZ   Agnese Geoghegan

Baim Collection   020-7486 1450
                                      Richard Jeffs

Barnardos   020-8550 8822
Tanners Lane, Barkingside   Fax 020-8551 6870
Ilford, Essex IG6 1QG   Stephen Pover

BBC Information & Archives   020-8576 9669
Room 7012, Television Centre   Natalie Dewar
Wood Lane, London W12 7RJ

BBC Motion Gallery   020-8433 2861
Media Centre   Fax 020-8433 2939
201 Wood Lane, London W12 7TQ   Sylva Onisiforou
www.bbcmotiongallery.com

BFI Archival Footage Sales   020-7957 4842
21 Stephen Street   Fax 020-7957 8968
London W1T 1LN   Sarah Wilde
www.bfi.org.uk/afs

Black Diamond Films   020-7240 4071
15 Bedford Street   Fax 020-7836 6339
London WC2E 9HE   Jim Odoire

Britain On View   020-7578 1000
1 Palace Street   Fax 020-7578 1001
London SW1E 5HX

British Defence Film Library   01494-878278
Chalfont Grove, Narcot Lane   Fax 01494-878007
Chalfont St Peter, Bucks SL9 8TN   Robert Dungate

British Movietonews   01895-833071
Denham Media Park, North Orbital Road Fax 01895-834893
Denham, Middx UB9 5HQ   Barry Florin

Brunswick Formula One   020-8960 0066
26 Macroom Road   Fax 020-8960 4997
London W9 3HY   Rohan Tully

The CCTV Archive   07850-926637
14 Ardilaun Road   Bill Rudgard
London N5 2QR

Clips & Footage   020-7278 1007
Studio 6, Albion Buildings   Fax 020-7278 1009
1 Back Hill, London EC1R 5EN   Jenny Coan

COI Archive @ BFI   020-7957 4842
21 Stephen Street   Fax 020-7957 8968
London W1T 1LN   Sarah Wilde
www.bfi.org.uk/afs

Duke International   01624-640020
Champion House   Fax 01624-640001
Douglas, Isle Of Man IM99 1DD   Jon Quayle

Environmental Investigation Agency 020-7354 7960
62-63 Upper Street   Fax 020-7354 7961
London N1 0NY   Bill Dishington

A story in every frame.

Mr Footage

Film & video stock footage shot on 35mm, HDTV & SD
by award winning cameramen

STOCK FOOTAGE • ONLINE VIDEO • HDTV • 35mm FILM

Team Sports, Soccer, Aerials, World Locations, Natural History,
Historical Footage Web Preview and FTP Download

info@mrfootage.com • stock.mrfootage.com
UK +44 (0)20 8419 8222
DE +49 (0)8151 555 0551 • SE +46 (0)8 559 24 555

Framepool　　　　　　**020-7014 3671**
Studio 506　　　　　　Fax 020-7014 3672
31 Clerkenwell Close, London ECIR 0AT　　Christina Kay
www.framepool.com

Getty Images　　　　　**0800-279 9255**
101 Bayham Street　　　　Fax 020-7544 3347
London NW1 0AG

GMTV Library Sales　　　**020-7827 7363**
London Television Centre　　Fax 020-7827 7043
Upper Ground, London SE1 9TT　Sandra Bamborough

Huntley Film Archives　　　**020-7226 9260**
22 Islington Green　　　　Fax 020-7359 9337
London N1 8DU　　　　　Amanda Huntley

Images Of War　　　　　**020-8446 2233**
108 Woodhouse Road　　　Fax 020-8492 8555
London N12 0RL　　　　　Derek Blades

IMG Media Archive　　　**020-8233 5500**
McCormack House　　　　Fax 020-8233 6476
3 Burlington Lane, London W4 2TH　James Durie

Index Stock Shots　　　　**01753-785099**
Pinewood Studios, Pinewood Road　　Philip Hinds
Iver Heath, Bucks SL0 0NH

ITN Source　　　　　　**020-7430 4480**
200 Grays Inn Road　　　　Fax 020-7430 4453
London WC1X 8XZ　　　　Simon Wood

Library Media Solutions　　**020-7659 2348**
77 Oxford Street　　　　　Fax 020-8498 9985
London W1D 2ES　　　　　Patrick Smith

Maverick Enterprises　　　**020-8459 3858**
31 Dobree Avenue　　　　Ghizela Rowe
London NW10 2AD

Moving Image Communications　**0845-257 2968**
9 Faversham Reach　　　　Fax 01795-534306
Faversham, Kent ME13 7LA　　Michael Maloney

MrFootage Stock Footage Video Library　**020-8419 8222**
78 York Street　　　　　Fax 020-7681 2286
London W1H 1DP　　　　Johan Sundberg
http://stock.mrfootage.com

National Motor Museum　　**01590-614664**
Beaulieu　　　　　　Fax 01590-612655
Brockenhurst, Hants SO42 7ZN　Stephen Vokins

National Screen & Sound Archive Of Wales　**01970-632533**
The National Library Of Wales　Fax 01970-632544
Aberystwyth SY23 3BU　　　Iestyn Hughes

North West Film Archive　　**0161-247 3097**
Minshull House　　　　　Fax 0161-247 3098
47-49 Chorlton Street, Manchester M1 3EU　Jo Abley

Olympic Television Archive Bureau　**020-8233 5353**
McCormack House　　　　Fax 020-8233 5354
1 Burlington Lane, London W4 2TH　Ross Arnold

Oxford Scientific (OSF)　　**020-7836 5591**
83-84 Long Acre　　　　　Fax 020-7379 4650
London WC2E 9NG　　　　James Cape

Publishing Factory　　　**020-7243 8453**
121 Notting Hill Gate　　　Fax 020-7792 4034
London W11 3LB　　　　　Robert Prior

Royal Mail Film Archive　　**01795-426465**
PO Box 145　　　　　　Fax 01795-437988
Sittingbourne, Kent ME10 1NH　Barry Wiles

RSPB　　　　　　　**01767-680551**
The Lodge　　　　　　Fax 01767-683262
Sandy, Beds SG19 2DL　　　Mike Pinhorn

Sky News Library Sales　　**020-7585 4485**
BSkyB, Grant Way　　　　Fax 020-7585 4454
Isleworth, Middx TW7 5QD　　Kev Smalley

Skyworks　　　　　　**020-8878 1177**
T30 Tideway Yard　　　　Fax 020-8878 6777
121 Mortlake High Street, London SW14 8SN　Damian Keogh

South West Film & Television Archive　**01752-202650**
Melville Building, Royal William Yard　Fax 01752-205025
Stonehouse, Plymouth PL1 3RP　Bob Sharpe

Specialist Stock　　　　**01275-375520**
1 Glen Cottages　　　　　Fax 07050-613938
Sandy Lane, Bristol BS8 3SE　Tom Walmsley

Splash News & Picture Agency　**0870-934 2666**
105-107 Farringdon Road　　Fax 0870-934 2669
London EC1R 3BU　　　　Raj Valley

Travel Television Productions　**020-8390 9909**
PO Box 260　　　　　　Nicholas Rogovsky
Teddington, Middx TW11 9TP

TRL　　　　　　　　**01344-773131**
Crowthorne House, 9 Mile Ride　Fax 01344-770356
Wokingham, Berks RG40 3GA　Geoff Helliwell

BFI

discover film

High Definition History

The BFI National Archive is the world's leading collection of moving images and chronicles all aspects of life and times since the invention of film in the late nineteenth century. New collections are constantly being acquired and popular material regularly remastered to HD Video.

Bring your next production to life.

BFI Footage Sales
21 Stephen Street
London W1T 1LN
+44 (0) 20 7957 4842
footage.films@bfi.org.uk

bfi.org.uk/afs

Dining Bus Services (DBS)	**01895-672381**
7 The Mallows	Fax 01895-636101
Ickenham, Middx UB10 8BX	Martin Porter
www.diningbusservices.com	
Eurostar International	**01895-435111**
The Old Coal Yard, Tavistock Road	Fax 01895-443561
West Drayton, Middx UB7 7QT	Willie Fonfe
Fatts	**0121-555 8530**
4 Laurel Gardens, Bittell Road	Fax 0121-555 8969
Barnt Green, Birmingham B45 8RP	Tom Hatcher
www.fattsltd.co.uk	
Fews Marquees	**01527-821789**
Ditchford Bank Road, Hanbury	Fax 01527-821118
Bromsgrove, Worcs B60 4HS	Ian Few
www.fewsmarquees.co.uk	
Film Flow	**020-8438 9919**
The Yard	Fax 020-8438 9929
Adrian Avenue, London NW2 1LX	Alan Hayter Karen Hayter
www.filmflow.co.uk	
Four Jays Group	**01622-843135**
Barling Farm, East Sutton	Fax 01622-844410
Maidstone, Kent ME17 3DX	Sarah Worsfold
G & H Film & Television Services	**028-9039 7808**
182A Church Road	Fax 028-9042 7921
Holywood, Co Down BT18 9RN	Alan Crozier
GT Caterers & Facilities	**0113-253 7773**
Unit 2, Howley Park Close	Fax 0113-252 6773
Morley, Leeds LS27 0BW	Danny Janes
www.gtcaterers.com	
HNA Facilities	**0161-202 1199**
Unit 6, Vale Park Industrial Estate	Fax 0161-202 2299
Hazelbottom Road, Manchester M8 0GF	Mike Cohen
John Anderson Hire	**0845-658 1451**
Unit 5, Smallford Works	Fax 01727-822886
Smallford Lane, St Albans, Herts AL4 0SA	Richard Crawley
www.superloo.co.uk	
Just Unique	**01293-540255**
5 Lamberhurst Walk	Gordon Skeggs
Crawley, W Sussex RH10 6SN	
Lays International	**01784-432100**
Delta Way, Thorpe Industrial Estate	Fax 01784-433200
Egham, Surrey TW20 8RX	Paul Lay
www.laysint.com	
Lift & Shoot	**020-7223 8166**
99 Bolingbroke Grove	Fax 020-7924 2879
London SW11 1DB	Adam Mitton
Location Facilities	**01784-436444**
Delta Way, Thorpe Industrial Estate	Fax 01784-430117
Egham, Surrey TW20 8RX	Ray Redrup
www.locationfacilities.com	

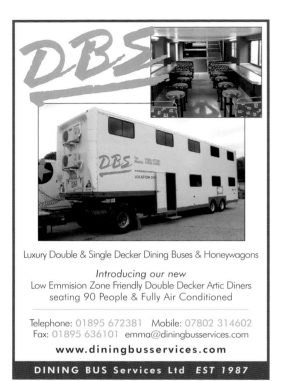

Luxury Double & Single Decker Dining Buses & Honeywagons

Introducing our new
Low Emmision Zone Friendly Double Decker Artic Diners
seating 90 People & Fully Air Conditioned

Telephone: 01895 672381   Mobile: 07802 314602
Fax: 01895 636101   emma@diningbusservices.com

www.diningbusservices.com

DINING BUS Services Ltd   EST 1987

The Loo Company	**01753-866267**
Culverden, Crimp Hill	Tom Daly
Old Windsor, Berks SL4 2RA	
Mac Rental	**0800-612 8104**
Unit 136, 61 Victoria Road	Patrick
Surbiton, Surrey KT6 4GX	
www.macrental.org.uk	
Midland International (Hire) Services	**024-7633 6411**
Wall Hill Road	Fax 024-7633 8007
Coventry CV5 9EL	Sarah Jeynes-Newey
Movie Makers Facilities	**01932-828888**
Woburn Park Farm, Addlestone Moor	Fax 01932-844738
Addlestone, Surrey KT15 2QF	Mel Dunne
www.mmuk.tv	
NGP Film Services	**07787-158630**
Kaitlin House, Padfield Court Business Park	Neville Padfield
Tonyrefail, Porth, Mid Glam CF39 8HQ	
Ones & Twos Location Loos	**01763-250692**
2 The Tanyard, Bassingbourn	James McMeechan
Royston, Herts SG8 5NH	
www.onesandtwos.net	
On-Set Location Services	**01763-244886**
Brook Orchard, Brook Road	Fax 01763-244663
Bassingbourn, Royston, Herts SG8 5NS	Nigel Howard

FILMFLOW TRANSPORT & LOCATION FACILITIES

American Trailers
Production Office
Dining Buses & Honey Wagons
Wardrobe & Hair & Make-up Vehicles

Call Alan Hayter on 020-8438 9919
Fax: 020-8438 9929   Mobile: 07831-831 964   **www.filmflow.co.uk**

Ott Film & TV Transport	**07720-972699**
8 Station Estate Road	John Ott
Feltham, Middx TW14 9BQ	
The Powerline	**01225-892336**
Knowle Hill Farm, Beeks Lane	Fax 01225-892336
Marshfield, Chippenham, Wilts SN14 8BB	Alistair Gregson
www.thepowerline.co.uk	
Site Unit Rentals	**01865-747025**
Watlington Road	Fax 01865-774562
Cowley, Oxford OX4 6SR	Denise Page
Squarewheels On Location	**01234-766476**
2 Howes Drive, Woburn Road	Fax 01234-766472
Marston Moretaine, Beds MK43 0FG	Ivan Silverstein
Time Marquees	**0118-973 6444**
Magnolia House, Fleet Lane	Robert Christmas
Wokingham, Berks RG40 4RN	
www.time-marquees.co.uk	
Translux International	**01494-520050**
Mill End Road	Fax 01494-459318
High Wycombe, Bucks HP12 4AX	Scott Johnson
Up & Running Facilities	**0161-292 7231**
21 Wrights Bank	Fax 0161-292 7231
Stockport, Cheshire SK2 5LY	Tony Colclough

Vroom With A View	**07973-432003**
Unit 12, The Business Village	Fax 01753-442002
Wexham Road, Slough, Berks SL2 5HF	Nicky Clarke
Wagon Wheels On Location	**07974-765792**
19 Tewkesbury Avenue	Steve Colegrave
Pinner, Middx HA5 5LQ	
Wheal's Far-go	**020-8965 8200**
Unit 5	Fax 020-8965 0699
13-15 Sunbeam Road, London NW10 6JP	Alan Wheal
www.whealsfargo.com	
Winnebago Hire	**0870-112 1121**
9 Brunel Close, Drayton Fields	Fax 0870-241 5615
Daventry, Northants NN11 8RB	Simon Leith
www.winnebagohire.co.uk	

LOCATION - SUPPORT

Ant's Makeup Mirrors	**020-7373 6767**
13 Childs Place	Fax 020-7373 7748
London SW5 9RX	Anthony Jordan
www.antsmakeupmirrors.com	
AW Smith & Partner (Calor Gas)	**01895-236781**
41 Oxford Road	Fax 01895-233026
New Denham, Middx UB9 4DB	John Smith
www.awsmith-calorgas.co.uk	

C & M Location Services	**01279-433979**
178 Willowfield	Fred Kelly
Harlow, Essex CM18 6RY	
Herts Traffic Management	**01753-785350**
Pinewood Studios, Pinewood Road	Fax 01753-785391
Iver Heath, Bucks SL0 0NH	Paul Masters
Location Hire	**07765-327418**
	Stephen Line
Makin Movies	**01895-832490**
Copse Hill Farm, Southlands Road	Fax 01895-835318
Iver Heath, Bucks SL0 0PG	Nick Waldron
Mask It	**020-7460 6484**
31 Lancaster Road	Fax 020-7460 6484
London W11 1QJ	
The Organisation Group	**01962-774034**
Burcot Farm, East Stratton	Fax 01962-774036
Winchester, Hants SO21 3DZ	Roger Irwin
Packexe	**01392-438191**
9-13 Marsh Green Road	Fax 01392-438371
Exeter EX2 8NY	Abbie Heart
Place Invaders	**01322-615030**
16 Farm Avenue	Fax 01322-665714
Swanley, Kent BR8 7JA	David Fowle
Protecta Screen	**0870-121 8670**
Unit 5, Driberg Way	Fax 0870-121 8680
Braintree, Essex CM7 1NB	
Screenflex UK	**01684-773111**
Cheynes House, Main Road	Fax 01684-773301
Bredon, Tewkesbury, Glos GL20 7EG	Alex Ayres
SP Location Rental	**01708-709633**
77 Ardleigh Green Road	Fax 01708-709633
Hornchurch, Essex RM11 2LE	Charlie Pigram
Traction Equipment	**01785-223355**
Glover Street	Fax 01785-211074
Stafford ST16 2NY	Tim Bloomer
Trio Plus Distribution	**01372-747555**
Unit 1, 85 Hook Road	Fax 01372-741240
Epsom, Surrey KT19 8TP	Richard Scrannage

LOCATION - TEMPORARY ROADWAYS & GROUND PROTECTION

Autotrak Portable Roadways	**01869-248952**
Bricknells Farm, Fringford Road	Fax 01869-250686
Caversfield, Oxon OX27 8TJ	Michael Fox

Eve Trakway	**0870-076 7676**
Bramley Vale	Fax 0870-073 7373
Chesterfield, Derbys S44 5GA	
Grassform Plant Hire	**01277-353686**
Little Woodbarns Farm Yard, Green Street	Fax 01277-356890
Fryerning, Ingatestone, Essex CM4 0NT	Mark Dunning
www.grassform.co.uk	
Terra Firma Roadways	**01235-868835**
Willowbrook Farm, Hanney Road	Fax 0871-900 5699
Steventon, Oxon OX13 6BE	Hugh Robertson
TPA Portable Roadways	**0870-240 2381**
Dukeries Mill, Claylands Avenue	Fax 0870-240 2382
Worksop, Notts S81 7DJ	Paul Murdoch
Trac - Temporary Roadway & Access	**01483-768485**
Morrison House, 3A Monument Way West	Fax 01483-767928
Woking, Surrey GU21 5EN	Nick Russell

LOCATIONS - SCOUTING & MANAGEMENT

Airspace	**020-7607 3030**
16A Crane Grove	Fax 020-7607 2190
London N7 8LE	Rosemary Harrison
Amazing Space	**020-7251 6661**
74 Clerkenwell Road	Fax 020-7251 6808
London EC1M 5QA	Jonny Levy
Clearspace Locations	**020-8673 2588**
62 Balham Park Road	Fax 020-8673 2588
London SW12 8DU	Tessa Evelegh
The Collective	**020-7284 8901**
7-8 Jeffreys Place	Fax 020-7485 4907
London NW1 9PP	Antony Iredale
www.location-collective.co.uk	
Cornish Locations	**07866-758285**
1 The Grey House, Heavitree Road	Salina Hatfield
Kingsand, Cornall PL10 1NP	
Film It Locations	**01395-443881**
Clinton Devon Estates, Rolle Estate Office	Fax 01395-446126
Bicton Arena, East Budleigh, Devon EX9 7BL	John Wilding
The Film Office	**020-8980 8771**
221 Bow Road	Fax 020-8981 2272
London E3 2SJ	Michelle Myrie
Great Northern Locations	**0161-236 2620**
Studio 6	Zoe Wassall
10 Canal Street, Manchester M1 3EZ	
Itasca Locations	**020-7494 0888**
42 Old Compton Street	Fax 020-7287 2855
London W1D 4TX	Louise Styles Holly Brightwell
www.itascalocations.com	

JJ Locations — 020-7749 0500
Fax 0844-774 6243
Unit 17D, Perseverance Works
25-27 Hackney Road, London E2 8DD — Johnny Jones

Lake District Locations — 01900-823927
Fax 01900-823927
The Mansion House, Main Street
Greysouthen, Cockermouth, Cumbria CA13 0UG — Elaine Wise

Lavish Locations — 0333-700 7007
Fax 020-3002 7255
PO Box 59517
London SE21 9AH — Helen Marsden

Light Locations — 01380-860589
Fax 01380-860643
Studio 2B, The Old Estate Yard, Chandlers Lane
Bishop Cannings, Devizes, Wilts SN10 2JZ — Sophie Hitchens

Locality — 020-7812 9144
Fax 0870-128 2298
Unit G2, Northside Studios
16-29 Andrews Road, London E8 4QF — Emma Plimmer

Locate A Location — 07786-631320
Nina Howe-Davies
46 Ray Mill Road West
Maidenhead, Berks SL6 8SQ

Locate Productions — 020-7978 1688
Fax 020-7978 2469
Unit 49, Spaces Business Centre
Ingate Place, London SW8 3NS — Luke Jackson
www.locateproductions.com

The Location Partnership — 020-7734 0456
Fax 020-7734 5411
82 Berwick Street
London W1F 8TP — Eddy Pearce
www.locationpartnership.com

Location Production — 07957-434387
Graham Aza
40 Formosa Street
London W9 2JP

Location Scotland — 0131-561 0120
Fax 0131-467 5614
Mitchell House
5 Mitchell Street, Edinburgh EH6 7BD — Michelle Methven

Location25 — 020-7720 6514
Fax 020-7498 0040
25 Clapham Common Southside
London SW4 7AB — Nicola Scott
www.location25.com

Locationinc — 01303-862154
Edward Sharp
Brook Forstal Cottage, Stowting
Ashford, Kent TN25 6AU

LocDown South — 01323-520215
Paul Dix
15 Spring Close
Eastbourne, E Sussex BN20 9HD

Lovely Locations — 07714-727276
Ben Carter
5 Oaklands Mews
Carlingford Road, London N15 3AS

Max Locations — 020-7993 2984
Fax 01689-872836
94 Poverest Road
Orpington, Kent BR5 2DQ — Carina McCarthy

Ascot Racecourse   **0870-727 8765**
Ascot   Fax 0870-460 1248
Berks SL5 7JX   Anna Retka
www.ascot.co.uk

Beachyhead   **01323-423906**
The Gilbert Estate Office, Upper Street East   Fax 01323-423906
Dean, E Sussex BN20 0BY   Charlie Davies-Gilbert

Bentwaters Parks   **01394-460655**
Control Tower, Bentwaters Parks   Fax 01394-460355
Rendlesham, Woodbridge, Suffolk IP12 2TW   Sarah Brown
www.bentwatersparks.com

Bizspace   **07921-370347**
Sovereign House   Gregg Sheen
Albert Place, London N3 1QB

Blackbushe Airport   **01252-879449**
Camberley   Fax 01252-743182
Surrey GU17 9LQ   Mick Lambert

Bluebell Railway   **01825-720811**
Sheffield Park Station   Fax 01825-720804
Sheffield Park, E Sussex TN22 3QL   Chris Knibbs

Bressingham Steam Experience   **01379-686900**
Bressingham   Fax 01379-686907
Diss, Norfolk IP22 2AA   Howard Stephens

Brocket Hall   **01707-335241**
Welwyn   Fax 01707-333309
Herts AL8 7XG   Melanie Hickey

Canary Wharf Group   **020-7418 2000**
1 Canada Square   Fax 020-7418 2222
Canary Wharf, London E14 5AB

Castle Gibson   **020-8211 8690**
18A/B Manor Road   Fax 020-8211 8690
London N16 5SA   Joyce Gibson Jackie Marshall
www.castlegibson.com

Castle Gibson - The Depository   **020-8211 8690**
18A Manor Road   Fax 020-8211 8690
London N16 5SA   Joyce Gibson Jackie Marshall
www.castlegibson.com

Castle Gibson - The House Next Door   **020-8211 8690**
18D Manor Road   Fax 020-8211 8690
London N16 5SA   Joyce Gibson Jackie Marshall
www.castlegibson.com

Castle Gibson - MC Motors   **020-8211 8690**
28 Millers Avenue   Fax 020-8211 8690
London E8 2DS   Joyce Gibson Jackie Marshall
www.castlegibson.com

Cheltenham Racecourse & The Centaur   **01242-539538**
Prestbury Park   Fax 01242-224227
Cheltenham, Glos GL50 4SH   Susie Bradshaw

Chessgrove Day Spa — **01527-821789**
Ditchford Bank Road, Hanbury — Fax 01527-821118
Bromsgrove, Worcs B60 4HS — Ian Few
www.chessgrove.co.uk

Chessington World Of Adventure — **01372-731528**
Leatherhead Road — Maria Hamilton
Chessington, Surrey KT9 2NE

City Of London — **020-7332 3202**
PO Box 270 — Fax 020-7332 1797
Guildhall, London EC2P 2EJ — Joanna Burnaby-Atkins

City Of Westminster — **020-7641 2390**
Special Events, City Hall — Fax 020-7641 2640
64 Victoria Street, London SW1E 6QP

Clearwell Caves & Ancient Iron Mine — **01594-832535**
The Rock — Fax 01594-833362
Clearwell, Glos GL16 8JR — Jon Wright

The Collective — **020-7284 8901**
7-8 Jeffreys Place — Fax 020-7485 4907
London NW1 9PP — Antony Iredale
www.location-collective.co.uk

Coughton Court — **01789-400777**
Alcester — Fax 01789-765544
Warwicks B49 5JA — Lucy Reid

County Hall	020-7981 2550
Westminster Bridge Road	Fax 020-7981 2555
London SE1 7PB	Emma Wass

The Crown Estate - Windsor Great Park	01753-847519
The Crown Estate, The Great Park	Fax 01753-624107
Windsor, Berks SL4 2HT	Gino Caiafa Nick Day
www.theroyallandscape.co.uk	

Curious Science	020-8961 3113
Units 5 & 7	Fax 020-8961 7427
Commercial Way, London NW10 7XF	David Burns
www.curiousscience.com	

Cutty Sark Trust	020-8858 2698
2 Greenwich Church Street	Fax 020-8858 6976
London SE10 9BG	Richard Doughty

Ditchford Bank Farm	01527-821789
Ditchford Bank Road, Hanbury	Fax 01527-821118
Bromsgrove, Worcs B60 4HS	Ian Few
www.chessgrove.co.uk	

Docklands Light Railway	020-7363 9530
Castor Lane	Fax 020-7363 9919
London E14 0DS	Debra Cox

Dorset County Council	01305-221000
County Hall	Fax 01305-225190
Dorchester, Dorset DT1 1XJ	Lara Nixey

London Borough Of Enfield	**0845-402 2998**
Enfield Filming Office, Chiswick Town Hall	Fax 0845-402 2997
Heathfield Terrace, London W4 4JN	Dennis Firminger
London Borough Of Greenwich	**020-8921 6146**
Civic House	Fax 020-8921 8322
20 Grand Depot Road, London SE18 6SJ	Suzanne Hutchinson
London Borough Of Hackney	**020-8356 3541**
Town Hall	Fax 020-8356 3118
Mare Street, London E8 1EA	Rebecca Staffolani
London Borough Of Hammersmith & Fulham	**020-8753 2171**
Room 47, Town Hall	Fax 020-8741 2685
King Street, London W6 9JU	Janet Potter
www.lbhf.gov.uk/filming	
London Borough Of Haringey	**020-8489 6903**
Haringey Film Office	Fax 020-8489 2689
639 High Road, London N17 8BD	David Waterson
London Borough Of Harrow	**020-8825 7575**
West London Film Office, Perceval House	Fax 020-8825 7667
14-16 Uxbridge Road, London W5 2HL	Mike Liddall
London Borough Of Havering	**01706-432001**
Town Hall, Main Road	Fax 01706-432002
Romford, Essex RM1 3BD	Elizabeth Aelberry

NATURAL BEAUTY
IN THE HEART OF LONDON

Panoramic views of London
Picturesque lakes, water features & bridges
Formal gardens & tree lined avenues
Historic woodlands & vast open spaces
Hundreds of buildings, statues & memorials

THE
ROYAL
PARKS

London Borough Of Hillingdon	**01895-277452**
Civic Centre, High Street	Fax 01895-250493
Uxbridge, Middx UB8 1UW	Judith Dickson
London Borough Of Hounslow	**0845-402 2998**
Hounslow Filming Office, Chiswick Town Hall	Fax 0845-402 2997
Heathfield Terrace, London W4 4JN	Dennis Firminger
London Borough Of Islington	**020-8980 8771**
Film Office	Fax 020-8981 2272
221 Bow Road, London E3 2SJ	Dominic Reeve-Tucker
London Borough Of Kensington & Chelsea	**020-7341 5133**
Council Offices	Fax 020-7368 0341
37 Pembroke Road, London W8 6PW	Adrian Hodgson
London Borough Of Kingston-Upon-Thames	**020-8547 5016**
The Guildhall, High Street	Fax 020-8547 5012
Kingston-upon-Thames, Surrey KT1 1EU	Gail Daly
London Borough Of Lambeth	**020-8980 8771**
Film Office	Fax 020-8981 2272
221 Bow Road, London E3 2SJ	Jessica Wright
London Borough Of Lewisham	**0845-833 1523**
64 Borough High Street	Fax 0845-833 1524
London SE1 1XF	Andrew Pavord
London Borough Of Merton	**020-8545 3434**
Civic Centre, London Road	Fax 020-8545 0446
Morden, Surrey SM4 5DX	Andy Thompson
London Borough Of Newham	**020-8430 2261**
The Old Town Hall	Fax 020-8430 1255
29 The Broadway, London E15 4BQ	Sue Russo
London Borough Of Redbridge	**020-8708 3766**
Lynton House, 255-259 High Road	Fax 020-8708 3983
Ilford, Essex IG1 1NN	Kirsty Tobin
London Borough Of Richmond	**020-8487 5157**
York House, Richmond Road	Fax 020-8891 7718
Twickenham, Middx TW1 3AA	Sue Lewis
London Borough Of Southwark	**0845-833 1523**
64 Borough High Street	Fax 0845-833 1524
London SE1 1XF	Karen Everett
London Borough Of Sutton	**020-8770 6096**
Civic Centre, St Nicholas Way	Fax 020-8770 5404
Sutton, Surrey SM1 1EA	Robert Bownes
London Borough Of Tower Hamlets	**020-8980 8771**
Film Office	Fax 020-8981 2272
221 Bow Road, London E3 2SJ	Dominic Reeve-Tucker
London Borough Of Waltham Forest	**020-8496 4858**
Town Hall	Fax 020-8496 4504
Forest Road, London E17 4JF	Melissa Hoskins
London Borough Of Wandsworth	**020-8871 7119**
Battersea Park	Fax 020-7223 7919
London SW11 4NJ	Maria Horn

London City Airport	**020-7646 0132**
City Aviation House	Fax 020-7473 3105
Royal Docks, London E16 2PB	Geraldine Nolan
The London Eye	**0870-220 2777**
Riverside Building, County Hall	Fax 0870-990 8882
Westminster Bridge Road, London SE1 7PB	Sahrette Saayman
London Fire Brigade	**020-8536 5922**
Press Office	
169 Union Street, London SE1 0LL	
London Marriott Kensington	**020-7835 1398**
147C Cromwell Road	Fax 020-7835 0634
London SW5 0TH	Tracy Wood
London Transport Museum	**020-7379 6344**
Covent Garden Piazza	Fax 020-7565 7254
London WC2E 7BB	
London Underground	**020-7918 0003**
172 Buckingham Palace Road	Fax 020-7918 3489
London SW1W 9TN	Kate Reston
London Zoo	**020-7449 6363**
Regents Park	Fax 020-7586 6171
London NW1 4RY	Rowena Fisher
Longleat	**01985-845415**
The Estate Office, Longleat	Fax 01985-844885
Warminster, Wilts BA12 7NW	Steve Mytton
Metropolitan Police - Film Unit	**020-7918 3032**
200 Buckingham Palace Road	Fax 020-7918 3097
London SW1W 9TJ	PC Alan Cousins
Mid Hants Railway	**01962-733810**
The Railway Station	Fax 01962-735448
Alresford, Hants SO24 9JG	Colin Chambers
Millbrook Proving Ground	**01525-404242**
Millbrook	Fax 01525-408404
Bedford MK45 2JQ	Nick Wignall
Millennium Stadium	**0870-013 8600**
Gate 4	Fax 029-2082 2474
Westgate Street, Cardiff CF10 1NS	Vici Williams
Ministry Of Defence	**020-7218 9836**
3-M-39 Ministry Of Defence Main Building	Fax 020-7218 7579
Horseguards Avenue, Whitehall, London SW1A 2HB	Tony Burlton
National Maritime Museum	**020-8312 8522**
Greenwich	Fax 020-8312 6533
London SE10 9NF	David Taylor
National Trust	**020-7799 4547**
32 Queen Annes Gate	Harvey Edgington
London SW1H 9AB	
National Trust For Scotland	**0844-493 2412**
Wemyss House	Fax 0844-493 2102
28 Charlotte Square, Edinburgh EH2 4ET	Ian Gardner

LOCATIONS

Natural History Museum — 020-7942 5215
Cromwell Road — Fax 020-7942 5070
London SW7 5BD

Nene Valley Railway — 01780-784444
Wansford Station, Stibbington — Fax 01780-784440
Peterborough, Cambs PE8 6LR — Cris Rees

Network Rail — 020-7904 7164
1 Eversholt Street — Rachel Bettes
London NW1 2DN

New Wimbledon Theatre — 020-8545 7900
93 The Broadway — Fax 020-8543 6637
London SW19 1QG — Samantha Bain

Newmarket Racecourses — 01638-675505
Westfield House, The Links — Fax 01638-663044
Newmarket, Suffolk CB8 0TG — Gemma Hussey

Nina's Hair Parlour — 07511-548873
Alfies Antique Market — Nina Butkovich-Budden
13-25 Church Street, London NW8 8DT

North Weald Airfield — 01992-564200
Merlin Way, North Weald — Fax 01992-523054
Epping, Essex CM16 6HR — Darren Goodey
www.eppingforestdc.gov.uk

O2 Academy Brixton — 020-7771 3000
211 Stockwell Road — Fax 020-7738 4427
London SW9 9SL — Nigel Downs

Olympia — 020-7385 1200
Hammersmith Road
London W14 8UX

One Great George Street — 020-7665 2323
1 Great George Street — Fax 020-7976 0697
London SW1P 3AA — Lisa Fisher

Patchetts Equestrian Centre — 01923-852255
Hilfield Lane, Aldenham — Fax 01923-859289
Watford, Herts WD25 8PE — Derek Lea

Pippingford Park — 01825-712966
Pippingford Manor, Pippingford Park — Richard Morriss
Nutley, E Sussex TN22 3HW
www.pippingford.co.uk

The Plaza Shopping Centre — 020-7637 8811
120 Oxford Street — Fax 020-7436 3944
London W1N 1LT — Keith Brushneen

Port Of London Authority — 01474-562366
London River House, Royal Pier Road — Fax 01474-562398
Gravesend, Kent DA12 2BG — Martin Garside

Powderham Castle — 01626-890243
Kenton — Fax 01626-890729
Exeter EX6 8JQ — Simon Fishwick

North Weald Airfield

www.eppingforestdc.gov.uk

On a site that covers almost 400 acres there's more than just flying available at the historic North Weald Airfield !

With superb access to the M11 and within easy reach of central London this former Battle of Britain Fighter Station is the ideal location for photographic shoots and filming.

Boasting acres of both hard standing and grassed areas that offer open and clear aspects North Weald Airfield is simply an outstanding shoot location.

If you're looking for a large indoor space we have aircraft hangars available too !

North Weald Airfield offers flexibility, competitive rates and friendly, helpful staff who will do their best to accommodate your requests.

If you are interested in filming at North Weald Airfield then please contact the General Manager on 01992-564501.

To view our information leaflet go to:
http://www.eppingforestdc.gov.uk/
Library/Leisure/NWA/NorthWeald
A5Leaflet.pdf

North Weald Airfield

Epping Forest District Council

Merlin Way, North Weald, Epping, Essex CM16 6HR

**T: 01992 564200   F: 01992 523054
E: dgoodey@eppingforestdc.gov.uk**

195

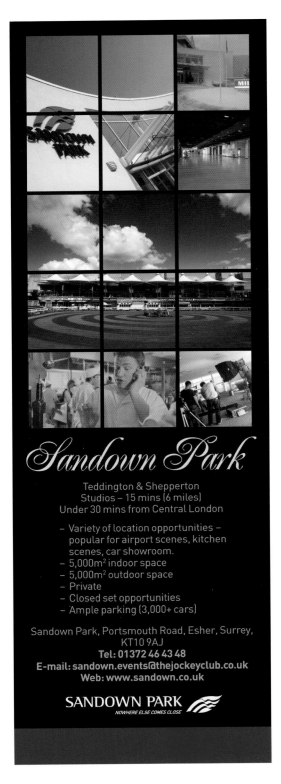

Premier Marinas (Brighton)	**01273-819919**
West Jetty, Brighton Marina	Fax 01273-675082
Brighton, E Sussex BN2 5UP	Phil Godfrey
Really Useful Theatres	**020-7240 0880**
22 Tower Street	Fax 020-7240 1292
London WC2H 9TW	Michael Townsend
Reel Film Locations	**0845-402 2998**
Chiswick Town Hall	Fax 0845-402 2997
Heathfield Terrace, London W4 4JN	Dennis Firminger
www.reelfilmlocations.com	
RIBA	**020-7307 3888**
66 Portland Place	Fax 020-7307 3763
London W1B 1AD	Lisa Lightfoot
Richmond Theatre	**0871-297 5454**
The Green	Fax 020-8332 4509
Richmond, Surrey TW9 1QJ	Kate Wrightson
Royal Mail	**020-7250 2468**
100 Victoria Embankment	Fax 020-7250 2244
London EC4Y 0HQ	
Royal Parks	**020-7298 2089**
Rangers Lodge	Fax 020-7298 2005
Hyde Park, London W2 2UH	Niki Duignan
www.royalparks.org.uk/film	
Saint Hill Manor	**01342-326711**
Saint Hill Road	Fax 01342-317057
East Grinstead, W Sussex RH19 4JY	Liz Ostermann
Sandown Park Racecourse	**01372-464348**
Portsmouth Road	
Esher, Surrey KT10 9AJ	
www.sandown.co.uk	
Science Museum	**020-7942 4350**
Exhibition Road	Fax 020-7942 4401
London SW7 2DD	Elizabeth Lahey
www.sciencemuseum.org.uk	
Scottish Screen Locations	**0141-302 1724**
249 West George Street	Fax 0141-302 1711
Glasgow G2 4QE	Belle Doyle
www.scottishscreenlocations.com	
Severn Valley Railway	**01299-403816**
The Railway Station	Fax 01299-400839
Bewdley, Worcs DY12 1BG	Dewi Jones
Slough Borough Council	**01753-875176**
Town Hall, Bath Road	Fax 01753-875087
Slough, Berks SL1 3UQ	
Slough Trading Estate	**01753-537171**
234 Bath Road	Fax 01753-820585
Slough, Berks SL1 4EE	David Drummond
Somerset House	**020-7845 4644**
Strand	Fax 020-7836 7613
London WC2R 1LA	Steven Doherty

Stags End Equestrian Centre	01582-794700
Gaddesden Lane	James Dickson
Hemel Hempstead, Herts HP2 6HN	
Stansted Airport	07956-340486
Enterprise House	Kim Ruskin
Stansted Airport, Essex CM24 1QW	
Stockers Farm	01753-662418
Blanchards Farm, Sevenhills Road	
Iver Heath, Bucks SL0 0NY	
Stoke Park	01753-717171
Park Road	Fax 01753-717181
Stoke Poges, Bucks SL2 4PG	Julia Buxton
www.stokepark.com	
Swanage Railway	01929-425800
Station House	Fax 01929-426680
Swanage, Dorset BH19 1HB	Martin Payne
Tate Enterprises	020-7887 8867
The Lodge	Fax 020-7887 8805
Millbank, London SW1P 4RG	Chris Webster
Tenerife Film Commission	+34 647 346 462
Alcalde José Emilio Garcia Gómez 9	Fax +34 922 237 872
38005 Santa Cruz de Tenerife, Canary Islands	Concha Diaz
www.tenerifefilm.com	
Thorpe Park	01932-577130
Staines Road	Sarah Morris
Chertsey, Surrey KT16 8PN	
Three Rivers District Council	01923-776611
Three Rivers House, Northway	Fax 01923-896119
Rickmansworth, Herts WD3 1RL	Kevin Snow
Tower Bridge	020-7940 3960
Tower Bridge Road	Fax 020-7403 4477
London SE1 2UP	James Sansom
Trafalgar Square	020-7983 4750
City Hall	Fax 020-7983 4137
The Queens Walk, London SE1 2AA	Sarah Hall

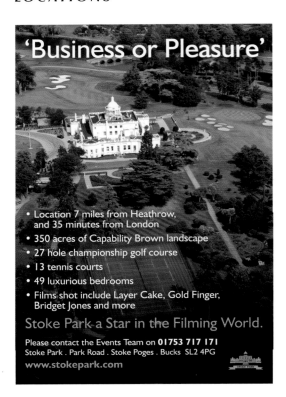
The Trafford Centre	**0161-746 7777**
Management Suite	Fax 0161-749 1599
Trafford Centre, Manchester M17 8AA	
Valley Site	**01923-232966**
Oxhey Hall	Fax 0923-232966
Oxhey, Herts WD19 4NU	
Victoria & Albert Museum	**020-7942 2841**
Cromwell Road	Fax 020-7942 2645
London SW7 2RL	Rachel Lloyd
www.vam.ac.uk	
Waddesdon Manor	**01296-653232**
Waddesdon	Fax 01296-653208
Aylesbury, Bucks HP18 0JH	Suzy Barron
Walpole Bay Hotel	**01843-221703**
Fifth Avenue, Cliftonville	Fax 01483-297399
Margate, Kent CT9 2JJ	Jane Bishop
www.walpolebayhotel.co.uk	
Wembley Arena	**020-8782 5500**
Arena Square, Engineers Way	Fax 020-8782 5501
Wembley, Middx HA9 0AA	
Wembley Stadium	**0844-980 8001**
Wembley Stadium	Fax 020-8795 9601
Wembley, Middx HA9 0WS	Sarah Hedges

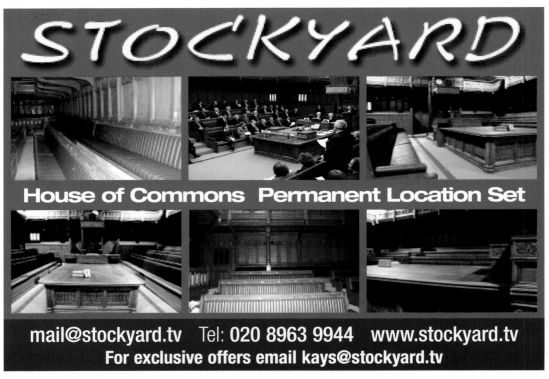

West Country Beaches	07866-758285
I The Grey House, Heavitree Road Kingsand, Cornwall PL10 1NP	
West Ham United	020-8548 2762
Boleyn Ground, Green Street Upton Park, London E13 9AZ	Fax 020-8586 8224
Westway Development Trust	020-8962 5737
I Thorpe Close London W10 5XL www.westway.org	Fax 020-8969 5936 Chris Bailey
Westway Sports Centre	020-8962 5737
I Crowthorne Road London W10 6RP www.westway.org	Fax 020-8969 5936 Haylie Durose
Whiteleys Shopping Centre	020-7229 8844
Centre Management Suite Queensway, London W2 4YN	Fax 020-7792 8921 Dean Allen
Wookey Hole Caves	01749-672243
The Mill, Wookey Hole Wells, Somerset BA5 1BB	Fax 01749-677749 Daniel Medley
Wrotham Park	020-8441 0755
Barnet Herts EN5 4SB	Fax 020-8449 9359

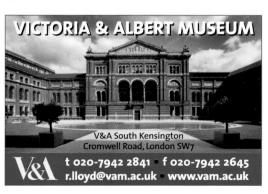

Trading Post	020-8903 3727
1 Beresford Avenue	Fax 020-8900 2565
Wembley, Middx HA0 1NU	Tim Oake
www.tradingposthire.co.uk	

Traditional Charter	07811-469505
The Holt, Butt Lane	Michael Emmett
Maldon, Essex CM9 5HD	

MARQUEES & CANOPIES

Academy Marquees	01276-64666
34 Upper Park Road	Fax 01276-22698
Camberley, Surrey GU15 2EF	Ed Buchanan
www.marqueehire.tv	

Andy Dixon Facilities	01656-725560
3 Squire Drive, Brynmenyn Industrial Estate	Fax 01656-725194
Bridgend, Mid Glam CF32 9TX	Andy Dixon Steve Haines
www.andydixonfacilities.co.uk	

Andy Dixon Facilities	07768-436768
Longcross Studios, Chobham Lane	Andy Dixon
Chertsey, Surrey KT16 0EE	
www.andydixonfacilities.co.uk	

Armoury Marquees	01753-656606
Pinewood Studios, Pinewood Road	Clive Shaw
Iver Heath, Bucks SL0 0NH	
www.thearmourygroup.com	

Bees Marquees	023-9255 4976
Overlord Office, 155 Daedalus	Fax 023-9255 6051
Chark Lane, Lee-on-Solent, Hants PO13 9NY	
www.beesmarquees.co.uk	

Carnival Marquees	01905-767680
North Farm	Stephen James
Little Malvern, Worcs WR14 4JN	

Chichester Canvas	01243-641164
Sidlesham Common	Fax 01243-641888
Chichester, W Sussex PO20 7PY	Robert Callaway-Lewis

City B Group   01782-744961
Unit 9, Stoke Business Park   Fax 01782-845375
Woddhouse Street, Stoke-on-Trent, Staffs ST4 1EZ   Steve Grimshaw

Classic Canvas   01524-222551
Storrs Cottage   Fax 01524-222551
Arkholme, Lancs LA6 1BB   Lewis Evans
www.classiccanvas.co.uk

Custom Canopies   01786-449519
Unit 6, 10 Munro Road   Fax 01786-449788
Springkerse Industrial Estate, Stirling FK7 7UU   Martyn Philip
www.customcanopies.co.uk

CW Garden Marquees   01568-613011
Unit 4, Southern Avenue   Fax 01568-613213
Leominster, Herefordshire HR6 0QF   Colin Watts

Cygnet Marquees   01268-521999
28 Hardys Way   Fax 01268-699988
Canvey Island, Essex SS8 9PT   Mark Hyam

The Devon Marquee Company   01647-433530
Fairview, Murchington   Fax 01647-433530
Chagford, Devon TQ13 8HJ   George Lyon-Smith

Dorset Canopy Sales & Hire   01258-837631
Unit 12, Milborne Business Centre   Richard Nicholson
Blandford Hill, Milborne St Andrew, Dorset DT11 0HZ

Faversham Marquees   01428-727089
Falkeners House, Rectory Lane   Peter Stuart
Bramshott, Hants GU30 7QZ

Fews Marquees   01527-821789
Ditchford Bank Road, Hanbury   Fax 01527-821118
Bromsgrove, Worcs B60 4HS   Ian Few
www.fewsmarquees.co.uk

Gazebo Shop   01295-269333
Unit 6B, Thorpe Drive   Fax 01295-273276
Thorpe Way Industrial Estate, Banbury, Oxon OX16 4UZ   Luigi Pannozzo
www.gazeboshop.co.uk

GL Events Owen Brown   01332-850000
Station Road   Fax 01332-850005
Castle Donington, Derbys DE74 2NL   Alex Robertson

We specialise in the most unique concept for Film & Television

The optimum quality of our Indian Traditional Tents & Marquees boast of innovative designs & magical colour combinations. This elite collection of traditional tents & marquees adds glory to your production, gardens or events. They are well versed with the changing trends.

We specialise in any custom size you can imagine..... The end result is an exquisite blend of bespoke hand crafted Bedouin tents, food, music & lush interiors.

Please contact
Trina Arcari
on 01873 850100

Four Seasons Film Set

27 Maes-Y-Llarwydd
Abergavenny
Monmouths NP7 5LQ

labellemaison@btconnect.com
www.labelle-maison.co.uk

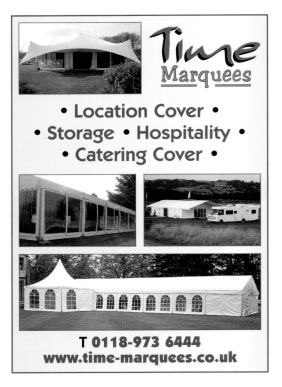

Time Marquees

• **Location Cover** •
• **Storage** • **Hospitality** •
• **Catering Cover** •

T 0118-973 6444
www.time-marquees.co.uk

Instant Marquees	**01275-371400**
Unit D, Highfield Road	Fax 01840-212909
Camelford, Cornwall PL32 9RA	John Fack
Key Structures	**020-8944 9633**
Unit 2	Fax 020-8947 1369
Gresham Way, London SW19 8ED	Ben Telford
La Belle Maison	**01873-850100**
27 Maes Y Llarwydd	Fax 01873-850100
Abergavenny, Monmouths NP7 5LQ	Trina Arcari
www.labelle-maison.co.uk	
LPM Bohemia - Tent Company	**0870-770 7185**
The Aga Buildings, Lamberhurst Road	Fax 0870-770 7186
Horsmonden, Kent TN12 8DP	Graham Cresswell
Mayflower Marquees	**01494-718800**
Unit 6, Penn Street Works	Fax 01494-718111
Penn Street, Amersham, Bucks HP7 0PU	Mike Read
Piggotts	**01277-363262**
43 London Road, Stanford Rivers	Fax 01277-365162
Ongar, Essex CM5 9PJ	Nick McLaren
Seaholme Marquees	**01273-857577**
Colemans Park, Shaveswood Lane	Fax 01273-857977
Albourne, W Sussex BN6 9DY	Olly Brown
SLS Group	**01256-764994**
Unit 9, Fosters Business Park	Fax 01256-763970
Old School Road, Hook, Hants RG27 9NY	Giles Stanford
The Stockyard	**020-8963 9944**
Unit A, Genesis	Fax 020-8963 9955
Rainsford Road, London NW10 7RG	Ron Painter
www.stockyard.tv	
Time Marquees	**0118-973 6444**
Magnolia House, Fleet Lane	Robert Christmas
Wokingham, Berks RG40 4RN	
www.time-marquees.co.uk	
TT Tents - The Marquee People	**01256-397551**
North Waltham Business Centre, North Waltham	Fax 01256-397082
Basingstoke, Hants RG25 2DJ	Anthony Wickham
WAAP Event Services	**01273-777272**
Brighton Media Centre, 9-12 Middle Street	Fax 01273-777022
Brighton, E Sussex BN1 1AL	Mark Pate

MATTE ARTISTS

Mattes & Miniatures Visual Effects	**01628-506626**
Bray Film Studios, Down Place	Pinewood 01753-656554
Water Oakley, Windsor, Berks SL4 5UG	Leigh Took
www.mattesandminiatures.com	

MEDICAL SERVICES

Action Back Care	**020-8922 9870**
Pinewood Studios, Pinewood Road	Jonathan Cohen
Iver Heath, Bucks SL0 0NH	
www.actionbackcare.com	
Alliance-Pioneer Group	**0845-539 5309**
PO Box 189	Fax 0845-539 5308
Plymouth PL6 5ZR	Matthew Davey
www.alliance-pioneer.co.uk	
Ambu-Kare (UK)	**01733-560972**
Unit 14, Wharf Road Industrial Estate	Fax 01733-286914
Peterborough, Cambs PE7 1AB	
AMS Services	**07767-215186**
22 Manfield Road	Fax 01252-323477
Ash, Surrey GU12 6NE	Adrian Hirons
County Paramedic Services	**07758-127999**
31 Ontario Close	Jamie Webb
Worthing, W Sussex BN13 2TE	
Docfarla Medical Suport	**07939-589805**
25 Tudor Gardens	Elton Farla
Twickenham, Middx TW1 4LE	
Doctors Direct	**020-8416 1444**
Buckingham House East, The Broadway	Fax 0870-486 4771
Stanmore, Middx HA7 4EB	Greg Smith
Event Medical Services	**01535-670648**
Suite 4, Craven Hall	Fax 0844-335 0582
Sackville Street, Skipton, N Yorks BD23 2PB	Tony Howsen
Events Medical Services	**0844-586 6009**
PO Box 4741	Fax 0844-586 6008
Coventry CV6 9EW	Matt Robbins
Fleet Street Travel Clinic	**020-7353 5678**
29 Fleet Street	Fax 020-7353 5500
London EC4Y 1AA	Richard Dawood
Lifecare Medics Southern	**0871-560 5112**
PO Box 181	Fax 0844-567 9718
Cranleigh, Surrey GU6 9AF	
Location Medical Services	**0870-750 9898**
Shepperton Studios, Studios Road	Fax 0870-750 9897
Shepperton, Middx TW17 0QD	Daniel Melhuish
www.locationmedical.com	
Location Medics	**07887-575611**
51 Preston Crowmarsh	Rob Field
Wallingford, Oxon OX10 6SL	
Manchester Medical Services	**07894-294548**
8 Merridale Road, Broadhurst Manor	Fax 0161-682 3339
Moston, Manchester M40 0AD	David Mylett
Media Medics	**01245-328062**
Deben House, Chapel Row	Fax 01245-329363
Woodham Ferrers, Essex CM3 8RN	John Cormack

MEDICAL SERVICES

Medicar European	**01233-660999**
Ascot Barn, Hinxhill Estate	Fax 01233-610721
Hinx Hill, Ashford, Kent TN25 5NR	Lyn Snoad
Medics UK	**07837-210050**
South Tees Motor Sport Park, Dormor Way	Fax 01642-706021
South Bank, Middlesbrough TS6 6XH	Ken Lumley
Medifilm	**07961-009898**
14 Leavesley Road	Steve Ogden
Blackpool, Lancs FY1 2QP	
Mediforce	**0845-456 2223**
Unit 28, Slough Business Park	Fax 0845-456 2122
97 Farnham Road, Slough, Berks SL1 3FQ	Dickie Henderson
Mediprop	**0161-344 1234**
21 Peterborough Close	Fax 0161-330 3084
Ashton-under-Lyne, Lancs OL6 8XW	Jonathan Carter
www.mediprop.com	
Nomad Travel	**0845-310 4470**
Unit 34, Redburn Industrial Estate	Fax 0845-310 4475
Woodall Road, Enfield, Middx EN3 4LE	Paul Goodyer
On Set Medical Support Services	**01753-630388**
Pinewood Studios, Pinewood Road	Fax 01753-630399
Iver Heath, Bucks SL0 0NH	Paul Cooke
Paramedic Services	**01273-888899**
25 Beach Green	Fax 01273-455095
Shoreham-by-Sea, W Sussex BN43 5YG	
Rowan Medical Services	**01242-232724**
216 Alstone Lane	Fax 01242-691633
Cheltenham, Glos GL51 8HZ	Ken Griffiths
SP Services	**01952-288999**
Unit D4, Hortonwood 7	Fax 01952-606112
Telford, Shropshire TF1 7GX	Jane Wilson
Want Medical Services	**0844-357 8214**
Douglas House, East Street	Wayne Sturt
Portslade, E Sussex BN41 1DL	
X9 Services	**020-7739 3777**
255 Hackney Road	Jannet Hammond
London E2 8NA	

MERCHANDISING

Doppelgangers	**01883-743324**
3 Fountain Cottages, Cuckseys Lane	David Mayo
Bletchingley, Surrey RH1 4NH	
Event! Merchandising	**01932-593005**
Shepperton Studios, Studios Road	Sue Sharphouse
Shepperton, Middx TW17 0QD	
Imprint Promotions	**01895-238675**
1A Villier Street	Andrew Shiolou
Uxbridge, Middx UB8 2PU	
www.imprintpromotions.co.uk	
Merchandise Mania	**0845-202 2388**
6 Elstree Way	Fax 0845-202 2389
Borehamwood, Herts WD6 1RN	Simon Patnick
MJ Services	**01932-593574**
Shepperton Studios, Studios Road	Fax 01932-593534
Shepperton, Middx TW17 0QD	Ian Wicks
Promotion Ideas	**01245-400303**
West View Lodge, Main Road	Paul Cooper
Rettendon Common, Chelmsford, Essex CM3 8DJ	
Threads	**020-7263 1924**
104 Belgravia Workshops	Fax 020-7281 1563
157-163 Marlborough Road, London N19 4NF	Mike Filer

MOBILE PHONES

AAA Wavevend Radio Communications	**020-7266 1280**
17B Pindock Mews	Fax 020-7266 1290
London W9 2PY	Melvin Lind
www.wavevend.co.uk	
Adam Phones	**0800-123000**
2-3 Dolphin Square	Fax 0500-001230
Edensor Road, London W4 2ST	Adam Toop
Audiolink	**020-8955 1101**
17 Iron Bridge Close	Fax 020-8955 1111
London NW10 0UF	Andrew Morgan John Morgan
www.audiolink.co.uk	
Audiolink	**01753-656692**
Pinewood Studios, Pinewood Road	Fax 020-8955 1111
Iver Heath, Bucks SL0 0NH	Andrew Morgan John Morgan
www.audiolink.co.uk	
Intercity Mobile Communications	**0121-643 7373**
101-114 Holloway Head	Fax 0121-643 6160
Birmingham B1 1QP	
Melvin Lind Radio Communications	**020-7266 1280**
17B Pindock Mews	Fax 020-7266 1290
London W9 2PY	Melvin Lind
www.wavevend.co.uk	

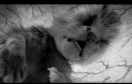
MODELMAKERS

2D:3D	**020-8998 3199**
263 Abbeydale Road	Fax 020-8998 7767
Wembley, Middx HA0 1TW	Rob Edkins
3D Eye	**020-8992 7777**
41-49 Stirling Road	Fax 020-8993 7050
London W3 8DJ	Sally Regis
3D Studios - Food Models	**020-7735 7932**
2 Bedlam Mews	Paul Baker
London SE11 6DF	
5th Axis	**020-8977 2772**
129-135 Fulwell Road	Fax 020-8977 2200
Teddington, Middx TW11 0RJ	Robert Smith
www.5th-axis.co.uk	
Advanced Fabrications	**020-8795 1188**
500 Sunleigh Road	Fax 020-8795 1171
Wembley, Middx HA0 4NF	Michael Wright
Agog Special Effects	**01869-345556**
Unit 14, Green Farm	07966-448282
Fritwell, Oxon OX27 7QU	Jason Troughton
www.agog.tv	
Alchemy	**01293-550107**
Starvemouse Farm, Parish Lane	Jason Kearsley
Pease Pottage, Crawley, W Sussex RH10 5NY	
Animal Instincts	**020-8390 0660**
78 King Charles Road	Steve Strath
Surbiton, Surrey KT5 8QG	
Applied Arts	**020-7739 3155**
22-27 The Oval	Bob Saunders
London E2 9DT	
www.appliedarts.co.uk	
Artem	**020-8997 7771**
Perivale Park, Horsenden Lane South	Fax 020-8997 1503
Perivale, Middx UB6 7RH	Frank Steggall
www.artem.com	
Artem (Scotland)	**0141-427 5775**
64-68 Brand Street	Fax 0141-427 1199
Govan, Glasgow G51 1DG	Joanna Dewar Gibb
www.artem.com	
Articole Props	**01462-835640**
9 Alexander Road, Stotfold	Fax 01462-834896
Hitchin, Herts SG5 4NA	Steve Articole
Asylum Models & Effects	**020-8871 2988**
20 Thornsett Road	Fax 020-8874 8186
London SW18 4EF	Mark Ward
www.asylumsfx.com	

Aztec Modelmakers   020-8977 2010

129-135 Fulwell Road   Fax 020-8977 2200
Teddington, Middx TW11 0RJ   Allan Smith
www.aztec-modelmakers.co.uk

Bandit Studio   0117-951 3922

Unit 13   Simon Peeke
Merton Road Industrial Estate, Bristol BS7 8TL

Breakaway Effects   01932-592446

Shepperton Studios, Studios Road   Fax 01932-580880
Shepperton, Middx TW17 0QD   Neil Upington

Brian Smithies Special Effects   01344-843251

1 Lyne Close Cottages, Lyne Close   Brian Smithies
Virginia Water, Surrey GU25 4EA

Camouflage   020-8742 9292

Totom House   Fax 020-8749 7347
70 Stanley Gardens, London W3 7SZ   Ray Churchouse
www.camouflage-it.com

Centaur Studios   020-8318 4677

12 Elliot Vale   Fax 020-8318 4677
London SE3 0UW   Graham High

Cinesite Production Services   01932-592425

Shepperton Studios, Studios Road   Fax 01932-568944
Shepperton, Middx TW17 0QD
www.cinesiteproductionservices.com

The CNC Factory   01753-656975

Pinewood Studios, Pinewood Road   Edward Hladio
Iver Heath, Bucks SL0 0NH
www.thecncfactory.com

Cnc-It   01403-823628

CNC House, Guildford Road   Fax 01403-823857
Bucks Green, Rudgwick, W Sussex RH12 3JJ   Paul Godden
www.cnc-it.co.uk

Cod Steaks   0117-980 3910

2 Cole Road   Fax 0117-972 8999
Bristol BS2 0UG   Renae Cronin

Complete Fabrication   020-8694 9666

Unit B110, Faircharm Trading Estate   Fax 020-8694 9669
8-12 Creekside, London SE8 3DX   Nick Corker

Cordek   01403-799600

Spring Copse Business Park   Fax 01403-791718
Slinfold, W Sussex RH13 0SZ   Sarah Teversham
www.cordek.com

Creations Online   0191-386 3755

22 Dolton Crescent   Scott Eland
Sheriton Park, Durham DH1 4FB

Cubic Design & Construction   01493-332031

Ventureforth House, South Denes Road   Fax 01493-745120
Great Yarmouth, Norfolk NR30 3PT   Stephanie Woolston

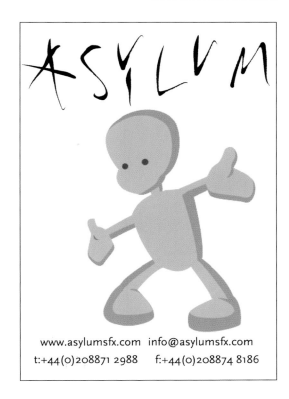
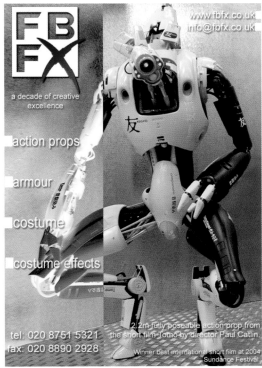

CUTcnc — 01895-237668
Bay D, Bridge Works
Iver Lane, Uxbridge, Middx UB8 2JG
www.cutcnc.co.uk
Fax 01895-237649
Mark Davis

Cutts Arts — 01892-783682
The Hall, Cousley Wood
Wadhurst, E Sussex TN5 6EY
Fax 01892-783682
George Cutts

DB Props — 01932-592733
Shepperton Studios, Studios Road
Shepperton, Middx TW17 0QD
www.dbprops.co.uk
Dean Brooks

Denny Plastics — 020-8964 9368
Unit 16, Mitre Bridge Industrial Estate
Mitre Way, London W10 6AU
Fax 020-8964 9369
Jim Males

Devon Metal Crafts — 01395-272846
2 Victoria Way
Exmouth, Devon EX8 1EW
Fax 01395-276688
Trevor Ford

DHfx Company — 020-8558 8655
Unit 3, Lee Park Trading Estate
Warley Close, London E10 7LF
Fax 020-8558 8655
Patrick O'Sullivan

Elements Special Effects — 020-8961 4244
Unit P04, Acton Business Centre
School Road, London NW10 6TD
www.elementsfx.co.uk
Fax 020-8961 4255
Johnny Rafique

FBFX — 020-8751 5321
Unit 1, Dockwells Estate
Central Way, Feltham, Middx TW14 0RX
www.fbfx.co.uk
Fax 020-8890 2928
Grant Pearmain

Ferox Effects — 07951-724992
Denham Media Park, North Orbital Road
Denham, Middx UB9 5HQ
Ben Hall

Film & TV Sculptors — 07768-440750
Colney Park House, 100 Harper Lane
Radlett, Herts WD7 9HG
www.filmandtvsculptors.com
Fax 01727-823087
Gideon Howarth

Freemont Baxter — 01291-673020
Unit 3, Woodside Industrial Estate
Usk, Monmouths NP15 1SS
Richard Higgs

Gerry Judah — 07831-464360
35 Inkerman Road
London NW5 3BT
Gerry Judah

Glueworks Studio — 01473-326888
Unit 8, Manorfarm Business Centre
Manor Lane, Ipswich IP9 2TG
Derek Bell

Godfrey Design — 01787-223322
The Lodge, Colne Heights
Brook Street, Colchester, Essex CM77 8EU
Fax 01787-223084
Kevin Godfrey

Graham Sweet Studio — 029-2052 2510
Unit 7, Clos Menter, Excelsior Industrial Estate
Western Avenue, Cardiff CF14 3AY
Fax 029-2052 2459
Graham Sweet

Hamilton Ice Sculptors	**020-8944 9787**
Unit 33, Wimbledon Stadium Business Centre	Duncan Hamilton
Riverside Road, London SW17 0BA	
Heron & Driver	**020-7394 8688**
Unit 7, Dockley Road Industrial Estate	Fax 020-7394 8680
Dockley Road, London SE16 3SF	Rolf Driver
Ice Work	**01892-722522**
Lamberhurst Road, Horsmonden	Fax 01892-722578
Tonbridge, Kent TN12 8DP	Robin Boon
Imagination 3D	**020-8904 0121**
3D Studios, 12 Poplar View, East Lane Business Park	Fax 020-8904 0121
East Lane, Wembley, Middx HA9 7RD	Shashi Patel
James Held Modelmaking	**07977-552258**
2A Pembroke Mansions	James Held
1-3 Oakfield Road, Bristol BS8 2AH	
Jeff Cliff Model Effects	**0117-944 5721**
Unit 3, Montpelier Central	Jeff Cliff
Station Road, Bristol BS6 5EE	
Jeremy King	**07850-901103**
43 Berkeley Court, Oatlands Drive	Jeremy King
Weybridge, Surrey KT13 9HX	
www.jeremykingfx.com	
John Wright Modelmaking	**0117-927 2854**
Studio 1, Centre Space	Fax 0117-927 2606
6 Leonard Lane, Bristol BS1 1EA	John Wright
JsM Industrial Modelmaking	**01672-512305**
Unit 3, Homefarm Studios	Fax 01672-512305
Mildenhall, Marlborough, Wilts SN8 2LR	Jay Sheppard
Justin Illusions Creative Studio	**01560-700208**
Blackwood Farm, Grassyards Road	Justin Wilson
Kilmarnock, Ayrshire KA3 6HY	
Keir Lusby Props	**01932-561717**
Shepperton Studios, Studios Road	Fax 01932-565898
Shepperton, Middx TW17 0QD	Keir Lusby
www.keirlusby.com	
Krintech	**020-8958 6111**
104 Hillside Gardens	Kalpesh Patel
Edgeware, Middx HA8 8HD	
www.krintech.co.uk	
Machine Shop Special Effects	**020-8961 5888**
180 Acton Lane	Fax 020-8961 5885
London NW10 7NH	Paul Mann
www.machineshop.co.uk	
Mackinnon & Saunders	**0161-929 4441**
148 Seamons Road	Fax 0161-929 1441
Altrincham, Cheshire WA14 4LJ	Peter Saunders
Mastermodels	**01753-681234**
5 David Road, Poyle Trading Estate	Fax 01753-682681
Colnbrook, Berks SL3 0DB	Debbie Barr

Machine Shop Special Effects
LONDON

Specsavers

Cadbury

Hancock Musuem

SKY HD

Rachel Whiteread

Contact our team

Tel: 020 8961 5888
Fax: 020 8961 5885
info@machineshop.co.uk
www.machineshop.co.uk

Model Makers | Food Replica | Sculpture | Props | costume

Mattes & Miniatures Visual Effects	**01628-506626**
Bray Film Studios, Down Place	Pinewood 01753-656554
Water Oakley, Windsor, Berks SL4 5UG	Leigh Took
www.mattesandminiatures.com	
Metro Models	**020-7252 4545**
2-6 Occupation Road	Fax 020-7252 5111
London SE17 3BE	Richard Guy
Mike & Rosi Compton	**020-8680 4364**
11 Woodstock Road	Fax 020-8681 3126
Croydon, Surrey CR0 1JS	Mike Compton
Mimesis	**020-7582 4303**
1 Bedlam Mews	Martin Kanter
London SE11 6DF	
Model Magic	**020-8909 2859**
1 Mount Stewart Avenue	Naomi Iny
Kenton, Middx HA3 0JR	
Model Solutions	**020-8881 2333**
72X Clarence Road	Fax 020-8881 2233
London N22 8PW	Danny Brook
www.modelsolutions.co.uk	
Modelworks	**01932-565433**
Shepperton Studios, Studios Road	Fax 01932-565433
Shepperton, Middx TW17 0QD	Peter Boys
NE3D	**01429-838899**
Unit 6, Wingate Grange Industrial Estate	Fax 0560-114 3393
Wingate, Co Durham TS28 5AH	Gary Thwaites
Paragon Creative	**01904-608020**
Unit 8, Harrier Court	Fax 01904-608011
The Airfield, Elvington, York YO41 4EA	Mark Pyrah
Paul Robbens Models & Props	**01628-672140**
94 Cordwallis Road	Paul Robbens
Maidenhead, Berks SL6 7BB	
Pipers	**020-7250 0530**
27-35 Bevenden Street	Fax 020-7251 0134
London N1 6BH	Carlos Sousa
Plunge Productions	**01273-227663**
Unit 10, Workhaus	Fax 01273-227663
18A Arthur Street, Hove, E Sussex BN3 5FD	Tim Simpson
Promotional Props & Costumes	**0115-947 4440**
Unit 14, Chaucer Court Workshops	Liz Johnson
Chaucer Street, Nottingham NG1 5LP	
www.promotionalpropsandcostumes.co.uk	
Propshop Modelmakers	**01753-785133**
Pinewood Studios, Pinewood Road	Fax 01753-656267
Iver Heath, Bucks SL0 0NH	James Enright
www.propshopmodelmakers.com	
Prototype Projects	**01763-249760**
1 Greenfield	Fax 01763-249382
Royston, Herts SG8 5HN	Justin Pringle

Rainbow Productions	**020-8254 5300**
Unit 3, Greenlea Park	Fax 020-8254 5306
Prince Georges Road, London SW19 2JD	Simon Foulkes

Robert Allsopp & Associates	**020-8654 4391**
4 Woodside Avenue	Fax 020-8654 4391
London SE25 5DJ	Robert Allsopp
www.raprops.com	

Rodney Forss Design	**01386-700429**
Ginger House, High Street	Rodney Forss
Blockley, Glos GL56 9EX	

Rorschach PropFX	**07980-242189**
Unit 4.7, Wembley Commercial Centre	Tim Wildgoose
East Lane, Wembley, Middx HA9 7UR	
www.rorschachpropfx.com	

Russell Beck Studio	**020-3241 0000**
Unit 11, Vale Industrial Park	Russell Beck
170 Rowan Road, London SW16 5BN	

ScaryCat Studio	**0117-972 1155**
Unit 6.1, The Paintworks	Gary Jackson
275 Bath Road, Bristol BS4 3EH	

S-F-X.com	**01663-741154**
info@s-f-x.com	07860-208432
www.s-f-x.com	Scott MacIntyre

Side Effects	**020-7587 1116**
92 Fentiman Road	Patrick Vigne
London SW8 1LA	

Skulls Direct	**01702-478251**
8 Dynevor Gardens	Simon Kemp
Leigh-on-Sea, Essex SS9 2RG	

Special Art Effects	**07508-640086**
86 Annandale Road	Paul Carey
London SE10 0JZ	

Specialist Engineering Services	**01252-544188**
22 Stake Lane, Cove	Fax 01252-544188
Farnborough, Hants GU14 8NP	Dave Wilson

Specialist Models & Displays	**029-2039 7788**
Unit 1	Fax 029-2039 7121
Hedel Road, Cardiff CF11 8DJ	Kristian Movahed

Spraytech Paint Services	**0845-459 9740**
Unit 57, The Arches	Fax 0845-459 9741
Alma Road, Windsor, Berks SL4 3HY	Paul Munden

Spur Creative Workshop	**01435-873755**
Unit 1A, North Yard	Phil Jarman
Pennybridge Lane, Mayfield, E Sussex TN20 6QB	

st modelmakers	**07818-023880**
Barton End House, Bath Road	William Sumpter
Nailsworth, Glos GL6 0QQ	

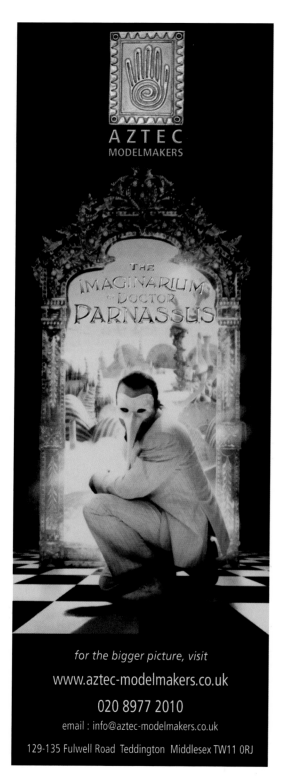

Stephen Greenfield Model Makers	**020-8393 8770**
The Downs Farm, Reigate Road	Fax 020-8394 2803
Ewell, Surrey KT17 3BY	Stephen Greenfield

Steve Wilsher Creative Effects	**020-8943 1066**
Church Road Studios, 30 Church Road	Fax 020-8943 1065
Teddington, Middx TW11 8PB	Steve Wilsher

Talbot Designs	**020-8346 8515**
225 Long Lane	Fax 020-8349 0294
London N3 2RL	Charles Woolff

Tarver Productions	**020-8813 8450**
1B Witley Works, Witley Gardens	Sophie Tarver
Norwood Green, Middx UB2 4ES	

Theatricks	**01994-419723**
Swn-y-Gan, Cefn-y-Pant	Karl Evans
Llanboidy, Carmarthens SA34 0TR	
www.theatricks.co.uk	

Theme Traders	**020-8452 8518**
The Stadium	Fax 020-8450 7322
Oaklands Road, London NW2 6DL	David Jamilly
www.themetraders.com	

Thorp Model Makers	**01344-876776**
24-26 High Street	Fax 01344-628028
Sunningdale, Berks SL5 0NG	Alec Saunders

Tim Weare & Partners	**01580-860808**
The Old Court House, 46-48 London Road	Fax 01580-860068
Hurst Green, E Sussex TN19 7QP	Tim Weare

Warwick Boole	**01869-343463**
The Cottage, School Lane	Warwick Boole
Middleton Stoney, Oxon OX25 4AW	

Whetton & Grosch	**020-8893 3660**
100 Colne Road	Fax 020-8893-3992
Twickenham, Middx TW2 6QE	Karen Grosch

Wingfield Studios	**01442-832951**
126 Flaunden	Fax 01442-834519
Hemel Hempstead, Herts HP3 0PL	Michael Fleming
www.wingfield-studios.com	

MODELMAKERS - PUPPETS

Promotional Props & Costumes	**0115-947 4440**
Unit 14, Chaucer Court Workshops	Liz Johnson
Chaucer Street, Nottingham NG1 5LP	
www.promotionalpropsandcostumes.co.uk	

Robert Allsopp & Associates	**020-8654 4391**
4 Woodside Avenue	Fax 020-8654 4391
London SE25 5DJ	Robert Allsopp
www.raprops.com	

Theatricks	01994-419723
Swn-y-Gan, Cefn-y-Pant	Karl Evans
Llanboidy, Carmarthens SA34 0TR	
www.theatricks.co.uk	

MODELMAKERS SUPPLIES

Adhesive Brokers	01494-868870
3 Whitefield Lane	Fax 0560-047 8208
Great Missenden, Bucks HP16 0BH	Nicola Brown
www.adhesivebrokers.co.uk	

Brodie & Middleton	020-7836 3289
68 Drury Lane	Fax 020-7497 0554
London WC2B 5SP	Andrew Milne Home
www.brodies.net	

Colorite Paint Company	020-8579 3381
169 Boston Road	Fax 020-8567 5158
London W7 3QJ	Irene Condon
www.colorite.co.uk	

Dirty Down	07926-196471
screenproducts@yahoo.co.uk	Fax 0845-299 2299
www.dirtydown.co.uk	Alan Taylor

EMA Model Supplies	01932-228228
Unit 2, Shepperton Business Park	Fax 01932-253766
Govett Avenue, Shepperton, Middx TW17 8BA	Jan Rawstron

Essex Tube Windings	01375-851613
Macanie House, Dock Road	Fax 01375-851717
Tilbury, Essex RM18 7PT	Gareth Thomas-Impey

Flint Hire & Supply	020-7703 9786
Queens Row	Fax 020-7708 4189
London SE17 2PX	Alasdair Flint
www.flints.co.uk	

Jacobson Chemicals	01420-86934
Unit 4, Newman Lane Industrial Estate	Fax 01420-549574
Alton, Hants GU34 2QR	Mike Cooper
www.jacobsonchemicals.co.uk	

MacGregor Industries	01628-760430
Cordwallis Street	Fax 01628-760435
Maidenhead, Berks SL6 7GF	Kevin Crozier

Precision Plastic Ball Company	01943-831166
70 Main Street, Addingham	Fax 01943-831240
Ilkley, W Yorks LS29 0PL	Jan Garth
www.theppb.co.uk	

Vacuum Coatings	020-8520 5353
66 Barrett Road	Fax 020-8520 5353
London E17 9ET	Terry Pearce
www.scientificmirrors.co.uk	

Yarwood Leather	0113-252 1014
Treefield Industrial Estate, Gelderd Road	Fax 0113-252 7391
Morley, Leeds LS27 7JU	Matthew Nicholls

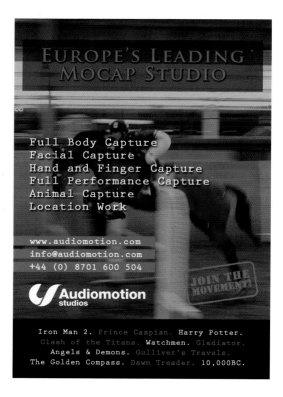

MOTION CAPTURE

2h3D	**01753-533343**
The Coach House, St Georges Meadow	Guy Hauldren
Mill Road, West Drayton, Middx UB7 7EQ	
www.2h3d.co.uk	
Audiomotion Studios	**0870-160 0504**
Holywell House	Fax 01865-728319
Osney Mead, Oxford OX2 0EA	Mick Morris
www.audiomotion.com	
Centroid	**01753-630202**
Pinewood Studios, Pinewood Road	Phil Stilgoe
Iver Heath, Bucks SL0 0NH	
Kontrol Freax	**020-8992 8222**
Unit 6, Westpoint Trading Estate	Fax 020-8992 8222
Alliance Road, London W3 0RA	Steve Scammell Nicola Heslop
www.kontrolfreax.com	

MOTION CONTROL

EMP Designs	**0845-603 3181**
Unit 9, Hercules Way	Fax 0845-603 3182
Aeropark Industrial Estate, Farnborough, Hants GU14 6UU	Dan Stanton
Jackson Woodburn Controls	**0161-439 1047**
9 Brampton Road, Bramhall	Fax 0161-439 9970
Stockport, Cheshire SK7 3BS	Geoff Jackson
Kontrol Freax	**020-8992 8222**
Unit 6, Westpoint Trading Estate	Fax 020-8992 8222
Alliance Road, London W3 0RA	Steve Scammell Nicola Heslop
www.kontrolfreax.com	
Mark Roberts Motion Control	**01342-334700**
Unit 3, South East Studios	Fax 01342-334701
Blindley Heath, Surrey RH7 6JP	Assaff Rawner
Mattes & Miniatures Visual Effects	**01628-506626**
Bray Film Studios, Down Place	Pinewood 01753-656554
Water Oakley, Windsor, Berks SL4 5UG	Leigh Took
www.mattesandminiatures.com	

UC Print Ltd, incorporating Y.C.E. Danwood, provide high quality large and small multi-function devices tailored to your needs.

Black and white or colour printing and copying, scan to email, faxing, stapling, scan to folder, double sided, collating and booklet finishing

We also supply:
Paper (white and tints), shredders and fax machines

24 hour phone support •
4 hour call out •
Weekly rentals available •
No contracts •

Now with offices at
Pinewood Studios and
Longcross Studios

Please contact Dan or Grant

Longcross Studios, Building 112, Chobham Lane, Chertsey, Surrey KT16 0EE
t: +44 (0)1753 657220 f: +44 (0)1753 657240 www.ucprint.co.uk

Topcopy	**01279-321717**
18 Newton Drive	Fax 01279-321718
Sawbridgeworth, Herts CM21 9HE	Toby Davies

TSM Copiers	**0845-375 2018**
Hurst House, 157-169 Walton Road	Fax 0845-375 2019
East Molesey, Surrey KT8 0DX	Jackie Torbett

UC Print	**01753-657220**
Longcross Studios, Building 112	Fax 01753-657240
Chobham Lane, Chertsey, Surrey KT16 0EE	Dan Higgins Grant Sproat
www.ucprint.co.uk	

OFFICE FURNITURE

Andrews Office Furniture	**020-8558 2364**
Unit 8, Estate Way	Fax 020-8988 2920
Church Road, London E10 7JN	Tony Andrews

CORT Furniture Rental	**020-8397 9344**
Unit 28, Barwell Business Park	Fax 020-8974 1440
Leatherhead Road, Chessington, Surrey KT9 2NY	Tim Swaddle

Herman Miller	**0845-226 7201**
Methuen Park	Fax 0845-430 9250
Chippenham, Wilts SN14 0GF	Luke Dawson

Park Royal Office Furniture	**020-8838 1500**
186 Acton Lane	Fax 020-8838 1501
London NW10 7NH	John Bresnahan
www.parkroyalofficefurniture.com	

Wagstaff Group	**020-8432 1000**
Wagstaff Centre, 15 Wharfside	Fax 020-8432 1111
Rosemont Road, Wembley, Middx HA0 4PE	Richard Amstell

OPTICAL EFFECTS & TITLING

Screen Opticals	**020-8997 6107**
6 Wadsworth Road	Fax 020-8810 8881
Perivale, Middx UB6 7JJ	Mike Reeves

Time Slice Films	**020-3004 0762**
9 Lydden Road	Tim Macmillan
London SW18 4LT	

OSTEOPATHS

Action Back Care	**020-8922 9870**
Pinewood Studios, Pinewood Road	Jonathan Cohen
Iver Heath, Bucks SL0 0NH	
www.actionbackcare.com	

PACKAGING

Acorn Packaging Supplies	**020-8992 6366**
101 Shakespeare Road	Fax 020-8992 9660
London W3 6SA	Lee Prentice

Brooks Packaging	**020-8961 2733**
37-39 North Acton Road	Fax 020-8965 9841
London NW10 6PF	Nick Horwood

Holman & Williams Packaging	**020-8879 1100**
Unit 9, Riverside Yard	Fax 020-8944 5162
Riverside Road, London SW17 0BB	Rob Mattock

PAYROLL SERVICES

Sargent-Disc	**01753-630300**
The Coach House, Pinewood Studios	Fax 01753-655881
Pinewood Road, Iver Heath, Bucks SL0 0NH	Laurence Sargent
www.sargent-disc.com	

Tentoo Payroll Services	**01895-810831**
Riverside House, 10-12 Victoria Road	Fax 01895-231499
Uxbridge, Middx UB8 2TW	Persha Sethi

PERSONAL FITNESS & HEALTH

Action Back Care	**020-8922 9870**
Pinewood Studios, Pinewood Road	Jonathan Cohen
Iver Heath, Bucks SL0 0NH	
www.actionbackcare.com	

The Anderson Clinic	**01993-708583**
41A Corn Street	Mark Anderson DC BSc MCC
Witney, Oxon OX28 6BT	

Tara Stoll	**020-8905 3833**
85 Hartland Drive	
Edgware, Middx HA8 8RJ	

PHOTOGRAPHIC EQUIPMENT

Calumet	**020-7383 5127**
93-103 Drummond Street	Fax 020-7383 0841
London NW1 2HJ	Simon Browitt

Hire A Camera	**01435-873028**
Unit 5, Wellbrook Farm	Fax 01435-874841
Berkeley Road, Mayfield, E Sussex TN20 6EH	Sales Team
www.hireacamera.com	

Photographic Hire (David French)	**020-8993 7655**
Unit 15, Alliance Court	Fax 020-8993 7656
Alliance Road, London W3 0RB	David French
www.photohire.co.uk	

VMI	020-8922 1222
Unit 1, Granville Industrial Estate	Fax 020-8922 1114
146-148 Granville Road, London NW2 2LD	Barry Bassett
www.vmi.tv	

PHOTOGRAPHIC TRANSLIGHTS

Artist Backcloths	020-8963 9944
Unit A, Genesis	Fax 020-8963 9955
Rainsford Road, London NW10 7RG	Ron Painter
www.stockyard.tv	
Imaginators	**01992-890800**
51 Hillgrove Business Park, Nazeing Road	Fax 01992-890900
Nazeing, Essex EN9 2HB	Matt Tydeman
Jumbocolor	**01840-213580**
Trekeek Farm	Fax 01840-213054
Camelford, Cornwall PL32 9UB	Mike Elsey
www.jumbocolor.com	
Rosco	**020-8659 2300**
Kangley Bridge Road	Fax 020-8659 3153
London SE26 5AQ	
www.rosco.com	
Rutters	**01223-833522**
Unit 6, South Cambridge Business Park	Fax 01223-833543
Babraham Road, Sawston, Cambridge CB2 4JH	Paul Rutter
www.translights.com	

PLAYOUT FACILITIES

Advanced Broadcast Services	020-8838 6188
11 Metro Centre	Fax 020-8838 1173
Britannia Way, London NW10 7PA	Rob Keith
Kentish Town Studios	**020-7691 3787**
Regis Road	Fax 020-7691 3801
London NW5 3EG	Peter Piddock
www.kentishtownstudios.tv	

FH Media — 020-3176 0072
Unit 1.08, The Wenlock — Adam Baxter
50-52 Wharf Road, London N1 7EU

Fifty Fifty Post — 020-7292 0920
24 D'Arblay Street — Fax 020-7292 0921
London W1F 8EH — Tim Whitehead

Films At 59 — 0117-906 4300
59 Cotham Hill — Fax 0117-923 7003
Bristol BS6 6JR — Gina Fucci

Finish — 020-7734 9110
6A Poland Street — Fax 020-7734 9001
London W1F 8PT — Justine White

Finishing Post Productions — 01895-834490
Denham Media Park, North Orbital Road — Fax 01895-832332
Denham, Middx UB9 5HQ — Neil Meredith

Finishing Post Creative — 0115-945 8800
Giltbrook Studios, 10 Giltway — Fax 0115-945 8801
Giltbrook, Nottingham NG16 2GN — Mark Harwood

First Cut Digital Post Production — 0117-903 0600
4 St Pauls Road — Fax 0117-903 0604
Bristol BS8 1LT — Jon Lomas

Flix Facilities — 0161-834 8808
Invicta House — Fax 0161-834 8807
2-4 Atkinson Street, Manchester M3 3HH — Leo Casserly

Framestore — 020-7208 2600
9 Noel Street — Fax 020-7208 2626
London W1F 8GH — Simon Whalley

Framestore — 020-7344 8000
19-23 Wells Street — Fax 020-7344 8001
London W1T 3PQ

Freakworks — 0131-555 3456
9 Waters Close — Fax 0131-555 1346
The Shore, Edinburgh EH6 6RB — Hamish Allison

Fugitive Studios — 020-7637 0060
72-73 Margaret Street — Simon Dowling
London W1W 8LN

Fullrange — 0121-224 7600
Studio 26, Fazeley Studios — Fax 0121-224 7613
191 Fazeley Street, Birmingham B5 5SE — Lee Kemp

Gizmo Animation — 01243-543697
19 Brittens Cottages, Brittens Lane — Fax 01243-543697
Fontwell, W Sussex BN18 0ST — Steve Whiteley
www.gizmoanimation.co.uk

Glassworks — 020-7434 1182
33-34 Great Pulteney Street — Fax 020-7434 1183
London W1F 9NP

Goldcrest Post Production — 020-7220 2800
1 Lexington Street — Fax 020-7437 5402
London W1F 9AF — Leigh Harrison

Golden Square Post Production — 020-7300 3555
11 Golden Square — Fax 020-7494 3288
London W1F 9JB — Ewan Macleod

The Hall Post Production — 01608-641592
Oddfellows Hall, London Road — Fax 01608-641969
Chipping Norton, Oxon OX7 5AR — Ann Burchell

Halo Post Production — 020-7436 8262
80 Great Portland Street
London W1W 7NW

Hat Factory Post — 020-7734 9942
16-18 Hollen Street — Fax 020-7734 3747
London W1F 8BQ — David Trezise

HD Heaven — 0121-224 7555
8 Allcock Street — Fax 0121-224 7557
Birmingham B9 4DY — Tony Quinsee-Jover

Holloway — 020-7494 0777
21-25 St Annes Court — David Holloway
London W1F 0BJ

Home Post Production — 020-7292 0200
12 Richmond Buildings — Fax 020-7292 0201
London W1D 3HG — Portia Napier

Hub+ — 020-7863 9400
191 Old Marylebone Road
London NW1 5DW

Hullabaloo Studios — 0161-929 6755
Unit J, Altrincham Business Park — Fax 0161-929 5990
Tribune Avenue, Altrincham, Cheshire WA14 5RX — David Porter

Hyperactive Broadcast — 01252-519191
5 The Royston Centre, Lynchford Lane — Fax 01252-513939
Ash Vale, Surrey GU12 5PQ — James Gander Liam Wife
www.hyperactivebroadcast.com

ilab — 020-7287 9520
55 Poland Street
London W1F 7NN
www.ilabuk.co.uk

Imagine TX — 0191-233 1153
65 Westgate Road — Fax 0191-230 0485
Newcastle-upon-Tyne NE1 1SG — Susan Underwood

Independent Post Company — 020-8746 2060
2 Goldhawk Mews — Fax 020-8749 8635
London W12 8PA — Simon Frodsham

International Broadcast Facilities — 020-7497 1515
13-15 Monmouth Street — Fax 020-7379 8562
London WC2H 9DA — David Carstairs

JCA TV Facilities — 020-8357 5400
Monarch House — Fax 020-8357 5450
Victoria Road, London W3 6UR — Perry Foran

The Joint	**020-7734 1674**
Wedgwood Mews	Fax 020-7734 1391
12-13 Greek Street, London W1D 4BA	Sarah Mackay
Light Illusion	**07765-400908**
The Granary, Throcking	Steve Shaw
Buntingford, Herts SG9 9RU	
Lipsync Post	**020-7534 9123**
Screen House	Fax 020-7534 9124
123 Wardour Street, London W1F 0UW	Lisa Jordan
Loaded Dice	**020-7494 4244**
3 Newburgh Street	Helena Evans
London W1F 7RE	
Lola Post Production	**020-7907 7878**
14-16 Great Portland Street	Fax 020-7907 7879
London W1W 8QW	Robert Harvey
M8media	**0141-420 2080**
95 Morrison Street	Fax 0141-420 1444
Glasgow G5 8BE	Jim Allison
Marall-Smith Multimedia Productions	**020-8567 9032**
The Studio	Fax 020-8566 3521
Cambridge Road, London W7 3PB	Alan Smith
Masterpiece	**020-7371 0700**
16 The Talina Centre	Fax 020-7384 1750
Bagleys Lane, London SW6 2BW	Lizzie Osbourn
Mayflower Studios	**020-7437 4421**
118-120 Wardour Street	Fax 020-7437 4461
London W1F 0TU	Lionel Strutt
www.mayflowerstudios.com	
MBP Facilities	**01403-741620**
Saucelands Barn, Coolham	Fax 01403-741647
Horsham, W Sussex RH13 8QG	Nick Stucke
Media Junction	**020-7434 9919**
2 Archer Street	Rob Nixon
London W1D 7AW	
mediahouse	**020-8233 5400**
3 Burlington Lane	Fax 020-8233 5401
London W4 2TH	Cherry Portbury
www.mediahouse.tv	
Mere Mortals	**0191-224 2333**
The Old Forge, Hoults Estate	Fax 0870-460 1456
Walker Road, Newcastle-upon-Tyne NE6 1AB	Lisa Musgrove
Met Film Post	**020-8832 1937**
Ealing Studios	Fax 020-8280 9111
Ealing Green, London W5 5EP	Patrick Fischer
Method	**020-7131 6431**
Film House	Fax 020-7878 7800
142 Wardour Street, London W1F 8DD	Drew Jones

The Mews	**020-7734 4501**
Portland House	Fax 020-7734 7034
12-13 Greek Street, London W1D 4DL	Gareth Mullaney
The Mill	**020-7287 4041**
40-41 Great Marlborough Street	Fax 020-7287 8393
London W1F 7JQ	
Molinare	**020-7478 7200**
34 Fouberts Place	Fax 020-7478 7199
London W1F 7PX	Steve Milne
Molinare	**020-7758 0500**
16 D'Arblay Street	Fax 020-7758 0501
London W1F 8EA	Robert Newlove
The Moving Picture Company	**020-7434 3100**
127 Wardour Street	Fax 020-7287 5187
London W1F 0NL	
MWNCI	**029-2039 9800**
20 Cathedral Road	Fax 029-2039 9700
Cardiff CF11 9LJ	Richard Moss
Mytherapy	**020-7636 6636**
28 Margaret Street	Fax 0871-433 0436
London W1W 8RZ	Dado Valentic
Naisbitt & Co	**020-7287 6536**
Hammer House	Fax 020-7287 5830
117 Wardour Street, London W1F 0UN	Ivan Naisbitt

Nice Biscuits	**020-7855 3619**
177 Wardour Street	Fax 020-7734 0828
London W1F 8WX	Danny Jones
Ntegrity	**020-7734 6767**
Paramount House	Fax 020-7734 7878
162-170 Wardour Street, London W1F 8ZX	Ian Sutherland
Offline Central	**028-9068 2211**
52 Elmwood Avenue	Gerard Brady
Belfast BT9 6AZ	
The Offline Editing Company	**020-7439 3321**
12-13 Poland Street	Fax 020-7439 3341
London W1F 8QB	Vanessa Myrie
Omas Media	**07786-198892**
60 Crawfordstown Road	Joe Marcus
Drumaness, Co Down BT24 8LZ	
Online Post Production	**020-7837 3333**
375 City Road	Fax 020-7833 2185
London EC1V 1NB	Kathy Kenyon
out post sound	**01273-556894**
Link House, Link Place	Rob Speight
Upper Hollingdean Road, Brighton, E Sussex BN1 7GA	
www.outpostsound.co.uk	
OutPost Facilities	**01753-630770**
Pinewood Studios, Pinewood Road	Fax 01753-630771
Iver Heath, Bucks SL0 0NH	Nigel Gourley
Paul Miller Post	**07778-853817**
1 Lexington Street	Paul Miller
London W1F 9AF	
Peepshow Post Production	**020-7434 9555**
58 Frith Street	Fax 020-7434 9444
London W1D 3JQ	Flora Atkinson
Pepper Post Production	**020-7836 1188**
14 Greek Street	Fax 020-7497 9305
London W1D 4DP	Kerry Franks
The Picture House	**028-9076 9800**
Cunningham House	Fax 028-9076 1984
429 Holywood Road, Belfast BT4 2LN	Stephen Petticrew

Pinewood Studios	**01753-651700**
Part of the Pinewood Studios Group	Fax 01753-656219
Pinewood Road, Iver Heath, Bucks SL0 0NH	
www.pinewoodgroup.com	
Platform Post Production	**020-7287 6766**
6 D'Arblay Street	Fax 020-7287 2028
London W1F 8DN	David Tasker
Plato Video	**01202-554382**
3 Poole Road	Fax 01202-557742
Bournemouth, Dorset BH2 5QJ	Lionel Fynn
Pogo Films	**020-7292 0650**
10-11 Moor Street	Fax 020-7292 0651
London W1D 5NF	Olivier Lauchenauer
The Pop Factory	**01443-688500**
Porth	Fax 01443-688501
Rhondda CF39 9PP	Emyr Afan Davis
The Post Factory	**020-7183 1600**
Newcombe House	Fax 020-7727 8509
45 Notting Hill Gate, London W11 3LQ	Markus Sorsa
www.postfactory.co.uk	
Prime Focus	**020-7565 1000**
37 Dean Street	Shail Shah
London W1D 4PT	
www.primefocusworld.com	
Prime Focus	**020-7437 2626**
58 Old Compton Street	Shail Shah
London W1D 4UF	
www.primefocusworld.com	
Quadrillion	**01628-487522**
The Old Barn, Kings Lane Business Park	Victor Jamison
Kings Lane, Cookham Dean, Berks SL6 9AY	
Rapid Pictures	**020-8743 8053**
21-25 Goldhawk Road	Fax 020-8749 9713
London W12 8QQ	Elouise Bell
Run VT	**020-7580 5625**
29 Newman Street	Fax 020-7323 5625
London W1T 1PS	Balvinder Sanghera
Rushes Post Production	**020-7437 8676**
66 Old Compton Street	Fax 020-7734 3002
London W1D 4UH	Joce Capper
Salon	**020-8746 7611**
Salon House	Fax 020-8746 7613
Swainson Road, London W3 7XB	Nick Long
www.salonrentals.com	
Sapex Scripts	**020-8236 1600**
Elstree Studios, Shenley Road	Fax 020-8324 2771
Borehamwood, Herts WD6 1JG	Paul Sattin
www.sapex.co.uk	

sohonet

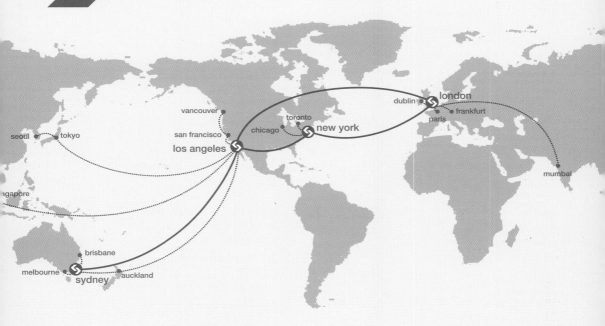

nabling global workflow for the worldwide media community

honet is the leading expert in connectivity and data management, working exclusively
r the media and entertainment industry. We offer clients worldwide an extensive range
services that enable pan-global collaboration within the media community, backed up
unrivalled support and expertise.

e growing popularity of tapeless production and global collaboration is leading to
pidly increasing demands on bandwidth, data security and expertise in workflows
d techniques. At Sohonet we have the perfect balance of technical skill and industry
derstanding to facilitate this trend.

POST PRODUCTION

Satellite Broadcast Facilities	020-8965 5599		**Suite**	020-7636 4488
Unit 20	Fax 0870-777 7800		28 Newman Street	Fax 020-7636 0444
Commercial Way, London NW10 7XF	Oliver Shawo		London W1T 1PR	Shelley Fox

Sequence Post Production — 020-7148 7100
37-38 Newman Street
London W1T 1QA
Ben Foakes

Sumners — 0161-228 0330
Suite 401, Barclay House
35 Whitworth Street West, Manchester M1 5NG
Fax 0161-228 0770
Andy Sumner

Serious Facilities — 0141-440 6940
Film City Glasgow
11 Merryland Street, Glasgow G51 2QF
Fax 0141-440 6950
Katie Whiteford

Swordfish — 020-7734 2428
7 Poland Street
London W1F 8PU
Naomi McNally

The Shed — 020-3100 7800
22 Dean Street
London W1D 3RX
Fax 020-3100 7799
Jason Elliot

Tangram Post Production — 020-7637 2727
1 Charlotte Street
London W1T 1RB
Simon Rose

Silverglade Associates — 020-7827 9510
2.05 Enterprise House
1-2 Hatfields, London SE1 9PG
Fax 020-7827 9511
Charles Frater

Tarmak Films — 020-7100 7458
585A Fulham Road
London SW6 5UA
Dana Trometer

Smoke & Mirrors — 020-7468 1000
57-59 Beak Street
London W1F 9SJ
Fax 020-7468 1001
Amanda Duncan

Technicolor Creative Services — 020-7319 4900
28-32 Lexington Street
London W1F 0LF
Matt Adams

Sohonet — 020-7292 6900
60 Poland Street
London W1F 7NT
www.sohonet.co.uk
Fax 020-7292 6901
Richard Linecar

Technicolor Media Services — 020-8799 0555
Perivale Park, Horsenden Lane South
Perivale, Middx UB6 7RL
Fax 020-8799 0579
George Kilpatrick

Spike — 020-7734 9297
12 Moor Street
London W1D 5NG
Fax 020-7734 9298

Ten Three Editing — 020-7287 0842
5 Newburgh Street
London W1F 7RG
Natalie Bright

Spiritlevel Post — 020-7014 1777
27 Cowper Street
London EC2A 4AP
Elio Espana

Terry Jones Post Production — 020-7434 1173
1 Lexington Street
London W1F 9AF
Fax 020-7437 5402
Terry Jones

Spot Post — 020-7291 9363
34-35 Eastcastle Street
London W1W 8DW
Guy Davis

Traffik — 020-7612 1234
23-31 Great Titchfield Street
London W1W 7PA
Fax 020-7323 4143
Katie Grayson

Stanley Productions — 020-7439 0311
147 Wardour Street
London W1F 8WD
www.stanleysonline.co.uk
Fax 020-7437 2126
Steve Langston Mick Pruce

Triangle Post — 020-7255 5222
81 Whitfield Street
London W1T 4HG
Fax 020-7255 5216
Sinead Gaffney

The Station — 020-7292 9595
46 Bloomsbury Street
London WC1B 3QJ
Fax 020-7292 9596
Jenny Field

Trinity Post — 020-8960 8777
Trinity Mews
Cambridge Gardens, London W10 6JH
Fax 020-8960 6700
Lawrence Smith

Steam Motion & Sound — 020-7734 9530
5 D'Arblay Street
London W1F 8DL
Naomi Stevens

TVC Soho — 020-7734 6840
34 Great Pulteney Street
London W1F 9NP
Fax 020-7734 2938
Simon Ward

Studio Alba — 01851-701125
54A Seaforth Road
Stornoway, Isle Of Lewis HS1 2SD
www.studioalba.com
Fax 01851-701094
Willie Macleod

Uncle — 020-3100 7700
1-7 Livonia Street
London W1F 8AD
Fax 020-3100 7701
Jason Elliott

Subterraneanfish — 028-9268 9268
12B Main Street
Hillsborough, Co Down BT26 6AE
Andrew Stewart

Unit Post — 020-7494 5700
16 Carlisle Street
London W1D 3BT
Fax 020-7494 5720

University Of Surrey Television — 01483-689991
University Of Surrey
Guildford, Surrey GU2 7XH
Brian Johnson

VCL Video	**020-7729 6967**
43-44 Hoxton Square	Fax 020-7613 0544
London N1 6PB	Giles Elwes
VET	**020-7505 4700**
Lux Building	Fax 020-7505 4800
2-4 Hoxton Square, London N1 6US	
Visionworks Television	**028-9024 1241**
Vision House	Fax 028-9024 1777
56 Donegall Pass, Belfast BT7 1BU	Alan Morton
VTR North	**0113-261 5858**
The Old Brewery	Fax 0113-261 5859
High Court, Leeds LS2 7ES	Zoe Tinsley
West Digital	**020-8743 5100**
65 Goldhawk Road	Fax 020-8743 2345
London W12 8EG	
Wheelers	**020-7243 3047**
4 Hansard Mews	Simon Wheeler
London W14 8BJ	
The Whitehouse Post Production	**020-7432 4300**
21-23 Meard Street	Fax 020-7432 4301
London W1F 0EY	Lisa Kenrick
Widei Films	**07958-707232**
Ealing Studios	
Ealing Green, London W5 5EP	
Williams Editing	**020-7439 1091**
15 Bateman Street	Fax 020-7437 8902
London W1D 3AQ	Derek Williams
XPtv	**020-7437 8182**
12 D'Arblay Street	Richard Meadowcroft
London W1F 8DU	
Yellow Moon Post Production	**028-9042 1826**
30 Shore Road	Fax 028-9042 8710
Holywood, Co Down BT18 9HX	Greg Darby

POST PRODUCTION - AUDIO

2nd Sense Broadcast	**020-8236 1133**
Elstree Studios, Shenley Road	Fax 020-8236 1113
Borehamwood, Herts WD6 1JG	Steve Presto
5A Studios	**020-8969 0914**
5A Scampston Mews	Cristina Aragon Michael Koderisch
London W10 6HX	
www.5astudios.co.uk	
750 mph	**020-7534 9999**
20 Golden Square	Fax 020-7534 9988
London W1F 9JL	Nancy O'Brien
Abstracts	**07702-948827**
30 Stronsa Road	Charlie Dodd
London W12 9LB	

Air Post Production	**020-7426 5100**
Picture House	Fax 020-7613 5293
Singer Street, London EC2A 4BQ	Rona McHugh
Alchemy Soho	**020-7248 2777**
12 Cock Lane	Neale Laxton
London EC1A 9BU	
Angell Sound Studios	**020-7478 7777**
Film House	Fax 020-7478 7700
142 Wardour Street, London W1F 8ZU	Nick Angell
APS	**0161-448 9990**
Old Town Hall, Lapwing Lane	Fax 0161-448 2023
Didsbury, Manchester M20 2NR	
Aquarium Studios	**020-7734 1611**
122 Wardour Street	Fax 020-7494 1962
London W1F 0TX	Ben Baird
The Audio Suite (UK)	**0121-224 8234**
8 Allcock Street	Neil Hillman
Birmingham B9 4DY	
BBC Studios & Post Production	**020-8225 6000**
Television Centre	Fax 020-8576 8806
Wood Lane, London W12 7RJ	
www.bbcstudiosandpostproduction.com	
Boom Post	**020-7478 8600**
27-29 Berwick Street	Fax 020-7478 8601
London W1F 8RQ	Paul Hamblin
CKUK Spoken Words	**020-8991 1855**
The Courtyard	Fax 020-8998 3382
Selby Road, London W5 1LX	Christopher Kent
www.ckuk.com	
Clarity Post Production Sound	**020-7287 2414**
27-29 Berwick Street	Fax 020-7478 8616
London W1F 8RQ	Tim Alban
De Lane Lea	**020-7432 3800**
75 Dean Street	Fax 020-7432 3838
London W1D 3PU	Alice Crosby
Digital Media Rentals	**0845-607 6635**
179 Wardour Street	Fax 020-7534 3411
London W1F 8WY	Duncan Napier-Bell
www.digitalmediarentals.co.uk	
Elite Television	**0113-262 3342**
248 Meanwood Road	Fax 0113-262 3798
Leeds LS7 2HZ	Stuart Josephs
www.elitetv.co.uk	
The Exchange	**020-7485 0530**
42 Bruges Place	Fax 020-7482 4588
London NW1 0TX	Mike Hinton
Factory	**020-7580 5810**
54-55 Margaret Street	Fax 020-7580 5811
London W1W 8SH	Lou Allen

Finesplice	020-8564 7839	**Jumbuck**	020-7287 7550
1 Summerhouse Lane	Fax 020-8759 9629	31-32 Eastcastle Street	Glenn Calder
Harmondsworth, Middx UB7 0AW	Ben Turner	London W1W 8DL	
Fitzrovia Post	020-7209 3474	**Loftus Audio**	020-8740 4666
33 Gresse Street	Fax 020-7209 3484	2A Aldine Street	Jo Coombs
London W1T 1QU	Lucy Considine	London W12 8AN	
Gemini Audio	020-7734 8962	**London Audio Labs**	020-8567 0961
Hammer House	Fax 020-7439 3122	Canalot Studios	Fax 020-8567 4512
117 Wardour Street, London W1F 0UN	Lance England	222 Kensal Road, London W10 5BN	David Cohen
Grand Central Sound Studios	020-7306 5600	**Marmalade Studios**	020-7534 5885
51-53 Great Marlborough Street	Fax 020-7306 5616	143 Wardour Street	Fax 020-7534 5884
London W1F 7JT	Chris Lagden	London W1F 8WA	Kate Pengilley
H2O Enterprises	020-7326 9460	**Mayflower Studios**	020-7437 4421
Sphere Studios	Fax 020-7326 9499	118-120 Wardour Street	Fax 020-7437 4461
2 Shuttleworth Road, London SW11 3EA	Simon Bohannon	London W1F 0TU	Lionel Strutt
		www.mayflowerstudios.com	
Hackenbacker	020-7734 1324		
10 Bateman Street	Fax 020-7439 1236	**mediahouse**	020-8233 5400
London W1D 4AQ	Nigel Heath	3 Burlington Lane	Fax 020-8233 5401
		London W4 2TH	Cherry Portbury
Hyperactive Broadcast	01252-519191	www.mediahouse.tv	
5 The Royston Centre, Lynchford Lane	Fax 01252-513939	**Mint Post**	020-8965 5491
Ash Vale, Surrey GU12 5PQ	James Gander Liam Wife	Unit 2, Europa Studios	Mark Verner
www.hyperactivebroadcast.com		Victoria Road, London NW10 6ND	

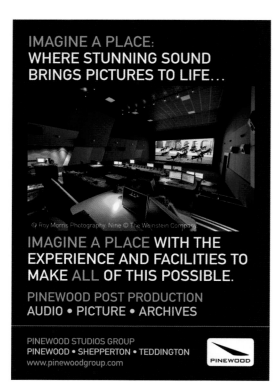

out post sound   **01273-556894**

Link House, Link Place   Rob Speight
Upper Hollingdean Road, Brighton, E Sussex BN1 7GA
www.outpostsound.co.uk

PDSoundDesign   **020-7220 2069**

65-66 Dean Street   Paul Davies
London W1D 4PL

Phoenix Sound   **01753-785495**

Pinewood Studios, Pinewood Road   Peter Fielder
Iver Heath, Bucks SL0 0NH
www.phoenixsound.net

Pinewood Studios   **01753-651700**

Part of the Pinewood Studios Group   Fax 01753-656219
Pinewood Road, Iver Heath, Bucks SL0 0NH
www.pinewoodgroup.com

Prime Focus   **020-7437 2626**

58 Old Compton Street
London W1D 4UF
www.primefocusworld.com

Red Facilities   **0131-555 2288**

61 Timberbush   Fax 0131-555 0088
Edinburgh EH6 6QH   Max Howarth

Redwood Studios   **020-7287 3799**

20 Great Chapel Street   Andre Jacquemin
London W1F 8FW

Reelsound   **01753-656372   020-7148 3800**

Pinewood Studios, Pinewood Road   Fax 01753-653351
Iver Heath, Bucks SL0 0NH Max Hoskins Michael Wabro
www.reelsound.com

SADiE UK   **01353-648888**

The Old School, High Street   Fax 01353-648867
Stretham, Cambs CB6 3LD   Jody Thorne

Side UK   **020-7631 4800**

14-18 Great Titchfield Street   Fax 020-7631 4801
London W1W 8BD   Andy Emery

Silk Sound   **020-7434 3461**

13 Berwick Street   Fax 020-7494 1748
London W1F 0PW   Paula Ryman

Sound 24   **01753-654124**

Pinewood Studios, Pinewood Road   Fax 01753-650213
Iver Heath, Bucks SL0 0NH   Glenn Freemantle

The Sound Company   **020-7580 5880**

23 Gosfield Street   Fax 020-7580 6454
London W1W 6HG   Amy Oliver

The Sound Design Company **07973-842593**

Synxspeed House, Denham Media Park   Steve Felton
North Orbital Road, Denham, Middx UB9 5HL

The Sound House   **0161-832 7299**

Astley House   Fax 0161-832 7266
23 Quay Street, Manchester M3 4AE   Mike Stewart

Sound Works	**029-2033 1010**
1-2 Mount Stuart Square	Fax 029-2033 1011
Cardiff CF10 5EE	Simon Jones
The Soundhouse	**020-8743 2677**
Unit 11, Goldhawk Industrial Estate	Fax 020-8740 9122
2A Brackenbury Road, London W6 0BA	Freddy Henry
Sounding Post	**0115-945 9433**
Giltbrook Studios, 10 Giltway	Richard Mowatt
Giltbrook, Nottingham NG16 2GN	
Sounds In Motion	**029-2059 0521**
The Media Centre	Fax 029-2059 0471
Culverhouse Cross, Cardiff CF5 6XJ	Ralph Evans
Soundtracks Studios	**020-8964 9696**
29 Elkstone Road	Adrian Sear
London W10 5NT	
Splice TV	**020-7033 9944**
21A Perseverance Works	Ramit Anchal
London E2 8DD	
Stationhouse	**020-7602 9906**
2 Russell Road	Jim Betteridge
London W14 8JA	
Synxspeed Post Production	**01895-830670**
Synxspeed House, Denham Media Park	Fax 01895-830671
North Orbital Road, Denham, Middx UB9 5HL	Nick Pocock
Tamborine	**020-7434 1812**
14 Livonia Street	Fax 020-7434 1813
London W1F 8AG	Siobhan Schulz
Trident Sound Studio	**020-7734 6198**
17 St Annes Court	Peter Hughes
London W1F 0BQ	
Universal Sound	**01494-723400**
Old Farm Lane, London Road East	Fax 01494-723500
Amersham, Bucks HP7 9DH	Phillip Barrett
The Voice & Music Company	**020-7494 3000**
33 Soho Square	Fax 020-7494 8222
London W1D 3QU	Kim Goody
Warwick Sound	**020-7437 5532**
111A Wardour Street	Fax 020-7439 0372
London W1F 0UJ	Ernest Marsh
Waterside Sound Studios	**0121-633 3545**
Waterside House	Fax 0121-633 0480
46 Gas Street, Birmingham B1 2JT	Robin Ward
Wave Recording Studios	**020-7439 8080**
32 Great Pulteney Street	Fax 020-7439 8090
London W1F 9NW	Jenny Standish
Wise Buddah Studios	**020-7307 1600**
74 Great Titchfield Street	Fax 020-7307 1601
London W1W 7QP	Neil Wease
www.wisebuddahstudios.com	

Wounded Buffalo	**0117-946 7348**
19 Hampton Lane	Fax 0117-970 6900
Bristol BS6 6LE	Helen Anderson
Zoo Studios	**020-7734 2000**
145 Wardour Street	Fax 020-7734 2200
London W1F 8WB	Graham Ebbs

POST PRODUCTION - DIGITAL INTERMEDIATE

Framestore	**020-7208 2600**
9 Noel Street	Fax 020-7208 2626
London W1F 8GH	Simon Whalley
ilab	**020-7287 9520**
55 Poland Street	
London W1F 7NN	
www.ilabuk.co.uk	
Molinare	**020-7478 7200**
34 Fouberts Place	Fax 020-7478 7199
London W1F 7PX	Steve Milne

POST PRODUCTION - NEG CUTTING

ilab	**020-7287 9520**
55 Poland Street	
London W1F 7NN	
www.ilabuk.co.uk	
Professional Negative Cutting	**020-7437 2605**
8 Dean Street	Fax 020-7437 2025
London W1D 3RL	Steve Farman
Reel Skill Film Cutting	**020-7836 1201**
3 Nottingham Court	Andrew Robinson
Covent Garden, London WC2H 9AY	

POST PRODUCTION EDITORS

Final Cut	**020-7556 6300**
Fenton House	Fax 020-7287 2824
55-57 Great Marlborough Street, London W1F 7JX	Michelle Corney
Marshall Street Editors	**020-7434 0101**
8-9 Carlisle Street	Kath Sawszak
London W1D 3BP	
The Quarry	**020-7437 4961**
26-28 Brewer Street	Tor Adams
London W1F 0SP	
Satusfaction	**020-7691 3898**
13-15 Monmouth Street	Fax 020-7691 4526
London WC2H 9DA	Satu Lawrence

Soho Editors	**020-7734 1286**
80 Berwick Street	Fax 020-7734 1287
London W1F 8TU	

Speade	**020-7734 6901**
Swan House	Fax 020-7734 6765
52-53 Poland Street, London W1F 7NH	Rebecca Boswell

Sue Moles Editing	**020-7494 3383**
1 Marlborough Court	Sue Moles
London W1F 7EE	

Work	**020-7845 6220**
10-11 St Martins Court	Fax 020-7240 5415
London WC2N 4AJ	

POST PRODUCTION EQUIPMENT - RENTAL

Digital Media Rentals	**0845-607 6635**
179 Wardour Street	Fax 020-7534 3411
London W1F 8WY	Duncan Napier-Bell
www.digitalmediarentals.co.uk	

Hiring Post	**01932-255525**
Unit 4, Shepperton Business Park	Fax 01932-260646
Govett Avenue, Shepperton, Middx TW17 8BA	Tasha Smith

Hyperactive Broadcast	**01252-519191**
5 The Royston Centre, Lynchford Lane	Fax 01252-513939
Ash Vale, Surrey GU12 5PQ	James Gander Liam Wife
www.hyperactivebroadcast.com	

Prime Focus	**020-7437 2626**
58 Old Compton Street	
London W1D 4UF	
www.primefocusworld.com	

The Post Factory	**020-7183 1600**
Newcombe House	Fax 020-7727 8509
45 Notting Hill Gate, London W11 3LQ	Markus Sorsa
www.postfactory.co.uk	

Salon	**020-8746 7611**
Salon House	Fax 020-8746 7613
Swainson Road, London W3 7XB	Nick Long
www.salonrentals.com	

Video Europe	**020-7494 1818**
8 Golden Square	Fax 020-7494 1717
London W1F 9HY	Matt Marner
www.videoeurope.co.uk	

Video Europe Wales	**029-2059 5111**
The Television Centre	Fax 029-2059 5222
Culverhouse Cross, Cardiff CF5 6XJ	Tom McNally
www.videoeurope.co.uk	

XTFX	**020-7636 7855**
12 Stephen Mews	Fax 020-7908 7240
London W1T 1AH	James Hamilton-Hislop
www.xtfx.co.uk	

POST PRODUCTION MANAGEMENT

Mayflower Studios	**020-7437 4421**
118-120 Wardour Street	Fax 020-7437 4461
London W1F 0TU	Lionel Strutt
www.mayflowerstudios.com	

Phil Brown PRC	**020-7380 3962**
Suffolk House	Phil Brown
1-8 Whitfield Place, London W1T 5JU	

Schedule 2	**0844-880 2282**
11-13 Broad Court	Fax 0844-880 2283
London WC2B 5PY	Rebecca Hawkes

Steeple Post Production Services	**01753-654942**
Pinewood Studios, Pinewood Road	Fax 01753-654958
Iver Heath, Bucks SL0 0NH	Steve Harrow

POWER

Aggreko UK	**08458-24 7 365**
14 Sandiford Road, Kimpton Industrial Estate	Fax 01543-476006
Sutton, Surrey SM3 9RD	Marcus Starling
www.aggreko.co.uk	
ARRI Lighting Rental	**01895-457200**
4 Highbridge, Oxford Road	Fax 01895-457201
Uxbridge, Middx UB8 1LX	Sinead Moran
ARRI Rental	**0161-736 8034**
Units 6-8	Fax 0161-745 8023
Orchard Street Industrial Estate, Manchester M6 6FL	Bob McGregor
PKE Lighting	**01942-678424**
Unit E7 Walter Leigh Way, Moss Industrial Estate	Fax 01942-678423
St Helens Road, Leigh, Lancs WN7 3PT	James Pollard
www.pkelighting.com	
Power Rental	**0151-282 4023**
Strand Road, Washington Parade	Fax 0151-922 8747
Bootle, Merseyside L20 1AA	
The Powerline	**01225-892336**
Knowle Hill Farm, Beeks Lane	Fax 01225-892336
Marshfield, Chippenham, Wilts SN14 8BB	Alistair Gregson
www.thepowerline.co.uk	
SLD Pumps & Power	**01322-350088**
2 Ness Road	Peter Sparley
Erith, Kent DA8 2LD	
The Technical Department	**01483-238050**
The Old Forge, Guildford Road	Fax 01483-238055
Normandy, Surrey GU3 2AR	Chantal Jacobs

PR

Braben	**020-7566 2990**
18 Soho Square	Fax 020-7025 8100
London W1D 3QL	Sarah Locke
Chicane	**01753-650004**
Pinewood Studios, Pinewood Road	Fax 01753-639288
Iver Heath, Bucks SL0 0NH	Gary Barak
DDA	**020-7932 9800**
192-198 Vauxhall Bridge Road	Fax 020-7932 4950
London SW1V 1DX	
Empica	**01275-394400**
1 Lyons Court, Long Ashton Business Park	Fax 01275-393933
Yanley Lane, Long Ashton, Bristol BS41 9LB	Martin Powell
Francesca Smith Publicity	**01803-868444**
Church Barn, Harberton	Fax 01803-868444
Totnes, Devon TQ9 7SH	Francesca Smith
Freud Communications	**020-7580 2626**
55 Newman Street	Fax 020-7637 2626
London W1T 3EB	Cathy Dunkley

Good Relations	020-7861 3030	**Daily Telegraph**	020-7931 2371
Holborn Gate	Fax 020-7861 3131	111 Buckingham Palace Road	Neil Midgley
26 Southampton Buildings, London WC2A 1PQ	Anne Fossey	London SW1W 0DT	
Ian Johnson Publicity	020-7836 3030	**Evening Standard**	020-7938 6000
8 Flitcroft Street	Ian Johnson	Northcliffe House	Fax 020-7937 2648
London WC2H 8DL		2 Derry Street, London W8 5TT	Gideon Spanier
Katinka Allender	01491-571402	**Financial Times**	020-7873 3000
PO Box 4745		1 Southwark Bridge	Fax 020-7873 3929
Henley-on-Thames, Oxon RG9 9DE		London SE1 9HL	
Milk Publicity	020-7520 1087	**Guardian**	020-3353 2000
8-14 Vine Hill	Fax 020-7608 0377	Kings Place	Fax 020-7837 2114
London EC1R 5DX	Victoria Brooks	90 York Way, London N1 9GU	
Premier PR	020-7292 8330	**Independent**	020-7005 2000
91 Berwick Street	Fax 020-7734 2024	Northcliffe House	Fax 020-7005 2864
London W1F 0NE	Sara Keene	2 Derry Street, London W8 5TT	David Lister
Public Eye Communications	020-7349 5021	**Mail On Sunday**	020-7938 6000
Suite 313, The Plaza	Sarah Hammond	Northcliffe House	Fax 020-7937 7488
535 Kings Road, London SW10 0SZ		2 Derry Street, London W8 5TT	
Red Lorry Yellow Lorry	020-7403 8878	**MovieScope Magazine**	0845-094 6263
Elm Court	Fax 020-7403 7834	Unit 3.02, Lafone House, The Leathermarket	Fax 0854-094 3846
156 Bermondsey Street, London SE1 3TQ	Rob Ettridge	11-13 Weston Street, London SE1 3HN	Rinaldo Quacquarini
Single Minded Promotions	07860-391902	**Network Nine News**	01753-656423
1 Lyric Square	Tony Byrne	Pinewood Studios, Pinewood Road	Wendy Laybourn
London W6 0DB		Iver Heath, Bucks SL0 0NH	
Verve Public Relations	01908-275271	**Observer**	020-3353 2000
Park House, 8 Grove Ash	Fax 01908-275272	Kings Place	Fax 020-7837 2114
Mount Farm, Milton Keynes, Bucks MK1 1BZ	Theo Chalmers	90 York Way, London N1 9GU	
The WhiteOaks Consultancy	01252-727313	**The People**	020-7293 3000
24 West Street	Fax 01252-727314	1 Canada Square	Fax 020-7293 3517
Farnham, Surrey GU9 7DR	Susanne Griffiths	Canary Wharf, London E14 5AP	Caroline Waterston

PRESS & PUBLICATIONS

		Programme News	020-7575 1938
		45 Fouberts Place	Fax 020-7575 1931
		London W1F 7QH	Adam Hampton
American Cinematographer	+1 323 969 4333	**Spotlight**	020-7437 7631
1782 North Orange Drive, Hollywood	Fax +1 323 876 4973	7 Leicester Place	Fax 020-7437 5881
CA 90028, USA	Saul Molina	London WC2H 7RJ	Laura Albery
		www.spotlight.com	
Britflicks	01303-271999	**Sun**	020-7782 4322
384 Cheriton Road	John Baker	1 Virginia Street	Fax 020-7782 4029
Folkestone, Kent CT19 4DX		London E98 1SN	Lorna Carmichael
Daily Express	0871-434 1010	**Sunday Express**	0871-434 1010
Northern & Shell Building		Northern & Shell Building	Jane Clinton
10 Lower Thames Street, London EC3R 6EN		10 Lower Thames Street, London EC3R 6EN	
Daily Mail	020-7938 6000	**Sunday Times**	020-7782 5000
Northcliffe House	Baz Bamingboye	1 Pennington Street	Fax 020-7782 5776
2 Derry Street, London W8 5TT		London E1 9XN	Helen Hawkins
Daily Mirror	020-7293 3000	**Times**	020-7782 5000
1 Canada Square	Fax 020-7293 3834	1 Virginia Street	Fax 020-7782 5203
Canary Wharf, London E14 5AP	Jonathan Clements	London E98 1RL	Sarah Vine

PRE-VISUALISATION

Painting Practice	**020-8948 2787**
2 Richmond Hill	Daniel May
Richmond, Surrey TW10 6QX	
Robert Finlay Films	**07961-451912**
Elstree Studios, Shenley Road	Robert Finlay
Borehamwood, Herts WD6 1JG	

PRINTING & PHOTOCOPYING

Lefa Print	**020-8302 2555**
Enterprise Works, LEFA Business Park	Fax 020-8302 1333
Edgington Way, Sidcup, Kent DA14 5BH	Richard Pizzey
Print Inc	**020-8605 1000**
37-39 Rookwood Avenue	Fax 020-8605 1011
New Malden, Surrey KT3 4LY	Richard Laws
The Production Copier Company	**07956-596415**
Elstree Studios, Shenley Road	Fax 020-8324 2771
Borehamwood, Herts WD6 1JG	Penny Sattin
www.productioncopiers.co.uk	
Spot On Design & Print	**01295-709988**
Pearl House, Butchers Row	Fax 01295-709990
Banbury, Oxon OX16 8JH	Samantha Miller
UC Print	**01753-657220**
Longcross Studios, Building 112	Fax 01753-657240
Chobham Lane, Chertsey, Surrey KT16 0EE	Dan Higgins Grant Sproat
www.ucprint.co.uk	
Xerox	**01895-843030**
Bridge House, Oxford Road	Fax 01895-843166
Uxbridge, Middx UB8 1HS	Jill Aldous

PRODUCT PLACEMENT

1st Place	**01223-894949**
The Old Bank, 30 High Street	Fax 01223-894971
Linton, Cambridge CB21 4HS	Liza Read
Bellwood Media	**0844-801 8010**
46 Jerningham Road	Fax 020-8635 8116
London SE14 5NW	Kellie Belle
Brand Exposure	**020-7924 9122**
Suite 206, Bon Marche Centre	Fax 020-7274 8676
241-251 Ferndale Road, London SW9 8BJ	Simon Key
Contemporary Props	**01753-655766**
Pinewood Studios, Pinewood Road	Fax 01753-655118
Iver Heath, Bucks SL0 0NH	James Warren

Hatched Brands	**0845-456 1085**
77 Heyford Park	Fax 0845-456 1086
Upper Heyford, Oxon OX25 5HD	Peter Thompson
www.hatchedbrands.com	
JBAW	**01753-651700**
Pinewood Studios, Pinewood Road	Fax 01753-653271
Iver Heath, Bucks SL0 0NH	Alan Wyatt
Production Profiles	**01276-850080**
Oak Tree Cottage, New Road	Fax 01276-300100
Windlesham, Surrey GU20 6BJ	Delena Keenan
Prop Portfolio	**01933-402464**
3 Faraday Court, Park Farm	Fax 01933-402474
Wellingborough, Northants NN8 6XY	Tony Birt
Scenario (UK)	**01279-842303**
Westfield, Westland Green	Fax 01279-841459
Little Hadham, Herts SG11 2AL	Geraldine Coyle
Seesaw Media	**020-8343 2022**
Baveno House	Fax 020-8371 6546
235 Regents Park Road, London N3 3LF	Simon Ritterband
Spotlight	**020-7922 5798**
117 Waterloo Road	Fax 020-7921 0574
London SE1 8UL	John Kellaway

PRODUCTION COMPANIES

116 Films 07885-705379
14 Maldon Road Richard Denton
London W3 6SU
Television

12 Yard Productions 020-7156 5750
131-151 Great Titchfield Street Fax 020-7849 9433
London WIW 5BB
Television

123 Productions 020-7263 4199
154 Corbyn Street Sue Crockford
London N4 3DB
Television

1410 Degrees 020-7287 1410
16 Dufours Place Fax 020-7287 4578
London WIF 7SP Robin Clarkson
Television

186 Media 0161-408 1861
Enterprise House Fax 0161-226 9995
Lloyd Street North, Manchester M15 6SE Michael Fox
Corporate

1871 Productions 020-3170 5545
20 Mortlake High Street Fax 020-8392 6677
London SW14 8JN Gaby Montanaro
Corporate

IA Productions 01360-620855
Langshot Farm, Acre Valley Road Norman Stone
Torrance, Glasgow G64 4DL
Television

247 Television 01753-650000
Pinewood Studios, Pinewood Road Fax 01865-890504
Iver Heath, Bucks SLO 0NH David Broscombe
Television

2AM Films 020-7292 9600
National House Fax 020-7292 9601
60-66 Wardour Street, London WIF 0TA Amanda Martin
Commercial

2BU Productions 01884-855627
Way Farm Elspeth Penny
Thorverton, Exeter EX5 5LN
Television

2Hotfilms 020-7231 1952
28 Fortune Place Dean Charles
London SE1 5JP
Promo

The 39 Production Company 01438-814150
The Estate Offices, Knebworth House Henry Cobbold
Knebworth, Herts SG3 6PY
Feature

3DD Group 020-7380 8100
8-12 Camden High Street Fax 020-7380 8118
London NW1 0JH Lyndy Saville
Television

3Di TV 0113-274 4933
77 Cardigan Road Fax 0113-274 4933
Leeds LS6 IEB Gerry Troyna
Television

400Blows Productions 020-8693 9782
24 Heber Road Andy Kimpton-Nye
London SE22 9LA
Feature

421 Productions 07971-123874
4 The Grove Gordon Egglestone
Lancaster LA1 3AL
Television

5 Lamps Media 01332-383322
36 Friar Gate Fax 01332-291268
Derby DE1 1DA Nick Waring
Corporate

76 020-7287 8739
59 Rupert Street Fax 020-7287 8751
London WID 7PN Mark Murrell
Commercial

A38 Films 01752-318358
26 Pounds Park Road Mick Catmull
Plymouth PL3 4QR
Television

Abacus Television 01603-812800
Fresh Fields Studio, Great Melton Road Jane Scarfe
Little Melton, Norwich NR9 3NR
Corporate

Acacia Productions 020-8341 9392
80 Weston Park Edward Milner
London N8 9TB
Television

Academy Films 020-7395 4155
16 West Central Street Fax 020-7240 0355
London WC1A 1JJ Lizie Gower
Commercial

Accentuate UK 01403-738262
64 Bamborough Close Fax 01403-738398
Southwater, W Sussex RH13 9XG Colin Newman
Corporate

Access Moving Image 0113-294 8166
The Media Place Craig Lawson
655A Roundhay Road, Leeds LS8 4BA
Television

Acrobat Television	**0161-477 9090**
107 Wellington Road North	Fax 0161-477 9191
Stockport, Cheshire SK4 2LP	David Hill
Television	

Actaeon Films	**020-8769 3339**
50 Gracefield Gardens	Fax 0870-134 7980
London SW16 2ST	Daniel Cormack
Feature	

Active Pictures (Film & Television)	**0113-389 1176**
Prospect House	Nick Hancock
32 Sovereign Street, Leeds LS1 4BJ	
Television	

Activelight	**01245-237445**
Wonder Street, Pleshy	John Culleton
Chelmsford, Essex CM3 1HQ	
Corporate	

Activideo Communications	**0161-228 6324**
Hotspur House	Brian Barnes
2 Gloucester Street, Manchester M1 5QR	
Corporate	

Ad:commercials	**020-8960 8777**
Townhouse Studios	Fax 020-8960 6700
52 Wallingford Avenue, London W10 6PY	Tula Skott
Commercial	

Adam Media	**020-8876 3333**
21 Dungarvan Avenue	Fax 020-8876 3333
London SW15 5QU	John McAdam
Television	

Addictive TV	**020-7700 0333**
The Old House	Nick Clarke
39A North Road, London N7 9DP	
Television	

Adrian Rowbotham Films	**01892-750201**
Bohemia, Eridge Park	Fax 01892-750978
Eridge Green, Tunbridge Wells, Kent TN3 9HA	Adrian Rowbotham
Commercial	

Advantage Productions	**01256-327244**
37 Heritage Park, Hatch Warren	Fax 01256-327244
Basingstoke, Hants RG22 4XT	Andrew Salter
Corporate	

Adventure Pictures	**020-7613 2233**
6 Blackbird Yard	Fax 020-7256 0842
Ravenscroft Street, London E2 7RP	Christopher Sheppard
Feature	

Aficionado Films	**0845-329 6945**
84 Nithsdale Road	Alan de Pellette
Glasgow G41 5RA	
Television	

PRODUCTION COMPANIES

Agile Films　　　　　**020-7000 2882**
Unit I　　　　　　　　　Fax 020-7729 3375
68-72 Redchurch Street, London E2 7DP　　Myles Payne
Commercial

Airwaves Media Productions　　**01489-578850**
58 Warsash Road　　　　Steve Ancsell
Southampton, Hants SO31 9JA
Television

Alan Johnson AV　　　　**01256-325419**
154 Pack Lane　　　　　Alan Johnson
Basingstoke, Hants RG22 5HR
Corporate

Alan More Films　　　　**01753-642628**
Pinewood Studios, Pinewood Road　　Alan More
Iver Heath, Bucks SL0 0NH
Television

Alan Zafer & Associates　　**020-7723 0106**
47-48 Chagford Street　　Fax 020-7724 6163
London NWI 6EB　　　　Alison Webb
Corporate

Alex Myers & Associates　　**020-7379 5124**
Apartment 25　　　　　Fax 020-7379 0269
9 Kean Street, London WC2B 4AY　　Alex Myers
Commercial

Alive Events　　　　　**020-8959 4178**
Athene House　　　　　Simon Coote
86 The Broadway, London NW7 3TD
Corporate

Almega Projects　　　　**020-7479 7410**
6 Newburgh Street　　　Fax 020-7287 4628
London WIF 7RQ　　　　Angus Aynsley
Feature

Alpha Productions　　　**07850-314379**
37 Furze Common Road, Thakeham　　Paul Cave
Pulborough, W Sussex RH20 3EG
Corporate

Alpha Star Films　　　　**07791-890669**
9 Caversham Close　　　Simon Cox
Nuneaton, Warwicks CVII 6UR
Feature

Alto Films　　　　　　**01273-747837**
18B Cross Street　　　　Toni Harman
Hove, E Sussex BN3 1AJ
Feature

Amaranth Film Partners　　**020-8211 1888**
PO Box 44636　　　　　Fax 020-8211 0222
London N16 5WP　　　　Paul Hills
Feature

Amarillo Films　　　　**020-7287 7476**
5 Dean Street　　　　　Fax 020-7287 7844
London WID 3RQ　　　　Tom Shard
Commercial

Amatis Films　　　　　**01737-215077**
PO Box 21　　　　　　David Pollock
Tadworth, Surrey KT20 5XZ
Corporate

Amazing Productions　　　**020-7602 5355**
31 Royal Crescent　　　Bassem Abdallah
London WII 4SN
Television

Amber Films　　　　　**0191-232 2000**
5-9 Side　　　　　　　Annie Robson
Newcastle-upon-Tyne NEI 3JE
Television

AMC Pictures　　　　　**01753-646280**
Little Hemmingford, Beaconsfield Road　Fax 01753-648222
Farnham Common, Bucks SL2 3LZ　Alistair Maclean-Clark
Feature

Amethyst Television　　　**01954-718900**
Bandileg Barn, Fox Road　　Des O'Brien
Bourn, Cambs CB23 2TX
Corporate

AMG Television Productions　　**0161-427 9001**
24 Brookdale Avenue
Marple, Cheshire SK6 7HP
Television

Ammonite　　　　　　**0117-942 1102**
85 Springfield Road　　　Martin Dohrn
Bristol BS6 5SW
Television

AMP　　　　　　　　**07976-746447**
Lynx House, School Lane　　Andy Matthews
Hadlow Down, E Sussex TN22 4JE
Feature

An Acquired Taste TV　　　**020-8686 1188**
Brickesley Cottage, 51 Croham Road　Fax 020-8686 5928
Croydon, Surrey CR2 7HD　　Colin Bennett
Television

Ancient Mariner Productions　　**020-7274 3110**
3 Inglis Street　　　　Paul Bush
London SE5 9QT
Television

Angel Eye Media　　　　**0845-230 0062**
9 Rudolf Place　　　　Fax 0845-230 9562
London SW8 IRP　　　　Richard Osborne
Television

Angel Productions	**0844-415 5534**
8 Hillside Gardens	Stephen Engelhard
London N6 5ST	
Corporate	
Angelic Films	**0845-094 1138**
Block A, Commercial Square	Fax 01296-696323
Leigh Street, High Wycombe, Bucks HP11 2RH	Adam Coop
Promo	
Angst Productions	**020-7631 4259**
Kenilworth House	Fax 020-7631 4279
79-80 Margaret Street, London W1W 8TA	Dan Patterson
Television	
Animals On Blue	**020-7794 3711**
38 Fitzjohns Avenue	Farokh Khorooshi
London NW3 5NB	
Commercial	
Annex Films	**020-7440 1400**
8 Ganton Street	Fax 020-7437 7507
London W1F 7QP	Jack Robinson
Commercial	
Anonymous Content	**020-7927 9400**
7-8 Bourlet Close	Fax 020-7927 9401
London W1W 7BW	Jani Guest
Commercial	
Another Direction	**01989-565059**
PO Box 422	Stephen Broadfield
Ross-on-Wye, Herefordshire HR9 5ZB	
Corporate	
Another Film Company	**020-7307 7750**
14-17 Wells Mews	Fax 020-7307 7755
London W1T 3HF	Tim Marshall
Commercial	
Antena Productions	**01286-662202**
Unit 2, Cibyn Industrial Estate	Fax 01286-678594
Caernarfon, Gwynedd LL55 2BD	Gill Bowen
Television	
Antix Productions	**0161-975 6172**
Houldsworth Mill, Houldsworth Street	Fax 0161-975 6173
Reddish, Stockport, Cheshire SK5 6DA	Karl Beattie
Television	
Anton Corbijn	**020-8743 9997**
10 Poplar Mews	Monica Axelsson
London W12 7JS	
Promo	
ANV Productions	**020-7262 3074**
47A Kendal Street	Antony Norris
London W2 2BU	
Corporate	

PRODUCTION COMPANIES

AP Digital   **0161-613 8756**
Eaton Place Business Centre   Fax 0161-613 1998
114 Washway Road, Sale, Cheshire M33 7RF   David Owen
Corporate

Apis Films   **020-7978 8586**
27 Gubyon Avenue   Fax 020-7978 8586
London SE24 0DU   Ben Hughes
Feature

APMS Productions   **01202-670666**
17 Church Street   Paul Sarony
Poole, Dorset BH15 1JP
Feature

Apollo Media   **020-7253 4516**
96-98A Curtain Road   Fax 020-7729 0138
London EC2A 3AA   Gavin Poolman
Feature

Applecross Productions   **01753-656196**
Pinewood Studios, Pinewood Road   Iain Smith
Iver Heath, Bucks SL0 0NH
Feature

Aquarius Films   **020-7291 1065**
9 Wimpole Street   Terence Potter
London W1G 9SR
Feature

Aquila Films   **020-8340 9500**
19 Bishops Road   Andrea Florence
London N6 4HP
Television

AR Communications   **0844-585 5959**
18 Church Road   Fax 0844-585 5958
Tunbridge Wells, Kent TN1 1JP   Alan Rustad
Corporate

ARC   **0141-420 0900**
40 Dalintober Street   Fax 0141-429 3723
Glasgow G5 8NW   John Rocchiccioli
Television

Arcadia Films   **020-8422 4885**
Flat 7   Fax 020-7402 5330
84 Westbourne Terrace, London W2 6QE   Marina Gratsos
Feature

Archer's Mark   **020-7426 5160**
120-124 Curtain Road
London EC2A 3SQ
Commercial

Aries Productions   **01372-457724**
Tyrrells, Effingham Common   Fax 01372-456184
Effingham, Surrey KT24 5JE   Brenda Ennis
Television

Artangel   **020-7713 1400**
31 Eyre Street Hill   Fax 020-7713 1401
London EC1R 5EW
Television

Artsview Productions   **020-8444 2001**
46 Ossulton Way   Claudine Hughes
London N2 0LB
Television

Arturi Films   **01453-884974**
PO Box 370   Elizabeth Morgan-Hemlock
Stroud, Glos GL6 1EJ
Television

ASA Productions (UK)   **020-8464 7929**
Ashleigh House, 42 Hammelton Road   Stephen Saunders
Bromley, Kent BR1 3PY
Television

ASAT Productions   **01631-567192**
Dunstaffnage Mains Farm   Fax 01631-567192
Dunbeg, Argyll PA37 1PZ   Peter Amsden
Television

ASD Lionheart   **020-7437 3898**
Unit G06, Clerkenwell Workshops   Fax 020-7014 3811
31 Clerkenwell Close, London EC1R 0AT   Nick Sutherland-Dodd
Commercial

ASF Productions   **07770-277637**
38 Clunbury Court, Manor Street   Fax 01442-872536
Berkhamsted, Herts HP4 2FF   Malcolm Bubb
Commercial

Ashford Entertainment Corporation   **020-8668 8188**
20 The Chase   Fax 0870-116 4142
Coulsdon, Surrey CR5 2EG   Frazer Ashford
Television

Aspect   **020-8282 7575**
Solar House   Fax 020-8282 7576
915 High Road, London N12 8QJ   Ben Hillson
Corporate

Aspect Television   **01989-770285**
Radnor House, Greenwood Close   Rob Finighan
Cardiff Gate Business Centre, Cardiff CF23 8AA
Television

Asylum Pictures   **01450-379416**
Cavers Garden Farm, Denholm   Robin MacPherson
Hawick, Roxburghshire TD9 8LN
Television

Atlantic Picture Company   **07970-884168**
49 Roundhill Crescent   Kirk Weddell
Brighton, E Sussex BN2 3FQ
Feature

Atlantic Productions   020-8735 9300

Brook Green House   Fax 020-8735 9333
4 Rowan Road, London W6 7DU   Anthony Geffen
Television

Atlas Films   01594-516996

Oakdean Studios, High Street   Graham Evans
Blakeney, Glos GL15 4DY
Corporate

Atoll Productions   020-8540 0700

64 Gore Road   Roy Perkins
London SW20 8JL
Television

Attaboy TV   020-7740 3000

Unit 1   Fax 020-7740 3008
23A Blue Anchor Lane, London SE16 3UL   Andrew Shaw
Television

Atticus Finch   020-7247 6600

Unit 7   Jim Waters
7A Plough Yard, London EC2A 3LP
Commercial

ATV Productions   0800-358 2933

Rossett Cottage, Beedon Common   Adrian Cubitt
Newbury, Berks RG20 8TU
Corporate

Aurora Films   01208-851810

Trenarlett, St Tudy   Beatrix Milburn
Bodmin, Cornwall PL30 3PR
Television

Autonomi   0141-357 7288

Studio 8   Marie Oleson
333 Woodlands Road, Glasgow G3 6NG
Television

AV Interactive   01789-761331

Minerva Mill Innovation Centre, Station Road   Marc Edwards
Alcester, Warwicks B49 5ET
Corporate

AV Sightline   01483-861555

Dylan House, Town End Street   Fax 01483-861516
Godalming, Surrey GU7 1BQ   Keith Thomas
Corporate

Available Light Productions   0117-908 4433

The Victorian Arcade   Fax 0117-908 4434
3A Boyces Avenue, Bristol BS8 4AA   David Parker
Television

Avalon Television   020-7598 2000

4A Exmoor Street   Fax 020-7598 7281
London W10 6BD
Television

Avanti Television   01443-688500

The Pop Factory, Jenkin Street   Fax 01443-688501
Porth, Rhondda CF39 9PP   Emyr Afan
Television

AVC Media Enterprises   01224-248007

Wellington Circle   Fax 01224-248407
Altens, Aberdeen AB12 3JG
Television

AVC Productions   01753-567377

242-243 Gresham Road   Fax 01753-525516
Slough, Berks SL1 4PH   Sara Hill
Corporate

AVT Connect   01273-299001

7 Stone Street   Fax 01273-299002
Brighton, E Sussex BN1 2HB   Steve Affleck
Television

Axiom Films   020-7243 3111

87 Notting Hill Gate   Fax 020-7243 3152
London W11 3JZ   Douglas Cummins
Feature

Axis Creative Communication   01524-849010

Cameron House   Andrew Daykin
White Cross, Lancaster LA1 4XF
Corporate

Baby Cow   020-7612 3370

33 Foley Street   Fax 020-7612 3352
London W1W 7TL
Television

Back2back Productions   01273-227700

10 Boyces Street   Fax 01273-227777
Brighton, E Sussex BN1 1AN   David Notman-Watt
Television

Balagan Films   07970-130912

Elstree Studios, Shenley Road   Jonathan Weissler
Borehamwood, Herts WD6 1JG
Feature

Baldovan Films   01932-881144

71A Manor Road   Ewa Weston
Walton-on-Thames, Surrey KT12 2NX
Television

Banana Split Productions   020-8200 8200

11 Carlisle Road   Fax 020-8200 1414
London NW9 0HD   Laura Trail
Television

Bang   020-7692 4444

43-45 Camden Road   Marcelina Majczynska
London NW1 9LR
Commercial

Bard Entertainments	**020-7043 9749**
57 Walnut Tree Walk	Margaret Matheson
London SE11 6DN	
Feature	

The Bare Film Company	**020-7758 4170**
Dewhurst House	Fax 020-7734 5507
3-6 Winnett Street, London W1D 6JY	Helen Hadfield
Commercial	

Barford Productions	**020-7324 1466**
206-212 St Johns Street	Tim Mein
London EC1V 4JY	
Corporate	

Barrie Joll Associates	**020-7437 9965**
58 Frith Street	Fax 020-7434 9444
London W1D 3JQ	Barrie Joll
Commercial	

Basilisk Communications	**020-7566 4065**
Suite 232, Kemp House	Fax 020-7566 3935
152-160 City Road, London EC1V 2NX	James Mackay
Feature	

Bazooka	**07860-681945**
37 Newman Street	Barry Glazer
London W1T 1QA	
Corporate	

BBC Natural History Unit	**0117-974 2114**
Broadcasting House	Fax 0117-973 3583
Whiteladies Road, Bristol BS8 2LR	Andrew Jackson
Television	

BBC Worldwide	**020-8433 2000**
Media Centre	Wayne Garvie
201 Wood Lane, London W12 7TQ	
Television	

BCA Films	**0118-977 6900**
26 Rose Street	Fax 0118-977 6400
Wokingham, Berks RG40 1XU	Jonathan Edwards
Corporate	

BDP Media	**020-7492 6900**
Aldwych House	Fax 020-7492 6909
81 Aldwych, London WC2B 4HN	Danny O'Neill
Corporate	

Bees Nees Media	**01413-526666**
19 Woodside Crescent	Fax 01413-526667
Glasgow G3 7UL	Alisdair MacCuish
Television	

Believe Media	**020-3145 0960**
17-18 Margaret Street	Fax 020-7580 5582
London W1W 8RP	Fiona Gillam
Commercial	

Bentley Productions	**01753-656594**
Pinewood Studios, Pinewood Road	Fax 01753-652638
Iver Heath, Bucks SL0 0NH	Jamie Felstead
Television	

BerginLake	**020-7727 0273**
Medius House	Fax 0870-051 9699
2 Sheraton Street, London W1F 8BH	Mark Bergin
Corporate	

Besom Productions	**028-7137 0303**
26-28 Bishop Street	Fax 028-7137 0728
Derry BT48 6PP	Margo Harkin
Television	

Betty TV	**020-7290 0660**
The Heals Building	Fax 020-7290 0679
8 Alfred Mews, London W1T 7AA	Sophy Walker
Television	

Between The Eyes	**020-7240 2414**
1 Brook Mews	Ben Pugh
Flitcroft Street, London WC2H 8DJ	
Promo	

Beyond The Frame	**020-8201 9820**
27 Old Gloucester Street	Victor Schonfeld
London WC1N 3XX	
Feature	

Big Bear Films	**020-7229 5982**
18-24 Turnham Green Terrace	Fax 020-7221 0676
London W4 1QP	Marcus Mortimer
Television	

Big Break-tv	**020-8960 8777**
London Townhouse	Fax 020-8960 6700
52 Wallingford Avenue, London W10 6PY	Scamps Miller
Television	

Big Heart Media	**020-7608 0352**
32 Clerkenwell Green	Fax 020-7250 1138
London EC1R 0DU	Colin Izod
Television	

Big Picture Communications	**020-7307 3560**
29 Museum Street	Fax 020-7307 3569
London WC1A 1LH	Jim Wilson
Corporate	

Big Red Button	**07890-268260**
The Old Truman Brewery	Johnny Burns
91 Brick Lane, London E1 6QL	
Commercial	

Big Talk Productions	**020-7255 1131**
26 Nassau Street	Fax 020-7255 1132
London W1W 7AQ	Matthew Justice
Television	

Big Time Pictures	**01753-785675**
Pinewood Studios, Pinewood Road	Tony Allen
Iver Heath, Bucks SLO ONH	
Corporate	

Big Wave Productions	**01243-532531**
156 St Pancras	Fax 01243-532153
Chichester, W Sussex PO19 7SH	Sarah Cunliffe
Television	

Big Yellow Feet Production Company	**01483-285928**
Dunley Hill Farm, Ranmore	Fax 01483-284406
Dorking, Surrey RH5 6SX	Gregory Mandry
Corporate	

BigBalls	**020-7434 3436**
Film House	Chris Kelly
142 Wardour Street, London W1F 8ZU	
Commercial	

Bikini Films	**020-7692 7340**
43-45 Camden Road	Fax 020-7323 0661
London NW1 9LR	Kate Elson
Commercial	

Bill Kenwright Films	**020-7446 6200**
106 Harrow Road	Fax 020-7446 6222
London W2 1RR	
Feature	

Billi Productions	**01236-826555**
Lovat House	Fax 01236-825560
Gavell Road, Fife G65 9BS	Tessa Hartman
Television	

Bino Honda Productions	**020-8878 7102**
63 White Hart Lane	Fax 020-8392 8510
London SW13 0PP	Bino Honda
Commercial	

Bite Yer Legs / Sniffer	**020-7631 2045**
Balfour House	Fax 020-7631 2040
46-54 Great Titchfield Street, London W1W 7QA	
Television	

Black Camel Pictures	**0141-339 2059**
55 Partickhill Road	Arabella Page-Croft
Glasgow G11 5AB	
Feature	

Black Dog Films	**020-7437 7426**
42-44 Beak Street	Fax 020-7734 4978
London W1F 9RH	Svana Gisla
Promo	

Blackbird Productions	**020-7924 6440**
6 Molasses Row	Sally Bell
Plantation Wharf, London SW11 3UX	
Television	

Blakeway	**01332-206888**
23 St James Street	Fax 01332-206999
Derby DE1 1RF	Charles Hunter
Television	

Blakeway	**020-7428 5000**
6 Anglers Lane	Fax 020-8743 2141
London NW5 3DG	Fiona Stourton
Television	

Blanche Marvin Agency	**020-7722 2313**
21A St Johns Wood High Street	Fax 020-7722 2313
London NW8 7NG	Blanche Marvin
Feature	

Blast! Films	**020-7267 4260**
Unit 2, Imperial Works	Fax 020-7485 2340
Perren Street, London NW5 3ED	Claire Bosworth
Television	

Blaze Films	**020-8688 1979**
House 2B, Saint Peters Road	Johanna Salomaki
Croydon, Surrey CR0 1HD	
Feature	

B-Line Productions	**020-8444 9574**
135 Sydney Road	Fax 020-8365 3664
London N10 2ND	Annie Moore
Television	

Blink Productions	**020-7494 0747**
181 Wardour Street	Fax 020-7494 3771
London W1F 8WZ	James Studholme
Commercial	

Blow By Blow Productions	**01522-754901**
Stocke House, 9 The Green	Andrew Blow
Nettleham, Lincoln LN2 2NR	
Corporate	

Blue Dolphin Films	**020-7255 2494**
40 Langham Street	Fax 020-7580 7670
London W1W 7AS	Joseph D'Moras
Feature	

Blue Egg Productions	**01873-851885**
Pen y Wyrlod Farm, Llanvetherine	Fax 01873-821704
Abergevenny, Gwent NP7 8RG	
Television	

Blue Heaven Productions	**01983-855689**
Macrocarpa, Macrocarpa Road	Fax 01983-855689
Ventnor, Isle Of Wight PO38 1EB	Graham Benson
Television	

Blue Thread	**01442-865528**
12 Hall Park Gate	Fax 01442-879046
Berkhamsted, Herts HP4 2NJ	Sheridan Dudley
Corporate	

Blueprint Pictures   020-7580 6915

43-45 Charlotte Street   Fax 020-7580 6934
London W1T 1RS   Mya Abrahams
Feature

Bona Broadcasting   0131-558 1696

9 Gayfield Square   Fax 0131-558 1694
Edinburgh EH1 3NT   Turan Ali
Television

Bonza TV   07973-224021

72 Cranbrook Road   Chris Lethbridge
London W4 2LH
Television

Boomerang   029-2055 0550

218 Penarth Road   Fax 029-2055 0551
Cardiff CF11 8NN   Dafydd Richards
Television

Bowens Productions   07767-824912

1 Hinchley Way, Hinchley Wood   Patrick Bowens
Esher, Surrey KT10 0BD
Corporate

Box Productions   01865-311040

28 St Margarets Road   Sean McPhilemy
Oxford OX2 6RX
Television

Box TV   020-7297 8040

151 Wardour Street   Fax 020-7297 8041
London W1F 8WE
Television

Brandcast Media   020-3358 0070

91 New Cavendish Street   Fax 020-3358 0071
London W1W 6XE   Lauren Owens
Corporate

Break Thru Films   020-7580 3688

25 Newman Street   Fax 020-7580 4445
London W1T 1PN   Alex Schinasi
Feature

Brechin Productions   020-8876 2046

7 High Park Road   Clive Doig
Kew, Surrey TW9 4BL
Television

The Bridge   0141-552 8384

The Jacobean Building   Fax 0141-552 2480
49-53 Virginia Street, Glasgow G1 1TS   Simon Stewart
Commercial

Bright Spark Studios   0845-257 7278

Sparkhouse Studios   Andrew Deptford
Ropewalk, Lincoln LN6 7DQ
www.brightsparkstudios.com
Corporate

Brighter Pictures   0870-333 1700

Shepherds Building Central   Fax 0870-333 1800
Charecroft Way, London W14 0EE
Television

British Film Corporation   01753-651700

Pinewood Studios, Pinewood Road   Fax 01753-656844
Iver Heath, Bucks SL0 0NH   John Hough
Television

Broadcast Media Com   020-7491 9144

21 South Molton Street   Fax 020-7491 7445
London W1K 5QZ   Alistair Boyd
Corporate

Broadview Communications   020-3179 2000

102-108 Clerkenwell Road   Fax 020-3179 2001
London EC1M 5SA   Stuart Maister
Corporate

Broadway Films   07710-504752

1-2 Alfred Place   Toby Courlander
London WC1E 1EB
Commercial

Brook Lapping Productions   020-7428 3100

6 Anglers Lane   Fax 020-7284 0626
London NW5 3DG   Andrew McKerlie
Television

Brown Eyed Boy   020-7117 6667

5 Gordon House Road   Nick Berry
London NW5 1LM
Television

Brown Films   020-8992 4795

11 Spencer Road   Fax 020-8993 4099
London W3 6DN   Iain Brown
Feature

Buffalo Pictures   020-8600 2532

Grove House   Fax 020-8600 2501
27 Hammersmith Grove, London W6 0JL   Philippa Braithwaite
Television

Bullseye TV Productions   020-3189 3000

Network House   Fax 020-3189 3030
1 Ariel Way, London W12 7SL   Lucie Harris
Television

Burder Films   01202-295395

37 Braidley Road   John Burder
Bournemouth, Dorset BH2 6JY
Corporate

The Bureau   020-7033 0555

18 Phipp Street   Fax 020-7033 9383
London EC2A 4NU   Bertrand Faivre
Feature

Burning Gold Productions   **0117-923 7774**

103 Whiteladies Road   Fax 0117-923 9700
Bristol BS8 2PB   Victoria Coules
Television

Burt Films   **01753-859276**

Commercial   Terence Bulley

Business Affair Productions   **020-7235 4495**

3 Bradbrooke House   Fax 020-7235 4495
Studios Place, London SW1X 8EL   Davina Belling
Television

BVC (Bath)   **01225-428777**

Kingston House   Fax 01225-429111
2 Combe Park, Bath BA1 3NP   Geoff Todd
Corporate

Bwark Productions   **020-7749 9510**

35-47 Bethnal Green Road   Fax 020-7749 9511
London E1 6LA
Television

Cactus TV   **020-7091 4700**

Cactus Studios   Fax 020-7091 4901
373 Kennington Road, London SE11 4PS   Simon Ross
Television

Cadburys UK   **0121-458 2000**

PO Box 12, Bournville Lane   Fax 0121-451 4320
Bournville, Birmingham B30 2LU   Nigel Proctor
Corporate

Caledonia TV   **0141-564 9100**

147 Bath Street   Fax 0141-564 9200
Glasgow G2 4SQ   Sajid Quayum
Television

Calliope Media   **0117-923 2026**

26 Archfield Road   Fax 0117-923 2026
Bristol BS6 6BE   Mark Kidel
Television

Cambridge Film & Television Productions   **01733-319303**

9 Westwood Park Road   Lester Milbank
Peterborough, Cambridge PE3 6JL
Television

Campaign Productions   **020-7258 9688**

35 Homer Street   Fax 020-7258 9689
London W1H 4NQ   Michael Stewart
Corporate

Campbell Lloyd Video   **01277-225818**

Swallowfields, Friars Close   Mike Lloyd
Shenfield, Brentwood, Essex CM15 8HX
Corporate

Can Communicate   **020-3274 1011**

Stable Yard, 52 Worple Way   Fax 020-8948 1216
Richmond, Surrey TW10 6DF   David Wooster
Television

Capricorn Film Productions   **0141-440 6750**

Film City Glasgow   Suzanne Reid
401 Govan Road, Glasgow G51 2QJ
Feature

Capricorn Productions   **01622-766998**

23-29 Albion Place   Fax 01622-673787
Maidstone, Kent ME14 5DY   Ernie Brennan
Television

Capriol Films   **01263-862263**

The Old Reading Room, The Street   Tony Britten
Brinton, Melton Constable, Norfolk NR24 2QF
Television

Cara Music Productions   **020-8886 5743**

PO Box 28286   Michael McDonagh
London N21 3WT
Promo

Caramel Pictures   **01303-220230**

6 Seascape, Gough Road   Fax 01303-220230
Sandgate, Kent CT20 3BF   Mark Hickmott
Commercial

Carbon Media   **020-7324 0700**

18-20 Farringdon Lane   Fax 020-7324 0749
London EC1R 3AU   Joe McLusky
Television

Carnival Film & Television   **020-7307 6600**

Oxford House   Fax 020-7307 6666
76 Oxford Street, London W1D 1BF   Gareth Neame
Television

Caroline Barrett Commercials   **020-7727 5702**

58 Princedale Road   Caroline Barrett
London W11 4NL
Commercial

Catherine Bailey   **020-7483 3330**

110 Gloucester Avenue   Fax 020-7483 2155
London NW1 8JA   Catherine Bailey
Feature

Caveman Films
020-7287 4859

20 Romilly Street
London W1D 5AE
Feature

Jonathan Cavendish

Celador Films
020-7845 6802

39 Long Acre
London WC2E 9LG
Feature

Fax 020-7845 6901
Cassie Mclean

Celtic Broadcasting
01463-234000

Flowerdale House
14 Lochalsh Road, Inverness IV3 8HS
Corporate

Fax 01463-231800
Morag Grant

Celtic Films Entertainment
020-7494 6886

3-4 Portland Mews
London SW3 5AH
Feature

Fax 020-7494 9134
Steven Russell

Centini
0161-776 4377

3 Bredbury Business Park
Stockport, Cheshire SK6 2SW
Television

Christopher Bisson

Centre Screen Productions
0161-832 7151

Eastgate
Castle Street, Manchester M3 4LZ
Corporate

Fax 0161-832 8934
Sarah Jackson

Century Aspect Films
020-7379 9060

27 Maiden Lane
London WC2E 7JS
Television

Fax 020-7379 9061

Century Films
020-7378 6106

Studio 32, Clink Street Studios
1 Clink Street, London SE1 9DG
Television

Fax 020-7407 6711
Brian Hill

Cerulean Television
0113-250 3467

4 St Josephs Court, Woodlands Drive
Rawdon, W Yorks LS19 6JZ
Television

Alan Hydes

Chameleon Television
0113-205 0040

Church House, 14 Town Street
Horsforth, Leeds LS18 4RJ
Television

Fax 0113-281 9454
Allen Jewhurst

Channel K
0161-237 9088

Fourways House
Manchester M1 2EJ
Television

Fax 0161-236 5814
Matt Tiller

Channel Television
01534-816880

Television Centre
St Helier, Jersey JE1 3ZD
Corporate

Fax 01534-816817
Mike Elsey

Channel X
0845-900 2940

4 Candover Street
London W1W 7DJ
Television

Fax 020-7566 8161
Gary Matsell

Chawton Wood Films
01753-651700

Pinewood Studios, Pinewood Road
Iver Heath, Bucks SL0 0NH
Feature

Dean La-Vey

Cheeky Monkey Enterprises
020-8878 4226

33 Eleanor Grove
London SW13 0JN
Feature

Fax 020-8876 3864
Katherine Robinson

Cheerful Scout Productions
020-7291 0444

25-27 Riding House Street
London W1W 7DU
Corporate

Fax 020-7291 0445
Gary Fitzpatrick

Cheetah Television
0870-333 1700

Shepherds Building Central
Charecroft Way, London W14 0EE
Television

Colette Foster

Chevron
020-7719 4451

1 Westferry Circus
London E14 4HA
Corporate

Fax 020-7719 5104
Mark Grady

Chief TV
0161-832 6001

Lloyds House
22 Lloyd Street, Manchester M2 5WA
Commercial

Fax 0161-832 6003
Martin Offland

Chocolate Films
020-7793 4287

Southbank House
Black Prince Road, London SE1 7SJ
Television

Mark Currie

Chris Chadwick Associates
020-7386 0254

Unit 29C, The Quadrangle
49 Atalanta Street, London SW6 6TU
Corporate

Fax 020-7381 0773
Chris Chadwick

Chris Horton Productions
020-8741 3337

19 Aldensley Road
London W6 0DH
Commercial

Fax 020-8741 9996
Chris Horton

The Christmas TV & Film Company
020-8673 2818

Communications House
26 York Street, London W1U 6PZ
Television

Fax 020-8675 7244
Lucy Gorham

Christopher Swann Associates
020-8746 2300

89 Wendell Road
London W12 9SB
Television

Fax 020-8740 9306
Frances Peters

Christopher Sykes Productions	**020-8748 8748**
18 Byfeld Gardens	Lotte Sykes
London SW13 9HP	
Television	

Chromatic Productions	**020-8943 3377**
Kingsgate House, 2 King Edwards Grove	Fax 020-8943 3358
Teddington, Middx TW11 9LU	Steve Nolan
Television	

Chromavision Worldwide	**020-8488 8800**
16 Brookwood Road	Nick Williams
London SW18 5BP	
Corporate	

Chrome Productions	**020-7148 7288**
2 Prince Arthur Mews	Joel Mishcon
Perrins Lane, London NW3 1RD	
Commercial	

Church Of England Communications	**020-7898 1326**
Church House	Fax 020-7898 1636
Great Smith Street, London SW1P 3AZ	Peter Crumpler
Corporate	

Chwarel Cyf	**01766-523522**
52 High Street	Sioned Morys
Cricieth, Gwynedd LL52 0EY	
Television	

Cicada Productions	**020-7266 4646**
39 Praed Street	Fax 020-7706 1355
London W2 1NR	Frances Berrigan
Television	

Cineflix Productions	**020-3179 0099**
1 Lorenzo Street	Fax 020-3179 0098
London WC1X 9DJ	
Television	

Clan Productions	**020-7428 8715**
Spectrum House	Fax 020-7428 8727
32-34 Gordon House Road, London NW5 1LP	Neil Cameron
Television	

Clapshot	**020-7923 0417**
40 De Beauvoir Place	George Gallaccio
1-3 Tottenham Road, London N1 4EP	
Television	

Clarendon Film Productions	**020-7498 3838**
1A Rectory Grove	Nigel Goldsack
London SW4 0DX	
Feature	

Classic Media Group	**01932-592016**
Shepperton Studios, Studios Road	Fax 01932-592046
Shepperton, Middx TW17 0QD	Lyn Beardsall
Television	

Classlane Media	**01430-472055**
The Coach House, Newpost Grange	Dave Beasley
Main Road, Newport, E Yorks HU15 2PR	
Promo	

Clear Focus Productions	**01865-744722**
53 Lime Walk	Fax 01865-744722
Oxford OX3 7AB	Phil Gauron
Television	

Clearcut Communications	**0161-427 3052**
7 Longhurst Lane, Mellor	Robin Anderson
Stockport, Cheshire SK6 5AE	
Television	

Clerkenwell Films	**020-7608 2726**
82 Clerkenwell Road	Fax 020-7608 2226
London EC1M 5RF	Andy Baker
Television	

Cloak Productions	**0191-549 4466**
The Quadrus Centre, Woodstock Way	Fax 0191-519 7201
Boldon, Tyne & Wear NE35 9PF	Graeme Spencer
Television	

Clockhouse	**020-7436 7702**
118 Braybrooke Road	Tony Fox
Hastings, E Sussex TN34 1TG	
Corporate	

Clouds Hill Imaging	**01823-481894**
Rock House, Curland	David Spears
Taunton, Somerset TA3 5SB	
Television	

Cloudscape Communications	**0121-506 9190**
BV Innovation Centre, Blythe Valley Business Park	Martin Head
Solihull, W Midlands B90 8AJ	
Television	

COAST	**020-7436 4481**
33 Gresse Street	Fax 020-7436 4725
London W1T 1QU	Elaine Andrew
Commercial	

Coastal Productions	**0191-222 3160**
25B Broadchare	Fax 0191-222 3169
The Quayside, Newcastle-upon-Tyne NE1 3DQ	Sandra Jobling
Television	

Collingwood O'Hare Productions	**020-8993 3666**
10-14 Crown Street	Fax 020-8993 9595
London W3 8SB	Tony Collingwood
Television	

Colonial Pictures	**01534-743678**
The Waterfront	Fax 01534-746613
St Aubin, Jersey JE3 8AB	Alastair Layzell
Television	

PRODUCTION COMPANIES

Colony Media 020-8677 7971
3 Mortimer Close Mario Cavalli
London SW16 1AQ
Commercial

The Comedy Unit 0141-220 6400
53 Botheel Street Fax 0141-220 6444
Glasgow G2 6TJ
Television

Commercials Unlimited 020-7470 8791
Garden Studios Fax 020-7470 8792
11-15 Betterton Street, London WC2H 9BP Neil Molyneux
Commercial

Communicator 020-7700 0777
Omnibus Business Centre Paul Drew
39-41 North Road, London N7 9DP
Corporate

Company Pictures 020-7380 3900
Suffolk House Fax 020-7380 1166
1-8 Whitfield Place, London W1T 5JU Suzan Harrison
Television

Complicite 020-7485 7700
14 Anglers Lane Fax 020-7485 7701
London NW5 3DG Fiona Stewart
Television

Comtec 0844-880 5238
Tandridge Court Farm, Tandridge Lane Fax 0844-880 5239
Oxted, Surrey RH8 9NJ Danny Edwardson
Corporate

Concept Productions 01224-894242
2A Craigshaw Road Fax 01224-870022
Aberdeen AB12 3AQ Mike Lloyd-Wiggins
Corporate

Connected Pictures 020-7580 1420
2 Percy Street Fax 020-7436 9740
London W1T 1DD Peter Penny
Commercial

Contentment Worldwide 020-7287 4501
30 Brewer Street Fax 020-7439 3075
London W1F 0SS Danny Fleet
Television

Cool World Films 07973-600584
39 Etchingham Park Road Gary Morris
London N3 2DU
Commercial

Coolabi 020-7258 7080
48 Broadley Terrace Fax 020-7258 7090
London NW1 6LG Julian Scott
Television

The Core Team 07870-646789
32 Craven Gardens Jo Freely
London SW19 8LU
Corporate

Cork Films 020-8962 0100
Unit 403 Fax 020-8962 0100
22 Notting Hill Gate, London W11 3JE Emily Corcoran
Feature

Cornucopia Productions 020-7062 1060
4 Scout Lane Fax 020-7062 1148
London SW4 0LA Daniella Wilson
Television

Couchman Communications 01438-812100
61 London Road Nick Couchman
Knebworth, Herts SG3 6JE
Corporate

Cougar Films 020-7292 6610
Paramount House Fax 020-7734 7878
162-170 Wardour Street, London W1F 8ZX Georgie Baker
Feature

Countrywise Communication 01933-272400
103 Main Road Josephine Rodgers
Wilby, Northants NN8 2UB
Corporate

Courtyard Productions 01732-700324
Little Postlings Farmhouse, Four Elms Toni Yardley
Edenbridge, Kent TN8 6NA
Television

Coy Communications 020-7434 0557
14 Newburgh Street Sara Cummins
London W1F 7RT
Commercial

CPL 020-7240 8101
38 Long Acre Fax 020-7836 9633
London WC2E 9JT Heather Hampson
Television

Crazy Lady Film Productions 07967-813645
18 Baltimore Close Sarah Ridley
Cardiff CF23 8PX
Feature

Create Media Partners 01420-561144
The Studio, 39 Telegraph Lane Fax 01420-560020
Four Marks, Alton, Hants GU34 5AX Mike Sanders
Commercial

Creation Company 020-8332 2200
7C Blake Mews Fax 020-8332 2230
Kew, Surrey TW9 3GA Steve Montgomery
Television

CreationVideo   **020-8987 9363**
The Barley Mow Centre   Fax 0871-277 2981
10 Barley Mow Passage, London W4 4PH   Mark Slocombe
Corporate

Creative Film Company   **07770-756730**
18 Soho Square   Ruth Shaw
London WID 3QL
Feature

Creative Media International   **01494-601049**
Victoria House, 28-32 Desborough Street   Fax 01494-863609
High Wycombe, Bucks HP11 2NF   Malcolm Bood
Corporate

Creative Video   **01484-303090**
1 Maplin Drive   Fax 01484-303090
Huddersfield, W Yorks HD3 3GT   Roy Plum
Corporate

Crevasse Films   **01608-645258**
The Elm Coach House, Church Lane   Francine Heywood
Chipping Norton, Oxon OX7 5NS
Feature

Cricket   **020-7845 0300**
Medius House   Fax 020-7845 0303
63-69 New Oxford Street, London WC1A 1EA   Justin Leahy
Corporate

Critter Productions   **01603-776444**
Swan Yard   James DuGard
68-74 King Street, Norwich NR1 1PG
Commercial

Croft Television   **01628-668735**
Croft House, Progress Business Centre   Fax 01628-668791
Whittle Parkway, Slough, Berks SL1 6DQ   Nick Devonshire
Corporate

Croft Video Productions   **01886-821599**
The Barn House   Cynthia Waterman
Whitbourne, Worcester WR6 5RT
Corporate

Crossroads Films   **020-7395 4848**
83 Long Acre   Fax 020-7395 4849
London WC2E 9NG   Carly Stone
Commercial

Crowfoot Films   **07770-864161**
82 Berwick Street   Fax 020-7734 5411
London W1F 8TP   Beth Sanders
Feature

Crown Business Communications   **020-7605 4500**
Shepherds Studios West   Fax 020-7605 4501
Rockley Road, London W14 0EH   Nicky Havelaar
Corporate

T: +44 (0) 20 8567 6655
W: www.ealingstudios.com

CTN Communications   **020-7395 4460**
114 St Martins Lane   Fax 020-7395 4461
London WC2N 4BE   Tristan Allsop
Corporate

CTVC   **020-7940 8480**
9-10 Copper Row   Fax 020-7940 8490
Tower Bridge Piazza, London SE1 2LH   Clare Hocter
Television

Cunning   **020-7099 0900**
Hoxton Studios   Leah Bazalgette
12-18 Hoxton Street, London N1 6NG
Commercial

Cutting Edge Productions   **020-8780 1476**
27 Erpingham Road   Julian Norridge
London SW15 1BE
Corporate

CWA Marketing Communications   **0116-232 7400**
Ashleigh Road   Fax 0116-232 7444
Leicester LE3 8DA   Patrick Veasey
Corporate

Cwmni Da   **01286-685300**
Cae Llenor, Lon Parc   Fax 01286-685301
Caernarfon, Gwynedd LL55 2HH   David Evans
Television

Dab Hand Media   **020-7637 0131**
Linton House   Fax 020-7637 0133
24 Wells Street, London W1T 3PH   Dominic Delaney
Commercial

Dai 4 Films   **01570-471368**
Penwern   Neil Davies
Temple Bar, Cerddigion SA48 8BD
Television

Dair   **01242-271970**
The Crescent Bakery, St Georges Place   Fax 01242-271979
Cheltenham, Glos GL50 3PN   Simon Tate
Corporate

Daisybeck Productions	**0113-262 3342**
248 Meanwood Road	Fax 0113-262 3798
Leeds LS7 2HZ	Paul Stead
Television	

Dan Films	**020-7916 4771**
249 Grays Inn Road	Fax 020-7916 4773
London WC1X 8QC	Julie Baines
Feature	

Dandy Productions	**020-7903 5200**
Gainsborough House	Andy Williams
81 Oxford Street, London W1D 2EU	
Television	

Dangerous Films	**020-7395 3670**
8 New Row	Fax 020-7395 3671
London WC2N 4LJ	Mike Kemp
Television	

Dareks Production House	**020-8658 2012**
58 Wickham Road	Fax 020-8325 0629
Beckenham, Kent BR3 6RQ	David Crossman
Corporate	

Dark Horse Graphics	**07831-729670**
102 Kirkstall Road	Chaz McAlpin
Leeds LS3 1JA	
Corporate	

Dark Horse Media	**01874-665435**
The Mill House, Pencelli	Fran Groves
Brecon, Powys LD3 7LX	
Corporate	

Darlow Smithson Productions	**020-7482 7027**
900 Highgate Studios	Fax 020-7482 7039
53-79 Highgate Road, London NW5 1TL	Ulla Streib
Television	

Darrall Macqueen	**020-8614 2061**
Teddington Studios, Broom Road	Fax 020-8614 2153
Teddington, Middx TW11 9NT	Maddy Darrall
Television	

Dash Films	**020-8995 8016**
9 Temple Road	David Hickman
London W4 5NW	
Television	

Dave Knowles Films	**023-8084 2190**
34 Ashleigh Close, Hythe	Jenny Knowles
Southampton, Hants SO45 3QP	
Corporate	

Davey Inc	**020-7209 0385**
20 Denmark Street	Fax 020-7209 0385
London WC2H 8NA	Gail Davey
Commercial	

David Paradine Productions	**020-7371 3111**
346 Kensington High Street	Fax 020-7602 0411
London W14 8NS	Trevor Poots
Television	

Dawson Film	**020-8444 6854**
40 Springfield Avenue	Sue Dawson
London N10 3SY	
Television	

Daylight Moving Image	**0161-839 9088**
72 Tib Street	Matt Smith
Manchester M4 1LG	
Corporate	

DBI Communication	**01926-497695**
Kenilworth Business Centre, 131 Warwick Road	David Impey
Kenilworth, Warwicks CV8 1HY	
Corporate	

DCD Media	**020-7297 8000**
151 Wardour Street	Fax 020-7297 8001
London W1F 8WE	Nahid Burke
Television	

DCTS Digital Media Group	**01296-656732**
RAF Halton	Fax 01296-656006
Aylesbury, Bucks HP22 5PG	Prakash Morjaria
Corporate	

Deep Water Films	**01932-592384**
Shepperton Studios, Studios Road	Fax 01932-592854
Shepperton, Middx TW17 0QD	Maria Slough
Feature	

DEFRA	**020-7238 6000**
Nobel House	Fax 020-7238 6609
17 Smith Square, London SW1P 3JR	
Corporate	

Democracy Productions	**020-7494 1841**
3 Meard Street	Fax 020-7494 1609
London W1F 0EL	Denise Haire
Commercial	

Demus Productions	**0141-342 4959**
44 Devonshire Terrace Lane	Fax 0141-357 5519
Glasgow G12 9XT	Nick Low
Television	

Denham Productions	**01752-345444**
Boydell House, Quay West Studios	Fax 01752-345448
Old Newnham, Plymouth PL7 5BH	Grace Kitto
Television	

Denman Productions	**020-8891 3461**
60 Mallard Place, Strawberry Vale	Anthony Gambier-Parry
Twickenham, Middx TW1 4SR	
Commercial	

DESQ — 0114-221 0185
The Workstation
Fax 0114-221 0205
15 Paternoster Row, Sheffield S1 2BX
Deborah Mills
Television

Destination Productions — 020-8445 3178
1 Golfside Close
Fax 020-8446 8070
London N20 0RD
Barry Weitz
Corporate

Devon Dickson — 07774-947746
Studio 10, Clink Street Studios
Devon Dickson
1 Clink Street, London SE1 9DG
Commercial

Dialogics Consultancy — 020-8960 6069
249-251 Kensal Road
Peter Osborn
London W10 5DB
Television

Dibb Directions — 020-8748 1579
27 Lillian Road
Mike Dibb
London SW13 9JG
Television

Dibgate Productions — 020-7722 5634
Studio 4, Parkstead Lodge
Nicholas Parsons
31 Upper Park Road, London NW3 2UL
Television

Diesel Films — 020-7729 6967
43-44 Hoxton Square
Fax 020-7613 0544
London N1 6PB
Shaun Fenton
Television

Digital Broadcast Media Solutions — 01295-788390
Pinewood Cottage, Blenheim Farm
Fax 01295-788390
Shutford, Oxon OX15 6HD
Alan Joy
Corporate

Digital Cinema Media — 020-7534 6363
12 Golden Square
Fax 020-7534 6464
London W1F 9JE
Angela Garton
Commercial

Dinamo Productions — 029-2047 0480
3 Mount Stuart Square
Aron Evans
Cardiff CF10 5EE
Television

Diplomat Films — 0161-929 1603
Oakdene House, Parkfield Road
Fax 0161-929 1604
Altrincham, Cheshire WA14 2BT
Keith Thompson
Television

Dive Out Productions — 07710-941730
17 Wolstonbury Walk
Rob Hayter
Shoreham-by-Sea, W Sussex BN43 5GU
Television

Diverse Productions — 020-3189 3000
1 Ariel Way
Fax 020-3189 3200
London W12 7SL
Paul Sowerbutts
Television

Divine Productions — 020-8348 5885
71 Priory Gardens
Fax 020-8348 5885
London N6 5QU
Carrie Kirkpatrick
Television

DLT Entertainment UK — 020-7631 1184
10 Bedford Square
Fax 020-7636 4571
London WC1B 3RA
John Bartlett
Television

DNA Films — 020-7292 8700
15 Greek Street
Fax 020-7292 8701
London W1D 4DP
Ryan Delaney
Feature

Dog Man Productions — 020-8303 8087
5 Orchard Close
Stephen Dipre
Bexleyheath, Kent DA7 4RP
Feature

Don Productions — 020-7254 0044
2 Foskett Mews
Fax 07092-273283
Shacklewell Lane, London E8 2BZ
James Harper
Corporate

Done & Dusted — 020-7297 8060
151 Wardour Street
Fax 020-7494 8001
London W1F 8WE
Simon Pizey
Television

Done Dog Productions — 020-8968 5513
52 Wallingford Avenue
James Hayward
London W10 6PY
Feature

Doris Inc — 07802-784826
14 Wells House
Bob Baldwin
London EC1R 4TR
Feature

Dot To Dot Productions — 020-8400 7744
27 Pyrmont Road
Fax 020-8580 0935
London W4 3NR
Jo Killingley
Television

Double Band Films — 028-9024 3331
3 Crescent Gardens
Fax 028-9023 6980
Belfast BT7 1NS
Michael Hewitt
Television

Double E Productions — 01769-580583
The Manse, New Street
Fax 01769-580583
Chulmleigh, Devon EX18 7DB
Sarah Errington
Television

Dox Productions	020-7602 3094
84 Addison Gardens	Fax 020-7602 3771
London W14 0DR	David Sington
Television	

Dragonfly Film & Television Productions	020-7033 2300
120-124 Curtain Road	Fax 020-7729 3086
London EC2A 3SQ	Francesca Newby
Television	

Dragons Productions Wales	07794-868448
23 Machen Place	Martin Pennell
Cardiff CF11 6ER	
Feature	

Dragons Tale Films	07876-527303
44 Marlborough Road	James DuGard
Norwich NR3 4PH	
Television	

Drake AV	029-2056 0333
89 St Fagans Road	Fax 029-2055 4909
Cardiff CF5 3AE	Ian Lewis
Corporate	

The Drama House	01278-733336
The Clock House, St Mary Street	Jack Emery
Nether Stowey, Somerset TA5 1LJ	
Television	

Dreamfinder Productions	07768-344307
114 Abbey Foregate	Natasha Carlish
Shrewsbury, Shropshire SY2 6BA	
Feature	

Dreaming Spires Productions	01494-772197
3 Bury Lane	Fax 07801-304805
Chesham, Bucks HP5 1HX	Robin Marriott
Television	

Duke & Earl	020-7580 7070
17-18 Margaret Street	Fax 020-7636 8815
London W1W 8RP	Bryony Timm
Commercial	

Duplexx Productions	0161-792 4144
14 Riverview Court, Moor End Avenue	Mick Cookson
Salford, Manchester M7 3NX	
Commercial	

DVS Productions	01767-601398
Prospect House, Lower Caldecote	David Smyth
Biggleswade, Beds SG18 9BA	
Promo	

EI Kids	020-7907 3773
120 New Cavendish Street	Fax 020-7907 3777
London W1W 6XX	Laura Clunie
Television	

Eagle & Eagle	020-8995 1884
15 Marlborough Road	Fax 020-8995 5648
London W4 4EU	Catharine Alen-Buckley
Television	

Eagle Films	01372-844484
Lakewood, Heathfield	Katrina Moss
Cobham, Surrey KT11 2QY	
Feature	

Eagle Rock Entertainment	020-8870 5670
22 Armoury Way	Fax 020-8874 2333
London SW18 1EZ	Terry Shand
Television	

Eagle Vision	020-7436 2707
20 Hanson Street	John Court
London W1W 6UF	
Corporate	

Eagles Productions	0141-639 4217
6 Titwood Road	Henry Eagles
Mearnskirk, Glasgow G77 6RP	
Television	

Earp & Partners	020-8265 3473
30 Alderbrook Road	Eddie Earp
London SW12 8AE	
Commercial	

Eastern Associates	01603-457654
85 Gipsy Lane	Ted Williams
Norwich NR5 8AX	
Corporate	

Eclipse Corporate Communications	0121-452 5070
111 Hagley Road	Fax 0121-452 5071
Edgbaston, Birmingham B16 8LB	Peter Dallow
Corporate	

Eclipse Presentations	020-8662 6444
5 Chaffinch Business Park, Croydon Road	Fax 020-8650 4635
Beckenham, Kent BR3 4AA	John Gibbons
Corporate	

Ecosse Films	020-7371 0290
Brigade House	Fax 020-7736 3436
8 Parsons Green, London SW6 4TN	Douglas Rae
Television	

The Edge Picture Company	020-7836 6262
20-22 Shelton Street	Fax 020-7836 6949
London WC2H 9JJ	Philip Blundell
Corporate	

Effective Presentations	01453-833221
Highlands, Pinfarthings	Bob Lawson
Amberley, Stroud, Glos GL5 5JJ	
Corporate	

Effingee Productions   0141-443 9301

13 Colquhoun Avenue   Fax 0141-882 5003
Hillington Park, Glasgow G52 4BN   Lesley Kiernan
Television

Elastic Films   07801-782725

Snowden Barn, Timble   David Bell
Harrogate, N Yorks LS21 2NN
Commercial

Electric Sky Productions   01273-224260

1 Clifton Mews, Clifton Hill   Fax 01273-224270
Brighton, E Sussex BN1 3HR   Ann Parker
Television

Element Productions   029-2047 2122

Crichton House   Fax 029-2047 2230
11-12 Mount Stuart Square, Cardiff CF10 5EE   Richard Edwards
Television

Elemental Films   0141-423 1237

34 Regent Park Square   Owen Thomas
Glasgow G41 2AG
Feature

Elephant Hide TV   020-8505 5536

381 High Road   Patrick Bedeau
Woodford Green, Essex IG8 9QH
Commercial

Elgin Media   07769-682927

81 Abbotsbury Road   Peter Swain
London W14 8EP
Television

ELT New Media & Video   01865-556767

Oxford University Press   Fax 01865-353622
Great Clarendon Street, Oxford OX2 6DP   James Magrane
Corporate

Emel Video Productions   01276-858262

96A High Street   Mike Lewin
Chobham, Surrey GU24 8LZ
Corporate

Endboard Productions   0121-429 9779

114A Poplar Road   Fax 0121-429 9008
Bearwood, Birmingham B66 4AP   Sunandan Walia
Television

Endemol UK   0870-333 1700

Shepherds Building Central   Fax 0870-333 1800
Charecroft Way, London W14 0EE
Television

Endor Productions   020-7851 1300

20 Greek Street   Fax 020-7851 1301
London W1D 4DU   Nick Blake
Television

Energy Films   020-7352 4132

16 Lots Road   Fax 020-7351 7971
London SW10 0QF   Melyssa Stokes
Television

Enterprise Productions   01303-892830

44 Minter Avenue, Densole   Barry Fletcher
Folkestone, Kent CT18 7DU
Corporate

Entertainment Film Productions   020-7930 7744

Eagle House   Fax 020-7930 9399
108-110 Jermyn Street, London SW1Y 6HB   Trevor Green
Feature

Eon Productions   020-7493 7953

Eon House   Fax 020-7408 1236
138 Piccadilly, London W1J 7NR   Barbara Broccoli
Feature

Eon Visual Media   01482-484850

1-7 Thomas Street   Fax 01482-339701
Hull HU9 1EH   Tim Evison
Corporate

EPM Production   01968-660984

Paulswell   Fax 01968-660984
West Linton, Peeblesshire EH46 7BH   Ken Andrew
Corporate

Epoch London   020-7908 6060

112-114 Great Portland Street   Rob Godbold
London W1W 6PA
Commercial

Equaville   01628-525210

Elmsmead, Princes Road   Terence Sharkey
Bourne End, Bucks SL8 5HZ
Corporate

ESA Films   020-7638 6333

33-34 Chiswell Street   Corine Long
London EC1Y 4SF
Feature

Essential Film & Television   **01344-627996**
140-146 Drummond House, Chobham Road   Richard Wawman
Sunningdale, Berks SL5 0HU
Feature

Euroart (Media)   **020-7931 9476**
11 Cambridge Street   Fax 020-7931 9476
London SW1V 4PP   Trisha Clarke
Television

Evans Woolfe   **020-8744 1012**
7A York Street   Fax 020-8892 5557
Twickenham, Middx TW1 3JZ   Harvey Woolfe
Television

Experience   **020-7554 1111**
85 Strand   Fax 020-7554 1110
London WC2R 0DW   Clare Foot
Corporate

Expose   **01423-520425**
Chadwick House, The Old Stables   Ian Watson
Harrogate, N Yorks HG1 2AN
Commercial

Extreme Entertainment   **020-7244 1000**
245 Old Marylebone Road   Fax 020-7244 0101
London NW1 5QT   Alistair Gosling
Television

Eye Film & Television   **0845-621 1133**
Epic Studios   Charlie Gauvain
112-114 Magdalen Street, Norwich NR3 1JD
Television

Eye-Cue Online Video Adverts   **020-8133 2687**
27 Old Gloucester Street   Benjamin Johns
London WC1N 3XX
Commercial

Eyeline Media   **01224-633628**
7 Crimon Place   Fax 01224-642847
Aberdeen AB10 1RX   Terry Wolsey
Television

Eyeworks   **020-7644 0000**
68 Salusbury Road   Fax 020-7644 0001
London NW6 6NU   Paul Jackson
Television

Face Films International   **020-8898 6328**
16 Dean Road   Yavar Abbas
Hounslow, Middx TW3 2EZ
Feature

Face Television   **01256-350022**
Parkgate House, 42B Hackwood Road   Fax 01256-350046
Basingstoke, Hants RG21 3AE   Paul Friend
Television

Faction Films   **020-7690 4446**
26 Shacklewell Lane   Fax 020-7690 4447
London E8 2EZ   Sylvia Stevens
Television

Factory Films   **020-7291 6130**
30 Bloomsbury Street   Fax 020-7291 6140
London WC1B 3QJ   Paul Fennelly
Promo

Falcon Hill Films   **01789-550624**
57 Avon Crescent   Fax 01789-550624
Stratford-upon-Avon, Warwicks CV37 7EZ   Michael Rolfe
Television

The Farnham Film Company   **01252-710313**
34 Burnt Hill Road, Lower Bourne   Fax 01252-725855
Farnham, Surrey GU10 3LZ   Ian Lewis
Television

Fayrestede Productions   **01895-835212**
Fayrestede, Village Road   Fax 01895-835212
Denham, Bucks UB9 5BH   Stan Long
Feature

Feature Films   **01258-839000**
Milborne Business Centre, Blandford Hill   Fax 01258-839111
Milborne St Andrew, Dorset DT11 0HZ   Simon Curtis
Feature

Feel Films   **020-7612 0666**
4 Market Place   Fax 020-7462 0058
London W1W 8AD   Nick Hirschkorn
Commercial

Feelgood Fiction   **020-8746 2535**
49 Goldhawk Road   Fax 020-8740 6177
London W12 8QP   Laurence Bowen
Television

Festival Film & TV   **020-8297 9999**
Festival House   Fax 020-8297 1155
Tranquil Passage, London SE3 0BJ   Ray Marshall
Television

Fettis Films   **07974-979373**
Little Haigh, Flaxton Road   Andrew Fettis
Strensall, York YO32 5XQ
Television

Fever Media   **020-7428 5760**
35 Inverness Street   Fax 020-7267 3730
London NW1 7HB   Tamsin Foyle
Television

Fflic TV   **029-2040 9000**
59 Mount Stuart Square   Fax 029-2040 9001
Cardiff CF10 5LR   Gwenda Griffith
Television

Fiction Factory Films   **029-2030 0320**
1-2 Mount Stuart Square   Fax 029-2030 0321
Cardiff CF10 5EE
Television

Fighting Films   **0845-408 5836**
PO Box 2405   Fax 0117-929 4540
Bristol BS1 9BA   Daniel Hicks
Television

Film & Music Entertainment   **020-7478 7527**
34 Fouberts Place   Fax 020-7691 9712
London W1F 7PX   Mike Downey
Feature

Film Nova   **0191-272 7035**
Newcastle House, Albany Court   Fax 0191-272 7036
Monarch Road, Newcastle-upon-Tyne NE4 7YB   Peter Brown
Corporate

Film Partners   **020-7610 0862**
1 Musard Road   Chris Rose
London W6 8NR
Commercial

Filmart Productions   **020-7792 2014**
100 Kensington Church Street   Fax 020-7229 0734
London W8 4BU   Ayman Mokhtar
Feature

Films Of Record   **020-7286 0333**
6 Anglers Lane   Fax 020-7284 0626
London NW5 3DG   Jane Bevan
Television

Final Draft Films   **020-8560 4900**
The Old Wall, 6 Upper Butts   Sabita Kumari-Dass
Brentford, Middx TW8 8DA
Television

Finestripe Productions   **0141-440 6774**
Film City Glasgow   Sue Summers
Summertown Road, Glasgow G51 2LY
Television

Finola Dwyer Productions   **020-7734 7065**
53 Greek Street   Fax 020-7734 4250
London W1D 3DR   Bennett McGhee
Feature

Firecracker Films   **020-7349 3400**
The Chambers   Fax 020-7351 3318
Chelsea Harbour, London SW10 0XF   Claire Mason
Television

Firehouse Productions   **020-7439 2220**
25 Beak Street   Peter Granger
London W1F 9RT
Corporate

The Firewater Partnership   **020-8830 5391**
41 Caddington Road   Fax 020-8450 1623
London NW2 1RP   Simon Kennedy
Television

The First Film Company   **020-7436 9490**
3 Bourlet Close   Fax 020-7637 1290
London W1W 7BQ   Roger Randall-Cutler
Feature

First Freedom Productions   **020-7916 9355**
99 Crawford Street   Graham Addicott
London, London W1H 2HN
Television

Fitch Live   **020-7544 7500**
121-141 Westbourne Terrace   Fax 020-7352 7906
London W2 6JR   Jane Mehta
Corporate

Fizz Films   **0121-633 7592**
90 Royal Arch, The Mailbox   Fax 0121-633 7583
Wharfside Street, Birmingham B1 1RG   James Rupp
Television

Flame Television   **020-7598 7372**
4A Exmoor Street   Fax 020-7598 7373
London W10 6BD   Roger Bolton
Television

Flashback Television   **020-7253 8768**
58 Farringdon Road   Fax 020-7253 8765
London EC1R 3BP   Taylor Downing
Television

Fluid Moves Productions   **07710-941730**
Fast Helicopter Building, Hangar 4   Paul Cave
Shoreham Airport, Shoreham-by-Sea, W Sussex BN43 5FF
Television

Flying Brick Films   **020-7249 7440**
41 Beck Road   Fax 020-7249 7440
London E8 4RE   Tomasz Pobog-Malinowski
Television

Flynn Productions   **020-7251 6197**
Pitfield House   Fax 020-7251 6272
31-35 Pitfield Street, London N1 6HB
Promo

Focal Point Television   **01428-684468**
1 Capital Park, Combe Lane   Fax 01428-684089
Wormley, Godalming, Surrey GU8 5TJ   Sebastian Bone
Television

Focus Films   **020-7435 9004**
Rotunda Studios   Fax 020-7431 3562
116-118 Finchley Road, London NW3 5HT   Jonny Kemp
Feature

Focus On Film	020-8392 9292	**Frame On Frame**	020-8563 1676
Mortlake Court	Fax 020-8392 9495	Hammersmith Studio	Trevor Hughes
28 Sheen Lane, London SW14 8LW	David Prys-Owen	63 Hammersmith Grove, London W6 0NE	
Commercial		Corporate	

Focus Productions — 0117-230 9726
4 Leopold Road
Bristol BS6 5BS
Television
Martin Weitz

Free Range Films — 020-7292 4702
2-3 Duck Lane
London W1F 0AX
Television
Fax 020-7434 1531
Kevin Loader

Focus Productions — 020-7359 4786
44A Queens Head Street
London N1 8NG
Corporate
Fax 020-7688 0771
Deborah Hillaire

Free Spirit Films — 0117-908 3934
7 Maurice Road
Bristol BS6 5BZ
Television
Paul Reddish

Focus Pullers — 01273-600610
145 Ditchling Rise
Brighton, E Sussex BN1 4QQ
Promo
David Peck

Free@Last TV — 020-7242 4333
47 Farringdon Road
London EC1M 3JB
Television
Fax 020-7242 7910
Barry Ryan

Footloose Films — 020-7435 1330
17 Langland Gardens
London NW3 6QE
Feature
Charles Harris

Freedom Pictures — 020-8743 5330
10 Rylett Crescent
London W12 9RL
Feature
Tim White

Footstep Productions — 020-7836 9990
2 Goldstone Close
Hove, E Sussex BN3 7PD
Television
Fax 020-7240 7168
Colette Thomson

Fremantle Media — 020-7691 6000
1 Stephen Street
London W1T 1AL
Television
Fax 020-7691 6100

Form Films — 01962-870173
15 Charlecote Mews
Winchester, Hants SO23 8SR
Television
Jonah Weston

Fresh Film Productions — 020-7580 6646
50 Great Portland Street
London W1W 7ND
Commercial
Fax 020-7580 6690
Kim Griffin

Formosa Films — 020-8709 8700
3 Mills Studios
Three Mill Lane, London E3 3DU
Feature
Fax 020-8709 8701
Kellie Stevenson

Fresh One Productions — 020-7017 0760
19-21 Nile Street
London N1 7LL
Television
Fax 020-7017 0770
Ada Onyekwelu

Formula Communications — 01442-250247
2 Austins Place
Hemel Hempstead, Herts HP2 5HN
Corporate
Fax 01442-261358
Steve Arnold

Fresh Paint Pictures — 07725-765161
2 Water Works
Croydon, Surrey CR0 4HY
Feature
Fax 020-7117 1872
Alec Bruce

The Foundation TV Productions — 01622-684632
The Maidstone Studios, Vinters Park
Maidstone, Kent ME14 5NZ
Television
Fax 01622-684421
Vanessa Hill

Fulcrum TV — 020-3326 6999
14 Bowden Street
London SE11 4DS
Television

Fractured Films — 01273-677139
Unit 23, Level 6, New England House
New England Street, Brighton, E Sussex BN1 4GH
Promo
Will Jewell

Fulmar Television — 029-2045 5000
Pascoe House
54 Bute Street, Cardiff CF10 5AF
Television
Fax 029-2045 5111
Val Croft

Fragile Films — 020-8567 6655
Ealing Studios
Ealing Green, London W5 5EP
Feature
Fax 020-8758 8576
Barnaby Thompson

The Fyzz — 020-7388 7868
94 Cleveland Street
London W1T 6NW
Feature
Wayne Marc Godfrey

Gainsbury & Whiting	**020-7729 0773**
Unit 301, Curtain House	Fax 020-7729 7307
134-146 Curtain Road, London EC2A 3AR	Anna Whiting
Promo	

Gala Productions	**020-8741 4200**
25 Stamford Brook Road	Fax 020-8741 2323
London W6 0XJ	Beata Romanowski
Commercial	

Galleon Films	**020-8310 7276**
Greenwich Playhouse	Alice de Sousa
189 Greenwich High Road, London SE10 8JA	
Feature	

Gallowgate Productions	**020-7297 8280**
16-18 Beak Street	Fax 020-7297 8281
London W1F 9RD	Charlotte Hanbury
Television	

The Gamma Project	**020-7323 1409**
26 Bloomsbury Street	Fax 020-7631 1946
London WC1B 3QJ	Hugh Whitworth
Television	

Gannet Films	**07957-304244**
8A Woodside	Ben Kellett
London SW19 7AR	
Feature	

The Gate Films	**0161-832 4888**
109 Timber Wharf	Fax 0161-832 5666
Manchester M15 4NX	Sarah Jarvis
Commercial	

GB Films	**020-7404 2351**
26 Ormonde Mansions	Jonathan Ruffle
110A Southampton Row, London WC1B 4BS	
Feature	

Gemini Pictures	**020-8977 3399**
Studio 9, The Business Park	Fax 020-8977 5554
Station Road, Teddington, Middx TW11 9BQ	Martin Stockham
Television	

Generator Films	**020-7631 0044**
114 New Cavendish Street	Fax 020-7631 2401
London W1W 6XT	Matt Brown
Commercial	

Gerard De Thame Films	**0845-201 1154**
Albany House	Fax 020-7266 7991
324-326 Regent Street, London W1B 3HH	Fabyan Daw
Commercial	

GHA	**020-7439 8705**
33 Newman Street	Fax 020-7437 5880
London W1T 1PY	Roddy Gye
Corporate	

Giant Film & TV	**020-7604 3003**
10-14 Lonsdale Road	Fax 020-7604 4144
London NW6 6RD	Alice Huzar
Television	

Giant Film & TV	**020-7604 3003**
10-14 Lonsdale Road	Fax 020-7604 4144
London NW6 6RD	Ashley Bothwell
Television	

Giant Films	**020-7290 0765**
24 Hanway Street	Fax 020-7290 0774
London W1T 1UH	Lulu O'Hagan
Feature	

Ginger Productions	**020-7535 7250**
Garfield House	Fax 020-7535 7285
86-88 Edgware Road, London W2 2EA	Ed Stobart
Television	

Gizmo Animation	**01243-543697**
19 Brittens Cottages, Brittens Lane	Fax 01243-543697
Fontwell, W Sussex BN18 0ST	Steve Whiteley
www.gizmoanimation.co.uk	
Commercial	

Glass Page	**0116-249 2199**
15 De Montfort Street	Fax 0116-249 2188
Leicester LE1 7GE	Susan Mitchell
Corporate	

Glasshead	**020-8742 6800**
1 Clifton Walk	Fax 020-8742 6810
146 Kings Street, London W6 0QE	Lambros Atteshlis
Television	

Gloss Media	**020-7494 5760**
17 Carlisle Street	Fax 020-7494 5761
London W1D 3BU	Yvette Colegrave
Commercial	

GME TV & Film Productions	**01457-764319**
35 Church Road, Hollingworth	Geoff Mellor
Hyde, Cheshire SK14 8PG	
Commercial	

Gnius Communications	**0844-669 6224**
Hamilton House, Kew Place	Fax 0870-460 5627
High Wycombe, Bucks HP11 1QW	Debbie Hollinson
Corporate	

Golant Media Ventures	**0844-884 9230**
Suite 311	Patrick Towell
19-21 Crawford Street, London W1H 1PJ	
Feature	

Goldhawk Media	**01273-885633**
32 Westbourne Gardens	Bernadette Bos
Hove, E Sussex BN3 5PP	
Television	

The Good Film Company   **020-7794 6222**

5-6 Eton Garages   Fax 020-7794 4651
Lambolle Place, London NW3 4PE   Yanina Barry
Commercial

Good Films   **020-7292 3006**

8 Dean Street   Paul Brennan
London W1D 3RL
Feature

Gordon Films   **01525-860248**

April Cottage, 9 The Green   Nigel Lesmoir-Gordon
Clophill, Beds MK45 4AD
Television

Gorgeous Enterprises   **020-7287 4060**

11 Portland Mews   Fax 020-7287 4994
London W1F 8JL   Paul Rothwell
Commercial

Grace Productions   **01935-385904**

Innovation Centre, Barracks Close   Fax 01935-385904
Copse Road, Yeovil, Somerset BA22 8RN   Ray Tostevin
Television

The Grade Company   **020-7435 2860**

5 Osprey Court   Marcia Stanton
256-258A Finchley Road, London NW3 7AA
Feature

Grand Visual   **020-3205 0011**

9A Margaret Street   Fax 020-7681 2838
London W1W 8RJ   Neil Morris
Commercial

Grant Corporate Media   **07970-610316**

43 St Georges Drive   Alasdair Grant
London SW1V 4DG
Corporate

Grant Naylor Productions   **01932-592175**

Shepperton Studios, Studios Road   Helen Norman
Shepperton, Middx TW17 0QD
Television

Grasshopper Productions   **020-7937 0980**

23 Hamilton House   Joy Whitby
Vicarage Gate, London W8 4HL
Television

Great Guns   **020-7692 4444**

43-45 Camden Road   Fax 020-7692 4422
London NW1 9LR
Commercial

Great Meadow Productions   **020-7733 7621**

38 Trinity Gardens   Kate Triggs
London SW9 8DP
Television

Green Bay Media   **029-2064 2370**

Talbot Studios   Fax 029-2023 2210
1 Talbot Street, Cardiff CF11 9BW   Maureen Watkins
Television

Green Inc Film & Television   **028-9057 3000**

47A Botanic Avenue   Fax 028-9057 0057
Belfast BT7 1JL   Stephen Stewart
Television

Green Umbrella   **0117-970 6584**

59 Cotham Hill   Nigel Ashcroft
Bristol BS6 6JR
Television

Greenlight Television   **01624-611601**

Tromode   Fax 01624-611602
Isle Of Man IM4 4QJ   David Beynon
Television

Greenlit Rights   **020-7287 3545**

14-15 D'Arblay Street   Fax 020-7439 6767
London W1F 8DZ
Television

Greenpoint Films   **020-7228 5465**

3 Avenue Mansions   Ann Scott
Sisters Avenue, London SW11 5SL
Feature

Groovy Movies   **01273-730000**

23 York Road   Mark Cribb
Brighton, E Sussex BN3 1DJ
Promo

Grosvenor Television Productions   **020-7439 4440**

22 Golden Square   Fax 020-7439 0429
London W1F 9AD   Des Good
Television

Ground Zero Productions   **0870-950 0222**

5 The Oaks Business Village, Revenge Road   Fax 0870-950 0220
Lordswood, Chatham, Kent ME5 8LF   Trevor Davies
Corporate

Guardian Films   **020-3353 2000**

Kings Place   Jacqui Timberlake
90 York Way, London N1 9GU
Television

Gumball 3000   **020-8964 7878**

303-315 Latimer Road   Fax 020-8964 7879
London W10 6RA   Patrick Fischer
Feature

H2 Business Communication   **01932-593717**

Shepperton Studios, Studios Road   Fax 01932-593718
Shepperton, Middx TW17 0QD   Julie Knight
Corporate

Hamma & Glamma Productions   **020-7199 0031**
19 Heathmans Road   William Mann
London SW6 4TJ
Television

Hammer & Tongs   **020-7684 0011**
Poppy, Holborn Studios   Fax 020-7684 3810
49-50 Eagle Wharf Road, London N1 7ED   Nick Goldsmith
Commercial

Hammerwood Film Productions   **01273-277333**
110 Trafalgar Road   Ralph Harvey
Portslade, E Sussex BN41 1GS
Feature

Handle & Spout   **020-7100 2758**
175-185 Grays Inn Road   Paul Shuttleworth
London W1X 8UP
Television

Handstand Productions   **0151-708 7441**
13 Hope Street   Fax 0151-709 3515
Liverpool L1 9BH   Han Duijvendak
Television

HANraHAN   **020-7388 9404**
68 Grafton Way   Fax 020-7388 9402
London W1T 5DS   Mark Hanrahan
Commercial

Hanrahan TV Productions   **01789-298899**
1 Scholars Lane   Will Hanrahan
Stratford-upon-Avon, Warwicks CV37 6HE
Television

Hardcash Productions   **020-7253 2782**
35 Waterside   Fax 020-7253 2761
44-48 Wharf Road, London N1 7UX
Television

Hardy Pictures   **020-8607 7255**
Twickenham Film Studios, St Margarets   Fax 020-8607 8974
Twickenham, Middx TW1 2AW   Lucy Bassnett-McGuire
Television

Hartswood Films   **020-8607 8736**
Twickenham Film Studios, St Margarets   Fax 020-8607 8744
Twickenham, Middx TW1 2AW   Debbie Vertue
Television

Hat Trick Productions   **020-7184 7777**
33 Oval Road   Fax 020-7184 7778
London NW1 7EA
Television

HCA Entertainment   **020-7287 7622**
18 Soho Square   Fax 01367-810741
London W1D 3QL   Henry Cole
Corporate

HCVF Television   **01463-224788**
Wells Street Studios   Fax 01463-711460
33 Wells Street, Inverness IV3 5JU   Jim Eglinton
Corporate

Head Gear Films   **020-7734 3566**
3 Richmond Buildings
London W1D 3HE
Feature

Headline Pictures   **0191-261 8808**
5 Charlotte Square   Fax 0191-261 8809
Newcastle-upon-Tyne NE1 4XF   Stewart MacKinnon
Feature

Headline Pictures   **020-7220 2985**
1 Lexington Street   Fax 020-7220 2965
London W1F 9LX   Stewart MacKinnon
Feature

Health & Safety Laboratories   **01298-218000**
Harpur Hill   Fax 01298-218272
Buxton, Derbys SK17 9JN   Steve Graham
Corporate

Heavy Entertainment   **020-7494 1000**
111 Wardour Street   Fax 020-7494 1100
London W1F 0UH   David Roper
Corporate

Heritage Theatre   **020-7243 2750**
43 Portland Road   Clare Rich
London W11 4LJ
Television

Hero Media   **020-7432 0540**
54 Poland Street   Fax 020-7432 0545
London W1F 7NJ
Commercial

Heyday Films   **020-7836 6333**
5 Denmark Street   Fax 020-7836 6444
London WC2H 8LP   Andrew Gow
Feature

Hijinx London	020-7836 9338
48 Dean Street	Sally Newsom
London WID 5BF	
Commercial	

Hillbilly Television	020-7861 8065
20-21 Newman Street	Polly Leys
London WIT IPG	
Television	

HLA	020-7299 1000
35 Adam & Eve Mews	Fax 020-7299 1001
London W8 6UG	Mike Wells
Commercial	

HMX Corporate Communication	01296-642070
The Stable Block, The Firs, High Street	Fax 01296-640345
Whitchurch, Aylesbury, Bucks HP22 4SJ	Tim Horrox
Corporate	

Holywood Films	028-9042 3160
14 Seapark Road	John T Davis
Holywood, Co Down BT18 0LH	
Television	

Home Corp	020-7439 3093
Fenton House	Fax 020-7439 3192
55-57 Great Marlborough Street, London WIF 7JX	Emily Bliss
Commercial	

Home Video	020-8582 7515
269 Long Drive	Fax 020-8582 7515
Ruislip, Middx HA4 0HT	Srith Arans
Television	

HomeRun Film Productions	020-7259 2595
77 Queens Gate	Fax 020-7259 2595
London SW7 5JU	Mark Crowdy
Feature	

Hopscotch Films	0141-440 6740
Film City Glasgow	John Archer
401 Govan Road, Glasgow G51 2QJ	
Television	

Hotbed Media	0121-248 3900
16 Regent Place	Fax 0121-248 4900
Birmingham B1 3NJ	Johannah Dyer
Television	

Hothouse Productions	020-7386 8343
11 Delaford Street	Fax 020-7610 3701
London SW6 7LT	Nick Fellows
Television	

Hotsauce TV	020-7298 0289
2-6 Rainsford Street	Fax 020-7298 0288
London W2 1PY	Adam Hays
Television	

Hotshot Films	028-9065 6023
49 Earlswood Road	Fax 0871-900 5304
Belfast BT4 3EA	Brendan Byrne
Television	

Hotspur & Argyle	020-7439 3130
30 Brewer Street	Fax 020-7439 3075
London WIF 0SS	Danny Fleet
Commercial	

Hourglass Productions	020-8540 8786
27 Princes Road	Martin Chilcott
London SW19 8RA	
Television	

House Media	020-8944 5147
Studio 87	Alasdair Hunter
87 Ridgway, London SW19 4ST	
Corporate	

HRH Productions	020-7439 1155
90 Dean Street	Fax 020-7439 1125
London WID 3SX	Bella Bunce
Commercial	

HRTV	020-7598 9430
10 D'Arblay Street	Fax 020-7494 0383
London WIF 8DS	Jerry Hibbert
Television	

HSI London	020-7637 3377
Newlands House	Fax 020-7291 7799
40 Berners Street, London WIT 3NA	Nicola Doring
Commercial	

Hubub Media	01273-470531
29 Prince Edwards Road	Fax 01273-470531
Lewes, E Sussex BN7 IBL	Martin Jangaard
Television	

Hungryman	020-7239 4550
1-2 Herbal Hill	Fax 020-7239 4589
London ECIR 5EF	Katie MacCormack
Commercial	

Hunkydory Productions	020-8440 0820
The Studio, 57 Alan Drive	Adrian Hilliard
Barnet, Herts EN5 2PW	
Corporate	

Hurricane Films	0151-707 9700
17 Hope Street	Fax 0151-707 9149
Liverpool LI 9BQ	Sol Papadopoulos
Feature	

Hybrid Eye	020-7226 2756
HG13 Aberdeen Centre	Brandon Beck
22-24 Highbury Grove, London N5 2EA	
Corporate	

Hyphen Films   020-7734 0632
101 Wardour Street   Nasreen Kabir
London W1F 0UN
Television

i2i Digital   01684-541885
PO Box 147   Fax 01684-541886
Malvern, Worcs WR13 6YP   Keith Duddy
Television

Iambic Productions   0117-923 7222
89 Whiteladies Road   Fax 0117-923 8343
Bristol BS8 2NT   Chris Hunt
Television

Iceni Productions   0845-680 9910
The Studio, Bell House Lane   Fax 01283-741393
Anslow, Staffs DE13 9PA   Andrew Jepson
Corporate

Icon Films   0117-317 1717
1-2 Fitzroy Terrace   Fax 0117-973 3890
Bristol BS6 6TF   Harry Marshall
Television

ID2   01260-299024
Moody House, 6 Moody Street   Fax 01260-299059
Congleton, Cheshire CW12 4AP   Mark Poole
Corporate

Igloo   01932-223843
Halliford Studios, Manygate Lane   Fax 01932-246336
Shepperton, Middx TW17 9EG   Rigby Andrews
Commercial

Ignition Films   0117-909 9941
4 Somerset Street   Alison Sterling
Bristol BS2 8NB
Feature

Illumina Digital   020-8600 9300
8 Canham Mews   Fax 020-8600 9333
London W3 7SR   Andrew Chitty
Television

Illuminations Television   020-7288 8400
19-20 Rheidol Mews   Fax 020-7288 8488
Rheidol Terrace, London N1 8NU   John Wyver
Television

Image Impact   01275-814348
The Old Rectory, Wood Lane   Fax 01275-846723
Clapton-in-Gordano, Bristol BS20 7RQ   Nigel Marven
Television

Images First   020-8579 6848
10 Hereford Road   Tony Freeth
London W5 4SE
Television

Imagicians Television   020-8374 4429
34 Fouberts Place   Fax 020-8374 4436
London W1F 7PX   Alan Scales
Television

Imagination   020-7323 3300
25 Store Street   Fax 020-7462 2885
London WC1E 7BL   Sushil Hunjan
Corporate

Imagine Media Productions   028-9066 6696
621 Lisburn Road   Fax 028-9066 6679
Belfast BT9 7GT   Sheila Friel
Television

Imari Entertainment   01494-677147
PO Box 158   Jonathan Fowke
Beaconsfield, Bucks HP9 1AY
Corporate

IMG Sports Media   020-8233 5300
McCormack House   Fax 020-8233 5301
3 Burlington Lane, London W4 2TH   John Hollywood
Television

Impact Image   01483-278640
Smithbrook Kilns   Fax 01483-278643
Cranleigh, Surrey GU6 8JJ   Robert Hayes
Corporate

Impossible Pictures   020-7636 4401
12 Great Portland Street   Fax 020-7436 6868
London W1W 8QN   Tim Haines
Television

Impossible Television   01273-737477
5 Frederick Terrace, Frederick Place   Peter Scott
Brighton, E Sussex BN1 1LH
Television

In Video Veritas   07941-073892
37 High Road   Stuart Fenegan
Hockley, Essex SS5 4SY
Feature

Independent   020-7927 9400
7-8 Bourlet Close   Fax 020-7927 9401
London W1W 7BW   Jani Guest
Commercial

Independent Image   01883-654867
The High, Old Stables   Fax 01883-653290
Kent Hatch Road, Oxted, Surrey RH8 0TA   David Wickham
Television

Indigo Television   020-7486 4443
76 Marylebone High Street   Fax 020-7486 3020
London W1U 5JU   Andy Bates
Television

Indus Films	029-2039 9555
20 Cathedral Road	Fax 029-2039 9777
Cardiff CF11 9LJ	Gwenllian Hughes
Television	

Indus Television	029-2039 5702
17 Cathedral Road	Fax 029-2019 5413
Cardiff CF11 9HA	Bethan Haf
Television	

Indyuk Films	07775-768531
13 Mountview	Stuart St Paul
Northwood, Middx HA6 3NZ	
Feature	

Infinity Productions	020-7636 3443
37 Great Portland Street	Mark Stothert
London W1W 8QH	
Commercial	

Inflight Productions	020-7400 0700
15 Stukeley Street	Fax 020-7400 0707
London WC2B 5LT	Tony Taverner
Corporate	

Infocus Television	0114-289 0173
1 Crawshaw Mews, Dronfield Woodhouse	Fax 0114-289 0830
Dronfield, Derbys S18 8WG	Rob Brown
Television	

Infonation Media	020-7370 1082
272A Earls Court Road	Fax 020-7370 1082
London SW5 9AS	Ron Blythe
Television	

Initial	0870-333 1700
Shepherds Building Central	Fax 0870-333 1800
Charecroft Way, London W14 0EE	
Television	

INP Media	01932-859960
Mill House, 58 Hamm Moor Lane	Fax 01932-857416
Weybridge, Surrey KT15 2SF	Bryn Downing
Corporate	

Input Media	020-8735 4300
191A Askew Road	Fax 020-8746 0811
London W12 9AX	Richard Markell
Television	

insidejobproductions	020-7033 2170
Willow House	Naomi Delap
72-74 Paul Street, London EC2A 4NA	
Corporate	

Inside-Out Branding	01422-825222
Upper Woodhead, Barkisland	Fax 01422-824433
Halifax, W Yorks HX4 0EQ	Nick Turley
Corporate	

Intelligent Television & Video	01723-500767
ITVV House, Norwood Street	Fax 01723-501208
Scarborough, N Yorks YO12 7EQ	Nick Grindley
Corporate	

Intense Productions	07970-651252
Unit 1-2-4, The Barracks	Chee Keong Cheung
White Cross, South Road, Lancaster LA1 4XQ	
Feature	

Interlink	020-7916 9595
23 Great Queen Street	Fax 020-7916 9596
London WC2B 5BB	Paul Lucas
Corporate	

International Programme Marketing	020-7515 5100
15 Skylines	Fax 020-7538 4484
Limeharbour, London E14 9TS	Craig Goldman
Television	

Intrepido	020-8123 9997
1A Waldron Road	Fax 020-8879 7320
London SW18 3TB	Paola Minazzato
Feature	

Intro	020-7324 3244
42 St Johns Street	Fax 020-7324 3245
London EC1M 4DL	Katy Richardson
Commercial	

IPH Associates	020-7207 2966
2 Cholmley Terrace, Portsmouth Road	Fax 020-8398 9928
Thames Ditton, Surrey KT7 0XX	Jed Leventhall
Television	

Ipso Facto Films	020-7240 6166
11 Denmark Street	Christine Alderson
London WC2H 8LS	
Feature	

Isis Media	0845-456 9936
PO Box 8209	Fax 0845-456 9937
Knowle, W Midlands B93 0EN	Ben Robinson
Television	

Itch Film	020-7609 6909
1 Mackenzie Road	Fax 020-7700 7402
London N7 8QZ	Charlie Paul
Commercial	

Ivory Tower Entertainment	01753-657174
Pinewood Studios, Pinewood Road	Jim Groom
Iver Heath, Bucks SL0 0NH	
Feature	

IWC Media	0141-353 3222
St Georges Studios	Fax 0141-353 3221
93-97 St Georges Road, Glasgow G3 6JA	Hamish Barbour
Television	

Jacaranda — 020-8741 9088
6 Studland Street
London W6 0JS
Corporate
Fax 020-8748 5670
Katy Eyre

Jack Morton Worldwide — 020-8735 2000
Units 16-18, Acton Park Estate
The Vale, London W3 7QE
Corporate
Fax 020-8735 2020
Julian Pullan

Jaffa Productions — 028-9084 0007
12 Sherwood Parks
Glengormley, Co Antrim BT36 5FY
Television
Fax 028-9084 3339
Stuart Lambe

JAM Pictures — 020-7638 2030
8 Hanover Street
London W1S 1YE
Television
Fax 020-7256 6818
Jane Walmsley

Jazz Films — 020-7735 3251
166B Old South Lambeth Road
London SW8 1XX
Feature
Fax 020-7735 3251
Mary Davies

Jelly — 020-7323 3307
9-10 Charlotte Mews
London W1T 4EF
Commercial
Fax 020-7636 2455
Charlie Sells

Jellytree Productions — 01483-569295
74 Bushy Hill Drive, Merrow
Guildford, Surrey GU1 2UJ
Promo
Craig Hills

The Jim Lee Film Company — 020-7589 6539
71 Sumner Place Mews
London SW7 3EF
Feature
Jim Lee

JK Productions — 020-8940 5270
74 Sheen Park
Richmond, Surrey TW9 1UP
Television
Fax 020-8940 5270
Janice Kay

The JMS Group — 01603-811855
Park Farm Studios
Hethersett, Norwich NR9 3DL
Commercial
Fax 01603-812255
Francesca Towner

JN Production — 020-7278 8800
16-24 Underwood Street
London N1 7JQ
Commercial
Fax 020-7608 1876
Lucinda Gil

John Crome Pictures — 01725-518601
Berrymead, Mintys Hill
Rockbourne, Hants SP6 3NA
Television
Fax 01725-518601
Maggie Shannon

John Hemson Associates — 01908-583062
37 Vicarage Street, Woburn Sands
Milton Keynes, Bucks MK17 8RE
Corporate
Fax 01908-281035
John Hemson

Jolly Decent Video Productions — 01733-223331
36 Tintern Rise, Eye
Peterborough, Cambs PE6 7YL
Corporate
Patrick Boyns

Jonathan Greenwood Productions — 020-8958 3807
7 The Grove
Edgware, Middx HA8 9QA
Corporate
Fax 020-8958 3807
Jonathan Greenwood

Joyrider — 020-7183 4224
28 Margaret Street
London W1W 8RZ
Commercial
Fax 020-7183 4273
Spencer Friend

Juice Moving Images — 01367-244878
The Byres, Wicklesham Lodge Farm
Faringdon, Oxon SN7 7PN
Corporate
Fax 01367-243630
Alan Poole

Junction Films — 0131-220 3377
45 Frederick Street
Edinburgh EH2 1EP
Television
Fax 0131-220 3550
Jemma Rodgers

Juniper Communications — 020-7407 9292
52 Lant Street
London SE1 1RB
Television
Fax 020-7407 3940
Paula Prynn

Just Film — 01923-269599
7 Barnsway
Kings Langley, Herts WD4 9PW
Corporate
Chris Pettit

JWP TV Productions — 020-7284 5919
Vineyards, The Business Centre
36 Gloucester Avenue, London NW1 7BB
Corporate
James Ward

Karen Hamilton Productions — 020-7503 1640
1 Foskett Mews
Shacklewell Lane, London E8 2BZ
Television
Fax 020-7503 1659
Karen Hamilton

Karpus Projects — 0141-946 1463
25 Kelvinside Terrace South
Glasgow G20 6DW
Television
Cassandra McGrogan

Kay Film Productions — 01753-651171
Pinewood Studios, Pinewood Road
Iver Heath, Bucks SL0 0NH
Feature
Simon Paige

Kaybee Pictures	020-8903 1330
Unit 8, Stanley House	Renu Patel
Stanley Avenue, Wembley, Middx HA0 4JE	
Feature	

Kemistry	020-7729 3636
43 Charlotte Road	Fax 020-7749 2760
London EC2A 3PD	Richard Churchill
Commercial	

Keo Films	020-7490 3580
101 St Johns Street	Fax 020-7490 8419
London EC1N 4AS	Andrew Palmer
Television	

The Kestrel Film Company	020-8788 6244
11 Landford Road	Fax 020-8780 9323
London SW15 1AQ	Bill Shapter
Feature	

Kickback Media	01580-890107
Silverlocks, Cradducks Lane	Fax 01580-890107
Staplehurst, Kent TN12 0DN	John Bullivant
Television	

Kindle Entertainment	020-7748 5277
1A Goldsmith Row	Fax 020-7749 0758
London E2 8QA	Melanie Stokes
Television	

Kindred Productions	0845-634 0067
Communications House, 12 Craufurd Rise	Glenn Pearce
Maidenhead, Berks SL6 7LS	
Corporate	

KMA Productions	01983-852031
Castle Cliff, Castle Road	Mike Kirby
Ventnor, Isle Of Wight PO38 1LQ	
Corporate	

Knifedge	020-7436 5434
4 Margaret Street	Fax 020-7436 5431
London W1W 8RF	Jonathan Brigden
Corporate	

Knucklehead	020-7292 7950
22-23 Archer Street Studios	Fax 020-7734 7584
10-11 Archer Street, London W1D 7AZ	Matthew Brown
Commercial	

Komedia Entertainment	01273-647947
44 Gardner Street	Fax 01273-647102
Brighton, E Sussex BN1 1UN	Ruth Macarthy
Television	

Kronfli Duliba Productions	01625-536606
Harefield South Lodge, Alderley Road	Fax 01625-536603
Wilmslow, Cheshire SK9 1RA	Edward Duliba
Commercial	

Kudos Film & Television	020-7812 3270
12-14 Amwell Street	Fax 020-7812 3271
London EC1R 1UQ	Stephen Garrett
Television	

La Belle Allee Productions	0141-287 9668
61 Holland Street	Fax 0141-287 9577
Glasgow G2 4NJ	Karen Smyth
Feature	

La Plante Productions	020-7734 6767
Paramount House	Fax 020-7734 7878
162-170 Wardour Street, London W1F 8ZX	Liz Thorburn
Television	

LA Productions	0151-933 8282
Old St Lawrence School	Fax 0151-922 4736
Westminster Road, Liverpool L4 3TQ	Colin McKeown
Television	

Lambent Productions	01273-648380
Brighton Media Centre, 21-22 Old Steyne	Fax 01273-648385
Brighton, E Sussex BN1 1EL	Emma Wakefield
Television	

Landmark Films	01865-297220
12 Evelyn Court	Nicholas O'Dwyer
267B Cowley Road, Oxford OX4 1GY	
Television	

Landscape Film & TV Productions	020-7228 9734
PO Box 35	Andrew Davie
London SW11 3LB	
Corporate	

Landseer Productions	020-7794 2523
27 Arkwright Road	Derek Bailey
London NW3 6BJ	
Television	

Lara Films	020-7727 7169
54 Ladbroke Grove	Fax 020-7792 0874
London W11 2PB	Nicolas Kullmann
Feature	

Large Scale	0116-242 2920
Workspace 18, Phoenix Square	Steve Friendship
4 Midland Street, Leicester LE1 1TG	
Feature	

Last Ditch Television	01603-660922
5 Kingsgate Court	Andy Murrow
Pottergate, Norwich NR2 1TS	
Television	

Latitude Films	07977-450673
The Cottage, 260 New Church Road	Howard Ford
Brighton, E Sussex BN3 4EB	
Commercial	

MJW Productions — 020-7713 0400
5 Warner House
43-49 Warner Street, London EC1R 5ER
Television
Fax 020-7713 0500
Anne Beresford

MJZ — 020-7434 4000
45A Brewer Street
London W1F 9UE
Commercial
Fax 020-7434 4010
Debbie Turner

MNE TV — 0141-300 3800
Pacific Quay
Glasgow G51 1PQ
Television
Fax 0141-300 3888
Allan MacDonald

The Mob Film Company — 020-7580 8142
10-11 Great Russell Street
London WC1B 3NH
Commercial
Fax 020-7255 1721
John Brocklehurst

Mob North — 0161-236 4010
12 Hilton Street
Manchester M1 1JF
Commercial
Fax 0161-236 4888
Serena Prosser

Model Robot — 020-7619 3859
71B Crouch Hill
London N4 4AJ
Commercial
Sean Miles

Modern Life? — 01323-842730
116 Teal Court, Observatory View
Hailsham, E Sussex BN27 2PP
Feature
Phil Hobden

Modern Television — 029-2066 4555
North Chambers
Castle Arcade, Cardiff CF10 1BX
Television
Fax 029-2066 4569
Simon Mansfield

Momoco — 020-7287 0776
22 Carnaby Street
London W1F 7DB
Commercial
Nic Benns

Monkey Kingdom — 020-7749 3110
Biscuit Building
10 Redchurch Street, London E2 7DD
Television
Fax 020-7749 3199
Harry Eastwood

Monterosa Productions — 020-7659 0320
21-22 Great Castle Street
London W1G 0HY
Television
Fax 020-7493 8416

Moon — 020-7751 4215
Studio 12
39 Tadema Road, London SW10 0PZ
Commercial
Fax 020-7349 7409
Linda Peryer

Moondance Films — 020-7323 6458
55 Charlotte Street
London W1T 4PB
Television
Fax 020-7580 4687
Anne MacGregor

Moonstone Films — 020-8144 9940
5 Linkenholt Mansions
Stamford Brook Avenue, London W6 0YA
Television
Fax 0870-005 6839
Tony Stark

Moonstone Productions — 01761-416703
Wesleyan Chambers, Park Road
Paulton, Bristol BS39 7QQ
Television
Fax 01761-411962
Martin Roberts

Mortal Films — 01285-650339
The Old School, Daglingworth
Cirencester, Glos GL7 7AQ
Feature
Fax 01285-650339
Alasdair Ogilvie

Mosaic Films — 020-7923 2994
Shacklewell Studios
28 Shacklewell Lane, London E8 2EZ
Television
Fax 020-7923 2994
Andy Glynne

Move A Mountain Productions — 020-8743 3017
5 Ashchurch Park Villas
London W12 9SP
Television
Fax 020-8749 8199
Elizabeth McKay

Move On Up — 01381-600777
Laurel House
High Street, Cromarty IV11 8YR
Television
Fax 01381-600778
Don Coutts

Moxie Pictures — 020-7291 1100
12 Percy Street
London W1T 1DW
Commercial
Fax 020-7631 1134
Dawn Laren

MST Television — 020-7724 8917
5A Cuthbert Street
London W2 1XT
Corporate
Fax 020-7262 8353
Clive Hayden

Music On Earth
01536-744070

5 Osborne Close
Oakley Vale, Northants NN18 8PJ
Television

Paul Balmer

Mustard
020-7434 2282

NCP Building
32 Brewer Street, London W1F 0ST
Commercial

Fax 020-7434 2292
John Doris

Myriad Media
020-7684 5050

50 Buttesland Street
London N1 6BY
Corporate

Fax 020-7684 1010
James Thompson

Naeve Films
01843-852934

Carlton Cinema, St Mildreds Road
Westgate-on-Sea, Kent CT8 8RE
Feature

Elaine Wickham

Neal Street Productions
020-7240 8890

26-28 Neal Street
London WC2H 9QQ
Feature

Fax 020-7240 7099
Pippa Harris

Nebraska Productions
020-8444 5317

12 Grove Avenue
London N10 2AR
Commercial

Brian Harding

Neon Productions
0141-429 6366

Studio 2
19 Marine Crescent, Glasgow G51 1HD
Television

Fax 0141-429 6377
Robert Noakes

New Edge Productions
01949-861848

The Manor House, Main Street
Aslockton, Notts NG13 9AL
Corporate

Richard Flewitt

New London Films
020-7609 5643

52 Anson Road
London N7 0AA
Television

Michael Grenville

New Moon Television
020-7479 7010

63 Poland Street
London W1F 7NY
Television

Fax 020-7479 7011
Caroline Rowland

New Town Films
01702-328248

Gateway Building, 10 Elmer Approach
Southend-on-Sea, Essex SS1 1LW
Feature

Terry Bird

Nexus Productions
020-7749 7500

113-114 Shoreditch High Street
London E1 6JN
Commercial

Fax 020-7749 7501

NFH
020-7240 4546

7 Denmark Street
London WC2H 8LZ
Feature

Fax 020-7240 9431
Hannah Boschi

Nice Shirt Films
020-7436 6913

41-42 Foley Street
London W1W 7TR
Commercial

Fax 020-7436 6915
Richard Martin

Noel Gay Television
01932-592569

Shepperton Studios, Studios Road
Shepperton, Middx TW17 0QD
Television

Fax 01932-592172
Lesley Armitage

Nois
020-3091 6052

Unit 27
London Lane, London E8 3PR
Commercial

Alex Carvalho

Nomadic Films
020-7221 7775

144 Portobello Road
London W11 2DZ
Commercial

Andrea Kleanthous

North One Television
020-7502 6000

46-52 Pentonville Road
London N1 9HF
Television

Fax 020-7502 5600
Amanda Smith

North One Television Midlands
0121-697 1900

5-6 Progress Works
Alcock Street, Birmingham B9 4DY
Television

Fax 0121-697 1999

Not To Scale
020-7734 4575

13 Manette Street
London W1D 4AP
Commercial

Dan O'Rourke

Notting Hill Movies
020-8962 8842

Suite 17
2-4 Exmoor Street, London W10 6BD
Feature

Andy Isaac

Novel Entertainment
01865-811562

Oxford Centre For Innovation
Mill Street, Oxford OX2 0JX
Television

Fax 01865-793165
Michael Watts

NSPCC
0116-234 7200

3 Gilmour Close
Beaumont Leys, Leicester LE4 1EZ
Corporate

Fax 0116-234 0464
David Ward

Number 9 Films
020-7323 4060

Linton House
24 Wells Street, London W1T 3PH
Feature

Fax 020-7323 0456

Numiko 0113-202 1400
46 The Calls Fax 0113-301 0223
Leeds LS2 7EY David Eccles
Television

Nutshell Productions 01491-575017
3 Westfield Cottage, Westfield Fax 01491-579335
Medmenham, Marlow, Bucks SL7 2HQ Madelaine Westwood
Television

Nyac 020-8802 2395
88 Gladesmore Road Richard Vizor
London N15 6TD
Feature

Objective Productions 020-7202 2300
Riverside Building, County Hall Fax 020-7202 2301
Westminster Bridge Road, London SE1 7PB Michael Vine
Television

Ocicat 020-8995 8991
The Courtyard Fax 020-8995 8992
Evelyn Road, London W4 5JL Paul Fabricius
Corporate

October Films 020-7284 6868
Lyme House Studios Fax 020-7284 6869
30-31 Lyme Street, London NW1 0EE Adam Bullmore
Television

Off The Fence Productions 0117-307 8107
Basement Suite Fax 0117-307 8111
6 St Pauls Road, Bristol BS8 1LT Allison Bean
Television

Olga TV 020-7151 0151
Aldwych House Fax 020-7151 0100
71-91 Aldwych, London WC2B 4HN Clare Barton
Television

Omni Productions 0117-954 7176
16 Wilson Place Fax 0117-955 7068
Bristol BS2 9HJ Sam Hearn
Television

Omnivision 01753-656329
Pinewood Studios, Pinewood Road Fax 01753-421045
Iver Heath, Bucks SL0 0NH Christopher Morris
Television

ON Communication 01235-537400
The Media Lab, 5 East St Helen Street Fax 01235-530581
Abingdon, Oxon OX14 5EG Martine Benoit
Corporate

On Screen Productions 01291-636300
Ashbourne House, 33 Bridge Street Fax 01291-636301
Chepstow, Monmouths NP16 5GA Richard Cobourne
Corporate

One Box Productions 01772-827766
The Watermark, 9-15 Ribbleton Lane Fax 01772-827733
Preston, Lancs PR1 5EZ David Langdon
Corporate

One Small Step 020-7490 2001
30D Great Sutton Street Fax 020-7490 2010
London EC1V 0DU Dan Kreeger
Commercial

One Ten Productions 020-7202 2488
Unit 316, Whiteleys Centre Fax 0871-661 3102
151 Queensway, London W2 4YN Christina Sayers
Television

One World Films 07970-936529
10 Orchid Close, Bure Park Alexander Finbow
Bicester, Oxon OX26 3WT
Feature

Onward Film Company 0141-332 0589
Trinity House James Jeffreys
20 Linedoch House, Glasgow G3 6EF
Commercial

Open Media 020-7603 9029
The Mews Studio Laura Cook
8 Addison Bridge Place, London W14 8XP
Television

Open Mike Productions 020-7434 4004
Hammer House Fax 020-7434 4045
113-117 Wardour Street, London W1F 0UN Andrew Beint
Television

Open Mind Productions 0845-890 9192
27 York Road Fax 0870-092 9192
Teddington, Middx TW11 8SL Clare Hepper
Television

Open Shutter Productions 01753-841309
100 Kings Road John Bruce
Windsor, Berks SL4 2AP
Television

Optomen Television 020-3227 5900
102 St Pancras Way Fax 020-3227 5901
London NW1 9ND Patricia Llewellyn
Television

OR TV 020-7437 1336
5-6 Portland Mews Fax 020-7440 3436
London W1F 8JG Elizabeth Hall
Television

Orca Media 01753-656093
Pinewood Studios, Pinewood Road Fax 01753-656839
Iver Hearth, Bucks SL0 0NH Jon Paul Careless
Corporate

Orchard Communications	**01483-769000**
May Court, The Links Business Centre	Fax 01483-769003
Old Woking Road, Woking, Surrey GU22 8BF	Martine Goddard
Corporate	

Original Film & Video Productions	**020-7731 0012**
84 St Dionis Road	Boyd Catling
London SW6 4TU	
Corporate	

Orion TV	**0845-077 2877**
Southbank House	Bob Whittaker
Black Prince Road, London SE1 7SJ	
Television	

Otmoor Productions	**01865-744844**
9 Turret House	John Edginton
New High Street, Oxford OX3 7BA	
Television	

Out There News	**020-8365 7811**
27 Pages Lane	Paul Eedle
London N10 1PU	
Television	

Outlaw	**020-7580 3039**
11-12 Tottenham Mews	Fax 020-7580 2232
London W1T 4AG	Bill James
Commercial	

Outline Productions	**020-7424 7600**
315 Highgate Studios	Fax 020-7424 7601
53-79 Highgate Road, London NW5 1TL	Laura Mansfield
Television	

Outrageous	**0845-505 5757**
57 Hatherley Road	Fax 01962-859033
Winchester, Hants SO22 6RR	Grenville Houser
Corporate	

Outrider International	**020-7723 6021**
92 Star Street	Fax 020-7706 1084
London W2 1QF	Michael Harris
Corporate	

Outsider	**020-7636 6666**
41-42 Foley Street	Fax 020-7323 0242
London W1W 7TS	Robert Campbell
Commercial	

Oval Films	**020-7424 8838**
31 Oval Road	Fax 020-7424 8839
London NW1 7EA	Tim Jones
Television	

Ovation Productions	**020-8340 4256**
The Gatehouse	Fax 020-8340 3466
Highgate Village, London N6 4BD	John Plews
Corporate	

Oxford Film & TV	**020-7483 3637**
Leeder House	Fax 020-7483 3567
6 Erskine Road, London NW3 3AJ	Lauren Jacobs
Television	

Oxford Scientific Films	**020-7317 1330**
47-57 Marylebone Lane	Fax 020-7317 1331
London W1U 2NT	Clare Birks
Television	

P4 Films	**01242-542760**
Cheltenham Film Studios, Hatherley Lane	Phil Partridge
Cheltenham, Glos GL51 6PN	
Television	

Pabulum Productions	**020-7235 3030**
77 Eaton Square	Fax 020-7235 7966
London SW1W 9AW	Zoe Wales
Television	

Pacific	**020-7691 2225**
5-7 Anglers Lane	Fax 020-7691 2226
London NW5 3DG	Carl Green
Television	

Pacifica Films	**020-8748 2733**
78 Yeldham Road	Fax 020-8748 2733
London W6 8JG	Christine Booth
Television	

Paladin Pictures	**020-8994 6451**
Belle Vue House	Fax 020-8747 0101
Chiswick Mall, London W4 2PJ	Clive Syddall
Television	

Palm Pictures	**020-7229 3000**
8 Kensington Park Road	Fax 020-7221 8899
London W11 3BU	Cassie Williams
Feature	

Palm Tree Entertainment	**01753-656424**
Pinewood Studios, Pinewood Road	Fax 01753-657086
Iver Heath, Bucks SL0 0NH	Robbie Moffat
Feature	

Pandora Productions	**020-7221 4222**
20 Ossington Street	Fax 020-7221 9688
London W2 4LY	Lynda Myles
Feature	

Panoramic Pictures	**01326-241719**
Halsephron House, Gunwalloe	Roger Thorp
Helston, Cornwall TR12 7QD	
Feature	

Pantechnicon Creative Services	**020-7228 1133**
The Glass Mill	Fax 020-7326 8398
1 Battersea Bridge Road, London SW11 3BZ	John Landon
Corporate	

Paper Moon Productions
01628-829819

Wychwood House, Burchetts Green Lane
Littlewick Green, Maidenhead, Berks SL6 3QW
Television

David Haggas

Parallel Film & TV Productions
020-7580 6888

107-109 Great Portland Street
London WIW 5NA
Television

Vicki Kisner

Parallel Pictures
01753-655191

Pinewood Studios, Pinewood Road
Iver Heath, Bucks SL0 0NH
Feature

Bill Chamberlain

Paramount Entertainment UK
020-3184 2100

Building 5, Chiswick Park
566 Chiswick High Road, London W4 5YF
Feature

Fax 020-3184 2101

Park Village Productions
020-7387 8077

I Park Village East
London NWI 7PX
Commercial

Fax 020-7388 3051
Tom Webb

Parliamentary Films
020-7827 9510

Enterprise House
1-2 Hatfield, London SEI 9PG
Television

Fax 020-7827 9511
Charles Frater

Parthenon Entertainment
01923-286886

Parthenon House, 5 Station Approach
Chorleywood, Herts WD3 5PF
Television

Fax 01923-286686
Danny Tipping

Partizan
020-7851 0200

40-42 Lexington Street
London WIF 0LN
Promo

Fax 020-7851 0249
Sasha Nixon

Passion Pictures
020-7323 9933

33-34 Rathbone Place
London WIT IJN
Commercial

Fax 020-7323 9030
Hugo Sands

Patricia Murphy Films
020-7267 0007

14 Lawfords Wharf
Lyme Street, London NWI 0SF
Commercial

Fax 020-7485 0555

Patrick Cahill & Associates
020-7589 0155

9 Wellington Court
116 Knightsbridge, London SWIX 7PL
Commercial

Patrick Cahill

Patrick Dromgoole Productions
01465-871219

Penkill Castle
Girvan, Ayrshire KA26 9TQ
Television

Fax 01465-871215
Patrick Dromgoole

Paul Knight Film & Television
020-7734 7042

26 St Annes Court
London WIF 0BL
Television

Fax 020-7734 9270
Paul Knight

PDI Media
0161-831 7575

Deansgate Quay
Deansgate, Manchester M3 4LA
Television

Fax 0161-831 7474
Kevin Hinde

Pelicula Films
0141-287 9522

59 Holland Street
Glasgow G2 4NJ
Television

Fax 0141-287 9504
Mike Alexander

Performance Communications
01494-670505

2B The Broadway, Penn Road
Beaconsfield, Bucks HP9 2PD
Corporate

Fax 01494-672263
Paul Kent

Peter Batty Productions
020-8942 6304

Claremont House, Renfrew Road
Kingston-upon-Thames, Surrey KT2 7NT
Television

Peter Batty

Peter Frow Productions
01483-486888

10 Victoria Road, Knaphill
Woking, Surrey GU21 2AH
Feature

Fax 01483-486888
Peter Frow

Peter Williams Television
01227-751171

Key Cottage, South Street
Boughton, Faversham, Kent ME13 9NR
Television

Fax 01227-751171
Peter Williams

Pett Productions
01737-647007

Fintrax House, Station Road North
Merstham, Surrey RHI 3ED
Television

Erica Leonard

Phil McIntyre Entertainment
020-7439 2270

35 Soho Square
London WID 3QX
Television

Fax 020-7439 2280
Phil McIntyre

Picture Coverage
0161-745 8686

23 The Crescent
Salford, Manchester M5 4PF
Commercial

Fax 0161-745 8998
David Gerrard

Picture Palace Films
020-7586 8763

13 Egbert Street
London NWI 8LJ
Feature

Fax 020-7586 9048
Malcolm Craddock

Picture Production Company
020-7439 4944

19-20 Poland Street
London WIF 8QF
Commercial

Fax 020-7434 9140
Steve O'Pray

Pidgin Productions — 0151-708 5708

35-47 Windsor Street
Liverpool L8 IXE
Television

Fax 0151-708 6006
Bea Freeman

Pier Productions — 01273-691401

8 St Georges Place
Brighton, E Sussex BNI 4GB
Television

Peter Hoare

Pilgrim Productions — 01233-750056

The Old Saw Mill, Hastingleigh
Ashford, Kent TN25 5HN
Television

Caroline Gilson

Pilot Film & Television Productions — 020-8960 2771

The Old Studio
18 Middle Row, London W10 5AT
Television

Fax 020-8960 2721
Rosemary Francis

Pioneer Productions — 020-8748 0888

Voyager House
32 Galena Road, London W6 0LT
Television

Fax 020-8748 7888
Stuart Carter

Pipedream Pictures — 020-7916 3345

56 Rochester Road
London NWI 9JG
Feature

Fax 020-7916 3345
Paul Smith

Pirate Productions — 0131-669 9432

I Portobello High Street
Edinburgh EH15 IDW
Television

Fax 0560-116 0471

Pixel Foundry — 01654-761461

Creative Unit 8, Aberystwyth Art Centre
Penglais, Aberystwyth SY23 3DE
Television

Pete Telfer

Planet Television — 020-8974 6050

7 Feltham Avenue
Hampton Court, Surrey KT8 9BJ
Television

Patrick Kirby

Platinum Films — 01753-651275

Pinewood Studios, Pinewood Road
Iver Heath, Bucks SLO 0NH
Television

Fax 01753-654082
Nigel Stone

Play It By Ear — 01342-326234

I The Jordans
East Grinstead, W Sussex RH19 4BX
Corporate

Martin Buchanan

Plum Films — 0131-555-1604

100B Constitution Street
Edinburgh EH6 6AW
Television

Fax 0131-553 7955
Tina Foster

Poisson Rouge Pictures — 020-7736 2200

Hurlingham Studios
Ranelagh Gardens, London SW6 3PA
Feature

Christopher Granier-Deferre

Poquito — 01507-525692

The Grange, West Ashby
Horncastle, Lincs LN9 5QB
Corporate

Matthew Rose

Portobello Pictures — 020-7605 1396

12 Addison Avenue
London WII 4QR
Feature

Fax 020-7605 1391
Kristin Irving

Poseidon Films — 020-7734 4441

Hammer House
117 Wardour Street, London WIF 0UN
Feature

Fax 020-7437 0638
Frixos Constantine

Positive Image — 01753-842248

25 Victoria Street
Windsor, Berks SL4 IHE
Corporate

Fax 01753-830878
Ben Moore

Poster Pictures — 07778-854873

Pinewood Studios, Pinewood Road
Iver Heath, Bucks SLO 0NH
Feature

Fax 020-7328 6197
Rick Senat

Powercorp International — 020-7323 0070

34 Gresse Street
London WIT IQX
Television

Fax 020-7323 0060
Eloise Tooke

Pozzitive Television — 020-7734 3258

Paramount House
162-170 Wardour Street, London WIF 8AB
Television

Fax 020-7437 3130
David Tyler

Presentable — 029-2057 5729

46 Cardiff Road
Cardiff CF5 2DT
Television

Fax 029-2057 5605
Chris Stuart

Pretty Clever Pictures — 01730-817899

Hurst Cottage, Old Buddington Lane
Easebourne, Midhurst, W Sussex GU29 0QN
Corporate

Gelly Morgan

Pretzel Films — 020-7580 9595

11-12 Tottenham Mews
London WIT 4AG
Corporate

Fax 020-7580 2232
Peter Shuttleworth

Price Western Associates — 01242-255515

Cedar Lodge, Cranham Road
Cheltenham, Glos GL52 6BQ
Corporate

Fax 01242-255515
Nancy Price Western

Princess Productions	**020-7985 1985**
Whiteleys Centre	Fax 020-7985 1986
151 Queensway, London W2 4YN	Henrietta Conrad
Television	

Prism Entertainment	**020-8969 1212**
220 Latimer Road	Fax 020-8969 1012
London W10 6QY	Mark Bishop
Television	

The Prisons Video Magazine	**020-7916 7707**
PVM Studios	Fax 020-7916 7488
7 Anglers Lane, London NW5 3DG	Antonio Ferrara
Television	

The Producers	**020-7636 4226**
8 Berners Mews	Fax 020-7636 4099
London W1T 3AW	Jenny Edwards
Television	

Production International	**020-7631 2400**
114 New Cavendish Street	Fax 020-7631 2401
London W1W 6XT	Charlotte Fuller
Commercial	

Production Network Worldwide	**020-8324 2669**
Elstree Studios, Shenley Road	Fax 020-8953 9063
Borehamwood, Herts WD6 1JG	Jay Ellis
Corporate	

Professional Medical Communications	**020-8381 1819**
1 High Street	Fax 020-8381 1816
Edgware, Middx HA8 7TA	Michael Wong
Corporate	

Projectile Productions	**07778-363492**
17 Shaw Court	Gerard Tierney
Cornwallis Road, London N19 4JJ	
Feature	

Projector Pictures	**020-7861 8000**
20-21 Newman Street	Polly Cork
London W1T 1PG	
Television	

Prolingua Productions	**020-8741 5157**
9 Cambridge Grove	Martin Williamson
London W6 0LA	
Corporate	

Prominent Television	**020-7497 1100**
34 Tavistock Street	Fax 020-7497 1133
London WC2E 7PB	Steve Abbott
Television	

Propeller Productions	**029-2037 7128**
PO Box 486	Fax 029-2037 7128
Cardiff CF24 4YB	George Auchterlonie
Television	

Prospect Cymru Wales	**029-2064 2395**
Talbot Studios	Rhys John
1 Talbot Street, Cardiff CF11 9BW	
Television	

Prospect Pictures	**020-8563 9393**
Glen House	Fax 020-8741 7214
22 Glenthorne Road, London W6 0NG	Louise Doffman
Television	

Prospectus	**020-8743 9707**
8 Flanchford Road	Richard Duplock
London W12 9ND	
Corporate	

The Proudfoot Company	**020-7253 5666**
104A St John Street	Fax 020-7253 5663
London EC1M 4EH	Michael Proudfoot
Television	

PSAfilms	**0161-924 0011**
52 The Downs	Fax 0161-924 0022
Altrincham, Cheshire WA14 2QJ	Ben Swift
Commercial	

Pukka Films	**020-7866 0000**
22 D'Arblay Street	Fax 020-7866 0011
London W1F 8EQ	Andrew de Lotbiniere
Corporate	

Pulse Films	**020-7240 2414**
1 Book Mews	Fax 020-7240 3244
Flitcroft Street, London WC2H 8DJ	Thomas Benksi
Commercial	

Pulse8media	**01582-766500**
2 Kinsbourne Court	Fax 01582-766525
Harpenden, Herts AL5 3BL	Paul Musselle
Television	

Pure Magic Films	**0141-416 0799**
61 Holland Street	Robbie Fraser
Glasgow G2 4NJ	
Feature	

Purple Flame Media	**020-7635 0732**
16 Aspinall Road	Phil Knox
London SE4 2EQ	
Corporate	

Qd	**020-7462 1700**
93 Great Titchfield Street	Fax 020-7636 0653
London W1W 6RP	Julie Hawkins
Commercial	

Qi Commercials	**020-7631 4084**
26 Market Place	Fax 020-7637 1707
London W1W 8AN	Stephen Gash
Commercial	

Quadrant Media & Communications   **029-2069 4900**
Greenmeadow Springs   Fax 029-2069 4999
Tongwynlais, Cardiff CF15 7NE   William Jenkins
Television

Quadrant Television   **07831-280333**
17 West Hill   Nik Cookson
London SW18 1RB
Corporate

Quanta   **01908-560674**
Old Forge House, Rodbourne Road   Nicholas Jones
Corston, Wilts SN16 0HA
Television

Quickfire Media   **0117-330 5462**
32 Alma Road   Fax 0845-307 2058
Bristol BS8 2DB   Mark Fielder
Television

Quicksilver Media   **01865-596223**
60 St Aldates   Fax 01865-596191
Oxford OX1 1ST   Lesley Cherry
Television

Quiet Storm Films   **020-7907 1140**
15-16 Margaret Street   Fax 020-7907 1150
London W1W 8RW   Kate Pirouet
Commercial

Quintessence Films   **01453-884651**
Hill House, Brownshill   Fax 01453-884651
Stroud, Glos GL6 8AQ   Matthew Lingard
Television

Radley Yeldar   **020-7033 0700**
24 Charlotte Road   Fax 020-7033 0800
London EC2A 3PB   Carl Radley
Corporate

Rafford Films   **020-7478 5151**
36 Marshall Street   Fax 020-7734 3189
London W1F 7EY   Joan Thompson
Feature

Ragdoll Productions   **01789-404100**
Timothys Bridge Road   Fax 01789-404178
Stratford-upon-Avon, Warwicks CV37 9NQ   Chris Wood
Television

Rainmakerfilms   **020-7493 4400**
12 St George Street   Georgina Townsley
London W1S 2FB
Feature

Ralphs Productions   **020-7284 2615**
7 Highcroft   Fax 020-7284 2615
170 Highgate Road, London NW5 1EJ   Mark Riley
Commercial

The Raspberry Picture Company   **020-7407 4506**
64 Dean Street   Fax 020-7434 1129
London W1D 4QQ   Barry Matthews
Feature

Rattling Stick Productions   **020-7851 2000**
39-43 Brewer Street   Fax 020-7851 2001
London W1F 9UD   Johnnie Frankel
Commercial

Raw Cut Television   **020-7287 1050**
35 Great Pulteney Street   Bill Rudgard
London W1F 9NR
Television

Raw Nerve Productions   **028-7126 0562**
7-8 Magazine Street   Fax 028-7137 1738
Derry BT48 6HJ   Pearse Moore
Feature

Raw Productions   **07921-858356**
23 Huberd House   Sal Anderson
Manciple Street, London SE1 4DN
Feature

Raw TV   **020-7017 1650**
13-27 Brunswick Place   Dimitri Doganis
London N1 6DX
Television

Razor Productions   **020-3102 5091**
103 New Oxford Street   Gary Chitty
London WC1A 1DD
Corporate

Razzmatazz Productions   **020-7722 2065**
48C Primrose Gardens   Jeremy Hoare
London NW3 4TP
Television

RDF Media Group   **020-7013 4000**
Gloucester Building, Kensington Village   Fax 020-7013 4001
Avonmore Road, London W14 8RF   David Frank
Television

Readers Digest   **020-7715 8000**
11 Westferry Circus   Fax 020-7715 8722
Canary Wharf, London E14 4HE
Corporate

Real Life Media Productions   **0113-237 1005**
Chapel Allerton House   Fax 0113-288 8523
114 Harrogate Road, Leeds LS7 4NY   Jenny Scott
Television

Realisation Marketing Services   **020-8878 3344**
Unit 13, The Old Power Station   Fax 020-8876 0125
121 Mortlake High Street, London SW14 8SN   Nick Gale
Commercial

Really Useful Group   020-7240 0880
22 Tower Street
London WC2H 9TW
Feature
Fax 020-7240 1204
Andy Hall

Recorded Picture Company   020-7636 2251
24 Hanway Street
London WIT IUH
Feature
Fax 020-7636 2261
Matthew Baker

Red Admiral   01865-331111
Grayling House, Merton
Bicester, Oxon OX25 2NF
Television
Fax 01865-331120
Graeme Bowd

Red Bee Media   020-8495 5521
Room BC2D6, Broadcast Centre
201 Wood Lane, London W12 7TP
Promo
Fax 020-8495 5399
Laura Gould

Red Box Media Productions   028-9077 3854
3 Ardrigh Court
737C Antrim Road, Belfast BT15 4EL
Corporate
Liam Creagh

Red Earth Studio   020-7613 1000
27 Phipp Street
London EC2A 4NP
Television
Fax 020-7613 1060

Red Fox Productions   01508-482630
Street Farm
Topcroft, Suffolk NR35 2BL
Television
Keith Tutt

Red Handed Television   01803-732038
Unit 10, Coombe Park
Ashbrington, Devon TQ9 7DY
Television
Sam Usher

Red Mullet   020-7702 5580
Unit 22, Waterside Studios
44-48 Wharf Road, London N1 7UX
Feature
Fax 020-7702 5581
Tara Smith

Red Planet Accidental   020-8520 6191
106 Hilton Grove Centre
Hatherley Mews, London E17 4QP
Corporate
Keir Husband

Red Production Company   01619-526284
Granada Television
Quay Street, Manchester M60 9EA
Television

Red Wave Films UK   020-7753 7200
31-32 Soho Square
London W1D 3AP
Feature
Fax 020-7753 7201
Uberto Pasolini

Redders Television   01438-832474
61 High Street
Kimpton, Herts SG4 8PU
Television
Bill Redway

Redhouse Lane   020-7462 2600
14 Bedford Square
London WC1B 3JA
Corporate
Fax 020-7462 2601
Jeremy Redhouse

Redoka   020-8488 8831
4 Court Hill
Sanderstead, Surrey CR2 9NA
Television
Ben Hole

Redshark   020-7729 0030
Zetland House
32 Paul Street, London EC2A 4LF
Corporate
Karen Davies

Redweather Productions   0117-941 5854
Easton Business Centre
Felix Road, Bristol BS5 0HE
Television
Fax 0117-941 5851
Ann Pugh

Reef Television   020-7539 2000
1 New Oxford Street
London WC1A 1NU
Television
Fax 020-7242 8685
Richard Farmbrough

Remedy Productions   020-8964 4408
Unit 1
9 Thorpe Close, London W10 5XL
Television
Fax 020-8964 4421
Sarah Corbett

Remvision   020-7713 1141
388 City Road
London EC1V 2QA
Corporate
Ed Lindfield

Renaissance Vision   01603-260280
256 Fakenham Road
Taverham, Norfolk NR8 6QW
Corporate
Brian Gardner

Renown Pictures   01923-290555
Strawplait Barn Studios, Croft Lane
Chipperfield, Herts WD4 9DX
Feature
Fax 01923-290556
Sarah Cronin-Stanley

Replay Media   01753-421055
Pinewood Studios, Pinewood Road
Iver Heath, Bucks SL0 0NH
Corporate
Fax 01753-651006
Chris Edmonds

Republic Productions   0131-557 1288
16 Calton Road
Edinburgh EH8 8DL
Corporate
Fax 0131-557 1232
Marnie Anderson

Retail Therapy Television   01784-256777

Unit 20A, Littleton House
Ashford Road, Middx TW15 1UU
Television

Retina Productions   020-7272 4448

6 Mount Pleasant Crescent   Bella Goyarts
London N4 4HP
Corporate

Revere Entertainment Company   020-7292 7390

91 Berwick Street   Fax 020-7292 7391
London W1F 0NE   John Goldstone
Feature

Revolution Films   020-7566 0700

9A Dallington Street   Fax 020-7566 0701
London EC1V 0BQ   Andrew Eaton
Feature

Revolution Productions   028-9336 4313

7 Watch Hill Road, Ballynure   Gordon Cross
Ballyclare, Co Antrim BT39 9QW
Corporate

Rich Productions   01935-826639

4 School Close   Fax 01935-825842
Tintinhull, Somerset BA22 8PX   Nigel Rich
Corporate

Richard Attenborough Productions   020-8940 7234

Beaver Lodge, The Green   Fax 020-8940 4741
Richmond, Surrey TW9 1NQ   Gabriel Clare-Hunt
Feature

Richmond Films & Television   020-7722 6464

PO Box 33154   Sandra Hastie
London NW3 4AZ
Television

Ricochet   01273-224800

Pacific House, 126 Dyke Road   Fax 01273-770350
Brighton, E Sussex BN1 3TE
Television

Ricochet   020-7239 1010

2 Holford Yard   Fax 020-7239 1011
London WC1X 9HD   Nick Southgate
Television

Riposte Pictures   020-7267 5213

16 Lupton Street   Fax 020-7267 5213
London NW5 2HT   Andrew Lambert
Television

Rival Media   020-8987 5450

1 Blue Lion Place   Fax 020-8987 5451
237 Long Lane, London SE1 4PU   Steve Wynne
Television

Riverhouse Productions   020-8979 0679

75A Walton Road   Colin Webb
East Molesey, Surrey KT8 0DP
Corporate

Rob Harris Productions   020-8748 2430

The Studio   Fax 020-8748 9489
310 King Street, London W6 0RR   Rob Harris
Corporate

Robert Golden Pictures   01308-421325

Three Chimneys, Pymore Lane   Fax 01308-421325
Dottery, Dorset DT6 5PS   Robert Golden
Feature

Robert Stigwood Organisation   01983-280676

Barton Manor   Fax 01983-293923
East Cowes, Isle Of Wight PO32 6LB
Feature

Rocket Pictures   020-7603 9530

1 Blythe Road   Fax 020-7348 4830
London W14 0HG
Feature

Rod Natkiel Associates   0121-355 2197

5 Vesey Road   Fax 0121-355 8033
Sutton Coldfield, W Midlands B73 5NP   Rod Natkiel
Corporate

Rodney Read Productions   020-8891 2875

45 Richmond Road   Rodney Read
Twickenham, Middx TW1 3AW
Promo

Roebuck Productions   01937-835900

Commer House, Station Road   Fax 01937-835901
Tadcaster, N Yorks LS24 9JF   Howard Hesling
Corporate

Rogue Films   020-7907 1000

2-3 Bourlet Close   Fax 020-7907 1001
London W1W 7BQ   Charlie Crompton
Commercial

Rokkit   020-7240 7900

Scriptor Court   Fax 0845-544 0164
155-157 Faringdon Road, London EC1R 3AD   Luke Jacobs
Commercial

Rollem Production Company   0113-275 1830

6 Weetwood Lane   Fax 0113-275 4779
Far Headingley, Leeds LS16 5LS   Anna Heathcoate
Television

Rolls-Royce   01332-247490

PO Box 31   Simon Pank
Derby DE24 8BJ
Corporate

Rondo Media   01286-675722
Moreia, Penrallt Isaf   Robin Evans
Caernarfon, Gwynedd LL55 1NS
Television

Roof Raic   07906-162968
25 Ardmore Avenue   Carol Murphy
Belfast BT7 3HD
Feature

Rooftop Productions   020-7523 2299
PO Box 100   Fax 020-7523 2441
London SE1 7RT   Sophie Chalk
Television

Roughcut TV   020-7299 4400
32 Newman Street   Fax 020-3205 0078
London W1T 1PU   Bertie Peek
Television

Royal National Lifeboat Institution   01202-663112
West Quay Road   Fax 01202-663287
Poole, Dorset BH15 1HZ   James Ellerton
Corporate

RPM Arts   0141-778 1633
7 Bowling Green Road   Bob Morton
Glasgow G32 0SR
Commercial

RPTA   020-3008 6511
Lyric Square   Margo Faith
London W6 0NB
Feature

RS Productions   07710-064632
191 Trewhitt Road   Mark Lavender
Newcastle-upon-Tyne NE6 5DY
Television

RSA Films   020-7437 7426
42-44 Beak Street   Fax 020-7734 4978
London W1F 9RH   Garfield Kempton
Commercial

Rubberductions   0845-680 0850
35 King Street   Matt Golding
Bristol BS1 4DZ
Commercial

Ruby Films   020-7833 9990
26 Lloyd Baker Street   Fax 020-7837 5862
London WC1X 9AW   Faye Ward
Feature

Rumble Productions   0141-956 2020
20 Lilac Wind   Mark Budd
Cambusleng, Glasgow G72 7GJ
Corporate

Running Bare Pictures   020-7428 8400
Block B, Imperial Works   Fax 020-7428 8401
Perren Street, London NW5 3ED   John Noel
Television

Rushmore   020-7439 4944
19-20 Poland Street   Sinead O'Leary
London W1F 8QF
Commercial

Sally Head Productions   020-8607 8730
Twickenham Film Studios, St Margarets   Fax 020-8607 8964
Twickenham, Middx TW1 2AW   Sally Head
Television

Salt Pictures   020-7478 0560
4 Golden Square   Daniel Fagerson
London W1F 9HT
Commercial

The Salvation Army   020-7367 4975
101 Newington Causeway   Fax 020-7367 4722
London SE1 6BN   John Anscombe
Corporate

Sarah Radclyffe Productions   020-7483 3556
10-11 St Georges Mews   Fax 020-7586 8063
London NW1 8XE   Sarah Radclyffe
Feature

Sarah Shuter Productions   020-7501 9919
2 Chaucer Road   Fax 020-7501 9926
London SE24 0NU   Sarah Shuter
Corporate

Sassi Productions   028-9334 4422
Hollybank Business Park, Hollybank Road   Fax 028-9334 1772
Parkgate, Belfast BT39 0DL   Colin Lewis
Television

Satellite Productions   020-7373 3966
4A Marloes Road   Fax 020-7373 3952
London W8 5LJ   Nicholas Kelsey
Corporate

Saxholm Media Communications
023-8076 8274

203 Bassett Avenue, Bassett
Southampton, Hants SO16 7HD
Corporate

Fax 023-8076 8915
Tony Pitcher

Scala Productions
020-7637 5720

37 Foley Street
London W1W 7TN
Feature

Nik Powell

Scallywag Pictures
01932-592496

Shepperton Studios, Studios Road
Shepperton, Middx TW17 0QD
Television

Fax 01932-592050
Neil Blewett

Scarab Films
020-7482 3433

St Martins Chapel
Bayham Street, London NW1 0BD
Feature

Fax 020-7482 2015
Jamil Dehlavi

Scenic Route Productions
020-7060 1471

52 Knollys Road
London SW16 2JX
Corporate

Jinne Stiksma

Scimitar Films
020-7734 8385

219 Kensington High Street
London W8 6BD
Feature

Fax 020-7602 9217
Michael Winner

Scope Productions
0141-221 4312

180 West Regent Street
Glasgow G2 4RW
Corporate

Laura Kingwell

Screen First
01825-712034

The Studios, Funnells Farm
Down Street, Nutley, E Sussex TN22 3LG
Television

Paul Madden

Screenhouse Productions
0113-266 8881

9 The Drive
Roundhay, Leeds LS8 1JF
Television

Fax 0113-266 8882
Paul Bader

ScreenProjex
020-7193 4745

Suite 3, 32 Montpelier Crescent
Brighton, E Sussex BN1 3JL
Feature

Fax 0870-235 6014
Ivan Clements

Screenscope
01797-226608

Ryeside, Farm Lane
Camber, E Sussex TN31 7QY
Promo

Michael Brandt

Scripture Union
01908-856000

207-209 Queensway, Bletchley
Milton Keynes, Bucks MK2 2EB
Corporate

Fax 01908-856111
Eddie Nock

September Films
020-8563 9393

Glen House
22 Glenthorne Road, London W6 0NG
Television

Fax 020-8741 7214
David Green

Serendipity Picture Company
0117-908 2711

Media Cabin
11 Lyndhurst Road, Bristol BS9 3QY
Television

Tony Yeadon

Serious Pictures
020-7792 4477

1A Rede Place
London W2 4TU
Commercial

Fax 020-7792 4488
Donnie Masters

Seven Stones Media
01594-530708

The Old Butchers Shop, High Street
St Briavels, Glos GL15 6TA
Television

Fax 01594-530094
Adam Alexander

Seventh Art Productions
01273-777678

63 Ship Street
Brighton, E Sussex BN1 1AE
Television

Fax 01273-323777
Phil Grabsky

Seventh House Films
01603-661353

13 Phillipa Flowerday Plain
Norwich NR2 2TA
Television

Clive Dunn

SGTV
01425-628772

32 Ashley Common Road
New Milton, Hants BH25 5AR
Television

Simon Golding

Shed Films
020-7608 2437

39 Featherstone Street
London EC1Y 8RE
Commercial

David Stewart

Shed Productions
020-7239 1010

2 Holford Yard
London WC1X 9HD
Television

Fax 020-7239 1011
Brian Park

Shell Film & Video Unit
020-7934 3318

Shell Centre
London SE1 7NA
Corporate

Fax 020-7934 7490
Jane Poynor

Shine
020-7985 7000

Primrose Studios
109 Regent Park Road, London NW1 8UR
Television

Fax 020-7985 7001
Elisabeth Murdoch

Shine North
0161-233 2100

Suite 302, Barclay House
35 Whitworth Street West, Manchester M1 5NG
Television

Fax 0161-233 2101

Shining Light Productions 01702-393758
PO Box 5520 Ryan Driscoll
Westcliff, Essex SS0 7WR
Feature

Shinobi Films 020-8590 8050
50-54 Farnham Road, Seven Kings Fax 020-8590 8099
Ilford, Essex IG3 8QD
Feature

Shooting Pictures 020-7378 7988
Studio 18, Blue Lion Place Fax 020-7378 8040
237 Long Lane, London SE1 4PU David Williams
Television

short-films 020-7287 3575
117 Wardour Street Holly Hartley
London W1F 0UN
Commercial

ShowReal Media 020-7193 5162
24 Lansdowne Crescent Tim Daukes
London W11 2NS
Commercial

Sigma Films 0141-445 0400
Film City Glasgow Fax 0141-445 6900
401 Govan Road, Glasgow G51 2QJ Brian Coffey
Feature

Silco Productions 07866-758285
4 Trinity Mews Rocco De Lucz
Cambridge Gardens, London W10 6PY
Television

Silver Films 020-7923 0700
4 Quebec Wharf Janey de Nordwall
315 Kingsland Road, London E8 4DJ
Commercial

Silver Light Media 01865-250400
19 Hilltop Road David Marlow
Oxford OX4 1PB
Feature

Silver Productions 01722-336221
Bridge Farm, Lower Road Fax 01722-336227
Britford, Wilts SP5 4DY Ethem Cetintas
Feature

Silver River 020-7307 2720
Brook House Fax 020-7907 3411
2-16 Torrington Place, London WC1E 7HN Daisy Goodwin
Television

Sindibad Films 020-7259 2707
226 Cromwell Road Omar Al-Qattan
London SW5 0SW
Feature

Sixteen Films 020-7734 0168
187 Wardour Street Rebecca O'Brien
London W1F 8ZB
Feature

Sixth Sense Media 0845-680 0966
107 Hallowell Road Tim Duck
Northwood, Middx HA6 1DY
Television

Skibbly TV 07973-321852
The Technocentre Fax 024-7623 6131
Puma Way, Coventry CV1 2TT Chris Jones
Television

Skylet Andrew 020-7692 0909
7 The Shrubberies Fax 020-7692 0910
George Lane, London E18 1BD Stella Brockway
Corporate

Skyline Films 07836-275584
Suite 316, East Block Steve Clark-Hall
County Hall, Forum Magnum Square, London SE1 7GN
Feature

Skyline Productions 0131-556 2026
10 Scotland Street Leslie Hills
Edinburgh EH3 6PS
Television

Skywalk Pictures 020-8549 4619
37 Upper Park Road David Skynner
Kingston-upon-Thames, Surrey KT2 5LB
Feature

Slate Films 020-7734 7372
9 Greek Street Fax 020-7287 5228
London W1D 4DQ Andrea Calderwood
Feature

Sledge 020-7380 4380
5-12 Mandela Street Fax 020-7387 3777
London NW1 0DU Nic Cooper
Commercial

Slingshot 020-7535 6720
1A Adpar Street Fax 020-7563 7283
London W2 1DE Arvind David
Feature

Slinky Productions 07779-794354
99 The Postbox Steve Mackie
Birmingham B1 1LJ
Television

Sly Fox Films 01580-752839
The Far Barn, Foxhole Lane Linda James
Cranbrook, Kent TN18 5NJ
Feature

Small World Productions   029-2034 1122

28 The Balcony   Justyn Jones
Castle Arcade, Cardiff CF10 1BY
Television

Smith & Jones Films   07771-784851

16-19 Southampton Place   Fax 020-7504 8010
London WC1A 2AJ   Philippa Smith
Commercial

Smith & Watson Productions   01803-863033

The Gothic House, Fore Street   Fax 01803-864219
Totnes, Devon TQ9 5EH   Nick Smith
Television

Smoking Dogs Films   020-7249 6644

26 Shacklewell Lane   Fax 020-7249 6655
London E8 2EZ   David Lawson
Feature

Smuggler   020-7636 7665

6-10 Great Portland Street   Fax 020-7637 4667
London W1W 8QL   Chris Barrett
Commercial

Sneezing Tree Films   020-7436 8036

37 Great Portland Street   Fax 020-7580 1957
London W1W 8QH   Brock van den Bogaerde
Commercial

So Television   020-7960 2000

18 Hatfields   Fax 020-7960 2095
London SE1 8GN
Television

Software Production Enterprises   020-7960 6044

Suite 523   Fax 020-7222 5184
10 Greycoat Place, London SW1P 1SB   Jeff Vicarioli
Corporate

Soho Films   020-7025 8777

18 Soho Square   Fax 020-7313 4665
London W1D 3QL   Lee Thomas
Feature

Somethin Else   020-7250 5500

20-26 Brunswick Place   Fax 020-7250 0937
London N1 6DZ   Jez Nelson
Television

Songbird   020-7249 1477

79 Albion Road   Bob Bentley
London N16 9PL
Television

Sonny   020-7734 8124

68 Wardour Street   Gabi Kay
London W1F 0TB
Commercial

Sound & Picture House   0121-429 5462

The Coach House, 29 Woodbourne Road   Edward Duffield
Edgbaston, Birmingham B17 8BY
Commercial

Sous Productions   07976-881196

55 Countess Road   Duncan Souster
Amesbury, Wilts SP4 7AS
Corporate

Space City Productions   020-7371 4000

77 Blythe Road   Fax 020-7371 4001
London W14 0HP   Victor Van Amerongen
Commercial

Spafax Inflight Entertainment   020-7906 2001

The Pumphouse   Fax 020-7906 2003
13-16 Jacobs Well Mews, London W1U 3DY   Ed Oppe
Corporate

Spank   020-7287 5502

8-18 Smiths Court   Fax 020-7287 5503
Great Windmill Street, London W1D 7DN   John Golley
Commercial

Speakeasy Productions   01738-828524

Wildwood House   Fax 01738-828419
Stanley, Perth PH1 4PX   Jim Adamson
Corporate

Special Treats Production Company   020-7851 1111

Grafton House   Fax 020-7494 4480
2-3 Golden Square, London W1F 9HR   Colin Burrows
Feature

Specific Films   020-7580 7476

25 Rathbone Street   Michael Hamlyn
London W1T 1NQ
Feature

Spectrecom Films   020-3405 2260

Waterloo Film Studios   Fax 020-3405 2279
27-31 Webber Street, London SE1 8QW   Andrew Greener
Corporate

Spice Factory   01273-739182

14 Regent Hill   Fax 01273-749122
Brighton, E Sussex BN1 3ED   Michael Cowan
Feature

Spiffing Films   020-8429 2672

64 Love Lane   Daniel Grant
Pinner, Middx HA5 3EX
Feature

Spike Productions   01534-738263

Hilgrove House, Hilgrove Street   Warren Mauger
St Helier, Jersey JE2 4SL
Corporate

Spirit Media	**020-8960 0108**
Canalot Studios	Fax 020-8960 1227
222 Kensal Road, London W10 5BN	Anthony Levene
Corporate	

Splash Media	**020-7255 5434**
1 Bedford Avenue	Fax 020-7255 5443
London WC1B 3AU	Jane Lush
Television	

Split Second Films	**01933-382289**
The Manor House, Station Road	Fax 01933-384669
Irthlingborough, Northants NN9 5SP	Milner Schmueck
Feature	

Spoke Films	**020-7734 5508**
14 Livonia Street	Fax 020-7434 2104
London W1F 8AG	Alison Cooper
Commercial	

Spoken Image	**0161-236 7522**
Studio 6, Riverside Mews	Fax 0161-832 3708
4 Commercial Street, Manchester M15 4RQ	Geoff Allman
Television	

Spoton Film & TV	**028-9023 6111**
Ormeau Business Park	Fax 028-9023 6068
8 Cromac Avenue, Belfast BT7 2JA	Micky O'Neill
Commercial	

Spudnick Productions	**01582-831119**
Beech Hyde Farm, Dyke Lane	Fax 01582-831937
Wheathampstead, Herts AL4 8EN	Fiona O'Mahoney
Television	

Spun Gold TV	**0870-164 7470**
Tabernacle Court	Fax 0870-164 7471
16-28 Tabernacle Street, London EC2A 4DD	Nick Bullen
Television	

Stagescreen Productions	**020-7481 4810**
Suite 92	Jeffrey Taylor
1 Prescot Street, London E1 8RL	
Feature	

Stampede	**01582-727330**
The Hat Factory, 65-67 Bute Street	Mike Chamberlain
Luton, Beds LU1 2EY	
Television	

Standfast Films	**020-8466 5580**
The Studio, 14 College Road	Anthony van der Elst
Bromley, Kent BR1 3NS	
Feature	

Star Quality Video Productions	**020-8769 6425**
36 Mount Ephraim Lane	Fax 020-8769 6425
London SW16 1JD	Don Reeve
Corporate	

Starfield Productions	**07710-380612**
18 Sheendale Road	Paul Raphael
Richmond, Surrey TW9 2JJ	
Feature	

Station Film	**020-7291 3125**
24 Wells Street	Fax 020-7637 0133
London W1T 3PH	Adam Lyne
Commercial	

Steadfast Television	**020-7471 9250**
Shepherds Building Central	Fax 020-7471 9380
Charecroft Way, London W14 0EE	Charles Thompson
Television	

Steam	**020-7609 3977**
Studio A, Mica House	Fax 020-7609 3978
Barnsbury Square, London N1 1RN	Geoff Stickler
Commercial	

Steel Mill Pictures	**020-7287 9882**
60 Berwick Street	Fax 020-7287 9882
London W1F 8SU	Ken Marshall
Feature	

Steel Spyda	**01638-554664**
9 & 10 Lanwades Business Park	Fax 020-7681 1651
Kennet, Suffolk CB8 7PN	Kay Hill
Television	

Stephen Arnold	**020-8444 8282**
Unit 1	Antony Arnold
Bedford Mews, London N2 9DF	
Commercial	

Sterling Pictures	**07956-529489**
7 Denmark Street	Michael Riley
London WC2H 8LZ	
Feature	

Steve Boulton Productions	**0161-200 8100**
23 Nicholas Street	Fax 0161-237 9222
Manchester M1 4EN	Dorothy Flynn
Television	

Stillking Films	**07919-845732**
127 Wardour Street	James Hatcher
London W1F 0NL	
Commercial	

Stingray Productions	**020-7220 2994**
Suite 4	Trevor Rogers
1 Lexington Street, London W1F 9AF	
Commercial	

Stink Productions	**020-7462 4000**
1 Alfred Mews	Fax 020-7462 4001
London W1T 7AA	Robert Herman
Commercial	

Stirling Film & Television Productions	028-9033 3848
137 University Street	Fax 028-9043 8644
Belfast BT7 IHP	Anne Stirling
Television	

Stone City Films	020-7405 9111
37 Johns Mews	Fax 020-7405 9137
London WCIN 2NS	Susie Strong
Television	

Straandlooper	028-9188 3756
150 Warren Road	Tim Bryans
Donaghadee, Co Down BT21 0PQ	
Television	

Straker Films	020-8605 2012
3 St Marks Place	Fax 020-8605 2121
London SW19 7ND	Nick Straker
Corporate	

Strange Beast	020-7462 0333
33-34 Rathbone Place	Fax 020-7323 9030
London WIT IJN	Nicola Finn
Commercial	

Streetlight Films UK	020-7434 1535
The Hat Factory	Fax 020-7434 1898
16-18 Hollen Street, London WIF 8BQ	Adrian Harrison
Commercial	

Stuart Josephs Associates	0113-262 3342
248 Meanwood Road	Fax 0113-262 3798
Leeds LS7 2HZ	Stuart Josephs
Commercial	

Studio AKA	020-7434 3581
30 Berwick Street	Fax 020-7437 2309
London WIF 8RH	Sue Goffe
Commercial	

Studio Lambert	020-7432 3141
42 Beak Street	Fax 020-7432 3142
London WIF 9RH	Sophie Clarke
Television	

Studio Scotland	01383-420397
The Studio, Johnston Park	Deborah Forrest
Inverkeithing, Fife KYII IBT	
Feature	

STV Group	0141-300 3000
Pacific Quay	
Glasgow G51 IPQ	
Television	

Suffolk Films	01986-875875
The Beeches, Wenhastan	Patrick Redsell
Halesworth, Suffolk IPI9 9ED	
Corporate	

Summer Films	020-8996 5550
Lamb House	Fax 020-8996 5551
Church Street, London W4 2PD	Emma Dunne
Television	

Sunipa Pictures	07798-600571
34 Albion Hill	Mat Sunderand
Brighton, E Sussex BN2 9NW	
Promo	

Sunset + Vine APP	01865-260200
18 Beaumont Street	Fax 01865-244458
Oxford OXI 2ND	Laura Garcia
Television	

Sunset + Vine Productions	020-7478 7300
Elsinore House	Fax 020-7478 7407
77 Fulham Palace Road, London W6 8JA	John Leach
Television	

Sunstone Films	020-7554 8755
Hamilton House	Alan Ereira
Mabledon Place, London WCIH 9BB	
Television	

Super Umami	01786-834349
Old Telephone Exchange, Fountain Road	Garry Marshall
Bridge of Allam, Stirling FK9 4ET	
Television	

Superfad	020-7734 5840
21A Noel Street	
London WIF 8GR	
Commercial	

Superkrush Films	0191-233 2001
20A Nun Street	Chris Taylor
Newcastle-upon-Tyne NEI 5AQ	
Promo	

Supernova	01273-323311
4 Cambridge Grove	Fax 01273-326624
Hove, E Sussex BN3 3ED	Vincent Thompson
Corporate	

The Sweet Shop	020-7636 1449
13A Tottenham Mews	Rudy Tajuri
London WIT 4AQ	
Commercial	

Swingbridge Video	0191-232 3762
41 Stowell Street	Hugh Kelly
Newcastle-upon-Tyne NEI 4YB	
Corporate	

Swiss Film London	020-7607 9488
20 Lowman Road	Hans-Peter Bertschy
London N7 6DD	
Corporate	

Synchronicity Films	**0141-244 0056**
18 Westminster Terrace	Fax 0141-221 7111
Glasgow G3 7RU	Claire Mundell
Feature	

Tabard Productions	**020-7497 0830**
Adam House	Fax 020-7497 0850
7-10 Adam Street, London WC2N 6AA	John Herbert
Corporate	

Table Top Productions	**020-8994 1269**
1 The Orchard	Fax 020-8742 0507
London W4 1JZ	Alvin Rakoff
Feature	

Table Twelve Media	**0161-737 3004**
25 The Crescent	Hannah Stevenson
Salford, Manchester M5 4PF	
Television	

Take 3 Productions	**020-7637 2694**
72-73 Margaret Street	Richard Smith
London W1W 8ST	
Corporate	

Take One Business Communications	**01494-898 919**
Media House, 12 Manor Courtyard	Fax 01494-898 910
High Wycombe, Bucks HP13 5RE	John Groves
Corporate	

Talent Television	**020-7822 3900**
13-19 Vinehill	Fax 020-7822 3949
London EC1R 5DW	Jonathan Glazier
Television	

Talent TV South	**0845-355 0858**
Wessex House, Upper Market Street	Kate Beal
Eastleigh, Hants SO50 9FD	
Television	

TalkBack Thames	**020-7861 8000**
20-21 Newman Street	Fax 020-7861 8001
London W1T 1PG	Lorraine Heggessey
Television	

Talking Pictures	**01753-655744**
Pinewood Studios, Pinewood Road	Fax 01865-890504
Iver Heath, Bucks SL0 0NH	David Broscombe
Corporate	

Tambuti Films	**020-8747 4099**
4 Antrobus Road	Fax 020-8747 4099
London W4 5HY	Cecile Trijssenaar
Television	

Tandem Creative	**01442-261576**
Charleston House, 13 High Street	Andrew Denbury
Hemel Hempstead, Herts HP1 3AA	
Corporate	

Tandem Entertainment	**020-7652 4922**
5 Cambridge Road	Fax 020-7652 8019
London SW11 4RT	Sue Birbeck
Television	

Tandem Films	**020-7688 1717**
26 Cross Street	Fax 020-7688 1718
London N1 2BG	Mike Bell
Commercial	

Tangerine Films	**01753-655099**
Pinewood Studios, Pinewood Road	Fax 01753-631188
Iver Heath, Bucks SL0 0NH	Linda McKenzie
Corporate	

Tantrum Productions	**020-7240 5086**
24 Litchfield Street	Fax 020-7240 6686
London WC2H 9NJ	Connor Hollman
Commercial	

Tantrwm	**01685-876700**
Venture House, Depot Road	Andrew Chainey
Aberdare, Mid Glan CF44 8DL	
Corporate	

Tapestry Productions	**0121-764 4487**
41 Kineton Green Road	Fax 0121-711 3159
Solihull, W Midlands B92 7DX	Jonathan Trace
Corporate	

The Television Company	**020-7713 6579**
8 Henley Prior	Ben Challis
Collier Street, London N1 9JU	
Television	

Television Junction	**0121-248 4466**
Waterside House	Fax 0121-248 4477
46 Gas Street, Birmingham B1 2JT	Yvonne Davies
Television	

Television Projects	**01702-480488**
17 Lord Roberts Avenue	Charles Sharman-Cox
Leigh-on-Sea, Essex SS9 1ND	
Corporate	

Televisionary	**01548-830081**
Suite 4, Modbury House	Jeremy Hibbard
New Mills Business Park, Devon PL21 0TP	
Television	

Telly Juice Productions	**020-7490 8045**
63 Charterhouse Street	Niall Towl
London EC1M 6HJ	
Commercial	

Ten Alps	**020-8740 4780**
6 Anglers Lane	Fax 020-7284 0626
London NW5 3DG	Andrew McKerlie
Television	

Ten Alps Vision   0191-580 0015

Old Brewery Court   Sam Morton
156 Sandyford Road, Newcastle-upon-Tyne NE2 IXG
Corporate

Tern Television Productions   01224-211123

73 Crown Street   Fax 01224-211199
Aberdeen AB11 6EX   David Strachan
Television

Testimony Films   0117-925 8589

12 Great George Street   Fax 0117-925 7668
Bristol BS1 5RH   Steve Humphries
Television

Th2ng   020-7439 7966

199 Wardour Street   Fax 020-7437 8211
London W1F 8JP   Hannah Cooper
Commercial

Thatcham Media Services   01635-868855

Motor Insurance Research Centre, Colthrop Way   Fax 01635-871346
Thatcham, Berks RG19 4NR   Simon Thackeray
Corporate

Therapy Films   020-7436 5191

26 Market Place   Fax 020-7637 1707
London W1W 8AN   Barry Hughes
Commercial

Thin Man Films   020-7734 7372

9 Greek Street   Fax 020-7287 5228
London W1D 4DQ
Feature

Third Light Films   01580-891531

58 Corner Farm Road   Leon Chambers
Staplehurst, Kent TN12 0PS
Feature

Thirdman   01752-331404

9 Branson Court   Fax 01752-346530
Roddick Way, Plymouth PL7 2WU   Ian Stockdale
Television

Thomas Thomas Films   020-7437 1112

3-4A Little Portland Street   Fax 020-7437 1113
London W1W 7JB   Trent Simpson
Commercial

Three Stones Media   020-8983 5702

36 Ellesmere Road   Greg Boardman
London E3 5QX
Television

Thumbs Up Productions   020-7902 9880

90-92 Great Portland Street   Fax 020-7633 9058
London W1W 7NT
Television

Tiara Productions   01564-742520

Timbers Court   Tom Ross
Tanworth-in-Arden, Warwicks B94 5AJ
Television

Tiger Aspect Productions   020-7434 6700

5 Soho Square
London W1D 3QA
Television

Tigerlily Films   020-7729 9845

35-47 Bethnal Green Road   Atessa Hoomani
London E1 6LA
Television

Tigervision   020-7438 9960

27 Maiden Lane   Fax 020-7438 9980
London WC2E 7JS   Stephen Hervieu
Corporate

Tigress Productions   0117-933 5600

2 St Pauls Road   Fax 0117-933 5666
Bristol BS8 1LT   Nicola Haycocks
Television

Tilling Productions   01895-824022

12 Park Place, Newdigate Road   Fax 01895-824026
Harefield, Middx UB9 6EJ   Ed Swatman
Television

Tinopolis   01554-880880

Park Street   Fax 01554-880881
Llanelli, Dyfed SA15 3YE   Glynog Davies
Television

Tinpan Films   020-7240 6018

7 Denmark Street   Ed Blum
London WC2H 8LZ
Feature

TMB Marketing & Communications   01306-877000

Milton Heath House, Westcott Road   Fax 01306-877777
Dorking, Surrey RH4 3NB   Cara Meldrum
Corporate

Toast   020-7437 0506

10 Frith Street   Fax 020-7439 8852
London W1D 3JF   Michael Stitchman
Commercial

Tomboy Films   020-8962 3456

The Old Dairy   Fax 020-8962 3457
13A Hewer Street, London W10 6DU   Glynis Murray
Commercial

Tony Staveacre Productions   01761-462161

Channel View   Tony Staveacre
Blagdon, Somerset BS40 7TP
Television

Top Banana	**01562-700404**
The Studio, Broome	Fax 01562-700930
Stourbridge, W Midlands DY9 0HA	Kathryn Ray
Corporate	

Topical Television	**023-8071 2233**
Devonshire House, 61 Devonshire Road	Fax 023-8033 9835
Southampton, Hants SO15 2GR	Chris Riley
Television	

Topspin Communications	**01926-881419**
15 Dormer Place	Nick Fulford
Leamington, Warwicks CV32 5AA	
Corporate	

Touch Productions	**01225-484666**
18 Queen Square	Fax 01225-483620
Bath BA1 2HN	Malcolm Brinkworth
Television	

Touchpaper Television	**020-7013 4406**
3-6 Kenrick Place	Fax 020-7013 4401
London W1U 6HD	Rob Pursey
Television	

Townhouse Productions (UK)	**0117-946 7979**
13 Trelawney Road	Antony Draper
Bristol BS6 6DX	
Corporate	

Trademark Films	**020-7478 5167**
36 Marshall Street	David Parfitt
London W1F 7EY	
Feature	

Trading Pictures	**01943-603254**
4 Cowpasture Road	John Thirlwell
Ilkley, W Yorks LS29 8SR	
Corporate	

Trafalgar 1	**020-7722 7789**
153 Burnham Towers	Fax 020-7483 0662
Fellows Road, London NW3 3JN	Hasan Shah
Feature	

TransAtlantic Films	**01497-831428**
Cabalva Studios	Corisande Albert
Whitney-on-Wye, Herefordshire HR3 6EX	
Television	

Transparent	**020-7388 0202**
125 Parkway	Fax 020-7388 0203
London NW1 7PS	Eilon Kennet
Commercial	

Triangle Production	**020-7255 5222**
81 Whitfield Street	Fax 020-7255 5216
London W1T 4HG	Richard Baker
Commercial	

Tricorn Associates	**07736-601727**
11 Wellesley Road	Elizabeth Bennett
London W4 4BS	
Television	

Trifield Productions	**020-7739 1927**
23 Charlotte Road	Fax 020-7739 1907
London EC2A 3PB	
Commercial	

Triple Echo Productions	**01540-673170**
The Birches, Old Glen Road	Richard Else
Newtonmore, Inverness-shire PH20 1EB	
Television	

True North Productions	**0113-394 5494**
Marshalls Mill	Fax 0113-394 5495
Marshall Street, Leeds LS11 9YP	Carol McKenzie
Television	

True TV & Film	**0141-554 1196**
2 Whitehill Street	Fax 0141-554 1196
Glasgow G31 2LJ	Barbara Orton
Television	

True Vision Productions	**020-8742 7852**
49A Oxford Road South	Fax 020-8742 7853
London W4 3DD	Ruth McCarthy
Television	

Tubedale Films	**0151-282 9646**
Talgarth House	Fax 0151-282 9602
15 Crosby Road South, Liverpool L22 1RG	John Maxwell
Feature	

Tundra	**020-7729 8001**
2 Blackall Street	Espen Haslene
London EC2A 4AD	
Promo	

Turn On Television	**0161-247 7700**
Unit 2B	Fax 0161-923 4940
22 Lever Street, Manchester M1 1EA	Angela Smith
Television	

Turnround	**01242-224360**
Barn Studios, Chapel Farm	Ross Lammas
Over Old Road, Hartpury, Glos GL19 3BJ	
Television	

TV 6	**01892-536999**
75 High Street	Fax 01892-536062
Tunbridge Wells, Kent TN1 1XZ	George Hodges
Television	

TV Choice	**020-8464 7402**
PO Box 597	Fax 020-8464 7845
Bromley, Kent BR2 0YB	Christopher Barnard
Television	

The TV Department	01625-538835
31 Chapel Lane	Fax 01625-526621
Wilmslow, Cheshire SK9 5HW	Neil Armstrong
Commercial	

tv e	020-7901 8855
21 Elizabeth Street	Fax 020-7901 8856
London SW1W 9RP	Janine Honour
Television	

TV House Productions	01483-574545
45A Whitemore Road	Robert Golding
Guildford, Surrey GU1 1QU	
Corporate	

TVA	01423-531727
1A Kent Avenue	Fax 01423-567727
Harrogate, N Yorks HG1 2ES	Alan Davies
Corporate	

Twentieth Century Fox	020-7437 7766
Twentieth Century House	Fax 020-7434 2170
31-32 Soho Square, London W1D 3AP	
Feature	

Twenty Twenty Television	020-7284 2020
20 Kentish Town Road	Fax 020-7284 1810
London NW1 9NX	Tim Carter
Television	

Twist & Shout Communications	0844-335 6715
31 Rutland Street	
Leicester LE1 1RE	
Corporate	

Two Four Digital	01752-727400
Twofour Studios	Fax 01752-725450
Plymouth PL6 7RG	Dave Patton
Television	

Two Hand Productions	020-7924 7800
6 Leeward House	Fax 020-7924 7962
Plantation Wharf, London SW11 3TX	Luke Gallie
Television	

Twofour	020-7438 1800
6-7 St Cross Street	Fax 020-7438 1850
London EC1N 8UA	Charles Mills
Television	

Twothreefive	0845-054 2550
The Picture House, High Street	Fax 01825-760593
Uckfield, E Sussex TN22 1AS	Kevin Markwick
Feature	

Tyburn Film Productions	01753-516767
Cippenham Court, Cippenham Lane	Fax 01753-691785
Cippenham, Berks SL1 5AU	
Feature	

Tympani Productions	01494-878550
Chalfont Grove, Narcot Lane	Penny King
Chalfont St Peter, Bucks SL9 8TW	
Corporate	

Tyro Films & Television	020-8943 4697
The Coach House, 20A Park Road	Simon Passmore
Teddington, Middx TW11 0AQ	
Television	

Ubiquity Communications	01252-622800
13 Grove Road, Church Crookham	Fax 01252-622000
Fleet, Hants GU52 6DX	Tim Juby
Corporate	

Uden Media	07968-145889
42 Rochester Place	Patrick Uden
London NW1 9JX	
Television	

Ugly Duckling Films	020-8392 8500
The Studio	Fax 020-8876 4879
20 Barnes High Street, London SW13 9LW	Lene Bausager
Feature	

Umbrella Entertainment	020-7267 8834
11 St Marks Crescent	Sandy Lieberson
London NW1 7TS	
Feature	

UMTV	020-7424 7600
315 Highgate Studios	Fax 020-7424 7601
53-79 Highgate Road, London NW5 1TL	Chris Gillett
Television	

Undercurrents	01792-455900
The Old Telephone Exchange	Fax 01792-480400
Pier Street, Swansea SA1 1RY	Paul O'Connor
Television	

Underground Media (UK)	0845-838 6081
26 Old Gloucester Street	Fax 0845-838 6082
London WC1N 3AN	Steve Lanning
Television	

Union Commercials	020-7734 5555
25 Beak Street	Fax 020-7494 0604
London W1F 9RT	Jonathan Murphy
Commercial	

Unique Factuals	0161-874 5700
100 Talbot Road	Fax 0161-888 2242
Old Trafford, Manchester M16 0PG	Charlie Rodger
Television	

Unique Television	020-8987 6400
Studio G.09, Power Road Studios	Fax 020-8987 6401
114 Power Road, London W4 5PY	Vijay Amarnani
Television	

UniTal Films	**020-7734 4313**
6 Brewer Street	Fax 020-7734 4313
London W1H 0SD	Debi Nethersole
Feature	

United Television Artists	**020-7831 4433**
Baird House	Fax 020-7831 6633
15-17 St Cross Street, London EC1N 8UW	Bill Kerr Elliott
Television	

Unity Film & Video Production	**0845-226 5826**
PO Box 38	Mike Sumner
London W1A 4WW	
Corporate	

Up	**020-8986 2635**
27 Cleeve House	Jamie Balliu
Calvert Avenue, London E2 7JJ	
Commercial	

Update	**01727-568373**
12 Queens Crescent	Ian Absolon
St Albans, Herts AL4 9QG	
Corporate	

Uppercut Films	**020-7478 7507**
34 Fouberts Place	Fax 020-7478 7199
London W1F 7PX	Chris Terrill
Television	

Upset Media	**020-7377 9457**
The Old Truman Brewery	Matt Cook
91 Brick Lane, London E1 6QL	
Commercial	

Upstart Films	**020-7240 7411**
23 Denmark Street	Fax 020-7240 9311
London WC2H 8NH	Anita Mahal
Commercial	

Urban Canyons	**0161-237 9046**
1 Stevenson Square	Fax 0161-923 6933
Manchester M1 1DN	Sebastian Peiter
Television	

V Point TV	**0115-969 3636**
1 First Avenue	Fax 0115-969 3434
Sherwood Rise, Nottingham NG7 6JL	Ian Sterling
Corporate	

Vanity Projects	**020-7428 8400**
Unit B, Imperial Works	Fax 020-7428 8401
Perren Street, London NW5 3ED	John Noel
Television	

Vashca	**020-7324 7212**
2 Printing House Yard	Fax 020-7033 9955
London E2 7PR	
Television	

Velvet Pictures	**01590-610327**
Badgers Wood, Sway Road	Claire Cottrell
Lymington, Hants SO41 8LR	
Commercial	

Vera Productions	**020-7292 1480**
165 Wardour Street	Fax 020-7292 1481
London W1F 8WW	Phoebe Wallace
Television	

Vertigo Films	**020-7428 7555**
The Big Room Studios	Fax 020-7485 9713
77 Fortess Road, London NW5 1AG	Allan Niblo
Feature	

Viasat Broadcasting UK	**01895-433433**
Horton Road	Fax 01895-446606
West Drayton, Middx UB7 8JD	
Television	

Video Arts	**020-7400 4800**
6-7 St Cross Street	Fax 020-7400 4900
London EC1N 8UA	Martin Addison
Corporate	

Video Enterprises	**01494-534144**
12 Barbers Wood Road	Maurice Fleisher
High Wycombe, Bucks HP12 4EP	
Corporate	

Video Inn Production	**01604-864868**
Glebe Farm, Wootton Road	Fax 01604-864344
Quinton, Northants NN7 2EE	
Corporate	

Videoactive	**01948-780564**
Mill House Studios, Higher Wych	Fax 01948-780566
Malpas, Cheshire SY14 7JR	Chris Smith
Corporate	

Videotel Productions	**020-7299 1800**
84 Newman Street	Fax 020-7299 1818
London W1T 3EU	Kathrein Guenther
Corporate	

Vidox Video Productions	**01227-781155**
Unit 1B, Dane John Works	John McLeod
Gordon Road, Canterbury, Kent CT1 3PP	
Corporate	

The View From The North	**0113-249 3001**
456A Roundhay Road	Fax 0113-249 3006
Leeds LS8 2HU	Kathryn Hall
Television	

Viewpress TV	**01903-534141**
Woods Way	Dominic Dellow
Goring-by-Sea, W Sussex BN12 4QY	
Television	

Visability Productions	**01322-400175**
Kingsland House, 23 Raeburn Avenue	Fax 01322-294746
Dartford, Kent DA1 3BQ	Derek Wheeler
Corporate	

VisaVis Productions	**01727-854447**
PO Box 530	Georgia Maytum
St Albans, Herts AL1 1WB	
Corporate	

Viscom Aberdeen	**0845-345 1987**
430 Clifton Road	Fax 01224-663520
Aberdeen AB24 4EJ	Bruce Milne
Corporate	

Visible Ink Television	**01968-661291**
Nine Mile Burn	Fax 01968-661291
Penicuik, Midlothian EH26 9LX	Martin Fisher
Television	

Vision Associates	**07888-667321**
2 The Mill, Mill Lane	Tim Johnston
Little Shrewley, Warwicks CV35 7HN	
Corporate	

Vision Challenge	**020-8741 3669**
Portobello Studios	Fax 020-7221 2528
138 Portobello Road, London W11 2DZ	John Paul Davidson
Television	

Vision In Production	**01784-461147**
93 London Road	Len Evans
Staines, Middx TW18 4HN	
Feature	

Visual Motions	**01274-678342**
111 Wibsey Park Avenue	Gohar Nisar
Bradford, W Yorks BD6 3QD	
Corporate	

Viva Films	**020-8444 5064**
46 Cascade Avenue	John Goldschmidt
London N10 3PU	
Feature	

Volcano Films	**020-7424 0146**
47 Woodsome Road	Fax 020-7424 0143
London NW5 1SA	John Dollar
Television	

Vox Pops International	**020-8786 8855**
Bank House, 42 High Street	Fax 020-8393 9240
Ewell, Surrey KT17 1RW	John Earnshaw
Corporate	

W3KTS	**01904-647822**
10 Portland Street	Chris Wood
York YO31 7EH	
Corporate	

Waddell Media	**028-9042 7646**
7-12 St Helens Business Park	Fax 028-9042 7922
Holywood, Co Down BT18 9HQ	Jannine Waddell
Television	

Wag TV	**020-7688 1711**
2D Leroy House	Fax 020-7688 1702
436 Essex Road, London N1 3QP	Martin Durkin
Television	

Walker George Films	**020-8743 7733**
65-69 Shepherds Bush Green	Fax 020-8743 7774
London W12 8QE	Stephen Walker
Television	

Wall To Wall Television	**020-7485 7424**
8-9 Spring Place	Fax 020-7267 5292
London NW5 3ER	
Television	

Walnut Media	**0113-285 7906**
4 Sadler Close	Gary Nutland
Leeds LS16 8NN	
Corporate	

Walsh Bros	**020-8858 6870**
29 Trafalgar Grove	John Walsh
London SE10 9TB	
Feature	

Wardour Motion Pictures	**01474-853538**
Flints Studios, Knatts Valley	Mike Sutton
Sevenoaks, Kent TN15 6XY	
Corporate	

Warner Bros Productions	**01923-685222**
Leavesden Studios, South Way	Fax 01923-685221
Leavesden, Herts WD25 7LT	Roy Button OBE
Feature	

Warner Sisters	**020-8567 6655**
Ealing Studios	Fax 020-8758 8658
Ealing Green, London W5 5EP	Lavinia Warner
Television	

Wave Marketing & Communications	**0118-988 3333**
26-28 Southampton Street	Fax 0118-958 1604
Reading, Berks RG1 2QL	Beckie Cotton
Corporate	

Wavelength Films	**01603-283510**
The Royal	Fax 01603-628280
2 Bank Plain, Norwich NR2 4SF	Patrick McGrady
Television	

Weilands	**020-7287 6900**
14 Newburgh Street	Fax 020-7434 0146
London W1F 7RT	Ivana Bohuslavova
Commercial	

The Weinstein Company	**020-7494 6180**
39 Beak Street	Fax 020-7287 1305
London W1F 9SA	
Feature	

West Park Pictures	**020-8563 9393**
Glen House	Fax 020-8741 7214
22 Glenthorne Road, London W6 0NG	Pat Footer
Television	

Westside Video Productions	**01753-890400**
20 High Beeches	Stuart Johnson
Gerrards Cross, Bucks SL9 7HX	
Corporate	

Westway Film Productions	**028-7130 8383**
42 Clarendon Street	Fax 028-7130 9393
Derry BT48 7ET	Joe Mahon
Television	

White Hart Multimedia	**01291-650761**
Upper Glyn Farm, Devauden	John Brooks
Chepstow, Monmouths NP16 6PN	
Corporate	

White Lantern Film	**0870-054 3322**
The Enterprise Pavillion, Sern Barrow	Fax 0870-052 6120
Poole, Dorset BH12 5HH	Rob Sharp
Feature	

Whizz Kid Entertainment	**020-7440 2550**
4 Kingly Street	Fax 020-7440 2599
London W1B 5PE	Tracey Lloyd
Television	

Wide Angle	**07768-612040**
52 Bell Lane	Nick Da Costa
Little Chalfont, Bucks HP6 6PF	
Commercial	

Wide Eye Pictures	**020-7793 7740**
35 Heyford Avenue	Christina Burnett
London SW8 1EA	
Television	

Wide Vision Productions	**07887-691241**
87 Elm Park Mansions	Rob Shepherd
Park Walk, London SW10 0AP	
Television	

Wide-Angle	**01732-220500**
10A Swan Street	Fax 01732-220500
West Malling, Kent ME19 6LP	David Brazier
Corporate	

Wild Dream Films	**029-2009 9897**
Mount Stuart House	Fax 029-2009 9896
Mount Stuart Square, Cardiff CF10 5FQ	Stuart Clarke
Television	

Wild Iris Films	**020-7686 0324**
59 Brewer Street	Joe Matthews
London W1R 3FB	
Commercial	

Wild Pictures	**020-7428 5620**
15 Apollo Studios	Fax 020-7428 5626
Charlton Kings Road, London NW5 2SB	
Television	

Wild Productions	**01372-379069**
Randalls Farmhouse, Randalls Road	Fax 01372-375183
Leatherhead, Surrey KT22 0AL	Simon Cowell
Television	

Wild Rover Productions	**028-9050 0980**
112-114 Lisburn Road	Fax 028-9050 0970
Belfast BT9 6AH	Philip Morrow
Television	

Wildcard Production	**020-8998 1114**
10 Arlington Road	Fax 020-8741 5296
London W13 8PE	
Television	

Wilder	**020-7631 3417**
21 Little Portland Street	Richard Batty
London W1W 8BT	
Corporate	

Wildfire Television	**020-8735 5333**
49 Goldhawk Road	Fax 020-8743 4328
London W12 8QP	Philip Clarke
Television	

Wildlight Films UK	**0113-216 5958**
23 Eddison Walk	Lizzie Rymer
Adel, Leeds LS17 8DA	
Feature	

William Martin Productions	**01865-390258**
The Studio, Tubney Warren Barns	Fax 01865-390148
Tubney, Oxon OX13 5QJ	Lisa Woodward
Corporate	

Wilton Films	**020-7428 3100**
6 Anglers Lane	Fax 020-7284 0626
London NW5 3DG	Paul Mitchell
Television	

Windfall Films	**020-7251 7676**
1 Underwood Row	Fax 020-7253 8468
London N1 7LZ	Kristina Obradovic
Television	

Winged Lion Productions	**020-8969 7622**
55 Wallingford Avenue	Mark Ezra
London W10 6PZ	
Feature	

Wingspan Production	**020-7428 8700**
Unit 5, Spectrum House	Fax 020-7428 8727
32-34 Gordon House Road, London NW5 1LP	Archie Baron
Television	

Wire Films	**07802-635241**
3 Duxford Road	Fax 01223-280323
Whittlesford, Cambs CB22 4NQ	Michael Kelk
Feature	

WiseGuy	**020-7407 2007**
Studio 54, Clink Street Studios	Steve Callanan
1 Clink Street, London SE1 9DG	
Commercial	

Wish Films	**020-8324 2308**
Elstree Studios, Shenley Road	Fax 020-8324 2696
Borehamwood, Herts WD6 1JG	Helen Cadwallader
Television	

WMR Productions	**020-8600 7910**
3 Angel Walk	Alan Griffiths
London W6 9HX	
Television	

Woodcross	**023-8045 8854**
12 Marina Drive, Hamble	Fax 023-8045 8854
Southampton, Hants SO31 4PJ	William Cartlidge
Feature	

Working Title Films	**020-7307 3000**
26 Aybrook Street	Fax 020-7307 3002
London W1U 4AN	
Feature	

The Works Music & Sound	**020-3012 0234**
Albany House	Nick Payne
324-326 Regent Street, London W1B 3HH	
Commercial	

World Of Wonder	**020-7199 9211**
182 Hercules Road	Fax 020-7401 7801
London SE1 7LD	
Television	

World Productions	**020-3179 1800**
32 Lasenby House	Fax 020-3179 1801
Kingly Street, London W1B 5QQ	Helen Saunders
Television	

World Television	**020-7243 7350**
33 Astley House	Fax 020-7627 7768
Nottinghill Gate, London W11 3JQ	Toby Low
Corporate	

World Wide Pictures	**020-7613 6580**
Unit 30	Fax 020-7613 6581
10-50 Willon Street, London EC2A 4BH	Chris Courtenay Taylor
Corporate	

Worlds End Television	**020-7386 4900**
16-18 Empress Place	Fax 020-7386 4901
London SW6 1TT	
Television	

Wren Media Productions	**01992-471620**
50 Rodney Crescent	John Perkins
Hoddesdon, Herts EN11 9EW	
Corporate	

WRG	**0845-313 0000**
The Tower, Deva Centre	Fax 0161-920 9600
Trinity Way, Manchester M3 7BF	Sam Pole
Commercial	

Yap Films	**0113-243 7100**
141 Kirkstall Road	Fax 0113-234 3421
Leeds LS3 1JJ	Pauline Duffy
Television	

Yellow Communications	**01254-246160**
Field Barn, Old Langho Road	Guy Middleton
Blackburn, Lancs BB6 8AW	
Corporate	

Young Films	**020-7292 8716**
15 Greek Street	Christopher Young
London W1D 4DP	
Feature	

YTKO	**01223-421470**
St Johns Innovation Centre	Fax 01223-421471
Cowley Road, Cambridge CB4 0WS	Peter White
Corporate	

Zafer Associates	**020-7723 0106**
47-48 Chagford Street	Fax 020-7724 6163
London NW1 6EB	Alan Zafer
Corporate	

Zanzibar Film Productions	**01425-472892**
30 Meadow Road	Fax 01425-472892
Ringwood, Hants BH24 1RU	Chris Bradley
Feature	

Zap Productions	**020-7580 6900**
37 Great Portland Street	Mark Parsons
London W1W 8QH	
Commercial	

ZCZ Films	**020-7284 0521**
Linton House	Fax 020-7267 1225
39-51 Highgate Road, London NW5 1RS	Waldemar Januszczak
Television	

Zenith Corporate Communications	**020-8675 4455**
41 Balham High Road	Fax 020-8673 9585
London SW12 9AN	Deborah Roslund
Corporate	

Zephyr Films	**020-7255 3555**
33 Percy Street	Fax 020-7255 3777
London W1T 2DF	Chris Curling
Feature	

Zeppotron	**0870-333 1700**
Shepherds Building Central	Fax 0870-333 1800
Charecroft Way, London W14 0EE	
Television	

Zig Zag Productions	**020-7017 8755**
13-14 Great Sutton Street	Fax 020-7017 8750
London EC1V 0BX	Nicola Ellis
Television	

Zip TV	**029-2021 0889**
109 Heol Isaf	Richard Pawelko
Cardiff CF15 8DW	
Television	

ZKK	**020-7482 5885**
152-156 Kentish Town Road	Fax 020-7482 5884
London NW1 9QB	Colleen Hannah
Television	

Zygon Films	**01798-869452**
Burton Mill House, Burton Park Road	Fax 01798-869429
Petworth, W Sussex GU28 0JR	Stephen White
Television	

PRODUCTION DESIGN

AllSet	**020-8665 6566**
Unit 41, Neville Court	Fax 020-8665 6566
Neville Road, Croydon, Surrey CR0 2DS	Richard Ward

Anna Burns Studio	**07905-890514**
Shop 81	
81 Goldsmiths Row, London E2 8QR	

Art Department	**020-7372 3701**
Chase 55	Fax 020-7657 4141
55 Chase Road, London NW10 6LU	Michael Mulligan
www.michaelmulligan.net	

Department Purple	**020-8451 0213**
104 Brondesbury Park	Fax 020-8830 4330
London NW2 5JR	Russell de Rozario

Design Arrival	**020-7739 2758**
12 Waterson Street	Fax 020-7739 2821
London E2 8HL	Matt Gates

Design For Film	**01753-785295**
Pinewood Studios, Pinewood Road	Fax 01753-785929
Iver Heath, Bucks SL0 0NH	Daniel Rogers
www.designforfilm.net	

E & P Associates	**020-7278 4272**
52 Berwick Street	Fax 020-7437 8176
London W1F 8SL	Rob Machin

Einsteins Octopus	**020-8985 9850**
22 Clapton Square	Tony Pletts
London E5 8HP	

Elemental Design	**020-7733 7793**
Shakespeare Business Centre	Fax 020-7733 0883
245A Coldharbour Lane, London SW9 8RR	Gary Porter

eye-catching design	**020-8973 3933**
Teddington Studios, Broom Road	Fax 020-8973 3939
Teddington, Middx TW11 9NT	Nik Callan

FDI - Film Design International	**01753-651700**
Pinewood Studios, Pinewood Road	Terry Ackland-Snow
Iver Heath, Bucks SL0 0NH	
www.filmdi.com	

The FX Team	**07956-520901**
1 Tregaron Avenue	John Mackie
London N8 9HA	

Hedz	**0845-838 7358**
The Custard Factory	Stuart Styles
Gibb Street, Birmingham B9 4AA	

Ian Fogden Design	**020-7821 0888**
149A Grosvenor Road	Fax 020-7834 9470
London SW1V 3JY	Ian Fogden

Ingenius Productions	**020-8971 7888**
Unit 16, Wimbledon Stadium Business Centre	Fax 020-8947 2616
Riverside Road, London SW17 0BA	Mike McMillan

Red Rhino	**020-8854 4472**
Fairlawn, Ashwood Road	Fax 01483-750415
Woking, Surrey GU22 7JN	Jane Cecchi

S2 Events	**020-7928 5474**
3-5 Valentine Place	Fax 020-7928 6082
London SE1 8QH	Wolter Dammers
www.s2events.co.uk	

Set To Set	**020-8677 0100**
6A Greyhound Lane	Fax 020-8677 0100
London SW16 5SD	Simon Godfrey

T: +44 (0) 20 8567 6655
W: www.ealingstudios.com

Wizzard	020-7287 2356
Europa House	Fax 020-7734 7597
54 Great Marlborough Street, London WIF 7JU	Sharn Holland

PRODUCTION MANAGEMENT & CONSULTANCY

Ewart Needham Broadcast Consultant	01656-881068
West Farm	Fax 01656-880152
Southerndown, Mid Glam CF32 0PY	Ewart Needham

Help Unlimited	01932-592364
Shepperton Studios, Studios Road	Fax 01932-569527
Shepperton, Middx TW17 0QD	Vicki Manning

International Movie Management	020-8788 5152
28 Dover Park Drive	Nigel Wooll
London SW15 5BG	

Lionel Strutt	020-7437 4421
118-120 Wardour Street	Fax 020-7437 4461
London WIF 0TU	Lionel Strutt
www.mayflowerstudios.com	

Olsberg SPI	020-7402 1300
4 Junction Mews	Fax 020-7402 6111
London W2 IPN	Olsberg Jonathan

Personnel Advisory Services	0118-986 0244
9 Selsey Way, Lower Earley	Fax 0118-931 4334
Reading, Berks RG6 4DL	Gareth Morgan

Planispheres	020-7602 2038
Sinclair House	Malcolm Moore
2 Sinclair Gardens, London W14 0AT	

PRODUCTION OFFICES

3 Mills Studios	020-7363 3336
Three Mill Lane	Fax 0871-594 4028
London E3 3DU	Melanie Faulkner
www.3mills.com	

Canalot Studios	020-8960 8580
222 Kensal Road	Fax 020-8960 8907
London W10 5BN	Barbara Acheampong

The Custard Factory	0121-224 7777
Gibb Street	Fax 0121-604 8888
Birmingham B9 4AA	

Ealing Studios	020-8567 6655
Ealing Green	Fax 020-8758 8658
London W5 5EP	John Abbott
www.ealingstudios.com	

MEPC Leavesden	01923-894400
Estate Office, 5 Hercules Way	Fax 01923-894555
Leavesden Park, Herts WD25 7GS	Anna Murkowski

Park Royal Partnership	020-3110 2300
Monarch House	Fax 020-3110 2301
Victoria Road, London W3 6UR	Rena Kazinou

The Sharp Project	0161-205 5508
Thorp Road	John Mariner
Manchester M40 5BJ	

Studio Alba	01851-701125
54A Seaforth Road	Fax 01851-701094
Stornoway, Isle Of Lewis HS1 2SD	Willie Macleod
www.studioalba.com	

Studio81	0113-246 7390
Leeds Production Centre, Studio 81	Fax 0113-242 5261
Kirkstall Road, Leeds LS3 ILH	Martin Cook
www.leedsis.biz	

PRODUCTION SERVICES

Indian Summer Films	07000-262377
31 Camplin Street	Fax 07000-262377
London SE14 5QX	Joshua Clement

Just Shoots	0161-745 8462
4 Acton Square	Fax 0161-736 1222
The Crescent, Manchester M5 4NY	Eileen Gartside

Kream	020-7612 1770
31 Vernon Street	Sally Blackburn
London W14 0RN	

Mistral Films	020-7284 2300
31 Oval Road	Fax 020-7284 0547
London NW1 7EA	Takashi Sudo

The Production Factory	020-7395 8660
49 Neal Street	Fax 020-7379 4885
London WC2H 9PZ	Anthony Chebabo

UK Film Productions	020-7494 3337
6 Brewer Street	Fax 020-7494 3338
London WIF 0SD	David Choudhry

PROJECTION EQUIPMENT

EMF Technology	**0118-988 7647**
Unit 1A, Thurley Business Units, Pump Lane	Fax 0118-988 7651
Grazeley, Reading, Berks RG7 1LL	Julia Roberts
Event Projection	**020-7232 1748**
Unit 6, Rotherhithe Business Estate	Fax 020-7232 5063
Rotherhithe New Road, London SE16 3EH	
www.eventprojection.co.uk	
The Projection Partnership	**01787-221628**
Unit 14A, Wakes Hall Business Centre	Fax 01787-221639
Colchester Road, Wakes Colne, Essex CO6 2DY	Thomas Conlon

PROMPTING EQUIPMENT

Anthony's Autocues	**020-7373 6767**
13 Childs Place	Fax 020-7373 7748
London SW5 9RX	Anthony Jordan
www.anthonysautocues.com	
Autocue	**020-8665 2992**
Unit 3, Puma Trade Park	Fax 020-8687 4869
145 Morden Road, Mitcham, Surrey CR4 4DG	Frank Hyman
Autoscript	**020-8891 8900**
Unit 2, Heathlands Close	Fax 020-8891 8901
Twickenham, Middx TW1 4BP	Brian Larter
CueBox Bristol	**0845-880 1290**
Imagist Studios, Units 8 & 9	Fax 0845-880 1280
Second Way, Avonmouth, Bristol BS11 8DF	Jonathan Saunders
www.cuebox.com	
CueBox London	**0845-880 1270**
Unit 11, Dares Farm	Fax 0845-880 1280
Farnham Road, Ewshot, Surrey GU10 5BB	Ros Ince
www.cuebox.com	
CueBox Manchester	**0845-880 1290**
www.cuebox.com	Fax 0845-880 1280
	Stacey Bliss

CueBox Wales	**0845-880 1290**
Television Centre	Fax 0845-880 1280
Culverhouse Cross, Cardiff CF5 6XJ	Louise Jones
www.cuebox.com	
First Take Autocue	**020-8898 8807**
info@first-take.tv	Chris Myers
www.first-take.tv	
Liz McGuffie Prompting Services	**01442-843961**
Pear Tree House, Beacon Road	Liz McGuffie
Ringshall, Herts HP4 1ND	
Portaprompt	**01494-450414**
1 Spearmast Industrial Park, Lane End Road	Fax 01494-437591
Sands, High Wycombe, Bucks HP12 4JQ	Helen Kingsbury
ScotPrompt	**0131-449 2384**
194 Lanark Road West	Norma Bone
Edinburgh EH14 5NX	
Telescript Prompting	**01985-844461**
Handpost Farmhouse, Cocks Lane	Avril Voller
Maidens Green, Berks RG42 6JE	

PROMPTING EQUIPMENT SUPPLIES

Vacuum Coatings	**020-8520 5353**
66 Barrett Road	Fax 020-8520 5353
London E17 9ET	Terry Pearce
www.scientificmirrors.co.uk	

PROP FINDING & STYLING

Prop Solutions	**07870-702178**
91A Acton Lane	Maya Crome
London NW10 8UT	
Propped Up	**07956-200648**
52A Tavistock Road	Hannah Penfold
London W11 1AW	

Stylebox	**020-7729 8183**
43 Temple Street	Angelina Read
London E2 6QQ	
Unconventional Productions	**020-8450 6148**
3 Heber Road	Fax 020-8450 1574
London NW2 6AB	Louise de Ville Morel

PROPS - ACTION VEHICLES

1st AAA @ Dream Cars	**01737-765050**
82 Holmethorpe Avenue	Fax 01737-236179
Redhill, Surrey RH1 2NL	Stewart Homan
www.dreamcars.co.uk	
1st Defense Fire & Rescue Services	**01483-200911**
The South Wing, Building 140	Fax 01483-200994
Dunsfold Park, Cranleigh, Surrey GU6 8TB	Peter Edwards
www.1stdefensefire.co.uk	
1st Position Vehicles	**0870-609 3441**
27 Old Gloucester Street	John Noel
London WC1N 3XX	
www.1stpositionvehicles.co.uk	
4u2 Drive	**07947-069418**
Maytree Cottage, 34 North Street	Martin Sismey
Rothersthorpe, Northampton NN7 3JB	
70's & 80's Vehicles	**01233-714767**
MPV Windrush, Egghill Road	Deborah Holmes
Charing, Kent TN27 0HG	
99 Cars	**01923-266373**
Hyde Meadow Farm, Hyde Lane	Fax 01923-260852
Hemel Hempstead, Herts HP3 8SA	David Hammatt
www.nineninecars.com	
Aces High	**01483-200057**
Dunsfold Aerodrome, Stovolds Hill	Fax 01483-201088
Cranleigh, Surrey GU6 8TB	Mike Woodley
www.aceshigh-aviation.com	
Action @ TLO Film Services	**01753-862637**
Longclose House, Common Road	Fax 01753-841998
Eton Wick, Windsor, Berks SL4 6QY	Mark Oliver
www.tlofilmservices.tv	
Action Bus	**020-8893 5569**
90-95 Waterside Centre	Fax 020-8571 6505
Trumpers Way, London W7 2QD	Gerard Boath
www.actionbus.co.uk	
Action Cars	**01753-785690**
Pinewood Studios, Pinewood Road	Fax 01753-652027
Iver Heath, Bucks SL0 0NH	Steven Royffe
Action Classic Cars	**01883-740377**
Bransfield Cottage, Church Lane	Miles Pinniger
Godstone, Surrey RH9 8BW	

The Action Factory   **01753-656588**

Pinewood Studios, Pinewood Road   Graham Kelly
Iver Heath, Bucks SL0 0NH

Action Vehicles   **0845-888 7000**

Hangar 5, Redhill Aerodrome   Darren Litten Gary Litten
Redhill, Surrey RH1 5JY
www.actionvehicles.com

The Aircraft Restoration Company   **01223-835313**

Duxford Airfield   Fax 01223-837290
Cambridge CB22 4QR   Anna McDowell

American 50s Convertibles Car Hire   **01268-735914**

Claygate, Enfield Road   Garry Darby
Shotgate, Wickford, Essex SS11 8SD

American Dreams   **0800-848 8032**

47 Wilsons Lane, Marks Tey   Paul Nash
Colchester, Essex CO6 1HP

B & B Autos Tanks & Jeeps   **01279-871437**

The Jaguars, Dunmow Road   Fax 01279-871638
Bishops Stortford, Herts CM22 6SJ   Barry Knee

B17 Preservation   **01638-721304**

PO Box 92   Fax 01638-720506
Bury St Edmunds, Suffolk IP28 8RR   Elly Sallingboe

ACTIONBUS

Mobile 07768 164888 or 07866 493941
Works 020 8893 5569
Fax 020 8571 6505

90-95 Waterside Centre
Trumpers Way
Hanwell, London. W7

Hire of buses, trains and transport related props

Bus stops, Bus shelters,
Ticket machines, Uniforms,
Platform seats, Timetables,
Posters, Roudels,
Underground props.

WWW.ACTIONBUS.CO.UK

Bailey Balloons   **01275-375300**
44 Ham Green   Fax 01275-375660
Bristol BS20 0HA   Jo Bailey
www.baileyballoons.co.uk

Ben Ford Horses & Carriages   **01363-877766**
Higher Parks, Morchard Bishop   Maria Bisset
Crediton, Devon EX17 6NW

Bettys Classic & Vintage Cars & Bikes   **07727-653363**
Courtlands Stables, Chamlers Road   Jessica Lynch
Banstead, Surrey SM7 3HF

Bianchi Aviation Film Services   **01494-449810**
Wycombe Air Park, Booker   Fax 01494-461236
Marlow, Bucks SL7 3DP   Tony Bianchi

Bicycles Unlimited   **0121-350 0685**
522 Holly Lane   Doug Pinkerton
Erdington, Birmingham B24 9LY

Big Boys & Their Toys   **01642-645645**
Handley Cross, Leven Bank   Fax 01642-645647
Yarm, Stockton-on-Tees, N Yorks TS15 9JL   Bill Bates

Bikes On Film   **020-8877 9922**
5 St Georges Court   Fax 020-8870 5533
131 Putney Bridge Road, London SW15 2PA   Mark George

Burts Cycles   **020-8979 2124**
77-79 High Street   Fax 020-8941 7612
Hampton Hill, Middx TW12 1NH   Roger Hitchman
www.burtscycles.co.uk

Bygone Transport Services   **01274-881640**
42 Coniston Avenue, Queensbury   Fax 0870-094 0075
Bradford, W Yorks BD13 2JD   Keith Jenkinson

Caristhestar   **01482-881881**
8 Short Hill   Tony Wilson
Beverley, E Yorks HU17 8NY

Carriages Vehicle Agency   **01737-373737**
147 Nork Way   Fax 01737-353926
Banstead, Surrey SM7 1HR   Norman Hodkinson

Cars For Stars   **01883-742822**
Days Garage, Ivy Park   David Stamp
Ivy Mill Lane, Godstone, Surrey RH8 9NT

Cars Of The Stars   **01768-772090**
Standish Street   Peter Nelson
Keswick, Cumbria CA12 5LS

Centaur Horsedrawn Carriages   **01869-349000**
The Old Dairy   Andy Spatcher
Duns Tew, Oxon OX25 6JS

The Classic Car Shop   **01672-511911**
Cadley Garage, Cadley   Fax 01672-511755
Marlborough, Wilts SN8 4NE   Jonathan Horsley

Classic Hot Air Ballooning   **01622-858956**
1 Home Farm Cottages, Lenham Heath Road   Fax 01622-853817
Sandway, Maidstone, Kent ME17 2HX   Glen Everett

Cravens Classic Motorcycles   **01904-400493**
Brockfield Villa   Fax 01904-400493
Stockton-on-the-Forest, York YO32 9UE   Dick Craven

Cumbria Classic Coaches   **01539-623254**
Bowber Head, Ravenstonedale   Fax 01539-623254
Kirkby Stephen, Cumbria CA17 4NL   Alison Morris

The Devils Horsemen   **01296-720854**
Wychwood Stud, Salden   Fax 01296-720855
Mursley, Bucks MK17 0HX   Gerard Naprous
www.thedevilshorsemen.com

Donovans Ice Cream Vans   **020-8472 7932**
61-65 Grangewood Street   Fax 020-8821 9001
London E6 1HB   Margaret Donovan

Dreamcarhire   **0844-800 0195**
Unit 1C, Whitehorse Business Park   Fax 01367-710480
Ware Road, Stanford-in-the-Vale, Oxon SN7 8NY   Tony Rodia

ELS Action   **020-8599 1318**
James Lovell Business Park, Selinas Lane   Fax 020-8599 1318
Dagenham, Essex RM8 1RX   Paul Weller
www.elsaction.com

LA Stretch Limos	**020-8554 9292**
115 Beehive Lane	Fax 020-8554 9393
Gants Hill, Essex IG1 3RW	Carl Westwood
Lambo Genie	**01254-854414**
Carr Wood Business Centre, Higher Walton	Fax 01254-915709
Preston, Lancs PR5 4EL	Chris Regan
The Left Hand Drive Place	**01256-461173**
Whitney Road, Daneshill	Fax 01256-811541
Basingstoke, Hants RG24 8NS	Maggie Woodhouse
Locamotion	**07958-700160**
Pippingford Manor, Pippingford Park	Andy Ellis
Nutley, E Sussex TN22 3HW	
www.locamotion.com	
The London Cab Company	**020-8530 1578**
49 Raymond Avenue	Fax 020-8530 1578
London E18 2HF	Gary Zylberszac
www.thelondoncabcompany.com	
London Classic Bus Hire	**01474-353896**
Grove Road	Fax 01474-358475
North Fleet, Kent DA11 9AX	Susan Mee
London Recumbents - Bikes	**020-8299 6636**
Rangers Yard, Dulwich Park	Fax 020-8299 6636
College Road, London SE21 7BQ	Nigel Frost
Marine Film Services	**020-8224 9246**
15 Church Road	Fax 020-8224 9265
East Molesey, Surrey KT8 9DR	Richard Carless
www.marinefilm.co.uk	
Media Bus Hire	**07860-332339**
19 Greenway, Harold Park	Fax 020-8651 1051
Romford, Essex RM3 0HH	Tony Peters
Memory Lane Vintage Omnibus	**01628-825050**
78 Lillibrooke Crescent	Mike Clarke
Maidenhead, Berks SL6 3XQ	
Mercator Military Vehicles	**01634-370883**
Bowen House, Bredgar Road	Fax 01634-263328
Gillingham, Kent ME8 6PL	Les Langridge
MGM Cars	**020-8324 2664**
Elstree Studios, Shenley Road	Fax 020-8324 2345
Borehamwood, Herts WD6 1JG	Ben Dillon Tom Dillon
www.mgmcars.com	
Midland Fire Protection Services	**024-7636 7766**
Unit 6	Fax 024-7645 0923
Bayton Way, Coventry CV7 9ER	Liam Smith
www.midlandfire.co.uk	
Modded Motors	**07737-598184**
10 Chalfont House, Chenies Way	Danny Cross
Watford, Herts WD18 6UR	
Moore Large & Co	**01332-274200**
Sinfin Industrial Estate, Sinfin Lane	Fax 01332-274203
Sinfin, Derbys DE24 9GL	Gary Mather

Bushwood Antiques	01582-794700
Stags Head Equestrian Centre, Gaddesden Lane	Fax 01582-792299
Redbourn, Herts HP2 6HN	Anthony Bush

Camden Attic	0117-941 1969
Location House	Fax 0117-955 2480
5 Dove Lane, Bristol BS2 9HP	Gene Lowson

Casper Slieker	020-7751 5577
Studio 1	Fax 020-7751 5577
65-69 Lots Road, London SW10 0RN	Casper Slieker

Castle Gibson	020-8211 8690
18A/B Manor Road	Fax 020-8211 8690
London N16 5SA	Joyce Gibson Jackie Marshall
www.castlegibson.com	

Catering Linen Hire	020-8575 1844
Unit E7, Aladdin Business Centre	Fax 020-8575 9025
Long Drive, Greenford, Middx UB6 8UH	Maureen Cooper
www.cateringlinenhire.co.uk	

Celtic Prop Hire	029-2068 9686
Units 52-53, Lambourne Crescent	Fax 029-2068 9910
Cardiff Business Park, Llanishen, Cardiff CF14 5GG	Sian Bundy

Chase 55 Accessories	0871-231 0900
55 Chase Road	Fax 020-8965 8107
London NW10 6LU	Andy Wills
www.chase55.com	

Chase 55 Furniture	0871-231 0900
55 Chase Road	Fax 020-8965 8107
London NW10 6LU	Tony Hardacre
www.chase55.com	

Cheekytiki	020-7241 0742
Unit C	Anjy Cameron Jamie Wilson
2 Leswin Place, London N16 7NJ	
www.cheekytiki.com	

China & Co Props Hire	020-8740 9588
2C Macfarlane Road	Fax 020-8740 8873
London W12 7JY	Paula Webster
www.chinaandco.com	

Chinasearch	01926-512402
4 Princes Drive	Fax 01926-859311
Kenilworth, Warwicks CV8 2FD	David Ward
www.chinasearch.co.uk	

City Furniture	01733-208162
Unit 3A, 35 Benwick Road	Fax 01733-205784
Whittlesey, Cambs PE7 2HD	Martin Wilson

Clockprops.com	020-8944 0473
Unit 11, Wimbledon Stadium Business Centre	Fax 020-8947 3752
Riverside Road, London SW17 0BA	Roger Lascelles
www.clockprops.com	

Clutter Props   **020-8961 9556**
Unit B2   Fax 020-8961 9229
St Leonards Road, London NW10 6ST   George Francis

Compuhire   **020-3137 0599**
mark@compuhire.com   Fax 020-8819 6010
www.compuhire.com   Mark Jordan

David Edmonds   **020-8453 1112**
The Old Sub Station   David Edmonds
Acton Lane, London NW10 8UR

De Parma   **020-7736 3384**
Core 1, The Gas Works
2 Michael Road, London SW6 2AD

Design Matters Furniture Hire   **0118-978 7666**
10 Twycross Road   Fax 0118-978 7999
Wokingham, Berks RG40 5PE   David Dyche

Don Speake & Co   **020-8992 8668**
49 Churchfield Road   Fax 020-8992 8678
London W3 6AY   Eileen Driscoll
www.donspeake.4t.com

DR Prop Supplies   **028-9081 3700**
Unit 2, Edgar Industrial Estate   Fax 028-9081 3707
Comber Road, Carryduff, Co Down BT8 8AN   Paul Fitzsimons

Chase55.com

55 Miles of set solutions
250,000 sq ft
2,000,000 productions

Trading Post - always a great deal

Theatricks	**01994-419723**
Swn-y-Gan, Cefn-y-Pant	Karl Evans
Llanboidy, Carmarthens SA34 0TR	
www.theatricks.co.uk	
Theme Traders	**020-8452 8518**
The Stadium	Fax 020-8450 7322
Oaklands Road, London NW2 6DL	David Jamilly
www.themetraders.com	
Thorns Group	**020-8801 4444**
Unit C	Fax 020-8801 4445
125 Brantwood Road, London N17 0DX	Claire Whitecross
Trading Post	**020-8903 3727**
1 Beresford Avenue	Fax 020-8900 2565
Wembley, Middx HA0 1NU	Tim Oake
www.tradingposthire.co.uk	
Trevor Howsam	**020-8838 6166**
182 Acton Lane	Fax 020-8838 6167
London NW10 7NH	Marcus Howsam
www.retrowallpaper.co.uk	
Trevor Howsam	**01205-356010**
The Granary, Grove Street East	Fax 01205-366411
Boston, Lincs PE21 6TE	Trevor Howsam Tim Howsam
www.retrowallpaper.co.uk	
Unique Glass International	**01621-850058**
Station Road	Fax 01621-840219
Maldon, Essex CM9 4LQ	Paul Antony
Vintage By Zana	**0844-884 8569**
60 Asker Lane	Sarah Marsh Graupera
Matlock, Derbys DE4 5LA	
Vintage Touch	**028-9042 1990**
10 Park Avenue	Laura Menary
Holywood, Co Down BT18 9LS	
Walpole Bay Hotel	**01843-221703**
Fifth Avenue, Cliftonville	Fax 01483-297399
Margate, Kent CT9 2JJ	Jane Bishop
www.walpolebayhotel.co.uk	

Wimbledon Sewing Machines	**020-8767 4724**
292-312 Balham High Road	Fax 020-8767 4726
London SW17 7AA	Warren Rushton
Woodmans World	**01666-824932**
Wayside, Tetbury Hill Gardens	Fax 01666-824932
Malmesbury, Wilts SN16 9JP	Carl Sadler
www.woodmansworld.co.uk	

PROPS - FUTURISTIC

Bob's Bits	**01442-400588**
56 Beechfield Road	Fax 01442-400588
Hemel Hempstead, Herts HP1 1PP	Bob Thorne
www.bobsbits.tv	
The Stockyard	**020-8963 9944**
Unit A, Genesis	Fax 020-8963 9955
Rainsford Road, London NW10 7RG	Ron Painter
www.stockyard.tv	

PROPS - GAMING & CASINO EQUIPMENT

Ace Of Diamonds	**01277-841011**
Unit 1-2, Kings Head Business Park	Karl Rank
Stock Road, Ingatestone, Essex CM4 9PH	
Cabaret Casino Associates	**0845-000 8007**
Ten Acre Farm, Stonehill Road	Fax 0870-754 5545
Ottershaw, Surrey KT16 0AQ	Les Squires Mikael Brown
www.cabaretcasino.co.uk	
Glen Francis Poker Events	**07734-721129**
26 York Street	Glen Francis
London W1U 6PZ	
Viva Vegas Casino Hire	**020-7820 0999**
144A Old South Lambeth Road	Fax 020-7820 0998
London SW8 1XX	David Gant
www.viva-vegas.co.uk	

PROPS - GOLD PLATING

City Gold Plating	**020-7831 8825**
City House	Fax 020-7242 1403
72-80 Leather Lane, London EC1N 7TR	Manny Good

PROPS - GOVERNMENT SURPLUS

Anchor Supplies	**01773-570139**
Peasehill Road	Fax 01773-570537
Ripley, Derbys DE5 3JG	Alison Knight

FNG Supplies	**01344-451563**
PO Box 3513	Lee Money
Bracknell, Berks RG12 7XL	
H & M Sales	**07973-627988**
Templewood Estate, Stock Road	Matt Turnidge
West Hanningfield, Chelmsford, Essex CM2 8LA	
www.hmsales.co.uk	
The Stockyard	**020-8963 9944**
Unit A, Genesis	Fax 020-8963 9955
Rainsford Road, London NW10 7RG	Ron Painter
www.stockyard.tv	

PROPS - GRAPHIC

Acme Graphics	**020-8395 5130**
35 Wick Road	Fax 020-8395 5129
Teddington, Middx TW11 9DN	Nick Hellman
www.acmegraphics.co.uk	
Coloursonic	**020-7286 4766**
40 Chippenham Mews	Fax 020-7286 1139
London W9 2AW	Paul Chandler
Data Reprographics	**01784-243996**
Unit 1, West Surrey Estate	Fax 01784-256290
Ashford Road, Ashford, Middx TW15 1XB	John Lindsay
www.datarepro.co.uk	
Design 108	**07831-866979**
The Pie Factory, 101 Broadway	Stephen Bradshaw
Salford Quays, Manchester M50 2EQ	
www.design108.tv	
Digital Ceramic Systems	**01782-512843**
The Old School House, Outclough Road	Fax 01782-517026
Brindley Ford, Stoke-on-Trent, Staffs ST4 2EJ	Stuart Jones
Euan MacGregor Calligraphy	**01323-641008**
School House, College Road	Euan MacGregor
Eastbourne, E Sussex BN21 4JH	
Eyecandy Art Group	**01628-785206**
2 St Peters Road	Fax 01628-639194
Maidenhead, Berks SL6 7QU	Mark Blackburn
www.eyecandyartgroup.com	
Handwritten Letters & Documents	**01626-833975**
41 Mary Street	Susanne Haines
Bovey Tracey, Devon TQ13 9HQ	
Keir Lusby Props	**01932-561717**
Shepperton Studios, Studios Road	Fax 01932-565898
Shepperton, Middx TW17 0QD	Keir Lusby
www.keirlusby.com	
Mina Lima	**07770-887234**
7 Goodge Place	07962-077635
London W1T 4SF	Miraphora Mina Eduardo Lima
www.minalima.com	

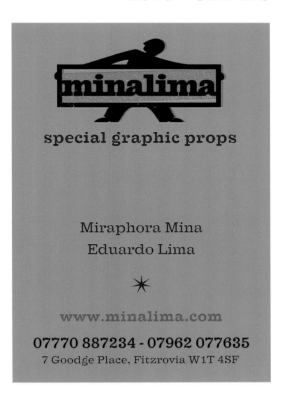

Paul Antonio Scribe   020-7720 8883

Studio 6C, Clapham North Arts Centre   Paul Antonio
26-32 Voltaire Road, London SW4 6DH

Photographics   01923-894591

Unit 5, Hill Farm Avenue Industrial Estate   Fax 01923-894599
Leavesden, Herts WD25 7SD   David Holmes

Printed Word   020-8965 4044

Unit 9, Europa Studios   Fax 020-8965 4089
Victoria Road, London NW10 6ND   Barbara Horne
www.printed-word.co.uk

richindesign   07788-441432

27 Braycourt Avenue   Richard Lloyd-Jones
Walton-on-Thames, Surrey KT12 2AZ

Soda Art   0845-644 0212

Somerset House, Somerset Road   Mark Crowther
Teddington, Middx TW11 8RL

PROPS - GREENERY & FLOWERS

Act On Impulse Flowers   020-8896 0222

1A King Street   Hazel Jordan
London W3 9LA

Amazon Exhibitions & Landscapes   020-7371 4664

The Old Forge, Wendens Ambo   Fax 01799-542055
Saffron Walden, Essex CB11 4JL   Jane Somerville

Ambius   0800-037 0128

Ebony House, Castlegate Way   Fax 0121-521 2294
Dudley, W Midlands DY1 4TA

Artificial Grass Solutions   0845-603 5751

Unit 1C, South March   Libby Parratt
Long March Industrial Estate, Daventry, Northants NN11 4PH

Avant Gardener   020-7978 4253

16 Winders Road   James Fraser
London SW11 3HE

Burston Nurseries   01727-853015

North Orbital Road   Fax 01727-844244
St Albans, Herts AL2 2DS   Paul Young

Clapro Bamboo   020-8949 4963

2A Sussex Road   Fax 020-8949 7517
New Malden, Surrey KT3 3PY   Ian Cave

Clifton Nurseries   020-7289 6851

5A Clifton Villas   Fax 020-7286 4215
London W9 2PH   Stephen Davis

Deedman Tropical Plant Hire   01204-577000

Deedman House, 3K Longcauseway   Fax 01204-577770
Kearsley, Bolton, Lancs BL4 9BS   Butch Deedman
www.deedman.co.uk

Detta Phillips Floral Design	**020-7498 2728**
274 Queenstown Road	Fax 020-7498 8805
London SW8 4LP	Emma Harvey
The Dutch Nursery	**01707-653372**
Great North Road, Brookmans Park	Fax 01707-647196
Hatfield, Herts AL9 6ND	Richard Henn
EFG	**01789-470847**
The Tree House	Fax 01789-470897
Charlecote, Warwicks CV35 9GZ	Clare Holloway
Egmont Water Garden Centre	**020-8337 9605**
132 Tolworth Rise South	Fax 020-8330 6916
Surbiton, Surrey KT5 9NJ	James Sadler
Fake Landscapes	**020-7835 1500**
164 Old Brompton Road	Fax 020-7370 6895
London SW5 0BA	Shaun Skelly
Filmscapes	**020-8398 9151**
Ditton Nursery, Summerfield Lane	Fax 020-8398 6260
Surbiton, Surrey KT6 5DZ	Lucinda Mclean
www.filmscapes.co.uk	
Flirty	**020-8960 9191**
9 Halstow Road	Amanda Willgrave
London NW10 5DB	

Floral Symphonies by Nichlas Vilsmark   **0844-561 7670**

Unit 109, Saga Centre	Fax 07092-866482
326 Kensal Road, London W10 5BZ	Nichlas Vilsmark
www.floralsymphonies.com	

Florally Yours   **07904-517205**

10 Hawthorne Farm Avenue	Fax 020-8965 8107
Northolt, Middx UB5 5QG	Kerry McLoughlin
www.florallyyours.com	

Forestry Commission   **01483-326261**

Bucks Horn Oak	07778-110349
Farnham, Surrey GU10 4LS	Pam Eastwood
www.forestry.gov.uk	

Hanging Garden   **01256-880647**

Wildmoor Lane, Sherfield-on-Loddon	Fax 01256-880651
Hook, Hants RG27 0JD	Nick Kirby

Hiden Floral Design   **020-7224 0564**

26 Paddington Street	Marco Arrichiello
London W1U 5QY	

Isabella   **020-8876 9640**

203 Upper Richmond Road West	Fax 020-8876 9800
London SW14 8QT	Micaela Quinn

ISS Waterers Landscape   **0845-057 6200**

ISS House, Genesis Business Park	Fax 0871-429 6200
Albert Drive, Woking, Surrey GU21 5RW	Jeremy Schomberg

Jayne Copperwaite Flowers   **020-8675 1888**

Unit 15, Zennor Road Industrial Estate	Fax 0560-125 7382
Zennor Road, London SW12 0PS	Jayne Copperwaite
www.jaynecopperwaiteflowers.com	

Jenny Tobin Flowers (Period Modern Silk)   **07802-338599**

1-3 Telford Way	Fax 01628-476126
London W3 7XS	Jenny Tobin
www.jennytobinflowers.co.uk	

Living Props   **01895-835100**

Sevenhills Road	Fax 01895-835757
Iver Heath, Bucks SL0 0PA	Karen Maychell Michael Lambert
www.livingprops.co.uk	

Millfields   **01702-554981**

Solbys Lane, Hadleigh	Fax 01702-554981
Benfleet, Essex SS7 2NG	Peter Brackin

Orlando Hamilton Floral Design   **020-8962 8944**

59 St Helens Gardens	Orlando Hamilton
London W10 6LN	

Palmbrokers   **01628-663734**

Cenacle Nursery, Taplow Common Road	Fax 01628-661047
Burnham, Bucks SL1 8NW	Mat Campbell Steve Taylor
www.palmbrokers.com	

Paul Bromfield Aquatics   **01462-457399**

Maydencroft Lane, Gosmore	Fax 01462-422652
Hitchin, Herts SG4 7QD	Deborah Edwards

Peter Dowle Plants & Gardens	**01531-820345**
The Old Malt House, High Street	Fax 01531-820382
Newent, Glos GL18 1AY	Peter Dowle

Peter Harvey Floral Art Products	**01494-533244**
Unit 1, Hughenden Avenue	Fax 01494-443222
High Wycombe, Bucks HP13 5FT	Darren Broxup

The Plant People	**020-8398 8813**
Ditton Nursery, Summerfield Lane	Fax 020-8398 8814
Surbiton, Surrey KT6 5DZ	Malcolm Smith

Rebel Rebel	**020-7254 4487**
5 Broadway Market	Fax 020-7254 4438
London E8 4PH	Mai Read

Roger Radish	**01202-735022**
27A Vale Road, Parkstone	Roger Holden
Poole, Dorset BH14 9AT	

RVH Floral Design	**020-7720 6774**
8 Tun Yard	Fax 020-7720 9568
Peardon Street, London SW8 3HT	Zelica Ensah

Sells First Impressions	**020-7720 9070**
Units 72-74, Flower Market	Fax 020-7720 4186
New Covent Garden, London SW8 5NJ	Jenty Whitbread

The Silk Forest	**01530-231241**
Main Street	Fax 01530-231240
Bagworth, Leics LE67 1DN	Graham Aldred Judi Robinson
www.thesilkforest.com	

Sophie Hanna Flowers	**020-7720 0841**
Arch 49	Fax 020-7720 1756
New Covent Garden, London SW8 5PP	Sophie Hanna

Sugavision Cannabis Props	**07968-754813**
190 Dumbarton Court	Marko Waschke
Brixton Hill, London SW2 5LR	

Theme Traders	**020-8452 8518**
The Stadium	Fax 020-8450 7322
Oaklands Road, London NW2 6DL	David Jamilly
www.themetraders.com	

TopiaryHire.co.uk	**020-7125 0215**
London Head Office & Depot	
Unit 439, 40 Warren Street, London W1T 6AF	
www.topiaryhire.co.uk	

TopiaryHire.co.uk	**01279-876300**
South East Office & Depot	Fax 0845-230 6009
Bretts, Chelmsford Road	Dan Parker-Bowles
White Roding, Great Dunmow, Essex CM6 1RF	
www.topiaryhire.co.uk	

TopiaryHire.co.uk	**0845-230 6008**
Midlands Office & Depot	
Tweeds Nursery, Priory Dumble, Priory Road	
Thurgarton, Nottingham NG14 7GT	
www.topiaryhire.co.uk	

Trulawn - Artificial Grass Experts	**01252-819695**
sales@trulawn.co.uk	Ian Parry
www.trulawn.co.uk	

Veevers Carter	**020-7237 8800**
Units B3 & B4, Galleywall Road Trading Estate	Fax 020-7237 7788
Galleywall Road, London SE16 3PB	Hilda Carr

Wild At Heart	**020-7229 1174**
54 Pimlico Road	Fax 020-7792 8302
London SW1W 8LP	Kirsty Frost

Worlds End Nurseries	**020-7351 3343**
441-457 Kings Road	James Lotery
London SW10 0LR	

PROPS - INDUSTRIAL

Bob's Bits	**01442-400588**
56 Beechfield Road	Fax 01442-400588
Hemel Hempstead, Herts HP1 1PP	Bob Thorne
www.bobsbits.tv	

Men At Work	**020-8893 5569**
90-95 Waterside Centre	Fax 020-8571 6505
Trumpers Way, London W7 2QD	Gerard Boath
www.menatwork.co.uk www.americanprops.co.uk	

The Stockyard	**020-8963 9944**
Unit A, Genesis	Fax 020-8963 9955
Rainsford Road, London NW10 7RG	Ron Painter
www.stockyard.tv	

PROPS - INFLATABLES

Airtechs	**01986-835724**
Unit 18, Halesworth Business Centre	Fax 01986-874466
Norwich Road, Halesworth, Suffolk IP19 8QJ	Isobel Harries

Art Of Air	**0845-644 1568**
Holly Tree Farm	Fax 0845-166 2596
Newton Poppleford, Devon EX10 0BZ	Dave Taylor

Baconinflate	**01604-766500**
20 Osyth Close	Fax 01604-760890
Brackmills Industrial Estate, Northampton NN4 7DY	Gary Bennett

Bubblehouse	**020-8854 5236**
61B 4th Floor, 2 Faraday Way	Fax 020-8854 5236
Westminster Industrial Estate, London SE18 5TR	Gareth Whitham

Lucid Productions	**020-7739 0240**
407 Greenheath Business Centre	Fax 020-7739 0240
3 Golds Lane, London E2 6JB	Chas Branson

Party Plus	**020-8994 1674**
4 Acton Lane	Stephen Wilson
London W4 5NB	
www.partyplus.co.uk	

PROPS - KITCHENS

Home Economist Prop Hire   01932-592364

Shepperton Studios, Studios Road   Fax 01932-569527
Shepperton, Middx TW17 0QD   John Manning
www.home-economist.co.uk

Park Royal Salvage   020-8961 3627

Lower Place Wharf   Fax 020-8961 3627
Acton Lane, London NW10 7AB   Ray Cullup
www.parkroyalsalvage.co.uk

PROPS - LIGHTING

Ancient Lights & Props   01932-570652

Hardwick Park Farm, Hardwick Lane   Fax 01932-570652
Lyne, Surrey KT16 0AA   Claire Grainger
www.ancientlightsandprops.co.uk

Bodomo Chandeliers   0845-643 2047

Anvil House, Kingsingfield Road   Richard Sekula
West Kingsdown, Kent TN15 6LJ

Farley   020-8749 9925

1-17 Brunel Road   Fax 020-8749 8372
London W3 7XR   Mark Farley
www.farley.co.uk

Mirrorball Paul   07989-522871

                                                Paul Cornwall

Newman Hire Company   020-8743 0741

Lewis Scher House   Fax 020-8749 3513
16 The Vale, London W3 7SB   Terry Poole Raven King
www.newmanhire.co.uk

Party Lights   020-8892 3444

Saville House, 2 Saville Road   Richard Sawkins
Twickenham, Middx TW1 4BQ

Shok London   0871-282 0500

34 Riggindale Road   Graham Jones
London SW16 1QJ

The Stockyard   020-8963 9944

Unit A, Genesis   Fax 020-8963 9955
Rainsford Road, London NW10 7RG   Ron Painter
www.stockyard.tv

PROPS - MEDICAL & SCIENTIFIC

Bob's Bits   01442-400588

56 Beechfield Road   Fax 01442-400588
Hemel Hempstead, Herts HP1 1PP   Bob Thorne
www.bobsbits.tv

Colco Scientific   01932-349141

6 Peatmore Close   Fax 01932-349141
Woking, Surrey GU22 8TQ   Colin Shandley

Curious Science   020-8961 3113

Units 5 & 7   Fax 020-8961 7427
Commercial Way, London NW10 7XF   David Burns
www.curiousscience.com

Film Medical Services   020-8961 3222

Units 5 & 7   Fax 020-8961 7427
Commercial Way, London NW10 7XF   Erskine Berry
www.filmmedical.co.uk

Gillian Gould Antiques   020-8458 7675

38 Denman Drive South   Gillian Gould
London NW11 6RH

Medinet Film Hire   0800-281912

Unit 18, Park Royal Business Centre   Fax 020-8694 1880
9-17 Park Royal Road, London NW10 7LQ   Dr Anthony MacDermott
www.medinetfilmhire.com

Mediprop   0161-344 1234

21 Peterborough Close   Fax 0161-330 3084
Ashton-under-Lyne, Lancs OL6 8XW   Jonathan Carter
www.mediprop.com

Mediscene   07973-385654

9 Croffets   Fax 07977-112152
Tadworth, Surrey KT20 5TX   Carlton Jarvis
www.mediscene.co.uk

ARTHOUSE|HIRE

Clearance-free art collection for the Film and TV industry
Studio 10, Europa Studios, Victoria Road, London, NW10 6ND
T: 020 8838 0436   F: 020 8453 0920   www.arthousehire.com

Bobo Funn Co	**020-8991 5666**
Unit 5, Nagi Business Centre	Fax 020-8991 5888
Marsh Road, Wembley, Middx HA0 1ES	Harmesh Sethi
Farley	**020-8749 9925**
1-17 Brunel Road	Fax 020-8749 8372
London W3 7XR	Mark Farley
www.farley.co.uk	
Funky Floors	**01702-556878**
34 Homestead Gardens	Fax 01702-711808
Hadleigh, Essex SS7 2AB	Matt Letley
Lewis & Kaye	**020-8749 2121**
1-17 Brunel Road	Fax 020-8749 9455
London W3 7XR	Mark Allday
www.farley.co.uk	
Mentzendorff & Co	**020-7840 3600**
Prince Consort House	Fax 020-7840 3601
27-29 Albert Embankment, London SE1 7TJ	Chloe Craven
www.mentzendorff.co.uk	
Non-Stop Party Shop	**01932-864452**
35 High Street	Fax 01932-868660
Cobham, Surrey KT11 3DP	Nick Pearce
Party Plus	**020-8994 1674**
4 Acton Lane	Stephen Wilson
London W4 5NB	
www.partyplus.co.uk	
Partymoods	**020-8931 1234**
250 Greenford Avenue	07748-727082
London W7 3AA	Suresh Nath
www.partymoods.com	
PartyWorks	**01403-865000**
North Lodge, 122 Cowfold Road	James Feary
West Grinstead, W Sussex RH13 8LU	
The Stockyard	**020-8963 9944**
Unit A, Genesis	Fax 020-8963 9955
Rainsford Road, London NW10 7RG	Ron Painter
www.stockyard.tv	

Truly Scrumptious Chocolate Fountains	**020-8398 2141**
22 Greenwood Close	Fax 020-8339 0040
Thames Ditton, Surrey KT7 0BG	Brian Davey
www.trulyscrumptiouschocolatefountains.com	

PROPS - PICTURE FRAMING

Frinton Gallery Frames	**01255-673707**
80-82 Pole Barn Lane	Fax 01255-677307
Frinton-on-Sea, Essex CO13 9NH	Edward Adkins
www.frintonframes.co.uk	
J White Framing	**020-8960 2660**
489 Latimer Road	Fax 020-8960 2660
London W10 6RD	John White
Lookin' Glass	**020-8896 1920**
389 Uxbridge Road	Fax 020-8992 5779
London W3 9SA	Ken Seager
www.lookin-glass.co.uk	

PROPS - PICTURES & ART

Art4Film	**020-8795 4954**
13 Princes Court	Tanya Smijth Windham
Wembley, Middx HA9 7JJ	
Arthouse Hire	**020-8838 0436**
Studio 10, Europa Studios	Fax 020-8453 0920
Victoria Road, London NW10 6ND	Jane Henwood
www.arthousehire.com	
Eyecandy Art Group	**01628-785206**
2 St Peters Road	Fax 01628-639194
Maidenhead, Berks SL6 7QU	Mark Blackburn
www.eyecandyartgroup.com	
Lucyart	**0845-659 0660**
29 Station Road	Rob Haigh
Ossett, W Yorks WF5 8AY	
Pictures Props Company	**020-8749 2434**
Brunel House	Fax 020-8740 5846
12-16 Brunel Road, London W3 7XR	Jane Owen
www.propascene.com	
Spiller	**020-8743 8747**
1-17 Brunel Road	Fax 020-8354 1866
London W3 7XR	Simon Russell
www.farley.co.uk	

PROPS - SHOP DISPLAY & MANNEQUINS

Adel Rootstein Display Mannequins	**020-7381 1447**
9 Beaumont Avenue	Fax 020-7386 9594
London W14 9LP	Edward Stammers

BJK Shop Equipment — **020-8692 2325**

Units 3-5, Blackhorse Business Park — Fax 020-8694 2391
Blackhorse Road, London SE8 5HY — Chris Edwards
www.bjkshopequipment.co.uk

Bus Stop Mannequins — **07588-867161**

17 Hawarden Grove — Fax 020-7652 1853
London SE24 9DQ — Howard Tong
www.busstopmannequins.co.uk

Don Speake & Co — **020-8992 8668**

49 Churchfield Road — Fax 020-8992 8678
London W3 6AY — Eileen Driscoll
www.donspeake.4t.com

Exhibition & Retail Supplies (EARS)

020-8979 0358 Mobile 07773-744021
Fax 020-8224 1153
Email: eric@earsuk.com
www.earsuk.com
48 Molesham Way, West Molesey, Surrey KT8 1NX
Contact: Eric Ponsford
The hire and sale of shopfitting i.e. shelving, clothes rails,
mannequins, cheval mirrors, showcases, tailors dummies,
dump bins, etc.

Mannequin World — **0161-480 5595**

Unit 1, Ajax Works — Fax 0161-480 8320
White Hill Street, Stockport, Cheshire SK4 1NT — Mike Ball

Proportion > London — **020-7251 6943**

9 Dallington Street — Fax 020-7250 1798
London EC1V 0LN — Bianca Wint

Props Galore — **020-8746 1222**

1-17 Brunel Road — Fax 020-8354 1866
London W3 7XR — Naomi Leigh
www.farley.co.uk

PROPS - SPORTS EQUIPMENT

Academy Billiard Company — **01932-352067**

5 Camphill Industrial Estate — Fax 01932-353904
West Byfleet, Surrey KT14 6EW — Robert Donnachie
www.games-room.com

Black Country Saddles — **01922-626936**

59-61 Wednesbury Road — Nikki Newcombe
Walsall, W Midlands WS1 4JL

Farley — **020-8749 9925**

1-17 Brunel Road — Fax 020-8749 8372
London W3 7XR — Mark Farley
www.farley.co.uk

Hire Fitness — **0845-226 1233**

Unit 93, 24-28 St Leonards Road — Fax 0845-226 0068
Windsor, Berks SL4 3BB — Paul Healey

Hubble & Freeman   01622-691071
11-12 Granada House, Lower Stone Street   Fax 01622-683434
Maidstone, Kent ME15 6JP   Peter Ludgate

Ice Rink HIre   01253-827092
PO Box 57   Vivien Robinson
Poulton-Le-Fylde, Lancs FY6 8GN

Mayfair Gym Equipment Hire   020-8903 7005
Unit 20, Popin Business Centre   Fax 020-8900 2025
South Way, Wembley, Middx HA9 0HF   Barry Ditton

Ringcraft Boxing Services   0870-077 7777
Unit 21, Briar Close Business Park   Fax 01386-422617
Evesham, Worcs WR11 4JT   Mike Goodall

PROPS - STREET SCENES

Lesters TV & Film Services   01494-448689
Lane End Road, Sands   Fax 01494-527552
High Wycombe, Bucks HP12 4HG   Mick Piggot
www.lesterstvandfilm.com

Men At Work   020-8893 5569
90-95 Waterside Centre   Fax 020-8571 6505
Trumpers Way, London W7 2QD   Gerard Boath
www.menatwork.co.uk   www.americanprops.co.uk

The Period Petrol Pump Company   01379-740254
The Cottage, Bridge Road   Lee Trevail
Scole, Diss, Norfolk IP21 4DP

RAC Signs   0845-610 6466
PO Box 10   Fax 01777-709878
Retford, Notts DN22 7EE

The Stockyard   020-8963 9944
Unit A, Genesis   Fax 020-8963 9955
Rainsford Road, London NW10 7RG   Ron Painter
www.stockyard.tv

Trading Post   020-8903 3727
1 Beresford Avenue   Fax 020-8900 2565
Wembley, Middx HA0 1NU   Tim Oake
www.tradingposthire.co.uk

Trevors Petrol Pumps   01634-361231
2 Cement Cottages, Station Road   Trevor Hoare
Rainham, Kent ME8 7UF

PROPS - TAPESTRIES

Farley   020-8749 9925
1-17 Brunel Road   Fax 020-8749 8372
London W3 7XR   Mark Farley
www.farley.co.uk

The Grove Music Studios	020-8960 9601
Unit 10	Alistair Fincham
Latimer Road, London W10 6RQ	

The Playground	020-8960 0110
Unit 8	Fax 020-8960 0110
Latimer Road, London W10 6RQ	Caitriona McLaughlin

Rambert Dance Company	020-8630 0601
94 Chiswick High Road	Fax 020-8747 8323
London W4 1SH	

REMOTE HEADS

A & C	020-8427 5168
83 Headstone Road	Fax 020-8861 2469
Harrow, Middx HA1 1PQ	Frank Fletcher

Aerial Camera Systems (ACS)	01483-426767
Innovation House, Douglas Drive	Fax 01483-413900
Godalming, Surrey GU7 1JX	Matthew Coyde
www.acsmedia.com	

Camera Corps	01932-592299
Shepperton Studios, Studios Road	Fax 01932-592674
Shepperton, Middx TW17 0QD	Matt Frost
www.cameracorps.co.uk	

Camera Revolution	01932-592322
Shepperton Studios, Studios Road	Fax 01932-592202
Shepperton, Middx TW17 0QD	Ian Speed
www.camerarevolution.com	

Chapman UK	01923-265953
Unit 5, Kingley Park	Fax 01923-268315
Station Road, Kings Langley, Herts WD4 8GW	Dennis Fraser
www.chapmanleonard.com	

Dan Greenway Minicam Specialist	020-856 00 856
dg@dangreenwayltd.co.uk	07711-903990
www.dangreenwayltd.co.uk	Dan Greenway

Dynamic Mounts International	01932-592348
Shepperton Studios, Studios Road	Fax 01932-592138
Shepperton, Middx TW17 0QD	Dan Gillham

Kontrol Freax	020-8992 8222
Unit 6, Westpoint Trading Estate	Fax 020-8992 8222
Alliance Road, London W3 0RA	Steve Scammell Nicola Heslop
www.kontrolfreax.com	

Transmission (TX)	020-8783 1972
Shepperton Studios, Studios Road	Fax 01932-592571
Shepperton, Middx TW17 0QD	Steve Lloyd
www.ttx.co.uk	

The Visual Effects Company	020-7637 4832
4 Bourlet Close	Rob Delicata
London W1W 7BJ	
www.thevfxco.co.uk	

RESEARCH SERVICES

Attentional	**01823-322829**
33-39 Bridge Street	Fax 01823-323093
Taunton, Somerset TA1 1TP	Fiona Keene

Broadcasters Audience Research Board	**020-7529 5529**
18 Dering Street	Fax 020-7529 5530
London W1S 1AQ	

FRPS	**020-8670 2959**
PO Box 28045	Fax 020-8670 1793
London SE27 9WZ	Amanda Dunne

The Information Bureau	**020-7924 4414**
41 The Business Centre	Fax 020-7738 2513
103 Lavender Hill, London SW11 5QL	Jane Hall

Reid & Casement Research	**020-7240 4550**
7 New Row	Fax 020-7836 6339
London WC2N 4LH	Simon Carpenter

The Researchers	**01732-365446**
62 Quarry Hill Road	Elizabeth Dawson
Tonbridge, Kent TN9 2PE	

Riley Research	**020-8968 7236**
190 Ladbroke Grove	Ursula Riley
London W10 5LZ	

RIGGING & SCAFFOLDING

A One Rigging Co	**01753-785352**
A Specialist Rigging Company, Pinewood Studios	07767-775760
Pinewood Road, Iver Heath, Bucks SL0 0NH	Kevin Mathews
www.specialist-wire-rigs.co.uk	

Beaver 84	**01708-861821**
Watson Close, Oliver Road	Fax 01708-869537
West Thurrock, Essex RM20 3EF	Gary Westbrook

Blitz Hire	**07931-377502**
3 Mills Studios	Fax 020-8534 4221
Sugar House Lane, London E15 2QS	Paul Skipper
www.blitz-rigging.co.uk	

Bob Wiesinger	**07000-wirefx (947339)**
10 Blaydon Court, Sussex Crescent	Fax 07968-253071
Northolt, Middx UB5 4DW	Bob Wiesinger

C & D Rigging	**01753-785414**
Pinewood Studios, Pinewood Road	Fax 01753-785971
Iver Heath, Bucks SL0 0NH	Chris Sayers
www.cdrigging.co.uk	

CMS Rigging	**01784-240441**
85 Elizabeth Avenue	Fax 01784-240441
Staines, Middx TW18 1JN	Colin Seers

Concept Staging	**01282-777600**
Wellington Mill, Ribble Street	Fax 01282-777602
Padiham, Burnley, Lancs BB12 8DQ	Gary Hilton
www.conceptstaging.co.uk	
Extreme Locations Rigging	**01753-785815**
Pinewood Studios, Pinewood Road	Fax 01753-655564
Iver Heath, Bucks SL0 0NH	Robin Earle
Gwizz	**01344-635435**
Longcross Studios, Chobham Lane	Fax 01344-635165
Chertsey, Surrey KT16 0EE	Grant Wiesinger
JC Rigging	**07768-012419**
29 Crockford Park Road	Fax 07768-019078
Addlestone, Surrey KT15 2LF	John Cooling
Media Structures	**020-8683 3131**
87-91 Beddington Lane	Fax 020-8683 3111
Croydon, Surrey CR0 4TD	Geoff Tyler
Metro Rigging & Drape Hire	**07973-115216**
metrorigging@hotmail.com	Fax 020-8341 1318
www.metrorigging.co.uk	Vince Shaw Lee Sherlock
Nippy Industries	**01487-773003**
Grange Farm, Abbots Ripton	Fax 01487-773733
Huntingdon, Cambs PE28 2PH	Sue Miller
Outback Rigging	**020-8993 0066**
Unit 5, Kendal Court	Fax 020-8752 1753
Western Avenue Trading Estate, Kendal Avenue, London W3 0RU	
Rigging Services	**0121-333 4409**
Unit E, Dartmouth Industrial Estate	Fax 0121-333 4909
Bracebridge Street, Birmingham B6 4NE	David Rogers
www.riggingservices.co.uk	
Rigging Services	**020-8215 1240**
3 Mills Studios	Fax 020-8215 1243
Three Mill Lane, London E3 3DU	Bob Dean
www.riggingservices.co.uk	
Rigging Services	**01925-251040**
21 Rivington Court	Fax 01925-813120
Warrington, Cheshire WA1 4RT	Dirk Van Hoof
www.riggingservices.co.uk	

S2 Events	**020-7928 5474**
3-5 Valentine Place	Fax 020-7928 6082
London SE1 8QH	Wolter Dammers
www.s2events.co.uk	
Skyhook Rigging	**07813-800637**
Wayside Cottage, 10 Cowbridge Road	Russell Hall
Brynsadler, Cardiff CF72 9BT	
www.skyhookrigging.co.uk	
Specialist Rigging	**01895-850454**
57 Richmond Avenue	Fax 01895-850454
Hillingdon, Middx UB10 9BH	Roy Elston
Summit Steel	**01622-745977**
Clockhouse Farm, Heath Road	Fax 01622-746370
Coxheath, Maidstone, Kent ME17 4PB	Jon Bray
UK Rigging	**01204-391343**
Units 7-9, Undershore Business Park	Fax 01204-363238
Brookside Road, Bolton, Lancs BL2 2SE	Chris Sinnott
Unusual	**01604-830083**
The Wharf	Fax 01604-831144
Bugbrooke, Northants NN7 3QB	Denis Bramhall
Vertigo Rigging	**020-8694 6033**
Unit 10, Elizabeth Industrial Estate	Fax 020-8694 6066
Juno Way, London SE14 5RW	

ROSTRUM CAMERAS

Animops	**07905-168226**
64 Kingswood Avenue	Ray Clayton
Bromley, Kent BR2 0NY	
Elite Television	**0113-262 3342**
248 Meanwood Road	Fax 0113-262 3798
Leeds LS7 2HZ	Stuart Josephs
www.elitetv.co.uk	
Frameline	**020-7636 1303**
38 Bedford Square	Fax 020-7436 8878
London WC1B 3EL	Nick Summers
Ken Morse	**020-8749 0245**
King Camera Services	**020-7439 7445**
73A Beak Street	Fax 020-7439 7166
London W1F 9SR	Chris King
Peter Jones Rostrums	**07885-282968**
38 Bedford Square	Peter Jones
London WC1B 3EL	

ROYALTY MANAGEMENT

Bevis & Co	**01372-840280**
Apex House, 6 West Street	Fax 01372-840282
Epsom, Surrey KT18 7RG	Chris Bevis

MMG @ MGR	**020-7625 4545**
55 Loudoun Road	Fax 020-7625 5265
London NW8 0DL	Paul Simnock

RUBBISH COLLECTION

Chrispy Clean	**01932-858171**
25 Pear Tree Road	Fax 01932-858171
Addlestone, Surrey KT15 1SR	Debbie Millis
www.chrispyclean.co.uk	
Scenery Salvage	**01494-866110**
Middlegrove Farm, Chesham Road	07831-455583
Great Misenden, Bucks HP16 0RD	Hugo Keating
www.scenerysalvage.com	

SATELLITE LINKS

AAA Wavevend Radio Communications	**020-7266 1280**
17B Pindock Mews	Fax 020-7266 1290
London W9 2PY	Melvin Lind
www.wavevend.co.uk	
Ascent Media Network Services	**020-7131 6131**
1 Stephen Street	Fax 020-7691 6919
London W1T 1AL	Margaret Davies

Audiolink	**020-8955 1101**
17 Iron Bridge Close	Fax 020-8955 1111
London NW10 0UF	Andrew Morgan John Morgan
www.audiolink.co.uk	

Audiolink	**01753-656692**
Pinewood Studios, Pinewood Road	Fax 020-8955 1111
Iver Heath, Bucks SL0 0NH	Andrew Morgan John Morgan
www.audiolink.co.uk	

Globecast UK	**020-7430 4400**
200 Grays Inn Road	Fax 020-7753 3601
London WC1X 8XZ	Francis Rolland

Melvin Lind Radio Communications	**020-7266 1280**
17B Pindock Mews	Fax 020-7266 1290
London W9 2PY	Melvin Lind
www.wavevend.co.uk	

SIS LIVE	**01908-865500**
2 Whitehall Avenue, Kingston	Fax 01908-865501
Milton Keynes, Bucks MK10 0AX	Donna Palumbo
www.sislive.tv	

SNG	**020-7819 2800**
6 Union Court	Fax 020-7819 2801
20-22 Union Road, London SW4 6JP	

SCENERY DISPOSAL

Scenery Salvage	**01494-866110**
Middlegrove Farm, Chesham Road	07831-455583
Great Misenden, Bucks HP16 0RD	Hugo Keating
www.scenerysalvage.com	

Waste King	**0800-141 2778**
3 Homefield Road	Fax 01442-216784
Hemel Hempstead, Herts HP2 4BZ	Glenn Currie

SCENERY HIRE

Deedman Tropical Plant Hire	**01204-577000**
Deedman House, 3K Longcauseway	Fax 01204-577770
Kearsley, Bolton, Lancs BL4 9BS	Butch Deedman
www.deedman.co.uk	

Set Supermarket	**020-8133 0573**
Chase 55	Michael Mulligan
55 Chase Road, London NW10 6LU	
www.setsupermarket.com	

The Stockyard	**020-8963 9944**
Unit A, Genesis	Fax 020-8963 9955
Rainsford Road, London NW10 7RG	Ron Painter
www.stockyard.tv	

SCREENING ROOMS

3 Mills Studios	**020-7363 3336**
Three Mill Lane	Fax 0871-594 4028
London E3 3DU	Melanie Faulkner
www.3mills.com	
BAFTA	**020-7292 5811**
195 Piccadilly	Fax 020-7734 1009
London W1J 9LN	Jenny Bones
BBFC Preview Theatre	**020-7440 1590**
3 Soho Square	Fax 020-7287 0141
London W1D 3HD	
Century Preview Theatre	**020-7753 7135**
31-32 Soho Square	Nick Ross
London W1D 3AP	
Digital Media Rentals	**0845-607 6635**
179 Wardour Street	Fax 020-7534 3411
London W1F 8WY	Duncan Napier-Bell
www.digitalmediarentals.co.uk	
Eon Productions	**020-7493 7953**
Eon House	Fax 020-7408 1236
138 Piccadilly, London W1J 7NR	Ray Aguilar
Soho Screening Rooms	**020-7437 1771**
14 D'Arblay Street	
London W1F 8DY	

SCREENS - LARGE FORMAT

Anna Valley Displays	**020-8941 4500**
9 Mount Mews, High Street	Fax 020-8941 0077
Hampton, Middx TW12 2SH	Tim Oliver
AVC Big Screen	**01753-567377**
242-243 Gresham Road	Fax 01753-691843
Slough, Berks SL1 4PH	Nick Pask
Bay TV	**01446-720727**
Unit A3, Atlantic Gate Trading Estate	Alan Carter
Hayes Road, Barry, Vale Of Glamorgan CF63 3RF	
CT London	**01293-582000**
Unit E2, Sussex Manor Business Park	Fax 01293-582010
Gatwick Road, Crawley, W Sussex RH10 9NH	
Electrosonic	**01322-222211**
Hawley Mill, Hawley Road	Fax 01322-282282
Dartford, Kent DA2 7SY	
Event Projection	**020-7232 1748**
Unit 6, Rotherhithe Business Estate	Fax 020-7232 5063
Rotherhithe New Road, London SE16 3EH	
www.eventprojection.co.uk	
Harkness Screens	**01438-725200**
Unit A, Norton Road	Fax 01438-344400
Stevenage, Herts SG1 2BB	David Harrison

Joys Production Services	**020-8678 9790**
Unit 2A	Peter Joy
Birkbeck Place, London SE21 8JU	

SCRIPT SERVICES

Help Unlimited	**01932-592364**
Shepperton Studios, Studios Road	Fax 01932-569527
Shepperton, Middx TW17 0QD	Vicki Manning
Industrial Scripts	**020-7183 8907**
324-326 Regent Street	Evan Leighton-Davis
London W1B 3BL	
The London Script Consultancy	**020-8983 4563**
1 Penpoll Road	Colin Sorrell
London E8 1EX	
Sapex Scripts	**020-8236 1600**
Elstree Studios, Shenley Road	Fax 020-8324 2771
Borehamwood, Herts WD6 1JG	Paul Sattin
www.sapex.co.uk	
Take 1 Transcription	**0800-085 4418**
456-458 Strand	Fax 01580-715208
London WC2R 0DZ	Louise Tapia
www.take1.tv	

SCRIPT WRITING SOFTWARE

Moviesoft	**020-7060 9025**
26 York Street	Fax 0845-094 6061
London W1U 6PZ	Francois Farrugia
www.moviesoft.co.uk	
Sapex Scripts	**020-8236 1600**
Elstree Studios, Shenley Road	Fax 020-8324 2771
Borehamwood, Herts WD6 1JG	Paul Sattin
www.sapex.co.uk	
The Screenwriters Store	**0845-094 6061**
Unit 3.02, Lafone House, The Leathermarket	Fax 0845-094 3846
11-13 Weston Street, London SE1 3HN	Rinaldo Quacquarini

SCULPTORS

Aden Hynes Sculpture Studios	**01268-418837**
3 Hornsby Square, Southfields Industrial Park	Aden Hynes
Laindon, Essex SS15 6SD	
Figurative Sculpture Studio	**020-8850 4624**
2 Eltham Park Gardens	Steve Hunter
London SE9 1AW	
Film & TV Sculptors	**07768-440750**
Colney Park House, 100 Harper Lane	Fax 01727-823087
Radlett, Herts WD7 9HG	Gideon Howarth
www.filmandtvsculptors.com	

SECURITY

The A Team Film & TV Agency	**020-8958 8617**
100 Fairmead Crescent	Fax 020-8958 8617
Edgware, Middx HA8 8YP	Joe Gibson
Able Security	**020-8317 6899**
117 Waverly Road	Fax 020-8317 6899
London SE18 7TH	Tom Gandl
Alliance-Pioneer Group	**0845-539 5309**
PO Box 189	Fax 0845-539 5308
Plymouth PL6 5ZR	Matthew Davey
www.alliance-pioneer.co.uk	
Business & Entertainment Security	**01603-441806**
38 Ashtree Road	Fax 01603-441807
Norwich NR5 0LS	Sean Stone
G4S Security Services	**0845-900 0447**
Sutton Park House, 15 Carshalton Road	Rhian Woolrych
Sutton, Surrey SM1 4LD	
Gallowglass Security	**0845-257 5648**
1-5 Beehive Place	Fax 0845-257 5649
London SW9 7QR	Stuart Rae

Gauntlet Security Management	**029-2002 6416**
214 Whitchurch Road	Fax 029-2002 6417
Cardiff CF14 3ND	Tony Evans
Octaga Security Services	**01753-639263**
Pinewood Studios, Pinewood Road	Fax 01753-656593
Iver Heath, Bucks SL0 0NH	David Allison
SPA Security & Events	**0844-543 0954**
Spa House, Soloms Court Road	Fax 0844-543 0959
Banstead, Surrey SM7 3QG	Tim Price
Tex's Rangers Security Services	**01424-447737**
102 Ashburnham Road, Clivevale	Fax 01424-447737
Hastings, E Sussex TN35 5JH	Tex Avery
Vanguard Film & TV Security	**01934-419399**
35 Bridge Road	Fax 01934-429779
Weston-super-Mare, Somerset BS23 3PN	Gail Parsons

SIGNS & GRAPHICS

Acme Graphics	**020-8395 5130**
35 Wick Road	Fax 020-8395 5129
Teddington, Middx TW11 9DN	Nick Hellman
www.acmegraphics.co.uk	
Amersham Sign Design	**01494-432007**
9 The Business Centre, Corinium Industrial Estate	Fax 01494-432677
Raans Road, Amersham, Bucks HP6 6FB	Perry Brahan
Archer Signs	**020-8891 2666**
Crown House, 80 Crown Road	Fax 020-8891 3666
St Margarets, Twickenham, Middx TW1 3ER	Nathan Bowman
Artbox Inc	**01296-730215**
Winters Tale Farm Studio, Old Blackmoor Hill	Will Hodgins
Steeple Claydon, Bucks MK18 2EZ	
C & P Graphics	**01753-656515**
Pinewood Studios, Pinewood Road	Fax 01753-656045
Iver Heath, Bucks SL0 0NH	Peter Wright Andy Wright
Clive Ingleton	**01753-880322**
Woodside, Old Amersham Road	Clive Ingleton
Gerrards Cross, Bucks SL9 7BG	
Data Reprographics	**01784-243996**
Unit 1, West Surrey Estate	Fax 01784-256290
Ashford Road, Ashford, Middx TW15 1XB	John Lindsay
www.datarepro.co.uk	
David Copping	**01787-377006**
90 East Street	
Sudbury, Suffolk CO10 2TP	
Design 108	**07831-866979**
The Pie Factory, 101 Broadway	Stephen Bradshaw
Salford Quays, Manchester M50 2EQ	
www.design108.tv	

E Solar Trading	**0800-731 2259**
72 Bond Street	Fax 0845-004 2259
London W1S 1RR	Lewis Critchley
Electro Signs	**020-8521 8066**
97 Vallentin Road	Fax 020-8520 8127
London E17 3JJ	Chris Bracey
www.electrosigns.co.uk	
Francis Martin	**020-8809 7583**
78 Hermitage Road	Fax 020-8809 7583
London N4 1LY	
Furnells	**020-8880 2771**
Unit 5, Crusader Industrial Estate	Fax 020-8880 2333
167 Hermitage Road, London N4 1LZ	Wes Taylor
www.furnells.com	
graffitiartist	**0870-224 4104**
104 Stoner Road	David Brown
Hall Green, Birmingham B28 0QS	
Graphics Euro	**020-8575 7444**
Unit B6, Aladdin Business Centre	Fax 020-8813 2153
Long Drive, Greenford, Middx UB6 8UH	Steve Wright
Ian Robinson Design	**0115-845 7695**
27 Owthorpe Grove	Fax 0115-986 1007
Nottingham NG5 2LX	Ian Robinson

Jaysigns	**020-8443 5400**
1A North Road	Fax 020-8443 5800
London N9 7QX	Andy Sellick
Keir Lusby Props	**01932-561717**
Shepperton Studios, Studios Road	Fax 01932-565898
Shepperton, Middx TW17 0QD	Keir Lusby
www.keirlusby.com	
Neon Circus	**01799-598080**
Wrights Yard, Top Road	Fax 01799-598081
Wimbish Green, Saffron Walden, Essex CB10 2XJ	Mike Harradine
www.neoncircus.com	
Peels Of London	**020-8948 0689**
63 Ham Street	Fax 020-8948 0689
Richmond, Surrey TW10 7HW	Rod Kitchen
Pentagon London	**0800-907 1254**
Unit 4, Hazel Green Works	Fax 020-8275 8551
Edward Road, Barnet, Herts EN4 8AZ	Martin Westney
www.pentagonlondon.co.uk	
Phil McGill Signs & Police Crests	**01494-482288**
Highfield View, Park Lane	Fax 01494-483152
Stokenchurch, Bucks HP14 3TQ	Phil McGill
Print Sign Design	**020-8961 2004**
55 Chase Road	Fax 0560-312 7241
London NW10 6LU	Attila Raczkevy
Pullinger Signs	**01932-565340**
Maywood, Green Road	Fax 01932-568375
Thorpe, Surrey TW20 8QW	Bob Pullinger
Purlfrost	**020-8961 7337**
180 Park Avenue	Fax 0871-733 4587
London NW10 7XH	Emmanuel Baumard
Spectrum Signs	**01895-676333**
Long Lane Farm, Long Lane	Mark Josling
Ickenham, Middx UB10 8QT	
www.spectrumsignsuk.co.uk	
Steven Hedinger	**01344-624528**
9 Beech Hill Road	Fax 01344-627461
Sunningdale, Berks SL5 0BN	
Tony Statham Studio	**01843-825762**
Unit 3	Tony Statham
100 Vauxhall Walk, London SE11 5EL	

SINGING COACHES

Jo Thompson	**020-8992 6257**
3 Derwentwater Road	Fax 020-8992 6983
London W3 6DE	

SOUND - RENTAL

Beat About The Bush	**020-8960 2087**
Unit 23, Enterprise Way, Triangle Business Centre	Fax 020-8969 2281
Salter Street, London NW10 6UG	Adrian Purbrick
www.beataboutthebush.com	
Better Sound	**020-7482 0177**
31 Cathcart Street	Fax 020-7482 2677
London NW5 3BJ	
Dimension Audio	**01293-582005**
Unit E2, Sussex Manor Business Park	Fax 01293-582006
Gatwick Road, Crawley, W Sussex RH10 9NH	Mark Boden
FAB Sound	**020-8947 7738**
Unit 8, Rufus Business Centre	Fax 020-8947 6608
Ravensbury Terrace, London SW18 4RL	Geoff Horne
FX Rentals	**020-8746 2121**
38-40 Telford Way	Fax 020-8746 4100
London W3 7XS	Peter Brooks
Genesis Plus	**020-7391 9200**
Suffolk House	Fax 020-7391 9201
1-8 Whitfield Place, London W1T 5JU	Tim Banks
www.genesis-plus.com	
Hand Held Audio	**01992-719078**
Unit 8, Waterways Business Centre	Fax 01992-763860
Navigation Drive, Enfield, Middx EN3 6JJ	Mick Shepherd
Hawthorn Theatrical	**01664-821101**
Crown Business Park	Fax 01664-821119
Old Dalby, Leics LE14 3NQ	Leisa Tomaselli
www.hawthorns.uk.com	
Hyperactive Broadcast	**01252-519191**
5 The Royston Centre, Lynchford Lane	Fax 01252-513939
Ash Vale, Surrey GU12 5PQ	James Gander Liam Wife
www.hyperactivebroadcast.com	
Lightning Media	**020-8998 9911**
Unit 32, Sheraton Business Centre	Fax 020-8998 2781
20 Wadsworth Road, Perivale, Middx UB6 7JB	Lee Patel
www.lightningmedia.co.uk	
MAC Sound Hire	**0161-969 8311**
1-2 Attenburys Park, Park Road	Fax 0161-962 9423
Altrincham, Cheshire WA14 5QE	Clem Rawling
Picture Canning North	**0191-265 0061**
156 Brinkburn Street	Jamie Hutchinson
Newcastle-upon-Tyne NE6 2AR	
www.picturecanningnorth.co.uk	
RG Jones Sound Engineering	**020-8971 3100**
16 Endeavour Way	Fax 020-8971 3101
London SW19 8UH	John Carroll
Richmond Film Services	**0845-644 1640**
The Old School, Park Lane	Fax 020-8948 8326
Richmond, Surrey TW9 2RA	Nigel Woodford

Salon	**020-8746 7611**
Salon House	Fax 020-8746 7613
Swainson Road, London W3 7XB	Nick Long
www.salonrentals.com	

Sound Hire	**020-8644 1248**
Unit 7, Kimpton Trade & Business Centre	Fax 020-8644 6642
Minden Road, Sutton, Surrey SM3 9PF	Richard Lienard

SSE Audio	**020-8569 0100**
Units 10 & 11, Abenglen Industrial Estate	Fax 020-8569 0300
Betam Road, Hayes, Middx UB3 1SS	Luther Edmonds

Stronghire	**020-7426 5178**
120-124 Curtain Road	Fax 020-7613 5293
London EC2A 3SQ	Alex Green

Tacet	**07836-345092**
41 Shakespeare Road	Simon Bishop
London W7 1LT	

Television Film Services (TFS)	**0114-249 5902**
151 Knowle Lane	Fax 0114-221 4496
Sheffield S11 9SN	Keith Silva

Tickle Music	**020-8964 3399**
The Old Dairy	Fax 020-8964 0428
133-137 Kilburn Lane, London W10 4AN	Tad Barker

VME	**01565-652202**
Unit D, Marlborough Close	Fax 01565-652203
Parkgate Industrial Estate, Knutsford, Cheshire WA16 8XN	Bill Hyman

Warehouse Sound Services	**0131-555 6900**
23 Water Street	Fax 0131-555 6901
Edinburgh EH6 6SU	Pete Harris

SOUND - SALE

AES Pro Audio	**01932-872672**
North Lodge, Stonehill Road	Fax 01932-874364
Ottershaw, Surrey KT16 0AQ	Michael Stockdale

Appleworld Distribution	**01753-422744**
Pinewood Studios, Pinewood Road	Fax 01753-656683
Iver Heath, Bucks SL0 0NH	Rod Aaron
www.appleworld-distribution.com	

Audio	**01494-511711**
Audio House, Progress Road	Fax 01494-539600
Sands, High Wycombe, Bucks HP12 4JD	Kishore Patel

Audio Developments	**01922-457007**
23 Portland Road, Aldridge	Fax 01922-457008
Walsall, W Midlands WS9 8NS	Tom Cryan

Audio Engineering	**020-8341 3500**
Micron House	Fax 020-8341 5100
3 New Road, London N8 8TA	

Broadcast Bionics	**01444-473999**
Brooklands Barn, Brooklands Farm	Fax 01444-473888
Rocky Lane, Haywards Heath, W Sussex RH16 4RR	Kirsten Smith
www.bionics.co.uk	

Clive Cowan Recording (CCR)	**01702-460451**
217 Elm Road	Clive Cowan
Leigh-on-Sea, Essex SS9 1SA	

Dolby Laboratories	**01793-842100**
Interface Park	Fax 01793-842101
Wootton Bassett, Wilts SN4 8QJ	Jenny Warner

Electracoustic	**020-8297 0318**
127 Brightfield Road	Fax 020-8297 0218
London SE12 8QG	Jon Trotter

Everything Audio	**020-8324 2726**
Elstree Studios, Shenley Road	Fax 020-8324 2775
Borehamwood, Herts WD6 1JG	Roger Patel

HHB Communications	**020-8962 5000**
73-75 Scrubs Lane	Fax 020-8962 5050
London NW10 6QU	Steve Angel

Nagra Kudelski (GB)	**01727-810002**
3U Long Spring, Porters Wood	Fax 01727-837677
St Albans, Herts AL3 6EN	John Rudling

Pink Noise Systems	**0845-219 0107**
Rose Tree Cottage, The Street	John McCombie
Coaley, Glos GL11 5EB	

Planet Audio	**01753-422750**
Pinewood Studios, Pinewood Road	Fax 01753-656683
Iver Heath, Bucks SL0 0NH	Rod Gammons
www.planetaudiosystems.co.uk	

Prism Sound	**01353-648888**
The Old School, High Street	Fax 01353-648867
Stretham, Cambs CB6 3LD	Jody Thorne

Sennheiser UK	**01494-551551**
3 Century Point, Halifax Road	Fax 01494-551550
High Wycombe, Bucks HP12 3SL	

Solid State Logic	**01865-842300**
25 Springhill Road	Fax 01865-842118
Begbroke, Oxon OX5 1RU	Philippe Guerinet

Sound Technology	**01462-480000**
17 Letchworth Point	Fax 01462-480800
Letchworth, Herts SG6 1ND	Gary Dent

Soundkit

029-2034 2907 Fax 029-2023 1235
Email: martyn@soundkit.co.uk
www.soundkit.co.uk
12 Earle Place, Cardiff CF5 1NZ
Contact: Martyn Richards
Sales of television and film sound equipment. Let us quote for all your mics, boompoles, mixers, radio mics, etc. Give me a call or visit the website at www.soundkit.co.uk

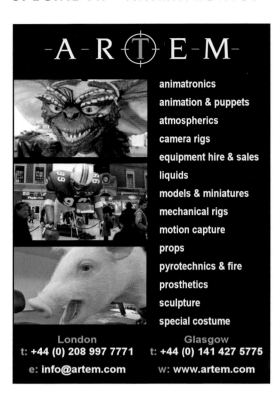

Total Audio	01527-880051
Unit 65, Basepoint Business Centre	Fax 01527-880052
Isidore Road, Bromsgrove, Worcs B60 3ET	Peter Knowles

WS Steele	0141-353 3393
Unit 5/05, Oakbank Industrial Estate	Fax 0141-353 3396
Garscube Road, Glasgow G20 7LU	Stuart McArthur

SPECIAL FX - ANIMATRONICS

Artem	020-8997 7771
Perivale Park, Horsenden Lane South	Fax 020-8997 1503
Perivale, Middx UB6 7RH	Frank Steggall
www.artem.com	

Artem (Scotland)	0141-427 5775
64-68 Brand Street	Fax 0141-427 1199
Govan, Glasgow G51 1DG	Joanna Dewar Gibb
www.artem.com	

Asylum Models & Effects	020-8871 2988
20 Thornsett Road	Fax 020-8874 8186
London SW18 4EF	Mark Ward
www.asylumsfx.com	

CG Effects	01932-841144
56A Hamm Moor Lane	Fax 01932-841177
Addlestone, Surrey KT15 2SF	Colin Gorry
www.cg-sfx.com	

Cinesite Production Services	01932-592425
Shepperton Studios, Studios Road	Fax 01932-568944
Shepperton, Middx TW17 0QD	
www.cinesiteproductionservices.com	

Crawley Creatures	01280-815300
Unit 8, Swan Business Centre	Fax 01280-813010
Osier Way, Buckingham MK18 1TB	Jez Gibson-Harris
www.crawley-creatures.com	

Pirate	020-8930 5000
Disraeli Road	Fax 020-8930 5001
London NW10 7AX	Martin Godward
www.pirate.co.uk	

Propshop Modelmakers	01753-785133
Pinewood Studios, Pinewood Road	Fax 01753-656267
Iver Heath, Bucks SL0 0NH	James Enright
www.propshopmodelmakers.com	

S-F-X.com	01663-741154
info@s-f-x.com	07860-208432
www.s-f-x.com	Scott MacIntyre

Wingfield Studios	01442-832951
126 Flaunden	Fax 01442-834519
Hemel Hempstead, Herts HP3 0PL	Michael Fleming
www.wingfield-studios.com	

SPECIAL FX - ATMOSPHERICS & PYROTECHNICS

4D Effects	**07921-619966**
20 Thirlmere Avenue	Dean Ford
Burnham, Bucks SL1 6ED	
Agog Special Effects	**01869-345556**
Unit 14, Green Farm	07966-448282
Fritwell, Oxon OX27 7QU	Jason Troughton
www.agog.tv	
All Effects	**0118-977 6666**
Unit 1, Berkyn Manor Farm, Stanwell Road	Fax 0118-977 6666
Horton, Slough, Berks SL3 9PE	Chris Reynolds
Any Effects	**01497-831436**
Ton Farm	07774-217282
Hay-on-Wye, Herefordshire HR3 5HL	Tom Harris
www.anyeffects.com	
Armoury In Action	**07702-205809**
www.armouryinaction.co.uk	Neil A Mountain
Artem	**020-8997 7771**
Perivale Park, Horsenden Lane South	Fax 020-8997 1503
Perivale, Middx UB6 7RH	Frank Steggall
www.artem.com	

Artem (Scotland)	**0141-427 5775**
64-68 Brand Street	Fax 0141-427 1199
Govan, Glasgow G51 1DG	Joanna Dewar Gibb
www.artem.com	
Asylum Models & Effects	**020-8871 2988**
20 Thornsett Road	Fax 020-8874 8186
London SW18 4EF	Mark Ward
www.asylumsfx.com	
Bubble Incorporated	**020-8350 0362**
26 Mansfield Avenue	Sam Heath
London N15 4HW	
CG Effects	**01932-841144**
56A Hamm Moor Lane	Fax 01932-841177
Addlestone, Surrey KT15 2SF	Colin Gorry
www.cg-sfx.com	
Cinesite Production Services	**01932-592425**
Shepperton Studios, Studios Road	Fax 01932-568944
Shepperton, Middx TW17 0QD	
www.cinesiteproductionservices.com	
Concept Engineering	**01628-825555**
7 Woodlands Business Park, Woodlands Park Avenue	Fax 01628-826261
Maidenhead, Berks SL6 3UA	Trevor Dunnington

Confetti Magic   01582-723502

Rocket Park
Luton, Beds LU1 4LL
www.confettimagic.com

Fax 01582-485545
Ian Woodroof

Darkside FX   07000-327574

Pinewood Studios, Pinewood Road
Iver Heath, Bucks SL0 0NH

Fax 07002-327574
Joss Williams

David Harris Special Effects   07831-227005

Model Farm, Gorelands Lane
Chalfont St Giles, Bucks HP8 4AB

David Harris

Effective Actions   01753-676651

46 The Limes, Dedworth Road
Windsor, Berks SL4 4US
www.easfx.co.uk

Jonathan Bullock Mark Roberts

Elements Special Effects   020-8961 4244

Unit P04, Acton Business Centre
School Road, London NW10 6TD
www.elementsfx.co.uk

Fax 020-8961 4255
Johnny Rafique

Emergency House   0161-339 1362

21 Peterborough Close
Ashton-under-Lyne, Lancs OL6 8XW
www.emergencyhouse.co.uk

Fax 0161-330 3084
Jonathan Carter

Enterprises Unlimited SFX	**01780-752166**
Unit 10, Glen Industrial Estate	Fax 01780-752167
Essendine, Stamford, Lincs PE9 4LE	Harry Stokes
The Especial Effects Company	**07000-433332**
86 Woodhurst Avenue	Fax 01689-837251
Petts Wood, Kent BR5 1AT	Phil Anderson
HA & C Rowley	**0113-257 4415**
46A Oaklands Road	Fax 0113-257 4415
Leeds LS13 1LQ	Ian Rowley
HVFX	**020-7060 4839**
Velt House, Velt House Lane	Fax 020-7117 3065
Elmore, Gloucester GL2 3NY	Mark Turner
www.hvfx.com	
Jeremy King	**07850-901103**
43 Berkeley Court, Oatlands Drive	Jeremy King
Weybridge, Surrey KT13 9HX	
www.jeremykingfx.com	
Le Maitre Events	**020-8646 2222**
6 Forval Close, Wandle Way	Fax 020-8648 1955
Mitcham, Surrey CR4 4NE	Karen Haddon
www.lemaitreevents.com	
Live Action FX	**01635-529078**
119 Dene Way, Donnington	Stephen Miller
Newbury, Berks RG14 2JN	
Machine Shop Special Effects	**020-8961 5888**
180 Acton Lane	Fax 020-8961 5885
London NW10 7NH	Paul Mann
www.machineshop.co.uk	
MTFX	**01452-729903**
Velt House, Velt House Lane	Fax 01452-729904
Elmore, Gloucester GL2 3NY	Mark Turner
www.mtfx.com	
MTFX Cardiff	**029-2141 4141**
Television Centre	Mark Turner
Culverhouse Cross, Cardiff CF5 6XJ	
www.mtfx.com	
Neil Corbould Special Effects	**01753-656415**
Pinewood Studios, Pinewood Road	Fax 01753-656147
Iver Heath, Bucks SL0 0NH	Gail Corbould
North Star Special Effects	**028-4272 9743**
3 Ballyblack Road	Fax 028-4272 9897
Portaferry, Co Down BT22 1PY	Martin Neill
Peter Hutchinson Special Effects	**01256-771000**
Copse Farm, South Litchfield	Peter Hutchinson
Overton, Basingstoke, Hants RG25 3BP	
Quicksilver	**0800-015 2264**
17 Hyde Road	Fax 0161-335 9871
Denton, Manchester M34 3AF	Darren Wallis
www.quicksilversfx.co.uk	

S-F-X.com	**01663-741154**
info@s-f-x.com	07860-208432
www.s-f-x.com	Scott MacIntyre
SFX-Ltd	**01753-656653**
Pinewood Studios, Pinewood Road	Andy McVean
Iver Heath, Bucks SL0 0NH	
Skyhigh FX	**01795-830383**
The Old Gun Site, Hole Street Farm	Fax 01795-830127
Kingsdown, Sittingbourne, Kent ME9 0QX	Ellie Beadle
Snow Business International	**01453-840077**
The Snow Mill, Bridge Road	Fax 01453-840077
Ebley, Stroud, Glos GL5 4TR	Andrew Carruthers
www.snowbusiness.com	
Special Effects (GB)	**01932-592416**
Shepperton Studios, Studios Road	Fax 01932-592415
Shepperton, Middx TW17 0QD	Neal Champion
Special Effects UK	**01753-650658**
Pinewood Studios, Pinewood Road	Fax 01753-650659
Iver Heath, Bucks SL0 0NH	Paul Dunn
Steve Bowman SFX	**07973-719837**
Unit 1, Berkyn Manor Farm, Stanwell Road	Fax 020-8568 7661
Horton, Slough, Berks SL3 9PE	Steve Bowman
Water Sculptures	**01524-37707**
Unit 4, Stevant Way	Fax 01524-37717
White Lund, Morecambe, Lancs LA3 3PU	Alasdair Elliot

SPECIAL FX - CONFETTI

Confetti Creations	**01452-888540**
Velt House, Velt House Lane	Fax 01452-729904
Elmore, Gloucester GL2 3NY	Mark Turner
www.confetticreations.co.uk	
Confetti Magic	**01582-723502**
Rocket Park	Fax 01582-485545
Luton, Beds LU1 4LL	Ian Woodroof
www.confettimagic.com	

SPECIAL FX - CONSTRUCTION

Cinesite Production Services	**01932-592425**
Shepperton Studios, Studios Road	Fax 01932-568944
Shepperton, Middx TW17 0QD	
www.cinesiteproductionservices.com	

SPECIAL FX - FIREWORKS

Asylum Models & Effects	**020-8871 2988**
20 Thornsett Road	Fax 020-8874 8186
London SW18 4EF	Mark Ward
www.asylumsfx.com	

Celebration Displays	**0161-723 4422**
Unit 9A, Bealey Industrial Estate	Fax 0161-723 4433
Radcliffe, Manchester M26 2BD	Maurice Bent

CG Effects	**01932-841144**
56A Hamm Moor Lane	Fax 01932-841177
Addlestone, Surrey KT15 2SF	Colin Gorry
www.cg-sfx.com	

Cinesite Production Services	**01932-592425**
Shepperton Studios, Studios Road	Fax 01932-568944
Shepperton, Middx TW17 0QD	
www.cinesiteproductionservices.com	

Dragon Fireworks	**01932-872424**
Wey Farm, Guildford Road	Fax 01932-874758
Ottershaw, Surrey KT16 0QW	Noah Le Mare

Fantastic Fireworks	**01582-485555**
Rocket Park, Halfmoon Lane	Fax 01582-485545
Pepperstock, Luton, Beds LU1 4LL	

Fireworks International	**01283-704849**
Donington Park Race Track, Donington Park	Fax 01283-704064
Castle Donington, Derbys DE74 2RP	Julian Garner

Kimbolton Fireworks	**01480-860988**
7 High Street, Kimbolton	Fax 01480-861277
Huntingdon, Cambs PE28 0HB	Simon Page

Le Maitre Events	**020-8646 2222**
6 Forval Close, Wandle Way	Fax 020-8648 1955
Mitcham, Surrey CR4 4NE	Karen Haddon
www.lemaitreevents.com	

MTFX	**01452-729903**
Velt House, Velt House Lane	Fax 01452-729904
Elmore, Gloucester GL2 3NY	Mark Turner
www.mtfx.com	

MTFX Cardiff	**029-2141 4141**
Television Centre	Mark Turner
Culverhouse Cross, Cardiff CF5 6XJ	
www.mtfx.com	

Pains Fireworks	**01794-884040**
Romsey Road, Whiteparish	Fax 01794-884015
Salisbury, Wilts SP5 2SD	David Alvis

Quicksilver	**0800-015 2264**
17 Hyde Road	Fax 0161-335 9871
Denton, Manchester M34 3AF	Darren Wallis
www.quicksilversfx.co.uk	

S-F-X.com	**01663-741154**
info@s-f-x.com	07860-208432
www.s-f-x.com	Scott MacIntyre

Skyburst - The Firework Company	**0800-074 4636**
11 Nelson Parade	Fax 0117-923 1377
East Street, Bristol BS3 4JA	Alan Christie

SPECIAL FX - GLASS

Asylum Models & Effects	**020-8871 2988**
20 Thornsett Road	Fax 020-8874 8186
London SW18 4EF	Mark Ward
www.asylumsfx.com	

Glass Designs	**01296-688901**
Unit 4, Manor Farm Courtyard	Fax 01296-688901
Rowsham, Aylesbury, Bucks HP22 4QP	Ray Priem

Pentagon London   **0800-907 1254**
Unit 4, Hazel Green Works   Fax 020-8275 8551
Edward Road, Barnet, Herts EN4 8AZ   Martin Westney
www.pentagonlondon.co.uk

SPECIAL FX - LASERS & HOLOGRAPHY

Definitive Special Projects   **01438-869005**
PO Box 169   Fax 01438-869006
Ardeley, Herts SG2 7SG   Steve Hitchins

Holograms - 3D   **020-7370 2239**
286 Earls Court Road   Fax 020-7373 2511
London SW5 9AS   Jonathan Ross

Laser Visuals   **01539-552138**
940 Cornforth Drive, Kent Science Park   Julie Moore
Sittingbourne, Kent ME9 8PX

LCI Production   **020-8741 5747**
55 Merthyr Terrace   Fax 020-8748 9879
London SW13 8DL   Luke Bennett

LM Productions   **01323-432170**
Unit 6H, Southbourne Business Park   Fax 01323-432171
Courtlands Road, Eastbourne, E Sussex BN22 8UY   Stephen Harvey

SPECIAL FX - MAGIC

Consultant Magician   **07738-971077**
67 De Tany Court   Tony Middleton
St Albans, Herts AL1 1TX
www.consultantmagician.com

SPECIAL FX - MAKE-UP & PROSTHETICS

Altered States FX   **01932-562611**
Shepperton Studios, Studios Road   Fax 01932-568989
Shepperton, Middx TW17 0QD   David White

Animated Extras   **01932-592347**
Shepperton Studios, Studios Road   Fax 01932-569605
Shepperton, Middx TW17 0QD   Nik Williams

Applied Arts   **020-7739 3155**
22-27 The Oval   Bob Saunders
London E2 9DT
www.appliedarts.co.uk

Artem   **020-8997 7771**
Perivale Park, Horsenden Lane South   Fax 020-8997 1503
Perivale, Middx UB6 7RH   Frank Steggall
www.artem.com

Artem (Scotland)	**0141-427 5775**
64-68 Brand Street	Fax 0141-427 1199
Govan, Glasgow G51 1DG	Joanna Dewar Gibb
www.artem.com	

Asylum Models & Effects	**020-8871 2988**
20 Thornsett Road	Fax 020-8874 8186
London SW18 4EF	Mark Ward
www.asylumsfx.com	

Clive Kay	**020-7834 7296**
4 Warwick Way	Fax 020-7834 2310
London SW1V 1RU	Gerry Price
www.specialeyeeffects.com	

Coulier Creatures FX	**07973-115018**
Unit 2.4, Building A, Wembley Commercial Centre	Mark Coulier
East Lane, Wembley, Middx HA9 7UR	
www.couliercreatures.com	

Creature Effects	**01895-251107**
Unit 2, 549 Eskdale Road	Fax 01895-251102
Uxbridge, Middx UB8 2RT	Cliff Wallace
www.creature-effects.com	

Fangs FX	**01494-713807**
The Studio, Sheepcote Dell Road	Fax 01494-719070
Beamond End, Amersham, Bucks HP7 0QS	Chris Lyons

Glynn McKay Masks	01728-723865
11 Mount Pleasant, Framlingham	Fax 01728-723865
Woodbridge, Suffolk IP13 9HQ	Glynn McKay

Hybrid Enterprises	01277-654862	0113-217 1300
London & Leeds		Mike Bates
www.hybridfx.com		

Image FX	01753-656598
Pinewood Studios, Pinewood Road	Bob Keen
Iver Heath, Bucks SL0 0NH	

Karl Derrick	020-8575 7550
PO Box 140	Fax 020-8578 7880
Greenford, Middx UB6 9AL	Karl Derrick

Kristyan Mallett Make-Up Effects	01923-805656
Unit 4, Riverside Works	07733-334446
Riverside Road, Watford, Herts WD19 4HY	Kristyan Mallett
www.kristyanmallett.com	

Millennium FX	01494-775576
Unit 6, Springfield Road	Fax 01494-775526
Chesham, Bucks HP5 1PW	Neill Gorton

The Reel Eye Company	01923-850207
365-367 Watling Street	Fax 01923-850738
Radlett, Herts WD7 7LB	Jemma Scott

Robert Smith (Special Make-Up Effects)	020-8651 1230
11 Ashdown Gardens	Robert Smith
Sanderstead, Surrey CR2 9DR	

S-F-X.com	01663-741154
info@s-f-x.com	07860-208432
www.s-f-x.com	Scott MacIntyre

Sherman Make-Up Effects	020-8559 1942
17 Tomswood Road	Aaron Sherman
Chigwell, Essex IG7 5QP	

Silicone Prosthetics	020-8840 1168
1 Park Road	Conor O'Sullivan
London W7 1LY	
www.siliconeprosthetics.com	

Theatricks	01994-419723
Swn-y-Gan, Cefn-y-Pant	Karl Evans
Llanboidy, Carmarthens SA34 0TR	
www.theatricks.co.uk	

SPECIAL FX - MECHANICAL

Agog Special Effects	01869-345556
Unit 14, Green Farm	07966-448282
Fritwell, Oxon OX27 7QU	Jason Troughton
www.agog.tv	

Any Effects	01497-831436
Ton Farm	07774-217282
Hay-on-Wye, Herefordshire HR3 5HL	Tom Harris
www.anyeffects.com	

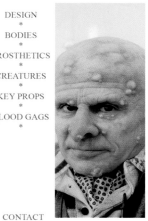
Artem	020-8997 7771
Perivale Park, Horsenden Lane South	Fax 020-8997 1503
Perivale, Middx UB6 7RH	Frank Steggall
www.artem.com	

Artem (Scotland)	0141-427 5775
64-68 Brand Street	Fax 0141-427 1199
Govan, Glasgow G51 1DG	Joanna Dewar Gibb
www.artem.com	

Asylum Models & Effects	020-8871 2988
20 Thornsett Road	Fax 020-8874 8186
London SW18 4EF	Mark Ward
www.asylumsfx.com	

CG Effects	01932-841144
56A Hamm Moor Lane	Fax 01932-841177
Addlestone, Surrey KT15 2SF	Colin Gorry
www.cg-sfx.com	

Cinesite Production Services	01932-592425
Shepperton Studios, Studios Road	Fax 01932-568944
Shepperton, Middx TW17 0QD	
www.cinesiteproductionservices.com	

MTFX	01452-729903
Velt House, Velt House Lane	Fax 01452-729904
Elmore, Gloucester GL2 3NY	Mark Turner
www.mtfx.com	

MTFX Cardiff	029-2141 4141
Television Centre	Mark Turner
Culverhouse Cross, Cardiff CF5 6XJ	
www.mtfx.com	

S-F-X.com	01663-741154
info@s-f-x.com	07860-208432
www.s-f-x.com	Scott MacIntyre

SPECIAL FX - RIGGING & WIRE

Any Effects	01497-831436
Ton Farm	07774-217282
Hay-on-Wye, Herefordshire HR3 5HL	Tom Harris
www.anyeffects.com	
Bob Schofield	**01895-258253**
179 Park Road	Fax 01895-258253
Uxbridge, Middx UB8 1NP	Bob Schofield
Bob Wiesinger	**07000-wirefx (947339)**
10 Blaydon Court, Sussex Crescent	Fax 07968-253071
Northolt, Middx UB5 4DW	Bob Wiesinger
Flying By Foy	**020-8236 0234**
Unit 4, Borehamwood Enterprise Centre	Fax 020-8236 0235
Theobald Street, Borehamwood, Herts WD6 4RQ	Stephen Wareham

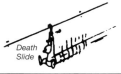

Kirbys AFX   **020-8723 8552**

8 Greenford Avenue   Andy Sutton
London W7 3QP

MTFX   **01452-729903**

Velt House, Velt House Lane   Fax 01452-729904
Elmore, Gloucester GL2 3NY   Mark Turner
www.mtfx.com

MTFX Cardiff   **029-2141 4141**

Television Centre   Mark Turner
Culverhouse Cross, Cardiff CF5 6XJ
www.mtfx.com

Specialist Wire Rigs   **01753-785352**

Pinewood Studios, Pinewood Road   07767-775760
Iver Heath, Bucks SL0 0NH   Kevin Mathews
www.specialist-wire-rigs.co.uk

Stunt Rigging Services   **01753-522219**

Black Potts, Pococks Lane   07552-698621
Eton, Windsor, Berks SL4 6HW   Kevin Welch
www.stuntrigging.com

SPECIAL FX - WATER SCREENS

Aquagraphics   **01452-883308**

Velt House, Velt House Lane   Fax 01452-729904
Elmore, Gloucester GL2 3NY   Mark Turner
www.aquagraphics.com

SPECIAL FX EQUIPMENT

Agog Special Effects   **01869-345556**

Unit 14, Green Farm   07966-448282
Fritwell, Oxon OX27 7QU   Jason Troughton
www.agog.tv

Any Effects   **01497-831436**

Ton Farm   07774-217282
Hay-on-Wye, Herefordshire HR3 5HL   Tom Harris
www.anyeffects.com

Artem   **020-8997 7771**

Perivale Park, Horsenden Lane South   Fax 020-8997 1503
Perivale, Middx UB6 7RH   Frank Steggall
www.artem.com

Artem (Scotland)   **0141-427 5775**

64-68 Brand Street   Fax 0141-427 1199
Govan, Glasgow G51 1DG   Joanna Dewar Gibb
www.artem.com

Asylum Models & Effects   **020-8871 2988**

20 Thornsett Road   Fax 020-8874 8186
London SW18 4EF   Mark Ward
www.asylumsfx.com

CG Effects   01932-841144
56A Hamm Moor Lane
Addlestone, Surrey KT15 2SF
www.cg-sfx.com
Fax 01932-841177
Colin Gorry

Cinesite Production Services   01932-592425
Shepperton Studios, Studios Road
Shepperton, Middx TW17 0QD
www.cinesiteproductionservices.com
Fax 01932-568944

Confetti Magic   01582-723502
Rocket Park
Luton, Beds LU1 4LL
www.confettimagic.com
Fax 01582-485545
Ian Woodroof

Machine Shop Special Effects   020-8961 5888
180 Acton Lane
London NW10 7NH
www.machineshop.co.uk
Fax 020-8961 5885
Paul Mann

MTFX   01452-729903
Velt House, Velt House Lane
Elmore, Gloucester GL2 3NY
www.mtfx.com
Fax 01452-729904
Mark Turner

MTFX Cardiff   029-2141 4141
Television Centre
Culverhouse Cross, Cardiff CF5 6XJ
www.mtfx.com
Mark Turner

SPECIAL FX SUPPLIES

ACC Silicones   01278-411400
Amber House, Showground Road
Bridgwater, Somerset TA6 6AJ
Fax 01278-411444
Chris Dawson

Adhesive Brokers   01494-868870
3 Whitefield Lane
Great Missenden, Bucks HP16 0BH
www.adhesivebrokers.co.uk
Fax 0560-047 8208
Nicola Brown

Alec Tiranti   0845-123 2100
3 Pipers Court, Berkshire Drive
Thatcham, Berks RG19 4ER
Fax 0845-123 2101
Robert Chenery

Bentley Chemicals   01562-515121
Frederick Road, Hoo Farm Industrial Estate
Kidderminster, Worcs DY11 7RA
Fax 01562-515847
Richard Watson

BMA Supplies   01784-483480
Moon Rakers, Friary Island
Wraysbury, Middx TW19 5JS
Fax 01784-483480
Brian Ahern

Brodie & Middleton   020-7836 3289
68 Drury Lane
London WC2B 5SP
www.brodies.net
Fax 020-7497 0554
Andrew Milne Home

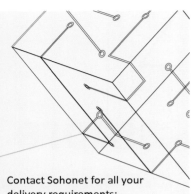

Contact Sohonet for all your
delivery requirements:

»   Live Streaming

»   Video-over-IP

»   SFTP/FTP

»   CDN

»   Submission Services

Pinewood: 01753 656565

Soho: 020 7292 6900

www.sohonet.co.uk

sohonet ↘

Mac Universe	01753-422750
Pinewood Studios, Pinewood Road	Fax 01753-656683
Iver Heath, Bucks SL0 0NH	Rod Gammons
www.macuniverse.com	

TipTop Media	020-8503 3644
i0 Unity Works	Fax 020-8503 3655
Sutherland Road, London E17 6JW	Colin Edwards

STREAMING

Adstream	020-7539 8400
Berkshire House	Fax 020-7836 1065
168-173 High Holborn, London WC1V 7AA	

Beam TV	020-7208 8190
40-41 Great Marlborough Street	Fax 020-7287 8393
London W1F 7JQ	

Chillibean	0845-054 4004
10 Livonia Street	Peter Godden
London W1F 8AF	

Digital Rapids	01428-751012
Passfield Business Centre, Lynchborough Road	Fax 01428-751013
Passfield, Hants GU30 7SB	Kerr Duffy
www.digital-rapids.com	

Groovy Gecko	**020-7240 0900**
126 Long Acre	Fax 020-7240 9699
London WC2E 9PE	Craig Moehl
i2i Media	**01444-240180**
The Forum, 277 London Road	Philip Radley-Smith
Burgess Hill, W Sussex RH15 9QU	
IMD	**020-7468 6868**
10 John Princess Street	Fax 020-7468 6889
London WIG 0JW	Sebastian Mattern
Joose	**020-7278 7072**
51-53 Mount Pleasant	Fax 020-7713 6000
London WC1X 0AE	Eddie McCaffrey
SIS LIVE	**01908-865500**
2 Whitehall Avenue, Kingston	Fax 01908-865501
Milton Keynes, Bucks MK10 0AX	Donna Palumbo
www.sislive.tv	
Sohonet	**020-7292 6900**
60 Poland Street	Fax 020-7292 6901
London W1F 7NT	Richard Linecar
www.sohonet.co.uk	
Stream UK	**020-7387 6091**
1 Water Lane	Joe Bray
London NW1 8NZ	

STRUCTURAL ENGINEERS

Pole Structural Engineers	**020-8944 9955**
24 High Street	Simon Pole
London SW19 5DX	

STUDIO DESIGN & INSTALLATION

AKA Design	**020-8829 9100**
2 Kingfisher Place	Fax 020-8829 9148
Clarendon Road, London N22 6XF	Guy Wilson
Custom Consoles	**01525-379909**
Leedon House, Billington Road	Fax 01525-370237
Leighton Buzzard, Beds LU7 4TN	Gary Fuller
First Choice Solutions	**01483-302333**
1L Merrow Business Centre, Merrow Lane	Fax 01483-306789
Guildford, Surrey GU4 7WA	Jim Inskip
www.firstchoicesolutions.co.uk	
Jigsaw Systems	**03332-400222**
The Old Mill	Fax 03332-409202
High Church Street, Nottingham NG7 7JA	Lewis Brown
www.jigsaw24.com/broadcast	
Lund Halsey	**01296-489964**
Gatehouse Close	Fax 01296-392284
Aylesbury, Bucks HP19 8DE	Caroline Winton

Mitcorp UK	**020-8380 7400**
23 Shield Drive, West Cross Industrial Estate	Fax 020-8380 7410
Brentford, Middx TW8 9EX	Mark Forth
www.mitcorp.co.uk	
MW Video Systems	**01869-345222**
64 North Street	Fax 01869-346002
Fritwell, Oxon OX27 7QR	Brian Speck
The Studio Wizard Organisation	**07092-123666**
Sawmill Cottage, Melton Park	Fax 07092-123666
Melton Constable, Norfolk NR24 2NJ	Howard Turner
T4 Group	**0845-500 6644**
The Farmhouse, Latchford Farm	Fax 0845-500 6645
Latchford, Ware, Herts SG11 1QZ	Paul Vanlint
www.t4-group.com	
Westcountry Broadcast	**0845-634 5906**
17 Woodland Park	Fax 07092-195677
Northam, Devon EX39 2RP	Nick Beer
White Mark	**0870-075 7767**
Bredfield Lodge, Bredfield Road	Fax 01394-385655
Woodbridge, Suffolk IP12 1JB	David Bell
Winsted	**01905-770276**
Units 7-8, Lovett Road	Fax 01905-779791
Hampton Lovett Industrial Estate, Droitwich, Worcs WR9 0QG	

STUDIOS

3 Mills Studios	**020-7363 3336**
Three Mill Lane	Fax 0871-594 4028
London E3 3DU	Melanie Faulkner
www.3mills.com	
3sixtymedia - The Manchester Studios	**0161-952 6000**
Quay Street	Paul Bennett
Manchester M60 9EA	
Arqiva	**01494-878548**
Chalfont Grove, Narcot Lane	Fax 01494-878006
Chalfont St Peter, Bucks SL9 8TW	Stan Hollins
Audiomotion Studios	**0870-160 0504**
Holywell House	Fax 01865-728319
Osney Mead, Oxford OX2 0EA	Mick Morris
www.audiomotion.com	
BBC Northern Ireland	**028-9033 8710**
Broadcasting House	Fax 028-9033 8934
Ormeau Avenue, Belfast BT2 8HQ	Helen Thompson
BBC Studios & Post Production	**020-8225 6000**
Television Centre	Fax 020-8576 8806
Wood Lane, London W12 7RJ	
www.bbcstudiosandpostproduction.com	
Bentwaters Parks	**01394-460655**
Control Tower, Bentwaters Parks	Fax 01394-460355
Rendlesham, Woodbridge, Suffolk IP12 2TW	Sarah Brown
www.bentwatersparks.com	
Black Island Studios	**020-8956 5600**
9-11 Alliance Road	Fax 020-8956 5604
London W3 0RA	Steve Giudici
www.islandstudios.net	
Bray Film Studios	**01628-622111**
Down Place, Water Oakley	Fax 01628-623000
Windsor, Berks SL4 5UG	Naomi Hendricks
Bristol Film Studios	**0117-939 7773**
Universal House	Fax 0117-939 7778
Ebenezer Street, Bristol BS5 8EF	
Broadley Studio	**020-7725 5858**
48 Broadley Terrace	Fax 020-7725 5859
London NW1 6LG	Mark French
Calvert Studios	**01525-853700**
Enterprise Way, Grovebury Road	Fax 01525-852111
Leighton Buzzard, Beds LU7 4SZ	Kevin Calvert
Camberwell Studios	**020-7737 0007**
Block A, Chartwell Business Park	Andy Woodruff
61-65 Paulet Road, London SE5 9HW	
The Camden Studio	**020-7482 4340**
Unit 6, St Pancras Commercial Centre	Fax 020-7267 3972
63 Pratt Street, London NW1 0BY	Peter Gregory

Discover London's Largest Studios

14 stages | 20 acres

"3 MILLS STUDIOS IS **THE BEST KEPT SECRET** FILM STUDIO IN LONDON".

Danny Boyle, director,
28 Days Later and Sunshine

14 STAGES | 200+ PRODUCTION OFFICES | 10 REHEARSAL ROOMS
PROP STORES & PAINT SHOPS | WORKSHOPS | SCREENING ROOM
DRESSING & MAKE UP ROOMS | LOCATIONS & PRISON SET
RESTAURANT & BAR | MEDIA VILLAGE AND MORE

3 Mills Studios
Three Mill Lane, London, UK, E3 3DU

T: +44 (0) 20 7363 3336   F: +44 (0) 87 1594 4028   E: info@3mills.com   W: www.3mills.com

SUPPORTED BY
LONDON
DEVELOPMENT
AGENCY
WORKING FOR THE MAYOR OF LONDON

Central Studios	0117-955 4777
Location House	Fax 0117-955 2480
5 Dove Lane, Bristol BS2 9HP	Gene Lowson

Centrestage Studios	020-7288 4599
8-10 Colebrooke Place	Fax 020-7288 4598
London N1 8HZ	Saul Barrington
www.centrestagestudios.co.uk	

Clapham Road Studios	020-7582 9664
161 Clapham Road	Fax 020-7582 9933
London SW9 0PU	Matthew Day

Denmark Studios	020-8364 3132
28 The Grangeway	Fax 020-8360 4618
London N21 2HG	Mark Brennan
www.denmarkstudios.co.uk	

Dragon Studios	0117-934 2771
Llanilid Pencoed	David Ferris
Bridgend, Mid Glam CF35 5L	

Dukes Island Studios	020-8956 5600
2 Dukes Road	Fax 020-8956 5604
London W3 0SL	Steve Giudici
www.islandstudios.net	

Dumbarton Studios	01389-736511
BBC Scotland	Neil Mac
Overburn Avenue, Dumbarton G82 2AP	

Dunsfold Park Studios	01483-542224
Cranleigh	Fax 01483-200555
Surrey GU6 8TB	Peter Farnfield
www.dunsfoldpark.com	

Ealing Studios	020-8567 6655
Ealing Green	Fax 020-8758 8658
London W5 5EP	John Abbott
www.ealingstudios.com	

Edinburgh Film Studios	07956-307381
Nine Mile Burn	Donald Mitchell
Midlothian, Edinburgh EH26 9LT	

Elite Television	0113-262 3342
248 Meanwood Road	Fax 0113-262 3798
Leeds LS7 2HZ	Stuart Josephs
www.elitetv.co.uk	

Elstree Studios	020-8953 1600
Shenley Road	Fax 020-8905 1135
Borehamwood, Herts WD6 1JG	Roger Morris

EPIC Studios	01603-727727
112-114 Magdalen Street	Simon Coward
Norwich NR3 1JD	

ETV	020-7820 4470
8 Park Place	Fax 020-7820 4471
Lawn Lane, London SW8 1UD	Justine Collins

www.denmarkstudios.co.uk

Stage 50 x 45 x 15 · CYC · 1000 Amps
· Sound Proofed · Green Room
· Make-up Room · Kitchen

Tel: 0208 364 31
Mobile: 07836 6393
Email: mark@denmarkstudios.co.

Farm Studio Bristol	**01275-395333**
Manor Farm	Nick Pitt
Green Lane, Bristol BS8 3TP	
Film City Glasgow	**0141-445 7244**
401 Govan Road	Fax 0141-445 6900
Glasgow G51 2QJ	Kelly Tiernan
Fleetwood Film Studios	**0118-933 3797**
Butlers Lands Farm, Mortimer	Keith Hicks
Reading, Berks RG7 2AG	

Fountain Studios

020-8900 5800   Fax 020-8900 5802
Email: enquiries@ftv.co.uk
www.ftv.co.uk
128 Wembley Park Road, Wembley, Middx HA9 8HQ
Contact: Sarah Joyce
Fully equipped broadcast studios with HD and SD capability. Flexible hire from 3,000 - 13,000sqft, with HD/SD TX lines, audience seating, on-site set storage and parking. Credits include: The X Factor, Britain's Got Talent, The Cube and Over The Rainbow.

Giltbrook Studios	**0115-945 8800**
10 Giltway	Mark Harwood
Giltbrook, Nottingham NG16 2GN	
Green Screen Soho	**020-7434 9919**
2 Archer Street	Fax 020-7439 0794
London W1D 7AW	Sophie Goddard
Greenford Studios	**020-8956 5600**
5-11 Taunton Road	Fax 020-8956 5604
Greenford, Middx UB6 8UQ	Steve Giudici
www.islandstudios.net	
Halliford Studios	**01932-226341**
Manygate Lane	Fax 01932-246336
Shepperton, Middx TW17 9EG	Rigby Andrews Callum Andrews
www.hallifordfilmstudios.co.uk	
Hampshire Street Studios	**020-7485 6999**
1 Hampshire Street	Fax 020-7485 4785
London NW5 2TE	Max Yeomans
The Hospital Club Studios	**020-7170 9110**
24 Endell Street	Fax 020-7170 9102
London WC2H 9HQ	Anne Marie Phelan
Imagist Studios	**0117-938 2000**
Units 8 & 9, Second Way	Emma Curtis
Avonmouth, Bristol BS11 8DF	
www.imagiststudios.com	
Island Studios	**020-8956 5600**
2 Dukes Road	Fax 020-8956 5604
London W3 0SL	Steve Giudici
www.islandstudios.net	

Kentish Town Studios	**020-7691 3787**
Regis Road	Fax 020-7691 3801
London NW5 3EG	Peter Piddock
www.kentishtownstudios.tv	

Leavesden Studios	**01923-685060**
South Way	Fax 01923-685061
Leavesden, Herts WD25 7LT	Daniel Dark

Litestructures Live Studio	**01977-659888**
Langthwaite Business Park, South Kirby	Fax 01977-659801
Wakefield, W Yorks WF9 3NR	Adam Bettley

Liverpool Film Studios	**0151-225 0134**
105 Boundary Street	Fax 0151-225 0155
Liverpool L5 9YJ	Chris Thurston

London Stock Exchange Studios	**020-7797 2040**
Media & Business Complex	Fax 020-7920 4770
10 Paternoster Square, London EC4M 7LS	

The London Studios	**020-7157 5555**
Upper Ground	Fax 020-7157 5757
London SE1 9LT	Kathy Schulz

Longcross Studios	**01344-635631**
Chobham Lane	Fax 01344-635559
Chertsey, Surrey KT16 0EE	Bob Terry

Macmillan Media	**028-9043 6550**
Broadcast Centre Belfast, Venture Gate	Fax 028-9032 5490
32-36 Dublin Road, Belfast BT2 7HN	

Macmillan Media	**0141-352 8620**
Broadcast Centre Glasgow	Fax 0141-333 0943
1 Woodside Place, Glasgow G3 7QF	

The Maidstone Studios	**01622-691111**
Vinters Park	Fax 01622-684411
Maidstone, Kent ME14 5NZ	Emma Norris

Malcolm Ryan Studios	**020-8947 4766**
Unit 48, Wimbledon Stadium Business Centre	Fax 020-8947 9517
Riverside Road, London SW17 0BA	Luke Ryan
www.mrstudios.co.uk	

Meadows Farm Studios	**01491-577789**
Marlow Road	Fax 01491-410504
Henley-on-Thames, Oxon RG9 3AA	Richard Pinches

MediaCityUK	**0161-660 3710**
The Pie Factory, 101 Broadway	Andy Waters
Salford Quays, Manchester M50 2EQ	

mediahouse	**020-8233 5400**
3 Burlington Lane	Fax 020-8233 5401
London W4 2TH	Cherry Portbury
www.mediahouse.tv	

Millbank Studios	**020-7233 2020**
4 Millbank	Fax 020-7233 3158
London SW1P 3JA	Caroline Bloomfield

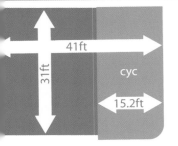

Mount Pleasant Studio	**020-7837 1957**
51-53 Mount Pleasant	Fax 020-7168 3106
London WC1X 0AE	Mark Dunn
www.mountpleasantstudio.com	
MTV Studios	**020-7284 7866**
17-19 Hawley Crescent	Fax 020-7284 7641
London NW1 8TT	Jane Anderson
Pacific Quay	**0141-422 6830**
BBC Scotland	Natalie Adams
40 Pacific Quay, Glasgow G51 1DA	
Panalux Island Studios	**01204-794000**
Manchester Road, Kearsley	Fax 01204-571877
Bolton, Lancs BL4 8RL	Colin Smart
Park Royal Studios	**020-8965 9778**
1 Barretts Green Road	Fax 020-8963 1056
London NW10 7AE	Scott Chambers
The Pie Factory	**0161-660 3600**
101 Broadway	Andy Sumner
Salford Quays, Manchester M50 2EQ	
www.thepiefactory.co.uk	
Pinewood Studios	**01753-651700**
Part of the Pinewood Studios Group	Fax 01753-656219
Pinewood Road, Iver Heath, Bucks SL0 0NH	
www.pinewoodgroup.com	

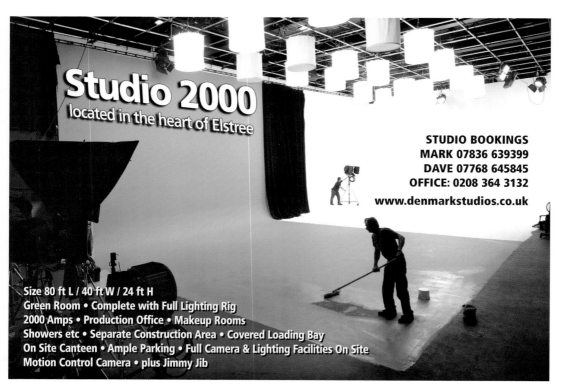

STUDIO, HD POST PRODUCTION, SUBTITLING, PRODUCTION OFFICES

Studio Alba, 54a Seaforth Road, Stornoway, HS1 2SD
01851 701125/701200   info@studioalba.com
www.studioalba.com

Plough Studios	**020-7622 1939**
Units 4-5	Tim Edwards
9 Park Hill, London SW4 9NS	
Portland TV	**020-7308 5351**
4 Selsdon Way	Fax 020-7308 6001
London E14 9GL	
Riverside Television Studios	**020-8237 1000**
Crisp Road	Fax 020-8237 1121
London W6 9RL	Bobbi Blackman
Sands Film Studios	**020-7231 2209**
119 Rotherhithe Street	Fax 020-7231 2119
London SE16 4NF	Olivier Stockman
Sassy Films Studio	**020-8905 2345**
Unit 407, Centennial Park	Juliette Linton
Centennial Avenue, Elstree, Herts WD6 3TN	
Savoir Faire Studios	**01603-765005**
50-52 Bessemer Road	Julian Sandiford
Norwich NR4 6DQ	
Shepperton Studios	**01932-562611**
Part of the Pinewood Studios Group	Fax 01932-568989
Studios Road, Shepperton, Middx TW17 0QD	
www.pinewoodgroup.com	
South Manchester Studios	**0161-432 9000**
Battersea Road, Heaton Mersey	Fax 0161-443 1325
Stockport, Cheshire SK4 3EA	Robert Topliss
Stephen Street Studios	**020-7691 6555**
1 Stephen Street	Tony Shepherd
London W1T 1AL	
The Studio	**020-7228 5228**
21 Cabul Road	Fax 020-7228 9975
London SW11 2PR	Simon Tobias
Studio 2000	**020-8364 3132**
5 Elstree Way	Fax 020-8360 4618
Borehamwood, Herts WD6 1SF	Mark Brennan
www.denmarkstudios.co.uk	

Studio Alba	**01851-701125**
54A Seaforth Road	Fax 01851-701094
Stornoway, Isle Of Lewis HS1 2SD	Willie Macleod
www.studioalba.com	
Studio81	**0113-246 7390**
Leeds Production Centre, Studio 81	Fax 0113-242 5261
Kirkstall Road, Leeds LS3 1LH	Martin Cook
www.leedsis.biz	
Summit Studios	**020-8799 6199**
Summit House	
100 Hangar Lane, London W5 1EZ	
Teddington Studios	**020-8977 3252**
Part of the Pinewood Studios Group	Fax 020-8943 4050
Broom Road, Teddington, Middx TW11 9NT	
www.pinewoodgroup.com	
Twickenham Film Studios	**020-8607 8888**
St Margarets	Fax 020-8607 8889
Twickenham, Middx TW1 2AW	Caroline Tipple
Waterfall House	**020-8746 2000**
Unit 2, Silver Road	Fax 020-8746 0180
White City Industrial Estate, London W12 7SG	Ann Fairclough
Waterloo Film Studios	**020-3405 2260**
27-31 Webber Street	Sabelo Mcanyana
London SE1 8QW	
Westminster Live	**020-7587 3450**
Westminster Tower	Fax 020-7587 3618
3 Albert Embankment, London SE1 7SP	Daniel Mason

STUDIOS - ANIMAL

Amazing Animals	**01608-683389**
Heythrop Zoological Gardens, Heythrop	Fax 01608-683420
Chipping Norton, Oxon OX7 5TU	Jim Clubb
www.amazinganimals.co.uk	

STUDIOS - PHOTOGRAPHIC

Amberroom	**020-7228 0220**
Studio 3	Fax 020-7228 2090
2-18 Yelverton Road, London SW11 3QG	Phil Conrad
Basement Photographic	**01628-529900**
Unit 11, Wooburn Industrial Park	Fax 01628-851039
Wooburn Green, High Wycombe, Bucks HP10 0PE	Jacquie Higham
BigSky London	**020-7619 6600**
29-31 Brewery Road	Fax 020-7619 6611
London N7 9QH	Melanie Elliott
Film Plus	**020-8969 0234**
77-81 Scrubs Lane	Fax 020-8969 0567
London NW10 6QW	Arun Soni

Holborn Studios	**020-7490 4099**
49-50 Eagle Wharf Road	Fax 020-7253 8120
London N1 7ED	Billy McCartney
Hoxton Street Studios	**020-7033 1984**
12-18 Hoxton Street	Fax 020-7033 1985
London N1 6NG	Fatima Ianno
Hungry Tiger Studios	**020-7751 8600**
Unit 16, The Piper Building	Fax 020-7751 8618
Peterborough Road, London SW6 3EF	Steve Jackson
Jasmine Studios	**020-7751 1157**
186-188 Shepherds Bush Road	Fax 020-7751 1156
London W6 7NL	Matthew Honey
PPL	**01243-555561**
William Bookers Yard, The Street	Fax 01243-555562
Walberton, Arundel, W Sussex BN18 0PF	Barry Pickthall
Premier Park Studios	**0844-815 6624**
Unit 10, Premier Park	Fax 020-8965 9290
Premier Park Road, London NW10 7NZ	Ritchie Garrod
Sola Studio	**020-8960 1121**
3 Latimer Place	Fax 020-7117 1930
London W10 6QT	Mike Parker
Spot Studios	**020-7354 9955**
Canonbury Yard	Fax 020-7354 8333
202 New North Road, London N1 7BJ	James Rudland
Spring Studios	**020-7267 8383**
Spring House	Fax 020-7267 8481
10 Spring Place, London NW5 3BH	Verien Wiltshire
Street Studios	**020-7923 9430**
2 Dunston Street	Fax 020-7923 9429
London E8 4EB	Alec McGhie
Unit Studio	**07970-371897**
Unit 40, Cromwell Industrial Estate	Sam Mercer
Staffa Road, London E10 7QZ	
The Worx	**020-7371 9777**
10 Heathmans Road	Fax 020-7371 9888
London SW6 4TJ	Michelle Henochsberg

STUDIOS - UNDERWATER

Pinewood Studios Underwater Stage	**01753-651700**
Part of the Pinewood Studios Group	Fax 01753-656219
Pinewood Road, Iver Heath, Bucks SL0 0NH	
www.pinewoodgroup.com	
The Underwater Studio	**01268-270171**
Archers Fields, Burnt Mills Estate	Fax 01268-270156
Basildon, Essex SS13 1DL	Geoff Smith
www.theunderwaterstudio.com	

STUNT CO-ORDINATORS

Action Inc	07711-375928
www.abbicollins.com	Abbi Collins
Vic Armstrong	01344-483326
Mobile 07771-932088	
Gary Arthurs	07710-056511
Bailey Balloons	01275-375300
Mobile 07976-523530	Jo Bailey
www.baileyballoons.co.uk	
Andy Bennett	01249-446624
Mobile 07785-717970	
Dani Biernat	01737-554955
Mobile 07710-021128	
Andy Bradford	020-7435 2856
Mobile 07831-281320	
Richard Bradshaw	01707-872396
Mobile 07798-866303	
Terry Cade	01536-711583
Mobile 07808-928966	
Marc Cass	07860-776978
Gary Connery	07768-696369
David Cronnelly	01923-286446
Mobile 07831-880182	
Clive Curtis	01476-530572
Mobile 07831-850295	
Ray de Haan	07831-820195
The Devils Horsemen	01296-720854
Mobile 07808-901428	Gerard Naprous
www.thedevilshorsemen.com	
Nrinder Dhudwar	01634-842519
Mobile 07860-889500	
Jim Dowdall	01580-880322
Mobile 07836-204228	
Sadie Eden	01344-884664
Mobile 07816-315214	
Steve Emerson	020-8858 2096
Mobile 07831-858572	
Royston Farrell	020-8904 4978
Neil Finnigan	07836-666140
Elaine Ford	07836-633877
Dean Forster	07818-887328
Mark Franklin Henson	01273-857036
Mobile 07768-580595	

Sarah Franzl	01442-253018
Mobile 07831-465650	
Nick Gillard	01273-680575
Mobile 07775-912366	
Steve Griffin	07860-711009
Richard Hammatt	01923-266373
Mobile 07836-642074	
www.nineninecars.com	
Paul Heasman	01932-862484
Mobile 07885-877281	
Frank Henson	01273-857657
Mobile 07860-208583	
Paul Herbert	01438-716813
Mobile 07785-983983	
Jeff Hewitt-Davis	01279-422736
Mobile 07785-574467	
Nick Hobbs	020-8950 1199
Mobile 07768-056114	
William Hobbs	07884-253295
David Holland	020-8743 2904
Mobile 07774-908907	
Sy Hollands	07831-392589
Rob Inch	01494-439850
Mobile 07973-307095	
Rowley Irlam	01923-263600
Mobile 07710-057887	
Steve James	01372-372680
Paul Jennings	07889-041663
Dave Judge	07774-101448
www.stuntjudge.co.uk	
Crispin Layfield	01494-513953
Mobile 07850-193774	
Derek Lea	01344-843063
Mobile 07850-150890	
Wendy Leech	01344-483326
Mobile 07771-932087	
Mark Lisbon	0121-378 1001
Mobile 07831-890793	
Tom Lucy	07802-600950
Wayne Michaels	01344-882122
Mobile 07836-225031	
Gareth Milne	020-7686 1891
Mobile 07836-278778	

Chrissy Monk	01342-321321
Mobile 07831-819191	
Valentino Musetti	020-7387 2595
Mobile 07836-248079	
Gerard Naprous	01296-720854
Mobile 07860-321284	
www.thedevilshorsemen.com	
Ray Nicholas	01744-604495
Mobile 07885-948824	
Peter Pedrero	01908-368072
Mobile 07956-273108	
Dinny Powell	020-8851 9063
Mobile 07866-129469	
Gary Powell	01737-371787
Mobile 07831-803273	
Greg Powell	01737-242788
Mobile 07785-705874	
Doug Robinson	01344-310853
Mobile 07789-811754	
Denise Ryan	01425-472377
Mobile 07785-998454	

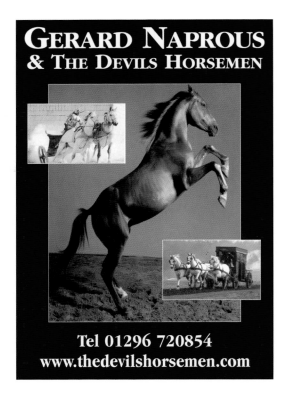

GERARD NAPROUS
& THE DEVILS HORSEMEN

Tel 01296 720854
www.thedevilshorsemen.com

Lee Sheward	**01403-780595**
Mobile 07831-474829	
Colin Skeaping	**07860-756708**
Andy Smart	**020-8393 6646**
Mobile 07866-470236	
Julian Spencer	**07885-743334**
Stuart St Paul	**07775-768531**
Alan Stuart	**01243-674477**
Mobile 07836-231129	
Steve Truglia	**020-8989 2801**
Tony Van Silva	**01273-775685**
Mobile 07831-488190	
Chris Webb	**01903-786500**
Mobile 07973-465154	
Bill Weston	**01980-862222**
Mobile 07836-517844	
Paul Weston	**01590-670660**
Mobile 07860-878800	
Steve Whyment	**01394-380203**
Mobile 07831-556527	

Roderick Woodruff	**01932-789358**
Mobile 07850-059005	

STUNT - PERFORMERS

Action Inc	**07711-375928**
www.abbicollins.com	Abbi Collins
Lucy Allen	**020-8555 2334**
Mobile 07831-185549	
Stephanie Carey	**07979-958176**
Tracey Caudle	**01342-312366**
Mobile 07956-539642	
Stuart Clark	**01784-483751**
Mobile 07831-467235	
Wayne de Strete	**01273-230214**
Mobile 07970-976381	
Tracey Eddon	**01344-882122**
Mobile 07812-381243	
Cecily Fay Harris	**07866-894630**
David Garrick	**07802-256282**
Paul Hornsby	**020-8981 4884**
Mobile 07867-614929	
Jason Hunjan	**020-8644 7892**
Mobile 07932-035633	
Dave Judge	**07774-101448**
www.stuntjudge.co.uk	
Vincent Keane	**01923-855805**
Mobile 07831-840749	
Paul Kennington	**07710-319929**
Maurice Lee	**07956-539047**
Erol Mehmet	**07770-934916**
Peter Miles	**01761-435894**
Mobile 07968-777884	
Mark Mottram	**07850-779315**
Daniel Naprous	**01296-720854**
Mobile 07860-149415	
www.devilshorsemen.co.uk	
Brian Nickels	**07702-211907**
Bean Peel	**01494-439850**
Mobile 07970-737739	
Jim Ryan	**0161-437 6505**
Mobile 07802-900095	

Kiran Shah	**020-8572 7671**
Mobile 07718-898269	
CC Smiff	**07976-298507**
Lyndal Smith	**07770-983868**
Leonard Woodcock	**07740-985899**
Zero-g	**020-7561 0404**
07900-696919	Dave Judge Keiko Nagai
www.zero-gfilms.com	

STUNT ENGINEERING

99 Cars

01923-266373 Mobile 07785-382448
Fax 01923-260852
Email: david@nineninecars.com
www.nineninecars.com
Hyde Meadow Farm, Hyde Lane, Hemel Hempstead,
Herts HP3 8SA
Contact: David Hammatt
Stunt engineering and mechanical effects - Action vehicle
preparation and controlled stunt effects using hydraulics and
cables - Complete action vehicle, tracking vehicle, low loader
and logistic services.

Artem	**020-8997 7771**
Perivale Park, Horsenden Lane South	Fax 020-8997 1503
Perivale, Middx UB6 7RH	Frank Steggall
www.artem.com	
Artem (Scotland)	**0141-427 5775**
64-68 Brand Street	Fax 0141-427 1199
Govan, Glasgow G51 1DG	Joanna Dewar Gibb
www.artem.com	
Dave Judge	**07774-101448**
dave@stuntjudge.co.uk	
www.stuntjudge.co.uk	
MGM Cars	**020-8324 2664**
Elstree Studios, Shenley Road	Fax 020-8324 2345
Borehamwood, Herts WD6 1JG	Ben Dillon Tom Dillon
www.mgmcars.com	
Stunt Rigging Services	**01753-522219**
Black Potts, Pococks Lane	07552-698621
Eton, Windsor, Berks SL4 6HW	Kevin Welch
www.stuntrigging.com	

STUNT EQUIPMENT

Screen Stunt Supplies	**07860-711009**
Stonepits Manor, Marringdean Road	Steve Griffin
Billingshurst, W Sussex RH14 9HE	

SUBTITLING

1st Transnational	**020-7629 2787**
180 Piccadilly	Fax 020-7329 5004
London W1J 9HF	Christine Wittl
www.1sttransnational.com	
Independent Media Support (IMS)	**020-7440 5400**
10 Carlisle Street	Fax 020-7440 5410
London W1D 3BR	Melvin Angell
ITFC	**020-8752 0352**
28 Concord Road	Fax 020-8993 6393
London W3 0TH	Liz Clarke
www.itfc.com	
Joanna Clarkson	**020-8569 7098**
126 Linkfield Road	Joanna Clarkson
Isleworth, Middx TW7 6QJ	
Sapex Scripts	**020-8236 1600**
Elstree Studios, Shenley Road	Fax 020-8324 2771
Borehamwood, Herts WD6 1JG	Paul Sattin
www.sapex.co.uk	
Screen Subtitling Systems	**01473-831700**
The Old Rectory, Church Lane	Fax 01473-830078
Claydon, Suffolk IP6 0EQ	
Screentext	**01957-711863**
38 Setters Hill Estate, Baltasound	Fax 01957-711863
Unst, Shetland XE2 9DU	David Packham
SDI Media UK	**020-8237 7900**
Cambridge House	Fax 020-8237 7950
100 Cambridge Grove, London W6 0LE	
Studio Alba	**01851-701125**
54A Seaforth Road	Fax 01851-701094
Stornoway, Isle Of Lewis HS1 2SD	Willie Macleod
www.studioalba.com	
Subti	**020-7495 7494**
48 Albemarle Street	Fax 020-7409 0605
London W1S 4JP	Federico Spoletti

TECHNICAL ADVISORS

Consultant Magician	**01727-838656**
67 De Tany Court	07738-971077
St Albans, Herts AL1 1TX	Tony Middleton
www.consultantmagician.com	
Magic	
Foxtrot Firearms	**020-8964 3555**
3B Brassie Avenue	Fax 020-8960 3811
London W3 7DE	Richard Howell
www.foxtrot-productions.co.uk	
Police & Military	

Griffin Historical   01686-624439

Upper Weeg, Dolfor   Mark Griffin
Newtown, Powys SY16 4AT
Historic Reconstruction

Medinet Film Hire   0800-281912

Unit 18, Park Royal Business Centre   Fax 020-8694 1880
9-17 Park Royal Road, London NW10 7LQ   Dr Anthony MacDermott
www.medinetfilmhire.com
Medical

Military Advisory Services   01672-851826

The Old Rectory, Alton Barnes   Fax 01672-851150
Marlborough, Wilts SN8 4LB   David Carson
Military

Police Advisory Service   01923-823716

20 Ardross Avenue   Malcolm Cooper
Northwood, Middx HA6 3DS
Police

TELECINE

BBC Studios & Post Production   020-8225 6000

Television Centre   Fax 020-8576 8806
Wood Lane, London W12 7RJ
www.bbcstudiosandpostproduction.com

Cintel International   01920-463939

Watton Road   Fax 01920-460803
Ware, Herts SG12 0AE   Simon Clark
www.cintel.co.uk

ilab   020-7287 9520

55 Poland Street
London W1F 7NN
www.ilabuk.co.uk

ITN Video Facilities   020-7430 4303

200 Grays Inn Road   Fax 020-7430 4381
London WC1X 8XZ   David Price

Prime Focus   020-7565 1000

37 Dean Street   Shail Shah
London W1D 4PT
www.primefocusworld.com

Stanley Productions   020-7439 0311

147 Wardour Street   Fax 020-7437 2126
London W1F 8WD   Steve Langston Mick Pruce
www.stanleysonline.co.uk

TKone   020-7240 7040

35 Bedfordbury   Fax 020-7240 2232
London WC2N 4DU   David Yeo

VideoStation   020-8987 6035

Suite 33   Joseph Faul
10 Barley Mow Passage, London W4 4PH

TELEVISION STATIONS - CABLE DIGITAL & SATELLITE

AL JAZEERA

HEAD OFFICE
I Knightsbridge, London SWIX 7XW
020-7201 2887
http://english.aljazeera.net

Bureau Chief	Muftah Al-Suwaidan
Head of Communications	Satnam Matharu

Launched November 2006 Al Jazeera English is a 24-hour English language news and current affairs TV channel headquartered in Doha, Qatar. It is the sister channel of Al Jazeera Arabic TV and the world's first global English language news channel to be based in the Middle East. The station broadcasts factual programming including news features and analysis documentaries, live debates, current affairs, business and sport. News management rotates daily around four broadcast centres based in Kuala Lumpur, Doha, London and Washington DC 'following the sun'. They are supported by 21 bureaus that gather and produce news. The channel aims to provide both a regional voice and a fresh global perspective on international news to a worldwide English speaking audience. The channel currently reaches 140 million homes making it one of the three biggest global English language 24 hour news channels. Al Jazeera English is available in the UK and Ireland on Sky's digital satellite platform on channel 514.

ARY DIGITAL

HEAD OFFICE
65 North Acton Road, London NWI0 6PJ
020-8838 6300 Fax 020-8838 6122
www.arydigital.tv

Primarily an Asian channel providing family entertainment 24 hours a day including news, drama and talk shows.

AT THE RACES

HEAD OFFICE
9 Kingsway, London WC2B 6XF
020-7954 3000 Fax 020-7954 3001
www.attheraces.com

Chief Executive Officer	Matthew Imi
Chief Financial Officer	Kevin Robertson
Legal Director	Teresa Walsh
Head of Commercial Development	Tony Sweeney
Executive Producer	Rob Dakin
Head of Marketing	James Singer
Head of Online	Matthew Taylor

B4U

HEAD OFFICE
19 Heather Park Drive, Wembley, Middx HA0 ISS
020-8795 7171 Fax 020-8795 7181
www.b4utv.com

B4U MOVIES showcases star studded premieres, Bollywood blockbusters and an exclusive mix of behind-the-scenes programming.

B4U MUSIC is the number one Asian channel in the UK, with the biggest hits, star interviews and exclusives that count.

THE

b a b y

CHANNEL

BABY CHANNEL

HEAD OFFICE
Bentima House, 169-172 Old Street, London ECIV 9BP
020-7608 8672
www.babychanneltv.com

Chief Executive	Henry Scott

RAI Amsterdam

Conference 9-14 September : Exhibition 10-14 September

IBC2010
Experience the
state-of-the-art

2010

IBC is the premier annual event for professionals engaged in the creation, management and delivery of entertainment and news content worldwide.

- **45,000+ attendees** from 140+ countries
- **1300+** key international technology suppliers across 11+ exhibition halls
- **world-class demonstrations** of groundbreaking technology such as stereo 3D
- **agenda-setting conference** with 300+ high-profile international speakers

- **NEW Connected World** for IPTV, Mobile & Digital Signage (Hall 9)
- **FREE hands-on training;** Production Village (Hall 11) and Post Production (Hall 7)
- **FREE Exhibition Business Briefings**
- **FREE movies screenings** in the IBC Big Screen
- **FREE entry** to the prestigious awards ceremony on Sunday 12 September

Register now at www.ibc.org/register

www.ibc.org

IBC Fifth Floor International Press Centre 76 Shoe Lane London EC4A 3JB UK
T. +44 (0) 20 7832 4100 **F.** +44 (0) 20 7832 4130 **E. info@ibc.org**

The Baby Channel is the only channel aimed exclusively at pregnant women and parents of pre-school children. The key themes and topics featured on the channel are: pregnancy and health, child health and nutrition, early learning, first aid and safety in the home. The channel incorporates a 'Baby Channel Shop', which retails a range of products to consumers during teleshopping airtime, which may also be purchased online.

BBC NEWS CHANNEL

HEAD OFFICE

Television Centre, Wood Lane, London WI2 7RJ

020-8743 8000

www.bbc.co.uk/news

Controller, BBC News Channel   Kevin Bakhurst

Britain's most-watched news channel, delivering breaking news and analysis all day, every day.

BBC THREE / FOUR

BBC CORPORATE & BBC RADIO HEADQUARTERS

Broadcasting House, Portland Place, London WIA IAA

020-7580 4468 Fax 020-7637 I630

BBC NEWS & BBC TELEVISION HEADQUARTERS

Television Centre, Wood Lane, London WI2 7RJ

020-8743 8000 Fax 020-8749 7520

www.bbc.co.uk

Channel Controller, BBC3   Danny Cohen

Channel Controller, BBC4   Richard Klein

BBC THREE aims to offer an intelligent, ambitious mix of programmes which reflect the things that matter to young British adults. The channel is committed to a mixed schedule of news, current affairs, music, documentaries, arts and coverage of international issues, as well as to high quality innovative drama, comedy and entertainment.

BBC FOUR is for audiences in search of even greater depth and range in their viewing. With an ambition to be British televisions most intellectually and culturally enriching channel, BBC Four balances a distinctive mix of arts, music, culture and knowledge programmes.

BFBS

HEAD OFFICE

Chalfont Grove, Narcot Lane, Chalfont St Peter, Bucks SL9 8TN

01494-878304 Fax 01494-874429

www.bfbs.com

Chief Executive   Nick Pollard

Controller of TV   Helen Williams

Head of Scheduling & Acquisitions   Richard Hulme

Head of Newsgathering   Laura Rhea

BIOGRAPHY CHANNEL

HEAD OFFICE

Grant Way, Isleworth, Middx TW7 5QD

0870-240 3000 Fax 020-7941 5187

www.thebiographychannel.co.uk

Managing Director   Tom Davidson

Bio is famous for telling people's stories. Its programmes are all about people with incredible tales to tell, be they the rich and famous or ordinary people with extraordinary lives.

BOOMERANG

LONDON OFFICE

Turner Broadcasting System Europe

Turner House, I6 Great Marlborough Street, London WIF 7HS

020-7693 I000 Fax 020-7693 I00I

www.boomerangtv.co.uk

President	Jeff Kupsky
Turner Broadcasting System Europe	
Senior VP & General Manager	Pete Flamman
Turner Broadcasting System EMEA	
Senior VP, Digital Media	Casey Harwood
VP, Network Operations	Gabby Redfern

Boomerang offers an exciting mix of family favourite cartoons such as Scooby-Doo, Tom & Jerry, The Garfield Show, Pink Panther & Pals and Looney Tunes. Boomerang is available 24 hours a day on digital cable and satellite in the UK and has localised services throughout Europe, the Middle East and Africa where it is available in 11 languages and in over 35 million homes. Boomerang is operated by Turner Broadcasting System Europe, a Time Warner Company.

BRAVO

HEAD OFFICE
160 Great Portland Street, London WIW 5QA
020-7299 5000 Fax 020-7299 6000
www.bravo.co.uk

Director of Programming	Daniela Neuman
Channel Editor	David Clarke
Senior Commissioning Editor	Amy Barham

Bravo has been entertaining men since 1985, and is the UK's leading entertainment destination for men. It premieres an eclectic and award-winning blend of cutting edge original productions from the top rating Brits Behind Bars: America's Toughest Jail to gritty factual documentary series Danny Dyer's Deadliest Men, Chris Ryan's Elite Police and MacIntyre's World's Toughest Towns. It is the exclusive sporting home of TNA Wrestling and cult ratings Dog The Bounty Hunter.

CARTOON NETWORK

LONDON OFFICE
Turner Broadcasting System Europe
Turner House, 16 Great Marlborough Street, London WIF 7HS
020-7693 1000 Fax 020-7693 1001
www.cartoonnetwork.co.uk

For Key Personnel see BOOMERANG

Cartoon Network is a leading commercial kids' TV network in the UK, which broadcasts a range of popular comedy and action-adventure animation. Hit shows include Ben 10, Star Wars: The Clone Wars, Bakugan Battle Brawlers, Storm Hawks, World Of Quest, Johnny Test, Ed, Edd & Eddy and the Grim Adventures Of Billy and Mandy. Cartoon Network can also be experienced through it's award-winning website, via games, VOD, mobiles and through an array of licensing and merchandising. Since launching as a pan-European channel in 1993, Cartoon Network now has localised services throughout Europe, the Middle East and Africa where it is available in 14 languages and in over 57 million homes. Cartoon Network is operated by Turner Broadcasting System Europe, a Time Warner Company.

CBBC

HEAD OFFICE
Television Centre, Wood Lane, London WI2 7RJ
020-8743 8000
www.bbc.co.uk/cbbc

Controller, CBBC	Damian Kavanagh
Head of CBBC In-House Production	Steven Andrew

CBBC is for primary school children aged 6-12 years. We want to reflect the lives of the audience and to give them multi-platform content which is innovative, challenging and infectious. CBBC's tone is funny, energetic, unpredictable, upbeat and fun. We give audiences opportunities to participate, learn something new and laugh out loud. We want CBBC content talked about in the playground and we want our content to empower and stimulate children.

CBEEBIES

HEAD OFFICE
Television Centre, Wood Lane, London WI2 7RJ
020-8743 8000
www.bbc.co.uk/cbeebies

Controller, CBeebies — Kate Benbow

Head of CBeebies Production — Alison Stewart
Animation & Acquisitions

Executive Producer, Independents — Sarah Colclough

CBeebies offers high quality, mostly UK-produced programmes to educate and entertain the BBC's youngest audience. The channel provides a range of programming designed to encourage learning through play in a consistently safe environment for children aged 6 or under. By developing programmes which are creative, imaginative, stimulating and trusted, CBeebies seeks to enrich young children's lives through a range of topics and tales that grab their interest, empower them to try something new and encourage them to be active.

CHALLENGE

HEAD OFFICE

160 Great Portland Street, London W1W 5QA

020-7299 5000 Fax 020-7299 6000

www.challenge.co.uk

Channel Controller — David Clarke

Commissioning Editor — Rebecca Johnson

Senior PR Manager — Jakki Lewis

It's Saturday night, every night on Challenge. Challenge is the home of game show entertainment, combining mad cap cult shows with world famous quiz formats and game shows galore.

CHINESE CHANNEL

HEAD OFFICE

Teddington Studios, Broom Road, Teddington,

Middx TW11 9NT

020-8614 8300 Fax 020-8943 0982

www.chinese-channel.co.uk

Assistant General Manager — Lawrence Ma

Programme & Production Manager — Harry Cheung

TVBS-Europe is a chinese-language channel, which is broadcast via satellite to 48 countries in Europe.

CITV

HEAD OFFICE

200 Grays Inn Road, London WC1X 8HF

020-7157 3000

www.itv.com

Commercial Director, ITV Channels — Jonathan Rogers

Director of Digital Channels & Acquisitions — Zai Bennett

Controller, Digital Channels — Emma Tennant

ITV's dedicated childrens channel has gone from strength to strength since its launch in 2006. Aimed at younger viewers it is on air every day between 6.00am and 6.00pm. The channel features a range of UK and imported children's programming such as Pocoyo, Horrid Henry, Art Attack and My Parents Are Aliens.

CNBC

LONDON OFFICE

10 Fleet Place, London EC4M 7QS

020-7653 9300 Fax 020-7653 5756

www.cnbc.com

President & CEO — Mick Buckley

Director of Operations — John Turner

VP, News & Programming — Barbara Stelzner

VP, Marketing & Communications — Charlotte Westgate

CNBC is the leading global broadcaster of live business and financial news and information, reporting directly from the major financial markets around the globe, with three regional networks in Asia, EMEA and the US. In EMEA, CNBC is the only real-time, pan-regional business and financial news network dedicated to CEOs, senior corporate executives, the financial services industry and EMEA investors. The channel is available in approximately 130 million homes, 1,400 banks and financial institutions and leading hotels across Europe, The Middle East and Africa.

CNN INTERNATIONAL

EUROPEAN HEAD OFFICE

Turner House, 16 Great Marlborough Street, London WIF 7HS

020-7693 1000 Fax 020-7693 1001

www.cnn.com

President - TBS Europe	Jeff Kupsky
CNNI Managing Director, EMEA	Tony Maddox

CNN is the world's leading global 24-hour news network, delivered across a range of multimedia platforms including television, mobile phones and internet. The channel's output comprises its trademark breaking news, business news, sports news, current affairs and analysis, documentaries and feature programming. CNN is a Time Warner Company.

COMMUNITY CHANNEL

HEAD OFFICE

Riverwalk House, 157-161 Millbank, London SWI 4RR

020-7217 3717

www.communitychannel.org

Director of Digital Media	Mark Dodd

Community Channel is the UK's only television channel that is dedicated to highlighting the issues that surround both the local and international communities as well as the voluntary sector.

DISCOVERY CHANNEL

HEAD OFFICE

Discovery House, Building 2, Chiswick Park,

566 Chiswick High Road, London W4 5YB

020-8811 3000 Fax 020-8811 3100

www.discoverychannel.co.uk

Acting General Manager UK	Sahar Elhabashi
VP, Programming	Dan Korn
Press & PR	Claire McCormack

Discovery Communications is the world's number one non-fiction media company reaching more than 1.5 billion cumulative subscribers in more than 170 countries. Discovery empowers people to explore their world and satisfy their curiosity through 100-plus worldwide networks led by Discovery Channel.

DISNEY CHANNEL

HEAD OFFICE

Building 12, Chiswick Park, 566 Chiswick High Road,

London W4 5BN

020-8222 1000 Fax 020-8222 1144

www.disneychannel.co.uk

VP, Programming Disney Channels UK & Ireland	Jonathan Boseley
VP, Brand Marketing Disney Channels EMEA	Nicoletta Gelli

E4

HEADQUARTERS

124 Horseferry Road, London SWIP 2TX

020-7396 4444

www.e4.com

Head of E4	Angela Jain

E4 is Channel 4's digital entertainment channel and features a mix of new commissions, acquisitions and repeats of the best of recent Channel 4 programmes. The new commissions should have a 'Channel 4' attitude and be entertainment programmes, although the definition of entertainment is very broad stretching from arts and youth culture documentaries to new comedy to reality formats. The commissions are important in forging an identity for E4 and as such should be innovative, imaginative and intelligent. As a digital channel E4 is keen to use interactive digital technology where appropriate and want programmes that use the internet to its full potential.

EURONEWS

HEAD OFFICE
114 St Martins Lane, London WC2N 4BE
020-7240 8717 Fax 020-7240 8718
www.euronews.net

CEO	Philip Cayla
Head of Programming	Lucian Sarb

EuroNews, the pan-European news channel launched in January 1993. It offers international news from a European perspective and simultaneously broadcasts in nine languages through cable digital platforms and terrestrial TV in 146 countries in Europe, the Middle East, the American and the African continents to 331 million homes. Every 30 minutes, EuroNews provides a constantly updated bulletin containing in-depth coverage of the day's top news, sport, business and European affairs, together with a comprehensive weather forecast. EuroNews also brings a wide range of current affairs and lifestyle features.

EXTREME SPORTS

HEAD OFFICE
105-109 Salusbury Road, London NW6 6RG
020-7328 8808 Fax 020-7751 7270
www.extreme.com

Managing Director	Phil Jones
Head of Scheduling & Operations	Nesta Owens
Head of Acquisitions	Alex Barnes
Head of Programming	Kathy Fairbairn

Extreme Sports Channel is the world's first television channel totally dedicated to the world's fastest growing participatory sports and the music, fashion and way of life that accompanies them. Exteme is available in more than 50 countries across Europe, the Middle East and North Africa. It transmits in 10 languages and broadcasts 24/7.

FILM 4 PRODUCTIONS

HEADQUARTERS
124 Horseferry Road, London SWIP 2TX
020-7396 4444
www.film4.com

Controller of Film4 & Drama	Tessa Ross

Film4 Productions is Channel 4 Television's feature film division. The company develops and co-finances film productions and is known for working with the most innovative talent in the UK, whether new or established. Film4 is a founding partner of the Warp X digital studio.

GOD TV

UK OFFICE
Angel House, Borough Road, Sunderland SRI IHW
0191-568 0800 Fax 0191-568 0808
www.god.tv

Founders	Rory Alec Wendy Alec

The GOD Channel features a variety of Christian programming; presenting an array of powerful preachers, life-changing conferences and vibrant youth events, also including contemporary Christian music, films, fascinating documentaries, discussions, kid's shows and a range of exclusive interviews with prominent Christian leaders from around the globe.

HALLMARK CHANNEL

HEAD OFFICE
Prospect House, 80-110 New Oxford Street, London WCIA IHB
020-7079 6000 Fax 020-7631 2802

www.hallmarkchannel.co.uk

Managing Director, UK Channels	Lawrence Dawkin-Jones
Head of Marketing	Faye Harcourt
Senior Press Officer	Anna Morgan

HISTORY CHANNEL

HEAD OFFICE

Grant Way, Isleworth, Middx TW7 5QD

0870-240 3000 Fax 020-7941 5187

www.history.co.uk

Managing Director	Tom Davidson
Channel Director	James Pestell

ITV2 / ITV3 / ITV4

HEAD OFFICE

200 Grays Inn Road, London WC1X 8HF

0844-881 8000

www.itv.com

ITV's family of digital channels - ITV2, ITV3, ITV4 and CITV - are broadcast free-to-air on Freeview, digital satellite and cable, and are entirely funded by advertising and sponsorship.

ITV2 launched in 1998 is the UK's most popular digital channel and is particularly targeted at the younger 16-34 year old demographic. The schedule includes a mix of original commissions, spin-offs from ITV1 programming, movies, US acquired series and repeats. Original commissions for the channel include What Katie Did Next and Secret Diary Of A Call Girl, and spin-off programming include The Xtra Factor and Britain's Got Talent. Exclusive acquisitions include The Vampire Diaries, American Idol and Hell's Kitchen USA. ITV2's share of the viewing across 2009 was 2.4%, up from 2.1% in 2008.

ITV3 is aimed at an upmarket audience with a schedule including repeated ITV drama, acquired programming, films

and some original content. Programming which performs well on the channel includes Lewis, Agatha Christie's Poirot and A Touch Of Frost. ITV3 was the UK's second largest multichannel station in terms of its share of commercial impacts in 2009 and the third largest in terms of total viewing.

ITV4 targets young male viewers, with a schedule including live football, IPL cricket, Tour de France cycling, classic repeated drama and US acquisitions. ITV4 grew its volume of impacts by 8% in 2009.

LIVINGTV

HEAD OFFICE

160 Great Portland Street, London W1W 5QA

020-7299 5000 Fax 020-7299 6000

www.livingtv.co.uk

Director of Programming	Claudia Rosencrantz
Head of Commissioning	Mark Sammon

Commissions like Britain's Next Top Model, Dirty Dancing - The Time Of Your Life and Living With Kimberly Stewart have emerged as some of the UK's most talked-about programmes. As the home of the paranormal Living airs cult phenomena Most Haunted and the hugely successful Most Haunted Live. Living has also built a reputation for identifying and out-manoeuvring its rivals to the best acquired shows out there such as Grey's Anatomy, Criminal Minds and America's Next Top Model.

MORE4

HEADQUARTERS

124 Horseferry Road, London SW1P 2TX

020-7396 4444

www.channel4.com/programmes/tags/more4

Head of More4	Hamish Mykura

More4 is a digital channel which Channel 4 launched in 2005 on Freeview and other digital platforms. It features brand new documentaries, film, drama and current affairs and provides viewers with more of the high-quality intelligent programming for which Channel 4 is known and loved. At the heart of the schedule are the True Stories strand and viewers also have another chance to see the most talked about Channel 4 shows from the main channel.

MTV NETWORKS EUROPE

HEAD OFFICE
17-29 Hawley Crescent, London NW1 8TT
020-7284 7777 Fax 020-7284 7788
www.mtveurope.com

Executive VP & Managing Director	David Lynn
Executive VP, Content & Creative Director of Television	Heather Jones
Senior VP, Digital Media	Phillip Bourchier O'Ferrall
VP, Programming	Vanessa Brookman
Director Talent & Music	Matt Cook

MTV Networks is the largest television network in the world and a leading creator of programming and content across all media platforms. MTV Networks' brands are seen globally in 642 million households in 163 countries and 34 languages via 168 locally programmed and operated TV channels and more than 400 digital media properties. MTV Networks UK & Ireland operates 3 channel groups - Comedy, Kids and Music. Our ten branded music and entertainment channels comprise of MTV, MTV+1, MTV Rocks, MTV Classics, MTV Shows, MTV Hits, MTV Dance, MTV Base, VH1 and VIVA. They feature the best in music alongside popular shows such as Pimp My Ride, The Hills, Laguna Beach, My Super Sweet 16, Punk'd and Cribs. MTV Networks' music channels are available on Sky, Virgin Media and Freeview.

NATIONAL GEOGRAPHIC CHANNEL

HEAD OFFICE
Shepherds Building East, Richmond Way, London W14 0DQ
020-7751 7700
www.nationalgeographic.co.uk

General Manager (UK)	Simon Bohrsmann
Head of Programming	Jamil Ahmed

NICKELODEON

HEAD OFFICE
15-18 Rathbone Place, London W1T 1HU
020-7462 1000 Fax 020-7462 1030
www.nick.co.uk

Director of Channels	Howard Litton

Nickelodeon is the number 1 advertising-funded TV network in the UK. Launched in 1993, it comprises six dedicated award-winning entertainment channels for kids aged 2-12: Nickelodeon, NickToons, NickToonsters, Nick Jr, Nick Jr 2 and Nick Replay. The Nickelodeon network now reaches more than 10 million viewers a month and is available in 12.7 million cable and satellite homes.

PLAYBOY TV

HEAD OFFICE
Aquis House, Station Road, Hayes, Middx UB3 4DX
020-8581 7000 Fax 020-8581 7007
www.playboytv.co.uk

Head of European Marketing	Richard Gale

QVC

HEAD OFFICE
Marco Polo House, 346 Queenstown Road, Chelsea Bridge, London SW8 4NQ
020-7705 5600 Fax 020-7705 5601
www.qvcuk.com

Chief Executive Officer   Dermot Boyd

Director of Broadcasting   Brian Farrelly

QVC began broadcasting in the US in 1986. QVC UK was launched in 1993, QVC Germany in 1996 and QVC Japan in 2001. It reaches 166 million homes across the globe. QVC is Britain's first 24/7 365 days a year shopping channel.

REVELATION TV

HEAD OFFICE

Genesis House, Cocks Crescent, New Malden, Surrey KT3 4TA

020-8972 1400 Fax 020-8942 4367

www.revelationtv.com

Founders   Howard Conder Lesley Conder

Revelation TV is a Judeo Christian television service bringing live and pre-recorded discussion, music and educational programmes to both Christians and non-Christians.

SKY I

HEAD OFFICE

Grant Way, Isleworth, Middx TW7 5QD

0870-240 3000 Fax 020-7705 3030

www.skyl.sky.com

Head of Channel   Stuart Murphy

Head of Drama   Elaine Pyke

Head of Factual   Celia Taylor

Commissioning Editors, Drama   Annie Baxter
            Sarah Conroy
          Huw Kennair-Jones

Commissioning Editor, Entertainment   Duncan Gray

Senior Acquisitions   Louisa Forsyth
            Julia Stuart

Sky 1 is the most watched non-terrestrial channel in Sky homes, attracting more than 19m unique viewers every month. Sky 1 distinguishes itself from rival networks with award-winning exclusive US drama, home grown drama, talked about entertainment formats and distinctive factual entertainment programming.

SKY ARTS

HEAD OFFICE

New Horizons Court 4, 0Grant Way, Isleworth,

Middx TW7 5QD

0870-240 3000

www.skyarts.co.uk

Channel Director   John Cassy

Head of Programming   James Hunt

Head of Production   Laura Green

Head of Acquisitions   Philip Barnsdall-Thompson

Head of New Media   Sinead Hughes

Channel Scheduler   Tracy To

Marketing Controller   Georgina Seddon

Sky Arts 1's schedule is crammed full of the best contemporary arts programming, such as live rock concerts, documentaries and films.

Sky Art 2 is the home of Sky Arts more classical arts content, featuring the best of the world's operas, the big names from the Jazz world, an eclectic mix of contemporary and classical dance and concerts with the great conductors.

Sky Arts 1 HD and Sky Arts 2 HD simulcast all content from their standard definition channels, delivering spectacular clarity on the channel's visual art and live performance genres.

SYFY

HEAD OFFICE

Prospect House, 80-110 New Oxford Street, London WCIA IHB

020-7079 6000 Fax 020-7079 6500

www.syfy.co.uk

Reaching over 3 million people each week, SCI FI features a continuous stream of cinematic hits, British TV premiere series and special events, bringing viewers the best content from the worlds of the fantasy, paranormal and horror programming. SCI FI is a channel service of NBC Universal Global Networks, a division of NBC Universal.

TRAVEL CHANNEL

HEAD OFFICE
64 Newman Street, London WIT 3EF
020-7636 5401 Fax 020-7636 6424
www.travelchanneltv.com

Chief Executive	Richard Wolfe
Director of Broadcast	Steve Fright

Launched in 1994, Travel Channel broadcasts in 16 languages to 117 countries across Europe, the Middle East and Africa. Entertaining, informative and inspirational, Travel Channel presents a uniquely panoramic and objective perspective on the travel experience. Programmes transport viewers to every corner of the globe, on backpacking adventures, culinary quests, eco-friendly holidays and exclusive luxury getaways.

TURNER CLASSIC MOVIES - TCM

LONDON OFFICE
Turner Broadcasting System Europe
Turner House, 16 Great Marlborough Street, London WIF 7HS
020-7693 1000 Fax 020-7693 1001
www.tcmuk.tv

For Key Personnel see BOOMERANG

TCM (Turner Classic Movies) is a 24-hour cable, satellite and digital terrestrial film channel that launched in the US in 1994 and in the UK, Europe, the Middle East and Africa in 1999 as part of the Time Warner Group. Ensuring that film lovers are fully catered for is at the heart of TCM, whether it's quirky comedies such as Hannah And Her Sisters or Austin Powers: The Spy Who Shagged Me, horror greats like The Shining, acclaimed Westerns like Unforgiven, or crime dramas such as Goodfellas. TCM also shows family favourites such as Superman and The Wizard Of Oz as well as Oscar-winning epics like Gone With The Wind. TCM is available throughout EMEA in 50 million homes.

UKTV

HEAD OFFICE
160 Great Portland Street, London WIW 5QA
020-7299 6200 Fax 020-7299 5412
www.uktv.co.uk

Controller of Channels	Matthew Littlewood
Editor, UKTV Style & Style Gardens	Catherine Catton
Editor, UKTV Food & Bright Ideas	Paul Moreton
Editor, UKTV Gold & G2	James Newton
Editor, UKTV People	Steven North
Editor, UKTV Documentary & History	Adrian Wills
Editor, UKTV Drama	Richard Kingsbury

VIRGIN I

HEAD OFFICE
160 Great Portland Street, London WIW 5QA
020-7299 5000 Fax 020-7299 6000
www.virginl.co.uk

Director of Programmes	Daniela Neumann
Head of Commissioning	Mark Sammon
Senior PR Manager	Jakki Lewis

Virgin1 is a vibrant, mainstream, populist multi-platform entertainment channel packed with top drama premieres, movies, humour and compelling factual entertainment.

ZEE NETWORK

HEAD OFFICE
Unit 7, Belvue Business Centre, Belvue Road, Northolt,
Middx UB5 5QQ
020-8839 4000 Fax 020-8841 9550
www.zeetv.co.uk

Head of Programming   Shaney Burney

One of the world's largest Indian media and entertainment conglomerates, Zee Network reaches more than 500 million viewers in over 167 countries. Zee was the first South Asian television broadcaster to launch in the UK with its flagship channel Zee TV. Today it has expanded to five channels in the UK and one in Russia. Zee TV, the UK's most popular South Asian family entertainment channel, showcases gripping dramas, soaps, Bollywood blockbuster movies, reality shows and news. Zee Cinema has the largest library of Bollywood movies in the world with latest blockbusters and renowned classics. Zee Punjabi targets the punjabi speaking audience and broadcasts daily religious sermons, films, drama, comedy and music shows. Free-to-air channel Zing showcases the best of Bollywood and British Asian music with lifestyle and entertainment shows. Whilst Zee Cafe showcases for a Bengali and Marathi audience international cricket and regional programming with English subtitles.

TELEVISION STATIONS - TERRESTRIAL

BRITISH BROADCASTING CORPORATION

BBC CORPORATE & BBC RADIO HEADQUARTERS
Broadcasting House, Portland Place, London WIA IAA
020-7580 4468 Fax 020-7637 1630

BBC NEWS & BBC TELEVISION HEADQUARTERS
Television Centre, Wood Lane, London WI2 7RJ
020-8743 8000 Fax 020-8749 7520

BBC WORLDWIDE & BBC RESOURCES
Woodlands, 80 Wood Lane, London WI2 OTT
020-8433 2000
www.bbc.co.uk

BBC TRUST

Chairman	Sir Michael Lyons
Vice Chairman	Chitra Bharucha
	Diana Coyle
	Anthony Fry
	Alison Hastings (England)
	Patricia Hodgson
	Rotha Johnston (N Ireland)
	Janet Lewis-Jones (Wales)
	David Liddiment
	Mehmuda Mian
	Jeremy Peat (Scotland)
	Richard Tait

The BBC Trust consists of the Chairman, Vice-Chairman and ten members or 'trustees'. Four Trustees take special responsibility for England, Scotland, Wales and Northern Ireland. Their backgrounds and experience is wide, ranging from broadcasting, regulation, competition, business, the public sector and engagement with the public, to programme-making and journalism. They are appointed by the Queen on advice from ministers after an open selection process.

The role of the BBC Trust is to ensure, on behalf of all licence fee payers, that the BBC provides high quality output and good value for all UK citizens, and to protect the independence of the BBC. To achieve this, the Trustees must keep in close contact with licence fee payers, being aware of and understanding their expectations of the BBC. They do this via research, direct engagement with the public and through the work of the BBC Audience Councils.

The arrival of the BBC Trust marks a revolution in the way the BBC is governed. The BBC Trust will ensure greater transparency of how the BBC does its business and for the first time the public will have a say in setting the strategic direction of the BBC. The trust will be independent of BBC managment and any external body, leaving it free to meet its clear responsibility to operate only in the interest of all licence fee payers.

BBC EXECUTIVE BOARD

Director-General	Mark Thompson
Deputy Director-General	Mark Byford
Director, Audio & Music	Tim Davie
Director, Vision	Jana Bennett
Director, Marketing & Communications	Sharon Baylay
Director, Future Media & Technology	Eric Huggers
Director, BBC People	Lucy Adams
Director, BBC North	Peter Salmon
Group Finance Officer	Zarin Patel
Chief Operating Officer	Caroline Thomson

DIRECTORS

Director, News	Helen Boaden
Director, Archive Content	Roly Keating
Director, London 2012	Roger Mosey

Director, Global News	Peter Horrocks
Creative Director	Alan Yentob
Controller, BBC 1	Jay Hunt
Controller, BBC 2	Janice Hadlow
Controller, BBC 3	Danny Cohen
Controller, BBC 4	Richard Klein
Controller, BBC English Regions	David Holdsworth
Director, BBC Northern Ireland	Peter Johnston
Director, BBC Scotland	Ken MacQuarrie
Director, BBC Wales	Menna Richards

PROGRAMMING

Controller, Programme Acquisitions	George McGhee

COMMISSIONING

CHILDRENS

Controller, CBBC	Damian Kavanagh
Controller, CBeebies	Kay Benbow

DAYTIME

Controller, Daytime	Liam Keelan
EXECUTIVE EDITORS	
Daytime	Lindsay Bradbury
Daytime	Carla-Maria Lawson
Daytime	Jacqueline Hewer

DRAMA

Head of Drama Commissioning	Ben Stephenson
COMMISSIONING EDITORS	
Head of Drama	Polly Hill
Independent Drama	Lucy Richer
Independent Drama	Juliette Howell
Head of Drama, N Ireland	Stephen Wright
Head of Drama, Scotland	Anne Mensah
Head of Drama, Wales	Poers Wenger

ENTERTAINMENT

Controller, Entertainment Commissioning	Mark Linsey
Controller, Comedy Commissioning	Cheryl Taylor
EXECUTIVE EDITORS - ENTERTAINMENT	
Saturday Night	Jo Wallace
Comedy BBC1 & BBC2	Suzanne Gilfillan
BBC3 & Comedy BBC1	Karl Warner
Factual	Mirella Breda
Nations & Lottery	Alan Tyler
EXECUTIVE EDITORS - COMEDY	
Comedy	Simon Lupten

FACTUAL

Head of Knowledge Commissioning	Emma Swain
COMMISSIONING EDITORS	
Documentaries	Charlotte Moore
Features & Formats BBC1 & BBC2	Alison Kirkham
Features, Formats & Specialist Factual BBC3	Harry Lansdown
History & Business	Martin Davidson
Science & Natural HIstory	Kim Shillinglaw
Arts	Mark Bell
Religion	Aaqil Ahmed
Music & Events	Jan Younghusband
Current Affairs & Investigations	Clive Edwards

SPORT

Director of Sport	Barbara Slater

MULTI-PLATFORM

Head of Knowledge	Ayesha Mohideen
COMMISSIONING EDITORS	
Fiction & Entertainment	Victoria Jaye
Comedy	Martin Trickey
Drama	Sarah Clay
Science & Natural History	Lisa Sargood
Childrens	Rebecca Shallcross
History & Business Factual	Max Gadney
Arts	Nick Cohen

SCOTLAND
Broadcasting House, Queen Margaret Drive, Glasgow GI2 8DG
0I4I-339 8844
40 Pacific Quay, Glasgow G5I IDA
0I4I-422 7000

WALES
Broadcasting House, Llantrisant Road, Cardiff CF5 2YQ
029-2032 2000

NORTHERN IRELAND
Broadcasting House, Ormeau Avenue, Belfast BT2 8HQ
028-9033 8000

MIDLANDS & EAST
Broadcasting Centre, Pebble Mill Road, Birmingham B5 7QQ
0I2I-432 8888

SOUTH
Broadcasting House, Whiteladies Road, Bristol BS8 2LR
0II7-973 22II

NORTH
New Broadcasting House, Oxford Road, Manchester M60 ISJ
0I6I-200 2020

CHANNEL 4

HEADQUARTERS

124 Horseferry Road, London SWIP 2TX

020-7396 4444 Fax 020-7306 8116

www.channel4.com

Director of Television	Kevin Lygo
Head of Channel 4	Julian Bellamy

PROGRAMMING

Controller, Broadcasting	Rosemary Newell
Head of Acquisitions	Gill Hay
Head of Daytime	Helen Warner

COMMISSIONING

EDUCATION

Head of Education & Managing Editor, Commissioning	Janey Walker
Commissioning Editors, Education	Jo Twist
	Alice Taylor

DOCUMENTARIES

Head of Documentaries	Hamish Mykura
Deputy Head of Documentaries	Simon Dickson
Commissioning Editors, Documentaries	Mark Raphael
	Aysha Rafaele
Commissioning Editor, Arts & Performance	tbc

DRAMA

Controller, Film4 & Drama	Tessa Ross
Head of Drama	Camilla Campbell
Commissioning Editors, Drama	Roberto Troni
	Robert Wulff-Cochrane

ENTERTAINMENT & COMEDY

Head of Comedy	Shane Allen
Head of Entertainment	Justin Gorman
Commissioning Editors, Entertainment	Madeleine Knight
	Syeda Irtizaali
Commissioning Editor, Comedy	Nerys Evans
Commissioning Editor, Comedy Entertainment	Darren Smith

FACTUAL ENTERTAINMENT & FEATURES

Head of Features & Factual Entertainment	Sue Murphy
Deputy Head of Factual Entertainment	Liam Humphries
Deputy Head of Features	Andrew Jackson
Commissioning Editor, Factual Entertainment	Dominique Walker
Commissioning Editor, Features	Kate Techman

MUSIC & YOUTH

Head of T4 & Music	Neil McCallum

NEWS & CURRENT AFFAIRS

Head of News & Current Affairs	Dorothy Byrne
Deputy Head of News & Current Affairs	Kevin Sutcliffe
Commissioning Editor, News & Current Affairs	Siobhan Sinnerton

SPECIALIST FACTUAL

Head of Specialist Factual	Ralph Lee
Commissioning Editor, Specialist Factual	Tanya Shaw
Commissioning Editor, Science	David Glover
Commissioning Editor, History	Julia Harrington

CHANNEL FIVE

HEAD OFFICE

22 Long Acre, London WC2E 9LY

020-7550 5555 Fax 020-7550 5554

www.five.tv

CHANNEL TELEVISION

HEAD OFFICE

Television Centre, La Pouquelaye, St Helier, Jersey JEI 3ZD

01534-816816 Fax 01534-816817

Executive Chairman	Michael Desmond
Chief Executive	Rowan O'Sullivan
Managing Director, Commercial	Mike Elsey
Managing Director, Broadcast	Karen Rankine
Director of Transmission & Resources	Kevin Banner

INDEPENDENT TELEVISION NEWS

HEADQUARTERS

200 Grays Inn Road, London WCIX 8XZ

0844-881 8000

www.itn.co.uk

CEO	John Hardie
Editor in Chief, ITV News	David Mannion
Editor, Channel 4 News	Jim Gray

ITN is one of the world's leading news and multimedia content companies creating, packaging and distributing news, entertainment, factual and corporate content on multiple platforms to customers around the globe. The news programming produced for ITV and Channel 4 reaches nearly 10 million people every day, providing comprehensive, impartial news provision for the British public. ITN's news is also watched by millions of viewers worldwide, through partnerships with global news outlets such as Reuters, CNN and NBC and online partners such as Livestation, YouTube and MSN.

ITV NETWORK

HEAD OFFICE

200 Grays Inn Road, London WCIX 8HF

0844-881 8000

www.itv.com

ITV Broadcasting operates ITV's family of channels: ITV1, ITV2, ITV3, ITV4 and CITV.

ITV1 is the largest commercial television channel in the UK in terms of both audience share and advertising revenues. In peak viewing time, ITV1 attracts the largest audience of any UK broadcaster, including BBC1. ITV's digital channels are available on all multi-channel platforms and continue to grow their audiences year-on-year.

Across its channels, ITV invests around £1 billion each year in network and regional programming, with the majority spent on UK production.

ITV's channels are delivered free of charge to consumers, funded by advertising and sponsorship revenues, which totalled £1,350 million in 2009. As well as national advertising, ITV offers companies the opportunity to advertise on television at a regional or local level. Programming on ITV channels also generates revenue through viewer competitions and voting.

Chief Executive	Adam Crozier
Director of Strategy & Development	Carolyn Fairbairn
Director of Television	Peter Fincham

COMMISSIONING

ENTERTAINMENT

Director of Entertainment & Comedy	Elaine Bedell
Controller, Entertainment	John Kay-Cooper
Controller, Entertainment	Layla Smith
Commissioning Editor, Entertainment	Claire Zolkwer
Commissioning Editor, Comedy	Michaela Hennessey-Vass

DRAMA

Director of Drama	Laura Mackie
Controller, Drama Commissioning	Sally Haynes
Development Editor	Ben McGrath

FACTUAL & DAYTIME

Director of Factual & Daytime	Alison Sharman
Controller, Popular Factual	Jo Clinton-Davies
Commissioning Editor, Factual	Diana Howie

NEWS SPORT & CURRENT AFFAIRS

Director of News, Sport & Current Affairs	Michael Jermey
Controller, Sport	Niall Sloane
Controller, Regions & Current Affairs	Ian Squires
Director of ING Events & Projects	Guy Phillips

DIGITAL CHANNELS & ACQUISITIONS

Director of Digital Channels & Acquisitions	Zai Bennett
Controller, Digital Channels	Emma Tennant

ITV ANGLIA

Anglia House, Norwich NRI 3JG

01603-615151 Fax 01603-631032

ITV CENTRAL - WEST MIDLANDS
Central Court, Gas Street, Birmingham BI 2JT
0844-881 4000

ITV GRANADA
Granada Television Centre, Quay Street, Manchester M60 9EA
0161-952 1000 Fax 0161-952 6319

ITV LONDON
London Television Centre, Upper Ground, London SEI 9LT
020-7157 3000

ITV MERIDIAN
Forum One, Solent Business Park, Whitely, Hants POI5 7PA
0844-881 2000

ITV TYNE TEES & BORDER
Television House, The Watermark, Gateshead,
Tyne & Wear NEII 9SZ
0844-881 5000

ITV WALES
Television Centre, Culverhouse Cross, Cardiff CF5 6XJ
0844-881 0100

ITV WEST COUNTRY
Television Centre, Bath Road, Bristol BS4 3HG
0117-972 2722 Fax 0117-972 2400

ITV YORKSHIRE
Television Centre, Leeds LS3 IJS
0113-243 8283 Fax 0113-244 5107

Winston Roddick

SENIOR STAFF

Chief Executive	Iona Jones
Director of Commissioning	Rhian Gibson
Director of Communications	Garffild Lloyd Lewis
Director of Policy	Elin Morris

CONTENT EDITORS

Head of Content	Meirion Davies
Head of Childrens Services	Sian Eirian
Content Editor, Sport	Geraint Rowlands
Content Editor, Culture	Rob Nicholls
Content Editor, Entertainment	Gaynor Davies
Content Editor, Fiction	Bethan Eames

Independent television companies are responsible for producing the majority of S4C's programmes. The BBC provides over 10 hours a week of programming. ITV Wales also makes programmes for the channel. A variety of programmes are broadcast on S4C, including live national events, sport, music, news, drama, entertainment, children, culture, rural and lifestyle. In 2009 the Government will switch off the analogue signal in Wales. At that time, S4C will become a wholly Welsh-language service. English language Channel 4 programmes will no longer be broadcast on S4C as that channel will be freely available in Wales.

S4/C

S4C

HEADQUARTERS
Parc Ty Glas, Llanisien, Cardiff CFI4 5DU
029-2074 7444 Fax 029-2075 4444
www.s4c.co.uk

THE WELSH FOURTH CHANNEL AUTHORITY

Chair	John Walter Jones
Members	Bill Davies
	Cenwyn Edwards
	Dyfrig Jones
	Dr Glenda Jones
	John Davies
	Sir Roger Jones OBE
	Rheon Tomos

STV

STV CENTRAL
Pacific Quay, Glasgow G5I IPQ
0141-300 3000 Fax 0141-300 3030

STV NORTH
Craigshaw Business Park, West Tullos, Aberdeen ABI2 3QH
01224-848848 Fax 01224-848800

Chief Executive, STV Group plc	Rob Woodward
Director of Broadcasting & Regulatory Affairs	Bobby Hain
Director of Content	Alan Clements
Commercial Director	David Connolly

STV Group plc comprises STV, Scotland's most popular peak time TV station, and production companies STV Productions and Ginger Productions. Broadcasting since 1957, STV's broadcasting business incorporates two licenses, one for the north of Scotland and one for central Scotland. STV delivers a diverse schedule comprising network and Scottish programming to over 3.5m viewers across Scotland each week. The channel is fully supported online at st.tv, home of the STV video player and comprehensive news, sport and entertainment services.

UTV

HEAD OFFICE

Ormeau Road, Belfast BT7 IEB

028-9032 8122 Fax 028-9024 6695

www.u.tv

DIRECTORS

Chairman	John B McGuckian
Group Chief Executive	John McCann
Board Members	Jim Downey
	Roy Baillie
	Paul OBrien
	Helen Kirkpatrick
	Kevin Lagan
	Scott Taunton
	Shane Reihill

OFFICERS

Group Finance Director	Norman McKeown
Managing Director, UTV Television	Michael Wilson
Head of News & Content	Rob Morrison
Head of Communication	Orla McKibbin

UTV is part of the ITV network. A strong network schedule coupled with ever-popular regional programming, makes UTV one of the most powerful mediums in the country. It has the highest penetration of all media in Northern Ireland, with more than 90% of the population reached over a 4 week period and UTV is also available in 70% of homes in the Republic of Ireland. This makes UTV unbeatable for those companies with a total Ireland perspective.

TRADE SHOW & CONFERENCE FURNITURE

Europa International	**0845-430 3015**
Europa House	Fax 0845-430 3016
Meaford Way, London SE20 8RA	Stephen Murphy
www.europainternational.com/kays	

Penny Banks	**01480-498498**
2 Bank Road	Fax 01480-498499
St Ives, Cambs PE27 3EZ	

TRADE SHOWS & FESTIVALS

Doc/Fest Sheffield	**0114-276 5141**
The Workstation	Fax 0114-272 1849
15 Paternoster Row, Sheffield S1 2BX	Chris Black

Edinburgh International Film Festival	**0131-228 4051**
88 Lothian Road	Fax 0131-229 5501
Edinburgh EH3 9BZ	

IBC	**020-7832 4100**
International Press Centre	Fax 020-7832 4130
76 Shoe Lane, London EC4A 3JB	Kelly Hyde
www.ibc.org	

International Advertising Festival	**020-7728 4040**
Greater London House	
Hampstead Road, London NW1 7EJ	

MediaGuardian International TV Festival	**020-7278 9515**
117 Farringdon Road	Fax 020-7278 9495
London EC1R 3BX	

Raindance Festival	**020-7287 3833**
81 Berwick Street	Fax 020-7439 2243
London W1F 8TW	Elliot Grove

Reed Midem	**020-7528 0086**
Walmar House	Fax 020-7895 0949
296 Regent Street, London W1B 3AB	Peter Rhodes

Wildscreen Festival	**0117-328 5950**
PO Box 366	Fax 0117-328 5955
Bristol BS99 2HD	Sarah Mitchell

TRAINING COURSES

01zero-one	**020-7025 1985**
Westminster Kingsway College	Fax 020-7025 1991
Peter Street, London W1F 0HS	Pollyanna Lindley

Academy Class	**0800-043 8889**
99 Waterloo Road	Fax 0870-330 5722
London SE1 8UL	Sarah Paton

Actors Studio	**01753-650951**
Pinewood Studios, Pinewood Road	Fax 01753-655622
Iver Heath, Bucks SL0 ONH	
Art Department Training	**01844-218072**
Stable Studios, 15 Priest End	Fax 01844-217558
Thame, Oxon OX9 2AE	Shaun Moore
The Arts Institute At Bournemouth	**01202-533011**
Wallisdown	Fax 01202-537729
Poole, Dorset BH12 5HH	Stewart Bartholomew
BBC Training & Development	**0370-010 0264**
Avon Wing, Wood Norton	Fax 0370-010 0265
Evesham, Worcs WR11 4YB	Andrew Carmichael
Brighton Film School	**01273-302166**
13 Tudor Close, Dean Court Road	Franz von Habsburg
Rottingdean, E Sussex BN2 7DF	
Brit School	**020-8665 5242**
60 The Crescent	Fax 020-8665 8676
Croydon, Surrey CR0 2HN	Dean Peckett
Brushstroke Make-Up School & Agency	**01932-592463**
Shepperton Studios, Studios Road	Fax 01932-592023
Shepperton, Middx TW17 0QD	Cheraine Bell
Bucks New University	**01494-522141**
Queen Alexandra Road	Fax 01494-524392
High Wycombe, Bucks HP11 2JZ	Ruth Gunstone

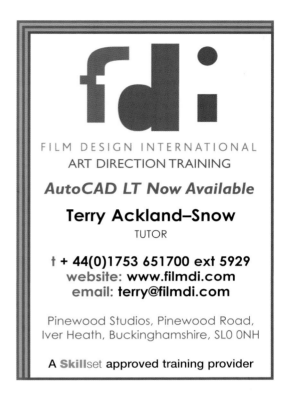

Cadschool	**01962-711907**
Westwood, Twyford Moors	Steve Bran
Winchester, Hants SO21 1RN	

Central St Martins College Of Art	**020-7514 2154**
Department Of Fine Art	Fax 020-7514 7208
107-109 Charing Cross Road, London WC2H 0DU	

Chi Coaching	**0844-567 4065**
27 Old Gloucester Street	William Pennington
London WC1N 3AX	

City Of Westminster College	**020-7723 8826**
Paddington Basin Campus	Fax 020-7258 2700
North Wharf Road, London W2 1LF	

Cyfle	**029-2046 5533**
33-35 Westbute Street	Fax 029-2046 3344
Cardiff CF10 5LH	Iona Williams

Delamar Academy Of Make-Up	**020-8579 9511**
Ealing Studios	Fax 020-8579 9511
Ealing Green, London W5 5EP	Leda Shawyer

Edinburgh College Of Art	**0131-221 6138**
Lauriston Place	Fax 0131-221 6004
Edinburgh EH3 9DF	Colette Nelson

Edinburgh Napier University	**0845-260 6040**
2A Merchiston Avenue	Fax 0131-455 2538
Edinburgh EH10 4NU	Michele Marcoux

Escape Studios	**020-7348 1920**
Shepherds Building	Fax 020-7348 1921
Rockley Road, London W14 0DA	

FDI - Film Design International	**01753-651700**
Pinewood Studios, Pinewood Road	Terry Ackland-Snow
Iver Heath, Bucks SL0 0NH	
www.filmdi.com	

FDMX	**01707-285310**
School Of Creative Arts, University Of Hertfordshire	Martina Porter
Hatfield, Herts AL10 9AB	
www.go.herts.ac.uk/creativelearning	

Film Education	**020-7292 7330**
91 Berwick Street	Fax 020-7287 6970
London W1F 0BP	Jane Dickson

Four Corners Film & Photography	**020-8981 6111**
121 Roman Road	Fax 020-8983 7866
London E2 0QN	Lyn Turner

Foxtrot Firearms	**020-8964 3555**
3B Brassie Avenue	Fax 020-8960 3811
London W3 7DE	Richard Howell
www.foxtrot-productions.co.uk	

Futureworks	**0161-237 7570**
87-89 Mosley Street	
Manchester M2 3LR	

Greasepaint Make-Up Placement Agency	**020-8840 6000**
143 Northfield Avenue	Fax 020-8840 3983
London W13 9QT	Hannah Cruttenden

International Film School Wales	**01633-432210**
University Of Wales, Caerleon Campus	Fax 01633-432610
Lodge Road, Newport, Gwent NP18 3QT	Chris Morris

James Watt College	**01475-724433**
Finnart Street	Fax 01475-888079
Greenock, Renfrewshire PA16 8HF	

Leicester College	**0116-224 2000**
Freemans Park Campus	Marisol Martinez-Lees
Aylestone Road, Leicester LE2 7LW	

Liverpool Institute For Performing Arts	**0151-330 3000**
Mount Street	Fax 0151-330 3131
Liverpool L1 9HF	

London College Of Communication	**020-7514 6500**
Elephant & Castle	Fax 020-7541 6848
London SE1 6SB	Cathy Greenhalgh

London College Of Fashion	**020-7514 7446**
20 John Princes Street	Fax 020-7514 7580
London W1G 0BJ	

The London Film Academy	**020-7386 7711**
52A Walham Grove	Fax 020-7381 6116
London SW6 1QR	Daisy Gili

London Film School	**020-7836 9642**
24 Shelton Street	Fax 020-7497 3718
London WC2H 9UB	Shirley Streete-Bharath

Manchester Metropolitan University	**0161-247 1931**
School Of Art, Ormond Building	Rachel Davies
Lower Ormond Street, Manchester M15 6BR	

Met Film School	**020-8280 9127**
Ealing Studios	Fax 020-8280 9111
Ealing Green, London W5 5EP	

National Film & Television School	**01494-671234**
Beaconsfield Studios, Station Road	Fax 01494-674042
Beaconsfield, Bucks HP9 1LG	

Newham College Of Further Education	**020-8257 4446**
High Street South	Fax 020-8257 4308
London E6 6ER	Ray Banton

North Warwickshire & Hinckley College	**024-7624 3000**
Hinckley Road	Martin Shelton
Nuneaton, Warwicks CV11 6BH	

Northern Media School	**0114-225 2863**
2418 Harmer Building	Fax 0114-225 3161
City Campus, Sheffield S1 1WB	Ruth Fox

Plymouth Art	**01752-203434**
Tavistock Place	Fax 01752-203444
Plymouth, Devon PL4 8AT	Dave Hotchkiss

Ravensbourne College Of Design	**020-3040 3500**
6 Penrose Way	
London SE10 0EW	
SAE Institute	**020-7923 9159**
297 Kingsland Road	Fax 020-7691 7653
London E8 4DD	Matthias Postel
Salisbury College	**01722-344344**
Southampton Road	Fax 01722-344345
Salisbury, Wilts SP1 2LW	Ian Smith
Sargent-Disc	**01753-630300**
The Coach House, Pinewood Studios	Fax 01753-655881
Pinewood Road, Iver Heath, Bucks SL0 0NH	Laurence Sargent
www.sargent-disc.com	
Sheffield Independent Film & Television	**0114-272 0304**
5 Brown Street	Bridget Kelly
Sheffield S1 2BS	
Skillset	**020-7713 9800**
21 Caledonian Road	Fax 020-7713 9801
London N1 9GB	
Soho Editors Training	**020-7839 2410**
20 York Buildings	Fax 020-7839 6995
London WC2N 6JU	
Sphere VFX	**01633-790211**
36 Coolgreany Crescent	Matt Leonard
Newport, Gwent NP20 6EQ	
TAPS	**01932-592151**
Shepperton Studios, Studios Road	Fax 01932-592233
Shepperton, Middx TW17 0QD	Jill James
University College Falmouth	**01326-370400**
Tremough Road	Paul Inman
Penryn, Cornwall TR10 9EZ	
University For The Creative Arts	**01252-722441**
Falkner Road	Fax 01252-892787
Farnham, Surrey GU9 7DS	Claire Barwell
University Of Bristol	**0117-331 5088**
Department Of Drama Film & Television	Fax 0117-331 5082
Cantocks Close, Woodland Road, Bristol BS8 1UP	Kate Withers
University Of Chester	**01925-530000**
Department Of Media, Warrington Campus	Fax 01925-816077
Crab Lane, Cheshire WA2 0DB	Brendan O'Sullivan
University Of Portsmouth	**023-9284 5465**
School Of Creative Technologies, Eldon Building	Searle Kochberg
Winston Churchill Avenue, Portsmouth, Hants PO1 2DJ	
University Of Westminster	**020-7911 5000**
School Of Media Arts & Design, Watford Road	Fax 020-7911 5943
Northwick Park, Harrow, Middx HA1 3TP	Sally Feldman
The Video College	**020-8964 2641**
1 Thorpe Close	Sarah Martin
London W10 5XL	

VMI	**020-8922 1222**
Unit 1, Granville Industrial Estate	Fax 020-8922 1114
146-148 Granville Road, London NW2 2LD	Barry Bassett
www.vmi.tv	
West Herts College	**01923-812000**
School Of Art Design & Media, Hempstead Road	Fax 01923-812556
Watford, Herts WD17 3EZ	Colin Humphrey
Wiltshire College	**01249-465261**
Interactive Media Centre, Cocklebury Road	Fax 01249-465326
Chippenham, Wilts SN15 3QD	Paul Bryant
York St John University	**01904-624624**
Lord Mayors Walk	Fax 01904-612512
York YO31 7EX	Rob Edgar-Hunt

TRANSCRIPTION

1st Transnational	**020-7629 2787**
180 Piccadilly	Fax 020-7329 5004
London W1J 9HF	Christine Wittl
www.1sttransnational.com	
A Way With Words	**020-7022 4814**
Central House	Fax 0845-280 2854
1 Ballards Lane, London N3 1LQ	Adam Kossowski

Eco-Transcriptions	**020-3012 0076**
78 York Street	Fax 020-3012 0076
London W1H 1DP	Nicky Terrett
Express Transcripts	**01895-237256**
219 Long Lane	Jilly Lloyd
Hillingdon, Middx UB10 9JW	
Orchid Video & Crewing	**0117-924 5687**
11 Sommerville Road	Fax 0117-924 7323
Bristol BS7 9AD	Naomi Knott
Production Services Group	**020-7533 6666**
Crown House	Fax 020-7533 6667
72 Hammersmith Road, London W14 8TH	
Sapex Scripts	**020-8236 1600**
Elstree Studios, Shenley Road	Fax 020-8324 2771
Borehamwood, Herts WD6 1JG	Paul Sattin
www.sapex.co.uk	
Take 1 Transcription	**0800-085 4418**
456-458 Strand	Fax 01580-715208
London WC2R 0DZ	Louise Tapia
www.take1.tv	

TRANSLATION

1st Transnational	**020-7629 2787**
180 Piccadilly	Fax 020-7329 5004
London W1J 9HF	Christine Wittl
www.1sttransnational.com	
1st Transnational	**0121-607 8657**
Aspect Court	Fax 0121-607 8658
4 Temple Row, Birmingham B2 5HG	
1st Transnational	**0117-900 0004**
St Nicholas House	Fax 0117-900 0005
31-34 High Street, Bristol BS1 2AW	
1st Transnational	**029-2029 0083**
Sophia House	Fax 029-2029 0084
28 Cathedral Road, Cardiff CF11 9LJ	
1st Transnational	**0131-278 0190**
1 St Colme Street	Fax 0131-278 0191
Edinburgh EH3 6AA	
1st Transnational	**0161-930 8214**
The Triangle	Fax 0161-930 8215
Exchange Square, Manchester M4 3TR	
American Pie	**020-7278 9490**
197 Kings Cross Road	Fax 020-7000 1365
London WC1X 9DB	Josephine Bacon
APA Translations	**020-8752 1944**
91 Princes Avenue	Fax 020-8752 1918
London W3 8LY	Ana Soto

Biznet Translation & Voiceovers	**020-7565 0909**
63 Abingdon Villas	Fax 020-7565 0111
London W8 6XA	David Levin

CKUK Spoken Words	**020-8991 1855**
The Courtyard	Fax 020-8998 3382
Selby Road, London W5 1LX	Christopher Kent
www.ckuk.com	

Danusia Stok	**020-8847 2078**
42 Chandos Avenue	
London W5 4ER	

German Accurate Translations	**020-8459 5023**
81 Chambers Lane	Fax 020-8459 5023
London NW10 2RN	Michael Mertl

Hebrew Translation	**020-8876 4451**
11 First Avenue	Fax 020-8241 0958
London SW14 8SP	Yaffa Clarke

Inter-Com Translations	**020-7731 8000**
Hurlingham Studios	Fax 0870-094 1954
Ranelagh Gardens, London SW6 3PA	Carolina Lehrian

ITFC	**020-8752 0352**
28 Concord Road	Fax 020-8993 6393
London W3 0TH	Liz Clarke
www.itfc.com	

Lesley Howard Languages	**020-7267 2677**
27 Ryland Road	Lesley Howard
London NW5 3EH	

Marguet & Ball Translations	**020-7732 1741**
45 Endwell Road	Catherine Marguet
London SE4 2PQ	

Password	**020-8144 9980**
17 The Quadrant	Xavier Fernandez
135 Salusbury Road, London NW6 6RJ	

Take 1 Transcription	**0800-085 4418**
456-458 Strand	Fax 01580-715208
London WC2R 0DZ	Louise Tapia
www.take1.tv	

Take A Note Translation	**020-8348 5137**
13 Glasslyn Road	Monica Bloxam
London N8 8RJ	

thebigword	**0870-748 8000**
Link Up House	Fax 0870-748 8001
Lower Wortley, Leeds LS12 6AB	Bernadette Byrne

Universal Translations	**020-7248 8707**
80-83 Long Lane	Fax 0870-429 2748
London EC1A 9ET	Tom Wesel

UPS Translations	**020-7224 1220**
111 Baker Street	Fax 020-7486 3272
London W1U 6RR	Bernard Silver

TRANSPORT - CHAUFFEUR DRIVEN

Black & White Cars	**020-8891 4434**
208-212 Amyand Park Road, St Margarets	Fax 020-8891 0643
Twickenham, Middx TW1 3HY	Malcolm Holland

Cars & Bikes	**020-8962 2222**
Unit 18, Oliver Business Park	Fax 020-8961 2277
Oliver Road, London NW10 7JB	Jay Patel

CB Chauffeur Drive	**01753-655528**
9 Swallowdale	Colin Burge
Iver Heath, Bucks SL0 0EU	

Chauffeur Drive Services	**0844-850 6070**
Unit 423, Channelsea Business Centre	Craig Freedman
Canning Road, London E15 3ND	

Chauffeur Select	**01753-657144**
Pinewood Studios, Pinewood Road	Rick Aggio
Iver Heath, Bucks SL0 0NH	

The Civilised Car Hire Company	**020-7738 7788**
365 Clapham Road	Fax 020-7738 7799
London SW9 9BT	Toby Hobson Vek McGuire
www.londoncarhire.com	

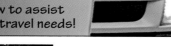

Crawfords Cars	**020-8896 3030**
CDS House, 8 Concord Business Centre	Fax 020-8896 3300
Concord Road, London W3 0TR	Dave Roberts
Hallmark Executive Travel Services	**01582-722600**
Hallmark House, Dallow Road	Fax 01582-400645
Luton, Beds LU1 1TW	
Hatchford Cars	**01483-281968**
17 Overbrook	Les Heaton
West Horsley, Surrey KT24 6BH	
International Executive Car Services	**020-7183 9551**
3A Princes Parade	Jeff Howard
London NW11 9PS	
Limolux Transportation	**020-7286 7555**
3 Harrow Lodge	Fax 020-7286 7555
St Johns Wood Road, London NW8 8HR	Michael Marks
MJ Executive Cars	**01442-400475**
26 Crossways	Fax 01442-400475
Hemel Hempstead, Herts HP3 8PU	Malcolm Theedam
MJB Chauffeur Services	**0161-945 2255**
659 Altrincham Road	Fax 0161-945 1441
Manchester M23 9AA	Mike Bevan
www.mjb24.com	

Multi-Media Transport	**020-8560 2111**
Brentford Station House, Boston Manor Road	Fax 020-8560 2123
Brentford, Middx TW8 8DT	Steve Edwards
Pinnacle Chauffeur Transport	**0800-783 4107**
14 Lucerne Close	Alan Pinner
London N13 4QJ	
Professional Chauffeur Services	**0845-223 2000**
1 Fair Oak Lane	Fax 0845-223 2020
Runcorn, Cheshire WA7 3DU	
Roadsmith	**07939-539182**
47 Dalmain Road	Jason Mortlock
London SE23 1AR	
UK Chauffeur Services	**020-8998 8099**
37B New Cavendish Street	Fax 020-8998 7099
London W1G 8JR	Nazir Choudhry
Westgate Chauffeurs	**020-8538 1304**
Vista Centre, 50 Salisbury Road	Fax 020-8538 0186
Hounslow, Middx TW4 6JQ	Jason Taylor
Wyndhams Cars	**020-8752 8015**
CDS House, 8 Concord Business Centre	Fax 020-8752 8058
Concord Road, London W3 0TR	Graham Waxman

TRANSPORT - COACHES & MINI-BUSES

Bliss Travel	**020-7730 5290**
3 Eccleston Place	Fax 020-7730 6492
London SW1W 9NF	Andrew Bliss
The Civilised Car Hire Company	**020-7738 7788**
365 Clapham Road	Fax 020-7738 7799
London SW9 9BT	Toby Hobson Vek McGuire
www.londoncarhire.com	
Hills Coaches	**01932-254795**
129 Burwood Road	Fax 01932-222671
Hersham, Surrey KT12 4AN	Danny Hill
Howard Ray Executive Travel	**01753-785790**
Pinewood Studios, Pinewood Road	Fax 01753-785791
Iver Heath, Bucks SL0 0NH	Gavin Saunders
Jay-Cee Coaches	**07860-460056**
Loring Road	John Dreelan
Windsor, Berks SL4 5NH	
Kings Ferry Travel Group	**0845-257 9913**
The Travel Centre, Eastcourt Lane	Fax 01634-370656
Gillingham, Kent ME8 6HW	Steve O' Neill
Lee's Travel Company	**01708-344766**
7 Harold Court Road, Harold Park	Lee Cartwright
Romford, Essex RM3 0YU	
www.leestravelcompany.com	

Link Line Coaches   020-8965 2221
1 Wrottesley Road   Fax 020-8961 3680
London NW10 5XA   Tim Russell

MK Travel   01892-838089
Homecroft, Whetsted Road   Fax 01892-832315
Five Oak Green, Tonbridge, Kent TN12 6RT   Malcolm Hill

Mullanys Coaches   01923-279991
Brookdell Transport Yard, St Albans Road   Kevin Crawford
Watford, Herts WD25 0GB

Parkhurst Self Drive Hire   020-8547 3355
69-71 Richmond Road   Fax 020-8547 3354
Kingston-upon-Thames, Surrey KT2 5BP   Richard Maskew
www.parkhurst.biz

Parkhurst Self Drive Hire   020-8979 2067
Island Farm Road   Fax 020-8979 8452
West Molesey, Surrey KT8 2UU   Richard Maskew
www.parkhurst.biz

Potters Bar Coach Hire   01707-652706
70 Baker Street   Fax 01707-652706
Potters Bar, Herts EN6 2EQ   Kevin Wills

PPH Coaches   01753-546375
Pinewood Studios, Pinewood Road   Fax 01753-749969
Iver Heath, Bucks SL0 0NH   Rachel Colahan

Practical Car & Van Hire   01895-232788
43 Arundel Road   Kate Labak
Uxbridge, Middx UB8 2RP
www.practical.co.uk/locations/england/london/uxbridge/

Readybus   0800-587 4066
Pinewood Studios, Pinewood Road   Fax 01753-657169
Iver Heath, Bucks SL0 0NH   Mark Bugden

Trans-Executives   020-8381 0020
PO Box 57646   Fax 020-8906 1491
London NW7 0FB   George Maile

TRANSPORT - CONSTRUCTION & PROPS

Amber Transport   020-8807 7117
Unit 8, Orbital Business Park   Fax 020-8807 7171
Argon Road, London N18 3BZ   Kate Prendergast

Anystate International   020-7732 7772
Unit 25, Arch 121, Astbury Business Park   Fax 020-7732 7772
Station Passage, London SE15 2JR   Colin Brown

Brunels Removals   0117-907 7855
20A Warner Lane   Simon Hippisley
Kingswood, Bristol BS15 4JG

Cavalier Transport   01932-222896
38 Rydens Road   John Cornelius
Walton-on-Thames, Surrey KT12 3DL

The Collectors   020-8961 9382
100 Longstone Avenue   Nick Cutler
London NW10 3UD

Eurotrux   07803-758547
Norrington Lane, Broughton Gifford   Philip Allen
Melksham, Wilts SN12 8LT

Film Flow   020-8438 9919
The Yard   Fax 020-8438 9929
Adrian Avenue, London NW2 1LX   Alan Hayter Karen Hayter
www.filmflow.co.uk

Flash Film Transport   07778-668137
58 Wincanton Road   Lorenzo Macchiarola
London SW18 5TY

Gee Whizz Transport   07860-385227
14 Cheriton Close   Fax 020-8930 9115
London W5 1TR   James Hall

Keep On Movin'   07969-693369
Unit 696   Brian Douglas
456-458 Strand, London WC2R 0DZ

Keptset Logistics   020-8367 2820
Beech Barn Farm, The Ridgeway   07831-455583
Enfield, Middx EN2 8AF   Hugo Keating
www.keptsetlogistics.com

Laxtons (UK2)   020-8335 3207
47 Woodlands Avenue   Fax 020-8335 3209
Worcester Park, Surrey KT4 7AL   Mike Ridge

Lays International   01784-432100
Delta Way, Thorpe Industrial Estate   Fax 01784-433200
Egham, Surrey TW20 8RX   Paul Lay
www.laysint.com

Lesters TV & Film Services   01494-448689
Lane End Road, Sands   Fax 01494-527552
High Wycombe, Bucks HP12 4HG   Mick Piggot
www.lesterstvandfilm.com

Loaded Logistics   07710-562365
Compound 14, Woodside Trading Estate   Fax 01992-560962
Thornwood Common, Epping, Essex CM16 6LJ   Lloyd Haste
www.loadedlogisticslimited.com

Mandata Contracts   0161-220 8111
The Dresser Centre   Phil Lines
Whitworth Street, Manchester M11 2NE

Movie Makers Facilities	**01932-828888**
Woburn Park Farm, Addlestone Moor	Fax 01932-844738
Addlestone, Surrey KT15 2QF	Mel Dunne
www.mmuk.tv	
Northern Lightweights	**01625-858101**
Coppice Farm, Coppice Road	Simon Taylor
Poynton, Cheshire SK12 1SP	
Palletways Manchester	**07823-555111**
Unit 2, Rhodes Business Park	Paul Taylor
Silburn Way, Middleton, Manchester M24 4NE	
Prop Hire & Deliver	**020-8903 7005**
Unit 20, Popin Business Centre	Fax 020-8900 2025
South Way, Wembley, Middx HA9 0HF	Barry Ditton
Propajob Transport	**020-8248 6662**
43 Ashfield Road	Fax 020-8248 6662
London W3 7JF	Philip El-Kadhi
Property Logistics	**07831-430595**
5 Kennet Drive	Steve Hammick
Hayes, Middx UB4 9SP	
Roger Royce Film Services	**020-8743 5544**
Unit A1, Impress House	Fax 020-8749 7365
Mansell Road, London W3 7QH	Roger Royce

FILMFLOW
TRANSPORT & LOCATION FACILITIES

**Prop Construction & SFX Transport
All with experienced Drivers**

PHONE ALAN HAYTER

Tel: 020-8438 9919
Fax: 020-8438 9929 Mobile: 07831-831 964

Set Transport	**01494-872221**
Stone House, 12 High Street	Charlie Villiers-Smith
Chalfont St Giles, Bucks HP8 4QA	
Set2It Transport	**07837-815432**
103 High Street	R. "Chipz" Chipping
Northwood, Middx HA6 1ED	
Squeeky Wheels	**020-8367 2820**
Beech Barn Farm, The Ridgeway	07768-613204
Enfield, Middx EN2 8AF	Mark Thomas
www.squeekywheels.co.uk	
Vanorama	**01932-780161**
2 Rooksmead Road	Fax 01932-780161
Lower Sunbury, Middx TW16 6PD	Dick Burgess
Warners & Hare Transport	**020-7586 6060**
55 Chase Road	Fax 020-8965 8107
London NW10 6LU	Daniel Dunphy
Wheal's Far-go	**020-8965 8200**
Unit 5	Fax 020-8965 0699
13-15 Sunbeam Road, London NW10 6JP	Alan Wheal
www.whealsfargo.com	
Wrap-Pac Transport Company	**07974-698872**
5 Mead Platt	David Kibble
Stokenchurch, Bucks HP14 3PZ	
Your Choice Props	**07960-959831**
6 Maundsey Close	Paul Elston
Dunstable, Beds LU6 3LZ	

TRANSPORT - EXHIBITIONS ROADSHOWS & CREWS

Conference Haul International	**01344-873232**
Longcross Studios, Building 103	Fax 01344-873228
Chobham Lane, Chertsey, Surrey KT16 0EE	Terry Goodwin
EST	**020-7055 7200**
Bell Lane	Fax 020-7055 7201
North Woolwich Road, London E16 2AB	Del Roll

Fieldings	**01245-422333**
Highwood Road, Writtle	Fax 01245-422888
Chelmsford, Essex CM1 3PT	Tony Fielding
Luckings	**0845-603 8211**
Boston House, 69 Boston Manor Road	Fax 020-8847 8677
Brentford, Middx TW8 9JJ	
Pulleyn Transport	**0118-984 0300**
Church Lane, Three Mile Cross	Fax 0118-984 0301
Reading, Berks RG7 1HB	Scott Pulleyn
Redburn Transfer	**020-8804 0027**
Redburn House, Stockingswater Lane	Fax 020-8804 8021
Enfield, Middx EN3 7PH	Chris Redburn
Stage Truck	**020-8569 4444**
Speed House, Green Lane	Fax 020-8569 4194
Hounslow, Middx TW4 6BY	Robert Hewett
Stagefreight	**0113-238 0805**
Unit B	Fax 0113-238 0806
Gildersome Spur, Leeds LS27 7JZ	Peter Cresswell

TRANSPORT - LOW LOADERS

99 Cars	**01923-266373**
Hyde Meadow Farm, Hyde Lane	Fax 01923-260852
Hemel Hempstead, Herts HP3 8SA	David Hammatt
www.nineninecars.com	

TRANSPORT - SELF DRIVE

1st Direct Vehicle Rental Company	**020-8679 5110**
628 Streatham High Road	Fax 020-8679 6869
London SW16 3QL	Simon Bates
www.1stdirectvehiclerentals.co.uk	
55 Car Rental	**020-8890 0155**
St Giles Hotel, Hounslow Road	Fax 020-8893 2729
Feltham, Middx TW14 9AD	Chris Renton-Rose
Aim Rent A Car	**020-8987 2802**
Hardwicke Road	Fax 020-8742 8944
London W4 5EA	Robert Speirs
Arnold Clark Car & Van Rental	**0141-849 7879**
Film & TV Division, 16-30 Murray Street	Fax 0141-848 1920
Paisley, Renfrewshire PA3 1QQ	
Avis Rentacar	**0844-544 5555**
Avis House, Park Road	
Bracknell, Berks RG12 2EW	
Blue Chip Car Hire	**020-7278 7833**
66 York Way	Adrian Nyack
London N1 9AG	

Budget Car & Van Rental

96-102 Great Victoria Street
Belfast BT2 7BE

028-9023 0700
Fax 028-9023 0550
Jim Close

The Civilised Car Hire Company

365 Clapham Road
London SW9 9BT
www.londoncarhire.com

020-7738 7788
Fax 020-7738 7799
Toby Hobson Vek McGuire

Europcar UK

Europcar House, Aldenham Road
Watford, Herts WD23 2QQ

01923-811000
Fax 01923-811010

Express Vehicle Rentals

2 Bayham Street
London NW1 0ES

020-7387 5028
Fax 020-7388 0002

Film Transport

Shepperton Studios, Studios Road
Shepperton, Middx TW17 0QD

07802-284777
Peter Devlin

Goodmans Hire

16-20 Shenley Road
Borehamwood, Herts WD6 1DS

020-8953 3005
Fax 020-8386 3041
Peter Hedges

Heathrow Rent A Truck

Unit 4, Falcon Way
Feltham, Middx TW14 0XJ

020-8844 2070
Fax 020-8831 9977
Alan Smith

Lays International	**01784-432100**
Delta Way, Thorpe Industrial Estate	Fax 01784-433200
Egham, Surrey TW20 8RX	Paul Lay
www.laysint.com	
Matt Snowball Music	**020-7700 6555**
Unit 2	Fax 020-7700 6990
3-9 Brewery Road, London N7 9QJ	Matt Snowball
Meridian Vehicle Hire	**020-8686 8088**
Norflex House, Anchor Business Park	Stuart Riddick
102 Beddington Lane, Croydon, Surrey CR0 4YX	
Moving Space	**020-8205 2503**
Unit C4, Connaught Business Centre	Fax 020-8905 9373
Hyde Estate Road, London NW9 6JP	Nick Yeatman
Parkhurst Self Drive Hire	**020-8547 3355**
69-71 Richmond Road	Fax 020-8547 3354
Kingston-upon-Thames, Surrey KT2 5BP	Richard Maskew
www.parkhurst.biz	
Parkhurst Self Drive Hire	**020-8979 2067**
Island Farm Road	Fax 020-8979 8452
West Molesey, Surrey KT8 2UU	Richard Maskew
www.parkhurst.biz	
Practical Car & Van Hire	**01895-232788**
43 Arundel Road	Kate Labak
Uxbridge, Middx UB8 2RP	
www.practical.co.uk/locations/england/london/uxbridge/	
SHB Hire	**01794-511458**
18 Premier Way, Abbey Park Industrial Estate	Fax 01794-511468
Romsey, Hants SO51 9DQ	Paul Street
Star Rentals	**028-9083 2232**
34 Roughfort Road	Fax 028-9084 5070
Mallusk, Co Antrim BT36 4RE	Donald Reith
Tigertours	**020-8902 1006**
81-83 Wembley Hill Road	Kieran Barry
Wembley, Middx HA9 8BU	
U-Drive	**0800-980 9966**
48-56 Old Wareham Road	Fax 01202-741883
Poole, Dorset BH12 4QR	Dean Smith

TRANSPORT - TAXIS

Computer Cab	**020-7908 0286**
66-68 College Road	Fax 020-7908 0050
Harrow, Middx HA1 1BE	Andrew Robson
Dial-A-Cab	**020-7251 0581**
Dial-A-Cab House	Fax 020-7553 7293
39-47 East Road, London N1 6AH	Allen Togwell
Lancaster Private Hire	**020-8452 1122**
Cardiff House	Fax 020-8452 1131
Tilling Road, London NW2 1LJ	Ernest Hill

TRANSPORT - VEHICLE TRANSPORTERS

99 Cars	**01923-266373**
Hyde Meadow Farm, Hyde Lane	Fax 01923-260852
Hemel Hempstead, Herts HP3 8SA	David Hammatt
www.nineninecars.com	

TRAVEL AGENTS

Access Bookings	**0870-855 5777**
53A Tamworth Road	Fax 0870-950 5907
Lichfield, Staffs WS14 9HG	Patricia Barnes
www.accessbookings.com	
Anderson Business Travel	**01932-222002**
Shepperton Marina, Felix Lane	Fax 01932-246140
Shepperton, Middx TW17 8NS	Susie Lyons
BCD Travel	**020-7262 5040**
Marble Arch House	Fax 020-7724 9883
66-68 Seymour Street, London W1H 5AF	
Capable Travel	**020-7489 8787**
31 Old Bailey	Fax 020-7236 7901
London EC4M 7QJ	George Herrera
Scallywag Travel	**01932-593082**
Shepperton Studios, Studios Road	Fax 01932-592050
Shepperton, Middx TW17 0QD	Sue Roberts
www.scallywagtravel.com	
Screen & Music Travel	**01753-764050**
Colne House, High Street	Fax 01753-764051
Colnbrook, Berks SL3 0LX	Colin Doran
Sky Media Travel	**01753-783340**
Pinewood Studios, Pinewood Road	Fax 01753-656623
Iver Heath, Bucks SL0 0NH	Ezra Arwas
Travel Harbour	**020-8949 4427**
180-186 Kingston Road	Fax 020-8949 8287
New Malden, Surrey KT3 3RD	Michael O'Mara

T-SHIRT PRINTING

Imprint Promotions	**01895-238675**
IA Villier Street	Andrew Shiolou
Uxbridge, Middx UB8 2PU	
www.imprintpromotions.co.uk	

TV ADMIN

The Traffic Bureau	**020-7372 2223**
173 West End Lane	Fax 020-7372 2226
London NW6 2LY	Lisa Lavender

UNDERWATER SERVICES

Aquarius Marine Group	**01458-834734**
Mill Lane, The Beckery	Fax 01458-834734
Glastonbury, Somerset BA6 9NT	Tony Wynes
Aquatic Purification Systems UK	**07785-562743**
Nightingale House, Coolham Road	Peter Taylor
Horsham, W Sussex RHI3 8QE	
Asylum Models & Effects	**020-8871 2988**
20 Thornsett Road	Fax 020-8874 8186
London SWI8 4EF	Mark Ward
www.asylumsfx.com	

Cameras Underwater	**01404-812277**
East Island Farmhouse, Slade Road	Fax 01404-812399
East Hill, Ottery St Mary, Devon EXII IQH	Jenny Rosenfeld
Cinesite Production Services	**01932-592425**
Shepperton Studios, Studios Road	Fax 01932-568944
Shepperton, Middx TWI7 0QD	
www.cinesiteproductionservices.com	
Commercial Diving & Marine Services	**01904-744424**
Malt Kiln Lane	Fax 01904-744724
Appleton Roebuck, York YO23 7DT	Steve Fila
Croxley Divers	**01923-777700**
125 New Road	Tim Hickling
Croxley Green, Herts WD3 3EN	
CSD Specialised Diving	**01202-580007**
Units 7 & 8, Barnes Business Park	Fax 01202-578971
Barrack Road, Ferndown, Dorset BH22 8UB	Phil Richards
Diving Services UK	**01753-785401**
Pinewood Studios, Pinewood Road	Fax 01753-785379
Iver Heath, Bucks SL0 0NH	David Shaw
DV Diving	**028-9186 1686**
138 Mount Stewart Road	Fax 028-9186 1686
Newtownards, Co Down BT22 2ES	David Vincent

Eyewitness Hazardous Facilities   01794-322500

The Drove, Sherfield English Road   Fax 01794-323601
Plaitford, Hants SO51 6EF   Slim MacDonnell

GK Diving Services   01279-410303

50 Purford Green   Fax 01279-454329
Harlow, Essex CM18 6HN   Gary Kirby

Greenaway Marine   01793-814992

Basset Down   Fax 01793-813973
Swindon, Wilts SN4 9QP   Gerald Greenaway

Immages   07860-544417

www.scubacam4hire.com   Michael Barnes

Indepth Solutions   0118-948 1783

17 Wolsey Road, Caversham   Mike Seares
Reading, Berks RG4 8BY

Marine Film Services   020-8224 9246

15 Church Road   Fax 020-8224 9265
East Molesey, Surrey KT8 9DR   Richard Carless
www.marinefilm.co.uk

Professional Diving Academy   01369-701701

Unit 19, Sandbank Business Park   Fax 01369-701700
Sandbank, Dunoon, Argyll PA23 8PB

Rob Franklin Underwater   07973-196002

8 Upper Winchendon   Rob Franklin
Aylesbury, Bucks HP18 0EH

Safety Diving Services   07866-801156

28 Poplar Avenue   Alexandra Davis
Altrincham, Cheshire WA14 1LF

Scubacam   01923-822872

Unit 2, Battlerswells Farm   Mark Dalton
Jackets Lane, Harefield, Middx UB9 6PZ

Subsea ROV Services   01324-555056

33 Macdonald Court, Larbert   Steven Borthwick
Falkirk, Stirlingshire FK5 4FR

Underwater Marketing Company   07973-117862

18 Glossop Way, Church End   Rosemary Lunn
Arlesey, Beds SG15 6YG

The Underwater Studio   01268-270171

Archers Fields, Burnt Mills Estate   Fax 01268-270156
Basildon, Essex SS13 1DL   Geoff Smith
www.theunderwaterstudio.com

Watertight Film Productions   020-7644 3717

77 Beak Street   Fax 020-7439 3330
London W1F 9DB   Trevor Evans

Zero-g   020-7561 0404

118 Piccadilly   Fax 020-7272 8675
London W1J 7NW   Dave Judge Keiko Nagai
www.zero-gfilms.com

USB DUPLICATION

Adaptatech   020-8987 6161

Unit 2, Bell Industrial Estate   Fax 0870-458 2659
Cunnington Street, London W4 5HB   John Farrant
www.adaptatech.co.uk

Multi Media Replication   01264-336330

Unit 4, Balksbury Estate   Fax 01264-336694
Upper Clatford, Andover, Hants SP11 7LW   Philip Hall

VIDEO ASSIST

Buddy Video Services   020-7221 1978

57 Blenheim Crescent   Buddy Blackwell
London W11 2EG

Chris Warren & Associates   020-8337 6760

72 Riverview Road   Chris Warren
Ewell, Surrey KT19 0JU

Inbox Solutions   020-8903 5449

66 Robin Hood Way   Fax 020-8903 5449
Greenford, Middx UB6 7QN   Steve Campbell

Kellys Eye   07950-902196

Sunnybank Cottage, Bullocks Farm Lane   Fax 01494-881247
Wheeler End, High Wycombe, Bucks HP14 3NQ   Lizzie Kelly

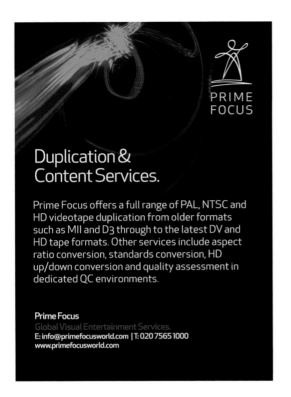

**Duplication &
Content Services.**

Prime Focus offers a full range of PAL, NTSC and
HD videotape duplication from older formats
such as MII and D3 through to the latest DV and
HD tape formats. Other services include aspect
ratio conversion, standards conversion, HD
up/down conversion and quality assessment in
dedicated QC environments.

Prime Focus
Global Visual Entertainment Services.
E: info@primefocusworld.com | T: 020 7565 1000
www.primefocusworld.com

Monitor Video	020-8868 7546
49 Cannonbury Avenue	Fax 020-8868 7546
Pinner, Middx HA5 1TP	Peter Hodgson

VIDEO DUPLICATION

Adaptatech	020-8987 6161
Unit 2, Bell Industrial Estate	Fax 0870-458 2659
Cunnington Street, London W4 5HB	John Farrant
www.adaptatech.co.uk	

BBC Studios & Post Production	020-8225 6000
Television Centre	Fax 020-8576 8806
Wood Lane, London W12 7RJ	
www.bbcstudiosandpostproduction.com	

Broadcast Services	0845-130 3950
The Coach House, Ruxbury Road	Fax 01932-570443
Chertsey, Surrey KT16 9EP	Peter Scrutton
www.broadcast-services.co.uk	

Elite Television	0113-262 3342
248 Meanwood Road	Fax 0113-262 3798
Leeds LS7 2HZ	Stuart Josephs
www.elitetv.co.uk	

Intervideo	020-7624 1711
87 Boundary Road	Fax 020-7624 2683
London NW8 0RG	Trevor Nash

Prime Focus	020-7565 1000
37 Dean Street	Shail Shah
London W1D 4PT	
www.primefocusworld.com	

Soho Transfer	020-7292 5151
5 D'Arblay Street	Paul Smith
London W1F 8DL	

Stanley Productions	020-7439 0311
147 Wardour Street	Fax 020-7437 2126
London W1F 8WD	Steve Langston Mick Pruce
www.stanleysonline.co.uk	

TTV Pictures	020-7419 9555
32-34 Gordon House Road	Fax 020-7419 9556
London NW5 1LP	Torquil Boyd

Vanderquest	020-8977 1743
7 Latimer Road	Fax 020-8943 4812
Teddington, Middx TW11 8QA	Nick Maingay

Video Duplicating Company	020-8963 3555
Units 3 & 4, Nucleus Business Centre	Fax 020-8965 9412
Central Way, London NW10 7XT	Sanjay Mohindra

VIDEOTAPE RECYCLING

Creative Video Associates	01454-410253
CVA House, 2 Cooper Road	Fax 01454-281868
Thornbury, Bristol BS35 3UP	Mark Jones

VISAS

Visa World	020-8959 6161
627 Watford Way	Fax 020-8959 2888
London NW7 3JN	Chris Webber

VISUAL EFFECTS

Cinesite (Europe)	020-7973 4000
Medius House	Fax 020-7973 4040
2 Sheraton Street, London W1F 8BH	
www.cinesite.com	

Double Negative	020-7534 4400
77 Shaftesbury Avenue	Fax 020-7534 4452
London W1D 5DU	

Framestore	020-7208 2600
9 Noel Street	Fax 020-7208 2626
London W1F 8GH	Simon Whalley

Jellyfish Pictures	**020-7580 8154**
66-68 Margaret Street	Fax 020-7580 8158
London WIW 8SR	Sophie Orde

Mattes & Miniatures Visual Effects	**01628-506626**
Bray Film Studios, Down Place	Pinewood 01753-656554
Water Oakley, Windsor, Berks SL4 5UG	Leigh Took
www.mattesandminiatures.com	

mediahouse FX	**020-8233 5716**
3 Burlington Lane	Andrew Gould
London W4 2TH	
www.mediahousefx.com	

Men-From-Mars	**020-7478 7221**
34 Fouberts Place	Simon Frame
London WIF 7PX	

MFX London	**020-7268 0068**
32 Rathbone Place	Fax 020-7268 0069
London WIT IJJ	Megan Guy

The Mill	**020-7287 4041**
40-41 Great Marlborough Street	Fax 020-7287 8393
London WIF 7JQ	

Mobius MC	**020-3384 1740**
II D'Arblay Street	Rod Mcfall
London WIF 8DT	

Munky	**020-7494 3777**
77 Dean Street	Fax 020-7851 6992
London WID 3SH	Georgina Isherwood

Peerless Camera Company	**020-7836 3367**
32 Bedfordbury	Fax 020-7240 2143
London WC2N 4DS	Diane Kingston

Prime Focus	**020-7565 1000**
37 Dean Street	Shail Shah
London WID 4PT	
www.primefocusworld.com	

The Senate	**020-8607 8890**
Twickenham Film Studios, St Margarets	Fax 020-8607 8779
Twickenham, Middx TWI 2AW	Sarah Hemsley

UFX	**020-7268 0068**
32 Rathbone Place	Fax 020-7268 0069
London WIT IJJ	Jonathan Cheetham

VISUAL EFFECTS - 2D-3D CONVERSION

Prime Focus	**020-7565 1000**
37 Dean Street	Shail Shah
London WID 4PT	
www.primefocusworld.com	

VISUAL EFFECTS - 3D SCANNING

2h3D	**01753-533343**
The Coach House, St Georges Meadow	Guy Hauldren
Mill Road, West Drayton, Middx UB7 7EQ	
www.2h3d.co.uk	

Surface Development & Engineering	**01621-744900**
Alpha, Kitchener Road	
North Fambridge, Essex CM3 6NJ	

VISUAL EFFECTS - STEREOSCOPIC

Cinesite (Europe)	**020-7973 4000**
Medius House	Fax 020-7973 4040
2 Sheraton Street, London W1F 8BH	
www.cinesite.com	

VISUAL EFFECTS SUPPLIES

Bristol (UK)	**01923-779333**
Unit 3, Sutherland Court	Fax 01923-779666
Tolpits Lane, Watford, Herts WD18 9SP	Mark Chapman

Brodie & Middleton	**020-7836 3289**
68 Drury Lane	Fax 020-7497 0554
London WC2B 5SP	Andrew Milne Home
www.brodies.net	

Chromakey-Hire.com	**07831-871565**
15 Glenham Road	Graham Caulfield
Thame, Oxon OX9 3WD	
www.chromakey-hire.com	

Screens UK	**01932-560175**
Shepperton Studios, Studios Road	Fax 01932-560175
Shepperton, Middx TW17 0QD	Gary Handley
www.screensuk.com	

VOICE OVER AGENCIES

1st Transnational	**020-7629 2787**
180 Piccadilly	Fax 020-7329 5004
London W1J 9HF	Christine Wittl
www.1sttransnational.com	

Another Tongue Voices	**020-7494 0300**
10-11 D'Arblay Street	Fax 020-7494 7080
London W1F 8DS	John Love

Calypso Voices	**020-7734 6415**
25-26 Poland Street	Fax 020-7437 0410
London W1F 8QN	Jane Savage

Castaway	**020-7240 2345**
Suite 3	Fax 020-7240 2772
15 Broad Court, London WC2B 5QN	Sheila Britten

CKUK Spoken Words	**020-8991 1855**
The Courtyard	Fax 020-8998 3382
Selby Road, London W5 1LX	Christopher Kent
www.ckuk.com	

Diamond Management	**020-7631 0400**
31 Percy Street	Fax 020-7631 0500
London W1T 2DD	Harry Jones

englishvoiceover	**07976-326222**
31 Stickleback Road	John Calvert
Calne, Wilts SN11 9RB	

Foreign Voices	**020-7517 3550**
24 Hawgood Street	James Bonallack
London E3 3RU	

Harvey Voices	**020-7952 4361**
58 Woodlands Road	Emma Harvey
London N9 8RT	

Junior Model Management	**0845-838 8985**
PO Box 61667	Fax 0845-838 8985
London SE9 9AT	Olivea James
www.juniormm.com	

Lip Service Casting	**020-7734 3393**
National House	Fax 020-7734 3373
60-66 Wardour Street, London W1F 0TA	Alex Mactavish

Mooncraft Productions	**01279-813514**
43 Chapel Hill	Fax 01279-817672
Stansted Mountfitchet, Essex CM24 8AD	Martin West

Mumbojumbo	**020-7100 7189**
152 Iverson Road	
London NW6 2HH	

MW Voice	**07795-102991**
mjwestney@hotmail.com	Martin Westney

Rabbit Vocal Management	**020-7287 6466**
18 Broadwick Street	Fax 020-7287 6566
London W1F 8HS	Rebecca Fuller

Rhubarb Voices	**020-8742 8683**
IA Devonshire Road	Fax 020-8742 8693
London W4 2EU	Johnny Garcia
Spanish Voice Over Talent	**07855-293992**
50 Chetwynd Road	Jacqueline Vitali
London NW5 IBY	
Speak-Easy	**01604-686100**
PO Box 648	Kate Moon
Draughton, Northants NN6 9XT	
SueTerryVoices	**020-7434 2040**
18 Broadwick Street	Fax 020-7434 2042
London WIF 8HS	Sue Terry
Talking Heads	**020-7292 7575**
Argyll House	Fax 020-7292 7576
All Saints Passage, London SW18 IEP	John Sachs
Tongue & Groove	**0161-228 2469**
Manchester House	Fax 0161-237 1809
84-86 Princess Street, Manchester MI 6NG	Beverley Ashworth
Voice & Script International	**020-7692 7700**
132 Cleveland Street	Fax 020-7692 7711
London WIT 6AB	Norman Dawood
Voice Shop	**020-8742 7077**
IA Devonshire Road	Fax 020-8742 7011
London W4 2EU	Maxine Wiltshire
Voice Squad	**020-8450 4451**
I Kendal Road	Neil Conrich
London NW10 IJH	
VoiceBank	**0161-874 5741**
100 Talbot Road	Fax 0161-888 2242
Old Trafford, Manchester M16 0PG	Elinor Stanton
Voicebookers	**020-7402 2649**
45 Gloucester Square	
London W2 2TQ	
The Voiceover Gallery	**0161-881 8844**
Paragon House, 48 Seymour Grove	Kath Owen
Old Trafford, Manchester M16 0LN	
www.thevoiceovergallery.co.uk	
The Voiceover Gallery	**020-7987 0951**
The Cobalt Building	Marylou Thistleton-Smith
19-20 Noel Street, London WIF 8GW	
www.thevoiceovergallery.co.uk	
Voiceovers-UK	**01524-792020**
Shireshead Studio, Shireshead Old Church	Fax 01524-792305
Stony Lane, Forton, Lancs PR3 IDE	Martin Hughes

VOICE OVER STUDIOS

1st Transnational	**020-7629 2787**
180 Piccadilly	Fax 020-7329 5004
London WIJ 9HF	Christine Wittl
www.1sttransnational.com	
5A Studios	**020-8969 0914**
5A Scampston Mews	Cristina Aragon Michael Koderisch
London W10 6HX	
www.5astudios.co.uk	
AI Vox	**020-7434 4404**
20 Old Compton Street	Fax 020-7434 4414
London WID 4TW	Sarah Goldstone
Annette Witte (German)	**01225-766889**
The White House, 25 Westwood Road	
Trowbridge, Wilts BA14 9BR	
Apex Studios	**020-8968 5885**
Studio 10, Saga Centre	Mak Johnson
326 Kensal Road, London W10 5BZ	
CKUK Spoken Words	**020-8991 1855**
The Courtyard	Fax 020-8998 3382
Selby Road, London W5 ILX	Christopher Kent
www.ckuk.com	

5A STUDIOS • BRINGING YOUR SOUND TO LIFE

ADR • stereo and 5.1 mixing • sound design • voice-overs • Foley • Dolby encoding

Ladbroke Grove • Kentish Town • 020 8969 0914 • www.5astudios.co.uk

Nostairway Media	**020-8255 4614**
Teddington Studios, Broom Road	Fax 020-8614 2651
Teddington, Middx TW11 9NT	Rob Marshall
out post sound	**01273-556894**
Link House, Link Place	Rob Speight
Upper Hollingdean Road, Brighton, E Sussex BN1 7GA	
www.outpostsound.co.uk	
The Voiceover Gallery	**0161-881 8844**
Paragon House, 48 Seymour Grove	Kath Owen
Old Trafford, Manchester M16 0LN	
www.thevoiceovergallery.co.uk	
The Voiceover Gallery	**020-7987 0951**
The Cobalt Building	Marylou Thistleton-Smith
19-20 Noel Street, London W1F 8GW	
www.thevoiceovergallery.co.uk	

WALKIE TALKIES

AAA Wavevend Radio Communications	**020-7266 1280**
17B Pindock Mews	Fax 020-7266 1290
London W9 2PY	Melvin Lind
www.wavevend.co.uk	
Audiolink	**020-8955 1101**
17 Iron Bridge Close	Fax 020-8955 1111
London NW10 0UF	Andrew Morgan John Morgan
www.audiolink.co.uk	
Audiolink	**01753-656692**
Pinewood Studios, Pinewood Road	Fax 020-8955 1111
Iver Heath, Bucks SL0 0NH	Andrew Morgan John Morgan
www.audiolink.co.uk	
Audiosend Communications	**020-8876 8553**
39 Leinster Avenue	Fax 020-8876 9381
London SW14 7JW	Bridget Hayes
Comsco	**0800-369 9123**
Pickwood Hall	Fax 01538-388238
Leek, Staffs ST13 5BZ	Sharon Chauveau
Melvin Lind Radio Communications	**020-7266 1280**
17B Pindock Mews	Fax 020-7266 1290
London W9 2PY	Melvin Lind
www.wavevend.co.uk	
National Radio Bank	**01778-393938**
Pinfold Road	Fax 01778-421603
Bourne, Lincs PE10 9HT	Mike Bailey
The Radio Hire Company	**0800-374916**
26 Station Road	Fax 01883-625700
Whyteleafe, Surrey CR3 0EP	Neil Shafto
Riedel Communications	**01753-785805**
Pinewood Studios, Pinewood Road	Fax 01753-785806
Iver Heath, Bucks SL0 0NH	Simon Beesley
www.riedel.net	

Nibble

Contact Sohonet for information on our

»   Uncontended
»   Symmetric
»   Future-proof
»   Dedicated fibre

Internet services

Pinewood: 01753 656565
Soho: 020 7292 6900
www.sohonet.co.uk

sohonet

WEATHER

Fugro Geos Weather Services	**01491-820515**
Fugro House, Hithercroft Road	Fax 01491-820516
Wallingford, Oxon OX10 9RB	Trevor Pitt
Met Office	**0870-900 0100**
Fitzroy Road	Fax 0870-900 5050
Exeter EX1 3PB	
Oxford Scientific Services	**01865-872327**
Orchard House, 9 Butts Road	Martin Harris
Horspath, Oxon OX33 1RH	
Weather 2 Travel	**01753-650880**
Pinewood Studios, Pinewood Road	Jon Nigel
Iver Heath, Bucks SL0 0NH	
Weather Action	**020-7939 9946**
Delta House	Fax 020-7939 9901
175-177 Borough High Street, London SE1 1HR	Piers Corbyn
Weather Forcast	**07866-758285**
PO Box 277	Simon Roy
London W1T 5EY	
Weather Services International	**0121-233 7600**
22-24 Vittoria Street	Fax 0121-233 7666
Birmingham B1 3PE	

WEB CONNECTIVITY

Sohonet	**020-7292 6900**
60 Poland Street	Fax 020-7292 6901
London W1F 7NT	Richard Linecar
www.sohonet.co.uk	

WEB DESIGN

21st Century New Media	**0844-844 2428**
Elstree Studios, Shenley Road	Clifford White
Borehamwood, Herts WD6 1JG	
Blue Sea Media	**01424-892287**
1 Ninfield Gate, Frickley Lane	Tim Macpherson
Catsfield, Battle, E Sussex TN33 9LU	
eClick Marketing Websites	**01840-213580**
Trekeek Farm	Fax 01840-213054
Camelford, Cornwall PL32 9UB	Mike Elsey
www.eclickmarketing.com	
Fifth Dimension Productions	**020-8864 0155**
36 Byron Hill Road	Philip Campbell
Harrow-on-the-Hill, Middx HA2 0HY	
LBI	**020-7063 6465**
Atlantis Building, Trueman Brewery	Fax 020-7063 6001
146 Brick Lane, London E1 6RU	
MLS Media	**01753-656384**
Pinewood Studios, Pinewood Road	Jeanette Lloyd-Stern
Iver Heath, Bucks SL0 0NH	
Sapient Nitro	**020-7786 4500**
Eden House	Fax 020-7786 4600
8 Spital Square, London E1 6DU	
Warp Interactive	**07946-401180**
New Media Studios	Timothy Deighton
21 Claverdale Road, London SW2 2DJ	
www.warp-i.com	
Worth	**01273-207555**
20 Middle Street	Fax 01273-201840
Brighton, E Sussex BN1 1AL	Mark Ralphs

WEB SHOWREELS

Kays Internet Services - KIS	**01753-651171**
Pinewood Studios, Pinewood Road	Fax 01753-656844
Iver Heath, Bucks SL0 0NH	Bernard Kay
www.kays.co.uk	
TVbuz	**0845-130 8285**
Unit 3.19, The Plaza	Denis Maryk
535 Kings Road, London SW10 0SZ	

WIGS & FACIAL HAIR

A & A Studios	**0131-556 7057**
8-10 Tanfield	Fax 0131-556 3223
Edinburgh EH3 5HF	Nicky Sefdar
Angels Wigs	**020-8202 2244**
1 Garrick Road	Fax 020-8202 1820
London NW9 6AA	Ben Stanton
Derek Easton	**01273-588262**
1 Dorothy Avenue	Fax 01273-588262
Peacehaven, E Sussex BN10 8LP	Derek Easton
Diversity Hair	**01582-469757**
PO Box 528	Jenna Richards
Harpenden, Herts AL5 9FD	
Hairaisers	**020-8965 2500**
9-11 Sunbeam Road	Fax 020-8963 1600
London NW10 6JP	
Le Postiche	**028-8224 0980**
14 Creevangar Road, Fireagh	Patricia Strong
Omagh, Co Tyrone BT78 1SH	
London Wigs	**020-7721 7095**
Unit 107, Blackfriars Foundry	Fax 020-7721 7026
156 Blackfriars Road, London SE1 8EN	Jan Archibald
www.wigslondon.com	
Ray Marston Wig Studio	**020-7739 3900**
4 Charlotte Road	Fax 020-7739 8100
London EC2A 3DH	Ray Marston
Sarah Weatherburn & Co	**020-8808 2171**
Unit 11, Tottenham Green Co-Operative Workshops	Fax 020-8808 2157
2 Somerset Road, London N17 9EJ	Sarah Weatherburn
Shepperton Wig Company	**01932-225796**
Halliford Studios, Manygate Lane	Gillian Little
Shepperton, Middx TW17 9EG	
www.sheppertonwigs.co.uk	
Wig Specialities	**020-7262 6565**
173 Seymour Place	Fax 020-7723 1566
London W1H 4PW	Richard Mawbey
The Wig Store	**020-8575 0097**
Wigginton House, 1-4 Rockware Avenue	Fax 020-8575 2697
Greenford, Middx UB6 0AA	Philippa Devon
Wigs Up North	**0161-236 5483**
Unit 8, Royal Mills	Fax 0161-236 6843
17 Redhill Street, Manchester M4 5BA	Jackie Sweeney

Art

DEPARTMENT

ACTION VEHICLE CO-ORDINATORS

Martin Alderdice   01753-862637 Mobile 07974-725996
Fax 01753-841998
The King's Speech (feature), Attack The Block (feature), Hot Fuzz (feature).
www.tlofilmservices.tv

Paul Bickers   01449-761300 Mobile 07831-132009
Fax 01449-760614
Harry Potter & The Deathly Hallows (feature), Angels & Demons (feature), Coronation Street (TV drama).

Ian Clarke   Mobile 07778-260720
Green Zone (feature), Quantum Of Solace (feature).

Ben Dillon   020-8324 2664 Mobile 07931-795308
Fax 020-8324 2345
Kick-Ass (feature), The Kid (feature), Blitz (feature).
www.mgmcars.com

David Hammatt   01923-266373 Mobile 07785-382448
Fax 01923-260852
The Boat That Rocked (feature), Franklyn (feature), Is There Anybody There? (feature).
www.nineninecars.com

Milton Homan   01737-765050 Mobile 07973-400327
Fax 01737-236179
Flight 93 (feature), National Treasure (feature), Ghostbusters (video game).
www.dreamcars.co.uk

Stewart Homan   01737-765050 Mobile 07973-400245
Fax 01737-236179
Mission: Impossible (feature), Louis Vuitton (stills), How To Lose Friends & Alienate People (feature).
www.dreamcars.co.uk

Graham Kelly   01753-656588 Mobile 07770-650650
Green Zone (feature), Quantum Of Solace (feature), The Bourne Ultimatum (feature).

Alex King   01932-250966 Mobile 07850-237081
Green Zone (feature), National Treasure: Book Of Secrets (feature), RocknRolla (feature).

Marion Lamb   Mobile 07791-282034
Children Of Men (feature).

Steve Lamonby   01489-895559 Mobile 07885-619783
Atonement (feature), Blood Diamond (feature), Band Of Brothers (TV drama).

Darren Litten   0845-888 7000 Mobile 07836-734477
Harry Potter & The Deathly Hallows (feature), Casino Royale (feature), The Da Vinci Code (feature).
www.actionvehicles.com

John Noel   0870-609 3441 Mobile 07860-373799
Nowhere Boy (feature), The Business (feature), The Mummy (feature).
www.1stpositionvehicles.co.uk

Mark Oliver   01753-862637 Mobile 07831-428837
Fax 01753-841998
The Special Relationship (feature), EastEnders (TV drama), Hereafter (feature).
www.tlofilmservices.tv

Steven Royffe   01753-785690 Mobile 07831-611533
Fax 01753-652027
Stormbreaker (feature), Mission London (feature), Ashes To Ashes (TV drama).

Rodney Rushton   Mobile 07768-265911

ARMOURERS

Simon Atherton   01494-883100 Mobile 07973-179060
Fax 01494-883750
Clash Of The Titans (feature), Robin Hood (feature), The Pacific (TV drama).

Jon Baker   020-8574 7700 Mobile 07976-913503
Stormbreaker (feature), Die Another Day (feature), Underworld (feature).

Charles Bodycomb   020-7221 6730 Mobile 07973-830076
Fax 020-7221 6730
Prince Of Persia (feature) (2nd unit), Quantum Of Solace (feature), In Bruges (feature).

Peter Christopher   Mobile 07817-782485
Prince Of Persia (feature) (2nd unit).

Greg Corke   Mobile 07901-945206
Prince Of Persia (feature).

Ivo Coveney   01706-813026 Mobile 07850-508618
Gulliver's Travels (feature), Kingdom Of Heaven (feature).

Stephen Cummings   01608-810788 Mobile 07808-721752
Robin Hood (feature), Green Zone (feature), Eragon (feature).

Jim Elliott   Mobile 07775-920189
New Town Killers (feature).

ARMOURERS

David Evans   01483-569279 Mobile 07879-882271
Bonded By Blood (feature), Prince Of Persia (feature), Children Of Men (feature).

Kenneth Garside   020-8672 2770 Mobile 07931-295544
Fax 020-8672 2770
Cold Mountain (feature), Charlotte Gray (feature), The Four Feathers (feature).

Rob Grundy   01494-563519 Mobile 07703-289300
Fax 01494-563942
Layer Cake (feature), Reign Of Fire (feature), Hidalgo (feature).

Alan Hausmann   01784-452238 Mobile 07870-263484
Robin Hood (feature), Green Zone (feature), Sahara (feature).

Richard Hooper   0845-395 4786 Mobile 07887-983747
Prince Of Persia (feature), In Bruges (feature), Children Of Men (feature).

Richard Howell   020-8964 3555 Mobile 07801-418867
Fax 020-8964 3555
www.foxtrot-productions.co.uk

Nick Jeffries   Mobile 07958-472340
The Wolfman (feature), The Golden Compass (feature).

Nicholas Komornicki   01288-355797
Mobile 07768-438645
Clash Of The Titans (feature), Blood Diamond (feature), Black Hawk Down (feature).

Catriona Maccann   Mobile 07714-033855
John Carter Of Mars (feature).

Scott MacIntyre   01663-741154 Mobile 07860-208432
Dog House (feature), Dead Man Running (feature), Real Crime (TV docu drama).
www.s-f-x.com

Tracey Millar   Mobile 07900-906520
Prince Of Persia (feature).

Neil A Mountain   Mobile 07702-205809 Fax 07050-079587
I Deal (TV drama), Paradox (TV drama), Land Girls (TV drama).
www.armouryinaction.co.uk

John Nixon   Mobile 07966-386278
Robin Hood (feature), The Bourne Ultimatum (feature), Blood Diamond (feature).

Robert Partridge   0845-003 8795 Mobile 07770-793533
Fax 0845-003 8796
Ultimate Force (TV drama), Murphy's Law (TV drama), Revolver (feature).

Les Powell   01909-723100 Mobile 07836-273322
Fax 01909-721465
The League Of Gentlemen (tour), Shooters (feature), Life On Mars (TV drama).

Mark Shelley   01535-637838 Mobile 07973-321090
Fax 01535-636536
Doctor Who (TV drama), The Outsiders (TV drama), Torchwood (TV drama).

David Sillery   01707-332520 Mobile 07747-305471
Robin Hood (feature), Hellboy 2: The Golden Army (feature).

Joss Skottowe   01923-832066 Mobile 07831-868709
Prince Of Persia (feature) (2nd unit), Quantum Of Solace (feature), Casino Royale (feature).

Dominic Weisz   01323-899516 Mobile 07950-404076
John Carter Of Mars (feature).

Mike Wild   Mobile 07719-764231

ART DEPARTMENT ASSISTANTS

Sian Alaw Jones   Mobile 07876-103799
Your Highness (feature) (Assistant Set Decorator), Occupation (TV drama), Small Island (TV drama).

Rebecca Amissah   Mobile 07930-745873
St Trinian's (feature), How To Be (feature), Street Dance (feature).

Lindy Anderson   Mobile 07908-626881
The Saturdays (promo) (Art Director), Calvin Harris (promo), Girls Aloud (promo).

Maudie Andrews   Mobile 07788-102530
Merlin (TV drama), The Fixer (TV drama), Mistresses (TV drama).

Katia Aprille   Mobile 07972-700002
MTV Brazil (TV light entertainment).

Grant Bailey   Mobile 07717-217629
It's A Wonderful Afterlife (feature), Junior Apprentice (TV reality).

Ida Ballerini   Mobile 07531-590987

Laura Barnes   Mobile 07832-167377
Nineteen Seventy-Four (TV film) (Graphic Designer), Scallywagga (TV light entertainment), Massive (TV comedy drama).

Gwyneth Binyon   Mobile 07811-811112
A Bunch Of Amateurs (feature), Song Of Songs (feature), The Queen (feature).

Abby Bowers   Mobile 07739-023581

Sophie Bridgman   Mobile 07968-694696
Inception (feature), Centurion (feature), Moon (feature).

Philip Brown   Mobile 07881-955353
Desperate Romantics (TV drama), Survivors (TV drama), Hollyoaks (TV drama).

Carlene Clarke   01442-827592 Mobile 07708-901145
Nanny McPhee & The Big Bang (feature), Home Time (TV comedy drama).

Alexandra Collins   Mobile 07814-123316
W.E. (feature).

Celyn Cooke   020-8458 7821 Mobile 07960-667574
My Life As A Popat (TV drama), Popo Gigi (promo), Substitute (promo).

James Corker   020-8542 4002 Mobile 07716-235296
Oh Baby (short), The Black Dinner (short).

Lizzie Mary Cullen   Mobile 07904-110866
Harry Potter & The Half-Blood Prince (feature), Flea (short).

Matt Deely   01634-319925 Mobile 07779-892948
Exodus (feature), Closer (feature), Proof (feature).

Juliette Digonnet   Mobile 07722-198482

Florence Dixon   Mobile 07921-077038
Peter (feature), Numerous commercials, Numerous promos.

Luke Edwards   Mobile 07736-451319
Robin Hood (feature), Body Of Lies (feature), Kingdom Of Heaven (feature).

Laochlainn Fotheringham   Mobile 07985-482388
Clone (TV comedy drama), Posh Bingo (commercial).

Nina Fowler   Mobile 07734-081884
EastEnders (promo), The Fixer (TV drama), The Wolfman (feature).

Zoe Franklin   Mobile 07749-891828

Dan Gardner   Mobile 07799-066289

Liam Georgensen   Mobile 07789-861677
Paul Carter Of Mars (feature), Prince Of Persia (feature), Harry Potter & The Deathly Hallows (feature).

Sarah Ginn   Mobile 07515-664016
Robin Hood (feature), John Carter Of Mars (feature).

Heather Gordon   01753-680645 Mobile 07815-507083
Emma (feature), Dr Who (TV drama), Ashes To Ashes (TV drama).

Saskia Green   Mobile 07956-675544
Sahara (feature), Possession (feature), Chocolat (feature).

Carlos Gris   Mobile 07857-284333
The Firm (feature), Quantum Of Solace (feature), Star Wars: Episode II - Attack Of The Clones (feature).

Becky Grove   Mobile 07815-725474
Powder (feature) (Prop Buyer), Hollyoaks (TV drama) (Standby Art Director).

Katya Guy   020-7272 4322 Mobile 07753-615621
Good Arrows (TV film), The Pacific (TV drama), Suicide Brothers (short).

Jake Hall   Mobile 07875-015327
John Carter Of Mars (feature), Gulliver's Travels (feature).

Kate Halsall   Mobile 07881-962107
The Dark (feature), A Number (TV drama), The Oxford Murders (feature).

Deena Hargreaves   01296-682344 Mobile 07801-702810
Fax 01296-682197
Wests (commercial), British Telecom (commercial), Channel 4 Literacy Campaign (commercial).

Sean Robert Hogan   Mobile 07828-156496
Primeval (TV drama) (Graphic Artist).

Michelle Hosier   Mobile 07786-437083
Hotel Babylon (TV drama), Goal! (feature), The Bourne Ultimatum (feature).

Pippa Howes   01935-823823 Mobile 07719-799248
Clothes In The Wardrobe (TV drama), Sleepers (TV drama), EastEnders (promo).

Tara Ilsley   01923-677912 Mobile 07793-867039
Clash Of The Titans (feature), The Wolfman (feature), Mamma Mia! (feature).

Helen Jones   01905-771848 Mobile 07921-159145
Hustle (TV drama), Kingdom (TV drama), Doctors (TV drama).

Kira Kemble   Mobile 07516-561176
Midsomer Murders (TV drama).

Chryssanthy Kofidou   Mobile 07788-434705

James Lees   Mobile 07875-523771

Pip Longson   Mobile 07914-488092
Robin Hood (feature), Blitz (feature), From Time To Time (feature).

Emma Lovell   Mobile 07984-409442
Stormbreaker (feature), Charlie & The Chocolate Factory (feature), Phantom Of The Opera (feature).

Charlotte Malynn   Mobile 07737-000103
Clash Of The Titans (feature).

ART DEPARTMENT ASSISTANTS

Gary McMonnies   01252-879000 Mobile 07747-686779
Harry Potter & The Half-Blood Prince (feature), Pushing Daisies (TV drama), Atonement (feature).

Amy Meakin   Mobile 07909-902709

Sophia Millar   020-7751 1653 Mobile 07974-005149
We Are Mongrels (TV light entertainment), Mike Leigh - Untitled 09 (feature), Law & Order (TV drama).

Simon Mills   Mobile 07985-689560
The Commander (TV drama), Trial & Retribution (TV drama).

Mel Mitchell   Mobile 07956-981131
Hollyoaks (TV drama), Demolition Dad (TV childrens), The Milkshake Show (TV childrens).

Belle Mundi   Mobile 07957-558879
Robin Hood (feature) (Prop Maker), Pray (short) (Production Designer), Seven Days (short) (Art Director).

Kelly Neary   Mobile 07791-996559

Sophie Neil   020-7700 5236 Mobile 07809-127470

Eva Onsrud   Mobile 07981-133938
Gulliver's Travels (feature), The King's Speech (feature), Blackberry (commercial).

Amy Padmore   Mobile 07930-491761
The Defender (feature), Dot Kill (feature).

Shona Paton   Mobile 07796-696487
Taggart (TV drama), New Town Killers (feature) (Production Buyer).

Lewis Peake   020-7272 6956 Mobile 07888-696733

Daisy Popham   Mobile 07817-444762

Olivia Portman   Mobile 07740-930911

Amandeep Rahi   Mobile 07841-597700
Run Fat Boy Run (feature) (Assistant Set Decorator), City Rats (feature), It's A Wonderful Afterlife (feature) (Assistant Production Buyer).

Jenny Ray   Mobile 07706-887717
Robin Hood (feature).

Anabel Reed   01473-736613 Mobile 07704-786468
Cheryl Cole (promo) (Set Decorator), Expose (feature), Ollie Kepler's Expanding Purple World (feature).

Dominee Reid   Mobile 07738-366501
Silent Witness (TV drama), Criminal Justice (TV drama), The Kevin Bishop Show (TV light entertainment).

Carla Rennie-Nash   Mobile 07730-595397
Harry Potter & The Deathly Hallows (feature), Nine (feature).

Rosie Rose   Mobile 07940-280075

Chris Rosser   Mobile 07590-506317
Hotel Babylon (TV drama).

Scott Salter   Mobile 07841-158693
The Golden Compass (feature) (Runner).

Johanna Sansom   020-8979 3142 Mobile 07712-628376
London Boulevard (feature).

Patrick Scalise   Mobile 07506-412159
Don McKay (feature), Step Up 3-D (feature), The Other Guys (feature).

Luke Stevens   Mobile 07951-604001
A Cock & Bull Story (feature), The Mutant Chronicles (feature), Dangerous Parking (feature).

Kate Stubbs   01364-72593 Mobile 07977-777869
Wittgenstein (TV film), The South Bank Show (TV arts), Elton John (promo).

Mia Summerville   Mobile 07712-184246
Tamara Drewe (feature), Dead Man Running (feature) (Standby Props), Beyond The Rave (feature) (Standby Art Director).

Chris Tooth   Mobile 07970-793438
The Wolfman (feature), RocknRolla (feature), Alice In Wonderland (feature).

Kiera Tudway   Mobile 07720-289509
Nanny McPhee & The Big Bang (feature).

Richard Usher   020-8449 0861 Mobile 07818-831388
Robin Hood (feature), Babylon AD (feature) (Set Decorator), Hustle (TV drama) (Art Department Runner).

Hannah Waheed   Mobile 07872-642964
Dagenham Girls (feature), Hovis (commercial), Shameless (TV drama).

Rebecca Walker   Mobile 07805-787577
Robin Hood (feature).

Jack Wilkinson   Mobile 07527-485296
Nine (feature) (Draughtsman), London Boulevard (feature), Miss Potter (feature).

Elen Williams   Mobile 07527-900740

Sophie Windsor Clive   020-7731 1997
Mobile 07970-617126
Re-uniting The Rubins (feature) (Standby Propertyman), Prodigy (promo) (Assistant Art Director), Nokia (commercial).

Tom Wingrove   Mobile 07811-542831
Robin Hood (feature).

Sophie Worley   Mobile 07841-824769
Robin Hood (feature), Dorian Gray (feature), Green Zone (feature).

ART DEPARTMENT CO-ORDINATORS

Jennifer Bowes   Mobile 07985-116497
Clash Of The Titans (feature), Prince Of Persia (feature), The Dark Knight (feature).

Gabi Dolenska   020-8889 0101   Mobile 07960-067587
The Wolfman (feature), Casino Royale (feature), Sherlock Holmes (feature).

Katie Gabriel   01784-479684   Mobile 07885-484994
Gulliver's Travels (feature), The Bourne Ultimatum (feature), Children Of Men (feature).

Jodie Jackman   020-8993 5262   Mobile 07957-384111
Harry Potter & The Order Of The Phoenix (feature), Harry Potter & The Half-Blood Prince (feature), Harry Potter & The Deathly Hallows (feature).

Heather Noble   Mobile 07970-462970
Robin Hood (feature), Prince Of Persia (feature).

Alanna Riddell   Mobile 07748-184181
Your Highness (feature), Your Highness (feature).

Sarah Robinson   Mobile 07710-761705
Prince Of Persia (feature) (Costume Co-Ordinator), Casino Royale (feature), The Dark Knight (feature).

Sally Ross   Mobile 07850-585085
Sweeney Todd (feature), Wimbledon (feature), Flyboys (feature).

Tamazin Simmonds   Mobile +1 323 384 9515
Quantum Of Solace (feature), The Golden Compass (feature).

Anna Skrein   Mobile 07970-128877
Quantum Of Solace (feature), Elizabeth: The Golden Age (feature), Inkheart (feature).

Lavinia Waters   020-8749 8613   Mobile 07768-005421
John Carter Of Mars (feature), Nine (feature), Stardust (feature).

Zoe Wilson   Mobile 07799-521874
Robin Hood (feature), Green Zone (feature), Children Of Men (feature).

ART DIRECTORS

Andrew Ackland-Snow   01628-522782
Mobile 07976-430765
Harry Potter & The Deathly Hallows (feature), The World Is Not Enough (feature), Titanic (feature).

Charmian Adams   020-8977 0143   Mobile 07710-513137
Fax 020-8977 0143
Shadow In The North (TV drama) (Production Designer), Nowhere Boy (feature), Hilary & Jackie (feature).

David Allday   01494-721469   Mobile 07778-183021
Robin Hood (feature), Prince Of Persia (feature), Prince Caspian (feature).

Dave Allen   01949-844118   Mobile 07801-014355
Coffee (short), Chainmail (short), Carcass (feature).

Sue Anderson   Mobile 07976-969015
Holby City (TV drama) (Production Designer), Boy Meets Girl (TV drama), Drop Dead Gorgeous (TV drama).

Eddy Andres   020-8740 4823   Mobile 07973-413863
Five Children & It (feature), Face (feature), Jason & The Argonauts (TV film).

Ben Ansell   Mobile 07961-114426
Kingdom Of Heaven (feature), Robbie Williams (concert), Sony (commercial).

Lucy Anstey   Mobile 07825-348578

Grant Armstrong   01606-782421   Mobile 07973-637431
The Bourne Ultimatum (feature), Miss Potter (feature), Closer (feature).

Huw Arthur   Mobile 07710-487335
W.E. (feature) (Standby), London Boulevard (feature) (Standby), Little Dorrit (TV drama).

Julian Ashby   +1 323 256 0199   Mobile +1 323 481 7653
Transformers: Revenge Of The Fallen (feature), National Treasure: Book Of Secrets (feature), Troy (feature).

Suzanne Austin   020-8973 1447   Mobile 07711-427732
Nanny McPhee & The Big Bang (feature), Last Chance Harvey (feature), Bleak House (TV drama).

Neil Barnes   01494-452709   Mobile 07768-760260
Big Top (TV comedy drama), Life Begins (TV drama), The Catherine Tate Show (TV light entertainment).

Ian Barratt   Mobile 07973-625817
Nikon (commercial), Credential (commercial), Ann Summers (commercial).

Kat Berry   Mobile 07720-886840
Britain's Best Dish (TV light entertainment), Strictly Come Dancing (TV light entertainment), Let's Dance For Comic Relief (TV light entertainment).

Simon Bishop   Mobile 07974-713112
EastEnders (promo), Holby City (TV drama), Death In Holy Orders (TV drama).

Tim Blake   020-8374 5446   Mobile 07771-530545
From Time To Time (feature) (Standby), Cuckoo (feature), Into The Storm (TV film) (Art Department Assistant).

Nick Blanche   Mobile 07961-869601
Kingdom (TV drama), Whitechapel (TV drama), Foyle's War (TV drama).

Steven Blundell   Mobile 07931-537715
Unmade Beds (feature), No Where Fast (feature) (Production Designer), Mini (commercial).

Paul Booth   01628-629288   Mobile 07976-383903
Ultimate Force (TV drama), Midsomer Murders (TV drama), The Tenth Kingdom (TV drama).

Dennis Bosher   01895-235296   Mobile 07770-384886
Fax 01895-235296
Oliver Twist (feature) (Draughtsman), Tomb Raider II (feature), Jason & The Golden Fleece (TV film).

Roger Bowles   01249-814453   Mobile 07808-470769
Alexander (feature), High Heels & Low Lifes (feature), Below (feature).

Andy Brightman   Mobile 07766-760162

Bill Brown   0117-973 3099   Mobile 07778-852934
Fax 0117-973 3099
Breathless (TV drama), Armstrong & Miller (TV light entertainment), Being Human (TV drama).

Thomas Brown   020-8979 9834   Mobile 07788-601580
The Boat That Rocked (feature), Robin Hood (feature) (Assistant), Brideshead Revisited (feature).

Tom Browne Jones   020-8968 5513   Mobile 07866-758285
Fax 020-8960 6700
Got There (TV drama), Striking Oil (TV drama), New Horizons (TV drama).

Tim Browning   01628-660279   Mobile 07813-816639
Alice In Wonderland (feature), The Wolfman (feature) (Assistant), In Bruges (feature) (Assistant).

Katie Buckley-Driscoll   01494-488179
Mobile 07831-765469
Tamara Drewe (feature) (Graphic Designer), The Queen (feature) (Graphic Designer), Charlie & The Chocolate Factory (feature).

Peter Bull   01202-290096   Mobile 07974-349350
Captain Corelli's Mandolin (feature), The Forsyte Saga (TV drama), The Brit Awards (party).

Alastair Bullock   020-8943 4138   Mobile 07801-491367
Harry Potter & The Deathly Hallows (feature), Harry Potter & The Goblet Of Fire (feature), Harry Potter & The Half-Blood Prince (feature).

Nick Burnell   020-8788 3987   Mobile 07711-334432
Fax 020-8788 3987
Doctor Who (TV drama), Torchwood (TV drama), Battleships (commercial).

Debbie Burton   Mobile 07939-052730
The Rapture (feature), Nearly Famous (TV drama), EastEnders (promo).

Ed Butcher   Mobile 07768-287420
Land Rover (commercial), HSBC (commercial), Army Recruitment (commercial).

Catherine Byrne   Mobile 07714-234704
The Diary Of Anne Frank (TV drama), Miss Potter (feature) (Assistant), Notes On A Scandal (feature) (Assistant).

Neal Callow   Mobile 07958-958174
Nine (feature), Quantum Of Solace (feature) (2nd unit), RocknRolla (feature).

Alex Cameron   020-8542 0300   Mobile 07713-260339
Robin Hood (feature) (Assistant), Fred Claus (feature), Stardust (feature).

Claudio Campana   029-2047 2663   Mobile 07703-775277
The Prisoner (TV drama), Rome (TV drama), Batman Begins (feature) (Assistant).

Jamie Campbell   020-7722 0017   Mobile 07932-153723
Sea Monsters (short), The Mutant Chronicles (feature), Space Odyssey (TV drama doc).

Stephen Campbell   Mobile 07966-192661
Robin Hood (TV drama), Sixty Six (feature), Nanny McPhee (feature).

John Campling   Mobile 07957-668962   STA 020-7729 7477
Wanted (feature), Reverb (feature), Mister Lonely (feature).

Anthony Caron-Delion   Mobile 07775-787792
Robin Hood (feature), Hellboy 2: The Golden Army (feature), Charlie & The Chocolate Factory (feature).

Steve Carter   01273-778515 Mobile 07973-384118
Crusoe (TV drama), Doomsday (feature), The Flood (feature).

Antony Cartlidge   020-7223 6277 Mobile 07976-683959
New Tricks (TV drama), Love Soup (TV drama), Jonathan Creek (TV drama).

Alan Cassie   01628-523234 Mobile 07713-541534
Fax 01628-523234
Hitchhiker's Guide To The Galaxy (feature), Restoration (feature), Muppet Treasure Island (feature).

Julia Castle   01491-413165 Mobile 07885-836565
Run Fat Boy Run (feature), Stormbreaker (feature), Mrs Henderson Presents (feature).

Rhian Cemlyn   01248-490677 Mobile 07810-488481
Uned 5 (TV magazine), Cer I Greu (TV childrens), Gwyl Cerbb Dant (TV light entertainment).

Ray Chan   01446-772805 Mobile 07973-132034
Robin Hood (feature), Blood Diamond (feature), Fools Gold (feature).

Jan Chaney   01326-212434 Mobile 07787-125284
Darwin (TV film), Wycliffe (TV drama), Hornblower (TV drama).

Netty Chapman   020-8778 5706 Mobile 07940-560666
Sherlock Holmes (feature), Bright Star (feature), Atonement (feature) (Standby).

Tony Charalambous   020-7735 5468 Mobile 07968-754810
Fax 020-7735 5468
Hermes (party), Metrosexuality (TV drama), Saving Grace (feature) (Propertymaster).

Diana Charnley   020-8948 2761 Mobile 07799-694062
Fax 020-8948 2761
The Dawning (feature), High Hopes (feature), Defence Of The Realm (feature).

Cheeky   Mobile 07956-579460 AD 020-7428 0500
3 Mobile (commercial), KFC (commercial).

Shaun Clark   01977-661155 Mobile 07721-373537
Fax 0113-222 7225
Heartbeat (TV drama), The Royal (TV drama), Emmerdale (TV drama).

Sam Clark-Hall   Mobile 07803-593683
Little Devil (TV drama), Freezing (TV drama) (Production Designer), Mouth To Mouth (TV drama) (Production Designer).

Dom Clasby   Mobile 07748-010616
Best House In The Street (TV doc), The Charlotte Church Show (TV light entertainment), Big Brother (TV reality).

Andrea Coathupe   Mobile 07970-833701
Tess Of The D'Urbervilles (TV drama), Pierrepoint (TV film), Sex Traffic (TV drama).

Rachel Cocks   Mobile 07966-138250
Bear Behaving Badly (TV childrens), The Basil Brush Show (TV childrens), Globo Loco (TV childrens).

Laura Conway-Gordon   Mobile 07870-270340
A Short Stay In Switzerland (TV drama) (Standby).

Louise Corcoran   Mobile 07957-240665

Gareth Cousins   Mobile 07789-403819
Skellig (feature), Last Chance Harvey (feature) (Assistant), Chat Room (feature).

Rob Cowper   020-7384 9615 Mobile 07958-466223
Prince Of Persia (feature), The Bourne Ultimatum (feature), Body Of Lies (feature).

Amanda Craggs   Mobile 07930-396461
Four Seasons (TV drama), The Roman Mysteries (TV childrens), The Last Enemy (TV drama).

Bill Crutcher   01935-814389 Mobile 07977-433025
Nanny McPhee & The Big Bang (feature), Creation (feature), Me & Orson Welles (feature).

Miranda Cull   01603-631666 Mobile 07710-429795
Ballet Shoes (TV drama), Poirot (TV drama), Miss Marple (TV drama).

Philippa Culpepper   Mobile 07739-802863

Adam Cutts   Mobile 07968-843255
Elmina's Kitchen (TV drama), Function At The Junction (short), H (short).

Russell Daly   020-8761 3911 Mobile 07957-320652

Wolter Dammers   020-7928 5474 Fax 020-7928 6082
www.s2events.co.uk

Diane Dancklefsen   020-8674 0436 Mobile 07970-594986
Caught In A Trap (TV comedy drama), Party Animals (TV drama), The Way We Live Now (TV drama).

Simon Davis   Mobile 07930-562467

Adam Dawe   Mobile 07958-200268

Nick Dent   Mobile 07958-387905
Slave (feature), Nanny McPhee & The Big Bang (feature), In The Loop (feature).

Stephen Dobric   020-8940 9093 Mobile 07771-951003
Spy Game (feature), Troy (feature), The Nutcracker (ballet).

ART DIRECTORS

Robbie Doig Mobile 07774-854367
Paul Smith (stills), Dolce & Gabbana (stills), Hugo Boss (stills).

Laura Donnelly 0141-550 2821 Mobile 07710-513527
Revolver (feature), Young Adam (feature), Meet The Magoons (TV comedy drama).

Martyn Doust Mobile 07956-605717
Benidorm (TV comedy drama), The Bill (TV drama), Ladies Of Letters (TV drama).

Richard Downes 01943-604969 Mobile 07976-683943
Unforgiven (TV drama), Sunshine (feature), Five Days (feature).

Paul Drake 01273-549677 Mobile 07931-756997
Hell's Kitchen (TV reality), Dancing On Ice (TV light entertainment), Big Brother (TV reality).

Andy Drummond 0141-563 4930 Mobile 07710-495474
Outpost (feature), Stone Of Destiny (feature), Waybuloo (TV childrens).

Paul Drummond 020-8241 1842 Mobile 07973-367633

Keith Dunne Mobile 07909-708791
Doctor Who (TV drama), Torchwood (TV drama), MI High (TV childrens).

Richard Earl 020-8560 7182
Pirates Of The Caribbean: The Curse Of The Black Pearl (feature), Evita (feature), The Boxer (feature).

Jonnie Elf Mobile 07776-156389
Daz (commercial), Magicians (feature) (Production Buyer), The Mutant Chronicles (feature) (Production Buyer).

Russell Ellams Mobile 07880-706798
Souled Out (feature), A Thing Called Love (TV drama), Life Isn't All Ha Ha Hee Hee (TV drama).

Philip Elton 020-8959 2359 Mobile 07710-458493
Fax 020-8959 2359
Resident Evil (feature), Merlin (TV drama), Control (feature).

Alex Evans 01453-810024 Mobile 07796-950877
Holby City (TV drama), The Giblet Boys (TV childrens), Casualty (TV drama).

Frederic Evard 01423-500751 Mobile 07850-775315
Green Zone (feature), A Good Year (feature), Confetti (feature).

Kate Evenden 020-7923 4985 Mobile 07767-810005
Margaret (TV drama), Enid (TV drama), Margot (TV drama).

Daniela Faggio Mobile 07976-764677
Bonded By Blood (feature).

Robinia Farnaby 01748-850277 Mobile 07956-280140
Fax 01748-850277
Wuthering Heights (feature), Fat Slags (feature), The League Of Gentlemen (tour).

John Fenner 01628-523000 Mobile 07850-641889
Fax 01628-523000
Phantom Of The Opera (feature), Tomb Raider II (feature), The Talented Mr Ripley (feature).

Sue Ferguson Mobile 07976-431322
Shooting Fish (feature), EastEnders (promo) (Production Designer), The Bill (TV drama) (Production Designer).

Jacqueline Fey 020-7358 6893 Mobile 07956-894029

Richard Field 01728-663347 Mobile 07767-684825
Primeval (TV drama), Gracie (TV drama), Bouquet Of Barbed Wire (TV drama).

Joanna Foley Mobile 07836-550165
Mrs Henderson Presents (feature), United 93 (feature), The Bourne Ultimatum (feature).

Martin Foley 01784-438889 Mobile 07957-470690
Harry Potter & The Deathly Hallows (feature), Harry Potter & The Half-Blood Prince (feature), Harry Potter & The Order Of The Phoenix (feature).

Nicholas Foley-Oates 01273-478088
Mobile 07976-609517
Orange (commercial), Adidas (commercial), Phones 4U (commercial).

James Foster 01483-769060 Mobile 07956-398164
Clash Of The Titans (feature), Quantum Of Solace (feature), City Of Ember (feature).

Pilar Foy 020-7638 1297 Mobile 07787-154307
The Turn Of The Screw (TV drama), Emma (feature), Merlin (TV drama).

Peter Francis Mobile 07767-780850
Shanghai (feature), Hellboy 2: The Golden Army (feature), Casino Royale (feature).

John Frankish 020-8741 4084 Mobile 07798-525481

Gary Freeman 01372-465141 Mobile 07785-353577
Fax 01372-465141
Prince Of Persia (feature), Sweeney Todd (feature), National Treasure: Book Of Secrets (feature).

Paul Frost Mobile 07976-359333
House Of Saddam (TV drama), Rabbit Fever (feature) (Production Designer), Ladies In Lavender (feature) (Draughtsman).

Georgia Fuller   Mobile 07702-842750
Green Wing (TV comedy drama), The Green Green Grass (TV comedy drama), Canterbury Tales (TV drama).

Tom Gander   Mobile 07957-121029

Matt Gant   020-7503 6535   Mobile 07718-586393
Hotel Babylon (TV drama).

Sandy Garfield   020-8450 2225   Mobile 07710-212477
Little Britain (tour), Children's Party At The Palace (TV light entertainment), Dame Edna (TV light entertainment).

Ali Gartshaw   Mobile 07976-917097

Lorna Gay Copp   Mobile 07771-573620
Dummy (TV drama), Dutch Bird (short).

Rae George   020-8949 2060   Mobile 07958-492271
If (TV drama doc), Love On A Saturday Night (TV light entertainment), The Very Best Of Candid Camera (TV light entertainment).

Paul Ghirardani   Mobile 07713-074702
Brighton Rock (feature), Little Dorrit (TV drama), Into The Storm (TV film).

Nikki Gibbard   Mobile 07790-007283
A Quiet Drink (short), Later With Jools Holland (TV light entertainment), The Late Edition (TV light entertainment).

Alan Gilmore   020-8742 3117   Mobile 07710-434776
The Wizarding World Of Harry Potter (theme park), The Bourne Ultimatum (feature), United 93 (feature).

Jim Glen   020-7821 8671   Mobile 07970-375655
Wild Target (feature), Mutual Friends (TV drama), Shameless (TV drama) (Production Designer).

Nick Gottschalk   Mobile 07850-109269
Sherlock Holmes (feature), Atonement (feature), Miss Pettigrew Lives For A Day (feature).

Matt Gray   Mobile 07702-852182
Prince Caspian (feature), The Other Boleyn Girl (feature), Charlie & The Chocolate Factory (feature).

Caroline Grebbell   Mobile 07974-923352
Glorious 39 (feature), This Is England (feature), Neds (feature).

Annie Gregson   Mobile 07956-231814
Franz Ferdinand (promo), Dido (promo), Eurostar (commercial).

Sophie Griffiths   Mobile 07785-916368

Kate Grimble   020-8579 0265   Mobile 07808-579909
Harry Potter & The Deathly Hallows (feature), From Time To Time (feature), Into The Storm (TV film).

Ben Grounds   Mobile 07949-261181

Owen Gundry   Mobile 07769-650504
Celebrity Big Brother (TV reality), Volvic (commercial).

Kate Guyan   Mobile 07764-190992

Tony Halton   01400-230099   Mobile 07831-113936
Wimbledon (feature), I'll Sleep When I'm Dead (feature), Spy Game (feature).

James Hambidge   01494-711675   Mobile 07976-288493
John Carter Of Mars (feature), Mannerheim (feature), Princess Ka'lulani (feature).

Nick Harding   020-8568 6106   Mobile 07815-073587
Broken News (TV comedy drama), Waking The Dead (TV drama), Great News (TV comedy drama).

Stephen Hargreaves   01296-682344   Mobile 07970-753142
Fax 01296-682197

Caroline Harper   020-8670 1297   Mobile 07712-007003
The Catherine Tate Show (TV light entertainment), Kingdom (TV drama), Telstar (feature).

Henry Harris   01883-715038   Mobile 07774-412410
Withnail & I (feature), East Is East (feature), The Warrior (feature).

Lynda Harris   Mobile 07957-295574
Holby City (TV drama), Casualty (TV drama), In The Night Garden (TV childrens) (Standby).

Mark Harris   01628-823894   Mobile 07776-192621
John Carter Of Mars (feature), Quantum Of Solace (feature), Red Dwarf: Back To Earth (TV comedy drama).

Beckie Harvey   Mobile 07850-383052
A Room With A View (feature), Fallen Angel (TV drama), The Last Detective (TV drama).

Katy Harvey   Mobile 07747-751109
The Other Boleyn Girl (feature), Hippie Hippie Shake (feature), Venus (feature).

Philip Harvey   01932-576486   Mobile 07768-844298
John Carter Of Mars (feature), Nine (feature), The Wolfman (feature).

James Hatt   Mobile 07816-424160
Homebase (commercial), Cadbury (commercial), Burger King (commercial).

Rachel Heady   Mobile 07831-667809
Whistleblowers (TV drama), Skins (TV drama), The Last Detective (TV drama).

Rebecca Hemy   01727-850665 Mobile 07957-134483
Doctor Who (TV drama) (Standby), Titanic: Birth Of A Legend (TV drama), Early Doors (TV drama).

David Hindle   Mobile 07710-019897
Bright Star (feature), Wild Child (feature), Ladies In Lavender (feature).

Joseph Hodges   Mobile 07977-988152
John Carter Of Mars (feature).

Catherine Holmes   01869-347795 Mobile 07768-790167
Cold Comfort Farm (TV film), The Fast Show (TV light entertainment), EastEnders (promo).

Rebecca Holmes   020-8579 5918 Mobile 07802-887677
Mamma Mia! (feature), Dirty Pretty Things (feature), Birthday Girl (feature).

Marc Homes   Mobile 07850-726851
Robin Hood (feature), Prince Of Persia (feature), Angels & Demons (feature).

Mags Horspool   0141-424 0242 Mobile 07973-203972
Hope Springs (TV drama), Book Of Blood (feature), Rebus (TV drama).

Christian Huband   01628-781681 Mobile 07956-442991
Bright Star (feature), Prince Caspian (feature), Elizabeth: The Golden Age (feature).

Steve Hudson   020-8452 1814 Mobile 07963-320705
Daily Mail (commercial), Action For Children (commercial), Miracle-Gro (commercial).

Cliff Hughes   Mobile 07714-428852
Hollyoaks (TV drama), The Beat Goes On (TV drama), Brookside (TV drama).

Jo Hughes   029-2049 8139 Mobile 07774-685623
Pobol Y Cwm (TV drama), A Life Less Ordinary (feature) (animation unit), Casualty (TV drama).

Molly Hughes   Mobile 07734-106036
Harry Potter & The Deathly Hallows (feature), Harry Potter & The Half-Blood Prince (feature) (Assistant), Harry Potter & The Order Of The Phoenix (feature).

Lynne Huitson   Mobile 07976-726732
Brideshead Revisited (feature), The Last King Of Scotland (feature), Nanny McPhee (feature).

Dominic Hyman   01491-612630 Mobile 07775-681539
The Pacific (TV drama), Rome (TV drama), Tom Brown's School Days (TV drama).

Paul Inglis   020-8546 7048 Mobile 07966-275014
Game Of Thrones (TV drama), Quantum Of Solace (feature), The Young Victoria (feature).

Sarah Jenneson   Mobile 07973-343331

Claire Johnston   020-8241 0386 Mobile 07798-600110
Not Going Out (TV comedy drama), Judge John Deed (TV drama), The Catherine Tate Show (TV light entertainment).

Gemma Jones   Mobile 07841-126491

Henry Jones   020-7231 7067 Mobile 07973-317809
Fax 020-7231 7635

Samantha Jones   Mobile 07711-327859
Captain Scarlet (TV drama), Anna & The King (feature) (Draughtsman), Eyes Wide Shut (feature) (Art Department Assistant).

Victoria Jones   Mobile 07866-758285

Chris Kay   Mobile 07941-302614
Clay (TV drama), Blue Murder (TV drama), The Good Samaritan (TV drama).

Stuart Kearns   020-8541 4044 Mobile 07768-667125
1408 (feature), Agora (feature), Batman Begins (feature).

Tim Keates   020-8785 9725 Mobile 07836-781498
2012 (commercial), Dark Corners (feature), Tour De France (commercial).

Andrew Kelly   Mobile 07816-203739

Michael Kelm   01442-400648 Mobile 07904-085431
The Descent 2 (feature), The Colour Of Magic (TV film), Hitchhiker's Guide To The Galaxy (feature).

Jean Kerr   0141-334 8097 Mobile 07768-946790
Fax 0141-334 8097
River City (TV drama), The Magdalene Sisters (feature).

Sami Khan   Mobile 07956-982868
Nineteen Eighty (TV film), Celebrity Pop Factor (TV light entertainment), Fonejacker (TV light entertainment).

Joanna King   020-8487 0027 Mobile 07710-347255
The Life Of Riley (TV comedy drama), After You've Gone (TV comedy drama), Vivian Vile (TV comedy drama).

John King   01895-253396 Mobile 07802-536628
John Carter Of Mars (feature), Robin Hood (feature), Quantum Of Solace (feature).

Matthew King   Mobile 07973-573932
In Love With Barbara (TV drama), Happiness Lies In The Garden (TV drama), A Real Summer (TV drama) (Standby).

Paul Kirby　　020-8541 1991　Mobile 07768-384164
The Brothers Bloom (feature), Phantom Of The Opera (feature), Green Zone (feature).

Jason Knox-Johnston　　Mobile 07802-812875
AD 020-7428 0500
Centurion (feature), Agora (feature), Prince Caspian (feature).

Dinos Laftsidis　　Mobile 07732-415490
Angus Thongs & Perfect Snogging (feature), It's A Wonderful Afterlife (feature).

Neil Lamont　　020-8674 2924　Mobile 07977-988415
AD 020-7428 0500
Harry Potter & The Deathly Hallows (feature), The World Is Not Enough (feature), The English Patient (feature).

Simon Lamont　　Mobile 07836-221353
John Carter Of Mars (feature), Nine (feature), The Dark Knight (feature).

Catherine Land　　Mobile 07968-958545

Paul Laugier　　Mobile 07785-392077
Inception (feature), Crusoe (TV drama), Hellboy 2: The Golden Army (feature).

Steve Lawrence　　01753-840449　Mobile 07779-352997
John Carter Of Mars (feature) (CAD Draughtsman), The Dark Knight (feature), Casino Royale (feature).

Madelaine Leech　　Mobile 07973-513449
Ashes To Ashes (TV drama), Primeval (TV drama), City Lights (TV drama).

Gavin Lewis　　01623-491346　Mobile 07790-709058
Britannia High (TV drama), The Street (TV drama), Longford (TV drama) (Standby).

David London　　Mobile 07899-041568

Chris Lowe　　020-8362 8199　Mobile 07889-218626
Quantum Of Solace (feature), In Bruges (feature), The Golden Compass (feature).

Mari Lucaccini　　020-8991 9837　Mobile 07708-324349
1066 (TV film) (Production Designer), Swinging With The Finkels (feature) (Standby), Casualty 1906 (TV drama).

John Lucas　　+34 95 251 6429
Angel (feature) (Production Designer), Light Years Away (feature), Braveheart (feature).

Emma MacDevitt　　Mobile 07774-424973
The Other Boleyn Girl (feature), Venus (feature), Hotel Rwanda (feature).

Stuart Mackay　　Mobile 07792-629852

Anna Magrath　　Mobile 07801-801213
Byker Grove (TV childrens), Paradise (short), Welsh Water (commercial).

Adam Makin　　020-8671 4865　Mobile 07976-892197
Luther (TV drama), Spooks (TV drama), Trinity (feature).

Choi Ho Man　　020-8299 2121　Mobile 07973-542027
Fax 020-8299 2121
Silent Witness (TV drama), Double Zero (feature), Alibi (TV drama).

Kamlan Man　　020-8769 6883　Mobile 07976-984105
The Mutant Chronicles (feature), Alien Autopsy (feature), Silent Witness (TV drama).

Richard Maris　　020-8533 8282　Mobile 07956-290576

Dominic Masters　　Mobile 07967-292459
Shanghai (feature), Casino Royale (feature), The Debt (feature).

Giles Masters　　01932-867513　Mobile 07710-762483
The Da Vinci Code (feature), The Mummy Returns (feature), Van Helsing (feature).

Andrea Matheson　　020-8693 5340　Mobile 07957-254361
Fax 020-8693 5340
Wedding Belles (TV drama), Perfect Day (TV film), Ratcatcher (feature).

Daniel May　　020-8948 2840　Mobile 07788-740219
The Day Of The Triffids (TV drama) (visual fx), Hitchhiker's Guide To The Galaxy (feature), Quantum Of Solace (feature) (Pre-Vis Supervisor).

Les McCallum　　020-8560 3974　Mobile 07940-280268
The Vicar Of Dibley (TV comedy drama), Only Fools & Horses (TV comedy drama), The Green Green Grass (TV comedy drama).

Tom McCullagh　　Mobile 07795-626421
Your Highness (feature).

Iain McFadyen　　+1 310 310 8102　Mobile +1 213 400 8935
Transformers: Revenge Of The Fallen (feature), Stardust (feature), Munich (feature).

Althea McGhie　　0141-339 6767　Mobile 07788-923733
Dalziel & Pascoe (TV drama), Legend Of Loch Lomond (feature), Winter Solstice (TV drama).

John McHugh　　Mobile 07774-601998
A Closed Book (feature), Holy Waters (feature), New Tricks (TV drama).

Jonathan McKinstry +34 96 526 9611
Mobile +34 66 768 6046
Prince Of Persia (feature), The Garden Of Eden (feature), Love In The Time Of Cholera (feature).

Rod McLean 020-7636 2668 Mobile 07768-774532
Inkheart (feature), Stardust (feature), Munich (feature).

Drogo Michie Mobile 07973-746559 WZ 020-7437 2055

Tanya Miller Mobile 07867-507655
Vexed (TV drama), Octavia (TV drama), What We Did On Our Holidays (TV drama).

David Minty 01344-622489 Mobile 07742-478756
In The Night Garden (TV childrens), Band Of Brothers (TV drama), Son Of The Pink Panther (feature).

Stephen Morahan 0118-971 2903 Mobile 07944-606112
Sunshine (feature), Batman Begins (feature) (Assistant), Die Another Day (feature) (Assistant).

David Morison 01784-436945 Mobile 07802-412587
AD 020-7428 0500
It's A Wonderful Afterlife (feature), Angus Thongs & Perfect Snogging (feature), Doctor Who (TV drama) (Set Decorator).

Deborah Morley 0117-971 5863 Mobile 07831-615338
Silent Witness (TV drama), These Foolish Things (feature), In A Land Of Plenty (TV drama).

Niall Moroney Mobile 07866-730110
Sherlock Holmes (feature), Atonement (feature), Separate Lies (feature).

Hannah Moseley 020-8994 2169 Mobile 07958-646322
Fax 020-7603 5743
London Boulevard (feature) (Draughtsman), Notes On A Scandal (feature), Closer (feature).

Rachel Munday Mobile 07752-841703

Andrew Munro Mobile 07826-717716 DA 020-7437 4551
Mansfield Park (TV film), Breakfast On Pluto (feature), Gormenghast (TV drama).

Nicholas Murray Mobile 07985-471517
Doctor Who (TV drama), The Restaurant (TV reality), Holby City (TV drama).

Julian Nagel Mobile 07734-692183 STA 020-7729 7477
Puritan (feature), School Of Life (short), Jetson (feature).

Nandie Narishkin Mobile 07855-477709
Hollyoaks (TV drama), Casualty (TV drama).

Victoria Nelson 020-8748 1934 Mobile 07973-890303
Fax 020-8748 1934
The Ruth Rendell Mysteries (TV drama), The Weakest Link (TV light entertainment), As If (TV drama).

Matthew Nevin Mobile 07792-944832
The Bill (TV drama), Babydoll (short), Fear Of Music (promo).

Andy Nicholson 020-7168 5692 Mobile 07899-904848
Alice In Wonderland (feature), The Wolfman (feature), RocknRolla (feature).

Julian Nix Mobile 07932-599346
Lewis (TV drama), Spooks (TV drama), Hustle (TV drama).

Alice Norris 020-8442 9955 Mobile 07957-622762
Fax 020-8442 9955
Lesbian Vampire Killers (feature), A Short Stay In Switzerland (TV drama), Ways To Live Forever (feature).

Andy Norris Mobile 07973-828606
Paul McCartney (promo), Nationwide (commercial), Virgin Mobile (commercial).

Stephanie Oakley Mobile 07977-010360
Apparitions (TV drama), Lilies (TV drama), Bodies (TV drama).

Adam O'Neill 01604-686381 Mobile 07973-791340
The Nutcracker (ballet), Troy (feature), Billy Elliot (feature).

Emer O'Sullivan Mobile 07961-163012
Lip Service (TV drama), Sea Of Souls (TV drama), Doomsday (feature).

Robyn Paiba Mobile 07968-711879
Hitchhiker's Guide To The Galaxy (feature) (Standby), Son Of Rambow (feature), The Day Of The Triffids (TV drama).

Keith Pain 01372-465733 Mobile 07776-195101
Valkyrie (feature), Oliver Twist (feature), Gladiator (feature).

Nic Pallace Mobile 07831-193554
A Short Stay In Switzerland (TV drama), Mr Harvey Lights A Candle (TV film), Love Again (TV film).

Nick Palmer Mobile 07778-242040
Mamma Mia! (feature), Eastern Promises (feature), The Hours (feature).

Sarah Pasquali Mobile 07976-747588
Bunny & The Bull (feature), Submarine (feature), Miss Pettigrew Lives For A Day (feature).

Aimee Paton Mobile 07802-852689
Dionne Bromfield (promo), Nintendo Wii (commercial).

Tristan Peatfield   01335-350476   Mobile 07799-846617
Fax 01335-350476
Doctor Who (TV drama), The Bill (TV drama).

Siobhan Pemberton   Mobile 07702-156488
Outnumbered (TV comedy drama), Heartbeat (TV drama), The Kumars (TV light entertainment).

Mike Perry   01622-791543   Mobile 07860-795445
Auf Wiedersehen Pet (TV drama).

Amy Pickwoad   Mobile 07967-712356
Spooks (TV drama) (Standby), Primeval (TV drama) (Standby), The Broken (feature).

Rachel Pierce   0161-941 2840   Mobile 07720-296894
Burn It (TV drama), The Royle Family (TV comedy drama), Cold Feet (TV drama) (Assistant).

Rebecca Pilkington   Mobile 07711-417313
Breaking The Mould (feature), The Curse Of Steptoe (TV drama).

Tony Pletts   020-8985 9850   Mobile 07976-353676

Nigel Pollock   Mobile 07973-767482
Miss Conception (feature), Waz (feature), The Secret Life Of Words (feature).

James Price   Mobile 07968-206248
Bullet Boy (feature), Dustbin Baby (TV drama), Grow Your Own (feature).

Karl Probert   Mobile 07768-424939
Survivors (TV drama), Hotel Babylon (TV drama), The Wyvern Mystery (TV film).

Kate Purdy   Mobile 07811-217997
Recovery (TV drama) (Standby), Torn (TV drama), Losing It (TV drama).

Mark Raggett   020-8960 7306   Mobile 07889-441225
Fax 020-8964 2335
W.E. (feature), London Boulevard (feature), 1408 (feature).

Natasha Rand   01932-858857   Mobile 07930-417781

Joe Rappaport   0117-980 3840   Mobile 07800-914708
Modern Toss (TV light entertainment), The Business (feature) (Prop Maker).

Ian Reade-Hill   Mobile 07767-481226
Hostile Waters (feature), Ultraviolet (TV drama), Red Dwarf (TV comedy drama).

John Reid   Mobile 07973-798547
Three & Out (feature), St Trinian's (feature), Penelope (feature).

Hauke Richter   020-8340 1274   Mobile 07775-565338
U Be Dead (TV film), City Of Vice (TV drama), Mrs Henderson Presents (feature).

Emma Robens   01949-20232   Mobile 07973-297323
Fax 01949-21124
Dido (promo), Mr Inbetween (feature) (Production Buyer).

Darren Robinson   Mobile 07729-325772

Danny Rogers   01753-785295   Mobile 07966-373819
Fax 01753-785929
Mes Amis Mes Amoures (feature), Inkheart (feature), Spy Game (feature).

Patrick Rolfe   020-8977 5696   Mobile 07836-599747
The Libertine (feature), 28 Weeks Later (feature), Jane Eyre (feature).

Stuart Rose   01932-563077   Mobile 07860-301924
Prince Of Persia (feature), Children Of Men (feature) (vehicles), Alexander (feature).

David Rosen   Mobile 07931-598126
Amy Winehouse (promo), Kellogg's (commercial), Razorlight (promo).

Andrew Rothschild   020-8960 3386   Mobile 07768-720066
Fax 020-8960 3386
Deep Blue Sea (feature), Mike Leigh - Untitled 09 (feature), The Long Walk To Finchley (TV film).

Graham Russell   01273-205610   Mobile 07974-018357
Diamond Geezer (TV drama), The Only Boy For Me (TV film), Down To Earth (TV drama).

Peter Russell   01525-375146   Mobile 07802-412648
Gulliver's Travels (feature), Stardust (feature), Gladiator (feature).

Anthony Rutter   Mobile 07713-769668
Looking For Eric (feature), Monarch Of The Glen (TV drama), Beethoven (TV drama).

Alistair Saunders   020-7502 1561   Mobile 07932-632719
Fax 020-7502 1561

Vivienne Schadinsky   020-7209 9945
Mobile 07775-781162
Foyle's War (TV drama), The Murder Room (TV drama), Silent Witness (TV drama).

Tino Schaedler   Mobile 07817-681244
Prince Of Persia (feature) (visual fx unit).

ART DIRECTORS

Denis Schnegg   Mobile 07932-600645
The Imaginarium Of Dr Parnassus (feature), The Constant Gardener (feature), Sunshine (feature).

Verity-Jane Scott   01280-860014   Mobile 07814-869978
Fax 01280-860014
A Very British Sex Scandal (TV docu drama), True Stories (TV docu drama), Nowhere Left To Hide (TV docu drama).

Mark Scruton   Mobile 07889-190231   AD 020-7428 0500
Gulliver's Travels (feature) (Assistant), Angus Thongs & Perfect Snogging (feature), The Bank Job (feature).

Samantha Selby   020-8664 6095   Mobile 07768-613304
The Bill (TV drama), The Knock (TV drama), London's Burning (TV drama).

Jenny Selden   020-8965 2666   Mobile 07956-538327

Barbara Shaw   01904-488520   Mobile 07973-265472
Fax 01904-488520
Emmerdale (TV drama), How We Used To Live (TV childrens).

Sandie Shepherd   01723-367781   Mobile 07785-252644
Trial & Retribution (TV drama), My Family (TV comedy drama), The Commander (TV drama).

Julia Sherborne   020-7731 7444   Mobile 07831-485589
AD 020-7428 0500   Fax 020-7731 4245

Gregg Shoulder   Mobile 07949-635927

Astrid Sieben   020-7704 9731   Mobile 07767-830765
Criminal Justice (TV drama), Shooting Dogs (feature), The Wedding Date (feature).

Phil Sims   Mobile 07931-572390
Gulliver's Travels (feature) (visual fx), Angels & Demons (feature), Prince Caspian (feature).

Troy Sizemore   Mobile 07827-893590
Clash Of The Titans (feature).

Keith Slote   020-8207 3267   Mobile 07887-578331
Children Of Men (feature) (Standby), Proof (feature), Stage Beauty (feature).

Ben Smith   020-8678 7494   Mobile 07967-833853
An Education (feature), The Queen (feature), Dean Spanley (feature).

Kajsa Soderlund   Mobile 07929-888789
Huge (feature).

Carrie Southall   Mobile 07779-025659

Fabrice Spelta   020-8892 7387   Mobile 07958-027596
Harry Brown (feature), Tormented (feature).

Lucy Spink   Mobile 07776-395169
Free Agents (TV drama), Jonathan Creek (TV drama) (Standby), Campus (TV comedy drama).

Jan Spoczynski   020-8715 0885   Mobile 07860-240035
Shanghai (feature), Matchpoint (feature), Stage Beauty (feature).

Margaret Spohrer   020-8677 7327   Mobile 07976-631225
Fax 020-8677 7327
Outnumbered (TV comedy drama), Benidorm (TV comedy drama), That Mitchell & Webb Look (TV light entertainment).

Mike Stallion   01892-782204   Mobile 07785-377272
Quantum Of Solace (feature), Robin Hood (feature), Children Of Men (feature).

Elaine Starks   01273-464853   Mobile 07768-077410
Murder City (TV drama), Doc Martin (TV drama), Red Cap (TV drama).

Hayley Stephens   Mobile 07734-859924
Home & Away (TV drama), My Kitchen Rules (TV reality), Spirited (TV drama).

Toby Stevens   Mobile 07957-453006

Tom Still   Mobile 07778-480786
Robin Hood (feature) (Assistant), Prince Of Persia (feature), The Nutcracker (ballet).

Jamie Stimpson   Mobile 07956-496716
British Airways (commercial), Vogue Homme (magazine), Vanity Fair (feature).

Sam Stokes   0117-902 0304   Mobile 07973-191682
Fax 0117-902 0304
The Shooter (feature), Revolver (feature), Vanity Fair (feature).

Malcolm Stone   020-8642 8616   Mobile 07836-772230
Fax 020-8642 6731
Ironclad (feature), The Company (TV film), In The Night Garden (TV childrens).

Mark Stonehouse   Mobile 07514-007608
Survivors (TV drama), Bad Girls (TV drama), Cutting It (TV drama).

Emily Straight   01304-369070   Mobile 07734-392453

Alan Sullivan   Mobile 07967-823011
Hell's Kitchen (TV reality), Later With Jools Holland (TV light entertainment), The Bill (TV drama) (Standby).

Lucienne Suren   020-8838 0894   Mobile 07970-016849
Run Fat Boy Run (feature).

Mark Swain Mobile 07790-346679
Robin Hood (feature), Green Zone (feature), Prince Of Persia (feature).

Maddy Swinglehurst 01784-459351 Mobile 07736-384241
DIY Hard (short), Cold & Dark (feature).

Cheryl Tarbuck Mobile 07973-859597
Toblerone (commercial), Five Alive (commercial), Fairy Liquid (commercial).

Daniel Taylor Mobile 07801-539260
Cass (feature) (Production Designer), Freestyle (feature) (Production Designer), Wallander (TV drama).

Gareth Thomas Mobile 07796-956360
Swinging With The Finkels (feature), British Telecom (commercial), NC Aggro (promo).

Robert Thomas 020-8567 8262 Mobile 07971-045490
Hackers (feature), The Borrowers (feature).

Mel Thompson 020-8348 5014 Mobile 07711-719030
EastEnders (promo), Jonathan Creek (TV drama), LD 50 (feature).

Andrew Thomson 01436-678007 Mobile 07712-674205
Fax 01436-678007
Elizabeth: The Golden Age (feature), Inception (feature), Centurion (feature).

Lucinda Thomson 020-7253 9470 Mobile 07785-333939
Don't Be Afraid Of The Dark (feature), Where The Wild Things Are (feature), Rogue (feature).

Sam Tidman Mobile 07720-528458

Gary Tomkins 01296-632024 Mobile 07778-325430
Harry Potter & The Deathly Hallows (feature), Harry Potter & The Half-Blood Prince (feature), Harry Potter & The Goblet Of Fire (feature).

Yvonne Toner Mobile 07970-898933
Knife Edge (feature), Coming Of Age (TV comedy drama), Mrs In-Betweeny (TV comedy drama).

Remo Tozzi 020-8510 9695 Mobile 07966-406219
Robin Hood (feature), Sunshine (feature) (Standby), Batman Begins (feature) (Draughtsman).

Madeleine Turnbull Mobile 07771-924621
Emmerdale (TV drama) (Production Designer), Murphy's Law (TV drama), Canterbury Tales (TV drama).

Katy Tuxford Mobile 07967-398644
Bone Kickers (TV drama), Echo Beach (TV drama), Cape Wrath (TV drama).

Sloane U'Ren Mobile 07906-472496
Harry Potter & The Half-Blood Prince (feature), Shanghai (feature), Tsunami: The Aftermath (TV drama).

Oli van der Vijver Mobile 07930-407148
Heartless (feature), Nanny McPhee & The Big Bang (feature), The Disappearance Of Alice Creed (feature).

Norman Vertigan 020-8932 1995 Mobile 07831-581264
Fax 020-8932 1996
British Telecom (commercial), British Airways (commercial), Dulux (commercial).

Karen Wakefield 020-7978 1389 Mobile 07831-669889
Fax 020-7978 1389
Robin Hood (feature), The Duchess (feature), The Kingdom (feature).

Alexandra Walker Mobile 07976-212683
Harry Potter & The Order Of The Phoenix (feature), Incendiary (feature), The Young Victoria (feature).

Leigh Walker 01386-841155 Mobile 07774-190020
Fax 01386-841155
Law & Order (TV drama), Lark Rise To Candleford (TV drama), Mrs Ratcliffe's Revolution (feature).

Frank Walsh 01494-875921 Mobile 07760-176160
Inception (feature), Prince Caspian (feature), Elizabeth: The Golden Age (feature).

Justin Warburton-Brown 020-7326 4930
Mobile 07973-854665
Alien Vs Predator (feature), Love Actually (feature), The Nutcracker (ballet).

Dave Warren 020-8941 9835 Mobile 07710-043970
The Imaginarium Of Dr Parnassus (feature), Sweeney Todd (feature), 10,000 BC (feature).

Kellie Waugh Mobile 07973-307560
The Walker (feature), Jekyll (TV drama), Sense & Sensibility (feature).

Lisa Westwell Mobile 07958-964365
Mortal Kombat - Annihilation (feature), Coronation Street (TV drama), Mr Kipling (commercial).

Susan Whitaker 020-8896 9557 Mobile 07831-186182
Prince Of Persia (feature), Angels & Demons (feature), Valkyrie (feature).

Iain White 020-8441 0409 Mobile 07779-606687
Sleuth (feature), The Magic Flute (feature), As You Like It (feature).

ART DIRECTORS

Fleur Whitlock   020-8948 0016 Mobile 07831-415780
Fax 020-8948 0016
Wuthering Heights (feature), Krod Mandoon & The Flaming Sword Of
Fire (TV drama), 10,000 BC (feature).

Olly Williams   Mobile 07949-034585

Ben Wilson   Mobile 07866-775826
Ashes (short), Private Life (short), Kodak (commercial).

Stephen Wong   Mobile 07710-752022
A Thing Called Love (TV drama), The Secret Life Of Mrs Beeton (TV
drama), Babylon AD (feature).

Jeffrey Woodbridge   01932-562611 Mobile 07796-333987
Fax 01932-568989
Gladiators (TV light entertainment), Secrets (TV drama), Dire
Straits (promo).

Kevin Woodhouse   01732-300081 Mobile 07903-152971
Law & Order (TV drama), House Of Saddam (TV drama), The
Children (feature).

Kate Woodman   020-8659 8787 Mobile 07931-798606

Mike Wright   01582-572041 Mobile 07832-268938
The Paul O'Grady Show (trailer), Strictly Come Dancing (TV
light entertainment), Friday Night With Jonathan Ross (TV light
entertainment).

Stephen Wright   01273-685483 Mobile 07850-485189
Fax 01273-601904
Rosemary & Thyme (TV drama), EastEnders (promo) (Production
Designer), Last Of The Summer Wine (TV comedy drama).

Christopher Wyatt   Mobile 07939-122324
Tamara Drewe (feature), Fish Tank (feature), Alien Autopsy
(feature).

Jacqueline Zoppi-Tighe   01737-773366
Mobile 07966-394955
Desperados (TV childrens), Bleak House (TV drama), Are You Looking
At Me? (TV film).

ART DIRECTORS - ASSISTANT

Antonia Atha   01872-553269 Mobile 07817-631425
Cranford (TV drama), Little Dorrit (TV drama), Somers Town
(feature).

Louise Begbie   020-7359 2233 Mobile 07967-626453
Gulliver's Travels (feature), Easy Virtue (feature), The Descent 2
(feature).

Andrew Bennett   Mobile 07715-369463
John Carter Of Mars (feature), Clash Of The Titans (feature) (Set
Designer), Sherlock Holmes (feature).

Alex Beverly   Mobile 07802-253717
Missing (TV doc), Monday Monday (TV drama), Holby Blue (TV
drama).

Sophie Boddington   01326-210846 Mobile 07967-525461
The Russian Bride (TV drama), The Inspector Lynley Mysteries (TV
drama).

Guy Bradley   020-8876 2305 Mobile 07931-351293
John Carter Of Mars (feature), Robin Hood (feature), Prince Of
Persia (feature).

Toby Britton   020-7908 1909 Mobile 07980-912421
John Carter Of Mars (feature), Prince Of Persia (feature)
(Draughtsman), The Dark Knight (feature).

Cara Brower   Mobile 07875-736583
Never Let Me Go (feature), The Eagle Of The Ninth (feature).

Emma Caplin   Mobile 07957-221324
Nanny McPhee (feature), Dirty Pretty Things (feature), Jericho (TV
drama) (Standby).

Sion Clarke   Mobile 07803-124842
Apparitions (TV drama), Fattest Man In Britian (TV drama), Casualty
1909 (TV drama).

Dean Clegg   Mobile 07939-572506
Quantum Of Solace (feature), Mamma Mia! (feature) (Art Director),
Elizabeth: The Golden Age (feature).

Susan Collin   Mobile 07932-761613
Doomsday (feature).

Ben Collins   Mobile 07813-181134
Gulliver's Travels (feature), The Boat That Rocked (feature), Ondine
(feature).

Rachel Corbould   01372-454088 Mobile 07809-441662
John Carter Of Mars (feature), Saxondale (TV comedy drama)
(Runner).

Jordan Crockett   Mobile 07872-997796
Prince Of Persia (feature), Green Zone (feature), Robin Hood
(feature).

Julia Dehoff   Mobile 07973-853676
1408 (feature), The Dark Is Rising (feature) (Art Director), Harry
Potter & The Deathly Hallows (feature).

Peter Dorme   020-8873 0056 Mobile 07889-214717
John Carter Of Mars (feature), Prince Of Persia (feature), The Dark
Knight (feature).

Katrina Dunn   Mobile 07789-152947
Hippie Hippie Shake (feature) (Draughtsman), Happy-Go-Lucky (feature), 28 Weeks Later (feature).

Anna Ekholm   Mobile 07956-007754

Gavin Fitch   01892-527759   Mobile 07958-351982
Gulliver's Travels (feature), Prince Of Persia (feature), Quantum Of Solace (feature).

Joy Fonderson   Mobile 07861-708815

Dalia Gellert   Mobile 07985-397227
Dogging (feature), Britain's Next Top Model (TV light entertainment), The F Word (TV doc).

Luke Gledsdale   Mobile 07932-796994
A Lonely Place to Die (feature), Bonded By Blood (feature), Dead Cert (feature).

Maria Goldmann   Mobile 07767-846093
Jenny & The Worm (short), Detective Mafahiro (short), Boves El Urogallo (feature).

Andrew Grant   020-7708 5254   Mobile 07976-715809
Fax 020-7708 5254
Vera Drake (feature), The Dark (feature) (Art Director), Nicholas Nickleby (feature).

Austin Harris   Mobile 07711-699348
Discovering Ancient Egypt (TV drama doc), A Rather English Marriage (TV drama), East Is East (feature).

Jane Harwood   020-7286 9967   Mobile 07957-574858
Dagenham Girls (feature), Kick-Ass (feature), Robin Hood (feature) (Draughtsman).

Jemima Hawkins   Mobile 07989-972580
Four Seasons (TV drama), Whitechapel (TV drama), Foyle's War (TV drama).

Sophie Hervieu   Mobile 07967-372015
Albert's Memorial (TV drama), Bunny & The Bull (feature), Samsung (commercial).

Patricia Johnson   01784-431970   Mobile 07747-180951
Robin Hood (feature), Prince Of Persia (feature), The Da Vinci Code (feature).

Katherine Law   Mobile 07799-333050
Brighton Rock (feature), Cemetery Junction (feature), Little Dorrit (TV drama).

Daniel Maclagan   Mobile 07787-564637
Numerous commercials & promos.

Elizabeth Marcussen   01633-420884
Mobile 07866-605179
Collision (TV drama), Lark Rise To Candleford (TV drama) (Production Buyer), Tess Of The D'Urbervilles (TV drama) (Production Buyer).

Catriona McKail   Mobile 07771-755681
Tess Of The D'Urbervilles (TV drama), Lark Rise To Candleford (TV drama), Britz (TV drama).

Daryn McLaughlan   Mobile 07967-100820
44 Inch Chest (feature), Nineteen Eighty (TV film), Miss Pettigrew Lives For A Day (feature).

Georgina Millett   Mobile 07779-113691
Atonement (feature), Hippie Hippie Shake (feature), Taking The Flack (TV comedy drama).

Yrsa Palmer   01803-605089   Mobile 07939-228489
Impact (TV film), Trial & Retribution (TV drama), Murder Most Horrid (TV drama).

Sandra Phillips   020-8566 0671   Mobile 07958-733481
Quantum Of Solace (feature), Clash Of The Titans (feature) (Set Designer), The Eagle Of The Ninth (feature) (Draughtsman).

Matt Robinson   020-8533 7475   Mobile 07931-149533
Robin Hood (feature) (Art Director), Little Dorrit (TV drama), Sherlock Holmes (feature).

Nina Ross   Mobile 07940-501168
Between Two Rivers (TV drama) (Art Director), Minzy (feature), Derailed (feature).

Emma Saunders   Mobile 07812-654054
Miss Potter (feature), The Edge Of Love (feature), Poppy Shakespeare (TV film).

Richard Selway   Mobile 07939-115045
The Wolfman (feature).

Lucy Spofforth   Mobile 07730-507900
Tess Of The D'Urbervilles (TV drama), Cranford (TV drama), Identity (TV drama).

Stephen Swain   01296-651019   Mobile 07989-332229
Harry Potter & The Deathly Hallows (feature), Harry Potter & The Goblet Of Fire (feature) (Draughtsman), Harry Potter & The Half-Blood Prince (feature).

Andy Tomlinson   Mobile 07941-048148
Sixty Six (feature), Death At A Funeral (feature) (Standby), Nanny McPhee (feature) (Draughtsman).

James Wakefield   Mobile 07834-777376
Nanny McPhee & The Big Bang (feature), Creation (feature), Miss Marple (TV drama).

CONCEPT ARTISTS

Ravi Bansal Mobile 07973-871821
Star Wars: Episode II - Attack Of The Clones (feature), Batman Begins (feature), Tin Tin (feature).

Max Berman Mobile 07850-151712

Adam Brockbank 020-8995 9501 Mobile 07957-281020
Harry Potter & The Order Of The Phoenix (feature), Harry Potter & The Goblet Of Fire (feature), Sleepy Hollow (feature).

Ian Bunting Mobile 07811-536920
Torchwood (TV drama), Doctor Who (TV drama), Captain Scarlet (TV drama).

Julian Caldow 020-8654 1922 Mobile 07867-982022
Prince Of Persia (feature), Casino Royale (feature), Children Of Men (feature).

Neil Campbell Ross 020-7281 4579
Mobile 07961-976268
The Golden Compass (feature), Charlie & The Chocolate Factory (feature), Corpse Bride (feature).

Paul Catling Mobile 07703-357479
The Wolfman (feature), The Golden Compass (feature), Spiderman II (feature).

Rory Collins 01234-870605 Mobile 07808-765162
Nine (feature), Children Of Men (feature), Layer Cake (feature).

Ross Dearsley 01344-301972 Mobile 07817-153166
Harry Potter & The Order Of The Phoenix (feature), Harry Potter & The Goblet Of Fire (feature), Harry Potter & The Half-Blood Prince (feature).

Ben Dennett 01736-810558 Mobile 07952-264481
Harry Potter & The Goblet Of Fire (feature).

Stephen Forrest-Smith 020-8355 5553
Mobile 07801-628372
Fred Claus (feature), Alien Vs Predator (feature), Resident Evil (feature).

Alex Fort Mobile 07743-294732
Torchwood (TV drama), Doctor Who (TV drama), Hitchhiker's Guide To The Galaxy (feature).

Kim Frederiksen Mobile 07868-730411
GI Joe: The Rise Of Cobra (feature), Prince Of Persia (feature).

Tom Garwood Mobile 07780-601808
Adventures With Pirates (feature), The Life & Death Of Peter Sellers (feature), The Nutcracker (ballet).

Achilleas Gatsopoulos Mobile 07787-182912
Charlie & The Chocolate Factory (feature), Absolut Vodka (corporate), Pet Shop Boys (promo).

Geoffrey Huband 01736-711832 Mobile 07746-960392
Harry Potter & The Goblet Of Fire (feature).

Kevin Hunter Mobile 07968-841325
Saving Private Ryan (feature), The Nutcracker (ballet), The Mutant Chronicles (feature) (Assistant Art Director).

Sevendalino Khay Mobile 07901-885635
The Golden Compass (feature), Hitchhiker's Guide To The Galaxy (feature), The Matrix III (feature).

Eva Kuntz Mobile 07876-366177
Made In Dagenham (feature), London Boulevard (feature), Sherlock Holmes (feature).

Dominic Lavery 01865-891234 Mobile 07889-549471
Gulliver's Travels (feature), Stardust (feature), Captain Scarlet (TV drama) (also Director).

Paul McGill 020-7249 0166 Mobile 07974-210632
Robin Hood (feature), Quantum Of Solace (feature), Charlie & The Chocolate Factory (feature).

Simon McGuire 01788-576818 Mobile 07979-551661
Sweeney Todd (feature), Fred Claus (feature), Children Of Men (feature).

Peter Mckinstry Mobile 07929-442330
Harry Potter & The Half-Blood Prince (feature), Harry Potter & The Deathly Hallows (feature), Dr Who (TV drama).

Cyrille Nomberg 020-7254 9471 Mobile 07710-510347
Gulliver's Travels (feature), The Golden Compass (feature), The Wolfman (feature).

Lee Oliver 01582-602448 Mobile 07786-512564
The Golden Compass (feature), Stardust (feature), Casino Royale (feature).

Kimberley Pope 01525-240560 Mobile 07890-229747
Agora (feature), Stormbreaker (feature), Hitchhiker's Guide To The Galaxy (feature).

Dermot Power 020-8206 2484 Mobile 07957-625998
Harry Potter & The Goblet Of Fire (feature), Beowulf & Grendel (feature), Star Wars: Episode II - Attack Of The Clones (feature).

Lee Ray 0115-985 5698 Mobile 07818-081406
Hounded (TV childrens) (Digital Art).
www.lee-ray.com

Simon Roberts 01225-317151 Mobile 07968-556568
Skins (TV drama) (Graphic Designer), Adidas (commercial).
www.sr-illustration.com

Neil Ross Mobile 07961-976268
Prince Of Persia (feature).

Neil Ross   Mobile 07961-976268
Prince Of Persia (feature).

Silvana Sacco   Mobile 07764-636375
Green Zone (feature), Lord Of The Rings (feature), Alexander (feature).

Gert Stevens   Mobile 07761-716789
City Of Ember (feature), Stardust (feature), Charlie & The Chocolate Factory (feature).

Howard Swindell   01753-655587 Mobile 07791-720517
Skellig (feature), 10,000 BC (feature), Stardust (feature).

Simon Thorpe   01580-850367 Mobile 07775-558709
The Green Lantern (feature) (costumes), Stardust (feature), Alexander (feature).

Mike Trim   01227-860488 Mobile 07711-296562
Agent Crush (feature), Thunderbirds (feature), UFO (TV drama).

Dan Walker   Mobile 07967-205662
John Carter Of Mars (feature), Robin Hood (feature), Prince Of Persia (feature).

Norman Walshe   Mobile 07800-658043
Gulliver's Travels (feature), Your Highness (feature), Inkheart (feature).

CONSTRUCTION BUYERS

Hillery Cope   01872-863396 Mobile 07710-975522
Charlie & The Chocolate Factory (feature), Phantom Of The Opera (feature), Band Of Brothers (TV drama).

Jack Dyer   020-8953 5718 Mobile 07956-577003
Angels & Demons (feature), Wanted (feature), The Da Vinci Code (feature).

Garry Hayes   Mobile 07886-615362
Harry Potter & The Deathly Hallows (feature), Harry Potter & The Half-Blood Prince (feature), Harry Potter & The Order Of The Phoenix (feature).

Richard Lyon   Mobile 07932-767311
Notting Hill (feature), Tomb Raider II (feature), Quills (feature).

Mark Russell   01206-532678 Mobile 07732-556912
Prince Of Persia (feature).

CONSTRUCTION CO-ORDINATORS

Laura Davison   Mobile 07974-215961
John Carter Of Mars (feature), Robin Hood (feature).

Catherine Haugh   Mobile 07967-466894
Gulliver's Travels (feature), Quantum Of Solace (feature).

Jenny Hawkins   01932-588950 Mobile 07774-759442
Quantum Of Solace (feature), The Dark Knight (feature), Nanny McPhee & The Big Bang (feature).

Tracy Low   Mobile 07957-650515
Nanny McPhee & The Big Bang (feature), The Wolfman (feature).

Julia Newell   01923-210318 Mobile 07506-959264
The Wolfman (feature).

Nancy Scott   020-8969 9884 Mobile 07917-533882
Prince Of Persia (feature).

Nicola Short   Mobile 07971-854502
Clash Of The Titans (feature).

CONSTRUCTION MANAGERS

Dave Allen   020-7635 9155 Mobile 07973-523379
Fax 020-7277 5120
Wild Target (feature), In The Loop (feature), The Mutant Chronicles (feature).

Rob Anderson   020-8694 0223 Mobile 07973-443861
Hippie Hippie Shake (feature), Venus (feature), The Lost Prince (TV drama).

Callum Andrews   01932-226341 Mobile 07967-593735
Fax 01932-246336
Dead Set (TV drama), Metamorphosis (short), Nike (commercial).
www.hallifordfilmstudios.co.uk

Ray Barrett   01494-485202 Mobile 07860-818013
The Da Vinci Code (feature), Sahara (feature), Van Helsing (feature).

Steve Bedford   0161-973 1427 Mobile 07976-657751
Fax 0161-973 1427
The Bad Mother's Handbook (TV drama), See No Evil (TV drama), Cold Blood (TV drama).

Marc Beros   01403-730658 Mobile 07798-825044
Shanghai (feature).

John Bohan   020-8299 1990 Mobile 07831-767109
Fax 020-8299 1766
Gulliver's Travels (feature), The Wolfman (feature), The Bourne Ultimatum (feature).

Steve Bohan   020-8658 8977 Mobile 07831-767110
Fax 020-8402 9290
Nanny McPhee & The Big Bang (feature), Nine (feature), Quantum Of Solace (feature).

ART

CONSTRUCTION MANAGERS

Phil Bowen Mobile 07974-114294
PAs (TV drama), Doomsday (feature).

Perry Cella Mobile 07956-324566
Fashion Babylon (TV drama), City Of Vice (TV drama), A Harlot's Progress (TV drama).

Alan Chesters 01491-413165 Mobile 07860-929761
Bright Star (feature), Stormbreaker (feature), Mrs Henderson Presents (feature).

Dan Crandon 020-8561 4108 Mobile 07973-664973
The Libertine (feature), 28 Weeks Later (feature), The Duchess (feature).

Dave Creed 01932-858458 Mobile 07764-190914
Fax 01932-858458
Eastern Promises (feature), Cassandra's Dream (feature), Half Light (feature).

Robert Crewe Mobile 07976-629579

Gene D'Cruze 020-8759 5333 Mobile 07917-855052
Fax 020-8897 4496
W.E. (feature), London Boulevard (feature), The Young Victoria (feature).

Brian Dowling 020-8855 6888 Mobile 07976-282684
Fax 020-8855 9888
Hot Fuzz (feature), Goldfrapp (promo), Barclays Bank (commercial).

Paul Duff 01536-722491 Mobile 07778-113332
Fax 01536-722491
Quantum Of Solace (feature), The Bourne Ultimatum (feature) (HOD Carpenter), Casino Royale (feature) (HOD Carpenter).

Trevor Dyer 01923-253469 Mobile 07831-885948
Little Dorrit (TV drama), Fred Claus (feature), The Da Vinci Code (feature).

Brian Eatough Mobile 07831-275268

Steve Ede 020-8857 3766 Mobile 07976-708031
Miss Potter (feature), Keeping Mum (feature).

Andy Evans 01923-894579 Mobile 07831-675783
The Golden Compass (feature), Children Of Men (feature), Charlie & The Chocolate Factory (feature).

Colin Fraser 01786-870348 Mobile 07973-737929
Valkyrie (feature), 1408 (feature).

David Garbe 0117-955 5538 Mobile 07973-833449
Fax 0117-955 2480
Deal Or No Deal (TV light entertainment), Mistresses (TV drama), Merlin (TV drama).

Leigh Gilbert 01628-669388 Mobile 07836-580222
Fax 01628-667143
John Carter Of Mars (feature), Robin Hood (feature), The Dark Knight (feature).
www.leighgilbert.co.uk

David Gray 01784-433962 Mobile 07850-826962
Fax 01784-437895
Love Soup (TV drama), The Libertine (feature), War Bride (feature).
www.fabrytrading.com

Tony Graysmark 01895-232776 Mobile 07768-208958
Shanghai (feature), Hellboy 2: The Golden Army (feature), Munich (feature).

Ian Green 020-8440 1613 Mobile 07719-815009
Speed Racer (feature), Ninja Assassin (feature), The Golden Compass (feature) (Assistant).

Stephen Hargreaves 01296-682344 Mobile 07970-753142
Fax 01296-682197

Kevin Harris Mobile 07967-671041
Brighton Rock (feature), Desperate Romantics (TV drama), Little Dorrit (TV drama).

Tony Harris 020-8607 8769 Mobile 07889-045301
Fax 020-8607 7284
2012 Olympics (TV comedy drama), Push The Button (TV light entertainment), Blue Peter (TV childrens).
www.keepforseriesltd.com

Jo Hawthorne 020-7272 3750 Mobile 07973-386334
Sense & Sensibility (feature), Into The Storm (TV film), From Time To Time (feature).

Paul Hayes 01296-651925 Mobile 07734-060251
Harry Potter & The Deathly Hallows (feature), Harry Potter & The Half-Blood Prince (feature), Die Another Day (feature).

Stephen Hayward 020-8953 1745 Mobile 07768-965857
Fax 020-8953 9044

Paul Jones 0118-986 9719 Mobile 07711-579900
The Magic Flute (feature) (Assistant), Phantom Of The Opera (feature) (Assistant).

Alan King 01449-674126 Mobile 07785-511705
Fax 01449-674126
Sheila's Wheels (commercial), Center Parcs (commercial), Land Rover (commercial).

John Kirsop Mobile 07956-577754
Clash Of The Titans (feature), City Of Ember (feature).

Warren Lever   Mobile 07961-428510 Fax 0871-989 5820
A Bunch Of Amateurs (feature), Miss Austin Regrets (TV drama),
Take That: Shine (promo).
www.constructscenery.co.uk

Colt MacInnes   Mobile 07786-895050
New Town Killers (feature).

John Maher   01753-654157 Mobile 07836-242551
Fax 01753-654157
Prince Of Persia (feature), Breaking & Entering (feature), The
Holiday (feature).

Tom Martin   020-8299 2851 Mobile 07785-704796
Fax 020-8299 2191
The Boat That Rocked (feature), Dorian Gray (feature), Sunshine
(feature).

Eamon McLoughlin   01895-465846 Mobile 07747-691127
Fax 01895-465846
Gulliver's Travels (feature), The Wolfman (feature) (Assistant),
Death Defying Acts (feature).

Sam Mercer   Mobile 07970-371897
Intel (commercial), Man Stroke Woman (TV light entertainment),
Gucci (stills).

Harry Metcalfe   020-7702 7337 Mobile 07831-720054
Fax 020-7702 7334
Thunderbirds (feature), What A Girl Wants (feature), 102
Dalmatians (feature).

Jono Moles   020-7231 7067 Mobile 07973-377475
Fax 020-7231 7635
Angus Thongs & Perfect Snogging (feature), Easy Virtue (feature),
The Descent 2 (feature).

Barry Moll   Mobile 07710-444759
Cranford (TV drama), To The Ends Of The Earth (TV drama), Topsy-
Turvy (feature).

Brian Neighbour   01923-267546 Mobile 07774-713407
Prince Of Persia (feature), Green Zone (feature), National Treasure:
Book Of Secrets (feature).

Dave Paley   01923-857320 Mobile 07831-234557
Mean Machine (feature), Telstar (feature), Headless (TV drama).

John Park   Mobile 07973-145084
The Nutcracker (ballet), Eragon (feature), The Truth About Love
(feature).

Jamie Powell   Mobile 07515-360632
The Golden Compass (feature), Home Of The Brave (feature).

Steve Protheroe   01992-445755 Mobile 07711-424030
Bad Girls (TV drama).

Jason Reilly   Mobile 07711-094220 Fax 01784-462877
Merlin (TV drama), Foyle's War (TV drama), Ashes To Ashes (TV
drama).

Mike Rickard   01932-227210 Mobile 07966-370738
Confessions (feature), The Lion In Winter (TV film), Five Children
& It (feature).

Malcolm Roberts   01753-573115 Mobile 07802-738402
Elizabeth: The Golden Age (feature), Gladiator (feature), Harry
Potter & The Chamber Of Secrets (feature).

Antoine Robin   020-7354 8131 Mobile 07887-983543
In Bruges (feature), Murder In Mind (TV drama), The Passion (TV
drama).

Paul Sansom   Mobile 07702-241246
The Commander (TV drama), Spooks (TV drama), My Family (TV
comedy drama).

David Sawyer   Mobile 07913-491897
Huge (feature).

Joe Sheehan   020-8607 8769 Mobile 07789-117133
Fax 020-8607 7284
Absolute Power (TV drama), Judge John Deed (TV drama), Last Of
The Summer Wine (TV comedy drama).
www.keepforseriesltd.com

Hugo Slight   020-8742 9292 Mobile 07767-684136
Fax 020-8749 7347
4.3.2.1 (feature), Garrow's Law (TV drama), Lark Rise To Candleford
(TV drama).
www.totom.co.uk

Christopher Spurling   Mobile 07973-383704

Peter Steward   Mobile 07710-798415
Three & Out (feature), St Trinian's (feature), Penelope (feature).

Glenn Taylor   01252-879013 Mobile 07831-448893
Fax 01252-879013
Midsomer Murders (TV drama), A & E (TV drama), Blue Dove (TV
drama).

John Thorpe   01943-465040 Mobile 07860-394586
Fax 01943-465040
Lark Rise To Candleford (TV drama), Tess Of The D'Urbervilles (TV
drama), Law & Order (TV drama).

Roger Tyrrell   01707-335558 Mobile 07860-599059
Children Of Men (feature).

David Wescott   01296-712257 Mobile 07956-125993
Harry Potter & The Half-Blood Prince (feature), Harry Potter
& The Order Of The Phoenix (feature), City Of Ember (feature)
(Assistant).

ART

CONSTRUCTION MANAGERS

Roger Wilkins   01784-437855 Mobile 07802-412259
Pickles (TV film), Born & Bred (TV drama), State Of Play (TV drama).

Peter Williams   020-7229 2012 Mobile 07786-693229
Batman Returns (feature), The World Is Not Enough (feature), Titanic (feature).

Denis Wilson   01883-732209 Mobile 07973-560802
Fax 01883-732209
RocknRolla (feature), The Four Feathers (feature), Snatch (feature).

Bob Windle   020-8578 2627 Mobile 07968-598584
Fax 020-8578 2425
The Russell Brand Show (TV light entertainment), Extras (TV comedy drama).
www.sia-trading.co.uk

Gus Wookey   01633-420832 Mobile 07775-691889
Poirot (TV drama), Outlaw (feature), The Roman Mysteries (TV childrens).

CONSTRUCTION SUPERVISORS

Steve Deane   01908-662645 Mobile 07970-300657
Fax 01908-672489
Ruby In The Smoke (TV film), Elizabeth The Virgin Queen (TV drama), The Murder Room (TV drama).

Eddie Murphy   01932-700486 Mobile 07956-244148
In Bruges (feature), Shaun Of The Dead (feature), Rogue Trader (feature).

John Paterson   0118-947 8102 Mobile 07989-967428
Flight Of The Phoenix (feature), Seven Years In Tibet (feature), The Mummy (feature).

Dave Reed   020-8896 3131 Mobile 07767-326917
Fax 020-8896 3232
St Trinian's (feature), The Broken (feature), Penelope (feature).

Nicholas Sargent   01784-211561 Mobile 07778-173742
Quantum Of Solace (feature), The Dark Knight (feature), In Bruges (feature).

DRAPESMEN

Graham Caulfield   Mobile 07831-871565
Inception (feature), Prince Of Persia (feature), Shanghai (feature).
www.grahamcaulfield.co.uk

Laurent Ferrie   Mobile 07976-852995
Robin Hood (feature), Harry Potter & The Deathly Hallows (feature).

Colin Fox   01628-529009 Mobile 07831-642960
Fax 01628-529009
John Carter Of Mars (feature), Robin Hood (feature), The Other Boleyn Girl (feature).

Daniel Handley   01932-560175 Mobile 07795-053376
Fax 01932-560175
Harry Potter & The Deathly Hallows (feature), Gulliver's Travels (feature), Clash Of The Titans (feature).
www.sheppertondrapes.co.uk

Gary Handley   01932-560175 Mobile 07831-871071
Fax 01932-560175
Harry Potter & The Deathly Hallows (feature), Gulliver's Travels (feature), Clash Of The Titans (feature).
www.sheppertondrapes.co.uk

Frank Howe   01753-656245 Mobile 07976-938961
Fax 01753-656202
www.pinewoodgroup.com

Jesse Jones   01932-560175 Mobile 07810-651288
Fax 01932-560175
Harry Potter & The Deathly Hallows (feature), Gulliver's Travels (feature), Clash Of The Titans (feature).
www.sheppertondrapes.co.uk

Chris Lewry   0113-284 2958 Mobile 07808-138863
Sex & The City 2 (feature), Gulliver's Travels (feature), Harry Potter & The Deathly Hallows (feature).

Mark McCabe   Mobile 07773-299232
Robin Hood (feature), Quantum Of Solace (feature), The Duchess (feature).

Cleo Nethersole   01932-560175 Mobile 07831-198127
Fax 01932-560175
Quantum Of Solace (feature), Gulliver's Travels (feature), Clash Of The Titans (feature).
www.sheppertondrapes.co.uk

Colin Pearce   01753-654403 Mobile 07787-560731
Fax 01753-654403
Clash Of The Titans (feature), Cranford (TV drama), Shakespeare In Love (feature).

Chris Seddon   Mobile 07889-132546
Nine (feature), The Wolfman (feature), Prince Caspian (feature).

Anthony Szuch   07543-630313 Mobile 07795-418317
Inkheart (feature), Little Dorrit (TV drama), Dorian Gray (feature).
www.anthony-szuch.com

Maria Vasaiou   020-8297 8485 Mobile 07890-651699
Robin Hood (feature), Sweeney Todd (feature), The Duchess (feature).

Karl Wilson   020-8324 2666 Mobile 07515-352239
Fax 020-8324 2694
www.elstreedrapes.com

Patrick Worsley   01462-455298 Mobile 07767-726171
The Dark Crystal (feature), A Village Affair (TV drama), What Rats Won't Do (feature).

DRAUGHTSMEN

Roxana Alexandru   Mobile 07515-396590
Nanny McPhee & The Big Bang (feature), The Secret Of Moonacre (feature).

Ted Ambrose   01628-521963
Mission: Impossible (feature), Die Another Day (feature), Thunderbirds (feature).

Hideki Arichi   Mobile 07941-480729
Batman Begins (feature), Star Wars: Episode III - Revenge Of The Sith (feature), Moon (feature).

Virginia Bain   01603-624203 Mobile 07986-103601
Lost In Space (feature), Nemo (feature), Bramwell (TV drama) (Assistant Art Director).

Denise Ball   01844-238564 Mobile 07770-763968
Gulliver's Travels (feature), Shanghai (feature), Harry Potter & The Half-Blood Prince (feature).

Jim Barr   01462-612367 Mobile 07958-404307
Inception (feature), Robin Hood (feature), Prince Caspian (feature).

Alice Biddle   01932-887720 Mobile 07961-325606
The Wolfman (feature), Project Strongarm (theme park), The Golden Compass (feature).

Mike Bishop Anderson   01920-484227
Mobile 07754-500827
Star Wars: Episode I - The Phantom Menace (feature), The World Is Not Enough (feature), Die Another Day (feature).

Anna Bregman   Mobile 07779-093790
John Carter Of Mars (feature), Robin Hood (feature), The Wolfman (feature).

Oliver Carroll   020-8963 1567 Mobile 07790-909335
Robin Hood (feature), Your Highness (feature), 10,000 BC (feature).

Will Coubrough   Mobile 07855-246320
Me & Orson Welles (feature) (Assistant Art Director), Hellboy 2: The Golden Army (feature), Prince Of Persia (feature).

Teri Fairhurst   Mobile 07968-218051
Into The Storm (TV film), Tales Of The Riverbank (feature), See No Evil (TV drama).

Jo Finkel   Mobile 07830-169787
John Carter Of Mars (feature) (Assistant), Harry Potter & The Deathly Hallows (feature), Quantum Of Solace (feature).

Jim Gaffney   020-8810 9829 Mobile 07862-274883
Tintin In Tibet (theatre), Vernon God Little (theatre), Quantum Of Solace (feature).

Heidi Gibb   020-8347 0900 Mobile 07971-551229
The Bourne Ultimatum (feature), Eragon (feature), Alexander (feature).

Oliver Goodier   Mobile 07930-406294
Robin Hood (feature), Prince Of Persia (feature), Hellboy 2: The Golden Army (feature).

Rod Gorwood   Mobile 07768-506801

Rosie Hardwick   Mobile 07768-892812
The Other Boleyn Girl (feature), Children Of Men (feature), Harry Potter & The Goblet Of Fire (feature) (Assistant Art Director).

Nicholas Henderson   01727-847997
Mobile 07890-564044
Harry Potter & The Deathly Hallows (feature) (Digital Art), Quantum Of Solace (feature), National Treasure: Book Of Secrets (feature).

Jonathan Houlding   020-8694 6556 Mobile 07979-654745
Phantom Of The Opera (feature), Band Of Brothers (TV drama).

Christine Ivall   01344-317815 Mobile 07767-262224
Sweeney Todd (feature), Stardust (feature), Sleepy Hollow (feature).

Gary Jopling   Mobile 07751-340434
Your Highness (feature), Nanny McPhee & The Big Bang (feature) (Art Director), Creation (feature) (Art Director).

Adam Kincaid   01273-720819 Mobile 07789-347784
Green Street (feature) (Assistant Art Director), Alexander (feature), Troy (feature).

Ashley Lamont   Mobile 07786-981186
Harry Potter & The Deathly Hallows (feature), Harry Potter & The Half-Blood Prince (feature), Harry Potter & The Order Of The Phoenix (feature).

DRAUGHTSMEN

Charles Leatherland Mobile 07775-521565
Sherlock Holmes (feature) (Assistant Art Director), Prince Caspian (feature), The Golden Compass (feature).

Amanda Leggatt Mobile 07841-626016
Harry Potter & The Deathly Hallows (feature), Harry Potter & The Half-Blood Prince (feature), The Tudors (TV drama).

Alexis Lemonis 020-7375 1520 Mobile 07941-019049
Prince Of Persia (feature) (CAD/Maya Operator), Stardust (feature) (Maya Operator), Breaking & Entering (feature) (Graphics Assistant).

Elizabeth Loach Mobile 07879-494349
Robin Hood (feature), Sherlock Holmes (feature), Harry Potter & The Half-Blood Prince (feature).

Poppy Luard 020-8740 4543 Mobile 07768-981798
Fantastic Mr Fox (feature), Corpse Bride (feature), Elizabeth (feature).

Andrew Palmer Mobile 07751-223271
Harry Potter & The Deathly Hallows (feature), Green Zone (feature), The Imaginarium Of Dr Parnassus (feature).

Catherine Palmer Mobile 07746-364223
Freedom: A History Of Us (TV doc), The Sinking Of The Laconia (TV drama doc), Heaven & Earth (feature).

Andrew Proctor Mobile 07881-783332
Robin Hood (feature), Moon (feature), Harry Potter & The Deathly Hallows (feature).

Carly Reddin Mobile 07949-134724
Hard Shoulder (feature) (Art Director), Green Zone (feature).

Anthony Rimmington 020-8998 1990
Babylon AD (feature), City Of Ember (feature), The Magic Flute (feature).

Quinn Robinson Mobile 07779-602490
U Be Dead (TV film) (Standby Art Director), Phantom Of The Opera (feature), Die Another Day (feature).

Jane Shepherd 020-8740 5558 Mobile 07710-511547
Penelope (feature), Merlin (TV drama), World Cup Football (TV sport).

Alex Smith 020-7381 5157 Mobile 07970-267849
John Carter Of Mars (feature), Harry Potter & The Half-Blood Prince (feature), Casino Royale (feature).

Molly Sole 01753-841249 Mobile 07909-837423
John Carter Of Mars (feature) (assistant), Harry Potter & The Deathly Hallows (feature), The Dark Knight (feature).

Hattie Storey 020-7241 1812 Mobile 07779-096315
Harry Potter & The Deathly Hallows (feature), Sweeney Todd (feature), Harry Potter & The Order Of The Phoenix (feature).

Daniel Swingler 020-7502 6543 Mobile 07899-905142
Sherlock Holmes (feature), The Imaginarium Of Dr Parnassus (feature), The Wizarding World Of Harry Potter (theme park).

Toad Tozer 020-8749 7439 Mobile 07798-828997
Thunderbirds (feature), Chocolat (feature), Harry Potter & The Philosopher's Stone (feature).

Darren Tubby 01603-748958 Mobile 07940-588252
Children Of Men (feature), Nanny McPhee (feature).

Emma Vane Mobile 07961-444261
Harry Potter & The Deathly Hallows (feature), The Bourne Ultimatum (feature), Atonement (feature).

Ruth Wallington 01296-660339 Mobile 07766-238470
The Golden Compass (feature), Harry Potter & The Prisoner Of Azkaban (feature), Harry Potter & The Goblet Of Fire (feature).

Damian Watts Mobile 07760-369549
The Escort (short).

Tom Whitehead 020-7792 2294 Mobile 07971-817724
Clash Of The Titans (feature), Atonement (feature), Charlie & The Chocolate Factory (feature).

Catherine Whiting 01494-816354 Mobile 07817-283357
John Carter Of Mars (feature) (Assistant), Robin Hood (feature), How To Lose Friends & Alienate People (feature).

Philip Wilding Mobile 07834-150672
English National (ballet), Royal Opera House (opera), Bloomburg News (TV news & current affairs).

DRAUGHTSMEN - JUNIOR

Rhys Ifan Mobile 07971-888818
John Carter Of Mars (feature), Prince Of Persia (feature).

Bethan Jones Mobile 07733-360636
Prince Of Persia (feature), National Treasure: Book Of Secrets (feature), Robin Hood (feature).

Chris Ledger Mobile 07892-693045
Little Dorrit (TV drama), Christmas At The Riviera (TV drama), Last Battle Dreamer (feature).

Laura Ng Mobile 07876-564887
Your Highness (feature).

Mark Niedenthal Mobile 07855-081243
Casino Royale (feature), The Dark Knight (feature), John Carter Of Mars (feature).

Edward Symon   01753-867376 Mobile 07970-955997
Harry Potter & The Deathly Hallows (feature), Harry Potter & The Half-Blood Prince (feature), Harry Potter & The Order Of The Phoenix (feature).

Ketan Waikar   Mobile 07941-972672
John Carter Of Mars (feature) (Modelmaker), Harry Potter & The Deathly Hallows (feature), Harry Potter & The Half-Blood Prince (feature).

Dorrie Young   Mobile 07939-103022
Harry Potter & The Deathly Hallows (feature), The Imaginarium Of Dr Parnassus (feature), Miss Pettigrew Lives For A Day (feature).

GLASS FIBRE MOULD MAKERS

Michael Fleming   0845-658 8787 Fax 0845-658 8788
Robin Hood (feature), John Carter Of Mars (feature), Batman Begins (feature).
www.wingfield-studios.com

GRAPHIC DESIGNERS

Frances Bennett   020-7607 4740 Mobile 07976-350545
Miss Potter (feature), Shakespeare In Love (feature), Quills (feature).

Stephen Bradshaw   Mobile 07831-866979
A Touch Of Frost (TV drama) (Art Director), Coronation Street (TV drama), Being Human (TV drama).
www.design108.tv

Philippa Broadhurst   Mobile 07817-305664
Proof (feature), Hotel Babylon (TV drama), An Education (feature).

Dan Burke   Mobile 07967-183043
The Holiday (feature), Charlie & The Chocolate Factory (feature), Breaking & Entering (feature).

Hannah Capron   Mobile 07939-588038
Hippie Hippie Shake (feature), Scoop (feature).

Jolanta Damski   Mobile 07711-481119
Ashes To Ashes (TV drama), Spooks (TV drama), Hustle (TV drama).

Anita Dhillon   020-7209 1756 Mobile 07957-169121
Fax 020-7209 1756
The Wolfman (feature), Kinky Boots (feature), Sunshine (feature).

Laura Dishington   Mobile 07966-428723
London Boulevard (feature), Sherlock Holmes (feature), Green Zone (feature).

Jools Faiers   01394-274628 Mobile 07941-841984
Amazing Grace (feature), Munich (feature), Love Actually (feature).

Neil Floyd   AD 020-7428 0500
www.neildesignsstuff.com

Sarah Hauldren   Mobile 07775-582284
Crusoe (TV drama), Lark Rise To Candleford (TV drama), Tess Of The D'Urbervilles (TV drama).

Kathy Heaser   Mobile 07932-065035
Clash Of The Titans (feature), The Duchess (feature), Charlie & The Chocolate Factory (feature).

Felicity Hickson   020-8508 1912 Mobile 07740-308216
Franklyn (feature), Me & Orson Welles (feature), Creation (feature).

Natalie Jackson   Mobile 07980-886080
Emmerdale (TV drama), The Royal (TV drama), EastEnders (promo).

Helen Koutas   Mobile 07974-142868
Prince Of Persia (feature), Mamma Mia! (feature), Alexander (feature).

Carol Kupisz   020-8997 2896 Mobile 07799-007294
W.E. (feature), The Imaginarium Of Dr Parnassus (feature), Children Of Men (feature).

Martin Lang   020-8245 6751 Mobile 07909-880986
Brick Lane (feature), Bleak House (TV drama), North & South (TV drama).

Eduardo Lima   Mobile 07962-077635
Harry Potter & The Half-Blood Prince (feature), Harry Potter & The Deathly Hallows (feature), City Of Ember (feature).
www.minalima.com

Emily Lutyens   Mobile 07867-503249
Into The Storm (TV film), The History Boys (feature), Vanity Fair (feature).

Mary Mackenzie   020-7209 1239 Mobile 07779-094423
John Carter Of Mars (feature), Shanghai (feature), Casino Royale (feature).

Miraphora Mina   Mobile 07770-887234
Harry Potter 1-8 (feature), The Golden Compass (feature), Sweeney Todd (feature).
www.minalima.com

Alan Payne   020-8962 1604 Mobile 07770-507159
Gulliver's Travels (feature), Prince Of Persia (feature), Elizabeth: The Golden Age (feature).

rob morris

qualified chef | food stylist | recipe development | home economist

An experienced passionate and creative food stylist with a great knowledge and love for food. Working in all aspects of still-life photography from editorial, packaging, advertising to TV commercials and live events. With his skills and ability as a trained chef he works closely with many companies in the development of recipes and writing of food articles. His attention to detail, unfailing patience and unflappable style are almost legendary with his clients.

for information regarding bookings call pha creative management on

tel: 0161 273 4444   **mobile:** 07970 663380
fax: 0161 273 4567   **email:** creatives@pha-agency.co.uk
web: pha-agency.co.uk   **web:** robmorrislang.com

Heather Pollington   Mobile 07834-184312
Nanny McPhee & The Big Bang (feature), Quantum Of Solace (feature), The Golden Compass (feature).

Joanna Pratt   020-7326 1225 Mobile 07773-721020
The Dark Knight (feature), Casino Royale (feature), Mrs Henderson Presents (feature).

Pippa Roberts   Mobile 07751-129774
Fade To Black (feature), It's A Boy Girl Thing (feature), Being Julia (feature).

Dominic Sikking   Mobile 07832-251460
Green Zone (feature), Prince Of Persia (feature), Sex & The City 2 (feature).

George Simons   Mobile 07769-705371
Penelope (feature), Babylon AD (feature), Nathan Barley (TV drama).

Jim Stanes   01404-841723 Mobile 07703-437874
Fax 01404-841266
Robin Hood (feature), The Young Victoria (feature), The Golden Compass (feature).

Andrew Tapper   020-7737 0459 Mobile 07960-890738
A Mighty Heart (feature), Babylon AD (feature), Dead Set (TV drama).

Rebecca Todd   Mobile 07725-230654
Hippie Hippie Shake (feature) (Assistant).

Julian Walker   01923-240697 Mobile 07751-954450
Casino Royale (feature), Batman Begins (feature), Harry Potter & The Philosopher's Stone (feature).

Andy Watson   Mobile 07855-366323
Powder (feature), Red Riding (TV drama), Life On Mars (TV drama).

HOME ECONOMISTS & FOOD STYLISTS

Jennie Berresford   HERS 0844-811 6811

Kate Blinman   HERS 0844-811 6811

Janet Brinkworth   HERS 0844-811 6811

Madeline Cameron   0161-428 1280 Mobile 07785-932807
Fax 0161-283 8062

Lynne Clayton   Mobile 07774-113989
Magnum (commercial).

Gina Craig   01323-502123 Mobile 07710-317198
Never Let Me Go (feature), Creation (feature), The Boat That Rocked (feature).

Martha Dunkerley   HERS 0844-811 6811

Gizzi Erskine   HERS 0844-811 6811

Clare Ferguson   HERS 0844-811 6811

Katie Giovanni   HERS 0844-811 6811

Christine Greaves   HERS 0844-811 6811

Carole Handslip   HERS 0844-811 6811

Seiko Hatfield   HERS 0844-811 6811

Bethany Heald   HERS 0844-811 6811

Marie-Ange Lapierre   HERS 0844-811 6811

Mary Luther   HERS 0844-811 6811

Caroline Marson   01296-631287 Mobile 07989-358855
HERS 0844-811 6811

Rob Morris   Mobile 07970-663380 PHA 0161-273 4444
www.robmorrislang.com

Jane Oddie   Mobile 07802-402165
Super Quin (commercial), Algieda Ice Cream (commercial), Sainsbury's (commercial).

Stephen Parkins-Knight   HERS 0844-811 6811

Kathy Roche   020-7286 5383   Mobile 07836-288222
Fax 020-7286 6947

Rosie Scott   HERS 0844-811 6811

Lesley Sendall   HERS 0844-811 6811

Sue Townsend   01799-541588   Mobile 07901-925013
Fax 01799-542568
Best (magazine), 1408 (feature), Bernard Matthews (commercial).

Dagmar Vesely   HERS 0844-811 6811

LETTERING DESIGN & CALLIGRAPHY

Paul Antonio   020-7720 8883   Mobile 07951-196275

Ann Bowen   01737-246171   Mobile 07803-840948
Fax 01737-246171
Bleak House (TV drama), Wimbledon (feature), Amazing Grace (feature).

Denise Hagon   01789-264114   Mobile 07811-845018
Fax 01789-264114
Under The Greenwood Tree (TV film), Bleak House (TV drama), Samuel Johnson The Dictionary Man (TV docu drama).

Deborah Hammond   020-7278 0822   Mobile 07866-347021
Fax 020-7278 0822
Elizabeth: The Golden Age (feature), The Other Boleyn Girl (feature), The Diary Of Anne Frank (TV drama).

Mark L'Argent   01992-629307   Mobile 07786-143430
Fax 01992-629307
Bright Star (feature), Bleak House (TV drama), The Libertine (feature).

Julian Walker   01923-240697
Mobile 07751-954450
Moon (feature), Robin Hood (feature), Nine (feature).

Tim Wilson   020-8348 2699   Mobile 07952-867818
The World Is Not Enough (feature), The End Of The Affair (feature), The Borrowers (feature).

MODELMAKERS

David Allum   01753-888170   Mobile 07799-012153
Casino Royale (feature), Children Of Men (feature), Batman Begins (feature).

Mark Angus   Mobile 07863-552889
Hot Fuzz (feature), Sony HD (commercial).

David Atkinson   01753-831432   Mobile 07711-294009
Fax 01753-831432
Quantum Of Solace (feature), Children Of Men (feature), Mrs Henderson Presents (feature).

Jolyon Bambridge   01344-453575   Mobile 07973-113412
Fax 01344-453575
Star Wars: Episode I - The Phantom Menace (feature), The World Is Not Enough (feature), Goldeneye (feature).

Robert Bean   01276-500454   Mobile 07710-945940
Prince Of Persia (feature), The Last Dragon (TV drama doc), The Brothers Grimm (feature).

Hannah Biggs   01442-870172   Mobile 07944-154361
Kingdom Of Heaven (feature), Harry Potter & The Chamber Of Secrets (feature), The World Is Not Enough (feature).

Doug Bishop   01227-794439   Mobile 07702-173808
Charlie & The Chocolate Factory (feature), Harry Potter & The Prisoner Of Azkaban (feature), V For Vendetta (feature).

Pierre Bohanna   01628-783599   Mobile 07770-976440
The Dark Knight (feature), Harry Potter & The Goblet Of Fire (feature), Star Wars: Episode I - The Phantom Menace (feature).

Matt Boyton   01483-574847   Mobile 07812-159707
V For Vendetta (feature), Waking The Dead (TV drama), Charlie & The Chocolate Factory (feature).

Ben Cain   020-8563 0681   Mobile 07740-621342
Fax 020-8563 0681
The Bourne Supremacy (feature), Tomorrow Never Dies (feature).

Nadia Drizi   Mobile 07748-310460

Simon Gosling   Mobile 07966-283822
The Colour Of Magic (TV film).

Richard Grant   01280-848820   Mobile 07802-987147
Alien Vs Predator (feature), Five Children & It (feature), Band Of Brothers (TV drama).

Sarah Hardy   Mobile 07801-946505
Dream Team (TV drama), Kingsland (feature).

Toby Hawkes   020-8241 0695   Mobile 07973-740276
The Wolfman (feature), Charlie & The Chocolate Factory (feature), Die Another Day (feature).

ART

MODELMAKERS

Chris Hayes 01895-904628 Mobile 07966-209210
Hitchhiker's Guide To The Galaxy (feature), Alien Vs Predator (feature), Harry Potter & The Philosopher's Stone (feature).

Oliver Hodge Mobile 07956-180118
Charlie & The Chocolate Factory (feature), Troy (feature), Die Another Day (feature).

Mark Holdcroft Mobile 07967-366143
Stardust (feature), Sunshine (feature), Charlie & The Chocolate Factory (feature).

Penny Howarth 0118-934 3847 Fax 07900-242024
Doctor Who (TV drama), Corpse Bride (feature), Die Another Day (feature).

Steve Howarth 01457-762144 Mobile 07769-513513
Hitchhiker's Guide To The Galaxy (feature), Five Children & It (feature), Alien Vs Predator (feature).

George Hughes 020-8395 7381
Harry Potter & The Goblet Of Fire (feature), Harry Potter & The Prisoner Of Azkaban (feature), Die Another Day (feature).

Robert Jose 01256-767010 Mobile 07971-486851
Prince Of Persia (feature).

Paul Knight 01482-869159 Mobile 07771-914219
Harry Potter & The Goblet Of Fire (feature), The World Is Not Enough (feature), Die Another Day (feature).

William Lawlor Mobile 07866-167438
Five Children & It (feature), Revolver (feature), The Dark (feature).

Rob Lee 01865-726914 Mobile 07973-618490
Batman (feature), Sleepy Hollow (feature), Charlie & The Chocolate Factory (feature).

Rufus Marsh 01273-507993

Duncan McDevitt 01322-287734 Mobile 07876-785450
Prince Of Persia (feature) (HOD).

Marcus Murray Mobile 07866-606377
The Hills Have Eyes II (feature), Batman Begins (feature), Charlie & The Chocolate Factory (feature).

Stephen Onions 01628-477290 Mobile 07800-753489
Prince Of Persia (feature).

Jill Paskins Mobile 07957-331462
CBeebies (TV childrens), Stardust (feature), Curse Of The Were-Rabbit (feature).

Bill Pearson 020-8974 5980 Mobile 07967-472551
Hitchhiker's Guide To The Galaxy (feature), Five Children & It (feature), Casino Royale (feature).

Ty Senior 01993-773736 Mobile 07979-607474
Children Of Men (feature), Kingdom Of Heaven (feature), Die Another Day (feature).

Keith Shannon 01252-838420 Mobile 07762-600576
Charlie & The Chocolate Factory (feature).

Toby Shears 01962-862218 Mobile 07713-165260
The Golden Compass (feature), Black Hawk Down (feature), Gladiator (feature).

Francesca Thorborn 01932-227737
Mobile 07738-064014
Inkheart (feature), Little Shop Of Horrors (promo), The Golden Compass (feature).

Derek Tomblin 01582-840802 Mobile 07974-079017
Fax 01582-840802
Sleepy Hollow (feature), Mortal Kombat - Annihilation (feature), Judge Dredd (feature).

Chris Trice 01689-875551 Mobile 07801-286093
Hitchhiker's Guide To The Galaxy (feature), Five Children & It (feature), Alien Vs Predator (feature).

Paula Vine Mobile 07703-437905
The Colour Of Magic (TV film).

John Weller 01483-839550 Mobile 07973-518283
Fax 01483-839550
The World Is Not Enough (feature), Harry Potter & The Prisoner Of Azkaban (feature), Star Wars: Episode I - The Phantom Menace (feature).

Scott Wescombe 01708-526997 Mobile 07976-154291
The Golden Bowl (feature), Quills (feature), A Midsummer Night's Dream (feature).

Richard Windley 01432-378166 Mobile 07974-537083
Ancient Discoveries (TV doc).

Mark Woollard 01344-429275 Mobile 07973-256057
Fax 01344-429275
Harry Potter & The Philosopher's Stone (feature), The World Is Not Enough (feature), Captain Scarlet (TV drama) (Director).

PAINTERS

Gary Crosby Mobile 07771-525657
Nanny McPhee & The Big Bang (feature) (HOD), Quantum Of Solace (feature).

Trevor Eve Mobile 07798-516834
City Of Ember (feature).

490

Michael Guyett   Mobile 07976-202172
Shanghai (feature) (HOD).

Kavin Hall   020-8848 1605 Mobile 07762-485092
The Magic Flute (feature), Tomb Raider II (feature), Judge Dredd (feature).

Robert Harper   01932-336563
Charlie & The Chocolate Factory (feature), Tomb Raider II (feature).

Jo Monks   020-8429 4243 Mobile 07956-809249
Prince Of Persia (feature) (HOD).

Doug Regan   01932-353565 Mobile 07778-532439
Children Of Men (feature).

Adrian Start   01753-652617 Mobile 07734-689302
Prince Of Persia (feature) (HOD).

Clive Ward   Mobile 07880-713304
Gulliver's Travels (feature) (HOD), The Wolfman (feature).

Peter Western   01494-722931 Mobile 07970-256861
Charlie & The Chocolate Factory (feature), Wimbledon (feature), Tomb Raider II (feature).

PLASTERERS

Alex Aitken   01494-762510 Mobile 07985-421411
Prince Of Persia (feature) (HOD).

Douglas Allam   01895-621309 Mobile 07932-624102
Robin Hood (feature), John Carter Of Mars (feature).

Ken Barley   Mobile 07775-655653
Prince Of Persia (feature) (HOD).

Ray Churchouse   020-8742 9292 Mobile 07958-513161
Fax 020-8749 7347
Sherlock Holmes (feature), Atonement (feature), Me & Orson Welles (feature).
www.camouflage-it.com

Neil Clark   01932-782979 Mobile 07790-520165
Phantom Of The Opera (feature), The Magic Flute (feature), Tomb Raider II (feature).

Allan Croucher   020-8894 3825 Mobile 07721-939913
Sleepy Hollow (feature), Band Of Brothers (TV drama), Charlie & The Chocolate Factory (feature).

Richard McCarthy   Mobile 07956-873347
Nanny McPhee & The Big Bang (feature) (HOD).

Michael Spence   01276-469882 Mobile 07711-179784
Casino Royale (feature), The Brothers Grimm (feature).

Steve Tranfield   01784-247989 Mobile 07774-144543
Gulliver's Travels (feature) (HOD), The Wolfman (feature), Gladiator (feature).

Kenny Wilson   01895-237422 Mobile 07931-597669
Clash Of The Titans (feature) (HOD), City Of Ember (feature).

PORTRAIT ARTISTS

Gill Andrae-Reid   020-8979 6857 Mobile 07973-313814
Phantom Of The Opera (feature), The Da Vinci Code (feature), The Last King Of Scotland (feature).

Sally Dray   01932-842538 Mobile 07817-355146
Fax 01932-842538
Children Of Men (feature), Elizabeth: The Golden Age (feature), Harry Potter & The Order Of The Phoenix (feature).

Jane Gifford   020-7359 5663 Mobile 07957-396232
Mrs Henderson Presents (feature), Harry Potter & The Prisoner Of Azkaban (feature), Carrington (feature).

PRE-VISUALISATION

Paul Cousins   Mobile 07881-636687
The Golden Compass (feature).

Pawl Fulker   020-8372 0063 Mobile 07751-094350
The Golden Compass (feature).

Richard Perry   Mobile 07730-533486
The Golden Compass (feature).

Anthony Zwartouw   Mobile 07796-424899
Harry Potter & The Order Of The Phoenix (feature).

PRODUCTION BUYERS

Pushkin   01903-776050 Mobile 07768-977720
Fax 01903-776050
Bad Blood (TV film), Perfect (short), Casualty (TV drama).

Sandi Adams   01458-831232 Mobile 07734-034370
Spinal Tap Reunion (TV film), Eurythmics (promo), Dire Straits (promo).

Sara Aghdami   Mobile 07855-789646
Quantum Of Solace (feature) (Product Placement), The Dark Knight (feature), Casino Royale (feature).

Liz Ainley   01737-221186 Mobile 07768-807782
Fax 01737-221186
From Time To Time (feature), Into The Storm (TV film), Pride & Prejudice (feature).

Ebonie Allard   Mobile 07957-427917

Clone (TV comedy drama), Hotel Babylon (TV drama), Secret Diary Of A Call Girl (TV drama).

Terry Allen   020-8549 1824 Mobile 07774-444822

Fax 020-8547 3882

The Bill (TV drama), Mud (TV childrens), Trial & Error (TV drama doc).

Marshall Aver   Mobile 07976-750683

Bouquet Of Barbed Wire (TV drama), Nanny McPhee & The Big Bang (feature), Einstein & Eddington (TV film).

Fiona Bambrough-Stott   01296-655784

Mobile 07949-086316 Fax 01296-655784

Judge John Deed (TV drama), The IT Crowd (TV comedy drama), Holby City (TV drama).

Sam Barbic   Mobile 07973-118089

How To Lose Friends & Alienate People (feature), Pure (feature), Kiss Of Life (feature).

Nicola Barnes   Mobile 07887-681165

Gulliver's Travels (feature) (Researcher), Matchpoint (feature) (Assistant Set Decorator), Phantom Of The Opera (feature).

Nick Barnett   020-8810 0327 Mobile 07973-631363

Fax 020-8810 0327

New Tricks (TV drama), The Inspector Lynley Mysteries (TV drama), Love Soup (TV drama).

Bob Bayne   0113-250 7965 Mobile 07831-422689

Heartbeat (TV drama), The Chase (TV drama), Sweet Medicine (TV drama).

Richard Bennett   Mobile 07774-720481

Being Human (TV drama), Waking The Dead (TV drama), Afterlife (TV drama).

Graham Bishop   01525-377509 Mobile 07774-185616

Robin Hood (feature), Shanghai (feature), Hellboy 2: The Golden Army (feature).

Sally Black   01624-845271 Mobile 07624-495480

Kingdom Of Heaven (feature), Body Of Lies (feature), The Cottage (feature).

Terry Black   Mobile 07501-131418

Bill Bonner   01923-773486 Mobile 07885-526888

EastEnders (promo), Holby City (TV drama).

Tim Bonstow   Mobile 07768-393028

Lewis (TV drama), Poirot (TV drama), Miss Marple (TV drama).

Suzy Bourke   Mobile 07825-812607

Sue Bowcott   +33 5 53 56 49 68

Mobile +33 6 37 92 56 20

The Kite Runner (feature), For Queen & Country (feature), When The Whales Came (feature).

Leanda Bowden-Smith   0117-908 9068

Mobile 07836-596659

Lark Rise To Candleford (TV drama), Mistresses (TV drama), The Portrait Of A Lady (feature).

Paul Boyle   Mobile 07970-620925

Shameless (TV drama), Cutting It (TV drama), The Royal (TV drama).

Sophie Bridgman   Mobile 07968-694696

Moon (feature).

Corina Burrough   020-8694 2091 Mobile 07801-588155

Fax 020-8694 2091

The King's Speech (feature), Eastern Promises (feature), Hannibal Rising (feature).

Nicola Burrough Knight   020-8840 2671

Mobile 07957-660219

Holby City (TV drama).

Beverley Butcher   01252-850094 Mobile 07860-733577

Speed Racer (feature), V For Vendetta (feature), No Heroics (TV comedy drama).

Alison Cardy   Mobile 07810-367977

Atonement (feature) (Assistant), Silent Witness (TV drama), Sherlock Holmes (feature) (Assistant).

Anne Carlyle-Gall   020-8995 9974 Mobile 07973-683720

Fax 020-8996 9055

Shoot On Sight (feature), Sainsbury's (commercial), Woolworths (commercial).

Jacki Castelli   Mobile 07879-842229

The Broken (feature), How To Lose Friends & Alienate People (feature), Cashback (feature).

Maddie Chesterton   Mobile 07974-330390

Harry & Paul (TV light entertainment), The John Culshaw Show (TV light entertainment).

Jennifer Clapcott   020-8391 1678 Mobile 07970-902679

That Mitchell & Webb Look (TV light entertainment), Life Bites (TV light entertainment), The Kylie Show (TV light entertainment).

Sue Claybyn   01753-663984 Mobile 07831-654805

Fax 01753-663984

Ashes To Ashes (TV drama), Spooks (TV drama), Canterbury Tales (TV drama).

Fergus Clegg   Mobile 07976-693159
Clash Of The Titans (feature) (Assistant Set Decorator), Quantum Of Solace (feature) (Assistant Set Decorator), The Golden Compass (feature) (Assistant Set Decorator).

Dave Copus   01737-768790 Mobile 07850-982984
Pen Taler (TV drama), Dunkirk (TV drama doc), Rosemary & Thyme (TV drama).

Cathy Cosgrove   01296-339540 Mobile 07831-392848

Ann Marie Coulter   0141-423 1012 Mobile 07976-403947
God On Trial (TV drama), Hope Springs (TV drama), The Flying Scotsman (feature).

Gina Cromwell   020-8408 1952 Mobile 07711-420811
Cranford (TV drama), Fingersmith (TV drama), Tipping The Velvet (TV drama).

Charlotte Crosbie   Mobile 07813-873624
Gulliver's Travels (feature) (Assistant), Sherlock Holmes (feature) (Set Decorating Co-ordinator), Alice In Wonderland (feature) (Assistant).

Lesley Cross   Mobile 07768-201815
Rendition (feature), The Golden Compass (feature), Sixty Six (feature).

Chris Cunningham   01278-671313 Mobile 07850-292277
Midsomer Murders (TV drama), Walk Away & I Stumble (TV drama), Casualty (TV drama).

Mandy Cuttill   Mobile 07718-904514
Swinging With The Finkels (feature), Miranda (TV comedy drama), Katy Brand's Big Ass Show (TV light entertainment).

Emma Dalton   0151-606 0148 Mobile 07719-653147
Ingenious (TV drama), Hollyoaks (TV drama), Grange Hill (TV childrens).

Rachel Danbury   01784-483599 Mobile 07761-187370
The Commander (TV drama) (Assistant), My Family (TV comedy drama), Trial & Retribution (TV drama) (Assistant).

Emma Davis   Mobile 07808-401420 Fax 020-7724 7343
Celebration (TV film), United 93 (feature), Made Of Honor (feature).

Nicola de Fresness   020-8835 8112 Mobile 07971-662351
Victoria Wood Xmas Special (TV light entertainment), Demons (TV drama), Lark Rise To Candleford (TV drama).

Celia De La Hey   020-7229 6069 Mobile 07887-654062
Mistress Of Spices (feature), Penelope (feature), St Trinian's (feature).

Trevor Devoy   01253-865324 Mobile 07768-600378

Gell Dove-Higginson   020-8943 2323
Mobile 07876-192085
Kerching! (TV childrens), EastEnders (promo), The Bill (TV drama).

Katrina Duce   Mobile 07785-730114
Hitchhiker's Guide To The Galaxy (feature), The Catherine Tate Show (TV light entertainment), Nighty Night (TV comedy drama).

Judy Ducker   020-8997 7957 Mobile 07831-342785
Fax 020-8998 8763
GI Joe: The Rise Of Cobra (feature), The Golden Compass (feature), Oliver Twist (feature).

Sarah Duncan   Mobile 07736-858461
A Good Year (feature) (Assistant), Kingdom Of Heaven (feature) (Assistant), Bleak House (TV drama) (Assistant).

Billy Edwards   020-7727 7239 Mobile 07956-642292
Fax 020-7727 7239
Cemetery Junction (feature), Body Of Lies (feature), Babylon AD (feature).

Lisa Engel   Mobile 07958-579892

Hannah Evans   020-7485 8829 Mobile 07958-528738
Ashes To Ashes (TV drama), Magicians (feature), Cass (feature).

Lucy Eyre   020-7703 5768 Mobile 07811-040484
Robin Hood (feature) (Assistant), John Adams (TV drama), Foyle's War (TV drama).

Kimberley Fahey   Mobile 07899-751844
Incendiary (feature), The Children (feature), The Last King Of Scotland (feature).

Gill Farr   020-8995 2526 Mobile 07860-358266
The Wolfman (feature), Mamma Mia! (feature), The Bourne Ultimatum (feature).

Cathy Featherstone   Mobile 07952-691513
Bonded By Blood (feature), Nineteen Eighty-Three (TV film), Dead Man Running (feature).

Sarah Forbes   Mobile 07957-345027
Mutual Friends (TV drama), Nanny McPhee & The Big Bang (feature) (Assistant), Creation (feature) (Assistant Set Decorator).

Laura Forsyth   Mobile 07768-765742
Bremner Bird & Fortune (TV light entertainment), Ponderland (TV light entertainment), Hear The Silence (TV drama).

Mary-Ann Foster   Mobile 07753-661768
Puritan (feature), Dream Team '80's (TV drama).

Stella Fox   Mobile 07595-053551
Misfits (TV comedy drama), Bright Star (feature).

Mary-Rose Fox-Ness   020-8376 5804
Mobile 07957-640571
My Spy Family (TV childrens), Thieves Like Us (TV drama), EastEnders (promo).

George Francis   Mobile 07813-097248

Bronwyn Franklin   Mobile 07981-778323
Hustle (TV drama), Primeval (TV drama), The Changeling (feature).

Sarah Frere   Mobile 07976-895542
Other People (TV comedy drama), Oil Of Olay (commercial), 50 Cent (promo).

Polly Fullman   Mobile 07793-198975
Tonight's The Night (TV light entertainment), The Bill (TV drama), Rude Tube (TV light entertainment).

Lisa Gandy   Mobile 07796-675100
Little Britain (tour) (Assistant), Casanova (feature) (Assistant).

Carrie Garner   Mobile 07711-007993

Amanda George   01483-272131 Mobile 07850-631807
Fax 01483-272131
Hotel Babylon (TV drama), EastEnders (promo), The Catherine Tate Show (TV light entertainment).

Marvin George   020-8293 5008 Mobile 07774-495255
Only Fools & Horses (TV comedy drama), Footballers' Wives (TV drama), Gabriel & Me (feature).

Antonia Gibbs   Mobile 07747-628670
Collision (TV drama), It's A Wonderful Afterlife (feature), Danone Activia (commercial).

Christine Gibson   Mobile 07941-246595
Ooglies (TV childrens), Mission: 2110 (TV childrens), Stone Of Destiny (feature).

Annie Gilhooly   Mobile 07787-115133
Nanny McPhee & The Big Bang (feature), Dean Spanley (feature), The Other Man (feature).

Rose Gilman   Mobile 07769-707710
Harry Potter & The Half-Blood Prince (feature) (Assistant).

Emma Godwin   Mobile 07956-367565
Robin Hood (feature), Kick-Ass (feature), A Short Stay In Switzerland (TV drama).

John Gooch   Mobile 07967-304786
Casualty (TV drama), Skins (TV drama), Coal House (TV drama).

Claire Grainger   01932-400689 Mobile 07768-410329
Fax 01932-400689
The Colour Of Magic (TV film), The Dark (feature), Agent Cody Banks II (feature).

Emma Jane Grainger   Mobile 07941-154769
Sunshine (feature), Moving On (TV drama), Grange Hill (TV childrens).

Barry Greaves   01276-677873 Mobile 07831-877362
Fax 01276-677873
Casino Royale (feature), Keeping Mum (feature), Batman Begins (feature).

Adrian Greenwood   Mobile 07970-718188
Trinity (feature), Sainsbury's (commercial).

Sara Grimshaw   020-8977 4386 Mobile 07836-318157
Fax 020-8977 4386
Sex Drugs & Rock 'n' Chips (TV comedy drama), Tess Of The D'Urbervilles (TV drama), Sex Traffic (TV drama).

Abi Groves   020-8398 0989 Mobile 07747-610191
The Magic Flute (feature), As You Like It (feature), The Imaginarium Of Dr Parnassus (feature).

Anita Gupta   Mobile 07802-604012
The 51st State (feature), Route Irish (feature), Looking For Eric (feature).

Colin Harris   01503-230104 Mobile 07860-553863
Fax 01895-622175
Casualty (TV drama), Dream (feature), Last Of The Summer Wine (TV comedy drama).

Alison Harvey   Mobile 07976-910299
Sherlock Holmes (feature), Miss Pettigrew Lives For A Day (feature), Atonement (feature).

Jayne Hatfield   020-8960 8777 Mobile 07866-758285
Fax 020-8960 6700
Found (TV drama), High Tide (TV drama), Always & Forever (TV film).

Jo Hellerman   Mobile 07767-484672
EastEnders (promo), My Life As A Popat (TV drama), The Paul O'Grady Show (trailer).

Ted High   01205-723335 Mobile 07831-490190
Murder On The Orient Express (feature), Holby City (TV drama), Max & Paddy (TV drama).

Zoe Hoare   020-8772 9793 Mobile 07903-522369
Fax 020-8772 9793
Housefull (feature), The Scouting Book For Boys (feature), Demons (TV drama).

Tamsin Holmes   0114-266 9149   Mobile 07798-830184
Heartbeat (TV drama), Sweet Medicine (TV drama), Principles Of Lust (feature).

Clare Holton   020-8847 2484   Mobile 07812-360399
The Turn Of The Screw (TV drama), Emma (feature), The Wolfman (feature) (Assistant).

Karen How   020-7652 5649   Mobile 07956-369111

Prue Howard   Mobile 07905-115234

Esther Jenkins   Mobile 07717-178727
Kingdom (TV drama) (Assistant), Malice In Wonderland (feature) (Assistant Art Director).

Marje Jennings   020-8748 3451   Mobile 07976-546339
Fax 020-8748 3451
Gavin & Stacey (TV comedy drama), Saxondale (TV comedy drama), EastEnders (promo).

Robert Jones   01985-301158   Mobile 07778-468553
Cambridge Spies (TV drama), The Queen (feature), My Boy Jack (TV film) (Set Decorator).

Terry Jones   Mobile 07831-784195
Holby City (TV drama), The Last Detective (TV drama), Dunkirk (TV drama doc).

Anna Kasabova   Mobile 07958-906145
Free Agents (TV drama).

Kate Kilroy   020-8969 8430   Mobile 07785-957631

Michael King   01494-672738   Mobile 07770-424765
John Carter Of Mars (feature), Gulliver's Travels (feature), Quantum Of Solace (feature).

Hannah Knowlton   020-8548 9820   Mobile 07530-329265
Mao's Last Dancer (feature), Fools Gold (feature), Superman Returns (feature).

Jo Kornstein   Mobile 07801-816389
Persuasion (feature), Margot (TV drama), Enid (TV drama).

Chris Lake   Mobile 07971-814445

Maura Laverty   020-8767 3710   Mobile 07831-654806
Fax 020-8355 8785
Dead Ringers (TV comedy), Cold Comfort Farm (TV film), Outnumbered (TV comedy drama).

Ray Lee   020-8769 3141   Mobile 07831-571051
Fax 020-8677 7127
Gosford Park (feature), The Reckoning (feature), Sword Of Honour (TV drama).

Jon Lewis   020-8966 9948   Mobile 07811-863994
Swinging With The Finkels (feature), U Be Dead (TV film), Cuckoo (feature).

David Livsey   0161-794 1047   Mobile 07768-464403
Fax 0161-794 1047
True Dare Kiss (TV drama), My Beautiful Son (TV film), The Forsyte Saga (TV drama).

Charlie Lynam   01252-812021   Mobile 07779-247948
Lewis (TV drama), Silent Witness (TV drama), Brick Lane (feature) (Assistant).

Claudia Lyster   Mobile 07940-502240

Bert Mackay   01423-508799   Mobile 07836-705323
A Passionate Woman (TV drama), The Royal (TV drama), The Chase (TV drama).

Alison Macmillan   01364-643971   Mobile 07919-594775
This Is The Sea (feature), Bad Girls (TV drama), Midsomer Murders (TV drama).

Janice Macrae   Mobile 07941-545146
The Last Word (feature), Outcast (feature), Hallam Foe (feature).

Melissa Magna   Mobile 07940-982925
Sweeney Todd (feature), Franklyn (feature), The Boat That Rocked (feature).

Syreeta Makan   020-8800 9287   Mobile 07967-220370
Bad Girls (TV drama) (Assistant), Hot Fuzz (feature) (Assistant), Fur TV (TV comedy drama).

Laura Marsh   Mobile 07525-813626
Harry & Paul (TV light entertainment), The Thick Of It (TV comedy drama), Stewart Lee's Comedy Vehicle (TV light entertainment).

Kay McGlone   020-8510 9180   Mobile 07860-404675
John Adams (TV drama), Run Fat Boy Run (feature), The Secret Of Moonacre (feature).

Sue McLean   Mobile 07949-078079

Elaine McLenachan   0141-579 2449   Mobile 07939-014004
Fiona's Story (TV drama), Miss Potter (feature), The Street (TV drama).

David Medlycott   0191-285 4191   Mobile 07976-291361
Fax 0191-285 4191
The Revenge Files of Alastair Fury (TV childrens), Drop Dead Gorgeous (TV drama), The Class Apart (TV drama).

Craig Menzies   0141-959 2352   Mobile 07785-392853
The Diary Of Anne Frank (TV drama), The Mark Of Cain (feature), Monarch Of The Glen (TV drama).

Clementine Miller Mobile 07779-803828
Green Zone (feature) (Assistant), Robbie Williams (concert), Barclays Bank (commercial).

Emma Mitchell 01279-778997 Mobile 07802-449709
Fax 01279-777200
Carmen (opera), Midsomer Murders (TV drama), EastEnders (promo).

Sian Molloy Mobile 07729-335378
W.E. (feature), London Boulevard (feature) (Assistant Set Decorator), Nativity (feature).

Naomi Moore Mobile 07951-484075
Poirot (TV drama) (Assistant), Miss Marple (TV drama) (Assistant).

Tony Moore 020-8847 1182 Mobile 07774-147964
EastEnders (promo), Benidorm (TV comedy drama).

Linda Morgan Mobile 07768-344460
Wire In The Blood (TV drama), Waterloo Road (TV drama), Eleventh Hour (TV drama).

Ben Morris Mobile 07813-791531
Doctor Who (TV drama), Torchwood (TV drama).

Sue Morrison 0141-956 3215 Mobile 07702-189303
Young Adam (feature), Rebus (TV drama), The Jacket (feature).

Dennis Murphy 0151-428 7965 Mobile 07813-825131
Fax 0151-428 7965
A Touch Of Frost (TV drama), Diamond Geezer (TV drama), The Marchioness Disaster (TV drama).

George Noonan 01753-542964 Mobile 07807-898356
Dr Dolittle (feature), Murder On The Orient Express (feature), Star Wars (feature).

Oli Novadnieks 020-8769 8699 Mobile 07860-791259
Body Of Lies (feature), Ripley Under Ground (feature), Keen Eddie (TV drama).

Nina Ogden Mobile 07956-421749

Harriet Orman 020-7223 6907 Mobile 07973-822746
Sex & The City (feature), Green Zone (feature), Alexander (feature).

John O'Shaughnessy 020-7371 6917 Mobile 07774-818188
Fax 020-7371 6917
Clash Of The Titans (feature), Nine (feature), Me & Orson Welles (feature).

Nicola Painter Mobile 07973-562053
The Vicar Of Dibley (TV comedy drama), Conclusion (feature), The Fast Show (TV light entertainment).

Carol Payne 01670-791949 Mobile 07710-353434
The Street (TV drama), Wire In The Blood (TV drama), Britannia High (TV drama).

Hannah Penfold Mobile 07956-200648
Timewatch (TV doc), Fox Kids Europe (promo).

Jane Pincham 01372-463852 Mobile 07710-170065
Fax 01372-463852
Armstrong & Miller (TV light entertainment), The Kumars (TV light entertainment).

Shelly Pond Mobile 07885-967826
Britain's Got The Pop Factor (TV light entertainment), The Parole Officer (feature) (Set Decorator), Housewife 49 (TV drama) (Set Decorator).

Lee Porter 0141-341 0706 Mobile 07957-371149
This Is England (feature), Ae Fond Kiss (feature), Sweet Sixteen (feature).

Geraint Powell Mobile 07958-319439
The Tudors (TV drama), The Mutant Chronicles (feature) (Set Decorator), Wild Target (feature) (Set Decorator).

Ron Pritchard Mobile 07768-464885
Moll Flanders (TV drama), Life On Mars (TV drama), Paradox (TV drama).

Kathryn Pyle Mobile 07976-520520
28 Weeks Later (feature), Sunshine (feature), The Boat That Rocked (feature).

Martin Radmall Mobile 07825-403672
Emmerdale (TV drama), At Home With The Braithwaites (TV drama), Last Of The Summer Wine (TV comedy drama).

Katie Ralph Mobile 07875-413290
John Carter Of Mars (feature) (Assistant).

Tom Rea Mobile 07939-013993
Harry Hill's TV Burp (TV light entertainment), Beautiful People (TV comedy drama), Jam & Jerusalem (TV comedy drama).

Lynda Reiss 01624-882224 Mobile 07624-484300
Fax 01624-882224
Eagle Eye (feature), Big Nothing (feature), American Beauty (feature).
www.lyndaspropshop.com

Laura Richardson 020-8810 0260 Mobile 07968-068259
Fax 020-8840 2374
Broken Glass (TV film), Momento Mori (TV film), Hour Of The Pig (feature).

Joanna Robinson   Mobile 07710-319823
Open House (TV magazine), Today With Des & Mel (TV magazine) (Art Director), The Alan Titchmarsh Show (TV light entertainment) (Art Director).

Caroline Roemmele   0141-357 5090 Mobile 07767-688291
New Town Killers (feature), Sea Of Souls (TV drama), How Not To Live Your Life (TV comedy drama).

Malcolm Rougvie   020-8545 1083 Mobile 07970-265458
Fax 020-8545 0764
A Mind To Kill (TV drama), Jinnah (feature), The Bill (TV drama).

Justin Rumbelow   01275-866206 Mobile 07803-605464
Casualty (TV drama), Holby City (TV drama), Lighthouse (feature).

Robin Rumbelow   01275-818775 Mobile 07860-393432
Skins (TV drama), Rebecca (TV drama), Casualty (TV drama).

Peter Rutherford   +351 91 348 8488
Mobile 07774-940507
Ladies In Lavender (feature), Beethoven (TV drama), The Truth About Love (feature).

Charlotte Sammons   01494-714036 Mobile 07796-265296
Fax 01494-718571
Comic Relief (TV light entertainment), Restoration (feature), The Office (TV comedy drama).

Zoe Scivoletto   Mobile 07779-123201 Fax 020-8859 6777
Amazing Grace (feature), Flyboys (feature), Confetti (feature).

Kate Scopes   Mobile 07702-124822
Bad Girls (TV drama), Titty Bang Bang (TV light entertainment), Survivors (TV drama).

Derek Scriminger   Mobile 07973-271925

Pauline Seager   020-8567 2762 Mobile 07831-665019
Spooks (TV drama), Primeval (TV drama), Saddam's Tribe (TV drama).

Ellie Shanks   Mobile 07905-025250
Son Of Rambow (feature).

Carol Sheeran   020-8948 8226 Mobile 07817-451581

Amanda Smith   01590-681126 Mobile 07956-808451
He Kills Coppers (TV drama), Prime Suspect (TV drama), Pierrepoint (TV film).

Francis Smith   01386-761882 Mobile 07986-283041
Fax 01386-761882
Miss Marple (TV drama), As Time Goes By (TV comedy drama).

Mike Smith   01622-678723 Mobile 07860-389742
Fax 01622-678723
Murderland (TV drama), A Room With A View (feature), Fallen Angel (TV drama).

Shonagh Smith   0151-726 0249 Mobile 07779-639488
Lark Rise To Candleford (TV drama), Messiah (TV drama), Shameless (TV drama).

Ussal Smithers   01424-422323 Mobile 07713-886585
Fax 01424-422323
The Last Days Of Lehman Brothers (TV drama), The Street (TV drama), The Libertine (feature).

Clare Solly   020-8567 2923 Mobile 07976-707245
EastEnders (promo), Our Mutual Friend (TV drama), The Bill (TV drama).

Michael Standish   020-8789 9275 Mobile 07711-421678
The Duchess (feature), Topsy-Turvy (feature), About A Boy (feature).

Theresa Stevens   Mobile 07966-411851
EastEnders (promo), Ladies Of Letters (TV drama), Nuclear Race (TV docu drama).

Deborah Stokely   01245-361392 Mobile 07889-413416
Fax 01245-361392
National Treasure: Book Of Secrets (feature), Harry Potter & The Goblet Of Fire (feature), Star Wars: Episode I - The Phantom Menace (feature).

Lucinda Sturgis   020-7267 8007 Mobile 07973-470468
Fax 020-7267 8007
Harry Potter & The Half-Blood Prince (feature), Munich (feature), Closer (feature).

Dorothy Sullivan   020-8346 3364 Mobile 07940-587648
Mike Leigh - Untitled 09 (feature) (Assistant), Criminal Justice (TV drama), Is There Anybody There? (feature) (Assistant Set Decorator).

Charlotte Taylor   020-8876 9085 Mobile 07836-708904
Chemical Wedding (feature), Lewis (TV drama), Murder Prevention (TV drama).

Fanny Taylor   01865-552172 Mobile 07710-412972
Miss Marple (TV drama), Lock Stock & Two Smoking Barrels (feature), 28 Days Later (feature) (Set Decorator).

Lucy Taylor   01372-279345 Mobile 07710-098249

Sarah Teasdale   01932-827075 Mobile 07711-103040

Sue Templar   01548-831289 Mobile 07721-460792
Skins (TV drama), Waking The Dead (TV drama), Crash (TV doc).

PRODUCTION BUYERS

Kate Thomas   Mobile 07970-724408
The Damned United (feature), Heartbeat (TV drama), Millions (feature) (Assistant).

Holly Thurman   Mobile 07890-966463

Paul Tormey   Mobile 07831-403340
Holby City (TV drama), Lark Rise To Candleford (TV drama), Above Suspicion (TV drama).

Ian Tully   Mobile 07973-641786
The Cottage (feature), Life On Mars (TV drama), Merlin (TV drama).

Sophie Tyler   Mobile 07899-990032
Sherlock Holmes (feature) (Assistant Set Decorator), Hippie Hippie Shake (feature), Miss Pettigrew Lives For A Day (feature) (Assistant Set Decorator).

Kate Venner   020-7371 6510   Mobile 07768-362572
Fax 020-7371 6510
Red Tails (feature), The Young Victoria (feature), Prince Of Persia (feature).

Vanda Vivian   01300-320409   Mobile 07785-397141
Fax 01300-320409

Maddy Walmsley   01925-838874   Mobile 07889-428978
Fax 01925-838874
Coronation Street (TV drama), Revenger's Tragedy (feature), About A Girl (short).

Bob Warans   020-8576 1220   Fax 020-8225 7084
Strictly Come Dancing (TV light entertainment), Horrible Histories (TV childrens), The Inbetweeners (TV comedy drama).

Roger Williams   Mobile 07958-729571

Krissi Williamson   01753-865722   Mobile 07956-269600
Fax 01753-832902
W.E. (feature), London Boulevard (feature), Hereafter (feature).

Janet Willmott   01372-279467   Mobile 07774-452280
Fax 01372-279467
Missing (TV doc), Hustle (TV drama), Buy Borrow Steel (feature).

Deborah Wilson   01442-876362   Mobile 07973-507480
Fax 01442-876362
Brighton Rock (feature), Little Dorrit (TV drama), Sense & Sensibility (feature).

Lizzi Wilson   Mobile 07817-194093
Dr Who (TV drama), Harry Potter & The Philosopher's Stone (feature).

Duncan Windram-Wheeler   01422-843407
Mobile 07831-130841
Hush (feature), My Summer Of Love (feature), Mischief Night (feature).

Brian Winterborn   Mobile 07919-888757
Lucky Break (feature), Warriors (TV film), Wild Flowers (feature).

Jackie Yau   020-7460 0753   Mobile 07799-411617
AD 020-7428 0500
Clash Of The Titans (feature), Sherlock Holmes (feature), Venus (feature).

Sue Youll   Mobile 07850-712779
Emmerdale (TV drama).

PRODUCTION DESIGNERS

Jacqueline Abrahams   020-7923 3539
Mobile 07961-416614   DA 020-7437 4551
Wallander (TV drama), Pop Art (short), White Girl (TV drama).

Belinda Ackermann   020-7688 0914   Mobile 07973-622240

Terry Ackland-Snow   01895-639256
Mobile 07885-468625
Batman (feature), Inspector Morse (TV drama), Soldier Soldier (TV drama).
www.filmdi.com

Sir Ken Adam OBE   020-7589 9372   Fax 020-7584 7090
The Madness Of King George (feature), In & Out (feature), Taking Sides (feature).

Anthony Ainsworth   01323-645463   Mobile 07973-442704
UA 020-3214 0800
Primeval (TV drama), Spooks (TV drama), Doc Martin (TV drama).

Jess Alexander   Mobile 07890-185983
Mum & Dad (feature), Wintering (short), Hotel Babylon (TV drama) (Assistant Art Director).

Melanie Allen   Mobile 07973-435736   UA 020-3214 0800
A Bunch Of Amateurs (feature), Bullet Boy (feature), Desperate Romantics (TV drama).

Caroline Amies   Mobile 07973-411379   CM 020-7287 4450
Copying Beethoven (feature), Ladies In Lavender (feature), In The Name Of The Father (feature).

John Anderson   01584-810099   Mobile 07778-784663
Children In Need (TV light entertainment), The Tony Ferrino Phenomenon (TV light entertainment), The Dark Ages (TV comedy drama).

Luciana Arrighi   Mobile 07932-713772 ITG 020-7636 6565
Howards End (feature), From Time To Time (feature), Into The Storm (TV film).

Dave Arrowsmith   01261-861885 Mobile 07967-020229
CMM 020-8584 5363
Father & Son (TV drama), Under The Greenwood Tree (TV film), My Boy Jack (TV film).

John Asbridge   020-8948 6659 Mobile 07850-007424
BA 020-7836 1112 Fax 020-8948 6659
The Cazalets (TV drama), New Tricks (TV drama), Jonathan Creek (TV drama).

Julie Ash   Mobile 07969-700168
The Crunch (TV childrens), QVC (channel).

Humphrey Bangham   020-8994 8533
Mobile 07973-317363 Fax 020-8384 3765
Family Business (TV drama), Arthur's Dyke (feature), Pinocchio II (feature).

Philip Barber   01494-782590 Mobile 07973-684244
Fax 07967-044896
Prehistoric Park (TV docu drama), Primo (TV film), Dummy (TV drama).

Sarah Beaman   Mobile 07701-002951
Thin Ice (TV drama), Holby City (TV drama), Devil's Gate (feature).

John Beard   020-7485 8320 Mobile 07802-183474
ITG 020-7636 6565 Fax 020-7267 6729
Inkheart (feature), How To Lose Friends & Alienate People (feature), The Skeleton Key (feature).

Sophie Becher   CM 020-7287 4450
The Secret Of Moonacre (feature), Run Fat Boy Run (feature), To Kill A King (feature).

Max Bellhouse   Mobile 07889-861749

Joseph Bennett   020-8208 2639 Mobile 07860-783612
Rome (TV drama), Deep Blue Sea (feature), Event Horizon (feature).

Simon Beresford   020-7357 7880 Mobile 07989-856693
MM 020-8995 4747 Fax 020-7357 7880
The Long Walk To Finchley (TV film), Out Of Season (feature), Bradford Riots (TV film).

Amanda Bernstein   020-7792 2108 Mobile 07774-740689
Fax 020-7792 2108
Nuremberg: Goering's Last Stand (TV drama), Pompeii: The Last Day (TV drama), Daniel & The Superdogs (feature).

Dan Betteridge   Mobile 07973-467468 WZ 020-7437 2055
Flashbacks Of A Fool (feature) (Art Director).

David Bevin   01483-750415 Mobile 07932-559153
Fax 01483-750415
The Slammer (TV childrens), Frost Over The World (TV news & current affairs), Dick & Dom In Da Bungalow (TV childrens).

Eli Bo   BA 020-7836 1112
Menace (TV drama), Room To Rent (feature), Insomnia (feature).

Gavin Bocquet   Mobile 07774-877356 MM 020-8995 4747
Gulliver's Travels (feature), The Bank Job (feature), Stardust (feature).

Richard Booth   0115-961 0871 Mobile 07887-705031
Peak Practice (TV drama), Prove It (TV childrens), Bernard's Watch (TV childrens).

Sue Booth   Mobile 07836-608206
O Jerusalem (feature), Goldplated (TV drama), Booze Cruise III (TV film).

David Bowes   01484-667012 Mobile 07710-038065
Britain's Got The Pop Factor (TV light entertainment), Shameless (TV drama), Where The Heart Is (TV drama).

Simon Bowles   Mobile 07774-852777 MM 020-8995 4747
Centurion (feature), The Descent (feature), Doomsday (feature).

Tom Bowyer   020-8998 0700 Mobile 07774-804843
The Dinner Party (TV drama), The Last Resort (TV drama), Cracker (TV drama).

Francesca Boyd   Mobile 07718-742339 CM 020-7287 4450
The Criminal (TV film), Beyond Fear (TV film), Sony Playstation (commercial).

Candida Boyes   01928-791079 Mobile 07767-214233
Fax 01928-751353
Moving On (TV drama), Hollyoaks (TV drama), Crossroads (TV drama).

Francis Boyle   020-8299 0907 Mobile 07768-038151
Land Girls (TV drama), Doctors (TV drama), Afternoon Plays (TV drama).

John Bramble   020-8340 3814 Mobile 07973-560291
AD 020-7428 0500
The Act In Question (feature), Soulscapes (TV drama), Bacon (TV film).

Byron Broadbent   Mobile 07769-653167
Fax 07092-151636
Basement (feature), The Last Thakur (feature), Re-uniting The Rubins (feature).

PRODUCTION DESIGNERS

Kay Brown   01245-403201 Mobile 07974-221492
GEMS 029-2071 0770
Beacon 77 (feature), EastEnders (promo), Torchwood (TV drama).

Robin Brown   Mobile 07973-174512
Honda (commercial), Guinness (commercial), Levi's (commercial).

Tom Brown   01296-668301 Mobile 07980-743541
Apparitions (TV drama), Highlander: The Source (feature), Green Street (feature).

David Bryan   Mobile 07774-294726
0-800-Love (feature), Coming Up (feature), The Hurt Locker (feature).

Bill Bryce   01633-815636 Mobile 07885-379150
Daddy's Girl (feature), Trial & Retribution (TV drama), Mind Games (TV drama).

David Buckingham   020-8993 5736 Mobile 07778-471803
Fax 020-8993 5736
Loop (feature), Born Kicking (TV film), Human Traffic (feature).

Richard Bullock   Mobile 07956-468239 AD 020-7428 0500
The Space Race (TV drama doc), The Lazarus Child (feature), Pelican Blood (feature) (Production Designer).

Jon Bunker   020-7603 5317 Mobile 07785-318081
Fax 020-7371 1879
Miguel & William (feature), Croupier (feature), Vertical Limit (feature).

Christopher Burke   01929-425967 Mobile 07732-186524
Fax 01929-425967
Widows (TV drama), Red Fox (TV drama), Great Trafalgar River Race (TV drama doc).

Milly Burns   020-8749 1202 Mobile 07770-843346
Time Bandits (feature), The Armando Iannucci Show (TV light entertainment), Vipere Au Poing (feature).

Paul Burns   Mobile 07968-798266 DD 020-7851 3575
Good Arrows (TV film), When Women Ruled The World (TV reality), The Business (feature).

Tony Burrough   ITG 020-7636 6565
Richard III (feature), A Knight's Tale (feature), The Waterhorse (feature).

Tom Burton   Mobile 07774-689612 DA 020-7437 4551
1980 (TV drama), Money (TV drama), The Wedding Date (feature).

David Butterworth   Mobile 07710-916032
The Street (TV drama), Vincent (TV drama), Cutting It (TV drama).

Matt Button   Mobile 07956-588199
Bonded By Blood (feature), The Rise Of The Foot Soldier (feature), The Defender (feature).

Maurice Cain   020-8567 9144 Mobile 07778-214996
CMM 020-8584 5363 Fax 020-8567 9144
Skellig (feature), House Of Saddam (TV drama), Foyle's War (TV drama).

Nik Callan   020-8973 3933 Mobile 07973-781971
Fax 020-8973 3939

Allan Cameron   01372-457724 Fax 01372-456184
Angels & Demons (feature), The Da Vinci Code (feature), Sahara (feature).

Roger Cann   01308-426553 Mobile 07977-042745
ITG 020-7636 6565
Foyle's War (TV drama), Tom Jones (TV drama), The Buddha Of Suburbia (TV drama).

Jason Carlin   Mobile 07768-254389 MM 020-8995 4747
The Roman Mysteries (TV childrens), Johnny & The Bomb (TV childrens), Yasmin (feature).

Michael Carlin   Mobile 07831-293096 CM 020-7287 4450
The Eagle Of The Ninth (feature), Red Tails (feature), The Duchess (feature).

Jane Carroll   Mobile 07973-405813

Maggie Carroll   020-8983 9839 Mobile 07775-518954
Holby City (TV drama), Morecambe & Wise (TV light entertainment), Film 2008 (TV light entertainment).

Cristina Casali   Mobile 07957-215878
Nineteen Seventy-Four (TV film), In The Loop (feature), Criminal Justice (TV drama).

Jane Cecchi   020-8854 4472 Mobile 07956-616704
Fax 01483-750415
TMi (TV childrens), SMart (TV childrens), Police Bravery Awards (TV light entertainment).

Chris Chesney   020-8968 5908 Mobile 07973-759146
AC/DC (promo), Hearts & Minds (TV drama), Sanex (commercial).

Martin Childs   020-7401 7773 ITG 020-7636 6565
W.E. (feature), London Boulevard (feature), The Boy In The Striped Pyjamas (feature).

Maria Chryssikos   020-8579 5121 Mobile 07817-739614
The Oxford Murders (feature) (Art Director), Rimmell (commercial), Audi (commercial).

Ged Clarke   0118-944 8090 Mobile 07860-239398
Fax 0118-944 9080
The Fall (feature).

Clare Clarkson   020-7731 5549 Mobile 07885-515575
AD 020-7428 0500 Fax 020-7348 7574
Volkswagen (commercial), Guinness (commercial), One 2 One (commercial).

Jim Clay   020-8940 9450 CM 020-7287 4450
Shanghai (feature), The Brothers Bloom (feature), Children Of Men (feature).

Fergus Clegg   Mobile 07976-693159
Looking For Eric (feature), It's A Free World (feature), The Wind That Shakes The Barley (feature).

Caroline Cobbold   020-7625 5875 Mobile 07831-580172
Jiro & Masako (TV drama), The Fever (feature), Nostalgia Oma Fast (Art House Film Installation).

Joel Collins   Mobile 07956-856087 MM 020-8995 4747
Hitchhiker's Guide To The Galaxy (feature), Son Of Rambow (feature), The Day Of The Triffids (TV drama).

John Collins   Mobile 07860-186204
Waterloo Road (TV drama), Conviction (TV drama), Wire In The Blood (TV drama).

Stephane Collonge   020-8985 9283 Mobile 07958-906956
Puritan (feature), Lisa & The Pilot (feature), Unrelated (feature).

Linda Conoboy   Mobile 07968-339559
Holby City (TV drama), One Foot In The Grave (TV comedy drama), Casualty (TV drama).

Tom Conroy   +353 87 261 3204
The Tudors (TV drama), Breakfast On Pluto (feature), East Is East (feature).

Darrell Cooke   Mobile 07958-563724

Maggie Coombes   0161-445 6476 Mobile 07779-263633
Cold Feet (TV drama), Blue Murder (TV drama), Cold Blood (TV drama).

Fran Cooper   Mobile 07973-911131
0-800-Love (feature) (Art Director), Coming Up (feature) (Art Director), Bookaboo (TV childrens).

Paul Cowell   01590-673625 Mobile 07770-353612
Midsomer Murders (TV drama), Ultimate Force (TV drama), The Ruth Rendell Mysteries (TV drama).

Alex Craig   020-7286 6716 Mobile 07958-326353
Children In Need (TV light entertainment), The Office (TV comedy drama), Shooting Stars (TV light entertainment).

Stuart Craig   SK 020-7434 9055
Harry Potter & The Half-Blood Prince (feature), The English Patient (feature), The Mission (feature).

Paul Cripps   020-8748 1934 Mobile 07768-404243
The Scouting Book For Boys (feature), Never Let Me Go (feature), Bones (TV drama).

Paul Cross   020-8986 6666 Mobile 07774-482367
Babylon AD (feature), Luther (TV drama), Spooks (TV drama).

Tim Dann   020-7352 8689 Mobile 07973-137716
Fax 020-7352 8689

Anna Dargavel   020-8992 1723 Mobile 07802-241965
EastEnders (promo), Grange Hill (TV childrens), BBC World Service (TV news & current affairs).

Suzie Davies   01844-274156 Mobile 07850-533411
Fax 01844-274156
The Children (feature), Kingdom (TV drama), The Cost Of Living (TV drama).

Dennis De Groot   020-7625 4677 Mobile 07831-217490
Fax 020-7624 4468
The IT Crowd (TV comedy drama), Black Books (TV comedy drama), I'm Alan Partridge (TV comedy).

Russell de Rozario   020-8451 0213 Mobile 07831-893427
Fax 020-8830 4330
Kick-Ass (feature), The Kid (feature), Telstar (feature).

John Demetri   020-8445 6918 Mobile 07828-154301

Emma Dibb   0161-881 6072 Mobile 07973-451309
We Are Klang (TV comedy drama), Massive (TV comedy drama), The Visit (TV drama).

James Dillon   020-7585 2284 Mobile 07831-501514
The Crystal Maze (TV light entertainment), The Mighty Boosh (TV light entertainment), My Friend Joe (feature).

Eileen Diss   020-7937 8794 Mobile 07836-548143
Jeeves & Wooster (TV drama), Longitude (TV film), A Dance To The Music Of Time (TV film).

Maria Djurkovic   020-8743 5653 Mobile 07831-286488
ITG 020-7636 6565 Fax 020-8743 5653
Mamma Mia! (feature), Vanity Fair (feature), Cassandra's Dream (feature).

Alison Dominitz   020-8968 0143 Mobile 07788-871191
AD 020-7428 0500
Mrs Harris (feature), Hotel Splendide (feature), Casanova (feature).

Laurence Dorman   MM 020-8995 4747
Me & Orson Welles (feature), Franklyn (feature), Flashbacks Of A Fool (feature).

PRODUCTION DESIGNERS

Richard Drew   Mobile 07774-759047
French & Saunders (TV light entertainment), The Inbetweeners (TV comedy drama), Nationwide (commercial).

John Ebden   020-7836 0066   Mobile 07831-235510
AD 020-7428 0500

Simon Elliott   Mobile 07973-842733
Nanny McPhee & The Big Bang (feature), The Passion (TV drama), Bleak House (TV drama).

Eryl Ellis   Mobile 07968-488745
The Bill (TV drama), BBC Proms: Doctor Who Special (TV light entertainment), Young Musician Of The Year (TV light entertainment).

Graham Ellis   Mobile 07976-266921
EastEnders (promo), Holby City (TV drama), Stella Street (TV comedy drama).

John Ellis   Mobile 07802-494346   CVH 020-8741 7647
A Boy Called Dad (feature), Mischief Night (feature), The Death Of Klinghoffer (TV film).

Nick Ellis   020-8892 0334   Mobile 07831-668397
AD 020-7428 0500
Bend It Like Beckham (feature), Angus Thongs & Perfect Snogging (feature), It's A Wonderful Afterlife (feature).

Derek Evans   01483-285307   Mobile 07778-006671
Children In Need (TV light entertainment), Keeping Up Appearances (TV comedy drama), Little & Large (TV light entertainment).

Ricky Eyres   Mobile 07980-606424
Solomon Kane (feature), Heartless (feature), Stormbreaker (feature).

David Ferris   020-8398 2353   Mobile 07889-861666
Home Time (TV comedy drama), Gavin & Stacey (TV comedy drama), Saxondale (TV comedy drama).

Graham Ferris   01749-671225
2001: A Space Odyssey (feature), The Ghost Of Greville Lodge (TV film), Yellow Submarine (feature).

Tony Ferris   01727-832209   Mobile 07979-804130
Fax 01727-832209
My Parents Are Aliens (TV childrens), Kiss Me Kate (theatre), Feel The Force (TV comedy drama).

Will Field   Mobile 07812-196175
The Maccabees (promo), Daylight Robbery (feature), Phoo Action (TV film).

Peter Findley   01206-337338   Mobile 07850-080590
Nine (feature) (Art Director), Tchaikovsky (TV drama doc), Titanic: Birth Of A Legend (TV drama).

Ian Fisher   01384-390137   Mobile 07831-102361
The Commander (TV drama), Trial & Retribution (TV drama), My Family (TV comedy drama).

Michael Fleischer   020-8441 6619   Mobile 07977-464011
Fax 020-8441 6619
Whatever It Takes (TV drama), Hotel Babylon (TV drama), Joy Division (feature).

Nicholas Foley-Oates   01273-478088
Mobile 07976-609517
Orange (commercial), Adidas (commercial), Phones 4U (commercial).

Robert Foster   020-7348 3773   Mobile 07850-318363
Spooks (TV drama), Silent Witness (TV drama), Nuclear Race (TV docu drama).

Julian Fullalove   020-8614 4387   Mobile 07970-541507
Fax 020-8977 7939
Trinity (feature).

Charles Garrad   ITG 020-7636 6565
I Really Hate My Job (feature), Waiting For Godot (feature), The Englishman Who Went Up A Hill (feature).

Norman Garwood   020-8891 2239   Mobile 07881-644253
SMM +1 310 285 0303
Brazil (feature), Hook (feature), Glory (feature).

Carol Golder   020-8892 8832   Mobile 07956-239482
Fax 020-8892 8832

Daniel Gomme   +1 310 927 7253   Mobile 07773-647245
The Dead (feature), Mainline Run (feature), Skinner (feature).

Peter Gordon   Mobile 07980-586529
Nigel Slater's Simple Suppers (TV light entertainment), Big Brother (TV reality), The Day Britain Stopped (TV drama).

Max Gottlieb   Mobile 07860-546136
Blitz (feature), Mr Nice (feature), The Full Monty (feature).

Jim Grant   020-8579 1119   Mobile 07976-272241
Fax 020-8579 1119
A Room With A View (feature), The Last Detective (TV drama), Neville's Island (TV drama).

Jonathan Paul Green   01923-850870
Mobile 07831-348719   Fax 07092-248719
Mobo Awards (TV light entertainment), Top Gear (TV light entertainment), Qi (TV light entertainment).

Sarah Greenwood   Mobile 07973-507403
ITG 020-7636 6565
Sherlock Holmes (feature), Atonement (feature), Pride & Prejudice (feature).

Caroline Greville-Morris   01460-55995
Mobile 07768-012040 STA 020-7729 7477 Fax 01460-55995
Boogie Woogie (feature), Wild Target (feature), The Mutant Chronicles (feature).

Venita Gribble   029-2040 4371 Mobile 07968-179374
Fax 029-2065 1452
Wire In The Blood (TV drama), Young Dracula (TV childrens), Carrie's War (TV film).

Steve Groves   020-7622 8166 Mobile 07771-651915
Jinx (TV childrens), Powerful Texts (TV doc), My Spy Family (TV childrens).

Lisa Marie Hall   Mobile 07813-785457
Somers Town (feature), Malice In Wonderland (feature), Dangerous Parking (feature).

Roger Hall   01285-841419 Mobile 07785-222502
AD 020-7428 0500 Fax 01285-841385

Imogen Hammond   020-7735 5353 Mobile 07771-574003
Jamie's Fowl Dinners (TV doc), Dizzee Rascal (promo), Timewatch (TV doc).

Luana Hanson   Mobile 07831-708334 CM 020-7287 4450
Collision (TV drama), The Diary Of Anne Frank (TV drama), The Mark Of Cain (feature).

Christopher Hardinge   020-8789 7339
Mobile 07932-669279 Fax 020-8789 7339

Andy Harris   0141-945 5270 Mobile 07831-851295
ITG 020-7636 6565
The Strange Case Of Sherlock Holmes & Arthur Conan Doyle (TV drama), Nina's Heavenly Delights (feature), Rebus (TV drama).

Julie Harris   Mobile 07887-480285
Honest (TV drama), The Office (TV comedy drama), Beehive (TV light entertainment).

Rob Harris   Mobile 07710-369207 DA 020-7437 4551
Britannic (feature), St Ives (feature), Housewife 49 (TV drama).

Roger Harris   020-8747 8545 Mobile 07885-723433
GEMS 029-2071 0770 Fax 020-8747 8545
Shoot On Sight (feature), Private Moments (feature), Salaam-E-Ishq (feature).

Philip Harrison   01784-482192 Mobile 07817-179420
Fax 01784-483882
Outland (feature), Stakeout (feature), The Core (feature).

Penny Harvey   Mobile 07850-396938
Irish Jam (feature) (Art Director), The Truth About Love (feature) (Art Director), Torchwood (TV drama).

Guy Hendrix Dyas   +1 213 309 0933
Mobile +1 323 276 0807
Agora (feature), Indiana Jones: The Kingdom Of The Crystal Skull (feature), Elizabeth: The Golden Age (feature).

James Hendy   Mobile 07976-701264
The Outsiders (TV drama) (Art Director), Can't Buy Me Love (TV drama), Grange Hill (TV childrens).

Jon Henson   Mobile 07973-937696 CM 020-7287 4450
Chat Room (feature), Last Chance Harvey (feature), Brothers Of The Head (feature).

Stevie Herbert   020-8177 8806 Mobile 07973-423998
CCM 020-8743 7337
Maxwell (TV docu drama), Ashes To Ashes (TV drama), Wide Sargasso Sea (TV film).

Alice Herrick   020-7739 9723 Mobile 07976-831869
Life Translated (feature), The Truth Game (feature), Paradise Grove (feature).

Grant Hicks   020-8891 2228 Mobile 07831-642785
DD 020-7851 3575 Fax 020-8891 2228
Nighty Night (TV comedy drama), The Race (feature), The Tall Guy (feature).

Anna Higginson   Mobile 07774-746746
CMM 020-8584 5363
Cemetery Junction (feature), Party Animals (TV drama), Mistresses (TV drama).

Bruce Hill   Mobile 07836-203871
Sainsbury's (commercial), Renault (commercial), BBC (ident).

Rob Hinds   01404-892950 Mobile 07774-150950
Fax 01404-892950
The Grid (TV drama), Our Friends In The North (TV drama), The Tenth Kingdom (TV drama).

David Hitchcock   020-8943 2857 Mobile 07885-284536
Fax 020-8943 2857
Sex Drugs & Rock 'n' Chips (TV comedy drama), To The Manor Born (TV comedy drama), The Green Green Grass (TV comedy drama).

Richard Hogan   Mobile 07802-813024
Poirot (TV drama), Casualty (TV drama), Death In Holy Orders (TV drama).

Simon Holland   01398-323419 Mobile 07768-060117
CM 020-7287 4450 Fax 01398-323419
Greyfriars Bobby (feature), Leprechauns (feature), Tales Of The Riverbank (feature).

Grenville Horner　　　　Mobile 07956-843350
CM 020-7287 4450
Krod Mandoon & The Flaming Sword Of Fire (TV drama), Married Single Other (TV drama), Wuthering Heights (feature).

Andrew Howe Davies　　　　020-8932 3928
Mobile 07710-349388 Fax 020-8932 3928
The League Of Gentlemen (tour), Little Britain (tour), The Vicar Of Dibley (TV comedy drama).

Duncan Howell　　　　Mobile 07770-883098
In The Night Garden (TV childrens), Shameless (TV drama), The Royal (TV drama).

Ant Howells　　　　Mobile 07973-217717
Bear Behaving Badly (TV childrens), Hi-5 (TV childrens), The Bill (TV drama).

Mark Hudson　　　　01952-603896 Mobile 07721-625763
Peak Practice (TV drama), Grease Monkeys (TV drama), Dalziel & Pascoe (TV drama).

Richard Hudson　　　　Mobile 07906-461057
The Englishman (feature), Tuesday (feature), Devilwood (short).

Will Hughes-Jones　　　　Mobile 07774-709801
JCA 020-7434 4143
Small Island (TV drama), Criminal Justice (TV drama), Survivors (TV drama).

Alison Humphries　　　020-8873 1721 Mobile 07885-780692
Fax 020-8873 1721

Charlotte Humpston　　01749-890610 Mobile 07976-166454
Forever (feature), A Child In The Forest (TV drama), Out Of Order (feature).

Mick Hurd　　　　020-7354 4826 Mobile 07831-362919
AD 020-7428 0500
Slime Across The UK (TV childrens), Saturday Night Divas (TV light entertainment), Miss Naked Beauty (TV light entertainment).

Tim Hutchinson　　　020-8994 3157 Mobile 07836-245625
Fax 020-8987 2761
The Garden Of Eden (feature), Mansfield Park (TV film), Tom Brown's School Days (TV drama).

Robert Ide　　　　020-8977 5247 Mobile 07984-327033
Fax 020-8977 5247
The Real Thing (theatre), Rosemary & Thyme (TV drama), The Complete Works Of William Shakespeare (TV film).

Gemma Jackson　　　020-7289 4981 Mobile 07798-844745
ITG 020-7636 6565 Fax 020-7289 3148
John Adams (TV drama), Finding Neverland (feature), Iris (feature).

Humphrey Jaeger　　020-8946 6811 Mobile 07850-712776
BA 020-7836 1112 Fax 020-8946 6811
Miss Conception (feature), Wide Blue Yonder (feature), Relative Values (feature).

Simon Jago　　　　Mobile 07850-771493

Henry Jaworski　　020-8993 3952 Mobile 07778-039869
Fax 020-8993 3952
The Tenth Kingdom (TV drama), Survivors (TV drama), Casualty (TV drama).

Alison Jeffery　　Mobile 07970-619727 Fax 01258-860265
Keep Your Enemies Close (TV light entertainment), Raven (TV childrens), Comedy Showcase (TV childrens).

Martyn John　　　Mobile 07774-952749 ITG 020-7636 6565
Foyle's War (TV drama), Whitechapel (TV drama), Four Seasons (TV drama).

Mike Joyce　　　　020-8874 6779 Mobile 07885-300013
The Milkshake Show (TV childrens), Hornblower (TV drama), Sharpe (TV drama).

Peter Joyce　　　　01932-223766 Mobile 07947-765675
The Professionals (TV drama), Where Eagles Dare (feature), The Bill (TV drama).

Gerry Judah　　　　Mobile 07831-464360

Michael Kane　　　Mobile 07712-190948 PS 020-8883 1616
Sick House (feature), Once Were Warriors (feature), Broken Lines (feature).

Kitty Kaye　　　　020-8960 8777 Mobile 07866-758285
Fax 020-8960 6700
New Beginnings (TV drama), At Last (TV drama), Rewards (TV film).

John-Paul Kelly　　Mobile 07770-390161 DA 020-7437 4551
Hippie Hippie Shake (feature), The Other Boleyn Girl (feature), Venus (feature).

Morgan Kennedy　　　　Mobile 07973-491091
WZ 020-7437 2055
Cashback (feature), The Broken (feature).

Claire Kenny　　　020-8995 9659 Mobile 07889-770277
ITG 020-7636 6565
Einstein & Eddington (TV film), Place Of Execution (TV drama), David Kelly (TV drama).

Stephen Keogh　　　020-8569 7892 Mobile 07941-486468
Missing (TV doc), Madson (TV drama), Holby Blue (TV drama).

Jennifer Kernke   Mobile 07956-506411 DA 020-7437 4551
The Baker (feature), Dear Frankie (feature), In My Father's Den (feature).

Andrew Kiff   01625-535355 Mobile 07973-204739

Buffy Kimm   020-8549 2728 Mobile 07990-502400
Holding On (TV drama), Live & Kicking (TV childrens), Run The Risk (TV childrens).

Simon Kimmel   020-8441 9247 Mobile 07850-007427
Fax 020-8441 9247
The Royal Variety Performance (TV light entertainment), Noel's HQ (TV light entertainment), This Is Your Life (TV light entertainment).

Kyz Kistell   Mobile 07956-400033
EastEnders (promo), Gavin & Stacey (TV comedy drama), Saxondale (TV comedy drama).

George Kyriakides   Mobile 07947-125169
Night & Day (TV drama), A Touch Of Frost (TV drama), Urban Gothic (TV drama).

Martin Laing   +1 213 447 9666
Mobile 07827-893591
Captain Nemo (feature), Clash Of The Titans (feature), Terminator Salvation (feature) (Art Director).

Peter Lamont   01753-644898 Mobile 07887-998070
Casino Royale (feature), Die Another Day (feature), Titanic (feature).

James Lapsley   Mobile 07789-301382
New Town Killers (feature), Skeletons (feature), The Week We Went To War (TV light entertainment).

David Laskey   020-8995 0979 Mobile 07973-727238
Fax 020-8995 0979
BBC Election (TV news & current affairs), New Year's Eve Live (TV news & current affairs).

Ken Ledsham   01753-866342 Mobile 07778-555660
Fax 01753-830398
Judge John Deed (TV drama), Devil's Advocate (TV drama), The Colour Of Justice (TV drama).

David Lee   020-8740 4543 Mobile 07860-683010
The Dark Is Rising (feature), Batman Begins (feature) (Art Director), Star Wars: Episode III - Revenge Of The Sith (feature) (Art Director).

Jonathan Lee   01784-471233 Mobile 07836-689731
SMM +1 310 285 0303 Fax 01784-436838
The Flood (feature), Stealth (feature), Crusoe (TV drama).

Mark Leese   0141-554 5852 Mobile 07855-788659
ITG 020-7636 6565
This Is England (feature), Neds (feature), Glorious 39 (feature).

Jamie Leonard   020-7249 6262 Mobile 07799-898118
Desert Flower (feature), Complicity (feature), Tom & Viv (feature).

James Lewis   Mobile 07710-410755 CMM 020-8584 5363
Swinging With The Finkels (feature), Material Girls (TV drama), City Of Vice (TV drama).

Chris Lightburn-Jones   Mobile 07779-150059
VW Golf (commercial), Egg (commercial), Dead Set (TV drama).

Hugo Luczyc-Wyhowski   Mobile 07802-259287
DA 020-7437 4551
I Love You Philip Morris (feature), Flash Of Genius (feature), Mrs Henderson Presents (feature).

Rob Lunn   Mobile 07973-479081
Shadowscan (short).

Patrick Lyndon-Stanford   Mobile 07989-953977

Tracey Macario   Mobile 07958-413230
Holby City (TV drama), Born To Win (TV light entertainment), Aquila (TV childrens).

Alan MacDonald   ITG 020-7636 6565
The Edge Of Love (feature), The Queen (feature), The Jacket (feature).

Jo Manser   Mobile 07710-349784
The Gunpowder Plot (TV docu drama), Oceans (TV docu drama), Global Health (TV drama doc).

Adele Marolf   020-8941 5312 Mobile 07850-551170
The Bill (TV drama), Ivanhoe (TV drama), House Of Elliot (TV drama).

Adam Marshall   020-8676 8503 Mobile 07850-468449
Random Quest (TV drama), Number 13 (TV drama), The Plot Against Harold Wilson (TV drama doc).

Hayden Matthews   01548-581315 Mobile 07778-178922
Casualty 1909 (TV drama), The Street (TV drama), Skins (TV drama).

Eve Mavrakis   Mobile 07767-486787
UA 020-3214 0800
Imagine Me & You (feature), Lock Stock & Two Smoking Barrels (feature), Bandit Queen (feature).

Andrew McAlpine   020-7289 4981 Mobile 07970-588596
CM 020-7287 4450 Fax 020-7289 3148
An Education (feature), Aeon Flux (feature), The Piano (feature).

Amanda McArthur   020-7243 4411 Mobile 07831-889418
St Trinian's (feature), Penelope (feature), Driving Lessons (feature).

Stuart McCarthy   01730-827258 Mobile 07860-912714
EastEnders (promo), The Bill (TV drama), The Treasure Seekers (TV film).

David McHenry   01242-820813 Mobile 07887-728007
Love & Death On Long Island (feature), Jackboots On Whitehall (feature), Chosyu 5 (feature).

Murray McKeown   Mobile 07711-790488
4.3.2.1 (feature), Adulthood (feature), Kidulthood (feature).

Jonnie Mead   020-8516 8879 Mobile 07941-177259
Runaway (TV drama), EastEnders (promo), The Bill (TV drama).

Catrin Meredydd   Mobile 07973-862812 BA 020-7836 1112
Vexed (TV drama), Spirit Warriors (TV childrens), New Tricks (TV drama).

James Merifield   Mobile 07770-753220
CMM 020-8584 5363
Little Dorrit (TV drama), Sense & Sensibility (feature), The Walker (feature).

Martin Methven   +33 4 90 28 94 18
Mobile 07775-948027
The Inspector Alleyn Mysteries (TV drama), The Precious Blood (feature), The Face At The Window (TV childrens).

Gillian Miles   020-8390 2389 Mobile 07768-278262
Fax 020-8390 2389
Blessed (TV comedy drama), Fat Friends (TV drama), Little Miss Jocelyn (TV comedy drama).

Kristian Milsted   Mobile 07956-395505
Unmade Beds (feature), Secret Diary Of A Call Girl (TV drama), Huge (feature).

Sarah Milton   020-8361 0532 Mobile 07958-592439
Fax 020-8361 0532
Jackanory (TV childrens), Zingzillas (TV childrens), Relic (TV childrens).

Colin Monk   Mobile 07785-110324
The Knock (TV drama), Murder In Mind (TV drama), Waking The Dead (TV drama).

Grant Montgomery   Mobile 07973-864659
UA 020-3214 0800
A Passionate Woman (TV drama), Unforgiven (TV drama), Lewis (TV drama).

Christina Moore   020-7435 6164 Mobile 07976-752934
Fax 020-7435 6164
Exodus (feature), The Other Man (feature) (Supervising Art Director), John Adams (TV drama) (Supervising Art Director).

Shaun Moore   01844-218072 Mobile 07909-521754
Fax 01844-217558
NEWSX - Delhi & Mumbai (TV news & current affairs), The Summerhouse (feature), ADTV/EMI National Newsroom (TV news & current affairs).

Brian Morris   ITG 020-7636 6565
Pirates Of The Caribbean: The Curse Of The Black Pearl (feature), The Insider (feature), Firewall (feature).

Richard Morris   020-8940 4774 Mobile 07850-469486
Fax 020-8940 8336
Today With Des & Mel (TV magazine), Ronnie Corbett Live (DVD), Loose Women (TV light entertainment).

Gabriel Mossa   020-7636 4588 Mobile 07973-844701
Fax 020-7636 4588
Discovery Channel (ident), Dating In The Dark (TV reality), The Gallows (promo).

Michael Mulligan   Mobile 07958-961249
www.michaelmulligan.net

Paul Munting   020-8973 3803 Mobile 07802-291827
BA 020-7836 1112
Dispatches (TV doc), Jonathan Creek (TV drama), Nelson (TV doc).

Gerald Murphy   029-2049 4381 Mobile 07860-297420
Fax 029-2049 4382
Only Connect (TV light entertainment), Kill It Cook It Eat It (TV reality), Anatomy For Beginners (TV reality).

Roger Murray-Leach   01249-782920 Mobile 07831-421087
Fax 01249-782774
Local Hero (feature), A Fish Called Wanda (feature), Defence Of The Realm (feature).

Peter Murton   020-8346 8180
Stargate (feature), The Lion In Winter (TV film), Superman III (feature).

Ben Myhill   Mobile 07714-343730 Fax 020-8985 8662

Julian Nagel   Mobile 07734-692183 STA 020-7729 7477
Tormented (feature), One Night In Emergency (TV drama), Goodbye Cruel World (short).

Anthea Nelson   Mobile 07973-952235 DD 020-7851 3575
The Innocence Project (TV drama), The Illustrated Mum (TV drama), Uncle Dad (TV drama).

Juliet Nichols   Mobile 07976-744114

3's A Crowd (TV light entertainment), Fame Academy (TV reality), Here Comes The Sun (TV light entertainment).

Tony Noble   020-8977 3459   Mobile 07956-414227

Moon (feature), Rendition (feature) (Art Director), Baker Street Irregulars (TV drama) (Art Director).

Alice Normington   DA 020-7437 4551

Brideshead Revisited (feature), Proof (feature), And When Did You Last See Your Father? (feature).

Nicole Northridge   Mobile 07899-924363

Extras (TV comedy drama) (Art Director), Casualty (TV drama), EastEnders (promo).

Candida Otton   Mobile 07767-496747

Pierrepoint (TV film), Tess Of The D'Ubervilles (TV drama), Sex Traffic (TV drama).

Glyn Owen   Mobile 07976-707267

Bill Palmer   01647-231465   Mobile 07970-527150

Fax 01647-231465

Casualty (TV drama), Down To Earth (TV drama), Rumpole Of The Bailey (TV drama).

Kalpesh Patel   020-8958 6111   Mobile 07767-808599

Audi (commercial), Guinness (commercial), Rolex (commercial).

Cath Pater-Lancucki   020-8806 3352

Mobile 07774-863809   Fax 020-8880 8722

The Apprentice (TV reality), The Culture Show (TV arts), The Lily Allen Show (TV light entertainment).

Charlotte Pearson   Mobile 07811-453360

The Pit (short), Rush Hour (TV light entertainment).

Kevin Phipps   01932-730003   Mobile 07885-478647

Blood & Chocolate (feature), The Nutcracker (ballet), V For Vendetta (feature) (Art Director).

Michael Pickwoad   01865-511106   Mobile 07790-103272

CM 020-7287 4450

The Prisoner (TV drama), The Old Curiosity Shop (TV drama), Longford (TV drama).

Colin Pigott   020-7589 4260   Mobile 07770-693320

Fax 020-7589 4260

The Trial Of Gemma Lang (TV drama), Live At The Apollo (TV light entertainment), Commercial Breakdown (TV light entertainment).

Anthony Pratt   020-7272 4322   Mobile 07904-652137

SMM +1 310 285 0303   Fax 020-7281 8294

Phantom Of The Opera (feature), The End Of The Affair (feature), Band Of Brothers (TV drama).

Clem Price Thomas   WZ 020-7437 2055

Mercedes (commercial), Orange (commercial), Barclays Bank (commercial).

Mark Pritchard   01458-259793   Mobile 07976-910330

Prada (stills), Yves St Laurent (commercial), Louis Vuitton (stills).

Marco Puig   Mobile 07961-100530

Johnnie Walker (commercial), Boots (commercial), Madonna (promo).

Andrew Purcell   0117-985 7917   Mobile 07770-430327

The Diary Of A Nobody (TV drama), Afterlife (TV drama), Being Human (TV drama).

Jon Pusey   01603-504515   Mobile 07885-466522

Fax 01603-504515

Kave Quinn   Mobile 07957-165552   CM 020-7287 4450

Harry Brown (feature), Is There Anybody There? (feature), Trainspotting (feature).

Michael Ralph   Mobile 07981-778326   CCM 020-8743 7337

Primeval (TV drama), Hustle (TV drama), Sea Of Souls (TV drama).

Sara Ranieri   Mobile 07546-352741

Erik Rehl   020-7249 7459   Mobile 07977-570809

Fax 020-7249 7459

The Infidel (feature), Shifty (feature), When Boris Met Dave (TV docu drama).

Norman Reynolds   01242-216771

Raiders Of The Lost Ark (feature), Star Wars (feature), Empire Of The Sun (feature).

Sally Reynolds   Mobile 07889-056657

Sunshine (feature), The Royle Family (TV comedy drama), Early Doors (TV drama).

Jason Richards   Mobile 07977-274649

Aida (opera), Crazy For You (theatre), Fame (theatre).

Chris Richmond   Mobile 07837-327195

Control (feature), Magic Boys (feature), Dubplate Drama (TV drama).

Fiona Riddick   Mobile 07711-514152

Unleashed (feature), Night People (feature), River City (TV drama).

Sam Riley   020-8743 8086   Mobile 07973-877906

Steve Ritchie   020-7274 9339   Mobile 07976-854043

Sexy Beast (feature), Modern Toss (TV light entertainment), Genie In The House (TV childrens).

Alison Riva   Mobile 07767-371337

Empire (TV film), Affinity (TV film).

Phil Roberson　　01273-720680　Mobile 07973-223726
Knife Edge (feature), Flick (feature), The Taming Of The Shrew (TV film).

Bernadette Roberts　　Mobile 07956-552163
Desperados (TV childrens), Everytime You Look At Me (TV film), Always & Everyone (TV drama).

Dominic Roberts　　Mobile 07803-597783
EastEnders (promo), Merlin (TV drama), The Bill (TV drama).

John Roberts　　01373-462892
Photo Finish (feature), The Butterfly Effect (feature), The Mirror Cracked (feature) (Art Director).

Rachel Robertson　　Mobile 07968-968511
Boogie Woogie (feature) (Art Director), Make Me A Supermodel (TV reality), Living It (TV drama).

David Roger　　020-8969 8354　Mobile 07930-421625
Fax 020-8969 8354
Fanny Hill (TV drama), Persuasion (feature), Low Winter Sun (TV drama).

Chris Roope　　Mobile 07976-659038　ITG 020-7636 6565
Nativity (feature), Control (feature), The Upside Of Anger (feature).

Paul Rowan　　0161-941 2840　Mobile 07885-332869
Burn It (TV drama), Wuthering Heights (feature), Murder On The Orient Express (feature).

Marcus Rowland　　Mobile 07710-169960
Scott Pilgrim Vs The World (feature), Shaun Of The Dead (feature), Hot Fuzz (feature).

Caroline Russell　　020-8299 6122　Mobile 07976-710022
Fax 020-8299 4893
V Graham Norton (TV light entertainment), Sit Up (TV light entertainment), Girl Eats Boy (promo).

Ian Russell　　020-8395 9141　Mobile 07802-259959
The Bill (TV drama), The Canterville Ghost (TV film), Burnside (TV drama).

Ken Ryan　　01200-440095
The Prisoner (TV drama), Ring Of Bright Water (feature), Spitting Image (TV light entertainment).

Crispian Sallis　　01932-225700　Mobile 07850-413109
Fax 01932-231928
Keeping Mum (feature), Colour Me Kubrick (feature), My Little Eye (feature).

Andrew Sanders　　020-7736 8649　Mobile 07802-501140
AD 020-7428 0500　Fax 020-7736 8649
The White Countess (feature), Spider (feature), The Witches (feature).

Sabina Sattar　　Mobile 07976-272176
The First Men In The Moon (TV drama), Crooked House (TV drama), EastEnders (promo).

Helen Scott　　Mobile 07973-563201
Fish Tank (feature), Red Road (feature).

Sid Scott　　Mobile 07785-795421　Fax 029-2021 4869
Mosgito (TV childrens), Y Garej (TV childrens), Planed Plant (TV childrens).

Stephen Scott　　020-8883 7750　Mobile 07776-257118
Hellboy 2: The Golden Army (feature), Doom (feature), Hellboy (feature).

Christopher Seagers　　Mobile 07831-787762
ITG 020-7636 6565
Deja Vu (feature), Man On Fire (feature), The Taking Of Pelham 1 2 3 (feature).

Michael Seymour　　020-7727 7836
Alien (feature), Eureka (feature), Beverley Hills Cop III (feature).

Amelia Shankland　　029-2021 7598　Mobile 07771-905860
Fax 029-2021 7598
Skins (TV drama), The Giblet Boys (TV childrens), Casualty (TV drama).

Stephen Sharratt　　01494-880570　Mobile 07831-528400
Prince Of Persia (feature) (Set Decorator), Hellboy 2: The Golden Army (feature) (Set Decorator), Holby City (TV drama).

Greg Shaw　　Mobile 07958-781145
Sorry I've Got No Head (TV comedy drama), Clone (TV comedy drama), Secret Diary Of A Call Girl (TV drama).

Jacqueline Smith　　Mobile 07770-234476　BA 020-7836 1112
Filth: The Mary Whitehouse Story (TV drama), Life Isn't All Ha Ha Hee Hee (TV drama), Marian Again (TV drama).

Morley Smith　　01707-656564
The Shooting Party (feature), The House That Mary Bought (TV film), Dusty Death (TV film).

Steve Smithwick　　020-8874 5383　Mobile 07836-551730

Nick Somerville　　020-8579 1959　Mobile 07850-556716
Love Me Still (feature), Taste Of Life (TV drama), The Bombmaker (TV film).

Alan Spalding　　020-8997 6400　Mobile 07850-315350
The Space Race (TV drama doc), The Mirror Cracked (feature).

Paul Spriggs   01242-520640 Mobile 07889-322578
Lewis (TV drama), Hustle (TV drama), Spooks (TV drama).

Adam Squires   01667-404797 Mobile 07976-378024
The Chase (TV drama), 16 Years Of Alcohol (feature), Meet The Magoons (TV comedy drama).

Stewart Starkin   Mobile 07770-885474
Goodbye Lover (feature), Undressed (TV light entertainment).

Chris Stephenson   01772-726819 Mobile 07971-818028
Fax 01772-726819
Clocking Off (TV drama), Peak Practice (TV drama), BAFTA Awards (TV light entertainment).

John Stevenson   CM 020-7287 4450
The Last Enemy (TV drama), Five Days (feature), My Summer Of Love (feature).

Eve Stewart   01442-874318 Mobile 07778-490849
Topsy-Turvy (feature), De Lovely (feature), Vera Drake (feature).

Caroline Story   Mobile 07970-571464 PS 020-8883 1616
Sugarhouse Lane (feature), Surveillance (feature).

Graeme Story   01628-417610 Mobile 07957-140690
Outnumbered (TV comedy drama), The Worst Week Of My Life (TV comedy drama), Bedtime (TV drama).

Rod Stratfold   020-7221 5026 Mobile 07774-920601
New Tricks (TV drama), The Jump (TV drama), The Alchemist (TV film).

Tony Stringer   Mobile 07711-066059
Exitz (feature), Gypsy Woman (feature), Crust (feature).

Paul Sudlow   Mobile 07860-363311

Jo Sutherland   020-8446 9245 Mobile 07778-210475
The IT Crowd (TV comedy drama), Spaced (TV comedy drama), The Catherine Tate Show (TV light entertainment).

Roger Swanborough   020-8693 1681
Mobile 07956-536699 Fax 020-8693 1681
Altroids (commercial), Schweppes (commercial), Nike (commercial).

Brian Sykes   Mobile 07976-439146 DD 020-7851 3575
Psychoville (TV comedy drama), Echo Beach (TV drama), Life On Mars (TV drama).

Nigel Talamo   020-7242 1668 Mobile 07793-816888
Adidas (commercial), British Airways (commercial), O2 (commercial).

Robin Tarsnane   020-8349 1449 Mobile 07802-713772
CCM 020-8743 7337
Simon & Emily (feature), Lewis (TV drama), The Brief (TV drama).

Jonathan Taylor   020-7703 5158 Mobile 07774-698847
SPA 01932-571044
Waking The Dead (TV drama), My Night With Reg (TV drama), Tracy Beaker (TV childrens).

Jeff Tessler   020-7609 1097 Mobile 07860-415603
ITG 020-7636 6565
Poirot (TV drama), Miss Marple (TV drama), Ballet Shoes (TV drama).

Rudi Thackray   Mobile 07966-423861
Ponderland (TV light entertainment), The One Show (TV magazine), Deal Or No Deal (TV light entertainment).

Edward Thomas   01792-233804 Mobile 07850-331548
CMM 020-8584 5363
Doctor Who (TV drama), Torchwood (TV drama), Berserker (feature).

Rosy Thomas   020-8961 0879 Mobile 07968-165396
Fur TV (TV comedy drama), Look Around You (TV light entertainment), Suburban Shootout (TV drama).

James Thompson   Mobile 07788-752094
Big Babies (TV childrens), Hounded (TV childrens), The Wrong Door (TV light entertainment).

Malcolm Thornton   020-8462 6811 Mobile 07831-654804
ITG 020-7636 6565
Our Mutual Friend (TV drama), The Long Firm (TV drama), Lark Rise To Candleford (TV drama).

Anne Tilby   01707-644620 Mobile 07775-925490
Opera At Covent Garden (opera), Opera At The ENO (opera), Come & Have A Go (TV light entertainment).

Mark Tildesley   Mobile 07768-418192
28 Weeks Later (feature), The Constant Gardener (feature), Sunshine (feature).

Jane Tomblin   Mobile 07885-183924
Bad Girls (TV drama), Bombshell (TV drama), Titty Bang Bang (TV light entertainment).

Leslie Tomkins   01923-260900 Mobile 07831-883996
Fax 01923-260900
Prince Of Persia (feature) (Art Director), Eyes Wide Shut (feature), Charlie & The Chocolate Factory (feature) (Art Director).

Michael Trevor   020-8876 7739 Mobile 07785-907285
The Scolds Bridle (TV drama), The Ice House (TV drama), Pyramid (TV docu drama).

Chris Truelove   01524-273857 Mobile 07831-481499

PRODUCTION DESIGNERS

Ed Turner 020-8390 6369 Mobile 07956-484138
CMM 020-8584 5363
MI High (TV childrens), Top Buzzer (TV drama), As If (TV drama).

Adrian Uwalaka 020-8960 7239 Mobile 07802-706286
Fax 020-8960 7239
Olympic Games (TV sport), World Championship Athletics (TV sport), Commonwealth Games (TV sport).

Tom Wales Mobile 07973-614966
Sony (commercial), TetraPak (commercial), Orange (commercial).

Jan Walker 020-8368 8011 Mobile 07974-658505

Stuart Walker 020-8740 5431 Mobile 07710-147664
CM 020-7287 4450
Cosi (feature), Above Suspicion (TV drama), Saddam's Tribe (TV drama).

Eric Walmsley 01494-673802 Mobile 07925-287279
Fax 01494-673802
King Lear (theatre), The Merchant Of Venice (feature), Oklahoma! (TV film).

Marko Waschke Mobile 07968-754813
Children Of Men (feature), Saving Grace (feature).

Simon Waters 01483-747981 Mobile 07711-425227
MM 020-8995 4747 Fax 01483-747981
The Truth About Love (feature), Jonathan Toomey (feature), Irish Jam (feature).

David Weare Mobile 07956-347680
Banzuke (TV childrens), Great British Menu (TV light entertainment), Feasts (TV light entertainment).

Julian Weaver 020-8523 5138 Mobile 07976-737574
Bunnytown (TV childrens), Machines Time Forgot (TV doc), Dream Team (TV drama).

Chris Webster 020-8985 4560 Mobile 07860-364104
Fax 020-8986 1409
Hell's Kitchen (TV reality), Too Much Too Young (feature), Any Dream Will Do (TV light entertainment).

Peter Wenham 020-8940 5650 Mobile 07860-480293
The Queen (feature), Blood Diamond (feature), The Bourne Ultimatum (feature).

Gordon Whistance Mobile 07940-499594
Smirnoff (commercial), Lead Balloon (TV comedy drama), School Of Comedy (TV light entertainment).

Lynne Whiteread Mobile 07866-260698
DA 020-7437 4551
Sold (TV drama), Fear Of Fanny (TV drama), Lawless Heart (feature).

Ash Wilkinson 0191-285 8012 Mobile 07885-322205
Fax 0191-285 8012
The Return Of Tracy Beaker (TV drama), Northern Lights (TV drama), Bunnytown (TV childrens).

Laurence Williams 020-8973 3933 Mobile 07831-679179
Fax 020-8973 3939
Casualty At Holby City (TV drama), Dragon's Den (TV light entertainment), The Inspector Alleyn Mysteries (TV drama).

Phil Williams 029-2049 3665 Mobile 07774-613451
Fax 029-2049 0658
Grandpa In My Pocket (TV childrens), BAFTA Craft Awards (TV light entertainment), The Tom Jones Show (TV light entertainment).

Susannah Williams 020-7687 7317 Mobile 07973-407849
Baby Juice Express (feature).

Gary Williamson 020-8567 6457 Mobile 07831-405799
ITG 020-7636 6565
Lipstick On Your Collar (TV drama), Wah Wah (feature), Bunny & The Bull (feature).

Charles Wood Mobile 07976-615528
Fools Gold (feature), Amazing Grace (feature), Flyboys (feature).

Donal Woods Mobile 07831-713641 ITG 020-7636 6565
Cranford (TV drama), State Of Play (TV drama), To The Ends Of The Earth (TV drama).

Marcus Wookey 01460-55995 Mobile 07775-763947
STA 020-7729 7477 Fax 01460-55995
Outlaw (feature), Earthquake (feature), Sexy Beast (feature).

Tony Woollard 020-7736 2717

Michael Young 020-8748 4715

James Zafar 020-8348 7784 Mobile 07940-560592
Fax 020-8348 7784
Holby City (TV drama), Masterchef (TV light entertainment), The Charlotte Church Show (TV light entertainment).

Adam Zoltowski Mobile 07968-091883

PROPERTYMASTERS

John Allenby 01438-350415 Mobile 07774-844231
From Time To Time (feature), Into The Storm (TV film), Sahara (feature).

Laurence Archer Mobile 07815-088420
Jonathan Creek (TV drama), Extras (TV comedy drama), Love Soup (TV drama).

Kenneth Augustin   020-7625 9376 Mobile 07860-315816
Fax 020-7625 9376
Doc Martin (TV drama), Twentyfour: Seven (feature).

Gari Bacon   01438-311294 Mobile 07984-603393
Hotel Babylon (TV drama), Silent Witness (TV drama), Wall Of
Silence (TV drama).

Alan Bailey   01483-579072 Mobile 07831-544368
London Boulevard (feature), Love In The Time Of Cholera (feature),
Munich (feature).

Simon Bailey   Mobile 07769-731000
Moon (feature), This Is England (feature), Joe's Palace (TV drama).

David Balfour   Mobile 07774-787039
Sweeney Todd (feature), Prince Of Persia (feature), The Da Vinci
Code (feature).

Colin Bayliss   01296-655784 Mobile 07947-125847
Fax 01296-655784
28 Weeks Later (feature), Bleak House (TV drama), Sunshine
(feature).

Andy Beales   Mobile 07836-588686 Fax 020-8960 4036
Benidorm (TV comedy drama), The Catherine Tate Show (TV light
entertainment), Saxondale (TV comedy drama).

Patrick Begley   023-8055 0086 Mobile 07979-095844
Doctor Who (TV drama), Father Ted (TV comedy drama), In Deep
(TV drama).

Michael Betts   0113-295 9219 Mobile 07962-260109
The Kid (feature), Hustle (TV drama), Brideshead Revisited (feature)
(Propertyman).

Bruce Bigg   01895-235085 Mobile 07785-713576
Fax 01895-237039
David Cronenberg Untitled 2006 (feature), The Young Victoria
(feature), Me & Orson Welles (feature).

Nick Bowering   020-7639 5677 Mobile 07889-730866
BE 01727-841177 Fax 020-7639 5677

Paul Bradburn   020-8897 6630 Mobile 07976-283711
Ladies In Lavender (feature), The Descent (feature), Spirit Trap
(feature).

Colin Bradbury   01489-582849 Mobile 07831-239824
Minder (TV drama), Afterlife (TV drama), New Tricks (TV drama).

Chris Brett   01737-215056 Mobile 07973-538065
Fax 01737-215056

John Brown   0121-476 6438 Mobile 07802-433611
Fax 0121-475 2794
Lark Rise To Candleford (TV drama), A Boy Called Dad (feature),
Sunshine (feature).

Mark Burgess   01494-464517 Mobile 07867-533000
BFF (commercial), Lloyds TSB (commercial), Half Broken Things (TV
drama).

Christopher Burton   Mobile 07796-252010
The One Show (TV magazine), Ant & Dec's Saturday Night (TV light
entertainment), This Morning (TV magazine).

Paul Carter   020-8923 8786 Mobile 07771-616652
Freefall (TV drama), Dive (TV drama), Daughters (TV drama).

Craig Cheeseman   Mobile 07973-282971
Chat Room (feature), Skins (TV drama), Alien Vs Predator
(feature).

R. "Chipz" Chipping   Mobile 07837-815432
Love Me Still (feature), Come Dine With Me (ident).

John Chisholm   Mobile 07941-087446
Death Wish (feature), Love & Bullets (feature), A View To A Kill
(feature).

John Condron   0161-799 7460 Mobile 07764-687865
Fax 0161-799 6671
Fiona's Story (TV drama), Lost In Austen (TV drama), The Roman
Mysteries (TV childrens).

Brian Cornish   01767-631351 Mobile 07976-203661
EastEnders (promo), Holby City (TV drama), Casualty (TV drama).

Noel Cowell   023-8024 3838 Mobile 07973-156086
Creation (feature), Lesbian Vampire Killers (feature), Alien Vs
Predator (feature).

David Crawford   01752-330491 Mobile 07702-878365
Jenny's Dream (TV drama), Parting Shots (feature), Dinotopia (TV
drama).

Chris Cull   Mobile 07976-955728
Dorian Gray (feature), Inkheart (feature), Franklyn (feature).

Trevor Daniels   01932-821119 Mobile 07973-839329
Jane Eyre (feature), Filth: The Mary Whitehouse Story (TV drama),
Oliver Twist (feature).

Gary P Dawson   01923-839990 Mobile 07956-255348
Robin Hood (feature).

Roy Dawson   01243-672963 Mobile 07860-294757
Always & Everyone (TV drama), Trial & Retribution (TV drama), Fire
Boy (TV film).

Paul de Csernatony   01784-248552 Mobile 07831-233000
Harry & Paul (TV light entertainment), The Omid Djalili Show (TV
light entertainment), Pulling (TV comedy drama).

Marc Dillon   020-7435 1276 Mobile 07963-833182
The Detectives (TV light entertainment), Women In Love (TV film),
Thunderbirds (feature).

Ron Downing   +52 33 3617 6438
The Great Raid (feature), Somersby (feature), Last Of The Mohicans
(feature).

Simon Drew   020-8993 6653 Mobile 07980-898428
Above Suspicion (TV drama), Nineteen Eighty (TV film), Trial &
Retribution (TV drama).

Paul Emerson   01276-670198 Mobile 07802-265264
Lewis (TV drama), He Kills Coppers (TV drama), Pride & Prejudice
(feature).

Gordon Fitzgerald   0141-334 6466 Mobile 07850-106357
Fax 0141-334 6466
The Dark Is Rising (feature), 1408 (feature), Amazing Grace
(feature).

Mike Fowlie   01296-489228 Mobile 07714-719553
The Ten Commandments (TV film), Barry Lyndon (feature), Shout At
The Devil (feature).

Barry Gibbs   01508-536652 Mobile 07970-171160
Inception (feature), Quantum Of Solace (feature), The Golden
Compass (feature).

Muffin Green   01255-503303 Mobile 07967-136056
Centurion (feature), The Eagle Of The Ninth (feature), The Duchess
(feature).

John Greenham   020-8950 1645 Mobile 07976-164947
Fax 020-8950 4344
My Worst Week (TV light entertainment), Holby City (TV drama),
EastEnders (promo).

Duncan Griffiths   01924-450482 Mobile 07970-023916
Albert's Memorial (TV drama), Diamond Geezer (TV drama), A Touch
Of Frost (TV drama).

Peter Hallam   01959-522274 Mobile 07979-907979
Nanny McPhee & The Big Bang (feature), Brick Lane (feature),
Rendition (feature).

Russell Hanson   020-8408 1484 Mobile 07973-146693
BE 01727-841177

Geoffrey Hartman   01932-240768 BE 01727-841177
Oliver (feature), The Life Of Brian (feature), The Sea Wolves
(feature).

Tony Henshaw   0161-682 3406 Mobile 07930-555714
Fax 0161-682 3406
Casualty 1909 (TV drama), Casualty 1907 (TV drama), The 39 Steps
(TV film).

Richard Hindson   0121-354 5045 Mobile 07802-936767
Fax 0121-354 5045
Above Suspicion (TV drama), Lark Rise To Candleford (TV drama),
Trial & Retribution (TV drama).

Malcolm Holt   020-8689 6083 Mobile 07973-392669
Primeval (TV drama), Silent Witness (TV drama), Parents Of The
Band (TV comedy drama).

Ray Holt   01923-675846 Mobile 07850-373248
Fax 01923-675846
Luther (TV drama), Misfits (TV comedy drama).

Dean Humphrey   020-7405 0380 Mobile 07860-240725
Fax 020-7405 0380
Star Stories (TV light entertainment), Little Britain (tour), Green
Wing (TV comedy drama).

Doug Irvine   023-8077 0696 Mobile 07775-656563
Fax 023-8077 0696
Place Of Execution (TV drama), Greenfingers (feature), The Glass
(TV drama).

Paul Jefferies   01869-277606 Mobile 07767-667664
BE 01727-841177

Adrian Jendrosz   +34 62 070 1920 Mobile 07973-428539
EXEC 01753-646677
Guinness (commercial), John Smith's (commercial), Fosters
(commercial).

Maurice Jones   01753-859623 Mobile 07974-691963
Fax 01753-859623
Charlie & The Chocolate Factory (feature) (blue screen), Nouvelle
France (feature), The Queen's Sister (TV drama).

Robert Judd   Mobile 07941-954533
Street Dance (feature), Footballers' Wives - Extra Time (TV
drama).

Paul Kearney   023-8081 1754 Mobile 07711-256362
Midsomer Murders (TV drama), Ultimate Force (TV drama), Fat
Friends (TV drama).

Richard Kelloway   Mobile 07831-719480
Love In A Cold Climate (TV drama).

John Knight   0141-942 2249 Mobile 07885-238994
Hope Springs (TV drama), New Town Killers (feature), Elizabeth
(feature).

Andy Leach   020-8789 2440 Mobile 07956-366573
Fax 020-8789 2440
Outnumbered (TV comedy drama), Dead Ringers (TV comedy), The
Worst Week Of My Life (TV comedy drama).

Judy Lewis   Mobile 07876-162589

Brian Lofthouse   020-8203 7718 Mobile 07976-464112
Fax 020-7607 5928
The Constant Gardener (feature), Once Upon A Time In The Midlands (feature), Helen West (TV drama).

Ben Lofts   Mobile 07949-253050
The Green Green Grass (TV comedy drama), Hustle (TV drama), Water's Rising (feature) (Standby Art Director).

Mike Malik   01443-225924 Mobile 07850-447138
Fax 01443-225924
0-800-Love (feature), The Shooting Of Thomas Hurndall (TV drama), The Hurt Locker (feature).

Joe Malone   Mobile 07802-265260
Garrow's Law (TV drama), Psychoville (TV comedy drama), Life On Mars (TV drama).

Jim Marlow   01255-812666 Mobile 07850-139518
Marks & Spencer (commercial), Asda (commercial), Tesco (commercial).

Toby Marrow   Mobile 07949-778639
The Inbetweeners (TV comedy drama), Sex & Drugs & Rock & Roll (feature).

Adam McCreight   Mobile 07976-850480
The Heavy (feature), Jiro (feature).

Maxie McDonald   020-8953 8199 Mobile 07710-328693
Mamma Mia! (feature), Gladiator (feature), Saving Private Ryan (feature).

Ray McNeill   Mobile 07973-616109
Going Postal (TV film), Solomon Kane (feature), The Colour Of Magic (TV film).

Dave Merchant   020-8422 2509 Mobile 07776-381222
Food Of Love (feature).

Laurie Miller   020-8398 4615 Mobile 07831-709663
The Tenant Of Wildfell Hall (TV drama), Persuasion (feature), Cold Comfort Farm (TV film).

Paul Miller   01491-871508 Mobile 07774-808756

John Mills   01737-361664 Mobile 07850-487652

Richard Mills   01442-878374 Mobile 07885-676727
Fax 01442-878374
United 93 (feature), Vera Drake (feature), Revolver (feature).

Simon Morrissey   020-7221 5575 Mobile 07768-864658
Fax 020-7221 5575
Control (feature), Beowulf & Grendel (feature), Lock Stock & Two Smoking Barrels (feature).

Rory O'Connor   0113-216 9672 Mobile 07885-464627
At Home With The Braithwaites (TV drama), Bodies (TV drama).

Bob Orr   0131-445 2050 Mobile 07778-062106
The Mark Of Cain (feature), Lost In Austen (TV drama), Britz (TV drama).

Steve Parnell   Mobile 07970-887639
Run Fat Boy Run (feature).

Clive Pegg   Mobile 07956-365307

Ray Perry   01908-640165 Mobile 07836-702624
City Of Ember (feature), Doom (feature), The Brothers Grimm (feature).

Tom Pleydell-Pearce   0117-924 4939 Mobile 07973-135940
Fax 0117-924 4939
Finding Neverland (feature), Iris (feature), Dirty Pretty Things (feature).

Allen Polley   01737-841086 Mobile 07778-524784
The Queen (feature), Miss Potter (feature), The Bourne Ultimatum (feature).

Mike Povey   0117-961 3480 Mobile 07831-836789
Submerged (feature), Last Orders (feature), The Grid (TV drama).

Mike Power   0117-944 6459 Mobile 07802-822688
Cranford (TV drama), Foyle's War (TV drama), The Children (feature).

Craig Price   Mobile 07973-194742
Egypt (TV drama doc), The Thick Of It (TV comedy drama), The Chatterley Affair (TV drama).

Simon Price   0117-908 0884 Mobile 07770-688889
Dead Clever (TV film), Wired (TV drama), The Street (TV drama).

Tony Price   01727-866761 Mobile 07778-179990
EXEC 01753-646677 Fax 01727-866761

Graeme Purdy   01442-264132 Mobile 07836-778262
Black Hawk Down (feature), Gladiator (feature), Kingdom Of Heaven (feature).

Steven Register   Mobile 07712-048593
Pandorum (feature), RocknRolla (feature), Incendiary (feature).

Dave Reilly   01932-561512 Mobile 07778-476531
Fax 01932-561512
Secret Diary Of A Call Girl (TV drama), The Walker (feature), Mr Eleven (TV comedy drama).

Mike Roberts   01484-861399 Mobile 07850-439332
Fax 01484-861399
Stig Of The Dump (TV childrens), In Denial Of Murder (TV drama), This Little Life (TV film).

Ewan Robertson   Mobile 07867-593598
Fax 020-8802 4626
Micro Men (TV drama), Trinity (feature), Magic Boys (feature).

Scott Rogers   020-8866 7206 Mobile 07968-970208
Fax 020-8866 7206
City Of Vice (TV drama), Wild Target (feature), A Harlot's Progress (TV drama).

Anthony Rycyk   01704-501469 Mobile 07782-348594
Where The Heart Is (TV drama), O Jerusalem (feature), My Kingdom (feature).

Nigel Salter   0117-942 3535 Mobile 07850-050100
I Could Never Be Your Woman (feature), The Libertine (feature), Dead Fish (feature).

Peter Saunders   01406-370013 Mobile 07802-273430

Jason Scott   Mobile 07950-294395
Shooting Stars (TV light entertainment), Titty Bang Bang (TV light entertainment), Bad Girls (TV drama).

Steve Short   01905-621296 Mobile 07831-470432
EXEC 01753-646677 Fax 01905-621296
Walkers Crisps (commercial), Crunchy Nut Cornflakes (commercial), John Smith's (commercial).

Paul Smith   01285-771285 Mobile 07850-198186
Waking The Dead (TV drama), The Queen's Nose (TV childrens), Skins (TV drama).

Ray Spencer   01273-550462 Mobile 07860-441022
BE 01727-841177

David Springer Horrill   Mobile 07778-147681
St Trinian's (feature), Hot Fuzz (feature), The Other Boleyn Girl (feature).

Graham Stickley   01784-450452 Mobile 07711-265430
Fax 01784-450452
Behaving Badly (TV drama), Spitting Image (TV light entertainment), Covington Cross (TV drama).

Terry Tague   01840-213030 Mobile 07771-606947
Split Second (feature), Tom's Midnight Garden (TV film), Treasure Island (Trilogy).

Ty Teiger   020-8579 9315 Mobile 07768-012766
Wanted (feature), The Wolfman (feature), Nine (feature).

Nick Thomas   01656-865515 Mobile 07850-568216
Fax 01656-865515
Mr Nice (feature), Dagenham Girls (feature), 28 Weeks Later (feature).

Colin Thurston   01753-887910 Mobile 07957-929834
Beverly Hills Chihuahua (feature), Dragonball (feature), Vantage Point (feature).

Nick Turnbull   020-8540 6721 Mobile 07710-043405
BE 01727-841177 Fax 020-8540 6721
Doomsday (feature), Star Wars: Episode II - Attack Of The Clones (feature), Colditz (TV drama).

Andie Vining   01225-466588 Mobile 07771-712399
Fax 01225-466588
Benidorm (TV comedy drama), The IT Crowd (TV comedy drama), Little Britain (tour).

Nick Walker   020-7976 6456 Mobile 07976-329039
Enid (TV drama), Margot (TV drama), Fanny Hill (TV drama).

Keith Warwick   01760-440632 Mobile 07836-355513
Fax 01760-440632
Kingdom (TV drama), Little Britain (tour) (Propertyman), Green Wing (TV comedy drama) (Propertyman).

Gary Watson   01707-393267 Mobile 07774-964567
Fax 01707-393267
Spooks (TV drama), Law & Order (TV drama), Kingdom (TV drama).

Matt Wells   Mobile 07906-475599
Bunny & The Bull (feature), The Unloved (feature), Oranges & Sunshine (feature).

Terry Wells Snr   01234-831975 Mobile 07831-188641
Fax 01234-831975
Robin Hood (feature), Green Zone (feature), American Gangster (feature).

Stephen Wheeler   01932-229222 Mobile 07768-362132
Harry Brown (feature), Little Dorrit (TV drama), Sense & Sensibility (feature).

Arthur Wicks   01371-859831 Mobile 07836-677194
Fax 01371-859831
W.E. (feature), London Boulevard (feature), Shanghai (feature).

Barry Wilkinson   020-8440 4961 Mobile 07860-465820
Harry Potter & The Deathly Hallows (feature), Harry Potter & The Half-Blood Prince (feature), Harry Potter & The Order Of The Phoenix (feature).

Jamie Wilkinson   020-8449 3023 Mobile 07887-647984
John Carter Of Mars (feature), Clash Of The Titans (feature), The Dark Knight (feature).

Dennis Wiseman   020-8529 9899 Mobile 07785-940020
Sherlock Holmes (feature), Atonement (feature), Starter For Ten (feature).

Jason Wood   01273-231559 Mobile 07973-272355
Merlin (TV drama), Demons (TV drama), Albatross (feature).

Terry Wood   020-8574 1697 Mobile 07976-255974
Fax 020-8574 1697
Robin Hood (feature), Brideshead Revisited (feature), The Upside Of Anger (feature).

Tim Youngman   Mobile 07920-129221
Gavin & Stacey (TV comedy drama), Red Dwarf (TV comedy drama), Phoenix Nights (TV drama).

PROPERTYMEN

Brian Aldridge   01753-526438 Mobile 07786-121288
Batman Begins (feature), Charlie & The Chocolate Factory (feature), Ladies In Lavender (feature).

Keith Amey   01454-633157 Mobile 07966-273795
The Street (TV drama), Lark Rise To Candleford (TV drama), Shameless (TV drama).

Barry Arnold   020-8386 1691 Mobile 07790-816602
Harry Potter & The Deathly Hallows (feature), Kick-Ass (feature), Robin Hood (feature).

Chris Arnold   Mobile 07941-836868
Above Suspicion (TV drama), The Wolfman (feature), Shanghai (feature).

Gerry Atkinson   01753-832211 Mobile 07855-303803
An Education (feature), Quantum Of Solace (feature), Shanghai (feature).

Lawrie Ayres   01737-769963 Mobile 07768-848961
Fax 01737-218378
Harry Potter & The Goblet Of Fire (feature), Cold Mountain (feature), Band Of Brothers (TV drama).

Will Ayres   Mobile 07725-165719
Clash Of The Titans (feature) (Greensman), Creation (feature), The Wolfman (feature) (Greensman).

Ken Bacon   0115-923 3798 Mobile 07702-256180
Charlie & The Chocolate Factory (feature), Troy (feature), Tomb Raider II (feature).

Scott Bailey   01483-579072
London Boulevard (feature).

Eddie Baker   020-8953 5296 Mobile 07802-748612
Robin Hood (feature), Stardust (feature), Phantom Of The Opera (feature).

Mike Bartlett   01753-865722 Mobile 07956-500468
Money (TV drama), Trial & Retribution (TV drama), Nineteen Eighty (TV film).

Roy Beeston   01603-413862 Mobile 07710-620633
Malice In Wonderland (feature), Born Romantic (feature), All The King's Men (feature).

Mat Bergel   020-8698 0340 Mobile 07778-910062
Robin Hood (feature) (2nd unit), Prince Of Persia (feature), Blitz (feature).

Peter Bigg   01628-526695 Mobile 07778-281038
The Young Victoria (feature), Eastern Promises (feature), Gladiator (feature).

Paul Biggs   029-2040 4973 Mobile 07970-474046
Solomon & Gaenor (feature), A Way Of Life (feature), Bhaji On The Beach (feature).

Brian Bird   Mobile 07771-752711
Clash Of The Titans (feature), Green Zone (feature), The Duchess (feature).

Simon Blackmore   0117-942 8184 Mobile 07774-240887
These Foolish Things (feature), The Office (TV comedy drama) (Propertymaster), Not Going Out (TV comedy drama) (Propertymaster).

Mike Booys   01525-872228 Mobile 07976-659190
Spooks (TV drama), Pride & Prejudice (feature), Waking The Dead (TV drama).

Alex Boswell   01276-476277 Mobile 07711-142456
Quantum Of Solace (feature), The Duchess (feature), The Golden Compass (feature).

John Botton   020-8870 5597 Mobile 07885-611161
Quantum Of Solace (feature), Robin Hood (feature).

Alan Briant   020-8224 5021 Mobile 07767-253522
Fax 020-8224 8672
Shanghai (feature), Emma (feature), Glorious 39 (feature).

James Brooker   Mobile 07787-766389
The Letters (feature), No Ordinary Trifle (feature), Round Ireland With A Fridge (feature).

Giles Brown   020-8811 1901 Mobile 07905-348374
St Trinian's (feature), Desperate Romantics (TV drama), Hippie Hippie Shake (feature).

Haydn Buckingham-Jones   Mobile 07802-208881
Ashes To Ashes (TV drama), Spooks (TV drama), The Princess & The Warrior (feature).

Paul Bufton   020-8207 1347 Mobile 07956-806286
Robin Hood (feature), Mamma Mia! (feature), Little Dorrit (TV drama).

Simon Buret   020-8337 0522 Mobile 07792-648760
Midsomer Murders (TV drama), The Ghost (feature), Cemetery Junction (feature).

Alfie Burgess   01932-571620 Mobile 07973-491861
And When Did You Last See Your Father? (feature), The Upside Of Anger (feature), Swept Away (feature).

Damian Butlin   Mobile 07776-130152
Foyle's War (TV drama), Wild Child (feature), The Other Man (feature).

Eddie Campbell   020-8207 1681 Mobile 07973-801212
Spooks (TV drama), Ashes To Ashes (TV drama), Hornblower (TV drama).

Tristan Carlise-Kitz   020-8560 8920
Mobile 07970-615598
Robin Hood (feature), Prince Of Persia (feature), Inkheart (feature).

Olly Cassidy   0131-623 5682 Mobile 07766-807327
Waybuloo (TV childrens), New Town Killers (feature).

Graham Chalk   Mobile 07866-295915
Green Zone (feature), The Golden Compass (feature), The Queen (feature).

Barry Chapman   020-8581 4858 Mobile 07977-132315
Harry Brown (feature), Chat Room (feature), Sense & Sensibility (feature).

Richard Cheal   Mobile 07770-870548
John Carter Of Mars (feature).

Bruce Cheesman   01438-216699 Mobile 07909-694006
Harry Potter & The Goblet Of Fire (feature), Harry Potter & The Prisoner Of Azkaban (feature), Band Of Brothers (TV drama).

David Cheesman   Mobile 07767-324004
Prince Of Persia (feature), Green Zone (feature), Sweeney Todd (feature).

Paul Cheesman   01727-865756 Mobile 07957-146748
Harry Potter & The Deathly Hallows (feature), Harry Potter & The Half-Blood Prince (feature), Harry Potter & The Goblet Of Fire (feature).

David Chisholm   Mobile 07976-443625
Tamara Drewe (feature), Get Him To The Greek (feature), Kick-Ass (feature).

Matt Chisholm   0118-973 2557 Mobile 07941-228447
Harry Potter & The Half-Blood Prince (feature), Harry Potter & The Prisoner Of Azkaban (feature), Stage Beauty (feature).

Dave Clarke   020-8979 2060 Mobile 07984-011223
Out Of Africa (feature), Full Metal Jacket (feature), Hear My Song (feature).

Simon Clifft   020-8289 2412 Mobile 07889-074718
AD 020-7428 0500
Hitchhiker's Guide To The Galaxy (feature), The Calcium Kid (feature).

Marlon Cole   020-7386 7319 Mobile 07710-472699
Your Highness (feature), Prince Of Persia (feature), Sweeney Todd (feature).

Stephen Conway   01438-228993 Mobile 07884-010291
Sherlock Holmes (feature), Mamma Mia! (feature), The Magic Flute (feature).

Kelvin Cook   Mobile 07976-442652
Tamara Drewe (feature), Get Him To The Greek (feature), Prince Of Persia (feature).

Stan Cook   Mobile 07810-442005
Alice In Wonderland (feature), The Dark Knight (feature), Green Zone (feature).

Matt Cooke   Mobile 07958-596014
Harry Potter & The Deathly Hallows (feature), Harry Potter & The Half-Blood Prince (feature), Harry Potter & The Goblet Of Fire (feature).

Sean Michael Cuddy   020-8445 7768
Mobile 07801-702434
Woody Allan's Summer Project (feature), Munich (feature), Love In The Time Of Cholera (feature).

Christopher Cutler   01275-791501 Mobile 07976-380232
The Libertine (feature), Teachers (TV drama), Afterlife (TV drama).

Paul Cutler   020-8579 6770 Mobile 07973-601436
Fax 020-8579 6770
Secrets & Lies (feature), Institute Benjamenta (feature).

Ged Dale   01753-645003 Mobile 07798-697525
Fax 01753-645003
The Young Victoria (feature), Hitchhiker's Guide To The Galaxy (feature), The Bourne Ultimatum (feature).

Stuart Daniels   01932-821119 Mobile 07950-432846
Fax 01932-821119
Cemetery Junction (feature), My Almost Famous Family (TV comedy drama), Sex Drugs & Rock 'n' Chips (TV comedy drama).

John Dashfield   01622-880458 Mobile 07831-396262
Holby Blue (TV drama), The Basil Brush Show (TV childrens), After Thomas (TV drama).

Mark Daubney   020-8332 9670 Mobile 07850-008324
Charlie & The Chocolate Factory (feature).

Jamie Davidson   01691-610329 Mobile 07775-655955
Doctor Who (TV drama), Perfectly Frank (TV drama), Holby City (TV drama).

Quentin Davies   01932-885787 Mobile 07958-547184
Casino Royale (feature), The Boat That Rocked (feature), Clash Of The Titans (feature).

Jerry Davis   01286-872264 Mobile 07774-282604
Loch Ness (feature), B-Monkey (feature), Prince Valiant (feature).

Garry D Dawson   Mobile 07710-356161
Little Dorrit (TV drama), Is There Anybody There? (feature), Green Street (feature).

Gary S Dawson   01923-839990 Mobile 07958-778584
Robin Hood (feature), Body Of Lies (feature), Prince Of Persia (feature).

Kevin Day   020-8883 0940 Mobile 07956-260400
Is There Anybody There? (feature), The Day (feature), Hot Fuzz (feature).

Noel Deegan   020-8715 6446 Mobile 07710-507490
Wuthering Heights (feature), Cemetery Junction (feature), Oliver Twist (feature).

Joe Dipple   01727-823375 Mobile 07768-801603
Robin Hood (feature), Green Zone (feature), Body Of Lies (feature).

Jonathan Downing   Mobile 07951-721519
Clash Of The Titans (feature), Green Zone (feature), The Bourne Ultimatum (feature).

Patrick Dunne   01992-503041 Mobile 07866-493851
Mutual Friends (TV drama), 100 Years Of Mills & Boon (TV doc), Walter's War (TV drama).

Colin Ellis   Mobile 07976-735405
The Golden Compass (feature), Bridget Jones's Diary II (feature), Little Voice (feature).

Francis Ewen   020-8773 9521 Mobile 07958-578378
Fax 020-8773 9521
The Inspector Lynley Mysteries (TV drama), The Green Green Grass (TV comedy drama), Primeval (TV drama).

Dave Fisher   Mobile 07867-942946
1408 (feature), Derailed (feature), Thunderbirds (feature).

Natalie Fitzgerald   01344-449824 Mobile 07939-056881
Phantom Of The Opera (feature), Dinotopia (TV drama), The Importance Of Being Earnest (feature).

Kevin Fleet   0117-932 4048 Mobile 07976-611464
Foyle's War (TV drama).

Michael Fleming   Mobile 07956-599355
The Young Victoria (feature), Me & Orson Welles (feature), The Dark Knight (feature).

Andy Forrest   020-8690 8724 Mobile 07977-410387
Creation (feature), Chat Room (feature), Vera Drake (feature).

Matt Foster   020-8749 9020 Mobile 07973-362585
Fax 020-8749 9020
Gulliver's Travels (feature), The Wolfman (feature), Nine (feature).

Hugh Fottrell   020-8995 5974 Mobile 07956-824628
Kingdom Of Heaven (feature), First Daughter (feature), Rough Footage (feature).

John Fox   020-8386 1486 Mobile 07956-828627
Paul Carter Of Mars (feature), Clash Of The Titans (feature), Green Zone (feature).

Pip Fox   Mobile 07879-690433
The Dark Knight (feature), Green Zone (feature), Clash Of The Titans (feature).

Mark Fruin   020-7813 1143 Mobile 07850-660424
Fax 020-7813 1143
W.E. (feature), Hotel Babylon (TV drama), London Boulevard (feature).

Anthony Fryer   Mobile 07958-487606
How To Lose Friends & Alienate People (feature), Band Of Brothers (TV drama), Lorna Doone (TV film).

Jack Garwood   Mobile 07799-730714
Clash Of The Titans (feature), The Dark Knight (feature), The Mummy Returns (feature).

Barry Gates   01395-442912 Mobile 07970-461994
Sahara (feature), Wimbledon (feature), Band Of Brothers (TV drama).

Mark Geeson   01932-789420 Mobile 07970-668579
Green Zone (feature), Sex & The City 2 (feature), Prince Of Persia (feature).

Alan Stuart Gipp   020-8332 2042 Mobile 07967-390213
Fax 020-8332 2042

Douglas Glen   Mobile 07831-877789
Mistress Of Spices (feature), The Last Legion (feature), Elizabeth The Virgin Queen (TV drama).

PROPERTYMEN

Brad Godwin 020-8953 6834 Mobile 07989-386588
Lewis (TV drama), Kingdom (TV drama), Fanny Hill (TV drama).

Max Grant 023-8078 3014 Mobile 07899-985753
Murderland (TV drama), New Tricks (TV drama), Jonathan Creek (TV drama).

Colin Gray Mobile 07774-259405
Agent Cody Banks II (feature), Nanny McPhee (feature), Gladiator (feature).

Brian Green 01268-782227 Mobile 07778-835661
Law & Order (TV drama), Doc Martin (TV drama), Judge John Deed (TV drama).

Arthur Griggs Mobile 07718-224779
Tomb Raider (feature), Alfie (feature), The Dark Knight (feature).

Steve Hammick Mobile 07831-430595
Quantum Of Solace (feature) (Action Vehicle Driver), Harry Brown (feature), Hippie Hippie Shake (feature).

Shane Harford Mobile 07932-542293
Shanghai (feature), The Colour Of Magic (TV film), The Oxford Murders (feature).

William Hargreaves 01344-457285 Mobile 07885-737482
The Golden Compass (feature), Gladiator (feature), About A Boy (feature).

Samantha Harley Mobile 07740-365714
Pulling (TV comedy drama), Hyperdrive (TV comedy drama), The Thick Of It (TV comedy drama).

Andy Harris 023-8047 3097 Mobile 07802-790203
Fax 023-8047 3097
Torchwood (TV drama), New Tricks (TV drama), Phantom Of The Opera (feature).

David Hayden 0191-284 6598 Mobile 07702-203818
Shameless (TV drama), Moving Wallpaper (TV drama), Mansfield Park (TV film).

Justin Hayzelden 01932-349115 Mobile 07966-274223
Sold (TV drama), Children Of Men (feature), Mutual Friends (TV drama).

Bernard Hearn 01483-222309 Mobile 07803-129789
Nine (feature), The Wolfman (feature), Wanted (feature).

Paul Hearn Mobile 07768-174874
The Wolfman (feature), Fanny Hill (TV drama), Stardust (feature).

Mike Hennessey 0161-720 7446 Mobile 07976-523742
Sparkle (feature), Sunshine (feature), The Diary Of Anne Frank (TV drama).

Vincent Henshaw 01457-829193 Mobile 07957-552281
Casualty 1909 (TV drama), The 39 Steps (TV film), Housewife 49 (TV drama).

Kevin Herbert 01932-562105 Mobile 07802-482886
Fax 01932-562105
Son Of Rambow (feature), Harry Potter & The Half-Blood Prince (feature), I Want Candy (feature).

Ron Higgins 01727-841899 Mobile 07943-259503

Rob Hill 01923-821890 Mobile 07973-324388
Your Highness (feature), Prince Of Persia (feature), Sweeney Todd (feature).

Dennis Hopperton 01749-673170 Mobile 07831-267754
Fax 01749-671466
Robin Hood (feature), Munich (feature), Kingdom Of Heaven (feature).

Jason Hopperton 01483-702109 Mobile 07887-587207
Gulliver's Travels (feature), Quantum Of Solace (feature), The Young Victoria (feature).

Barry Howard-Clarke 020-8401 6270
Mobile 07932-531311
Mistresses (TV drama), Cemetery Junction (feature), Jonathan Creek (TV drama).

Paul Humbles 01923-491933 Mobile 07775-913080
Batman Begins (feature), Die Another Day (feature), The Queen (feature).

Derek Ixer 020-8207 3524 Mobile 07850-660428
Robin Hood (feature), Green Zone (feature), Stardust (feature).

Gary Ixer 020-8440 2972 Mobile 07711-032756
Harry Potter & The Goblet Of Fire (feature), Harry Potter & The Order Of The Phoenix (feature), Titanic (feature).

Charlie Johnson 01488-72406 Mobile 07973-794018
Fax 01488-72406
Bouquet Of Barbed Wire (TV drama), Stuart: A Life Backwards (TV drama), Tess Of The D'Urbervilles (TV drama).

Martin Kane Mobile 07956-998908
The Wolfman (feature), Clash Of The Titans (feature), Creation (feature).

Scott Keery 0141-424 3431 Mobile 07968-248612
Fax 0141-424 3431
Sweeney Todd (feature), The Da Vinci Code (feature), Prince Of Persia (feature).

Rick Kenton   01245-260014   Mobile 07979-681502
Fax 01245-260014
London Bridge (TV drama) (Propertymaster), Interview With The Vampire (feature), Jane Eyre (feature).

Mark Kimber   020-8207 2677   Mobile 07931-740384
Robin Hood (feature), Body Of Lies (feature), Stardust (feature).

Martin Kingsley   01895-636463   Mobile 07773-188035
Gulliver's Travels (feature), Nine (feature), The Wolfman (feature).

Barry Kirkham   0161-794 2751   Mobile 07832-288973
Wuthering Heights (feature), Mistresses (TV drama), Jekyll (TV drama).

Paul Lambie   Mobile 07796-445126
The Last Word (feature), Book Of Blood (feature), Doomsday (feature).

Dougie Lankston   020-8200 3632   Mobile 07973-271801
Agent Cody Banks II (feature), Bright Young Things (feature), Shackleton (TV drama).

Jack Lee   0161-737 0844   Mobile 07850-551469
Fax 0161-737 0844
Shameless (TV drama), The Royal (TV drama), Wire In The Blood (TV drama).

Shay Leonard   020-7485 3432   Mobile 07966-166460
Fax 020-7485 3432
Hippie Hippie Shake (feature), Hot Fuzz (feature), Shaun Of The Dead (feature).

Neil Levy   029-2071 1373   Mobile 07778-800308
I Want You (feature), Downtime (feature).

Joe Linfield   Mobile 07801-334222
Merlin (TV drama), Albatross (feature).

Roy Linnett   01767-600029   Mobile 07889-998151
Fax 01767-600029
Holby City (TV drama), Wild West (TV drama), Wilde (feature).

Rob Macpherson   Mobile 07771-934389
Atonement (feature), Death Defying Acts (feature), The Other Man (feature).

Gary Martin   020-8866 1798   Mobile 07939-395249

Stephen McDonald   01438-350653   Mobile 07867-530340
Sahara (feature), What A Girl Wants (feature), Mission: Impossible (feature).

Karl McGovern   Mobile 07971-699087
The IT Crowd (TV comedy drama), Benidorm (TV comedy drama), The Mighty Boosh (TV light entertainment).

Colin McKenzie   Mobile 07958-660831
Britain's Got Talent (TV light entertainment), The X Factor (TV light entertainment), Primeval (TV drama).

Kieron McNamara   020-8386 7642   Mobile 07768-841301
Little Dorrit (TV drama), Miss Potter (feature), Gladiator (feature).

Paul McNamara   Mobile 07855-099653
The Acid House Trilogy (feature), Trainspotting (feature), Mission: Impossible II (feature).

Paul Michel   01737-279016   Mobile 07887-934434
Loser (TV drama), Ashes To Ashes (TV drama), Spooks (TV drama).

David Midson   01923-857376   Mobile 07956-528143
Fax 01923-469455
Prince Of Persia (feature), Hellboy 2: The Golden Army (feature), Reign Of Fire (feature).

Nick Milner   01494-473137   Mobile 07712-780627
Robin Hood (feature), Cold Mountain (feature), Man On Fire (feature).

Campbell Mitchell   0141-946 6686   Mobile 07973-890392
Foyle's War (TV drama), The Other Man (feature), Cherie (feature).

Paul Mitchell   0161-682 0787   Mobile 07712-366914
Casualty 1907 (TV drama), The 39 Steps (TV film), Casualty 1909 (TV drama).

John Moore   020-8995 6082   Mobile 07956-991695
Harry Potter & The Deathly Hallows (feature), Harry Potter & The Prisoner Of Azkaban (feature), Alfie (feature).

Neil Murrum   020-8579 0265   Mobile 07788-475812
Nine (feature), Gulliver's Travels (feature), The Wolfman (feature).

Colin Mutch   Mobile 07970-714492
The Da Vinci Code (feature), The Bourne Ultimatum (feature), Green Zone (feature).

Ian Newton   Mobile 07976-160862
Spooks (TV drama), Law & Order (TV drama), Vanity Fair (feature).

Stuart Newton   020-8789 0910   Mobile 07976-274294
Fax 020-8789 0910
Silent Witness (TV drama), Waking The Dead (TV drama), Judge John Deed (TV drama).

Mitch Niclas   01865-331071   Mobile 07818-015231
Quantum Of Solace (feature), Speed Racer (feature), The Golden Compass (feature).

Gerald O'Connor   020-8953 0611 Mobile 07932-464516
Harry Potter & The Half-Blood Prince (feature), Harry Potter & The Prisoner Of Azkaban (feature), Band Of Brothers (TV drama).

Martin O'Loughlin   020-8861 0574 Mobile 07932-677938
Waking The Dead (TV drama), The Worst Week Of My Life (TV comedy drama), EastEnders (promo).

John Palmer   020-8449 8287 Mobile 07939-045658
Fax 020-8449 8287
Kick-Ass (feature), Harry Potter & The Deathly Hallows (feature), Tamara Drewe (feature).

Kenny Palmer   023-8044 4411 Mobile 07973-617221
New Tricks (TV drama), Murderland (TV drama), Place Of Execution (TV drama).

Mark Papworth   01737-240301 Mobile 07973-833071
RocknRolla (feature), The Line Of Beauty (TV drama), Fallen Angel (TV drama).

Darryl Paterson   020-8542 7199 Mobile 07831-262337
Quantum Of Solace (feature), The Golden Compass (feature), Hannibal Rising (feature).

Steven Payne   01344-457495 Mobile 07747-694492
Robin Hood (feature), Agora (feature), The Nutcracker (ballet).

Wesley Peppiatt   01403-783460 Mobile 07860-672998
BE 01727-841177
John Carter Of Mars (feature), Clash Of The Titans (feature), Quantum Of Solace (feature).

Carl Peters   Mobile 07779-473775
Quantum Of Solace (feature), The Golden Compass (feature), Bridget Jones's Diary II (feature).

Keith Pitt   01895-256155 Mobile 07748-943859
Star Wars: Episode I - The Phantom Menace (feature), Spy Game (feature), Alexander (feature).

Paul Pitts   020-8949 7450 Mobile 07753-612626
Party Animals (TV drama), Alien Autopsy (feature), Extras (TV comedy drama).

Adrian Platt   Mobile 07765-882371
Atonement (feature), The Boat That Rocked (feature), Sherlock Holmes (feature).

Neil Poley   Mobile 07905-694580
The Colour Of Magic (TV film), Bride & Prejudice (feature), Stormbreaker (feature).

Mickey Pugh   020-8953 2569 Mobile 07932-788470
Fax 020-8953 2569
Agora (feature), Hellboy 2: The Golden Army (feature), Love In The Time Of Cholera (feature).

Todd Quattromini   020-8446 3379 Mobile 07930-522661
Fax 020-8446 3379
Harry Potter & The Chamber Of Secrets (feature), Charlotte Gray (feature), Eyes Wide Shut (feature).

Darren Reynolds   Mobile 07799-073714
John Carter Of Mars (feature).

Mark Reynolds   Mobile 07931-390690
The Bourne Ultimatum (feature), Looking For Eric (feature), From Time To Time (feature).

Simon Riley   Mobile 07966-368017
Inkheart (feature), Vanity Fair (feature), Band Of Brothers (TV drama).

Ray Rose   01753-593661 Mobile 07702-243074
The Wolfman (feature), Batman Begins (feature), Children Of Men (feature).

Terry Royce   01707-655181 Mobile 07860-885284
Fax 01707-655181
From Time To Time (feature), The Wolfman (feature), The Pillars Of The Earth (TV drama).

Lucien Sands   Mobile 07813-480646
The Apprentice (TV reality), Re-uniting The Rubins (feature), Sainsbury's (commercial).

Don Santos   01422-847465 Mobile 07941-652784
United 93 (feature), Vera Drake (feature), Cranford (TV drama).

Kevin Scarrott   Mobile 07974-393501
The Damned United (feature), Moon (feature), This Is England (feature).

Bob Sherwood   01389-606939 Mobile 07831-497960
Robin Hood (feature), Agora (feature), 1408 (feature).

Christian Short   01923-267731 Mobile 07721-775775
Harry Potter & The Deathly Hallows (feature), Harry Potter & The Half-Blood Prince (feature), The Dark Knight (feature).

Dave Simpson   Mobile 07771-633134
Albatross (feature), Merlin (TV drama), Head Of The Class (TV drama).

Andrew Skipsey   020-8207 3373 Mobile 07970-808287
Clash Of The Titans (feature), Alice In Wonderland (feature), The Dark Knight (feature).

Jim Skipsey   020-8207 4174 Mobile 07710-201452
Wimbledon (feature), Harry Potter & The Goblet Of Fire (feature), Phantom Of The Opera (feature).

Alfie Smith   01895-237791 Mobile 07710-256255
The Wolfman (feature), Phantom Of The Opera (feature), Hamlet (feature).

Ted Stickley   023-9246 1289 Mobile 07768-453848
Sons & Lovers (TV drama), Phantom Of The Opera (feature), Hornblower (TV drama).

Warren Stickley   01256-765336 Mobile 07836-675192
Basic Instinct II (feature), Colour Me Kubrick (feature), Goal! II (feature).

Terry Stinson   020-7813 0760 Mobile 07958-441165
An Education (feature), The Kid (feature), Brideshead Revisited (feature).

Eric Strange   020-8953 2920 Mobile 07957-632878
Gulliver's Travels (feature), Nine (feature), The Wolfman (feature).

Nicolas Stubbings   01273-388284 Mobile 07981-032951
Rendition (feature), Outlaw (feature), Breaking & Entering (feature).

Danny Sullivan   020-8997 2953 Mobile 07719-813240
Fax 020-8997 2953
EastEnders (promo), The Bill (TV drama), Mother Love (TV drama).

Ron Sutcliffe   01932-227247 Mobile 07732-415175
Kick-Ass (feature), Primeval (TV drama), Persuasion (feature).

Micky Swift   01753-792874 Mobile 07710-499786
Clash Of The Titans (feature), City Of Ember (feature), The Wolfman (feature).

Bob Thorne   01525-383215 Mobile 07713-077293
Charles Dickens Little Diary (TV drama), Bad Girls (TV drama), Shanghai (feature).

Trevor Tilney   01372-725670 Mobile 07956-805384
Hustle (TV drama), Blackpool (TV drama), Silent Witness (TV drama).

Bradley Torbett   01582-461331 Mobile 07710-019360
Fax 01582-461331
Prince Of Persia (feature), The Wolfman (feature), Sweeney Todd (feature).

Jason Torbett   Mobile 07710-019373
Harry Potter & The Deathly Hallows (feature), Harry Potter & The Half-Blood Prince (feature), Sweeney Todd (feature).

Paul Turley   01884-841758 Mobile 07710-556386
Gladiator (feature), Victoria Wood Xmas Special (TV light entertainment), Magners Cider (commercial).

Paul Turner   01923-852715 Mobile 07751-414041
The Colour Of Magic (TV film), Miss Potter (feature), The Queen (feature).

Libby Uppington   Mobile 07968-243577
Sunshine (feature), The Boat That Rocked (feature), Last Chance Harvey (feature).

Mark Venn-McNeil   01397-712056 Mobile 07919-525405
Hotel Babylon (TV drama), Robin Hood (feature), Phantom Of The Opera (feature).

Bruce Vincent   01923-857868 Mobile 07939-286742
Fax 01923-857868
Secret Diary Of A Call Girl (TV drama), DFS (commercial), Hornby (commercial).

Lloyd Vincent   Mobile 07957-293652 Fax 01923-857868
It's A Wonderful Afterlife (feature), Sherlock Holmes (feature), Easy Virtue (feature).

Keith Vowles   020-8440 2808 Mobile 07946-410974
W.E. (feature), Hotel Babylon (TV drama), Green Zone (feature).

Peter Watson   020-8566 0971 Mobile 07976-726646
The Wolfman (feature), Nine (feature), Gulliver's Travels (feature).

Steve Watson   020-7837 9449 Mobile 07778-289830
Spooks (TV drama), Law & Order (TV drama), Trial & Retribution (TV drama).

Jake Wells   020-8441 1529 Mobile 07761-231505
The Dark Knight (feature), Stardust (feature), Green Zone (feature).

John Wells   020-8953 0457 Mobile 07956-279703
Your Highness (feature), Prince Of Persia (feature), Sweeney Todd (feature).

Terry Wells Jnr   020-8953 5508 Mobile 07946-350656
Robin Hood (feature), Green Zone (feature), Body Of Lies (feature).

Steve Westley   020-8651 4541 Mobile 07729-250113
Robin Hood (feature).

Kevin Wheeler   Mobile 07855-486373
Quantum Of Solace (feature), Miss Potter (feature), The Bourne Ultimatum (feature).

Greg White   Mobile 07970-551183
Robin Hood (feature), Poppy Shakespeare (TV film), Survivors (TV drama).

Penny White   Mobile 07811-340116
St Trinian's (feature), The Other Boleyn Girl (feature), Bright Star (feature).

Rod Whiting   0113-224 2556 Mobile 07768-581239
In Bruges (feature), 1066 (TV film), Mansfield Park (TV film).

PROPERTYMEN

Ben Wilkinson   020-8447 5535 Mobile 07957-273370
The Dark Knight (feature), Harry Potter & The Deathly Hallows (feature), Saving Private Ryan (feature).

Simon Wilkinson   01727-868375 Mobile 07958-375334
Harry Potter & The Goblet Of Fire (feature), The Dark Knight (feature), Titanic (feature).

Clive Wilson   01895-674760 Mobile 07958-348488
The Wolfman (feature), John Carter Of Mars (feature), Body Of Lies (feature).

Julian Wilson   Mobile 07799-521390
Stardust (feature), Children Of Men (feature), Charlie & The Chocolate Factory (feature).

Monty Wilson   01932-243942 Mobile 07990-915035
Vera Drake (feature), The Duchess (feature), Cranford (TV drama).

Peter Wood   020-7738 3984 Mobile 07956-451409
Bright Star (feature), St Trinian's (feature), Hot Fuzz (feature).

Nigel Woodford   Mobile 07957-251848
Run Fat Boy Run (feature).

Mickey Woolfson   020-8386 3860 Mobile 07957-386386
W.E. (feature), My Life In Ruins (feature), London Boulevard (feature).

Matt Wyles   01992-551224 Mobile 07507-525679
It's A Wonderful Afterlife (feature), Star Wars: Episode III - Revenge Of The Sith (feature).

Ian Young   Mobile 07590-754099
Shanghai (feature), City Of Ember (feature), Doom (feature).

PROPERTYMEN - GREENSMEN

Fatiha Aitbadi   01202-735022 Mobile 07789-938099
Children Of Men (feature), Kingdom Of Heaven (feature), Cold Mountain (feature).

Roger Holden   01202-735022 Mobile 07831-119702
The Wolfman (feature), Children Of Men (feature), The Black Dahlia (feature).

Will Holden   01202-657593 Mobile 07990-575635
The Wolfman (feature), Tales Of The Riverbank (feature), Children Of Men (feature).

Charles Hooper   Mobile 07957-621672

Jon Marson   Mobile 07929-155237
Prince Of Persia (feature), Prince Caspian (feature), Sleepy Hollow (feature).

Dicken Warner   0845-260 0899 Mobile 07885-305693
Fax 0871-989 6378
Robin Hood (feature), Gardeners' World (TV light entertainment), A Good Year (feature).
www.brandonthatchers.co.uk

RIGGERS

Simon Alderton   020-8386 4483 Mobile 07956-101799
The World Is Not Enough (feature), Casino Royale (feature), Stardust (feature).

Rob Armstrong   Mobile 07816-402680
Revolver (feature), Footballers' Wives (TV drama), Shaun Of The Dead (feature).

Paul Barker   01245-258716 Mobile 07977-470515
Fred Claus (feature), Bad Girls (TV drama), Shaun Of The Dead (feature).

Leslie Beaver   020-8207 4484 Mobile 07958-293221
Fax 020-8207 4484
The World Is Not Enough (feature), Tomorrow Never Dies (feature), Captain Corelli's Mandolin (feature).

William Beenham   01428-684843 Mobile 07879-688771
Batman Begins (feature), The Da Vinci Code (feature), Love Actually (feature).

William Bimpson   01375-643103 Mobile 07971-565191
Casino Royale (feature), Children Of Men (feature), The Golden Compass (feature).

Harry Boxell   020-8286 0382 Mobile 07770-917991
The Da Vinci Code (feature), Casino Royale (feature), The Golden Compass (feature).

Steve Challis   01438-358808 Mobile 07973-560626
Die Another Day (feature), The World Is Not Enough (feature), Harry Potter & The Prisoner Of Azkaban (feature).

Nobby Clarke   020-8788 9150 Mobile 07976-310351
Fax 020-8788 9150
Charlie & The Chocolate Factory (feature), The Magic Flute (feature), Gladiator (feature).

John Cooling   Mobile 07768-012419 Fax 07768-019078

Mike Coveney   01708-478847 Mobile 07976-880961
Fax 01708-464696
Spooks (TV drama), Waking The Dead (TV drama), Bleak House (TV drama).

Gary Dormer   020-8979 0650   Mobile 07946-323763
Die Another Day (feature), Batman Begins (feature), Tomb Raider II (feature).

Simon Dutton   01784-461884   Mobile 07850-155054
Clash Of The Titans (feature) (HOD), City Of Ember (feature), Harry Potter & The Goblet Of Fire (feature).

Roy Elston   01895-850454   Mobile 07768-857375
Fax 01895-850454
Atonement (feature), Miss Pettigrew Lives For A Day (feature), Me & Orson Welles (feature).

Darren Flindall   01442-395309   Mobile 07890-365498
The World Is Not Enough (feature), Dinotopia (TV drama), Die Another Day (feature).

Raymond Flindall   01442-253003   Mobile 07790-039008
Gosford Park (feature), The World Is Not Enough (feature), Five Children & It (feature).

Paul Garratt   Mobile 07885-625091
Children Of Men (feature), Die Another Day (feature), Batman Begins (feature).

Clive Goble   01865-763105   Mobile 07768-037643
Fax 01865-763105
Harry Potter & The Order Of The Phoenix (feature), Harry Potter & The Goblet Of Fire (feature), Harry Potter & The Prisoner Of Azkaban (feature).

John Goble   01865-423163   Mobile 07751-792998
Harry Potter & The Goblet Of Fire (feature), Die Another Day (feature).

Martin Goddard   020-8768 0253   Mobile 07931-802041
Charlie & The Chocolate Factory (feature), Vanity Fair (feature), Around The World In 80 Days (feature).

Damon Graham   Mobile 07796-697717
Bride & Prejudice (feature), Dead Fish (feature), Thunderpants (feature).

Bryan Griffiths   029-2021 2409   Mobile 07778-994609
Fax 029-2021 2409
Doctor Who (TV drama).

Pat Hagarty   Mobile 07885-353030
1408 (feature), Harry Potter & The Order Of The Phoenix (feature), 28 Days Later (feature).

Richard Harris   01628-770411   Mobile 07715-490731
Sahara (feature), Enigma (feature), Superman (feature).

Peter Hawkins   020-8677 2421   Mobile 07775-603039
Gulliver's Travels (feature), Quantum Of Solace (feature), The Wolfman (feature).

Steve Howe   01491-575601   Mobile 07768-834299
Fax 01491-575601
Hotel Babylon (TV drama), Thunderpants (feature), The Magic Flute (feature).

William Howe   Mobile 07811-589484
Doom (feature), Phantom Of The Opera (feature), The Magic Flute (feature).

Pat Killeen   01372-462132   Mobile 07778-415136
Fax 01372-462132
Strange (TV drama), The Crying Game (feature).

James Knox   01582-840780   Mobile 07802-325088
The Hours (feature), Harry Potter & The Chamber Of Secrets (feature), Harry Potter & The Goblet Of Fire (feature).

Mark Looker   01869-246897   Mobile 07799-037057
Fax 01869-246897
The Da Vinci Code (feature), Harry Potter & The Prisoner Of Azkaban (feature), Die Another Day (feature).

Iain Lowe   01923-567313   Mobile 07976-310353
Prince Of Persia (feature) (HOD).

Charlie Macher   020-8330 0879   Mobile 07850-260099
Daniel Deronda (TV drama), May 33rd (TV film), Born & Bred (TV drama).

Stephen Macher   Mobile 07836-545684
Die Another Day (feature), Tomb Raider II (feature), The Da Vinci Code (feature).

Danny Madden   020-8568 5582   Mobile 07950-362504
Harry Potter & The Goblet Of Fire (feature), Alfie (feature), Five Children & It (feature).

Kevin Mathews   01753-785352   Mobile 07767-775760
Pirates Of The Caribbean: On Stranger Tides (feature), Quantum Of Solace (feature), The Dark Knight (feature).
www.specialist-wire-rigs.co.uk

Ginger McCarthy   01865-873116   Mobile 07973-562389
Harry Potter & The Goblet Of Fire (feature), Die Another Day (feature), Harry Potter & The Prisoner Of Azkaban (feature).

Anthony Murphy   01708-472135   Mobile 07956-378815
Hitchhiker's Guide To The Galaxy (feature).

Steven Pollecutt   020-8236 0710   Mobile 07949-129857
Sleepy Hollow (feature), Band Of Brothers (TV drama), Phantom Of The Opera (feature).

Russell Prosser   Mobile 07768-841314   Fax 020-8236 0089
Entrapment (feature), The Mummy Returns (feature), Spy Game (feature).

RIGGERS

John Robertson   01753-888569 Mobile 07976-310352
Stormbreaker (feature), Bridget Jones's Diary (feature), The Hours (feature).

Ian Rolfe   01753-520041 Mobile 07946-192435
Children Of Men (feature), Tomb Raider II (feature), Die Another Day (feature).

Vince Shaw   Mobile 07973-115216 Fax 020-8341 1318
Quantum Of Solace (feature), Kick-Ass (feature), The Duchess (feature).
www.metrorigging.co.uk

Colin Smith   020-7378 9023 Mobile 07971-565160
Band Of Brothers (TV drama), Tomorrow Never Dies (feature), The Da Vinci Code (feature).

Martin Smith   Mobile 07971-286007
Sunshine (feature), Bleak House (TV drama), Harry Potter & The Order Of The Phoenix (feature).

Frankie Webster   01923-264389 Mobile 07775-688771
Fax 01923-264389
Harry Potter & The Goblet Of Fire (feature), Gladiator (feature).

Kevin Welch   01753-522219 Mobile 07552-698621
Harry Potter & The Deathly Hallows (feature), The World Is Not Enough (feature), Tomb Raider (feature).
www.stuntrigging.com

David Weller   0118-986 7471 Mobile 07889-951397
Fax 0118-986 7471
Doom (feature), The Brothers Grimm (feature), Love Actually (feature).

Bob Wiesinger   07000-wirefx (947339)
Mobile 07973-662393 Fax 07968-253071
The Nutcracker (ballet), The Holiday (feature), Harry Potter & The Goblet Of Fire (feature).

Grant Wiesinger   01344-635435 Mobile 07921-000677
Fax 01344-635165

SCENIC ARTISTS

Chris Bradley   01588-620460 Mobile 07790-403458
Fax 01588-620460
Clash Of The Titans (feature), Casanova (feature), 102 Dalmatians (feature).

Susannah Brough   020-7435 4635 Mobile 07766-066242

Chris Clark   Mobile 07775-778914 Fax 020-8342 0917
Aida (opera), Into The Storm (TV film), The Brit Awards (party).

Liz Clark   Mobile 07885-400552 Fax 020-8342 0917
Big Brother (TV reality), Phantom Of The Opera (feature), Edward Scissorhands (ballet).

Stuart Clarke   01926-332844 Mobile 07831-567228
The Tudors (TV drama), The Fifth Element (feature), Trainspotting (feature).

Robert Dugdale   020-8656 6781 Mobile 07958-604892
Fax 020-8405 1506
Gulliver's Travels (feature), Eastern Promises (feature), In The Loop (feature).

Sally Fletcher   01932-227679 Mobile 07778-370571
E Bay (commercial), Hex (TV drama).

James Gemmill   Mobile 07889-508888
Prince Of Persia (feature), The Wolfman (feature), Angels & Demons (feature).

Liana Goatman   Mobile 07932-021162
Godzilla (feature), Time (nightclub), Lutyens (restaurant).

Fred Gray   01803-605655 Mobile 07831-417479

Simon Hague   Mobile 07778-471056
Little Dorrit (TV drama), Elizabeth: The Golden Age (feature), Alexander (feature).

Rohan Harris   Mobile 07974-792183
Clash Of The Titans (feature), The Imaginarium Of Dr Parnassus (feature), Agora (feature).

Nigel Hughes   Mobile 07973-659091
Quantum Of Solace (feature), Cranford (TV drama), The Libertine (feature).

Tom Jolliffe   Mobile 07867-602160
Robin Hood (feature), Clash Of The Titans (feature), Children Of Men (feature).

Grahame Menage   +1 678 230 4033 Mobile 07767-250227
Glory Road (feature), Babe II (feature), Enemy Of The State (feature).

Roy Monk   01923-856338 Mobile 07860-285594
Prince Of Persia (feature), Alexander (feature), City Of Vice (TV drama).

David Nicoll   020-8386 8137 Mobile 07949-646559
Alexander (feature), The World Is Not Enough (feature), Harry Potter & The Philosopher's Stone (feature).

Gilly Noyes-Court   01628-472122
Interview With The Vampire (feature), Hamlet (feature), Moonraker (feature).

Russell Oxley   020-8802 4211 Mobile 07710-497677
Fred Claus (feature), Atonement (feature), The Da Vinci Code (feature).

David Packard   Mobile 07971-546377
Casino Royale (feature), Batman Returns (feature), The Bourne Ultimatum (feature).

Cosmo Sarson   Mobile 07958-277885
Sweeney Todd (feature), Dorian Gray (feature), The Wolfman (feature).

Laura Skinner   01753-652967 Mobile 07957-582206
The Wolfman (feature) (miniatures), Batman Begins (feature) (miniatures), Harry Potter & The Half-Blood Prince (feature).

Matthew Walker   01923-256515 Mobile 07836-385365
The Colour Of Magic (TV film), Harry Potter & The Half-Blood Prince (feature), Harry Potter & The Order Of The Phoenix (feature).

Howard Weaver   Mobile 07968-618690
Valkyrie (feature), Miss Potter (feature), Notes On A Scandal (feature).

Marie White   Mobile 07980-303311
Eurovision Song Contest (TV light entertainment), The Lion The Witch & The Wardrobe (feature), MTV Music Awards (TV light entertainment).

Marcus Williams   01372-809611 Mobile 07769-697260
Harry Potter & The Half-Blood Prince (feature), Harry Potter & The Order Of The Phoenix (feature), Harry Potter & The Goblet Of Fire (feature).

Timna Woollard   Mobile 07710-132602
My Zinc Bed (TV film), Alexander (feature), Miss Marple (TV drama).

SCULPTORS

John Blakeley   Mobile 07802-672402
John Carter Of Mars (feature) (HOD), Robin Hood (feature) (HOD), The Magic Flute (feature).

Jody Brothers   020-8429 0874 Mobile 07889-032314
Robin Hood (feature), Nine (feature), Batman Begins (feature).

Eddie Butler   020-7485 7260 Mobile 07977-546859
Alexander (feature), Star Wars: Episode I - The Phantom Menace (feature), 102 Dalmatians (feature).

Anna Claxton   020-7249 4916 Mobile 07947-049956
Alexander (feature), Harry Potter & The Prisoner Of Azkaban (feature), Charlie & The Chocolate Factory (feature).

Bryn Court   020-8362 1107 Mobile 07702-963088
Harry Potter & The Prisoner Of Azkaban (feature), The World Is Not Enough (feature), The Mummy Returns (feature).

David Darby   020-8367 3175 Fax 01753-656218
Charlie & The Chocolate Factory (feature).

Steve Deahl   020-8949 4357 Mobile 07780-603122
Charlie & The Chocolate Factory (feature), Harry Potter & The Philosopher's Stone (feature), Die Another Day (feature).

Nicholas Dutton   Mobile 07814-622175
The Golden Compass (feature), Pride & Prejudice (feature), Alexander (feature).

Fred Evans   Mobile 07050-095969
Die Another Day (feature), Harry Potter & The Philosopher's Stone (feature), Captain Corelli's Mandolin (feature).

Luke Furlonger   Mobile 07803-005423
Charlie & The Chocolate Factory (feature), Alexander (feature).

Andy Garner   020-8442 1688 Mobile 07939-543647
Charlie & The Chocolate Factory (feature), 28 Weeks Later (feature), Munich (feature).

Bruce Gordon   Mobile 07881-552428
The Wolfman (feature), Stardust (feature), The Da Vinci Code (feature).

Emma Hanson   Mobile 07767-356228
Charlie & The Chocolate Factory (feature), The Golden Compass (feature), Phantom Of The Opera (feature).

Wesley Harland   Mobile 07903-402693
John Carter Of Mars (feature).

Derek Howarth   01727-822845 Mobile 07831-305338
Fax 01727-823087

Gideon Howarth   Mobile 07768-440750 Fax 01727-823087
www.filmandtvsculptors.com

Aden Hynes   01268-418837 Fax 01268-414118

Emma Jackson   01252-717465 Mobile 07932-316680
John Carter Of Mars (feature).

Sarah Mayfield   Mobile 07968-430240
Die Another Day (feature), Tomb Raider (feature), The Reckoning (feature).

Rob Mayor   Mobile 07899-985407
Kingdom Of Heaven (feature), Gladiator (feature), Saving Private Ryan (feature).

Jonny Moore   Mobile 07946-355548
Clash Of The Titans (feature) (HOD).

Brian Muir 01442-246835 Mobile 07968-590610
Alexander (feature), Tomb Raider II (feature), Die Another Day (feature).

Anthony Parker Mobile 07957-168627
Blood Diamond (feature), From Hell (feature), Kingdom Of Heaven (feature).

Max Patte Mobile 07770-966153
Harry Potter & The Order Of The Phoenix (feature), Batman Begins (feature), Troy (feature).

Justin Pitkethly 020-8867 7263 Mobile 07752-598864
Kingdom Of Heaven (feature), Star Wars: Episode I - The Phantom Menace (feature), Sleepy Hollow (feature).

John Robinson 01275-817883 Mobile 07798-693966
Gladiator (feature), Harry Potter & The Philosopher's Stone (feature), Aliens (feature).

Roy Rodgers 020-8385 7735 Mobile 07831-588711
Harry Potter & The Goblet Of Fire (feature), The Mummy Returns (feature), Stormwalker (feature).

Julien Short Mobile 07813-051679
Alexander (feature), Harry Potter & The Prisoner Of Azkaban (feature), Star Wars: Episode I - The Phantom Menace (feature).

Keith Short 01923-400569 Mobile 07788-423533
Fax 01923-400569
Alexander (feature), Die Another Day (feature), The Mummy (feature).

Colin Shulver Mobile 07866-681781
Charlie & The Chocolate Factory (feature), Hitchhiker's Guide To The Galaxy (feature), Prehistoric Park (TV docu drama).

Richard Smith 020-8968 3662 Mobile 07712-005985
Fax 020-8968 3662
Charlie & The Chocolate Factory (feature), Children Of Men (feature), Alexander (feature).

Roland Stevenson 01273-501053 Mobile 07971-277220
Prince Caspian (feature), Kingdom Of Heaven (feature), Gladiator (feature).

Roger Walker 020-8746 0312 Mobile 07961-193681
Fax 020-8740 7430
Alexander (feature), Troy (feature).

Sophie Wills 020-8694 9765 Mobile 07956-481582
Nanny McPhee (feature), Alexander (feature), Charlie & The Chocolate Factory (feature).

Christine Withers 01932-422995

SET DECORATORS

Rebecca Alleway 020-8964 5745 Mobile 07973-210773
The Eagle Of The Ninth (feature), The Duchess (feature), The Last King Of Scotland (feature) (UK).

Clare Andrade 020-8678 5250 Mobile 07973-552482
Fax 020-8678 5250
Wuthering Heights (feature), Nineteen Eighty (TV film), Oliver Twist (feature).

Jille Azis 01428-645966 Mobile 07850-509900
CMM 020-8584 5363
Rendition (feature), Oliver Twist (feature), Gladiator (feature).

Ben Barrington-Groves Mobile 07971-371321
Green Zone (feature) (Assistant), Sex & The City 2 (feature) (Assistant), Thunderbirds (feature) (Assistant).

Carlotta Barrow 01929-425967 Mobile 07850-313910
Fax 01929-425967
Mrs Dalloway (feature), Poirot (TV drama), Bramwell (TV drama).

Jo Barrs 01398-324409 Mobile 07778-156106
Layer Cake (feature), Keen Eddie (TV drama), Down To Earth (TV drama) (Production Buyer).

Kate Beckly Mobile 07771-892993
Hitchhiker's Guide To The Galaxy (feature).

Ute Bergk 020-7326 4930 Mobile 07713-252407
Bruno (feature), The Dark Knight (feature) (Assistant), Die Another Day (feature) (Assistant).

Celia Bobak 020-8947 2817 Mobile 07836-236467
Fax 020-8947 3720
W.E. (feature), London Boulevard (feature), Shanghai (feature).

John Bush 020-8946 5372 Mobile 07850-205949
Fax 020-8946 9640
The Wolfman (feature), Munich (feature), Vera Drake (feature).

Peta Button 020-7722 4692 Mobile 07885-810809
Three Blind Mice (feature), Labyrinth (feature), The Fourth Angel (feature).

Robert Cameron 01273-624746 Mobile 07790-766687
Gulliver's Travels (feature) (Assistant), Fred Claus (feature) (Assistant), Elizabeth: The Golden Age (feature) (Assistant).

Dominic Capon 020-8969 8331 Mobile 07801-067217
Your Highness (feature), Creation (feature), The Boat That Rocked (feature).

Sophia Chowdhury   020-7243 3170   Mobile 07958-955693
Fax 020-7243 3170
The Long Walk To Finchley (TV film), The Edge Of Love (feature) (Assistant), The Bourne Ultimatum (feature) (Assistant).

Lisa Chugg   Mobile 07767-690766
Agora (feature), Inception (feature), Hereafter (feature).

Tamsin Clarke   Mobile 07772-782771

Caroline Cobbold   020-7625 5875   Mobile 07831-580172
How To Lose Friends & Alienate People (feature), Wuthering Heights (feature), Wimbledon (feature).

Jane Cooke   Mobile 07771-597776   AD 020-7428 0500
Full Metal Jacket (feature), Sexy Beast (feature), Goal! (feature).

Cathy Cosgrove   01296-339540   Mobile 07831-392848

Niamh Coulter   020-8378 6284   Mobile 07973-878338
AD 020-7428 0500
Inkheart (feature), Easy Virtue (feature), Dorian Gray (feature).

Penny Crawford   020-7419 0199   Mobile 07860-403319
Fax 020-7419 0199
Alfie (feature), To Kill A King (feature).

Francesca Cross   020-8986 6666   Mobile 07985-927668
Spooks (TV drama), Luther (TV drama), Babylon AD (feature).

Belinda Cusmano   020-7625 6507   Mobile 07904-125630
Fax 020-7625 6507
Dead Man Running (feature), Dead Cert (feature), Vanity Fair (feature) (Assistant).

Helen Dagger   01278-671313   Mobile 07770-688892
White (TV comedy drama) (Art Director), Pobol Y Cwm (TV drama) (Art Director), Murder In Mind (TV drama).

Emma Davis   Mobile 07808-401420   Fax 020-7724 7343
Secret Diary Of A Call Girl (TV drama), Somers Town (feature), This Life +10 (TV drama).

Nicola de Fresnes   020-8835 8112   Mobile 07971-662351
Children Of Men (feature) (Assistant), I Want Candy (feature), Class Of 76 (TV drama).

Gillie Delap   01598-741106   Mobile 07973-797277
Fax 01598-741196
The Merchant Of Venice (feature), I'll Sleep When I'm Dead (feature), Croupier (feature).

Belinda Delyle-Turner   020-8741 9600
Mobile 07710-037285   Fax 020-8748 9100
Asda (commercial), Nintendo (commercial), Twinings (commercial).

Trisha Edwards   020-8675 3830   Mobile 07956-207424
Cranford (TV drama), Finding Neverland (feature), Iris (feature).

Lucy Eyre   020-7703 5768   Mobile 07811-040484
Me & Orson Welles (feature) (Assistant), The Duchess (feature) (Assistant), Notes On A Scandal (feature) (Assistant).

Judy Farr   01295-770676   Mobile 07836-753311
Ondine (feature), Eastern Promises (feature), Death At A Funeral (feature).

Alice Felton   Mobile 07702-272015
The Boat That Rocked (feature) (Assistant), Your Highness (feature) (Assistant), The Last Enemy (TV drama).

Rosie Goodwin   Mobile 07891-434336
Harry Potter & The Deathly Hallows (feature) (Assistant), Harry Potter & The Half-Blood Prince (feature) (Assistant), Harry Potter & The Order Of The Phoenix (feature).

Lee Gordon   Mobile 07771-757995
Solomon Kane (feature), The Colour Of Magic (TV film), Stormbreaker (feature).

Jo Graysmark   020-8755 4549   Mobile 07721-442550

Elli Griff   01494-882864   Mobile 07774-639816
Prince Of Persia (feature), Hellboy 2: The Golden Army (feature), Love In The Time Of Cholera (feature).

Liz Griffiths   020-8969 0669   Mobile 07831-713883
Fax 020-8969 0669
It's A Wonderful Afterlife (feature), Angus Thongs & Perfect Snogging (feature), Hot Fuzz (feature).

Andy Grogan   01923-333001   Mobile 07860-205067
Hotel Babylon (TV drama), Cemetery Junction (feature), Glorious 39 (feature).

Philippa Hart   020-8740 7845   Mobile 07802-160842
The Hours (feature), Love Is The Devil (feature), The Gathering Storm (TV film).

Barbara Herman-Skelding   020-8800 5132
Mobile 07973-139397
Nowhere Boy (feature), Mamma Mia! (feature), And When Did You Last See Your Father? (feature).

Careen Hertzog   020-7328 2365   Mobile 07973-209578
Trauma (feature), The Borrowers (feature).
www.grangerhertzog.com

Lucy Howe   020-8979 0591   Mobile 07973-264958
AD 020-7428 0500   Fax 020-8979 0591
Easy Virtue (feature), 24 Hour Party People (feature), Two Men Went To War (feature).

Graham Wyn-Jones Mobile 07979-622179
Ultramarines: The Movie (3D animated), Heavenly Sword (video game), Moon (feature).

STYLISTS - ART DEPARTMENT

Kate Abrahams Mobile 07850-454094

Ali Allen Mobile 07976-984128

Trish Appleton 01367-850175 Mobile 07973-909304

Melinda Ashton Turner 020-7288 0017
Mobile 07931-597025

Suzie Attaway Mobile 07939-144815
Christy Towels & Bedlinen (stills), Hobbycraft (stills), House Beautiful (magazine).

Jocelyn Bailey 020-8441 9111 Mobile 07910-262433

Jo Barnes 020-7225 0522 Mobile 07766-303071

Poppy Bartlett Mobile 07816-874073

Tess Bartlett Mobile 07970-767872
Mui Mui (stills), Armani (stills).

Catherine Bates 020-8992 0956 Mobile 07973-412686
AD 020-7428 0500

Shannon Beare 01372-462623 Mobile 07850-967334
Tesco (commercial), Waitrose (commercial), Safeway (commercial).

Liz Belton Mobile 07957-364374

Lucy Benson Mobile 07990-591797

Julia Bird Mobile 07710-808313

Carolyn Boult 020-8288 9366 Mobile 07970-089592
AD 020-7428 0500

Abi Boura Mobile 07974-677718
Elle Decoration (magazine), Sony (commercial), Habitat (commercial).

Richard Bradbury Mobile 07768-352100

Ali Bradshaw Mobile 07949-850428

Carl Braganza 020-8988 9774 Mobile 07939-560898

Niki Brodie Mobile 07768-954505

Chloe Brown Mobile 07881-827604

Lisa Brown Mobile 07768-592297

Malena Burgess Mobile 07968-722663

Clare Carter 020-8964 4804 Mobile 07870-632123

Charlie Cave Mobile 07715-093705

Lizzie Chambers Mobile 07946-604694

Tina Charad 020-8838 2505 Mobile 07919-854790
Robin Hood (feature).

Rachel Christensen Mobile 07734-466434

Diana Civil Mobile 07971-841859

Penny Clark Mobile 07958-516606

Susie Clegg Mobile 07956-469581

Sally Conran Mobile 07980-240967

Katie Cordell 020-8521 8870 Mobile 07947-197791

Jane Crow 020-8941 1752 Mobile 07973-403632
Fax 020-8941 1752

Sharron Daly 020-8932 8758 Mobile 07831-766092
Barclays Bank (commercial), Ford (commercial), Sony (commercial).

Alison Davidson Mobile 07768-298347

Rebecca De Boehmler Mobile 07721-866783

Louise de Ville Morel 020-8450 6148
Mobile 07966-173913 Fax 020-8450 1574

Marianne de Vries HERS 0844-811 6811

Sally Denning Mobile 07968-302211

Helen Downes Mobile 07932-713997

Rebecca Du Pont De Bie 020-8208 2639
Mobile 07860-484655

Matt Duddleston Mobile 07968-326798

Sam Duffy Mobile 07887-733163

Diane Edwards 020-7736 7966 Mobile 07836-226823
Fax 020-7736 7966

Lucy Elworthy HERS 0844-811 6811

Suzie Finch Mobile 07831-651919 HERS 0844-811 6811
Handpicked Hotels (stills), Marriott Hotels (commercial), De Vere Hotels (stills).

Natasha Freeman 020-7275 0747 Mobile 07739-968368

Laura Fulmine Mobile 07968-802322

Bay Garnett Mobile 07984-560715

Martin Gaskell Mobile 07939-628459

Seana Gavin Mobile 07759-606897

Katie Gibbs 020-8220 2296 Mobile 07976-415008
DFS (commercial), Next (stills), Homebase (commercial).

Karen Granger 020-8960 5412 Mobile 07831-529676
AD 020-7428 0500
The Borrowers (feature), Fierce Creatures (feature), Backbeat (feature).
www.grangerhertzog.com

Louisa Grey Mobile 07970-259022

Stefanie Grieve Mobile 07977-580709
TetraPak (commercial), Ikea (commercial), British Airways (commercial).

Dan Griffiths Mobile 07974-188905 CM 020-7287 4450

Julia Griffiths 020-7352 4008 Mobile 07774-694140
HERS 0844-811 6811
American Express (commercial), Pepsi-Cola (commercial), Mercedes (commercial).

Samantha Grigg Mobile 07984-862023

Hilary Guy 020-7281 0620 Mobile 07831-365946
Fax 020-7281 0620

Christine Harding Mobile 07855-325722

Deena Hargreaves 01296-682344 Mobile 07801-702810
Fax 01296-682197
Nintendo (commercial), Currys (commercial), Robinson Crusoe (feature).

Kasha Harmer Mobile 07802-895333

Jane Harris 020-7586 2403 Mobile 07976-612887
Fax 020-7586 2403

Jo Harris Mobile 07850-478072

Becky Harvey Mobile 07752-651114

Nel Haynes Mobile 07970-708477

Jenny Heel Mobile 07740-153361

Jane Henwood 020-7727 5832 Mobile 07831-537003

Emily Hill Mobile 07957-634415
Vogue (magazine), Nike (commercial), Nicole Farhi (stills).

Sue Hollis 01428-652981 Mobile 07973-617447
Fax 01428-652981

Rosie Hopper 020-8892 1172 Mobile 07831-539517
Fax 020-8892 1172

Tony Hornecker Mobile 07944-289734

Sarah Hubacher Mobile 07949-080984
10,000 BC (feature).

Catherine Huckerby 01273-747531 Mobile 07970-792249

Clare Hunt 020-8671 6320 Mobile 07836-643367
HERS 0844-811 6811 Fax 020-8674 1544

Tony Hutchinson 020-8785 9443 Mobile 07770-918662
Fax 020-8785 9443

Twig Hutchinson Mobile 07956-622150

Labeena Ishaque Mobile 07971-604438

Pippa Jameson 020-7613 2395 Mobile 07973-185594
John Lewis (commercial), JJB (commercial), CSL (commercial).

Emily Jewsbury Mobile 07976-298946

Sam Johnson 01628-632517 Mobile 07721-621013
Fax 01628-632717

Rachel Jukes Mobile 07990-591923

Alison Landy Mobile 07775-787466

Jenny Lawrence-Smith Mobile 07989-350205
Viper In The Fist (feature), Mean Machine (feature), Eurostar (commercial).

Penny Legg 020-8995 1624 Mobile 07879-683267

Fraser Leggate Mobile 07973-156241

Sue Leighton 020-8876 8497 Mobile 07973-321474
Fax 020-8876 9755
Diet Coke (commercial), Hoseasons (commercial), Center Parcs (commercial).

Tracey Lester Mobile 07831-556335

Monica Loudon 0131-667 6309 Mobile 07968-176774
The Dalmore (stills), Midori (commercial), SNP (commercial).

Ashlie Love 020-8245 8717 Mobile 07779-099273

Juliana Loveday Mobile 07957-667920

Paula Lovell Mobile 07785-353900 HERS 0844-811 6811

Sarah Lovett 020-8674 0335 Mobile 07976-272590
Hippie Hippie Shake (feature) (Prop Maker), The Brit Awards (party) (Prop Maker), ITV 3 (ident).

Katy Lynne   020-8365 7540 Mobile 07956-249396
Fax 020-8365 7540

Penny Markham   020-8995 5255 Mobile 07831-527020

Geraldine Marks   Mobile 07932-741767

Juliet Mawtus   Mobile 07889-442332

Sarah May   Mobile 07812-575760

Sally McEwan   020-8299 4295 Mobile 07903-019591
House Of Fraser (stills), John Lewis (commercial), Harrods (stills).

Jo McGuinness   Mobile 07956-926605

Charlotte Melling   Mobile 07951-041092

Victoria Metcalf   Mobile 07957-433886

Milena Mihic   Mobile 07815-786682

Blake Minton   020-7249 6332 Mobile 07770-274303
Fax 020-7249 6332

Portland Mitchell   Mobile 07740-766261

Melanie Molesworth 020-8747 4848 Mobile 07976-721429

Lucyina Moodie   020-8961 0429 Mobile 07703-229996

Kevin Moran   Mobile 07932-490979

Claire Morgan   Mobile 07932-042615

Stella Nicolaisen 020-7281 4651 Mobile 07813-956386

Mary Norden   Mobile 07887-714407
Red (magazine), Laura Ashley (stills), Boden (catalogue).

Gillian O'Brien   Mobile 07980-933443

Karin Otte   020-7286 6149 Mobile 07850-271536
Fax 020-7289 1213

Sarah Pletts   020-8985 9850

Harriet Porter   020-8678 6468 Mobile 07831-690673

Sue Quimby   01527-857495 Mobile 07831-215488

Angelina Read   020-7729 8183 Mobile 07980-647796

Hannah Read Baldrey   Mobile 07977-297303
Elle (magazine), Flashbacks Of A Fool (feature), The Bank Job (feature).

Andie Redman   Mobile 07710-443416

Chloe Richardson   Mobile 07903-125056

Lesley Richardson 020-7354 0374 Mobile 07713-410921

Sophie Robinson   Mobile 07970-672805
60 Minute Makeover (TV light entertainment), Cowboy Builders (TV light entertainment).

Vicky Robinson   Mobile 07941-230965

Timna Rose   020-8882 9448 Mobile 07860-161627

Cath Rossner   Mobile 07976-381310
Head & Shoulders (commercial), Oil Of Olay (commercial), Samsung (commercial).

Sue Rowlands   Mobile 07836-660365

Nina Russell-Cowan   020-8874 4734
Mobile 07870-646691 Fax 020-8874 4734

Nadine Sanders   Mobile 07958-325702

Faye Sawyer   Mobile 07050-112859
The X Factor (TV light entertainment), This Morning (TV magazine).

Vicky Sheard   Mobile 07970-075758

Hannah Simmons   Mobile 07771-801364

Gail Smith   Mobile 07831-381513 Fax 020-8255 4571

Karen Smith   Mobile 07956-463299

Emma Thomas   Mobile 07973-227998

Leonora Trafford   Mobile 07940-581650
Saturday Telegraph (magazine), Habitat (commercial).

Baz Troubridge   020-7370 3912 Mobile 07976-848637

Catherine Tully 020-7837 2960 Mobile 07973-286174

Mary Wadsworth   Mobile 07885-367668
Waitrose (commercial), Lombok (stills), Debenhams (stills).

Nicki Walkinshaw 01494-675046 Mobile 07850-978971
Babies R Us (stills), Mattel Toys (stills).

Fanny Ward   Mobile 07973-265477
Heals (stills), Laura Ashley (stills), Harrods (stills).

Miranda Watchorn   Mobile 07816-817213
HERS 0844-811 6811

Suzanne Webster 01628-825405 Mobile 07931-387033

Jenny Weeks   Mobile 07855-541914

Dawn Weller   Mobile 07966-014580

Tamsin Weston   HERS 0844-811 6811

Charis White   0118-954 6706 Mobile 07771-871994

Laura Ashley (stills), Marks & Spencer (commercial), Mothercare (stills).

Tuula Whitlow   Mobile 07973-838655

Dulux (commercial), Woolworths (commercial), Marks & Spencer (commercial).

Gill Wright   0161-442 0807 Mobile 07980-431285

Fax 0161-442 0807

Lucy Wright   020-7352 7718 Mobile 07711-515168

Nicola Yeoman   Mobile 07957-275347

Lizzi Zita   Mobile 07966-431007

Chloe (stills), Marks & Spencer (commercial), Frank (magazine).

Camera DEPARTMENT

AERIAL CAMERA PILOTS

Philip Amadeus   01737-823700 Mobile 07768-100900
Fax 01737-823737
The Apprentice (TV reality), Jekyll (TV drama), Sahara (feature).

Ian Evans   Mobile 07976-688002
Nanny McPhee & The Big Bang (feature), Numerous commercials, The Royal (TV drama).

Alistair Gwilt   Mobile 07767-614419 Fax 01268-769610
Coast (TV doc), World Rally Championship (TV sport), 28 Weeks Later (feature).

BEST BOYS

Tony Allen   Mobile 07973-188747
From Time To Time (feature).

Chris Allkins   Mobile 07956-413188
Bad Girls (TV drama), Footballers' Wives (TV drama), Half Broken Dreams (TV drama) (Rigger).

Steve Anthony   Mobile 07778-031672
Johnny English (feature), Stormbreaker (feature), Little Dorrit (TV drama).

Andy Bell   Mobile 07810-080800
Robin Hood (feature) (2nd unit).

Sonny Burdis   020-8368 9696 Mobile 07889-990001
Shanghai (feature), 1408 (feature).

Terry Eden   01204-571456 Mobile 07966-415938
Life On Mars (TV drama), Gladiator (feature), Birthday Girl (feature).

Lee Eldred   Mobile 07956-413339
Miss Marple (TV drama), Starter For Ten (feature).

William Finch   01424-773181 Mobile 07752-730019
Kingdom Of Heaven (feature), Harry Potter & The Order Of The Phoenix (feature), The Bourne Ultimatum (feature).

Mark Funnel   Mobile 07850-194724
Nanny McPhee & The Big Bang (feature), Green Zone (feature), Amazing Grace (feature).

Sam Kite   020-8662 0452 Mobile 07711-047490
Friends & Crocodiles (TV drama), Gideon's Daughter (TV drama), Murder In Suburbia (TV drama).

Jamie Knight   Mobile 07740-101459
Gulliver's Travels (feature).

Vince Madden   020-8400 7551 Mobile 07831-845852
Fax 020-8400 7551
Harry Potter & The Goblet Of Fire (feature) (2nd unit), Five Children & It (feature), Sky Captain & The World Of Tomorrow (feature).

Bill Merrell   020-8335 3066 Mobile 07770-367944
Fax 020-8335 3066
City Of Ember (feature), Harry Potter & The Goblet Of Fire (feature), Troy (feature).

Guy Minoli   020-8360 3467 Mobile 07973-262975
Miss Potter (feature).

Stewart Monteith   01708-456048 Mobile 07931-752896
Star Wars: Episode I - The Phantom Menace (feature), Star Wars: Episode II - Attack Of The Clones (feature), Star Wars: Episode III - Revenge Of The Sith (feature).

Richard Potter   020-8568 3246 Mobile 07703-599677
The Thick Of It (TV comedy drama), Law & Order (TV drama), Spooks (TV drama).

Jon Scadden   Mobile 07710-816811
Messiah (TV drama), Amnesia (TV drama), Tough Love (TV drama).

Ronny Shane   020-8930 5166 Mobile 07976-433793
Harry Brown (feature), Anna & The King (feature), Band Of Brothers (TV drama).

Paul Sharp   Mobile 07802-774099
London Boulevard (feature).

David Staton   01706-212353 Mobile 07811-669731
Inspector George Gently (TV drama), Hotel Babylon (TV drama).

Aaron Walters   020-8555 2422 Mobile 07813-324063
Downton Abbey (TV drama), Fanny Hill (TV drama).

Andrew Watson   Mobile 07976-745113
Shanghai Knights (feature), Bridget Jones's Diary II (feature), Reign Of Fire (feature).

Shawn White   01628-531901 Mobile 07768-847042
Prince Of Persia (feature) (Gaffer - visual fx unit), The Golden Compass (feature).

Jonathan Yates   Mobile 07764-193303
Born & Bred (TV drama), Bend It Like Beckham (feature), Captain Corelli's Mandolin (feature).

CAMERA OPERATORS

Steven Alcorn   01895-622697 Mobile 07974-070713
Lewis (TV drama), Inspector Morse (TV drama), Dalziel & Pascoe (TV drama).

John Attwell   01702-478328 Mobile 07718-099312
SC 01932-252577
Beacon 77 (feature), Exam (feature).

Ossie Bacon   Mobile 07876-346934 DYA 020-7386 0310

Chas Bain   020-7602 7779 Mobile 07973-833781
ARRI 01895-457180 Fax 020-7602 7779
Nine (feature), Clash Of The Titans (feature), Quantum Of Solace (feature).

Roddy Barron   01424-447554 Mobile 07774-655555
CB 01932-592572 Fax 01424-447554
The Wolfman (feature), National Treasure: Book Of Secrets (feature), The Mummy Returns (feature).

Perry Barwick   Mobile 07973-253090
Heroes & Villains (feature), Fighting The Red Baron (TV docu drama), Ancient Rome: The Rise & Fall Of An Empire (TV drama).

Peter Batten   01235-764194 Mobile 07768-432646
ARRI 01895-457180
Fakers (feature), Hustle (TV drama), Atonement (feature) (additional photography).

Nick Beeks-Sanders   01926-335375 Mobile 07980-988161
Nativity (feature), The Edge Of Love (feature), Tess Of The D'Urbervilles (TV drama).

Julie Bills   Mobile 07802-443067 Fax 0131-556 8357
The Eagle Of The Ninth (feature), Neds (feature), Book Of Blood (feature).

Bob Binnall   Mobile 07774-723738
Clash Of The Titans (feature), Knife Edge (feature) (Director Of Photography - 2nd unit), Bronson (feature).

Joe Blackwell   020-7226 2410 Mobile 07880-711249
Primeval (TV drama), Life On Mars (TV drama), Waking The Dead (TV drama).

Lucy Bristow   020-7690 1216 Mobile 07973-822916
Me & Orson Welles (feature), It's A Wonderful Afterlife (feature), Into The Storm (TV film).

David Byrne   Mobile 07802-250456
Free Spirits (feature), Those Without Shadows (feature), The Vanguard (feature).

Robert Carter   Mobile 07712-050014
Shameless (TV drama), Skins (TV drama), The Bill (TV drama).

Ben Chads   01730-890147 Mobile 07973-137110
SC 01932-252577

Ian Clark   01454-321900 Mobile 07973-521248
Skellig (feature), Starter For Ten (feature), A Bunch Of Amateurs (feature).

Ben Coles   0117-965 7126 Mobile 07921-384362
Bad Girls (TV drama), Footballers' Wives (TV drama), Young Dracula (TV childrens).

Roberto Contreras   01603-447686 Mobile 07530-435866
Robin Hood (feature), Prince Of Persia (feature) (2nd unit), Casino Royale (feature).

Trevor Coop   01296-625414 Mobile 07885-097406
Fax 01296-696323
Julie & Julia (feature), Charlie Wilson's War (feature), Harry Potter & The Goblet Of Fire (feature).

Colin Corby   01895-834095

Rod Cumberbatch   020-7657 2567 Mobile 07957-646543
LSD (TV drama), Midnight Madness (TV drama), Lion Stove For Lesotho (TV doc).

Tim Dodd   01980-621917 Mobile 07831-379667
Fax 01980-621917
Wild Target (feature), A Line In The Sand (TV drama), Face (feature) (1st Assistant).

Paul Donachie   +1 424 558 1420 Mobile 07973-889208
Desperate Romantics (TV drama), The Other Boleyn Girl (feature), Spooks (TV drama).

Desmond Dubber   Mobile 07768-165286
Channel 4 News (TV news & current affairs), Sky Sport (TV sport).

Graeme Dunn   Mobile 07973-412014 Fax 07970-097686
Dear Frankie (feature), Sugar Rush (TV drama), Mastercard (commercial).

Jason Ellis   020-8968 4695 Mobile 07712-895357

Stephen Emerson   020-8770 7330 Mobile 07803-879871
BBC News (TV news & current affairs).

Craig Feather   0161-434 5526 Mobile 07768-624534
The Prisoner (TV drama), House Of Saddam (TV drama).

Nick Fenwick   Mobile 07990-970178
Blues & Twos (TV doc), Ski Sunday (TV sport), Revealing Secrets (TV doc).

Simon Finney   020-7435 6430 Mobile 07949-833456
ITG 020-7636 6565
Cemetery Junction (feature), Shanghai (feature) (B camera), The Pacific (TV drama) (blue unit).

Martin Foley 01483-893697 Mobile 07778-126947
CB 01932-592572
The Daisy Chain (feature), Greyfriars Bobby (feature), Prime Suspect (TV drama).

Mike Fox 020-8992 7268 Mobile 07740-475398
Shadow Of The Vampire (feature), Dangerous Liaisons (feature), Hope & Glory (feature).

Ken Garraway 020-8428 2007 Mobile 07831-211706
Fax 020-8428 2007

Jeremy Gee 020-8947 9261 Mobile 07850-387510
Fax 020-8947 9261
Charlotte Gray (feature), The Wind That Shakes The Barley (feature), Sliding Doors (feature).

Adam Gillham 020-8977 2701 Mobile 07973-383857
Fax 020-8977 2701
Spooks (TV drama), To The Ends Of The Earth (TV drama), Life & Lyrics (feature).

David Gopsill 020-7735 8495
The Stepdaughter (TV drama), Countdown To War (TV drama).

Dan Greenway 020-856 00 856 Mobile 07711-903990
www.dangreenwayltd.co.uk

Rodrigo Gutierrez 020-8744 9787 Mobile 07973-503837
PS 020-8883 1616
Sahara (feature) (2nd unit), Wimbledon (feature), The Van (feature).

Steven Hall Mobile 07836-335604
A Good Murder (TV drama), Gladiator (feature), Wedding Belles (TV drama).

Jamie Harcourt 0118-948 4150 Mobile 07973-893774
Ways To Live Forever (feature), Kiss Of Death (TV drama), Miss Marple (TV drama).

Paul Hardy Mobile 07958-611099

Gordon Hayman 01491-612918 Mobile 07787-504096

Jeremy Hiles 01798-869207 Mobile 07973-214126
ARRI 01895-457180
Harry Potter & The Half-Blood Prince (feature), Harry Potter & The Order Of The Phoenix (feature), Sex Traffic (TV drama).

Peter "Skip" Howard 020-8948 0031
Mobile 07976-565386
Ashes To Ashes (TV drama), Survivors (TV drama).

Gareth Hughes 020-7703 7522 Mobile 07973-540486
CC 01932-568268 Fax 020-7703 7522
Lark Rise To Candleford (TV drama), The Pillars Of The Earth (TV drama), Metamorphosis (short).

Martin Hume 01753-884696 Mobile 07803-048781
ARRI 01895-457180 Fax 01753-891088

Clive Jackson 020-8441 2255 Mobile 07785-268128
Robin Hood (feature), Prince Of Persia (feature) (2nd unit), Casino Royale (feature).

Ian Jackson 01494-725299 Mobile 07976-236628
Holby City (TV drama), RKO 281 (TV film), Jonathan Creek (TV drama).

Mark Jackson 01305-826082 Mobile 07768-256356
Mirror Signal Manoeuvre (TV doc), Asian Poker Open (TV sport), Ramsay's Kitchen Nightmares (TV reality).

Sam Jackson Mobile 07836-622392
Built From Disaster (TV doc), Gillette World Sport (TV sport), The Culture Show (TV arts).

Nigel Kirton 020-7272 4833 Mobile 07767-263904

Paul Langridge Mobile 07909-981267
The Bill (TV drama), Saved (TV drama), Headwig & The Angry Inch (feature) (2nd unit).

Dan Lightening Mobile 07768-615242
Blue Murder (TV drama), The Mutant Chronicles (feature) (Director Of Photography - 2nd unit), Cold Blood (TV drama) (1st Assistant).

Ken Lowe 01243-263859 Mobile 07973-618880
Primeval (TV drama), Holby Blue (TV drama), The Commander (TV drama).

Nick Lowin 01628-850912 Mobile 07973-226719
William & Mary (TV drama), A Class Apart (TV drama) (2nd unit), Walk Away & I Stumble (TV drama) (2nd unit).

Lee Mander 01932-354518 Mobile 07931-684049

John Maskall   0113-203 7256 Mobile 07836-240964
Fax 0113-203 7256
A Touch Of Frost (TV drama), Diamond Geezer (TV drama), The Quest (TV drama).

Michael McCleery   020-8892 8256 Mobile 07946-284090
Fax 020-8892 8256
Band Of Gold (TV drama), The Vietnamese (TV doc), Sainsbury's (commercial).

Mark McQuoid   Mobile 07906-557967
Apparitions (TV drama), Law & Order (TV drama), The Crew (feature) (B camera).

Luke Menges   Mobile 07973-324068
London Boulevard (feature).

Michael Metcalfe   01273-772800 Mobile 07802-969498
SC 01932-252577
B & Q (commercial), BBC Electric Proms (TV light entertainment), Live From Abbey Road (TV light entertainment).

Darren Miller   01274-586867 Mobile 07973-452898
Fax 01274-586867
A Touch Of Frost (TV drama), All The Small Things (TV drama), Waterloo Road (TV drama).

Mike Miller   01449-720593 Mobile 07939-093198
Fax 01449-720593
It's A Wonderful Afterlife (feature) (2nd unit), Staffroom Monologues (TV educational) (Director Of Photography), Primo (TV film).

Nic Milner   01886-833306 Mobile 07973-158627
PS 020-8883 1616 Fax 01886-833306
Harry Potter & The Half-Blood Prince (feature) (2nd unit), Equilibrium (feature), Colour Me Kubrick (feature).

Mark Milsome   Mobile 07813-786875 PS 020-8883 1616
Your Highness (feature) (B camera), Quantum Of Solace (feature) (B camera), Skellig (feature).

Darren Montague   Mobile 07796-446468
Kylie Minogue (concert), Genesis (concert), Party In The Park (events).

David Morgan   020-8360 9189 Mobile 07775-908050
Harry Potter & The Deathly Hallows (feature), The Golden Compass (feature) (2nd unit), The Last Legion (feature).

Karl Morgan   Mobile 07956-274029
Prince Of Persia (feature), Casino Royale (feature), V For Vendetta (feature).

Julian Morson   020-8675 2988 Mobile 07831-391224
SPA 01932-571044 Fax 020-8673 6603
Kick-Ass (feature), Dorian Gray (feature), RocknRolla (feature).

James Moss   020-8997 1014 Mobile 07966-373701
ARRI 01895-457180 Fax 0870-133 1187
Monday Monday (TV drama), Torchwood (TV drama), Silent Witness (TV drama).

Stephen Murray   01480-469139 Mobile 07713-458196
Fax 01480-469139
Poirot (TV drama), Apparitions (TV drama), The Street (TV drama).

Zac Nicholson   Mobile 07770-864979 UA 020-3214 0800
Glorious 39 (feature), The Boat That Rocked (feature), John Adams (TV drama).

Doug O'Neons   01372-723748 Mobile 07801-746346
Fax 01372-722029
Bad Boys (feature), Lolita (feature), Hanging Up (feature).

John Palmer   01494-862246 Mobile 07787-543606
Fax 01494-868411
Charlie & The Chocolate Factory (feature) (bluescreen), The World Is Not Enough (feature), 102 Dalmatians (feature).

Roger Pearce   01761-490611 Mobile 07831-110883
Fax 01761-490611
Goldeneye (feature), Casino Royale (feature), The Legend Of Zorro (feature).

Richard Philpott   020-8546 2735 Mobile 07771-664275
ARRI 01895-457180

John Piggott   020-8650 5158 Mobile 07956-125948
The Fixer (TV drama), Hotel Babylon (TV drama), Moving Wallpaper (TV drama).

Chris Pinnock   01372-451292 Mobile 07979-256814
Where Love Reigns (feature), The Tell-Tale Heart (TV film), Numerous commercials.

Mike Proudfoot   01984-640745 Mobile 07956-267590
Harry Potter & The Deathly Hallows (feature), Blood Diamond (feature), Defiance (feature).

Neil Purcell   Mobile 07976-702798
Red Dwarf: Back To Earth (TV comedy drama), Hell's Kitchen (TV reality), This Morning (TV magazine).

Alastair Rae   01288-361179 Mobile 07850-627230
SC 01932-252577
The Debt (feature), The Eagle Of The Ninth (feature), Cherie (feature).

Wayne Ratcliffe   Mobile 07831-608270 CCR 0845-634 5910
Royal Opera House (opera), The Nutcracker (ballet), Dancing On Ice (TV light entertainment).

CAMERA

Luke Redgrave 020-7351 3203 Mobile 07919-554550
ARRI 01895-457180
Mamma Mia! (feature), The Boat That Rocked (feature), The Other Boleyn Girl (feature) (2nd unit).

George Richmond BSC Mobile 07768-366633
ITG 020-7636 6565
Burn After Reading (feature), Clash Of The Titans (feature), Quantum Of Solace (feature).

Brian Rose 020-8868 1729 Mobile 07768-635788

Jane Rousseau Mobile 07971-850923
Life On Mars (TV drama), 24 Hour Party People (feature), Cops (TV drama).

Donald Russell 020-8693 0817 Mobile 07186-968040
Fax 020-8693 0817
Mayo (TV drama), Law & Order (TV drama), Six Degrees (TV drama).

John Ryan 01684-772330 Mobile 07774-851085
LL 020-8426 2200
Rachel Allen Bake (TV light entertainment), Rolf On Art (TV light entertainment), Scrapheap Challenge (TV light entertainment).

Xandy Sahla Mobile 07802-174955 PS 020-8883 1616
The Philanthropist (TV drama), Diamonds (TV drama), Agent Cody Banks II (feature).

Jerry Sandler 020-7684 1123 Mobile 07909-951190
Numerous commercials, B-Monkey (feature) (2nd unit).

Sean Savage 01491-834521 Mobile 07973-195144
PS 020-8883 1616
Clash Of The Titans (feature), Easy Virtue (feature), St Trinian's (feature).

Andrew Sheard 01347-838538 Mobile 07939-075034
Coronation Street (TV drama), Emmerdale (TV drama), Doctors (TV drama).

Bob Shipsey 01763-852127 Mobile 07973-385818
Fax 01763-852127
Wallander (TV drama), Trial & Retribution (TV drama), Blackpool (TV drama).

Philip Sindall 020-8998 7703 Mobile 07931-398466
SPA 01932-571044
Mamma Mia! (feature), Ladies In Lavender (feature), Nanny McPhee & The Big Bang (feature).

Loren Slater 01229-586818 Mobile 07813-051392
Daylight Hole (short), Death In The Bay (TV doc), The Drill (short).

Mark Smeaton 01453-833242 Mobile 07973-801646
Life On Mars (TV drama), Mistresses (TV drama), Lark Rise To Candleford (TV drama).

Bob Smith 01372-467955 Mobile 07774-133709
Fax 01372-467955
Kingdom Of Heaven (feature), Stardust (feature), Withnail & I (feature).

Rob Southam 0121-249 3445 Mobile 07941-010698
Sherlock Holmes (feature), Elizabeth: The Golden Age (feature), Broken Thread (feature).

Gary Spratling 01753-662913 Mobile 07946-518612
BE 01727-841177
Robin Hood (feature) (2nd unit), Quantum Of Solace (feature), Speed Racer (feature).

Stefan Stankowski Mobile 07754-871557
EXEC 01753-646677
Harry Potter & The Half-Blood Prince (feature) (2nd unit), Harry Potter & The Goblet Of Fire (feature), Harry Potter & The Prisoner Of Azkaban (feature).

Jon Stephen Mobile 07970-700911
Waterloo Road (TV drama), Shameless (TV drama), Love Soup (TV drama).

Martin Stephens 029-2052 0755 Mobile 07831-404009
ARRI 01895-457180 Fax 029-2052 0755
Dad Savage (feature), Doctor Who (TV drama), The River King (feature).

James Swanson 01428-645484 Mobile 07973-519794
Volvo (commercial), Kia (commercial), 600 Kg Of Pure Gold (feature).

Jonathan Sykes Mobile 07850-065916
Dust (feature), The Lost Prince (TV drama), City Lights (TV drama).

Peter Taylor 01727-832738 Mobile 07850-708691
EXEC 01753-646677
Kick-Ass (feature), Robin Hood (feature), Harry Potter & The Goblet Of Fire (feature).

Phil Taylor 01392-200340 Mobile 07976-655990

Dean Thompson 01749-672692 Mobile 07710-338357
Ironclad (feature), Ford (commercial), The Damned United (feature).

David Tondeur Mobile 07593-643023
The Two Mrs Grenvilles (feature), City Of Stone (feature), Shadow Of The Vampire (feature).

Daniel Trapp ARRI 01895-457180

CAMERA

Peter Versey   020-8873 7271   Mobile 07973-345378
ARRI 01895-457180
Little Dorrit (TV drama), The Brothers Grimm (feature) (model unit), Trial & Retribution (TV drama).

Malcolm Vinson BSC   Mobile 07811-085638
Fax 01276-678327
Harry & The Wrinklies (TV childrens), Die Another Day (feature) (action unit), Hollyoaks (TV drama).

Brett Walker   Mobile 07752-826626
Channel U (TV music), Eurosport (TV sport).

Geraint Warrington   020-8546 1060
Mobile 07831-624321 SC 01932-252577

Peter Welch   01932-254055   Mobile 07976-254347
Outnumbered (TV comedy drama), Little Britain (tour), Sting (promo).

Stefan Whatcott   Mobile 07876-654436
Young Dracula (TV childrens), MI High (TV childrens), Dream Team (TV drama).

Des Whelan   +353 1 235 0636
Sherlock Holmes (feature), Prince Of Persia (feature), The Wolfman (feature).

Peter Wignall   020-7482 2283   Mobile 07710-061127
Kick-Ass (feature), Telstar (feature) (Director Of Photography), Stardust (feature).

Ben Wilson   01491-629584   Mobile 07798-601401
ARRI 01895-457180
Clash Of The Titans (feature), The Pacific (TV drama), Elizabeth: The Golden Age (feature).

Tony Woodcock   01424-437221   Mobile 07710-276273
Fax 01424-437221
Peak Practice (TV drama), Poirot (TV drama), A Dance To The Music Of Time (TV film).

David Worley   01423-810780   Mobile 07956-263442
EXEC 01753-646677
The Wolfman (feature) (2nd unit), V For Vendetta (feature), An American Haunting (feature).

CAMERAMEN - 1ST ASSISTANT

Kirsti Abernethy   Mobile 07798-525878   WZ 020-7437 2055
The Broken (feature), Cashback (feature), Ginger Gora & The Gentles (short).

Christian Abomnes   Mobile +33 6 61 00 87 75
Asterix At The Olympic Games (feature), Babylon AD (feature), La Vie En Rose (feature).

Rene Aderfarasin   Mobile 07824-777145
Robin Hood (feature) (2nd unit), Shanghai (feature), Fred Claus (feature).

Tim Allan   Mobile 07866-769288   SC 01932-252577

Eva Arnold   Mobile 07986-580209
Shank (short), Huge (feature), St Trinian's (feature).

Marc Atherfold   01375-393280   Mobile 07909-961660
Harry Potter & The Deathly Hallows (feature), Quantum Of Solace (feature), The Golden Compass (feature).

John Bailie   020-7586 7008   Mobile 07973-742127
The Day Of The Triffids (TV drama), Doom (feature), Colour Me Kubrick (feature).

Chris Bain   Mobile 07973-820946
Clash Of The Titans (feature), Quantum Of Solace (feature), City Of Ember (feature).

Andrew Banwell   Mobile 07970-548013
Ghost Squad (TV drama), 55 Degrees North (TV drama), Conviction (TV drama).

Sam Barnes   020-8293 3991   Mobile 07973-955474
City Lights (TV drama), Amazing Grace (feature), Casino Royale (feature).

Terry Bartlett FRPS   029-2061 6414   Mobile 07831-709778
Fax 029-2061 6414
Ironclad (feature), Merlin (TV drama), Lark Rise To Candleford (TV drama).

Peter Bateson   Mobile 07899-946056
Mr Eleven (TV comedy drama), The Lives Of The Saints (feature), The Message (TV light entertainment).

Ben Battersby   Mobile 07977-105075   ARRI 01895-457180
Little Dorrit (TV drama).

Tim Battersby   020-8961 9395   Mobile 07976-278145
EXEC 01753-646677   Fax 020-8691 9395
Harry Brown (feature), Ironclad (feature), Sex Drugs & Rock & Roll (feature).

Steven Battley   01483-200687   Mobile 07973-560852
Fax 01483-200782
Underworld (feature), Hamish Macbeth (TV drama), Miss Marple (TV drama).

Jon Beacham   Mobile 07768-904590
Lewis (TV drama), Pride & Prejudice (feature), Spooks (TV drama).

David Bell   01204-884539 Mobile 07946-813168
Eleventh Hour (TV drama), Survivors (TV drama), Byron (TV drama).

Richard Bevan   01909-518006 Mobile 07774-453965
Ways To Live Forever (feature), All The Small Things (TV drama), A Touch Of Frost (TV drama).

Kelvin Billing   01932-567511 Mobile 07774-745745
Hotel Babylon (TV drama), Holby City (TV drama), Silent Witness (TV drama).

Jim Bishop   Mobile 07831-354970 SR 020-7736 7786

Paddy Blake   01753-662692 Mobile 07970-694862
GEMS 029-2071 0770
Driving Lessons (feature), Run Fat Boy Run (feature), Flawless (feature).

Craig Bloor   01753-887887 Mobile 07771-927413
EXEC 01753-646677
The Wolfman (feature) (2nd unit), Kingdom Of Heaven (feature) (2nd unit), The Imaginarium Of Dr Parnassus (feature).

Ashley Bond   020-7586 0737 Mobile 07774-862131
Mamma Mia! (feature), Robin Hood (feature), Creation (feature).

Harry Bowers   01865-728704 Mobile 07976-237476
Your Highness (feature) (B camera), Into The Storm (TV film) (B camera), Quantum Of Solace (feature) (B camera).

Roger Bowles   Mobile 07976-221036 ARRI 01895-457180
Unmade Beds (feature), Kings (feature), Waz (feature).

Catherine Brandish   01753-647051 Mobile 07973-164690
Holby City (TV drama), Footballers' Wives (TV drama), Casualty (TV drama).

Richard Brierley   01932-853680 Mobile 07710-450970
Sharpe's Peril (TV drama), Foyle's War (TV drama), Miss Marple (TV drama).

Jessie Brough   020-7328 6175 Mobile 07973-436075
WZ 020-7437 2055 Fax 020-7328-6175
Jimmy's Farm (TV doc) (Camera Operator).

Catharine Brown   01424-712216 Mobile 07958-767904
SC 01932-252577
Numerous commercials, features & promos, The Reeds (feature), Madonna (promo).

Neil Brown   01494-868340 Mobile 07973-751514
Fax 01494-868340

Warren Buckingham   01273-327394
Mobile 07802-846035 SC 01932-252577

Julian Bucknall   01932-852532 Mobile 07768-960363
Your Highness (feature) (B camera), Sherlock Holmes (feature), The Wolfman (feature).

James Burgess   Mobile 07979-813063 SC 01932-252577
Defiance (feature), The Wolfman (feature) (2nd unit), Stardust (feature) (2nd unit).

Steve Burgess   Mobile 07968-393047
Prince Of Persia (feature), The Wolfman (feature) (2nd unit), The Da Vinci Code (feature) (2nd unit).

Peter Byrne   Mobile 07968-628954 ARRI 01895-457180
The Special Relationship (feature), The King's Speech (feature), The Boat That Rocked (feature).

Ciro Candia   020-8543 5414 Mobile 07711-001600
WZ 020-7437 2055

Sue Cane   01297-444995 Mobile 07733-230423
F59 0117-906 4300
Death Of A President (feature), No Heroics (TV comedy drama), The Palace (TV drama).

Billy Charlton   020-8671 2056 Mobile 07961-382248
Spooks (TV drama), Trial & Retribution (TV drama), The Fixer (TV drama).

Julian Charrington   020-8747 4744 Mobile 07795-342842
Fax 020-8995 0665
Last Of The Summer Wine (TV comedy drama), Carriani A Courtesan (TV drama), Madhur Jaffrey's Far East Cookery (TV light entertainment).

Giles Christopher   020-8979 9401 Mobile 07768-946656

Shaun Cobley   020-8888 0494 Mobile 07958-669025
ARRI 01895-457180
Wild Child (feature), Gulliver's Travels (feature) (2nd unit), Hitchhiker's Guide To The Galaxy (feature) (2nd unit).

Ian Coffey   Mobile 07966-155573
From Time To Time (feature).

Philippe Cointepas   Mobile 07905-107851
ARRI 01895-457180
Eden Lake (feature), Britannia High (TV drama).

Chris Cole   020-8657 2379 Mobile 07880-795101

Adam Coles   01932-250219 Mobile 07931-155098
The Day Of The Triffids (TV drama), The Damned United (feature), Cranford (TV drama).

Sean Connor   01494-872500 Mobile 07976-364049

Jason Coop   Mobile 07718-747447
Adulthood (feature), 1408 (feature), Party Animals (TV drama).

CAMERA

Richard Copeman Mobile 07974-412166
Jackboots On Whitehall (feature), Harry Potter & The Half-Blood Prince (feature), The Wolfman (feature).

David Cozens 01932-229414 Mobile 07711-638115
ARRI 01895-457180
Clash Of The Titans (feature), Green Zone (feature), Prince Of Persia (feature).

Carlos De Carvalho 01923-853024 Mobile 07870-519471
Harry Potter & The Half-Blood Prince (feature), Sahara (feature), Atonement (feature).

John Deaton 01923-222001 Mobile 07850-013705
Harry Potter & The Chamber Of Secrets (feature), Anna & The King (feature), Les Miserables (feature).

Robert Dibble 020-8883 8487 Mobile 07803-131823
Fax 020-8883 8487
Harry Potter & The Deathly Hallows (feature), Blood Diamond (feature), Defiance (feature).

Chris Dodds Mobile 07932-749592
Marks & Spencer (commercial), Huge (feature).

Oliver Driscoll 01494-488179 Mobile 07815-145767
The Hurt Locker (feature), The Special Relationship (feature), Green Zone (feature).

Jonathan Earp Mobile 07771-823577
The Wolfman (feature), Lewis (TV drama), New Tricks (TV drama).

Dan Edwards Mobile 07790-259221
Centurion (feature), Die Another Day (feature), Basic Instinct II (feature).

Tobias Eedy Mobile 07770-928673 ARRI 01895-457180
Basic Instinct II (feature), Stormbreaker (feature), Harry Potter & The Philosopher's Stone (feature).

John Ellis Evans Mobile 07779-574424
ARRI 01895-457180
Hamlet (feature), Five Daughters (TV drama), Wild Target (feature).

Charlie England 020-7700 1344 Mobile 07976-936710
Defiance (feature), Cranford (TV drama), Survivors (TV drama).

Miles Evans 020-7263 4009 Mobile 07956-544112
Fax 020-7263 4009
The Inspector Lynley Mysteries (TV drama), The Glass (TV drama), Appetite (feature).

Shaun Evans 01245-251828 Mobile 07946-391308

John Ferguson 01273-509510 Mobile 07831-371566
Harry Potter & The Half-Blood Prince (feature) (2nd unit), Harry Potter & The Prisoner Of Azkaban (feature), Sleepy Hollow (feature).

Russell Ferguson Mobile 07973-400262
ARRI 01895-457180
Nanny McPhee & The Big Bang (feature) (2nd unit), The Other Boleyn Girl (feature), Bleak House (TV drama).

Francesco Ferrari Mobile 07956-976717
Little Dorrit (TV drama), Harry Potter & The Order Of The Phoenix (feature), Waking The Dead (TV drama).

Neil Flaherty Mobile 07947-578649

Adam Forrester 01460-62770 Mobile 07774-700066
Fax 01460-62770

James Foster Mobile 07968-149901
Primeval (TV drama), Bronson (feature).

John Foster 01494-527608 Mobile 07881-613236
EXEC 01753-646677 Fax 01494-527608
The Golden Compass (feature), Nanny McPhee (feature), Flyboys (feature).

Guy Frost 01621-869044 Mobile 07812-100946
Troy (feature), Harry Potter & The Chamber Of Secrets (feature), Chocolat (feature).

Dan Gadd Mobile 07884-252864
Ian Brown (promo), Castrol (commercial), Powder (feature).

John Gamble 01932-222538 Mobile 07885-294875
Robin Hood (feature), Nine (feature), Quantum Of Solace (feature) (2nd unit).

Sarah Gardiner 020-8567 0262 Mobile 07770-500543
EXEC 01753-646677
Outnumbered (TV comedy drama), From Time To Time (feature), Band Of Brothers (TV drama).

Steven Gardner 0114-249 3915 Mobile 07931-715891
GEMS 029-2071 0770
Four Lions (feature), The Secret Diaries Of Miss Anne Lister (TV drama), Shameless (TV drama).

Jonathan Garwes Mobile 07768-698315
Doomsday (feature), The Descent 2 (feature).

Ben Gibb 020-8395 0060 Mobile 07932-737493
SC 01932-252577
Miss Marple (TV drama), Ballast (feature) (2nd Assistant), Poirot (TV drama).

Leigh Gold 020-7502 3489 Mobile 07801-287453
RED 020-8374 3074
An Education (feature), Last Chance Harvey (feature), Casino Royale (feature).

Sam Goldie 020-7226 6717 Mobile 07958-517623
WZ 020-7437 2055

Michael Green 01865-872820 Mobile 07770-592968
Christmas At The Riviera (TV drama), Poirot (TV drama), Below (feature).

George Grieve 020-8883 8398 Mobile 07956-185641
Spooks (TV drama), Hustle (TV drama), The Brief (TV drama).

Kenny Groom 020-8449 7998 Mobile 07966-165890
Street Fighter: The Legend of Chun-Li (feature), The Golden Compass (feature).

Tristan Haley Mobile 07786-260600 WZ 020-7437 2055

Kash Halford ARRI 01895-457180

Paul Hanning 01423-506783 Mobile 07899-081656

Tom Harding 01840-261339 Mobile 07768-815705
Fax 01840-261339

John Harper 020-8354 1742 Mobile 07980-981261
The 39 Steps (TV film), Secret Diary Of A Call Girl (TV drama), God On Trial (TV drama).

Elly Harrowes Mobile 07958-259218
Doctor Who (TV drama), Walkers Crisps (commercial), The Queen's Nose (TV childrens).

Rawdon Hayne 0118-984 3097 Mobile 07836-238704
Gulliver's Travels (feature), In Bruges (feature), Atonement (feature).

Guy Hazel Mobile 07803-139124 SC 01932-252577
Audi (commercial), Mastercard (commercial), Jaguar (commercial).

Simon Heck 01442-872124 Mobile 07966-472998
Prince Of Persia (feature) (visual fx unit), The Wolfman (feature), Wanted (feature) (2nd unit).

David Hedges 020-8543 8192 Mobile 07710-271708
Fax 020-8543 8192
Miss Marple (TV drama), Doc Martin (TV drama), Last Orders (feature).

Charlie Herranz Mobile 07981-066595 SC 01932-252577
Clash Of The Titans (feature), Numerous commercials, Prince Of Persia (feature) (2nd unit).

Dermot Hickey 01628-473724 Mobile 07970-104220
Fax 01628-473724
The Duchess (feature), Shanghai (feature), 1408 (feature).

Leo Holba Mobile 07980-621757 ARRI 01895-457180
Smirnoff (commercial), Ford (commercial), Huge (feature).

Robin Horn 01225-471887 Mobile 07958-428472
SC 01932-252577
Numerous commercials.

Alex Howe 020-7703 0466 Mobile 07885-305804
Fax 020-7703 0466

Peter Hughes 01628-475397 Mobile 07752-844193

Karl Hui Mobile 07941-954968
Soul Boy (feature), Third Star (feature), Samsung (commercial).

Simon Hume 01494-718988 Mobile 07976-817483
ARRI 01895-457180 Fax 01494-718988
Robin Hood (feature), Kingdom Of Heaven (feature), Troy (feature).

Chris Hutchinson 01457-874148 Mobile 07720-708242
Blue Murder (TV drama), Shameless (TV drama), Cold Blood (TV drama).

Anna James Mobile 07779-090079
Hotel Babylon (TV drama), Boy Meets Girl (TV drama), Torchwood (TV drama).

Cedric James 01932-342878 Mobile 07860-681640
Shergar: The Hunted (TV drama), Event Horizon (feature), First Knight (feature).

Stephen Janes 020-8285 1049 Mobile 07958-684289
Holby City (TV drama), The Daisy Chain (feature), Numerous commercials.

John Jordan 01798-865598 Mobile 07932-165206
GAS 020-8813 1999
Harry Potter & The Half-Blood Prince (feature), Sahara (feature), Tomb Raider (feature).

Tony Kay Mobile 07747-801948 SC 01932-252577
Fish Tank (feature).

Steve Kemp 020-7350 0917 Mobile 07955-170097
Hamish Macbeth (TV drama), Delicate & Damned (TV drama).

Mary Kyte 01628-660679 Mobile 07973-341429
ARRI 01895-457180 Fax 0845-391 4960
Emma (feature), Ashes To Ashes (TV drama), Pure Mule (TV drama).

CAMERAMEN - 1ST ASSISTANT

Brad Larner   01923-854414 Mobile 07771-558824
Fax 01923-854414
The Dark Knight (feature), Shakespeare In Love (feature), Gosford Park (feature).

Josh Lee   Mobile 07771-665539
Midsomer Murders (TV drama), City Lights (TV drama), Minder (TV drama).

Oliver Longcraine   020-7263 4378 Mobile 07770-874373
W.E. (feature), The Young Victoria (feature), Green Zone (feature).

Sally Low   Mobile 07855-756936
All Good Children (feature), A Boy Called Dad (feature), The Children (feature).

Paul Mackay   020-8693 6632 Mobile 07958-770227
SC 01932-252577
Little White Lies (feature), Eden Lake (feature), The Escapist (feature).

Clive Mackey   01483-481277 Mobile 07976-318538
GAS 020-8813 1999
Batman Begins (feature), Inception (feature), The Way Back (feature).

Mark Maidment   01932-232456 Mobile 07973-827623
Wallander (TV drama), Shrooms (feature), Messiah (TV drama).

Nathan Mann   Mobile 07973-263042 ARRI 01895-457180
Chalet Girl (feature), Poirot (TV drama), 28 Weeks Later (feature).

Joe Maples   020-8986 8917 Mobile 07801-341034
Wuthering Heights (feature), Angel (feature), Heartbreak Hotel (feature).

Rod "The Vicar" Marley   020-8748 0736
Mobile 07734-713846 ARRI 01895-457180
Being Human (TV drama), 28 Days Later (feature), Bright Star (feature) (2nd camera).

David McDowall   Mobile 07930-472536
Trial & Retribution (TV drama), Mitsubishi (commercial), British Telecom (commercial).

Keith McNamara   020-7837 3666 Mobile 07976-852303
Robin Hood (feature), Prince Of Persia (feature) (2nd unit), Kingdom Of Heaven (feature).

Simon Mills   01753-857887 Mobile 07854-648327
Harry Potter & The Goblet Of Fire (feature) (underwater), The Four Feathers (feature), The Dark Is Rising (feature).

Jon Mitchell   020-8953 5454 Mobile 07976-407856
SC 01932-252577

Rory Moles   020-8755 4549 Mobile 07973-383306
Spooks (TV drama), The Other Boleyn Girl (feature), Hustle (TV drama).

Ray Moore   01273-692874 Mobile 07932-154482
Fax 01273-692874
Strength & Honour (feature), Botched (feature), The Pinocchio Effect (feature).

Phil Mullally   Mobile 07867-914037
Your Highness (feature), High Heels & Low Lifes (feature), The Flood (feature).

Spencer Murray   020-8207 2644 Mobile 07970-473678
Quantum Of Solace (feature) (2nd unit), Back In Business (feature), Die Another Day (feature) (action unit).

Ros Naylor   01438-714793 Mobile 07973-600804
SC 01932-252577 Fax 01438-714793
Finding Neverland (feature), Harry Potter & The Philosopher's Stone (feature), The Clandestine Marriage (feature).

Gabi Norland   Mobile 07974-147106 SC 01932-252577
The Unloved (feature), Live From Abbey Road (TV light entertainment), Madonna - Confessions (concert).

Eamonn O'Keeffe   Mobile 07849-440669
Harry Potter & The Half-Blood Prince (feature) (2nd unit), Mississippi Burning (feature), Eragon (feature).

Jason Olive   020-7383 0968 Mobile 07958-221681

Jenny Paddon   Mobile 07977-262827
Nowhere Boy (feature), The First Grader (feature), Sahara (feature).

Robert Palmer   01494-712812 Mobile 07798-601054
Fax 01494-712352
Prince Of Persia (feature), Green Zone (feature), Hippie Hippie Shake (feature).

Rob Paterson   01629-760135 Mobile 07973-333693
Nike (commercial), Tetley's (commercial), Iceland (commercial).

Marcus Pavett   01628-626896 Mobile 07956-439731

Martin Payne   Mobile 07968-030492
Dalziel & Pascoe (TV drama), Pie In The Sky (TV drama), Soldier Soldier (TV drama).

Nigel Permane   01628-626412 Mobile 07977-939298
The Wolfman (feature) (visual fx unit), The Golden Compass (feature) (visual fx unit), Harry Potter & The Goblet Of Fire (feature) (2nd unit).

Derrick Peters   01753-654573 Mobile 07710-947933
The Last Word (feature), Here (feature), Four Lions (feature).

Barney Piercy   020-8874 5735 Mobile 07778-649970
ARRI 01895-457180 Fax 020-8874 5735
RocknRolla (feature), The Edge Of Love (feature).

Timothy Potter   020-7639 3263 Mobile 07739-989333
BE 01727-841177 Fax 020-7729 8093
Dead Set (TV drama), The Disappearance Of Alice Creed (feature),
The Wedding Date (feature).

Oleg Poupko   01424-204788 Mobile 07713-322004
SC 01932-252577
Gorillaz (music), PG Tips (commercial), AC/DC (promo).

Matt Poynter   0117-9095787 Mobile 07976-815009
ARRI 01895-457180
RocknRolla (feature), Lesbian Vampire Killers (feature), The Shell
Seekers (TV drama).

Jon Priddle   Mobile 07905-175041
Sparkle (feature), Hotel Babylon (TV drama), The Brief (TV
drama).

Rupert Prince   Mobile 07976-393868

Clive Prior   020-8372 3241 Mobile 07803-048793
Fax 020-8372 3241
The Debt (feature), St Trinian's II: The Legend Of Fritton's Gold
(feature), Tamara Drewe (feature).

Miles Proudfoot   Mobile 07976-732762
Eragon (feature), From Time To Time (feature), The Colour Of Magic
(TV film).

Ralph Ramsden   020-8977 1472 Mobile 07850-765418
How To Lose Friends & Alienate People (feature), Centurion (feature),
The Da Vinci Code (feature).

Darren Ravenscroft   Mobile 07971-727597
Massive (TV comedy drama), Inspector George Gently (TV drama),
Numerous commercials.

Alex Reid   020-8735 0393 Mobile 07956-152358
SC 01932-252577
Married Single Other (TV drama), Sexy Beast (feature), Tales Of The
City (TV drama).

Sam Renton   Mobile 07973-425734 EXEC 01753-646677

Chris Reynolds   Mobile 07986-906140
Hotel Babylon (TV drama).

Iwan Prys Reynolds   020-8205 9710 Mobile 07966-383205
ARRI 01895-457180
Tyrannosaur (feature), 4.3.2.1 (feature), Submarine (feature).

Gavin Richards   01502-723525 Mobile 07762-881084
Hyperdrive (TV comedy drama), Catastrophes (TV doc), Engineering
Egypt (TV drama doc).

Jonathan Richmond 020-7604 3588 Mobile 07767-262722
EXEC 01753-646677 Fax 020-7604 3589
Clash Of The Titans (feature), Quantum Of Solace (feature), Nine
(feature).

Keith Roberts   Mobile 07973-553454
The Golden Compass (feature) (2nd unit).

Neil Robertson   020-8891 1109 Mobile 07768-434700
Inspector Morse (TV drama), Hornblower (TV drama), True Blue (TV
drama) (2nd Assistant).

Sarah Rollason   01424-447597 Mobile 07974-307299
SC 01932-252577
Flying Monsters 3D (feature), Intimacy (feature) (B camera).

Shirley Schumacher   Mobile 07957-751301
F59 0117-906 4300
Crash (TV drama), Dr Who (TV drama), The First Men In The Moon
(TV drama).

Hilda Sealy   07050-072388 Mobile 07734-294668
Swinging With The Finkels (feature), Death At A Funeral (feature),
Tormented (feature) (2nd unit).

Kim Seber   Mobile 07973-121988 ARRI 01895-457180
Harry Potter & The Order Of The Phoenix (feature), State Of Play (TV
drama), The Way We Live Now (TV drama).

Gordan Segrove   020-7924 4344 Mobile 07973-227638
Me & Orson Welles (feature), It's A Wonderful Afterlife (feature),
Mike Leigh - Untitled 10 (feature).

Sky Sharrock   020-7267 3170 Mobile 07956-277880
The Imaginarium Of Dr Parnassus (feature) (model unit),
Celebration (TV film).

Martin Shepherd   01237-478571 Mobile 07976-799691
The Nutcracker (ballet), Fingersmith (TV drama), In The Night
Garden (TV childrens).

Dan Shoring   Mobile 07710-037652
Touching The Void (TV doc), Jane Eyre (TV drama), Micro Men (TV
drama).

Basil Smith   Mobile 07767-676367
Prince Of Persia (feature) (2nd unit).

Matthew Smith   Mobile 07866-516811
Numerous commercials.

Mark Sneddon   Mobile 07940-180895
In The Loop (feature), The Inbetweeners (TV comedy drama).

CAMERA

Tony Stanier 01474-700339 Mobile 07968-070682
Devil's Playground (feature), Walter's War (TV drama), Agent Cody Banks II (feature).

Iain Struthers Mobile 07802-983086 ARRI 01895-457180
It's A Wonderful Afterlife (feature), Cemetery Junction (feature), Sherlock Holmes (feature).

Olly Tellett 01962-863652 Mobile 07976-362830
ARRI 01895-457180
Sherlock Holmes (feature), Sunshine (feature), The Constant Gardener (feature).

Hayden Thomas Mobile 07980-550051
The Seven Wonders Of The Solar System (TV doc), Hotel Babylon (TV drama), Little Dorrit (TV drama).

Simon Tindall Mobile 07775-658992
Bright Star (feature), Mighty Heart (feature), The Queen (feature).

Andy Todd Mobile 07730-796590
Hotel Babylon (TV drama).

Jonathan Tomes Mobile 07889-217385
Jonathan Creek (TV drama), Footballers' Wives (TV drama), Bad Girls (TV drama).

Axel Ulrich 01895-833762 Mobile 07776-232080
Fax 01895-833762
Creation (feature) (2nd unit), Action Star (feature), True North (feature).

Simon Walton 01392-428057 Mobile 07711-627893
Skins (TV drama), New Tricks (TV drama), Foyle's War (TV drama).

Stephen Warner 0113-250 9605 Mobile 07977-510027
Blue Murder (TV drama), Casualty 1909 (TV drama), A Passionate Woman (TV drama).

John Watters Mobile 07813-708846 SC 01932-252577
Casino Royale (feature) (2nd unit), Man On Fire (feature), Black Hawk Down (feature).

George Watts 01584-877025 Mobile 07754-775223
The Raging Moon (feature), The Slipper & The Rose (feature), Edward VII (TV drama).

Matthew Waving Mobile 07879-647206
Macbeth (TV film), The Hills Have Eyes II (feature) (2nd Assistant), The Descent (feature) (2nd Assistant).

Jon Webb 01293-226107 Mobile 07971-859453
SC 01932-252577
The Bourne Ultimatum (feature), Kick-Ass (feature), Revolver (feature).

Matt Wesson 01923-771609 Mobile 07973-226590
Clash Of The Titans (feature) (underwater unit), Prime Suspect (TV drama), Numerous commercials.

Fran Weston Mobile 07970-895130 WZ 020-7437 2055
Numerous commercials & promos, Rather You Than Me (TV drama), Clubbed (feature) (2nd unit).

Nathan Wiley 020-8333 0055 Mobile 07703-963220

Tom Wilkinson Mobile 07976-612343 ARRI 01895-457180
Freestyle (feature), Huge (feature), Holy Waters (feature).

Glyn Williams 01372-463389 Mobile 07831-622183
Robin Hood (feature), Amelia (feature) (aerial unit), Casino Royale (feature) (aerial unit).

Tom Williams Mobile 07944-796442
Shameless (TV drama), Holby City (TV drama), Love Soup (TV drama).

Gavin Wilson 01422-845030 Mobile 07973-677445
See No Evil (TV drama), Last Of The Summer Wine (TV comedy drama), No Angels (TV drama).

Matt Windon Mobile 07597-569521
Your Highness (feature).

Simon Woodards 01784-248134 Mobile 07763-555021

Jenny Woods 020-7801 0233 Mobile 07971-411773
Silent Witness (TV drama), The Film Programme (TV light entertainment), The Human Body (TV doc).

Joe Wright Mobile 07966-529502 CB 01932-592572
The Da Vinci Code (feature) (2nd unit), The Wolfman (feature) (2nd unit).

David Wyatt Mobile 07961-403309 SC 01932-252577
The League Of Gentlemen's Apocalypse (feature), Cape Wrath (TV drama), Shameless (TV drama).

CAMERAMEN - 2ND ASSISTANT

John Adefarasin Mobile 07920-460174
Amazing Grace (feature), The Jacket (feature), Vanity Fair (feature).

Stuart Anderson 0141-636 3813 Mobile 07904-098179
New Town Killers (feature), Doomsday (feature), Stone Of Destiny (feature).

Natasha Back Mobile 07799-032472

Sebastian Barraclough   Mobile 07974-725245
Clash Of The Titans (feature), Quantum Of Solace (feature), Nine (feature).

Jacob Barrie   Mobile 07966-220993 ARRI 01895-457180
Robin Hood (feature), Creation (feature), Shanghai (feature).

Rami Bartholdy   020-8675 5305 Mobile 07815-793449
London Boulevard (feature).

Louise Ben-Nathan   Mobile 07956-910141
ARRI 01895-457180
Primeval (TV drama), Ashes To Ashes (TV drama), The Big I Am (feature).

Alfie Biddle   Mobile 07769-885620
Green Zone (feature), From Time To Time (feature), Harry Potter & The Order Of The Phoenix (feature).

Alex Byng   Mobile 07960-936250

Alice Canty   01494-713761 Mobile 07974-025363
Midsomer Murders (TV drama), Housewife 49 (TV drama), Ironclad (feature).

Dan Carling   Mobile 07709-426940 SC 01932-252577
The Devil's Double (feature), Street Dance 3D (feature), Macbeth (TV film).

Abigail Catto   Mobile 07973-783476
London Boulevard (feature).

David Churchyard   Mobile 07939-678450
John Carter Of Mars (feature), Robin Hood (TV drama), Clash Of The Titans (feature).

Chris Clarke   020-8251 8577 Mobile 07921-189758
W.E. (feature), Clash (feature), Prince Of Persia (feature).

Matthew Cole   020-7249 3068 Mobile 07960-665822
WZ 020-7437 2055
Numerous commercials & promos.

Cat Cornes   Mobile 07957-763415
Little Dorrit (TV drama).

Sandra Coulson   0161-282 7147 Mobile 07860-384985
Foyle's War (TV drama), Fanny Hill (TV drama), Sharpe's Peril (TV drama).

Barny Crocker   020-7690 1539 Mobile 07813-694010
ARRI 01895-457180
Prince Of Persia (feature) (visual fx unit), Dean Spanley (feature), The Edge Of Love (feature).

Jason Cuddy   Mobile 07801-269561 CC 01932-568268
Freestyle (feature), Huge (feature).

Christopher Dale   Mobile 07956-379792
Sweeney Todd (feature), The Bourne Ultimatum (feature), Gulliver's Travels (feature) (2nd unit).

Mark Dempsey   Mobile 07930-371314
The Damned United (feature), Moon (feature), The Cottage (feature).

Jackie Dewe Mathews   Mobile 07813-312916
Stardust (feature) (2nd unit).

Camilla "Milly" Drennan   Mobile 07771-723020

Jason Dully   Mobile 07944-555213 ARRI 01895-457180
Sherlock Holmes (feature) (B camera), The Other Boleyn Girl (feature), London Boulevard (feature).

Emma Edwards   Mobile 07830-315155
Nanny McPhee & The Big Bang (feature) (2nd unit), Death Defying Acts (feature), Hancock & Joan (TV drama).

Tom Ellis   020-7159 2646 Mobile 07977-290193
SC 01932-252577

John Evans   Mobile 07798-601847 ARRI 01895-457180
Angus Thongs & Perfect Snogging (feature).

Richard Evans   Mobile 07973-478010
The Second Coming (TV drama), Bodies (TV drama), The Royle Family (TV comedy drama).

Stephen Evans   020-8931 2608 Mobile 07771-941417

Kate Filby   Mobile 07949-088973 ARRI 01895-457180
From Time To Time (feature), St Trinian's (feature), The Colour Of Magic (TV film).

Catherine Frift   01926-511427 Mobile 07768-057746
Servants (TV drama), Possession (feature), The Mummy Returns (feature) (2nd unit).

Natasha Gamper   Mobile 07961-438872
Little Dorrit (TV drama).

Andy Gardner   Mobile 07813-786875
Your Highness (feature).

Max Glickman   Mobile 07803-161731 RED 020-8374 3074

Magnus Graham   Mobile 07900-513360
Searchd: The Inaccessible Pinnacle (feature).

Brian Greenway   Mobile 07989-414884
In Bruges (feature) (2nd unit), Angus Thongs & Perfect Snogging (feature).

Woody Gregson   Mobile 07966-211314
Miss Marple (TV drama).

CAMERA

Alan Hall   Mobile 07770-784278
Iron Man II (feature), Gulliver's Travels (feature), Inception (feature).

Valdez Hanks   Mobile 07799-624291 SC 01932-252577

Michael Hannan   020-7727 2257 Mobile 07860-514671
Harry Potter & The Prisoner Of Azkaban (feature) (2nd unit), Children Of Men (feature) (2nd unit), Hippie Hippie Shake (feature) (2nd unit).

Kate Higgs   Mobile 07949-767282
The Commander (TV drama), Spooks (TV drama), Sharpe's Challenge (TV drama).

Andy Hill   ARRI 01895-457180

Alice Hobden   Mobile 07971-963589
Mamma Mia! (feature), Clash Of The Titans (feature) (2nd unit), 1408 (feature).

Jon Howard   Mobile 07768-793999 ARRI 01895-457180
Hunter (TV drama), Lewis (TV drama), Spooks (TV drama) (1st Assistant).

Lewis Hume   Mobile 07867-804306
Robin Hood (feature), The Wolfman (feature), Stardust (feature).

Will Humphris   Mobile 07789-654859
Clash Of The Titans (feature), Quantum Of Solace (feature) (2nd unit), Children Of Men (feature).

Gabriel Hyman   01923-239343 Mobile 07980-747133
ARRI 01895-457180
Lewis (TV drama), New Tricks (TV drama), Rosemary & Thyme (TV drama).

Jamie Jackson   Mobile 07798-505603

Jenny John-Chuan   020-8845 2269 Mobile 07973-830066
SC 01932-252577 Fax 020-8845 2269

Ed Jones   Mobile 07956-318882
Clash Of The Titans (feature), Casino Royale (feature), Kingdom Of Heaven (feature).

Sacha Jones   Mobile 07595-351625
Brighton Rock (feature), Woody Allan's Summer Project (feature), Kick-Ass (feature).

Chris Kane   Mobile 07932-749751 SC 01932-252577

Peter Keith   Mobile 07989-396015
New Town Killers (feature).

Russell Kennedy   01279-723368 Mobile 07976-725974
EXEC 01753-646677
The Hurt Locker (feature), Quantum Of Solace (feature), Nine (feature).

Alison Lai   020-7702 8840 Mobile 07931-761292
SC 01932-252577 Fax 020-7702 8840
Your Highness (feature), The Shell Seekers (TV drama), Primo (TV film).

Alison Lai   Mobile 07931-761292
Your Highness (feature) (B camera).

Danny Lee   Mobile 07791-645961
The Tenth Kingdom (TV drama), Mile High (TV drama), Night & Day (TV drama).

David Lee   Mobile 07947-811422
Waking The Dead (TV drama), Primeval (TV drama), Matchpoint (feature).

Joanne Lee   Mobile 07940-586873
Charlie & The Chocolate Factory (feature).

James Lewis   01923-897075 Mobile 07764-742184
Basic Instinct II (feature), Casino Royale (feature), The Dark Is Rising (feature).

Chaz Lyon   Mobile 07973-128310 ARRI 01895-457180
Green Zone (feature), The Queen (feature), The Bourne Ultimatum (feature) (2nd unit).

Iain Mackay   Mobile 07968-366642
Gulliver's Travels (feature), In Bruges (feature), Mamma Mia! (feature).

David Mackie   020-8546 3065 Mobile 07966-552168
Fax 07974-439150
Harry Potter & The Half-Blood Prince (feature), The Dark Knight (feature), Batman Begins (feature).

Bash Malik   Mobile 07939-579805 SC 01932-252577

Tobias Marshall   Mobile 07979-913989
Robin Hood (feature), Prince Of Persia (feature) (2nd unit).

Joseph Mastrangelo   ARRI 01895-457180

Kate McDonough   Mobile 07803-252027 SC 01932-252577

Tom McFarling   020-8835 8338 Mobile 07973-518011
ARRI 01895-457180
Malice In Wonderland (feature), The Boat That Rocked (feature), Stormbreaker (feature) (2nd unit).

Ross McNamara   01494-718841 Mobile 07968-718797
Prince Of Persia (feature) (2nd unit).

Ray Meere   020-8881 6290 Mobile 07968-367950
Green Zone (feature), Harry Potter & The Half-Blood Prince (feature) (2nd unit), Harry Potter & The Order Of The Phoenix (feature).

Pat Mellor   Mobile 07944-481569
Spooks (TV drama).

Tim Morris   Mobile 07779-639605 ARRI 01895-457180
Harry Potter & The Deathly Hallows (feature), Prince Of Persia (feature) (visual fx unit), Jane Eyre (feature).

Dean Morrish   01732-464106 Mobile 07747-751757
Quantum Of Solace (feature), City Of Ember (feature), Agent Crush (feature).

Dean Murray   Mobile 07890-826134

Vicci Orton   029-2066 6322 Mobile 07767-445231
Fax 029-2066 6322
Con Passionate (TV drama), Screen Gems (short), Belonging (TV drama).

Ben Perry   Mobile 07957-334520
The Dark Knight (feature), The Mummy (feature), Batman Begins (feature).

Danny Preston   Mobile 07931-774618
Numerous commercials.

Sam Rawlings   Mobile 07761-780056 SC 01932-252577
It's A Wonderful Afterlife (feature), B & Q (commercial), Peroni (commercial).

Matthew Rearden   Mobile 07968-111102 SC 01932-252577

Mike Rees   Mobile 07771-782535
The Queen's Sister (TV drama), Monarch Of The Glen (TV drama), The Vice (TV drama).

Nigel Seal   Mobile 07849-474090
The World Is Not Enough (feature), Anna & The King (feature), Oklahoma! (TV film).

Luke Selway   Mobile 07869-141259
Robin Hood (feature), Sherlock Holmes (feature), Harry Potter & The Half-Blood Prince (feature).

Chris Shaw   Mobile 07876-567501
Taggart (TV drama), Doomsday (feature), New Town Killers (feature).

Sam Smith   Mobile 07932-994624
Little Dorrit (TV drama), Into The Storm (TV film), Made Of Honor (feature).

Erin Stevens   Mobile 07944-427533

Dean Straffon   0161-795 2374 Mobile 07866-566684
Hollyoaks (TV drama), Shameless (TV drama), Survivors (TV drama).

Simon Surtees   020-8288 1091 Mobile 07974-392995
Quantum Of Solace (feature), In Bruges (feature), Hitchhiker's Guide To The Galaxy (feature).

Ryan Taggart   Mobile 07775-647379
Gulliver's Travels (feature), The Da Vinci Code (feature) (2nd unit), Sahara (feature).

Daniel Tubby   Mobile 07949-205318
The Mutant Chronicles (feature), The Midnight Man (TV drama), Blue Murder (TV drama).

Kim Vinegrad   Mobile 07974-434992
The Damned United (feature), Lost In Austen (TV drama), Unforgiven (TV drama).

Jimmy Ward   Mobile 07813-718473
Hotel Babylon (TV drama).

Emma Ware   Mobile 07973-410302
Waking The Dead (TV drama), Primeval (TV drama), The Commander (TV drama).

Brian Warner   Mobile 07808-843330
At Home With The Braithwaites (TV drama), Dalziel & Pascoe (TV drama), Casanova (feature) (2nd unit).

Paul Wheeldon   01628-528958 Mobile 07770-694191
EXEC 01753-646677 Fax 01628-528958
The Wolfman (feature) (2nd unit), Green Zone (feature), Miss Potter (feature) (2nd unit).

Scott Williams   020-8693 0545 Mobile 07866-742989
SC 01932-252577 Fax 020-8693 0545

Renee Willis   020-7289 5589 Mobile 07867-786312
GAS 020-8813 1999 Fax 020-7289 5589
Merlin (TV drama), Dead Set (TV drama), Criminal Justice (TV drama).

Sarah Woodward   01494-712812 Mobile 07810-207449
The Bourne Ultimatum (feature), The Wolfman (feature), The Imaginarium Of Dr Parnassus (feature).

Sally Wright   Mobile 07764-756363
Prince Of Persia (feature).

CAMERAMEN - 2ND UNIT

Jay Jay Odedra   Mobile 07956-559989
The Namesake (feature), Vanity Fair (feature), Walking With Cavemen (TV doc).

CAMERAMEN - AERIAL

Trevor Bassett Matthews 01305-775050
Mobile 07770-303964 Fax 01305-775050
West Sussex Cancer Association (corporate), Ring Out For An Alibi (TV drama), Water Board (corporate).

Chris Bonass 020-8894 6382 Mobile 07850-971491
World Cup Cricket (TV sport), The Air Show (TV magazine), International Rugby (TV sport).

Jeremy Braben 01895-833365 Mobile 07836-542906
Fax 01895-834523
The Boat That Rocked (feature), Angels & Demons (feature), The Bourne Identity / Supremacy / Ultimatum (feature).
www.helicopterfilm.tv

Adam Dale 01264-862222 Fax 01264-860033
Prince Of Persia: The Sands Of Time (feature), Harry Potter & The Deathly Hallows (feature), Sherlock Holmes (feature).

Robert Hayes 01483-278640 Fax 01483-278643
Eurofighter (corporate), SAAB (commercial), DHL (commercial).

John Marzano 01264-862211 Mobile 07785-277567
Fax 01264-860033
Body Of Lies (feature), Quantum Of Solace (feature), Amelia (feature).

David McKay 01494-729873 Mobile 07831-715909
Fax 01494-729873
The Descent 2 (feature), O2 (commercial), Life (TV doc).
www.tenthirteen.co.uk

Mike Parker 01362-684135 Mobile 07768-667361
Skellig (feature), Blue Murder (TV drama), World Cup Football (TV sport).
www.mpl-aerialfilming.co.uk

Simon Werry 01579-344087 Mobile 07971-020088
Life (TV doc), Nature's Great Events (TV doc), Stardust (feature).

CAMERAMEN - ANIMATION MODEL & MOTION CONTROL

Joe Dembinski 0161-439 1583 Mobile 07971-798225
Brambly Hedge (TV childrens), Bob The Builder (TV childrens), Rubber Dubbers (TV childrens).

Maxim Ford 020-8802 8791 Mobile 07966-139709
Fax 020-8211 8286
Critical Eye (TV doc), Voice From Afar (feature), Mel Del Plata (promo).

Mark Gardiner 01494-678218
Inkheart (feature), Band Of Brothers (TV drama).

Matthew Kitcat 01453-811489 Mobile 07767-202073
Tennent's (commercial), Chicken Run (feature), Lurpak (commercial).

CAMERAMEN - ASSISTANT

Richard Ackland Mobile 07970-425356

Joseph Alexander Mobile 07960-322016
Robin Hood (feature), Green Zone (feature), The Wolfman (feature).

Hamish Anderson 01367-860341 Mobile 07868-842763
Wimbledon (feature), Waiting (short), O2 (commercial).

Stephen Andrews 0117-377 0171 Mobile 07798-673610
Casino Royale (feature), Around The World In 80 Days (feature), East Is East (feature).

Adam Bowes HC 020-8742 1888
The X Factor (TV light entertainment), Britain's Got Talent (TV light entertainment), Over The Rainbow (TV light entertainment).
www.hotcam.tv

Glenn Coulman Mobile 07815-309977
The Hurt Locker (feature), John Carter Of Mars (feature), Green Zone (feature).

Pearce Crowley Mobile 07725-868507
Angus Thongs & Perfect Snogging (feature), Me & Orson Welles (feature), Run Fat Boy Run (feature).

Simon de Glanville Mobile 07734-052712
Extreme Andes (TV doc), Alien Oceans (TV doc).

Jess Doxey Mobile 07891-640426

Elliot Dupuy Mobile 07792-632155
The Special Relationship (feature), The King's Speech (feature), The Wolfman (feature).

Jean-Louis Farmer 01892-530402 Mobile 07966-286533
Kent County Council (corporate), Coming To England (feature), Old Neutral (corporate).

Phill Hardy Mobile 07941-421028
Robin Hood (feature) (2nd unit), Late Bloomers (feature), Prince Of Persia (feature) (2nd unit).

Tom Hooker 020-8943 2743 Mobile 07944-891654
In Bruges (feature) (Trainee).

Alex Jason Mobile 07711-952772

Neil Kent   Mobile 07884-191861
Unbreakable (TV doc), Extreme Dreams (TV doc), Brat Camp (TV reality).

Malcolm Keys   0161-231 7496   Mobile 07979-903643
Fax 0161-231 7496
See No Evil (TV drama), Shameless (TV drama), The Forsyte Saga (TV drama).

Stefan Krzysiak   Mobile 07845-547555
Wire In The Blood (TV drama), FAQ About Time Travel (feature).

Philip Martin   Mobile 07815-058484
The Colour Of Magic (TV film) (Trainee).

Rebecca McDonald   Mobile 07973-842208
LL 020-8426 2200
The X Factor (TV light entertainment), Green Wing (TV comedy drama).

Joanne McIvor   Mobile 07835-477164
Foyle's War (TV drama), Mutual Friends (TV drama), Fanny Hill (TV drama) (Trainee).

Ross Millard   Mobile 07815-956226   DG 020-7386 0310

Ben Richards   Mobile 07969-691383
Combat Chefs: Afghanistan (TV doc), Extreme Dreams (TV doc).

Pete Rowell   Mobile 07793-746252
Millionaires' Mission: Uganda (TV doc), Extreme Dreams (TV doc).

Adam Scarth   Mobile 07505-912025   WZ 020-7437 2055
The Arbor (feature), Dread (feature), KFC (commercial).

Paul Snell   Mobile 07968-041019
The Colour Of Magic (TV film) (2nd unit), The Edge Of Love (feature), The Other Boleyn Girl (feature).

Kat Spencer   Mobile 07838-169602
Robin Hood (feature).

Dean Straffon   0161-795 2374   Mobile 07866-566684
Hollyoaks (TV drama), Shameless (TV drama), Survivors (TV drama).

Sarah Tapsfield   020-7586 2600
Mobile 07710-767925
On The Run (TV doc), The River (TV doc), In Britain (TV doc).

Tom Taylor   020-8560 7450   Mobile 07748-631655
ARRI 01895-457180   Quantum Of Solace (feature), Children Of Men (feature), Fred Claus (feature).

Greg Therenot   Mobile 07967-993115
Luther (TV drama) (Lighting Cameraman), Spooks (TV drama).

Darren Vincent   Mobile 07989-604938
The Decameron (feature), Sixty Six (feature).

CAMERAMEN - DOCUMENTARY

David Atchison-Jones   020-8423 6056
Great Railway Journeys (TV doc), Modern Times (TV doc), Situation Vacant (TV doc).

Jean-Pierre Bassin   Mobile 07802-226135
The World Is Not Enough (feature), Bridget Jones's Diary II (feature).

William Best   020-8578 9003   Mobile 07717-473206
Malvern Mountain Bikes Event (TV doc), Bacardi (commercial), Windsurfing In Greece (TV doc).

Danny Bishop   Mobile 07815-853448
Jack Osbourne: Adrenaline Junkie (TV doc), Panorama (TV doc).

Richard Brereton   0117-986 0351   Mobile 07860-529831

Ian Burton   Mobile 07879-442133
Mountains With Griff Rhys Jones (TV doc), Nevis: A Land For All People (TV doc).

Anthony Buxton   01684-573830   Fax 01684-573830
American Gypsy (TV doc), Danger Money (TV doc), Country Ways (TV doc).

Mike Carling   Mobile 07768-590256
Austin Stevens Adventures (TV doc), Everest Last Secret (TV doc), Commando (TV light entertainment).

Timothy Chard   01908-678822   Mobile 07956-544291
Return To Gender (TV doc), Security Failures (TV doc), Cabinet Confidential (TV doc).

Julian Charrington   020-8747 4744   Mobile 07795-342842
Fax 020-8995 0665
Galahad Of Everest (feature), Around The World In 80 Days (feature), Flying Boats (TV docu drama).

Matt Conway   Mobile 07801-341413   LL 020-8426 2200
Duffy (promo), The Apprentice (TV reality), Giving Up Weed (TV doc).

Luke Cormack   Mobile 07941-974657
Living With Tigers (TV doc), Pacific Abyss (TV doc).

Andrew Dishman   01904-702395   Mobile 07973-172581
Spendaholics (TV doc), Cutting Edge (TV doc), Fred West (TV doc).

CAMERA

Anne Dodsworth Mobile 07768-682536
Timewatch (TV doc), The South Bank Show (TV arts), The Bill (TV drama).

Graham Dougall 020-8578 6623 Mobile 07976-293352
CX 020-8420 1444 Fax 020-8578 6623
Scrapheap Challenge (TV light entertainment), Turf Wars (TV light entertainment).

Stuart Dunn Mobile 07719-280804
Extreme Dreams (TV doc), Helicopter Missions: Vietnam (TV doc).

Nigel Dupont Mobile 07973-136715
Beyond Boundaries (TV doc), Rory & Paddy's Great British Adventure (TV doc).

David Evans Mobile 07976-283696
Survivor (TV reality), Danny Dares (TV doc).

Richard Farish Mobile 07900-554896
Extreme Dreams (TV doc), Escape To The Legion (TV doc), The Hottest Place On Earth (TV doc).

Simon ffrench 01453-840404 Mobile 07860-266591
Execution Of A Teenage Girl (TV doc), Alive: Escape From The Amazon (TV drama doc), This World (TV doc).

Robert Foster 0161-926 9808 Mobile 07974-151617
Fax 0161-929 9000
MCFC Live Shows (TV sport), Teachers Television (TV doc), Newsnight (TV news & current affairs).
www.broadcast-tv.co.uk

Tania Freimuth Mobile 07976-610672
Out At Lunch (TV doc), Treasure Of Albion (feature), Sacrifice (short).

Richard Gammons 020-8444 0435 Mobile 07770-852280

Peter George 01483-202565 Mobile 07768-156670
Fax 01483-203566
Novemthree (TV doc), Panorama (TV doc), Abused & Catholic (TV doc).

Simon Gilmour Mobile 07932-592482
Our World (TV doc), 46664 - A Concert For Nelson Mandela (concert).

Gordon Gronbach 01494-786862 Mobile 07850-055628

Pete Hayns Mobile 07977-538511
Raging Planet (TV doc), Altitude Everest Expedition (TV doc).

Keith Hunter 01622-820114 Mobile 07976-256646
GI 020-8324 2224
The Getty Dynasty (TV doc), Hospitals From Hell (TV reality), Mo Mowlam (TV doc).

Stephen Huntley 01245-225803 Mobile 07973-208461
Fax 01245-221674
Jimmy's Farm (TV doc), Watchdog (TV news & current affairs), Inside Out (TV news & current affairs).

Roger Laxon Mobile 07884-436572
Planet Action (TV doc), Challenge Anneka (TV light entertainment).

Casper Leaver 020-8673 6089 Mobile 07973-281555
Battle Stations (TV doc), Nissan (commercial), Top Gear (TV light entertainment).

Ian Livesey 01942-206476 Mobile 07971-106596
The Reluctant Ballet Dancer (TV doc), The Life Of Buddha (TV doc), Beauty School (TV doc).

Peter Loring 01923-283407 Mobile 07850-690058
Fax 01923-283407
Something Special (TV doc), Food Police (TV doc), Heaven & Earth (feature).

Angus Macfadyen Mobile 07973-936298
Correspondent (TV news & current affairs), Max's Big Tracks (TV doc).

Ray Marlow 020-7681 8766 Mobile 07768-981616
SC 01932-252577

Peter Meakin Mobile 07801-866405
Himalaya With Michael Palin (TV doc), Nefertiti Revealed (TV doc), Sahara With Michael Palin (TV doc).

Ashley Meneely Mobile 07956-646812 DG 020-7386 0310
The Battle For North America (TV doc), Wildest Dreams (TV doc), Hadrian (TV doc).

Ash Mills Mobile 07775-906634
Britain's Toughest Family (TV reality), 20th Century Battles (TV doc), Extreme Archaeology (TV doc).

Chris Morphet 020-7624 3479 Mobile 07771-537294
Fax 020-7625 7035
Jamie's School Dinners (TV doc), Don't Mess With Miss Beckles (TV doc), Derren Brown: The Heist (TV light entertainment).

Paul Mungeam Mobile 07710-908482
By Any Means (TV doc), Escape To The Legion (TV doc), The Hottest Place On Earth (TV doc).

Barbara Nicholls 020-8348 5792 Mobile 07798-525977
How To Look Good Naked (TV light entertainment), Children On The Frontline (TV doc), Tribal Wives (TV doc).

Chris Payne 01327-354754 Mobile 07711-239557
Fax 01327-353811
Rhythm Hunter (TV doc).

Geoff Perry   01706-372029 Mobile 07973-539698
The Money Programme (TV news & current affairs), Home Front (TV light entertainment), Panorama (TV doc).

Tim Platten   01462-420097 Mobile 07801-642434
Walking With Beasts (TV doc), The Real Good Life (TV doc), Horizon (TV doc).

Dave Prevost   Mobile 07971-295732 DG 020-7386 0310

Mike Robinson   020-7622 5060 Mobile 07768-096383
Road To Martyrdom (TV drama doc), The Umbrella Assassin (TV doc), Supergrass (TV drama doc).

Simon Rowles   Mobile 07702-364023
Extraordinary Animals (TV doc), The F Word (TV doc), Wreck Detectives (TV doc).

John Samuels   01458-860103 Mobile 07974-354660
Daily Planet (TV doc), The Politics Show (TV news & current affairs), Testament (TV doc).

Martin Saunders   Mobile 07709-540418
Fax 0117-924 4966
Life On Earth (TV doc), The Life Of Birds (TV doc), Wildlife Special - The Polar Bear (TV doc).

Brian Sewell   + 55 21 2205 3128
Mobile + 55 21 8115 7005 Fax + 55 21 2205 0477
World Cup Stories (TV doc), Trouble At The Top (TV doc), Natural Wonders Of The World (TV doc).

Mike Shelton   020-8578 7040 Mobile 07973-746562
Omnibus (TV doc), Record Breakers (TV childrens), Wild Garden (TV doc).

Stephen Standen   020-7631 1129 Mobile 07956-457799
Fax 020-7631 1130
Rasputin: The Devil In The Flesh (TV doc), Visions Of Space: Antoni Gaudi (TV doc), Bodyshock (TV doc).

John Tarby   020-7734 5021 Mobile 07860-327866
Newsnight (TV news & current affairs), Tricky (TV childrens), Demon Wheels (feature).

John Templeton   +974 583-5929 Mobile 07768-165989
Fax 07980-670572
Hotlinks (TV doc), BBC News 24 (TV news & current affairs), Vital Pulse (TV doc).

Michael Timney   Mobile 07721-384481
Songbirds (TV doc), Feltham Sings (TV doc), Falling Apart (TV drama).

Hedley Trigge   020-7372 7225 Mobile 07824-824482
Correspondent (TV news & current affairs), Foreign Correspondent (TV news & Current affairs), Saddam's Revenge (TV news & current affairs).

Neil Tugwell   01752-881744 Mobile 07831-823762
The Boat Show (TV light entertainment), Beating Retreat (TV doc), Peak Performance (TV doc).

Claudio von Planta   Mobile 07785-330616
Fax 07050-696243
A Long Way Round (TV doc), Dispatches (TV doc), Out Of The Shadows (TV doc).

Paul Walker   01928-571903 Mobile 07831-885247
Workshop Of The World (TV doc), Locks & Quays (TV doc).

Michael Ward   01633-422507 Mobile 07850-142294
Fax 01633-422507
John Charles (TV doc), Why Me God? (TV drama), Six Nations Rugby (TV sport).

David Wickham   Mobile 07870-635353
Survivor (TV reality), The Search (TV light entertainment).

Lee York   Mobile 07967-217365
Dangerous Adventures For Boys (TV light entertainment), The Hottest Place On Earth (TV doc).

CAMERAMEN - HIGH SPEED

Lawrence Bewsher   01923-225523 Mobile 07811-334845
Marks & Spencer (commercial), Sony Bravia (commercial).

John Hadfield   01844-217148 Mobile 07831-396266
Fax 01844-217148
Gulliver's Travels (feature), Nanny McPhee & The Big Bang (feature), The Damned United (feature).
www.greendoorfilms.co.uk

CAMERAMEN - POLECAM

Ian Barnes   01840-261327 Mobile 07836-228937
Small Town Gardens (TV light entertainment), Freestyle Kitchen (TV light entertainment).

CAMERAMEN - ROSTRUM

Chris King   020-7439 7445 Mobile 07858-425041
Fax 020-7439 7166
Pop Britannia (TV doc), Soul Britannia (TV doc), Who Do You Think You Are? (TV doc).

Ken Morse BSC   020-8749 0245

Nick Price   01372-723294

CAMERAMEN - SKYDIVING

Ian Barraclough   Mobile 07941-845385
One In A Million (TV doc), You Bet (TV light entertainment), Gravity Powered Adventure (corporate).

CAMERAMEN - SPECIAL FX

Stuart Galloway   01753-656728 Mobile 07768-403109
Sunshine (feature), Corpse Bride (feature), Scragg & Bones (TV childrens).

Jose F Granell   01932-592425 Mobile 07710-457154
Fax 01932-568944
Prince Of Persia (feature), Harry Potter & The Half-Blood Prince (feature), V For Vendetta (feature).
www.cinesiteproductionservices.com

Stefan Lange   Mobile 07973-506792
Alexander (feature), Lost In Space (feature) (2nd unit), Tomb Raider (feature).

Nigel Stone BSC   01494-485392 Mobile 07957-187885
Fax 01494-485392
V For Vendetta (feature), Harry Potter 1-6 (feature), Band Of Brothers (TV drama).

Peter Tyler   01946-724534 Mobile 07850-929063
Doctor Who (TV drama), Aliens (feature), Red Dwarf (TV comedy drama).

CAMERAMEN - STEADICAM

Andrei Austin   01604-759750 Mobile 07973-331371
EXEC 01753-646677 Fax 01604-759750
New Town Killers (feature), Honey & Sting (short), Waking The Dead (TV drama).

Simon Baker   01483-279784 Mobile 07768-085692
PS 020-8883 1616 Fax 01483-279784
Mamma Mia! (feature), Sleuth (feature), Pride & Prejudice (feature).

Joe Bullen   0151-928 1046 Mobile 07791-212263
GEMS 029-2071 0770

David Carey   01937-849362 Mobile 07831-442205
Fax 01937-849367
Lost In Austen (TV drama), Doc Martin (TV drama), Midsomer Murders (TV drama).

Dion Casey   01460-30005 Mobile 07831-441553
DD 020-7851 3575
Harry Brown (feature), Luna (feature), Sixty Six (feature).

Peter Cavaciuti   Mobile 07973-639709 ARRI 01895-457180
You Will Meet A Tall Dark Stranger (feature), How To Lose Friends & Alienate People (feature), The Wolfman (feature).

John Clarke   01444-881195 Mobile 07774-148207
ARRI 01895-457180
Harry Potter & The Half-Blood Prince (feature), Led Zeppelin (concert), The Heavy (feature).

Nigel Clarkson   01594-510912 Mobile 07761-701755
Mistresses (TV drama), Casualty (TV drama), Nina's Heavenly Delights (feature).

Mike Connelly   01372-742088 Mobile 07802-419830
The Keith Barret Show (TV light entertainment), Grandstand (TV sport), Breakfast With Frost (TV news & current affairs).

Barney Davis   Mobile 07733-108248

Paul Edwards   029-2076 1323 Mobile 07831-545164
ARRI 01895-457180 Fax 029-2076 1363
Harry Potter & The Half-Blood Prince (feature), Sunshine (feature), Phantom Of The Opera (feature).

Thomas English   Mobile 07970-025389 SC 01932-252577

Felix Forrest   020-7193 5384 Mobile 07831-826859
Storage (short), Scratch (short), Shank (short).

Alan Glover   01744-25017 Mobile 07713-047195
SC 01932-252577
Taggart (TV drama), Life On Mars (TV drama), Wire In The Blood (TV drama).

Dogan Halil   01789-262274 Mobile 07973-549739
Fax 01789-262274

Graham Hall   01494-864984 Mobile 07793-653394
Inception (feature), Gulliver's Travels (feature) (2nd unit), The Golden Compass (feature).

John Hembrough   Mobile 07973-149352
ARRI 01895-457180
The Last Enemy (TV drama), Little Dorrit (TV drama), Hunter (TV drama).

CAMERA

Stuart Howell   Mobile 07836-524714 ITG 020-7636 6565
The Last King Of Scotland (feature), Push (feature), Me & Orson Welles (feature).

Gareth Hughes   020-7703 7522 Mobile 07973-540486
Fax 020-7703 7522
Lark Rise To Candleford (TV drama), The Pillars Of The Earth (TV drama), Metamorphosis (short).

Dominic Jackson   020-7385 3108 Mobile 07850-341818
SC 01932-252577
Carmen (opera), Silent Cry (TV film), The Marriage Of Figaro (opera).

Tony Jackson   01372-722563 Mobile 07973-304748
EXEC 01753-646677 Fax 01372-722563
Ondine (feature), Swordfish (feature), Troy (feature).

Jim Littlehales   ARRI 01895-457180

Vincent McGahon   01904-706178 Mobile 07973-798814
Fax 01904-707381
The Damned United (feature), Sweeney Todd (feature), Sherlock Holmes (feature).

Christopher TJ McGuire   +1 661 839 7432
Mobile 07831-464407
Street Fighter: The Legend of Chun-Li (feature), Whiteout (feature), Harry Potter & The Order Of The Phoenix (feature).

Joe McNally   Mobile 07973-226532
Dr Who (TV drama), Sex Drugs & Rock & Roll (feature), Faithless (concert).

Pete Murray   020-8364 1818 Mobile 07973-152963
SC 01932-252577

Matt Norman   0117-962 1057 Mobile 07976-247652
F59 0117-906 4300 Fax 0117-962 1057
Rush It (feature), In This City (TV drama), Ancient Rome: The Rise & Fall Of An Empire (TV drama).

Martin Parry   Mobile 07973-462448
The Poet (feature), Sea Of Souls (TV drama).

Martyn Porter   01799-525723 Mobile 07973-112616
Fax 07971-048117
The X Factor (TV light entertainment), Green Wing (TV comedy drama), Pop Idol (TV light entertainment).

Rupert Power   020-8563 9109 Mobile 07768-698250
EXEC 01753-646677
Fair Game (feature), Shifty (feature), Shaun Of The Dead (feature).

Nathan Ridler   01249-783264 Mobile 07774-450060
Panda Week (TV doc), Andy's Wild Adventures (TV childrens), Accidental Angler (TV doc).

Peter Robertson   020-8374 4036 Mobile 07973-146592
PS 020-8883 1616
In Bruges (feature), Atonement (feature), Gulliver's Travels (feature).

Alexander Sahla   Mobile 07802-174955 PS 020-8883 1616
The Philanthropist (TV drama), Diamonds (TV drama), Agent Cody Banks II (feature).

Fabrizio Sciarra   Mobile 07904-707313 DD 020-7851 3575

Mike Scott   020-8398 2134 Mobile 07973-750113
GAS 020-8813 1999

Howard J Smith   +1 310 804 0973 Mobile 07768-147499
MKV 0161-850 0658
The Matrix II & III (feature), Asylum (feature) (Director Of Photography - 2nd unit), In America (feature) (Director Of Photography - 2nd unit).

Richard Stoddard   Mobile 07711-284187
Doctor Who (TV drama), Trinity (feature), Outpost (feature).

John Taylor   01663-751153   Mobile 07768-772302
SC 01932-252577
Doctor Who (TV drama), Street Dance (feature), The Descent (feature).

Roger Tooley   Mobile 07831-860416   WZ 020-7437 2055
The Deep (TV drama), Blitz (feature), Margot (TV drama).

Jason Torbitt   Mobile 07749-961604
Emmerdale (TV drama), News Of The World (commercial), Sky Sports News (TV news & current affairs).

Alf Tramontin   01453-873613   Mobile 07831-383052
Troy (feature), Harry Potter & The Goblet Of Fire (feature), Girl With A Pearl Earring (feature).

Gerry Vasbenter   020-3067 0061   Mobile 07973-194502
PS 020-8883 1616
The Duchess (feature), Your Highness (feature), Shanghai (feature).

Derek Walker   020-8568 0857   Mobile 07788-404396
ARRI 01895-457180
Lesbian Vampire Killers (feature), The Golden Compass (feature), The Broken (feature).

Rick Woollard   020-7738 1738   Mobile 07860-327674
CC 01932-568268
Red Riding (TV drama).

CAMERAMEN - TV & VIDEO

Robin Barrett   020-8876 6694   Mobile 07976-659333
One Foot In The Past (TV magazine), Omnibus (TV doc), Sergio Leone (TV doc).

Tom Basciano   Mobile 07830-023247
Celebrity Fame Academy (TV reality), Panorama (TV doc), Human Safari (TV doc).

Jon Baverstock   023-8081 3344   Mobile 07850-566503
Elton John (promo).

Mark Bloomfield   01892-528736   Mobile 07973-132734

Ian Boddie   01698-427893   Mobile 07836-574966
Champions League Football (TV sport), Don't Look Down (TV light entertainment), Scotland Today (TV news & current affairs).

Joel Bradley   Mobile 07973-674438
Never Mind The Buzzcocks (TV light entertainment), Perfect Getaways (TV doc), Pop World (TV light entertainment).

Philip Bradshaw   01628-521484   Mobile 07973-435763

Carolyn Burnley   01737-245404

Andy Calvert   020-8866 3937   Mobile 07973-129074
Morning Glory (TV light entertainment), Make Me A Supermodel (TV reality), Scrapheap Challenge (TV light entertainment).

Paul Cave   01798-812919   Mobile 07850-314379
Walkonair (commercial), Sailing The Skies (TV sport) (also Director), Passies Ponds (corporate) (also Director).

Tom Challis   01483-281633   Mobile 07973-147945
Stitch Up! (TV childrens), Saturday Kitchen (TV light entertainment), CD:UK (TV light entertainment).

Julian Charrington - J-PIX

020-8747 4744 Mobile 07795-342842
Fax 020-8747 4744   Fax 020-8995 0665
Email: juliancharrington@hotmail.com
2nd Cam. BAFTA win "Flying Boats". Filmed from Everest to 30m below. Skiing, trekking, scuba. Producer quote "Julian is dedicated, enthusiastic, professional and fun to be with".

Tim Collins   01780-470655   Mobile 07973-503605
Red Peppers (short), When Words Prevail (TV doc), Too Much Pressure (corporate).

Simon Curtis   01258-839000   Mobile 07770-763337
Fax 01258-839111
ITV Fixers (TV news & current affairs), Watchdog (TV news & current affairs), Comedy Connections (TV doc).

Martin Doyle   020-8567 4482   Mobile 07831-101654
MP3 Classic (commercial), The Trail Of The Mummy (TV doc), Illegal (short).

Mike Dugdale   Mobile 07973-321338   Fax 08701-294238
Jerry Springer - The Opera (theatre), Elton John At Radio City (concert), Celine Dion - Caesars Palace (concert).

Sarah Edwards   Mobile 07855-832544   DG 020-7386 0310
UKTV (promo), Grand Designs (TV doc), Torch (short).

Chris Evans   01903-884441   Mobile 07831-604338
Fat Doctor (TV doc), Property Developing Abroad (TV doc), Britain's Best Back Gardens (TV doc).

Andrew Fair   0161-486 0789   Mobile 07973-226227

Richard Faulkner   01332-824881   Mobile 07973-616343
East Midlands Today (TV news & current affairs), Midland Report (TV news & current affairs).

Robert Foster   0161-926 9808   Mobile 07974-151617
Fax 0161-929 9000
MCFC Live Shows (TV sport), Teachers Television (TV doc), Newsnight (TV news & current affairs).
www.broadcast-tv.co.uk

CAMERA

Steven Green   Mobile 07940-570377 ZDB 020-7604 4100
Ant & Dec's Saturday Night (TV light entertainment), The Oscars (TV light entertainment), Alex Zane's Guest List (TV light entertainment).

Warren Green   Mobile 07836-506085
Panorama (TV doc), Trading Up (TV doc), The Salvager (TV doc).

John Hadfield   01844-217148 Mobile 07831-396266
Fax 01844-217148
Gulliver's Travels (feature), Nanny McPhee & The Big Bang (feature), The Damned United (feature).
www.greendoorfilms.co.uk

John Hemson   01908-583062 Mobile 07762-922551
Fax 01908-281035
Cowes 2009 (TV sport), Travelling Painter In Greece (TV doc), Milton Keynes Theatre (TV doc).

Tim Hirst   01384-341650 Mobile 07831-440564
Coppers (TV doc), Watchdog (TV news & current affairs), Sky News (TV news & current affairs).

Richard Hookings   023-8086 6123 Mobile 07976-399959
Death By Excess (TV doc), UK Strongest Man 2005 (TV light entertainment), Evil Rajan (TV light entertainment).

Paul Kateley   020-8873 3611 Mobile 07985-272772
Tonight With Trevor McDonald (TV news & current affairs), The Culture Show (TV arts), The Great British Village Show (TV light entertainment).

Chris Kenny   01483-427995 Mobile 07973-223268
The F Word (TV doc), Supernanny (TV doc), Selling Houses (TV doc).

Pat Kingston   01453-886884 Mobile 07976-767681
Central News (TV news & current affairs), BBC News (TV news & current affairs), ITN News (TV news & current affairs).

Timothy Konewko   01275-843011 Mobile 07970-761646

Julian Langham   Mobile 07956-569758

George Leslie   01224-734811 Mobile 07836-355751
Songs Of Praise (TV religious), Country File (TV doc), Beechgrove Garden (TV doc).

Geoff Lewis   020-8549 0652 Mobile 07711-623621
Fax 020-8287 7761
The Politician's Wife (TV drama), Sarah (TV film), BBC News (TV news & current affairs).

Caroline Luguet   020-8316 1793 Mobile 07956-509018
Fax 020-8316 1793
S Club 7 (concert).

Graham Maunder   07000-345678 Mobile 07831-515678
Fax 07000-345679
Dancing On Ice (TV light entertainment), Six Days One June (TV drama), The Last Word Monologues (TV drama).

James McCallum   01249-701465 Mobile 07973-315451
SAS - A Soldier's Story (TV drama doc), Stella Does Tricks (feature), London's Burning (TV drama).

Ian McCann   0870-601 0139 Mobile 07778-641566
Fear (commercial), Watchdog (TV news & current affairs), This Morning (TV magazine).

David Meads   0115-924 1248 Mobile 07775-606012
The One Show (TV magazine), Restored To Glory (TV doc), Watchdog (TV news & current affairs).

John Nettleship   0113-284 3515 Mobile 07850-293180
The Cook Report (TV doc), Newsnight (TV news & current affairs), Sky Sport (TV sport).

Stuart Nicholls   01920-461265 Mobile 07850-810131
Derren Brown (TV light entertainment), BBC News (TV news & current affairs), Frost On Sunday (TV news & current affairs).

Terry Pearce   Mobile 07831-634863
Sky News (TV news & current affairs).

Jon Pijnen   0845-680 0038

Harry Rabbie   020-8202 8183 Mobile 07836-678744
Fax 020-8202 8183
BBC News (TV news & current affairs).

Andy Reik   020-7624 4545 Mobile 07971-492050
Glamour's 50 Best Dressed (TV light entertainment), Come Dine With Me (ident), Airline (TV reality).

Duncan Richmond   023-8067 9662 Mobile 07768-694890

Peter Rimington   01908-370516
What The Ancients Did For Us (TV doc), 15:1 (TV light entertainment), Hero School - Bomb Squad (TV doc).

Mark Robinson   Mobile 07973-559898 LL 020-8426 2200
Fantasy Rooms (TV light entertainment), Animal Park (TV doc), Restoration (feature).

Gordon Ross   01698-794100 Mobile 07831-867056
Born To Win (TV light entertainment), Kylie's Millions (TV light entertainment), Blue Peter (TV childrens).

Bruce Sabin   01527-821741 Mobile 07831-305457
33rd Americas Cup (TV sport).

Michael Sanders   Mobile 07976-269818
GMTV (TV news & current affairs), British Airways (commercial), Real Stories (TV doc).

Steve Shaw   020-8960 3733 Mobile 07941-310303
Fax 020-7286 0654
Spirit Of Trees (TV doc), Africa's Child (TV doc), Rebels Of A Forgotten World (TV doc).

Kate Sherwin   020-8392 9099 Mobile 07973-663232
The Travel Express (TV light entertainment), Europe A La Carte (TV light entertainment), London Tonight (TV news & current affairs).

Peter Simmons   020-8302 0788 Mobile 07850-825683
London Tonight (TV news & current affairs), Sky Sport (TV sport).

James Sloss   01252-628159 Mobile 07970-694673
Fax 01252-811809

Nic Small   01273-772990 Mobile 07860-863302
Fax 01273-774990
The Politics Show (TV news & current affairs), Inside Out (TV news & current affairs), Flog It! (TV light entertainment).

Alasdair Smith   Mobile 07836-225192
Kenyon Confronts (TV doc), Jamie Andrews (TV doc), Designer Homes (TV doc).

Tim Sutton   Mobile 07956-276170
Around The World In 80 Treasures (TV doc), Panorama (TV doc), The Culture Show (TV arts).

Arun Taylor   Mobile 07798-854085
Derren Brown (TV light entertainment), Sony Netjuke (commercial), Desperados (TV childrens).

Keith Taylor   01277-822033 Fax 01277-822033
Great Railway Journeys (TV doc), Fire (TV doc), Horizon (TV doc).

Garan Ormond Thomas   029-2023 0210
Mobile 07860-517070
The Ferret (TV News & Current Affairs), Wales This Week (TV news & current affairs).

Graeme Wall   023-8044 4218 Mobile 07850-503015
Scotland's Dark Heritage (TV doc), Super Bikes (TV sport), Commonwealth Games (TV sport).

Chas Watts   01276-858993 Mobile 07831-268545
The Green Green Grass (TV comedy drama), Coupling (TV comedy drama), Men Behaving Badly (TV comedy drama).

David Wilder   Mobile 07939-388797
BBC News (TV news & current affairs).

Rhys Williams   01286-673562 Mobile 07885-770566
Tsunami Disaster Sri Lanka (TV news & current affairs), Darfur Sudan (TV news & current affairs), West Bank (TV news & current affairs).

CAMERAMEN - UNDERWATER

Steve Axtell   01202-679430
Beach Lovers (TV doc), Tsunami The Killer Wave (TV doc), Lifeboat (TV doc).

Charlie Bennett   01635-250671 Mobile 07702-263952
Five Days (TV drama), Peep Show (TV comedy drama), In Deep (TV drama).

Jason Bulley   Mobile 07775-595559
Stormbreaker (feature), Harry Potter & The Goblet Of Fire (feature), Great Expectations (TV drama).

Dan Burton   01392-875446 Mobile 07767-446250
The F Word (TV doc), The One Show (TV magazine), Coast (TV doc).

Hugh Fairs   01306-889250 Mobile 07770-321940
DYA 020-7386 0310
Coronation Street (TV drama), Spooks (TV drama), Under The Molluccan Sea (TV doc).

Stephen Foote   01929-422457 Mobile 07831-857399
State Of The Apes (TV doc), Panorama (TV doc), Time Team (TV doc).

Rob Franklin   01296-658960 Mobile 07973-196002
DYA 020-7386 0310 Fax 01296-658960
The Human Body (imax), Madeira Tourism (commercial), Hanging By A Thread (TV docu drama).

Jose F Granell   01932-592425 Mobile 07710-457154
Fax 01932-568944
Prince Of Persia (feature), Harry Potter & The Half-Blood Prince (feature), V For Vendetta (feature).
www.cinesiteproductionservices.com

Slim MacDonnell   01794-322500 Mobile 07711-845108
Fax 01794-323601
Death Wish Live (TV light entertainment), Great Expectations (TV drama), Our Mutual Friend (TV drama).

Brian Marden-Jones   020-8679 2331 Mobile 07831-319480
Fax 020-8764 1923

John Miles   020-7602 1989 Mobile 07930-622964
Fax 020-7602 1989
Jaguar People (TV doc), Underworld (feature), Sharks (TV doc).

Franz Pagot   020-7281 8520 Mobile 07770-520757
Fax 020-7281 8520
Ocean Of Fear (TV drama), Jaws 1916 (TV drama doc), Love Honour & Obey (feature) (2nd unit).

Fabrizio Sciarra   Mobile 07904-707313 DD 020-7851 3575

Mike Seares   0118-948 1783 Mobile 07720-295984
You Only Breathe Twice (TV doc), British Sub Aqua Club (corporate), Scrapheap Challenge (TV light entertainment).

Mark Silk   01442-244414 Mobile 07831-520035
CB 01932-592572 Fax 01442-244414
Egyptian Tourist Board (commercial), Layer Cake (feature), Thunderbirds (feature).

Mike Valentine BSC   020-7351 1504 Mobile 07880-746292
Fax 020-7351 1504
Robin Hood (feature), Hereafter (feature), Bacardi (commercial).

Simon Wagen   0117-907 1747 Mobile 07808-887266
DG 020-7386 0310 Fax 0117-985 4482
Touching The Void (TV doc), Hamish Macbeth (TV drama), Journey Of Life (TV doc).

Ian Young   020-8569 8996 Mobile 07802-883943
Fax 020-8569 8996

CAMERAMEN - WILDLIFE

Andrew Anderson   01600-890374 Mobile 07745-162794
Fax 01600-891071
Animal Detectives (TV doc), Owls: Silent Hunters (TV doc), The Secret Garden (feature).

Barrie Britton   0117-968 5440 Mobile 07792-269861
Life (TV doc), Planet Earth (TV doc), The Life Of Birds (TV doc).

Neil Bromhall   01865-512561 Mobile 07771-786297
The Private Life Of Plants (TV doc), Giants (TV doc), Attenborough's Mammals (TV doc).

Steve Downer   0121-764 4727
Planet Earth (TV doc), Nadine (feature), Blue Planet (TV doc).

Kevin Flay   0117-949 7731 Mobile 07971-478761
The Natural World (TV doc), Blue Planet (TV doc), Wildlife On One (TV doc).

Graham Hatherley   01747-811320 Mobile 07775-783156
Nature Of Britain (TV doc), Nature's Calendar (TV doc), Life In The Undergrowth (TV doc).

Clive Lonsdale   01328-829546 Mobile 07787-124095
Fax 01328-829540
Norwegian Whaling (TV doc), A Desert Divided (TV doc), Animal Detectives (TV doc).

Justin Maguire   020-7354 1517 Mobile 07860-601691
Fax 0870-055 4916
Nature's Great Events (TV doc), Life In Cold Blood (TV doc), Planet Earth (TV doc).

Hugh Maynard   0117-968 1305 Fax 0117-968 1305
Life In The Freezer (TV doc), Blue Planet (TV doc), Big Cat Diary (TV doc).

Zane Webb   01386-870852 Mobile 07789-000803

DATA WRANGLERS

Giles Harding   Mobile 07957-323687
Prince Of Persia (feature).

William Snow   Mobile 07816-936950
John Carter Of Mars (feature), Gulliver's Travels (feature).

Sam Townend   Mobile 07921-708050
Prince Of Persia (feature) (Assistant).

Mike Woodhead   Mobile 07789-378665
Robin Hood (TV drama), Prince Caspian (feature), Prince Of Persia (feature).

DIRECTORS OF PHOTOGRAPHY - 2ND UNIT

Hamish Doyne-Ditmas   Mobile 07958-771488

DIRECTORS OF PHOTOGRAPHY & LIGHTING CAMERAMEN

Barry Ackroyd BSC   020-8800 9374 Mobile 07976-367082
UA 020-3214 0800 Fax 020-8800 9374
The Hurt Locker (feature), Green Zone (feature), United 93 (feature).

Jamie Acton-Bond   020-8892 7351 Mobile 07831-463453
Sky Football (TV sport), Sky TV (trailer), Primary Dance (CD).

Richard Adam   01932-232047 Mobile 07802-227447
History Of British Motorways (TV doc), Mountain Men (TV doc), The World Of Albert Kahn (TV doc).

John Adderley   020-8542 4847 Mobile 07973-730042
DYA 020-7386 0310 Fax 07970-088760
Disappearance At Sea (short), Horizon (TV doc), The Planets (TV doc).

Remi Adefarasin BSC   020-8997 7443
Mobile 07973-428973 CM 020-7287 4450
The Pacific (TV drama), Amazing Grace (feature), Elizabeth: The Golden Age (feature).

CAMERA

Ian Adrian   Mobile 07850-623912
Nanny McPhee & The Big Bang (feature) (2nd unit), Little Dorrit (TV drama), The Innocence Project (TV drama).

Federico Alfonzo   020-7607 0554   Mobile 07776-183631
WZ 020-7437 2055   Fax 020-7607 5784
E Bay (commercial), Nationwide (commercial), Dragon's Den (TV light entertainment).

Mik Allen   Mobile 07973-313991
Numerous commercials.

Alan Almond BSC   01263-577396   Mobile 07774-637522
UA 020-3214 0800
Desperate Romantics (TV drama), From Time To Time (feature), Little Dorrit (TV drama).

Edward Ames   Mobile 07973-389014
Your Mother Should Know (TV drama), Casualty (TV drama), Johnny Shakespeare (TV drama).

David Amphlett   ARRI 01895-457180

Simon Archer   Mobile 07968-753858   AMM 020-7244 1159
Ashes To Ashes (TV drama), Doc Martin (TV drama), The Bachelor (feature).

Lincoln Ascott   020-8450 1806   Mobile 07866-552507
Fax 020-8450 1806
Sugar Sugar (feature), Celtic Fists (TV doc) (Lighting Director), Darklands (feature) (Camera Operator - 2nd unit).

James Aspinall   020-7371 4153   Mobile 07747-631600
CM 020-7287 4450
Fanny Hill (TV drama), The Chatterley Affair (TV drama), Under The Greenwood Tree (TV film).

Howard Baker   020-8977 6538   Mobile 07860-882093
JCA 020-7434 4143   Fax 020-8977 6538
Trial & Retribution (TV drama), Dalziel & Pascoe (TV drama), Monsignor Renard (TV drama).

Derek Banks   01276-26013   Mobile 07774-126392
Decisions Decisions (TV doc), Strangeways Revisted (TV doc).

Graham Banks   Mobile 07957-693877
Grange Hill (TV childrens), Command Approved (feature), Kerching! (TV childrens).

Kristian Barrass   Mobile 07734-035247
Motorway Cops (TV reality), BBC News (TV news & current affairs), Sky Sports News (TV news & current affairs).

Dominic Bartels   Mobile 07957-585405   MY 01932-253325
Babyshambles (promo), The Rakes (promo), Barry White (promo).

Sarah Bartles-Smith   020-7263 9811   Mobile 07968-175995
ARRI 01895-457180
Doctor Who (TV drama), Five Days (TV drama), Bad Girls (TV drama).

David Bennett   020-8998 9418   Mobile 07785-990395
Human Traffic (feature), Fortune's Fool (feature), Endgame (feature).

Nick Bennett   Mobile 07710-074499

Mirko Beutler   01342-824781   Mobile 07775-651923
CB 01932-592572
Fanfarlo: Harold T Wilkins (promo), Stillborn (short), E4music (ident).

Ole Bratt Birkeland   Mobile 07931-327240
ARRI 01895-457180

Marcus Birsel   020-7602 0622   Mobile 07831-363032
SC 01932-252577

Peter Biziou BSC   020-7794 8803   WZ 020-7437 2055
Fax 020-7794 8803
Ladies In Lavender (feature), Mississippi Burning (feature), In The Name Of The Father (feature).

Stephen Blackman   Fax 020-7836 9543
Trigger Happy (feature), Strictly Sinatra (feature), The Cement Garden (feature).

Sean Bobbitt   CM 020-7287 4450
Cargo (feature), The Long Firm (TV drama), Wonderland (feature).

Balazs Bolygo   020-8453 1959   Mobile 07767-261474
MM 020-8995 4747   Fax 0870-913 7652
Life On Mars (TV drama), It's All Gone Pete Tong (feature), Stan (TV film).

Mark Bond   020-7263 7710   Mobile 07973-325392
PS 020-8883 1616
Bellamy's People (TV comedy drama), Secret Millionaire (TV reality), The Trouble With Working Women (TV doc).

Paul Bond   020-7737 3807   Mobile 07980-926945
Fax 020-7737 3807

Crighton Bone   Mobile 07767-767545
I Want Candy (feature), Half Moon (feature), Heroes & Villains (feature).

Roger Bonnici   01293-774038   Mobile 07976-529619
MY 01932-253325   Fax 01293-774038
Do Elephants Pray? (feature), The Poet (feature), London's Burning (TV drama).

Denis Borrow   01963-441151   Mobile 07831-403728
Fax 01963-441151
Piers Morgan On... (TV doc), Restoration Village (TV doc), Time Team (TV doc).

Andy Boulter   Mobile 07768-877686

Geoff Boyle   020-7748 3238   Mobile 07831-562877
BF 020-8450 6444
The Mutant Chronicles (feature), Dark Country (feature), Street Fighter: The Legend of Chun-Li (feature).

Jeremy Braben   01895-833365   Mobile 07836-542906
Fax 01895-834523
The Boat That Rocked (feature) (aerial unit), Angels & Demons (feature) (aerial unit), The Bourne Identity / Supremacy / Ultimatum (feature) (aerial unit).
www.helicopterfilm.tv

Keith Bradshaw   Mobile 07836-365563   GI 020-8324 2224
The European Poker Tour (TV sport), Polo World Series (TV sport), Shock Treatment (TV reality).

Darran Bragg   Mobile 07971-956347   STA 020-7729 7477
Numerous commercials & promos.

Henry Braham   020-7727 7785   CM 020-7287 4450
The Golden Compass (feature), Flyboys (feature), Nanny McPhee (feature).

Stephen J Brand   Mobile 07976-731725
War Stories (TV doc), Benjamin's Struggle (short), Hollyoaks (TV drama).

Martyn Bray   020-8758 1232   Mobile 07860-493538
Mazda Six (commercial), British Telecom (commercial), Lexus (commercial).

Mike Brewster   Mobile 07950-472575
Harry Potter & The Deathly Hallows (feature) (2nd unit), Five Children & It (feature), Animal Farm (TV film).

Stephen Brind   01444-454945   Mobile 07973-506068
Rosie & Jim (TV childrens), Frost Tonight (TV news & current affairs), The World Stands Up (TV light entertainment).

Ken Brinsley BSC   01622-862228   Mobile 07747-630078
Down To Earth (TV drama), Monarch Of The Glen (TV drama), Holby City (TV drama).

Damian Bromley   01494-672087   Mobile 07710-161000
The Business (feature), Spooks (TV drama), The Football Factory (feature).

Dan Bronks   020-8453 0832   Fax 020-8453 0832
Channel 4 (ident), Murphy's Law (TV drama), The Stretford Wives (TV film).

Steve Brooke Smith   020-3255 0142   Mobile 07803-602303
Zone Of The Dead (feature), Inkheart (feature) (visual fx unit), The Da Vinci Code (feature) (visual fx unit).
www.stevebrookesmith.com

Trevor Brooker   Mobile 07771-691643
DTG +1 310 201 6565
Senseless (feature), Razorfish (feature), The Borrowers (feature).

Phil Broom   0121-472 0313   Mobile 07831-490444
Mountains With Griff Rhys Jones (TV doc), Omnibus (TV doc), Blue Peter (TV childrens).

Bill Broomfield   01865-351670   Mobile 07973-134219
Fax 0871-522 7072
Dalziel & Pascoe (TV drama), The Bill (TV drama), Teachers (TV drama).

John Brown   0131-663 7651   Mobile 07774-454004

Sam Brown   Mobile 07860-557768

Tony Brown   Mobile 07958-371757   DD 020-7851 3575

Max Browne   020-8340 3036   Mobile 07966-436973
LL 020-8426 2200

Robin Browne BSC   +1 248 645 5298
Fax +1 248 645 5298
Gorillas In The Mist (feature) (animatronics photography), Milk Money (feature) (2nd unit), The Incorporate (feature).

Robert Brownhill   0117-962 0680   Mobile 07831-688788
Fax 0117-940 1292
Rigoletto (opera), Six Nations Rugby (TV sport), Ryder Cup Golf (TV sport).

Steve Buckland   01372-276245   Mobile 07710-549679
Shameless (TV drama), Holby City (TV drama), Hotel Babylon (TV drama).

Mike Bulley   01932-228108   Mobile 07711-008808
EXEC 01753-646677

Paul Bulley   020-8420 4340   Mobile 07973-358438
Hurricane Katrina (TV doc), Al Murray's Road To Berlin (TV doc), Derren Brown: The Heist (TV light entertainment).

Terence Bulley   Mobile +33 622 348 572
Lisa & The Pilot (feature), Belle La Vie (TV drama), Genie In The House (TV childrens).

Riki KJ Butland   +971 507 258068   Mobile 07871-462645
BF 020-8450 6444
Treasure Island (Trilogy) (feature), Middleton's Changeling (feature).

CAMERA

Melissa Byers   Mobile 07930-341250 PS 020-8883 1616
Corpse Bride (feature), Kaz (feature), Rare Books & Manuscripts (short).

Billy Caine   020-8968 5513 Mobile 07866-758285
Doom Bar (commercial), Westcountry Live (TV news & current affairs), Inspector Morse (TV drama).

Mike Caine   Mobile 07831-387009
Numerous commercials, Walking With Cavemen (TV doc).

Brian Cairney   Mobile 07831-201696
Black Prince (commercial), River City (TV drama), Misconceptions (TV drama).

Fredrik Callinggard 020-7602 8947 Mobile 07900-606269
MY 01932-253325 Fax 020-7751 1154

Alistair Cameron   HC 020-8742 1888
The X Factor (TV light entertainment), Britain's Got Talent (TV light entertainment), The South Bank Show (TV arts).
www.hotcam.tv

Grant Cameron   0141-334 7511 Mobile 07831-426460
Fax 0141-334 7511
Orphans (feature), Life On Mars (TV drama), Cutting It (TV drama).

Luke Cardiff   020-7272 6197 Mobile 07860-137066
Fax 020-7281 3651
Jonathan Meades: Off Kilter (TV doc), Aldi (commercial), Sainsbury's (commercial).

Mark Carey   Mobile 07973-614328 CB 01932-592572
Birds Eye (commercial), Barclays Bank (commercial).

Olivier Cariou   020-8968 4300 Mobile 07775-713843
MY 01932-253325

Sean Carswell   Mobile 07767-782832
Apollo 11 (TV doc), Munich: Mossad's Revenge (TV drama doc), Is Harry On The Boat? (TV film).

Mark Chan   Mobile 07973-461223 SD 020-8994 1199
Airport (TV doc), Animal Park (TV doc), Animal Cops (TV doc).

Julian Charrington 020-8747 4744 Mobile 07795-342842
Fax 020-8995 0665
Galahad Of Everest (feature), Around The World In 80 Days (feature), Flying Boats (TV docu drama).

David Chilton   020-7582 4067
Numerous commercials.

Andrea Chiozzotto 020-7193 5316 Mobile 07846-399162
The Tomb Robbery Papyrus: Notes of a Past (feature), Happy Day (feature), Casanova (feature).

John Christie   01728-723321 Mobile 07802-400115
The Great Nazi Cash Swindle (TV doc), Birth Of A Legend - Queen Mary II (TV doc), Seven Wonders Of The Industrial World (TV docu drama).

Colin Clarke   020-8876 4451 Mobile 07785-226432
Fax 020-8241 0958
Sergio Leone (TV doc), When The Moors Ruled In Europe (TV doc), Nefertiti - Search For The Lost Mummy (TV drama doc).
www.colclarke.co.uk

Gary Clarke   Mobile 07957-212384 PS 020-8883 1616
Simon Schama's Power Of Art (TV doc), 37 Uses For A Dead Sheep (TV doc), What Makes Us Human (TV doc).

Dominic Clemence   Mobile 07931-517569
ITG 020-7636 6565
Kingdom (TV drama), Messiah (TV drama), Tough Love (TV drama).

Richard Clutterbuck   Mobile 07778-599084
Fax 0117-904 0507
Horizon (TV doc), Nature Of Britain (TV doc), LPG Gas Pipeline (corporate).

Ray Coates   020-7498 9952 Mobile 07767-784553
MY 01932-253325

Tony Coldwell   01484-680067 Mobile 07860-639089
BF 020-8450 6444
Blue Murder (TV drama), Ghost Boat (TV drama), Falling Apart (TV drama).

Ben Cole   Mobile 07956-317902
One Giant Leap (feature), The Future Is Unwritten (feature), The Man Upstairs (feature).

Ken Coles   01932-222787 Mobile 07711-743494
Lost In Space (feature) (3rd unit), The Quest (TV drama), Harbour Lights (TV drama).

Mike Coles   020-8444 7909 Mobile 07968-158379
Hannibal (TV drama), Born With Two Mothers (TV drama), The Lost Leonardo (TV doc).

Eddie Collins   01494-681243 Mobile 07767-765687
Fax 01494-681243
Tomorrow Never Dies (feature) (2nd unit), Braveheart (feature) (2nd unit), Shadowlands (feature) (2nd unit).

Chris Connell   Mobile 07970-495080

Michael Connor   020-8845 6800 Mobile 07802-255620
EXEC 01753-646677 Fax 020-8845 3900
www.motioncontrol.co.uk

Miles Cooke　　01279-422908　Mobile 07812-047703
Looking For Richard (feature), Where Sleeping Dogs Lie (feature), Paradise Grove (feature).

Mick Coulter BSC　　MM 020-8995 4747
Notting Hill (feature), Love Actually (feature), Sense & Sensibility (feature).

Julian Court　　CM 020-7287 4450
Hawking (TV film), Men Only (TV drama).

Simon Cox　　01453-547435　Mobile 07771-596730
Grand Designs (TV doc), The Restaurant (TV reality), The Apprentice (TV reality).

Richard Craske　　020-8969 2642　Mobile 07770-755261
Creep (feature) (visual fx unit), The Tutankhamun Conspiracy (TV doc), The Phoenix & The Carpet (TV childrens) (2nd unit).

Mike Craven-Todd　　01491-838749　Mobile 07771-546321
Egypt Week Live (TV doc), The Trench (TV drama doc), Time Team (TV doc).

Lol Crawley　　Mobile 07540-621579　DA 020-7437 4551
Ballast (feature), Love Me Or Leave Me Alone (short), Field (short).

Denis Crossan BSC　　020-8995 2943　MM 020-8995 4747
I Know What You Did Last Summer (feature), Me Without You (feature), Agent Cody Banks (feature).

Neve Cunningham　　020-8691 4908　Mobile 07973-128671
BA 020-7836 1112
One Day In September (feature), Strictly Confidential (TV drama), Hornblower (TV drama).

Oliver Curtis BSC　　020-7433 3391　Mobile 07770-840975
ITG 020-7636 6565　Fax 020-7433 3391
Death At A Funeral (feature), The Wedding Date (feature), Owning Mahowny (feature).

Shane Daly　　020-8883 4071　Mobile 07973-445428
MM 020-8995 4747
Hostel (feature), The Street (TV drama), Alpha Male (feature).

John Daly BSC　　01932-562093　Mobile 07771-603567
DD 020-7851 3575　Fax 01932-562093
Life & Lyrics (feature), Cape Wrath (TV drama), 20,000 Streets Under The Sky (TV drama).

Nick Dance　　01488-685492　Mobile 07860-283274
SPA 01932-571044　Fax 01488-685492
Bodies (TV drama), Mansfield Park (TV film), Skins (TV drama).

Damian Daniel　　020-8778 3531　Mobile 07803-715042
Fax 020-8778 3531
Nathan Barley (TV drama), Emile (feature), Married/Unmarried (feature).

Jamie Daniels　　029-2055 2414　Mobile 07831-337694
Dispatches (TV doc), Bloody Towers (TV doc), Mine All Mine (TV drama).

Tony David　　020-7328 4815　Mobile 07956-602778
The X Factor (TV light entertainment), The Apprentice (TV reality), Masterchef (TV light entertainment).

Huw Davies　　01446-775854　Mobile 07850-887060

Ben Davis　　Mobile 07812-205823
Layer Cake (feature), Stardust (feature), Hannibal Rising (feature).

Keith Dawson　　01753-868595　Mobile 07976-272577
EastEnders (promo), Olympic Games (TV sport), Network Sport (TV sport).

Graham Day　　020-8991 5505　Mobile 07956-254244
F59 0117-906 4300
In The Wild (TV doc), Great Railway Journeys (TV doc), Doctors (TV drama).

Richard Day　　01256-703659　Mobile 07785-330470
Fax 01256-703659

John de Borman BSC　　020-7424 9616
Mobile 07836-620212　MM 020-8995 4747　Fax 020-7424 9618
Made In Dagenham (feature), An Education (feature), Tsunami: The Aftermath (TV drama).

Francis De Groote　　01327-264640　Mobile 07931-913219
Psychoville (TV comedy drama), The IT Crowd (TV comedy drama), Catterick (TV comedy drama).

Lester De Havilland　　Mobile 07973-895766
MY 01932-253325

Bruno de Keyzer BSC　　+33 2 31 87 14 99
Sunday In The Country (feature), Life & Nothing But (feature).

Roger Deakins BSC　　ICM +1 310 550 4474
Jarhead (feature), The Man Who Wasn't There (feature), Shawshank Redemption (feature).

Allen Della-Valle　　01923-233956　Mobile 07774-183366
CB 01932-592572　Fax 01923-224289
www.fuelfilm.co.uk

Roland Denning　　020-7267 8483　Mobile 07785-784492

Simon Dennis　　Mobile 07718-856626
New Town Killers (feature).

Noski Deville　　Mobile 07958-469093
Wintergarden (short), Loneliness & The Modern Pentathlon (short), Man & Mask (short).

CAMERA

Joel Devlin   01373-834834 Mobile 07968-191695
SC 01932-252577

Uinkar "Bobby" Dhillon   01926-745097
Mobile 07966-477262
HSBC (commercial), Samsung (commercial), Titan Watches (commercial).

Jimmy Dibling   01597-840697 Fax 01597-840697
Dreaming Of Joseph Lees (feature), Relative Values (feature), 31-12-99 (TV drama).

Richard Dodd   +39 04 34521363 Mobile 07860-555794
Ultimate Force (TV drama), Ny-Lon (TV drama), Cracker (TV drama).

Marcus Domleo   020-7625 9207 Mobile 07973-410818
SC 01932-252577

David Dunlap   020-8964 9349
Shaun Of The Dead (feature).

Alan Dunlop   020-8675 3863 Mobile 07802-704655
Bad Day (feature), Neil's Party (feature), The Killing Zone (feature).

Andrew Dunn BSC   020-8933 2222 Mobile 07976-377850
Miss Potter (feature), Gosford Park (feature), LA Story (feature).

Patrick Duval   020-7241 0683 Mobile 07973-233293
Sensitive Skin (TV comedy drama), Anorak Of Fire (TV film), Distant Voices Still Lives (feature).

Joe Dyer   020-7254 6374 Mobile 07860-292895
SC 01932-252577
Days That Shook The World (TV doc), Annie Lennox (promo), British Telecom (commercial).

Brendan Easton   Mobile 07976-752724 DG 020-7386 0310
Sugar Rush (TV drama) (Camera Operator), The Battle For Brixton (TV doc), The Real Vampire Chronicles (TV docu drama).

Roger Eaton   020-7565 5445 Mobile 07831-606310
Fax 0870-127 2165
Lava (feature), The Killing Of John Lennon (feature), Truck Of Dreams (feature).

Peter Edwards   Mobile 07973-541271

Damian Eggs   Mobile 07785-276674
Equinox (TV doc), Secret History (TV doc), Secrets Of The Dead (TV doc).

Marc Ehrenbold   020-8352 1125 Mobile 07956-275504
Fax 020-8352 1125

Mike Eley   020-7357 0102 Mobile 07831-381507
Nanny McPhee & The Big Bang (feature), Touching The Void (TV doc), He Knew He Was Right (TV drama).

Michael Elphick ACS   020-8332 6958
Mobile 07850-982962 BF 020-8450 6444
Don't Call Back (feature), Just Ines (feature), Back Home (TV film).

Mark Emberton   01525-242105 Mobile 07734-534368
SC 01932-252577

Paul Englefield   Mobile 07767-261827 BA 020-7836 1112
Rosemary & Thyme (TV drama), The Lives Of Animals (TV drama doc), The Van Boys (feature).

Ray Evans   01628-525354

Andy Fairgrieve   020-8549 0200 Mobile 07808-858656

Ross Fall   Mobile 07802-241509
Silence Becomes You (feature), Devil's Music (feature), Time Enough (feature).

Michael Farr   0161-445 1510 Mobile 07973-875340
Time Team (TV doc), Everyman (TV doc), Come Dine With Me (TV light entertainment).

Mike Fash BSC   +1 310 827 2766
Strong Medicine (TV film), Sarah (TV film), The Whales Of August (feature).

Faye   Mobile 07966-484980
No Ordinary Trifle (feature), King Lear (TV film), Southern Softies (feature).

Jaime Feliu-Torres   Mobile 07939-380061

John Fenner BSC   020-8883 3492 Mobile 07767-870412
AMM 020-7244 1159 Fax 020-8883 3492
Valiant (feature), Jack & The Beanstalk - The Real Story (feature), The Borrowers (feature).

Peter Field   Mobile 07778-215440 DD 020-7851 3575
Quantum Of Solace (feature), Hot Fuzz (feature) (2nd unit), Doomsday (feature) (2nd unit).
www.peterfielddop.com

Gavin Finney BSC   020-7624 5426 Mobile 07770-915660
MM 020-8995 4747
St Trinian's (feature), Keeping Mum (feature), Alex & Emma (feature).

Terry Flaxton   01749-890610 Mobile 07976-370984
Past Present Future Imperfect (feature), Living In Hope (feature), Out Of Order (feature).

Gerry Floyd　　01769-520434　Mobile 07801-257827
MY 01932-253325
Zinky Boys Go Underground (TV drama), Honeymooner (feature), Tomorrow La Scala (TV film).

Jon Ford　　01323-740621　Mobile 07810-670226
Fax 07977-153276
Ariel Gold (commercial), MTN Mobile (commercial), Guinness (commercial).

Trevor Forrest　　020-8968 3911　Mobile 07710-561556
Tormented (feature), Someone Else (TV drama), Huge (feature).

Cinders Forshaw BSC　　020-7226 1702
Mobile 07866-727867　ITG 020-7636 6565
Schweitzer (feature), Churchill: The Hollywood Years (feature), Anita & Me (feature).

Ian Foster　　01628-488293　Mobile 07515-928440
ARRI 01895-457180
Flyboys (feature), Alexander (feature), Sexy Beast (feature).

Robert Foster　　0161-926 9808　Mobile 07974-151617
Fax 0161-929 9000
MCFC Live Shows (TV sport), Teachers Television (TV doc), Newsnight (TV news & current affairs).
www.broadcast-tv.co.uk

Graham Fowler　　020-8508 0069　Mobile 07768-551532
South West 9 (feature), Dangerous Obsession (feature).

Colin Fox　　020-8876 7853　LL 020-8426 2200
Krakatoa 1883 (TV film), Anghiari (TV doc), Mega Yachts (TV doc).

Graham Frake　　MM 020-8995 4747
Waking The Dead (TV drama), POW (TV drama), Stig Of The Dump (TV childrens).

Conall Freeley　　020-8946 3268　Mobile 07831-442714
Murder In Paradise (TV doc), Wealth Of Men (TV doc), Escape To River Cottage (TV doc).

Ben Frewin　　020-8994 9412　Mobile 07973-324366

James Friend　　Mobile 07740-929799　CMM 020-8584 5363
Expose (feature), The Rapture (feature), Carmen's Kiss (feature).

Kathleen Friend　　0141-334 4401　Mobile 07770-484401
Shoebox Zoo (TV childrens) (2nd unit), Scrapheap Challenge (TV light entertainment), Horizon (TV doc).

Michael Frift　　01926-511427　PS 020-8883 1616
Little Dorrit (TV drama), In The Night Garden (TV childrens), Doc Martin (TV drama).

Martin Fuhrer BSC　　020-8964 9140　Mobile 07798-684480
STA 020-7729 7477　Fax 020-8964 9140
Perfume (feature), The Gathering (feature), Wilde (feature).

Mike Garner　　Mobile 07973-984202
The Victorians (TV doc), Autumnwatch (TV doc), How We Built Britain (TV doc).

Sam Garwood　　Mobile 07973-885268
Cheeky (feature) (2nd unit), Dracula (TV drama) (2nd unit), The Wedding Date (feature) (2nd unit).

Rickie Gauld　　01242-676003　Mobile 07860-598323
The Parent Trap (feature) (2nd unit), Horizon (TV doc), Dispatches (TV doc).

Paul Gavin　　0131-446 0444　Mobile 07785-258383
Fax 0131-446 0333
Gamerz (feature), River City (TV drama), The £Million Property Experiment (TV doc).

Martyn Gibson　　Mobile 07831-553063　LL 020-8426 2200
Location Location Location (TV doc), Calaisa (promo), Army Recruitment (commercial).

Sue Gibson BSC　　Mobile 07860-784088　MM 020-8995 4747
Riot At The Rite (TV film), Miss Marple (TV drama), Spooks (TV drama).

Clive Gill　　Mobile 07860-459565
Holby City (TV drama), Bad Girls (TV drama), Casualty (TV drama).

Eric Gillespie　　Mobile 07769-650187
Hearts & Bones (TV drama), At Home With The Braithwaites (TV drama), Rebus (TV drama).

Keith Goddard BSC　　01903-815140　Mobile 07836-285835
Twenty One (feature), Hussy (feature), Snazzer's Progress (feature).

CAMERA

Paul Godfrey　01503-220744　Mobile 07714-217536
Four Seasons (TV drama) (2nd unit), A & E (TV drama), Dream Team (TV drama).

Merritt Gold　020-8363 2030　Mobile 07973-908472
SC 01932-252577
The Stepfather (TV drama) (2nd unit), Don't Look Back (feature), Murder Squad (TV drama).

Stephen Goldblatt BSC　+1 510 549 9273
Mobile +1 650 773 3369
Closer (feature), Angels In America (TV film), Batman (feature).

John Golding　020-8749 3854　Mobile 07837-990069
Fax 020-8749 3854
Blackball (feature) (additional photography), Second Nature (TV film) (additional photography).

Nigel Goudge　01202-765203　Mobile 07785-227421
New Middle Classes (TV doc), The Guernica Children (TV doc), Loop (feature).

Len Gowing　0151-292 0600　Mobile 07973-210090
Revenger's Tragedy (feature), Moving On (TV drama), Sunshine (TV drama).

Stuart Graham　020-7328 6433　Mobile 07976-286920
Fax 07006-009287
Shell (commercial), Vodafone (commercial), BMW (commercial).
www.stuartgraham.tv

Matt Gray　0117-985 1833　Mobile 07900-697138
CM 020-7287 4450
Cold Feet (TV drama), Manchild (TV drama), Rescue Me (TV drama).

Steven Gray　Mobile 07711-009515　DYA 020-7386 0310
Guns Germs & Steel (TV docu drama), Britain's First Suicide Bombers (TV docu drama), Blood (short).

Peter Greenhalgh BSC　01425-402291
Mobile 07785-994060　SPA 01932-571044　Fax 01425-402291
Ballet Shoes (TV drama), Poirot (TV drama), Much Ado About Nothing (theatre).

Andy Greenwood　0191-233 0050　Mobile 07974-925477
Fax 0191-233 0052
Grumpy Old Women (TV light entertainment), Panorama (TV doc), Coast (TV doc).

Dominique Grosz　020-8743 6006　Mobile 07768-686810
MTV (commercial), Peugeot (commercial), Azzurro (feature).

Derek Gruszeckyj　01926-773485　Mobile 07595-023703
Quantum Of Solace (feature) (HDFX Camera Operator), Virgin Atlantic (TV doc), Bill Wyman's Blues Odyssey (TV doc).

Phil Gurney　Mobile 07967-211540

Chris Hall　01332-842062　Mobile 07920-043782
Killing Mum & Dad (TV doc), The Great Wall Of China (TV doc), Blood Ties (TV doc).

Lynda Hall　Mobile 07976-761231　SC 01932-252577

Doug Hallows　0161-980 8612　Mobile 07767-371910
Fax 0161-980 1271
Gavin & Stacey (TV comedy drama), Waterloo Road (TV drama), Northern Lights (TV drama).

Peter Hannan BSC　Mobile 07785-392780
WZ 020-7437 2055
Longitude (TV film), Withnail & I (feature), Children Of Men (feature) (2nd unit - also Director).

Stephanie Hardt　Mobile 07932-698760
As If (TV drama), Tracy Beaker (TV childrens), Telewest (commercial).

John S Harris BSC　01243-513789

Geoff Harrison　01483-421604　Mobile 07973-392913
Fax 01932-592246
Live From Abbey Road (TV light entertainment), Without Motive (TV drama), Jonathan Creek (TV drama).

Jonathan Harrison　020-8987 8810　Mobile 07860-825950
Thatcher: The Downing Street Years (TV doc), P & G (commercial).

Thomas Harrison　01803-839301　Mobile 07802-273603

Harvey Harrison BSC　020-8540 2590
Mobile 07836-616080　Fax 020-8287 3540
Eragon (feature), V For Vendetta (feature), Sahara (feature) (2nd unit).

Nick Hart　01562-886947　Mobile 07770-925025
Country File (TV doc), CD:UK (TV light entertainment).

Douglas Hartington　Mobile 07860-339937
CC 01932-568268
Spanish Flu: The Forgotten Fallen (TV drama), City Of Vice (TV drama), 1066 (TV film).

Peter Harvey　01296-681705　Mobile 07836-286752
Fax 01296-681705
Dwarfs (TV drama), In Search Of Shakespeare (TV drama doc), Mummy Autopsy (TV drama doc).

Simon Hawken　Mobile 07831-872723　WZ 020-7437 2055
Storytellers (TV light entertainment).

Martin Hawkins　01993-878567　Mobile 07831-252585
Outnumbered (TV comedy drama), Extras (TV comedy drama), Armstrong & Miller (TV light entertainment).

Mike Haynes   01603-746522 Mobile 07836-363686

Paul Hennessy   020-8876 6104

James Henry   0161-445 6080 Mobile 07973-826055
SC 01932-252577

Will Henshaw   Mobile 07770-920923
Mind Body & Kick Ass Moves (TV doc).

Gordon Hickie   020-8340 0557 Mobile 07939-209073
Red Cap (TV drama), Silent Witness (TV drama), The Inspector Lynley Mysteries (TV drama).

David G Hicks   020-3231 0073 Mobile 07710-419810
Hitchhiker's Guide To The Galaxy: Making Of (TV doc), Blake's Seven: Making Of (TV doc).

Neil Higginson   Mobile 07768-816366 DG 020-7386 0310
Horizon (TV doc), The Money Programme (TV news & current affairs), Panorama (TV doc).

Robin Higginson   029-2049 8799

Daf Hobson BSC   01248-716316 Mobile 07986-818766
Welcome To Sarajevo (feature), Fiona's Story (TV drama), The Street (TV drama).

Ben Hodgson   01628-485914 Mobile 07850-377000
Fax 01628-482439
Battlefield Detectives (TV doc), Timewatch (TV doc), Everyman (TV doc).

Brad Hogan   Mobile 07768-415801

John Hooper BSC   020-8998 3740 Mobile 07802-413804
David Hockney The Secret Knowledge (feature), Monarch Of The Glen (TV drama), Scarlet Pimpernel (TV drama).

Andrew Horner   020-8873 3092 Mobile 07973-197413
SC 01932-252577

Tania Hoser   01227-379550 Mobile 07977-212404
Fax 01227-379550
She Works Hard For The Money (TV doc), The Man That Drove With Mandela (TV drama), Amoy Noodles (commercial).

Chris Howard BSC   01227-272520 Mobile 07768-306537
New Tricks (TV drama), Doc Martin (TV drama), Red Light Runners (feature).

John Howarth   01296-715700 Mobile 07973-465017
Fax 01296-715700
The Last Dragon (TV drama doc), The Lost World (TV docu drama), Walking With Dinosaurs (TV doc).

Mark Howe   01295-275708 Mobile 07932-166193
The Magical Mystery Tour (TV doc), Crimewatch (TV doc), Ghosts & Werewolves (TV doc).

Ian Howes   020-8549 7301 Mobile 07973-164987
BF 020-8450 6444 Fax 020-8549 7301

Angus Hudson   020-7402 4299 Mobile 07973-669962
WZ 020-7437 2055
The Broken (feature), Cashback (feature), Hari Om (feature).

Duncan Humphreys   01483-579763 Mobile 07976-264136
The Knock (TV drama), Living With Lions (TV doc).

Jeremy Humphries   Mobile 07860-832447
DG 020-7386 0310
Coast (TV doc), Journeys From The Centre Of The Earth (TV doc), One Life (TV doc).

David Hunter   01494-783559 Mobile 07973-795380

Liam Iandoli   Mobile 07949-121701
The Slums Are Alive With The Sound Of Music (TV doc), Bale (short), Ralph (short).

John Ignatius   020-8943 4008 Mobile 07831-421521
ITG 020-7636 6565
Greyfriars Bobby (feature), Two Men Went To War (feature), The Water Giant (feature).

Tony Impey BSC   01834-811961 Mobile 07974-777108
Fax 01834-811961

Baz Irvine   020-7209 4907 Mobile 07866-568260
CM 020-7287 4450 Fax 020-7209 4907

Jeremy Irving   01483-856202 Mobile 07973-194810
DG 020-7386 0310 Fax 01483-856203
Suggs' Survivors (TV doc), The Machine That Made Us (TV doc), Kipling (TV doc).

Peter Jackson BSC   01423-560066 Mobile 07974-081117
Fax 01423-560066
A Touch Of Frost (TV drama), Micawber (TV drama), The Quest (TV drama).

Graham Jaggers   020-8977 5787 Mobile 07831-629314
Fax 020-8977 5787
Casualty (TV drama), Witch Hunt (TV drama), Holby City (TV drama).

Peter James   020-8542 0896 Mobile 07710-020438
WZ 020-7437 2055

Paul Jenkins   01342-302319 Mobile 07767-785409
Moonshot (TV docu drama), Blackbeard The Pirate (TV docu drama), 9/11 The Twin Towers (TV drama).

CAMERA

CAMERA

Neils Johansen   Mobile 07958-238312 PS 020-8883 1616
Aftersun (TV drama), Cold Feet (TV drama), Nynne (feature).

Andrew Johnson   020-7252 9008 Mobile 07968-656624
The Animator (TV drama), Soldier Husband Daughter Dad (TV doc),
Vodafone (commercial).

John Johnson   Mobile 07973-563990
The Late Show (TV arts), Whitbread (corporate), Vauxhall
(commercial).

Neil A Johnson   Mobile 07969-845523

Shelly Johnson   Mobile 07825-276227
The Wolfman (feature).

David Johnson BSC   020-7221 0851 Mobile 07785-258590
DA 020-7437 4551
On A Clear Day (feature), Hilary & Jackie (feature), Resident Evil
(feature).

David Jones   01263-734566 Mobile 07836-515745
Build A New Life (TV doc), Spooks: Access All Areas (TV doc).

Lawrence Jones   0161-794 5515 Mobile 07976-739447
CMM 020-8584 5363
In Denial Of Murder (TV drama), Hope Springs (TV drama), Waterloo
Road (TV drama).

Paul Kanwar   020-8997 0676 Fax 020-8997 2406

David Katznelson   020-7482 4450 Mobile 07961-170551
Driving Lessons (feature), Shoot The Messenger (TV drama), The
Queen's Sister (TV drama).

John Keedwell   020-8421 3672 Mobile 07831-209232
Mali Festival In The Desert (TV arts).

John Keen   01362-637669 Mobile 07767-405098
Fax 01362-637669
Don't Look Back (feature), The Bear Hunt (short).

Stephen Keith-Roach   01747-852429
Mobile 07885-665526 UA 020-3214 0800

Nina Kellgren BSC   020-7241 2417 Mobile 07971-288693
MM 020-8995 4747
Wondrous Oblivion (feature), The Private Life Of Samuel Pepys (TV
drama), Solomon & Gaenor (feature).

Michael Kennedy   Mobile 07932-780732
Got To Know Campaign (TV doc), Babies (TV doc).

John Kenway BSC   ITG 020-7636 6565
Perfect Day (TV film), Roman Road (TV film), Booze Cruise (TV
film).

Martin Kenzie   Mobile 07768-705109 ITG 020-7636 6565
Clash Of The Titans (feature), Easy Virtue (feature), The Boat That
Rocked (feature).

David Kerr   Mobile 07768-115232

Paul Kerrigan   01405-761145 Mobile 07831-839101
Panorama (TV doc), Horizon (TV doc), Dispatches (TV doc).

Dominic Kersey   020-8998 9484 Mobile 07850-009967
Fax 020-8998 9484
Apples & Oranges (feature), The Grey Man (TV drama), Totally Frank
(TV drama).

Sam Key   Mobile 07976-352681
Pampers (commercial), Dream Team (TV drama), Battle For The
Holocaust (TV doc).

Nick Kindon   Mobile 07815-286140

Charlie Kinross   Mobile 07973-428510 SC 01932-252577
Dizzee Rascal (promo), Cutting Edge (TV doc), Swatch
(commercial).

Alex Kinsman   Mobile 07909-526981 SD 020-8994 1199
Surveillance (feature), Britain's Got Talent (TV light entertainment),
Boots (commercial).

Ross Kirkman   020-8968 4523 Mobile 07860-100905

Rob Kitzmann   Mobile 07092-081201 Fax 0870-922 3936
The League Of Gentlemen's Apocalypse (feature), Pulling (TV comedy
drama), Thieves Like Us (TV drama).

Nic Knowland BSC   020-7226 2315 DA 020-7437 4551
Macbeth (TV film), Institute Benjamenta (feature), Al's Lads
(feature).

Simon Kossoff BSC   020-8992 0610 Mobile 07702-542121
DA 020-7437 4551
The Daisy Chain (feature), Fingersmith (TV drama), Sinners (TV
film).

Michael Kubicki   01372-458184 Mobile 07746-367366
Fax 01372-458184

Andrew Kuchanny   Mobile 07977-195697

Alwin Kuchler BSC   020-7388 2507 Mobile 07788-107303
UA 020-3214 0800

Mark La Femina   020-8954 8233 Mobile 07949-814298
Can You See The Sun? (feature), The Road (feature), Harting
(corporate).

Hugh Lambert   01202-717477   Mobile 07979-237649
DG 020-7386 0310
Francis Bacon (TV doc), Frank Bruno (TV doc), Scrapheap Challenge (TV light entertainment).

John Lamborn   01483-306067   Mobile 07836-625831
Fax 01483-306067
The Colours Of Infinity (TV doc), The Billy Fiske Story (TV doc), Mavala Beauty (corporate).

Brett Lamb-Shine   020-7622 8175   Mobile 07876-688899
Driving Miss Crazy (short), See You Next Monday (short), OAP Rebel (short).

Daniel Landin   020-7281 5105   Mobile 07796-950002
Fax 020-7281 5105
Sixty Six (feature), Starry Night (short), Baby (short).

Paul Lang   020-8568 2511   Mobile 07802-456660
DYA 020-7386 0310

Norman Langley BSC   01243-372195   Mobile 07831-566723
Fax 01243-372195
Poirot (TV drama).

Steve Lawes   Mobile 07976-238914   ARRI 01895-457180

Nic Lawson   01483-271465   Mobile 07973-317356
The Possession Of David O'Reilly (feature), Ashes To Ashes (TV drama), Tuesday (feature).

Vernon Layton BSC   01394-388640   Mobile 07879-625336
I Still Know What You Did Last Summer (feature), The Englishman Who Went Up A Hill (feature), The Young Americans (feature).

Anthony Leake   020-7622 0870   Mobile 07973-502349
Fax 020-7720 7875
The Dark Side Of Fame With Piers Morgan (TV doc), The Culture Show (TV arts), Ross Kemp On Gangs (TV doc).
www.bluefintv.com

Oli Ledwith   020-8325 9962   Mobile 07973-725137
Fax 020-8325 9962
Barclays Bank (commercial).

Piers Leigh   Mobile 07956-443674   ARRI 01895-457180

Piers Lello   01892-516194   Mobile 07968-066243
Holby City (TV drama), The Apprentice (TV reality), Half Man Full Life (TV doc).

Andy Leonard   Mobile 07973-321708
Johnny & The Bomb (TV childrens) (2nd unit), The Chop (TV drama).

Alvin Leong   Mobile 07976-206172   GEMS 029-2071 0770
Mersey Beat (TV drama), Offending Angels (feature), A Fistful Of Fingers (feature).

Stephen Ley   020-7254 4567   Mobile 07836-247406

Ian Liggett   Mobile 07973-676380   PS 020-8883 1616
Plus One (TV comedy drama), Moving Wallpaper (TV drama), The Somme (TV drama).

Martin Lightening   0161-969 2346   Fax 0161-282 8479
Secret Millionaire (TV reality), Alexi Sayle Liverpool (TV doc), My Family & Autism (TV doc).

Don Lord   01273-558888   Mobile 07774-450469
The Tenth Kingdom (TV drama) (2nd unit), Haunted (feature) (2nd unit), Before You Go (feature) (2nd unit).

Jorge Luengas   020-8351 2804   Mobile 07958-913959
Fax 020-8351 2804
Lost Cities Of The Ancients (TV drama doc), Hannibal (TV drama) (2nd unit), Waking The Dead (TV drama) (2nd unit).

David Luther   CM 020-7287 4450

Ronnie Maasz BSC   01984-624414   Mobile 07762-618408
We Are Seven (TV drama), Return Of The Native (TV film) (2nd unit), Seeking Somerset (TV drama doc).

Gordon MacGregor   0161-928 7165   Mobile 07813-944009
Fax 0161-928 7165
Casualty (TV drama), Waterloo Road (TV drama), New Street Law (TV drama).

Kenneth MacMillan BSC   020-8997 6557
CM 020-7287 4450   Fax 020-8997 6557
Henry V (feature), Dancing At Lughnasa (feature).

Rex Maidment BSC   01483-893319   Mobile 07836-634513
CM 020-7287 4450
Trial & Retribution (TV drama), Cider With Rosie (TV drama), Enchanted April (feature).

Hong Manley   020-8668 1210   Mobile 07946-398871
MM 020-8995 4747
Casanova's Love Letters (short), The Insatiable Mrs Kirsch (feature), The Untitled (short).

Laurence Manly   01491-576672   Mobile 07732-918873
CCA 020-7630 6303
Hitler's Irish Movies (TV doc), 7/7: Attack On London (TV drama doc), Asylum (feature) (2nd unit).

Bahram Manocheri   020-8785 9240   Fax 020-8785 9240
City Of Joy (feature) (2nd unit), The Pan Loaf (short), Boxed (feature).

CAMERA

Rick Manzanero   01895-631635 Mobile 07831-586362
Walking With Cavemen (TV doc), Terror Tourists (TV doc), Harry Hill's TV Burp (TV light entertainment).

Henry Marcuzzi   020-8657 5520 Mobile 07753-675656
Fax 020-8657 4374
Casualty (TV drama), Doctors (TV drama), The Bill (TV drama).

Mike Marmion   020-7703 1595 Mobile 07860-444343
LL 020-8426 2200
Ten Years Younger (TV light entertainment), Who Rules The Roost (TV doc), Selling Houses (TV doc).

David Marsh   020-8692 6007 Mobile 07767-617626
SPA 01932-571044
Poirot (TV drama), Fear Of Fanny (TV drama), The Illustrated Mum (TV drama).

Andrew Martin   01727-843036 Mobile 07850-303143
Fax 01727-863638
Cloud Cuckoo Land (feature), Never Play With The Dead (TV film), Fate & Fortune (short).

Graham Martyr   020-8968 8365 Mobile 07764-677370
Fax 020-8968 8365
Other Side Of The Game (feature).

Paul Marwaha   01753-859618 Mobile 07860-664037

Mick Mason   01727-859612 Mobile 07768-650464
Fax 01727-859612

Keith Massey   01904-707693 Mobile 07831-388407
The Flight (TV doc), Emmerdale (TV drama), Restoration (feature).

Miles Massey   01904-707693 Mobile 07831-388407
The Blair Years (TV doc), The Flight (TV doc), Football Focus (TV sport).

David Matches   Mobile 07970-855509 SC 01932-252577

John Mathieson BSC   020-7221 0476
Mobile 07831-389444 Fax 020-7243 4926
Robin Hood (feature), Phantom Of The Opera (feature), Gladiator (feature).

Vaughan Matthews   020-3286 3296 Mobile 07831-521875
DYA 020-7386 0310
Elgar: The Man Behind The Mask (TV doc), Lost Kingdoms Of Africa (TV doc), National Geographic (TV doc).

Mark Mayling   01494-712255 Mobile 07831-124628
LL 020-8426 2200

John McCallum   01227-274820 Fax 01227-274820

Duane McClunie   Mobile 07767-785757
Fax 020-8932 8216
It's Not Easy Being A Wolfboy (TV doc), History Of The Internet (TV doc), Ultimate Biker Challenge (TV sport).

Vince McConnachie   020-8673 1737 Mobile 07808-769869
WZ 020-7437 2055
Night & Day (TV drama), Here Today (short), Four Seasons Hotel (commercial).

Sam McCurdy   Mobile 07976-729367
Doomsday (feature).

Brian McDairmant   01228-560663 Mobile 07785-354130
Fax 01228-562299
The Longest Memory (TV drama), Ice World (TV drama doc), Galileo's Daughter (TV film).

Robin McDonald   0121-384 2093 Mobile 07831-890802

Roger McDonald   +33 4 91 73 44 74
Mobile +33 6 80 72 82 44

Andrew McDonnell   01943-872887 Mobile 07973-278085
Fax 01943-872887
Blue Murder (TV drama), Born & Bred (TV drama) (Camera Operator), Shameless (TV drama).

Seamus McGarvey BSC   CM 020-7287 4450
World Trade Center (feature), Charlotte's Web (feature), Atonement (feature).

John McGlashan BSC   020-8997 9449
Mobile 07931-540232
Monarch Of The Glen (TV drama), Jane Eyre (feature), Captain Jack (feature).

Kieran McGuigan   020-8348 4250 Mobile 07710-544294
Spooks (TV drama), The Other Boleyn Girl (feature), Bleak House (TV drama).

Ian McMillan BSC   01326-218575 Mobile 07969-768355
BA 020-7836 1112
Event Horizon (feature) (2nd unit), A Midsummer Night's Dream (feature) (2nd unit), Restoration (feature) (Additional Photography).

Phil Meheux BSC   020-7724 6979 Mobile 07981-258965
MM 020-8995 4747
Edge Of Darkness (feature), Casino Royale (feature), Around The World In 80 Days (feature).

Chris Menges BSC   01547-510276
Dirty Pretty Things (feature), The Reader (feature), Notes On A Scandal (feature).

Peter Menzies Mobile 07827-893582
Clash Of The Titans (feature).

Chris Merry 020-8299 4686 Mobile 07703-599012
European Life (TV doc), Science & The Swastika (TV doc), The Real Stephen Hawking (TV doc).

Chris Middleton 01295-760125 Mobile 07808-491562
Fax 01295-760125
Beg (feature), E=MC2 (feature).

Peter Middleton BSC + 33 2 35 36 18 74
The Jury (TV drama), Foyle's War (TV drama), Henry VIII (TV drama).

Michael Miles 07000-242628 Mobile 07860-319206
CC 01932-568268

Dave Miller Mobile 07710-406750
My Last Five Girlfriends (feature), Jamie Oliver (TV light entertainment).

Justin Mills 020-8452 9929 Mobile 07768-772829
SR 020-7736 7786

Doug Milsome BSC 01544-327123 Mobile 07970-558898

Zubin Mistry Mobile 07768-69420
ARRI 01895-457180
Killing Joe (short), Leo (feature).

Lynn Mitchell 020-8674 2818 Mobile 07973-178881
Fax 020-8674 2818

Brian Mitchison 020-8578 9003

Maxwell Modray 01494-481236 Mobile 07802-790590
Antonioni In London (feature), Daimler Chrysler (commercial), London Children's Ballet (TV doc).

Mike Molloy BSC ACS +61 2 9997 1282
Mobile +61 409 121 112 CM 020-7287 4450
The Fourth Angel (feature), Shiner (feature), Scandal (feature).

Toby Moore Mobile 07770-882540
Wish You Were Here (feature), V For Vendetta (feature), Timber Falls (feature).

Mark Moreve 01483-211063 Mobile 07976-327130
Love/Loss (feature), The Private Life Of A Masterpiece (TV doc), Homes Under the Hammer (TV light entertainment).

Peter Morgan 020-8948 7882 Mobile 07860-440498
BF 020-8450 6444
Bedtime (TV drama), Where The Heart Is (TV drama), Clocking Off (TV drama).

Mark Moriarty 01732-850362 Mobile 07917-715680
The Bourne Ultimatum (feature) (2nd unit), The Riddle (feature), Johnny Was (feature).
www.markmoriarty.co.uk

Sam Morris Mobile 07968-487421
The Sad Case (short), Grey Notes (short), Revolution (short) (Additional Photography).

Nic Morris BSC Mobile 07860-515154
Minotaur (feature), Spooks (TV drama), Longtime Dead (feature).

Peter Moseley 01452-814250 Mobile 07774-600924
Fax 01452-814530
The Magic Door (feature), Laurie Lee - Storytellers Landscape (TV doc), Corn Devils (TV drama).

Andrew Mott Mobile 07836-642609 DG 020-7386 0310
What The Past Did For Us (TV doc), The Secret Life Of The Mona Lisa (TV arts), The Culture Show (TV arts).

Richard Mott 020-7738 3581 Mobile 07770-850783
VAW 020-7439 4657
Nowhere Fast (feature), The One & Only Herb McGwyer Plays Wallis Island (short), Cold Water (short).

Wayne Mottershead Mobile 07973-323127
The Bill (TV drama), Holby City (TV drama).

Ben Moulden Mobile 07968-212459 MY 01932-253325

Caren Moy Mobile 07802-485705

Andrew Muggleton 020-7737 4423 Mobile 07802-722120
LL 020-8426 2200 Fax 020-7737 4423
The Queen (TV drama doc), Changing Climate Changing Times (TV drama), Kevin McCloud's Grand Tour Of Europe (TV doc).

Louis Mulvey 01254-672553 Mobile 07973-212863
SC 01932-252577
The History Of The Clash (feature), Dancing In The Street (TV doc).

Colin Munn 01628-627466 Mobile 07788-134124
CMM 020-8584 5363
Midsomer Murders (TV drama), Rockface (TV drama), Avalanche (feature).

Mike Muschamp 020-7095 9103 Mobile 07950-131659
Christina (feature), Chicken Tikka Masala (feature), Splinter (feature).

Jon Nash Mobile 07793-228187

Simon Niblett Mobile 07798-524545 DG 020-7386 0310
HD Atlas India (corporate), Peacocks (TV doc), The Tyre (short).

CAMERA

Clive North   01761-241538 Mobile 07831-879594
Horizon (TV doc), Battlefield Britain (TV doc), Hitler's Hidden Secret (TV doc).

Graham Norton   01873-810814 Mobile 07973-149909
CB 01932-592572
The Da Vinci Code (feature) (2nd unit), Calendar Girls (feature), Troy (feature).

Mattias Nyberg   Mobile 07970-718896
Ollie Kepler's Expanding Purple World (feature), The Wonderful World Of Death (short), Bacardi (commercial).

Eugene O'Connor   Mobile 07831-851220 MY 01932-253325
Beat Route (TV doc), The Beatles Anthology (TV doc), Father Ted (TV comedy drama).

Shaun O'Dell   01823-480479 Mobile 07785-775634
ITG 020-7636 6565
Gulliver's Travels (feature) (2nd unit), Quantum Of Solace (feature) (2nd unit), Fred Claus (feature) (2nd unit).

Chris O'Dell BSC   +353 28 37296
Mobile +353 86 806 5625
Lewis (TV drama), Goodnight Mr Tom (TV film), Hornblower (TV drama).

Tristan Oliver   020-8568 6079 Mobile 07775-531990
BA 020-7836 1112 Fax 020-8568 6079
Fantastic Mr Fox (feature), Chicken Run (feature), Curse Of The Were-Rabbit (feature).

Chris Openshaw   Mobile 07831-470942 DG 020-7386 0310
Power Of Art (TV art), Heat Wave (TV drama), Leonardo (TV drama doc).

Ray Orton   029-2066 6322 Mobile 07836-542848
Fax 029-2066 6322
Torchwood (TV drama), Belonging (TV drama), Casualty (TV drama).

Sam Osborne   020-8969 1479 Mobile 07831-849158
SC 01932-252577 Fax 020-8969 1479
The House (feature), Colin Brumby (short).

Mahmoud Oskoui   020-8933 2070 Mobile 07831-102260
Crash (TV doc), Tehran Hostage Crisis (TV news & Current affairs), UK Wildlife (TV doc).

Luke Palmer   Mobile 07973-637011 VAW 020-7439 4657

Tim Palmer   CM 020-7287 4450
Life On Mars (TV drama), England Expects (TV drama).

Bruce Parker   020-8398 9330 Mobile 07774-805460
The Bill (TV drama), Doctors (TV drama), British Airways (commercial).

Mike Parker   Mobile 07768-667361
The Escapist (feature) (2nd unit), A Very Social Secretary (TV drama) (2nd unit), Chasing Churchill (TV drama doc).

Steve Parker   01494-677801 Mobile 07774-699990

Terry Parker   Mobile 07776-200522
Planet Earth (TV doc), The First Emperor (TV drama doc) (2nd unit), The Tribe (feature).

Austin Parkinson   01403-752225 Mobile 07802-777392

Belinda Parsons   020-7837 3781 Mobile 07711-984779
Fax 01992-444851
Volvo City (TV doc), Thin Ice (TV drama), Back To The Floor (TV doc).

Robert Pascall   020-8994 5530 Mobile 07850-690028
Fax 020-8994 5530

Martin Patmore   01494-481425 Mobile 07977-470886
Fax 01494-481579
Behind Closed Doors (TV drama doc), Auschwitz: The Final Solution (TV drama doc), Battle Of The Somme (TV drama doc).

Mark Patten   020-7738 8808 Mobile 07775-656302
San Miguel (commercial), P & O Cruises (commercial), Nike (commercial).

Simon Paul   020-7266 2665 Mobile 07831-400850

Kevin Pearcy   0117-965 1694 Mobile 07973-173384
LL 020-8426 2200 Fax 0117-965 1694
The Firm (feature) (2nd unit), Spice Girls - Tour Story (TV doc), Servants (TV drama) (2nd unit).

Stephan Pehrsson   Mobile 07941-977565
PS 020-8883 1616
Five Days (TV drama), Hustle (TV drama), Dr Who (TV drama).

Jan Pester   0141-334 8887 Mobile 07831-875608
BF 020-8450 6444
Wicker Tree (feature), Shoebox Zoo (TV childrens), Dinosapien (TV drama).

Jim Peters   01360-550479 Mobile 07989-402360
Born & Bred (TV drama), Taggart (TV drama).

Graham Pettit   020-7272 9039 Mobile 07957-574004
Fax 020-7272 9039
Fantastic Mr Fox (feature), Rock Profile (TV light entertainment), Corpse Bride (feature).

Ben Philpott   Mobile 07785-935666

Tony Pierce-Roberts   01328-823474   Mobile 07831-855278
MM 020-8995 4747
Made Of Honor (feature), Underworld (feature), Howards End (feature).

Joe Piotrowski   Mobile 07973-621726
The Crystal Maze (TV light entertainment), Winter Olympics (TV sport), La Traviata (opera).

Tim Piper   01258-454985   Mobile 07836-211786

Charles Pitt   020-8398 7005   Mobile 07831-411918
Horizon (TV doc), Ultimate Guide (TV doc).

Chris Plevin   01494-783393   Mobile 07973-208942
ARRI 01895-457180
Robin Hood (feature), Band Of Brothers (TV drama).

Tony Poole   01403-254758   Mobile 07831-546369
Rough Science (TV doc), Horizon (TV doc), I'll Show Them Who's Boss (TV doc).

Dick Pope   ITG 020-7636 6565
It's A Wonderful Afterlife (feature), Me & Orson Welles (feature), Happy-Go-Lucky (feature).

Jeremy Porter   020-7252 5626   Mobile 07976-354379
Modern Times (TV doc), Equinox (TV doc).

Roger Pratt BSC   020-8348 4292   ZBB +1 310 859 6890
Fax 020-8347 6656
Harry Potter & The Chamber Of Secrets (feature), Troy (feature).

Christopher Preston   020-8531 0049   Mobile 07973-282314
Land Girls (TV drama), Casualty (TV drama), Holby City (TV drama).

Dan Rack   020-8444 7523   Mobile 07768-081355
SPA 01932-571044
The Blitz - London's Firestorm (TV drama doc), Loser's Anonymous (feature), AIWA (commercial).

David Rea   Mobile 07970-910478
Crimestrike (feature), Cutting It (TV drama).

David Read   01793-815487   Mobile 07771-580699
Room 36 (feature), Family Affairs (TV drama), The Bill (TV drama).

Jeremy Read   020-8289 9780   Mobile 07836-594832
Fax 020-8289 9780
Fever Road (TV doc), Adrian Munsey (promo).

Keith Reed   0115-937 6015   Mobile 07860-272282

John Rhodes   0141-942 7316   Mobile 07973-132583
CMM 020-8584 5363
16 Years Of Alcohol (feature), Victoria Wood Xmas Special (TV light entertainment), The Purifiers (feature).

Kelvin Richard   020-8421 4004   Mobile 07802-463154
BA 020-7836 1112
Walter's War (TV drama), Live From Abbey Road (TV light entertainment), Hustle (TV drama) (2nd unit).

Simon Richards   01761-431991   Mobile 07774-842771
UA 020-3214 0800
The Midnight Man (TV drama), The Murder Room (TV drama), Fallen Angel (TV drama).

Jan Richter-Friis   Mobile 07785-307367
WZ 020-7437 2055

Chris Roach   Mobile +33 637 948699
The Bill (TV drama), Family Affairs (TV drama), Night & Day (TV drama).

Philip Robertson   01506-855405   Mobile 07947-365005
AMM 020-7244 1159
Book Of Blood (feature), Frozen (feature), Jekyll (TV drama).

Paul Robinson   020-8682 4416   Mobile 07973-255815
The Apprentice (TV reality), The Impressionists (TV drama) (additional photography), Grey Wolf (TV drama doc).

Patrick Rowe   Mobile 07860-233948
The South Bank Show (TV arts), Timewatch (TV doc), Martians & Us (TV doc).

Peter Rowe   01923-777059   Mobile 07860-852957
FM (TV comedy drama), Taking The Flack (TV comedy drama), Star Stories (TV light entertainment).

Ashley Rowe BSC   01725-517056   Mobile 07956-207213
ITG 020-7636 6565
Starter For Ten (feature), Copying Beethoven (feature), Alfie (feature).

Edward Rutherford   Mobile 07973-844474
VAW 020-7439 4657
Run Fat Boy Run (feature) (2nd unit), Ladies In Lavender (feature) (2nd unit), Irish Jam (feature) (2nd unit).

Robbie Ryan   Mobile 07974-923340   MY 01932-253325

Dimitri Sabbagh   01303-259988

Nic Sadler   +1 310 623 0901
Trauma (feature) (additional photography), Pirates Of The Caribbean: At World's End (feature) (additional scene).

CAMERA

Paul Sadourian Mobile 07973-629441
Dark Corners (feature), Married/Unmarried (feature), Nike (commercial).

James Saligari Mobile 07774-114321
Abbot Ale (commercial), Inside MI5: The Real Spooks (TV doc), Green Street (feature).

Eric Samuel 020-8868 8653 Mobile 07860-636527
Fax 020-8866 8670
Wimbledon (feature), Crystal Computers (commercial), Merck Pharmaceuticals (corporate).

Steve Saunderson 01543-414045 Mobile 07831-416368
Fax 01543-411298
Living It (TV drama), Playing The Field (TV drama), Midsomer Murders (TV drama).
www.stevesaunderson.com

Nick Sawyer 01202-708772 Mobile 07802-644337
WZ 020-7437 2055
Orange Magic Markers (commercial), Spirit Trap (feature), REM (promo).

Alessandra Scherillo 020-7249 3349
Mobile 07976-675742 Fax 020-7249 3349
Stella Artois (commercial), Campari (commercial), Porsche (commercial).

David Scott 020-7837 3781 Mobile 07710-171891
Fax 01992-444851
Marpiccolo (feature), Il Giudice Ragazzino (feature), A Small Dance (TV film).
www.indfilms.co.uk

Owen Scurfield SR 020-7736 7786

Chris Seager BSC 020-8840 3564 Mobile 07801-353502
MM 020-8995 4747
Hamlet (feature), New In Town (feature), Five Daughters (TV drama).

Desmond Seal 01694-781444 Mobile 07814-670649
Fax 01694-781444
O'Shea's Big Adventure (TV doc), Days That Shook The World (TV doc), P Company (TV doc).

John Sennett 01491-612367 Mobile 07973-616180
Fax 01491-612367
Comin' Atcha (TV childrens), Bitesize (TV doc), Heaven & Earth (feature).

Ben Seresin 020-7289 0811 Mobile 07855-526694
Best Laid Plans (feature), A Good Woman (feature), Terminator III (feature) (2nd unit).

Jean-Paul Seresin 020-8960 8325 Mobile 07957-455944
Mercedes (commercial), Dead Cool (feature), Robbie Williams (concert).

Michael Seresin BSC 020-7224 9040 Fax 020-7224 9040
Angela's Ashes (feature), The Life Of David Gale (feature), Harry Potter & The Prisoner Of Azkaban (feature).

Antonio Serpini 01908-376912 Mobile 07973-316987
Distant Bridges (feature).

Robert Shacklady Mobile 07973-633402
ARRI 01895-457180
Life Goes On (feature), Stagknight (feature), Numerous commercials.

Gary Shaw Mobile 07836-600714 WZ 020-7437 2055
Vision Express (commercial), Vauxhall (commercial), Nissan (commercial).

Matt Shaw Mobile 07956-873645

Antony Shearn 020-7371 2327 Mobile 07973-261396
Fax 020-7371 2327
Luna (feature), Lestat (feature), Mirrormask (feature).

Jason Shepherd ARRI 01895-457180

Guy Sherborne 020-8567 4223 Mobile 07778-157402

Andrew Shillabeer Mobile 07767-233286
Life In Cold Blood (TV doc), India's Deadly Dozen (TV doc), Planet Earth (TV doc).

David Shillingford 020-8673 1818 Mobile 07702-334134
Harry Potter & The Half-Blood Prince (feature) (2nd unit).
www.davidshillingford.com

John Simmons 020-8740 4183 Mobile 07976-423130
DG 020-7386 0310
Chandos (promo), EMI (promo), LSO (promo).

Roger Simonsz Mobile +33 6 74 59 18 79
Nine Miles Down (feature), The Devil Wears Prada (feature) (2nd unit), The Happening (feature) (2nd unit).

Peter Sinclair 0118-976 7527 Mobile 07774-995912
Sinchronicity (TV drama), Britannia High (TV drama), Life Is Wild (TV drama).

Tony Slater-Ling 0161-969 4776 Mobile 07939-587794
Nanny McPhee & The Big Bang (feature), Spooks (TV drama), Shameless (TV drama).

Mark Sloper 020-8746 1400 Fax 020-8749 3755
Wedding Diaries (TV reality), Full Throttle Famous (TV light entertainment), Redemption TV (TV channel).

Alan Smith   020-8892 4945 Mobile 07850-690015
Fax 020-8255 0798
Ma France (TV doc), Dunkirk (TV drama doc), Diverse Orchestras (TV doc).

Arthur Smith   0161-962 9657 Mobile 07966-521407
Jake's Progress (TV drama), Self Catering (TV film), Fred Dibnah - Steeplejack (TV doc).

Jono Smith   Mobile 07973-625947
Hope Springs (TV drama), Sus (TV drama), The Fixer (TV drama).

Larry Smith BSC   020-7833 1351 Mobile 07802-181474
Fax 020-7833 1351
Miss Marple (TV drama), Eyes Wide Shut (feature), The Piano Player (feature).

Mark Smythe   020-7723 5765 Mobile 07710-348997

Howard Somers   0161-928 4124 Mobile 07801-480334
Gold (TV drama), Prime Suspect (TV drama), Cold Feet (TV drama).

John Sorapure   020-7267 6550 Mobile 07831-308110
Fax 020-7267 3082
Bunny & The Bull (feature), Fat Slags (feature), The Mighty Boosh (TV light entertainment).

Mike Southon BSC   CMM 020-8584 5363
Pursued (feature), RKO 281 (TV film), Little Man Tate (feature).

Andrew Speller   01453-832064 Mobile 07966-379764
Little Devil (TV drama), Perfect Day (TV film), Supernatural (TV drama).

Tim Spence   01403-751744 Mobile 07860-449036
Brazil (feature) (2nd unit), Hospital (TV light entertainment).

Mike Spragg   020-8749 3565 Mobile 07973-422567
Fax 020-8749 3565
Waking The Dead (TV drama), Hughie Green, Most Sincerely (TV film), Primeval (TV drama).

Tony Spratling BSC   01923-823761
The Saint (feature) (2nd unit), Alien III (feature) (2nd unit), Muppet Treasure Island (feature) (2nd unit).

Chris St John Smith 020-8979 2927 Mobile 07850-165469
Fax 020-8979 2927

Oliver Stapleton BSC   01364-653614 ITG 020-7636 6565
Fax 01364-653704
The Proposal (feature), The Shipping News (feature), Buffalo Soldiers (feature).

Kate Stark   Mobile 07973-322784
Clubbed (feature), Desserts (TV drama), Chasing Heaven (TV drama).

Simon Starling   020-8740 5532 Mobile 07973-191702
Fax 020-8740 5532
Daniel Deronda (TV drama) (2nd unit), Dalziel & Pascoe (TV drama).

George Steel   Mobile 07767-892537
Cast Offs (TV drama), Cleanskin (feature), Numerous commercials & promos.

Alan Stewart   01438-714793 Mobile 07774-699514
ARRI 01895-457180 Fax 01438-714793
Sherlock Holmes (feature) (2nd unit), Inkheart (feature) (2nd unit), Elizabeth: The Golden Age (feature) (2nd unit).

Richard Stewart   01932-253325 Mobile 07775-900742
MY 01932-253325

Witold Stok BSC   020-8847 2078 Mobile 07710-246953
MM 020-8995 4747
Close My Eyes (feature), Two Deaths (feature), Among Giants (feature).

Ivan Strasburg BSC   020-7328 2536 Mobile 07802-484759
DA 020-7437 4551
Treme (TV drama), Shooting Dogs (feature), Bloody Sunday (feature).

Rik Stratton   020-8940 8478
COI (commercial), HSBC (commercial).

Lukas Strebel   Mobile 07711-432860 UA 020-3214 0800
Wallander (TV drama), Little Dorrit (TV drama), See No Evil (TV drama).

Gavin Struthers   Mobile 07956-133301
CMM 020-8584 5363
Outpost (feature), Secret Diary Of A Call Girl (TV drama), Shameless (TV drama).

Dan Studley   HC 020-8742 1888
The X Factor (TV light entertainment), Britain's Got Talent (TV light entertainment), Over The Rainbow (TV light entertainment).
www.hotcam.tv

Adam Suschitzky Mobile 07968-528034 DA 020-7437 4551
Middletown (feature), Shadow In The North (TV drama), Life On Mars (TV drama).

Peter Suschitzky BSC   020-7624 3734 Fax 020-7625 6843
Star Wars: Episode V - The Empire Strikes Back (feature), Mars Attacks (feature), A History Of Violence (feature).

Chris Sutcliffe   0191-233 0050 Fax 0191-233 0052
Engineering Egypt (TV drama doc), Naked Science (TV doc), Edward Lear In The Balkens (TV doc).

CAMERA

Derek Suter BSC   01494-677341 Mobile 07802-232576
SPA 01932-571044 Fax 01494-677341
Walk Away & I Stumble (TV drama), Save Angel Hope (feature), The Last Detective (TV drama).

Katie Swain   020-8962 6364 Mobile 07711-624600
MM 020-8995 4747
Help (TV light entertainment), Little Britain (tour), Killing Hitler (TV drama).

David Swan   020-3249 0024 Mobile 07768-362476
Science Of Shark Attack (TV doc), Seconds From Disaster (TV doc), The Curse Of Tutankhamun (TV doc).

Fraser Taggart   01491-413194 Mobile 07973-632038
ITG 020-7636 6565 Fax 01491-413194
Vertical Limit (feature) (2nd unit), Prince Of Persia (feature) (2nd unit), Your Highness (feature) (2nd unit).

Peter Talbot   01494-483882 Mobile 07974-920450
Fax 01494-483882
The Wolfman (feature), Prince Of Persia (feature) (visual fx unit), Sunshine (feature) (2nd unit).

Fred Tammes BSC   +61 7 5564 6367 MM 020-8995 4747

Derik Tan   020-7284 0859 Mobile 07973-325361
Fax 020-7284 0859
Bullies (short), The Virus (short), The Audition (short).

John Tarby   020-7734 5021 Mobile 07860-327866
Newsnight (TV news & current affairs), Tricky (TV childrens), Demon Wheels (feature).

David Tattersall BSC   Mobile 07827-240546
MM 020-8995 4747
Gulliver's Travels (feature), Triple X II (feature), Star Wars: Episode III - Revenge Of The Sith (feature).

John Taylor   020-8994 0576 Mobile 07778-636065
SD 020-8994 1199

Rory Taylor   Mobile 07836-549230
Crash (feature), Doctor Who (TV drama), Torchwood (TV drama).

Nick Tebbet   Mobile 07956-379540 WZ 020-7437 2055
The Truth (feature), Elephant Palm Tree (short), The Fifth Element (feature).

Richard Terry   01803-322502 Mobile 07974-323408
Decoding Da Vinci (TV doc), Living With Wolves (TV doc), The Porn King Versus The President (TV doc).

Martin Testar   020-8874 4040 Mobile 07798-524040
RED 020-8374 3074
Numerous commercials.

Serge Teulon   Mobile 07883-086440

Anna Thew   020-7221 0457 Fax 020-7221 0457
LFMC Demolition (short), Broken Pieces (short), Minsk Girl (short).

Clive Thom   01257-265421 Mobile 07892-870408
John Meets Paul - A Mediterranean Journey (TV doc), No Sweat (TV drama).

Mike Thomson   JCA 020-7434 4143
Urban Gothic (TV drama), The Coral Island (TV drama), Harry & The Wrinklies (TV childrens).

Peter Thornton   020-8845 8755 Mobile 07976-725493
DD 020-7851 3575
Doctor Who (TV drama), Dalziel & Pascoe (TV drama), Robin Hood (TV drama).
www.peterthornton.info

Steve Tickner   Mobile 07836-765668
The Queen (feature) (2nd unit), Tales Of The Riverbank (feature) (2nd unit), Greyfriars Bobby (feature) (2nd unit).

Clive Tickner BSC   01502-723367 Mobile 07802-895616
MM 020-8995 4747
Twelfth Night (theatre), Trust Me (feature), Hidden Agenda (feature).

Frank Tidy BSC   020-8870 3570

George Tiffin   020-7793 0468 Mobile 07970-473359
Sketches Of Frank Gehry (feature), Chromophobia (feature).

Ben Todd   Mobile 07718-868154 VAW 020-7439 4657
Numerous commercials & promos.

Janet Tovey   020-7625 8361 Mobile 07818-425221
PS 020-8883 1616
The New Worst Witch (TV childrens), The Murder Game (TV light entertainment), Survivors (TV drama).

Mark Treays   01752-267669 Mobile 07973-287922
Fax 01752-267669

Neil Trierweiler   Mobile 07973-702159 SR 020-7736 7786

Vladimir Trivic   Mobile 07956-433829 PS 020-8883 1616
Soul Boy (feature), The Happiness Thief (short), Summer (feature).

Alan Trow BSC   Mobile 07710-458791
Tornado (feature), Little Pudding (TV film), Up N Under (feature).

Brian Tufano BSC   01491-652314 Mobile 07970-122874
MM 020-8995 4747

Patrick Turley   01932-852734 Mobile 07850-836995
Eyes Wide Shut (feature) (2nd unit), Witness (TV doc), Sony Playstation (commercial).

Brett Turnbull   020-8802 4484 Mobile 07796-953837
SC 01932-252577
Three Men In A Restaurant (feature), Kumbh Mela - The Greatest Show On Earth (TV doc).

Garry Turnbull   020-8671 5377 Mobile 07887-704666
DD 020-7851 3575 Fax 020-8671 5377
The Bus (feature), Reverb (feature), Everything's Going To Be OK (feature).

Jamie Turner   Mobile 07799-890281
Mist: Sheepdog Tales (TV childrens), The One Show (TV magazine), The Money Programme (TV news & current affairs).

Sean Van Hales   Mobile 07775-557535
Hotel Babylon (TV drama), Sparkle (feature), French Film (feature).

Zoran Veljkovic   ARRI 01895-457180

Bjorn Ventris   020-7387 3082 Mobile 07973-197987
SR 020-7736 7786
Microsoft (commercial), Menuhin's Children (TV doc).

Robin Vidgeon BSC   01932-848948 Mobile 07860-764907
BA 020-7836 1112 Fax 01932-848948
Octane (feature), A Touch Of Frost (TV drama).

Ernest Vincze BSC   020-7385 3413 Mobile 07711-664773
Doctor Who (TV drama), The Mystic Masseur (feature), Sea Of Souls (TV drama).

Alex Wakeford   01273-747837 Mobile 07890-393875
Pepsi-Cola (commercial), Credo (feature), Daddy's Boy (short).

John Walker BSC   01643-707456 Mobile 07779-870475
Respect (TV drama), Underworld (feature), The Vice (TV drama).

Nigel Walters BSC   020-8740 6732 Mobile 07774-115988
Fax 020-8354 0609
One Of The Hollywood Ten (feature), Queer As Folk (TV drama), Kavanagh QC (TV drama).

Chris Ward   01982-552724 Mobile 07754-838018
Good Parenting (TV magazine), Food & Drink (TV magazine), Pet Rescue (TV doc).

John Ward   020-8761 5431 Mobile 07768-451239
Final Cut (feature), To Die For (feature), Love Honour & Obey (feature).

Mark Waters   Mobile 07721-347891 ITG 020-7636 6565
Powder (feature), Doctor Who (TV drama), Torchwood (TV drama).
www.markwaters-dop.com

Karl Watkins   020-8889 2224 Mobile 07973-211873
SC 01932-252577 Fax 020-8374 8839
Prisoners Of The Sun (feature) (2nd unit), High Heels & Low Lifes (feature) (2nd unit), Blackball (feature) (2nd unit).

Colin Watkinson   020-8447 5479 Mobile 07710-080284
The Fall (feature).

Steve Watson   020-8257 5240 Mobile 07973-502640

Andy Watt   01932-842799 Mobile 07774-161291
Fax 01932-842799
Cher In Las Vegas (DVD), The Merchant Of Venice (feature), Jesus Christ Superstar (theatre).

Ian Watts   020-8333 6555 Mobile 07956-262808
DYA 020-7386 0310 Fax 020-8333 6555
Planet Mechanics (TV doc), Who Do You Think You Are? (TV doc), The Verdict (TV doc).

Simon Weekes   Mobile 07903-879130
Numerous commercials & promos.

James Welland   020-7275 0286 Mobile 07973-226065
CM 020-7287 4450 Fax 020-7275 0287
The Last Minute (feature), Spooks (TV drama), Palais Royale! (feature).

Andy Whale   01305-751723 Mobile 07774-190023
Esquire Magazine Online (corporate), No Ordinary Joe (short), Dirtbox (short).
www.andywhale.com

Paul Wheeler BSC   020-8878 7193 Mobile 07836-593740
CMM 020-8584 5363 Fax 020-8878 7193
Inspector Morse (TV drama), King Lear (theatre), Oklahoma! (TV film).

Winstan Whitter   020-3093 1091 Mobile 07957-208687
Cobra (commercial), Dizzee Rascal (promo).

Nigel Willoughby   020-8241 0749 Mobile 07712-837352
MY 01932-253325
It's A Free World (feature), Bridget Jones's Diary (feature) (2nd unit), The Magdalene Sisters (feature).

Paul Wilson BSC   01242-603855 Mobile 07973-327526
Die Another Day (feature), The World Is Not Enough (feature), Goldeneye (feature).

Mark Wolf   020-7722 5606 Mobile 07768-031122
Battle For Haditha (feature), Ghosts (feature), Inconceivable (feature).

Tim Wooster　01442-870519　Mobile 07976-689946
STA 020-7729 7477
Wanted (feature), Beacon 77 (feature), Exam (feature).

Trevor Wrenn　01494-881101　Mobile 07768-846833

Alan Wright　020-7687 2646　Mobile 07956-262304
BA 020-7836 1112
Holby City (TV drama), London's Burning (TV drama), Border Cafe
(TV drama).

Ed Wright　ARRI 01895-457180

John Wyatt　01844-350221　Mobile 07710-232349
Fax 01844-351165

Gary Young　01225-480751　Mobile 07966-372413
MY 01932-253325
JD Sports (commercial), NTL (commercial), Mercedes
(commercial).

Haris Zambarloukos　020-7935 9774
Mobile 07968-800098
Mamma Mia! (feature).

DIVERS

Alexandra Davis　0161-928 8770　Mobile 07866-801156
Coronation Street (TV drama), Hollyoaks (TV drama), Mischief Night
(feature).

GAFFERS - RIGGING

Guy Cope　Mobile 07792-446005
Hotel Babylon (TV drama).

Warren Evans　Mobile 07766-805381
Prince Of Persia (feature).

Ian Franklin　Mobile 07768-656379
Green Zone (feature).

Lee Martin　Mobile 07850-083984
Robin Hood (feature).

Raymond Mills　Mobile 07973-531513
Clash Of The Titans (feature).

GAFFERS & ELECTRICIANS

Edmund Alexander　020-8581 3341　Mobile 07956-499665
2000 Acres Of Sky (TV drama), A Many Splintered Thing (TV
drama).

John Atkins　01934-413736　Mobile 07710-028566

Phil Baker　Mobile 07774-999954

Ian Barwick　Mobile 07734-068961
From Time To Time (feature).

Brian Beaumont　0117-924 6827　Mobile 07710-297789
Hamlet (feature), Hunger (feature), Being Human (TV drama).

Paul Benson　Mobile 07779-490947

Chris Bird　Mobile 07966-475007
The Commander (TV drama).

Sam Bloor　01753-893027　Mobile 07810-532950
Kingdom Of Heaven (feature), Spy Game (feature), Evita (feature).

Reg Boddy　020-8878 6910　Mobile 07799-597132
The Golden Hour (TV drama), Around The World In 80 Days
(feature), The World Is Not Enough (feature).

Lou Bogue　01753-646642
The Golden Compass (feature).

Paul Borg　01628-637195　Mobile 07962-137007
Fax 01628-637195
The Da Vinci Code (feature), Death At A Funeral (feature), A Murder
Is Announced (TV drama).

Chris Brennan　Mobile 07775-727494

Mark Brennan　Mobile 07836-639399
Inside Out (TV news & current affairs), British Telecom (commercial),
Renault (commercial).

Paul Brennan　Mobile 07738-331845
Little Britain (tour), X-Box (commercial).

Paul Brewster　Mobile 07702-525032

Peter Brimson　Mobile 07973-344561
Murder In Suburbia (TV drama), The Inspector Lynley Mysteries (TV
drama), Confetti (feature).

Robert Brock　01784-451617　Mobile 07973-659047
Children Of Men (feature), Stardust (feature), The Golden Compass
(feature).

Geoff Brown　Mobile 07973-746381
In Deep (TV drama).

Micky Brown　020-8579 0896　Mobile 07774-264662
Fax 020-8579 0896
Wuthering Heights (feature), A Kiss Before Dying (feature), RKO
281 (TV film).

Michael Chambers　020-8941 2070　Mobile 07900-310946
1408 (feature).

Mark Clayton Mobile 07801-368462
Dead Man's Shoes (feature), Spooks (TV drama), Bleak House (TV drama).

Gary Colkett 020-8470 2024 Mobile 07957-207486
Tomb Raider II (feature), Die Another Day (feature), The World Is Not Enough (feature).

Steve Cortie Mobile 07967-395094
The Colour Of Magic (TV film).

Steve Costello 01273-561804 Mobile 07802-813728
Fax 01273-561804
Prince Of Persia (feature), Charlie & The Chocolate Factory (feature) (2nd unit), Alexander (feature).

Perry Cullen Mobile 07956-218736
Troy (feature), Harry Potter & The Chamber Of Secrets (feature), Kingdom Of Heaven (feature).

Pat Deveney 020-8466 1141 Mobile 07970-257152
Footballers' Wives (TV drama), Truly Madly Deeply (feature), Only Fools & Horses (TV comedy drama).

Mat Dowler 01296-625027 Mobile 07710-900108
Fax 0560-131 8165
Sliding Doors (feature), The Tenth Kingdom (TV drama), Midsomer Murders (TV drama).

Kevin Edland 020-8668 5123 Mobile 07802-775654
The Wolfman (feature), Children Of Men (feature), Alexander (feature).

Andrew Evans Mobile 07833-702419
Harry Potter & The Order Of The Phoenix (feature), Die Another Day (feature), Below (feature).

Mark "Giffer" Evans 01784-455170 Mobile 07710-941200
The Da Vinci Code (feature), Alfie (feature), Harry Potter & The Goblet Of Fire (feature).

Mark "Rocky" Evans 020-8948 6930
Mobile 07974-829984
The Da Vinci Code (feature), The Life & Death Of Peter Sellers (feature), Wimbledon (feature).

Perry Evans 01784-455116 Mobile 07831-552776
Clash Of The Titans (feature), The Da Vinci Code (feature), Harry Potter & The Prisoner Of Azkaban (feature).

Warren Ewen 020-8866 5221 Mobile 07904-319537
Fax 020-8866 5221
Troy (feature) (2nd unit), Harry Potter & The Goblet Of Fire (feature) (2nd unit), Nil By Mouth (feature).

Chuck Finch Mobile 07703-126295

Steve Finch Mobile 07956-561043
W.E. (feature), Harry Potter & The Goblet Of Fire (feature), Troy (feature).

Tommy Finch 020-8393 5446 Mobile 07909-644582
W.E. (feature), Closer (feature), De Lovely (feature).

Wick Finch 01424-773181 Mobile 07711-367832
Harry Potter & The Half-Blood Prince (feature) (2nd unit), X-Men II (feature), Kingdom Of Heaven (feature).

Kevin Fitzpatrick Mobile 07976-239814
Desperate Romantics (TV drama), Angus Thongs & Perfect Snogging (feature).

Michael Flynn 01932-789226

Stephen Foster 01243-587110 Mobile 07973-500549
Fax 01243-587260
The Wolfman (feature), Sex & The City (feature), The Day Of The Triffids (TV drama).

Mark Gay 020-8995 7054 Mobile 07970-682077
The Da Vinci Code (feature), Shaun Of The Dead (feature), Batman Begins (feature).

Dieter Geller 01895-633230 Mobile 07710-325826
Walk Away & I Stumble (TV drama), William & Mary (TV drama), Little Britain (tour).

Peter Goddard 020-8524 5505 Mobile 07956-303252
Run Fat Boy Run (feature), Harry Potter & The Goblet Of Fire (feature), Five Children & It (feature).

Vince Goddard 01753-538511 Mobile 07702-124956
Fax 01753-538511
Lewis (TV drama), The English Harem (TV drama), Snuff Box (TV drama).

Ronnie Green 01895-236722 Mobile 07977-886217
V For Vendetta (feature), Charlie & The Chocolate Factory (feature), Batman Begins (feature).

Mark Grew Mobile 07887-934047
Harry Potter & The Philosopher's Stone (feature), The World Is Not Enough (feature), Blade II (feature).

Brian Grint 01493-750039 Mobile 07710-616620
Softies (TV childrens), Mile High (TV drama), Hero To Zero (TV drama).

Mark Hanlon 020-8890 8159 Mobile 07890-248009
The Debt (feature), In Bruges (feature), The Queen (feature).

Paul Harris 020-8361 5085 Mobile 07786-302716
Christmas At The Riviera (TV drama), London Boulevard (feature).

Darren Harvey   020-8488 5889 Mobile 07850-054484
Bad Girls (TV drama), The Governess (feature), Footballers' Wives (TV drama).

Andy Hebden   01707-320127 Mobile 07957-646177
Fax 01707-320127
Holby City (TV drama), Serious & Organised (TV drama), Trial & Retribution (TV drama).

David Hedley   020-8968 6293 Mobile 07958-409506
Henry VIII (TV drama), New Tricks (TV drama), Foyle's War (TV drama).

John Higgins   020-7370 1185 Mobile 07836-552840
The Wolfman (feature), Children Of Men (feature), Stardust (feature).

Richard Holborow   01634-855898 Mobile 07957-588377

Ben Horsefield   0161-998 3578 Mobile 07747-808432
Kingdom Of Heaven (feature), Troy (feature), My Summer Of Love (feature).

Terry Hunt   Mobile 07860-718457
The Colour Of Magic (TV film), Miss Marple (TV drama).

Bob Jones   01758-770338 Mobile 07901-918991

Joe Judge   01204-437888 Mobile 07967-736151
Hotel Babylon (TV drama).

JP Judge   Mobile 07974-667283
Al's Lads (feature), Murphy's Law (TV drama), Born & Bred (TV drama).

Ossie Jung   01923-778653 Mobile 07971-818199
The Mutant Chronicles (feature), Seed Of Chucky (feature), The Englishman Who Went Up A Hill (feature).

Nikos Kalimerakis   Mobile 07829-887711
The Wolfman (feature).

Pip Keeling   01992-714329 Mobile 07850-102886
Harry Potter & The Goblet Of Fire (feature) (underwater), Tomb Raider (feature) (2nd unit).

John King   01753-663984 Mobile 07770-211506
Fax 01753-663984
Bridget Jones's Diary II (feature), The Mummy Returns (feature), The World Is Not Enough (feature).

Stuart King   020-8992 8770 Mobile 07850-660425
Little Dorrit (TV drama).

Dave Kirkwood   01525-221917 Mobile 07973-154170
Fax 01525-221917
Scrapheap Challenge (TV light entertainment), Changing Rooms (TV light entertainment), Big Kevin Little Kevin (TV light entertainment).

Steve Kitchen   01895-631502 Mobile 07850-217574
Pure (feature), There's Only One Jimmy Grimble (feature), Saving Grace (feature).

Eddie Knight   Mobile 07889-691848
Gulliver's Travels (feature).

Wayne Leach   01895-236090 Mobile 07802-963962
The Wolfman (feature), Stardust (feature), Children Of Men (feature).

Andy Long   01452-381179 Mobile 07973-742379
Fax 01452-381179
The Boy In The Striped Pyjamas (feature), In Bruges (feature), Death Defying Acts (feature).

Hugh Madden   020-8992 9513 Mobile 07961-314642
Die Another Day (feature), Harry Potter & The Prisoner Of Azkaban (feature).

Mal Maguire   020-8997 4406 Mobile 07802-441368
Haagen-Dazs (commercial), Andrex (commercial), Youngs (commercial).

Alan Martin   020-8950 4454 Mobile 07885-302495
Robin Hood (feature), Prince Of Persia (feature), Phantom Of The Opera (feature).

Michael McDermott   01276-21691 Mobile 07831-781132
Quantum Of Solace (feature) (2nd unit), The Decameron (feature), Franklyn (feature).

Paul McGeachan   01628-488401 Mobile 07770-756870
Pierrepoint (TV film), Dear Frankie (feature), Messiah (TV drama).

Liam McGill   020-8841 2242 Mobile 07973-634182
Pride & Prejudice (feature), Billy Elliot (feature), East Is East (feature).

Carl McGillivray   01784-455050 Mobile 07802-818263
Elizabeth The Virgin Queen (TV drama), The Line Of Beauty (TV drama), The Tenth Kingdom (TV drama).

Terry McGuinness   020-8421 5354 Mobile 07976-302821
Hotel Babylon (TV drama).

Campbell McIntosh   Mobile 07770-736231
Miss Marple (TV drama), Miss Potter (feature), Starter For Ten (feature).

Richard Merrell   Mobile 07841-571409
Harry Potter & The Goblet Of Fire (feature), Kingdom Of Heaven (feature), Troy (feature).

Patrick Miller   020-8573 8032   Mobile 07885-656201
Fax 020-8573 8032
United 93 (feature), V For Vendetta (feature), Incendiary (feature).

Jamie Mills   020-8930 4343   Mobile 07956-622751
Tomb Raider II (feature), Band Of Brothers (TV drama), What A Girl Wants (feature).

Shaun Mone   Mobile 07976-806595
From Time To Time (feature).

Robert Monger   01293-863939   Mobile 07850-945610
Harry Potter & The Philosopher's Stone (feature), Tomorrow Never Dies (feature), The World Is Not Enough (feature).

Terry Montague   020-8989 7391   Mobile 07889-448285
Robin Hood (feature), Prince Of Persia (feature), Wild & Wicked (feature).

Dave Moss   020-8841 7092   Mobile 07774-995601
The Da Vinci Code (feature), Batman Begins (feature), Harry Potter & The Prisoner Of Azkaban (feature).

Paul Murphy   Mobile 07710-313828
Nanny McPhee & The Big Bang (feature).

Andrew Nolan   Mobile 07901-643630
From Time To Time (feature).

Gary Nolan   Mobile 07973-416984
Batman Begins (feature), Pride & Prejudice (feature), Derailed (feature).

Dennis O'Connell   020-8644 2480   Mobile 07770-792137
Fax 020-8644 2480
Thunderbirds (feature), Alexander (feature), Batman Returns (feature).

Dave Oldroyd   Mobile 07973-423925
Friends & Crocodiles (TV drama), Like Minds (feature), Gideon's Daughter (TV drama).

Keith Osborn   020-7923 3101   Mobile 07815-460472
CBBC (TV childrens), Footballers' Wives (TV drama).

Tom O'Sullivan   020-8440 4020   Mobile 07931-319007

David Owen   Mobile 07956-451014
All About George (TV drama), William & Mary (TV drama), The Last Detective (TV drama).

Garry Owen   01934-733482   Mobile 07860-751108
Chinese Food In Minutes (TV light entertainment), Kill It Cook It Eat It (TV reality), Time Team (TV doc).

Ricky Pattenden   01727-850134   Mobile 07798-528789
Clash Of The Titans (feature), The Da Vinci Code (feature), Batman Begins (feature).

Ronnie Phillips   01929-480025   Mobile 07802-575176
Derailed (feature), Tomb Raider II (feature), Hitchhiker's Guide To The Galaxy (feature).

Ray Potter   01903-244268   Mobile 07860-370146
Fax 01903-244268
Casino Royale (feature) (2nd unit), Beyond Borders (feature), I'll Sleep When I'm Dead (feature).

Larry Prinz   020-8339 0051   Mobile 07958-670765
Fax 020-8339 0025
Ali G In Da House (feature), Poirot (TV drama), Gladiator (feature).

Mike Prior   Mobile 07624-481977
White On White (feature), Hound Of The Baskervilles (TV film), Island At War (TV drama).

Larry Randall   020-8422 1559   Mobile 07802-643984
The Golden Compass (feature).

Phil Reader   Mobile 07966-293206
Hotel Babylon (TV drama).

Dave Ridout   01895-232065   Mobile 07855-780111
Harry Potter & The Philosopher's Stone (feature), Notting Hill (feature), Harry Potter & The Prisoner Of Azkaban (feature).

Steve Roberts   020-7350 2762   Mobile 07976-701714
Prince Of Persia (feature), Doomsday (feature).

Peter Robinson   01747-812239   Mobile 07850-690051
Fax 01747-812239

James Roper   01784-252858
Harry Potter & The Philosopher's Stone (feature), Die Another Day (feature), Harry Potter & The Prisoner Of Azkaban (feature).

Jimmy Russell   020-8508 9726   Mobile 07973-613242
The Commander (TV drama).

John Saunders   Mobile 07939-541399
Little Dorrit (TV drama).

Carolina Schmidtholstein   020-7738 3314
Mobile 07788-784918
Brick Lane (feature), Hallam Foe (feature), Driving Lessons (feature).

CAMERA

Alex Scott   0117-962 9350 Mobile 07774-240656
Fax 0117-962 9350
28 Weeks Later (feature), All In The Game (TV film), Wimbledon (feature).

Paul Slatter   01726-833286 Mobile 07815-685332
Johnny Was (feature), The Bourne Ultimatum (feature) (2nd unit), Far Cry (feature).

David Smith   020-8989 2195 Mobile 07767-493212
Shanghai (feature), Miss Potter (feature), 1408 (feature).

Norman Smith   01895-635420 Mobile 07850-532585
Below (feature), Longtime Dead (feature), The Crying Game (feature).

Steve Smith   01296-614799 Mobile 07831-428015

Joe Spence   020-7727 6113 Mobile 07973-344436
Love Soup (TV drama), Jonathan Creek (TV drama), Murder In Mind (TV drama).

James Summers   020-8304 9056 Mobile 07900-896132
Spooks (TV drama).

Steve Swannell   020-8292 0107 Mobile 07774-159137
Poirot (TV drama), The Taming Of The Shrew (TV film), Kevin & Perry Go Large (feature).

Pat Sweeney   01698-801399 Mobile 07770-488832
Angus Thongs & Perfect Snogging (feature), St Trinian's (feature), London Boulevard (feature).

Barnaby Sweet   Mobile 07870-573772
Huge (feature).

Andrew Taylor   Mobile 07850-954854
Doomsday (feature).

Mark Thomas   Mobile 07977-504089
Casino Royale (feature), The Tenth Kingdom (TV drama), Hitchhiker's Guide To The Galaxy (feature).

Bill Tracey   0161-428 6359 Mobile 07957-233830
The Constant Gardener (feature) (Rigging Gaffer), The History Boys (feature) (Rigging Gaffer), Kinky Boots (feature) (Rigging Gaffer).

Gavin Walters   01487-823763 Mobile 07885-260940
Fanny Hill (TV drama).

Lee Walters   020-8519 1851 Mobile 07774-888946
Fax 020-7639 3105
Notes On A Scandal (feature), Sahara (feature), The Hours (feature).

Martin Welland   01252-542082 Mobile 07973-323111
Batman Begins (feature), Goal! (feature), Wimbledon (feature) (2nd unit).

David White   020-8959 0520 Mobile 07903-987734
John Carter Of Mars (feature).

Eddy White   Mobile 07831-151001
Invasion: Earth (TV drama), Scarlet Pimpernel (TV drama), Messiah (TV drama).

Julian White   020-7255 1027 Mobile 07880-554799
Venus (feature), Rescue Dawn (feature), Sleuth (feature).

Harry Wiggins   020-8741 2269 Mobile 07710-478475
Fax 020-8741 2269
Green Zone (feature), The Oxford Murders (feature), A Good Year (feature).

Tony Wilcock   Mobile 07710-459517
Robin Hood (feature) (2nd unit).

Dean Wilkinson   01628-819436 Mobile 07775-684125
Harry Potter & The Prisoner Of Azkaban (feature), Harry Potter & The Philosopher's Stone (feature), Proof Of Life (feature).

Iwan Williams   01895-234580 Mobile 07973-695683
I Could Never Be Your Woman (feature), Pride & Prejudice (feature) (Best Boy), Derailed (feature).

Steve Williams   01962-883359 Mobile 07778-001588

Gary Willis   01344-890009 Mobile 07788-673917
Fax 01344-890009
The Merchant Of Venice (feature).

Jimmy Wilson   Mobile 07968-007972
Amazing Grace (feature).

Micky Wilson   01932-229745 Mobile 07850-805392
Fax 01932-229745
First Knight (feature), Dinotopia (TV drama), Lost In Space (feature).

Danny Young   Mobile 07977-756262
Hotel Babylon (TV drama).

GRIPS

David Appleby   01923-855656 Mobile 07973-141360
BE 01727-841177 Fax 01923-859157
Clash Of The Titans (feature), Prince Of Persia (feature), Quantum Of Solace (feature).

John Arnold   01737-643003 Mobile 07768-876223
ARRI 01895-457180 Fax 01737-643003
The Young Victoria (feature), Fred Claus (feature), Amazing Grace (feature).

Ken Ashley-Johnson   01344-893845   Mobile 07970-197561
WZ 020-7437 2055
The Brit Awards (party), Robbie At Knebworth (concert), The Fifth
Element (feature).

Kenny Atherfold   01375-382866   Mobile 07774-681675
Fax 01375-382866
The Mummy: Tomb Of The Dragon Emperor (feature), Harry Potter &
The Deathly Hallows (feature), Quantum Of Solace (feature).

Craig Atkinson   0191-284 3922

Phil Aylward   Mobile 07050-261951
Victoria & Albert (TV drama).

Clive Baldwin   029-2079 1437   Mobile 07721-418040
Fax 029-2079 1437
Insiders (TV drama), Dreaming Of Joseph Lees (feature), Relative
Values (feature).

Rob Barlow   Mobile 07957-370619   SC 01932-252577
The Escapist (feature), The Deaths Of Ian Stone (feature), Freebird
(feature).

Stuart Bell   Mobile 07894-074377
Prince Of Persia (feature) (visual fx unit).

Anthony Benjamin   020-7639 5363   Mobile 07811-963874
SC 01932-252577

Guy Bennett   Mobile 07786-473246
From Time To Time (feature) (Trainee).

Mark Binnall   020-8845 2269   Mobile 07866-437523
EXEC 01753-646677   Fax 020-8845 2269
The Magic Flute (feature), Mission: Impossible (feature), Brassed
Off (feature).

James Boorer   020-8330 4661   Mobile 07778-262743
ARRI 01895-457180
Miss Potter (feature), Miss Marple (TV drama), King Arthur
(feature).

Paul Brinkworth   01483-211294   Mobile 07774-655655
Fax 01483-211294
Happiness (TV drama), Below (feature).

Ian Buckley   01296-770818   Mobile 07802-741134
Casino Royale (feature), Hitchhiker's Guide To The Galaxy (feature),
Harry Potter & The Philosopher's Stone (feature).

Matt Budd   Mobile 07766-143036
Johnny & The Bomb (TV childrens), Bodies (TV drama), Footballers'
Wives (TV drama).

Stuart Bunting   0141-638 1420   Mobile 07866-438474
Miss Potter (feature) (2nd unit), The Jacket (feature), Band Of
Brothers (TV drama).

David Cadwallader   01494-671542   Mobile 07774-888873
ARRI 01895-457180   Fax 01494-671542
Vanity Fair (feature).

Emmet Cahill   Mobile 07803-730622   SC 01932-252577

Barry Calvert   01438-353632   Mobile 07973-228396
SC 01932-252577
Hotel Babylon (TV drama).

Luke Chisholm   01923-261046   Mobile 07931-200765
St Trinian's (feature), London Boulevard (feature).

Craig Copple   0161-773 8918   Mobile 07944-482830
Gold (TV drama).

Paul Copple   0161-773 8918   Fax 0161-773 8918
Coronation Street (TV drama), Gold (TV drama), The John Lennon
Story (TV film).

James Coulter   0141-647 1892   Mobile 07771-775992
Fax 0141-647 1892
Regeneration (feature), Strictly Sinatra (feature), Taggart (TV
drama).

Alex Coverley   020-87471706   Mobile 07961-135448
The Commander (TV drama), Cutting It (TV drama), Down To Earth (TV drama).

David Cross   01375-386776   Mobile 07850-587004
SC 01932-252577   Fax 01375-386776
Quantum Of Solace (feature) (2nd unit), Starter For Ten (feature), Charlie & The Chocolate Factory (feature) (2nd unit).

Jim Crowther   01737-356209   Mobile 07973-491641
Prince Of Persia (feature), Quantum Of Solace (feature), City Of Ember (feature).

Nick Cupac   Mobile 07967-473139   ARRI 01895-457180
In Bruges (feature), Son Of Rambow (feature), Little Dorrit (TV drama).

Les Dash   01582-662197   Mobile 07774-234452
Fax 01582-656615
Alastair McGowan (TV light entertainment), Holby City (TV drama), EastEnders (promo).

Richard Davies   Mobile 07802-976706
From Time To Time (feature), Little Dorrit (TV drama).

Russell Diamond   01462-730946   Mobile 07802-484668
ARRI 01895-457180
Nanny McPhee & The Big Bang (feature), The Other Boleyn Girl (feature), Jane Eyre (feature).

Johnny Donne   020-8960 3690   Mobile 07831-351139
SC 01932-252577

Dave Draper   01252-522574   Mobile 07976-277679
GAS 020-8813 1999   Fax 01252-522574
Rosemary & Thyme (TV drama), Stardust (feature), Jericho (TV drama).

Warwick Drucker   Mobile 07887-856664
The Cottage (feature), Control (feature), Lewis (TV drama).

Peter Durbin   020-8661 1841   Mobile 07768-697009

Harry Eckford   020-8953 8526   Mobile 07950-422486
Fax 020-8953 8526

Andy Edridge   01494-676035   Mobile 07956-431292
CC 01932-568268   Fax 01494-674468
Tomb Raider (feature), Gunpowder Treason & Plot (TV film), Rehab (TV film).

Steve Ellingworth   01550-720032   Mobile 07860-805883
Fax 01550-720032
Harry Potter & The Order Of The Phoenix (feature), Stormbreaker (feature), Sex Traffic (TV drama).

Mark Ellis   01372-452107   Mobile 07798-676435
EXEC 01753-646677   Fax 01372-452107
Full Metal Jacket (feature), VW Golf (commercial), Ford (commercial).

Daniel Essex   Mobile 07973-439246   WZ 020-7437 2055

Robert Etherson   Mobile 07976-385554
New Town Killers (feature).

Steve Evans   01239-810760   Mobile 07836-748732
GAS 020-8813 1999   Fax 01239-810760
The Daisy Chain (feature), Scarlet Pimpernel (TV drama), Tom & Viv (feature).

Tony Fabian   01932-230255   Mobile 07966-232362
Fax 01932-262566
Mike Bassett: Manager (TV drama).

Bob Farrell   01753-621210   Mobile 07765-407297

John Flemming   01895-236839   Mobile 07850-576971
Fax 01895-253261
Gulliver's Travels (feature), The Wolfman (feature) (2nd unit), Stardust (feature).

Simon Fogg   020-7267 2676   Mobile 07976-835969
SC 01932-252577

Dennis Fraser   01923-265953   Mobile 07711-983298
Fax 01923-268315
www.chapmanleonard.com

Kevin Fraser   Mobile 07710-064955   EXEC 01753-646677
Kick-Ass (feature), Casino Royale (feature), The Legend Of Zorro (feature).

Andy Friswell   020-7486 1708   Mobile 07951-000141
The Da Vinci Code (feature) (2nd unit).

Dan Garlick   01628-664238   Mobile 07961-382932
ARRI 01895-457180
Little Dorrit (TV drama), The Queen (feature), The Upside Of Anger (feature).

Liam Garrett   Mobile 07950-779159
The Colour Of Magic (TV film) (Trainee).

Pat Garrett   020-8236 0254   Mobile 07793-750066
CB 01932-592572
The Colour Of Magic (TV film), Munich (feature), Rendition (feature).

Bill Geddes   01769-520488   Mobile 07710-018900
Fax 01769-520488
Basic Instinct II (feature), Eyes Wide Shut (feature), Wimbledon (feature).

Rob Gilman   Mobile 07950-230935
Green Zone (feature), The Commander (TV drama).

Colin Ginger   Mobile 07868-690831   SC 01932-252577
Huge (feature).

Lee Godfrey   Mobile 07779-583657
W.E. (feature), London Boulevard (feature).

Stuart Godfrey   01277-656759   Mobile 07973-217184
ARRI 01895-457180
W.E. (feature), Never Let Me Go (feature), The Young Victoria
(feature).

Ben Goode   01582-841354   Mobile 07738-062534
Harry Potter & The Half-Blood Prince (feature) (2nd unit).

Jimmy Grimes   020-8568 5547   Mobile 07850-690056

Ray Hall   01344-891197   Mobile 07710-488594
EXEC 01753-646677   Fax 01344-891197
Out Of Africa (feature), Gulliver's Travels (feature).

Ricky Hall   01753-831219   Mobile 07802-353850
EXEC 01753-646677   Fax 01753-831219
Midsomer Murders (TV drama), Rockface (TV drama), Die Another
Day (feature).

Vic Hammond   01895-624163   Mobile 07956-232757
Fax 01895-624163
The Da Vinci Code (feature), Troy (feature), Harry Potter & The
Chamber Of Secrets (feature).

Paul Hatchman   01246-211459   Mobile 07860-927349
EXEC 01753-646677
A Bunch Of Amateurs (feature), The Constant Gardener (feature),
Flashbacks Of A Fool (feature).

Tony Haughey   020-8953 6264   Mobile 07958-565418
SC 01932-252577
The Commander (TV drama).

Dickie Haw   Mobile 07836-361222
The Da Vinci Code (feature) (2nd unit).

Jonathan Head   0161-442 6695   Mobile 07957-540151

John Heald   Mobile 07885-066018
Little Dorrit (TV drama), The Descent (feature), Cape Wrath (TV
drama).

Niall Heuston   020-8994 9284   Mobile 07932-045334
SC 01932-252577

Kevin Higgins   029-2059 4694   Mobile 07899-942144
Band Of Brothers (TV drama), Plots With A View (feature), The I
Inside (feature).

Peter Hodge   Mobile 07831-733074
Sons Of The Wind (feature), London Suite (TV drama).

Darren Holland   020-8950 4217   Mobile 07976-266379
EXEC 01753-646677   Fax 01582-849439
Harry Potter & The Half-Blood Prince (feature) (2nd unit), Harry
Potter & The Order Of The Phoenix (feature).

David Holliday   01554-833009   Mobile 07973-136105
Fax 01554-833009
Skins (TV drama), Big Nothing (feature), Sahara (feature).

Andy Hopkins   020-8286 9323   Mobile 07768-116893
GAS 020-8813 1999   Fax 020-8286 9323
Inception (feature), Quantum Of Solace (feature), The Dark Knight
(feature).

David Hopkins   029-2048 5557   Mobile 07831-287345
Fax 029-2048 5557
Breaking & Entering (feature), Hitchhiker's Guide To The Galaxy
(feature), A Knight's Tale (feature).

Peter Hopkins   01784-243327   Mobile 07976-423548
Bounty (feature), The Prince & The Pauper (TV film).

Ian Horne   01803-558981   Mobile 07811-928313
Superman (feature), A Bridge Too Far (feature), Worzel Gummidge
(TV childrens).

Mike House   020-8977 7012   Mobile 07770-832903
The Nutcracker Prince (feature), The Madness Of King George
(feature), Endgame (feature).

Bob Howland   020-8964 0559   Mobile 07985-373994
SC 01932-252577

Allan Hughes   01492-876334   Mobile 07778-367104
Fax 01492-876334
Dalziel & Pascoe (TV drama), Dead Man's Cards (feature), Doctor
Who (TV drama).

Chunky Huse   01932-228080   Mobile 07746-849722
Mrs Henderson Presents (feature), Batman Begins (feature),
Alexander (feature).

Malcolm Huse   Mobile 07867-811097
Robin Hood (feature) (2nd unit), Prince Of Persia (feature).

Gary Hutchings   01344-457324   Mobile 07976-736757
Sahara (feature), Atonement (feature), The Hours (feature).

Gary Hymns   01895-632043   Mobile 07976-833989
Robin Hood (feature), The Wolfman (feature), St Trinian's
(feature).

Paul Hymns   Mobile 07968-972121
Robin Hood (feature), The Wolfman (feature), St Trinian's
(feature).

Dan Inman   0113-218 9494 Mobile 07545-210961
Oliver Twist (feature), The Mark Of Cain (feature), Ghost Boat (TV drama).

Mark Jones   0161-438 2908 Mobile 07817-396982
The Mutant Chronicles (feature).

Philip Jones   01323-648905
Good Morning Vietnam (feature), Sharpe (TV drama), Dempsey & Makepeace (TV drama).

Chris Jordan   Mobile 07876-473586
Hotel Babylon (TV drama), Holby City (TV drama).

Brendan Judge   0161-439 2768 Mobile 07973-850184
Fax 0161-439 2768
Casanova (feature), Northern Lights (TV drama), Vincent (TV drama).

Andy Kendall   01932-561710 Mobile 07860-607952
Fanny Hill (TV drama), Silent Witness (TV drama), Under The Greenwood Tree (TV film).

Jody Knight   Mobile 07947-696290
Nanny McPhee & The Big Bang (feature), Harry Potter & The Order Of The Phoenix (feature).

John Kolthammer   020-8335 0544 Mobile 07778-288894
Olympic Games (TV sport), Who Wants To Be A Millionaire? (TV light entertainment), The Brit Awards (party).

Kevin Lakin   0121-422 2518 Mobile 07976-270073
Fax 0121-422 2518
Casualty (TV drama), This Life (TV drama), Red Dwarf (TV comedy drama).

Ed Lancaster   Mobile 07899-655953

Paul Legall   Mobile 07880-544700
Harry Potter & The Half-Blood Prince (feature) (2nd unit).

Rupert Lloyd Parry   Mobile 07802-273987
How To Lose Friends & Alienate People (feature), Ondine (feature), Pride & Prejudice (feature).

Matt Lopez-Dias   Mobile 07810-288954 CB 01932-592572
McFly (promo), Kaiser Chiefs (promo), Cancer Research (commercial).

Ian Maghie   Mobile 07831-244428
Foyle's War (TV drama).

Keith Manning   01895-445753 Mobile 07885-348877
CB 01932-592572
Gulliver's Travels (feature), Agent Crush (feature), The Da Vinci Code (feature).

Joe Martin   020-8441 0230 Mobile 07889-031743
The League Of Gentlemen's Apocalypse (feature), Northanger Abbey (TV film), Inside I'm Dancing (feature).

Tom Maslen   Mobile 07789-090507
The Shell Seekers (TV drama).

David Maund   Mobile 07711-453213 ARRI 01895-457180
Nine (feature), The Boat That Rocked (feature), Batman Begins (feature) (visual fx unit).

Cassius McCabe   Mobile 07723-301838
Little Dorrit (TV drama).

Adrian McCarthy   Mobile 07973-256299 SC 01932-252577
Mamma Mia! (feature), The Reader (feature), Gladiator (feature).

Martin McCullough   028-8164 8562 Mobile 07788-832152
Agent Cody Banks II (feature), The Cook The Thief His Wife & His Lover (feature).

Alex Meacock   Mobile 07973-639045

Keith Mead   01483-751287 Mobile 07885-273186
Fax 01483-751287
Survivors (TV drama), Ruby In The Smoke (TV film), North & South (TV drama).

Nigel Mealing   0113-265 9576 Mobile 07590-695778
A Touch Of Frost (TV drama), My Parents Are Aliens (TV childrens), Emmerdale (TV drama).

Steve Morgan   Mobile 07768-120793 CC 01932-568268
Prince Of Persia (feature) (visual fx unit), Band Of Brothers (TV drama) (visual fx unit), The Brothers Grimm (feature) (visual fx unit).

Mark Morley   Mobile 07961-821967 GAS 020-8813 1999
Legacy (feature), The 39 Steps (TV film), Taggart (TV drama) (Crane Grip).

Dean Morris   Mobile 07970-825605 WZ 020-7437 2055

David Morrison   Mobile 07919-915699

Jem Morton   01753-885624 Mobile 07980-222492
SC 01932-252577 Fax 01753-886255
Numerous commercials & concerts, Harry Brown (feature), Venus (feature).

Jimmy Mullins   020-8977 5005 Mobile 07836-751080
Fax 020-8977 9388

Peter Muncey   020-8949 3871 Mobile 07973-218435
CC 01932-568268 Fax 020-8949 3871
Cold Comfort Farm (TV film), Harry Potter & The Philosopher's Stone (feature).

Ronan Murphy　　01295-670003　Mobile 07973-794341
SC 01932-252577
Greyfriars Bobby (feature), Charlie & The Chocolate Factory (feature), Keeping Mum (feature).

Greg Murray　　　　　Mobile 07851-939338
Fanny Hill (TV drama) (Trainee).

Phil Murray　　01727-839919　Mobile 07973-513830
EXEC 01753-646677
Quantum Of Solace (feature), City Of Ember (feature), Phantom Of The Opera (feature).

Peter Myslowski　　0121-453 9519　Mobile 07971-811980
Fax 0121-453 9519
Star Wars: Episode III - Revenge Of The Sith (feature), Closer (feature), Finding Neverland (feature).

Pete Nash　　Mobile 07810-748710　SC 01932-252577

Ben Nicholls　　　　Mobile 07912-673445
The Wolfman (feature) (Assistant).

Ron Nicholls　　　　Mobile 07769-702237
Harry Potter & The Deathly Hallows (feature), Quantum Of Solace (feature), The Mummy: Tomb Of The Dragon Emperor (feature).

Gary Norman　　01442-391243　Mobile 07976-245234
Hotel Babylon (TV drama), Bad Girls (TV drama).

Tom North　　01932-252577　Mobile 07739-719821
SC 01932-252577

Chris Ogden　　0161-224 9477　Mobile 07971-166057
Vacuuming Completely Nude In Paradise (TV drama), Steel River Blues (TV drama), The Royal (TV drama).

Terry Pate　　　　　Mobile 07944-301692

Mickey Patten　　01424-716384　Mobile 07976-848501
Fax 01424-716384
Tomb Raider II (feature) (2nd unit), Clocking Off (TV drama), Murphy's Law (TV drama).

Nick Pearson　　Mobile 07710-086047　EXEC 01753-646677
Pearl Harbor (feature), Mersey Beat (TV drama), Batman (feature).

James Philpott　　Mobile 07930-417882　ARRI 01895-457180

Les Pickering　　01493-377446　Mobile 07905-900233
Darkness Falls (feature), White On White (feature), Head In The Clouds (feature).

Toby Plaskitt　　01628-826744　Mobile 07884-232591
ARRI 01895-457180
National Treasure (feature), The Broken (feature), London Boulevard (feature).

Steve Pugh　　0117-9424138　Mobile 07860-580171
Game Of Thrones (TV drama), St Trinian's II: The Legend Of Fritton's Gold (feature), Green Zone (feature).

Darren Quinn　　01932-242910　Mobile 07977-340529
Fax 01932-246336
The Letters (feature), The Wolfman (feature), Underworld (feature).
www.independentgrip.co.uk

Daniel Rake　　Mobile 07793-201990　SC 01932-252577

John Rake　　020-8892 3736　Mobile 07710-073517
ARRI 01895-457180　Fax 020-8404 8310
Numerous commercials, A Short Stay In Switzerland (TV drama), The Libertine (feature).

Alan Rank　　01895-447335　Mobile 07956-421318
Fax 01895-422565
Spice World (feature), Bring Me The Head Of Mavis Davis (feature), Ivanhoe (TV drama).

Nick Ray　　01736-797706　Mobile 07973-550663
Fax 01736-797706
The Special Relationship (feature), Shanghai (feature), The League Of Extraordinary Gentlemen (feature).

Barry Read　　01923-775785　Mobile 07973-624185
Fax 01923-721328
Hustle (TV drama), Holby City (TV drama), Bleak House (TV drama).

David Rist　　01462-491293　Mobile 07885-427638
EXEC 01753-646677
Harry Potter & The Half-Blood Prince (feature) (2nd unit), Harry Potter & The Goblet Of Fire (feature), Spy Game (feature).

John D Robinson　　029-2046 4794　Mobile 07976-443656
Harry Potter & The Philosopher's Stone (feature), Doctor Who (TV drama), Lark Rise To Candleford (TV drama).

Nobby Roker　　01424-752276　Mobile 07976-742215
SC 01932-252577　Fax 01424-752276
Hotel Babylon (TV drama), MIT (TV drama), Sid & Nancy (feature).

Gary Romaine　　01628-602071　Mobile 07973-600251
CC 01932-568268
Prince Of Persia (feature), Quantum Of Solace (feature), The Bourne Ultimatum (feature).

Tony Rowland　　01932-347637　Mobile 07790-909771
GAS 020-8813 1999
Robin Hood (feature), An American Haunting (feature), Sky Captain & The World Of Tomorrow (feature).

John Rundle 0161-773 5154 Mobile 07831-570278
Messiah (TV drama), Funland (TV drama), The Street (TV drama).

Derek Russell 01895-270995 Mobile 07973-658114
EXEC 01753-646677 Fax 01895-270996
Gulliver's Travels (feature), Harry Potter & The Half-Blood Prince (feature) (2nd unit), Stardust (feature).

Tony Sankey 0121-427 1599 Mobile 07973-257597
Little Dorrit (TV drama), Dirty Filthy Love (TV drama), Elizabeth The Virgin Queen (TV drama).

Andy Sauer 01442-842383 Mobile 07971-294292
SC 01932-252577
Hotel Babylon (TV drama).

David Scott 01865-407591 Mobile 07973-729889
Dustbin Baby (TV drama), Enchanted (feature), Tomb Raider II (feature).

Gary "Gizza" Smith 020-8398 6326 Mobile 07973-785162
EXEC 01753-646677
Robin Hood (feature), The Wolfman (feature), The Golden Compass (feature).

Malcolm Smith Mobile 07773-283807
Life Begins (TV drama), Alexander (feature), Heidi (feature).

Stephen Smith 0113-286 0950 Mobile 07786-922140

Joe Smyth Mobile 07904-556183
The IT Crowd (TV comedy drama), The Mighty Boosh (TV light entertainment), Little Britain (tour).

Les Spring 020-8728 1331 Mobile 07930-848061

Robin Stone 0121-422 4142 Mobile 07973-363566
CC 01932-568268
The Full Monty (feature), Band Of Brothers (TV drama), Saving Grace (feature).

Colin Strachan 020-8892 8693 Mobile 07710-305955
Angus Thongs & Perfect Snogging (feature), Charlotte Gray (feature), Nicholas Nickleby (feature).

Derek Strachan 01628-524046 Mobile 07976-356544
Fax 01628-524046
Hotel Babylon (TV drama).

Alan Tabner 01908-675876 Mobile 07976-282626
Fax 01908-675876
MTV Music Awards (TV light entertainment), Extras (TV comedy drama).

Alex Tate 020-8943 3816 Mobile 07802-611630
SC 01932-252577

Brian Taylor Mobile 07932-554803
Around The World In 80 Days (feature) (2nd unit), Troy (feature), Harry Potter & The Goblet Of Fire (feature).

Tim Thompson 01562-852718 Mobile 07903-256359
Shameless (TV drama), Footballers' Wives (TV drama), Outlaws (TV drama).

Kirk Thornton Mobile 07958-405415 CB 01932-592572
Distant Shores (TV drama), The Purifiers (feature), Help (TV light entertainment).

Simon Thorpe Mobile 07899-846297
Prince Of Persia (feature) (visual fx unit), Angus Thongs & Perfect Snogging (feature), London Boulevard (feature).

Tony Turner 01403-823801 Mobile 07910-225290
Blood Diamond (feature), Derailed (feature), Beyond The Sea (feature).

Simon Ward 01344-882887 Mobile 07831-815470
WZ 020-7437 2055
The World Is Not Enough (feature) (3rd unit), Mission To Mars (feature) (2nd unit), High Heels & Low Lifes (feature).

Steve Weightman Mobile 07721-452876
Spooks (TV drama), Hotel Babylon (TV drama).

David Wells Mobile 07816-024485
Harry Potter & The Order Of The Phoenix (feature).

Jim Wilkinson 01823-652653 Mobile 07883-092560
Fax 01823-652653
Doctor Who (TV drama), Living In Hope (feature), Walk Away & I Stumble (TV drama).

Jim Will 0191-268 1841 Fax 0191-268 1841
The Uninvited (TV drama), Animal Ark (TV drama), Wycliffe (TV drama).

Terry Williams 020-7687 7317 Mobile 07850-419126
WZ 020-7437 2055
FAQ About Time Travel (feature), Lock Stock & Two Smoking Barrels (feature), A Room For Romeo Brass (feature).

Paul Worley Mobile 07771-968623

JIMMY JIB OPERATORS

Jon Budd Mobile 07973-675584
Top Of The Pops (TV light entertainment), Lenny Henry In Pieces (TV light entertainment), A Harlot's Progress (TV drama).

Phillip Covell 020-8770 7790 Mobile 07881-828355

Adrian Croome Mobile 07973-426659

Chris Hatcher   01291-620240 Mobile 07973-257350
Proms In The Park (TV light entertainment), V Festival (TV light entertainment), The Royal Wedding (TV news & current affairs).

Simon Priestman   Mobile 07971-217985
DG 020-7386 0310
Grease Is The Word (TV light entertainment), True North (feature).

Gary Tepper   01252-377481 Mobile 07973-757494
Superstars (TV light entertainment), World's Strongest Man (TV sport), Tennis Masters (TV sport).

LIGHTING DIRECTORS

Philip Burne   01603-812747 Mobile 07885-841913
Fax 01603-811954
Heartbeat (TV drama), Grange Hill (TV childrens).

Dennis Butcher   01784-457900 Mobile 07860-662733
Fax 01784-440240
BBC Proms (TV light entertainment), Cardiff Singer Of The World (TV light entertainment), Westminster Hall - Visit of Nelson Mandela (TV doc).

Andrew Dixon   020-8998 9514 Mobile 07885-731865
Fax 020-8998 9514
Daily Politics (TV news & current affairs), Primetime (TV light entertainment), Greek Royal Wedding (TV news & current affairs).

Merv Gagen   01553-670066 Mobile 07710-504214
CUMIS (corporate), Guitar Maestros (DVD), BBC News (TV news & current affairs).

Clive Gulliver   01628-522692 Mobile 07774-190737
Fax 01628-522692
The Bill (TV drama), Sky Medical (TV doc).

Jeremy Hoare   020-7722 2065 Fax 020-7722 2065
The Upper Hand (TV comedy drama), Blockbusters (TV light entertainment), The Price Is Right (TV light entertainment).

Martin Kempton   01628-674980 Mobile 07721-550285
Al Murray's Happy Hour (TV light entertainment), Harry Hill's TV Burp (TV light entertainment), Little Britain (tour).

David Kidd   020-8340 5869 Mobile 07818-063083
Fax 020-8341 0639

Tom Kinane   020-8449 2946 Mobile 07813-198549
French & Saunders (TV light entertainment).

Michael Lingard   020-8864 5067 Mobile 07973-264130
Fax 020-8422 2839
Ministry Of Mayhem (TV light entertainment), The Basil Brush Show (TV childrens), Big Brother (TV reality).

John Scarrott   01477-532231 Mobile 07885-870919
Coronation Street (TV drama), Hollyoaks (TV drama), My Parents Are Aliens (TV childrens).

REMOTE HEAD OPERATORS

Stuart Bush   01582-765501 Mobile 07836-702236
Fax 01582-765506
Ancient Rome: The Rise & Fall Of An Empire (TV drama), Ryder Cup Golf (TV sport), Andre Bocelli In Pisa (concert).

Joe Buxton   Mobile 07900-893024
Green Zone (feature).

Laurence Edwards   020-8330 3845 Mobile 07968-185611
Quantum Of Solace (feature), City Of Ember (feature).

David Freeth   Mobile 07802-344478
Harry Potter & The Half-Blood Prince (feature) (2nd unit), In Bruges (feature).

Dan Greenway   020-856 00 856 Mobile 07711-903990
www.dangreenwayltd.co.uk

Colin Hazell   020-8386 3465 Mobile 07710-725663
Prince Of Persia (feature), The Golden Compass (feature).

Russell O'Connor   01727-760417 Mobile 07710-725662
Miss Potter (feature), The Golden Compass (feature).

Adam Samuelson   020-8959 3082 Mobile 07831-805624
Fax 020-8906 3217
Harry Potter & The Goblet Of Fire (feature), Troy (feature), Love Actually (feature).

Ian Townsend   020-8573 2514 Mobile 07747-031191
Prince Of Persia (feature), The Mummy Returns (feature).

UNIT STILLS

Michael A'Court   023-8058 2301 Mobile 07075-110055
Fax 023-8058 2301

Eugene Adebari   Mobile 07973-623670
Angus Thongs & Perfect Snogging (feature).

David Appleby   01458-830493 Mobile 07778-934154
Robin Hood (feature), 1408 (feature).

Sophie Baker   020-8340 3850 Fax 020-8340 2315
Felicia's Journey (feature), Brassed Off (feature), Hideous Kinky (feature).

CAMERA

Joss Barratt   01963-23673 Mobile 07973-394926
The Wind That Shakes The Barley (feature), Ae Fond Kiss (feature), Faith (TV film).

Etienne Bol   020-7221 4227 Mobile 07836-361821
Fax 0870-051 5775

Nick Briggs   020-7278 0993 Mobile 07778-646602
Little Dorrit (TV drama).

Jaap Buitendijk   Mobile 07790-909561
In Bruges (feature), The Constant Gardener (feature), Children Of Men (feature).

Laurence Cendrowicz   Mobile 07973-729374
Fanny Hill (TV drama).

Julian Charrington   020-8747 4744 Mobile 07795-342842
Fax 020-8995 0665
Last Of The Summer Wine (TV comedy drama), Secrets Of The Lost Empires (TV doc), Around The World In 80 Days (feature).

Murray Close   Mobile 07834-771346
Babel (feature), Inkheart (feature), Harry Potter & The Order Of The Phoenix (feature).

Liam Daniel   020-8969 1448 Mobile 07966-159963
Nanny McPhee (feature), The Edge Of Love (feature), Trainspotting (feature).

Gautier Deblonde   020-7274 1762 Mobile 07958-779533
Bleak House (TV drama), Harry Potter & The Prisoner Of Azkaban (feature), Morvern Callar (feature).

Neil Genower   020-8299 4127 Mobile 07774-281498
Trial & Retribution (TV drama), Henry VIII (TV drama), The Commander (TV drama).

John Gott   01243-786245 Mobile 07860-297566
Fax 01243-780872
Kevin McCloud (stills).

Keith Hamshere   01442-863035 Mobile 07836-733630
Fax 01442-863347
City Of Ember (feature).

Jules Heath   Mobile 07734-649469
Cemetery Junction (feature).

Jo Hidderley   01225-719205 Mobile 07768-096008
Preston Front (TV drama), Famous Five (TV childrens), Billy Joel (TV doc).

Mike Hogan   Mobile 07764-941364
Spooks (TV drama).

Robbie Jack   020-8567 9616 Mobile 07774-235533
HEBS (commercial), The Armando Iannucci Show (TV light entertainment).

Luke Kelly   020-8878 2823
The Man Who Knew Too Little (feature).

Giles Keyte   020-8670 7848 Mobile 07958-616727
Fax 020-8670 7848
Death Defying Acts (feature), And When Did You Last See Your Father? (feature), Mr Bean's Holiday (feature).

Stephen Morley   01730-814535 Mobile 07860-733784
Bunnytown (TV childrens), Midsomer Murders (TV drama), Ready When You Are Mr McGill (TV film).

Roy Morris   01753-656168 Mobile 07718-785050
Fax 01494-675978
Planet Cook (TV childrens), Inferno (TV film), Tales From The Black Museum (TV doc).

Peter Mountain   020-8682 4818 Mobile 07802-461922
Pirates Of The Caribbean: Dead Man's Chest (feature), Charlie & The Chocolate Factory (feature), Fear & Loathing In Las Vegas (feature).

Angus Muir   Mobile 07970-838002
Fanny Hill (TV drama).

Tony Nutley   01489-582693 Mobile 07767-890686
Fax 01489-582693
Foyle's War (TV drama), Sharpe (TV drama), Inspector Morse (TV drama).

Seb Pearson   020-7221 2012 Mobile 07710-349101
Fax 020-7229 0914
Stardust (feature).

Kristin Perers   020-7729 4546
Elle Decoration (magazine), Country Living (magazine).

Keith Pettinato   020-7794 7989 Mobile 0845-987 2946
Fax 0845-258 2584

Barry Read   020-8330 4152 Mobile 07831-704926
James Blunt (promo), Deichmann Shoes (commercial), Freddie Le Grand (promo).

Chris Ridley   020-7286 4843 Mobile 07775-526586
Back To Reality (TV reality), A Doll's House (theatre), European History (TV doc).

Adrian Rogers   029-2070 2096 Mobile 07831-899513
Doctor Who (TV drama), Torchwood (TV drama), Casualty (TV drama).

Tony Russell   020-8530 4030 Mobile 07831-103843
Fax 020-8530 4030
Promoted To Glory (TV film), Never Never (TV drama), The Mayor Of Casterbridge (TV drama).

Amanda Searle   Mobile 07785-253163
Spooks (TV drama).

Anthony Souza   Mobile 07515-553719
W.E. (feature).

Laurie Sparham   020-8800 8594 Mobile 07778-190973
Fax 020-8809 7406
The Queen (feature), Bridget Jones's Diary II (feature), Hitchhiker's Guide To The Galaxy (feature).

Paul Tennant   020-8948 4460 Mobile 07860-295848
Fax 020-8878 4934
Half Light (feature), The Bill (TV drama), Black & Decker (commercial).

Mark Tillie   Mobile 07941-491163
Moon (feature), Gosford Park (feature), Boogie Woogie (feature).

Mike Vaughan   01753-524306 Mobile 07836-723991
Fax 01753-524306
The Green Green Grass (TV comedy drama), Prime Suspect (TV drama), Footballers' Wives (TV drama).

Nick Wall   Mobile 07778-290818
St Trinian's (feature).

Karen Whiteread   020-7561 0992 Mobile 07702-878965
Rose & Maloney (TV drama), Murphy's Law (TV drama), My Brother Tom (feature).

VIDEO ASSIST

Charles Bata   020-8673 3855 Mobile 07956-261312
Winter Olympics (TV sport), Sky TV (trailer), Reach Toothbrushes (commercial).

Buddy Blackwell   020-7221 1978 Mobile 07860-418376
EXEC 01753-646677

John Bowman   020-8449 8446 Mobile 07710-316735
Prince Of Persia (feature), Quantum Of Solace (feature), The Bourne Ultimatum (feature).

Bob Bridges   07050-649932 Mobile 07710-597772
EXEC 01753-646677 Fax 07050-649934
Harry Potter & The Deathly Hallows (feature), Harry Potter & The Half-Blood Prince (feature), St Trinian's (feature).

Stuart Bridges   01494-445013 Mobile 07879-457075
Harry Potter & The Order Of The Phoenix (feature).

Kevin Brookner   020-8201 5746 Mobile 07976-938323
The Four Feathers (feature), Die Another Day (feature), Band Of Brothers (TV drama).

Leon Buckley   Mobile 07881-934583
The Da Vinci Code (feature) (model unit), Breakfast On Pluto (feature), Troy (feature).

Steve Campbell   020-8903 5449 Mobile 07939-012249
Fax 020-8903 5449
Asian Music Awards (TV music), Stardust (feature), Dinotopia (TV drama).

Neil Chapelhow   Mobile 07738-086647
Miss Marple (TV drama).

Phillipe Clavier   Mobile 07973-906392

Ann-Marie Crotty   Mobile 07787-911222
St Trinian's (feature).

Ira Curtis-Coleman   01923-237575 Mobile 07710-247787
Fax 01923-237575

Tom Elgar   020-8441 5655 Mobile 07816-206033
Quantum Of Solace (feature) (Assistant).

Andrew Haddock   01202-673985 Mobile 07831-583391
Fax 01202-669886
The Wolfman (feature), Elizabeth: The Golden Age (feature), The Da Vinci Code (feature).

Luke Haddock   Mobile 07788-893764 Fax 01202-669886
Green Zone (feature), The Da Vinci Code (feature), The Bourne Ultimatum (feature).

Rob Hamiliton   Mobile 07796-874804
Angus Thongs & Perfect Snogging (feature).

Robert Hamilton   020-7350 1187 Mobile 07796-874804
London Boulevard (feature).

Dan Hartley   020-7461 9516 Mobile 07887-548640
Harry Potter & The Half-Blood Prince (feature) (2nd unit), Harry Potter & The Order Of The Phoenix (feature).

James Helps   01624-833208
Five Children & It (feature), Island At War (TV drama).

Peter Hodgson   020-8868 7546 Mobile 07831-399506
EXEC 01753-646677 Fax 020-8868 7546
The Colour Of Magic (TV film), King Arthur (feature), Kingdom Of Heaven (feature).

Demetri Jagger   Mobile 07796-853753
Star Wars: Episode III - Revenge Of The Sith (feature), Stardust (feature), Closer (feature).

Dylan Jones   01628-472803 Mobile 07976-631494
Children Of Men (feature), Kingdom Of Heaven (feature), Alexander (feature).

Finchley Judges   Mobile 07970-985453
Trigger Happy TV (TV light entertainment).

Lizzie Kelly   020-8279 7018 Mobile 07950-902196
28 Weeks Later (feature), 1408 (feature), Sunshine (feature).

Nick Kenealy   01920-821304 Mobile 07887-647899
EXEC 01753-646677 Fax 01920-821211
Eastern Promises (feature), Atonement (feature), Hot Fuzz (feature).

David Kirman   Mobile 07828-443403
The Wolfman (feature) (2nd unit).

Stephen Lee   020-8969 5409 Mobile 07771-534635
EXEC 01753-646677 Fax 020-8969 5409
Troy (feature), Love Actually (feature), Sahara (feature).

Ed Lindsley   Mobile 07899-847760 DG 020-7386 0310
Three Minute Moment (feature), Wire In The Blood (TV drama), For The Benefit Of Mr Parris (TV doc).

Jules Longdin-Prisk   Mobile 07960-093103

Ed Lousley   Mobile 07738-589824
From Time To Time (feature).

Guy McCormack   01223-368164 Mobile 07754-401702
W.E. (feature), Gulliver's Travels (feature), Miss Potter (feature).

Jeremy Nathan   020-8864 2228 Mobile 07956-893014
EXEC 01753-646677
British Telecom (commercial), Kellogg's (commercial), Daily Mirror (commercial).

Lucien Nunes-Vaz   020-8440 8962 Mobile 07976-252356
Fax 020-8440 8962
Gladiator (feature), Star Wars: Episode 1 - The Phantom Menace (feature).

Steve Petrie   0118-934 4833 Mobile 07931-300016
Harry Potter & The Order Of The Phoenix (feature).

Darryl Rose   020-8950 5666 Mobile 07970-624424
TOVS 020-7287 6110
I'm A Celebrity (TV light entertainment), Hell's Kitchen (TV reality), Premier Football (TV sport).

Sam Sale   020-8449 9771 Mobile 07708-398021
Harry Potter & The Half-Blood Prince (feature) (2nd unit), Harry Potter & The Order Of The Phoenix (feature).

Andy Sandom   020-8582 3950 Mobile 07976-270729

Richard Shean   Mobile 07899-912486
Harry Potter & The Half-Blood Prince (feature) (2nd unit).

Andy Shields   020-8671 1544 Mobile 07973-769935
EXEC 01753-646677 Fax 020-8671 1544
Quantum Of Solace (feature), City Of Ember (feature), Casino Royale (feature) (2nd unit).

Dan Simpson   Mobile 07841-534494
London Boulevard (feature).

Adrian Spanna   Mobile 07968-196012
Green Zone (feature), The Da Vinci Code (feature) (2nd unit).

Nick Stewart   020-8852 4254 Mobile 07759-280544
Fax 020-8852 4254
Piccadilly Jim (feature), Shanghai Knights (feature), Just One Of Those Things (feature).

Ross Taggart   0118-969 6632 Mobile 07973-286933
Fax 0118-969 6632

Martin Ward   01582-622655 Mobile 07976-265661
Gulliver's Travels (feature), 1408 (feature), Children Of Men (feature).

Chris Warren   020-8337 6760 Mobile 07831-420451
W.E. (feature), Miss Potter (feature), Keeping Mum (feature).

Zoe Whittaker   Mobile 07941-194318
The Wolfman (feature), Stardust (feature).

Sally Cairney   01932-842799 Mobile 07802-263549
GEMS 029-2071 0770 Fax 01932-842799
The Bill (TV drama).

Kate Carin   Mobile 07768-444497 DA 020-7437 4551
The 51st State (feature), Hideous Kinky (feature), Shallow Grave
(feature).

Brian Castle   0113-273 3855 Mobile 07768-688353
Fax 0113-273 3855
The Royal (TV drama), A Touch Of Frost (TV drama), Steel River
Blues (TV drama).

Alexandra Caulfield   0151-475 5642 Mobile 07889-502333
AMM 020-7244 1159
House Of Saddam (TV drama), The Mark Of Cain (feature), The
Parole Officer (feature).

Lilian Chapman   01244-372355 Mobile 07815-104219
Conan The Barbarian (feature) (Costume Maker), The Duke (short),
Act Of Grace (feature).

Maggie Chappelhow   0117-924 6827 Mobile 07767-357322
SPA 01932-571044
Sleep With Me (TV drama), The Other Boleyn Girl (feature), Casualty
(TV drama).

Rosie Cheshire   01737-350040 Fax 01737-350040
Shooting Stars (TV light entertainment).

Fiona Chilcott   020-8964 2406 Mobile 07973-366743
Huge (feature), Absolute Power (TV drama), The Abbey (TV comedy
drama).

Stephanie Collie   CM 020-7287 4450
Van Wilder II (feature), Layer Cake (feature), Lock Stock & Two
Smoking Barrels (feature).

Dinah Collin   Mobile 07836-694905 DA 020-7437 4551
Endgame (feature), Much Ado About Nothing (theatre), United 93
(feature).

Jo Conti   01570-423321 Mobile 07876-353323
Nightwatching (feature), The Royal Variety Performance (TV light
entertainment), Relic Hunter (TV drama).

Kandis Cook   Mobile 07967-505516
The Piano Tuner Of Earthquakes (feature).

Martine Cooper   01483-721239 Mobile 07860-586392
Fax 01483-721239
Trading Ages (TV doc), The King's Servant (TV doc), The Real Thomas
Beckett (TV doc).

Andrew Cox   Mobile 07785-395828
The Firm (feature), Faintheart (feature), The Business (feature).

Philip Crichton   020-8450 7311 Mobile 07714-342325
Twisted Tales (TV drama), Mile High (TV drama), Twentyfour: Seven
(feature).

Annie Curtis Jones   020-7226 5857 Mobile 07774-626366
Fax 020-7226 5857
Munich - The Hunt For Black September (TV drama doc), Tony Blair
Rockstar (TV drama doc), Sex Footballers & Scoring Goals (TV doc).

Liz Da Costa   020-8960 7845 Mobile 07962-926116
CMM 020-8584 5363
Starlight Express (theatre), Stick With Me Kid (TV film), Tosca
(opera).

Elvis Davis   Mobile 07769-971944 STA 020-7729 7477
Souled Out (feature), The Shepherd (feature).

Phoebe De Gaye   020-7354 1029 DA 020-7437 4551
Miss Marple (TV drama), Creep (feature), Five Children & It
(feature).

Fiona Dealey   020-7837 2644 Mobile 07774-114101
WZ 020-7437 2055 Fax 020-7837 2644
Britain's Got The Pop Factor (TV light entertainment), Diet Coke
(commercial), Pepsi-Cola (commercial).

Gaby Dean   Mobile 07811-322358

Odile Dicks-Mireaux   Mobile 07884-436543
CM 020-7287 4450
The Constant Gardener (feature), Dirty Pretty Things (feature),
Buffalo Soldiers (feature).

Kate Dixey   020-8960 9091 Fax 020-8960 9481
Homebase (commercial), Vidal Sassoon (commercial), Daily Express
(commercial).

Eric Doughney   Mobile 07790-551584
Doctors (TV drama), Cardiff Singer Of The World (TV light
entertainment), Grange Hill (TV childrens).

Pam Downe   01225-466588 Mobile 07768-614306
DA 020-7437 4551
The Baker (feature), Modigliani (feature), My Uncle Silas (TV
drama).

Nadia Dunn-Hill   Mobile 07802-441825 CB 01932-592572
Matchpoint (feature) (Costume Buyer), The Walker (feature)
(Costume Buyer), Wimbledon (feature) (Assistant).

Jacqueline Durran   Mobile 07961-171719
CM 020-7287 4450
Nanny McPhee & The Big Bang (feature), Atonement (feature), Pride
& Prejudice (feature).

COSTUME

Joanna Eatwell   020-7703 3533 Mobile 07850-363731
CM 020-7287 4450 Fax 020-7703 3533
Amnesia (TV drama), Hawking (TV film), Oliver Twist (feature).

Rosalind Ebbutt   01372-843473 Mobile 07774-863560
CCM 020-8743 7337 Fax 01372-843473
Fallen Angel (TV drama), Hotel Babylon (TV drama), To The Ends Of
The Earth (TV drama).

Nic Ede   01544-230700 Mobile 07774-211234
UA 020-3214 0800
Me & Orson Welles (feature), Bright Young Things (feature), Nanny
McPhee (feature).

Andy Edwards   020-7580 0209 Mobile 07887-852103
Fax 020-7580 0209
Planespotting (TV drama), Eleventh Hour (TV drama), Footloose
(theatre).

Nigel Egerton   020-8675 5655 Mobile 07770-694319
The Queen (feature) (Assistant), Blackball (feature), Three Blind
Mice (feature).

Ffion Elinor   01446-760736
Plots With A View (feature), Trauma (feature).

Morgan Elliott-Richards   01502-723525
Mobile 07889-141137
My Spy Family (TV childrens), Five Children & It (feature) (Assistant),
Hyperdrive (TV comedy drama).

Sarah-Jane Ellis   Mobile 07973-500542
The All Star Talent Show (TV light entertainment), If (TV drama
doc), Comic Relief (TV light entertainment).

Elizabeth Emanuel   020-7289 4545 Fax 020-7289 7584
Frankenstein The Modern Prometheus (ballet), Rosbeef (short),
Metamorphosis (short).

Gwenda Evans   020-8870 3208 Mobile 07771-793291
Rock & Roll Hymns (TV drama), Lois (TV drama), The First Child
(TV drama).

Dany Everett   01483-560166 Mobile 07704-977225
From Time To Time (feature) (Assistant), Jeeves & Wooster (TV
drama), A Dance To The Music Of Time (TV film).

Darren Finch   0161-446 1049 Mobile 07889-701194
Fax 0161-446 1049
Waterloo Road (TV drama), Wire In The Blood (TV drama), Phoenix
Nights (TV drama).

Kate Forbes   020-7241 2704 Mobile 07989-501416
STA 020-7729 7477
Nearly Famous (TV drama), Suburban Shootout (TV drama), The
Last Chancers (TV light entertainment).

Margie Fortune   Mobile 07775-842248
Prince Of Persia (feature) (Assistant), Ashes To Ashes (TV drama),
Doomsday (feature).

Mark Foster   Mobile 07778-234207
Casualty (TV drama), Ealing Comedy (feature), Charlie Noades RIP
(feature).

Kim Foster Dillon   020-8699 6322 Mobile 07798-831043
GEMS 029-2071 0770 Fax 020-8699 6322
The Wolfman (feature), The Bill (TV drama), Bear Behaving Badly
(TV childrens).

Robin Fraser-Paye   020-7584 5658 Mobile 07957-324335
CMM 020-8584 5363
Prisoners Of The Sun (feature), Driving Lessons (feature), Once
Upon A Time In The Midlands (feature).

Louise Frogley   Mobile 07900-582007
Quantum Of Solace (feature).

Emma Fryer   Mobile 07801-720830 BA 020-7836 1112
Grow Your Own (feature), Fear Of Fanny (TV drama), Elizabeth
David - A Life In Recipes (TV drama).

Jackie Galloway   020-7277 5650 Mobile 07973-259579
Fax 020-7277 5650
Pinter's People (theatre), Love Song (theatre), Saturday Night Fever
(theatre).

Tudor George   020-8994 6286 Mobile 07702-909851
Fax 020-8994 6286
Diamond Geezer (TV drama), Silent Witness (TV drama), Brass Eye
(TV light entertainment).

Tim Goodchild   020-7733 0967 Fax 020-7733 0967
The Look Of Love (TV drama), A Simple Man (TV drama), Fool On
The Hill (TV film).

Rebecca Gore   Mobile 07977-205196
Night Junkies (feature), The Calling (feature), Fallen Dreams
(feature).

Emma Greenstreet   Mobile 07791-102357
Audi (commercial), Volvo (commercial).

Jayne Gregory   029-2070 9790 Mobile 07973-197321
The Football Factory (feature), Lock Stock (TV drama), Rose &
Maloney (TV drama).

Steven Gregory   020-8693 9789 Mobile 07944-834331
Tonight Lola Blau (theatre), Cadbury (commercial).

Rosie Hackett   020-7249 9373 Mobile 07757-045133
CCM 020-8743 7337
Chasing Liberty (feature), Crime & Punishment (TV film), Canterbury
Tales (TV drama).

COSTUME

Debra Haggett   01495-310570 Mobile 07702-211423
Sea Of Souls (TV drama) (Costume Supervisor), Belonging (TV drama), A Mind To Kill (TV drama).

Rebecca Hale   Mobile 07770-914310
St Trinian's (feature), Dead Set (TV drama).

Kate Halfpenny   Mobile 07976-761166 WZ 020-7437 2055
Rimmell (commercial), Marks & Spencer (commercial), Amelia Fox (promo).

Sue Hallas   Mobile 07831-864423
Blue Murder (TV drama), New Tricks (TV drama), At Home With The Braithwaites (TV drama).

Jane Hamilton   020-8995 6275 Mobile 07771-786357
Fax 020-8995 6275
Phantom Of The Opera (feature), La Bastille (opera), Royal Opera House (opera).

Annie Hardinge   020-8789 7339 Mobile 07778-210388
DA 020-7437 4551 Fax 020-8789 7339
Run Fat Boy Run (feature), Hot Fuzz (feature), Shaun Of The Dead (feature).

Clare Harries   Mobile 07796-173171
Gordon's Gin (commercial), Reebok (commercial), Graff Diamonds (commercial).

Lyn Harvey   01784-433349 Mobile 07836-567924
Fax 01784-438141
Monday Monday (TV drama), Banglatown Banquet (TV drama), Johnny Shakespeare (TV drama).

Shuna Harwood   01435-883394 CM 020-7287 4450
Firewall (feature), Notting Hill (feature), Richard III (feature).

Verity Hawkes   020-7373 5600 Mobile 07966-399191
UA 020-3214 0800 Fax 020-7835 0269
Hippie Hippie Shake (feature), Inkheart (feature), Revolver (feature).

Linda Haysman   020-8992 5072 Mobile 07778-784601
Niagara Motel (feature), The Crouches (TV light entertainment), An Urban Ghost Story (feature).

Liz Healy   Mobile 07957-611570
Alive Baja (TV docu drama), This Life +10 (TV drama), Somebreak (short).

Lindy Hemming   020-7607 6107 Mobile 07860-493995
ITG 020-7636 6565 Fax 020-7607 6107
Clash Of The Titans (feature), Casino Royale (feature), The Dark Knight (feature).

John Hibbs   020-7636 0283 Mobile 07961-939743
Flashmob (opera), Blessed (TV comedy drama), Intimate Relations (feature).

Joe Hobbs   01929-471327 Mobile 07734-681521
DD 020-7851 3575 Fax 01929-471327
Primeval (TV drama), The Pacific (TV drama), Silent Witness (TV drama).

Karen Hobbs   020-7328 7741 Mobile 07973-294309
Fax 020-7328 7741
The Riddle Of The Sphinx (TV drama doc), Bremner Bird & Fortune (TV light entertainment), Babyfather (TV drama).

Charlotte Holdich   Mobile 07710-314421
ITG 020-7636 6565
The Long Walk To Finchley (TV film), 20,000 Streets Under The Sky (TV drama), The History Of Mr Polly (TV drama).

Ann Hollowood   01727-850680 Mobile 07956-992623
BA 020-7836 1112 Fax 01727-841361
The Ten Commandments (TV film), Merlin (TV drama), Hans Christian Andersen (TV film).

Ray Holman   029-2075 0258 Mobile 07831-091428
UA 020-3214 0800 Fax 029-2075 0258
Torchwood (TV drama), Sea Of Souls (TV drama), Place Of Execution (TV drama).

Diane Holmes   020-8977 8421 Mobile 07802-543341
Fax 020-8977 8421
The Little Riders (TV drama), Apocalypse Watch (TV film), Jewel In The Crown (TV drama).

Eileen Hubball   01530-413278 Mobile 07941-507565
Dalziel & Pascoe (TV drama), Crossroads (TV drama), Touching Evil (TV drama).

Sue Hunting   01372-372404 Mobile 07836-334440
Fax 01372-372421
Coronation Street (TV drama), The Bill (TV drama), Emmerdale (TV drama).

Bet Huws   01286-870092 Mobile 07774-125165
Fax 01286-870092
Tipyn O Stad (TV drama), Little Pork Pies (TV drama), Bryn Terfel Festival (TV light entertainment).

Vanessa John   020-7351 3263 Mobile 07768-017733
Casualty (TV drama), The Windsor Years (feature), Pride & Prejudice (feature).

Janet Johnson   Mobile 07885-273782
Heartbeat (TV drama), The Bill (TV drama), Coronation Street (TV drama).

COSTUME

Laura Johnson   Mobile 07958-577459

As If (TV drama), Hex (TV drama), Ladies In Lavender (feature) (Assistant).

Lisa Johnson   020-7419 2451 Mobile 07711-078544

Fax 020-7419 2451

Island At War (TV drama) (Costume Supervisor), Dangerous Parking (feature), Sub Down (feature).

Michael Johnson   Mobile 07973-137170

Hotel Babylon (TV drama), Cutting It (TV drama), True Dare Kiss (TV drama).

Joanna Johnston   ITG 020-7636 6565

Munich (feature), War Of The Worlds (feature), Love Actually (feature).

Mark Jones   020-8674 4043 Mobile 07956-503283

Alien Vs Predator (feature), Fat Slags (feature), Tooth (feature).

James Keast   DA 020-7437 4551

Bullet Boy (feature), The Line Of Beauty (TV drama), The Long Firm (TV drama).

Barbara Kidd   020-7249 5287 Mobile 07831-293058

Fax 020-7249 5287

Little Dorrit (TV drama), The Street (TV drama), Futureshock: Comet (TV drama).

Lorraine Kinman   020-7221 6285 Mobile 07973-749930

MCR 020-7720 6234 Fax 020-7221 9767

Mrs Meitlemeihr (short), Pantene (commercial), True Love Once Removed (short).

Franca Knight   01934-863209 Mobile 07801-140155

Fax 01934-863209

Kiss Of Death (TV drama), Common As Muck (TV drama), Casualty (TV drama).

John Krausa   Mobile 07973-469054 DA 020-7437 4551

Green Street (feature), Funland (TV drama), Bonkers (TV comedy drama).

Scott Langridge   Mobile 07736-881995

Bunnytown (TV childrens), Living With Two People (TV comedy drama), Britannia High (TV drama).

Les Lansdown   020-7607 0504 Mobile 07774-864405

CCM 020-8743 7337

Wide Sargasso Sea (TV film), Doc Martin (TV drama), The Chatterley Affair (TV drama).

Marlene Lawlor   020-8997 6995 Mobile 07976-922576

Fax 020-8997 6995

New Tricks (TV drama), The Commander (TV drama), The Student Prince (TV drama).

Jacky Levy   020-8755 1686 Mobile 07768-923727

Fax 020-8755 1686

The Girl In The Cafe (TV film), U Be Dead (TV film), Primeval (TV drama).

Mark Lewis   Mobile 07890-992623 WZ 020-7437 2055

John Lindlar   Mobile 07850-978844 CCM 020-8743 7337

The Best Man (feature), Lewis (TV drama), The Brief (TV drama).

Ros Little   020-8567 9616 Mobile 07860-187872

Fax 020-8567 9616

In The Loop (feature), Horrible Histories (TV childrens), Heroes & Villains (feature).

Sally Loughridge   020-7223 9378 Mobile 07973-286446

Fax 020-7223 9378

The Bill (TV drama).

Sarah Lubel   020-8888 1536 Mobile 07973-406005

Fax 020-8888 1536

Bad Girls (TV drama), Essex Boys (feature), Goodness Gracious Me (TV light entertainment).

Nadya Lubrani   01689-821889 Mobile 07721-527779

Cressy Luke   01730-231846 Mobile 07767-780544

The Darkening (CD), The Doherty Brothers (TV film), I Hate Christmas (TV film).

Justine Luxton   Mobile 07973-628266 ITG 020-7636 6565

Born Equal (TV drama), The History Boys (feature), Stuart: A Life Backwards (TV drama).

Iain MacAulay   020-7450 3238 Mobile 07710-038869

The Sixer (TV drama), Spooks (TV drama), Hustle (TV drama).

Veronica McAuliffe   020-7437 5488 Mobile 07831-248398

Fax 020-7437 5488

The International Face Of The Moon (feature), Breaking The Trade (TV drama doc), Samsung (commercial).

Tanya McCallin   020-7431 1663 Mobile 07989-273087

Fax 020-7431 2860

La Traviata (opera), Rigoletto (opera), The Marriage Of Figaro (opera).

Bobby McCulla   0131-661 4082 Mobile 07855-247226

New Town Killers (feature).

Karen McKinlay-Gunn   Mobile 07775-900482

55 Degrees North (TV drama), Touching Evil (TV drama), Dalziel & Pascoe (TV drama).

COSTUME

Lindsey McLean   020-8806 8017 Mobile 07885-102498
Fax 020-8880 0101
Graham Norton (TV light entertainment), Nike (commercial), Doc Martin (TV drama).

Katy McPhee   020-7723 9373 Mobile 07775-637103
AD 020-7428 0500
Consenting Adults (TV drama), History Of Venice (TV drama doc), Power Of Art (TV art).

Val Metheringham   020-8744 3131 Mobile 07889-778642
Stig Of The Dump (TV childrens), Urban Gothic (TV drama), Junk (TV drama).

Lance Milligan   01729-824528 Mobile 07966-773058
Falling (TV film), Booze Cruise (TV film), Strictly Confidential (TV drama).

Ali Mitchell   Mobile 07976-833097
Outpost (feature), Low Winter Sun (TV drama), Greyfriars Bobby (feature).

John Mollo   01235-868205
Event Horizon (feature), Jungle Book (feature), Hornblower (TV drama).

Michael Mooney   020-8675 9965 Mobile 07966-219336
Dread (feature).

Aideen Morgan   020-8964 4549 Mobile 07831-193014
Life Begins (TV drama), The Wyvern Mystery (TV film), Ladies Of Letters (TV drama).

Cat Morgan-Jones   020-7722 2541 Mobile 07973-619896

Charlotte Morris   Mobile 07771-734380 UA 020-3214 0800
Merlin (TV drama), Starter For Ten (feature), Silent Witness (TV drama).

Diana Moseley   020-7328 6116 Mobile 07710-170903
UA 020-3214 0800 Fax 020-7328 6116
Vincent (TV drama), May 33rd (TV film), Wild About Harry (feature).

Jillie Murphy   020-7289 1823 Mobile 07831-514393
Coca-Cola (commercial), Matalan (commercial), DFS (commercial).

Ita Murray   01273-720680 Mobile 07966-235691
Last Rights (TV drama), Bella & The Boys (TV drama), It's All Gone Pete Tong (feature).

Ruth Myers   020-7586 2029 Mobile 07977-988374
City Of Ember (feature), Stardust (feature), The Golden Compass (feature).

Kimie Nakano   01634-319925 Mobile 07791-657639
Fax 01634-319925
8 1/2 Women (feature), Basho (short), Parsifal (opera).

Sheena Napier   020-8994 1925 Mobile 07710-419626
ITG 020-7636 6565 Fax 020-8248 7101
Wild Target (feature), Wah Wah (feature), Poirot (TV drama).

June Nevin   020-7738 5461 Mobile 07767-496519
The Mighty Boosh (TV light entertainment), Tales From The Crypt (TV film), Beethoven (TV drama).

Anushia Nieradzik   020-7486 2072 Mobile 07778-277735
CM 020-7287 4450 Fax 020-7486 2072
Ex Memoria (short), Sex Traffic (TV drama), Wondrous Oblivion (feature).

Nadia Nigoumi   01243-552535 Mobile 07976-974711
Strictly Come Dancing (TV light entertainment), CBBC (TV childrens), The Bill (TV drama).

Steven Noble   Mobile 07767-337010
Severance (feature), Benidorm (TV comedy drama), Agent Cody Banks II (feature).

John Norster   020-8761 3471 Mobile 07711-643375
Fax 020-8761 3471
Prince Of Persia (feature), Evita (feature), King Arthur (feature).

Fiona O'Connor   020-7241 1021 Mobile 07941-037995

Michael O'Connor   020-7713 5436 Mobile 07973-392470
DA 020-7437 4551
The Duchess (feature), Miss Pettigrew Lives For A Day (feature), The Last King Of Scotland (feature).

Kate O'Farrell   020-7359 0274 Mobile 07973-365412
Fax 020-7359 0274
The Big Impression (TV light entertainment), Nostradamus (feature), The New Worst Witch (TV childrens).

Mike O'Neill   01725-553388 Mobile 07831-673608
ITG 020-7636 6565 Fax 01725-553388
The Damned United (feature), Elizabeth I (TV drama), Charles II (TV drama).

Louise Page   020-8459 8569 Mobile 07711-668541
Doctor Who (TV drama), The Wedding Date (feature).

Judy Pepperdine   01798-873597 Mobile 07818-034138
CMM 020-8584 5363 Fax 01798-873597
Cider With Rosie (TV drama), Mrs Dalloway (feature), Miss Marple (TV drama).

Sam Perry   020-7607 6749 Mobile 07958-366759
Born With Two Mothers (TV drama), Normal For Norfolk (short), Spoons (TV comedy drama).

COSTUME

COSTUME DESIGNERS

COSTUME

Suzy Peters 020-7794 5428 Mobile 07803-006994
Everything (feature), Just Like A Woman (feature), Mrs Caldicot's Cabbage War (feature).

Jane Petrie 020-7729 1544 Mobile 07973-963413
Moon (feature), Is There Anybody There? (feature), 28 Weeks Later (feature).

Caroline Pitcher 020-8677 8668 Mobile 07860-948404
Fax 020-8677 8088
Mutual Friends (TV drama), Armstrong & Miller (TV light entertainment), The Inbetweeners (TV comedy drama).

Sally Plum 020-7602 7398 Mobile 07941-069276
BA 020-7836 1112
School For Seduction (feature), The Worst Week Of My Life (TV comedy drama), Living It (TV drama).

Toni Porter 020-8980 2732 Mobile 07976-912316
Pop Idol (TV light entertainment), Ant & Dec's Saturday Night (TV light entertainment).

Anthony Powell 020-8852 0035
Miss Potter (feature).

Janet Powell Mobile 07767-456998
Emmerdale (TV drama), EastEnders (promo), A Touch Of Frost (TV drama).

Sandy Powell Mobile 07976-245192

Maria Price 01273-612272 Mobile 07932-493787
Jonathan Toomey (feature), Foyle's War (TV drama), Secrets & Lies (feature).

Sally Puttick 020-7502 2068 Mobile 07710-444908
MI High (TV childrens).

Jo Rainforth 01962-880180 Mobile 07050-043447
Dunkirk (TV drama doc), The Space Race (TV drama doc), My Family (TV comedy drama).

Rita Reekie 01372-470975
Shrink (short), Liza Minnelli Live At The Albert Hall (concert), Hotel Du Lac (TV film).

Mary-Jane Reyner 01273-675522 Mobile 07774-692118
ITG 020-7636 6565
Pierrepoint (TV film), Broken Thread (feature), The War Zone (feature).

Rebecca Rich 020-8968 3226 Mobile 07866-494142
WZ 020-7437 2055 Fax 020-8968 3226
Stella Artois (commercial), Egg (commercial), Magnum (commercial).

Janice Rider 0121-441 2702 Mobile 07714-545110
Fax 0121-441 2702
Almost Adult (feature), Room To Rent (feature), Macbeth On The Estate (TV drama).

Amy Roberts 020-8568 4023 Mobile 07875-735546
MM 020-8995 4747 Fax 020-8758 9364
Elizabeth The Virgin Queen (TV drama), Perfect Parents (TV film), Dracula (TV drama).

Pennie Robertson 0117-973 2224 Mobile 07956-889234
Fax 0117-973 2224
The Thin Blue Line (TV comedy drama), Mr Bean (TV light entertainment), The Vicar Of Dibley (TV comedy drama).

Jane Robinson 020-7262 7607 Mobile 07977-988145
ITG 020-7636 6565 Fax 020-7262 7607
From Time To Time (feature), My Zinc Bed (TV film), Celebration (TV film).

Delphine Roche-Gordon 01306-886288
Mobile 07885-452921 Fax 01306-886288
Rose & Maloney (TV drama), Berry's Way (TV drama), Down To Earth (TV drama).

Anne Rudd 01225-744367 Mobile 07970-279523
Fax 01225-744367
The Family (TV drama), Waterloo Road (TV drama), The Cry (TV drama).

Rhona Russell 0141-579 0787 Mobile 07748-968196
BA 020-7836 1112 Fax 0141-579 0787
Alien Autopsy (feature), Blind Flight (feature), Jekyll (TV drama).

Victoria Russell 020-7229 3939 Mobile 07788-817622
WZ 020-7437 2055
Colour Me Kubrick (feature), Keeping Mum (feature), Cashback (feature).

Emma Ryott 020-8348 0414 Mobile 07973-632384
Fax 020-8341 5022
Lulu Stuttgart (ballet), One Touch Of Venus (opera), Oedipus Rex (theatre).

Astrid Schulz 020-7388 2162 Mobile 07947-155611
Fax 020-7388 2162
Fly Fishing (feature), Holding On (TV drama), The Serpent (TV drama doc).

Sammy Sheldon Mobile 07973-320648
Gulliver's Travels (feature), Stardust (feature), V For Vendetta (feature).

Anna Sheppard 020-8743 2895 Mobile 07768-332411
ITG 020-7636 6565
Sahara (feature), The Pianist (feature), Schindler's List (feature).

Emma Skala   Mobile 07973-305150
Beast (TV comedy drama), Birds Of A Feather (TV comedy drama), Kerwhizz (TV childrens).

Joanne Slater   0191-455 2692 Mobile 07976-259495
Fax 0191-455 2692
Boy Meets Girl (TV drama), Bad Girls (TV drama), 55 Degrees North (TV drama).

Sue Smith   01484-862472 Mobile 07785-718634
My Parents Are Aliens (TV childrens), Time Treasures (TV educational), Adam's Family Tree (TV childrens).

Sue Snell   020-7589 3885 Mobile 07771-763042
Flight To Berlin (feature), Fords On Water (feature), Ghost Dance (feature).

Isolde Sommerfeldt 020-7232 1909 Mobile 07973-634810
Fax 020-7232 1909
Inside Waco (TV drama doc), Hannibal (TV drama), Pompeii: The Last Day (TV drama).

Yolanda Sonnabend   020-7286 9616 CMM 020-8584 5363
Fax 020-7286 9616
The Tempest (feature), Seven Deadly Sins (TV drama), Decadence (feature).

Jane Spicer   020-8892 6634 Mobile 07940-263176
The Colour Of Magic (TV film).

Marcia Stanton   020-8979 1792 Fax 020-8979 6155
Knowing Me Knowing You (TV light entertainment), The Frank Skinner Show (TV light entertainment), Johnny Vegas - 18 Stone Of Idiot (TV light entertainment).

Louise Stjernsward   020-7352 3311 Mobile 07775-994727
DA 020-7437 4551 Fax 020-7352 3311
Creation (feature), The Dreamer (feature), Sexy Beast (feature).

Anna Stubley   01895-833805 Mobile 07802-440546
Fax 01895-833805

Annie Symons   020-7263 5475 Mobile 07973-815608
Fax 020-7263 5475
Glorious 39 (feature), Dr Zhivago (TV film), Love Is The Devil (feature).

Jennie Tate   01953-454759 Mobile 07860-636179
Fax 01953-454759
Kingdom (TV drama), Dalziel & Pascoe (TV drama), The Roman Mysteries (TV childrens).

Jill Taylor   020-8879 6481 Mobile 07774-127523
Angus Thongs & Perfect Snogging (feature), The Life & Death Of Peter Sellers (feature), Matchpoint (feature).

Mecheal Taylor   020-7733 2495 Mobile 07798-625719
MM 020-8995 4747
The Shell Seekers (TV drama), The Rotter's Club (TV drama), Summer Solstice (TV drama).

Jany Temime   Mobile 07866-412284 MM 020-8995 4747
In Bruges (feature), Harry Potter & The Order Of The Phoenix (feature), Harry Potter & The Half-Blood Prince (feature).

Frances Tempest   01273-680750 Mobile 07850-710999
Fax 01273-680750
Miss Marple (TV drama), These Foolish Things (feature), Calendar Girls (feature).

Dawn Thomas Mondo   029-2066 6611
Mobile 07774-947700 Fax 029-2064 4668
The Chosen (TV drama), The Tulse Luper Suitcase (feature), In The Company Of Strangers (TV film).

Jo Thompson   020-7498 2175 Mobile 07973-308152
Somers Town (feature), Horne & Corden (TV light entertainment), This Is England (feature).

Sue Thomson   020-8673 5313 Mobile 07771-783277
BA 020-7836 1112 Fax 020-8673 5313
Mistresses (TV drama), The Haunted Airman (TV film), The Yellow House (TV film).

Jill Thornley   01446-421320 Mobile 07771-865041
Fax 01446-421320
Tracy Beaker (TV childrens), Young Dracula (TV childrens).

Jeremy Turner   020-7701 6506 Mobile 07949-123682
Martin Chuzzlewit (TV drama), Berkeley Square (TV drama), John Carter Of Mars (feature) (Assistant).

Jackie Vernon   020-8374 0201 Mobile 07860-899111
CCA 020-7630 6303 Fax 020-8374 0201
The Wrong Door (TV light entertainment), The Thick Of It (TV comedy drama), Meet The Magoons (TV comedy drama).

Joan Wadge   Mobile 07821-421083 BA 020-7836 1112
Festen (theatre), Ivanhoe (TV drama), House Of Elliot (TV drama).

Natalie Ward   020-8533 7125 Mobile 07973-733971
Last Chance Harvey (feature), The Debt (feature), 1408 (feature).

Tina Waugh   020-8378 9160 Mobile 07973-513801
Fax 020-8378 9160
Microsoap (TV childrens), The Law (TV drama), A Royal Scandal (TV drama).

Hazel Webb-Crozier 028-9079 9426 Mobile 07884-495986
Closing The Ring (feature), Mickeybo & Me (feature), Small Engine Repair (feature).

COSTUME

Saga Widen   020-7249 0599   Mobile 07811-906895
BMW (commercial), Silent Witness (TV drama).

Lynda Susan Wood   020-8998 4648   Mobile 07973-560691
Fax 020-8998 4648
The Royal Variety Performance (TV light entertainment), An Audience With (TV light entertainment), Strictly Come Ice-Skating (TV light entertainment).

Lucinda Wright   Mobile 07885-307622
Fanny Hill (TV drama).

Allison Wyldeck   020-8940 8379   Mobile 07775-558411
The Wolfman (feature) (Costume Supervisor), Notes On A Scandal (feature), The Good Shepherd (feature).

Janty Yates   020-8671 5869   Mobile 07836-641037
ITG 020-7636 6565
Robin Hood (feature), Kingdom Of Heaven (feature), Gladiator (feature).

COSTUME DESIGNERS - ASSISTANT

Jeeda Barford   Mobile 07768-627637
Casino Royale (feature), Eragon (feature) (Costume Buyer), Batman Begins (feature).

Karen Beale   020-8847 0306   Mobile 07976-619878
Fax 020-8932 1901
Scoop (feature), Rogue Trader (feature), Penelope (feature).

Penny Beard McDonald   020-7485 7167
Mobile 07885-842190
Nicholas Nickleby (feature), Star Wars: Episode III - Revenge Of The Sith (feature), Ella Enchanted (feature).

Camille Benda   020-7274 3360   Mobile 07814-058038
CB 01932-592572
City Of Ember (feature), The Golden Compass (feature), Bathory (feature).

Charlotte Bird   Mobile 07774-275680
Being Julia (feature), The Clandestine Marriage (feature), Joseph & His Amazing Technicolor Dream Coat (feature).

Kathryn Blight   Mobile 07711-313085
The Queen (feature), London Boulevard (feature).

Lucy Bowring   Mobile 07946-583271
Prince Of Persia (feature).

Emma Bull   Mobile 07855-793643
Kylie Minogue (concert), Flashbacks Of A Fool (feature), Trimming The Fat (short).

Joanna Campbell   Mobile 07867-554395
The Mutant Chronicles (feature).

Viveene Campbell   Mobile 07828-34918
Little Dorrit (TV drama).

Deborah Cantor   Mobile 07771-694264
Gladiators (TV light entertainment), Any Dream Will Do (TV light entertainment), Cirque De Celebrite (TV light entertainment).

Mauricio Carneiro   020-8374 0544   Mobile 07962-077636
Harry Potter & The Half-Blood Prince (feature), Harry Potter & The Order Of The Phoenix (feature), Harry Potter & The Goblet Of Fire (feature).

Rosina Catlin   01249-701327   Mobile 07881-533073
The Ghost Of Greville Lodge (TV film), The Sobering (feature), Firedance (theatre).

Martin Chitty   020-7603 0458   Mobile 07970-656118
W.E. (feature).

Jane Clive   020-7624 0028   Mobile 07801-702261
Oliver Twist (feature), Around The World In 80 Days (feature), Sahara (feature).

Claire Collins   Mobile 07967-097262
Miss Austin Regrets (TV drama), Hustle (TV drama), Miss Marple (TV drama).

Richard Cooke   Mobile 07976-666867
Easy Virtue (feature), Hustle (TV drama), MI High (TV childrens) (Costume Designer).

Gaia Cozzi   020-8432 3495   Mobile 07930-397862
Kingdom (TV drama) (Trainee), Christmas At The Riviera (TV drama).

Ellen Crawshaw   Mobile 07866-772080
London Boulevard (feature).

Sally Crees   01920-422536   Mobile 07753-619717
Munich (feature), Mrs Henderson Presents (feature), Bleak House (TV drama).

Andrea Cripps   020-7821 7061   Mobile 07711-790342
The Dark Knight (feature), Atonement (feature), Robin Hood (feature).

Richard Davies   020-7062 0026   Mobile 07976-350730
In Bruges (feature), Children Of Men (feature), Harry Potter & The Order Of The Phoenix (feature).

Kate Duffy   01844-291259   Mobile 07803-505127
Head Over Heels (TV drama), The Return Of Captain Invincible (feature), Beginners Guide To Coming Out (TV light entertainment).

COSTUME

Francoise Fourcade   020-7771 6709 Mobile 07947-716709
Harry Potter & The Prisoner Of Azkaban (feature), The Heart Of Me (feature), Robinson Crusoe (feature).

Rosie Grant   Mobile 07973-710843
Creation (feature), The Other Man (feature), Little Dorrit (TV drama).

Paul Gregory   0161-225 9974 Mobile 07850-247301
City Central (TV drama), Mersey Beat (TV drama), Casualty (TV drama).

Tina Hackett-James   01823-322254 Mobile 07808-791437
Fax 01823-322254
Dreaming Of Joseph Lees (feature), The Prince & The Pauper (TV film), Casualty (TV drama).

Jamie Harvey   Mobile 07921-538293
John Carter Of Mars (feature).

Jo Hayes   Mobile 07957-186882
Fanny Hill (TV drama).

Yvonne Hobbs   01929-471327 Mobile 07952-491130
Fax 01929-471327
Jiro (feature), Silent Witness (TV drama), D-Day (TV drama doc).

Carin Hoff   Mobile 07768-243181
I Capture The Castle (feature), The Man Who Cried (feature), Gormenghast (TV drama).

Caroline Hume   020-8854 2871
The Royal (TV drama), Madame Bovary (TV drama), Micawber (TV drama).

Natalie Humphries   Mobile 07773-767351
Hotel Babylon (TV drama), London Boulevard (feature).

Vivienne Jones   020-8690 1687 Mobile 07989-969055
Munich (feature) (Costume Buyer), Bridget Jones's Diary II (feature), Harry Potter & The Half-Blood Prince (feature).

Charlotte Kay   Mobile 07958-358165
Stardust (feature), Hellboy 2: The Golden Army (feature), V For Vendetta (feature).

Amanda Keable   01403-741483 Mobile 07966-540815
Death Defying Acts (feature), Dean Spanley (feature), The Colour Of Magic (TV film).

Colleen Kelsall   Mobile 07881-702711
Nine (feature), Sweeney Todd (feature), The Wolfman (feature).

Anna Kot   020-7622 3650 Mobile 07788-678985
Fax 020-7622 3650
The Duchess (feature), Gosford Park (feature), Alexander (feature).

Poli Kyriacou   020-8881 2443 Mobile 07879-882496
The Debt (feature).

Poli Kyriacou   020-8881 2443 Mobile 07879-882496
The Debt (feature).

Charlotte Law   Mobile 07799-601882

Susie Lewis   029-2061 2751 Mobile 07780-708761
Tracy Beaker (TV childrens), A Way Of Life (feature), The Bench (TV drama).

Gabriella Loria   Mobile 07880-623137
Nanny McPhee & The Big Bang (feature), Basic Instinct II (feature), Casino Royale (feature).

Heather MacVean   020-8533 7821 Mobile 07976-429340
Mayo (TV drama), Sold (TV drama), Grass (TV drama).

Kay Manasseh   020-8671 4509 Mobile 07768-693652
The Other Boleyn Girl (feature) (Costume Buyer), Sweeney Todd (feature) (Costume Buyer), Sylvia (feature).

Monique Mathieu   020-7771 0239 Mobile 07787-575543
San Antonio (feature), Family Affairs (TV drama), Othello (theatre).

Caroline McCall   020-8546 7424 Mobile 07957-438923
Fax 020-8546 7424
Little Dorrit (TV drama), Death Defying Acts (feature), As You Like It (feature).

Sara Meek   020-7708 5591 Mobile 07973-371423
Harry Potter & The Goblet Of Fire (feature), Young Adam (feature), Children Of Men (feature).

Heidi Miller   Mobile 07966-555432
Little Dorrit (TV drama).

Laura Morgan   Mobile 07539-200968

Clare Mould   0115-972 8030 Mobile 07714-196924
Coronation Street (TV drama), Pride & Prejudice (feature), Crossroads (TV drama).

Gerald Moulin   01962-761023 Mobile 07990-543737
Fax 01962-761023
The Space Race (TV drama doc), Band Of Brothers (TV drama), Enemy At The Gates (feature).

Caroline Nicholls   Mobile 07834-829228

Bojana Nikitovic   Mobile 07825-848497
The Wolfman (feature).

COSTUME

Maggie Partington-Smith   020-7727 5726
Mobile 07905-929855
The Young Victoria (feature), Judge John Deed (TV drama), Black Book (feature).

Livia Pascucci   020-7627 1404 Mobile 07710-316835
Notting Hill (feature), Sexy Beast (feature), Tomorrow Never Dies (feature).

Philip Rainforth   01962-880180 Mobile 07050-104598
Dunkirk (TV drama doc), Back Home (TV film), Braveheart (feature).

Magdalen Rubalcava   Mobile 07793-811206
The Lion In Winter (TV film), Being Julia (feature), Asylum (feature).

Pookie Russell   020-8299 6720 Mobile 07775-876402
Foyle's War (TV drama), The Girl In The Cafe (TV film).

Amber Ryder   Mobile 07843-006530
Cauldron Of Changes (TV drama).

Richard Sale   Mobile 07711-784161
Green Zone (feature).

Anna Sandler   Mobile 07958-967386
Little Dorrit (TV drama).

Debbie Scott   Mobile 07778-463795

Jan Simpson   0151-427 0359 Mobile 07778-179913
Like Minds (feature), Revenger's Tragedy (feature), The Forsyte Saga (TV drama).

Fola Solanke   020-8488 6782 Mobile 07966-389405
Fax 020-8488 6782
Shoot The Messenger (TV drama), Bullet Boy (feature), Bashment (theatre).

Oliver Southhall   Mobile 07780-674154
Spooks (TV drama).

Georgina Sparrow   Mobile 07801-948270
Hotel Babylon (TV drama).

Pamela Stewart   020-7610 4010
Hustle (TV drama).

Mark Sutherland   020-8969 4871 Mobile 07973-150580
Quantum Of Solace (feature), Spooks (TV drama).

Ann Taylor-Cowan   020-8541 0329 Mobile 07808-726822
The Man In The Iron Mask (feature), Restoration (feature), Mary Shelley's Frankenstein (feature).

Sally Turner   01844-218878 Mobile 07802-412643
Fax 01844-214655
Flawless (feature), Casanova (feature), Cranford (TV drama).

Robin Walker   020-8677 3746 Mobile 07973-198672
Fax 020-8677 3746
Zero To Hero (TV light entertainment), Family Affairs (TV drama), London's Burning (TV drama).

Hilary Watson   020-8537 2687
Mobile 07799-891920
Wish Baby (feature), Stage Beauty (feature), Randall & Hopkirk (Deceased) (TV drama).

Saffron Webb   020-8858 2565 Mobile 07793-317986
Ultimate Force (TV drama), Bad Girls (TV drama), Fanny Hill (TV drama) (Costume Supervisor).

Michelle Wickland   Mobile 07957-437154
Distant Shores (TV drama), Oliver Twist (feature) (Costume Buyer), Sahara (feature).

Robert Worley   01277-214014 Mobile 07774-689204
Fax 01277-214014
John Adams (TV drama), Kingdom Of Heaven (feature), The Wolfman (feature).

Chrissie Wrench   020-8943 2213 Mobile 07887-607948
The John Lennon Story (TV film), The Bill (TV drama).

Celia Yau   Mobile 07939-235761
The Wolfman (feature), A Mighty Heart (feature), Vera Drake (feature).

Paul Yeowell   Mobile 07976-844178
The Duchess (feature), Kingdom Of Heaven (feature), Alexander (feature).

COSTUME EFFECTS

Alexander Carey   01323-811636 Mobile 07970-040635
Fax 01323-811636
Defiance (feature), Sherlock Holmes (feature), Troy (feature).

Day Murch   020-8677 4656 Mobile 07957-798740
Harry Potter & The Prisoner Of Azkaban (feature), In The Night Garden (TV childrens), Batman Begins (feature).

Helen Perks   020-7439 4230 Mobile 07918-684335
The Wind In The Willows (TV film), Tosca (opera), Casino Royale (feature).

Tim Shanahan   020-7697 0122 Mobile 07841-819984
The Da Vinci Code (feature), Harry Potter & The Goblet Of Fire (feature), Kingdom Of Heaven (feature).

COSTUME

COSTUME MAKERS

Jennifer Alford   020-8376 5087   Mobile 07930-377749
Atonement (feature), Vera Drake (feature), Batman Begins (feature).

Ron Briggs   020-8444 8801   Mobile 07752-899945
Around The World In 80 Days (feature), Atonement (feature), Les Miserables (theatre).
www.ronbriggs.com

Lorraine Cooksley   020-8904 4003   Mobile 07929-487869
Charlie & The Chocolate Factory (feature), Genie In The House (TV childrens), The Colour Of Magic (TV film).

Rosy Coppola   020-8444 5410   Mobile 07710-451176
In Bruges (feature), The Duchess (feature), Children Of Men (feature).

Ian Costello   020-8478 2780   Mobile 07860-919688
Fax 020-8553 3336

Sara Creed   01273-206253   Mobile 07976-763873
Troy (feature), The Man In The Iron Mask (feature), Mansfield Park (TV film).

Lal d'Abo   020-8674 2249   Mobile 07796-267797
Fax 020-8671 4787
The Royal (TV drama), English National (ballet), Royal Opera House (opera).

Don Fearney   020-8806 6915   Mobile 07939-467550

Simone Feulner   Mobile 07796-437577
John Carter Of Mars (feature).

Dennis Fitzgerald   020-8850 7398   Mobile 07813-945295
Fax 020-8850 7398
Master & Commander (feature), A Few Good Men (theatre), A Man For All Seasons (theatre).

Shirley Fitzgerald   020-8850 7398   Mobile 07976-709586
Fax 020-8850 7398
David Bailey (stills), Hay Fever (theatre), Scrooge (theatre).

Nicola Foy   Mobile 07958-474122
John Carter Of Mars (feature).

Robbie Gordon   020-7474 4734   Mobile 07958-637647
Porgy & Bess (theatre), The Tempest (feature), Sleeping Beauty (ballet).

Georgina Greathead   01273-846961   Mobile 07747-657812

Jane Grimshaw   Mobile 07952-261253
Elizabeth: The Golden Age (feature), The Other Boleyn Girl (feature), Elizabeth (feature).

Naomi Isaacs   020-7226 7872

Harriet Johnson   Mobile 07967-029142
John Carter Of Mars (feature).

Alleyne Kirby-Davies   020-7602 5773
Mobile 07785-782332
Kingdom Of Heaven (feature), Alexander (feature), The Wolfman (feature) (Cutter).

Maria Liljefors   020-8838 1448   Mobile 07802-155593
Fax 020-8961 0752
Body Of Lies (feature), Robinson Crusoe (feature), Robin Hood (feature).

Christine Manning   020-8853 2024   Fax 020-8853 2024
Billy Elliot (feature), The Woman In White (theatre), National Lottery (commercial).

David McMurray   01692-581537   Fax 01692-581537
Phantom Of The Opera (feature), Troy (feature), Elizabeth (feature).

Caroline Mirfin   01675-443998   Mobile 07917-541663
Phantom Of The Opera (feature), Sleepy Hollow (feature), Harry Potter & The Chamber Of Secrets (feature).

Karen Mitchell   020-8856 2712   Mobile 07719-460300
Hitchhiker's Guide To The Galaxy (feature), Sahara (feature), Harry Potter & The Order Of The Phoenix (feature).

Andrea Moon   01424-717177   Mobile 07708-252118
Fax 01424-717177
Phantom Of The Opera (feature), Star Wars: Episode I - The Phantom Menace (feature), Gladiator (feature).

Tanya Mould   01483-237464   Mobile 07958-786891

Anne Nichols   01263-733081   Mobile 07887-847125
Fax 01263-733081
Charlie & The Chocolate Factory (feature), Mrs Henderson Presents (feature), Kingdom Of Heaven (feature).

Lucy Nye   0161-798 0944   Mobile 07894-201301
Don Giovanni (opera), Vanity Fair (feature), Phantom Of The Opera (feature).

Susanne Pavelkova   01303-813233   Mobile 07958-308125
The Clandestine Marriage (feature), Barbara Streisand (concert), English National (ballet).

Mein Roberts   029-2022 4132   Mobile 07866-558053
Fax 029-2034 2980
Oliver! (theatre), The Madness Of King George (feature), The Sound Of Music (theatre).

COSTUME MAKERS

Laura Rushton   01784-452067 Mobile 07801-552801
Prince Of Persia (feature), The Tempest (feature).

Carole Thompson   020-8858 6844
Wicked (theatre), Billy Elliot (feature), The Woman In White (theatre).

Trethanna Trevarthen   Mobile 07799-723555
John Carter Of Mars (feature).

Mervyn Wallace   01692-581537 Fax 01692-581537
Troy (feature), Pirates Of The Caribbean: The Curse Of The Black Pearl (feature), The Opera Ghost (feature).

Nicola Wheeler   01422-843407 Mobile 07772-166273
My Parents Are Aliens (TV childrens), The Summer Of Love (feature), The Full Monty (feature).

Nikki White   020-8992 1771 Mobile 07947-849728
Mamma Mia! (feature), Jesus Christ Superstar (theatre), Dutch National (ballet).

COSTUME SUPERVISORS

Joanna Beatty   01825-766221 Mobile 07769-972639
Ancient Rome: The Rise & Fall Of An Empire (TV drama), Warriors (TV film), Rosemary & Thyme (TV drama).

Allan Birkett   01492-871929 Mobile 07968-746520
Fax 01492-871929
Land Of The Blind (feature), Girls In Love (TV drama), Five Children & It (feature).

Joy Bondini   020-8965 6561 Mobile 07747-611765
Fax 020-8453 1652
The Producers (theatre), We Will Rock You (theatre), Chicago (theatre).

Liza Bracey   020-7250 4122 Mobile 07774-955939
Shanghai (feature).

Daryl Bristow   01727-852879 Mobile 07808-914212
Fax 01727-845775
Hannibal Rising (feature), Fred Claus (feature), Sahara (feature).

Rosemary Burrows   0118-934 5565 Mobile 07050-042300
Miss Potter (feature).

Billy Caine   020-8968 5513 Mobile 07866-758285
Doom Bar (commercial), Westcountry Live (TV news & current affairs), Inspector Morse (TV drama).

Sue Clewett   020-8992 6254 Mobile 07974-752766
Fax 020-8992 6254
Harry & Paul (TV light entertainment), The Catherine Tate Show (TV light entertainment), The Lost World (TV docu drama).

Natasha Cottier   Mobile 07932-631164
Summer Solstice (TV drama), Waking The Dead (TV drama), The Shell Seekers (TV drama).

Annie Crawford   020-8941 3405 Mobile 07510-296622
W.E. (feature), Robin Hood (feature), Children Of Men (feature).

David Crossman   01799-540020 Mobile 07702-615828
Robin Hood (feature), The Da Vinci Code (feature) (Assistant), Harry Potter & The Goblet Of Fire (feature).

Kenny Crouch   020-8367 5191 Mobile 07956-309931
Prince Of Persia (feature), Evita (feature), Mission: Impossible (feature).

Lee Croucher   Mobile 07775-637608
The Dark Knight (feature), United 93 (feature), A Good Year (feature).

David Culbert   01506-828590 Mobile 07796-226884
New Town Killers (feature).

Sophie Doncaster   0161-224 5043 Mobile 07885-105692
Casanova (feature), Once Upon A Time In The Midlands (feature), A Room For Romeo Brass (feature).

Louise Egan   Mobile 07968-856062
The Colour Of Magic (TV film), The Dark Is Rising (feature), It's A Free World (feature).

Lezli Everitt   Mobile 07961-427670
Souled Out (feature), Hotel Babylon (TV drama), Christmas Lights (TV drama).

Mark Ferguson   020-8623 9305 Mobile 07790-884527
Defiance (feature), Cranford (TV drama).

Charlotte Finlay   020-8245 2848 Mobile 07956-655335
Harry Potter & The Half-Blood Prince (feature), Inkheart (feature), Munich (feature).

Alan Flyng   020-7358 9724 Mobile 07831-756368
Dog House (feature), Richard III (feature), Ronin (feature).

Helen Godwin   020-8959 8692 Mobile 07770-576165
Fax 020-8959 8692
Britain's Got Talent (TV light entertainment), Cold Feet (TV drama), Holby City (TV drama).

Dan Grace   020-7833 9270 Mobile 07973-343365
Clash Of The Titans (feature), The Da Vinci Code (feature), The Dark Knight (feature).

Celia Griffiths   020-8977 2168 Mobile 07803-118853
The Commander (TV drama).

Laurent Guinci   Mobile 07956-561316
In Bruges (feature).

Jane Hamnett   020-8341 9475 Mobile 07774-618507
Hustle (TV drama), Spooks (TV drama), Holby City (TV drama).

Abigail Hicks   01737-226411 Mobile 07778-553035
Fax 01737-226411
The Bill (TV drama), Midsomer Murders (TV drama), Ultimate Force (TV drama).

Katie Hill   Mobile 07812-129478
Sense & Sensibility (feature), Lark Rise To Candleford (TV drama), Miss Potter (feature).

Thomas Hornsby   Mobile 07973-230935
Gulliver's Travels (feature) (2nd unit), Harry Potter & The Prisoner Of Azkaban (feature), Band Of Brothers (TV drama).

Heather Howell   020-8943 9946 Mobile 07850-104819
Fax 020-8943 9946
Foyle's War (TV drama), The Midnight Man (TV drama), Cape Wrath (TV drama).

Gary Hyams   020-8236 0813 Mobile 07762-615426
Band Of Brothers (TV drama), Harry Potter & The Goblet Of Fire (feature), EastEnders (promo).

Mary Judge   020-8444 5285 Mobile 07768-511131
Fax 020-8444 5285
The Long Walk To Finchley (TV film), Housewife 49 (TV drama), Midsomer Murders (TV drama).

Steve Kirkby   01438-367648 Mobile 07767-296889
Spy Game (feature), World Of Tomorrow (feature), The Saint (feature).

Ruth Kirton   020-7652 7234 Mobile 07785-756333
Fax 020-7652 7234
Mysterious Creatures (TV film), Five Days (feature), Life & Lyrics (feature).

Josef Kowalewski   020-8292 1799 Mobile 07799-798730
Prince Of Persia (feature) (Wardrobe Assistant), Kingdom Of Heaven (feature).

Anna Lau   Mobile 07974-973019
Stone Of Destiny (feature), Hope Springs (TV drama), Doomsday (feature).

Sharon Long   Mobile 07802-755903
Robin Hood (feature), Stormbreaker (feature), Mrs Henderson Presents (feature).

Joanna Macklin   Mobile 07703-580775
Trial & Retribution (TV drama), Prime Suspect (TV drama), The Commander (TV drama).

Jannie Marr   020-7402 5386 Mobile 07974-838178
Hotel Babylon (TV drama).

Gilly Martin   Mobile 07973-155846
Flyboys (feature), Nanny McPhee (feature), The Walker (feature).

Kay McIntosh   0161-998 5505 Mobile 07968-978957
Mobile (TV drama), Sorted (TV drama), Conviction (TV drama).

William McPhail   020-7328 3228 Mobile 07860-702330
Fax 020-7328 3228
The Golden Compass (feature), City Of Ember (feature), Dorian Gray (feature).

Shirley Nevin   020-7624 5134 Mobile 07887-575251
Fax 020-7624 5134
Alfie (feature), Calendar Girls (feature), Children Of Men (feature).

Lindsay Pugh   020-8968 5413 Mobile 07768-733143
Fax 020-8968 5413
Quantum Of Solace (feature), Mamma Mia! (feature), Cold Mountain (feature).

Natalie Richmond Elvy   020-8605 2122
Mobile 07973-397593
Miss Marple (TV drama), The Inspector Lynley Mysteries (TV drama), Cambridge Spies (TV drama).

Mark Ridley   01531-640291 Mobile 07941-740863
Afterlife (TV drama), Doctors (TV drama), Born & Bred (TV drama).

Cheryl Roberts   01273-269622 Mobile 07803-291778
Hollyoaks (TV drama), The Coral (promo), Brookside (TV drama).

Barbara Rutter   01795-890979 Mobile 07050-046469
Confetti (feature), Bright Young Things (feature), Hornblower (TV drama).

Dulcie Scott   020-8743 8511 Mobile 07831-594373
Fax 020-8743 8511
Black Book (feature), Valkyrie (feature), Cherie (feature).

Charlotte Sewell   020-7720 7136 Mobile 07768-156567
Hippie Hippie Shake (feature), St Trinian's (feature), Dead Set (TV drama).

Hazel Shrieves   01323-894836 Mobile 07941-071863
Dancing On Ice (TV light entertainment), Dame Edna (TV light entertainment), Britain's Got Talent (TV light entertainment).

Mike Skorepa   01932-706917 Mobile 07767-688870
Robin Hood (feature) (2nd unit).

Gabrielle Spanswick   020-7358 0467
Mobile 07957-177096
Layer Cake (feature), Poirot (TV drama), How To Lose Friends & Alienate People (feature).

COSTUME

COSTUME SUPERVISORS

Clare Spragge　　　　　　　　Mobile 07966-460018
Prince Of Persia (feature).

Lesley Tait　　　　01603-898638　Mobile 07799-245107
The Chief (TV drama), Wycliffe (TV drama), Trisha (TV light entertainment).

Sarah Touaibi　　　020-8341 0994　Mobile 07767-498858
Fax 020-8341 0994
Miss Potter (feature), Black Book (feature), Gladiator (feature).

Suzi Turnbull　　　　　　　　Mobile 07768-116017
Sweeney Todd (feature), Elizabeth: The Golden Age (feature), The New World (feature).

Lupt Utama　　　　　　　　Mobile 07825-135703
The Firm (feature), Outlaw (feature), Bradford Riots (TV film).

Marion Weise　　　020-7703 8439　Mobile 07802-603758
Fax 020-7703 8439
The Bank Job (feature), The Other Man (feature), United 93 (feature).

Bushy Westfallen　　　020-8674 4653　Mobile 07710-129643
Fax 020-8674 4653
Grease (theatre), Twelfth Night (theatre), Daisy Pulls It Off (theatre).

Lucy Williams　　　　　　　　Mobile 07885-105472
Hotel Babylon (TV drama).

Nicole Young　　　020-7790 4871　Mobile 07850-617681
Fax 020-7790 4871
Gulliver's Travels (feature), Pierrepoint (TV film), Sunshine (feature) (Assistant Costume Designer).

HAIR SUPERVISORS

Natasha Allegro　　　　　　　Mobile 07947-562056
Prince Of Persia (feature).

Nina Butkovich-Budden　　　　Mobile 07511-548873

John Henry Gordon　　01604-518034　Mobile 07968-496740
Prince Of Persia (feature).

Colin Jamison　　　01494-813292　Mobile 07831-366049
Harry Potter & The Order Of The Phoenix (feature), The Changeling (feature), Mr & Mrs Smith (feature).

Suzanne Stokes-Munton　　　　Mobile 07785-246061
Agora (feature), Hotel Rwanda (feature), 1408 (feature).

HAIRDRESSERS

Kevin Alexander　　　01273-325847　Mobile 07956-367863
Robin Hood (feature), Casino Royale (feature), Prince Caspian (feature).

Jan Archibald　　　020-7721 7095　Mobile 07976-262099
Fax 020-7721 7026
Prince Of Persia (feature), The Duchess (feature), La Vie En Rose (feature).
www.wigslondon.com

Faye Aydin Le Jeune　　　　　Mobile 07813-620337
Hollyoaks (TV drama), Walter's War (TV drama), Mobile (TV drama).

Candice Banks　　　　　　　Mobile 07768-913448
Robin Hood (feature).

Nina Butkovich-Budden　　　　Mobile 07511-548873

Nicola Clarke　　　020-7713 1509　Mobile 07961-352520
Prince Of Persia (feature), Babel (feature), Children Of Men (feature).

Carolyn Cousins　　　　　　Mobile 07831-340306
Little Dorrit (TV drama), Longford (TV drama), Sense & Sensibility (feature).

Francesca Crowder　　01932-563577　Mobile 07850-674847
SPA 01932-571044
Love & Other Disasters (feature), United 93 (feature), Lost In Space (feature).

Catherine Davies　　　029-2037 7554　Mobile 07768-344433
Prince Of Persia (feature), The Duchess (feature), The Edge Of Love (feature).

Mark English　　　020-7388 5903　Mobile 07973-739152
Closer (feature), Sylvia (feature), The Bridge Of San Luis Rey (feature).

Eithne Fennell　　　01753-539482　Mobile 07710-597040
Fax 01753-539482
The Princess Bride (feature), Mamma Mia! (feature), Quantum Of Solace (feature).

Matthew George　　　020-8699 1224　Mobile 07899-930699

Kay Georgiou　　　　　　　Mobile 07710-408834
The Departed (feature), Sylvia (feature), Syriana (feature).

Betty Glasow　　　01243-585723　Mobile 07905-740903
Harry Potter & The Goblet Of Fire (feature), Sylvia (feature), Harry Potter & The Prisoner Of Azkaban (feature).

Jon Gordon   Mobile 07968-496740
Stormbreaker (feature), Mrs Henderson Presents (feature), Amazing Grace (feature).

Iain Guthrie   020-8202 2496 Mobile 07813-704163
Doc Martin (TV drama), New Tricks (TV drama), Bones (TV drama).

Hilary Haines   01494-863034 Mobile 07808-488743
Fax 01494-863034

Janet Jamison   01494-813292 Mobile 07778-604522
Harry Potter & The Order Of The Phoenix (feature), Harry Potter & The Goblet Of Fire (feature), Die Another Day (feature).

Gerry Jones   020-8740 6746 Mobile 07885-297970
MIL 020-7729 9226 Fax 020-8740 6746
Marley & Me (feature), Green Zone (feature) (Assistant).

Elizabeth Lewis   020-7701 3440 Mobile 07714-768211
Harry Potter & The Prisoner Of Azkaban (feature), Hamlet (feature), The Golden Bowl (feature).

Sarah Love   01458-274688 Mobile 07710-065375
Shanghai (feature), Son Of Rambow (feature), Pride & Prejudice (feature).

Victoria Mactaggart   01534-498702
Mobile 07797-925710

Lauren Mathis   Mobile 07724-317859
WKD (commercial) (Assistant), Nintendo (commercial) (Assistant), Angus Thongs & Perfect Snogging (feature).

Donald McInnes   Mobile 07976-846794
Angus Thongs & Perfect Snogging (feature).

Chloe Meddings   Mobile 07900-265000
London Boulevard (feature).

Liz Michie   020-8346 9096 Mobile 07721-496980
Fax 020-8346 9096
St Trinian's (feature), Bride & Prejudice (feature), Gormenghast (TV drama).

Cheryl Mitchell   020-8241 7402 Mobile 07930-601218
Foyle's War (TV drama), Five Children & It (feature), Phantom Of The Opera (feature).

Paul Mooney   020-7450 3048 Mobile 07713-877718
Gulliver's Travels (feature), Matchpoint (feature), The Da Vinci Code (feature).

Anna Morena   01245-604948 Mobile 07802-544189
Elizabeth The Virgin Queen (TV drama), The Queen's Sister (TV drama), The Seagull (theatre).

Derek Morris   020-7495 7774 Mobile 07711-671350
Fax 020-7349 0239
Pantene (commercial), Head & Shoulders (commercial), Wella (commercial).

Pedro   020-7584 7130 Mobile 07816-908499
Organics (commercial), Walkers Crisps (commercial), Tesco (commercial).

Marc Pilcher   Mobile 07973-118311
W.E. (feature), Prince Of Persia (feature).

Jamie Pritchard   Mobile 07946-345534
St Trinian's (feature).

Jeanette Redmond   Mobile 07946-226639
Carmen (opera) (Wig Designer), Alexander (feature), Die Another Day (feature).

Peter Regan   0161-832 8000 Mobile 07836-344350
The Last Leprechaun (feature), The Jealous God (feature), Merlin - The Return (feature).

Jenna Richards   01582-469757 Mobile 07817-925371

Loulia Sheppard   01992-423872 Mobile 07958-214967
Fax 01992-423872
Amazing Grace (feature), Starter For Ten (feature), Phantom Of The Opera (feature).

Rupert Simon   Mobile 07717-713755
Prince Of Persia (feature), The Duchess (feature), Brideshead Revisited (feature).

Sandra Simons   020-8969 3735 Mobile 07946-544604
The Perfectionist (feature), Nescafe (commercial), Ferrero Rocher (commercial).

Tracey Smith   01923-231652 Mobile 07770-593776
Harry Potter & The Half-Blood Prince (feature), Harry Potter & The Order Of The Phoenix (feature), Die Another Day (feature).

Sharon Spob   0113-219 5020 Mobile 07778-803158
Fax 0113-219 5020
Revolver (feature), Brideshead Revisited (feature), The Bank Job (feature).

Zoe Tahir   020-8459 5556 Mobile 07958-625839
Fax 020-8459 5556
Quantum Of Solace (feature) (Hair Designer), Mamma Mia! (feature) (Hair Designer), Eragon (feature).

Barbara Taylor   01457-869431 Mobile 07836-748359
Fax 01457-869431
Prince Of Persia (feature), The Duchess (feature), Band Of Brothers (TV drama).

COSTUME

Lisa Tomblin   Mobile 07774-884475
Harry Potter & The Half-Blood Prince (feature), The Dark Is Rising (feature), Captain Corelli's Mandolin (feature).

Colin Watkins   01932-787623 Mobile 07878-340211
Fax 01932-787623
Blue Peter (TV childrens), This Morning (TV magazine), Exchange (TV light entertainment).

Tracey Wells   01273-593455 Mobile 07710-943107
Robin Hood (feature).

Felicity Wright   020-7485 1954 Mobile 07710-199216
Fax 020-7485 1954
The Wind In The Willows (TV film), The Upside Of Anger (feature) (Make-Up Artist), The End Of The Affair (feature).

Colin Wyatt   01225-312205 Mobile 07970-966827
Starter For Ten (feature), Amazing Grace (feature), The Bourne Ultimatum (feature).

HAIRDRESSERS - BARBERS

Tony Tahir   Mobile 07870-858987
Mamma Mia! (feature), Atonement (feature), De Lovely (feature).

MAKE-UP ARTISTS

Melissa Adams   Mobile 07760-556186

Sue Adams   020-8858 0225 Mobile 07710-626019
Fax 020-8858 0225
The Best Man (feature), State Of Mind (TV drama).

Clair Allison   Mobile 07831-379146
Sugar Rush (TV drama).

Marlene Andersson   020-8444 9530 Mobile 07957-137856
Fax 020-8444 9530
Radox (commercial), Sony (commercial), Lloyds TSB (commercial).

Sara Angharad   029-2031 2777 Mobile 07768-580579
Doctor Who (TV drama), Casualty (TV drama), Cutting It (TV drama).

Sharon Anniss   020-8607 9765 Mobile 07711-314310
Fax 020-8607 9765
Waking The Dead (TV drama), Born & Bred (TV drama), Holby City (TV drama).

Christina Baker   020-8567 6457 Mobile 07778-784549
Fax 020-8840 4315
Calendar Girls (feature), Wah Wah (feature), The Hangman (feature).

Tamsin Barbosa   01296-696979 Mobile 07831-558955
Nanny McPhee & The Big Bang (feature).

Judith Barkas   020-8450 7157 Mobile 07973-261637
Fax 020-8450 7157
Star Stories (TV light entertainment), Last Rights (TV drama), The Thick Of It (TV comedy drama).

Amanda Barker   023-8044 8533 Mobile 07968-064022
SC 01932-252577
Colman's Cook In Sauce (commercial), Birds Eye (commercial), Wrigley's (commercial).

Celia Baxter   020-7790 6322 Mobile 07831-508768
Strictly Come Dancing (TV light entertainment), Middlemarch (TV drama), Buccaneers (TV drama).

Michele Baylis   020-7224 5725 Mobile 07774-232850
Fax 020-7224 5725
Oliver Twist (feature), The Mutant Chronicles (feature), George Michael (tour).

Jane Beard   029-2076 1888 Mobile 07885-475576
Torchwood (TV drama), High Hopes (feature), Doctor Who (TV drama).

Cheraine Bell   01932-592463 Mobile 07860-354654
Fax 01932-592023
See It Saw It (TV childrens), Urban Myth Chiller (short).

Penny Bell   01784-483168 Mobile 07850-902384
Fax 01784-483168
Midsomer Murders (TV drama), An Unsuitable Job For A Woman (TV drama), The Sculptress (TV drama).

Chrissie Beveridge   01728-648745 Mobile 07881-623640
Syriana (feature), The Departed (feature), The Good Shepherd (feature).

Jacqueline Bhavnani   01245-460874
Mobile 07808-927007
Valkyrie (feature), The Boy In The Striped Pyjamas (feature), De Lovely (feature).

Kay Bilk   01442-833616 Mobile 07973-382848
In The Loop (feature), Hotel Babylon (TV drama), Bleak House (TV drama).

Allen Bills   0117-956 6556 Mobile 07840-847325
Fax 0117-956 6556

Madeleine Bills   0117-956 6556 Mobile 07840-847325
Fax 0117-956 6556
The Real Inspector Hound (theatre), Daily Mail (commercial).

Beverley Binda   020-7377 1164 Mobile 07802-310801
Bleak House (TV drama), Hellboy (feature), Stage Beauty
(feature).

Sarah Birkett   Mobile 07958-538872

Kirsty Birnstiel   Mobile 07801-480568
Waking The Dead (TV drama), Silent Witness (TV drama).

Sue Black   01494-563658 Mobile 07885-365357
Shine (feature), Crocodile Shoes (TV drama), The Vicar Of Dibley
(TV comedy drama).

Christine Blundell   020-7609 0395 Mobile 07970-796370
ITG 020-7636 6565 Fax 020-7609 0395
Casino Royale (feature) (Hair Designer), The Boat That Rocked
(feature), Sherlock Holmes (feature).

Linda Bodily   020-8876 7966 Mobile 07768-432667
The Da Vinci Code (feature), Entrapment (feature).

Clare Bonser   020-8877 9514 Mobile 07931-728065
Fax 020-8877 9514
Liquid News (TV light entertainment), Redemption Road (feature),
Kama Sutra (feature).

Corinne Bossu   Mobile 07856-541779
The Duchess (feature), King Kong (feature), Kidnapped (TV film).

Elisa Brandom   01442-384424 Mobile 07812-372931
Fax 01442-266995
Jam & Jerusalem (TV comedy drama), The IT Crowd (TV comedy
drama), Life Isn't All Ha Ha Hee Hee (TV drama).

Amelia Brauer   01825-733256 Mobile 07947-483057
Jonathan Toomey (feature), Before The Booker (TV light
entertainment), Sporting Talk (TV light entertainment).

Suzan Broad   020-8567 7293 Mobile 07710-286296
Hornblower (TV drama), Firelight (feature).

Lizzie Broadley   Mobile 07742-162931
Dead Man's Shoes (feature), Satsuma & Pumpkin (TV light
entertainment).

Jess Brooks   Mobile 07956-386355
Little Dorrit (TV drama).

Abi Brotherton   0117-377 4690 Mobile 07786-246062
Fax 0117-377 4690
The Libertine (feature), Breaking & Entering (feature), Charlie &
The Chocolate Factory (feature).

Laura Jane Brown   Mobile 07968-998667
Yves St Laurent (commercial), News Of The World Magazine
(stills).

Tina Brown   020-8289 0090 Mobile 07961-447201
Little Dorrit (TV drama), All About George (TV drama), Reversals
(feature).

Zoe Brown   Mobile 07980-898903
Valkyrie (feature), The Imaginarium Of Dr Parnassus (feature), The
Wolfman (feature).

Anita Burger   Mobile 07771-783167
Stardust (feature), Gosford Park (feature), Girl With A Pearl
Earring (feature).

Linda Burns   Mobile 07941-238663
Archers (commercial), Boots (commercial), British Telecom
(commercial).

Lois Burwell   020-8894 4018 ITG 020-7636 6565
War Of The Worlds (feature), Collateral (feature), Braveheart
(feature).

Nina Butkovich-Budden   Mobile 07511-548873

Jayne Buxton   Mobile 07860-742044
The Wolfman (feature), Miss Potter (feature), Notes On A Scandal
(feature).

Judy Cain   020-7350 2293 Mobile 07788-454749
Fax 020-7223 2120
The Two Ronnies (TV light entertainment), Miss UK (TV light
entertainment), Shoestring (TV drama).

Tricia Cameron   01923-836980 Mobile 07860-831454
EXEC 01753-646677
Last Chance Harvey (feature), 102 Dalmatians (feature), Death
Defying Acts (feature).

Elaine Carew   Mobile 07710-254892 WZ 020-7437 2055
From Time To Time (feature), My Beautiful Laundrette (feature),
Brazil (feature).

Joanna Casserley   Mobile 07802-458676
Later With Jools Holland (TV light entertainment), Persuasion
(feature), I Dreamed Of Africa (feature).

Linda Catlin   01932-223801
Hancock & Joan (TV drama).

Kirstin Chalmers   020-7263 1766 Mobile 07767-893786
UA 020-3214 0800 Fax 020-7263 1766
RocknRolla (feature), Lesbian Vampire Killers (feature), The Bank
Job (feature).

Sarah Cherry   020-8960 1447 Mobile 07769-704604
RED 020-8374 3074

Fiona Clegg   020-8940 8859 Mobile 07961-051342
The Crooked Man (TV drama), Sharpe (TV drama), Stella Does Tricks (feature).

Anna Cobley   Mobile 07973-368541
Memphis Belle (feature), Close My Eyes (feature), Casualty (TV drama).

Karen Cohen   020-8854 4648 Mobile 07971-020073
Fax 020-8854 4648
Prince Of Persia (feature), Wanted (feature), Children Of Men (feature).

Jane Cole   020-7937 1288 Mobile 07880-792317
Too Good To Be True (TV drama) (Assistant), Love Again (TV film) (Assistant), The Vice (TV drama).

Hanna Coles   Mobile 07831-353317
The Wedding Date (feature), Ali G In Da House (feature), Band Of Brothers (TV drama).

Cicely Connelly   Mobile 07767-366547
EastEnders (promo), Holby City (TV drama), The Bill (TV drama).

Louise Constad   020-7262 9553 Mobile 07958-621344
MCR 020-7720 6234 Fax 020-7262 9553
Sophie Ellis Bextor (promo), Max Factor (commercial), Nivea (commercial).

Nuala Conway   Mobile 07768-344020
Cold Mountain (feature), The Hours (feature), The Statement (feature).

Carol Cooper   01225-480708 Mobile 07831-504124
Lark Rise To Candleford (TV drama), Mistresses (TV drama), Housewife 49 (TV drama).

Hajera Coovadia   020-7402 3006 Mobile 07779-095924
Fax 020-7402 3006
Handle With Care (TV film), Such A Long Journey (feature), Bollywood Awards (TV light entertainment).

Donna May Cordery   Mobile 07958-518459
Loose Women (TV light entertainment), SM:tv (TV light entertainment), Pop Idol (TV light entertainment).

Pauline Cox   020-8398 8389 Mobile 07976-988658
From Time To Time (feature), The Divine Michelangelo (TV doc), Prunella Scales: Looking For Victoria (TV doc).

Ang Coxley Evans   Mobile 07789-763462
Boogie Woogie (feature).

Francoise Cresson   01728-830499 Mobile 07771-983876
Star Stories (TV light entertainment), Green Wing (TV comedy drama), Holby City (TV drama).

Linda Crozier   01423-521975 Mobile 07721-050235
Heartbeat (TV drama), Emmerdale (TV drama).

Julia Cruttenden   020-8579 4806 Mobile 07973-636778
Fax 020-8840 3983

Betsan Dafydd   Mobile 07825-339063
Rownd & Rownd (TV drama), Small Country (TV drama), The Real Mario Grey (TV drama).

Michelle Daniels   01923-681804 Mobile 07850-054634
Top Gear (TV light entertainment), This Morning (TV magazine), Petrolheads (TV light entertainment).

Julie Dartnell   01344-444983 Mobile 07801-354960
Fax 01344-444983
Gulliver's Travels (feature) (2nd unit), Miss Potter (feature), Breaking & Entering (feature).

Fay De Bremaeker   Mobile 07973-361751
The Girl In The Cafe (TV film), Hawking (TV film), Hustle (TV drama).

Carol De Vine   01273-719085 Mobile 07765-110543

Nicky Dell   01923-285881 Mobile 07711-023092
Foyle's War (TV drama), EastEnders (promo), Silent Witness (TV drama).

Linda Devetta   020-7722 4662 Mobile 07785-251420
Fax 020-7586 0546
Quantum Of Solace (feature), The Bridge Of San Luis Rey (feature), Closer (feature).

Naomi Donne   020-8969 6107 Mobile 07815-706710
Quantum Of Solace (feature).

Jo Drake   Mobile 07803-501983
Crimewatch (TV doc), Kirsty Young Interviews (TV light entertainment), Peroni (stills).

Lisa Dredge   Mobile 07885-305174 SR 020-7736 7786
T Mobile (commercial), Volvo (commercial), JB Whisky (commercial).

Emma-Dee Drew   01784-885406 Mobile 07702-252481
Land Of Leather (commercial), Sylvia (feature), Christian Dior (fashion).

Anna Dryhurst   01344-841173 Mobile 07860-422353
Hudson Hawk (feature), Hope & Glory (feature), Party Of Five (TV drama).

Kathy Ducker   0161-764 8429 Mobile 07885-258950
Fax 0161-764 5080
Sahara (feature), Longford (TV drama), Instinct (TV drama).

Jennifer Eades-England   020-8428 6121
Mobile 07956-312600 Fax 020-8428 6121
Pride & Prejudice (feature), EastEnders (promo).

Anne Edwards   020-8942 2131 Mobile 07801-884914

Bean Ellis   020-7371 5540 Mobile 07885-756779
WZ 020-7437 2055 Fax 020-7371 5540

Karen Evans   Mobile 07985-407534
Never Mind The Buzzcocks (TV light entertainment), Jonathan
Toomey (feature).

Melissa Evans   Mobile 07810-500858
Never Mind The Buzzcocks (TV light entertainment), Big Brother (TV
reality), Nike (commercial).

Sallie Evans   01344-773747 Mobile 07973-152505
Harry Potter & The Goblet Of Fire (feature), Harry Potter & The
Prisoner Of Azkaban (feature), Harry Potter & The Chamber Of
Secrets (feature).

Karen Farrell   0121-624 7958 Mobile 07931-164271

Marlene Farrell   Mobile 07710-444484
Adulthood (feature), Hit Me Baby One More Time (TV light
entertainment), Des & Mel (TV magazine).

Annette Field   020-7371 3695 Mobile 07930-667800
The Mutant Chronicles (feature).

Andrea Finch-Pennell   01932-354544
Mobile 07980-269202 Fax 01932-354544
Harry Potter & The Order Of The Phoenix (feature), Harry Potter &
The Goblet Of Fire (feature), The Mummy Returns (feature) (2nd
unit).

Louise Fisher   01834-844605 Mobile 07802-251369
Fax 01834-844605
The Wolfman (feature), The Young Victoria (feature), The Duchess
(feature).

Cathy Flesher   01962-863645 Mobile 07850-453904
The Vice (TV drama) (Make-Up Designer), Take A Girl Like You (TV
drama).

Charlotte Foster-Brown   01923-771998
Mobile 07899-973829 Fax 01923-771998
Absolutely Fabulous (TV comedy drama).

Margaret Fozard   01484-723677 Mobile 07833-378411
Coronation Street (TV drama), Prime Suspect (TV drama), A Touch
Of Frost (TV drama).

Julia Francis   Mobile 07803-121923
Hitchhiker's Guide To The Galaxy (feature), Bacardi (commercial),
Star Wars: Episode III - Revenge Of The Sith (feature).

Charmaine Fuller   01273-205959 Mobile 07831-500400
Fax 01273-205959
Elizabeth: The Golden Age (feature), The Golden Compass (feature),
David Cronenberg Untitled 2006 (feature).

Nikki Galan-Bamfield   01249-820053
Mobile 07986-552832
Dangerous Parking (feature).

Jennifer Gilling   01886-884398 Mobile 07903-824504
The Golden Sphere (short), Expresso (short), On A Roll
(corporate).

Clare Golds   0161-485 1988 Mobile 07966-233648
Apparitions (TV drama), The Forsyte Saga (TV drama), Early Doors
(TV drama).

Paul Gooch   Mobile 07850-152336
Gulliver's Travels (feature), The Other Boleyn Girl (feature),
Sweeney Todd (feature).

Debbie Gould   020-8985 8107 Mobile 07956-917772
Fax 020-8985 8107

Amanda Green   020-8295 1732 Mobile 07947-442796
Fax 020-8468 7648
Just The Two Of Us (TV light entertainment), Rolf Harris Star
Portraits (TV light entertainment), The British Comedy Awards (TV
light entertainment).

Shelley Greenham   020-8950 1645 Mobile 07802-447403
Fax 020-8950 4344
The Green Green Grass (TV comedy drama), My Family (TV comedy
drama), Holby City (TV drama).

Christine Greenwood   Mobile 07836-680892
Miss Marple (TV drama), Elizabeth (feature), Gormenghast (TV
drama).

Sarah Grispo   020-8977 8785 Mobile 07973-834135
The Commander (TV drama), The Brothers Grimm (feature), The
Vice (TV drama).

Sarah Grundy   020-8995 0624 Mobile 07957-422357
Somers Town (feature), Sharpe's Peril (TV drama), Foyle's War (TV
drama).

Felicity Hague   01273-390276 Mobile 07749-420217

Gill Hall   01753-622133 Mobile 07970-793203
Who Wants To Be A Millionaire? (TV light entertainment), CBBC (TV
childrens), Live 8 (TV light entertainment).

Cara Halstead   Mobile 07900-241374

Caroline Hamilton   0141-959 7011 Mobile 07990-581512
Fax 0141-959 7011
Wilbur Wants To Kill Himself (feature), Holby City (TV drama), The Four Feathers (feature).

Gabrielle Hamilton   0113-275 4871 Mobile 07768-238824
Fax 0113-275 4871
Blessed (TV comedy drama), Fat Friends (TV drama), My Family (TV comedy drama).

Faye Sarah Hammond   Mobile 07950-462220
Sky News (TV news & current affairs), Sky Sport (TV sport).

Maureen Hannaford-Naisbitt   020-8977 6538
Mobile 07802-323633 Fax 020-8977 6538
Rosemary & Thyme (TV drama), The Inspector Lynley Mysteries (TV drama), Hornblower (TV drama).

Jennifer Harty   Mobile 07813-323676
The Mutant Chronicles (feature).

Debra Hawkins   Mobile 07976-916912
Razorfish (feature), Tattoo (commercial), Rockface (TV drama).

Pat Hay   020-7263 0545 Mobile 07976-352409
Fax 020-7263 0545
St Trinian's (feature), Sherlock Holmes (feature), Doc Martin (TV drama).

Charlotte Hayward   Mobile 07748-732955
Prince Of Persia (feature).

Maureen Hetherington   020-8317 8084
Mobile 07774-952251 Fax 020-8317 8084
Closing The Ring (feature), Syriana (feature) (2nd unit), The Bourne Supremacy (feature).

Catherine Heys   01494-474540 Mobile 07702-563083
Harry Potter & The Half-Blood Prince (feature) (2nd unit), The Dark Is Rising (feature), The Last Samurai (feature).

Ashley Hill   Mobile 07850-596134
Bad Girls (TV drama).

Laura Hill   Mobile 07889-993270
Bad Girls (TV drama).

Lorraine Hill   Mobile 07956-308061
Minotaur (feature), The Merchant Of Venice (feature), Fish Tales (feature).

Joan Hills   Mobile 07802-753536
As You Like It (feature), Gormenghast (TV drama), The Borrowers (feature).

Belinda Hodson   01494-730576 Mobile 07761-301971
Fax 01494-730576
Love & Other Disasters (feature), Harry Potter & The Order Of The Phoenix (feature), Piccadilly Jim (feature).

Carol Hoffmann   020-7351 2926 Mobile 07956-556104

Russ Holloway   Mobile 07976-967755
Wings Of Angels (TV film), Harry & Cosh (TV drama), Everyone's Got One (TV light entertainment).

Sharon Holloway   020-8985 0843 Mobile 07966-303354
Krakatoa: The Last Days (TV docu drama), Saxon (feature), Black Kids (promo).

Jane Hope-Kavanagh   Mobile 07973-793519
Elizabeth I (TV drama), The Commander (TV drama), King Arthur (feature).

Joe Hopker   020-8567 4272 Mobile 07710-521849
The Young Victoria (feature), Elizabeth: The Golden Age (feature), Phantom Of The Opera (feature) (Assistant).

Brigitte Hopkins   01992-448241 Mobile 07979-426568
Red Cap (TV drama), Small World (short), Child Of The Jago (theatre).

Jill Hornby   Mobile 07771-783774

Charlie Hounslow   Mobile 07712-527292
The Firm (feature), The Hills Have Eyes II (feature), The Mutant Chronicles (feature).

Pauline Hudson   Mobile 07885-700767

Carmel Jackson   020-8856 1444 Mobile 07976-251918
Fax 020-8856 1444
Gulliver's Travels (feature), The Da Vinci Code (feature), Flyboys (feature).

Annabel Jardella   020-8964 2484 Mobile 07973-637885
Afterlife (TV drama), What A Girl Wants (feature), Alexander (feature).

Deborah Jarvis   01654-710336 Mobile 07968-040411
Hellboy 2: The Golden Army (feature), Munich (feature), Alexander (feature).

Jacquie Jefferies   01727-866530 Mobile 07778-454407

Anna Johnson   020-8813 2932 Mobile 07711-706665
Fax 020-8813 2932
Plotlands (TV drama), The Marriage Of Figaro (opera), Sky News (TV news & current affairs).

Clare Johnson   Mobile 07813-813205
Maximo Park (promo), London Fashion Week (fashion).

Helen Johnson   020-8395 1200 Mobile 07812-249887
The Madness Of King George (feature), St Trinian's (feature), Miss Potter (feature).

Graham Johnston   Mobile 07836-604661
Children Of Men (feature), Love Actually (feature), Bridget Jones's Diary II (feature).

Vikky Johnston   Mobile 07736-846366
Lawless (TV drama), Goal! (feature), Sarin (TV drama).

Claire Jones   01302-714452 Mobile 07050-225849
Fax 01302-714452
Mischief Night (feature) (Make-Up Designer), The Death Of Klinghoffer (TV film), Principles Of Lust (feature).

Debra Pia Jones   Mobile 07796-892576

Teresa Kelly   020-8543 1996 Mobile 07831-829230
Persuasion (feature), The Upside Of Anger (feature) (Hairdresser), My Family & Other Animals (TV drama).

Harriet Kennedy   020-8948 1952 Mobile 07973-332236
Everything Must Go (TV light entertainment), Silent Witness (TV drama) (Assistant), The Bill (TV drama).

Alex King   Mobile 07956-171454
Rogue Trader (feature), Love Is The Devil (feature), Gladiator (feature).

Mel Kinsman   020-7221 7021 Mobile 07785-990178
Ministry Of Sound (commercial), Oil Of Olay (commercial).

Anthony Kitcher   01253-310218 Mobile 07799-153790
Coronation Street (TV drama), Linda Nolan Video Diaries (TV doc), For One Night Only - Builders In Drag (TV doc).

Kathy Kneller   Mobile 07710-095150
Dalziel & Pascoe (TV drama), Murphy's Law (TV drama), The Colour Of Magic (TV film).

Amanda Knight   01293-863939 Mobile 07831-238830
Harry Potter & The Goblet Of Fire (feature), Harry Potter & The Prisoner Of Azkaban (feature), Harry Potter & The Chamber Of Secrets (feature).

Antonia Krieger   01737-249844 Mobile 07711-762142
Fax 01737-249844
OFI Sunday (TV light entertainment), Frankenstein (TV drama), Bubble & Squeak (TV childrens).

Stacey Kutzak   Mobile 07870-138156
Fathers Of Girls (feature), Reverb (feature), Rollin With The Nines (feature).

Cor Kwakernaak   HERS 0844-811 6811

Melissa Lackersteen   01932-828117 Mobile 07774-235681
Fax 01932-852711
Robin Hood (feature), Prince Caspian (feature), Casino Royale (feature).

Emma Jane Ladds   01205-722606 Mobile 07795-163562

Rebecca Lafford   020-8856 7879 Mobile 07785-533321
Fax 020-8856 7879
Prince Of Persia (feature), Rendition (feature), Proof (feature).

Mary Ellen Lamb   Mobile 07718-862239
Fly Fishing (feature), One 2 One (commercial).

Marese Langan   Mobile 07831-748324
A Mighty Heart (feature), The Boy In The Striped Pyjamas (feature), Kingdom Of Heaven (feature).

Stephanie Latty   01384-827600 Mobile 07814-096385
Scrooge (theatre), Expresso (short), The Golden Sphere (short).

Mai Layton   01923-827703 Mobile 07796-176709
Phantom Of The Opera (feature), Mrs Henderson Presents (feature).

Clare Le Vesconte   01736-732463 Mobile 07831-274326
Harry Potter & The Goblet Of Fire (feature), Harry Potter & The Prisoner Of Azkaban (feature), Harry Potter & The Chamber Of Secrets (feature).

Tracy Lee   020-7259 2251 Mobile 07785-565619
Pride & Prejudice (feature), Sylvia (feature), Austin Powers (feature).

Delia Letham   01786-464108 Mobile 07977-140712
Fax 01786-464108
Stone Of Destiny (feature), The Old Course (TV drama), The Baldy Man (TV comedy drama).

Tony Lilley   Mobile 07973-755186
Shaun Of The Dead (feature), Trauma (feature), Life Begins (TV drama).

Corinne Lucy-Howlett   01932-223140
Mobile 07956-808115
Marie Antoinette (feature), AOL (commercial), Live 8 (TV light entertainment).

Saleena Malik   020-8251 7885 Mobile 07944-153687

Keely Mangham   020-8761 5550 Mobile 07855-403172

Shelly Manser Cavanagh   020-8255 1105
Mobile 07931-780960
Silent Witness (TV drama), The Gunpowder Plot (TV docu drama), Jack The Ripper (TV docu drama).

Heather Manson   Mobile 07715-105927
Booked Out (feature) (Make-Up Designer), Nowhere Boy (feature), Creation (feature).

Kelly Marazzi   Mobile 07976-393604
Sleuth (feature), Alfie (feature), Angus Thongs & Perfect Snogging (feature).

Eva Marieges-Moore 020-8286 7181 Mobile 07778-556411
BA 020-7836 1112 Fax 020-8286 7181
Poirot (TV drama), Silent Witness (TV drama), Mayo (TV drama).

Sharon Martin   Mobile 07956-570153
Prince Of Persia (feature), In Bruges (feature), The Last King Of Scotland (feature).

Suzanna Martin   01937-531603 Mobile 07721-433176
Emmerdale (TV drama), Whatever Happened To Harold Smith? (feature), Stone Scissors Paper (TV film).

Carolyne Martini   Mobile 07889-305570
Grown Ups (TV comedy drama), 2 Pints Of Lager (TV comedy drama).

Sally Mason   01636-674557 Mobile 07973-549668

Sophia Mason   Mobile 07880-720013
Mysti (TV childrens), Science Of The Shroud (TV doc), Mission Implausible (TV light entertainment).

Karon Mathers   Mobile 07775-686041
The Colour Of Magic (TV film), Genie In The House (TV childrens).

Claire Matthews   01932-569975 Mobile 07778-058025
EastEnders (promo).

Nicola Matthews   Mobile 07973-558938
Wild Target (feature), Shanghai (feature), Keeping Mum (feature).

Nuria Mbomio   Mobile 07958-988384
Hippie Hippie Shake (feature), Sunshine (feature), Casino Royale (feature).

Marilyn McDonald   020-8995 3508 Mobile 07973-216883
Prince Of Persia (feature), Syriana (feature), The Bourne Ultimatum (feature).

Tara McDonald   Mobile 07785-767596
Goal! (feature), My Summer Of Love (feature), Robin Hood (TV drama).

Alexis McDougal   Mobile 07834-354741
Bad Girls (TV drama).

Ann McEwan   01349-862031 Mobile 07979-596076
Fax 01349-864616
Rebus (TV drama), Kevin & Perry Go Large (feature), Monarch Of The Glen (TV drama).

Maureen McGill   020-8876 2241 Mobile 07850-484419
Fax 020-8876 2241
Little Dorrit (TV drama), The Brothers Grimm (feature), Pirates Of The Caribbean: The Curse Of The Black Pearl (feature) (Hairdresser).

Lorna McGowan   01233-730867 Mobile 07957-115169
Children Of Men (feature), Flyboys (feature), Love Actually (feature).

Ian McIntosh   Mobile 07957-649587
Kept (TV reality), Pantene (commercial), The Osbornes (TV light entertainment).

Lois McIntosh   Mobile 07899-956600
Little Dorrit (TV drama).

Deborah McKinlay   Mobile 07768-796118

Lisa McNally   01892-652298 Mobile 07855-785113

Katie Meakin   020-8941 3051 Mobile 07702-991223
Bradford Riots (TV film), Perfect Parents (TV film), Planespotting (TV drama).

Karen Megranahan   0870-242 3628 Mobile 07774-728728

Dianne Millar   020-8941 1643 Mobile 07773-869458
Fax 020-8941 1643
Brahms (TV film), Charlie The Kid (TV film), Caucasion Chalk Circle (TV drama).

Ruth Mitchell   Mobile 07974-790732
The Duchess (feature), Doctor Who Tardisodes (TV drama), Curse Of The Were-Rabbit (feature).

Sarah Monzani   01895-236090 Mobile 07850-196038
LLM 01372-450135 Fax 01895-236367
The Magic Flute (feature), Evita (feature), Quest For Fire (feature).

Alison Mountford   Mobile 07836-549845
Booze Cruise (TV film), Footballers' Wives (TV drama).

John Munro   029-2037 3339 Mobile 07887-623734
Casualty (TV drama), Dr Who (TV drama), The Libertine (feature).

Michi Nakao   020-7243 1612 Mobile 07774-458338
London Underground (commercial), Carling (commercial), Canon (commercial).

Corina Nicut   Mobile 07854-483949

Caroline Noble   020-8255 3957 Mobile 07774-133852
CCM 020-8743 7337 Fax 020-8255 3957
The Diary Of Anne Frank (TV drama), Fiona's Story (TV drama), Sex Traffic (TV drama).

Rosie Octon   Mobile 07742-435971
The Amazing Mrs Pritchard (TV drama), Hotel Babylon (TV drama), Judge John Deed (TV drama).

Anne "Nosh" Oldham   020-7286 6631
Mobile 07768-512429
The Girl In The Cafe (TV film), To The Ends Of The Earth (TV drama), Jane Eyre (feature).

Prue Oliver   Mobile 07932-684917   SC 01932-252577

Suzi Owen   020-8568 0819   Mobile 07973-669686
The Colour Of Magic (TV film), Waking The Dead (TV drama), Saving Private Ryan (feature).

Ang Oxley-Evans   01342-892039   Mobile 07789-763462
Hotel Babylon (TV drama) (Hairdresser), Mysti (TV childrens), Spivs (feature).

Terri Pace   020-7613 5434   Mobile 07939-698999
OK (magazine), CD:UK (TV light entertainment).

Talli Pachter   Mobile 07950-825695
Little Dorrit (TV drama).

Nathalie Page   01952-586787   Mobile 07876-592671
Haunted Homes (TV light entertainment), Disappearing Britain (TV doc).

Kerin Parfitt   020-8993 2949   Mobile 07802-478820
Fax 020-8993 2949
Scarlet Pimpernel (TV drama), The Wings Of The Dove (feature), My Life So Far (feature).

Sue Parkinson   020-8891 0982   Mobile 07976-248152
Thunderbirds (feature), Poirot (TV drama), Miss Marple (TV drama).

Belinda Parrish   01980-671597   Mobile 07802-294539
In Bruges (feature), The Da Vinci Code (feature).

Talli Patcher   Mobile 07950-825695
Sensitive Skin (TV comedy drama), Little Dorrit (TV drama).

Natalie Pateman   Mobile 07973-292563
The Line Of Beauty (TV drama) (Assistant), Spooks (TV drama), Hotel Babylon (TV drama).

Jane Paterson   020-8882 4608   Mobile 07885-151120
28 Weeks Later (feature), Trial & Retribution (TV drama), Diamond Geezer (TV drama).

Jane Pearce   01761-490611   Mobile 07774-879589
Fax 01761-490611
Rome (TV drama), Casualty (TV drama), The 200 Year Old House (TV drama doc).

Ros Peat   020-8870 5068   Mobile 07976-813197
Primeval (TV drama), Judge John Deed (TV drama), Waking The Dead (TV drama).

Daniel Phillips   020-7700 1022   Mobile 07788-106665
UA 020-3214 0800
The Duchess (feature), The Queen (feature), Bleak House (TV drama).

Lisa Pickering   01784-248535   Mobile 07831-201851
Fax 01784-248535
Atonement (feature), The Magic Flute (feature), The Da Vinci Code (feature).

Vivien Placks   020-8207 5502   Mobile 07831-745884
Fax 020-8953 3819
Birds Of A Feather (TV comedy drama).

Paula Price   Mobile 07774-909310
Nanny McPhee & The Big Bang (feature), Stardust (feature), Munich (feature).

Jenny Quille   Mobile 07976-671309
Sophos (corporate), SAP Computers (corporate), Freddie Starr (TV doc).

Nikita Rae   01273-880660   Mobile 07973-221923
The Other Boleyn Girl (feature), Pirates Of The Caribbean: The Curse Of The Black Pearl (feature), Troy (feature).

Sara Raeburn   020-8969 5409   Mobile 07771-534636
Colour Me Kubrick (feature), Chromophobia (feature), Marks & Spencer (commercial).

Clare Ramsey   Mobile 07792-840150
Robin Hood (feature).

Wendy Rawson   Mobile 07979-816020
101 Dalmatians (feature) (animal), 102 Dalmatians (feature) (animal), Oliver Twist (feature) (animal).

Tinks Reding   020-8986 7746   Mobile 07711-355153
GEMS 029-2071 0770
Alien Autopsy (feature), Enduring Love (feature), Charlie & The Chocolate Factory (feature).

Gill Rees   01446-760115   Mobile 07887-987348
Band Of Brothers (TV drama), Crush (feature), Mike Bassett: England Manager (feature).

Natalie Reid   020-8699 9252   Mobile 07976-366315

Gemma Richards   Mobile 07748-347315
Robin Hood (feature), Miss Potter (feature).

Sian Richards   Mobile 07860-555235 CMM 020-8584 5363
Silent Witness (TV drama), Live From Baghdad (TV film), The Upside Of Anger (feature).

Sara Riesel   Mobile 07956-327920
Piccadilly Jim (feature), Revolver (feature), Hustle (TV drama).

Vivian Riley   020-8840 1238 Mobile 07860-940416
Little Dorrit (TV drama), Waking The Dead (TV drama) (Make-Up Designer), Pride & Prejudice (feature) (Assistant).

Peter Robb-King   01628-620236 Mobile 07831-169080
Fax 01628-414060
The Dark Knight (feature).

Sue Robb-King   01628-620236 Mobile 07887-640834
Fax 01628-414060
The Dark Knight (feature), Batman Begins (feature).

Kate Roberts   Mobile 07950-561341
The Office (TV comedy drama), Poirot (TV drama), Gavin & Stacey (TV comedy drama).

Tori Robinson   Mobile 07968-159003
The Mark Of Cain (feature), Christmas At The Riviera (TV drama), Spooks (TV drama).

Steff Roeg   020-7289 4073 Mobile 07770-607597
WZ 020-7437 2055
First Sign Of Madness (TV drama), Nescafe (commercial).

Morag Ross   020-7720 2497 Mobile 07768-891129
Indiana Jones & The Temple Of Doom (feature), The Aviator (feature), Sense & Sensibility (feature).

Avril Russell   01371-830803 Mobile 07746-421437

Jutta Russell   Mobile 07973-917885
Blackbeard The Pirate (TV docu drama), Ten Days To War (TV drama), Pompeii: The Last Day (TV drama).

Tapio Salmi   01273-604503 Mobile 07966-391992
The Duchess (feature), The Edge Of Love (feature), Becoming Jane (feature).

Laura Schalker   Mobile 07941-230318
Open Wide (TV drama), Five Children & It (feature), Alan Clark Diaries (TV drama).

Loz Schiavo   Mobile 07930-911247
Casino Royale (feature), Samsara (feature), Stratosphere Girl (feature).

Janine Schneider   020-8994 3304 Mobile 07956-300441
The Golden Compass (feature), Lord Of The Rings (feature), Nine (feature).

Sarah Scott   01634-842424 Mobile 07771-788698

Kerry Scourfield   0151-427 8145 Mobile 07973-159807
Vera Drake (feature), Shiny Shiny Bright New Hole In My Heart (TV film), Saddam's Tribe (TV drama).

Debbie Scragg   020-7736 4887 Mobile 07850-027910
ITN News (TV news & current affairs), Sky News (TV news & current affairs), Bid Up TV (TV light entertainment).

Kerry September   Mobile 07748-594442 SC 01932-252577
Prodigy (promo), Wild On Tara (TV light entertainment), Odabash & McDonald Show (fashion).

Laura Jane Sessions   Mobile 07740-777910
DYA 020-7386 0310
Sky Sport (TV sport), Iyi Seneler (feature), Anaphylaxis (feature).

Jan Sewell   020-8292 0107 Mobile 07779-234177
UA 020-3214 0800
Run Fat Boy Run (feature), Agora (feature), Poirot (TV drama).

Angela Seyfang   01424-843534 Mobile 07714-032050
Edward & Mrs Simpson (TV drama), Rumpole Of The Bailey (TV drama), This Is Your Life (TV light entertainment).

Jenny Sharpe   020-8994 6115 Mobile 07973-491066
The Dark Knight (feature), Batman Begins (feature), The Last Samurai (feature).

Leda Shawyer   020-8567 2061 Mobile 07958-366793
55 Degrees North (TV drama), Wire In The Blood (TV drama), Murder City (TV drama).

Emma Sheldrick   020-8669 1978 Mobile 07711-658227
Bridget Jones's Diary II (feature), Johnny English (feature), Gladiator (feature).

Karen Sherriff-Brown   01494-433232
Mobile 07802-712586 Fax 01494-433232
Stardust (feature), Layer Cake (feature), Calendar Girls (feature).

Anne-Marie Simak   HERS 0844-811 6811

Lesley Smith   01582-767269 Mobile 07770-986464
Fax 01582-767269
Stardust (feature), Alexander (feature), Iris (feature).

Nicky South   Mobile 07887-596947
Spooks (TV drama).

Jean Speak   020-8994 9096 Mobile 07798-624747
Doc Martin (TV drama), Tom Jones (TV drama), Angel Cake (TV drama).

Meg Speirs   0141-341 0930 Mobile 07711-541630
Fax 0141-341 0930
The 39 Steps (TV film), Book Of Blood (feature), Summer (feature).

Paul Spateri   020-8995 2786 Mobile 07976-586137
Harry Potter & The Deathly Hallows (feature), Harry Potter & The Half-Blood Prince (feature), Harry Potter & The Prisoner Of Azkaban (feature).

Mike Stringer   0113-217 1300 Mobile 07870-600273
Fax 01943-877615
Undercover Dads (TV childrens), The Neanderthal Code (TV docu drama), Dil Bole Hadippa (feature).
www.hybridfx.com

Michelle Taylor   01628-828997 Mobile 07768-363386
Fax 01628-828997
Closer (feature), Blade II (feature), The League Of Extraordinary Gentlemen (feature).

Cliff Wallace   01895-251107 Mobile 07771-757819
Fax 01895-251102
Hellboy 2: The Golden Army (feature), Kingdom Of Heaven (feature), 28 Weeks Later (feature).
www.creature-effects.com

Simon Webber   Mobile 07947-363687
Doom (feature), Charlie & The Chocolate Factory (feature), Hellboy (feature).

David White   01903-816217 Mobile 07973-193669
Robin Hood (feature), Prince Of Persia (feature).

MAKE-UP BUYERS

John Lambert   020-8883 7388 Mobile 07932-641818
Harry Potter & The Order Of The Phoenix (feature), Harry Potter & The Chamber Of Secrets (feature), Harry Potter & The Prisoner Of Azkaban (feature).

MAKE-UP CO-ORDINATORS

Belinda Green-Smith 01695-571230 Mobile 07967-587235
Reverb (feature), Popcorn (feature), Charlie Noades RIP (feature).

Lyn Nicholson   01344-310177 Mobile 07765-360174
Harry Potter & The Goblet Of Fire (feature), Star Wars: Episode I - The Phantom Menace (feature), Mission: Impossible (feature).

MAKE-UP DESIGNERS

Valerie Ackrill   020-8815 9466 Mobile 07890-137721
Fax 020-8815 9466
Holby City (TV drama), Bo Selecta (TV light entertainment), EastEnders (promo).

Sallie Adams   01635-26886 Mobile 07930-713473
AMM 020-7244 1159
Fanny Hill (TV drama).

Jo Allen   Mobile 07774-201903
Mister Lonely (feature), The Sea Inside (feature), The Hours (feature).

Sarita Allison   Mobile 07976-264111
Skins (TV drama), Touching The Void (TV doc), Churchill: The Hollywood Years (feature).

Christine Allsopp   Mobile 07973-406067
CMM 020-8584 5363
Incendiary (feature), The Long Walk To Finchley (TV film), Miss Marple (TV drama).

Lynda Armstrong   01582-715698 Mobile 07860-210858
The Secret Of Moonacre (feature), Feast Of The Ghost (feature), Michael Collins (feature).

Jane Atkinson   01246-231391 Mobile 07860-103347
Fax 01246-231391
Emmerdale (TV drama), Loose Women (TV light entertainment), A Mind To Kill (TV drama).

Benita Barrell   01702-465513 Mobile 07802-422153
House Of Elliot (TV drama), The Full Wax (TV light entertainment), A Bit Of Fry & Laurie (TV light entertainment).

Kate Benton   Mobile 07720-296934 Fax 020-8567 0005
That Mitchell & Webb Look (TV light entertainment), Armstrong & Miller (TV light entertainment), Children Of Men (feature).

Scott Beswick   01977-618885 Mobile 07974-157384
Fax 01977-618885
Like Minds (feature), Heidi (feature), Can't Buy Me Love (TV drama).

Paul Boyce   Mobile 07932-467331
Casualty 1907 (TV drama), Soviet War Scare 1983 (TV docu drama), Too Much Too Young (feature).

Veronica Brebner   020-8840 2860 Mobile 07860-622016
The Da Vinci Code (feature), The Life & Death Of Peter Sellers (feature), Becoming Jane (feature).

Karen Bryan-Dawson 01923-773961 Mobile 07770-921583
Fax 01923-773961
From Time To Time (feature), Mr Eleven (TV comedy drama), Moon (feature).

Ann Buchanan   020-7244 1159 Mobile 07973-724934
AMM 020-7244 1159
Prince Of Persia (feature), The Merchant Of Venice (feature), Shadow Of The Vampire (feature).

Kim Burns   020-8567 0100 Mobile 07812-055938
England My England (TV film), Reeves & Mortimer - A Nose Through Nature (TV doc), Russ Abbot (TV light entertainment).

Lucy Cain   020-8997 8717 Mobile 07768-608735
Life Isn't All Ha Ha Hee Hee (TV drama), The Office (TV comedy drama), The Kumars (TV light entertainment).

Christine Cant   020-8220 7682 Mobile 07785-956601

Lisa Cavalli-Green   Mobile 07831-513505
Trinity (feature), Beautiful People (TV comedy drama), The Children (feature).

Charlotte Connolly   01491-636212 Mobile 07974-315270
Strictly Come Dancing (TV light entertainment).

Daphne Croker-Saunders   Mobile 07754-743439
Fax 0117-924 4966
Monarchy (TV drama doc), Down To Earth (TV drama), The Heart Of Thomas Hardy (TV docu drama).

Lin Davie   Mobile 07778-317891
Apparitions (TV drama), Doctor Who (TV drama), Bodies (TV drama).

Sarah Dickinson   Mobile 07973-866692
My Parents Are Aliens (TV childrens), Hyperdrive (TV comedy drama), My Spy Family (TV childrens).

Janita Doyle   Mobile 07973-150013
Poppy Shakespeare (TV film), Britannia High (TV drama), 24 Hour Party People (feature).

Nadia El-Saffar   0191-284 4549 Mobile 07966-233491
Fax 0191-284 4549
Northern Lights (TV drama), Distant Shores (TV drama), Wire In The Blood (TV drama).

Paul Engelen   01483-274677 Mobile 07990-554422
Fax 01483-274677
Robin Hood (feature), Quantum Of Solace (feature), Munich (feature).

Sandra Exelby   020-8998 7494 Mobile 07721-623728
Back To The Secret Garden (TV film), Feris Bela Gawd (TV drama), The Brylcreem Boys (feature).

Ann Fenton   020-8877 1737 Mobile 07951-200084
Katy Brand's Big Ass Show (TV light entertainment), The Unusual Miss Nightingale (TV drama doc), CS Lewis: Beyond Narnia (TV docu drama).

Claire Ford   020-8840 4599 Mobile 07976-370550
Casino Royale (feature), The Da Vinci Code (feature), Stranger Than Fiction (feature).

Katy Fray   01903-608539 Mobile 07786-994120
Dangerous Parking (feature), BackWoods (feature), Stupid (TV drama).

Mandy Furlonger   01737-843065 Mobile 07941-325705
Outnumbered (TV comedy drama), Graham Norton (TV light entertainment), The Apprentice (TV reality).

Pamela Haddock   0117-924 9917 Mobile 07771-548181
MM 020-8995 4747
Tess Of The D'Urbervilles (TV drama), Lark Rise To Candleford (TV drama), Persuasion (feature).

Jill Hagger   01458-850193 Mobile 07860-325987
Fax 01458-850193
Mobile (TV drama), House Of Elliot (TV drama), The Lost World (TV docu drama).

Lesley Hamon   Mobile 07774-628000
The Green Green Grass (TV comedy drama), Christmas At The Riviera (TV drama).

Frances Hannon   01895-834517 Mobile 07836-281696
Gulliver's Travels (feature), The Da Vinci Code (feature), The Gathering Storm (TV film).

Jan Harrison Shell   020-8878 9048 Mobile 07976-263313
Fax 020-8878 9048

Karen Hartley Thomas   Mobile 07973-294001
Little Dorrit (TV drama), Sense & Sensibility (feature), Longford (TV drama).

Pauline Heys   01494-862246 Mobile 07787-543600
Fax 01494-868411
The Last Samurai (feature), Captain Corelli's Mandolin (feature), The League Of Extraordinary Gentlemen (feature).

Mary Hillman   Mobile 07710-412961
A Dance To The Music Of Time (TV film), The Magnificent Ambersons (feature), Chariots Of Fire (feature).

Jacqueline Holloway-Russon   01275-817076
Mobile 07889-595990 Fax 01275-817076
Casualty (TV drama), Thread Across The Ocean (TV drama), Magic Grandad (TV childrens).

Suzanne Jansen   01449-761812 Mobile 07973-320820
Fax 01449-761812
Mirrors (feature), Prince Of Persia (feature), Exodus (feature).

Sallie Jaye   020-7266 4635 Mobile 07974-402063
Fax 020-7266 4635
Prince Of Persia (feature), In Bruges (feature), Gosford Park (feature).

COSTUME

Vanessa Johnson   Mobile 07976-251727 Fax 07970-094256
Lewis (TV drama), Midsomer Murders (TV drama), Ultimate Force (TV drama).

Meinir Jones Lewis   01570-422170 Mobile 07747-697944
CCM 020-8743 7337
The Fixer (TV drama), Boy Meets Girl (TV drama), Cape Wrath (TV drama).

Clare Juhasz   Mobile 07968-359809
The Colour Of Magic (TV film).

Eileen Kastner-Delago   Mobile 07798-698287
Angus Thongs & Perfect Snogging (feature).

Marianne Kerr   020-8340 5789 Mobile 07775-870942
Fax 020-8340 5789

Peter King   01761-434442 Mobile 07800-632118
Nanny McPhee & The Big Bang (feature), The Golden Compass (feature), King Kong (feature).

Sara Kramer   Mobile 07711-615567
Holby City (TV drama).

Lizzi Lawson   Mobile 07811-350128
W.E. (feature), The Eclipse (feature), Defiance (feature).

Ailbhe Lemass   01895-833762 Mobile 07990-572374
LLM 01372-450135 Fax 01895-833762
Valkyrie (feature), King Arthur (feature), Evita (feature).

Anne Marie Lepretre 01869-351393 Mobile 07831-557828
12 In A Box (feature), Sony (commercial).

Anna Lubbock   01428-712848 Mobile 07774-165058
The Weakest Link (TV light entertainment), Test The Nation (TV light entertainment), Outtake TV (TV light entertainment).

Marilyn MacDonald 020-8995 3508 Mobile 07973-216883
Scarlet Pimpernel (TV drama), Keep The Aspidistra Flying (feature), Last Chance Harvey (feature).

Sam Marshall   Mobile 07976-702961
The Street (TV drama), Eleventh Hour (TV drama), Cutting It (TV drama).

Linda Morton   020-8744 0249 Mobile 07831-188441
Fax 020-8744 0249
Primeval (TV drama), Waking The Dead (TV drama), Judge John Deed (TV drama).

Susie Munachen   020-8682 5257 Mobile 07970-977726
Magicians (feature), Spooks (TV drama), Law & Order (TV drama).

Irene Napier   0131-669 2795 Mobile 07831-350660
Bad Girls (TV drama), Down To Earth (TV drama), The Inspector Lynley Mysteries (TV drama).

Fran Needham   020-8876 4552 Mobile 07778-165277
Shanghai (feature), Moving Wallpaper (TV drama), Hustle (TV drama).

Dorka Nieradzik   020-8992 3952 Mobile 07966-217835
Fax 020-8992 3952
Children Of Men (feature), Derailed (feature), Closer (feature).

Peter Owen   0117-9738 768 Mobile 07801-099160
Lord Of The Rings (feature), Dangerous Liaisons (feature), Charlie & The Chocolate Factory (feature).

Anita Perrett   01932-241637 Mobile 07778-146052
Totally Frank (TV drama), Family Affairs (TV drama), See It Saw It (TV childrens).

Gilly Popham   020-8579 0368 Mobile 07961-428188
Hi-5 (TV childrens), Strictly Come Dancing (TV light entertainment), Princess Ka'Iulani (feature).

Trefor Proud   Mobile 07768-603903 MIL 020-7729 9226
Eragon (feature), Copying Beethoven (feature), Kinky Boots (feature).

Catherine Scoble   020-8840 3494 Mobile 07850-163840
This Is England (feature), Dirty War (TV drama), Lock Stock & Two Smoking Barrels (feature).

Aileen Seaton   020-8675 7674 Mobile 07798-622932
Shanghai (feature), Sahara (feature), Shanghai Knights (feature).

Marella Shearer   020-7787 7860 Mobile 07785-548809
House Of Saddam (TV drama), Wuthering Heights (feature), Spooks (TV drama).

Maralyn Sherman   020-8559 1942 Mobile 07713-989295
LLM 01372-450135
Celebration (TV film), French & Saunders (TV light entertainment), The John Culshaw Show (TV light entertainment).

Jenny Shircore   01797-270254 Mobile 07802-939615
MM 020-8995 4747 Fax 01797-270254
W.E. (feature), Elizabeth (feature), Mrs Henderson Presents (feature).

Penny Smith   020-8769 9178 Mobile 07768-453276
GEMS 029-2071 0770 Fax 020-8769 9178
The Wind In The Willows (TV film), Psychoville (TV comedy drama), Gandhi My Father (feature).

Tara Smith   Mobile 07831-398774 MIL 020-7729 9226
Half Light (feature), Factotum (feature), Freaky Friday (feature).

Heather Squire   020-8514 1912 Mobile 07811-423266
The Last Detective (TV drama), Schweppes (commercial), Alastair McGowan (TV light entertainment).

COSTUME

Joan Stribling   Mobile 07791-758480
She Stoops To Conquer (feature), Van Gogh (TV drama), The Funny Ladies Of British Comedy (TV doc).

Liz Tagg   020-8995 6316 Mobile 07702-591241
Penelope (feature), Hitchhiker's Guide To The Galaxy (feature), Band Of Brothers (TV drama).

Jessica Taylor   Mobile 07976-374156
Boy A (feature), Life On Mars (TV drama), Britain's Got Talent (TV light entertainment).

Deanne Turner   020-7229 5837 Mobile 07889-424080
Fax 020-7229 5837
Prime Suspect (TV drama), Margaret (TV drama), Einstein & Eddington (TV film).

Karen ZM Turner   01753-840093 Mobile 07785-286232
GEMS 029-2071 0770
Donkey Punch (feature), Margaret (TV drama), Cranford (TV drama).

Alex Volpe   020-7385 7875 Mobile 07956-465775
A Good Woman (feature) (Chief Hairdresser), Comme T'y Es Belle (feature) (Chief Hairdresser), Colditz (TV drama).

Alyn Waterman   Mobile 07778-606478
Hustle (TV drama), Holby Blue (TV drama), Footballers' Wives (TV drama).

Sheelagh Wells   020-8847 6270 Mobile 07979-504393
Fax 020-8847 6270
Victoria Cross (TV doc), Doctor Who (TV drama), Blood On Our Hands (TV drama).

Lisa Westcott   +33 4 68 51 05 72 Mobile 07774-869901
The Wolfman (feature), Stage Beauty (feature), Iris (feature).

Samantha Wilding   Mobile 07710-779799
Minder (TV drama), The Bill (TV drama), Bad Girls (TV drama).

Carole Williams   01600-750234 Mobile 07711-517453
Big Nothing (feature), Heidi (feature), Up N Under (feature).

Sarah Wilson   0114-268 2051 Mobile 07957-699112
Doctor Who (TV drama), Bodies (TV drama), Fat Friends (TV drama).

Tory Wright   020-8560 0781 Mobile 07766-034442
Dangerous Parking (feature).

Lizzie Yianni-Georgiou   020-8441 8707
Mobile 07973-118148 Fax 020-8441 8707
Stoned (feature), A Very Social Secretary (TV drama), VW Golf (commercial).

MILLINERS

Sean Barrett   020-8546 6924 Fax 020-8546 6924
Mrs Henderson Presents (feature), Phantom Of The Opera (feature), Shakespeare In Love (feature).

Simon Dawes   01323-722495 Fax 01323-431098
Harry Potter & The Philosopher's Stone (feature), Master & Commander (feature), The Lion King (theatre).

Catherine Delaney   01580-761218 Mobile 07866-373588
The Mighty Boosh (TV light entertainment), Les Miserables (feature), Shakespeare's Globe (theatre).

Marie-Louise Lowcock   01582-756365
Mobile 07931-524735
Middlemarch (TV drama), House Of The Spirit (feature), The Living Daylights (feature).

Lil Scott   020-7387 1239 Mobile 07982-467158
Little Dorrit (TV drama), The Duchess (feature), Bleak House (TV drama).

Karen Shannon   020-7250 1177 Mobile 07745-861862
Fax 020-7250 0297
Elizabeth: The Golden Age (feature), King Lear (theatre), Swan Lake (ballet).

STYLISTS - COSTUME DEPARTMENT

Rachel Beaumont   Mobile 07957-172644
Comic Relief (TV light entertainment), EastEnders (promo).

Ceril Campbell   Mobile 07831-506968

Lucy Ewing   020-7792 1049 Mobile 07973-407976
Prada (stills).

Angela Gusty   01223-316348 Mobile 07788-643157
Fax 01223-463180
Q8 Oil Calendar (stills), Laura Ashley (stills), Doc Martens (stills).

Annabel Hodin   020-7431 8761

Becky John   020-8341 2368 Mobile 07778-518305

Kate Kelly   0131-225 1968 Mobile 07836-678600
British Airways (commercial), British Gas (commercial), Ribena (commercial).

Cressida Lewis   020-7249 1878 Mobile 07768-797784
Goal! III (feature).

Ali Moloney Mobile 07831-377711
British Airways (commercial), Sony (commercial), Sainsbury's (commercial).

El Newton Mobile 07970-167040
Strictly Come Dancing (TV light entertainment), The Apprentice (TV reality).

Amanda Nilmadhub 020-8679 4407
Mobile 07939-307347

Sigi Phyland Mobile 07977-274934

Louise Sykes Mobile 07961-170155
The Clothes Show (fashion), The Times (magazine).

Phill Tarling Mobile 07973-122639
Who Dares Sings (TV light entertainment), Britain's Got Talent (TV light entertainment), Britain Does The Funniest Things (TV light entertainment).

Lilia Toncheva-O'Rourke Mobile 07769-941968

Kimberley Watson 020-7241 4821 Mobile 07768-737371
Fax 020-7241 4821
Citibank (stills), Olympus Cameras (stills), Renault (commercial).

WARDROBE

Jill Avery 01278-722880 Mobile 07767-688214
The Libertine (feature), Around The World In 80 Days (feature), Shanghai Knights (feature).

Charlotte Child Mobile 07932-623812
Quantum Of Solace (feature), Mamma Mia! (feature), Charlie & The Chocolate Factory (feature).

Elena D'Cruze Reynolds Mobile 07980-757003
The Upside Of Anger (feature), Fred Claus (feature).

Philip Goldsworthy 020-8809 4739 Mobile 07976-809279
Prince Of Persia (feature), The Mummy (feature), Saving Private Ryan (feature).

Anna Houghton 01237-441559 Mobile 07748-544373
Elizabeth (feature), The Misadventures Of Margaret (feature), The Borrowers (feature).

Phil Lester Mobile 07836-315357
Shaun Of The Dead (feature), The Mighty Boosh (TV light entertainment), Black Books (TV comedy drama).

Judith More 01753-642628 Mobile 07768-846646

James Pavlou 020-8693 7179 Mobile 07939-541037
Wimbledon (feature).

Helen Scarsbrook 024-7654 5596 Mobile 07944-585784
Dalziel & Pascoe (TV drama), All Creatures Great & Small (TV drama), Howard's Way (TV drama).

Adrian Simmons 01278-722880 Mobile 07767-688197
Nine (feature), Alice In Wonderland (feature), The Boat That Rocked (feature).

Nuala Tester 01895-832373 Mobile 07884-424432
Entrapment (feature), The Gathering Storm (TV film).

Jenny Wentzel 020-8438 6677 Mobile 07958-609902
Harley Medical (commercial), TetraPak (commercial).

WARDROBE - ASSISTANT

Sam Brooke-Taylor 01273-245534 Mobile 07798-624247
Amazing Grace (feature), Life Begins (TV drama), De Lovely (feature).

Estelle Butler 020-7277 8650 Mobile 07966-222386
Fax 020-7277 8650
Wonderful You (TV drama), In A Land Of Plenty (TV drama), A Kind Of Hush (feature).

Anabel Campbell-Yates Mobile 07958-963930
Captain Corelli's Mandolin (feature), Harry Potter & The Philosopher's Stone (feature), Die Another Day (feature).

Melissa Cook Mobile 07785-112030
Born & Bred (TV drama), Sex Traffic (TV drama), The Mayor Of Casterbridge (TV drama).

Bruno de Santa 020-8968 5180 Mobile 07710-940582
Children Of Men (feature), Casanova (feature), Troy (feature).

Harriet Eaton Mobile 07779-916734
Alice In Wonderland (feature), Casualty 1907 (TV drama), Cuckoo (feature).

Peter Edmonds 020-7720 6828 Mobile 07771-700068
Me & Orson Welles (feature), Children Of Men (feature), The Da Vinci Code (feature).

David Evans 01202-256984 Mobile 07860-951095
Harry Potter & The Prisoner Of Azkaban (feature), Gladiator (feature), Saving Private Ryan (feature).

Shula Fitzgerald Mobile 07940-734909

Brendan Handscombe 020-8961 4092
Mobile 07989-333374
Batman Begins (feature), Munich (feature), Charlie & The Chocolate Factory (feature).

Zoe Harvey   020-8674 8950 Mobile 07929-005554
River Queen (feature), Ladies In Lavender (feature), The Importance Of Being Earnest (feature).

Andrew Hunt   Mobile 07770-236836
Atonement (feature), Valkyrie (feature), Kingdom Of Heaven (feature).

Stephen Hyams   01438-237657 Mobile 07732-756179
Hotel Babylon (TV drama), EastEnders (promo), Agent Cody Banks II (feature).

Vikki Illing   020-8342 8163 Mobile 07775-615745
Children Of Men (feature), Alexander (feature), Millions (feature).

Helen Ingham   01752-822842 Mobile 07973-468319
W.E. (feature), Nanny McPhee & The Big Bang (feature), The Other Boleyn Girl (feature).

Rosemary Lis   Mobile 07960-122202
Enigma (feature), Spy Game (feature), Shackleton (TV drama).

Emily Newbold   Mobile 07768-430029
Last Of The Summer Wine (TV comedy drama), The New World (feature), Eragon (feature).

Sophie Norinder   020-7937 1855 Mobile 07889-983361
Kingdom Of Heaven (feature), Vanity Fair (feature), Shakespeare In Love (feature).

David Otzen   020-8442 2349 Mobile 07939-028466
The Wolfman (feature), Kingdom Of Heaven (feature), Proof (feature).

Stephanie Paul   Mobile 07979-601416
Harry Potter & The Order Of The Phoenix (feature), Children Of Men (feature), Fingersmith (TV drama).

Maria Phelan   0131-332 6515 Mobile 07815-764932
Fax 0131-332 6515
Taggart (TV drama), My Fair Lady (theatre).

Luan Placks   020-8348 6132 Mobile 07961-324819
Little Dorrit (TV drama), Miss Marple (TV drama) (Costume Designer), Phantom Of The Opera (feature).

Sunny Rowley   020-8965 6892 Mobile 07958-334005
Sweeney Todd (feature), Children Of Men (feature), Troy (feature).

Sunny Rowley   020-8965 6892 Mobile 07958-334005
Sweeney Todd (feature), Children Of Men (feature), Troy (feature).

Georgiana Sayer   020-7627 8339 Mobile 07947-077974
Goal! (feature), Charlie & The Chocolate Factory (feature).

Lucilla Simbari   020-7603 8153 Mobile 07932-729590
Quantum Of Solace (feature), Speed Racer (feature), Wanted (feature).

Sunita Singh   020-7252 4613 Mobile 07976-732451
The Black Dahlia (feature), Kingdom Of Heaven (feature), Sylvia (feature).

Alyson Smith   020-8840 2503 Mobile 07776-007403
The Lost Prince (TV drama), Vanity Fair (feature), The Lazarus Child (feature).

Esther St John Gray   Mobile 07780-968213
Nanny McPhee & The Big Bang (feature).

Rupert Steggle   020-8340 6667 Fax 020-8340 6667
Valkyrie (feature), Prince Of Persia (feature), Harry Potter & The Half-Blood Prince (feature).

Pippa Thorne   01603-622770 Mobile 07753-424716
Hobson's Choice (theatre), Cats (theatre), Romeo & Juliet (theatre).

Amanda Trewin   01803-782713 Mobile 07770-920937
Kingdom Of Heaven (feature), The Golden Compass (feature), Gladiator (feature).

Justine Warhurst   Mobile 07968-799956
Quantum Of Solace (feature), Mamma Mia! (feature), The Hours (feature).

Joanna Wright   020-7729 9074 Mobile 07939-208275
Pierrepoint (TV film), Sunshine (feature), 20,000 Streets Under The Sky (TV drama).

Tamsin Wright   020-8453 0334 Mobile 07980-557318
Breaking & Entering (feature), Venus (feature), Hitchhiker's Guide To The Galaxy (feature).

WARDROBE MASTERS & MISTRESSES

Russell Barnett   Mobile 07836-642030
Hitchhiker's Guide To The Galaxy (feature), Alexander (feature), Braveheart (feature) (Assistant).

Chris Bradshaw   01492-621049 Mobile 07990-850876
Across The Universe (feature), Kinky Boots (feature), The Queen (feature).

Anthony Brookman   020-8981 3122 Mobile 07768-116018
Fax 020-8981 3122
Elizabeth: The Golden Age (feature), Eragon (feature), Phantom Of The Opera (feature).

Rob Brown   020-8889 0101 Mobile 07905-118365
Amazing Grace (feature), Kingdom Of Heaven (feature), Alexander (feature).

COSTUME

Laura Ergis   020-8400 7641 Mobile 07764-581148
Dorian Gray (feature), City Of Ember (feature), The Golden Compass (feature).

Shula Fitzgerald   Mobile 07940-734909

Carolyn Handscombe   Mobile 07980-744943
The Golden Compass (feature), Munich (feature), Charlie & The Chocolate Factory (feature).

Mark Holmes   020-7704 0980 Mobile 07736-715590
Prince Of Persia (feature), Pirates Of The Caribbean: At World's End (feature), The Bourne Ultimatum (feature).

Kevin Jones   0121-588 6801 Mobile 07775-623738
Fax 0121-588 6801
Dancing On Ice (TV light entertainment), The Royal Variety Performance (TV light entertainment), Liza Minnelli (TV light entertainment).

Anna Kovacevic   020-7708 3682 Mobile 07774-979814
Miss Potter (feature).

Jane Leonard   Mobile 07940-065088
The Wolfman (feature).

Helen Mattocks   01628-780091 Mobile 07767-265144
Batman Begins (feature), Casino Royale (feature), The Da Vinci Code (feature).

Neil Murphy   020-8840 2853 Mobile 07958-230191
Fax 020-8840 2853
Children Of Men (feature), Harry Potter & The Goblet Of Fire (feature), Kingdom Of Heaven (feature).

Helen O'Donnell   01628-780091 Mobile 07767-265144
The Da Vinci Code (feature).

Adam Roach   01285-653323 Mobile 07711-326207
Prince Of Persia (feature), Quantum Of Solace (feature).

Jimmy Smith   01895-271304 Mobile 07847-544099
Is There Anybody There? (feature), The Dark Knight (feature), Children Of Men (feature).

WARDROBE SUPERVISORS

Anna-Maria D'Amato   020-8342 1027
Mobile 07958-641470
Spooks (TV drama), Burn Up (TV drama), West 10 LDN (TV drama).

Gemma Davison   01276-24979 Mobile 07808-496567
Bedtime (TV drama), The Vice (TV drama), The Lazarus Child (feature).

Tami French   Mobile 07785-915985
Bride & Prejudice (feature), Hotel Rwanda (feature), Messiah (TV drama) (Assistant).

Gordon Harmer   020-8800 6726 Mobile 07710-380259
Robin Hood (feature), From Time To Time (feature).

Anne Lavender-Jones   Mobile 07771-637247
Agent Cody Banks II (feature), 28 Days Later (feature).

Steve O'Sullivan   Mobile 07879-630861
The Last Detective (TV drama), Elizabeth: The Golden Age (feature) (Assistant), Doc Martin (TV drama).

Faith Thomas   029-2019 5105 Mobile 07771-755781
Little Dorrit (TV drama), Revolver (feature) (Wardrobe Mistress), Alfie (feature).

Pat Williamson   01932-784368 Mobile 07889-537594
Fax 01932-784368
She's Gone (TV drama), Spy Game (feature), Shackleton (TV drama).

WIG DESIGNERS

Jan Archibald   020-7721 7095 Mobile 07976-262099
Fax 020-7721 7026
Prince Of Persia (feature), The Duchess (feature), La Vie En Rose (feature).
www.wigslondon.com

Linda Cooley   01932-225796
Twelfth Night (theatre), Land Girls (TV drama), Hustle (TV drama).
www.sheppertonwigs.co.uk

Joanne Foster   01932-225796
Twelfth Night (theatre), Land Girls (TV drama), Hustle (TV drama).
www.sheppertonwigs.co.uk

Felicite Gillham   Mobile 07802-955908
Persuasion (feature), Restoration (feature), VE Day Celebrations (TV light entertainment).

Gillian Little   01932-225796
Twelfth Night (theatre), Land Girls (TV drama), Hustle (TV drama).
www.sheppertonwigs.co.uk

Richard Mawbey   020-7262 6565 Mobile 07788-743349
Fax 020-7723 1566
Little Britain (tour), Hairspray (theatre), Guys & Dolls (theatre).

COSTUME

WIG DESIGNERS

Claire Smith   01628-525465 Mobile 07961-160767
Little Britain (tour), Alastair McGowan (TV light entertainment).

Rita Smith   01628-525465 Mobile 07778-280092

Marion Wilson   01367-241696 Mobile 07879-200787
Fax 01367-242438
The Saint (feature), Pygmallion (theatre), Wisdom Of Crocodiles (feature).

Editing

DEPARTMENT

EDITORS

Kevin Ahern   020-8892 8136   Mobile 07931-563618
The Da Vinci Code (feature), Inkheart (feature), Angels & Demons (feature).

George Akers   Mobile 07973-656773   BA 020-7836 1112
Imagining Argentina (feature), Method (feature), The Only Boy For Me (TV film).

John Alcorn   020-8597 3642   Mobile 07702-114100
Soccer AM (TV sport), Bands Reunited (TV doc), Trail Of Guilt (TV doc).

Robert Alon-Monks   0113-379 2890   Mobile 07976-251741
Fax 07976-068361
Hollyoaks (TV drama), Countdown (TV light entertainment), Emmerdale (TV drama).

Romesh Aluwihare   020-8960 6598   Mobile 07905-056081
Revolver (feature), As If (TV drama), The Bill (TV drama).

Jonathan Amos   Mobile 07796-173625
Scott Pilgrim Vs The World (feature), Ashes To Ashes (TV drama), Peep Show (TV comedy drama).

Tariq Anwar   Mobile 07719-459139
The Good Shepherd (feature), The Other Man (feature), Revolutionary Road (feature).

Rick Aplin   01794-301677   Mobile 07850-499475
Seven Wonders Of The Industrial World (TV docu drama), Prehistoric Park (TV docu drama), Super Slim Me (TV doc).

Tony Appleton   01920-423420   Mobile 07808-892348
Watchdog (TV news & current affairs), The One Show (TV magazine), Project Catwalk (TV reality).

Alex Archer   Mobile 07968-194048
Man On Earth (TV doc), Pakistan's Taliban Generation (TV doc), Dispatches (TV doc).

Tim Arrowsmith   01590-626207   Mobile 07742-218830
TOVS 020-7287 6110   Fax 01590-672720
Seven Wonders Of The Muslim World (TV doc), African RocknRoll Years (TV doc), The Woodlanders (feature) (Assembly).

Nick Arthurs   01494-437630   Mobile 07966-169679
Casanova (TV drama), White Noise (feature), Little Dorrit (TV drama).

Nick Arthurs   01494-437630   Mobile 07966-169679
Little Dorrit (TV drama).

Sadek Asha   01273-683858
Finding Memet (feature), McCabe & Mrs Miller (trailer), The Return Of The Living Dead (trailer).

Mick Audsley   Mobile 07712-575956   CM 020-7287 4450
Tamara Drewe (feature), Prince Of Persia (feature), Harry Potter & The Goblet Of Fire (feature).

Derek Bain   01494-785678   Mobile 07711-479356
UA 020-3214 0800
Midsomer Murders (TV drama).

Hayden Baldwin   01785-812905   Mobile 07802-783625
Can't Cook Won't Cook (TV light entertainment), Capital Floyd (TV light entertainment), House Invaders (TV light entertainment).

Paul Trevor Bale   020-8932 6465   Mobile 07980-941586
Tory! Tory! Tory! (TV doc), My Precious Valentine (TV drama), Dreams Lost Dreams Found (TV film).

Clive Barrett   01923-285458   Mobile 07989-976695
Fax 01923-285458
Life Begins (TV drama), Omagh (TV film), Monarch Of The Glen (TV drama).

David Barrett   Mobile 07973-199292
Dr Who (TV drama), Dangerous Parking (feature), Survivors (TV drama).

David Barry   01787-379232   Mobile 07771-766593
How Clean Is Your House? (TV light entertainment), Impaled (TV doc), Teletubbies (TV childrens).

Jake Bernard   020-7624 4183   Mobile 07799-412538
Fax 020-7624 4183
New Tricks (TV drama), A Dance To The Music Of Time (TV film), Dalziel & Pascoe (TV drama).

Aurelio Bernardino   Mobile 07974-371765
Fax 01737-642970
Transworld Sport (TV doc), Premier Football (TV sport).

Emma Black   Mobile 07946-894052
Watching Desmond Morris (TV doc), Scotts (TV doc), The Train You've Been Waiting For (TV doc).

Richard Blackburn   Mobile 07878-636577
ZDB 020-7604 4100
Lost: The End Is Nigh (TV light entertainment), Ibiza Rocks (TV music), Bullrun (TV reality).

David Blackmore   01296-614751   Mobile 07811-116152
CM 020-7287 4450
Bouquet Of Barbed Wire (TV drama), Poirot (TV drama), Homeland (TV drama).

Caroline Bleakley   020-8579 1256   Mobile 07788-660958
Sea Of Souls (TV drama), The Commander (TV drama), Dalziel & Pascoe (TV drama).

John Bloom   020-7352 7836   ITG 020-7636 6565
Fax 020-7351 7885
Charlie Wilson's War (feature), Angels In America (TV film), Closer (feature).

William Blunden   020-8744 0459   Mobile 07921-707202
Jackboots On Whitehall (feature), Shanghai (feature).

Valerio Bonelli   020-7262 6564   Mobile 07930-267951
Cemetery Junction (feature), Incendiary (feature), Hannibal Rising (feature).

Frances Bowen   01524-842871   Mobile 07905-233241
This Little Farmer Went To Market (TV doc), Equinox (TV doc), House Doctor (TV light entertainment).

Victoria Boydell   020-7689 3778   Mobile 07950-459911
CM 020-7287 4450
Africa United (feature), Hush (feature), Occupation (TV drama).

Peter Boyle   020-8788 3147
Shanghai (feature), 1408 (feature).

Michael Bradsell   020-8992 4266   Mobile 07711-941643
Henry V (feature), Wilde (feature), Local Hero (feature).

Ida Bregninge   CM 020-7287 4450
Holiday (TV doc).

Sarah Brewerton   Mobile 07957-440435
Five Days (feature), Criminal Justice (TV drama), Life On Mars (TV drama).

Vinca Brown   Mobile 07714-286579
One Hundred Years One Hundred Movies (TV doc), The Wedding Cake (short), Tramp (short).

Nigel Buck   0117-377 1001   Mobile 07831-449642
Life (TV doc), Galapagos (TV doc), The Natural World (TV doc).

Kate Buckland   020-8571 6952   Mobile 07710-768642
Fax 020-8571 6952
The Hidden City (TV drama), Thomas The Tank Engine (TV childrens), Cleopatra (TV film).

Gavin Buckley   Mobile 07976-714295
The 27 Club (feature), Sirens (feature), Ironclad (feature).

Lois Bygrave   Mobile 07818-064613
Skins (TV drama), Lost In Austen (TV drama), Miss Marple (TV drama).

Billy Caine   020-8968 5513   Mobile 07866-758285
Doom Bar (commercial), Westcountry Live (TV news & current affairs), Inspector Morse (TV drama).

Nigel Cattle   Mobile 07770-393663
This Life (TV drama), The Inspector Lynley Mysteries (TV drama), Judge John Deed (TV drama).

Lucien Clayton   020-7603 8736   Mobile 07958-685721
Peep Show (TV comedy drama), Green Wing (TV comedy drama), Teachers (TV drama).

Anne Coates   020-7341 4202
The Golden Compass (feature).

Fiona Colbeck   Mobile 07785-757001   SPA 01932-571044
A Passionate Woman (TV drama), Fallout (TV drama), Merlin (TV drama).

Joel Corby   Mobile 07900-550095

Jon Costelloe   020-8749 2944   Mobile 07712-836944
JCA 020-7434 4143
Conviction (TV drama), Belonging (TV drama), Wall Of Silence (TV drama).

Danny Coster   020-7304 4403   Mobile 07957-634413
Fax 020-7304 4400
Flybe (commercial), Mamma Mio (commercial), Gillette World Sport (TV sport).

Belinda Cottrell   JCA 020-7434 4143
Aftersun (TV drama), Shameless (TV drama), Sugar Rush (TV drama).

Peter Coulson   01608-652215   CCA 020-7630 6303
Lassie (feature), Gulliver's Travels (feature), Shackleton (TV drama).

Peter Cox   020-8541 3137   Mobile 07981-007193
Soviet Echoes (TV doc), Africa's Child (TV doc).

Catherine Creed   020-8692 3355   Mobile 07798-670865
BA 020-7836 1112
Runaway (TV drama), Empathy (TV drama), Doc Martin (TV drama).

John Daniels   01747-861502   Fax 01747-861720
Curse Of The Were-Rabbit (feature) (voice breakdown), The Cramp Twins (animation) (voice breakdown), Heidi (feature) (voice breakdown).

Rashid Davari   020-8368 0831 Mobile 07778-059828
Fax 020-8368 0831
The Life Of A £10 Note (TV doc), Children's Hospital (TV doc), The Station Master (TV drama).

Stuart Davidson   020-8740 0586 Mobile 07960-778453
The Apprentice (TV reality), Out Of The Shadows (TV doc).

Lois Davis   020-7801 9390 Mobile 07811-452030
A Week In Politics (TV news & current affairs), The Power List (TV doc), The Power Of Love (TV doc).

Paul Dawe   Mobile 07960-438237
Time Team (TV doc), 1914-18 (TV doc), EastEnders (promo).

Mark Day   01932-862313 Mobile 07956-602613
ITG 020-7636 6565
Harry Potter & The Half-Blood Prince (feature), Harry Potter & The Order Of The Phoenix (feature), Sex Traffic (TV drama).

Anuree De Silva   020-7387 8670 Mobile 07739-466106
Thr3e (feature), Blessed (TV comedy drama), Trouble In Paradise (TV drama).

Daniel de Waal   020-7435 8917 Mobile 07764-586700
Hop Skip & Jump (TV doc), What Did You Do In The Great War Daddy? (TV doc), The Miracle Of Stairwell B (TV doc).

Andrew Denny   01279-793380 Mobile 07970-255571
John Pilger - Breaking The Silence (TV doc), Shot At Dawn (TV docu drama), Cold War (TV doc).

Chris Dickens   Mobile 07778-357235
Goal! (feature), Slum Dog Millionaire (feature), Hot Fuzz (feature).

David Dickie   Mobile 07768-400401
The Woodlanders (feature), Shanghai Vice (TV doc), Burgundy (TV doc).

Ian Differ   020-8778 0612 Mobile 07802-548562
Clash Of The Titans (feature), Green Zone (feature), Revolver (feature).

Bill Diver   Mobile 07905-181041 JCA 020-7434 4143
This Little Life (TV film), Soundproof (TV drama), Twentyfour: Seven (feature).

Humphrey Dixon   020-8741 1060 Mobile 07939-143908
JCA 020-7434 4143
Wimbledon (feature), Enemy At The Gates (feature), Lawn Dogs (feature).

Paul Dosaj   020-7794 0176 Mobile 07905-260130
My Heart Belongs To Dad (TV doc), The Trouble With Mother (TV doc), Dreaming Lhasa (feature).

Ben Drury   Mobile 07976-727138
Come Rain Or Come Shine (TV drama), Ashes To Ashes (TV drama), Waterloo Road (TV drama).

Guy Ducker   020-8846 9234 Mobile 07956-859750
Fax 020-8846 9234
En Tu Ausencia (feature), Brecha (feature), Heath: A Life Beyond Politics (TV doc).

Anne Dummett   020-7603 7775 Mobile 07803-724283
Horsepower With Martin Clunes (TV doc), Opera Italia (TV doc), Arena (TV doc).

Luke Dunkley   01483-898514 Mobile 07976-289644
Spooks (TV drama), Real Men (TV drama), This Life (TV drama).

Martin Elsbury   0117-906 4300 Mobile 07970-816653
Planet Earth (TV doc), Blue Planet (TV doc).

Richard Elson   020-8896 2655 Mobile 07979-750718
Spooks: Code 9 (TV drama), Secret Diary Of A Call Girl (TV drama), Chromophobia (feature).

Paul Endacott   01767-640292 Mobile 07721-560740
AMM 020-7244 1159 Fax 01767-640292
Being Human (TV drama), Spooks (TV drama), Frozen (feature).

William Ennals   01275 393675 Mobile 07958-451254
Bob Hope - The Other Side Of The Road (TV doc), The Verdict (TV doc), Walk On By (TV doc).

Sim Evan Jones   Mobile 07525-810337
Shrek (feature), The Lion The Witch & The Wardrobe (feature), Nanny McPhee & The Big Bang (feature).

Colin Fair   020-8293 6011 Mobile 07866-481911
Shameless (TV drama), Mutual Friends (TV drama), Hotel Babylon (TV drama).

Don Fairservice   0117-974 4282 Mobile 07875-172827
Beautiful Thing (feature), A Very British Coup (TV doc), Chattahoochee (feature).

Ian Farr   Mobile 07798-905220 ITG 020-7636 6565
Criminal Justice (TV drama), 24 Hours In London (feature), Sleep With Me (TV drama).

Toby Farrell   01672-851052 Mobile 07702-627284
The Protestant Revolution (TV doc), Tribal Wives (TV doc), Secret Millionaire (TV reality).

Jenn Feray   020-7275 7000 Mobile 07973-830064
People's Hospital (TV doc), Last Man Standing (TV doc), Lost In The Snow (TV drama doc).

Les Filby   020-8422 1932 Mobile 07970-757967
What's Wrong With British Politics? (TV doc), Rossetti (TV doc), Death Of A Porn Star (TV doc).

EDITING

Tony Fish   020-8340 2014   Mobile 07958-722590
Fax 020-8340 2014

Ardan Fisher   01737-240112   Mobile 07702-353591

Scott Flyger   020-8659 5543   Mobile 07880-633779
Robbie Coltrane: B-Road Britain (TV reality), That Mitchell & Webb Look (TV light entertainment), Waterloo Road (TV drama).

Nick Follows   020-7585 1832   Mobile 07831-289081
MI High (TV childrens), Weddings & Beheadings (TV drama), Cutting Edge (TV doc).

Alice Forward   Mobile 07710-495886
History Of Britain (TV doc), Horizon (TV doc), Contemporary Visions (TV doc).

Charles Frater   020-7827 9510   Fax 020-7827 9511
African Railway (TV doc), My Kidnapper (TV doc), Come Dine With Me (ident).

Julia Frater   020-7827 9510   Fax 020-7827 9511
A Long Way Round (TV doc), Year Dot (TV doc), Come Dine With Me (ident).

David Gamble   020-7267 7933
Shop Girl (feature), Veronica Guerin (feature), Shakespeare In Love (feature).

Jill Garrett   01275-333232   Mobile 07936-374000
Planet Earth (TV doc), The Natural World (TV doc), National Geographic (TV doc).

Paul Garrick   020-8579 5441   Mobile 07971-009821
JCA 020-7434 4143
Lost In Austen (TV drama), Take A Girl Like You (TV drama), Poirot (TV drama).

Nicolas Gaster   020-7736 6216   Mobile 07967-562373
DA 020-7437 4551
Welcome To The Rileys (feature), Coriolanus (feature), Moon (feature).

Stuart Gazzard   Mobile 07747-802077   DA 020-7437 4551
Battle For Haditha (feature), Severance (feature), The Football Factory (feature).

Anne Goudie   020-7354 0837   Mobile 07941-377408
Girl Cops (TV doc), Who Rules The Roost (TV doc), The Three Bears (short).

Colin Goudie   020-7354 0837   Mobile 07917-638963
Monster (feature), Man Dancing (feature), Holy Cross (TV film).

John Gow   0141-339 4701   Mobile 07974-670577
JCA 020-7434 4143
Shameless (TV drama), Life On Mars (TV drama), Messiah (TV drama).

Adam Green   Mobile 07979-642859
The Roman Mysteries (TV childrens), Lassie (feature), Fakers (feature).

Colin Green   CM 020-7287 4450
Five Children & It (feature), Dream Keeper (feature), Merlin (TV drama).

Crispin Green   01992-420434   JCA 020-7434 4143
Doctor Who (TV drama), Bodies (TV drama), House Of Saddam (TV drama).

Anna Gregory   020-7431 0533   Mobile 07984-015434
Fax 020-7431 0533
Children Of Men (feature), Fighting Bears Of The Punjab (TV doc), The Saint Making Business (TV doc).

Jon Gregory   020-8998 8639   Mobile 07855-310207
ITG 020-7636 6565
The Road (feature), Donnie Brasco (feature), In Bruges (feature).

David Griffiths   01686-430307   Mobile 07970-601919
Chez Dudley (TV light entertainment), Y Byd Ar Bedwar (TV doc), Wales This Week (TV news & current affairs).

Paul Griffiths-Davies   0161-456 6169
Mobile 07931-564321
Hollyoaks (TV drama), Living It (TV drama), Holby City (TV drama).

Marius Grose   0117-955 3055   Mobile 07719-484771
Bill Bailey's Bird Watching Bonanza (TV doc), Dispatches (TV doc), Britain's Worst Learners (TV doc).

John Grover   01494-713421   Mobile 07710-496779
Fax 01494-713421
Licence To Kill (feature), Forest Of The Gods (feature), Labyrinth (feature).

Celia Haining   Mobile 07960-975194   STA 020-7729 7477
The Deaths Of Ian Stone (feature), Freebird (feature), Dead Man's Shoes (feature).

Martin Hale   020-8579 5892   Mobile 07855-790460
TOVS 020-7287 6110
Escape To The Country (TV light entertainment), Fantasy Football 2004 (TV light entertainment), Futbol Mundial (TV sport).

Richard Halladey   01737-772762   Mobile 07803-046271
The Smoking Room (TV light entertainment), Not Going Out (TV comedy drama), Extras (TV comedy drama).

Peter Hallworth   01457-762763   Mobile 07973-919026
Bodies (TV drama), The League Of Gentlemen (tour), Phoenix Nights (TV drama).

Anthony Ham   0161-439 6254 Mobile 07980-270868
Salvage (feature), New Tricks (TV drama), Queer As Folk (TV drama).

Jim Hampton   020-8275 8396 Mobile 07939-286663
Secret Diary Of A Call Girl (TV drama), Holby Blue (TV drama), Plus One (TV comedy drama).

Robert Hargreaves   Mobile 07813-812856
Modern Times (TV doc), Cutting Edge (TV doc), The Real Q (TV doc).

PJ Harling   020-8313 3452 Mobile 07956-604069
Casino Royale (feature), Thunderbirds (feature) (visual fx), Hitchhiker's Guide To The Galaxy (feature) (visual fx).

Jane Harris   0117-924 6363
Sea Fever (TV doc), Rude Britannia (TV doc), Cutting Edge (TV doc).

Jon Harris   Mobile 07973-231607 ITG 020-7636 6565
Kick-Ass (feature), The Descent (feature), Layer Cake (feature).

David Head   Mobile 07710-400272
Desperate Romantics (TV drama), Little Dorrit (TV drama), The State Within (TV drama).

Gareth Heal   Mobile 07949-254674
Dispatches (TV doc), The Following (feature), Cyderdelic (TV comedy drama).

Les Healey   01628-530413 Mobile 07768-514984
DA 020-7437 4551
Meant To Be (feature), Tracy Beaker (TV childrens), The Hessen Affair (feature).

Penny Heighes   020-8977 7579 Mobile 07788-105868
Property Ladder (TV doc), Jordan & Peter Laid Bare (TV light entertainment), Ann Maurice: Interior Rivalry (TV reality).

Monica Henriquez   020-7485 1189 Mobile 07808-471731
War Takes (TV doc), Rising From The Ashes (TV doc), Bethlehem Diary (TV doc).

Howard Heywood   0118-981 5982 Mobile 07850-236738

David Hill   Mobile 07956-569053
Love + Hate (feature), Randall & Hopkirk (Deceased) (TV drama), Out Of Control (TV drama).

Geoff Hogg   01932-343316 Mobile 07814-398158
Churchill: The Hollywood Years (feature), Rhythm & Blues (feature), Stella Street - The Movie (feature).

Rodney Holland   020-7229 4598 MM 020-8995 4747
Fax 020-7229 4598
Dungeons & Dragons (feature), Messiah (TV drama), The Company Of Wolves (feature).

Charles Holloway   01708-341963 Mobile 07941-245170
Fax 01078-341963

Peter Hollywood   Mobile 07973-121026
Command Performance (feature), The Adventures Of Baron Munchausen (feature), Maybe Baby (feature).

Nigel Honey   Mobile 07703-272681
Ghosthunters Scotland (TV doc), Seconds From Disaster (TV doc), Car Booty (TV light entertainment).

David J Hope   01223-208511 Mobile 07803-606254
Timewatch (TV doc), Journeys To The Bottom Of The Sea (TV doc), The Elvis Mob (TV doc).

Mike Houghton   020-8568 6498 Mobile 07761-604362
The Man Who Killed Caroline Dickinson (TV doc), Storm Alert (TV drama), Hetty Wainthropp Investigates (TV drama).

Gordon Howe   0161-881 1988 Mobile 07710-434589
How To Live A Simple Life (TV doc), Weird & Wonderful Hotels (TV doc), Fern Britton Meets... (TV doc).

Niven Howie   MM 020-8995 4747
Hitchhiker's Guide To The Galaxy (feature), Dawn Of The Dead (feature), Lock Stock & Two Smoking Barrels (feature).

Ollie Huddleston   01208-737777 Mobile 07947-515315
Sisters In Law (feature), The Last Peasants (TV doc), Dunkirk (TV drama doc).

James Hughes   Mobile 07763-381888
Skins (TV drama), Married Single Other (TV drama), Being Human (TV drama).

Glenn Hyde   01736-786526 Mobile 07850-674561
Neighbours At War (TV doc), Timewatch (TV doc), The Making Of Eden (TV doc).

Huw Jenkins   Mobile 07533-092803
In The Womb (TV doc), Bad Boy (TV doc), How The Earth Was Made (TV doc).

Michael Johns   01494-728892 Mobile 07801-657062
Fax 01494-728892
Framed (feature), A Feast At Midnight (feature), Double X (feature).

Alan Jones   01544-318522 Mobile 07770-612845
JCA 020-7434 4143 Fax 01544-318901
Lark Rise To Candleford (TV drama), Vital Signs (TV drama), New Tricks (TV drama).

Lou Jones   020-7603 9847 Fax 020-7603 4032
The Duke & The Dictator (feature), Best Of British (TV doc), My Favourite Nosh (TV light entertainment).

EDITING

Andy Kemp 01268-743254 Mobile 07748-192746
TOVS 020-7287 6110
Citizen Journalists (TV doc), Swinging: The Patty Edwards Story (TV comedy drama), The Catherine Tate Show (TV light entertainment).

John Kerry 020-7639 9093
This World (TV doc), Panorama (TV doc), Battle For Islam (TV doc).

Nick Kershaw 029-2021 8888 Mobile 07850-993157
Extreme Fishing With Robson Green (TV doc), Dr Who Confidential, Seconds From Disaster (TV doc).

Philip Kloss Mobile 07775-891892 JCA 020-7434 4143
The Mark Of Cain (feature), To The Ends Of The Earth (TV drama), Daniel Deronda (TV drama).

Adam Knight 020-8686 1188
Strictly Soho (TV doc), Shoot The Writers (TV light entertainment), RADA - Behind The Scenes (TV doc).

Paul Knight 020-8567 0301 Mobile 07968-324984
The Passion (TV drama), The Other Boleyn Girl (feature), Bleak House (TV drama).

Maggie Knox 01483-202015 Mobile 07909-563738
Fat Doctor (TV doc), French Exchange (TV doc), In My Experience (TV educational).

Annie Kocur Mobile 07803-128241 AMM 020-7244 1159
Kingdom (TV drama), The Wind In The Willows (TV film), Anita & Me (feature).

Jason Krasucki 020-8883 0766 Mobile 07831-139239
AMM 020-7244 1159
Strike Back (TV drama), Bleak House (TV drama), Generation Kill (TV drama).

Justin Krish 020-8340 1661 Mobile 07974-916530
DA 020-7437 4551
Angus Thongs & Perfect Snogging (feature), Nanny McPhee (feature), Bride & Prejudice (feature).

Anna Ksiezopolska 020-8883 6082 Mobile 07747-805111
Fax 020-8883 6082
Alive: Escape From Avalanche Alley (TV drama doc), The Queen's Wedding (TV doc), Victory Is Your Duty (TV doc).

Matthew Langmead 01386-765634

Ray Lau 01438-228219 Mobile 07956-519686
Fax 01438-228219
Doom (feature) (visual fx), Sleepy Hollow (feature) (visual fx), Tomb Raider (feature) (visual fx).

Simon Laurie 020-7482 1157 Mobile 07710-358178
The Piano Tuner Of Earthquakes (feature), Rogue Traders (TV news & current affairs), Joe Smeal's Wheels (short).

Tony Lawson 01544-260326 CM 020-7287 4450
Ondine (feature), The Brave One (feature), The End Of The Affair (feature).

Kevin Lester 020-8348 1977 Mobile 07974-361835
A Room With A View (feature), Jericho (TV drama), Blue Orange (TV film).

Andy Lewis 020-7381 3696 Mobile 07768-382999
Nightline (TV news & current affairs), World News (TV news & current affairs), 20/20 (TV news & current affairs).

Joanna Lincoln Mobile 07976-429114
The Apprentice (TV reality), Grand Designs (TV doc), The Restaurant (TV reailty).

Ewa J Lind MM 020-8995 4747
The Warrior (feature), River Queen (feature), Under The Skin (feature).

John Louvre 0191-270 0656 Mobile 07522-957524
Wild West Country (TV doc), Magnetic North (TV doc), The Dales Diary (TV doc).

Bob Lowery 01442-242837 Mobile 07768-941304
Short Stories (TV doc), Top Guns (TV doc), 6th Extinction (TV doc).

Fiona Macdonald 0131-556 8876 Mobile 07712-649525
One Thousand Pictures: RFK's Last Journey (TV doc), Britain's Lost Wilderness (TV doc), Pride & Priviledge (TV doc).

Alex Mackie 020-7267 7933 MM 020-8995 4747
Going Postal (TV film), CSI: Crime Scene Investigation (TV drama), St Trinian's (feature).

Fergus Mackinnon 0141-563 9634 Mobile 07821-810065
BA 020-7836 1112
Torchwood (TV drama), Waterloo Road (TV drama), The Book Group (TV drama).

Andrew MacRitchie Mobile 07710-358269
ITG 020-7636 6565
Doomsday (feature), Stormbreaker (feature), Sahara (feature).

Brian Mann 01494-728675
Hamlet (feature) (visual fx), The Borrowers (feature) (visual fx), Memphis Belle (feature) (visual fx).

Susan Manning 020-8968 5665
Victoria Wood - My Big Fat Documentary (TV doc), 100 Worst Moments In TV (TV light entertainment), Homes Under the Hammer (TV light entertainment).

EDITING

EDITING

Bruno Mansi   020-8340 0548 Mobile 07833-518466
Ancient Rome: The Rise & Fall Of An Empire (TV drama), Zero Hour (TV drama doc), Lost Cities Of The Ancients (TV drama doc).

Jean Manthorpe   020-7328 8088 Mobile 07721-647180
Time Team (TV doc), No Going Back (TV doc), Portillo's Progress (TV doc).

Stefania Marangoni   020-8889 3285 Mobile 07930-431143
Semi Skimmed (short), Reality Bites (corporate), Dinner For Six (short).

Tim Marchant   JCA 020-7434 4143
Messiah (TV drama), Wire In The Blood (TV drama), Confessions Of A Diary Secretary (TV drama).

David Martin   020-8743 5432 MM 020-8995 4747
The Josephine Baker Story (TV film), Sid & Nancy (feature), The Shell Seekers (TV drama).

Adam Masters   01372-467322 Mobile 07759-203195
Waterloo Road (TV drama), The Bill (TV drama), Casualty (TV drama).

Andrew McClelland   020-8995 5751 Mobile 07050-053956
UA 020-3214 0800
Canterbury Tales (TV drama), Merlin (TV drama), God On Trial (TV drama).

Jamie McCoan   Mobile 07899-791740 UA 020-3214 0800
Lewis (TV drama), Silent Witness (TV drama), Doctor Who (TV drama).

Nick McPhee   01794-388409 Mobile 07976-327727
Downton Abbey (TV drama), Lark Rise To Candleford (TV drama), Doc Martin (TV drama).

Yan Miles   020-8459 0023 Mobile 07976-947004
Rock & Roll Fuck'n'Lovely (feature), The Prisoner (TV drama), Rome (TV drama).

Alastair Mitchell   020-7381 4336 Mobile 07973-717641

Sue Moles   020-7494 3383 Mobile 07711-079229

John Moratiel   020-8361 6897 Mobile 07785-231902
Cutting Edge (TV doc), Dispatches (TV doc), Cults Of The Suicide Bomber (TV doc).

Jonathan Morris   020-8958 8471 Mobile 07904-209977
The Other Boleyn Girl (feature), Looking For Eric (feature).

Andy Morrison   Mobile 07855-745532
Hotel Babylon (TV drama), Whatever It Takes (TV drama).

James Moseley   020-8291 2326 Mobile 07984-700052
Horizon (TV doc), Secret History (TV doc), Black Bag (TV doc).

Philip Moss   01923-223518 Mobile 07973-413431
Pride Of Britain (TV light entertainment), I'm A Celebrity (TV light entertainment), Hell's Kitchen (TV reality).

Enda Mullen   Mobile 07906-437979
Seven Ages Of Britain (TV doc), The Culture Show (TV arts), Art Of Eternity (TV arts).

Ulrike Munch   Mobile 07767-457626
Take A Seat (TV doc), United 93 - The Families & The Film (TV doc), Echo Beach (TV drama).

Tim Murrell   020-8255 9995 Mobile 07885-832052
Street Dance (feature), My Boy Jack (TV film), The Children (feature).

Colin Napthine   020-8402 7695 Mobile 07941-892911
Building The Olympic Dream (TV doc), Cut Up Kids (TV doc), The Brain Hospital (TV doc).

Paul Newson   Mobile 07961-535041
In The Beginning (TV film), Mary & Jesus (TV drama), The Seventh Scroll (TV drama).

Michael Nollet   Mobile 07909-588690
Harris's List: 18th Century Prostitution (TV doc), The Conspiracy Files: 9/11 (TV doc), Savage (short).

Bryan Oates   020-8874 7769 Mobile 07747-611130
Song For A Raggy Boy (feature), Foyle's War (TV drama).

Philip O'Dea   Mobile 07771-714526

Melanie Oliver   CM 020-7287 4450
Elizabeth The Virgin Queen (TV drama), Faith (TV film), Bodily Harm (TV drama).

Jackie Ophir   Mobile 07966-198698 SPA 01932-571044
Merlin (TV drama), Shameless (TV drama), Britannia High (TV drama).

St John O'Rorke   CM 020-7287 4450
The Hamburg Cell (TV film), Tomorrow La Scala (TV film).

James Orton   029-2056 4080 Mobile 07771-898194
Fax 029-2066 6322
The Pier (TV doc), 04Wal (TV magazine), Cwpwrdd Dillad (TV magazine).

Barry Osment   Mobile 07712-893803
Derren Brown (TV light entertainment), The Vicar Of Dibley (TV comedy drama), Christmas At The Riviera (TV drama).

Oral Ottey   0161-485 7438 ITG 020-7636 6565
Alien Autopsy (feature), Rome (TV drama), Dear Frankie (feature).

Russell Oxenden   01322-866809 Mobile 07956-349572
Numerous commercials.

Emma Oxley   Mobile 07791-742388
Hotel Babylon (TV drama).

Andrew Page   020-8863 1827 Mobile 07914-309481
Extreme Phobias (TV doc), To Kidnap A Princess (TV drama doc), My Crazy Life (TV doc).

Keith Palmer   01308-867640 Mobile 07816-499146
Hornblower (TV drama), Oklahoma! (TV film), Sharpe (TV drama).

Kant Pan   Mobile 07764-170797
Forget Me Not (feature), Kicks (feature), Boogie Woogie (feature).

Steve Pang   Mobile 07966-181662
The Chronicles Of Narnia: The Voyage Of The Dawn Treader (feature) (visual fx), 10,000 BC (feature) (pre-vis & visual fx).

Frances Parker   CM 020-7287 4450
Rome (TV drama), Inside I'm Dancing (feature), Band Of Brothers (TV drama).

Michael Parker   MM 020-8995 4747
Made In Dagenham (feature), Run Fat Boy Run (feature), Calendar Girls (feature).

Nick Parker   Mobile 07775-600744
The Commander (TV drama), The F Word (TV doc), Holby City (TV drama).

Stephen Parry   Mobile 07798-676633
Everything's George (feature), True Tales Of Terror (TV drama), Fred Dibnah - Age Of Steam (TV doc).

Alex Payne   020-8637 0573 Mobile 07966-501862
Dream Team (TV drama).

Jamie Pearson   020-8883 6061 Mobile 07790-020633
Fax 020-8883 6061
Dr Who (TV drama), King Arthur (feature), Spooks (TV drama).

Denise Perrin   01275-333867 Mobile 07973-148699
Coal House (TV drama), My Life - Children Of The Road (TV doc), Lie Lab (TV doc).

Barry Peters   01753-883369 Mobile 07798-742836
Marco Polo (TV drama), Porterhouse Blue (TV drama), In The Beginning (TV film).

Alex Pikal   01582-462885 Mobile 07973-825549

Barney Pilling   Mobile 07870-600674
Hotel Babylon (TV drama).

Ian Pitch   01934-842942 Mobile 07836-325779
Timeshift (TV doc), Timewatch (TV doc), Marty Feldman - Six Degrees Of Seperation (TV doc).

Pamela Power   01344-623137 Mobile 07836-658163
Lewis (TV drama), The Duellists (feature), Hunger (feature).

Paul Rapley   020-8891 6613 Mobile 07979-692447
Tribe (TV doc), Teaching Empire (TV doc), Doctors & Nurses At War (TV doc).

Terry Rawlings   020-8953 7520 Mobile 07956-491383
Phantom Of The Opera (feature), Entrapment (feature), Goldeneye (feature).

Nick Rayner   01923-775098 Mobile 07899-904010
Swing Time (TV doc), Search For Peace (TV doc), How To Be Home Secretary (TV doc).

Adam Recht   JCA 020-7434 4143
Ghost Squad (TV drama), 20,000 Streets Under The Sky (TV drama), Miss Marple (TV drama).

Tania Reddin   Mobile 07956-190920 ITG 020-7636 6565
Luther (TV drama), Generation Kill (TV drama), Pierrepoint (TV film).

David Rees   01753-883569 Mobile 07779-492148
CMM 020-8584 5363
Compulsion (TV doc), Survivors (TV drama), Torn (TV drama).

John Richards   Mobile 07831-434046 ITG 020-7636 6565
The Prisoner (TV drama), It's A Boy Girl Thing (feature), Little Black Book (feature).

Julian Rodd   Mobile 07779-965775 MM 020-8995 4747
The Secret Of Moonacre (feature), The Walker (feature), Broken Thread (feature).

Alex Rodriguez   Mobile 07966-841633
Planet 51 (feature), Children Of Men (feature).

Polly Rose   Mobile 07788-577737
Life On The List (TV doc), Your Life In Their Hands (TV doc), Doctor Who Confidential (TV doc).

Simon Rose   020-7637 2727 Mobile 07968-694051
My New Home (TV doc), Sons Of Cuba (feature), You're Not Splitting Up My Family (TV doc).

Adam Ross   Mobile 07815-775845
My Kingdom (feature), New Year's Day (feature), Footballers' Wives (TV drama).

Calum Ross   0131-4661765 Mobile 07949-633209
Game Over (TV childrens), Summer In Transylvania (TV childrens), Half-Moon Investigations (TV childrens).

Robin Sales   01628-605753 Mobile 07952-597883
MM 020-8995 4747
Last Chance Harvey (feature), Miss Potter (feature), Mrs Brown (feature).

Steven Sander   Mobile 07967-122561
New Town Killers (feature).

EDITING

Paul Swinburne Mobile 07787-172829
Flyboys (feature), Underworld (feature), Snatch (feature).

David Trent 01932-853113
Road Kill (short), Martha Meet Frank Daniel & Laurence (feature).

Natasha Westlake Mobile 07903-775185
Prince Of Persia (feature).

Bridgette Williams Mobile 07736-718544
Atonement (feature), Mamma Mia! (feature), The Soloist (feature).

Neil Williams 020-8556 0227
Shop Girl (feature), Ella Enchanted (feature), The Beach (feature).

Rab Wilson Mobile 07818-463670 Fax 020-8674 1729
Wallander (TV drama), Kingdom Of Heaven (feature), Five Days (feature).

Jane Winkles 020-7928 1514 Mobile 07887-991746
Clash (feature), Easy Virtue (feature), The Dark Knight (feature).

EDITORS - MUSIC

Michael Higham 01932-223810 Mobile 07770-915602
Prince Of Persia (feature).

Gerard McCann AMPS Mobile 07775-688338
The Golden Compass (feature), Harry Potter & The Goblet Of Fire (feature), The Road (feature).

Graham Sutton 01727-857864 Mobile 07768-927542
Harry Potter & The Goblet Of Fire (feature), Evita (feature), Gosford Park (feature).

John Warhurst Mobile 07818-056157
Sweeney Todd (feature), Prince Of Persia (feature).

Yang Xu Mobile 07738-492171
The Invincible Hero (feature), The Dream Of My Family (feature), Good Girl & Bad Boy (feature).

EDITORS - SOUND

Ross Adams 01628-529965 Mobile 07771-571172
DYA 020-7386 0310
Event Horizon (feature), Best Laid Plans (feature), Band Of Brothers (TV drama).

Nick Adams AMPS 020-8806 1671 Mobile 07710-427013
Mamma Mia! (feature), The Constant Gardener (feature), Buffalo Soldiers (feature).

Paul Apted Mobile 07957-477685
Alice In Wonderland (feature), The Chronicles Of Narnia: The Voyage Of The Dawn Treader (feature), Shanghai (feature).

Brigitte Arnold AMPS 020-8451 3979
Mobile 07833-642284
Event Horizon (feature), Shakespeare In Love (feature), Shiner (feature).

Ian "Spike" Banks AMPS 029-2022 9588
Fax 029-2022 9588
Friends & Heroes (animation), Cuckoo (feature), Otherworld (feature).

Tim Barker Mobile 07870-215522
The Unloved (feature), The Arbor (feature), The Mark Of Cain (feature).

Harry Barnes 020-7241 2698 Mobile 07903-942658
Brighton Rock (feature), Sweeney Todd (feature), Children Of Men (feature) (Foley).

Peter Bond AMPS 01753-883153 Mobile 07900-062788

Amit Bose 020-8657 8442 Fax 020-8657 8442
Ransom (feature), Above The Clouds (feature), Five Puppets (TV childrens).

Debra Bowring 01873-851182 Mobile 07721-087244
The Killing Fields (feature) (Foley), A Room With A View (feature), White City (feature).

Philip Crisswell 0116-230 4505 Mobile 07779-913987
Dalziel & Pascoe (TV drama), Coast (TV doc), Seaside Rescue (TV doc).

Paul Davies Mobile 07773-776994
Morvern Callar (feature), Hunger (feature), The Queen (feature).

John Downer 01296-613612 Mobile 07931-164048
Veronica Guerin (feature), Lewis (TV drama), Shakespeare In Love (feature).

Richard Dunford Mobile 07747-682380
The Boy In The Striped Pyjamas (feature), Severance (feature), Cracker (TV drama).

Robert Gavin 020-8891 1795 Mobile 07802-583700
Band Of Brothers (TV drama), GI Jane (feature) (Dialogue), White Squall (feature) (Dialogue).

Joe Gilmore 020-8422 8359 Mobile 07941-205778
Country Of My Skull (feature) (Dialogue), The Tailor Of Panama (feature) (Dialogue), The Crucible (feature) (Dialogue).

Rodney Glenn AMPS 020-8892 6966
The Boy In The Striped Pyjamas (feature), Little Voice (feature), Brazil (feature).

Simon Gotel 020-7691 1812 Mobile 07976-719983
Horizon (TV doc), Walking With Dinosaurs (TV doc), Daniel Bedingfield (tour).

Zane Hayward Mobile 07958-621363
Hellboy 2: The Golden Army (feature), Vera Drake (feature), Billy Elliot (feature).

Catherine Hodgson AMPS 020-7350 1019
Mobile 07743-135799 Fax 020-7478 8601
Wallander (TV drama), Cranford (TV drama), Atonement (feature).

Mike J Hopkins AMPS 020-8942 7883
Mobile 07941-588661
The Last Emperor (feature), Blade Runner (feature), Rebel Heart (TV drama).

Nick Hosker 020-7229 6302 Fax 020-7229 6302

Eddy Joseph AMPS 01494-712610 Mobile 07798-723135
Fax 01494-715455
Charlie & The Chocolate Factory (feature), Casino Royale (feature), United 93 (feature).

Gerard Loret AMPS 020-8741 0746 Mobile 07932-770715
10,000 BC (feature), Entrapment (feature), Mr Bean's Holiday (feature).

Keith Marriner AMPS 01628-785164
Mobile 07778-159664
The Boys Are Back (feature), St Trinian's (feature), The Queen (feature).

Colin Miller AMPS 01344-627033 Mobile 07947-072960
Ned Kelly (feature), Chasing Liberty (feature), The Bone Collector (feature).

Nigel Mills AMPS 01428-645069 Mobile 07775-572672
Shanghai (feature), Derailed (feature), Hotel Rwanda (feature).

Alan Paley AMPS 020-8892 2205 Mobile 07984-203735
Fax 020-8892 2205
Withnail & I (feature), Colour Me Kubrick (feature), Saving Grace (feature).

William Parnell 01202-600971 Mobile 07811-847915
Fax 01202-600971
Phantom Of The Opera (feature), The Saint (feature) (Dialogue), Entrapment (feature) (Dialogue).

Sandra Portman 020-8292 1599 Mobile 07796-270876

John Poyner AMPS 020-8892 1438
The Dirty Dozen (feature), The Saint (feature) (Dialogue).

John Taylor 01536-310958
The Draughtsman's Contract (feature), The South Bank Show (TV arts), Bellamy's USA (TV doc).

William Trent 01932-848353 Mobile 07788-640312
Fax 01932-848353
The Borrowers (feature), The Gambler (feature), Secrets & Lies (feature).

Karen Warnock Mobile 07956-563308
Playing The Field (TV drama), Hard To Forget (TV drama), HMS Brilliant (TV doc).

EDITORS - SOUND ASSISTANT

Alistair Hawkins 020-7820 1938 Mobile 07941-008282
Prince Caspian (feature), Harry Potter & The Order Of The Phoenix (feature), Charlie & The Chocolate Factory (feature).

EDITORS - SUPERVISING

Charles Davies 020-7229 8631 Mobile 07743-187131
Fax 020-7221 4214
The Great Plague (TV drama doc), The Elephant The Emperor & The Butterfly Tree (TV doc), Bugworld (TV doc).

Paul Edmunds 020-8209 1022 Mobile 07775-893944
Factory: Manchester from Joy Division to Happy Mondays (TV doc), Ross Kemp In Afghanistan (TV doc), Iran & The West (TV doc).

Andy Francis 020-8715 8802 Mobile 07986-608607
The Ultimate Choice (corporate), The Health Book (corporate).

Stefan Henrix 020-8421 6150 Mobile 07771-595552
Alice In Wonderland (feature), Sweeney Todd (feature), Batman Begins (feature).

Rodney Holland 020-7229 4598 MM 020-8995 4747
Fax 020-7229 4598
Dungeons & Dragons (feature), Messiah (TV drama), The Company Of Wolves (feature).

David Jacobs 020-7924 1435 Mobile 07884-435936
Murder Blues (TV doc), Operatunity (TV doc), The House Of War (TV doc).

Terry Jones 020-7434 1173 Mobile 07939-583512
The Return: Bringing Balanchine Back (TV doc), Keeping Mum (feature).

EDITING

Angus Newton   01256-862323 Mobile 07785-745324
ICM +1 310 550 4474
Foyle's War (TV drama), Scandal (feature), The Crow Road (TV drama).

Michael Parkinson   01297-561378 Mobile 07775-973923
CCA 020-7630 6303
Century (feature), Close My Eyes (feature), Wilderness (feature).

EDITORS - VISUAL EFFECTS

Simon Burchell   Mobile 07710-611226
Harry Potter & The Deathly Hallows (feature), Harry Potter & The Half-Blood Prince (feature), Harry Potter & The Order Of The Phoenix (feature).

Derek Burgess   Mobile 07970-697357
Prince Of Persia (feature), Quantum Of Solace (feature), The Golden Compass (feature).

Matthew Glen   01494-814129 Mobile 07768-016399
Harry Potter & The Half-Blood Prince (feature), Harry Potter & The Order Of The Phoenix (feature), Harry Potter & The Goblet Of Fire (feature).

Russell Pawson   020-8668 0010 Mobile 07957-459141
Nanny McPhee & The Big Bang (feature), Heartless (feature), Goal! (feature).

FOLEY ARTISTS

Stan Fiferman   020-8426 2176 Mobile 07501-329028
The Importance Of Being Earnest (feature), Captain Scarlet (TV drama), The Beach (feature).

POST PRODUCTION SUPERVISORS

Stephen Barker   01494-812429 Mobile 07881-610222
Dangerous Parking (feature), Around The World In 80 Days (feature), The Four Feathers (feature).

Roy Benson   020-8671 2168 Mobile 07905-625798
Until Death (feature), Rambo (feature), To End All Wars (feature).

Alison Black   Mobile 07831-648833
Waybuloo (TV childrens), Tricky (TV childrens), The Bill (TV drama).

Robi Borgonovo   Mobile 07789-608499
Holby City (TV drama).

Moira Brophy   Mobile 07876-540290
Whitechapel (TV drama), Small Island (TV drama), The Devil's Whore (TV drama).

Clare Buxton   020-7231 3961 Mobile 07957-287378
Merlin (TV drama), Demons (TV drama), Footballers' Wives (TV drama).

Michelle Camp   Mobile 07939-527407
Hotel Babylon (TV drama).

Polly Duval   Mobile 07770-887553
An Education (feature), Made In Dagenham (feature), Another Year (feature).

Fleur Fontaine   Mobile 07973-295051
Rome (TV drama) (Co-Ordinator), Hollywood Flies (feature), Mean Machine (feature).

Shuna Frood   Mobile 07940-738807
Ae Fond Kiss (feature), Big Nothing (feature), New Town Killers (feature).

Neil Grimshaw   020-8866 5237 Mobile 07767-818030
Brighton Rock (feature), Robin Hood (TV drama), The Crimson Wing (feature).

Tim Grover   01628-528568 Mobile 07956-477294
Clash Of The Titans (feature), The Imaginarium Of Dr Parnassus (feature), Eragon (feature).

Jeanette Haley   Mobile 07973-504563
The Special Relationship (feature), Slum Dog Millionaire (feature), Glorious 39 (feature).

Deborah Harding   01234-771511 Mobile 07802-985036
The Soloist (feature), Hippie Hippie Shake (feature), Nanny McPhee & The Big Bang (feature).

Jonathan Haren   Mobile 07780-607090
Generation Kill (TV drama), The Last King Of Scotland (feature), Shooting Dogs (feature).

Mark Harris   Mobile 07717-436969
Saving Grace (feature), Separate Lies (feature), Vantage Point (feature).

Steve Harrow   01753-654942 Mobile 07768-143164
The Invention Of Lying (feature), Never Let Me Go (feature), Dread (feature).

Alistair Hopkins   Mobile 07961-102091
Tamara Drewe (feature), Brideshead Revisited (feature), In Bruges (feature).

Matthew Jackson   020-7686 0051

EDITING

EDITING

Miranda Jones   020-8740 0438   Mobile 07899-980555
The Disappearance Of Alice Creed (feature), Calendar Girls (feature), Stardust (feature).

Teresa Kelly   Mobile 07977-988417
Robin Hood (feature).

Lis Kern   Mobile 07920-273891
Sahara (feature) (Associate Producer), Tomb Raider (feature), Clear & Present Danger (feature) (Associate Producer).

James Lamb   Mobile 07788-747324
Psych: 9 (feature).

Howard Lanning AMPS   01707-656244
Mobile 07774-445749
In Deep (TV drama), Trial & Retribution (TV drama), The Governor (TV drama).

Peter Miller   01263-588110   Mobile 07885-516940
America: The Story Of Us (TV docu drama), West 10 LDN (TV drama), Totally Frank (TV drama).

Mick Monks   01670-786094   Mobile 07761-696174
An Awfully Big Adventure (feature), It's Only Rock & Roll (feature), Nil By Mouth (feature).

Chris Nixon   020-8800 3023   Mobile 07956-589050
The Bridge Of San Luis Rey (feature), My House In Umbria (TV film), Longtime Dead (feature).

Liz Pearson   020-8579 8495   Mobile 07711-087800
Misfits (TV comedy drama), Lark Rise To Candleford (TV drama), The Government Inspector (TV drama).

Katie Reynolds   Mobile 07747-035511
Harry Potter & The Deathly Hallows (feature), Harry Potter & The Half-Blood Prince (feature), Harry Potter & The Goblet Of Fire (feature).

Jess Rundle   Mobile 07957-301562
Little Dorrit (TV drama).

Michael Saxton   020-7724 1994   Mobile 07768-878066
Sweeney Todd (feature), Children Of Men (feature), Cold Mountain (feature).

Michael Solinger   Mobile 07778-347970
Green Zone (feature), Quantum Of Solace (feature), Hellboy 2: The Golden Army (feature).

Clare St John   020-7267 7477   Mobile 07831-210530
Never Let Me Go (feature), 28 Weeks Later (feature), Sunshine (feature).

Kate Stannard   020-8473 5040   Mobile 07967-032647
Miss Marple (TV drama).

Lionel Strutt   020-7437 4421   Mobile 07710-375355
Fax 020-7437 4461
Flick (feature), An American Haunting (feature), Tomorrow Never Dies (feature).
www.mayflowerstudios.com

Jessie Thiele   Mobile 07977-988259
Alice In Wonderland (feature), Harry Potter & The Prisoner Of Azkaban (feature), Batman Begins (feature).

Tony Tromp   Mobile 07956-809658
Fear Dot Com (feature), The Boys From County Clare (feature), Ripley Under Ground (feature).

Jackie Vance   020-8866 1431   Mobile 07768-794688
School For Seduction (feature), Human Traffic (feature), The Intended (feature).

Maria Walker   Mobile 07770-325580
Bonded By Blood (feature).

Alasdair Whitelaw   Mobile 07971-192505
Auf Wiedersehen Pet (TV drama), The Rotter's Club (TV drama), Poirot (TV drama).

Emma Zee   Mobile 07775-920140
Sherlock Holmes (feature), The King's Speech (feature), Unknown White Male (TV doc).

RESEARCHERS - PICTURE

Adam Ambery-Smith   01483-579074   Mobile 07799-051797
Obama - His Story (TV doc), Bill Gates: The Geek That Changed The World (TV doc), The Money Programme (TV news & current affairs).

Sheila Bailey   01905-360209   Mobile 07956-531796
Ian Hislop Goes Off The Rails (TV doc), Cabinet Confidential (TV doc), Brideshead Revisited (feature).

Rosalind Bentley   020-8658 3164   Fax 020-8658 3164
War Of The Worlds (feature), Churchill's Forgotten Years (TV doc), A Very British Coup (TV doc).

Jenny Borthwick   Mobile 07932-040899
Piers Morgan's Review Of The Year (TV light entertainment), What The Pythons Did Next (TV doc), The Duke: A Portrait Of Prince Phillip (TV doc).

Phil Clark   Mobile 07768-080497
Nowhere Boy (feature), Incendiary (feature), The Golden Compass (feature).

Lisa Clayton-Jones   020-8346 2561 Mobile 07715-710845
Edward VII - Prince Of Pleasure (TV doc), Simon Schama On Obama's America (TV doc), Dispatches (TV doc).

Maggi Cook   020-8693 9332 Fax 020-8693 9332
Savage Earth (TV doc), People's Century (TV doc), A Labour Of Love (TV doc).

Alex Cowan   01453-884860 Mobile 07768-213719
Fax 01453-884860
Dispatches (TV doc).

Nick Dodd   Mobile 07802-704503

Jacqui Edwards   Mobile 07867-808554
The Fallen (TV doc), The End Of The Line (feature), Seconds From Disaster (TV doc).

Val Evans   01883-373034 Mobile 07950-825953
Bremner Bird & Fortune (TV light entertainment), Mock The Week (TV light entertainment), Top 50 Celebrity Meltdowns (TV light entertainment).

Liz Fay   020-8691 0242 Mobile 07970-975537
Man On WIre (TV doc), America: The Story Of Us (TV docu drama), The Shot That Shook The World (TV doc).

Paul Gardner   Mobile 07958-462848
Thriller In Manila (TV doc), 9/11 - The Falling Man (TV doc), The Blitz - London's Firestorm (TV drama doc).

Karen Ghai   01344-893247
The Story Of... (TV doc).

Suzanne Gray   020-8567 9536 Mobile 07941-995548
The South Bank Show (TV arts), It'll Be Alright On The Night (TV light entertainment), Panorama (TV doc).

Libby Gregory   020-8699 6998 Mobile 07971-026817
The Story Of Light Entertainment (TV doc), 100 Greatest Cartoons (TV light entertainment), Michael Portillo's Great British Losers (TV doc).

Liz Heasman   020-7928 1328

Valerie Hetherington   020-7473 3760
Mobile 07712-531621
River Of Blood (TV doc), Panorama (TV doc), Story Of A Princess (TV doc).

James Hunt   Mobile 07812-164664
1970's A Decade In Detail (TV doc), Celebrities On Heat (TV doc), Secrets Of The CIA (TV doc).

Susan Huxley   020-8299 4156 Fax 020-8299 4156

Christine Kirby   020-8540 1027 Mobile 07952-597987

George Latymer   0118-986 9334

Mike Lewis   020-8567 9932 Mobile 07811-268343
Backstairs Billy (TV doc), Dispatches (TV doc), House Of Saddam (TV drama).

Alison McAllan   020-8567 4448
The Ascent Of Money (TV doc), Clash Of Worlds (TV doc), China (TV doc).

Stuart McKay   01273-326356 Mobile 07773-270336
Sinatra: Dark Star (TV doc), The History Of Football (TV doc), First World War (TV doc).

Jill McLoughlin   Mobile 07941-787602
Witness (TV doc), Class Clips (TV childrens).

Kate Newington   020-7274 1418 Mobile 07763-127345
Fax 020-7274 1418
Secret History (TV doc), The Stripper & The Bent Copper (TV drama), Have I Got News For You (TV light entertainment).

Judy Patterson   020-8340 1130
China's Capitalist Revolution (TV doc), The Qur'an (TV doc), Bodysong (feature).

Alf Penn   01303-844412 Mobile 07775-658815
Savage Skies (TV doc), People's Century (TV doc), Timewatch (TV doc).

Richard Philpott   020-7267 9990 Mobile 07785-355368

Tricia Power   Mobile 07884-063307
Drugs Inc (TV doc), The Story Of Science (TV doc), Underworld (feature).

Dinah Rogers   020-7254 2414 Mobile 07961-381528
Science Story (TV doc), Timewatch (TV doc), Reputations (TV doc).

Peter Scott   020-7701 3296 Mobile 07768-594701
D-Day To Berlin (TV doc), Who Do You Think You Are? (TV doc), The World's Greatest Sporting Legend (TV doc).

Diana Sedgwick   020-8567 8286 Mobile 07966-634464
Dispatches (TV doc), Panorama (TV doc), TV's Naughtiest Blunders (TV light entertainment).

John Shearlaw   01278-671316 Mobile 07748-353919
Glastonbury The Movie (feature), The Dreamer (feature), The Filth & The Fury (feature).

Gill Shepherd   020-7352 1770

Angela Spindler-Brown   020-8866 5271
Mobile 07733-008782
A Very British Olympics (TV doc), Do We Need A Union Jack? (TV doc), In Search Of A Lost Ark (TV doc).

EDITING

Victoria Stable   020-7226 3381 Mobile 07710-719837
Crude Britannia: The Story Of North Sea Oil (TV doc), The Satanic Verses Affair (TV doc), Hunting The Edge Of Space (TV doc).

Ernest Stoddart   020-8465 0121 Mobile 07968-023210
The Noughties...Was That It? (TV light entertainment), The Paul O'Grady Show (trailer), The Comedian's Comedian (TV doc).

Sue Tiplady   01929-554500 Mobile 07973-765109
Fax 01929-556050
Memoirs Of A Cigarette (TV doc), Tory! Tory! Tory! (TV doc), The Greatest Movie Cars (TV light entertainment).

Evelyn Velleman   020-8451 0311
The Art Of Conducting: Legendary Conductors Of A Golden Era (TV doc).

Karen Walsh   Mobile 07779-185948
Most Annoying People (TV light entertainment), Obama's People (TV doc), 100 Greatest Musicals (TV light entertainment).

Andy Wheatcroft   01565-632017 Mobile 07957-193913

Gerard Wilkinson   020-8809 7993 Mobile 07712-673325
Fax 020-8809 7993

David Wyatt   Mobile 07799-370325 Fax 020-8907 9188
It Shouldn't Happen To... (TV doc), The Way We Were (TV drama), Legends (TV doc).

Cy Young   Mobile 07984-435469 Fax 020-8968 9086
The Great British Black Invasion (TV doc), Unseen Eric Morecombe (TV doc), Heroes Of Comedy (TV doc).

Simon King   Mobile 07976-306422
Big Brother's Big Mouth (TV light entertainment), Blue Peter (TV childrens), Question Time (TV news & current affairs).

Sonia Lovett   020-7502 1773 Mobile 07721-519444
Promenade (concert), Masterchef (TV light entertainment), Glyndebourne (opera).

Mark Waring   Mobile 07973-840681
Sky Active (TV light entertainment), BBC News 24 (TV news & current affairs), The Big Breakfast (TV light entertainment).

VISION CONTROLLERS

David Harvey   020-8902 0147 Fax 020-8902 0147
Loose Women (TV light entertainment), V Graham Norton (TV light entertainment), My Family (TV comedy drama).

Alan White   01543-490415 Mobile 07836-797893

VISION MIXERS

Sarah Giles-Harling   Mobile 07714-331731
EastEnders (TV drama), BBC Proms (TV light entertainment), Big Cook Little Cook (TV childrens).

Kay Harrington   020-7228 9952 Mobile 07811-263970
Champions League Football (TV sport), Question Time (TV news & current affairs), BBC Proms (TV light entertainment).

Alison Jones   Mobile 07958-476183
Rory Bremner (TV light entertainment), The Shirley Bassey Show (TV light entertainment), Jean-Michel Jarre (concert).

Production
DEPARTMENT

ASSOCIATE PRODUCERS

Jules Baker-Smith   Mobile 07917-583112
Dangerous Parking (feature), Iron Man II (feature), Sherlock Holmes (feature).

Simon Godley   Mobile 07946-371838
Huge (feature).

Adam Kempton   020-7935 1676 Mobile 07726-893120
Fax 020-7935 1676
The Keeper (feature), Victoria & Albert (TV drama), The Ninth Gate (feature).

Alison Law   Mobile 07771-757654 SPA 01932-571044
People Like Us (TV light entertainment), Talk To Me (TV drama), Sorted (TV drama).

Ivor Powell   020-8977 1791 Mobile 07775-784581
Fax 020-8977 9441
Alien (feature), Blade Runner (feature), The Dreamer (feature).

Carol Rodger   020-7281 2622 Mobile 07774-275632
Where The Heart Is (TV drama), Murder On The Orient Express (feature), Heavy Hearts (feature).

Michael Wood   020-8747 0222 Fax 020-8747 0222
Raving Beauties (feature), The Witch's Daughter (TV film), The Steal (feature).

Hoe Yeoh   Mobile 07973-272465
Holby City (TV drama), Casualty (TV drama), EastEnders (promo).

DIRECTORS

Keith Ackrill   0121-445 3563 Mobile 07887-698074
Top Gear (TV light entertainment), Pebble Mill At One (TV magazine), Asian Arts (TV doc).

Zaheer Ahmad   020-7638 6333
Shell (commercial), Lloyds TSB (commercial), TGI Fridays (commercial).

James Allen   01308-897755
Winter War (TV doc), Counter Attack (TV doc), Stunt School USA (TV doc).

Gordon Anderson   CRC 020-7735 2933
The Inbetweeners (TV comedy drama), The Catherine Tate Show (TV light entertainment), Suburban Shootout (TV drama).

Moira Armstrong   020-7603 8248
The Last Detective (TV drama), Miss Marple (TV drama), Lark Rise To Candleford (TV drama).

Richard Attenborough   020-8940 7234
Fax 020-8940 4741
Gandhi (feature), Chaplin (feature), Cry Freedom (feature).

Rob Bailey   ITG 020-7636 6565
The Wire (TV drama), Without A Trace (TV drama), CSI: Crime Scene Investigation (TV drama).

Roberto Bangura   020-7702 4605 Mobile 07976-700882
Casualty (TV drama), Smack The Pony (TV light entertainment), Footballers' Wives (TV drama).

Otto Bathurst   020-7267 6033 Mobile 07973-386283
Margot (TV drama), Criminal Justice (TV drama), Five Days (TV drama).

Stephen Bayly   01580-752839
Richard III (feature), Mrs Dalloway (feature), Just Ask For Diamonds (feature).

Adrian Bean   01704-227787 Mobile 07831-448208
Murder In Mind (TV drama), Heartbeat (TV drama), Casualty (TV drama).

Jane Beckwith   0113-284 2495 Mobile 07711-167754
Scams Fiddles & Honest Claims (TV doc), Priest Idol (TV reality), Hypercondriacs (TV doc).

Alex Beetham   01638-500888
Border Wars (TV doc), Mark Williams' Big Bangs (TV doc), Secret History (TV doc).

Alan Bell   020-8398 8159 Mobile 07718-536066
Lost For Words (TV drama), Last Of The Summer Wine (TV comedy drama).

Peter Bell   01751-417147 Fax 01751-417804
Jazz Film (TV doc), Basil Bunting (TV doc), K491 (TV doc).

Colin Bennett   020-8686 1188 Fax 020-8686 5928
Strictly Soho (TV doc), Shoot The Writers (TV light entertainment), Women Of A Certain Age (TV drama).

Mike Berry   01797-344623 Mobile 07813-158702
Fax 01797-344181
Respect Yourself Protect Yourself (corporate), Dangerous Waters (TV doc), Super...Vision (corporate).

Indra Bhose   RS 020-7359 3900
Girls In Love (TV drama), Holby City (TV drama), Down To Earth (TV drama).

Bob Blagden   01628-526312 TA 020-7727 1346
My Brother Marvin: The Truth About Marvin Gaye (feature), Long Haul (short), Ashes & Sand (feature).

DIRECTORS

Neil Blewett   01932-592496 Mobile 07801-801016
Fax 01932-592050
Beyond The NFL (TV doc), Troy Story (TV doc), Fighting Back - Michael Watson (TV doc).

Emma Bodger   Mobile 07973-506007
New Street Law (TV drama), Casualty (TV drama), Boys Don't Cry (short).

Christine Booth   020-8748 2733 Mobile 07931-366275
Fax 020-8748 2733
Ways To Work (corporate), Wendy Ebsworth: Sign Language Interpreter (TV doc), The Fisher Boxing Club (TV doc).

Shirley Booth   020-7736 8058 Mobile 07984-789483
Grand Gourmet (TV doc), Silent Invasion (TV doc), Japan: Food For The Spirit (TV doc).

Sarah Boston   020-7625 5283
Cruel Separation (feature), Great Britain United (TV doc), Grapes Of Wrath Revisited (TV doc).

Christopher Bould   020-7263 9370 Mobile 07973-674246
Impossible Heists (TV reality), Nuclear Secrets (TV docu drama).

Dermot Boyd   020-7249 5498 ITG 020-7636 6565
Fax 020-7503 8508
New Tricks (TV drama), Waterloo Road (TV drama), Drop Dead Gorgeous (TV drama).

Janice Broxup   01825-873388 Mobile 07905-509983
Fax 01825-873388
Delhi Belly (TV light entertainment).

John Bruce   01753-841309
Sherlock Holmes (feature), Poirot (TV drama), Casualty (TV drama).

Paul Bryers   020-8675 3735 Mobile 07985-777376
TA 020-7727 1346
Seven Wonders Of The Industrial World (TV docu drama), Murder At Canterbury (TV doc), The Great Nazi Cash Swindle (TV doc).

Graham Buchan   020-7515 5021 Mobile 07702-587777
Fax 020-7515 5021
Emergency Planning (corporate), Recruitment (corporate), Multiple Sclerosis (corporate).

Jim Burge   020-7435 1332 Mobile 07768-077334
David Starkey's Monarchy (TV doc), Strange Landscape (TV doc) (Producer), What If? (TV doc).

Nicholas Burgess-Jones   Mobile 07773-287288
The Oasis Of Siwa (TV doc), The Golden Czech Balls (TV doc), Womack & Womack (promo).

Tim Burkinshaw   020-7727 9759 Mobile 07973-411380

Michael Burns   020-8942 5588
A Gentleman Cricketer (feature).

Judith Burrows   020-7272 6924 Mobile 07966-540610
Saving Grace (feature), Carwash (short), Pulse (short).

Jenny Byrom   Mobile 07932-727030
Secret Millionaire (TV reality), How The Other Half Live (TV doc), Dispatches (TV doc).

Simon Callow   CRC 020-7735 2933
Ballad Of The Sad Cafe (feature).

Anya Camilleri   Mobile 07970-428882 DA 020-7437 4551
Ny-Lon (TV drama), Satisfaction (feature), Jealousy (TV drama).

James Cellan-Jones   020-8940 8742 Mobile 07891-426048
Holby City (TV drama).

Barry Clayton   020-7354 8290

Sue Clayton   020-8800 7450 Mobile 07944-956516
The Disappearance Of Finbar (feature), Heart Songs (short), The Last Crop (TV drama).

Tanya Cochrane   01672-871196 Mobile 07850-220007
Haunted London (TV doc), War Heroes (TV doc), Mummy Autopsy (TV drama doc).

Paul Cole   01243-864169 Mobile 07946-582509
Jim & Jam & Sunny (TV childrens), Tweenies (TV childrens), Mike & Angelo (TV childrens).

Aletta Collins   CRC 020-7735 2933
The Girl In The Red Dress (short).

David Corcoran   020-8755 3784 Mobile 07973-837702
Fax 020-8755 3784
Behind The Scenes At The RSC (TV doc), Designing The Future (TV educational).

Paul Cordsen   020-8741 8428 Mobile 07724-771336

Katie Crawford   Mobile 07980-615543
World's Strictest Parents (TV doc), The Hottest Place On Earth (TV doc), Extreme Dreams (TV doc).

John Crome   01725-518601
Dream Team (TV drama), Joe's Box (short), Lovejoy (TV drama).

David Crossman   020-8658 2012 Mobile 07973-664189
City Of The Rich (TV drama), The Last Frontier (corporate) (Producer), Schofield's Quest (TV light entertainment).

John Paul Davidson   020-8741 3669 Mobile 07770-534660
Himalaya With Michael Palin (TV doc), Catherine The Great (TV drama), Stephen Fry In America (TV doc).

John Davies   020-8985 8879
Acceptable Levels (feature), Ursula & Glenys (TV drama), Behind The Eye (TV arts).

Terence Daw   Mobile 07774-292242
Surviving Evil (feature), Revenge (TV film), Thief Takers (TV drama).

Tristan de Vere Cole   01635-40945   ITG 020-7636 6565
Orion's Belt (feature), The Dive (feature), Howard's Way (TV drama).

David Drury   Mobile 07990-505620
Fallen Angel (TV drama), Marian Again (TV drama), Tough Love (TV drama).

Charles Dunstan   020-8994 2328   Fax 020-8994 2328
Conserving The Coast (TV doc), Acid From The Sky (TV doc), The Far Reaches (TV doc).

Julie Edwards   020-7226 5717   Mobile 07973-828485
Where The Heart Is (TV drama), The Bill (TV drama), Footballers' Wives (TV drama).

Stephen Engelhard   0844-415 5534
Bully Beware (corporate), Can You Hear Me? (corporate), Diverse Reports (TV doc).

David Evans   020-7609 5055   Mobile 07980-544821
Unforgiven (TV drama), Whitechapel II (TV drama), The Children (feature).

Matthew Evans   ITG 020-7636 6565
William & Mary (TV drama), Robin Hood (TV drama), Rebus (TV drama).

Rob Evans   Mobile 07973-550668
New Tricks (TV drama), Silent Witness (TV drama), Bonkers (TV comedy drama).

Peter Fairbrass   01483-225179   Mobile 07712-881101
The Web (TV drama), Surrey Police Authority (corporate).

Brett Fallis   Mobile 07976-725565
Bad Girls (TV drama), Casualty (TV drama), The Bill (TV drama).

Brian Farnham   01276-684727   Mobile 07831-700632
CM 020-7287 4450   Fax 01276-684727
Poirot (TV drama), All Quiet On The Preston Front (TV drama), Rosemary & Thyme (TV drama).

Richard Fawkes   020-8997 3996   Mobile 07947-352109
G F Watts - Victorian Visionary (TV doc), Tom Keating On Painters (TV doc), The Original Three Tenors (TV doc).

Mike Figgis   CRC 020-7735 2933
Miss Julie (feature), Time Code 2000 (feature), Leaving Las Vegas (feature).

Vic Finch   020-8240 1107   Mobile 07801-432953
The Big Bang (TV childrens), Boo Bah (TV childrens), Teletubbies (TV childrens).

Steve Finn   01795-470181   Mobile 07787-531656
The Bill (TV drama), London's Burning (TV drama), Holby City (TV drama).

Steven Forrester   01462-819362   Mobile 07961-329162
Toby's Odyssey (feature), A70 (feature), Desperate Pursuit (feature).

Henry Foster   020-8748 2202   Mobile 07711-510896
Casualty (TV drama), Coronation Street (TV drama), Emmerdale (TV drama).

Stephen Friendship   0116-242 2920   Mobile 07714-245312
Coda (short), Freerange (short), A Postcard From Sutton (short).

Ben Fuller   Mobile 07831-502091   STA 020-7729 7477
Ideal (TV light entertainment), That Mitchell & Webb Look (TV light entertainment), The IT Crowd (TV comedy drama).

Paul Gawith   01903-883720   Mobile 07770-236938
Burghley Horse Trials (TV sport), Tronji (TV childrens), Canoe Slalom World Championships (TV sport).

Sean Glynn   01590-688252   Mobile 07956-802019
Holby City (TV drama), Missing (TV doc), Hollyoaks (TV drama).

Mick Gold   020-7482 6098   Mobile 07766-712534
Watergate (TV doc), The Private Life Of A Masterpiece (TV doc), Endgame In Ireland (TV doc).

Garry Grant   01463-234000   Mobile 07860-663566
Fax 01463-231800
The Other Loch Ness Monster (TV doc), Boom Or Bust (TV doc), John Carpenter (TV doc).

Rodney Greenberg   01494-527973

Cavan Greenwood   020-8339 6868   Mobile 07866-750269
Emmerdale (TV drama), Hollyoaks (TV drama).

Jonathan Hacker   Mobile 07949-261787
This World (TV doc), Timewatch (TV doc), Britain's First Suicide Bombers (TV docu drama).

Trevor Hampton   01707-261285   Mobile 07976-955330
Fax 01707-818111
Trisha (TV light entertainment), BBC Proms (TV light entertainment), Alliance & Leicester (corporate).

Sarah Harding   Mobile 07831-122339   UA 020-3214 0800
Queer As Folk (TV drama), Compulsion (TV drama), Poirot (TV drama).

PRODUCTION

Charles Harris   020-7435 1330
Love Pic (short), Ghost Story (short), Sex Drugs & Dinner (TV doc).

Bob Harvey   01379-898107 Mobile 07841-849444
Raven (TV childrens), Stagecraft (TV arts).

John Hay   01273-508066 PFD 020-7344 1000
The Truth About Love (feature), Journey Through Midnight (feature), There's Only One Jimmy Grimble (feature).

Daniel Herd   Mobile 07590292691
Old Vic New Voices (theatre).

Jeremy Hunter   Mobile 07768-490907
On The Horizon (TV doc), The French Foreign Legion (TV doc).

Nick Hurran   Mobile 07785-290548
Little Black Book (feature), Girls' Night (TV film), It's A Boy Girl Thing (feature).

Metin Huseyin   020-8995 0846 Mobile 07710-537038
ITG 020-7636 6565
Anita & Me (feature), It Was An Accident (feature), Tom Jones (TV drama).

Michael Hutchinson   020-7381 5016
Mobile 07970-655798
Emporer Of The Seas (TV drama), Legend Detectives (TV doc), Grandfather Of The Masaai (TV doc).

Terry Iland   020-8365 2331 Mobile 07981-229576
Down To Earth (TV drama), Casualty (TV drama), The Bill (TV drama).

John Inglis   020-8783 1836

Maximillian Jacobson-Gonzalez   01604-702288
Fax 0845-127 4078
The Changing World (TV doc), Billie Piper (promo), Speedo (corporate).

Sandy Johnson   020-8743 3792 Mobile 07831-582296
DA 020-7437 4551
Harry & Paul (TV light entertainment), Benidorm (TV comedy drama), Love Soup (TV drama).

Lateif Jorephani   020-8339 0054 Mobile 07929-638484

Justin Kelly   Mobile 07788-441315
Trawlermen (TV doc), The Hottest Place On Earth (TV doc), Dangerous Adventures For Boys (TV light entertainment).

Michael Kerrigan   01622-858377
The Phoenix & The Carpet (TV childrens), The Secret Life Of Toys (animation), Woolworths (commercial).

Elliot Kew   020-8281 5098 Mobile 07930-333078
Missing (TV doc), Crash (TV doc), Heir Hunters (TV doc).

Ray Kilby   020-7242 5066
Never Play With The Dead (TV film), Girls' Weekend (TV film), More Than Love (TV drama).

Vivienne King   020-7229 3844 Fax 020-7229 3844
SOE - Special Operations Executive (TV doc), Horizon (TV doc), Equinox (TV doc).

Alex Kirby   01275-842726 Mobile 07714-259843
ITG 020-7636 6565
Hollyoaks (TV drama), In The Night Garden (TV childrens), The Worst Witch (TV childrens).

Paul Kirrage   01483-472658 Mobile 07850-622281
Dancing On Ice (TV light entertainment), Piers Morgan Life Stories (TV light entertainment), Rod Stuart One Night Only (TV light entertainment).

Lance Kneeshaw   Mobile 07973-327210
Bad Girls (TV drama), Holby City (TV drama), EastEnders (TV drama).

Alan Knight   Mobile 07881-821772
Back To Sarajevo (TV doc), Ghost Show (TV doc), The Art Of Survival (TV doc).

Patrick Lau   020-7490 2644 UA 020-3214 0800
Lark Rise To Candleford (TV drama), Sherlock Holmes (TV drama), Scarlet Pimpernel (TV drama).

Nick Laughland   Mobile 07956-697950
CBR 020-7393 4400
Amnesia (TV drama), Under The Greenwood Tree (TV film), Wild At Heart (TV drama).

Michael Leggo   Mobile 07860-727222
Lesley Garrett Tonight (TV light entertainment), The Richard Blackwood Show (TV light entertainment), The Monkey's Paw (TV drama).

Nigel Lesmoir-Gordon   01525-860248
Mobile 07770-628693
Clouds Are Not Spheres (TV doc), The Colours Of Infinity (TV doc), Remember A Day (feature).

Chris Lethbridge   Mobile 07973-224021
Who Killed Alexander The Great? (TV doc), Nazi Hunters (TV doc), How To Build A Human (TV doc).

Ian Lewis   01252-710313 Fax 01252-725855
Children Of The Lake (feature), The Chef's Apprentice (TV drama doc), Mona The Vampire (TV childrens).

Craig Lines   Mobile 07904-586084
Tracy Beaker (TV childrens), Casualty (TV drama), Footballers' Wives (TV drama).

PRODUCTION

Jim Loach   Mobile 07837-392329 CBR 020-7393 4400
Hotel Babylon (TV drama), Waterloo Road (TV drama), Shameless (TV drama).

Ian Lorimer   020-8876 8140 Mobile 07836-363066
Fax 020-8876 8140
Qi (TV light entertainment), Never Mind The Buzzcocks (TV light entertainment), Argumental (TV light entertainment).

Peter Lydon   Mobile 07976-792083
Garrow's Law (TV drama), Mistresses (TV drama), Shameless (TV drama).

Lorne Magory   01428-607697 Mobile 07958-509531
Fax 01428-607697
Press Gang (TV childrens), Emmerdale (TV drama), Life Force (TV drama).

Paul Marcus   020-8540 1335 Mobile 07801-650778
ITG 020-7636 6565 Fax 020-8540 1335
Lark Rise To Candleford (TV drama), The Roman Mysteries (TV childrens), Heidi (feature).

Nigel Maslin   01394-450799
Diana - The Week The World Stood Still (TV doc), Conquerors (TV doc), History's Turning Points (TV doc).

Simon Massey   Mobile 07778-754680 UA 020-3214 0800
Skins (TV drama), Strange (TV drama), Rough Diamond (TV drama).

Terry McDonough   Mobile 07973-203420
The Street (TV drama), Vincent (TV drama), Breaking Bad (TV drama).

Nancy Meckler   020-7289 3500 Fax 020-7266 5484
Sister My Sister (feature), Alive & Kicking (feature).

Geoff Mellor   01457-764319
Numerous commercials & promos.

Gavin Millar   020-7226 0210 Mobile 07806-210714
UA 020-3214 0800 Fax 020-7359 0292
Albert Schweitzer (feature), Housewife 49 (TV drama).

Laurence Moody   020-8390 3053 Mobile 07711-627177
Waterloo Road (TV drama), Ultimate Force (TV drama), Footballers' Wives (TV drama).

Andrew Morgan   020-7723 4507 Mobile 07713-680377
TA 020-7727 1346
Doctor Who (TV drama), Little Lord Fauntleroy (TV childrens), The Worst Witch (TV childrens).

Jenny Morgan   020-7328 0523 Mobile 07780-702547
The Real Charlotte Gray (TV doc), Performing Wonders In South Africa (TV doc), A Place In The City (TV doc).

Tim Morgan   01295-711007 Mobile 07770-743551
Space (TV doc), Cut The Mustard (TV drama), Mad Dog (TV doc).

Martin Morrison   Mobile 07941-727948
Elephant Graveyard (TV doc), Men In White (TV light entertainment), Grand Designs (TV doc).

Paul Morrison   020-8280 9125 Fax 020-8280 9111
Wondrous Oblivion (feature), Solomon & Gaenor (feature), The Night Show (TV drama).

Robin Nash   020-7402 4593 Fax 020-7402 4593
Harry Hill (TV light entertainment), Goodnight Sweetheart (TV comedy drama).

Paul Nelson   Mobile 07989-564484
The Gril Who Cries Blood (TV doc), Twin Town (TV doc), Catastrophes (TV doc).

Phil O'Shea   020-8969 1889 DA 020-7437 4551
Fax 020-7439 1355
Vampire Diary (feature), Kinsey (TV drama), The Crane (short).

Juliette Otterburn-Hall   020-7404 2351
Mobile 07973-159921
No 57 The History Of A House (TV drama doc), Gardens Through Time (TV doc), Restoration (feature).

Dan Outram   Mobile 07932-618017

Charles Palmer   ITG 020-7636 6565
Doctor Who (TV drama), Ghost Squad (TV drama), Miss Marple (TV drama).

Brian Percival   Mobile 07768-622599 ITG 020-7636 6565
North & South (TV drama), Downton Abbey (TV drama), A Boy Called Dad (feature).

Helen Petts   020-7229 2512 Mobile 07961-307830
Dance For The Camera (TV arts), The Late Show (TV arts), Without Walls (TV doc).

Tomasz Pobog-Malinowski   020-7249 7440
Mobile 07770-481977 Fax 020-7249 7440
The World Acccording To General Jaruzelski (TV doc), Fire-Water-Stone (TV doc), Dispatches (TV doc).

Stephen Poliakoff   020-7861 8000
Gideon's Daughter (TV drama), Glorious 39 (feature), The Lost Prince (TV drama).

Gerry Poulson   Mobile 07802-410906 BA 020-7836 1112
Murder In Mind (TV drama), The Knock (TV drama), Heartbeat (TV drama).

PRODUCTION

Tristram Powell   Mobile 07860-381092
Trial & Retribution (TV drama), The Commander (TV drama), Foyle's War (TV drama).

Melanie Price   Mobile 07973-908324
Tribal Wives (TV doc), Tiger Queen (TV doc), Everest Beyond The Limit (TV doc).

Sian Price   029-2031 5444 Mobile 07879-637324
Coal House (TV drama), Time Team (TV doc), Beyond Boundaries (TV doc).

Tony Price   Mobile 07973-842888

Nicholas Prosser   020-8871 0458 Mobile 07778-865628
Thief Takers (TV drama), House Of Elliot (TV drama), The Bill (TV drama).

Alvin Rakoff   020-8994 1269 Mobile 07808-401999
Fax 020-8742 0507
Requiem For A Heavyweight (TV film), Waiting For Gillian (TV film), A Dance To The Music Of Time (TV film).

Alastair Reid   01823-698645 Fax 01823-698645
Tales Of The City (TV drama), Nostromo (TV drama), Traffik (TV drama).

David Richards   020-7263 4713 Mobile 07748-116391
Fax 020-7272 5254
The Taming Of The Shrew (TV film), Messiah (TV drama), This Is Personal (TV drama).

Kate Robinson   0151-708 0250 Mobile 07785-904355
The Royal Today (TV drama), Putting Down The King (short), The Bill (TV drama).

Nic Roeg BSC   020-7257 8723

Michael Rolfe   01789-550624 Mobile 07814-446504
Fax 01789-550624
Hollyoaks (TV drama), Baubas Adventures (feature), Taxandria (feature).

Beata Romanowski   020-8741 4200 Fax 020-8741 2323
Andrea Bocelli Sentimento (promo), Hampton Court Palace Music Festival (music), QE2 (corporate).

Renny Rye   01753-885075 Mobile 07973-740613
ITG 020-7636 6565
Oliver Twist (feature), Midsomer Murders (TV drama), Cold Lazarus (TV drama).

Gwennan Sage   029-2062 6219 Mobile 07818-068844
Casualty (TV drama), The Ruth Rendell Mysteries (TV drama), Rosemary & Thyme (TV drama).

Stephen Saunders   020-8464 7929 Mobile 07860-542352
Lancaster At War (TV doc), Fighting The Blue (TV doc).

Philip Saville   020-7431 7700 Mobile 07973-741960
The Life & Loves Of A She-Devil (TV drama), Boys Of The Black Stuff (TV drama), The Gospel Of John (feature).

Caroline Sax   020-8348 2686 Mobile 07831-482943
DA 020-7437 4551
Past Imperfect (feature), The Fishmonger's Daughter (short).

Justin Sbresni   Mobile 07951-601948
The Worst Week Of My Life (TV comedy drama), The Worst Christmas Of My Life (TV drama), Worst Week (TV comedy drama).

Nick Shipley   0117-962 2439 Mobile 07803-593833
Fax 0117-962 2439
Great British Isles (TV doc), Bionic Bodies (TV doc), Artefacts (TV doc).

Simon Shore   UA 020-3214 0800
After Thomas (TV drama), Things To Do Before You're 30 (feature), Get Real (feature).

Frank Smith   01225-309086 Mobile 07973-228363
Murder In Mind (TV drama), Down To Earth (TV drama), Heartbeat (TV drama).

Harold Snoad   01932-785887 Mobile 07803-722618
Fax 01932-785887
Ever Decreasing Circles (TV comedy drama), Don't Wait Up (TV comedy drama), Keeping Up Appearances (TV comedy drama).

Barnaby Southcombe   ITG 020-7636 6565
Teachers (TV drama), Sold (TV drama), Harley Street (TV drama).

Minkie Spiro   Mobile 07956-236791
Skins (TV drama), Hustle (TV drama), No Angels (TV drama).

Maurice Stevens   01403-780315 Mobile 07710-124971
Spirit Of Teignmouth (corporate), Rolls Royce (corporate).

Philip Stevens   Mobile 07970-909534
News Bulletin (TV news & current affairs), Parliamentary Coverage (TV news & current affairs), Growing The Top Line (corporate).

Charles Stewart   01452-830500 Mobile 07802-967369

Colin Still   020-8858 2482 Mobile 07973-311635
Fax 020-8858 2717
No More To Say & Nothing To Weep For (TV doc), Arrows of Desire (TV arts), Letters From The Trenches (TV arts).

Claire Storey   0191-281 7289 Mobile 07802-160836
Grumpy Old Women (TV light entertainment), 100 Greatest War Movies (TV light entertainment), The Sound Of Music Children (TV doc).

Toni Strasburg   020-7328 2536 Mobile 07713-471817
Fax 020-7372 6649
Chain Of Hope (TV doc), An Act Of Faith (TV doc), Paying The Price (TV doc).

John Stroud   020-7229 5982 Fax 020-7221 0676
The Hairy Bikers' Cookbook (TV doc), Game On (TV comedy drama), My Hero (TV comedy drama).

David Thacker   020-8444 8436 Mobile 07775-945102
ITG 020-7636 6565
Faith (TV film), Waking The Dead (TV drama), The Mayor Of Casterbridge (TV drama).

Delyth Thomas   JD 020-8964 8811
The Revenge Files of Alastair Fury (TV childrens), Most Mysterious Murders (TV drama), Tracy Beaker (TV childrens).

Peter Thornhill   0115-911 6361 Mobile 07770-995541
Noel's Christmas Presents (TV light entertainment), Royal Navy (corporate), Audi (commercial).

Jim Threapleton   020-7912 1169
Vodafone (commercial), Sony Ericsson (commercial), Dark Realm (TV drama).

David Tucker   Mobile 07966-177147
Lark Rise To Candleford (TV drama), Dalziel & Pascoe (TV drama), The Last Detective (TV drama).

Roger Tucker   020-7352 5158 DA 020-7437 4551
Fax 020-7352 5158
Waiting For Dublin (feature), Deadly Recruits (TV film), Bombay Blue (TV drama).

Paul Unwin   Mobile 07771-794908 UA 020-3214 0800
The Blue Room (feature), Proof Of Life (feature), Elijah (TV film).

Jamie Wadhawan   020-7727 4194
Cain's Film (TV doc), All I Know (TV doc) (also Producer), Sheep (feature).

Charles Wallace   020-8547 0277
A Midsummer Nightmare (feature), The Astronomical Patrick Moore (TV doc).

Adam Byrne Walton   Mobile 07775-848654
Placebo (concert), Tour Of Britain (TV sport), V Festival (TV light entertainment).

Alan Wareing   01205-354022 Mobile 07775-885693
Fax 01205-350202
Coronation Street (TV drama), Emmerdale (TV drama), Casualty (TV drama).

Norman Warren   020-8579 3674 Mobile 07957-487167
Fax 020-8579 3674
Inseminoid (feature), Terror (feature), Person To Person (TV drama).

Derek Wheeler   01322-400175 Mobile 07774-943586
Fax 01322-294746
Mr World 2010 (TV light entertainment), The Paul O'Grady Show (TV light entertainment), The British Comedy Awards (TV light entertainment).

Camilla Whitby   01403-820299 Mobile 07860-405582

Frederic Wichert   Mobile 07947-570566
The Interface (short), Addicted 2 (short).

Emlyn Williams   029-2030 4489 Mobile 07766-557625
The Bench (TV drama), The Three Sisters (TV drama), Do Not Go Gentle (feature).

Herbert Wise   020-7272 5047 Mobile 07887-735067
CCA 020-7630 6303 Fax 020-7281 3767
I Claudius (TV drama), The Tenth Kingdom (TV drama), Breaking The Code (TV film).

Carol Wiseman   Mobile 07831-377276 ITG 020-7636 6565
Face The Music (feature), The Queen's Nose (TV childrens), Goggle-Eyes (TV film).

Stephen Woolfenden   01932-349133 Mobile 07850-312233
SPA 01932-571044
Harry Potter & The Deathly Hallows (feature) (2nd unit), Harry Potter & The Order Of The Phoenix (feature) (2nd unit), Echo Beach (TV drama).

Jonathan Wright Miller   01732-832773
Fair City (TV drama), The Antiques Road Show (TV light entertainment), Connoisseur (TV light entertainment).

Ian Wyatt   020-8287 8055 Mobile 07802-212483
The Law Machine (TV drama doc), Signals (TV arts), Executive Lifestyles (TV doc).

DIRECTORS - 1ST ASSISTANT

Jay Arthur   01730-890156 Mobile 07802-824384
SC 01932-252577
Psychoville (TV comedy drama), The Mighty Boosh (TV light entertainment), Nathan Barley (TV drama).

Howard Arundel   020-8399 2155 Mobile 07836-575027
Downton Abbey (TV drama), The Shell Seekers (TV drama), Doctor Who (TV drama).

PRODUCTION

Andrew Bainbridge   01325-377451 Mobile 07785-343023
WZ 020-7437 2055

Scott Bates   Mobile 07950-449244
Minder (TV drama), No Holds Bard (TV comedy drama), The Rise Of
The Foot Soldier (feature).

John Bennett   01332-831952 Mobile 07974-751758
Dr Who (TV drama), Wild At Heart (TV drama), The Street (TV
drama).

Peter Bennett   01932-886714 Mobile 07715-034537
Alexander (feature), The Mummy Returns (feature), The Mummy
(feature).

Jonathan Benson   020-8749 1202 Mobile 07742-310803
Colour Me Kubrick (feature), Chariots Of Fire (feature), A Fish
Called Wanda (feature).

Grietje Besteman   020-7275 7623 Mobile 07970-643989
Micro Men (TV drama), My Life As A Popat (TV drama), Elizabeth
David - A Life In Recipes (TV drama).

James Blackwell   01483-534631 Mobile 07887-704654
Little Dorrit (TV drama), Desperate Romantics (TV drama), Five
Days (feature).

Tamana Bleasdale   Mobile 07960-865299
Dead Man's Cards (feature), 28 Weeks Later (feature) (2nd unit).

Robert Blishen   Mobile 07973-461774 RED 020-8374 3074
Somers Town (feature), When I Was Twelve (TV film).

William Booker   020-8961 2896 EXEC 01753-646677
Inkheart (feature) (2nd unit), Elizabeth: The Golden Age (feature)
(2nd unit), The Holiday (feature) (2nd unit).

Phil Booth   Mobile 07768-400694
W.E. (feature), Ironclad (feature), Centurion (feature).

Harry Boyd   Mobile 07836-743159
Red Tails (feature), New Tricks (TV drama), Rebus (TV drama).

Kas Braganza   Mobile 07774-761977 Fax 020-8568 1844
Britannia High (TV drama), The Long Walk To Finchley (TV film),
Bodies (TV drama).

Bill Brennan   01603-664727 Mobile 07880-553365
Fax 01603-664727
North & South (TV drama), Foyle's War (TV drama), Warlock
(feature).

Edward Brett   020-7610 6144 Mobile 07860-443895
SPA 01932-571044
Wolverine (feature), The Golden Compass (feature), Alien Vs
Predator (feature).

David Brown   01887-820080 Mobile 07718-808558
Rebus (TV drama), Rough Diamond (TV drama), Separate Lies
(feature).

Nick Brown   020-8647 1356 Mobile 07973-430981
Being Human (TV drama), Messiah (TV drama), True Dare Kiss (TV
drama).

Grantly Butters   Mobile 07976-295232
Waking The Dead (TV drama), Jam & Jerusalem (TV comedy drama),
Sleep With Me (TV drama).

Patrick Cadell   020-7221 9127 Mobile 07785-300906
WZ 020-7437 2055

Ian Cameron   01288-361410 Mobile 07831-887455
CB 01932-592572 Fax 01288-361410
Equilibrium (feature), The Call (feature).

Paddy Carpenter   01453-860706
Event Horizon (feature) (2nd unit), Hamish Macbeth (TV drama).

Chris Carreras   01844-218878 Mobile 07590-806755
Fax 01844-214655
Green Zone (feature), United 93 (feature), Harry Potter & The
Goblet Of Fire (feature).

Matt Carver   Mobile 07904-109777
Sex & Drugs & Rock & Roll (feature), Misfits (TV comedy drama),
Adulthood (feature).

Marcus Catlin   01932-231178 Mobile 07768-124991
The Day Of The Triffids (TV drama), Primeval (TV drama), A Touch
Of Frost (TV drama).

Mark Challenor   Mobile 07767-365913
Law & Order (TV drama), Victoria Wood Xmas Special (TV light
entertainment), Primeval (TV drama).

Jamie Christopher   Mobile 07711-417577
Harry Potter & The Order Of The Phoenix (feature) (2nd unit).

Marco Ciglia   Mobile 07961-807391
Chat Room (feature), Eichmann (feature), Toast (TV drama).

Patrick Clayton   01727-811223 Fax 01727-811223
Doom (feature), Interview With The Vampire (feature), Event
Horizon (feature).

Andi Coldwell   Mobile 07973-380147
The Shell Seekers (TV drama), Life On Mars (TV drama).

David Crabtree   Mobile 07885-600150
Four Seasons (TV drama), Compulsion (TV doc), Poirot (TV drama).

Joanna Crow   Mobile 07966-235683
Spooks (TV drama), Life On Mars (TV drama), Dirty Filthy Love (TV
drama).

PRODUCTION

Ken Cumberland   01943-816200 Mobile 07710-125299
Freight (short), The Royal (TV drama), Diamond Geezer (TV drama)
(2nd unit).

David Daniels   01208-880468 Mobile 07973-732202
CCM 020-8743 7337
National Treasure: Book Of Secrets (feature), The Golden Compass
(feature) (2nd unit), Flyboys (feature).

Rawdon de Fresnes   Mobile 07971-052969
EXEC 01753-646677
Numerous commercials, Scenes Of A Sexual Nature (feature).

Mark Dean   01273-684085 Mobile 07901-552041
CB 01932-592572

Kristian Dench   01923-720028 Mobile 07956-640793
Footballers' Wives (TV drama), Bad Girls (TV drama), Waking The
Dead (TV drama).

Melanie Dicks   Mobile 07775-912955
St Trinian's II: The Legend Of Fritton's Gold (feature), From Time To
Time (feature), Run Fat Boy Run (feature).

John Dodds   020-8940 6670 Mobile 07801-441010
Flawless (feature), The Merchant Of Venice (feature), Red Mercury
(feature).

Tom Dunbar   Mobile 07976-614487
Taking The Flack (TV comedy drama), Nearly Famous (TV drama),
Spooks: Code 9 (TV drama).

Keith Duncan   01204-591541 Mobile 07970-713916
True Dare Kiss (TV drama), Heartbeat (TV drama), Cutting It (TV
drama).

Tony Dyer   01923-676568 Mobile 07970-200909
The Bill (TV drama), London's Burning (TV drama), Return To
Treasure Island (TV drama).

Annie East   Mobile 07771-993977
EastEnders (promo), Holby City (TV drama), Casualty (TV drama).

Mark Egerton   Mobile 07889-071765 EXEC 01753-646677
Alien Vs Predator (feature), 12 Monkeys (feature), Mao's Last
Dancer (feature).

Paul Elkins   01457-874845 Mobile 07970-548053
Casualty 1908 (TV drama), A Is For Acid (TV drama), Brides In The
Bath (TV drama).

Peter Errington   020-8979 0572 Mobile 07947-885999
Fax 020-8979 0572
The Bill (TV drama), Nine Dead Gay Guys (feature) (Producer), NIL
(feature).

Robert Fabbri   Mobile 07798-613917
Doc Martin (TV drama), Comet (TV film), Tales Of The Riverbank
(feature).

Mark Fenn   Mobile 07702-491883 SPA 01932-571044
Krod Mandoon & The Flaming Sword Of Fire (TV drama), Flutter
(feature), A Passionate Woman (TV drama).

Micky Finch   01932-354544 Mobile 07974-925657
STA 020-7729 7477 Fax 01932-354544
The Chronicles Of Narnia: The Voyage Of The Dawn Treader (feature)
(visual fx unit), Angels & Demons (feature) (visual fx unit), The
Imaginarium Of Dr Parnassus (feature) (visual fx unit).

Toby Ford   01932-859808 Mobile 07973-254152
Sherlock Holmes (TV drama), Push (feature), Occupation (TV
drama).

Jerome Franc   Mobile 07944-646967
The Three Musketeers (feature), Shadow Dancer (feature).

Grant Freeman   Mobile 07771-783708 WZ 020-7437 2055
Nintendo Wii (commercial), Flex (short), Capital Radio
(commercial).

Peter Freeman   01753-862226 Mobile 07774-700747
The Colour Of Magic (TV film), Miss Marple (TV drama), These
Foolish Things (feature).

Dominic Fysh   020-8398 8798 Mobile 07831-137146
Harry Potter & The Order Of The Phoenix (feature), Harry Potter &
The Deathly Hallows (feature), Victims (feature).

Gerry Gavigan   01243-268064 Mobile 07973-634184
BE 01727-841177 Fax 01243-268064
Valkyrie (feature) (2nd unit), Troy (feature), Die Another Day
(feature).

Marcia Gay   020-8202 6660 Mobile 07774-289209
CMM 020-8584 5363
Atlantis (TV film), The Whisky Robber (feature), Dalziel & Pascoe
(TV drama).

Joe Geary   Mobile 07958-727788
An Education (feature), Mr Nice (feature), Four Lions (feature).

Ben Gill   020-7249 9561 Mobile 07976-848887
CB 01932-592572
True Love Once Removed (short), I Could Read The Sky (feature).

Trevor Gittings   01454-294383 Mobile 07831-823951
Lark Rise To Candleford (TV drama), Genie In The House (TV
childrens), The Impressionists (TV drama).

Mark Goddard   020-8892 8650 Mobile 07831-166424
Basic Instinct II (feature), Shooting Dogs (feature), Endgame
(feature).

Richard Goodwin   020-7686 0216 Mobile 07956-174291
EXEC 01753-646677
Children Of Men (feature), Harmony (feature), The Mummy: Tomb Of The Dragon Emperor (feature).

Tommy Gormley   0141-945 1150 Mobile 07778-527866
The Golden Compass (feature), John Carter Of Mars (feature).

Cherry Gould   01798-869207 Mobile 07973-614901
Trial & Retribution (TV drama).

Mike Gowans   020-8841 0150

Richard Graysmark   Mobile 07778-524583
Shanghai (feature) (2nd unit), The Bourne Ultimatum (feature) (2nd unit), Trial & Retribution (TV drama) (2nd unit).

Griffin   Mobile 07973-500618
This Is England (feature), Dead Man's Shoes (feature).

Neil Grigson   01892-864424 Mobile 07831-672942
Fax 01892-860478
Numerous commercials.

Lee Grumett   Mobile 07768-372510 ITG 020-7636 6565
Sherlock Holmes (feature) (2nd unit), Jane Eyre (feature), Never Let Me Go (feature).

Sean Guest   Mobile 07770-533252
1408 (feature), Derailed (feature), Girl With A Pearl Earring (feature).

Marios Hamboulides   020-8992 0669
Mobile 07767-822300
Primeval (TV drama), Hustle (TV drama), Poirot (TV drama).

Cordelia Hardy   01403-790776 Mobile 07770-656615
BA 020-7836 1112
Crime & Punishment (TV film), Miss Marple (TV drama), After Thomas (TV drama).

Martin Harrison   01962-859133 Mobile 07931-596758
Nine (feature), Nanny McPhee & The Big Bang (feature), Stardust (feature).

Richard Hatherell   Mobile 07747-604463
Man Vs Wild (TV doc), Morris: A Life With Bells On (feature), The Rise Of The Foot Soldier (feature).

Ursula Haworth   01706-224089 Mobile 07718-978556
The Waiting Room (feature), Waterloo Road (TV drama), Lilies (TV drama).

Kate Hazell   01296-655824 Mobile 07768-774318
Spooks (TV drama), Hotel Babylon (TV drama), Whatever It Takes (TV drama).

Julian Hearne   01344-301000 Mobile 07973-619908
Irish Jam (feature), Waking The Dead (TV drama), Shaun Of The Dead (feature).

Monica Heath   01295-810839 Mobile 07850-990795
GEMS 029-2071 0770 Fax 01295-810839
Casualty (TV drama), The Roman Mysteries (TV childrens), Dalziel & Pascoe (TV drama).

Nick Heckstall-Smith   020-8830 7057
Mobile 07770-917842 CCM 020-8743 7337
The Wolfman (feature) (2nd unit), Mirrors (feature), Stormbreaker (feature).

Mark Hedges   Mobile 07767-496596
Swinging With The Finkels (feature), The Mighty Boosh (TV light entertainment), Bunny & The Bull (feature).

Guy Heeley   020-8749 9646 Mobile 07973-309032
Miss Potter (feature), Hannah (feature), Starter For Ten (feature).

Mike Higgins   01934-624358 Mobile 07963-867521
GEMS 029-2071 0770
Shoot On Sight (feature), Life Translated (feature), Bandit Queen (feature).

Ben Howarth   Mobile 07973-144207 EXEC 01753-646677
Hannibal Rising (feature), Woody Allan's Summer Project (feature), Sahara (feature) (2nd Assistant).

Ben Hughes   020-7274 3685 Mobile 07710-115135
EXEC 01753-646677 Fax 020-7978 8586
Broken Lines (feature), U Be Dead (TV film), Land Of The Blind (feature).

Jim Imber   Mobile 07956-500947
Spaced (TV comedy drama), Spooks (TV drama).

Michael Jelves   01273-722046 Mobile 07973-666050
Big Brother (TV reality) (Director), Father Ted (TV comedy drama), French & Saunders (TV light entertainment).

Eurwyn Jones   01253-354977 Mobile 07939-539279
Question Time (TV news & current affairs), Coronation Street (TV drama), Emmerdale (TV drama).

Paul Judges   01903-538936 Mobile 07966-265945
The Virgin Queen (TV drama), Poirot (TV drama), Fanny Hill (TV drama).

Max Keene   Mobile 07831-240295
Robin Hood (TV drama), Sherlock Holmes (feature), The Libertine (feature).

Chris Kelly   020-8459 3116 Mobile 07976-360126
SC 01932-252577
Numerous commercials & promos, Caz Underground (TV drama).

Jessica Hurles Laws   020-8743 3064
Mobile 07966-478087
I Could Never Be Your Woman (feature), Venus (feature), A Cock & Bull Story (feature).

Jon Jennings   Mobile 07968-735210
In The Loop (feature), Green Wing (TV comedy drama), The IT Crowd (TV comedy drama).

Dan John   01442-876926 Mobile 07976-688978
From Time To Time (feature), St Trinian's (feature), The Golden Compass (feature) (2nd unit).

Sarah Jane Jones   Mobile 07971-442603
Coronation Street (TV drama), New Street Law (TV drama), Shameless (TV drama).

Trevor Kaye   020-8954 2763 Mobile 07703-258595
Torn (TV drama), Nice Guy Eddie (TV drama).

Ben Lanning   Mobile 07968-837302
Gulliver's Travels (feature), Hellboy 2: The Golden Army (feature), Harry Potter & The Order Of The Phoenix (feature).

Bryn Lawrence   Mobile 07815-106767
The Boat That Rocked (feature), Nowhere Boy (feature), Wild Child (feature).

Olivia Lloyd   Mobile 07778-872238
The Debt (feature), The Other Boleyn Girl (feature), Amazing Grace (feature).

Sarah Macfarlane   Mobile 07977-239692
Never Let Me Go (feature), The Dark Knight (feature), St Trinian's (feature).

Sasha Mann   Mobile 07710-426018
Hustle (TV drama), Spooks (TV drama), Something Borrowed (feature).

James Manning   Mobile 07831-720987
Spooks (TV drama), Oranges & Sunshine (feature), Going Postal (TV film).

Andrew Mannion   Mobile 07771-666113
Wallander (TV drama), Sex & Drugs & Rock & Roll (feature), Mad Dogs (TV drama).

Candy Marlowe   Mobile 07974-354336
London Boulevard (feature), Bridget Jones's Diary II (feature), Vanity Fair (feature).

Anna Marsh   020-8464 3244 Mobile 07957-497450
Bellamy's People (TV comedy drama), Dead Ringers (TV comedy), Summer In Transylvania (TV childrens).

Lisa Marsh   01494-775995 Mobile 07971-260050
Fanny Hill (TV drama).

Pru Mettyer   Mobile 07973-155717 GEMS 029-2071 0770
Almost Adult (feature), The History Of Mr Polly (TV drama), Ian Fleming: A Life In Pictures (TV drama doc).

Michael Michael   Mobile 07785-288284
Robin Hood (feature), Green Zone (feature), Quantum Of Solace (feature).

Adam Morris   Mobile 07971-670073
Midsomer Murders (TV drama), The Firm (feature), Street Dance (feature).

Simon Morris   Mobile 07768-128130
Spooks (TV drama).

Justin Murphy   +353 86 053 0501 Mobile 07970-077460
Footballers' Wives (TV drama), Casualty (TV drama), Provoked (feature).

Adam O'Brien   Mobile 07803-011772
The Last Detective (TV drama), Monkey Trousers (TV light entertainment), The Bill (TV drama).

Emily Perowne   Mobile 07855-144302
Blitz (feature), Red Riding (TV drama), Oh! Happy Day (feature).

David Pinkus   020-8392 9765 Mobile 07802-304400
Robin Hood (feature), Prince Of Persia (feature), Doomsday (feature).

Samar Pollitt   020-8567 7264 Mobile 07968-860316
Clash Of The Titans (feature), The Wolfman (feature), The Other Boleyn Girl (feature).

Daniel Precious   020-8508 2287 Mobile 07956-494404
Star Stories (TV light entertainment), The Kevin Bishop Show (TV comedy drama), Roman's Empire (TV drama).

Deborah Pursey   020-8715 4162 Mobile 07779-281167

Charlie Reed   Mobile 07876-495428
Brighton Rock (feature), Cemetery Junction (feature), In Bruges (feature).

Christian Rigg   Mobile 07710-433956
Acts Of Godfrey (feature), Third Star (feature), Better Things (feature).

Derek Ritchie   Mobile 07715-595265
New Town Killers (feature).

Lance Roehrig   Mobile 07957-121805
In Bruges (feature), Amazing Grace (feature).

Tom Rye   Mobile 07821-555005
Tamara Drewe (feature), The Damned United (feature), Any Human Heart (TV drama).

PRODUCTION

Rebecca Semark   01992-574967 Mobile 07956-850330
Fairy Liquid (commercial), New Wave (TV childrens), Tomorrow Beginnings (TV doc).

Matthew Sharp   01344-291494 Mobile 07973-254770
Batman Returns (feature), Harry Potter & The Deathly Hallows (feature), Harry Potter & The Order Of The Phoenix (feature).

Nick Shuttleworth   Mobile 07970-914585
Green Zone (feature), The Bourne Ultimatum (feature), Goal! (feature).

Nick Simmonds   Mobile 07930-412227
Glorious 39 (feature), The Impressions Show With Culshaw & Stephenson (TV light entertainment), The Life & Death Of Peter Sellers (feature).

Michael Stevenson   020-7978 6348
Lawrence Of Arabia (feature), Dr Zhivago (TV film), Shadowlands (feature).

Chris Stoaling   020-8451 6699 Mobile 07977-448841
44 Inch Chest (feature), Nanny McPhee & The Big Bang (feature), Stardust (feature).

Emma Stokes   01276-472852 Mobile 07885-301930
Harry Potter & The Deathly Hallows (feature), Harry Potter & The Half-Blood Prince (feature) (2nd unit), Sweeney Todd (feature).

Catrin Strong   Mobile 07860-472394 Fax 020-7281 5555
Spaced (TV comedy drama), Black Books (TV comedy drama), Bring Me The Head Of Mavis Davis (feature).

Ben Sweet   Mobile 07787-552427
The Colour Of Magic (TV film), Miss Marple (TV drama).

Jeff Taylor   Mobile 07775-908201
John Carter Of Mars (feature), The Eagle Of The Ninth (feature), Quantum Of Solace (feature).

Paul Taylor   01865-331602 Mobile 07774-257128
Fax 01865-331602
Green Zone (feature), The World Is Not Enough (feature), Troy (feature).

Ciara Tinney   Mobile 07807-009703
Your Highness (feature).

Charlie Waller   Mobile 07973-256133
Green Zone (feature), Nine (feature), Angus Thongs & Perfect Snogging (feature).

Holly Watson   Mobile 07788-448875
Waking The Dead (TV drama), Judge John Deed (TV drama).

Dominique Wedge   Mobile 07766-203677
Casualty (TV drama), Missing (TV doc), The Bill (TV drama).

Kim Whittaker   Mobile 07734-793905
Children Of Men (feature), The Golden Compass (feature), Kingdom Of Heaven (feature).

Anthony Wilcox   020-8772 4124 Mobile 07957-415692
W.E. (feature), Angus Thongs & Perfect Snogging (feature), Hot Fuzz (feature).

Harriet Worth   Mobile 07814-376293
Doomsday (feature).

DIRECTORS - 2ND UNIT

Vic Armstrong   01344-483326 Mobile 07771-932088
Fax 01344-862038
War Of The Worlds (feature), Die Another Day (feature), Gangs Of New York (feature).

Tom Delmar   Mobile 07831-571127 Fax 07785-833373
Waar (feature), Star Wars: Episode II - Attack Of The Clones (feature).

Jimmy Devis BSC   01227-752715 Fax 01227-752715
Interview With The Vampire (feature), Super Mario Brothers (feature), For Your Eyes Only (feature).

Jim Dowdall   01580-880322 Mobile 07836-204228
Agent Cody Banks II (feature), Enduring Love (feature).

George Gerwitz   01905-772767 Mobile 07833-771495
Doctor Who (TV drama), Wire In The Blood (TV drama), Sea Of Souls (TV drama).

Dominic Leung   020-7608 0238
Hitchhiker's Guide To The Galaxy (feature).

Peter Macdonald BSC   Mobile 07976-282474
Wolverine (feature), Percy Jackson & The Olympians: The Lightning Thief (feature), Harry Potter 1-4 (feature).

Eddie Stacey   Mobile 07836-677337
Highlander: The Source (feature).

Paul Weston   01590-670660 Mobile 07860-878800
Messiah (TV drama), My Giant (feature), Death Train (feature).

Marc Wolff   +33 497 010 717 Mobile +33 6 19 78 60 32
BA 020-7836 1112 Fax +33 497 010 718
Amelia (feature), Doomsday (feature), The Flood (feature).

DIRECTORS - 3RD ASSISTANT

Helen Allibone   Mobile 07989-541826
The Baker (feature), Trial & Retribution (TV drama), The Grid (TV drama).

PRODUCTION

Joe Barlow Mobile 07833-780891
Sweeney Todd (feature), St Trinian's II: The Legend Of Fritton's Gold (feature), Quantum Of Solace (feature).

Adam Barrington Mobile 07710-185299
Kingdom (TV drama), Lilacs (feature), Sex Actually (TV light entertainment).

Sarah Brand Mobile 07717-811365
Robin Hood (feature).

Tom Brewster Mobile 07900-252950
London Boulevard (feature).

Hannah Brown Mobile 07929-291413
Prince Of Persia (feature), Get Him To The Greek (feature), Lesbian Vampire Killers (feature).

Adam Byles Mobile 07916-173355
Quantum Of Solace (feature) (2nd unit), Gulliver's Travels (feature) (2nd unit), Made Of Honor (feature).

Stephen Carney Mobile 07915-635329
Neds (feature), Single Father (TV drama), Burke & Hare (feature).

Caroline Chapman 01753-643750 Mobile 07775-605921
Breaking & Entering (feature), Mrs Henderson Presents (feature), Sylvia (feature).

Joey Coughlin Mobile 07974-325567
The Debt (feature), The Wolfman (feature).

Annie Dibling Mobile 07989-386445
Caerdydd (TV drama), A Child's Christmas In Wales (TV drama), Gavin & Stacey (TV comedy drama).

Stephen Dipre 020-8303 8087 Mobile 07974-314132
Double Zero (feature), Namaste London (feature).

Clare Glass Mobile 07958-403473
Robin Hood (feature), Hereafter (feature), Sherlock Holmes (feature).

Heidi Gower Mobile 07787-281492
Nanny McPhee & The Big Bang (feature), Stardust (feature).

Hanna Haffenden Mobile 07792-171516
Little Dorrit (TV drama).

Cara Higgins Mobile 07769-961127
Puritan (feature), Troy (feature) (2nd unit), Helen Of Troy (TV film).

Nathan Holmes 01282-841043 Mobile 07939-541492
The Brothers Grimm (feature), Band Of Brothers (TV drama), Hornblower (TV drama).

Sarah Hood Mobile 07980-885505
The Wolfman (feature).

Barney Hughes Mobile 07979-915969
Sherlock Holmes (feature), Robin Hood (feature), From Time To Time (feature).

Ian Hughes Mobile 07776-186474
Blitz (feature), Four Lions (feature), The Firm (feature).

Carley Lane Mobile 07879-641162
Sherlock Holmes (feature), The Imaginarium Of Dr Parnassus (feature), Never Let Me Go (feature).

Briana Lebold Mobile 07949-111755
Holby City (TV drama), Bad Girls (TV drama), Bear Behaving Badly (TV childrens).

Andy Madden Mobile 07827-893602
Clash Of The Titans (feature).

James McGrady Mobile 07748-115890
Robin Hood (feature), John Carter Of Mars (feature) (2nd unit), The Disappearance Of Alice Creed (feature) (2nd unit).

Paul Melton Mobile 07968-326381
Shaun Of The Dead (feature), Dead Fish (feature), Waking The Dead (TV drama).

James Mountain Mobile 07810-128864
Spooks (TV drama).

Tony Payne 01306-877198 Mobile 07813-781712
CB 01932-592572
Snatch (feature), Fisticuffs (feature), As If (TV drama).

Fiona Perry Mobile 07956-569527 Fax 01723-368005
Little Voice (feature), Harry Potter & The Goblet Of Fire (feature), Harry Potter & The Prisoner Of Azkaban (feature).

Lisa Radin Mobile 07876-567108
Miss Marple (TV drama).

Jane Ryan 01932-784223
Harry Potter & The Deathly Hallows (feature), Harry Potter & The Half-Blood Prince (feature), Harry Potter & The Order Of The Phoenix (feature).

Camilla Southwell Mobile 07958-001824

Nick Starr Mobile 07745-405226
Gulliver's Travels (feature), GI Joe: The Rise Of Cobra (feature), Hellboy 2: The Golden Army (feature).

Becky Symons Mobile 07932-654627
EastEnders (promo), Spooks (TV drama), Promoted To Glory (TV film).

Brett Thomas Mobile 07872-909043
Fanny Hill (TV drama).

PRODUCTION

Robert Willden   01923-720776 Mobile 07956-653635
More Than Love (TV drama), The Stuff Of Life (TV drama), 2 Pints Of Lager (TV comedy drama).

DIRECTORS ASSISTANTS

Alex Hodgson   Mobile 07980-925467
Hippie Hippie Shake (feature), Children Of Men (feature), Charlie & The Chocolate Factory (feature).

Alex Molden   020-8423 1815 Mobile 07732-260352
John Carter Of Mars (feature).

Oliver Raynor   Mobile 07789-548982
The Wolfman (feature), The Bourne Ultimatum (feature).

Nicole Volavka   Mobile 07734-430072
Piccadilly Jim (feature), Shooting Dogs (feature).

FLOOR MANAGERS

Marc Baker   020-8994 0084 Mobile 07710-429776
Fax 020-8181 6108
MTV Music Awards (TV light entertainment), Top Gear (TV entertainment), BAFTA Awards (TV light entertainment).

Grenville Bartlett   01727-893346 Mobile 07957-387119
The Green Green Grass (TV comedy drama), Harry Hill's TV Burp (TV light entertainment), Never Mind The Buzzcocks (TV light entertainment).

Steven Cass   Mobile 07973-657130
The Price Is Right (TV light entertainment), Time Team (TV doc), World Rally Championship (TV sport).

Polly Morgan   01252-819737 Mobile 07958-646365
The Big Breakfast (TV light entertainment), SM:tv (TV light entertainment), Disney (TV childrens).

Adrian Walsh   Mobile 07956-893981
Britain's Got Talent (TV light entertainment), Pop Idol (TV light entertainment), Ant & Dec's Saturday Night (TV light entertainment).

LINE PRODUCERS

Bruce Abrahams   020-7370 0473 Mobile 07768-363783
Dani's House (TV childrens), Escape From Scorpion Island (TV childrens), Holby City (TV drama).

Lee Alliston GLM   01227-264355 Mobile 07833-772722
The Tapes (feature) (Producer), House Full (feature), Three: Love, Lies, Betrayal (feature).

Ken Baker   020-8953 7276 Mobile 07778-416083
The Day Of The Triffids (TV drama), Colour Me Kubrick (feature), Summerhill (TV drama).

David Ball   029-2034 4111 Mobile 07831-606169
The Contractor (feature), Abraham's Point (feature), Big Nothing (feature).

Sara Banister   01892-536067 Mobile 07889-235632
Missing (TV doc), Family Affairs (TV drama), The Bill (TV drama).

Dominic Barlow   Mobile 07977-444481
CCM 020-8743 7337
Spooks (TV drama), Casualty (TV drama), Cape Wrath (TV drama).

Alison Barnett   01252-723649 Mobile 07850-827013
Fax 01252-821168
Bleak House (TV drama), Spooks (TV drama), Hustle (TV drama).

Don Bell   01548-852730 Mobile 07971-107590
The Shell Seekers (TV drama), Afterlife (TV drama), The Diary Of A Nobody (TV drama).

Bernard Bellew   Mobile 07770-918636
127 Hours (feature), Sunshine (feature), 28 Weeks Later (feature).

Hilary Benson   Mobile 07979-526882
Murphy's Law (TV drama), Robin Hood (TV drama), Spooks (TV drama).

Mairi Bett   Mobile 07774-478160
Green Zone (feature), Jane Eyre (feature), The Debt (feature).

James Biddle   Mobile 07940-577070
Attack The Block (feature), Adulthood (feature), Free Agents (TV drama).

Helen Booth   Mobile 07778-212598

Sarah Bradshaw   020-8960 5178 Mobile 07836-657338
Prince Of Persia (feature), Miami Vice (feature).

Danielle Brandon   020-7272 1510 Mobile 07973-558424
Happy-Go-Lucky (feature), Another Year (feature), Primeval (TV drama).

Averil Brennan   01603-664727 Mobile 07836-263486
Fax 01603-664727
Kingdom (TV drama), Spooks (TV drama), Foyle's War (TV drama).

David Brown   020-7993 2707 Mobile 07775-896451
ITG 020-7636 6565
The Waterhorse (feature), Flyboys (feature), Nanny McPhee (feature).

Adam Browne   020-8892 0135 Mobile 07802-822807
Primeval (TV drama), Wild At Heart (TV drama), Misfits (TV comedy drama).

Vikki McCraw   0131-337 9893 Mobile 07976-608555
Was Guckst Du?! (TV light entertainment), Audi A8 (commercial), Orange (commercial).

Donald McDonald   0141-334 7413 Mobile 07771-608978
Miss Potter (feature).

James Nash GLM   Mobile 07739-472874
Midsomer Murders (TV drama).

Mark O'Hanlon GLM   01204-886228 Mobile 07973-744571

Nick Oliver   Mobile 07946-514954
Stardust (feature), Sherlock Holmes (feature), Green Zone (feature).

Lee Robertson   Mobile 07787-122326
Nine (feature).

Andrew Ryland   Mobile 07811-433202

Amie Tridgell   Mobile 07903-674834
W.E. (feature), Happy-Go-Lucky (feature), Never Let Me Go (feature).

Mark Walledge   Mobile 07715-464643
The Commander (TV drama), Trial & Retribution (TV drama), Miss Marple (TV drama).

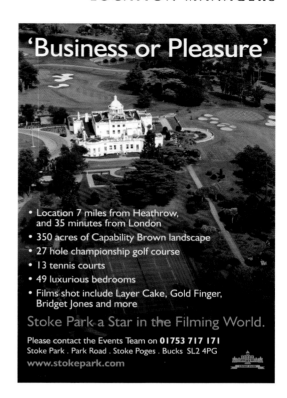
LOCATION MANAGERS

Ian Aegis   01437-532989 Mobile 07860-573025
55 Degrees North (TV drama), Bullet Boy (feature), Hear The Silence (TV drama).

Idris Ahmed   Mobile 07973-209979
Hex (TV drama), The Stepfather (TV drama), Clapham Junction (TV drama).

James Alexander GLM   Mobile 07720-706017
Lennon Naked (TV drama), Gulliver's Travels (feature), Made In Dagenham (feature).

Monty Allan   Mobile 07515-951431
The Secret Garden (feature), Survivors (TV drama), Reunited (short).

Jonathan Allott   Mobile 07885-653600
Being Human (TV drama), Doctor Who (TV drama), Skins (TV drama).

Rufus Andrews   01993-822434 Mobile 07836-222968
Lark Rise To Candleford (TV drama), William & Mary (TV drama), Dalziel & Pascoe (TV drama).

Graham Aza   Mobile 07957-434387
Nanny McPhee (feature), BMW (commercial), Expedia (commercial).

Tim Baish   +34 96 646 3965 Mobile +34 606 583341
Tom Brown's School Days (TV drama), Belonging (TV drama), Wall Of Silence (TV drama).

Linzi Baltrunas   Mobile 07778-772197
The Dark Knight (feature), The Other Boleyn Girl (feature), Miss Potter (feature) (Assistant).

Johnny Bamford GLM   01840-250445
Mobile 07770-915418
Doc Martin (TV drama), Saving Grace (feature), Being Julia (feature).

Caroline Barnes GLM   Mobile 07980-893795
The Bill (TV drama), HSBC (commercial), AA (commercial).

William Barringer GLM   01494-443859
Mobile 07836-672731
The Philanthropist (TV drama), The Nutcracker (ballet) (Production Manager), Miss Marple (TV drama).

Joanna Beckett   020-8566 0971 Mobile 07767-667707
Casino Royale (feature), Batman Begins (feature), Spy Game (feature).

John Bentham   01253-781994 Mobile 07785-505880

PRODUCTION

Brian Bilgorri GLM   01753-642980 Mobile 07785-568877
Saxondale (TV comedy drama), The Bill (TV drama), I Know You Know (feature).

Richard Blackburn GLM   01798-342453
Mobile 07973-264699

Terry Blyther   020-8941 3857 Mobile 07836-780089
Sex & The City 2 (feature), Green Zone (feature), The Golden Compass (feature).

David Boardman   01296-623732 Mobile 07836-642138
Casino Royale (feature), The World Is Not Enough (feature).

Eddie Booth   01624-676465 Mobile 07624-499289
Miss Potter (feature), Keeping Mum (feature), Big Nothing (feature).

Rupert Bray GLM   020-8892 9768 Mobile 07889-103030
Beyond The Sea (feature), The Da Vinci Code (feature) (2nd unit), V For Vendetta (feature).

Sam Breckman   01892-530995 Fax 01892-530995
The Bourne Ultimatum (feature), The Da Vinci Code (feature) (Production Manager), Agent Cody Banks (feature).

David Broder GLM   020-7378 0503 Mobile 07976-397466
Eastern Promises (feature), London Boulevard (feature), 44 Inch Chest (feature).

Frank Buckle GLM   020-8870 5942 Mobile 07885-663091
Channel 4 (ident), Telewest (commercial), KFC (commercial).

Chris Bunyan GLM   Mobile 07803-290917
Judge John Deed (TV drama), Love Again (TV film), The Crouches (TV light entertainment).

Simon Burgess   01895-233995 Mobile 07850-049841
Angus Thongs & Perfect Snogging (feature), Bride & Prejudice (feature), Tomb Raider II (feature).

Carn Burton GLM   01736-333423 Mobile 07973-886964
Solomon Kane (feature), Echo Beach (TV drama), Apocalypto (feature).

Roland Caine GLM   020-8673 4505 Mobile 07836-293493
Max Manus (feature), Soundproof (TV drama), VW Golf (commercial).

Ralph Cameron   01737-823722 Mobile 07515-889521
Honest (TV drama), Dangerous Parking (feature), Viva Blackpool (TV film).

Donald Cameron GLM   0131-466 3408
Mobile 07831-144557
Foyle's War (TV drama), Waking The Dead (TV drama), The Shell Seekers (TV drama).

Ben Carter GLM   Mobile 07714-727276
Numerous commercials.

Peter Chadwick GLM   01983-292936 Mobile 07974-058754
GEMS 029-2071 0770
The Bill (TV drama), The Riddle (feature), Only Fools & Horses (TV comedy drama).

Rob Champion GLM   01453-543876 Mobile 07939-042361
Five Daughters (TV drama), The Murdoch Mysteries (TV drama), NFU Mutual (corporate).

Holly Charlton   020-7978 1688 Mobile 07877-467369
Fax 020-7978 2469
Johnny English 2 (feature), Hewlett Packard (stills), Red Bull (event).
www.locateproductions.com

Tom Chisman   01590-672079 Mobile 07967-562283
Fax 01590-672079
Hear The Silence (TV drama), Trust (TV drama), Lad's Army (TV light entertainment).

Mally Chung   01228-546527 Mobile 07802-644072
Quantum Of Solace (feature), Robin Hood (feature), Across The Universe (feature).

Tony Clarkson   020-7737 6177 Mobile 07836-358883
And When Did You Last See Your Father? (feature), Scenes Of A Sexual Nature (feature), Mrs Henderson Presents (feature).

Daniel Connolly GLM   Mobile 07979-592113
The Shadow Line (TV drama), West Is West (feature), Bronson (feature).

Andrew Cooke GLM   01926-633788 Mobile 07774-106998
Robin Hood (feature), The Golden Compass (feature), Charlie & The Chocolate Factory (feature).

Lynsey Cosford   Mobile 07834-152808
New Tricks (TV drama), PhoneShop (TV comedy drama).

Alex Cox   01865-400624 Mobile 07973-141845
Nicholas Nickleby (feature), The Grid (TV drama), A Dance To The Music Of Time (TV film).

Tessa Crockett GLM   020-7267 6122 Mobile 07889-486336
The Navigators (feature), Second Sight (TV drama), London's Burning (TV drama).

Simon Crook   01793-870448 Mobile 07850-527663
Sex & The City 2 (feature), Alexander (feature), Prince Of Persia (feature).

Tom Crooke   Mobile 07787-113682
Sherlock Holmes (feature), Robin Hood (feature), Miss Potter (feature).

PRODUCTION

Grant Cummings GLM   Mobile 07779-110745
The Veteran (feature), The Escapist (feature), The Real Hustle (TV drama).

Rikke Dakin GLM   020-8766 8035 Mobile 07767-778138
Suburban Shootout (TV drama), Mistresses (TV drama), Bombshell (TV drama).

Andrew Dalmahoy   Mobile 07941-759140
Navid & Johnny (TV comedy drama), Albert's Memorial (TV drama), Victoria Wood Xmas Special (TV light entertainment).

Bill Darby   020-8740 8265 Mobile 07831-191558
Robin Hood (feature), National Treasure: Book Of Secrets (feature), Inkheart (feature).

Teresa Darby   020-8740 8265 Mobile 07768-737423
Robin Hood (feature), National Treasure: Book Of Secrets (feature), Inkheart (feature).

Nick Daubeny GLM   Mobile 07831-403290
Inception (feature), Elizabeth: The Golden Age (feature), The Pacific (TV drama).

Richard Dunmore   020-7607 3134 Mobile 07860-789274
PG 01753-651767 Fax 020-7607 3134
The Grid (TV drama), Incognito (feature), Shadowlands (feature).

Lloret Dunn   Mobile 07836-574927
Doomsday (feature).

Piers Dunn   Mobile 07973-175816
The Golden Compass (feature), The Da Vinci Code (feature).

Giles Edleston   Mobile 07850-366703
Green Zone (feature), Sherlock Holmes (feature), The Bank Job (feature).

Tom Elgood   020-8341 2368 Mobile 07860-376666
Brick Lane (feature), Identity (TV drama), Iris (feature).

Roger Elliott   01884-820888 Mobile 07774-428309
Stormy Years (TV drama), House Of The Sisters (TV drama), Curse This House (TV drama).

Fiona Elrington   Mobile 07990-570676
Foyle's War (TV drama), Casualty (TV drama), Kingdom (TV drama).

Clive Evans   Mobile 07971-837557
Ironclad (feature), Stanley Park (TV drama), The Bill (TV drama).

Midge Ferguson GLM   0121-434 5244
Mobile 07785-558880
A Thing Called Love (TV drama), Silent Witness (TV drama), Mayo (TV drama).

Duncan Flower   020-8453 0334 Mobile 07971-558748
Robin Hood (feature) (Assistant), Elizabeth: The Golden Age (feature), Miss Marple (TV drama).

Fiona Francombe GLM   0117-985 7917
Mobile 07770-430328
Lark Rise To Candleford (TV drama), Persuasion (feature), Afterlife (TV drama).

Nick Fulton   Mobile 07850-785045
Quantum Of Solace (feature), Gulliver's Travels (feature), Bridget Jones's Diary II (feature).

Stan Fus GLM   020-8993 1201 Mobile 07836-376230
Burn Up (TV drama), Casualty (TV drama), Shank (short).

Ian Galley   01697-475777 Mobile 07887-647138
Fax 01457-864063
The Street (TV drama), Donovan (TV film), Vincent (TV drama).

Phil Gates   Mobile 07779-797357
The Mutant Chronicles (feature).

Richard George   Mobile 07717-126245
London Boulevard (feature).

Alex Gladstone   020-8451 2522 Mobile 07774-758157
Get Him To The Greek (feature), The Imaginarium Of Dr Parnassus (feature), Saving Private Ryan (feature).

Ben Gladstone   020-7254 6429 Mobile 07860-299625
Fish Tank (feature), The Duchess (feature), Hot Fuzz (feature).

Mark Gladwin GLM   020-8299 4403 Mobile 07710-779485
Fax 020-8299 4403
Spooks (TV drama), Wedding Belles (TV drama), Sleep With Me (TV drama).

Synnove Godeseth   Mobile 07984-587375
Green Zone (feature) (Assistant), The Young Victoria (feature) (Assistant), The Wolfman (feature) (Assistant).

Richard Godfrey GLM   020-8886 7342
Mobile 07973-549137 Fax 07970-099048
Chalet Girl (feature), Huge (feature), Above Suspicion (TV drama).

Poppy Gordon Clark   01208-814601
Casualty (TV drama), Creation (feature).

Hugh Gourlay   0131-466 3089 Mobile 07889-160981
Nanny McPhee (feature), The Lazarus Child (feature), Solomon Kane (feature).

James Grant GLM   020-8878 3332 Mobile 07887-946301
Gulliver's Travels (feature), Quantum Of Solace (feature).

PRODUCTION

Mark Grimwade   Mobile 07860-682851

Perrier's Bounty (feature), Centurion (feature), Scaredy Cats (feature).

Michael Harm   Mobile 07956-317882

Bright Star (feature), Nine (feature), Matchpoint (feature).

Derek Harrington   01923-235510 Mobile 07831-308648

Judge John Deed (TV drama), Celebrity Scissorhands (TV reality), Stella Street - The Movie (feature).

Steve Hart GLM   Mobile 07831-351173

Robin Hood (feature), The Golden Compass (feature), Pirates Of The Caribbean: The Curse Of The Black Pearl (feature).

Michael Harvey GLM   0121-455 8667 Mobile 07721-500443

Phil Haselden   020-7734 0456 Mobile 07836-272359

Fax 020-7734 5411

Ford (commercial), Johnnie Walker (commercial), Falabella (commercial).

www.locationpartnership.com

Simon Hassard   Mobile 07970-719133 Fax 020-8670 2870

AA (commercial), Kings Of Leon (promo), Marks & Spencer (commercial).

Keith Hatcher   01895-255787 Mobile 07768-018763

Basic Instinct II (feature), 102 Dalmatians (feature), Harry Potter & The Philosopher's Stone (feature).

Bill Hayes   Mobile 07956-222162

Oh! Happy Day (feature), Animals (TV docu drama), The Candidate (TV reality).

Sally A Hendry   020-8874 2098 Mobile 07973-391498

Numerous commercials & promos.

Robin Higgs GLM   01865-311976 Mobile 07850-122425

The Dark Knight (feature), Pirates Of The Caribbean: At World's End (feature), Harry Potter & The Prisoner Of Azkaban (feature).

Richard Hill   Mobile 07881-585172

Waking The Dead (TV drama), The Other Man (feature), Gulliver's Travels (feature).

Neal Hirst GLM   Mobile 07966-459706

Wire In The Blood (TV drama), Touching Evil (TV drama), Distant Shores (TV drama).

Joel Holmes   Mobile 07711-055817

From Time To Time (feature), Into The Storm (TV film), Street Dance (feature).

Andy Holt   0161-445 2499 Mobile 07768-636141

Numerous commercials, The 51st State (feature).

Manus Home GLM   Mobile 07768-457585

Asylum (feature), Elizabeth: The Golden Age (feature), The Best Man (feature).

Tony Hood   Mobile 07841-997832

Age Of Heroes (feature), The Kid (feature), X-Men (feature).

Phil Hounam GLM   01865-375346 Mobile 07885-773304

Clash Of The Titans (feature), V For Vendetta (feature), Charlie & The Chocolate Factory (feature).

Thomas Howard GLM   Mobile 07973-934542

Last Chance Harvey (feature), Sex: The City & Me (TV drama), Little Britain (tour).

Adrian Hubbard   Mobile 07811-468616

Street Dance 3D (feature) (Assistant), Fosters (commercial) (Assistant).

Luke Jackson GLM   020-7978 1688 Mobile 07768-524778

Fax 020-7978 2469

Nokia (stills), Sky Sports News (promo), Promo Machine (commercial).

www.locateproductions.com

Ali James GLM   Mobile 07801-160411

The Wolfman (feature) (Assistant), Stardust (feature) (Assistant), The Golden Compass (feature) (Assistant).

Vinnie Jassal   Mobile 07792-323246

Sex & Drugs & Rock & Roll (feature), Attack The Block (feature), Heartless (feature).

Tom Jenkins   01875-830779 Mobile 07710-330670

New Town Killers (feature), Outcast (feature), Third Star (feature).

David Johnson   01225-852641 Mobile 07774-997002

Skins (TV drama), Casualty (TV drama), The Shell Seekers (TV drama).

Nick Jones GLM   0845-045 0608 Mobile 07811-180200

Fax 0845-045 0609

Martin Joy   01932-883526 Mobile 07956-139673

Hereafter (feature), Green Zone (feature), The Other Boleyn Girl (feature).

Pat Karam   020-8830 2147 Mobile 07850-972068

St Trinian's (feature), 1408 (feature), 28 Days Later (feature).

Sebastian Keep   020-7834 5048 Mobile 07850-045209

David Kellick   Mobile 07831-882402

The Mark Of Cain (feature), Waking The Dead (TV drama), Shooting Fish (feature) (Assistant).

James Khoury GLM   Mobile 07981-903233

Children Of Men (feature).

Paula Lamont   Mobile 07958-651883
The Inbetweeners (TV comedy drama), Bellamy's People (TV comedy drama), Cemetery Junction (feature).

Matthew Lane   020-8879 3239 Mobile 07989-983459
Down To Earth (TV drama), Waking The Dead (TV drama), The Golden Hour (TV drama).

Harriet Lawrence   020-8255 9121 Mobile 07802-885354
Fax 07854-990087
Glorious 39 (feature), Outnumbered (TV comedy drama), The Hole (feature).

Neil Lee   Mobile 07831-252252
Vera Drake (feature), De Lovely (feature), Topsy-Turvy (feature).

Sarah Lee GLM   020-7372 6469 Mobile 07831-130190
Fax 020-7372 6469
Starter For Ten (feature), The Hours (feature), Shaun Of The Dead (feature).

Jamie Lengyel   01225-852122 Mobile 07973-333110
Fax 01225-852122
The Invention Of Hugo Cabret (feature), Green Zone (feature), Children Of Men (feature).

Helene Lenszner   Mobile 07973-839956
Chat Room (feature), Franklyn (feature), East Is East (feature).

Nicholas Leslie   020-7793 9880 Mobile 07775-804984
Luther (TV drama), Above Suspicion (TV drama), Spooks (TV drama).

Angus Light GLM   020-7978 1688 Mobile 07788-725888
Fax 020-7978 2469
HSBC (stills), Ford (stills), Nike (stills).
www.locateproductions.com

Russell Lodge   01494-758769 Mobile 07831-403700
Fax 01494-758769
Harry Potter & The Deathly Hallows (feature), Harry Potter & The Half-Blood Prince (feature) (2nd unit), Harry Potter & The Prisoner Of Azkaban (feature).

Johnny Ludlow GLM   Mobile 07860-485699
The Rotter's Club (TV drama), Trebor (commercial), The Harry Enfield Show (TV light entertainment).

Douglas MacDonald GLM   Mobile 07836-774961
The Bill (TV drama), Emmerdale (TV drama).

Ben Mangham   020-8671 5550 Mobile 07974-243925
Pulling (TV comedy drama), Jam & Jerusalem (TV comedy drama), Horrible Histories (TV childrens).

Chris Martin   020-8348 0420 Mobile 07973-961718
GEMS 029-2071 0770
Red Light Runners (feature), The Secret Life Of Michael Fry (TV drama).

Tim Maw GLM   Mobile 07971-685323
The Wolfman (feature) (Assistant), Nutcracker & The Rat King (feature), Get Him To The Greek (feature).

Richard May   020-7274 2385 Mobile 07971-048422
Downton Abbey (TV drama), Bouquet Of Barbed Wire (TV drama), Cranford (TV drama).

Wayne McCoy   01753-886670
A Month In The Country (feature), Face (feature), Alice Through The Looking Glass (TV drama).

Darin McLeod GLM   Mobile 07792-513316
Hotel Babylon (TV drama).

Simon McNair-Scott 01840-261675 Mobile 07860-450376
Johnny English (feature), Eyes Wide Shut (feature), The Mummy Returns (feature).

Elliott Meddings   01344-884905 Mobile 07769-677772
Dangerous Parking (feature).

Clive Miles   01753-526221 Mobile 07785-551160
Five Children & It (feature), Johnny English (feature), Underworld (feature).

Chris Moore   Mobile 07966-508227
Intruders (feature), Hustle (TV drama).

Andy Morgan   Mobile 07930-544664
DCI Banks: Aftermath (TV film), Survivors (TV drama), Five Days (feature).

Chris Morgan GLM   Mobile 07973-295460
Remake (feature), Shooting Dogs (feature).

Steve Mortimore   020-7483 3529 Mobile 07990-542766
John Carter Of Mars (feature), The Imaginarium Of Dr Parnassus (feature), Eragon (feature).

Duncan Muggoch   01436-821587 Mobile 07976-983431
The Eagle Of The Ninth (feature), The Wolfman (feature), The Da Vinci Code (feature).

David Myatt   01695-731434 Mobile 07768-927167
Fax 01695-731434
Liverpool 1 (TV drama), There's Only One Jimmy Grimble (feature), The 51st State (feature).

Henry Neild   020-7384 4554 Mobile 07799-715974
Pride & Prejudice (feature), Habitat (commercial).

Simon Nixon Mobile 07989-533921
Gracie (TV drama), Tess Of The D'Ubervilles (TV drama), The Golden Compass (feature).

Spencer Normington 0118-912 2376
Mobile 07970-951144
Margot (TV drama), Above Suspicion (TV drama), Bird's Eye View (TV drama).

Paul O'Grady 01603-453504 Mobile 07973-827536

Mick O'Reilly GLM Mobile 07947-026546
Cashback (feature), Dream Team (TV drama), Dangerville (TV drama).

Alex Paysley-Tyler 020-7978 1688 Mobile 07909-963963
Fax 020-7978 2469
Ford (stills), HSBC (stills), Vodafone (stills).
www.locateproductions.com

Eddy Pearce 020-7734 0456 Mobile 07976-249699
Fax 020-7734 5411
John Lewis (commercial), Virgin Atlantic (commercial), Vodafone (commercial).
www.locationpartnership.com

Michelle Pianca Mobile 07770-917283
Brighton Rock (feature), 1408 (feature), Little Dorrit (TV drama).

Gary Pickering Mobile 07889-172303
Law & Order (TV drama), Monday Monday (TV drama), Coming Down The Mountain (TV drama).

Finlay Pile 020-8675 3872 Mobile 07769-694214
Gulliver's Travels (feature), The Wolfman (feature) (Assistant), Stardust (feature) (Unit Manager).

Emma Pill GLM Mobile 07710-038253
Alice In Wonderland (feature), Mamma Mia! (feature), The Wolfman (feature).

Alan Pinniger +39 081 285709 Mobile 07717-660821
The Brief (TV drama), Spider (feature), Inspector Morse (TV drama).

David Pinnington GLM 020-7924 0417
Mobile 07831-259704
Inception (feature), Quantum Of Solace (feature), The Golden Compass (feature).

Emma Plimmer 020-7812 9144 Mobile 07932-646480
Fax 0870-128 2298
The Boat That Rocked (feature), Ashes To Ashes (TV drama), The Golden Compass (feature).

Ian Pollington Mobile 07850-804112 Fax 07092-869345
Prime Suspect (TV drama), The Midnight Man (TV drama), Harley Street (TV drama).

Jonathan Posner Mobile 07050-099586
Stay Lucky (TV drama), The Bill (TV drama), Attachments (TV drama).

Susan Quinn 020-7223 9927 Mobile 07860-150627
Gosford Park (feature), Harry Potter & The Deathly Hallows (feature), Love Actually (feature).

Kevin Ramsay GLM 020-7252 8465 Mobile 07956-273291
The Bill (TV drama), Holby Blue (TV drama), Hustle (TV drama).

Mick Ratman GLM 020-7380 1128 Mobile 07836-208277
Hotel Rwanda (feature), Welcome To Sarajevo (feature), Joyriders (feature).

Garance Rawinsky GLM 0113-244 9906
Mobile 07771-893459
The Canterville Ghost (TV film), Rumpole Of The Bailey (TV drama), The Bill (TV drama).

Robert Rayner GLM Mobile 07831-123480
Kidulthood (feature), The Bill (TV drama), Feather Boy (TV film).

Adam Richards 020-8354 3334 Mobile 07774-279070
Sherlock Holmes (feature), Nanny McPhee & The Big Bang (feature), Pride & Prejudice (feature).

Alan Saywell Mobile 07970-868980
Bad Girls (TV drama).

David Seaton 01937-580202 Mobile 07973-725873
Shanghai (feature) (Assistant), Quantum Of Solace (feature) (Assistant), The Golden Compass (feature) (Assistant).

Graham Sewell 01737-363074 Mobile 07956-435162
Empathy (TV drama), Unmade Beds (feature), MI High (TV childrens).

Asha Sharma 020-8482 1741 Mobile 07958-061080
Hot Fuzz (feature), Wild Child (feature), The Descent 2 (feature).

Edward Sharp 01303-862154 Mobile 07785-552161

Michael Sharp 01463-790011 Mobile 07836-217550
Children Of Men (feature), Alexander (feature), Clash Of The Titans (feature).

Leonora Sheppard GLM 020-8969 7302
Mobile 07785-706707
BMW (stills), Land Rover (stills), Mercedes (commercial).

James Sherwood 020-8771 4968 Mobile 07973-334326
McDonalds (commercial), Currys (commercial), Benical (commercial).

PRODUCTION

Scott Sidey GLM   Mobile 07831-525630
Halifax (commercial), BBC iPlayer (ident), Miranda (TV comedy drama).

Kam Singh   Mobile 07944-123444

Karen Smythe   Mobile 07973-874219
Captain Jack (feature), Sword Of Honour (TV drama).

Jane Soans GLM   020-8969 0519 Mobile 07831-634380
W.E. (feature) (Supervising), Sherlock Holmes (feature), Me & Orson Welles (feature).

Charles Somers GLM   Mobile 07973-638228
Last Chance Harvey (feature), Green Zone (feature), Sherlock Holmes (feature).

Mark Somner   Mobile 07850-684410
Harry Potter & The Half-Blood Prince (feature), Sherlock Holmes (feature), Blood Diamond (feature).

Eddie Standish   020-7978 1688 Mobile 07768-025910
Fax 020-7978 2469
Layer Cake (feature), Hyundai (stills), BMW (stills).
www.locateproductions.com

Camilla Stephenson   Mobile 07931-386306
An Education (feature), London Boulevard (feature), Burke & Hare (feature).

Mark Stephenson   01931-714163 Mobile 07885-272770

Jeremy Stern GLM   Mobile 07941-930203
Tombola Bingo (commercial), Gatorade (commercial), The Brit Awards (trailer).

Amanda Stevens   020-8749 9646 Mobile 07860-688778
Made In Dagenham (feature), The Other Man (feature), Closer (feature).

Tom Stourton   020-8964 0755 Mobile 07973-829055
W.E. (feature).

Harriet Sutcliffe   Mobile 07776-183249
The Boat That Rocked (feature), The Green Green Grass (TV comedy drama), Atonement (feature).

Sian Sutherland GLM   Mobile 07624-430902
Fax 01624-877881
Hayes vs Ruiz (commercial), Albatross (feature), The Disappearance Of Alice Creed (feature).

Aurelia Thomas   020-7471 4630 Mobile 07957-254889
W.E. (feature), Gulliver's Travels (feature) (Assistant), Harry Potter & The Goblet Of Fire (feature) (Assistant).

Charlie Thompson   Mobile 07775-654339
Micro Men (TV drama), Small Island (TV drama), The Damned United (feature).

Cindy Thomson   0131-446 0444 Mobile 07887-571770
Fax 0131-446 0222
Daniel Deronda (TV drama), Driving Lessons (feature), Sharp Aquus HD Television (commercial).

Claire Tovey   Mobile 07889-028558
Blitz (feature), Life & Lyrics (feature), Britz (TV drama).

Peter Tullo   020-8874 8533 Mobile 07831-296904
The Day Of The Triffids (TV drama), After Thomas (TV drama), Goodbye Mr Chips (TV film).

Georgette Turner   Mobile 07787-429017
W.E. (feature) (Assistant).

Helen Turner   Mobile 07880-730131
National Treasure (feature), National Treasure: Book Of Secrets (feature), Hippie Hippie Shake (feature).

Russell Turner   Mobile 07956-306055

Bill Twiston-Davies   Mobile 07970-144790
New Tricks (TV drama), Spooks (TV drama), The Colour Of Magic (TV film).

Ian Vasey   0161-434 1902 Mobile 07768-200864
Fax 0161-614 0665
North & South (TV drama), With Or Without You (feature), I'm With Stupid (TV light entertainment).

Nick Wade   020-8314 1688 Mobile 07802-433206
Spooks (TV drama), Bleak House (TV drama), Hustle (TV drama).

Martin Wespestad   Mobile 07956-505059
Numerous commercials.

Jason Wheeler   Mobile 07801-627880
Brighton Rock (feature), Nowhere Boy (feature), Tomb Raider II (feature).

Christopher White   Mobile 07976-290915
Miss Marple (TV drama), Poirot (TV drama), Silent Witness (TV drama).

Daniel Whitty   Mobile 07901-587306
Nanny McPhee & The Big Bang (feature), Nine (feature), In Bruges (feature).

Jonathan Wicks   Mobile 07831-663701
All In The Game (TV film), Ruby In The Smoke (TV film), Better Things (feature).

PRODUCTION

Lucy Williams Mobile 07767-260992
About A Boy (feature), Shanghai (feature) (Assistant), Quantum Of Solace (feature) (Assistant).

Nick Williams 020-7978 1688 Mobile 07976-814868
Fax 020-7978 2469
Dulux (commercial), Sky Football (promo), BBC TV Radio (promo).
www.locateproductions.com

Andy Williamson Mobile 07984-183146
Everywhere & Nowhere (feature), Veer (feature), Fit (feature).

Emma Woodcock GLM Mobile 07957-343478
Whitechapel (TV drama), Looking For Eric (feature), Ashes To Ashes (TV drama).

Charlotte Wright Mobile 07904-955726
Nanny McPhee & The Big Bang (feature), Quantum Of Solace (feature), Children Of Men (feature).

Derek Yeaman 0141-949 0952 Mobile 07720-811376
How Not To Live Your Life (TV comedy drama), Centurion (feature), Miss Potter (feature).

PRODUCERS

Steve Abbott 020-7497 1100 Mobile 07714-960719
Fax 020-7497 1133
Himalaya With Michael Palin (TV doc), Michael Palin's New Europe (TV doc), Brassed Off (feature).

Eric Abraham 020-7605 1396 Fax 020-7605 1391
The Magic Flute (feature), Empties (feature), Embers (theatre).

Henry Adeane 020-7603 0714 Mobile 07836-509636

Christabel Albery 020-7243 8383 Mobile 07774-494999
Fax 020-7243 8543

Catharine Alen-Buckley 020-8995 1884
Mobile 07966-134380 Fax 020-8995 5648
Do You Speak American? (TV doc), Jihad (TV doc), The Relief Of Belsen (TV drama).

Ruhul Amin 020-8472 5001
A Kind Of English (feature), Moviewallah (TV doc), Frozen Moments (TV drama).

Jim Anderson 01925-765409
Premiership's Greatest Foreign Footballers (TV light entertainment), Of Time & The City (feature), Nike (commercial).

Robert Angell 020-7731 2999 Mobile 07714-819059
The Queen In 3D (TV doc) (Co-Producer), The Wandering Company (TV doc), The National Gallery (TV arts).

Sharon Baker Mobile 07956-975301
The Good Sex Guide (TV light entertainment), Turnabout (TV light entertainment), Art Of Design (TV light entertainment).

Madonna Baptiste Mobile 07976-945826
The Death Of Klinghoffer (TV film), Tina Goes Shopping (TV film), Tales From Pleasure Beach (TV film).

Ceri Barnes 020-8671 2444 Mobile 07957-606776
Dragons (TV drama doc), Guess With Jess (TV childrens), Ocean Odyssey (TV film).

Mark Bentley 020-7483 3637 Fax 020-7483 3567

Robert Bevan 020-7535 6710 Fax 020-7563 7283
Chromophobia (feature) (Executive Producer), Familia Rodante (feature), Cochochi (feature).

Matthew Bird 020-8291 0667 Mobile 07778-738306
Fax 020-8291 0667
Plus One (TV comedy drama), Worried About The Boy (TV drama), The Street (TV drama).

Andy Birmingham 01753-656254 Mobile 07711-223288
Fax 01753-656769
Beyond Friendship (feature), The Calling (feature), Mrs Caldicot's Cabbage War (feature).

Laurie Borg 01243-586626 Mobile 07836-235025
ITG 020-7636 6565
Asylum (feature), The Four Feathers (feature), Sense & Sensibility (feature).

Claire Bosworth 020-7267 4260 Fax 020-7485 2340
Hunger (feature), The Grandparent Diaries (TV doc), The Queen (TV drama doc).

David Broscombe 01753-655744 Mobile 07831-132942
Fax 01865-890504

Andrew Buchanan 01749-870404
Baby Planet (TV doc), Wild Sex (TV doc), Planet Action (TV doc).

Rosie Bunting 020-8392 2036
Microsoap (TV childrens), My Family (TV comedy drama), Cave Girl (TV childrens).

Timothy Burrill 020-7736 8673 Fax 020-7731 3921
The Pianist (feature), The Ghost (feature), La Vie En Rose (feature).

Chris Burt Mobile 07768-401322
Lewis (TV drama), Goodnight Mr Tom (TV film), Inspector Morse (TV drama).

Mark Bussell 01252-790908 Mobile 07976-714004
The Worst Week Of My Life (TV comedy drama), The Robinsons (TV comedy drama), Christmas At The Riviera (TV drama).

PRODUCTION

Elaine Cameron   020-8607 8736 Fax 020-8607 8744
Jekyll (TV drama), After Thomas (TV drama), Border Cafe (TV drama).

Luke Campbell   01737-223399 Mobile 07802-407384
Daredevils (TV doc), Half Ton Mum (TV doc), Karl Pilkington's Seven Wonders Of The World (TV comedy drama).

William Cartlidge   023-8045 8854 Mobile 07836-518253
Fax 023-8045 8854
An Ideal Husband (feature) (Director), Incognito (feature) (Co-Producer), Dinotopia (TV drama).

John Chapman   Mobile 07770-917751 ITG 020-7636 6565
Just William (TV childrens), The Street (TV drama), The Lost Prince (TV drama).

Richard Cobourne   01291-636300 Fax 01291-636301
Business Eye (commercial), Keeping Ahead Of The Competition (TV doc).

John Colville   020-8995 9049 Fax 020-8995 9049

Andrew Cooper   01626-872310
The Natural World (TV doc).

Louise Cowmeadow   Mobile 07970-616250
Project Catwalk (TV reality), Ant & Dec's Saturday Night (TV light entertainment), Most Haunted (TV doc).

Vivienne Cozens   020-7229 9776
Emmerdale (TV drama), Grange Hill (TV childrens), EastEnders (promo).

Malcolm Craddock   020-7586 8763 Fax 020-7586 9048
Sharpe (TV drama), Rebel Heart (TV drama), Kiszko (TV film).

Rob Craine   Mobile 07624-471376

Simon Crawford-Collins   020-7812 3270
Fax 020-7580 3271
Spooks (TV drama), Hustle (TV drama).

Robin Crichton   01896-831188 Fax 01896-831199
Sarah (TV film), Moonacre (TV film), Brave New World (TV drama).

David Cunliffe   020-8444 3337 Mobile 07836-200527
The Shell Seekers (TV drama).

Chris Curling   020-7255 3555 Mobile 07768-270513
Fax 020-7255 3777
It's A Wonderful Afterlife (feature), Penelope (feature), Hannibal Rising (feature).

Jonathan Curling   020-7733 6165 Mobile 07774-148239
Fax 020-7642 3095
The Clinic (TV drama), The Government Inspector (TV drama), Amongst Women (TV drama).

John Davis   01993-886843 Mobile 07768-314999
Fax 01993-886845
Kidnapped (TV film), 20,000 Leagues Under The Sea (TV film), David Copperfield (TV drama).

Margaret Dickinson   020-7485 1457 Fax 020-7482 6369
Sammy's Story (TV educational), City Swimmers (TV doc), Memories Of A Future (TV doc).

Han Duijvendak   0151-708 7441 Mobile 07771-660505
Fax 0151-709 3515

Richard Duplock   Mobile 07885-071109

Celia Duval   020-7241 0683 Mobile 07977-422209
CCM 020-8743 7337
Margot (TV drama), Christopher & His Kind (TV drama).

Josh Dynevor   0161-969 8560 Mobile 07836-512319
A Passionate Woman (TV drama), Boy Meets Girl (TV drama), Dead Clever (TV film).

Robert Eagle   020-8995 1884 Fax 020-8995 5648
The Solomon Treasures (TV doc), Robo Sapiens (TV doc), Big Questions (TV doc).

Adrian Edwards   0141-423 2055 Mobile 07885-675353
Woolamaloo (TV childrens), Our House (TV light entertainment), How 2 (TV childrens).

Bill Everett   020-8534 7850

Ohna Falby   020-8347 9837 Mobile 07768-512689
Baby (short), Son (short), Dad (short).

Becks Farhall   Mobile 07971-975664
Huge (feature).

Nicholas Farnes   01728-688374
Numerous commercials.

Rosalind Farrimond   01263-833933 Mobile 07774-712937

Stuart Fenegan   Mobile 07941-073892
Too Much Too Young (feature), Cargo (feature) (Co-Producer), Indecision (short).

Daniel Figuero   Mobile 07885-696322
The Bunker (feature), A Fistful Of Fingers (feature), The Scarlet Tunic (feature).

Patrick Fischer   020-8832 1927 Fax 020-8280 9111
3000 Miles (feature), Love Live Long (feature), Psychosis (feature).

Michelle Fox   020-8993 8354 Mobile 07778-224466
Fax 020-8993 7997
It's A Wonderful Afterlife (feature), Angus Thongs & Perfect Snogging (feature), Bones (TV drama).

PRODUCTION

Katterli Frauenfelder 020-7266 5766
Mobile 07977-988484 Fax 020-7266 9102
Charlie & The Chocolate Factory (feature) (Co-Producer).

Tony Freeth 020-8579 6848
Setting The Grassroots On Fire (TV doc), Ethiopia: My Hope My Future (TV doc), Fulfilling The Promise (TV doc).

Gin Godden Mobile 07976-722476

Nick Goldsmith 020-7684 0011 Fax 020-7684 3810
Son Of Rambow (feature), Hitchhiker's Guide To The Galaxy (feature).

Bridget Goodman Mobile 07973-306357
Family Affairs (TV drama), The Bill (TV drama), EastEnders (promo).

Katie Goodson 020-8451 1428 Mobile 07950-400063
Salvation (feature), Millions (feature), Thunderpants (feature).

Phil Grabsky 01273-777678 Fax 01273-323777
In Search Of Beethoven (TV doc), The Boy Who Plays On The Buddhas Of Bamiyan (TV film), The Great Artists (TV doc).

Alan Graves 01249-811777 Mobile 07980-666005
The Tournament (feature), Richo (corporate), Coca-Cola (commercial).

Bob Griffin 01943-879307 Mobile 07966-187243

Meg Guidon Mobile 07976-233497

Jeremy Gwilt Mobile 07747-602816
Torn (TV drama), The Little House (TV drama), Like Father Like Son (TV drama).

Christopher Hall 020-7349 9435 Mobile 07831-681283
Burn Up (TV drama), The Lost World (TV docu drama), Archangel (TV drama).

Jonathan R Hall 020-7722 7896 Mobile 07941-888012
Doctors (TV drama), In The Mood (short), Mr Thornton's Change Of Heart (short).

Suzan Harrison 020-7380 3900 Fax 020-7380 1166
White Teeth (TV drama), Shameless (TV drama), The Lakes (TV drama) (Executive Producer).

Annie Harrison-Baxter 0161-773 5154
Mobile 07802-176011 ITG 020-7636 6565
Conviction (TV drama), The Second Coming (TV drama), Clocking Off (TV drama).

Joe Hassell 0117-935 4831 Mobile 07971-959261
Fax 0117-935 4831
Inside Out (TV news & current affairs), The Antiques Road Show (TV light entertainment), Seaside Rescue (TV doc).

Geoffrey Helman 020-7373 6288
84 Charing Cross Road (feature), Superman (feature), The French Lieutenant's Woman (feature).

Mark Herbert 020-7612 7330

Peter Heslop 020-7381 3839 Mobile 07831-574150
The King's Speech (feature), 44 Inch Chest (feature), Control (feature).

Caroline Hewitt Mobile 07909-990645
The Eagle Of The Ninth (feature), Bright Star (feature), Hitchhiker's Guide To The Galaxy (feature).

David Heyman 020-7836 6333 Fax 020-7836 6444

Francine Heywood 01608-645258

Simon Hinkly 020-7502 1827 Mobile 07976-964102
CMM 020-8584 5363
Loop (feature), The Calling (feature).

Paul Hitchcock Mobile 07836-341298
Fred Claus (feature), Phantom Of The Opera (feature) (Executive Producer), The Man In The Iron Mask (feature) (Executive Producer).

Simon Holder Mobile 07850-884595
After Dark (TV news & current affairs), The French Revolution (TV doc).

Lynn Horsford 020-8968 4278
The Mark Of Cain (feature), Prime Suspect (TV drama), To The Ends Of The Earth (TV drama).

Sharon Houlihan Mobile 07973-726749
Down To Earth (TV drama), Holby City (TV drama), Bad Girls (TV drama).

Chris Hunt 0117-923 7222 Fax 0117-923 8343
The Michael Jackson Story (TV doc).

Diana Hunter Mobile 07966-227136

Sandra Jobling 0191-222 3160 Mobile 07778-480502
Fax 0191-222 3169
Place Of Execution (TV drama), Wire In The Blood (TV drama), Take Me (TV drama).

Maxine Julius 01784-741214 Mobile 07773-154639
Guantanamo (feature).

Matthew Justice 020-7255 1131 Mobile 07770-555666
Fax 020-7255 1132
Attack The Block (feature), Klimt (feature), Hallam Foe (feature).

PRODUCTION

Amanda Kean   020-8994 4398 Mobile 07702-459674
Lisa & Huey's Pet Nation (TV light entertainment), The British Comedy Awards (TV light entertainment).

Rebecca Knapp   Mobile 07966-372313
Rollin With The Nines (feature), Popcorn (feature), Frozen (feature).

Paul Knight   020-7734 7042
The Knock (TV drama), London's Burning (TV drama), Murder In Mind (TV drama).

Matthew Kuipers   020-7613 4241 Mobile 07768-825400
An American Haunting (feature), Slaughter (feature), Strictly Sinatra (feature).

Nicolas Kullmann   020-7727 7169 Mobile 07785-323952
Fax 020-7792 0874
Pasternak (TV drama), A Russia Of One's Own (TV doc).

Diana Kyle   020-8946 9865
Holby City (TV drama), Kidnapped (TV film), Silent Witness (TV drama).

Richard Leyland   01249-813701 Mobile 07770-916701
Enter The World Of James Cameron (TV light entertainment), Benicassim (concert), ITV At The Movies (TV light entertainment).

David Lindsay   020-8741 4200 Mobile 07768-078865
Fax 020-8741 2323

Jonathan Llewellyn   020-8567 8696 Mobile 07974-631075
Absolutely Fabulous (TV comedy drama), One Foot In The Grave (TV comedy drama), You Wish (TV light entertainment).

Georgina Lowe   Mobile 07973-553230
Another Year (feature), Tipping The Velvet (TV drama), Fingersmith (TV drama).

Paul Lowin   020-8977 0748 Mobile 07977-076809
Fax 020-8977 0150
The Nutcracker (feature), The Ten Commandments (TV film), The Lion In Winter (TV film).

Robin Lyons   029-2048 8400 Fax 029-2048 5962
Zoo Factor (TV childrens), Igam Ogam (TV childrens), Fireman Sam (TV childrens).

Lars Macfarlane   Mobile 07860-793219
Foyle's War (TV drama), Beneath The Skin (TV drama), Too Good To Be True (TV drama).

Raza Mallal   0113-295 8013
Quick Slip Me A Bride (feature), Licked (short), Crossed Lines (short).

Fiona Mascoll   020-8567 3147 Mobile 07775-583577
BBC News (TV news & current affairs), Reuters Television (TV news & current affairs), GMTV (TV news & current affairs).

Susan Mather   01494-785910 Mobile 07976-733957
SPA 01932-571044 Fax 01494-785910
EastEnders (TV drama), The Bill (TV drama), The Cry (TV drama).

Thomas Mattinson   020-7701 6404 Mobile 07976-354342
Dead Man Running (feature), Jonathan Toomey (feature), Irish Jam (feature).

Kath Mattock   Mobile 07977-920962
The Queen's Sister (TV drama).

Callum McDougall   020-7286 0911 Mobile 07774-989898
ICM +1 310 550 4474 Fax 020-7286 0911
Quantum Of Solace (feature), Casino Royale (feature), Harry Potter & The Prisoner Of Azkaban (feature).

Kirsten McFie   Mobile 07979-247404
Little Deaths (feature), The Shadow Line (TV drama), Kiss Me (short).

Julian Meers   020-8398 4526 Mobile 07778-917852
National Movie Awards (TV light entertainment), National Television Awards (TV light entertainment), The Green Green Grass (TV comedy drama).

Geoff Mellor   01457-764319
Numerous commercials & promos.

Hugo Middleton   01985-844820
Future Morph (short), Careers4u (commercial), Sharpe (TV drama) (Editor).

Simon Mills   020-8995 2526 Mobile 07720-593619
Fax 020-7681 2196
Derren Brown: The Heist (TV light entertainment), Derren Brown: Trick Or Treat (TV light entertainment), Navy In Action (feature).

Edward Milner   020-8341 9392
Vietnam: After The Fire (TV doc), No Easy Walk (TV doc), Spirit Of Trees (TV doc).

Margaret Mitchell   01562-710725 Mobile 07836-334357
Poirot (TV drama), Goodbye Mr Chips (TV film), Sirens (feature).

Simon Moseley   020-7431 7669 Mobile 07836-644815
Sleuth (feature), The Magic Flute (feature), As You Like It (feature).

David Nelson   0121-427 2231 Mobile 07803-724862
Fax 0121-427 4182
BBC News (TV news & current affairs), How Euro Are You? (TV news & current affairs), Birmingham - The History (TV light entertainment).

PRODUCTION

Peter Norris   Mobile 07711-034707 UA 020-3214 0800
Between The Lines (TV drama), Rough Diamond (TV drama), Ny-Lon (TV drama).

Rebecca O'Brien   020-7734 0168
Route Irish (feature), Looking For Eric (feature), It's A Free World (feature).

Isy Oliver   Mobile 07801-579051
Sneaker Seeker - The Legacy (TV doc), Soho Dolls (music).

Roger Owen   Mobile 07787-530678
Visions Of War (TV doc), 21st Century War Machines (TV doc), Road To Liberty (TV doc).

Tarquin Pack   Mobile 07788-665529
Kick-Ass (feature), Stardust (feature).

Barry Paine   01761-462256 Fax 01761-462256
The World About Us (TV doc), The Natural World (TV doc), Making Of A Continent (TV doc) (Scriptwriter).

Simon Passmore   020-8943 4697
Whose Baby? (TV drama), Foyle's War (TV drama), Forgive & Forget (TV film).

Grant Philpott   01702-713546 Mobile 07956-574633
Harry Hill's TV Burp (TV light entertainment), It'll Be Alright On The Night (TV light entertainment), The British Soap Awards (TV light entertainment).

Nick Pitt   Mobile 07976-295251 ITG 020-7636 6565
Garrow's Law (TV drama), Robin Hood (TV drama), My Life As A Popat (TV drama).

Bob Portal   Mobile 07866-367178
Red White & Blue (feature), In A Dark Place (feature), Mr Inbetween (feature).

Jules Powell   020-8960 9565 Mobile 07976-580434
The Toughest Girl In The World (short), Like Father (short), Kiss Me (short).

David Poyser   020-7609 1685 Mobile 07767-498040
Fax 020-7607 5058
The Question Is (TV educational), Local Heroes (TV doc), Tackling Tough Questions (DVD).

Ron Purdie   01488-682017 Mobile 07836-287669
Four Seasons (TV drama), Starting Over (TV drama), Circus (feature).

Stephanie Rafanelli   Mobile 07966-473731
The Mafia (TV doc), Modern Habits (TV doc).

Lucy Raffety   020-7737 1695 Mobile 07811-717826
Casualty (TV drama), Waterloo Road (TV drama), The Bill (TV drama).

Neville Raschid   020-8998 3591
Monica Ole (feature), Lost Dogs (feature).

Richard Raymond   Mobile 07920-888125
The Bridge (short).

Peter Richardson   Mobile 07831-177750
Fax 0161-743 1787
Booze Cruise II (TV film), Diamond Geezer (TV drama).

Sarah Ridley   Mobile 07967-813645

Selwyn Roberts   01442-862415 Mobile 07767-410141
Sizzle (feature), National Treasure: Book Of Secrets (feature), Shackleton (TV drama).

Alexander Ross   0131-620 4117 Mobile 07854-752918
Fax 0131-620 4117
E= (short), Miles To Dundee (TV doc), Science In The Flesh (animation).

Howard Ross   020-7638 5123
God: For & Against (TV religious), This Is A Man (TV film), Trial Of Patty Hearst (TV drama) (Director).

Andy Rowley   Mobile 07979-520080 DA 020-7437 4551
Harley's Angels (TV drama), Dalziel & Pascoe (TV drama), Jeopardy (TV drama).

Lee Ruette   020-8743 5353 Mobile 07740-306656
Chromophobia (feature), Things To Do Before You're 30 (feature), Ten Minutes Older (feature).

Jonathan Ruffle   020-7404 2351 Mobile 07770-737450
Secret Lives (TV doc), Never Mind The Buzzcocks (TV light entertainment), The Madness Of Modern Families (TV doc).

Charles Salmon   +66 2 663 2132 Mobile 07768-801061
Fax +66 2 663 2131
Flawless (feature), Marigold (feature), Malice In Wonderland (feature) (Co-Producer).

Helen Saunders   020-3179 1800
Cops (TV drama), This Life (TV drama), No Angels (TV drama).

Carl Schoenfeld   020-8838 2566 Mobile 07974-753838
The Living & The Dead (feature), My Brother Tom (feature), Sarajevo Diary (TV doc).

Bill Shapter   020-8788 6244 Fax 020-8780 9323
Rough Treatment (TV drama), Ultraviolet (TV drama), Beautiful Thing (feature).

Catherine Skinner   020-8442 8431

David Smith   0141-221 5290
Native Sun (short).

PRODUCTION

Jacky Holding Mobile 07889-014547
Harry Potter & The Order Of The Phoenix (feature), Harry Potter & The Goblet Of Fire (feature), Mona Lisa (feature).

Sarah Hunt 01932-565955 Mobile 07973-558628
Gulliver's Travels (feature), Elizabeth: The Golden Age (feature), Sweeney Todd (feature).

Elizabeth Hurley 01753-646630 Mobile 07917-889080
John Carter Of Mars (feature), Kick-Ass (feature), Hitchhiker's Guide To The Galaxy (feature).

Kelly Johnson Mobile 07736-171934
Inception (feature), From Time To Time (feature), In The Loop (feature).

Georgina Kelly Mobile 07956-271583
The Colour Of Magic (TV film).

Claire Kenny 01494-722943 Mobile 07776-232727
Quantum Of Solace (feature), Tomb Raider (feature), Robin Hood (feature).

Nichola Kerr 01784-446798 Mobile 07773-700954
Harry Potter & The Goblet Of Fire (feature), Harry Potter & The Order Of The Phoenix (feature).

Lisa-Kim Ling Kuan 020-7289 6882
Mobile 07785-922508
Sherlock Holmes (feature), Hellboy 2: The Golden Army (feature), Fred Claus (feature).

Jo Littlejohn Mobile 07808-864552
In Bruges (feature).

Sylvia Mackintosh Mobile 07970-901344
The Bourne Ultimatum (feature), Stormbreaker (feature), Sahara (feature).

Fry Martin 020-8989 0402 Mobile 07770-947442
PG 01753-651767
Bridget Jones's Diary II (feature), Skins (TV drama), Is This Love? (TV drama).

Ivan Mavor Mobile 07811-266299
The Brothers Grimm (feature), Cold Mountain (feature), Spy Game (feature).

Alastair McNeil 01753-654175 Mobile 07787-100109
Harry Potter & The Goblet Of Fire (feature), Harry Potter & The Order Of The Phoenix (feature), The Dark Knight (feature).

Justin Miller Mobile 07799-623097
Blitz (feature), Happy-Go-Lucky (feature), Goal! III (feature).

Claire Mitchell Mobile 07974-420560
Merlin (TV drama), Sharpe's Challenge (TV drama), Bad Girls (TV drama).

Debbie Moseley 020-8563 0209 Mobile 07831-331345
Atonement (feature), Phantom Of The Opera (feature), Tomb Raider (feature).

Julian Murray Mobile 07973-158706
The Debt (feature), Wallander (TV drama), The Boy In The Striped Pyjamas (feature).

Daniel Nixon Mobile 07972-666273
Quantum Of Solace (feature) (Panama).

Joyce Noakes 01628-666189
Quantum Of Solace (feature), The World Is Not Enough (feature), Tomorrow Never Dies (feature).

Angela Purdie 01488-682017 Mobile 07833-313283

Andrew Pyke 01494-863708 Mobile 07956-518302
Fax 01494-863708
Prince Of Persia (feature), The Ten Commandments (TV film), Exorcist: The Beginning (feature).

Louise Randall 01908-368072 Mobile 07775-530326
Fax 01908-368072
Harry Potter & The Philosopher's Stone (feature), Gangster No.1 (feature), Face (feature).

Jeremy Ranson Mobile 07957-408688
Island At War (TV drama), Kingdom Of Heaven (feature), Heartless (feature).

Frances Richardson 01892-723913
The Wolfman (feature), Children Of Men (feature), Alexander (feature).

Valerie Rosewell 01932-240051 Mobile 07730-167554
Sherlock Holmes (feature), An Education (feature), Into The Storm (TV film).

Angela Rowden Mobile 07939-200457
Harry Potter & The Goblet Of Fire (feature).

Isaac Sananes Mobile 07710-381610
Separate Lies (feature), The Other Boleyn Girl (feature), Sylvia (feature).

Paula Sargeant Mobile 07973-793350
Harry Potter & The Deathly Hallows (feature), Harry Potter & The Half-Blood Prince (feature), Harry Potter & The Order Of The Phoenix (feature).

Lara Sargent 01753-630300 Mobile 07977-474546
Fax 01753-655881
www.sargent-disc.com

Arno Seagrim Mobile 07957-570993
Bad Girls (TV drama), Hound Of The Baskervilles (TV film), Foyle's War (TV drama).

PRODUCTION

Emma Short   Mobile 07831-216171
Green Zone (feature), The Dark Knight (feature), Stormbreaker (feature).

Gemma Smithers   01753-853764   Mobile 07967-738027
W.E. (feature), Clash Of The Titans (feature), Nine (feature).

Sarah Stiff   01494-438486   Mobile 07713-812364
Alice In Wonderland (feature), The Debt (feature), Another Year (feature).

Celeste Talaszek   020-8808 7481   Mobile 07968-191898
Pirates Of The Caribbean: On Stranger Tides (feature), Get Him To The Greek (feature), 10,000 BC (feature).

Linda Taylor   020-8386 5825   Mobile 07776-191851
Harry Potter & The Order Of The Phoenix (feature), Harry Potter & The Goblet Of Fire (feature), Harry Potter & The Prisoner Of Azkaban (feature).

Margaret Teatum   020-8847 1976   Mobile 07815-600064
Johnny Vaughan Tonight (TV light entertainment), Shakespeare In Love (feature), The Wings Of The Dove (feature).

Jane Trower   01462-892329   Mobile 07801-537623
Vanity Fair (feature), 102 Dalmatians (feature), Basic Instinct II (feature).

John Udall   01923-404857   Mobile 07803-501334
Quantum Of Solace (feature).

Brendan Whiston   Mobile 07757-319647
Troy (feature), The Da Vinci Code (feature), Die Another Day (feature).

Sarah Wilson   Mobile 07775-783675
In Bruges (feature), Copying Beethoven (feature), Quantum Of Solace (feature).

Richard Wood   0113-368 2933   Mobile 07708-465684
Bouquet Of Barbed Wire (TV drama), Married Single Other (TV drama), Wuthering Heights (feature).

PRODUCTION ASSISTANTS

Rhiannon Andrews   01239-698252   Mobile 07780-787875
Wedi 7 (TV light entertainment), Soccer Night (TV sport).

Jill Barnes   020-7229 7675

Andrew Cameron   Mobile 07946-278651

Yvonne Craven   01483-480273   Mobile 07752-687467
Fax 01483-486334
World Music Awards (TV light entertainment), Have I Got News For You (TV light entertainment), BBC Proms (TV light entertainment).

Alicia Davies   Mobile 07824-332937
John Carter Of Mars (feature).

Stephen Deuters   Mobile 07775-746578
Pirates Of The Caribbean: The Curse Of The Black Pearl (feature), Pirates Of The Caribbean: Dead Man's Chest (feature), Charlie & The Chocolate Factory (feature).

Lorraine Edwards   Mobile 07922-649118
Gulliver's Travels (feature).

Hayley Gibbs   Mobile 07836-383311
Inception (feature), Hereafter (feature), Captain America (feature).

Tania Gordon   Mobile 07904-803443
Quantum Of Solace (feature), Clash Of The Titans (feature), Kick-Ass (feature).

Paula Hind   Mobile 07894-036578
Prince Of Persia (feature).

Andrew Holt   01252-725791   Mobile 07779-646998
On The Rails (TV doc), Massive Engines (TV doc).

Mondi Howard   Mobile 07896-834002
Gulliver's Travels (feature), Angels & Demons (feature), Numerous commercials.

Mondi Howard   Mobile 07896-834002
Gulliver's Travels (feature).

Susan Hubble   01872-862011   Mobile 07816-872565
Dispatches (TV doc), Horizon (TV doc), African Footsteps (TV doc).

Nicholas Kay   Mobile 07862-240457
The Wolfman (feature).

Tamara King   Mobile 07771-901765
In Bruges (feature).

Cathy Norton   020-8698 0528   Mobile 07887-882062
Fax 020-8698 0528
Blue Peter (TV childrens), Soccer AM (TV sport), 2000 Today (TV arts).

Maria Pudlowska   Mobile 07515-507672
Harry Potter & The Order Of The Phoenix (feature), John Carter Of Mars (feature), Clash Of The Titans (feature).

Andy Scott   Mobile 07769-644649
Prince Of Persia (feature).

Emily Ann Sonnet   Mobile 07973-184675
Proof (feature), The Life & Death Of Peter Sellers (feature), Sylvia (feature).

Toby Spanton   Mobile 07817-018428
The Wolfman (feature).

PRODUCTION

Bertie Spiegelberg Mobile 07887-722463
Get Him To The Greek (feature), Hereafter (feature), Quantum Of Solace (feature).

Kelly Taylor-Dias 01582-660747 Mobile 07932-045369
John Carter Of Mars (feature), Shanghai (feature), Munich (feature).

Melanie Ward 01952-771112 Mobile 07774-114510
Gardeners' World (TV light entertainment), Our House (TV light entertainment), The Archers (radio).

Victoria Worvell 020-8335 0641 Mobile 07940-501005
Finding Neverland (feature), Love Actually (feature).

PRODUCTION CO-ORDINATORS

Phyl Allarie 01753-662598 Mobile 07836-319553
Fax 01753-664301
Captain Scarlet (TV drama), Alexander (feature), Shiner (feature).

Carrie-Ann Banner Mobile 07747-060675
Hippie Hippie Shake (feature), Swinging With The Finkels (feature).

Mona Benjamin Mobile 07956-548703
Doomsday (feature), Casino Royale (feature), Half Light (feature).

Bee Benton 020-7229 0973
Kings (feature), Troy (feature), Die Another Day (feature).

Vicky Bishop Mobile 07961-164518
Harry Potter & The Order Of The Phoenix (feature).

Sam Black 01494-715927 Mobile 07721-589237
Clash Of The Titans (feature), Alice In Wonderland (feature), Elizabeth: The Golden Age (feature).

Jenny Brassett Mobile 07761-539553
Little Dorrit (TV drama).

Judy Britten 01727-847000 Mobile 07973-674461
Quantum Of Solace (feature) (2nd unit), Casino Royale (feature) (2nd unit), Harry Potter & The Prisoner Of Azkaban (feature).

Natalie Brook-Reynolds Mobile 07976-234840

Pat Bryan 01494-775366 Mobile 07831-494816
Fax 01494-775366
Lark Rise To Candleford (TV drama), Lewis (TV drama), Foyle's War (TV drama).

Zoe Burke 01727-853958 Mobile 07834-494921
Holby City (TV drama), The Impressions Show With Culshaw & Stephenson (TV light entertainment).

Jeremy Burnage Mobile 07808-177722
Moon (feature), Merlin (TV drama), The Curse Of Steptoe (TV drama).

Elaine Burt Mobile 07778-856840
Hotel Rwanda (feature), Lord Of The Rings (feature), Cold Mountain (feature).

Francesca Castellano 020-8896 0520
Mobile 07801-844959
The Other Boleyn Girl (feature), Notes On A Scandal (feature), Closer (feature).

Kate Chadderton Mobile 07967-819234
Bonded By Blood (feature).

Usha Chaman Mobile 07742-589895
Blood: The Last Vampire (feature), Casino Royale (feature) (Assistant), The Hills Have Eyes II (feature).

Chan Chau Mobile 07939-436992
Whitechapel (TV drama), Lennon Naked (TV drama), Vexed (TV drama).

Paige Chaytor Mobile 07767-345781
Quantum Of Solace (feature), The World Is Not Enough (feature) (2nd unit), Gulliver's Travels (feature).

Diane Chittell 020-8224 2874 Mobile 07736-528440
Miss Potter (feature), Poirot (TV drama), Captain Corelli's Mandolin (feature).

Niccolo Cioni 020-8991 9837 Mobile 07731-448387
1066 (TV film), Spanish Flu: The Forgotten Fallen (TV drama), Cuckoo (feature).

Valentina Coccia Mobile 07780-706131
Bel Ami (feature), From Time To Time (feature), St Trinian's (feature).

Hannah Collett Mobile 07818-817072
Burke & Hare (feature), Nanny McPhee & The Big Bang (feature), Dorian Gray (feature).

PRODUCTION

Richard Daldry   020-8992 3237 Mobile 07976-529015
Troy (feature), John Carter Of Mars (feature), Shanghai (feature).

Mandy Dalton   01494-432707
Like Father Like Son (TV drama).

Tony Davis   020-7607 3381 Mobile 07866-808673
Harry Potter & The Deathly Hallows (feature) (2nd unit), Sherlock Holmes (feature) (2nd unit), Harry Potter & The Half-Blood Prince (feature) (2nd unit).

Patsy de Lord   01932-229789 Mobile 07970-200203
Hannibal Rising (feature), Ladies In Lavender (feature), Sylvia (feature).

Mark Devlin   Mobile 07092-092923
Drop Dead Gorgeous (TV drama), Monarch Of The Glen (TV drama), The Tudors (TV drama).

Stephanie Dolker   Mobile 07941-416569
Goal! (feature), Goal! II (feature).

Francesca Dowd   020-8244 2993 Mobile 07775-657897
How To Lose Friends & Alienate People (feature), Matchpoint (feature), Billy Elliot (feature).

Rebecca Earl   01628-623630 Mobile 07790-005198
Einstein & Eddington (TV film), MI High (TV childrens), Confessions Of A Diary Secretary (TV drama).

Zoe Edwards   020-7350 1460 Mobile 07713-249288
The Queen's Sister (TV drama), The Queen (feature), Cracker (TV drama).

Jenny Elliott   01753-677891 Mobile 07778-832440
Miss Marple (TV drama), Rosemary & Thyme (TV drama), Footballers' Wives (TV drama).

Jill Forbes   Mobile 07810-483076
Law & Order (TV drama), Trinity (feature), Life Begins (TV drama).

Susanna Fyson   Mobile 07778-312082
The Last Days Of Lehman Brothers (TV drama), Above Suspicion (TV drama), The Commander (TV drama).

Kate Garbett   020-8607 9250 Mobile 07887-575569
Harry Potter & The Deathly Hallows (feature), Harry Potter & The Half-Blood Prince (feature) (2nd unit), Harry Potter & The Goblet Of Fire (feature) (2nd unit).

Fiona Garland   Mobile 07769-734867
Miss Potter (feature), Kingdom Of Heaven (feature).

Hannah Godwin   Mobile 07971-997804 PG 01753-651767
Hereafter (feature), The Invention Of Hugo Cabret (feature), Green Zone (feature).

Natasha Gormley   Mobile 07775-780898
Harry Potter & The Goblet Of Fire (feature) (2nd unit), Harry Potter & The Order Of The Phoenix (feature), Harry Potter & The Prisoner Of Azkaban (feature).

Jill Greenwood   01475-670670 Mobile 07900-603647
J K Rowling: A Year In The Life (TV doc), The Detonators (TV doc), Vera Brittain: A Woman At War (TV doc).

Victoria Hawden   Mobile 07760-191519
The Bourne Ultimatum (feature), Gulliver's Travels (feature), The Da Vinci Code (feature).

Nion Hazell   Mobile 07956-921976
Robin Hood (feature), The Wolfman (feature) (2nd unit), The Unloved (feature).

Claire Hildred   Mobile 07747-866860
Inspector George Gently (TV drama), Casualty (TV drama), Survivors (TV drama).

Una Hill   Mobile 07815-751643
1408 (feature).

Ben Holt   020-8946 7370 Mobile 07866-737711
Sleepy Head (feature), Spooks (TV drama), Father & Son (TV drama).

Lucy Hopkins   Mobile 07774-847849
Blackpool (TV drama), The Secret Life Of Mrs Beeton (TV drama), Maxwell (TV docu drama).

Sharon Howat   Mobile 07881-921328
Doomsday (feature), The Jacket (feature), Fiona's Story (TV drama).

Viviane Hurley   020-7820 9009 Fax 020-7820 9009

Polly Jefferies   020-8672 2279 Mobile 07770-752176
The Debt (feature), The Eagle Of The Ninth (feature).

Suzanne Jones   Mobile 07956-862667

Pamela Joyce   020-8995 0751 Mobile 07711-624428
Stardust (feature) (2nd unit), Night & Day (TV drama), Nine (feature).

Lisa Lake   Mobile 07976-743842 Fax 07970-092899
The Darkest Light (feature), Glastonbury The Movie (feature), The Punk & The Princess (feature).

Gabby Le Rasle   020-8993 9817 Mobile 07712-043300
Nine (feature), Stardust (feature), Brideshead Revisited (feature).

Ali Liddle   020-8998 7255 Mobile 07778-781739
Fax 020-8998 7255
The Private Life Of Samuel Pepys (TV drama), Sense & Sensibility (feature), The Inspector Lynley Mysteries (TV drama).

Bettina Lyster   Mobile 07788-740839
Sex & The City (feature), Downton Abbey (TV drama), Bride & Prejudice (feature).

Donna Mabey   Mobile 07919-181181
The Increasingly Poor Decisions Of Todd Margaret (TV comedy drama), Money (TV drama), Silent Witness (TV drama).

Vicki Manning   01932-592364 Fax 01932-569527
Miss Potter (feature), Mission: Impossible III (feature) (early prep), Keeping Mum (feature).

Miranda Marks   020-8960 7179 Mobile 07803-254524
Robin Hood (feature), The Golden Compass (feature), Driving Lessons (feature).

Phoebe Masters   020-8246 5565 Mobile 07899-992475
The Commander (TV drama), Batman Begins (feature) (miniatures), Trial & Retribution (TV drama).

Karen McLuskey   Mobile 07771-593696
The Brothers Grimm (feature), Things To Do Before You're 30 (feature), Band Of Brothers (TV drama).

Felicia McMdonald   Mobile 07967-552962
Holby City (TV drama), Spooks (TV drama).

Sam Mill   Mobile 07973-960632
Cemetery Junction (feature), Green Zone (feature), Hellboy 2: The Golden Army (feature).

Sanaz Missaghian   Mobile 07714-169849
Harry Potter & The Deathly Hallows (feature), Harry Potter & The Half-Blood Prince (feature), The Other Boleyn Girl (feature).

Amy Mobley   Mobile 07796-832324
Huge (feature), Swinging With The Finkels (feature), The Secret Diaries Of Miss Anne Lister (TV drama).

Sharon Moran   Mobile 07885-945589
The Day Of The Triffids (TV drama), Hotel Babylon (TV drama), Crime & Punishment (TV film).

Lulu Morgan   020-7731 2720 Mobile 07956-600909
Quantum Of Solace (feature), Eat Pray Love (feature), Casino Royale (feature).

Marilyse Morgan   020-8979 7966 Mobile 07831-588691
Fax 020-8979 7966
Event Horizon (feature), The Wind In The Willows (TV film), Haunted (feature).

Victoria Morgan   Mobile 07932-723550
Clash Of The Titans (feature), The Wolfman (feature), The Golden Compass (feature).

Fiona Murphy   Mobile 07891-096455

Monique Mussell   01722-782269 Mobile 07779-382652
I'll Sleep When I'm Dead (feature), Cracker (TV drama), Persuasion (feature).

Philippa Naughten   Mobile 07835-260091
W.E. (feature), Creation (feature), Gulliver's Travels (feature) (2nd unit).

Clarissa Newman   020-8969 9595 Mobile 07768-016356
Green Zone (feature), Quantum Of Solace (feature), Inkheart (feature).

Anji Oliver   Mobile 07961-915333
The Bourne Ultimatum (feature), The Da Vinci Code (feature), Batman Begins (feature).

Alex Protherough   Mobile 07968-911039
The Devil's Whore (TV drama), Wild At Heart (TV drama).

Holly Pullinger   Mobile 07765-403266
Dr Who (TV drama), Ashes To Ashes (TV drama), The Fixer (TV drama).

Louisa Rawlins   01342-843557 Mobile 07747-848737
Waking The Dead (TV drama), The Bill (TV drama), Neighbours (TV drama).

Matthew Sampson   01689-601006 Mobile 07957-140489
Fax 01689-810048
Captain America (feature), Robin Hood (feature), The Wolfman (feature).

Katryna Samut-Tagliaferro   Mobile 07785-747609
Sahara (feature), The Upside Of Anger (feature), Shanghai Knights (feature).

Jonathan Scott   01962-859469 Mobile 07771-628714
PSB 020-7434 2647 Fax 01962-859469
Robin Hood (feature), Brick Lane (feature), Sweeney Todd (feature).

Joy Scott   Mobile 07771-660565
Instant Restaurant (TV doc), Secret Millionaire (TV reality).

Lindsey Sharp   Mobile 07974-914182
Holby City (TV drama), Missing (TV doc), Scenes Of A Sexual Nature (feature).

Deryn Stafford   01483-274070 Mobile 07767-780860
Mamma Mia! (feature), Alfie (feature), Hitchhiker's Guide To The Galaxy (feature).

Jane Steel   020-8997 3081 Mobile 07903-390395

Eve Swannell   Mobile 07958-790150
Magicians (feature), The Walker (feature), Babylon AD (feature).

Nick Tanner   Mobile 07740-707249
Plus One (TV comedy drama), Spooks (TV drama).

Anastasia Timeneys 020-8372 1894 Mobile 07958-664704
Spooks (TV drama).

Jo Wallett   Mobile 07970-053108
London Boulevard (feature), Prince Of Persia (feature) (Assistant).

Winnie Wishart   01273-329686 Mobile 07714-706443
Fax 01273-329686
Harry Potter & The Order Of The Phoenix (feature), Harry Potter & The Goblet Of Fire (feature), Gosford Park (feature).

Aime Zola Lumbuyaka   Mobile 07931-624874
Really (feature), The Run (feature), Messages (feature).

PRODUCTION CO-ORDINATORS - ASSISTANT

Jake Bogert   Mobile 07976-262154
Children Of Men (feature).

Kate Bone   Mobile 07976-726759
Sherlock Holmes (feature), Leap Year (feature), Brighton Rock (feature).

Francesca Budd   Mobile 07906-638658
The King's Speech (feature), The Special Relationship (feature), From Time To Time (feature).

Cuong Dang   020-8342 8078 Mobile 07949-574129
Hot Fuzz (feature), Son Of Rambow (feature), In Bruges (feature).

Glenn Diot   Mobile 07951-413705
Robin Hood (feature), Any Human Heart (TV drama), Last Chance Harvey (feature).

Emily Dundas   Mobile 07968-841746
Spooks (TV drama), The Fixer (TV drama), The Outcasts (TV doc).

Scott Eaton   Mobile 07939-570707
A Mighty Heart (feature), Nine (feature), 0-800-Love (feature).

Tom Forbes   Mobile 07941-464021
Prince Of Persia (feature), Syriana (feature), Inception (feature).

Arabella Gilbert   Mobile 07813-243303
Inception (feature) (visual fx), Valkyrie (feature), Casino Royale (feature).

Andrew Gwyn Davies   Mobile 07989-216140
Robin Hood (feature), Mr Nice (feature), Me & Orson Welles (feature).

Suzie Hanson   Mobile 07790-607001
Skins (TV drama), Sorted (TV drama), Ghost Squad (TV drama).

Jonathan Houston   Mobile 07732-885245
The King's Speech (feature), Downton Abbey (TV drama), Nanny McPhee & The Big Bang (feature).

Matthew Jenkins   01844-260774 Mobile 07815-287020
Prince Of Persia (feature), Clash Of The Titans (feature), Medieval (feature).

Layla Mall   Mobile 07811-364480
Never Let Me Go (feature), Bright Star (feature), Green Zone (feature).

Lebo Boo Motjouadi   Mobile 07968-417960
Robin Hood (TV drama), The Golden Compass (feature), Charlie & The Chocolate Factory (feature).

Charlotte Piddington   Mobile 07832-228026
Clash Of The Titans (feature), The Wolfman (feature), The Golden Compass (feature).

Rebecca Rae   Mobile 07733-268073
Sherlock Holmes (feature), Gulliver's Travels (feature), The Wolfman (feature).

Nanw Rowlands   Mobile 07793-674758
Bonded By Blood (feature).

Geraldine Serafini   Mobile 07810-442069
Angus Thongs & Perfect Snogging (feature), Made Of Honor (feature), Bright Star (feature).

Helen Swanwick   Mobile 07761-185010
The Infidel (feature), Harmony (feature), Wuthering Heights (feature).

Kelly Taylor   01582-660747 Mobile 07932-045369
John Carter Of Mars (feature), Casino Royale (feature), Munich (feature).

Yuen Wai-Liu   Mobile 07795-551806
Sex & Drugs & Rock & Roll (feature), Cherry Tree Lane (feature), Silent Witness (TV drama).

David Zealey   Mobile 07789-885588
Clash Of The Titans (feature), The Wolfman (feature), The Golden Compass (feature).

PRODUCTION MANAGERS

Chris Alexander   Mobile 07703-170981
Bombshell (TV drama), Bad Girls (TV drama), Footballers' Wives (TV drama).

Jane Alexander   020-8891 6980 Mobile 07713-682578
Fax 020-8891 6980
The South Bank Show (TV arts), Under A Coloured Cap (TV doc).

Jim Allan   Mobile 07802-707071
Imagine Me & You (feature), Little Devil (TV drama), Minder (TV drama).

Jennifer Apps   Mobile 07770-636421
Skins (TV drama), Scrapheap Challenge (TV light entertainment), Victoria Cross (TV doc).

Keri Atkins   Mobile 07801-052386
Ross Lee's Ghoulies (TV childrens), Freak (TV drama), Derek Acorah's Ghost Town (TV light entertainment).

Abi Bach   020-7209 2446 Mobile 07979-597522
Fax 020-7209 2446
Bullet Boy (feature), Tina Goes Shopping (TV film), The Death Of Klinghoffer (TV film).

Terry Bamber   01483-285193 Mobile 07850-187742
Fax 01483-285193
Gulliver's Travels (feature) (2nd unit), Quantum Of Solace (feature) (2nd unit), City Of Ember (feature).

Alison Banks   020-8840 9587 Mobile 07778-112196
Street Dance (feature), The Descent 2 (feature), Three & Out (feature).

Tori Banks   020-8324 2133 Mobile 07890-792196
Bonded By Blood (feature).

Cate Barker   01444-443752 Mobile 07733-112799
Swan Lake (ballet), Queen Of Spades (opera).

Maddy Barrington-Amat   020-8675 1464
Mobile 07850-070071
BAFTA Awards (TV light entertainment), A Brief History Of Fun (TV doc), The Oscars (TV light entertainment).

Claire Barry   01869-331416 Mobile 07850-309231
Unreported World (TV doc), The Lost World (TV docu drama), Horrid Henry (animation).

Julia Beer   01296-641133 Mobile 07985-089886
Dyslexia (TV doc), Red Bomb (TV doc), Hardwick Village (TV doc).

Kate Beeston   Mobile 07710-040243
Casualty (TV drama), EastEnders (promo), Holby City (TV drama).

Erica Bensly   Mobile 07768-151635
The King's Speech (feature), The Boat That Rocked (feature), Atonement (feature).

Adam Berman   Mobile 07968-584556
Saxon Gold: Finding The Hoard (TV doc), Jack The Ripper (TV docu drama), My New Best Friend (TV drama).

Jane Bevan   020-7286 0333 Fax 020-7284 0626
Malaria (TV doc), Shaken Babies (TV doc), Global Crime (TV doc).

Loyce Blackmur   020-8998 9166 Mobile 07970-971207
The Longest Hatred (TV doc), Modern Times (TV doc), Jerusalem - City Of Heaven (TV doc).

Gerry Bourke   020-8207 1473

Emma Bowman   020-7272 1279 Mobile 07779-628755
True Face Of War (TV doc), Near Miss (TV doc), The Diagnosis (TV doc).

Alex Bridcut   Mobile 07778-787449
Zingzillas (TV childrens), My Family (TV comedy drama), The Friday Night Club (TV comedy drama).

Alison Brodie   020-7278 8144 Mobile 07831-235580
Tonight's The Night (TV light entertainment), Maestro (TV light entertainment), Liverpool Nativity (TV light entertainment).

Vivien Broome   Mobile 07906-814120

Helena Bullivant   Mobile 07973-509866
The Adventures Of English (TV doc), Pornography: The Secret History Of Civilisation (TV doc), The Genius Of Photography (TV doc).

Anne Cafferky   01372-465044 Mobile 07721-539688
The All Star Comedy Show (TV light entertainment), DNA (TV doc), The Real Brian Clough (TV doc).

Isa Campbell   Mobile 07810-052008
Dermot Meets... (TV doc), Ask The Chancellors (TV doc), Suchet's Music Hall Hero (TV doc).

Carolyn Carter   020-8692 3790 Mobile 07885-748892
Ideas That Changed The World (TV doc), The Salon (TV reality), Heroes Of Comedy (TV doc).

Peter Carter   01344-306284 Mobile 07751-669989
Fax 01344-306284
Poets Never Die (feature), Zeus (feature), Shirley Valentine (feature) (Location Manager).

PRODUCTION

Patricia Chacon Mobile 07976-247725
Versailles Stories (TV doc), Dispatches (TV doc), The Last Voyage Of Columbus (TV drama doc).

Stephen Cheers 0151-427 0541
Bodies (TV drama), Big Dippers (TV film), Sport One (commercial).

Jackie Chivers 020-7602 3765 Mobile 07714-049013
Chop Shop (TV light entertainment), Pete's PA (TV doc), Seconds From Disaster (TV doc).

Rebecca Christensen Mobile 07768-336466
Lunch Monkeys (TV comedy drama), Bremner Bird & Fortune (TV light entertainment), Turn Back Time (TV light entertainment).

Cormac Clarke Mobile 07785-797822
Ministry Of Defence (corporate), Videotel (corporate), Kingston Inmedia (corporate).

Joshua Clement 07000-262377 Mobile 07859-926709
Fax 07000-262377
Namaste London (feature), Matiuphoomi (feature), King Of Bollywood (feature).

Ray Corbett 020-8947 0623

Teri Corbett Mobile 07973-142875
School Of Silence (TV childrens), Rock Around The Block (TV reality), Johnny Vaughan Tonight (TV light entertainment).

Annie Crofts 020-8979 3410 Mobile 07941-308081
Fax 020-8941 2482
World Aids Day (concert), The Brit Awards (party), The Three Tenors (TV light entertainment).

Lesley Cruickshank Mobile 07764-604837
EastEnders (TV drama), Casualty (TV drama), Bad Girls (TV drama).

Joan Cuffy 020-8749 1487 Mobile 07958-737304
Britain's Hardest Man (TV light entertainment), The Kumars (TV light entertainment), My Family (TV comedy drama).

Caroline Daly 020-8286 1143 Mobile 07768-270358
Diameter Of The Bomb (feature), Perfect Scary Movie (TV doc).

Tina D'Arcy 01923-857785 Mobile 07958-444380
Betjeman & Me (TV doc), House Auction (TV light entertainment), The Real Bad Girls (TV doc).

Dawn Davis 020-8341 1461 Mobile 07971-197199
MTV Music Awards (TV light entertainment), The Word (TV light entertainment), Glastonbury (TV light entertainment).

Alice Dawson 020-7935 2700 Mobile 07715-448999
St Trinian's (feature).

Kevin de la Noy 020-8892 7525 Mobile 07836-766941
EXEC 01753-646677
Clash Of The Titans (feature) (Producer), Public Enemies (feature), Blood Diamond (feature).

Sara Desmond 020-8977 5337 Mobile 07973-412691
Will (feature), Creation (feature), Wimbledon (feature) (2nd unit).

Jennifer Dizio Mobile 07916-328918
First Light (feature), Little Deaths (feature) (Associate Producer), Huge (feature) (Associate Producer).

Andi d'Sa 020-7485 1989 Mobile 07711-087471
Paradise Hotel (TV reality), Compulsion (TV doc), Half Ton Hospital (TV doc).

Lucy Eagle 020-8671 1362 Mobile 07971-028837
I'm A Celebrity (TV light entertainment), Hell's Kitchen (TV reality).

Nicky Earnshaw Mobile 07966-102988
The Disappearance Of Alice Creed (feature), 10 Minute Tales (short), Attack The Block (feature).

Simon Emanuel Mobile 07798-795598
Harry Potter & The Order Of The Phoenix (feature), Harry Potter & The Half-Blood Prince (feature), Harry Potter & The Deathly Hallows (feature).

Justine Faram Mobile 07970-987130

Lorraine Fennell 01753-798692 Mobile 07850-350295
Mrs Henderson Presents (feature), Phantom Of The Opera (feature), Dinotopia (TV drama).

Emma Fenton 020-7372 7084

Guy Ferrington 0161-438 0383 Mobile 07711-188938
Fax 0870-133 8119
Pringles (commercial), Budweiser (commercial), HSBC (commercial).

Susie Field 020-7704 3300 Mobile 07785-766165
Fax 020-7704 3301

Pat Footer 01234-828940 Mobile 07785-346958
Fax 01234-828940
Kasparov: Game Over (feature), Wide Blue Yonder (feature), Stairway To Heaven (TV doc).

Joanna Ford Mobile 07971-095672
The World Wild Vet (TV doc), Inside: The Tiger Trade (TV doc), Long Way Down (TV doc).

Emma Fowler   020-7793 7515 Mobile 07957-426914
10 Days To War (TV drama), My Summer Of Love (feature), Bodysong (feature).

Sue Fowler   Mobile 07811-185756
50 Greatest Pop Videos (TV light entertainment), The Rob Brydon Show (TV light entertainment), Bang Goes The Theory (TV light entertainment).

Simon Fraser   020-7350 2173 Mobile 07834-487492
One Day (feature), Nanny McPhee & The Big Bang (feature), Atonement (feature).

Emma French   Mobile 07973-944127
Millionaires' Mission: Uganda (TV doc), Brat Camp (TV reality).

Samantha Frith   Mobile 07860-135748
Casualty (TV drama), EastEnders (promo), Coronation Street (TV drama).

Alan Gardner   Mobile 07970-936613

Tracy Garrett   020-8840 6809 Mobile 07802-751507
Young At Heart (feature), A Boy Called Alex (TV doc), George Melly's Last Stand (TV doc).

Richard Gates   01787-210432

Sharon Gold   BE 01727-841177

Simone Goodridge   020-8930 6548 Mobile 07956-916501
10,000 BC (feature), Prince Of Persia (feature), Pirates Of The Caribbean: On Stranger Tides (feature).

Susie Gordon   Mobile 07812-576932
River Of Blood (TV doc), Going Postal (TV film), War Of The Worlds (feature).

Nigel Gostelow   01494-882172 Mobile 07836-542065
The Wolfman (feature), The Da Vinci Code (feature), The Bourne Ultimatum (feature).

Shaheen Gould   01268-761969 Mobile 07956-189816
Honey I Ruined The House (TV reality), Bustamove (TV light entertainment), The Mind Masters (TV light entertainment).

Sarah Gowers   020-8997 1301 Mobile 07710-483471
Fax 020-8997 1301
Salvage Code Red (TV doc), The Outcasts (TV doc), The Death Squads (TV doc).

John Graham   020-8549 0367 Mobile 07802-802000
Fax 020-8549 0367
The Great British Village Show (TV light entertainment), Coach Trip (TV reality), LA 7 (TV childrens).

Penny Grant   01985-844513 Mobile 07778-615696
Live Heart Surgery (TV doc), International Rock Awards (TV light entertainment), Royal Bank Of Canada (corporate).

Dawn Gray   01276-858993 Mobile 07973-656936

John Gray   020-8749 6667 Mobile 07976-734564

Ben Greenacre GLM   Mobile 07973-726566
Fax 07970-098628
Franklyn (feature), 0-800-Love (feature), Shadows In The Sun (feature).

Marisa Guagenti   020-7207 2730 Mobile 07736-418134
The Frank Skinner Show (TV light entertainment), Comic Relief (TV light entertainment), V Festival (TV light entertainment).

Kathy Hale   Mobile 07887-612678
The National Trust (TV doc), Unknown White Male (TV doc).

Peter Hall   020-7630 0374 Mobile 07973-909247
Over The Rainbow (TV light entertainment), The Royal Variety Performance (TV light entertainment), Britain's Got Talent (TV light entertainment).

Alastair Hallett   01300-341154 Mobile 07850-214693
The Lesley Garrett Show (TV light entertainment), Jaguar (commercial).

Ann Hampsey   Mobile 07971-410338
The Last Aztec (TV doc), Situation Critical (TV doc), Extinct (TV doc).

Steven Harding   01923-773961 Mobile 07768-151634
EXEC 01753-646677
Fred Claus (feature), John Carter Of Mars (feature), Mission: Impossible III (feature) (China).

Sasha Harris   Mobile 07973-635109
Green Zone (feature), The Debt (feature), Jane Eyre (feature).

Annie Hart   Mobile 07956-452266
Adidas (commercial), Swatch (commercial), Sony (commercial).

Cathy Haslam   Mobile 07866-496543

Adam Hayes   020-7274 4828 Mobile 07715-169028
Friday Night With Jonathan Ross (TV light entertainment), Robot Wars (TV light entertainment), 11 O'Clock Show (TV light entertainment).

Fiona Henderson   Mobile 07050-287198
Room 101 (TV light entertainment), DOTSEC EcoCity (TV doc), Gametrac (TV drama).

Christian Holland   020-8969 2614 Mobile 07989-429247
Earth Wonders (TV doc), Living With The Tribe (TV doc), CSI Wild (TV doc).

PRODUCTION

Kelly Howard-Garde 020-8878 2479 Mobile 07941-308046
Spider (feature), Incendiary (feature), Last Chance Harvey (feature).

Sheila Humphreys 020-8769 3436 Mobile 07980-598899

Georgina Huxstep 020-8994 3321 Mobile 07973-396295
Hands Up (short), 12,000 Mile Dream (TV doc), Love Goddesses Of The World (TV doc).

Sophie Inman Mobile 07876-214003
Dream Team (TV drama), Hogfather (TV film), The Colour Of Magic (TV film).

Helen Jackson 020-8691 1125 Mobile 07973-835316
The Undercover Princes (TV doc), The Bigamists (TV doc), Streetmate (TV light entertainment).

Marianne Jenkins 020-8838 6330 Mobile 07977-988247
Prince Of Persia (feature).

Justin Johnson 020-8340 7041 Mobile 07860-786381
Holby City (TV drama), Tchaikovsky (TV drama doc), Wetin Dey (TV drama).

Selina Kay 020-8444 3611 Mobile 07710-198200
Fax 020-8444 3633

Chris Keats 01202-470850 Mobile 07910-529142

Andy Kelk 01322-294291 Mobile 07836-738368
I'm A Celebrity (TV light entertainment), An Audience With (TV light entertainment).

Paul Kelly 01400-250252 Mobile 07785-356944
The Price Is Right (TV light entertainment), Strike It Rich (TV light entertainment), Question Time (TV news & current affairs).

Samantha Knox-Johnston Mobile 07767-498894
Cherie (feature), Tamara Drewe (feature), Hippie Hippie Shake (feature).

Philip Kohler 020-8743 1196 Mobile 07774-292625
Fax 020-8743 1196
Speed Racer (feature), V For Vendetta (feature), Troy (feature).

Nikolas Korda 020-7602 5409 Mobile 07850-789248
Robin Hood (feature), The Golden Compass (feature), Charlie & The Chocolate Factory (feature).

Alexandra Kosevic Mobile 07971-193388
Skins (TV drama), Off The Hook (TV drama), Mission London (feature).

Mickey La Rosa Mobile 07930-365562
Sixth Sense With Colin Fry (TV light entertainment), Happiness (TV drama), Crime Files (TV doc).

Kaela Langan Mobile 07885-524153
Copycats (TV childrens), Safari 8 (TV childrens), A Question Of Sport (TV light entertainment).

Nick Laws Mobile 07796-694302
Blood Diamond (feature), The Constant Gardener (feature) (Production Supervisor), Bridget Jones's Diary II (feature).

Susan Lee Mobile 07971-676050
Dispatches (TV doc), Theo's Adventure Capitalists (TV light entertainment), The Seasons With Alan Titchmarsh (TV doc).

Denise Lesley 020-8851 6672 Mobile 07966-443034
Holloway (TV doc), In The Line Of Fire (TV doc), Execution Of A Teenage Girl (TV doc).

Sheena Logan Mobile 07971-565827
Bremner Bird & Fortune (TV light entertainment), Rome: The Model Empire (TV doc), Grease: The School Musical (TV reality).

Martin Long Mobile 07956-875387

Jonathan Lubert 020-7737 6929 Mobile 07932-075602
Missing (TV doc), Nigella Bites (TV light entertainment), Cash In The Attic (TV light entertainment).

Siobhan Lyons 020-7328 8144 Mobile 07976-714996
Robin Hood (feature), The Golden Compass (feature), The Truth (feature).

Jane Macaulay Mobile 07789-902327
Survivor (TV reality), Extinct (TV doc).

Emma Mager 020-8992 8770 Mobile 07710-056345
Fax 020-8896 9513
Mr Bean's Holiday (feature), Children Of Men (feature), Five Children & It (feature).

Nicola Mairs Mobile 07768-771056
The Firm (feature), Linear (promo).

Amy Mangion Mobile 07811-202483

Nigel Marchant 020-8992 3237 Mobile 07767-353296
The Philanthropist (TV drama), Charlie Wilson's War (feature), Sex & The City (feature).

Charlotte Markham Mobile 07956-498141

Laura Matthews Mobile 07880-600494

Sarah McBryde 020-7281 3500 Mobile 07775-845450
Kingdom (TV drama), Another Year (feature).

Donall McCusker Mobile 07050-053551
The Hurt Locker (feature).

Deborah McTaggart Mobile 07771-851901

PRODUCTION

Janine Modder   01494-758746   Mobile 07850-739244
EXEC 01753-646677 Fax 01494-758979
Casino Royale (feature), Gulliver's Travels (feature), Quantum Of Solace (feature).

Anne Moore   020-8367 1798   Mobile 07711-004276
Fax 020-8344 8414

Angus More-Gordon   020-7924 3673 Mobile 07831-362907
Fax 020-7924 3673
Green Zone (feature), Quantum Of Solace (feature), Amazing Grace (feature).

Katrina Moss   01372-844484 Mobile 07939-501228
Shaking Dream Land (feature), A Story Of The Heart (TV doc), Let's Do Lunch (short).

Mark Mostyn   01297-443611 Mobile 07850-654174
Fax 01297-443611
Sherlock Holmes (feature), Inception (feature), The Bourne Ultimatum (feature).

Anne Munyard   020-7223 8772
Millennium Mind (TV news & current affairs), Garden Rivals (TV light entertainment).

Michael Murray   01843-596696 Mobile 07967-183773
Batman Begins (feature), Fred Claus (feature), The Dark Knight (feature).

Rachel Neale   020-8943 0371 Mobile 07860-766363
London Boulevard (feature), The Other Boleyn Girl (feature), Notes On A Scandal (feature).

Hermione Ninnim   020-8248 3096 Mobile 07973-443083
Robin Hood (feature), The Young Victoria (feature), The Golden Compass (feature).

Tim O'Connor   01484-650362 Mobile 07974-030313
Coach Trip (TV reality), Kevin McCloud & The Big Town Plan (TV doc), Be A Good Grand Prix Driver (TV reality).

Isobel Oram   Mobile 07973-713124

Claire Otway   020-8352 4053 Mobile 07971-193736

Judy Owen   01295-811583 Mobile 07836-338780
Fax 01295-816008
Dispatches (TV doc), Equinox (TV doc), Hypotheticals (TV news & current affairs).

Gabriella Panas   020-8346 1288 Mobile 07775-891047
The South Bank Show (TV arts).

Ann Parker   023-8060 0155 Mobile 07860-832208
Running Man (TV doc), Meerkat Manor (TV doc), X Day - The Invasion Of Japan (TV doc).

Claire Perry   020-8883 0929 Mobile 07976-950114
Dog Fight Over Mig Alley (TV doc), The Seven Year Old Surgeon (TV doc), The Boy Who Will Never Grow (TV doc).

Emma Pike   Mobile 07973-723666
Layer Cake (feature), The Truth About Love (feature), Sharpe's Challenge (TV drama).

Cliff Pinnock   Mobile 07815-458208
The Bill (TV drama), Lovejoy (TV drama), Red Dwarf (TV comedy drama).

Rosemary Plum   Mobile 07785-378030

Tim Porter   020-8357 7456 Mobile 07973-531919
Nine (feature), Finding Neverland (feature), Iris (feature).

Vivien Pottersman   020-8540 0700
The Company Of Wolves (feature), The Fantasist (feature) (Associate Producer).

Justine Randle   Mobile 07973-241213
Armstrong & Miller (TV light entertainment), The Bill (TV drama), Bedtime (TV drama).

Caroline Richards   Mobile 07966-500307
Primeval (TV drama), The Roman Mysteries (TV childrens).

Glynis Robertson   020-8992 4795 Mobile 07710-175810
Fax 020-8993 4099
The American Future: A History (TV doc), Far Flung Floyd (TV light entertainment) (Producer), Nocturne (TV drama).

Melissa Robertson   01428-682430 Mobile 07973-843170
V Graham Norton (TV light entertainment), Big Brother (TV reality), Alastair McGowan (TV light entertainment).

Kirsty Robson   020-8249 3833 Mobile 07711-309652

Pauline Roenisch   Mobile 07956-664944
Michael Jackson: Search For His Spirit (TV doc), Michael Jackson: The Live Seance (TV light entertainment), Pakistan's War (TV doc).

Jayne Rowe   020-7419 0132 Mobile 07956-393464
Balderdash & Piffle (TV light entertainment), The Churchills (TV doc), Dispatches (TV doc).

Donald Sabourin   020-8525 0181 Mobile 07803-505649
Never Let Me Go (feature), Your Highness (feature), Killing Bono (feature).

Diana Salevourakis   020-8740 8005
Music Of The Outsiders (TV doc), Melina (TV doc), Pride Joy & Sorrow (TV doc).

Sarah Sapper   020-7272 4692 Mobile 07703-185111

Patrick Schweitzer   Mobile 07836-317688
Doctor Who (TV drama).

Julie Scott   020-7254 4104 Mobile 07790-568286

Yvonne Sellins   020-7487 5454 Mobile 07979-067319
Fax 020-7487 4660
French & Saunders (TV light entertainment), The Fugitives (TV childrens), What Katy Did (TV film).

Liz Seymour   Mobile 07803-006822

Jane Shackleton   020-8875 0536 Mobile 07850-510990

Richard Sharkey   Mobile 07850-621159
Season Of The Witch (feature), Doom (feature), Fantastic Four: Rise Of The Silver Surfer (feature).

Marnie Sirota   Mobile 07887-525525
I'm A Celebrity (TV light entertainment), Celebrity Big Brother (TV reality), The Tycoon (TV reality).

Ceri Smith   020-8749 7578 Mobile 07952-187096
America: The Story Of Us (TV docu drama), Cutting Edge (TV doc), I Shouldn't Be Alive (TV doc).

Janet Smyth   020-7692 6916 Mobile 07968-094914

Sam Somers   Mobile 07811-158360

Helen McAulay Stewart   029-2055 2414
Mobile 07778-175420
Everest ER (TV doc), The Private Life Of A Masterpiece (TV doc), A Light In The City (TV drama).

Emily Stillman   020-8993 4774 Mobile 07956-248497
Fax 020-8932 4422
Angus Thongs & Perfect Snogging (feature), Kingdom Of Heaven (feature), Pearl Harbor (feature).

Harry Storey   01932-221993 Mobile 07775-565000
Olympic Games (TV sport), Married With Children (TV comedy drama), The Nanny (TV comedy drama).

Linda Stradling   020-8244 2803 Mobile 07967-721129
Seconds From Disaster (TV doc), Two Men In A Trench (TV doc), Why Doctors Make Mistakes (TV doc).

Marion Sumerfield   020-8749 7450
The Amazing Race (TV light entertainment), Home Front (TV light entertainment), Funny Weekend (short).

Alex Sutherland   Mobile 07785-248002
Boogie Woogie (feature), Sharpe's Peril (TV drama), Sharpe's Challenge (TV drama).

Gilly Sykes   020-8450 1059 Mobile 07971-861572

Jacqueline Thorogood   Mobile 07768-415426
The Shell Seekers (TV drama), Mrs Ratcliffe's Revolution (feature), Summer Solstice (TV drama).

Gerry Toomey   01202-395931 Mobile 07831-761231
Fax 01202-395931
A Knight's Tale (feature), Evita (feature) (Production Supervisor), Angela's Ashes (feature).

Vanessa Tovell   020-7386 8084 Mobile 07973-607160

Susan Towner   Mobile 07500-795160
Clash Of The Titans (feature).

Lucy Trujillo   Mobile 07855-405855
By Any Means (TV doc), Long Way Round (TV doc).

Ngozi Ubaka   020-7229 9787 Mobile 07976-885393
Wasted (short), 57 Screaming Kids (TV doc), Marilyn On Marilyn (TV doc).

Piers Vellacott   Mobile 07921-299977
San Francisco (TV docu drama), Breakout (TV docu drama), Fugitive Chronicles (TV drama).

Marisa Verazzo   Mobile 07811-893858

Gerard Wall   01628-789899 Mobile 07887-566468
CB 01932-592572
Death Of The Revolution (short), Planet Cook (TV childrens).

Melanie Wangler   Mobile 07976-960447
Fax 020-7267 6525
Divine Magic (TV doc), The World Of Geo (TV doc), Art Crime (TV doc).

Vaughan Watkins   Mobile 07860-707199
Casualty (TV drama), Footballers' Wives (TV drama), Bad Girls (TV drama).

Julia Weedon   020-8699 6224 Mobile 07775-892111
Little Britain (tour), Comic Relief (TV light entertainment), Absolutely Fabulous (TV comedy drama).

Tim Wellspring   020-8977 1233 Mobile 07973-565414
Wild Child (feature), Easy Virtue (feature), Dorian Gray (feature).

Amanda Wilkie   01273-777678 Mobile 07973-512231

Jude Winstanley   020-8531 0517 Mobile 07702-694972
Christmas Tales (TV doc), Britain's Greatest Machines (TV doc), Iraq's Forgotten Conflict (radio).

Victoria Winter   020-8997 3570 Mobile 07971-565008
Bo Selecta (TV light entertainment), Blackout (TV light entertainment), Grand Designs (TV doc).

Tracie Wright   0115-849 4093 Mobile 07973-364304
Hawking (TV film), EastEnders (promo), Grease Monkeys (TV drama).

Frances Mable　　　　　Mobile 07768-760264
The Sarah Jane Adventures (TV drama), Missing (TV doc), Ultimate Force (TV drama).

Lisa Mail　　　01789-292975　Mobile 07768-340275
The Fixer (TV drama), Spooks (TV drama), Hustle (TV drama).

Tess Malone　　　　　Mobile 07968-187131
This Life +10 (TV drama), Murphy's Law (TV drama), Sunshine (feature).

Sharon Mansfield　　　　Mobile 07778-384664
Harry Potter & The Deathly Hallows (feature), My Angel (feature), Harry Potter & The Half-Blood Prince (feature) (2nd unit).

Elaine Matthews　　0117-960 7215　Mobile 07850-979610
Mistresses (TV drama), Five Daughters (TV drama), The Turn Of The Screw (TV drama).

Suzanne McGeachan　01628-488401　Mobile 07889-771062
Midsomer Murders (TV drama).

Laura Miles　　　　　Mobile 07901-717291
The Wolfman (feature) (2nd unit).

Helen Moran　　0161-798 8839　Mobile 07768-477205
Fax 0161-798 8839
Blue Murder (TV drama), Cold Feet (TV drama), New Street Law (TV drama).

Zoe Morgan　　　　　Mobile 07957-214937
The No. 1 Ladies' Detective Agency (TV drama), Bel Ami (feature), The Eagle Of The Ninth (feature).

Leigh Nicol　　020-8959 6792　Mobile 07879-411663
Grow Your Own (feature), Dream Team (TV drama), Saxon (feature).

Susi Oldroyd　　　　　020-7794 6967
Michelangelo: Season Of Giants (TV drama), All Men Are Mortal (feature), Death Wish III (feature).

Caroline O'Reilly　　020-8542 0464　Mobile 07778-384204
An Education (feature), Band Of Brothers (TV drama), Run Fat Boy Run (feature).

Sylvia Parker　　Mobile 07930-757109　STA 020-7729 7477
Jane Eyre (feature), Centurion (feature), The Bank Job (feature).

Annie Penn　　01753-869201　Mobile 07979-535636
EXEC 01753-646677　Fax 01753-869201
Gulliver's Travels (feature), Stardust (feature), The Da Vinci Code (feature).

Sian Prosser　　　　　Mobile 07980-137716
Foyle's War (TV drama), Hotel Babylon (TV drama), The Ten Commandments (TV film).

Vivianne Royal　　01753-531006　Mobile 07973-223262
GEMS 029-2071 0770　Fax 07970-536658
Midsomer Murders (TV drama), Ultimate Force (TV drama), Anna Karenina (feature).

Carol Saunderson　　020-7733 8663　Mobile 07778-052451
My Family & Other Animals (TV drama), Casanova (feature), Charles II (TV drama).

Janice Schumm　　020-8677 7986　Mobile 07932-790504
Little Dorrit (TV drama), The Mutant Chronicles (feature).

Simon Sharrod　　　　　Mobile 07703-648933
Desperate Romantics (TV drama), Money (TV drama), Little Dorrit (TV drama).

Annie Simpson　　01749-890689　Mobile 07973-818017
Fax 01749-890689
Eyes Wide Shut (feature), The Saint (feature).

Danuta Skarszewska　　　　0113-255 6949
Mobile 07768-643267　GEMS 029-2071 0770
Shadow Of The Vampire (feature), Attila The Hun (TV film), Egypt (TV drama doc).

Annie South　　020-7485 6258　Mobile 07774-103525
RED 020-8374 3074
Victoria Wood Xmas Special (TV light entertainment), The Comic Strip (TV light entertainment), Delia Smith's How To Cook (TV light entertainment).

Jayne Spooner　　020-8741 1871　Mobile 07785-791200
GEMS 029-2071 0770　Fax 020-8741 1871
The First Grader (feature), Hamlet (feature), The Other Boleyn Girl (feature).

Heather Storr　　020-8883 4167　Mobile 07973-686493
Fax 020-8883 4167
Another Year (feature), Bright Star (feature), It's A Wonderful Afterlife (feature).

Carole Taylor　　　　　Mobile 07958-192014
Doctors (TV drama), The Bill (TV drama), Casualty (TV drama).

Emma Thomas　　020-8894 4219　Mobile 07889-316126
Fax 020-8894 4219
The Boat That Rocked (feature), Luther (TV drama), Single Father (TV drama).

Carol Thompson　　020-8341 1179　Mobile 07790-762575
Fax 020-8340 2534
Poirot (TV drama), The Amazing Mrs Pritchard (TV drama), Bridget Jones's Diary (feature).

Alison Thorne　　020-8994 6286　Mobile 07860-876834
Fax 020-8994 6286

Lisa Vick   020-8783 9395 Mobile 07778-917630
EXEC 01753-646677
Clash Of The Titans (feature), The Wolfman (feature), Love Actually (feature).

Louise Wade   01273-480575 Mobile 07899-074247
EXEC 01753-646677
Clash Of The Titans (feature) (2nd unit), The Bourne Ultimatum (feature) (2nd unit), Green Zone (feature).

Liz West   020-8994 9291 Mobile 07973-316921
Sherlock Holmes (feature), Robin Hood (feature), United 93 (feature).

Beverley Winston   020-7431 1565 Mobile 07974-925860
EXEC 01753-646677
Prince Of Persia (feature), Children Of Men (feature), Wimbledon (feature).

Anna Worley   020-8255 3390 Mobile 07767-868125
EXEC 01753-646677
Harry Potter & The Deathly Hallows (feature), Inkheart (feature), Kingdom Of Heaven (feature).

Llinos Wyn-Jones   01443-239032 Mobile 07974-364146
Patagonia (feature), Torchwood (TV drama), Sherlock Holmes (TV drama).

SCRIPTWRITERS

David Ashton   020-8993 1783 Fax 020-8993 1783
God On The Rocks (TV film), Dalziel & Pascoe (TV drama), The Murder Room (TV drama).

Simon Beaufoy   Mobile 07050-186637
Yasmin (feature), The Full Monty (feature), Among Giants (feature).

John Bevan   01252-725843 Mobile 07815-716779
Fax 01252-725843
Blue Plaques (TV film), A British Artist In China (TV doc), No Time To Stand & Stare (TV drama).

Smita Bhide   020-7792 1769 CM 020-7287 4450
Fax 020-7792 1769

David Block   020-7486 1006 Mobile 07971-195632
Fax 0871-242 6162
Wish You Were Here (feature), A Town Called (feature), The Michael Aspel Show (TV light entertainment).

Robin Burr   020-8949 6970 Mobile 07932-152866
As Long As It Doesn't Rain (TV drama), Army Security Training (corporate).

Steven Butler   Mobile 07747-692683
Night Time (short), Apartment 106 (short), Mirror Mirror (feature).

Nick Crittenden   020-8998 0331 Mobile 07860-648281
Fax 0870-052 2428
EastEnders (promo), The Bill (TV drama).

Derek Cunningham   020-7385 0595 Mobile 07833-351208
Fax 020-7386 7686
Bullshot (feature), Sketches By Boz (TV drama), The Law Of Conflict (TV educational) (Director).

Richard Curtis   UA 020-3214 0800
The Boat That Rocked (feature), The Girl In The Cafe (TV film), Love Actually (feature).

Stephen Davis   01453-872531 Mobile 07974-754966
TA 020-7727 1346 Fax 01453-873735
Waking The Dead (TV drama).

Liana Dognini   01424-721797 Mobile 07989-491510
Daisy (feature), Lovely Bones (feature), Morvern Callar (feature).

Eugene Doyen   01474-873042

Grant Eustace   01306-883686 Mobile 07710-237241
Fax 01306-741594
World Media Festival (corporate), Treason (feature).

Susan Everett   0113-286 5001 Mobile 07946-519824
Fax 0113-286 5001
A Mind To Kill (TV drama), Mother Mine (short).

Gordon Hann   TA 020-7727 1346
The Black Velvet Gown (TV drama), Between The Lines (TV drama), The Love Child (feature).

Conrad Jarrett   Mobile 07932-073535

Peter Jukes   020-7209 2500 JD 020-8964 8811
In Deep (TV drama), The Inspector Lynley Mysteries (TV drama), Waking The Dead (TV drama).

Niall Leonard   020-8847 4072 Mobile 07973-797576
Monarch Of The Glen (TV drama), Wire In The Blood (TV drama), Hornblower (TV drama).

John Lubas   020-8858 9834 Mobile 07748-801415
Fax 020-8858 9834
Grave Misgivings (feature).

Pawan Mather   Mobile 07766-240223
Rendered (short), Common Grounds (short).

Anthony Matheson   020-7607 4239 Mobile 07973-167297
Fax 0870-134 3829

Tony McHale　　　01494-813183　Mobile 07850-910045
Waking The Dead (TV drama), Silent Witness (TV drama), Dalziel & Pascoe (TV drama).

Shaun McKenna　　020-8744 8355　Mobile 07778-241753
BA 020-7836 1112
Heartbeat (TV drama), Like Father Like Son (TV drama), The Crooked Man (TV drama).

John Milne　　　01206-514177　Mobile 07973-839682
TA 020-7727 1346
The Bill (TV drama), Waking The Dead (TV drama), Silent Witness (TV drama).

Philip Munnoch　　020-8221 1622　Fax 020-8221 1622
Friday Zone (TV childrens), Idiot Box (TV light entertainment), Giggly Bitz (TV childrens).

Kira-Anne Pelican　　　　　020-7243 6567

Philip Purser　　　　　01327-860274

Nico Rilla　　　　　Mobile 07973-201895

Simon Sharkey　　　　　RS 020-7359 3900
Murder In Mind (TV drama), Dalziel & Pascoe (TV drama), London's Burning (TV drama).

Richard Vizor　　　　　Mobile 07738-938285
The Trial (theatre), Cray (feature).

Robert Wade　　　　　CM 020-7287 4450
Quantum Of Solace (feature), Casino Royale (feature), Die Another Day (feature).

STAGE MANAGERS

Caroline Boocock　　　　　020-8748 4769
Top Of The Pops (TV light entertainment), Later With Jools Holland (TV light entertainment), Shooting Stars (TV light entertainment).

Sarah Daman　　020-8341 2456　Mobile 07973-296183
Hardware (TV comedy drama), Eyes Down (TV comedy drama), My Hero (TV comedy drama).

Nick Haffenden　　01375-484399　Mobile 07710-549612
The National (theatre), Night & Day (TV drama) (Set Decorator), The Merchant Of Venice (feature).

TRANSPORT CAPTAINS

Phil Allchin　　　01707-272710　Mobile 07836-204547
Fax 01707-272710
Quantum Of Solace (feature), Hereafter (feature), Inkheart (feature).

Simon Barker　　　　　Mobile 07721-343750
Kick-Ass (feature), Scaredy Cats (feature), The Awakening (feature).

Bryan Baverstock　　01908-661131　Mobile 07939-588057
The Wolfman (feature), Nanny McPhee & The Big Bang (feature), Green Zone (feature).

Mike Beaven　　　0118-981 4847　Mobile 07850-436116
Fax 0118-981 4847
Pride & Prejudice (feature), Closer (feature), Elizabeth: The Golden Age (feature).

Gary Birmingham　　020-8941 6255　Mobile 07973-848464
The Wolfman (feature), Night & Day (TV drama), London Boulevard (feature).

Steve Brigen　　　　　01784-251161

Peter Devlin　　　　　Mobile 07891-555666
Robin Hood (feature), The Da Vinci Code (feature), Charlie & The Chocolate Factory (feature).

Gerry Gore　　　0151-228 3155　Mobile 07860-683373
Fax 0151-228 3155
Prince Of Persia (feature), Syriana (feature), Sahara (feature).

Peter Graovac　　020-8398 4439　Mobile 07970-074627
Lord Of The Rings (feature), King Arthur (feature), Band Of Brothers (TV drama).

Robert Hempenstall　01753-891828　Mobile 07974-156605

Darren Leen　　　　　Mobile 07760-115569
Little Dorrit (TV drama).

David Rosenbaum　　020-8395 7773　Mobile 07802-580560
Harry Potter & The Deathly Hallows (feature), Harry Potter & The Goblet Of Fire (feature), Harry Potter & The Half-Blood Prince (feature).

Gerry Turner　　　01895-833708　Mobile 07785-727897
Fax 01895-833708
Quantum Of Solace (feature), Casino Royale (feature), Fred Claus (feature).

UNIT DRIVERS

Waseem Barlas　　Mobile 07976-813198　Fax 020-8270 7430
Alexander (feature), The Four Feathers (feature), Entrapment (feature).

Bob Beton　　　020-8818 0089　Mobile 07973-505925
Calendar Girls (feature), Thunderbirds (feature), Alexander (feature).

PRODUCTION

UNIT DRIVERS

Nigel Birtchnell   01753-675680 Mobile 07785-907781
Mamma Mia! (feature), Inkheart (feature), Harry Potter & The Order Of The Phoenix (feature).

Colin Burge   01753-655528 Mobile 07956-658272
Fax 01753-654457

Mike Elliot   Mobile 07778-978437
Death At A Funeral (feature), Rosemary & Thyme (TV drama), My Uncle Silas (TV drama).

Micky Grover   01634-314118 Mobile 07860-341391
Lewis (TV drama), The Glass (TV drama), Inspector Morse (TV drama).

Peter Harvey   Mobile 07802-229153
Harry Potter & The Deathly Hallows (feature), Harry Potter & The Philosopher's Stone (feature), Harry Potter & The Goblet Of Fire (feature).

Robert Hole   01268-492279 Mobile 07860-503005
The Boat That Rocked (feature), The Other Boleyn Girl (feature), The Holiday (feature).

John Hollywood   01844-351041 Mobile 07525-394917
Nine (feature), The Invention Of Hugo Cabret (feature), Spy Game (feature).

John Horan   020-8446 0988 Mobile 07831-888818
John Carter Of Mars (feature), Clash Of The Titans (feature), Batman (feature).

Tony Jayes   Mobile 07831-413198
Alexander (feature), Tomb Raider II (feature), War Bride (feature).

Phil Knight   020-8907 2736 Mobile 07836-597055
Fax 020-8621 0284
Sleepy Hollow (feature), The Mummy Returns (feature), Harry Potter & The Prisoner Of Azkaban (feature).

Niklas Kozma   01727-864249 Mobile 07714-333181
The Wolfman (feature), Gulliver's Travels (feature), Love Actually (feature).

Ed McLean   Mobile 07977-495915
Silent Witness (TV drama), Cranford (TV drama), Hustle (TV drama).

Jason Mortlock   Mobile 07939-539182
Harry Potter & The Deathly Hallows (feature), Harry Potter & The Half-Blood Prince (feature), Harry Potter & The Order Of The Phoenix (feature).

Barry Newell   020-8577 9416 Mobile 07860-700421
New Tricks (TV drama), Murderland (TV drama), The Girl In The Cafe (TV film).

David O'Connor   01923-775655 Mobile 07802-655888
Corpse Bride (feature), King Arthur (feature), Charlie & The Chocolate Factory (feature).

Brian Pitches   020-8940 0802 Mobile 07889-996474
The Da Vinci Code (feature), Charlie & The Chocolate Factory (feature), The Dark Knight (feature).

Terry Pritchard   0118-975 6986 Mobile 07831-506397
Fax 0118-975 6986
The Magic Flute (feature), As You Like It (feature), Five Children & It (feature).

Mark Richards   01932-242359 Mobile 07768-730887
Sweeney Todd (feature), Hereafter (feature), The Invention Of Hugo Cabret (feature).

Steve Rogers   020-8644 0801 Mobile 07932-165664
Cemetery Junction (feature), Harry Potter & The Deathly Hallows (feature), The Wolfman (feature).

John Smith   01371-859547 Mobile 07860-600489
London Boulevard (feature), Luther (TV drama), One Day (feature).

Alf Stone   020-8397 4171 Mobile 07798-835249
Fax 020-8397 4171
Two Men Went To War (feature), Harry Potter & The Chamber Of Secrets (feature), Foyle's War (TV drama).

Chris Streeter   01895-447680 Mobile 07836-736454
Harry Potter & The Deathly Hallows (feature), The Mummy Returns (feature), Star Wars: Episode I - The Phantom Menace (feature).

Tony Wadsworth   01628-602119 Mobile 07850-638423
Robin Hood (feature), The Bourne Ultimatum (feature), The Da Vinci Code (feature).

Paul Watson   0870-950 3377 Mobile 07939-999482
Calendar Girls (feature), Mansfield Park (TV film), Britz (TV drama).

Kitchener Young   01225-832410 Mobile 07719-589236
Fax 01225-832410
Harry Potter & The Deathly Hallows (feature), Harry Potter & The Half-Blood Prince (feature), Harry Potter & The Order Of The Phoenix (feature).

UNIT MANAGERS

David Bell   Mobile 07837-581806
London Boulevard (feature), The King's Speech (feature), Angus Thongs & Perfect Snogging (feature).

Greg Blank 020-8964 2831 Mobile 07932-256337
Hustle (TV drama).

David Campbell-Bell Mobile 07786-656662
Robin Hood (feature), Prince Of Persia (feature), Miss Potter (feature).

Danny Gulliver Mobile 07834-767677
Nanny McPhee & The Big Bang (feature).

John David Gunkle 01872-553630 Mobile 07773-208067
Hot Fuzz (feature), Apocalypto (feature), Grindhouse (feature).

Sally Hall 020-7249 7993 Mobile 07971-010913
The Garage (TV reality), What Makes Us Human (TV doc), Hit 40 UK (TV light entertainment).

Steve Harvey Mobile 07956-560198
Harry Potter & The Deathly Hallows (feature), In Bruges (feature), The Da Vinci Code (feature).

Ian Hutchinson 020-8202 5829 Mobile 07981-524010
St Trinian's (feature), Miss Marple (TV drama).

Joseph Jayawardena Mobile 07710-512145
Harry Potter & The Order Of The Phoenix (feature), The Da Vinci Code (feature).

Kevin Jenkins Mobile 07976-400141
Prince Of Persia (feature), Miss Potter (feature), Children Of Men (feature).

Matt Jones Mobile 07973-506939
Gulliver's Travels (feature).

Gavin Milligan 01628-671920 Mobile 07799-764839
Basic Instinct II (feature), The Da Vinci Code (feature) (2nd unit), Casino Royale (feature).

Nick Paolozzi 01234-341274 Mobile 07958-697010
Hotel Babylon (TV drama).

Bobby Prince Mobile 07970-958548
Burke & Hare (feature), Street Dance 3D (feature), From Time To Time (feature).

Bobby Prince Mobile 07970-958548
Burke & Hare (feature), Street Dance 3D (feature), From Time To Time (feature).

Charlie Simpson 020-8670 0090 Mobile 07774-821920
W.E. (feature), Sherlock Holmes (feature), Brighton Rock (feature).

Ed Smith Mobile 07810-271422
New Town Killers (feature), North & South (TV drama).

Dusty Symonds 01628-528683 EXEC 01753-646677
Fax 01628-528683
Phantom Of The Opera (feature), Sleepy Hollow (feature), Dinotopia (TV drama).

Nick Waldron 01895-932490 Mobile 07768-881222
Fax 01895-835318
Sahara (feature), King Arthur (feature), Band Of Brothers (TV drama).

Martin Walker Mobile 07876-124445
Trial & Retribution (TV drama), Robin Hood (feature), The Golden Compass (feature).

John Withers 01932-221882 Mobile 07774-444498
Being Human (TV drama), The Intimidation Game (feature).

UNIT PUBLICISTS

Kathryn Donovan Mobile 07710-656045
Gulliver's Travels (feature), Wanted (feature), The Wolfman (feature).

Linda Gamble Mobile 07768-082201
London Boulevard (feature).

Claudia Kalindjian Mobile 07957-361866
Nanny McPhee & The Big Bang (feature), From Time To Time (feature).

Stacy Mann Mobile 07768-966122
Robin Hood (feature).

PRODUCTION

Sound
DEPARTMENT

ADR SUPERVISORS

Paul Conway 020-8567 0822
Tsunami: The Aftermath (TV drama), United 93 (feature), Troy (feature).

BOOM OPERATORS

Christopher Atkinson Mobile 07961-198685
Inception (feature), Atonement (feature), Basic Instinct II (feature).

James Bain Mobile 07801-151896
Law & Order (TV drama), Little Dorrit (TV drama), Spooks (TV drama).

Alun Banks 020-8141 8296 Mobile 07768-478190
Fanny Hill (TV drama), Derailed (feature), Green Street (feature).

Orin Beaton Mobile 07785-565437
Harry Potter & The Deathly Hallows (feature), Harry Potter & The Half-Blood Prince (feature), Eastern Promises (feature).

Tony Bell AMPS 01494-875924 Mobile 07889-397344
Prince Of Persia (feature) (2nd unit), Eyes Wide Shut (feature), All Or Nothing (feature).

Jason Bennett Mobile 07809-046806
New Tricks (TV drama), Hotel Babylon (TV drama), A Bunch Of Amateurs (feature).

Simon Brown 01684-275990 Mobile 07900-225725
Wire In The Blood (TV drama), Land Of The Blind (feature), I Could Never Be Your Woman (feature).

Chris Cartwright 01260-252757 Mobile 07786-521658
Fax 01260-252757
Millions (feature), Cracker (TV drama), Casanova (feature).

John Coates 0115-972 2385 Mobile 07850-255365
Cracker (TV drama), Twentyfour: Seven (feature), Peak Practice (TV drama).

Tony Cook 0161-224 5043 Mobile 07831-305276
The Last Word (feature), Cranford (TV drama), The 39 Steps (TV film).

Paul Cridlin AMPS 020-8677 1704 Mobile 07808-578961
Charles II (TV drama), Friends & Crocodiles (TV drama), Entrapment (feature).

John Crossland 020-8874 5401 Mobile 07973-216253
Holby City (TV drama), Celebration (TV film), Panorama (TV doc).

St Clair Davis 020-8521 0057 Mobile 07973-559019
SC 01932-252577
Babylon AD (feature), My Beautiful Laundrette (feature), Sharpe (TV drama).

Matthew Desorgher AMPS 01529-497771
Mobile 07802-540985 Fax 01529-497771
The Lost Prince (TV drama), 101 Dalmatians (feature), Kundun (feature).

Gary Dodkin Mobile 07778-627948
The Wolfman (feature), Munich (feature), V For Vendetta (feature).

Mike Donald 01844-217568 Mobile 07766-913777
SC 01932-252577 Fax 01844-217294
Little Britain (tour), Young Indiana Jones (TV drama), Earth (feature).

Nathan Duncan 020-8286 8054
The Queen (feature).

Gavin Dunn Mobile 07973-549891
Casualty 1909 (TV drama), Boy Meets Girl (TV drama), Survivors (TV drama).

Peter Eusebe Mobile 07889-800119
Dorian Gray (feature), St Trinian's (feature), Hellboy (feature).

Arthur Fenn Mobile 07870-116061
Kick-Ass (feature), Nanny McPhee & The Big Bang (feature), Stardust (feature).

Steve Finn 020-8673 0694 Mobile 07885-864899
W.E. (feature).

Richie Finney AMPS 01553-828650 Mobile 07973-132753
Dunkirk (TV drama doc), True North (feature), Billy Elliot (feature).

Stephen Fish AMPS 01992-630282 Mobile 07973-265909
Jane Eyre (feature), Lewis (TV drama), Cambridge Spies (TV drama).

Robin Green Mobile 07885-854437
Chromophobia (feature), Hitchhiker's Guide To The Galaxy (feature), Stormbreaker (feature).

Andrew Griffiths Mobile 07956-375017
Van Helsing (feature), Black Hawk Down (feature), Die Another Day (feature).

Chris Gurney AMPS 020-8882 6462 Mobile 07860-834728
Fax 020-8882 8728
The Shouting Men (feature), Basic Instinct II (feature), Shooting Dogs (feature).

Loveday Harding AMPS 01840-261339
Mobile 07768-815706
Doc Martin (TV drama), Vera Drake (feature), Topsy-Turvy (feature).

James Harris 01932-563496 Mobile 07866-477793
Little Dorrit (TV drama), Kingdom Of Heaven (feature), Beneath The Skin (TV drama).

Tom Harrison Mobile 07713-627915
The Da Vinci Code (feature), Gavin & Stacey (TV comedy drama), Cold & Dark (feature).

Amber Howarth Mobile 07961-166593
Extras (TV comedy drama), Jam & Jerusalem (TV comedy drama).

Martin Ireland Mobile 07725-467425
Hope Springs (TV drama), Cowards (TV comedy drama), God On Trial (TV drama).

Richard Jay AMPS MIBS 020-8452 1329
Mobile 07836-252525 Fax 020-8452 1329
Foster (feature), Swinging With The Finkels (feature), Dracula (TV drama).

Robin Johnson 020-8392 1163 Mobile 07966-961949
Kick-Ass (feature), Nanny McPhee & The Big Bang (feature), Mamma Mia! (feature).

Richard Jupp 01628-530262 Mobile 07718-589026
Jonathan Creek (TV drama), Love Soup (TV drama), Crooked House (TV drama).

Garie Kan Mobile 07973-669898
RocknRolla (feature), Demons (TV drama), Merlin (TV drama).

Russell Keefe 01903-202649 Mobile 07930-312672
The Bill (TV drama), Holby City (TV drama), Dream Team (TV drama).

Michael Kent 01672-514852 Mobile 07710-597393
Fax 01672-514122
Water's Rising (feature), Man Woman (TV light entertainment), Quills (feature).

Mike Kneafsey Mobile 07968-762363
Bad Girls (TV drama).

Gordon Lester 01480-434362 Mobile 07977-490617
The Vice (TV drama), Silent Witness (TV drama), Holby City (TV drama).

John Lewis Aschenbrenner 01753-842756
Mobile 07976-238650
Hustle (TV drama), Colditz (TV drama), Klimt (feature).

Jeremy Lishman 020-8789 0858 Mobile 07956-620192
And When Did You Last See Your Father? (feature), Death Defying Acts (feature), State Of Play (TV drama).

Adam Margetts AMPS 01666-825846
Mobile 07802-747721 Fax 01666-825846
Being Human (TV drama), Afterlife (TV drama), This Life +10 (TV drama).

Peter Margrave 01234-781554 Mobile 07778-295486
Fax 01234-781554
Hamlet (feature), The Shell Seekers (TV drama), To The Ends Of The Earth (TV drama).

Jerome McCann AMPS 020-8802 5912
Mobile 07970-643288
Trial & Retribution (TV drama), Archangel (TV drama), Lawless Heart (feature).

Shaun Mills 01202-587675 Mobile 07850-281354
Green Zone (feature), Fred Claus (feature), Gosford Park (feature).

Kate Morath AMPS 01590-678766 Mobile 07770-231242
Prince Of Persia (feature), Miss Potter (feature), Notes On A Scandal (feature).

Clive Osborne Mobile 07801-337752
Children Of Men (feature).

Joe Paines Mobile 07879-426162
Miss Marple (TV drama).

Tim Partridge 01453-872545 Mobile 07813-906332
Luther (TV drama), The Last Detective (TV drama), The Inspector Lynley Mysteries (TV drama).

Steve Peckover 01642-781877 Mobile 07825-277774
Hotel Babylon (TV drama).

Dick Philip Mobile 07711-553160 Fax 020-8311 5517
The Daisy Chain (feature), The Roman Mysteries (TV childrens), The Hills Have Eyes (feature).

Richard Pilcher 01728-687534 Mobile 07714-014627
The Inbetweeners (TV comedy drama), The Catherine Tate Show (TV light entertainment), The Thick Of It (TV comedy drama).

June Prinz Mobile 07818-205075
Gulliver's Travels (feature), Star Wars: Episode 1 - The Phantom Menace (feature), Harry Potter & The Philosopher's Stone (feature).

Mike Reardon Mobile 07970-223464
Bleak House (TV drama), Life Begins (TV drama), Miss Marple (TV drama).

Ashley Reynolds   020-8883 5083 Mobile 07967-135175
Miss Marple (TV drama), Poirot (TV drama), Foyle's War (TV drama).

Andrew Rowe   Mobile 07811-403706 DG 020-7386 0310
Sugarhouse Lane (feature), The Walker (feature), Consent (TV drama doc).

Trevor Rutherford   020-8205 9012
Godfather III (feature), Murder On The Orient Express (feature), Good Morning Vietnam (feature).

Liam Ryan   01722-712611 Mobile 07971-784529
Ultimate Force (TV drama), Midsomer Murders (TV drama), Warriors (TV film).

Allan Sill   01388-608294 Mobile 07860-280409
Wire In The Blood (TV drama), Hollyoaks (TV drama), Byker Grove (TV childrens).

Martin Smith   0161-962 4947 Mobile 07976-969404
Goldplated (TV drama), The Street (TV drama), Coronation Street (TV drama).

Tim Surrey   Mobile 07880-550825
Mamma Mia! (feature), Desperate Romantics (TV drama), The Firm (feature).

Graham Tait   020-8384 3604 Mobile 07866-609879
The Golden Compass (feature), The Kevin Bishop Show (TV comedy drama), Holby City (TV drama).

Tristan Tarrant   Mobile 07976-299536
Nine (feature), The Golden Compass (feature), Sweeney Todd (feature).

Adrienne Taylor   020-7354 3847 Mobile 07769-700544
Dream Team (TV drama), Bleak House (TV drama), Piccadilly Jim (feature).

Will Towers   Mobile 07968-146360

Colin Wood AMPS   020-8953 1483 Fax 020-8387 0618
Wimbledon (feature), Tomorrow Never Dies (feature), The End Of The Affair (feature).

Stephen Wright   01992-558485 Mobile 07973-623563
Fax 01992-558485
Little Dorrit (TV drama), Kinky Boots (feature), Blackpool (TV drama).

PRODUCTION SOUND MIXERS

Mat Adams   Mobile 07931-350616
Secret Millionaire (TV reality), Shipwrecked (TV doc).

Martin Alimundo   Mobile 07831-356946
This Is Your Life (TV light entertainment), Wish You Were Here (feature), MacIntyre Undercover (TV doc).

Christopher Ashworth AMPS   01959-562509
Mobile 07774-140527 SPA 01932-571044
Glorious 39 (feature), Endgame (feature), Bleak House (TV drama).

Christopher Atkinson   01706-223533
Mobile 07836-784378
Cold Blood (TV drama), Survivors (TV drama), Boy Meets Girl (TV drama).

Mark Atkinson   0161-483 8887 Mobile 07958-901527
Billy Connolly: Journey To The Edge Of The World (TV light entertainment), Britain's Got The Pop Factor (TV light entertainment), Max & Paddy (TV drama).

John Avery   020-7686 1848 Mobile 07973-310645
Prometheus (feature), Surveillance (feature), The South Bank Show (TV arts).

Albert Bailey   020-8800 6523 Mobile 07973-285970
Fax 020-8800 6523
The Hills Have Eyes (feature), Blueberry (feature), Bloody Sunday (feature).

Ronald Bailey   Mobile 07956-378679
MI High (TV childrens), Bridget Jones's Diary (feature), Doctor Who (TV drama).

James Baker   Mobile 07956-379932
Escape From Experiment Island (TV light entertainment), Challenge Anneka (TV light entertainment).

Steph Baldini AMPS   Mobile 07958-350886
Robinson Crusoe (feature), An Urban Ghost Story (feature).

Fraser Barber   Mobile 07768-166089
Five Daughters (TV drama), House Of Saddam (TV drama), Little Dorrit (TV drama).

Steve Beech   01579-362301 Mobile 07836-263029
Grow Your Own Veg (TV doc), Gardeners' World (TV light entertainment), HMS Raleigh (TV doc).

Adrian Bell   Mobile 07836-322802 SPA 01932-571044
Merlin (TV drama), Hotel Babylon (TV drama), Demons (TV drama).

Nick Bennett   01749-346320 Mobile 07836-246700

Mike Bird   01275-858156 Mobile 07954-443399
Final Score (TV docu drama), BBC Sport (TV sport), World Cup Football (TV sport).

Simon Bishop AMPS 020-8579 3597 Mobile 07836-345092
SPA 01932-571044
Star Wars: Episode II - Attack Of The Clones (feature), Auf Wiedersehen Pet (TV drama), New Tricks (TV drama).

David Brabants Mobile 07850-690054
The Perfect Village (TV doc), Comedy Connections (TV doc), Drama Connections (TV doc).

Julian Brannigan Mobile 07850-325426
Iron Chef UK (TV light entertainment), Stephen Fry Manic Depressive (TV doc), The Boy Whose Skin Fell Off (TV doc).

Peter Brill 0141-357 0617 Mobile 07971-780572
Hallam Foe (feature), Cranford (TV drama), The 39 Steps (TV film).

Rudi Buckle AMPS 020-8778 1315 Mobile 07973-238785
ITG 020-7636 6565
Little Dorrit (TV drama), Spooks (TV drama), Hustle (TV drama).

Callum Bulmer Mobile 07956-424881
Ross Kemp On Gangs (TV doc), Nevis: Polar Challenge (TV doc).

Simon Burles Mobile 07836-681465 DG 020-7386 0310
Inside MI5: The Real Spooks (TV doc), Trawlermen (TV doc), V Festival (TV light entertainment).

George Camm 0115-932 1913 Mobile 07860-682910
Fax 0115-944 0011
War Against The French (TV doc), Loch Ness Monster (TV doc), A6 Murder (TV doc).

Ken Campbell 01727-861843 Mobile 07831-322642
The Palace (TV drama), Elizabeth I (TV drama), Apparitions (TV drama).

Dennis Cartwright 01260-252757 Mobile 07831-412408
Fax 01260-252757
Casanova (feature), The Street (TV drama), Longford (TV drama).

John Casali AMPS 01727-868025 Mobile 07973-755529
Fax 01727-868025
The Boy In The Striped Pyjamas (feature), Harry Potter & The Deathly Hallows (feature), Harry Potter & The Half-Blood Prince (feature) (2nd unit).

Dave Chapman 01442-230230 Mobile 07836-777737
Fax 01442-232583
Challenge Anneka (TV light entertainment), Holiday (TV doc), Jobs For The Boys (TV doc).

Julian Chatterjee 020-8962 9495 Mobile 07785-540282
SR 020-7736 7786
Top Gear (TV light entertainment), The X Factor (TV light entertainment), Masterchef (TV light entertainment).

Nigel Chatters 01904-411149 Mobile 07831-482417
SD 020-8994 1199
Timewatch (TV doc), The House That God Built (TV doc), Nation On Film (TV doc).

Simon Clark Mobile 07785-228588 SPA 01932-571044
Bouquet Of Barbed Wire (TV drama), Identity (TV drama), Waking The Dead (TV drama).

Murray Clarke 01530-563521 Mobile 07973-345115
Fax 01530-563524
Camel Trophy (TV sport), Jeremy Clarkson's Motorworld (TV doc), NFU Mutual (corporate).

Chris Clarkson 01937-529391 Mobile 07836-552133
Whicker's World (TV doc), Sherlock Holmes (feature), HSBC (commercial).

Colin Codner AMPS Mobile 07887-563290
Fred Claus (feature) (2nd unit), V For Vendetta (feature) (2nd unit), Kingdom Of Heaven (feature) (2nd unit).

Brian Comer 01278-455562 Mobile 07860-888205
Building The Dream (TV doc), Crash (TV doc), Dispatches (TV doc).

Nick Cook Mobile 07771-727454
Three Men Go To Ireland (TV doc), River Cottage (TV light entertainment), Country File (TV doc).

Clive Copland AMPS 020-8876 3728 Mobile 07956-374623
CMM 020-8584 5363 Fax 020-8876 3728
Acts Of Godfrey (feature), A Bunch Of Amateurs (feature), Made Of Honor (feature).

Rob Craig Mobile 07971-785179 SD 020-8994 1199

Phil Croal 0131-440 2335 Mobile 07836-786335
Robin Hood (TV drama), Low Winter Sun (TV drama), Monarch Of The Glen (TV drama).

Alistair Crocker 0117-974 3033 Mobile 07770-931015
CMM 020-8584 5363
In Bruges (feature), Sharpe's Challenge (TV drama), The Full Monty (feature).

John Currie 01273-324317 Mobile 07710-450794
SC 01932-252577
Little Britain (tour), Help (TV light entertainment), Home Front (TV light entertainment).

Tom Curry 020-7733 7654 Mobile 07976-271287
SR 020-7736 7786
Not Under My Roof (TV doc), The House That Lotto Built (TV doc), We Got A New Life (TV doc).

SOUND

Geoff Price   020-8567 7532 Mobile 07774-487870
SC 01932-252577
The National Trust (TV doc).

Billy Quinn   Mobile 07812-604562 ITG 020-7636 6565
Criminal Justice (TV drama), Dracula (TV drama), Consuming Passion (TV drama).

Keith Quirk   Mobile 07802-681279
The Disappearance Of Alice Creed (feature), Good Arrows (TV film), Island At War (TV drama).

Tamara Rawlingson Plant   Mobile 07979-690701
DYA 020-7386 0310
Grand Designs (TV doc), The Apprentice (TV reality).

Ian Richardson AMPS   029-2022 1938
Mobile 07973-263784
Tomorrow La Scala (TV film), Supernatural (TV drama), The Baker (feature).

Vaughan Roberts   Mobile 07887-504654
TOVS 020-7287 6110
Doctors (TV drama), ITN News (TV news & current affairs), Trauma (feature).

Nick Robertson   01273-241168 Mobile 07973-326745
SC 01932-252577
Help (TV light entertainment), Little Britain (tour).

John Rodda AMPS   Mobile 07785-504606
PS 020-8883 1616
Monte Carlo (feature), 28 Days Later (feature), National Treasure: Book Of Secrets (feature).

Keith Rodgerson   0117-973 3848 Mobile 07970-623262
F59 0117-906 4300 Fax 0117-923 7791
Dinner At Noon (feature), Secrets Of The Dead (TV doc), Elegant Universe (feature).

Mike Russell   020-8367 8109 Mobile 07990-503045
Den Of Lions (feature), Endangered Species (feature), Joy Division (feature).

Ian Sands AMPS   Mobile 07860-753717 Fax 01932-241694
The Bourne Ultimatum (feature) (2nd unit), Shanghai (feature) (2nd unit), Mirrormask (feature).

Rob Saunders   Mobile 07753-361951
The Sex Education Show (TV doc), Imagine (TV drama), Alesha Dixon (promo).

Adam Scourfield   020-7639 4237 Mobile 07050-039499
Parallel Worlds Parallel Lives (TV doc), Imagine (TV drama), Music Ophillia (TV light entertainment).

Tony Sercombe   01603-717885 Mobile 07941-716274
Seeds (TV film), Crime Punishment & A Tasty Morsel (feature), The City Programme (TV news & current affairs).

Ivan Sharrock AMPS   020-7267 3170
Mobile 07768-627856 Fax 020-7284 4250
Clash Of The Titans (feature), Blood Diamond (feature), The Da Vinci Code (feature).

Pasha Shilov   020-8993 8354 Mobile 07742-828100
The Naked Chef (TV light entertainment), Buffy The Vampire Slayer (TV drama), Winning London (feature).

Bryan Showell   01844-339316 Mobile 07711-181448
Ripping Yarns (TV drama), Omnibus (TV doc), To The Manor Born (TV comedy drama).

Keith Silva   Mobile 07831-666899 ARRI 01895-457180
Tormented (feature), The Gentleman Thief (TV drama), Like Minds (feature).

Brian Simmons AMPS   01932-226558
Mobile 07710-237065
Shanghai (feature), The Merchant Of Venice (feature), Star Wars: Episode III - Revenge Of The Sith (feature).

Andrew Sissons   01923-852146 Mobile 07976-897883
Fax 01923-852146
Foyle's War (TV drama), Miss Marple (TV drama), Poirot (TV drama).

Roger Slater AMPS   01684-565897 Mobile 07973-885363
Lark Rise To Candleford (TV drama), Midsomer Murders (TV drama), Dalziel & Pascoe (TV drama).

Michael Spencer AMPS   020-8567 6559
Mobile 07973-746434 CMM 020-8584 5363 Fax 020-8567 6559
Victoria Wood Xmas Special (TV light entertainment), Lead Balloon (TV comedy drama), Severance (feature).

Gary Stadden   0117-330 2031 Mobile 07970-667937
DG 020-7386 0310
The Restaurant (TV reailty), Grand Designs (TV doc), The X Factor (TV light entertainment).

Roger Stamp AMPS   Mobile 07887-554485
MIT (TV drama), The Golden Hour (TV drama), The Bill (TV drama).

Christopher Stanway   020-8950 1423
Mobile 07973-119217 Fax 020-8386 2446

David Steckler   01923-268954 Mobile 07801-555284
Symphony In G Minor (TV drama), Racing Game (TV doc), The Changeling (feature).

Tim Stephens   Mobile 07768-852555
Don't Die Young (TV doc), Gardeners' World (TV light entertainment), Grand Designs (TV doc).

David Stephenson AMPS   01276-857036
Mobile 07885-639332 ITG 020-7636 6565
London Boulevard (feature), The Wolfman (feature), Munich (feature).

Nick Stocker   01275-813966 Mobile 07939-369310
Fax 01275-813966
Minotaur (feature), Lost Dogs (feature), Married/Unmarried (feature).

Peter Stoddart   01760-723516 Mobile 07778-815344

Dave Stonestreet   01273-203191 Mobile 07710-601373
Fax 01273-203191
Here Comes The Bogeyman (TV doc), Big Brother (TV reality), Panadol Actifast (commercial).

Jonny Stothert   020-8855 1989 Mobile 07515-435266
The Apprentice (TV reality), The Altogether (feature) (Boom Operator).

Rosie Straker AMPS   020-7209 8950 Mobile 07973-445225
Pinochet In Suburbia (TV drama), Shooting Dogs (feature), Basic Instinct II (feature).

Chris Syner   01483-458120 Mobile 07831-514410
LL 020-8426 2200
Elizabeth David - A Life In Recipes (TV drama), The Year London Blew Up (TV drama), Who Do You Think You Are? (TV doc).

Ivor Talbot   Mobile 07775-711091
The Descent 2 (feature), Eden Lake (feature), Wonderland: The Man Who Eats Badgers (TV doc).

Darren Tate   01666-840418 Mobile 07831-666229
Ray Mears (TV doc), Serious Arctic (TV doc), Life Of Grime (TV doc).

Sean Taylor   Mobile 07831-592036
Fighting The War: Iraq (TV doc), Escape To The Legion (TV doc).

John Taylor AMPS   020-8840 1543 Mobile 07973-727631
ITG 020-7636 6565 Fax 07971-046656
Nativity (feature), The Great Ghost Rescue (feature), Charles II (TV drama).

Mike Thomas   0141-956 5003 Mobile 07785-250421
Fax 0141-956 5003
Blue Planet (TV doc), Secrets Of The Lost Empires (TV doc), History Of Slavery (TV doc).

Calum Thomson   Mobile 07968-436672
Extreme Dreams (TV doc), Panorama (TV doc).

Gordon Thomson AMPS   020-8845 7871
Mobile 07770-741707 CCA 020-7630 6303
Casualty (TV drama), Holby City (TV drama), The Bill (TV drama).

Chris Travers   HC 020-8742 1888
The X Factor (TV light entertainment), Britain's Got Talent (TV light entertainment), Over The Rainbow (TV light entertainment).
www.hotcam.tv

Martin Trevis AMPS   01344-771511 Mobile 07798-766171
The Last Station (feature), Into The Storm (TV film), Brighton Rock (feature).

Mike Turner AMPS   01706-846151 Mobile 07774-179606

Paul Vigars   Mobile 07768-820182
The South Bank Show (TV arts).

Ian Voigt AMPS   020-8941 0454 Mobile 07831-164465
MM 020-8995 4747 Fax 020-8224 9255
The Boat That Rocked (feature), Town Creek (feature), The Omen 666 (feature).

Nick Walker   Mobile 07973-198754 DG 020-7386 0310
Luminal (feature), Operatunity (TV doc).

Nick Ware   01483-222239 Mobile 07802-246088

Chris Watson   0191-233 0050 Fax 0191-233 0052
Life In The Undergrowth (TV doc), The Meerkats (feature), Life In Cold Blood (TV doc).

Mark Wellman   Mobile 07971-011510
Tiger Island (TV doc), Great British Summer (TV doc), Monkey Business (TV doc).

Tim White   020-8788 7944 Mobile 07785-366760
DD 020-7851 3575 Fax 020-8789 4659
9/11 The Twin Towers (TV drama), Magicians (feature), Moonshot (TV docu drama).

Rob Widger   01628-669171 Mobile 07973-491087
Masters Of The Sea (TV doc), The Bill (TV drama), Holby City (TV drama).

Alastair Widgery   01923-290051 Mobile 07774-236493

Dave Williams   020-8452 4549 Mobile 07850-735289
It's A Girl Thing (TV drama), Littlewoods (commercial), Space With Sam Neil (TV doc).

Lloyd Williamson   Mobile 07971-428670
71 Degrees North (TV reality), All At Sea (TV doc), Extreme Dreams (TV doc).

SOUND

Bruce Wills   01225-891972 Mobile 07973-304698
ITG 020-7636 6565 Fax 01225-892052
Miss Marple (TV drama), Blackpool (TV drama), Dr Zhivago (TV film).

Martin Wilson   020-8995 9392 Mobile 07813-609044
LL 020-8426 2200
Star Stories (TV light entertainment), The Queen (feature), Pete V Life (TV comedy drama).

Stuart Wilson AMPS   Mobile 07771-533816
Marie Antoinette (feature), Harry Potter & The Half-Blood Prince (feature), The Constant Gardener (feature).

Bob Withey   020-8339 6821 Mobile 07831-364986

Tim Worth   01784-258338 Mobile 07956-331320
LL 020-8426 2200 Fax 01784-258338
Casino Royale (feature), How Earth Made Us (TV doc), The Story Of Science (TV doc).

Jonathan Wyatt AMPS   01603-722673
Mobile 07968-192757 Fax 01603-722673
A Passionate Woman (TV drama), Waterloo Road (TV drama), Cuckoo (feature).

SOUND ASSISTANTS

Christian Bourne   Mobile 07970-256238
White Diamonds (TV doc), National Lottery (commercial), Goodyear (commercial).

Colin Bowman   01892-545285 Mobile 07973-640095
Britain Goes Wild (TV doc), Celebrity Fame Academy (TV reality), US Open Tennis (TV sport).

Jeremy Brown   Mobile 07734-086194
Dorian Gray (feature), The Duchess (feature), St Trinian's (feature).

Joe Carey   020-8446 4726 Mobile 07950-216379
Burke & Hare (feature), The King's Speech (feature), Spooks (TV drama).

James Gibb   Mobile 07725-269304
Kick-Ass (feature), Green Zone (feature), Nanny McPhee & The Big Bang (feature).

Sarah Howe   Mobile 07890-484560
From Time To Time (feature).

Gary Keller   Mobile 07812-942334
Dean Spanley (feature), Alice In Wonderland (feature), Robin Hood (feature).

Jim McBride   Mobile 07970-836770
John Carter Of Mars (feature), Valkyrie (feature), Quantum Of Solace (feature).

Chris Murphy   01727-864103 Mobile 07715-034999
Harry Potter & The Order Of The Phoenix (feature).

Rowan October   Mobile 07808-175697
This Is England (feature), Silent Witness (TV drama), Little Dorrit (TV drama).

Simon Pocock Schonning   Mobile 07900-953535
Being Julia (feature), The Life & Death Of Peter Sellers (feature), Tomb Raider II (feature).

Dave Sohanpal   Mobile 07958-075508
The Sally Lockhart Mysteries (TV drama), Billie Girl Of The Future (TV childrens).

SOUND MAINTENANCE ENGINEERS

Stephen Gilmour   Mobile 07710-891416
Children Of Men (feature), Harry Potter & The Chamber Of Secrets (feature), Death At A Funeral (feature).

James Harbour   020-7610 1952 Mobile 07732-228116
Run Fat Boy Run (feature).

Laurence O'Keefe   Mobile 07956-286686
Somers Town (feature), Hunger (feature), Miss Conception (feature).

Denise Yarde   Mobile 07980-570061
Robin Hood (feature), The Golden Compass (feature), The Good Night (feature) (Boom Operator).

SOUND RE-RECORDING MIXERS

Jim Betteridge   020-7602 9906
Azur Et Asmar (feature), Road Wars (TV doc), Human Cloning (TV doc).

Stephen Crawley   Mobile 07950-763589
Secret Millionaire (TV reality), Glamour Puds (TV light entertainment), Peter & Jordan (TV light entertainment).

Clive Derbyshire   020-8810 9406 Mobile 07778-277376
Hamlet (feature), The Singing Detective (TV drama), Agent Cody Banks II (feature).

Joao do Valle   Mobile 07956-363860 SD 020-8994 1199

SOUND

SPECIAL FX BUYERS

Lynne Corbould   Mobile 07956-245868
Inception (feature), The Dark Knight (feature), Quantum Of Solace (feature).

David Thomas   Mobile 07883-021368
Body Of Lies (feature), The Wolfman (feature).

SPECIAL FX DEPARTMENT CO-ORDINATORS

Jess Lewington   Mobile 07766-512226
Hellboy 2: The Golden Army (feature), The Da Vinci Code (feature), Green Zone (feature).

Phill Woodfine   01202-874995 Mobile 07973-135675
Sweeney Todd (feature), Charlie & The Chocolate Factory (feature), Kangaroo Jack (feature).

SPECIAL FX SUPERVISORS

Clive Beard   Mobile 07710-924336
Return Of Zoom (feature), The Gathering Storm (TV film), The Tailor Of Panama (feature).

Stuart Brisdon   020-8746 1056 Mobile 07860-682066
The Debt (feature), Stardust (feature), Bridget Jones's Diary II (feature).

Graham Brown   01923-270393 Mobile 07973-111700
Fax 01923-270115
Pride & Prejudice (feature), Silent Witness (TV drama), Waking The Dead (TV drama).

Neal Champion   01932-592416 Mobile 07802-637022
Fax 01932-592415
Ashes To Ashes (TV drama), Burke & Hare (feature), Little Dorrit (TV drama).

Jeff Clifford   01753-683824 Mobile 07850-684796
The Company (TV film), Underworld (feature), Hellboy (feature).

Richard Conway   01628-602693 Mobile 07802-946175
The Boat That Rocked (feature), 28 Weeks Later (feature), Sunshine (feature).

Ian Corbould   01494-883259 Mobile 07785-243880
John Carter Of Mars (feature), Inception (feature), The Wolfman (feature).

Neil Corbould   01753-656415 Mobile 07831-208995
Fax 01753-656147
Clash Of The Titans (feature), Defiance (feature), Gladiator (feature).

Paul Corbould   01932-561621 Mobile 07703-302455
The Wolfman (feature), 1408 (feature), Children Of Men (feature).

Mark Curtis   020-8871 2988 Fax 020-8874 8186
RAF: Tooled Up (commercial), Reebok (commercial), Son Of Rambow (feature).
www.asylumsfx.com

Paul Dunn   01753-650658 Mobile 07970-693228
Fax 01753-650659
Sony (commercial), Hannibal Rising (feature), Stormbreaker (feature).

Dave Eves   01420-475253 Mobile 07799-411614
Fax 01420-475253
Thomas The Tank Engine (TV childrens), The World Is Not Enough (feature), Black Hawk Down (feature).

Ricky Farns   01753-577751 Mobile 07702-431772
Harry Potter & The Deathly Hallows (feature), Wanted (feature), Sahara (feature).

George Gibbs   01753-853856 Mobile 07885-430100
Fax 01753-853856
Air America (feature), 101 Dalmatians (feature), Indiana Jones & The Temple Of Doom (feature).

Colin Gorry   01932-841144 Mobile 07836-294955
Fax 01932-841177
The Last Enemy (TV drama), Elizabeth The Virgin Queen (TV drama), Merlin (TV drama).
www.cg-sfx.com

Alex Gunn   01727-872352 Mobile 07778-934954
Conan (feature), John Rambo (feature), Valkyrie (feature).

Steve Hamilton   01932-830356 Mobile 07768-825327
Basic Instinct II (feature), Harry Potter & The Prisoner Of Azkaban (feature), Die Another Day (feature).

David Harris   Mobile 07831-227005 CCM 020-8743 7337
Route Irish (feature), The Magic Flute (feature), Kick-Ass (feature).

Tom Harris   01497-831436 Mobile 07774-217282
Top Gear (TV light entertainment), Doctor Who (TV drama), Spooks (TV drama).
www.anyeffects.com

Kevin Herd   Mobile 07971-277224
The Dark Knight (feature), Casino Royale (feature), Batman Begins (feature).

Bob Hollow   01784-456672   Mobile 07860-337650
The Imaginarium Of Dr Parnassus (feature), Harry Brown (feature), Double Zero (feature).

Mark Holt   020-8298 9438   Mobile 07836-246237
In Bruges (feature), Atonement (feature), Sherlock Holmes (feature).

Dave Hunter   020-8953 8153   Mobile 07970-234654
Harry Potter & The Deathly Hallows (feature), Gladiator (feature), Saving Private Ryan (feature).

Peter Hutchinson   01256-771000   Mobile 07836-641313
Batman Begins (feature) (miniatures), Phantom Of The Opera (feature), Hidalgo (feature).

Mike Kelt   020-8997 7771   Fax 020-8997 1503
Valhalla Rising (feature), The 39 Steps (TV film), Book Of Blood (feature).
www.artem.com

Peter Kersey   01494-675087   Mobile 07973-640688
Primeval (TV drama), Echo Beach (TV drama), Moving Wallpaper (TV drama).

Jeremy King   Mobile 07850-901103
Babylon AD (feature), Cuckoo (feature), City Of Vice (TV drama).
www.jeremykingfx.com

Paul Knowles   01293-786041   Mobile 07721-866758
Inception (feature), Casino Royale (feature) (workshop), Batman Begins (feature) (workshop).

Chris Lawson   01494-866983   Mobile 07774-873155
Fax 01494-866983
New Tricks (TV drama), Jonathan Creek (TV drama), Trial & Retribution (TV drama).

Graham Longhurst   0118-935 1089   Mobile 07785-390038
Fax 0118-935 1089
The Mutant Chronicles (feature), Mrs Henderson Presents (feature), Five Children & It (feature).

Paul Mann   020-8961 5888   Mobile 07973-752524
Fax 020-8961 5885
Silent Witness (TV drama), The Escapist (feature), Hyundai (commercial).
www.machineshop.co.uk

Colin Mapson   020-8943 2119   Mobile 07973-719670
Fax 020-8943 2119
French & Saunders (TV light entertainment), Dalziel & Pascoe (TV drama), Tumbledown (TV film).

John Markwell   01380-721102   Mobile 07768-891369
Photographing Fairies (feature), Band Of Brothers (TV drama).

Kevin Mathews   01753-785352   Mobile 07767-775760
Pirates Of The Caribbean: On Stranger Tides (feature), Quantum Of Solace (feature), The Dark Knight (feature).
www.specialist-wire-rigs.co.uk

Andy McVean   01753-656653   Mobile 07973-720305
Fax 01753-656192
The Night Detective (TV drama), Ant & Dec's Saturday Night (TV light entertainment), Ford Motorshow (corporate).

Digby Milner   01296-714490   Mobile 07970-452060
Fax 01296-713720
Harry Potter & The Deathly Hallows (feature), Deep Blue Sea (feature), Harry Potter & The Half-Blood Prince (feature).

Tom Murtagh   01753-662998   Mobile 07976-811020
The Intimidation Game (feature), The Dark Knight (feature), Inception (feature).

Trevor Neighbour   01753-682339   Mobile 07765-429634
Robin Hood (feature), Prince Of Persia (feature), Syriana (feature).

David Payne   020-8871 2988   Fax 020-8874 8186
John Rambo (feature), The Bourne Supremacy (feature) (underwater unit), Hogfather (TV film).
www.asylumsfx.com

John Pennicott   020-8871 2988   Fax 020-8874 8186
Skoda (commercial), Brylcreem (commercial), Ministry Of Sound (commercial).
www.asylumsfx.com

Graham Povey   01753-656808   Mobile 07789-936763
Jack Falls (feature).

John Richardson   Mobile 07977-988183
Harry Potter & The Deathly Hallows (feature), Harry Potter & The Half-Blood Prince (feature), Harry Potter & The Order Of The Phoenix (feature).

Brian Smithies   01344-843251   Mobile 07871-777215
Done (feature), The Dark Crystal (feature), Octopussy (feature).

Paul Stephenson   01326-317260   Mobile 07970-147720
Season Of The Witch (feature), Harry Potter & The Half-Blood Prince (feature).

SPECIAL FX

Simon Tayler   020-8997 7771 Fax 020-8997 1503
Sony (commercial), Ford (commercial), Animals In The Womb (TV doc).
www.artem.com

Bob Thorne   020-8997 7771 Fax 020-8997 1503
Sony Bravia (commercial), Babylon AD (feature), The Brothers Grimm (feature).
www.artem.com

Jason Troughton   01869-345556 Mobile 07966-448282
Fax 0870-112 5034
Coriolanus (feature), The Way Back (feature), Mirrors (feature).
www.agog.tv

Dominic Tuohy   020-8560 4929 Mobile 07710-116233
Gulliver's Travels (feature), The Da Vinci Code (feature), Sahara (feature).

Mark Turner   01452-729903 Mobile 07836-207522
Fax 01452-729904
Casualty (TV drama), Doctor Who (TV drama), Being Human (TV drama).
www.mtfx.com

Mark Ward   020-8871 2988 Fax 020-8874 8186
Tales Of The Riverbank (feature), Shell (commercial).
www.asylumsfx.com

Kit West   020-8878 6745 Mobile 07957-420247
BA 020-7836 1112 Fax 020-8392 2948
The Bourne Supremacy (feature), Around The World In 80 Days (feature), Enemy At The Gates (feature).

Bob Wiesinger   07000-wirefx (947339)
Mobile 07973-662393 Fax 07968-253071
The Nutcracker (ballet), The Holiday (feature), Harry Potter & The Goblet Of Fire (feature).

Andy Williams   Mobile 07770-936618
Beyond Borders (feature), King Arthur (feature), Rendition (feature).

Joss Williams   07000-327574 Mobile 07710-951115
Fax 07002-327574
Green Zone (feature), The Pacific (TV drama), Hellboy 2: The Golden Army (feature).

Ian Wingrove   01844-352210 Mobile 07774-720280
Fax 01844-352210
The Omen 666 (feature), Mission: Impossible (feature), Mirrors (feature).

Trevor Wood   01753-890035 Mobile 07808-865903
Robin Hood (feature), Prince Of Persia (feature), The Golden Compass (feature).

SPECIAL FX TECHNICIANS

Andy Aitken   01923-236458 Mobile 07973-273382
Quantum Of Solace (feature), The Dark Knight (feature), 1408 (feature).

Adam Aldridge   Mobile 07710-545660
Gulliver's Travels (feature), Sahara (feature), Prince Of Persia (feature).

Bruce Armstrong   01239-851497 Mobile 07887-574050

Scott Armstrong   01494-471934 Mobile 07990-940612
Quantum Of Solace (feature), Casino Royale (feature), Batman Begins (feature).

Robin Beavis   020-8342 1027 Mobile 07979-772175
Stardust (feature), Fred Claus (feature), Munich (feature).

Steve Benelisha   Mobile 07880-543286
John Carter Of Mars (feature), Clash Of The Titans (feature), The Dark Knight (feature).

Paul Bentman   Mobile 07968-361420
John Carter Of Mars (feature), Casino Royale (feature), The Da Vinci Code (feature).

Nick Bonathan   01276-471155 Mobile 07801-802868
The Dark Knight (feature), Gulliver's Travels (feature), John Carter Of Mars (feature).

Grant Boulton   020-8908 1743 Mobile 07790-518357
Children Of Men (feature), Inkheart (feature), The Bourne Ultimatum (feature).

Caimin Bourne   020-8893 2882 Mobile 07970-743589
Fax 0870-130 1148
The Wolfman (feature), Blood Diamond (feature), Children Of Men (feature).

Chris Brennan   01932-761160 Mobile 07780-617835
The Golden Compass (feature), Robin Hood (feature), Prince Of Persia (feature).

Julian Butterfield   01494-762715 Mobile 07803-014988
Fax 01494-762715
Fred Claus (feature), Clash Of The Titans (feature), Charlie & The Chocolate Factory (feature).

Gordon Cave   0151-252 1017 Mobile 07795-102024
Quantum Of Solace (feature), Casino Royale (feature), 1408 (feature).

Ryan Conder   Mobile 07734-461258
Prince Of Persia (feature), Children Of Men (feature), Casino Royale (feature).

Garry Cooper Mobile 07798-820074

Conan The Barbarian (feature), The Expendables (feature), Ninja Assassin (feature).

Keith Dawson Mobile 07970-057287

Green Zone (feature), Charlie & The Chocolate Factory (feature), Band Of Brothers (TV drama).

Paul Dimmer 01923-850040 Mobile 07950-298785

The Da Vinci Code (feature), Charlie & The Chocolate Factory (feature).

George Dunn Mobile 07747-791749

Push (feature), Robin Hood (feature), Prince Of Persia (feature).

Ronnie Durkan 01628-662082 Mobile 07808-760018

Harry Potter & The Deathly Hallows (feature), Harry Potter & The Prisoner Of Azkaban (feature), The Da Vinci Code (feature).

Alexander Fabre Mobile 07801-068528

John Carter Of Mars (feature).

James Ferguson 01235-751404 Mobile 07795-482530

Robin Hood (feature), Prince Of Persia (feature), The Golden Compass (feature).

Dean Ford Mobile 07921-619966

Michael Fox 01372-460177 Mobile 07710-593486

Quantum Of Solace (feature), Casino Royale (feature), Batman Begins (feature).

Joseph Geday 020-8954 6272 Mobile 07802-643946

Cold Mountain (feature), Band Of Brothers (TV drama), Black Hawk Down (feature).

Hugh Goodbody Mobile 07812-192060

Atonement (feature), Sherlock Holmes (feature), Nanny McPhee & The Big Bang (feature).

Joseph Halford Mobile 07748-654686

Robin Hood (feature), The Wolfman (feature), Children Of Men (feature).

Matthew Harlow Mobile 07753-833659

Harry Potter & The Philosopher's Stone (feature), Harry Potter & The Deathly Hallows (feature), Harry Potter & The Goblet Of Fire (feature).

Cat Hart Mobile 07880-565452

Shaun Of The Dead (feature), Hitchhiker's Guide To The Galaxy (feature).

Dan Homewood 020-8386 7547 Mobile 07930-645665

Quantum Of Solace (feature), Tomb Raider (feature), Die Another Day (feature).

Donald Joce 01344-777803 Mobile 07966-264425

Clash Of The Titans (feature), Kingdom Of Heaven (feature), Tomorrow Never Dies (feature).

Matt Johnson 01382-580038 Mobile 07712-190506

Inception (feature), Quantum Of Solace (feature), Batman Begins (feature).

Nick Joscelyne 01923-720335 Mobile 07789-866681

Harry Potter & The Half-Blood Prince (feature) (2nd unit), Harry Potter & The Order Of The Phoenix (feature).

Lee Kennealy Mobile 07710-353774

The Tailor Of Panama (feature), The Mummy Returns (feature).

Stuart Kerr Mobile 07951-787203

Fred Claus (feature), Kingdom Of Heaven (feature), 1408 (feature).

Terry Lathwell 020-8386 4808 Mobile 07764-363373

The Da Vinci Code (feature), Sahara (feature), Dinotopia (TV drama).

Roger Mann 020-8568 8635 Mobile 07747-605420

Inkheart (feature), Quantum Of Solace (feature), Children Of Men (feature).

Bruce Mayhew 01428-684547 Mobile 07884-438287

Robin Hood (feature), The Dark Knight (feature), Quantum Of Solace (feature).

Dave McGeary Mobile 07775-941837

Prince Of Persia (feature).

John McGoldrick 01753-819797 Mobile 07976-873047

Charlie & The Chocolate Factory (feature), The Bourne Ultimatum (feature), Phantom Of The Opera (feature).

Noah Meddings Mobile 07979-855207

Harry Potter & The Deathly Hallows (feature), The World Is Not Enough (feature), Harry Potter & The Half-Blood Prince (feature) (2nd unit).

Dominic Mewburn-Crook Mobile 07774-695539

Body Of Lies (feature), Robin Hood (feature), Troy (feature).

Dave Miller 01932-563268 Mobile 07976-775528

City Of Ember (feature), Entrapment (feature), Gladiator (feature).

Matthew Murray 01628-660550 Mobile 07894-462632

Charlie & The Chocolate Factory (feature).

Jamie Murrell Mobile 07771-528316

Kingdom Of Heaven (feature).

Terry Palmer Mobile 07989-055667

London Boulevard (feature), Brighton Rock (feature), Stardust (feature).

Simon Parker   01279-734235 Mobile 07833-373071
The Pacific (TV drama), The Matrix I II & III (feature), Charlie & The Chocolate Factory (feature).

Charlie Pedersen   Mobile 07841-285152
The Wolfman (feature), Prince Of Persia (feature), The Golden Compass (feature).

John Pilgrim   0118-932 1268 Mobile 07738-510591
Harry Potter & The Goblet Of Fire (feature), Harry Potter & The Order Of The Phoenix (feature), Black Hawk Down (feature).

Simon Quinn   01628-669283 Mobile 07786-072038
Gladiator (feature), The Day After Tomorrow (feature), Saving Private Ryan (feature).

Grant Rogan   01753-523186 Mobile 07721-643798
Robin Hood (feature), Prince Of Persia (feature), The Golden Compass (feature).

Shaun Rutter   01753-663727 Mobile 07917-756007
Kingdom Of Heaven (feature), King Arthur (feature), Black Hawk Down (feature).

Nigel Sinclair   Mobile 07832-214555
John Carter Of Mars (feature).

Conrad Sinclair-Peek   020-8224 2442
Batman Begins (feature), Die Another Day (feature), The World Is Not Enough (feature).

Harry Stokes   01780-752166 Mobile 07801-310468
Fax 01780-752167
Dean Spanley (feature), Raging Planet (TV doc), Control (feature).

Neil Todd   Mobile 07778-759273
Prince Of Persia (feature), Troy (feature), Phantom Of The Opera (feature).

Matt Veale   Mobile 07796-951276
Stardust (feature), The Magic Flute (feature), Syriana (feature).

Andrew Warner   Mobile 07967-640263
Quantum Of Solace (feature), Casino Royale (feature), The Dark Knight (feature).

Steve Warner   Mobile 07710-539317
1408 (feature), Kingdom Of Heaven (feature).

Barry White   01753-630006 Mobile 07770-402920
Inception (feature), Quantum Of Solace (feature), John Carter Of Mars (feature).

Mark White   Mobile 07778-325867
London Boulevard (feature).

Nigel Wilkinson   01483-825808 Mobile 07736-323964
Stardust (feature), Derailed (feature), Johnny English (feature).

Daniel Williams   01494-471593 Mobile 07834-737421
Gulliver's Travels (feature), Casino Royale (feature), The Wolfman (feature).

Hayley Williams   01628-670685 Mobile 07812-187955
Charlie & The Chocolate Factory (feature), Munich (feature), Elizabeth: The Golden Age (feature).

Mark Williams   020-7821 9059 Mobile 07855-765404
Children Of Men (feature).

Trevor Williams   01483-282154 Mobile 07956-382338
Fax 01483-282154
Cold Mountain (feature), Spy Game (feature), The League Of Extraordinary Gentlemen (feature).

Ashley Yallop   Mobile 07973-879132
The Pacific (TV drama), Charlie & The Chocolate Factory (feature), Troy (feature).

SPECIAL FX TECHNICIANS - ANIMATRONICS

Chris Barton   01280-850231 Mobile 07889-444714
Harry Potter & The Deathly Hallows (feature), The Fifth Element (feature), Harry Potter & The Chamber Of Secrets (feature).

Michael Fleming   0845-658 8787 Fax 0845-658 8788
Robin Hood (feature), John Carter Of Mars (feature), Batman Begins (feature).
www.wingfield-studios.com

Frank Guiney   01932-229688 Mobile 07836-682729
Harry Potter & The Chamber Of Secrets (feature), Harry Potter & The Order Of The Phoenix (feature), Harry Potter & The Prisoner Of Azkaban (feature).

Tamzine Hanks   020-8985 6987 Mobile 07711-420983
Harry Potter & The Goblet Of Fire (feature), Harry Potter & The Prisoner Of Azkaban (feature), Harry Potter & The Chamber Of Secrets (feature).

Gustav Hoegen   020-8699 8360 Mobile 07712-043216
Clash Of The Titans (feature), Charlie & The Chocolate Factory (feature), Hitchhiker's Guide To The Galaxy (feature).

Jamie Jackson-Moore 01442-877182 Mobile 07968-241934
Die Another Day (feature), Casino Royale (feature), Batman Begins (feature).

Andrew Lee   Mobile 07956-395621
Dog Soldiers (feature), Harry Potter & The Philosopher's Stone (feature), Star Wars: Episode II - Attack Of The Clones (feature).

Melissa Lenahan   01243-837091 Mobile 07050-050623
Hitchhiker's Guide To The Galaxy (feature), Harry Potter & The Chamber Of Secrets (feature), Harry Potter & The Philosopher's Stone (feature).

Esteban Mendoza   020-7272 7365 Mobile 07775-780042
Fax 020-7272 7365
Harry Potter & The Prisoner Of Azkaban (feature), Harry Potter & The Chamber Of Secrets (feature), Harry Potter & The Philosopher's Stone (feature).

Ian Mitchell   Mobile 07976-700878
John Carter Of Mars (feature).

Anton Prickett   Mobile 07798-516829
Gulliver's Travels (feature), The Da Vinci Code (feature), Harry Potter & The Chamber Of Secrets (feature).

Jason Reed   020-8979 1278 Mobile 07973-661675
Harry Potter & The Prisoner Of Azkaban (feature), Tomb Raider (feature), Die Another Day (feature).

Martin Reid   01379-677793
Star Wars: Episode I - The Phantom Menace (feature), Harry Potter & The Philosopher's Stone (feature).

Jim Sandys   Mobile 07979-504337
Harry Potter & The Prisoner Of Azkaban (feature), Harry Potter & The Chamber Of Secrets (feature), Harry Potter & The Philosopher's Stone (feature).

Andy Simm   01622-728050
Batman Begins (feature), Tomb Raider II (feature), The World Is Not Enough (feature).

Guy Stevens   Mobile 07956-923441
Hitchhiker's Guide To The Galaxy (feature), Harry Potter & The Goblet Of Fire (feature), Harry Potter & The Prisoner Of Azkaban (feature).

Phoebe Tait   Mobile 07989-404382
Harry Potter & The Order Of The Phoenix (feature), Harry Potter & The Goblet Of Fire (feature), Harry Potter & The Prisoner Of Azkaban (feature).

Mark Walker   01522-826788 Mobile 07940-705246
The Descent (feature), Cold & Dark (feature), Animal Makers (TV childrens).

Brian Wells   01753-518058 Mobile 07941-713228
Charlie & The Chocolate Factory (feature), Hitchhiker's Guide To The Galaxy (feature), Die Another Day (feature).

Simon Williams   01872-222159 Mobile 07957-633712
Harry Potter & The Goblet Of Fire (feature), Hitchhiker's Guide To The Galaxy (feature), Harry Potter & The Prisoner Of Azkaban (feature).

SPECIAL FX TECHNICIANS - ASSISTANT

Peter Britten   01179-659052 Mobile 07974-195363
John Carter Of Mars (feature).

Cliff Corbould   01598-753731
Blood Diamond (feature), Kingdom Of Heaven (feature), King Arthur (feature).

Christopher Corbould Jr   01932-561621
Mobile 07702-164909
Body Of Lies (feature), The Wolfman (feature), Gulliver's Travels (feature).

Mark Day   01932-565130 Mobile 07961-307014
John Carter Of Mars (feature).

Jaroslav Kolenic   Mobile 07915-212165
The Golden Compass (feature).

Huw Miller   02392-256164
Batman Begins (feature), Thunderbirds (feature), Tomb Raider II (feature).

David Roddham   Mobile +353 86 333 7566
Kingdom Of Heaven (feature).

Seb Sue   Mobile 07956-335727
The Brothers Grimm (feature), Die Another Day (feature), Harry Potter & The Philosopher's Stone (feature).

SPECIAL FX TECHNICIANS - COMPUTER EFFECTS

Paul Lada   +61 403 911 222
Harry Potter & The Prisoner Of Azkaban (feature), Tomb Raider II (feature), Dinotopia (TV drama).

SPECIAL FX TECHNICIANS - SENIOR

Graham Aikman   020-8509 2005 Mobile 07860-681856
Hornblower (TV drama), The Scarlet Tunic (feature), Devil's Gate (feature).

Jonathan Angell   01273-479021 Mobile 07973-220023
Sunshine (feature), Troy (feature), Band Of Brothers (TV drama).

John Arnitt   01483-727471 Mobile 07768-856165
John Carter Of Mars (feature), Inception (feature), Quantum Of Solace (feature).

Norman Baillie   01494-721946 Mobile 07788-921739
Fax 01494-433438
Harry Potter & The Deathly Hallows (feature), Harry Potter & The
Half-Blood Prince (feature), Blood Diamond (feature).

Ian Biggs   01872-571937 Mobile 07778-958065
The Da Vinci Code (feature) (2nd unit), Harry Potter & The Goblet
Of Fire (feature), Phantom Of The Opera (feature).

Nigel Brackley   01844-352640 Mobile 07778-578755
Fax 01844-351950
Harry Potter & The Deathly Hallows (feature), The World Is Not
Enough (feature), Tomorrow Never Dies (feature).

Terry Bridle   0118-971 4724 Mobile 07973-224911
Harry Potter & The Deathly Hallows (feature), Wanted (feature),
Sunshine (feature).

David Brighton   01932-564414 Mobile 07773-084911
Clash Of The Titans (feature), Blood Diamond (feature), Superman
Returns (feature).

Richard Brown   01932-336258 Mobile 07747-788191
Gulliver's Travels (feature), Quantum Of Solace (feature).

Mark Bullimore   Mobile 07970-033539
Harry Potter & The Deathly Hallows (feature), Harry Potter & The
Half-Blood Prince (feature), The World Is Not Enough (feature).

Jonathan Bullock   01753-676651 Mobile 07802-977651
Harry Potter & The Deathly Hallows (feature), Nine (feature), Harry
Potter & The Half-Blood Prince (feature).
www.easfx.co.uk

Andy Bunce   0118-976 1413 Mobile 07850-451614
Fax 0118-976 1413
Robin Hood (feature), Prince Of Persia (feature), Charlie & The
Chocolate Factory (feature).

Trevor Butterfield   01494-762715 Mobile 07710-325856
Fax 01494-762715
Harry Potter & The Goblet Of Fire (feature), Harry Potter & The
Prisoner Of Azkaban (feature), Harry Potter & The Chamber Of
Secrets (feature).

Paul Clancy   020-8972 9047 Mobile 07973-658117
Robin Hood (feature), Quantum Of Solace (feature), Batman Begins
(feature).

Simon Cockren   01895-462745 Mobile 07971-277228
Robin Hood (feature), Prince Of Persia (feature), The Golden
Compass (feature).

Gary Cohen   01895-231314 Mobile 07719-326442
Prince Of Persia (feature), Robin Hood (feature), Charlie & The
Chocolate Factory (feature).

Mike Dawson   07000-327574 Mobile 07973-165072
Fax 07002-327574
Troy (feature), Band Of Brothers (TV drama), Sleepy Hollow
(feature).

Stuart Digby   01494-716274 Mobile 07850-723908
Fax 01494-712625
Prince Of Persia (feature), Robin Hood (feature), The Invention Of
Hugo Cabret (feature).

Anthony Edwards   01494-445973 Mobile 07979-227177
Inception (feature), Prince Of Persia (feature), John Carter Of Mars
(feature).

Manex Effrem   01932-571970 Mobile 07970-173056
Blood Diamond (feature), Hellboy 2: The Golden Army (feature),
Sleepy Hollow (feature).

Dave Eltham   Mobile 07973-193211
John Carter Of Mars (feature), The Dark Knight (feature), Quantum
Of Solace (feature).

Raymond Ferguson   01235-751404 Mobile 07836-635124
Fax 01235-751404
Gladiator (feature), Saving Private Ryan (feature), Superman
(feature).

Peter Fern   01753-852952 Mobile 07780-668812
Robin Hood (feature), Prince Of Persia (feature), Babylon AD
(feature).

Nick Finlayson   020-8398 1333 Mobile 07973-258420
Fax 020-8398 1333
The Dark Knight (feature), Quantum Of Solace (feature), Casino
Royale (feature).

Terence Flowers   020-8589 9749 Mobile 07967-806552
The Pacific (TV drama), Troy (feature), Band Of Brothers (TV
drama).

Melvyn Friend   020-8444 4844 Mobile 07973-719986
Krakatoa: The Last Days (TV docu drama), Doctor Who (TV drama),
Hiroshima (TV docu drama).

Rodney Fuller   01784-431316 Mobile 07866-366440
Robin Hood (feature), Prince Of Persia (feature), The Golden
Compass (feature).

Terry Glass   Mobile 07885-369878
Robin Hood (feature), City Of Ember (feature), The League Of
Extraordinary Gentlemen (feature).

Garth Gutteridge   020-8580 2613 Mobile 07810-888235
Gulliver's Travels (feature), The Tourist (feature), The Da Vinci Code
(feature).

Darrell Guyon   01784-481091 Mobile 07847-303416
The Dark Knight (feature), Quantum Of Solace (feature), Casino Royale (feature).

Mark Haddenham   01262-850034 Mobile 07767-417747
Quantum Of Solace (feature), Stardust (feature).

John Hatt   01628-638894 Mobile 07802-247321
Fax 01628-638894
Die Another Day (feature), Blade II (feature), Enigma (feature).

Simon Hewitt   020-8423 1677 Mobile 07957-870930
Harry Potter & The Prisoner Of Azkaban (feature), The World Is Not Enough (feature), Harry Potter & The Goblet Of Fire (feature).

John Holmes   Mobile 07801-737431
Quantum Of Solace (feature), Batman Begins (feature), The World Is Not Enough (feature).

Ronald Hone   01494-531105 Mobile 07785-794010
Robin Hood (feature), Prince Of Persia (feature), Spy Game (feature).

Mark Howard   Mobile 07872-944321
Robin Hood (feature), Prince Of Persia (feature).

Steve Hutchinson   01420-86743 Mobile 07979-600050
Harry Potter & The Deathly Hallows (feature), Nine (feature), Harry Potter & The Half-Blood Prince (feature) (2nd unit).

David Keen   Mobile 07798-528595
Quantum Of Solace (feature), Tomb Raider II (feature), Tomb Raider (feature).

Steve Knowles   020-8773 3176 Mobile 07778-702074
Robin Hood (feature), Prince Of Persia (feature), Stardust (feature).

Steven Lewis   Mobile 07778-918966
The Dark Knight (feature), Quantum Of Solace (feature), Batman Begins (feature).

Steve Lloyd   Mobile 07775-992214
Charlie & The Chocolate Factory (feature), Troy (feature), Band Of Brothers (TV drama).

Raymond Lovell   020-8942 9299
Gladiator (feature), Saving Private Ryan (feature), The Mummy Returns (feature).

James Machin   01753-783779 Mobile 07973-855043
Quantum Of Solace (feature), Casino Royale (feature), Batman Returns (feature).

Jason Marsh   Mobile 07976-619314
Quantum Of Solace (feature), Children Of Men (feature), Sahara (feature).

Darren May   Mobile 07885-156963
Robin Hood (feature), Van Helsing (feature), Prince Of Persia (feature).

Jason McCameron   01753-856781 Mobile 07798-802129
The Wolfman (feature), Robin Hood (feature), Children Of Men (feature) (SFX Workshop Supervisor).

Doug Mccarthy   Mobile 07702-024010
Harry Potter & The Deathly Hallows (feature), Prince Of Persia (feature), City Of Ember (feature).

Mark Meddings   Mobile 07768-002211
Push (feature), The Brothers Bloom (feature), Black Hawk Down (feature).

Tim Mitchell   020-8815 0132 Mobile 07710-769174
Robin Hood (feature), Children Of Men (feature), Inkheart (feature).

John Morris   01753-822701
Harry Potter & The Deathly Hallows (feature), The Da Vinci Code (feature), Sahara (feature).

Brian Morrison   01628-529995 Mobile 07802-444094
Harry Potter & The Prisoner Of Azkaban (feature), Casino Royale (feature), United 93 (feature).

Luke Murphy   01525-402267 Mobile 07801-474674
Harry Potter & The Deathly Hallows (feature), Harry Potter & The Half-Blood Prince (feature) (2nd unit), Harry Potter & The Order Of The Phoenix (feature).

Roger Nichols   01895-630522 Mobile 07973-115923
Black Hawk Down (feature), The Nomad (feature), Sleepy Hollow (feature).

Nigel Nixon   01344-489029 Mobile 07920-282838
Robin Hood (feature), Prince Of Persia (feature), Troy (feature).

Peter Notley   01753-662410 Mobile 07778-370106
The Dark Knight (feature), Batman Begins (feature), Casino Royale (feature).

Stephen Paton   01753-652161 Mobile 07759-137111
W.E. (feature), Rambo (feature), Valkyrie (feature).

Peter Pickering   01296-612522
Harry Potter & The Deathly Hallows (feature), Harry Potter & The Half-Blood Prince (feature), Harry Potter & The Order Of The Phoenix (feature).

David Poole   01932-570955 Mobile 07889-615440
Clash Of The Titans (feature), Black Hawk Down (feature), Charlie & The Chocolate Factory (feature).

Roy Quinn   01628-669283 Mobile 07768-926054
Casino Royale (feature), Batman Begins (feature), Tomb Raider II (feature).

Mark Roberts   01753-676651 Mobile 07711-890182
Harry Potter & The Half-Blood Prince (feature), Tomb Raider (feature), Die Another Day (feature).
www.easfx.co.uk

Nick Smith   Mobile 07768-596161
The Mummy Returns (feature), My Giant (feature), Snow White (feature).

Paul Taylor   020-8207 1793 Mobile 07957-251198
Robin Hood (feature), Prince Of Persia (feature), The Da Vinci Code (feature).

Ian Thompson   01628-670988 Mobile 07050-051117
Gladiator (feature), Hellboy (feature), Triple X (feature).

Richard Todd   01787-227851 Mobile 07860-953522
Fax 01787-228200
The Dark Knight (feature), Casino Royale (feature), Quantum Of Solace (feature).

Colin Umpleby   020-8878 0717 Mobile 07973-195025
King Arthur (feature), The Day After Tomorrow (feature), Die Another Day (feature).

John van der Pool   020-7431 9857 Fax 020-7431 9857
Quantum Of Solace (feature), Casino Royale (feature), Batman Begins (feature).

Anne Marie Walters   01753-548159 Mobile 07721-311426
Clash Of The Titans (feature), Green Zone (feature), 44 Inch Chest (feature).

David Watkins   01628-666896 Mobile 07966-198813
Clash Of The Titans (feature), The Devil's Double (feature), Pirates Of The Caribbean: The Curse Of The Black Pearl (feature).

David Watson   Mobile 07956-418937
Charlie & The Chocolate Factory (feature), Troy (feature), Mission: Impossible (feature).

Les Wheeler   Mobile 07973-521532
Die Another Day (feature), The English Patient (feature), Goldeneye (feature).

Peter White   01299-401749 Mobile 07773-445930
Robin Hood (feature).

Terry Whitehouse   Mobile 07801-540444
Stardust (feature), Harry Potter & The Prisoner Of Azkaban (feature), Harry Potter & The Philosopher's Stone (feature).

Paul Whybrow   01895-673956 Mobile 07811-712945
Harry Potter & The Deathly Hallows (feature), A Knight's Tale (feature), Aliens (feature).

David Williams   01494-482760 Mobile 07787-501802
The World Is Not Enough (feature), Gladiator (feature), The Mummy Returns (feature).

Tori Williams   Mobile 07920-444996
The Pacific (TV drama), Band Of Brothers (TV drama), Green Zone (feature).

Gareth Wingrove   01844-352210 Mobile 07980-299378
Inception (feature), Body Of Lies (feature), Children Of Men (feature).

Lee Winter   020-8841 7124 Mobile 07802-840455
John Carter Of Mars (feature).

Stuart Wishart   Mobile 07921-161611
Doomsday (feature).

VISUAL EFFECTS ASSISTANTS

Luan Hall   01932-571954 Mobile 07876-332644
The Golden Compass (feature).

Nathan Kerry   Mobile 07793-799448
The Secret Of Moonacre (feature), The Golden Compass (feature).

Daniel Moody   Mobile 07891-016174
The Wolfman (feature).

VISUAL EFFECTS CO-ORDINATORS

Nicholas Atkinson   Mobile 07712-890728
Harry Potter & The Deathly Hallows (feature), Harry Potter & The Half-Blood Prince (feature), Harry Potter & The Prisoner Of Azkaban (feature).

Jeremy Engler   Mobile 07957-357322
Alexander (feature), Die Another Day (feature), The World Is Not Enough (feature).

Tracey Gibbons   01494-729101 Mobile 07976-732734
Gulliver's Travels (feature), X-Men: The Last Stand (feature), Kingdom Of Heaven (feature).

Peter Hartless   Mobile 07986-207631
Generation Kill (TV drama), Journey To The Centre Of The Earth (feature), Nanny McPhee & The Big Bang (feature).

Paul Ladd   Mobile 07739-183023
Scott Pilgrim Vs The World (feature), Hellboy 2: The Golden Army (feature), Children Of Men (feature).

Natalie Lovatt   Mobile 07932-040312
Clash Of The Titans (feature), The Golden Compass (feature), Quantum Of Solace (feature) (2nd unit).

Victoria McDowell   020-7494 4342 Mobile 07786-563599
Prince Of Persia (feature), John Carter Of Mars (feature).

Lindsay McFarlane   020-8783 9460 Mobile 07956-598636
Shanghai (feature), The Da Vinci Code (feature), Stardust (feature).

Dominic Ridley   Mobile 07800-655540
Nanny McPhee & The Big Bang (feature).

Rupert Smith   Mobile 07884-397520
The Chronicles Of Narnia: The Voyage Of The Dawn Treader (feature), The Wolfman (feature), Stardust (feature).

Jenny Weight   Mobile 07795-558595
Harry Potter & The Order Of The Phoenix (feature).

Gina Willis   Mobile 07961-422124
Charlie & The Chocolate Factory (feature), Troy (feature).

VISUAL EFFECTS PRODUCERS

Andrew Barker   020-7701 6189 Mobile 07778-759198
1408 (feature).

Alexandra Day   Mobile 07903-946082
Stormbreaker (feature), V For Vendetta (feature), Harry Potter & The Prisoner Of Azkaban (feature).

Tim Field   01494-564960 Mobile 07810-805938
Ironclad (feature), Stardust (feature), Batman Begins (feature).

Barrie Hemsley   Mobile 07786-801902
The Chronicles Of Narnia: The Voyage Of The Dawn Treader (feature), Angels & Demons (feature), The Da Vinci Code (feature).

Tim Keene   Mobile 07980-809520
Underdog (feature), Love Actually (feature), Die Another Day (feature).

Patrick Kelly   Mobile 07779-222925
Avatar (feature), The Wolfman (feature), The Golden Compass (feature).

Lucy Killick   020-7686 0072 Mobile 07836-608893
Children Of Men (feature), Hellboy 2: The Golden Army (feature), Nanny McPhee (feature).

Sharon Lark   020-7686 3302 Mobile 07970-258369
The Chronicles Of Narnia: The Voyage Of The Dawn Treader (feature), Casino Royale (feature), Prince Of Persia (feature).

Nikki Penny   Mobile 07970-462541
Sweeney Todd (feature), Gravity (feature), Clash Of The Titans (feature).

Rupert Porter   Mobile 07811-267030
In Bruges (feature), Casino Royale (feature), Children Of Men (feature).

Andy Taylor   Mobile 07976-635055
Kick-Ass (feature), Iron Man II (feature), Hellboy 2: The Golden Army (feature).

VISUAL EFFECTS SUPERVISORS

Laya Armian   Mobile 07947-750964
The Dark Knight (feature), Clash (feature), The Invention Of Hugo Cabret (feature).

Steve Begg   Mobile 07887-845016
The Golden Compass (feature), Batman Begins (feature), Tomb Raider (feature).

Angus Bickerton   Mobile 07802-214662
The Da Vinci Code (feature), Hitchhiker's Guide To The Galaxy (feature), Band Of Brothers (TV drama).

Richard Briscoe   Mobile 07711-006475
The Boat That Rocked (feature), Hot Fuzz (feature), In Bruges (feature).

Tim Burke   020-8348 9470 Mobile 07976-176975
Harry Potter & The Half-Blood Prince (feature), Harry Potter & The Prisoner Of Azkaban (feature), Gladiator (feature).

Peter Chiang   020-7534 4400 Mobile 07973-264141
Green Zone (feature), United 93 (feature), Stardust (feature).

Alan Church   020-8995 8169 Mobile 07903-933669
Fax 020-8995 8169
Prisoners Of The Sun (feature), The Hessen Affair (feature), Buffalo Soldiers (feature).

Frazer Churchill   Mobile 07989-401910
Scott Pilgrim Vs The World (feature), The Fast & The Furious (feature), Children Of Men (feature).

Hal Couzens   020-7249 7558 Mobile 07958-613466
Finding Neverland (feature), Batman Begins (feature), Doomsday (feature).

Neil Cunningham   Mobile 07802-419798
Thoda Pyaar Thoda Magic (feature).

VISUAL EFFECTS SUPERVISORS

Andrew Eio   01753-653456 Mobile 07710-597774
Fax 01753-654507

Simon Frame   020-7478 7221 Mobile 07957-105788
Little Dorrit (TV drama), Easy Virtue (feature), Solomon Kane
(feature).

Simon Giles   020-8995 8169 Mobile 07956-276328
Brighton Rock (feature), White Noise (feature), The Devil's Double
(feature).

Sally Goldberg   Mobile 07974-727309
Harry Potter & The Chamber Of Secrets (feature), The Nutcracker
(ballet), The Matrix (feature).

Christian Jelen   Mobile 07762-118736
4.3.2.1 (feature), Spirit Warriors (TV childrens), Gorillaz (music).

Chris McBride   0118-907 9701 Mobile 07973-822073
The Dark Knight (feature), Casino Royale (feature), Batman Begins
(feature).

Adam McInnes   01494-766537 Mobile 07974-245557
Generation Kill (TV drama), Nanny McPhee & The Big Bang
(feature).

Joe Pavlo   Mobile 07974-429029
Rome (TV drama), The Life & Death Of Peter Sellers (feature), Band
Of Brothers (TV drama).

Chris Shaw   Mobile 07887-642971
Harry Potter & The Deathly Hallows (feature), Harry Potter &
The Half-Blood Prince (feature), Harry Potter & The Order Of The
Phoenix (feature).

Leigh Took   Bray 01628-506626
Pinewood 01753-656554 Mobile 07836-278028
Angels & Demons (feature), The Descent (feature), The Imaginarium
Of Dr Parnassus (feature).
www.mattesandminiatures.com

Mike Turoff   Mobile 07768-824357
Rachel Getting Married (feature), Five Children & It (feature).

Kevin Mathews   01753-785352 Mobile 07767-775760
Pirates Of The Caribbean: On Stranger Tides (feature), Quantum Of
Solace (feature), The Dark Knight (feature).
www.specialist-wire-rigs.co.uk

Kevin Welch   01753-522219 Mobile 07552-698621
Harry Potter & The Deathly Hallows (feature), The World Is Not
Enough (feature), Tomb Raider (feature).
www.stuntrigging.com
Please see advertisement on page 739

Bob Wiesinger   07000-wirefx (947339)
Mobile 07973-662393 Fax 07968-253071
The Nutcracker (ballet), The Holiday (feature), Harry Potter & The
Goblet Of Fire (feature).

WIRE EFFECTS
CO-ORDINATORS

Steve Crawley   01753-652570 Mobile 07710-525587
Fax 01753-652570
The Dark Knight (feature), Quantum Of Solace (feature), Casino
Royale (feature).

SPECIAL FX

AD	Art Department	ITG	Independent Talent Group
AMM	Amanda McAllister Management	JCA	Jessica Carney Associates
ARG	Artists Rights Group	JD	Judy Daish Associates
ARRI	Arri Crew	LL	Linkline
BA	Berlin Associates	LLM	Linlee Management
BE	Bookends	MCR	Mandy Coakley Represents
BF	Bigfish Management	MIL	The Milton Agency
CB	Callbox	MM	McKinney Macartney Management
CBR	Curtis Brown	MY	MY Management
CC	Carlin Crew	PFD	PFD
CCA	CCA Management	PG	Production Guild
CCM	Caroline Cornish Management	PHA	PHA Creative Management
CCR	Camera Crew	PS	Princestone
CM	Casarotto Marsh	PSB	Production Switchboard
CMM	Creative Media Management	RED	Red Diary Service
CRC	Cruickshank Cazenove	RS	Rochelle Stevens & Co
CVH	Clare Vidal-Hall	SC	Suz Cruz
CX	Connections	SD	Stellas Diary
DA	Dench Arnold Agency	SK	Steve Kenis & Co
DD	Dinedor	SMM	Sandra Marsh Management (USA)
DG	The Digital Garage	SPA	Sara Putt Associates
DYA	The Diary Agency	SR	Stella Richards Management
EXEC	Exec Answering Service	STA	Screen Talent Agency
F59	Films At 59	TA	The Agency (London)
FBC	Firm Booking Company	TOVS	TOVS
GI	Grade One TV Personal	UA	United Agents
GAS	The Guild Answering Service	VAW	Vision@Wizzo
GEMS	Gems	WP	Warpaint
HC	HotCam	WZ	Wizzo & Co
HERS	HERS Agency	ZDB	Zero DB

ADVERTISERS INDEX

ADVERTISERS INDEX

ADVERTISERS INDEX

ADVERTISERS INDEX